Di[illegible]s

Edited by Susan Jones

AN Publications
Artic Producers

Artic Producers

Second Edition 1989
ISBN 0 907730 05

First edition published 1983

Design and production: **Richard Padwick**

Maps: **Alistair Hardy**

Printed: **E F Peterson**, 12 Laygate Lane, South Shields, Tyne & Wear tel 091 456 3493

Cover photograph: **Robin Forbes**
From the exhibition 'Our Space in Britain' shown at Camerawork, London and also at the Pavilion in Leeds.The exhibition resulted from workshops aimed at creating opportunities for migrant women to work together to make images which reflected their cultures and which were a *'reflection on our lives today'*. It brought together **Maria Luiza M Carvalho, Jacqueline Moran-Daubercies, Xenia Demetriou, Joy Kahumbu, Lucia Ines Molina, Mariagrazia Pecararo, Samena Rana, Catarina dos Santos** and **Lucy Ann Sylvester**. The catalogue is available from Camerawork *(see entry under London).*

Artists Newsletter Publications
Artic Producers Publishing Co Ltd
PO Box 23, Sunderland SR4 6DG tel 091 567 3589

Artic Producers is a non-profit distributing company. Its objective is to support and inform artists' practice.

The Directory of Exhibition Spaces has received financial assistance from Northern Arts in the form of an interest free loan.

Compilers

David Briers: Wales

Alice Bain: Scotland

Christopher Coppock: Ireland and Northern Ireland

Ruth Tott: Yorkshire

Daniel Dahl Cleveland, Cumbria, Durham, Tyne & Wear and Northumberland

Celia Cross, Debbie Newell, Susan Jones: Lancashire, Greater Manchester and Cheshire

Rosemary Christmas: Merseyside

Paul Swales: Derbyshire, Nottinghamshire, Leicestershire, Northamptonshire, Shropshire, Staffordshire, West Midlands, Warwickshire, Hereford & Worcester and Buckinghamshire

Janita Elton: Humberside & Lincolnshire

Tony Warner: Norfolk, Hertfordshire, Bedfordshire and Cambridgeshire

Jeremy Theophilus: Essex and Suffolk

Shirley Chubb: Kent, East Sussex and Surrey

Sarah Eckersley, Patricia Wressell: West Sussex, Isle of Wight, Hampshire, Berkshire, Oxfordshire and Wiltshire

Rupert Martin, Paul Swales, Patricia Wressell: Cornwall, Devon, Somerset, Dorset, Avon and Gloucestershire

Debbie Duffin, Rosemary Christmas, Shirley Chubb, Barbara Taylor: Greater London

With additional research by **Susan Jones, Richard Padwick, Patricia Wressell, Elizabeth Beech** and **Michelle Bowen**

Foreword

The completely revised and updated *Directory of Exhibition Spaces*, has been made possible because of the concerted efforts of a dedicated network of compilers, and thanks are due to all of them as well as to Patricia Wressell for her work as a 'sweeper' dealing with queries, loose ends and problems. Thanks also to Margo Ladell of Hertfordshire Arts for her help with spaces in Hertfordshire; Eastern Arts for enabling Jeremy Theophilus' research for the *Handbook for Essex and Suffolk Artists* to be used in this book; Cleveland Arts for their extensive lists; the Welsh Arts Council for access to the listing of *Art Galleries and Exhibition Spaces in Wales*; the regional arts associations and others who supplied source lists of galleries; Nich Pearson (Welsh Arts Council), Mike Sixsmith (Museums and Galleries Commission) and Eileen Healey (Arts Council) for their assistance in the compilation of the gallery questionnaire; Tricia Kerr Art Promotions who battled through the post strike and ensuing delays to sell the advertising and Robin Forbes for the cover photograph. And last but not least, the galleries, museums and exhibition spaces who provide the platform for contemporary visual arts, crafts and photography exhibitions and performance art events in England, Ireland, Northern Ireland, Scotland and Wales.

Contents

Introducing the Directory of Exhibition Spaces

Welcome to the completely revised and updated second edition of the *Directory of Exhibition Spaces*.

Since the first edition in 1985, over 500 galleries and exhibition spaces have been added, providing, we think, the most comprehensive gallery listing available.

In its pages you will find a wealth of information on museums; libraries; galleries in schools, colleges and universities; galleries run by artists in their studios or homes; galleries in community settings; display space in workshops, darkrooms and print studios; commercial galleries, private galleries and publicly-funded galleries; galleries for hire; specialist craft, photography, illustration or print galleries; exhibition space in nightclubs, theatres, cafés, bars, swimming pools, hospitals and other unusual settings; galleries in heritage centres, leisure centres and historic homes.

To provide this extensive reference book, we used a network of compilers to cover in detail England, Ireland, Northern Ireland, Scotland and Wales, our intention being to try to cover the places – however large or small, whether privately or publicly-funded, regardless of national or local status – where temporary exhibitions of contemporary visual arts, crafts, photography or performance art events took place.

Within this broad policy, however, there are exclusions. Omitted, for instance, are galleries who only show historical rather than contemporary work, galleries which are essentially shops and those showing the work of one artist in a changing display. There are, needless to say, anomolies.

Some galleries who we wished to list asked to be taken out. Some, despite our considerable research, have slipped through every net; some new galleries have just missed the final deadline for inclusion.

We hope with the *Directory of Exhibition Spaces* to give readers as broad a picture as possible, with the aim of assisting those wishing to visit galleries and exhibitions, aiding communication between gallery organisers wishing to tour and exchange exhibitions and, last but not least, to help artists, makers, photographers and performance artists to make informed choices about where to show their work.

Scouring the country!

A range of methods were used to research the book. Galleries first of all received a three-page questionnaire to which around 35% of galleries replied. Despite the delays caused by the post strike and subsequent the backlog on deliveries, compilers completed their areas using reminders, telephone surveys and a range of other sources of information and, before the book went to print the over 2000 galleries listed were sent a proof to confirm the text. This method, we hope, weeded out all the 'gone aways', changes of address, name or policy, as well as those which had closed down during the research period - a surprisingly large number!

The listings, largely based on what the galleries say about themselves, have, therefore, been published in good faith. So if you contact a gallery who purports to 'welcome applications' and they present a frosty face, or if a gallery described in glowing terms is, in fact, a damp and poorly-lit warehouse, let us know! Similarly, we need your help to find out when a gallery changes policy, ownership, address or simply fades away.

Using the book

The *Directory of Exhibition Spaces* has been organised by country - England, Ireland, Northern Ireland, Scotland, Wales, and the Channel Islands and the Isle of Man. Within each country, galleries are indexed by town which contains an Ordance Survey National Grid reference relating to the maps on pages 402 to 422. The indexes, in alphabetical order of gallery name and also in a county-by-county form, are included for ease of reference.

The title of the gallery is followed a sentence offering a thumb-nail description of what goes on there with an indication of the artforms shown. A key to these abbreviations, and others used in the listings, is contained on page 8 and 496. **'Policy'** tells you, where possible, more about the ideology of the gallery. **'The Space'** contains practical details of the size of rooms, lighting methods, humidity control and how works are fixed to the walls. This, and **'Exhibiting'** are of particular interest to artists. They can tell, for instance, from the abbreviation **[AW]** whether artists are welcome to apply to exhibit. **[EF]** denotes that an exhibition fee is payable to exhibitors, although this may not cover all artists and all exhibitions. We asked all galleries whether they supported the principle of Exhibition Payment Right - a description of which is contained on pages 430-432 – and some entries therefore contain *'Supports the principle of EPR'*.

Information on disabled access is based on details supplied by the galleries and disabled people and their companions are advised to check in advance of a visit. **[U]** indicates that there is unstepped access to the building; **[T]** that there is a toilet adapted for the disabled; **[L]** denotes a lift; **[F]** shows flat or one-step access to the galleries and **[S]** that there are 2-5 steps to negotiate. **[X]** denotes that there are many unavoidable steps or difficulties for wheelchair users.

Not only but also...

At the back of the book, you'll find, 'Making an Informed Choice', Debbie Duffin's practical guide for artists planning to apply for an exhibition. And for those curious about Exhibition Payment Right, there's a brief guide for artists and galleries of the national picture and an indication of how it could be developed into a fully-fledged 'Right' in the forseeable future. This is followed by 'Read On...', a substantial booklist plus a contacts, information and sources listing.

The *Directory of Exhibition Spaces*, might, for those artists marooned on a desert island, be considered the only book worth taking, so that the long, languid days spent waiting for the rescue squad or making art from driftwood and sand, could be constructively spent planning the next several years of exhibitions. For where else can such a wealth of information, in such a readable format, be found in one place?

Susan Jones
Editor

Key to codes used in listings

Arts council & regional arts association area

Arts funding bodies responsible for the town:

ACE Arts Council of Eire
ACNI Arts Council of N Ireland
BA Buckinghamshire Arts
EA Eastern Arts
EMA East Midlands Arts
GLA Greater London Arts
LHA Lincolnshire & Humberside
MA Merseyside Arts
NA Northern Arts
NWA North West Arts
NWaA North Wales Arts
SA Southern Arts
SEWaA South West Wales Arts
SWA South West Arts
WMA West Midlands Arts
WWaA West Wales Arts
YA Yorkshire Arts

For contacts and addresses see 'Read On...' pages 437-438.

For a map of arts council and regional arts areas see page 402.

Art forms shown

The codes indicate the main art forms shown by the gallery

VA Visual Arts consisting of:
- **Pa** Painting
- **Dr** Drawing
- **Il** Illustration
- **Pr** Print
- **Sc** Sculpture

Ph Photography
Fi Film
Vi Video
Ho Holography
LA Live Art
Ar Architecture

Cr Craft consisting of:
- **Ce** Ceramics
- **Je** Jewellery
- **Te** Textiles
- **Gl** Glass
- **Wo** Wood
- **Fu** Furniture
- **De** Design
- **Bo** Books

Torrington (Devon)

(SWA) Map 5 SS41

Plough Theatre

A gallery space in the foyer of a theatre in a converted pub. [VA,Ph,Cr]

Address: The Plough, Fore Street, Great Torrington, Devon EX38 8HQ tel 0805 22552
Contact: Theatre Director Jenny Neesham
Open: Tues-Sat 10-5 and 6.30-9
Policy: The monthly programme is predominantly work by local artists.
Sales: Work sold
The Space: The gallery has 16m linear hanging space with *'basic lighting', though improvements are 'scheduled'.*
Exhibiting: [AW] Apply to the Director. The theatre provides Insurance, transport, preview, list of exhibits and artists' expenses. Preview costs split equally between theatre and exhibitor. A commission of 25% is charged on sales.
Access: [U] Town centre location; BR Barnstable

Disabled access

Information on disabled access is based in details supplied by the gallery. Your are advised to check facilities for the disabled prior to a visit.

[U] Unstepped access to the building
[T] Toilet suitable for the disabled
[F] Flat or one-step access to some or all galleries
[L] Lift
[S] 2-5 steps
[X] Many unavoidable steps or dificulties for wheelchair users

Map reference

Codes locate the town on the maps on pages 404–421

Map 1 Northern Scotland pages 404-5
Map 2 Southern Scotland pages 406-7
Map 3 Northern England pages 408-9
Map 4 Wales/West Midlands pages 410-11
Map 5 East Midlands pages 412-13
Map 6 South West England pages 414-15
Map 7 South East England pages 416-17
Map 8 North of Ireland pages 418-19
Map 9 South of Ireland pages 420-421

The code following the map number is the Ordnance Survey National Grid Reference which locates the position of the town within the map and within any map employing the National Grid. ***See page 403 Key to Maps.***

Exhibiting

[AW] The gallery welcomes exhibition applications from artists
[EF] The gallery pays a fee to exhibiting artists for allowing public access to their work.

The inclusion of the phrase *'Supports the principle of EPR'* means the gallery agrees with the principle that artists should receive a payment *as of right* for publicly exhibiting their work. See 'Exhibition Payment Right' page 430.

Facing Page: Lamont Gallery, London

Accrington (Lancashire)

(NWA) Map3 SD72

Howarth Art Gallery

A gallery with one of the finest collections of Tiffany glass in the world, which also runs a temporary exhibition programme. [VA,Cr]

Address: Howarth Park, Manchester Road, Accrington, Lancashire BB5 tel 0254 33782
Contact: Curator
Open: Daily 2-5
Policy: The monthly exhibition programme is linked with exhibitions drawn from the permanent collection.

Aldeburgh (Suffolk)

(EA) Map5 TM45

Peter Pears Gallery

Supports the Aldeburgh Festival as a venue for specialist exhibitions, as well as hosting the Suffolk Craft Society. [Pa,Pr,Cr]

Address: Aldeburgh Foundation, High Street, Aldeburgh, Suffolk IP15 5AX tel 072885 2935
Contact: General Manager Kenneth Baird
Policy: Available for hire.
The Space: 16.7x10x4.8m, 36m linear hanging; comprehensive lighting, fans and central heating, alarmed. Space used for meetings, dinners, musical events.
Exhibiting: [AW] All terms negotiable. Supports EPR.
Access: [X] BR Saxmundham, bus link; Car parking nearby

Alnwick (Northumberland)

(NA) Map2 NU11

Bondgate Gallery

A gallery run by members of the society which shows art and craft in a wide variety of media every month. [VA,Ph,Cr]

Address: 22 Narrowgate, Alnwick, Northumberland NE66 2IG tel 0665 510777
Contact: Chairman I L August, Friars Well, Hulne Park, Alnwick, Northumberland NE66 2LJ
Open: Mon-Fri 11-1, 2-4.30, Sat 11-4
Policy: The gallery exists *'to illustrate the history of art and encourage its appreciation, to stimulate an interest in contemporary art in the area and at the same time provide facilities for artists to exhibit their work, usually in solo exhibitions, for the benefit of members, visitors, and local schools. Other activities include visits and lectures.*
Sales: Work sold
The Space: The gallery has 24m linear hanging space on 1.5m high hessian-covered plywood wall panels with direct fixing, spots with dimmer controls and electric heating with humidifiers. Maximum size of work is 2x1.5m. Craft showcase available. Gallery plans available.
Exhibiting: [AW] Contact the Exhibition Secretary Mrs R Young, The Beeches, Alnmouth Road, Alnwick, tel 0665 603178. Gallery provides insurance, publicity, printing and preview and takes 25% commission. Supports the principle of EPR.
Access: [U] Newcastle-Edinburgh coach stop 3 mins; Public car park 2 mins

Hill House Gallery

A commercial artist-run gallery with two exhibition areas one for solo exhibitions and the other for resident artists and makers. [VA,Ph,Cr]

Address: Corn Exchange Courtyard, 39 Bondgate Within, Alnwick, Northumberland NE66 1SX tel 0665 79275
Contact: J Cartmel-Crossley
Open: Mon-Fri 9.30-5, closed Wed afternoon; Open Sun July & August
Policy: Monthly exhibitions usually selected by personal contact mainly of non-figurative work *'though anything good considered... only real criteria is excellence'*. The audience is local residents and tourists. Other activities are lectures by artists, music events etc.
Sales: Work sold; Credit scheme
The Space: Hanging space is 14m or 22m using double banking on battened walls. Direct fixing to walls, adjustable spots, plinths and shelving for 3D work. Maximum size of work 100x74cm. Gallery plans available.
Exhibiting: [AW] Send slides of work or make an appointment. Gallery contributes to costs of insurance, publicity, preview and charges 33.3% commission (20% first exhibition). Previews are optional and are at the artists expense. Supports the principle of EPR.
Access: [U][T] Car park by gallery

Alresford (Hampshire)

(SA) Map7 TM02

Candover Gallery

A commercial art and craft gallery showing mainly ceramics and glass by British makers who are internationally recognised. [Pa,Sc,Cr]

Address: 22 West Street, Alresford, Hampshire SO24 9AE tel 0962 733200
Contact: Director Barbara Ling
Open: Mon-Sat 9.30-5.30
Policy: To show quality British makers in glass, ceramics and wood as well as paintings. It also identifies, encourages and supports newcomers by buying in their work. Most of the customers are serious collectors who travel far to the gallery which also sells a select range of jewellery, cards and Liberty goods. The exhibitions are normally shown for two to three weeks.
Sales: Work sold; Credit card
The Space: Ground floor gallery 7x8m devoted almost entirely to ceramics and glass. First floor gallery 6.4x3.9m with a linear run of 16.7x2.1m and Cellar gallery 4.8x4.5m with a linear run of 16.7x2m. Narrow access to first floor and cellar.
Exhibiting: [AW] By prior written application enclosing slides to Barbara Ling. The first floor and cellar are available for hire at £100 a week each. The gallery pays

for insurance, printing and mailing of publicity, list of exhibits, preview costs and a catalogue/card, and changes between 45%-55% commission.
Access: [F] Free parking; Bus service to Winchester

Hitchcocks

Commercial gallery (formerly Country Fare). [Je,Ce,Gl,Te,Wo]
Address: 11 East Street, New Alresford, Hampshire SO24 9EQ tel 0962 734 762
Contact: Partner Joyce Hitchcock
Open: Mon-Sat 9.30-1 & 2-5
Policy: Hitchcocks specialises in designer knitwear and hand-painted and printed silks by British makers including Lindean Mill, Michael Bolton, Sarah Burnett, Campbell & Kulagowski as well as showing knitwear and toys. The gallery seeks innovative work and most of the stock is bought outright so little space available for exhibitions which take place in their Bath gallery.
Sales: Work sold; Credit card
The Space: Small gallery space.
Access: Bus from BR Winchester or Alton

Alsager (Cheshire)

(NWA) Map4 SJ75

Alsager Gallery

The gallery is part of Crewe and Alsager College and provides a wide range of arts activities and events for the college and the general public. [VA,Cr,Ph,LA]
Address: Crewe & Alsager College of Higher Education, Hassall Road, Alsager, Cheshire ST7 2HL ST7 2HL tel 0270 882500
Contact: Senior Lecturer Dorothy Pickering
Open: Mon-Fri 9-5
Policy: The policy is to present exhibitions of living artists and makers often in conjunction with lectures and workshops. The programme of eight exhibitions a year includes touring shows, work by members of staff and that which reflects interest in historical and ethnic aspects.
Sales: Work sold
The Space: The gallery, which is a series of three connected exhibition spaces making up an area of 44x 41m, is lit by fluorescent and spot lighting with some natural light and work is hung by rod or direct fixing.
Exhibiting: [AW] Written applications with slides or black and white photographs are welcomed any time. These should be sent to Dorothy Pickering. The centre is responsible for costs of insurance, mailing and catalogue. 10% Commission taken on sales.
Access: [F] BR Alsager 15 mins; Car park 2 mins; Bus to Crewe and Hanley

Alston (Cumbria)

(NA) Map2 NY74

Gossipgate Gaslight Gallery

A commercial gallery run as a parallel business by 'countryside consultants' (architects and planners specialising in countryside projects). [VA,Ph,Cr,LA]
Address: The Butts, Alston, Cumbria CA9 3JU tel 0498 81806
Contact: Sonia Kempsey
Open: Mon-Sun 10-5
Policy: The gallery shows mixed exhibitions lasting six weeks. The aim is to promote the work of local artists and makers and selection is limited to those from the North of England and the Borders. They are looking for work of both quality and originality, particularly by younger artists and makers needing to get their work known by a wider audience. (See also Gossipgate Garden Gallery, Carlisle).
Sales: Work sold; Credit card
The Space: The main wall has 6m linear hanging space. There are four screens 2.4m high x 1.2m wide and two screens 2.4x.6m. The craft display area is 3 square metres plus two smaller areas about 1.4 square metres.
Exhibiting: [AW] Telephone Sonia Kempsey to arrange an appointment. Gallery finances insurance, publicity, list of exhibits, preview and charges 25-33.3% commission.
Access: [U][T] Keswick - Newcastle bus route; Public car parks and buses 5 mins

Alton (Hampshire)

(SA) Map7 SU73

Allen Gallery

Run by the Hampshire County Museums Service housing an English ceramics collection and a temporary exhibitions gallery. [VA,Ph,Cr]
Address: Church Street, Alton, Hampshire tel 0420 82802
Contact: Exhibitions Officer Jo Bailey, Hampshire County Museums Service, Chilcomb House, Chilcomb Lane, Winchester, Hampshire SO23 8RD tel 0962 846315
Open: Tues-Sat 10-5
Policy: This temporary exhibitions gallery is one of six galleries housed within museums throughout Hampshire. It receives six or seven touring exhibitions a year, about four of which include work by living artists or makers with a bias towards those living or working in or near Hampshire. It also holds two or three local exhibitions generated by local individuals or groups, such as camera clubs, art clubs and quilting groups. Exhibitions last five weeks and exhibiting artists are encouraged to give talks, demonstrations or workshops.
Sales: Work sold
The Space: An 'L' shaped gallery 8x7m on longest side with 25m linear hanging space, spot lights on track, direct fixing to hessian covered panels. Display cases and gallery plans available. Small garden occasionally available for outdoor displays.
Exhibiting: [AW] Applications in writing, accompanied by transparencies to Exhibitions Officer. The Museums Service pays for insurance, printing and mailing of publicity and transport. Commission is 20% plus VAT.
Access: [F] Temporary exhibitions gallery **[X]** Some permanent galleries. Near town centre; Public car park 2 mins

Altrincham (Cheshire)

(NWA) Map4 SJ78

South Manchester Gallery

A gallery on the Crafts Council's selected list which shows leading makers from throughout the country. [Cr]

Address: 140 Ashley Road, Altrincham, Cheshire WA14 2UN tel 061 941 6244
Contact: Audrey Love
Open: Mon-Sat 9.30-5.30
Policy: The regular displays are linked with a changing exhibition programme in the side gallery.
Access: BR Hale 10 mins

Ambleside (Cumbria)

(NA) Map3 NY30

Dexterity

Commercial gallery opened in 1988. [VA,Cr]

Address: Kelsick Road, Ambleside, Cumbria LA22 0BZ tel 05394 34045
Contact: Roger & Gillean Bell
Open: Daily 9.30-6; Closed Thurs out of season
Policy: The gallery aims to exhibit, facilitate commissions, and sell contemporary work by artists and makers from all over the UK, including 'adventurous work', appealing both to residents and visitors to the area. Framing service.
Sales: Work sold; Credit scheme; Credit card
The Space: The gallery is 8x8x3m high with 18m linear hanging space. Lighting is by spotlights and there are two showcases 1x2m high. Gallery plans available.
Exhibiting: [AW] Send photos or slides with details of size, medium and trade price or write or telephone for an appointment. Gallery provides insurance, publicity, list of exhibits and takes a commission of around 35%. Supports EPR in principle.
Access: [F] Gallery faces central car park; Bus station 5 mins

Dexterity: porcelain Bowl by Jane Smith, 24cm diameter

Amesbury (Wiltshire)

(SA) Map7 SU14

Amesbury Library

Gallery run by Wiltshire Library and Museum Service. [VA,Ph,Cr]

Address: Smithfield Street, Amesbury, Salisbury, Wiltshire SP4 7AL tel 0980 23491
Contact: Librarian
Open: Mon & Thurs 2-7, Tues & Sat 10-5, Fri 10-1 & 2-7
The Space: Gallery is 6x8m with 14m linear hanging space and four showcases. Hanging is by rods and there are spots and natural light. The space is also used for meetings. 15% commission charged.
Exhibiting: [AW].

Andover (Hampshire)

(SA) Map7 SU34

Andover Museum

Run by Hampshire County Museums Service. Contains galleries covering natural history, local history, English glass and the story of the Tasker Works. Next door to the Museum of the Iron Age. [VA,Ph,Cr]

Address: 6 Church Close, Andover, Hampshire SP10 1DP tel 0264 66283
Contact: Exhibitions Officer Jo Bailey, Hampshire County Museums Service, Chilcomb House, Chilcomb Lane, Winchester, Hampshire SO23 8RD tel 0962 846315
Open: Tues-Sat 10-5
Policy: This temporary exhibitions gallery is one of six galleries housed within museums throughout Hampshire, run by Hampshire County Council. It receives six or seven touring exhibitions per year, about four of which include work by living artists or craftspeople with a bias towards those living or working in or near Hampshire. It also holds two or three local exhibitions generated by local individuals or groups such as camera clubs, art clubs and quilting groups. The exhibitions are shown for five weeks. Exhibiting artists are encouraged to give talks, demonstrations or workshops.
Sales: Work sold
The Space: Gallery plans and display cases available. Direct fixing to hessian-covered panels. One gallery 8x5.5m, 24m linear hanging space. Spots on tracking.
Exhibiting: Applications in writing, accompanied by transparencies, welcome by Exhibitions Officer. The museums service covers cost of insurance, printing, mailing and transport. Commission on work sold 20% plus VAT on commission.
Access: [S] Temporary exhibitions gallery, **[X]** Some permanent galleries. Town centre site; Free parking

Hampshire County Library

A public library showing mostly paintings and drawings and small craft work by local artists. [Pa,Dr,Ph,Cr]

Address: Andover, Hampshire SP10 1LT tel 0264 52807

Open: Mon, Tues, Thurs, Fri 10-7, Sat 9.30-4
Policy: The primary aim of the exhibitions, which run for two to four weeks, is *'to enliven the library premises and to provide an outlet for local talent. Income generation is not the major consideration'* for an audience which is mainly the library clientele.
Sales: Work sold
The Space: An exhibition wall 8m long x 3m high, plus 3 double sided boards each 1.6x0.8m. 2 display cases.
Exhibiting: [AW] Applications to the Senior Librarian. Exhibitors are responsible for hanging their own work and the gallery charges 10% commission.
Access: [L]

Ashford (Kent)

(SEA) Map7 TR04

Ashford Library Gallery

This gallery has a broadly-based visual arts and crafts programme featuring artists who have a particular relevance or connection to the area as well as regional and national touring shows. [VA,Cr]
Address: Church Road, Ashford, Kent TN23 1QX tel 0233 620649
Contact: Group Librarian David Mole
Open: Mon-Tues 9.30-6, Thurs-Fri 9.30-7, Wed 9.30-5,Sat 9-5
Policy: The gallery aims to promote the work of living artists from the region in shows lasting approximately three weeks, about half of which are solo exhibitions. Designed to *'educate, inform and entertain'*, shows target an audience drawn from a cross-section of residents and visitors to Kent. There is an annual residency and related education programme.
Sales: Work sold
The Space: 11x6x3.5m with 50m linear hanging space by direct fixing or screen hanging with track-mounted spot lights.
Exhibiting: [AW] Apply to Group Librarian 15 months in advance enclosing slides/photographs and biography. The gallery finances insurance, list of exhibits and mail-out of publicity. Support in principle for EPR. Commission 15%.
Access: [X] BR Ashford 5 mins; Public car park 2 and 5 mins

Ashford-in-the-Water (Derbyshire)

(EMA) Map5 SK16

Tithe Barn Gallery

A private gallery promoting fine art and craft. [VA,Cr]
Address: Ashford-in-the-Water, Bakewell, Derbyshire DE4 1QF tel 062 981 2157
Contact: Jill Hopkins
Open: Mon-Sat 11-5, Sun 2-5 during exhibitions
Policy: *'To promote excellence in whatever form for living artists with an interpretive view.'*
Sales: Work sold
The Space: Work sold from within a permanent exhibition setting.
Exhibiting: Commission and costs charged.
Access: [F]

Ashington (Northumberland)

(NA) Map2 NZ28

Woodhorn Church Museum

Local authority museum with a permanent collection of local history and monthly exhibitions of visual arts and crafts. [VA,Cr,Ph]
Address: Woodhorn Village, Near Ashington, Northumberland NE63 tel 0670 817371
Contact: Chief Leisure and Publicity Officer Mr G R Stephenson, Wansbeck District Council, Town Hall, Ashington, Northumberland NE63 8RX tel 0670 81444
Open: Wed-Sun 10-12.30, 1-4
Policy: The programme is built up partly from established touring circuits and partly by negotiation with individual artists and makers. Whenever possible artists are invited to talk about their work. Demonstrations by leading makers, covering both traditional and contemporary crafts are a regular feature in the Museum. Educational visits by schools and colleges are an integral part of the exhibition programme.
Sales: Work sold
The Space: Two-dimensional work is mounted on 20 panels 2x1.3m. Craft work is shown in eight display cases. Tungsten spot lights and controlled environment.
Exhibiting: [AW] Applications in writing to the Chief Leisure and Publicity Officer. The Museum covers costs of insurance, printing and mailing of publicity. Commission is 15%.
Access: [U][T] Buses from Newcastle Haymarket; Car park on site

Aylesbury (Buckinghamshire)

(BA) Map7 SP81

Buckinghamshire County Museum

The gallery is run by Buckinghamshire County Council and is housed in the County Museum headquarters. [VA,Ph,Cr]
Address: Church Street, Aylesbury, Buckinghamshire HP20 tel 0296 82158
Contact: Exhibition Officer GE Peter Laws, Milton Keynes Exhibition Gallery, 555 Silbury Boulevard, Milton Keynes, MK9 3EL tel 0908 605536
Open: Mon-Fri 10am-5pm, Sat 10-5 closed 12.30-1.30
Policy: The programme covers a wide range of topics, history, natural history, scientific exhibitions, as well as contemporary art and historical art exhibitions. Approximately a quarter of the exhibitions feature the work of contemporary artists and makers.
Sales: Work sold
The Space: 10x4x3m gallery giving 32m linear hanging space with direct fixing and track lighting. Showcases are available and a grassed area to the rear of the building is occasionally used.
Exhibiting: [AW] Slides or photographs should be sent to the Exhibition Officer. The gallery provides insurance, publicity, mailing, transport, list of exhibits and preview.

A commission of 25% is charged on sales.

Access: **[S]** Car parks 10 mins; Bus station 10 mins; BR Aylesbury 15 mins

Queens Park Centre (The Gallery)

A community arts centre with a programme of participation activities and regular touring theatre. [VA,Cr,Ph,LA]

Address: Queens Park Road, Aylesbury, Buckinghamshire P21 7RT tel 0296 24332

Contact: MD Thackwray

Open: Mon-Sat 10-6

Policy: Two galleries in the centre are used for a wide variety of exhibitions. The centre specialises in being a 'first time' gallery for younger artists and makers particularly from the region. Great emphasis is put on making the exhibitions accessible to an audience lacking in 'fine art experience'.

Sales: Work sold; size 8x8x4m

The Space: The Gallery is the main space with good natural light, and good artificial lighting (8x8x4m). The Subway Gallery, which is 6x3x2m, has good artificial light. A large internally-lit showcase is available.

Exhibiting: **[AW]** Applications should be made to the Director. A commission of 15% is charged on sales, and the centre provides insurance, publicity and a list of exhibits.

Access: **[U][T]** Own car park; Town centre bus station and BR Aylesbury 5 mins

Aylsham (Norfolk)

(EA) Map5 TG12

Gallery at Bacon's Bookshop

Bookshop with gallery in large converted bakehouse behind. [Pa,Sc]

Address: 17 White Hart Street, Aylsham, Norfolk NR11 6HG tel 0263 734240

Contact: Partner Helen Bacon

Open: Mon-Sat 9-1 & 2-5 Wed 9-1

Policy: *'Essentially a local gallery, but artists coming from an increasingly wide area.'* All types of work considered but *'we have not been successful in selling abstract paintings.'* A continuing programme of three-week exhibitions by living artists.

Sales: Work sold

The Space: 11x3.45x2.35m high. 11m linear space available for solo shows, 5m reserved for work of gallery artists. Plus three blocks 0.46m square by 1.9m high. Unsuitable for exhibition of fragile objects.

Exhibiting: **[AW]** Write or telephone for an appointment. Two-year waiting list. Gallery pays for insurance, publicity costs and preview. Commission 30%.

Access: **[S]** Parking nearby

Banbury (Oxfordshire)

(SA) Map7 SP44

Mill (The)

A community arts centre for social, recreational and educational activities, with a commitment to community education. [VA,Ph,Cr,LA]

Address: Spiceball Park, Banbury, Oxfordshire OX16 8QE tel 0295 52050

Contact: Tony Snee

Open: Open most daytimes and evenings; closed Christmas Day & New Year's Day

Policy: The Mill is a resource for use by the local community in Banbury and the surrounding area, the development of the arts is seen as a priority. Support, encouragement and guidance are offered by the staff at the centre. The exhibitions normally run for three weeks and exhibitors are encouraged to take part in workshops, talks and demonstrations. The centre also houses meetings of local clubs and societies.

Sales: Sales referred to exhibitor

The Space: A range of different areas is available, the largest one being 9m square. There is no permanent hanging system or additional lighting and work must be capable of going up stairs and through normal-sized doors.

Exhibiting: Artists are responsible for installing and invigilating their own work and must take responsibility for security and staffing during their exhibitions. The gallery does not pay for any exhibition costs and takes 10% commission.

Access: **[U][T][L][X]** Close to BR station and bus station

Barnard Castle (Co Durham)

(NA) Map3 NZ01

Bowes Museum

Local authority museum housing a large collection of European paintings with an extensive decorative art collection. [VA,Cr,Ph]

Address: Barnard Castle, Co Durham DL12 8NP tel 0833 690606

Contact: Curator Elizabeth Conran

Open: Mon-Sat 10-5.30, Sun 2-5 May-Sept; closes 5 March, April & Oct; closes 4 Nov-Feb

Policy: Although the museum concentrates on the fine and decorative arts up to 1900, exhibitions of 20th century art are held. These are regional group exhibitions or solo shows by artists and makers working in Teesdale. There are five main exhibitions a year.

The Space: The space for temporary exhibitions is 9x6.7m with screens and showcases available. There are also other areas of the building in which *'very small exhibitions can be put on a few screens or showcases'.*

Exhibiting: **[AW]** Applications are welcomed when they are within the above policy. The Museum pays. insurance, transport, installation costs within limits, handlists. Commission is negotiable.

Access: **[U][T][L]** Buses from Darlington, Bishop Auckland and Richmond; Car park

Priors

A wholefood restaurant and art and craft gallery showing fine art and crafts with a monthly exhibition programme. [VA,Cr,Ph]

Address: 7 The Bank, Barnard Castle, Co Durham DH2 21D tel 0833 38141

Contact: Mark Prior

Open: Mon-Fri 10-5, Sat 10-6; Sun 12-6.30 (Easter-Christmas)

Policy: It is a retail outlet stocking a selection of each artist's work. Only professional Northern artists and makers are shown.

Sales: Work sold; Credit card

The Space: The gallery fronts the restaurant and continues around the restaurant walls with a large captive audience.

Exhibiting: [AW] Interested artists and makers should contact Mark Prior. Exhibitions often used to introduce new artists and makers to the gallery.

Access: [F] Buses to Barnard Castle from Darlington and Bishop Auckland

Barnsley (S Yorkshire)

(YA) Map3 SE30

Barnsley Central Library

Occasional temporary exhibitions are held in a multi-purpose hall in the library, including an annual exhibition by local art societies and other local groups and the annual exhibition of students work from Barnsley College of Art and Design. [Pa,Pr,Ph,Cr,LA]

Address: Shambles Street, Barnsley, S Yorkshire S70 2JF tel 0226 283241

Priors: wholefood restaurant and gallery

Contact: Chief Librarian C E Vickers, Mon, Wed 9.30-8, Tues,Thurs, Fri 9.30-6, Sat 9.30-5

Access: [U][T][L]

Cooper Gallery

A municipal gallery with a permanent collection of European art and exhibition spaces specifically for contemporary art. [VA,Ph,Cr,LA]

Address: Church Street, Barnsley, S Yorkshire S70 2AH tel 0226 242905

Contact: Curator Claire Slattery

Open: Wed-Sun 10-5.30; Tues 1-5.30

Policy: The gallery promotes a wide-ranging and varied programme of exhibitions and events by regional and national artists and makers. It *'actively encourages work from groups and individuals which includes a strong element of social relevance and whose work is interesting and relevant to all sections of the community'*. The exhibition programme is complemented by an outreach and education programme which aims to promote the wider enjoyment, appreciation and participation in the arts throughout the region. There are an average of 28 exhibitions a year, with an emphasis on thematic shows, and exhibitions last for five weeks. The galleries are also used for adult education classes, workshops and demonstrations, performances and dance activities.

Sales: Work sold

Cooper Gallery: 'She Sells She Shells' a performance by Sally Dawson from 'Along the Lines of Resistance'

The Space: There are five galleries with a total of 106m linear hanging space, the largest space being 32m linear and the smallest is 9m linear. In addition there are six 2m high show cases and three 2m high free-standing display cases. At the rear of the gallery there is an enclosed courtyard which is used for sculpture and performances. Gallery plans are available.
Exhibiting: [EF][AW] Slides, statement, CV and group publicity, statement and any relevant material to be directed to the Curator. The gallery supports the principal of EPR and takes 20% commission on works sold.
Access: [U][T][S] BR Barnsley 2 mins

North Lodge Gallery

A commercial gallery with a permanent collection of watercolours and ceramics by gallery artists and makers and occasional temporary exhibitions. [Pa,Cr,Ce]

Address: High Hoyland Lane, Cawthorne, Barnsley, S Yorkshire S75 4AX tel 0226 790634
Contact: Owner Clarke
Open: Thurs-Sun 10-5.30
Policy: The gallery aims to provide customers with high-quality ceramics and watercolours at reasonable prices and to *'raise the level of consciousness in the arts and crafts field in the immediate area'.* The gallery mounts solo shows as well as providing a continuous display of works by gallery artists and makers.
Sales: Work sold; Credit scheme
The Space: The gallery is 3.6x6x4.8m high and is limited to showing only domestic-size works.
Exhibiting: [AW] The gallery mainly draws on the gallery artists but the owner welcomes enquiries. The principle of EPR is supported and commission is 33.3%.
Access: [S] Bus routes 235 from Huddersfield, High Hoyland stop 5 mins; 236 Barnsley-Huddersfield, Country park stop 20 mins

Barnstaple (Devon)

(SWA) Map6 SS53

Blacksell Arts Centre

A gallery part of the arts centre and theatre complex in North Devon College.

Address: Arts Centre, North Devon College, Barnstaple, Devon EX31 2BQ tel 0271 5291
Contact: Head of Creative Arts Robin Wiggins
Open: Mon-Fri 9-5.30 term-time
Policy: Main emphasis is on the work of young artists and designers.
Sales: Sales referred to exhibitor
The Space: Maximum of 50 average sized works. Limited space for sculpture but two lockable showcases for small scale 3D work.
Exhibiting: [AW] Artists meet most of their own costs including insurance. Use of the space is free and no commission is charged.
Access: [S]

Barrow-in-Furness (Cumbria)

(NA) Map3 SD16

Furness Museum

Museum illustrating all aspects of the Furness area with temporary exhibitions.

Address: Ramsden Square Barrow, Cumbria LA14 1LL tel 0229 20650
Contact: Curator
Open: Mon,Tues,Wed, Fri 10-5, Thurs,Sat 10-4; closed bank holidays
Policy: Exhibitions of work by local artists or of local interest.
Sales: Sales referred to exhibitors
The Space: Mainly showcases of which there are a selection and Marler Haley screens, no wall space. Spot lighting.
Exhibiting: [AW] Local artists or organisations can apply. Museum insures work, no commission charged.

Barton upon Humber (S Humberside)

(LHA) Map3 TA02

Baysgarth Museum

18th Century Form House and park with permanent displays and changing exhibitions; run by Glamford Borough Council.

Address: Baysgarth Park, Caistor Road, Barton-upon-Humber, S Humberside DN18 6AH tel 0652 32318
Contact: Curator D Williams
Open: Thurs-Sun 10-4; open bank holidays
Access: [X] Car parking

Central Studio: a gallery in a sixth-form arts centre

Basildon (Essex)

(EA) Map7 TQ69

Pitsea Library

Exhibition space in a public library, available for hire. [VA,Cr]

Address: Community Centre, off Maydells, Pitsea, Essex SS13 3DU tel 0268 552884
Contact: Madeleine Fouch
Open: Mon 2-7, Tues, Sat 9-5, Wed, Fri 9-7
Sales: Work sold; Sales referred to exhibitor
The Space: Floor area of 20 square metres.
Exhibiting: [AW].
Access: [F]

Basingstoke (Hampshire)

(SA) Map7 SU65

Central Studio

A gallery within a sixth-form college arts centre and theatre showing Southern Arts touring exhibitions and other temporary exhibitions. [Pa,Pr,Dr,Ph]

Address: Cliddesden Road, Basingstoke, Hampshire RG14 3HF tel 0256 479221
Contact: Exhibitions Organiser Paul Tong tel 0256 20861 ext 158
Open: Mon-Fri 9-4 & 7.30-9.30
Policy: *'...the general policy is that the space is used for the exhibition of the work of living artists and makers working in a variety of media and contexts. Included are exhibitions by professionals as well as amateurs and students and as the space is open to the general public, theatre goers and sixth form students, it is a deliberate policy to show a wide range of work. Last year, of nine exhibitions of work by living artists, six were sold'.* The centre has close links with the local community and has a national reputation for theatre and performance.
Sales: Work sold
The Space: The corridor/foyer and bar area provides 10m linear hanging space plus 28.1m linear on boards which are divided in twelve panels. Spot lights are available throughout. The space is not presently suitable for sculpture. Gallery plans available.
Exhibiting: [AW] Contact the Exhibitions Organiser. The gallery pays for insurance, printing and mailing of publicity and a catalogue or exhibition card and provides licensed pay bar for previews. Commission is 10%.
Access: [F] Town centre 10 mins; Free car park

Willis Museum

Museum run by the Hampshire County Museums Service housing collections of clocks, watches, toys, embroideries, with a local history and natural history gallery, and showing temporary exhibitions. [VA,Ph,Cr]

Address: Market Place, Basingstoke, Hampshire tel 0256 465902
Contact: Exhibitions Officer Jo Bailey, Hampshire County Museums Service, Chilcomb House, Chilcomb Lane, Winchester, Hampshire SO23 8RD tel 0962 846315
Open: Tues-Fri 10-5, Sat 10-4
Policy: This temporary exhibitions gallery is one of six galleries housed within museums throughout Hampshire. It receives six or seven touring exhibitions a year, about four of which include work by living artists or makers with a bias towards those living or working in or near Hampshire. It also holds two or three local exhibitions generated by local individuals or groups, such as camera clubs, art clubs and quilting groups. Exhibitions last five weeks and exhibiting artists are encouraged to give talks, demonstrations or workshops.
Sales: Work sold
The Space: One gallery 7x9m with about 25m linear hanging space (undergoing improvements), direct fixing to hessian covered panels. Gallery plans and display cases available.
Exhibiting: [AW] Applications in writing, accompanied by transparencies to Exhibitions Officer. The Museums Service pays for insurance, printing and mailing of publicity and transport. Commission is 20% plus VAT.
Access: [S] Temporary exhibitions gallery, **[X]** Some permanent galleries. Town centre site; Public car park 5 mins

Bath (Avon)

(SWA) Map6 ST76

Artsite Gallery

A public gallery showing contemporary work by invited artists. [VA]

Address: Linley House, 1 Pierrepont Place, Bath, Avon BA1 1JY tel 0225 60394/61659
Contact: Director Sean Kelly
Open: Tues-Sun 10-30-7
Policy: Artsite's aims are to exhibit contemporary visual art of local national and international significance to the widest cross-section of the public. Artsite aims to enhance understanding and enjoyment and to encourage involvement and participation.
Sales: Work sold; Credit scheme
Access: BR Bath 2 mins

Beaux Arts

Beaux Arts is a commercial gallery dealing in Twentieth century British paintings, sculpture and ceramics. [Pa,Sc,Cr,Ce]

Address: 13 York Street, Bath, Avon BA1 1NG tel 0225 64850
Contact: Reg and Patricia Singh
Open: Mon-Sat 10-5
Policy: The gallery holds a continuous changing stock of work by prominent painters, sculptors and potters and stages eight solo exhibitions a year by well known and up-and-coming artists.
Sales: Work sold: Credit card
The Space: The gallery which comprises two storeys of a Georgian house in a terrace with white interiors and wooden floors uses four rooms, staircase and lobby for exhibitions. Gallery plans available.
Exhibiting: [AW] The gallery provides insurance, publicity, preview, list of exhibits, and catalogue/card.

Access: [F][X] City centre location close to Bath Abbey; BR Bath Spa 5 mins

CCA Galleries

A commercial gallery specialising in 'original limited edition prints'. [Pa,Pr,Sc]

Address: 5 George Street, Bath, Avon BA1 2EH tel 0225 448121

Contact: Charles Colmer

Open: Mon-Sat 9.30-6

Policy: The Bath gallery aims to *'make art as accessible to as wide an audience as possible'. 'The company is able to bring to their galleries a consistently stimulating mixture of work from artists of local and international stature, and to provide a platform for an enormous breadth of talent. The gallery will also present a regular programme of exhibitions featuring the work of contemporary artists.'*

Sales: Work sold; Credit card; Credit scheme

Exhibiting: **[AW]** A commission of 40-45% is charged on sales.

Access: **[F][S]**City centre site
centre

Cleveland Bridge Gallery

A commercial gallery with a changing display of work as well as regular monthly exhibitions. [Pa,Sc]

Address: 8 Cleveland Place East, Bath, Avon BA1 5DJ tel 0225 447885

Contact: Wayne Graham

Open: Tues-Sat 9.30am-5pm

Policy: The gallery *'attracts work from well established artists and sculptors internationally and represents younger artists working locally in smaller shows.'* The exhibition spaces are large enough to display substantial retrospective shows of academic importance and wide appeal.

Sales: Work sold; Credit card; Credit scheme

The Space: The gallery has 60m linear hanging space with spots and flood lighting. An extra 20-25m are also available in other rooms. Gallery plans available.

Exhibiting: **[AW]** Apply to Wayne Graham with slides and CV. The gallery provides insurance and publicity. A 40% commission is charged on sales.

Access: **[F]** City centre site

F Stop Photography Gallery

A community photography project with a 'non-political, non-discriminatory' policy for its exhibitions and darkrooms. [Ph]

Address: 2 Longacre, London Road, Bath, Avon BA1 5NL tel 0225 316922

Contact: Joint Co-ordinators Vicky Putler, Nic Smith

Open: Mon-Fri 10-5.30

Policy: The gallery generally shows young photographers' first or second exhibitions *'particularly for South West photographers'*. The programme contains one show a year for darkroom members, and one from foreign students. Regular courses and workshops are arranged for schools and handicapped groups with the work being exhibited during the year.

Sales: Work sold; Sales referred to exhibitor

The Space: Main Gallery has 16m linear hanging space and a further 13m linear on screens. Spots and natural light. Gallery plans available.

Exhibiting: **[AW]** Applications are considered once a year with a flexible late summer deadline. Insurance, publicity, transport and preview are provided by the gallery. EPR supported.

Access: **[U][T][F]** Bus 3 and 13 from bus station to Snow Hill; BR Bath Spa 20 mins

Glass Designs Gallery

A gallery on the Crafts Council's selected list specialising in exhibiting British studio glass. [Gl]

Address: 17 Barton Street, Bath, Avon BA1 1HQ tel 0225 462601

Contact: Director Martin Lusmore

Open: Mon-Fri 9.30-5.30, Sat 9.30-6; closed Mon Jan, Feb

Policy: The gallery houses the foremost collection of British studio glass. Normally the work of around 70 artists and studios, both established and newly-emerging is exhibited in an ever-changing display encompassing a wide variety of work, functional, decorative and sculptural. Four major exhibitions are held annually.

Sales: Work sold; Credit card

The Space: The gallery runs to 77 square metres and work is exhibited on glass shelving and plinths. Good artificial and natural lighting.

Exhibiting: **[AW]** Artists and makers are welcome to contact the gallery. Exhibition space is available to overseas artists in studio glass as well as those from the UK.

Access : **[F]** City centre site; Public car park 4 mins

Hitchcocks

A commercial gallery above a craft shop showing high-quality craftwork by contemporary makers. [Cr]

Address: 10 Chapel Row, Off Queen's Square, Bath, Avon BA1 1HN tel 0225 330646

Contact: F & J Hitchcocks

Open: Mon-Sat 10-5.30

Policy: The gallery has a varied programme of thematic and group exhibitions. Joyce and Fleur Hitchcock also run a shop in Alresford, Hampshire and try to *'reply as quickly as possible to being sent details of work'*. See also Alresford.

Sales: Work sold; Credit card

The Space: Gallery one is 2.6x1.4x2m with 6.9m linear hanging space, gallery two is 3x3.2x2m with 9.4m linear hanging space and gallery three is 4.9x3.7x2m with 12m linear hanging space. Low voltage halogen lighting.

Exhibiting: **[AW]** Avoid the Autumn/Christmas period when applying to exhibit. Insurance, publicity, preview, list of exhibits, catalogue/card provided by the gallery. A 33.3% commission is charged on sales.

Access: **[X]** Bath city centre 5 mins

Holburne Museum & Crafts Study Centre

Elegant 18th century building housing an excellent collection of 17th & 18th century fine art and decorative art as well as work by 20th century British makers including Bernard Leach. [Cr]

Address: Great Pulteney Street, Bath, Avon BA2 4DB tel 0225 66669
Contact: Curator Barley Roscoe
Open: Mon-Sat 11-5, Sun 2.30-6; closed mid-Dec to mid-Feb and Mons Nov to Easter
Policy: Temporary exhibitions are also shown.

Peter Hays Contemporary Art

A commercial gallery and studio complex with exhibitions, pottery demonstrations, poetry readings, puppet shows and music. [VA,Ph,Cr]

Address: 2 Cleveland Bridge, Bath, Avon BA1 5DH tel 0225 66215
Contact: Peter Hays
Open: Mon-Sat 9.30-5.30
Policy: The gallery is run *'as simply as possible using the expertise of others, and the artists themselves'* and promotes a stable of artists.
Sales: Work sold; Credit card
The Space: Top Gallery 5x6x2.5m giving 11m linear hanging space and the hallway and Lower Gallery have 9m linear hanging space.
Exhibiting: A 33.3% commission is charged on sales.
Access: [U][T][F] 15 mins city centre

Rooksmoor Gallery

A private gallery showing nine exhibitions a year predominantly solo shows by the gallery artists. Also ceramics and ceramic sculpture. [Pa,Sc,Pr,Ce]

Rooksmoor Gallery: 'Provencal Street' by Nigel Casseldine, oil on gesso

Address: 31 Brock Street, Bath, Avon BA1 2LN tel 0225 20495
Contact: Robin Lipsey
Open: Mon-Sat 10-5.30
Policy: Work shown *'is always by living artists who have a clearly-developed personal style. Work must be on a domestic scale of the kind that educated people with good taste like to live with'.*
Sales: Work sold; Credit card
The Space: The gallery has 18m linear hanging space with a height of 3m and track lighting and natural light. Three wall and two central display cases are available. The maximum picture size is 1.2x0.9m.
Exhibiting: [AW] Slides and CV required. Artist makes a contribution of £120 towards insurance, publicity, preview and catalogue/card. A 33.3% commission is charged on sales.
Access: [F] Situated close to the Circus and Crescent

RPS National Centre of Photography

The headquarters of the Royal Photographic Society, with collections and temporary exhibitions. [Ph,LA]

Address: Milsom Street, Bath, Avon BA1 1DN tel 0225 62841
Contact: Amanda Nevill
Open: Daily 9.30-5.30; last admission 5
Policy: A permanent collection of mainly 19th century work is displayed as well as temporary exhibitions of *'Contemporary greats, classical solo shows, touring exhibitions from major galleries, historical, theme/educational and young photographers'.* The centre runs an education programme of talks, lectures, films and workshops.
Sales: Work sold; Credit card
The Space: *'Too complex to outline'.* Environmental conditions are monitored. Gallery plans available.
Exhibiting: [AW] Contact Carole Sartain. The centre provides Insurance, transport, publicity, preview, list of exhibits and catalogue/card. EPR *'potentially supportable'.*
Access: [U][T][L] BR Bath Spa 10 mins

Saint James's Gallery

A commercial art and crafts gallery showing three group exhibitions a year with a changing display of work. At time of going to press this gallery was moving and looking for new premises. For information telephone 0225 337493. [Pa,Pr,Ce,Je]

Address: tel 0225 337493
Contact: Ron and Susan Sloman
Open: Mon-Sat 10-5.30

Sladebrook House

A 'country house gallery showing a personal selection of work including my own'. [Pa,Pr]

Address: 222 Englishcombe Lane, Bath, Avon BA2 2EP tel 0225 20180
Contact: John Trentham
Open: By appointment or as advertised in local press
Policy: The main exhibition is during the Bath Festival and it is possible to visit John Trentham's studio and

print workshop.
Sales: Work sold; Credit scheme
The Space: Room one is 4x6m, room two is 4.5x3m and the hallway has18m linear hanging space.
Exhibiting: Artists invited for exhibition receive publicity, preview, list of exhibits and catalogue/card. A 30% commission is charged on sales.
Access: [F] Bus 10 or 11 from city centre; Ample parking

Thursday Gallery

Commercial gallery showing contemporary paintings, sculpture, prints and ceramics. [Pa,Sc,Pr,Ce]
Address: 2a York Street, Bath, Avon BA1 1NG tel 0225 66904
Contact: Christine While
Open: Mon-Sat 10-5.30 & by appointment
Policy: The gallery shows contemporary work by new and established artists with five mixed shows a year as well as mixed exhibitions by gallery artists.
Sales: Work sold; Credit card
The Space: Three floors available for exhibitions, spot lighting.
Exhibiting: [AW] Artists should contact the gallery to make appointments. It covers insurance, printing and mailing of publicity and takes commission of 40% plus VAT on sales.
Access: BR Bath & bus station 2 mins; Parking

Underground Gallery

A commercial gallery specialising in 'work by Cornish and Scottish painters and sculptors, some ceramics'. [Pa,Pr,Ph]
Address: 72-74 Walcot Street, Bath, Avon BA1 5BD tel 0225 62546
Contact: Director Rupert Blunt
Open: Tues-Sat 10.30-4.30 and by appointment
Policy: *'It is our policy to seek out and promote painters and sculptors who we consider to be at a stage in their career where a one or possibly two man exhibition would be beneficial in advancing their career'.*
Sales: Work sold; Credit scheme
The Space: The gallery has two spaces each with 20m linear hanging space and variable lighting.
Exhibiting: [AW] Apply to the Director. The gallery is hired at £100 per week and insurance, publicity, preview, list of exhibits and a catalogue/card are provided. A commission of 33.3% is charged on sales and the gallery supports EPR.
Access: [X] City centre site

Victoria Art Gallery

A municipal gallery operated by Bath City Council with a permanent collection of fine and decorative art and a programme of temporary exhibitions. [VA]
Address: Bridge Street, Bath, Avon BA2 4AT tel 0225 461111 ext 2772
Contact: Curator Bath Museum Service Stephen Bird, 4 Circus, Bath, Avon tel 0225 461111 ext 2760
Open: Mon-Fri 10-6, Sat 10-5; Closed Suns and bank holidays
Policy: *'Eight to ten major exhibitions are held a year of fine and decorative art, both historic, thematic and contemporary'.* The *'small gallery is used for small-scale displays of work by individual artists, usually living, but generally of local connection or interest'.*
Sales: Work sold
The Space: The main gallery has 90m linear hanging space and the small gallery 27m linear hanging space with full environmental controls and direct fixing used. Gallery plans available.
Exhibiting: [AW] Apply to Victoria Barwell, Arts Officer, Victoria Gallery, Bridge Street, Bath with slides, photographs, catalogues of previous exhibitions and exhibition proposal. The gallery provides insurance, publicity, preview, list of exhibits, catalogue/card, transport and mailing. A 15% commission is charged on sales.
Access: [X] Walcot Street car park 5 mins; BR Bath Spa 10 mins

York Street Gallery

A commercial gallery with a changing display of work and occasional exhibitions of *'contemporary work by younger artists'. 'No particular locality, no prints, all original work.' [Pa,Sc]*
Address: 12 York Street, Bath, Avon BA1 1NS tel 0225 447399
Contact: J Bentham-Dinsdale
Open: Mon-Sat 10.30-5.30; or by appointment; closed Jan/Feb
Sales: Work sold; Credit card
Exhibiting: [AW] Apply to J Bentham-Dinsdale. The gallery provides insurance, publicity, preview, list of exhibits, catalogue/card, and charges a commission of 40% on sales.
Access: [F][X] City centre location

Batley (W Yorkshire)

(YA) Map3 SE22

Bagshaw Museum

A municipal museum with collections of ethnography, egyptology, oriental, fine and decorative arts and natural history and two galleries for temporary

Sladebrook House: 'Sladebrook House and the Magnolia tree' by John Trentham, oil 24"x3"

exhibitions. [VA,Ph,Cr]

Address: Wilton Park, Batley, W Yorkshire WF17 OAS tel 0924 472514

Contact: Curator Brian Haigh

Open: Mon-Sat 10-5; Sun 1-5

Policy: *'The museum displays a wide variety of objects which are the starting point for the temporary exhibitions but other shows of contemporary art have been organised which have used crafts from South East Asia and the Caribbean'.* Lectures, demonstrations, craft workshops and general educational activities are organised to complement the exhibitions of which there are an average of eight a year, three of which may be by contemporary artists and each exhibition lasts for six weeks.

The Space: There are two galleries of 9x8x7m high and 4.5x4.5x4m high. Additional flat, counter and upright showcases are available.

Exhibiting: [AW][EF] Slides and information should be sent to the Curator, the gallery covers exhibition costs and supports the principal of EPR.

Access: [U][T] Ground floor. BR Batley 30 mins; Buses 226,251,252,281,282,229,283,220

Batley Art Gallery

A municipal gallery run by Kirklees Leisure Services with changing exhibitions throughout the year. [Pa,Sc,Pr,Ph]

Address: Batley Library, Market Place, Batley, W Yorkshire WF17 5DA

Contact: Robert Hall, Huddersfield Art Gallery, Princess Alexander Walk, Huddersfield tel 0484 513808 ext 216

Open: Mon-Fri 10-6, Sat 10-4

Policy: The gallery tends to show work which has immediate local associations and hopes to encourage local artists and makers to show their work.

The Space: The exhibition space is 9x9m with 16m linear hanging space and direct fixing to walls, spots, fluorescent and natural light.

Exhibiting: [AW] Artists and makers should send slides to Robert Hall at Huddersfield Art Gallery. The gallery covers all exhibition costs and shares the cost of the preview and artists' travel expenses. The gallery takes l0% commission on works sold.

Access: [X] Parking

Oakwell Hall County Park

A municipal gallery and country park with responsibility for the care, display and maintenance of the historic hall and the permanent collection. [Ph,Cr]

Address: Nutter Lane, Birstall, Batley, W Yorkshire WF17 9LG tel 0924 474926

Contact: Senior Curator Jane Glaister

Open: Mon-Sat 10-5; Sun 1-5

Policy: The introduction of an exhibition programme into the hall is a new development and many areas of policy remain undefined. In the first year the hall showed a total of four exhibitions one of which was of contemporary art. It is the intention that each exhibition will run for a period of three months and should complement the permanent collection.

The Space: The exhibition space is divided into two rooms of 9x4m and 6x6m each with track lighting.

Exhibiting: The policy for inviting applications is under review.

Access: Car parking nearby

Beaford (Devon)

(SWA) Map6 SS51

Beaford Centre

A rural arts centre with residential courses, theatre and dance. [Pa,Pr,Dr,Ph,Cr,LA]

Address: Beaford, Winkleigh, Devon EX19 8LU tel 08053 201

Contact: Programme Manager Rick Bond

Open: Mon-Fri 9-5

Policy: The centre is *'very restricted by its year-round use by residential courses'.* Temporary exhibitions follow a theme and alternate with exhibitions from the Beaford photography archive. Demonstrations are arranged with exhibitions.

The Space: Depends on residential courses booked.

Exhibiting: [AW] The centre provides insurance, publicity, and transport. EPR supported.

Access: [F] Public transport from Exeter, Torrington and Barnstaple

Bebington (Merseyside)

(MA) Map4 SJ38

Bebington Central Library

Exhibition room with pegboard and hessian walls separate from and on first floor of large library showing work by local amateur artists and groups as well as taking exhibitions from North West Museum and Gallery Service and Merseyside Exhibitions. [VA,Ph,Cr]

Address: Bebington Civic Centre, Civic Way, Bebington, Merseyside L63 7PN tel 051 645 2080

Contact: Librarian Peter Sarjeant tel 051 645 2080 ext 4131

Open: Mon-Fri 10-8, Sat 10-5

Policy: Offers exhibition area for use by any person or body to promote or sell works of art and of educational interest. Most exhibitions are two weeks to one month long and feature living artists. A reasonable standard of work is desirable. The library has a permanent collection and offers a picture loan facility.

Sales: Sales referred to exhibitor

The Space: 25m linear run of 1.2m pegboard with track lighting. Room is occasionally used for local arts association functions. Gallery plans available.

Exhibiting: [AW] To Librarian. Library will provide list of exhibits. Commission is 15%.

Access: [X] Buses 10,18,110,112,119,164,165; Merseyrail Bebington station 15 mins; Car park at rear of library 2 mins

Bedford (Bedfordshire)

(EA) Map7 TL04

Bedford Central Library

Part of public library run by Bedfordshire Leisure Services. [VA,Ph,Cr]

Address: Harpur Street, Bedford, Bedfordshire MK40 1PG tel 0234 50931
Contact: Arts Officer or Group Librarian Su Kiteley or Nick Wilde
Open: Mon 11-7, Tues-Fri 9.30-7, Sat 9.30-4.30
Policy: *'To provide an accessible, widely-seen exhibition space for local artists at low cost and via touring exhibitions, to bring to Bedfordshire high-quality works of art which the public might otherwise not see.'* Programme of lectures and demonstrations by artists. Exhibitions run for three to four weeks, mainly mixed and group.
Sales: Sales referred to exhibitor
The Space: 5x5x2m high, total linear space 26m. Some movable walls. Two sets of spot lamps. Three glass-topped cases 1.5x0.75x0.25m deep. Suitable for *'C'* category exhibitions only. Gallery plans available.
Exhibiting: [AW] In writing with slides. Gallery pays printing and mailing of publicity. Hanging fee of £1 per item. No commission charged.
Access: [U][T][L] Bus stop outside, BR 10mins, Car park 5mins

Bromham Mill Art Gallery

Local authority owned, restored water mill. [VA,Cr,Ph]

Address: Bromham Mill, Bromham, Bedford, Bedfordshire MK43
Contact: Sue Readman, Leisure Services Department, Bedfordshire County Council, County Hall, Bedford MK42 9AP tel 0234 228342/228330
Open: Wed-Fri 10.30-4.30, Sat-Sun & Mon bank holiday 11.30-6 (April-October only)
Policy: Deliberate leaning towards non-commercial work by local professional artists, although *'outsiders'* are welcome. Local audience, including school groups but also advertises nationally. Artists are encouraged to work at the mill during exhibitions.
Sales: Sales referred to exhibitor
The Space: 12.5x4.75x2.5high & 10x2.6x2.5high. Total hanging space 20m. Three rows of battens at 2.25m, 1.75m, 1.5m. Two lighting tracks with floods and spots. Four small windows and a skylight.
Exhibiting: [AW] by letter with slides/photos. Finance available for publicity, mailing and catalogue. Commission 10%.
Access: [X] Buses 130,133,X3; On A428 Bedford-Cambridge

Cecil Higgins Art Gallery

Victorian mansion house with excellent permanent collection of arts and crafts. Adjoining extension with fine collections of watercolours, prints, drawings, ceramics, glass and lace. [VA,Cr]

Address: Castle Close, Bedford, Bedfordshire MK40 3NY tel 0234 211222
Contact: Curator Halina Grubert
Open: Tues-Fri 12.30-5, Sat 11-5, Sun 2-5
Policy: *'Nearly all the works on display are selected from our own collections'.* Exceptions may be considered for outside exhibitors.
Sales: Works not for sale
Access: [U][T][L] Adjacent large car park

Belford (Northumberland)

(NA) Map2 NU13

Brent Gallery

An artist-run commercial gallery with a changing display of work by wild-life artists. [VA,Cr]

Address: Fenham-le-Moor, Near Belford, Northumberland NE70 7PN tel 06683 533
Contact: David Binns
Open: Mon-Fri 10.30-6
Policy: Its policy is to *'exhibit the best in wild-life and make available the work of top artists in the North'* for *'people who appreciate and love the countryside and its living creatures, and collect works of art'.*
Sales: Work sold; Credit card
The Space: The gallery can hang 50 - 60 works of average size.
Exhibiting: [AW] Write or ring David Binns in the first instance. The gallery provides insurance, publicity, preview, and catalogue/card. The gallery takes a commission of 33.3%. Supports EPR in principle.
Access: [F]

Norselands Gallery (Studio Two)

A private gallery situated in the Old School. [VA,Cr]

Address: Warrenford, Near Belford, Northumberland NE70 7HY tel 066 83 465
Contact: Partners Mr & Mrs Rawlinson
Open: Daily 9-5 (9-9 summer season); Closed two weeks Christmas
Policy: A selection of professionally hand-made crafts, original paintings, drawings and etchings. The workshops of Studio Two Ceramics making figures is open to visitors.
Sales: Work sold; Credit card
The Space: Two gallery spaces.
Exhibiting: [AW] Please ring for an appointment or send several samples or photos of work.
Access: [F] ramp. Buses infrequent; Car park

Belper (Nottinghamshire)

(EMA) Map5 SK34

Fleet Arts Project

A community arts project offering a variety of art activities and projects including exhibitions. [VA,Ph]

Address: The Old School, The Fleet, Belper, Nottinghamshire DE5 1NU tel 0773 820484
Contact: Tam Draig/Catherine Bailes
Open: Mon, Tues, Thurs, Fri 9.30-5.30 & evenings, weekends for workshops and performances
Policy: Exhibitions are either an integral part of the

project programme, of particular local community interest or giving an opportunity to local artists who would not otherwise exhibit.
Sales: Work sold
The Space: Exhibitions can be held in the hall area 6x18m and meeting room 6x6.75m which are also used for other activities.
Exhibiting: [AW] Contact the project for details.
Access: [U] Main bus routes; On Derby/Matlock rail link; 10 miles north of Derby on A6

Berwick-upon-Tweed (Northumberland)

(NA) Map2 NT95

Berwick-upon-Tweed Museum & Art Gallery

A local history museum in 18th century barrack complex with occasional temporary exhibitions and a permanent collection including treasures from the Burrell Collection - including French work by Daubigny, Gericault, Degas, Monticelli, Boudin.
Address: The Clock Block, Berwick Barracks, Ravesdowne, Berwick, Northumberland TD15 1DQ tel 0289 330933
Contact: Curator Richard Doughty
Open: Mon-Sat 10-12.30, 1.30-6, Sun 11-1, 2-4 April - Sept; Tues-Sat 10-12.30, 1.30-4 Oct-March
Sales: Work sold
The Space: The temporary exhibition gallery has extensive hanging space.
Exhibiting: [AW] Will consider any approaches made by potential exhibitors but prefers local connections.
Access: [U][T] Ground floor. BR Berwick 10 mins; Car park adjacent

Sally Port Gallery

A commercial gallery housed in the same building as a wholefood shop and antiquarian bookstore. [Pa,Pr,Dr]
Address: 48 Bridge Street, Berwick-upon-Tweed, Northumberland TD15 1AQ tel 0289 307749
Contact: Director Derek Jones
Open: Mon-Sat 10-4; closed Thurs, Sun
Policy: The gallery has changing displays of realistic work, mainly of local views, by a group of artists; mostly watercolours but also some etchings and screenprints. The gallery also provides tuition in etching and figure drawing.
Sales: Work sold; Credit card
The Space: The gallery offers about 24m linear hanging space.
Exhibiting: [AW] Contact Derek Jones. Charges commission of 33.3%.
Access: [X]

Three Feathers Gallery

Commercial gallery showing a changing display of work.
Address: 83c Marygate, Berwick-upon-Tweed, Northumberland TD15 1BA tel 0289 307642
Sales: Work sold
Exhibiting: [AW] Open to approaches. They don't put on exhibitions but will find space for work they like.

Beverley (Humberside)

(LHA) Map3 TA03

Beverley Art Gallery & Museum

A municipal gallery.
Address: Champney Road, Beverley, N Humberside HU17 9BQ tel 0482 882255
Contact: Roy Gregory, Beverley Borough Council, The Hall, Lairgate, Beverley, N Humberside HU17 8HL
Open: Mon-Fri 9.30-5, Thurs 9.30-12, Sat 9.30-4
Policy: Exhibitions of contemporary work, schools, local artists and loan exhibitions.

Ladygate Gallery

A privately-run art and craft gallery specialising in painting, prints, ceramics, wood and jewellery which is on the Crafts Council's selected list. [Pa,Pr,Cr]
Address: 1 Ladygate, Beverley, Humberside HU17 8BH tel 0482 869715
Contact: Director Victoria Darvill
Open: Mon-Sat 10-5, closed Thurs
Policy: The gallery sells the best of British art and crafts, from both well-known practitioners and talented newcomers and reaches an audience of professionals and collectors between 21 and 55. Permanent exhibition programme showing a mixture of two and three-dimensional work. Also offers picture framing, restoration and interior design facilities.
Sales: Work sold; Credit card
The Space: Two galleries 8x5m and two galleries 5x5m. One showcase for jewellery, one for silver and precious artifacts.
Exhibiting: [AW] To the Directors, contacts as above. Gallery pays for insurance, printing and mailing of publicity, preview costs and catalogue. Gallery adds 38% commission.
Access: [F][S] BR Beverley 10 mins; Bus station 1 min; Public car parks 1 min

Billingham (Cleveland)

(NA) Map3 NZ42

Billingham Art Gallery

Municipal gallery with a programme of changing exhibitions. [VA,Cr,Ph]
Address: Queens Way, Billingham Town Centre, Billingham, Cleveland TS23 2LN tel 0642 555443
Contact: Curator J Warbrook, Gloucester House, Church Road, Stockton, Cleveland tel 670067 2783
Open: Mon-Sat 9.30-5; closed bank holidays
Policy: To provide a mixed medium exhibition programme featuring work from the local area, national and international touring exhibitions.
Sales: Work sold from some exhibitions
The Space: Large front gallery and smaller rear extension which can be separated if not required. Total 373 square metres, 23.6m linear hanging space plus

screens if needed. Track lighting, no natural light.
Exhibiting: [AW] Write to Curator at Gloucester House and enclose visual material. Full details will then be sent if applicable.
Access: [X]

Billingshurst (W Sussex)

(SEA) Map7 TQ02

Lannards Gallery

A gallery with restaurant and pottery. [Pa,Sc,Ce,Gl]
Address: Okehurst Lane, Billingshurst, W Sussex RH4 9HR tel 040 381 2692
Contact: Director
Open: Wed-Sun 11-5
Policy: Built of deal and pine wood, the gallery is an octagonal building overlooking the Sussex Weald. It also houses a pottery workshop, a licensed restaurant and serves afternoon teas. The gallery's specialities are sculpture, ceramics and glass. Special exhibitions are held of three-dimensional work by British Studio and Guild of Sussex Craftsmen members and fine art paintings are also on show.
Sales: Work sold
Access: 25 minutes from the M25 and a mile north of Billingshurst off the A29

Billingham Art Gallery: Contemporary Czechoslovakian Glass

Bilston (W Midlands)

(WMA) Map4 SO99

Bilston Museum & Art Gallery

The gallery is operated by Wolverhampton Museum and Art Gallery. [VA]
Address: Mount Pleasant, Bilston, Wolverhampton, W Midlands WV14 7LU tel 0902 409143
Contact: Keeper of Fine Art Brendan Flynn, Wolverhampton Museum and Art Gallery, Lichfield Street, Wolverhampton tel 0902 312 032
Open: Mon-Fri 10-5
Policy: The programme is mostly local and regional artists and makers. The gallery space is reputably one of the best in the West Midlands. It houses permanent collections of local history, fine English painted enamels and 19th century paintings.
Sales: Work sold
The Space: The galleries have recently been refurbished and offer 55m linear hanging space with direct fixing, artificial and daylight.
Exhibiting: [AW]
Access: [U] Town centre location next door to library; car parking

Bingley (W Yorkshire)

(YA) Map3 SE13

Bingley Arts Centre

A small community centre founded in order to provide a local venue for mounting shows and exhibitions. [VA]

Bilston Museum & Art Gallery: Artist Mick Thacker and his work at the gallery

Address: Main Street, Bingley, W Yorkshire BD16 2LZ tel 0274 567 982
Contact: Manager
Open: Mon-Fri 8.30-5
Policy: The centre is hired out to artists or groups wishing to put on shows.

Bingley Library

A public library which has a hanging space suitable for two-dimensional art works and cases for crafts. [Pa,Ph,Cr]
Address: Myrtle Walk, Bingley, W Yorkshire BD16 tel 0274 568697
Contact: M Davies
Open: Mon-Fri 9-7.30,Tues 9-1, Sat 9-5
Policy: The space is used by local societies and individual artists as a venue for exhibitions and provides a source of inspiration and interest for the public. There are twelve mixed and solo exhibitions a year.
Sales: Works for sale
The Space: The space is 12x6x6m high with a total of 54m linear hanging space. Paintings are hung with picture hooks and the works are spotlit. Three-dimensional work can be secured in two showcases.
Exhibiting: [AW] Local artists interested in exhibiting must apply to M Davies at the library. The library will cover the costs of the list of exhibits only and takes 15% commission.
Access: [L] BR Bingley 5 mins; Car park 2 mins

Birkenhead (Merseyside)

(MA) Map4 SJ38

Birkenhead Central Library

Large library with various exhibition spaces and display facilities, showing mainly work by local amateur artists and groups, but also taking professional shows from Merseyside Exhibitions and North West Museum and Art Gallery Service. [Pa,Ph,Cr]
Address: Borough Road, Birkenhead, Merseyside L41 tel 051 652 6106
Contact: Librarian
Open: Mon-Fri 10-8, Sat 10-1, 2-5
Policy: Exhibitions must be of general interest to library users. There is no selection policy as such, but shows with an overt commercial, political or religious message may be refused. Focus on local artists and activities to provide showcase for these which may not be available elsewhere.
Sales: Work sold
The Space: Hessian-covered wall boards 1.5x7m, and some Marler Haley boards and stands. Space available for exhibitor's own boards etc. Two display cases, 1.6x1x.6m.
Exhibiting: [AW] Apply anytime by telephone, letter or in person with as much notice as possible. Library does not charge for space or equipment, exhibitor has to mount, list and insure work. Commission is 15%.
Access: [U] no toilet On main Bus Route from Merseyrail Underground Hamilton Square; Buses 80,91,191,70,71,72,64,40,42; Merseyrail Birkenhead Central 10 mins; Car park opposite

Williamson Art Gallery & Museum

Municipal gallery with the majority of space given over to permanent collection of local history, which also runs over thirty temporary exhibits a year, about a third of which are contemporary work. [VA,Ph,Cr,LA]
Address: Slatey Road, Birkenhead, Wirral, Merseyside L43 4UE tel 051 652 4177
Contact: Curator David Hillhouse
Open: Mon-Sat 10-5, Sun 2-5,Thurs 10-9
Policy: *'Our aim is to involve the gallery directly with the community of which it is a part. Besides showing work by major local and national artists, we also believe that that we have a duty to provide an opportunity for younger artists and amateurs with at least a chance to exhibit here.'* Open exhibitions are selected but offer local involvement and the gallery also has a policy of showing occasional displays by community groups; disabled, schools, colleges etc. The gallery hosts large open exhibitions and has a regular programme of concerts, talks, meetings etc.
Sales: Work sold
The Space: Varies according to exhibitions, normally at least five large galleries, all suitable for sculpture, with spotlights, wooden floors, most with daylight.
Exhibiting: [AW] Apply to Curator. Commission is 15%. Gallery covers insurance, transport, preview and publicity.
Access: [U][T] Bus 91, 92 Oxton Circular 2 mins; Other routes 5 mins; Nearest Merseyrail stations, Birkenhead Park, Birkenhead Central at least 20 mins; Car park outside

Wirral Borough Council Department of Leisure Services & Tourism

As part of this department, Wirral Libraries runs a programme of touring exhibitions. [VA,Cr]
Address: Westminster House, Hamilton Street, Birkenhead, Merseyside L41 5FN
Contact: Assistant Director Libraries & Arts Ian Coles
Policy: The exhibition programme features work from Merseyside Exhibitions, North West Museum & Art Gallery Service and occasional self-generated shows. Branch libraries at Bromborough, Eastham, Ford, Greasby, Heswell, Hoylake, Irby, Leasowe, Moreton, Rock Ferry, Seacombe, St James, Upton, West Kirby, Woodchurch, Wallasey, Bebbington and Birkenhead have temporary exhibition space and are part of the touring network. (See also Bebbington Central Library, Birkenhead Central Library).
Exhibiting: For more information on the touring exhibitions programme, contact David Ewing, Woodchurch Library, Home Farm Road, Woodchurch, Wirral, Merseyside L49 7LN, tel 051 677 8068 or Paul Ivono, Wallasey Central Library, Earlston Road, Wallasey, Merseyside tel 051 639 2334.

Birmingham (W Midlands)

(WMA) Map4 SP08

Birmingham and Midland Institute

An independent self-supporting institution with a regular programme of meetings, lectures, conferences and recitals. [Pa,Sc,Ph,Cr]

Address: 9 Margaret Street, Birmingham, W Midlands B3 3BS tel 021 236 3591

Contact: Joe Hunt

Open: Mon-Fri 9.30-6.30

Policy: The monthly exhibitions are drawn mainly from local artists and societies. The institute's membership is over 1200 and a large daily audience attends meetings and conferences. Various specialist libraries are housed there as well as a restaurant and bar.

Sales: Work sold; Credit card

The Space: The Foyer Gallery can accommodate 30 paintings and the Chandos Gallery can accommodate 24 paintings. The Library has four 2x1m double-sided screens. Show cases are available for craft exhibitions, and gallery plans are available.

Exhibiting: [AW] A list of hire charges is available from the Administrator. Insurance, printing, publicity, mailing and a list of exhibits is provided by the institute and a commission of 15% is charged on sales.

Access: [U][T][L][X] Located in the city centre close to public car parks, buses and BR Birmingham New Street

Birmingham Museum & Art Gallery

'One of Britain's most important museums with rich varied collections in a spectacular Victorian building recently restored to its pristine style and elegance'. Birmingham Museum and Art Gallery comprises the Museum & Art Gallery, Museum of Science & Industry, four heritage buildings (Weoley Castle, Blakesley Hall, Sarehole Mill, Aston Hall), and Birmingham Nature Centre. [VA,Cr]

Address: Chamberlain Square, Birmingham, W Midlands B3 3DH tel 021 235 2834

Contact: Director Michael Diamond

Open: Mon-Sat 9.30-5, Sun 2-5

Policy: The excellent and wide-ranging permanent collections are supplemented by an extensive programme of temporary exhibitions covering fine art, crafts, historical and ethnographic exhibitions. In formulating a programme of exhibitions the museum achieves a balance *'between home-produced and touring shows (eg Arts Council), local, national and international content, contemporary and earlier material, popular and more specialist content, and the demands of temporary shows and the maintenance of permanent collection displays'*. An extensive and lively education programme is run throughout the year, including artists talks, tours, workshops and residencies. A craft showcase is used for the sale of high-quality contemporary work.

Sales: Work sold; Credit card

The Space: Grade A security with humidity and light level control. The temporary exhibition space is 242 square metres giving 62m linear hanging space with direct fixing or hanging rail used. Edmunds showcases available. Gallery plans available.

Exhibiting: [EF] The gallery *'rarely if ever exhibits work submitted through applications'* due to the shortage of space, and commitments to non-contemporary shows. Artists invited to exhibit are provided with publicity, insurance, mailing and transport. EPR supported.

Access: [U][T][L] City centre location; Car parks 5 mins; bus station and BR Birmingham New Street 10mins

Birmingham Polytechnic (Concourse)

The gallery is situated in the foyer of the fine art department and is used for a wide variety of fine art exhibitions. [VA]

Address: Birmingham Polytechnic, Department of Art, Margaret Street, Birmingham, W Midlands B3 3BX tel 021 331 5972

Contact: Jean Vaudeau

Open: Mon-Fri 10-5 (term-time.)

Policy: Exhibitions usually last three weeks, and cover staff shows, student shows, fellowship exhibitions and exhibitions from artists in the region or associated with the polytechnic. The gallery is seen as an educational facility, benefiting students through the practical side of exhibiting as well as running seminars. The programme also gives the public the opportunity to view *'a range of work not available otherwise in Birmingham'*.

Sales: Sales referred to exhibitors

The Space: 113 sqm giving 37m linear hanging space with artificial and daylight. Gallery plans available.

Exhibiting: [AW] The gallery produces a list of exhibits and publicity and it can sometimes provide help with transport. Insurance and preview costs are the responsibility of the artist. Gallery plans available.

Access: [X] City centre location; Close to car parks; BR Birmingham 10 mins

Birmingham University (Winterbourne House)

A gallery space in the foyer of the Department of Education and Continuing Studies showing mainly work from West Midlands artists and makers. [VA,Cr]

Address: School of Continuing Studies, Faculty of Education and Continuing Studies, Birmingham University, Birmingham, W Midlands B15 2TT tel 021 414 5613

Contact: Lucy-Anne Hunt, Dianne Barre

Open: Mon-Thurs 9-8, Fri 9-4

Policy: Two or three exhibitions are held each term, with half the shows being solo exhibitions. The main emphasis is on work by individuals and groups in the West Midlands. Winterbourne House hosts a variety of courses for graduates and continuing education students and is open to the public as well as those at the university.

Sales: Work sold

The Space: The 18x3m foyer is situated at the front of a turn-of-the-century building with daylight and artificial lighting. Work is hung from a rail, and free- standing work has to be situated against the wall.

Exhibiting: [AW] The gallery provides a handlist, publicity and mailing. The artist/maker is responsible for installation, transport, providing showcases and £10

towards insurance costs. Supports EPR.
Access: [U][T] Car park, Bristol Road buses 15 mins, BR University 10 mins

Building Sights

A community education and photography project funded by the City Council and West Midlands Arts to provide exhibitions, events, and activities in a wide range of community venues in the Balsall Heath and Sparkbrook area of Birmingham. [Ph]

Address: Tindal School, Tindal Street, Balsall Heath, Birmingham, W Midlands B12 9QS tel 021 440 1582
Contact: Jo Klaces
Open: 9-3.30 (School days)
Policy: Building Sights aims *'wherever possible to link exhibitions to place and occasion, with theatre performances, book stalls, seminars, community lunches as part of an informal wider learning experience'.* Exhibitions are usually laminated and shown in community centres, libraries, schools, churches and health centres. Building Sights provides advice and promotes *'the work of local photographers who have exhibitions, but no outlet for their work... All our exhibitions reflect the multi-cultural nature of our constituencies'.* A regular programme of community lunches with speakers addressing issues raised within the exhibitions is organised.
The Space: Three walls in the Community Rooms are used giving 11m linear hanging space.
Exhibiting: [AW][EF] Three to four months in advance to Jo Klaces. Insurance, publicity, mailing and list of exhibits are provided.
Access: [F] School car park, Bus 50 from city centre to Brighton Road

Carleton Gallery

A commercial gallery showing good-quality work from local and regional artists. It also sells prints, paintings and artists' materials. [VA,Cr]

Address: 91 Vivian Road, Harborne, Birmingham, W Midlands B17 tel 021 427 2487
Contact: D Dunnett
Open: Mon-Sat 10-5; Closed Wed
Sales: Work sold
The Space: 44 square metres with 50m linear hanging space.
Exhibiting: [AW] The gallery is responsible for insurance, framing, publicity and catalogue. The artist is responsible for mailing costs and transport. 33.3% commission is charged.

Cave (The)

A Black Arts Centre with an extensive programme of performance, drama, music and dance, funded by the probation service and West Midlands Arts. [VA,Ph,Cr]

Address: 156 Moseley Road, Balsall Heath, Birmingham, W Midlands B12 9AH tel 021 446 3742
Contact: Director Hermin MacIntosh
Policy: The gallery shows work from artists in the region and nationally.
Sales: Work sold
The Space: The gallery is 5x5m approx with track lighting. Direct fixing is used.
Exhibiting: [AW]
Access: [S] On the south side of the city centre; Bus 50

Central Library

A gallery space located within the busy purpose-built central library run by Birmingham City Council Public Libraries Department. [VA,Cr,Ph,LA]

Address: Chamberlain Square, Birmingham, W Midlands B3 3HQ tel 021 235 3392
Contact: Promotions Officer Dawn Wise
Open: Mon-Fri 9-8, Sat 9-5
Policy: The monthly exhibitions are selected to appeal to library users, and must be of a good standard and well-presented. Art and non-art exhibitions are mounted. The art exhibitions usually feature work by local or regional individuals and groups. The gallery space is situated in the main readers lounge.
Sales: Work sold; Sales referred to exhibitor
The Space: 11x3x2m with artificial lighting, the total hanging length including panels is 20m.
Exhibiting: [AW] Contact the Promotions Officer. The space is booked a year ahead. No charge is made for the space, and the artist or maker is responsible for hanging and all costs.
Access: [U][T][L] City centre location; Close to public car parking & buses; BR New Street 10 mins

Craftspace

A specialist gallery and touring service funded by West Midlands Arts in the Midlands Arts Centre. [Cr]

Address: Midlands Arts Centre, Cannon Hill Park, Birmingham, West Midlands B12 9QH tel 021 440 4221
Contact: Julia Ellis
Open: Daily 12-8pm
Policy: The gallery promotes high-quality craft exhibitions and educational events. It also produces touring shows which are largely thematic selling exhibitions. The gallery was sympathetically converted to provide a

Craftspace at Midlands Arts Centre: 'New Movement in Furniture' exhibition

specialist space for the exhibition of high-quality contemporary craft work. Each exhibition includes interpretive material and the shows are predominantly mixed and thematic. Exhibitors are new makers of high-quality, and established makers with national reputations. The touring exhibitions are all accompanied with extensive good-quality publicity and educational material, The gallery is able to arrange workshops or talks for venues hiring the touring shows.

Sales: Work sold

The Space: 100 square metres of gallery space with 30m linear hanging space. Four lockable purpose-built showcases are used each 0.7x0.73x1.2m. Additional showcases and plinths are available. Track lighting of floods and spots as well as natural light. Gallery and showcase plans available.

Exhibiting: [AW] Written applications with slides/photographs and CV to Julia Ellis. Individuals and groups are encouraged to apply, as are makers interested in educational work. Gallery covers exhibition costs except exhibition fee. Commission varies.

Access: [X] Car park at gallery; Buses 1,35,45,47 from city centre; Opposite Edgbaston cricket ground

Helios Pictures

A private gallery selling contemporary work from local and regional sources which also sells artists' materials and provides a good quality framing service. Exhibitions of work mostly by artists from Birmingham are held in the shop and occasionally other parts of the house. [Pa,Pr,Dr]

Address: 25 Valentine Road, Kings Heath, Birmingham, W Midlands B14 tel 021 444 1585

Contact: John Palmer

Sales: Work sold; Credit card

The Space: The gallery space is 4x7.5m with natural and artificial light.

Exhibiting: [AW]

Access: [S] Outside the city centre, just off the Alcester Road; Bus 50

Ikon

An independent gallery funded primarily by the Arts Council and Birmingham City Council. [VA,LA]

Address: 58-72 John Bright Street, Birmingham, W Midlands B1 1BN tel 021 643 0708

Contact: Director

Open: Tues-Sat 10-6; closed bank holidays and during exhibition change overs

Policy: The exhibition programme reflects current trends and issues in contemporary art. Solo, thematic and large touring exhibitions are shown. The gallery runs an extensive education programme alongside the exhibition programme, as well as a touring exhibitions service (see Ikon Touring listing). It has a small bookshop.

Sales: Work sold

The Space: Two floors each with 200 square metres and 125m linear hanging space with natural light and artificial light. Gallery plans available.

Exhibiting: [AW][EF] Contact the Director in writing. The gallery covers all exhibition costs, except framing.

Access: [U][T][X] City centre location; BR New Street 2 mins

Ikon Touring

Ikon Touring produces an annual programme of exhibitions designed to tour to non-gallery venues mainly in the West Midlands Arts region. [VA,Ph,Cr]

Address: 58-72 John Bright Street, Birmingham, W Midlands B1 1BN tel 021 643 0708

Contact: Touring Officers Myfanwy Johns, Deborah Robinson

Open: Various

Policy: The touring programme aims *'to increase the understanding and enjoyment of contemporary art and increase the opportunities for artists both inside and outside the region. The yearly programme usually has 60 bookings in a variety of venues. Information panels are provided and workshops and placements can be organised alongside the exhibitions. Exhibitions can be thematic or explore a particular discipline. The shows are displayed to a high standard and only tour for one year. For current exhibitions and venues information contact the Touring Officer'.*

Sales: Work sold

The Space: Exhibitions vary between 3.5 and 30 linear metres and direct hanging is used. The exhibitions are specially prepared and packed for non-gallery venues.

Exhibiting: [AW][EF] for solo and two-person shows. Applications should be sent to the Touring Officers and include a CV and up to ten slides or photographs. The programme is organised for April/May, though applications are *'welcome from artists throughout the year'.* Gallery provides insurance, transport, publicity, mailing and display. A commission of 33.3% is charged on sales and split between Ikon Touring and the venue.

Library Exhibition Hall

A multi-purpose building operated by Birmingham City Council Public Libraries Department in the centre of Birmingham. [VA,Cr,Ph,LA]

Address: Paradise Place, Birmingham, W Midlands B3 3HQ tel 021 235 4387

Contact: Commercial Officer Des Workman

Open: As required by hirer

Policy: The building can be hired for commercial and non-commercial exhibitions and events.

Sales: Work sold; Sales referred to exhibitor

The Space: 520sqm floor area with track lighting, lift, power points every 2m, display cases, 300 chairs, loading dock and lift (2.4x1.7m). Gallery plans available.

Exhibiting: Contact the Commercial Officer. Charges vary depending on length of hire and facilities required.

Access: [U] City centre location close to public car parks, bus routes; BR New Street 10 mins

Midlands Arts Centre

A purpose-built arts centre with a programme including cinema, theatre, music, dance, art classes, bookshop, bar, restaurant and puppet theatre. [VA,Ph,Cr]

Address: Cannon Hill Park, Birmingham, West Midlands

B12 9QH tel 021 440 4221
Contact: Gabrielle Oliver, Jo Kirk
Open: Daily 12-8
Policy: Although each department can use the exhibition spaces for special events, most of the exhibitions are fine art exhibitions. The exhibitions are mainly *'younger artists living in the region'*. Where possible, workshops are run in conjunction with the exhibitions.
Sales: Work sold
The Space: Cotton Gallery has 75m linear space on 20 different walls with a 2m hanging height, with track lighting and direct fixing.The Exhibition Foyer has 23m linear space with a varying wall height of 2.25-2.5m and raised platform suitable for plinths and free-standing sculpture and natural and spot lighting.The Inner Courtyard is approx 70 square metres which is glazed on all sides with natural light and a tree. Gallery plans available.
Exhibiting: **[AW]** Slides/photographs, statement and CV to Gabrielle Oliver for painting, and Jo Kirk for sculpture exhibitions. The gallery sometimes contributes to insurance, publicity, preview, transport, mailing and catalogue. A commission of 20% is charged on sales though this can vary.
Access: **[U]** Cotton Gallery only otherwise **[X]** Car park at the arts centre; Buses 1,35,45,47 from city centre

Public Art Commissions Agency

An agency for commissioning works of art, 'its principal resource is an extensive slide file'; a non-profit making charitable trust earning most of its running costs from consultancy fees. [VA,Ph,Cr,LA]
Address: 45/46 Guildhall Buildings, Navigation Street, Birmingham, W Midlands B2 4BT tel 021 643 4407
Contact: Director Vivien Lovell
Open: Mon-Fri 10-5
Policy: The agency is the principal commissions agency in the Midlands. Working with a wide variety of clients, it seeks to develop an increase in the understanding of good practice in public art *'through exhibitions, workshops, conferences and other educational events and activities'*. Exhibitions of proposed projects and other events are arranged in conjunction with clients or other organisations. Advice to artists is free.
The Space: A number of maquettes and working drawings are on display, and can be seen by appointment.
Exhibiting: **[AW]** Artists and makers may join the slide file by contacting the Director. EPR supported. The agency takes a consultancy fee on sales and commissions of between 10-20%.
Access: **[X]** City centre location; Car parks, bus station and BR Birmingham New Street 5 mins

Midlands Arts Centre: Exhibition Foyer

Royal Birmingham Society of Artists

A city centre space run by the society for its members, and available for hire. [VA,Ce]
Address: 69A New Street, Birmingham, W Midlands B2 4DU tel 021 643 3768
Contact: Secretary Mrs Priddey
Open: Mon-Sat 10.30-5
Policy: A varied yearly programme is made up of society exhibitions, shows by individuals and open exhibitions. A programme of talks, seminars, demonstrations and trips is also organised.
Sales: Work sold
The Space: Two rooms with direct fixing, spots and natural light and around 50m linear hanging space.
Exhibiting: Although usually heavily booked, some periods are occasionally available. Details of booking fee and dates can be obtained from Mrs Priddey. A 15% commission is charged on sales.
Access: **[X]** City centre location

Ten 8 Touring

A touring photography exhibition service for galleries, schools, colleges and community centres part funded by West Midlands Arts. [Ph]
Address: Unit 3, 137 Soho Road, Handsworth, Birmingham, W Midlands B21 9ST tel 021 554 2237
Contact: Touring Officer Richard Gagola
Policy: The exhibitions are *'primarily issue-based photography representing work by artists denied access to mainstream/commercial outlets. Afro-Caribbean, Asian, and women photographers have been especially encouraged, along with other independent photographers working with the local community'*. The touring service was established to promote the work of West Midlands photographers in the region and nationally. The shows are either framed or laminated panels, and talks and workshops can be arranged with the exhibitions.
The Space: Information on the venues currently showing the exhibitions is available on request.
Exhibiting: **[AW][EF]** Photographers are encouraged to contact the Touring Officer by post, *'having looked at* Ten 8 *magazine to see the kind of work we are interested in'*. A commission of 50% is charged on sales. Supports EPR.

Bishops Stortford (Hertfordshire)

(EA) Map7 TL42

Rhodes Memorial Museum & Commonwealth Centre

Gallery devoted to the life and times of Cecil John Rhodes (1853-1902).

Address: South Road, Bishops Stortford, Hertfordshire CM23 tel 0279 51746
Contact: Mr Parry
Open: Tues-Sat 10-4
Access: [X]

Bishops Waltham (Hampshire)

(SA) Map7 SU51

Old Granary

A 200-year-old building converted in 1976 into an art and craft centre now housing an art gallery and craft workshops for some 16 designer/makers. [Pa,Pr,Cr]

Address: Bank Street, Bishops Waltham, Southampton, Hampshire SO3 tel 048 934 700
Contact: The Directors G C & J M Mitchell
Open: Tues-Sat 10-5
Policy: Regular exhibitions are held of watercolours, pastels and oils with a continuous exhibition of contemporary prints.

Blackburn (Lancashire)

(NWA) Map3 SD62

Blackburn Museum & Art Gallery

A local authority run gallery and museum with a permanent collection of fine and decorative arts and a temporary exhibition programme. [VA,Cr]

Address: Library Street, Blackburn, Lancashire BB1 7AH tel 0254 667130
Contact: Exhibitions Officer
Open: Tues-Sat 10-5
Policy: The programme is based around *'a few regular annual exhibitions, with others being selected more often from applications than by invitation'*. See also entries for Lewis Textile Museum, Sunnyhurst Wood Visitor Centre and Witton Country Park Visitor Centre.
The Space: The temporary exhibition gallery has 43m linear hanging space with spot and flood lighting.
Exhibiting: [AW] Applications are welcome. The gallery pays for publicity and charges 10% commission on sales.

Lewis Textile Museum

A museum demonstrating the inventions of Kay, Hargreaves and Arkwright also showing temporary exhibitions. [Te]

Address: Exchange Street, Blackburn, Lancashire BB1 7JN
Contact: Exhibitions Officer Blackburn Museum & Art Gallery, Museum Street, Blackburn, Lancashire tel 0254 667130
Open: Tues-Sat 10-5
Policy: A regular programme of temporary exhibitions are held throughout the year. See also entry for Blackburn Museum & Art Gallery.
The Space: The upstairs gallery has 38m linear hanging space with spots and natural light.
Exhibiting: [AW] Applications are welcome. The gallery pays for publicity and charges 10% commission.

Street (The)

The gallery is part of Blackburn Central Library and concentrates on showing work of local artists. [VA]

Address: Blackburn Central Library, Town Hall Street, Blackburn Lancashire BB2 1AH tel 0254 661221
Contact: District Librarian J B Darbyshire
Open: Mon-Wed 9.30-8, Thurs-Fri 9.30-5, Sat 9.30-4
Policy: The gallery generally shows ten exhibitions a year. It sees its role as providing a venue for local artists to show their work and to be a focal point for public interest in local visual arts.
Sales: Work sold
The Space: There is 35m linear hanging space with a loop alarm system.
Exhibiting: [AW] Individual artists or groups should apply in writing to the District Librarian. The gallery will pay for list of exhibits.
Access: [U][T][L] BR Blackburn; Bus station and car park all within 2 mins

Sunnyhurst Wood Visitor Centre

A centre with changing displays on the history of Darwen which also shows temporary exhibitions. [VA,Cr]

Address: Sunnyhurst Wood, Darwen, Blackburn, Lancashire BB3 OLA tel 0254 71545
Open: Tues, Thurs, Sat, Sun & bank holidays 2-4.30
Policy: See also entry for Blackburn Museum & Art Gallery.
The Space: The centre has about 22m linear hanging space in the temporary exhibition space which has natural and flood lights.
Exhibiting: [AW] The centre pays for publicity and charges 10% commission on sales.
Access: [U]

Witton Country Park Visitor Centre

A centre with a display located in the stables showing harnesses, natural history and agricultural machinery with a temporary exhibition programme.

Address: Witton Country Park, Preston Old Road, Blackburn, Lancashire BB2 2TP tel 0254 55423
Contact: Senior Warden Mr R Wilson
Open: Thurs, Fri, Sat 1-5, Sun & bank holidays 11-5
Policy: See also entry for Blackburn Museum & Art Gallery.
Sales: Work sold
The Space: The space has 25m linear hanging space and natural light supplemented with flood lights.
Exhibiting: [AW] The centre will pay for publicity and charges 10% commission on sales.

Access: [X] Buses to Preston (via Old Road) and Chorley; BR Blackburn 1.5 miles, BR Mill Hill 1 mile

Blackpool (Lancashire)

(NWA) Map3 SD33

Grundy Art Gallery

A municipal gallery with four exhibition rooms that shows a changing programme of exhibitions and has a collection of early 20th Century English painting. [Pa,Dr,Ph,Cr]

Address: Queen Street, Blackpool, Lancashire FY1 tel 0253 23977
Contact: Assistant Keeper of Fine Art E Tomlinson
Open: Mon-Sat 10-5
Policy: *'As a public art gallery we aim to interest as wide an audience as possible. Local art societies have opportunities to exhibit their work but the solo shows are reserved for professional artists. Occasionally music recitals take place in the galleries'.* Around sixteen exhibitions shown a year.
Sales: Work sold
The Space: The gallery has three main rooms each with 32.30m linear hanging space, the fourth area has 23.16m linear hanging space. Hanging is by rail or direct fixing and lighting is by spots. Gallery plans available.
Exhibiting: [AW][EF] Applications should be sent to the Assistant Keeper and should include slides and a letter. The gallery will pay for insurance, publicity, list of exhibits and catalogue. Supports EPR. 15% Commission taken on sales.
Access: [U][T][L] BR Central 1 min; Bus stop 3 mins

Bodmin (Cornwall)

(SWA) Map6 SX06

Cornwall Crafts Association at Pencarrow

'Small and delightful craft gallery in the grounds of Pencarrow House' devoted to work by Cornwall Crafts Association members. [Cr]

Address: Pencarrow House, Washaway, Bodmin, Cornwall PL30 3AG tel 020 884 465
Contact: Margaret Way
Open: Sun-Thurs 1.30-5 Easter-15 Oct
Policy: See also Cornwall Crafts Association, Helston and Trelissick Gallery, Truro.
Sales: Work sold

Bolton (Lancashire)

(NWA) Map3 SD70

Bolton Institute of Higher Education (John Nicholson Gallery)

Established in September 1987, John Nicholson Gallery is part of the art and design department of Bolton Institute of Higher Education. [VA]

Address: Bolton Institute of Higher Education, Great Moor Street, Bolton, Lancashire BL3 tel 0204 28851 ext 3180
Contact: John Hannavy and Donald Taylor
Open: Mon-Fri 9.30-5
Policy: The gallery was conceived as a means of bringing work to the notice of students and of making the people of Bolton more aware of art and design within the institute.
Sales: Sales referred to exhibitor
Access: [U][T][L] BR Bolton 2 mins; Bus Station 2 mins

Bolton Library Service

The library service for Bolton. [VA,Cr]

Address: Bolton Central Library, Le Mans Crescent, Bolton, Greater Manchester BL2 tel 0204 22311
Contact: Chief Librarian
Policy: Although there are no facilities at the Central Library for showing exhibitions, small spaces are available at Farnworth Library, Harwood Library and Westhougton Library with the overall policy being to *'exhibit work with a local theme or work produced by local artists with target audiences being the library users and school and college groups.'* These are month-long exhibitions of which half are solo shows.
Sales: Work sold
The Space: Ask for details.
Exhibiting: [AW] For Farnwood and Harwood libraries contact K Beevers, Area Librarian, Farnworth Library, Market Street, Farnworth, Bolton BL4 7PG tel 0204 72790, or Mrs A J Smith, Area Librarian for Westhoughton Library, Library Street, Westhoughton, Bolton BL5 3AU tel 0942 811939.

Bolton Museum and Art Gallery

A municipal museum and art gallery run by Bolton Metropolitan Borough Council with permanent collections of fine and decorative arts and a varied exhibitions programme. [VA,Ph,Cr]

Address: Le Mans Cresent, Bolton, Greater Manchester BL1 1SE tel 0204 22311 ext 2194
Contact: Senior Keeper of Art David Morris
Open: Mon-Fri 9.30-5.30, Sat 10-5, closed Wed, Sun and bank holidays
Policy: The gallery mounts a varied programme of both historical and contemporary exhibitions. In 1987, 17 exhibitions were presented including eleven of living artists and six solo exhibitions. In recent years the gallery has had a policy of showing material from cultures outside the Western European mainstream, including that from Afro-Caribbean peoples and from Asia and the Soviet Union. *'We seek to show work of the highest quality, both technically and aesthetically and also work that communicates as directly as possible with our varied audience. We wish to foster an appreciation within the North West for arts from a wide range of cultures'.*
Sales: Work sold
The Space: The two galleries measure 16.7x8.5m and 17.6x8.5m giving up to 128m linear hanging space. Lighting is by dimmer controlled spots and fixing is by mirror plates. The galleries are fitted with humidifiers. Gallery plans are available.

Exhibiting: [AW][EF] Applications including slides and/or photographs should be sent to Senior Keeper of Art. Exhibition planning meetings are held quarterly. The gallery pays for insurance, printing and mail out of publicity, catalogue/card, preview costs, transport and artists expenses. A 10% sales commission is charged. Supports EPR.

Access: [U][T][L][F] In town centre; Public car park 2 mins; BR Bolton

Octagon Theatre

An exhibition space in the bar and lunch bar areas of a theatre. [Pa,Pr,Ph]

Address: Howell Croft South, Bolton, Lancashire BL1 1SB tel 0204 29407

Contact: Public Relations Officer

Open: Daily 12-2 & from 6 for theatre audiences

The Space: There is 19m linear hanging space with direct fixing, rods and rails with spots and natural light.

Exhibiting: [AW] Applications welcome and the theatre pays for insurance and mailing of publicity and takes 15% commission.

Turton Tower

An historic house run by Lancashire County Council Museum service, containing a number of period rooms and with a permanent collection of 17th to 19th Century furniture, arms and armour and also local history items. [Sc,Cr]

Address: Chapeltown Road, Bolton, Lancashire BL7 OHG tel 0204 852 203

Contact: Keeper Jocelyn Grigg

Open: Mon-Fri 10-12 1-5 Sat,Sun 1-5 May-Sept; Sat-Wed 2-5 Oct-March; Sun 2-5 Feb,Nov; Closed Dec-Jan

Policy: The house holds one self-initiated exhibition a year on either contemporary crafts or a local history theme. It also organises one or two touring exhibitions a year.

Sales: Work sold

The Space: Gallery one measures 7x7m, with a hanging height of approximately 2.5m and total of 15m linear space. Gallery two is suitable for three-dimensional objects only and measures 2.7x9.5x6m. Both galleries have natural light and spotlights.There is limited wallspace for two-dimensional work. Any exhibits must be carrried upstairs and through a 6.7m door. There is also exhibiting space in an eight-acre garden. Three to four standard display cases are available.

Exhibiting: The house covers the costs of insurance, publicity, preview and display costs plus transport and catalogue/card expenses. A 10% commission is charged. Supports EPR.

Access: [X] Buses 563 Bolton/Edgworth 5 mins; Bus to BR Bromley Cross

Boston (Lincolnshire)

(LHA) Map5 TF34

Blackfriars Arts Centre

Multi-programme arts centre with exhibition space in Foyer Gallery. [Pa,Pr,Dr,Ph]

Address: Spain Lane, Boston, Lincolnshire PE21 6HP tel 0205 63108

Contact: Director Paul Bisson

Open: Mon-Sat 10-6

Policy: A mixture of solo and touring shows and local amateur work excluding sculpture and three-dimensional craftwork. It is intended to *'provide a lively ever-changing selection of local, regional and national living artists'*.

Sales: Work sold; Credit card

The Space: The centre has 30 linear hanging metres of exhibition space. Work is mirror-plated to walls and lighting is by spots. Gallery plans available.

Exhibiting: [EF][AW] Applications to the director and selection takes place between August and October. The centre pays for insurance, printing of publicity, preview costs, transport, mailing and artists' expenses. Commission on sales is 20%-25% plus VAT. Applications to give lectures and workshops are also welcomed, particularly with reference to integrating with other arts centre activities, eg performances.

Access: [S] Town centre site; Car park

Guildhall Museum

A council-run 15th century building reflecting history of the town, with a monthly programme of exhibitions held in the entrance hall. [Pa,Dr,Cr]

Address: South Street, Boston, Lincolnshire PE21 6HT tel 0205 65954

Contact: Curator Andrew Crabtree

Open: Mon-Sat 10-5 (Sun 1.30-5 April-October)

Policy: *'To provide a wide variety of exhibitions to encourage local visitors to make repeat visits to the Guildhall Museum'*. Permanent collection of 18th and 19th century oil paintings and 19th and 20th century watercolours.

Sales: Work sold

The Space: Two areas 16.5x6.5x2.75m; 16.5x2.75m plus twelve free-standing screens 2.72 x1.25. Track lighting. UV protection to all windows. Standard lockable Edmonds showcases. Gallery plans available.

Exhibiting: [AW] One year in advance enclosing CV and slides to the Curator. Gallery pays for insurance, printing of publicity, preview costs, transport, mailing of publicity, catalogue. Commission on sales is 10%.

Access: [X] All bus routes 5 mins; BR Boston 20 mins; Public car park 5 mins

Bourton-on-the-Water (Gloucestershire)

(SWA) Map7 SP12

Chestnut Gallery

A commercial crafts gallery on the Crafts Council's selected list showing high-quality work by British makers. [Cr]

Address: High Street, Bourton-on-the-Water, Gloucestershire GL54 2AN tel 0451 20017

Contact: Mary & Peter O'Connor

Open: Mon-Sat 10-5; Suns and holidays 11.30-5; closed Mon &Wed Nov-May

Policy: The work shown *'tends to be at the traditional end of the market rather than the avant garde'*.

Sales: Work sold; Credit card
Access: **[F]** Town centres site; Buses from Cheltenham and Moreton-in-the-Marsh

Boxford (Suffolk)

(EA) Map7 TL94

Laurimore Gallery

Commercial gallery, formerly the Falcon House Gallery, with a special reputation for crafts of the highest quality and which is included on the Crafts Council selected list. [Pa,Sc,Pr,Cr]

Address: The Mews, 29 Swan Street, Boxford, Suffolk CO9 5NZ tel 0787 210138
Contact: Jon Laurimore
Open: Wed-Sat 10.30-1.30, 2.30-6 Sun 2.30-6 during exhibitions, other times by appointment
Policy: gallery specialises in work with *'a contemporary figurative feel'*, and has three major exhibitions a year.
Sales: Work sold
The Space: 85 square metres - on two floors.
Exhibiting: Selection is by invitation, although *'we are always interested in seeing new work from all over the country'*. Gallery covers insurance, publicity and catalogue, and shares the cost of mailing and private view, taking 30-40% commission.
Access: **[X]** About 14 miles from Colchester, Ipswich or Bury St Edmunds

Brackley (Northamptonshire)

(EMA) Map7 SP53

Brackley Library

See Northamptonshire Libraries. [VA,Ph,Cr,Ar]

Address: Manor Road, Brackley NN13 6AJ tel 0280 703455
Contact: District Librarian Miss Hudson
Open: Tues-Fri 10-1, 2-7, Sat 9.30-12.30; closed Mon
Sales: Work sold
The Space: 15 linear metres hanging space with one lockable display case and tape-slide equipment with track lighting. Display area 48 square metres.
Exhibiting: **[AW]** District Librarian. Publicity, insurance provided, as well as transport between libraries for touring exhibitions. Commission is 10%.
Access: **[F]** Bus services to Northampton and Banbury

Bracknell (Berkshire)

(SA) Map7 SU86

South Hill Park Arts Centre (Gallery at the Park)

A gallery within a publicly-funded multi-media arts centre and theatre, showing mainly two-dimensional work of interest to the local community from the region and elsewhere. [VA,Ph,Cr,LA]

Address: Bracknell, Berkshire RG12 4PA tel 0344 427272
Contact: Exhibitions Organiser Nicola Kennedy
Open: Mon-Fri 11-1, 2-5, 7-10, Sat 1-4 & 7-10, Sun 1-4
Policy: *'The gallery has a broad policy and a responsibility to the local community to present contemporary work of quality'*. Difficult exhibitions are counter-balanced with more accessible work. Exhibitions, which run for five weeks, are linked to activities including theatre, music, video and live art and also with workshops, artists in schools projects and occasional gallery talks. The centre also runs courses in visual arts and crafts. Crafts shop and monthly craft showcases.
Sales: Work sold; Credit card
The Space: The Main Gallery is 4m high with 17.6m linear hanging space broken by windows, a door and a fire place. Daylight can be excluded, but no environmental controls, with direct fixing to wall, fluorescent and spotlights. Stair Gallery has 10.9m linear hanging space with a mixture of direct fixing and hanging rods with single-track spotlights. The Long Gallery has 11m linear hanging space with direct fixing and single-track spotlights. Gallery plans available.
Exhibiting: **[AW]** Send slides of recent work, CV and an exhibition proposal to the Exhibitions Organiser. The gallery pays all costs except artists' expenses and charges 30% commission. Occasionally an exhibition is commissioned and the gallery supports EPR.
Access: **[L][F][X]** Bus from BR Bracknell; Car park

Bradford (W Yorkshire)

(YA) Map3 SE13

Bradford Community Arts Centre

A newly-established initiative between Bradford Community Arts Association and the Metropolitan Council to create a focus for developing creative opportunities in the community. [VA,Ph]

Address: The Old Quaker School, 17-21 Chapel Street, Bradford, W Yorkshire BD1 5DT tel 0274 721372
Contact: Jenny Wilson and Sue Beaumont
Open: Mon-Fri 10-4
Policy: The exhibition spaces will promote all types of community creativity and many of the future exhibitions will be initiated through community activities, including photography, textiles, printmaking and two and three-dimensional work. A significant exhibition last year was 'The Art of Disability'.
The Space: Limited wall space, although free-standing screens are available. Rooms are also let for meetings, performances and conferences.
Exhibiting: **[AW]** Community and voluntary groups are especially welcome to send applications to the House Committee. Commission is 15%.
Access: **[U][L]** Within easy walking distance from Bradford Metro Interchange

Cartwright Hall

A municipal gallery with permanent collection of late Victorian and Edwardian fine and decorative art and regular changing exhibitions of contemporary art. [VA,Ph,Cr,LA]

Address: Lister Park, Bradford, W Yorkshire BD9 4NS tel 0274 493313

Contact: Keeper of Exhibitions Caroline Krzesinska
Open: Tues-Sun 10-5 Oct-March; Tues-Sun 10-6 April-Oct
Policy: The gallery is dedicated to promoting contemporary art through exhibitions and educational activities. *'The programme aims to work alongside multi-cultural communities responding to ideas put forward by outside groups and creating a balanced programme of interest to all age groups and cultural backgrounds'.* Several touring exhibitions are generated from within the gallery and shows are also hired in from other venues. There are an average of 27 exhibitions mounted each year and each exhibition lasts for six to eight weeks. These include group shows and solo exhibitions.
Sales: Work sold
The Space: There are five exhibition spaces, two of 24x9x3.6m high with 66m linear hanging space, two of 9x6x6m high with 30m linear hanging space and one of 3.6x9x6m high with 84m linear hanging space, each has a mixture of spot and tube lighting, and humidity control. There are hexagonal, felt-lined cases 2.8m high and a variety of desk cases. Gallery plans are available.
Exhibiting: [AW][EF] Artists and makers should apply in writing to Caroline Krzesinska. The gallery covers all exhibition costs and takes 20% - 30% commission. Occasionally the gallery pays a commissioning fee for work. Supports the principle of EPR.
Access: [U][T][L] Buses 665-669 from Bradford Interchange

Hazelroyd Galleries

A commercial gallery offering a wide range of work but specialising in watercolours, pastels and etchings. [Pa,Pr,Ph]
Address: Number 4 Arch, Station Yard, Cheapside, Bradford, W Yorkshire BD1 tel 0274 309715
Contact: Owner David Wright
Open: 9-5 Mon-Sat
Policy: The gallery specialises in *'Northern landscapes, mountains and countryside subjects and maintains a friendly relationship with artists and customers'.* Space within the gallery has constantly changing displays and another is devoted to four solo exhibitions a year lasting six to eight weeks each.
Sales: Work sold
The Space: The gallery is 6x6x2.7m high giving 24m linear hanging space lit by Concord track lighting.
Exhibiting: [AW] Artists should send slides or photographs of their work to David Wright. The gallery covers the costs of printing publicity, list of exhibits, preview costs and usually buys some of the work and takes 25% commission.
Access: [U] BR Bradford Interchange 10 mins

Industrial Museum

A municipal museum dedicated to the care of the collection relating to Bradford's technological, industrial and social past and making the information relevant to the present through exhibitions and residency schemes. [Ph,Cr]
Address: Moorside Mills, Moorside Road, Bradford, W Yorkshire BD2 3HP tel 0274 631756
Contact: Keeper of Technology R McHugh
Open: Tues-Sun 10-5; Open bank holidays
Policy: Exhibitions are mounted which enhance the permanent collection but may not necessarily be directly linked to Bradford's heritage. The brief is wide and open to a variety of exhibitions relating to textiles, transport and industrial design. The museum is in the process of extending the displays relating to social history with the reconstruction of back-to-backs and a street-scape and has continual education support with activities and demonstrations. Exhibitions run for six weeks and the gallery has played host to musicians, dance groups and theatre companies.
The Space: The exhibition gallery is 15x7.5m and has overhead spotlights and tracking system with a number of display panels. Gallery plans are available.
Exhibiting: [AW] Artists and makers should send an application in writing to the Keeper or the Marketing Officer. The gallery covers the cost of insurance, printing of publicity, preview costs, display, transport, mailing out of publicity and a catalogue /card.
Access: [U][T][L][F] Buses 608,609,614,634 from Bank Street,614,634 from Market Street,Minibus 896 from Bradford Interchange; Car parking within the grounds

National Museum of Photography, Film & Television

Founded in 1983 by the Science Museum and Bradford Metropolitan Council, the museum is responsible for the care, maintenance and display of Britain's national collection relating to the history and art of film, television and photography. [Ph,Fi,TV]
Address: Prince's View, Bradford, W Yorkshire BD5 0TR tel 0274 727 488
Contact: Exhibitions Organiser Terry Morden
Open: Tues-Sat 11-6, Sun 2-5
Policy: It has a permanent interactive display and has been described as *'Britain's most dramatic and accessible new museum'.* It houses the country's first IMAX cinema with the biggest screen in Europe and with daily showings. The Kodak Museum, due to open in 1988/89, will tell the story of popular photography and cinematography. Two floors of the museum are devoted to temporary exhibitions relating to the collection and help promote, explore and inspire interest in the art of either film, photography or television. Generally there is a broad range of both contemporary and traditional exhibitions taking place, each lasting for up to ten weeks.
Sales: Works for sale
The Space: Two large L-shaped galleries measuring 370 square metres, with a variable linear hanging length, dependent on use of screens. Also a regular gallery of approximately 30m linear hanging space and several small display areas throughout the museum.
Exhibiting: [AW] Slides and application in writing to Terry Morden.
Access: [U][T][L] BR Bradford Interchange 5 mins; Pedestrian signposting

University of Bradford (Art Gallery)

A new gallery established in order to promote contemporary art to students, staff and the local community. [VA,Ph,Cr,LA]

Address: Chesham Building, Richmond Road, Bradford, W Yorkshire BD7 1DP tel 0274 733466 ext 8502 and 8494

Contact: Visual Arts Co-ordinator Carol McLaren, J B Priestley Library, University of Bradford, Richmond Road, Bradford

Open: Mon-Fri 8-8, Sat, Sun 10-6

Policy: The gallery's policy is to promote contemporary art *'mainly by young artists who have had a limited number of previous exhibitions - or none at all'* this is not to the exclusion of more established artists and makers. Talks are being planned for future exhibitions which number ten a year, each lasting one month. Most of the exhibitions are solo but group shows are also considered.

Sales: Work sold

The Space: The main display area is 18x15x9m high has a mixture of spot and natural light. Daylight coming from glass panels which run the total length of the outside wall. There are three show cases each 2m high. Gallery plans are available.

Exhibiting: [AW] Slides to be sent to Carol McLaren at the J B Priestley Library. The gallery covers insurance, printing of publicity, list of exhibits, preview costs, transport, mailing out of publicity and catalogue/card. Commission of 15%.

Access: [U][T][L][S] BR Bradford Interchange 20 mins; Bus 610; Car park within grounds

Braintree (Essex)

(EA) Map7 TL72

Artisans Gallery

Commercial art gallery stocking work from 1800 to the present day. [Pa,Pr,Dr]

Address: Finchingfield, Braintree, Essex CM7 4JS tel 0371 810709

Contact: Proprietors Peter & Christina Shore

University of Bradford Art Gallery: 'Objects on a Shelf' etching and aquatint print by Jeff Clarkson from his exhibition 'Glimpses of Vision' held in 1988

Open: Tues-Sat 10-5.30 Sun 2-5.30

Policy: The gallery holds a stock of some 150 oils, watercolours and prints. It also undertakes commissions to buy and sell at auction, and offers a bespoke framing service for contemporary and historical frames.

Sales: Work sold; Credit card

The Space: Floor area of 35 square metres with 22m linear hanging space and a height of 2.59m.

Exhibiting: [AW] Gallery covers: printing and mailing of publicity, list of exhibits, preview costs, display, catalogue/card. 33.3% commission on sales.

Access: [S] BR Braintree; Buses from Braintree and Saffron Walden

Town Hall Centre Art Gallery

Main gallery and two small side galleries administered by Braintree District Council. [VA,Cr]

Address: Town Hall, Braintree, Essex CM7 tel 43140

Contact: Gallery Manager John Fleetham

Open: Mon-Sat 10-5

Policy: To encourage exhibitions by local arts council, art societies and individual artists. Average of 20 exhibitions a year.

Sales: Work sold

The Space: Main gallery is 10x2.2m with block board and spot lights. The two side galleries are 5x3m with picture rail.

Exhibiting: [AW] Details of charges on request.

Access: [X]

Brentwood (Essex)

(EA) Map7 TQ59

Brandler Galleries

Commercial gallery specialising in modern British figurative art. [VA]

Address: 1 Coptfold Road, Brentwood, Essex CM14 4BM tel 0227 222269

Contact: J H Brandler

Open: Tues-Sat 10-5.30

Policy: Series of three to five-week mixed exhibitions, *'selling rather than display'*. Fee for commissioned work.

Sales: Work sold; Credit scheme; Credit card

Exhibiting: [AW] By post to the gallery, which takes a commission of 33.3%.

Access: [S] Own car park; BR Brentwood 400m

Shenfield Library

Exhibition area in public library, available for hire. [VA,Cr]

Address: Hutton Road, Shenfield, Brentwood CM15 8NJ tel 0277 225540

Contact: Deputy Area Librarian Cathy Downes

Open: Mon, Tues,Thurs, Fri 9-7, Sat 9-5

Policy: Exhibitions of art, craft, photography, painted china etc.

Sales: Work sold

The Space: Wall-mounted display board sized 11.90 square metres.

Exhibiting: [AW] Commission is 20%.
Access: [F]

Bridgewater (Somerset)

(SWA) Map6 ST33

Bridgewater

A commercial arts centre with a wide programme of music, theatre, film, and exhibitions. [VA,Ph,Cr]

Address: 11-13 Castle Street, Bridgewater TA6 3DD tel 0278 422700
Contact: Centre Director A Mortimer
Open: Tues-Sat 9.30-5, Mon-Sat 7-11
Policy: Exhibitions range from *'nudes to local artists work and schools exhibitions'*. The aim is to *'present work of local and national artists working in as many media as possible to focus the attention of the community to the wide aspects of art in general. This includes representation of local schools and national childrens painting'*.
Sales: Work sold; Credit card; Credit scheme
The Space: One room plus display cases. Gallery plans available.
Exhibiting: [AW] Apply to the Director. The centre provides insurance, publicity, and list of exhibits.
Access: [U] 5 mins BR Bridgewater

Bridlington (Humberside)

(LHA) Map3 TA1866

Sewerby Hall Art Gallery & Museum

A municipal gallery run by East Yorkshire Borough Council open to the general public only during the summer months which will become part of the middle-scale venue circuit in Lincolnshire and Humberside. [Pa,Dr]

Address: Sewerby Park YO15 1EA tel 0262 677874

Symondsbury Gallery

Contact: Keeper John Earnshaw
Open: Sun-Fri 10-6, Sat 1-6 (Easter-end September)
Policy: The gallery is at present *'developing a policy'*.
Sales: Work sold
The Space: 37m of hanging space in three rooms, with an additional 9m in a fourth room if required for larger exhibitions. The exhibitions are only of wall-based work and staffing and shortage facilities are limited. Pictures are fixed to wall-mounted battens except for one room which is panelled. Lockable full-height and desk cases in galleries. There is a stable block which is used for craft demonstrations. Gallery plans available.
Exhibiting: [AW] The Director of Tourism, Leisure Services Department, The Spa, South Marine Drive, Bridlington YO15 3JH. The gallery pays for printing and mailing of publicity, transport and charges 10% commission on sales.
Access: [X]

Bridport (Dorset)

(SWA) Map6 SY49

Symondsbury Gallery

A private art school with foundation and GCSE courses for resident students. [VA,Ph]

Address: The Art School, Symondsbury, Bridport, Dorset DT6 6HF tel 0308 27339
Contact: Ian Scott
Open: June/July & Nov/Dec
Policy: Exhibitions are held out of term-time and the gallery aims to *'introduce contemporary works of art to the West Dorset population'*.
Sales: Work sold
The Space: Two exhibition spaces are used both 7.5x5.75x4.75m plus a 10m corridor. Large gardens and grounds can be used for outdoor sculpture.
Exhibiting: [AW] Applications should be sent to the gallery committee. Insurance, preview, list of exhibits,and a catalogue/card are provided. A 20% commission is charged on sales.
Access: [F][S] On the main bus route from Bridport and Dorchester

Brighouse (W Yorkshire)

(YA) Map3 SE14

Smith Art Gallery

A municipal gallery and museum housing the Smith collection of nineteenth century oil paintings and playing host to a programme of changing exhibitions. [VA,Cr,Ph]

Address: Halifax Road, Brighouse, W Yorkshire HD6 2AF tel 0484 719222
Contact: Assistant Keeper, Calderdale Museums Service Brian Sheridan, Bankfield Museum, Boothtown Road, Halifax HX3 6HG tel 0422 54823/52334
Open: Mon-Sat 10-5, Sun 2.30-5 April-Sept
Access: [U][T] Ground floor only

Brighton (E Sussex)

(SEA) Map7 TQ30

Brighton College (Burstow Gallery)

A gallery exhibiting a variety of the visual arts with an emphasis on material of an educational nature. [VA,Cr,Ph]

Address: Brighton College, Eastern Road, Brighton, E Sussex BN2 2AL tel 027 369 7131

Contact: Director of Art Nicholas Bremer

Open: Mon-Sat 11.30-5, Sun 2-5

Policy: The gallery is situated in the college precincts and adjoins the main hall which has seating for between 300 and 400. Exhibitions can be arranged to coincide with concerts, seminars etc. The visual arts programme also includes touring shows as well as solo and group shows, often by local artists. About four exhibitions which are open to the public are presented each year, in addition to internal shows of students' work. One of the public exhibitions forms a major part of the Brighton Festival visual arts programme.

The Space: Approximately 274m square of hanging space is divided into two exhibition areas.

Exhibiting: Hire charges are by arrangement.

Access: [S]

Brighton Museum & Art Gallery

A local authority-run gallery showing a range of visual arts with a recent trend towards exhibitions with a theatrical theme. [VA,Ph,De]

Address: Church Street, Brighton, E Sussex BN1 1UE tel 027 360 3005

Contact: Exhibitions Officer John Filkin

Open: Tues-Sat 10-5.45, Sun 2-5, closed Mon

Policy: As part of the Royal Pavilion & Museums, the gallery's policy is to show and interpret a range of visual arts and design, including textiles, ethnographic items and visual arts from all periods. The permanent collection includes these areas, social history and the archaeology of Sussex. Each May, there is an exhibition linked to the Brighton Festival theme. Of the nine temporary exhibitions a year, around a third are by living artists and makers and the programme attracts the gallery-going public as well as moving towards the needs of new audiences. The education department has a continuous programme of lectures workshops and fun days.

Sales: Work sold; Sales referred to exhibitor; Credit card; Credit scheme

The Space: Three rooms 10x10x5m high with 109m of wall space, hanging is by mirror plates. Ceiling lights in two galleries with suspended lighting in the third. Showcases available and gallery plans on request.

Exhibiting: [AW] Gallery hire charges under review. Work is occasionally commissioned. Gallery covers insurance, printing and mail-out of publicity, catalogue/card and artists expenses. Support in principle for EPR. Commission is 33.3%.

Access: [X] BR Brighton 10 mins; Public car park 5 mins

Brighton Polytechnic Gallery

Run by the Faculty of Art and Design of Brighton Polytechnic, the programme links student shows with others of contemporary, historical or community interest. [VA,Ph,Cr,LA]

Address: Faculty of Art, Design & Humanities, Grand Parade, Brighton, E Sussex BN2 2JY tel 0273 604141 ext 251, 238

Contact: Exhibition Officer Julian Freeman

Open: Mon-Fri 9-5, extension by arrangement

Policy: The gallery is geared to course-related exhibitions which also aim to attract a wider audience than polytechnic users. Exhibitions, which run for three to four weeks are predominantly solo shows by living artists and makers. These are linked with historical exhibitions and shows which are of particular community interest.

Sales: Work sold

The Space: Main gallery with *'shop window'* front 21x5x5m high with one wall 21m high and the remainder divided by screens as appropriate. The separate foyer area is suitable for up to 40 framed works and video or audio visual works. Showcases available. Outdoor garden/quadrangle. Gallery plans on request.

Exhibiting: [AW][EF] Applications to Exhibition Officer. Gallery finances insurance, printing and mail-out of publicity, list of exhibits, transport and catalogue/card. Support in principle for EPR. Commission 25% and gallery may request one work from exhibition for polytechnic collection. Note above may change after April 1989. Details on request.

Access: [U][T][S] BR Brighton 10 mins; Public car parks 5 mins

Gardner Centre Gallery

This gallery shows a wide range of contemporary solo and touring and work by community groups, first shows by young artists and a major craft show annually. [VA,Cr,Ph,LA]

Address: University of Sussex, Falmer, Brighton, E Sussex BN1 9RA tel 027 368 5447

Contact: Visual Arts Organiser Hilary Lane

Open: Mon-Sat 10-6; closed bank holidays

Policy: Exhibitions in the gallery are regularly supported by day events with specialised speakers discussing related topics. The gallery is often visited by school and college groups. As part of the university arts centre the gallery aims to present new work to a wide and varied audience. Exhibitions normally show for one month and predominantly feature the work of living artists and makers.

Sales: Work sold

The Space: Foyer area 30m with hanging by rods and mirror plates, lighting by spots. Main gallery 100m, with a flexible screen system where work can be directly fixed to walls and lighting is by spots. Gallery plans available.

Exhibiting: [AW][EF] Exhibition proposals should be accompanied by slides or photographs and SAE. Gallery finances insurance, printing and mail-out of publicity and catalogue/card, transport, preview costs and artists' expenses. Support in principle for EPR.

Commission is 25%.
Access: [X] Buses from Lewes and Brighton; BR Falmer 5 mins; Public car park 2 mins

Hugo Barclay

This commercial gallery on the Crafts Council's selected list which promotes a changing display of work by selected artists as well as staging solo or group shows. [Ce,Pr,Je,Gl,Wo]

Address: 7 East Street, Brighton, E Sussex BN1 1HP tel 027 321 694
Contact: Hugo Barclay
Open: Mon-Sat 10-1, 2-5.30
Policy: The gallery shows an extensive collection of ceramics, prints, jewellery, glass and woodwork from both established and up-and-coming artists. About 125 makers are represented with four major exhibitions held a year. There is a large group 'Summer Show' and a jewellery promotion during the Christmas period.
Sales: Work sold; Credit card; Credit scheme
The Space: Lower and upper galleries each 4x7x3m high, tungsten and hallogen lighting with four large and eight smaller showcases available.
Exhibiting: [AW] Exhibition space is normally booked at least two years in advance. Gallery finances insurance, printing and mail-out of publicity, preview costs, display and part of the transport costs. Catalogue/card and biographies are also provided for customers. Commission charged at 50%.
Access: [F] BR Brighton 10 mins; Public car park 3 mins

Nexus

A commercial contemporary crafts gallery on the Crafts Council's selected list specialising in textiles, jewellery, wood and ceramics. [Cr]

Address: 14 Broad Street, Brighton, E Sussex BN2 1TJ tel 0273 684480
Contact: Owner Cynthia Cousens
Open: Wed-Sat 11-6
Policy: The gallery shows work of national and local well-established and new contemporary craftspeople. With a changing display of stock through the year and special theme, four or five group or solo exhibitions annually.

Red Herring Gallery: 'On All Fours' an installation by Bruce Williams

Sales: Work sold; Credit card
The Space: One gallery 3.5x7.5m, daylight boosted by spot lights, shelving, showcase and hanging space.
Exhibiting: [AW] Craftspeople should make initial contact sending information and visual material. Gallery covers cost of insurance, printing, publicity, preview and mailing out of publicity. Commission varies.
Access: [F] Town centre site

Pig & Fig

This gallery provides a showcase for mainly local artists and between exhibitions, there is a changing display of work for sale. [VA]

Address: 125 Kings Road Arches, Brighton, E Sussex BN1 2FA tel 027 356 4661
Contact: Richard Collett
Open: Mon-Sun 10-6
Policy: The gallery was set up to provide a show case for artists, many of whom are local. Its policy is to adjust fees and commission to suit each artist. In many cases fees are waived especially if the artist is able to help with invigilation. Well established artists are expected to pay the full fee, and those whose work has never been exhibited are shown commission-free. Exhibitions, mainly solo, are usually shown for two weeks.
Sales: Work sold
The Space: The upper and lower galleries approximately 5x5m and have natural daylight with extra lighting by spots and floods on tracks. Gallery plans available.
Exhibiting: [AW] Gallery finances insurance, hire charges and commission are negotiable.
Access: [F] **ground floor** [X] upper gallery. All buses to seafront; BR Brighton 15 mins

Red Herring Gallery

An artist-run gallery showing a broad range of works in all media in a mixture of individual, group and community based shows which consists of three different spaces which can be used in any combination. [VA,Ph,Cr,LA]

Address: 9-12 North Road, Brighton, E SussexBN1 1YF tel 027 368 4807
Contact: Gallery Co-ordinator Nannette Aldred, 24 North Place, Brighton, East Sussex, BN1 1YF
Open: Mon-Sun 10-6 (variable)
Policy: The aim of this gallery is to exhibit a range of contemporary art and craft, *'encompassing all forms of visual experiences that represent a realistic view of what is currently being produced, not necessarily one governed by the forces of fashion and commercial influence'*. To date, exhibitions have been predominantly by local artists but the gallery is keen to attract shows from further afield. Exhibitions normally show for nine days, but this is negotiable.
Sales: Sales referred to exhibitor
The Space: Main gallery 9x7x3m high, small gallery 10.5x2.5x3m high, both with shop window frontage and additional spot lighting. Basement gallery 9x7x2.5m high, lighting by track-mounted spots. Stairs restrict access of large works to basement. Gallery plans available.
Exhibiting: [AW] Studio members select from

applications quarterly, applicants should enquire for next review date from gallery co-ordinator. Slides or photographs and SAE should be enclosed with applications. Gallery finances preview costs, and charges a nominal hire fee. Where possible exhibitors are asked to invigilate their own shows. Supports EPR in principle. No commission taken on sales.
Access: [F] ground floor[X] basement. BR Brighton 10 mins; Public car park 2 mins

Studio Shop

This commercial gallery wishes to provide an outlet for emerging and established artists. [VA]

Address: Kensington Gardens, Brighton, E Sussex BN1 tel 027 369 6410
Contact: Sascha Swartz
Open: Mon-Sat 9-5
Policy: The Studio Shop which is situated in the busy North Lanes, Brighton, in the arcade of Kensington Gardens, offers an opportunity for professional and amateur artists and makers to submit their work for consideration.
The Space: [AW]

Window Gallery

A commercial gallery showing mainly figurative and representational work which is exhibited on consignment, 'no abstract work'. [Pa,Pr]

Address: 3 Dukes Lane, Brighton, E Sussex BN1 1BG tel 027 372 6190
Contact: Carole-Anne White or Mike Thompson
Open: Mon-Sat 10-6
Sales: Work sold
The Space: 36m linear hanging space with spots and natural lighting, hanging by rail and direct fixing.
Exhibiting: [AW] Gallery covers insurance, printing and mail-out of publicity and preview costs. Framing and transport costs are shared. Commission 40% including VAT.
Access: [S] BR Brighton 15 mins; Public car park 10 mins

Zap Club

Nightclub which since 1982 has been commissioning, producing and presenting cabaret, music, poetry, live art, dance and music. [Ph,Vi,LA]

Address: 17 Tichborne Street, Brighton, E Sussex BN1 1UR tel 027 372 7880
Contact: Director Dick Witts
Open: Mon-Sun evenings plus disco to 2 am, daytime opening during summer months
Policy: Zap is devoted to new and unfamliar work. It programmes performances into a network of South-East venues, provides programmes on request throughout the UK, creates major events throughout the UK and abroad, and organises workshops and events within the Brighton community.
The Space: The Zap club is being extended with a central performance area 7m square, audience capacity 300. One arch will comprise a café-bar with hanging space (2x 20m) lengths devoted to photography. Video exhibition facilities also available.
Access: [U]

Brimstage (Merseyside)

(MA) Map4 SJ38

Voirrey Embroidery Centre

Exhibition space in retail embroidery centre which sells a large range of specialist goods and runs instructional workshops and courses for beginners and others. [Cr,Te]

Address: Brimstage Hall, Brimstage, Wirral, Merseyside L63 6JA tel 051 342 3514
Contact: Partner Mrs Voirrey Branthwaite
Open: Mon-Sat 10-5; Open until 8pm first Thurs every month
Policy: *'To illustrate the many facets of embroidery and tapestry and to stretch the imagination of visitors.'* Exhibitions are intended to provide focus, generate ideas and encourage sales. The programme changes monthly, and covers work from past and present, designers, manufacturers, professional makers and also includes annual summer exhibition of work by *'customers'*. Most exhibitions are group shows and feature a more three-dimensional approach to display rather than traditional two-dimensional presentation.
The Space: Upstairs exhibition area of around 38 with an additional 18 square metres possible in summer months square metres.
Exhibiting: [AW] Initial enquiries to Mrs Voirrey Branthwaite. Centre covers insurance, printing and publicity.
Access: [X] to exhibition area; **[U]** to retail area Bus 185 or 186 from Heswall to Talbot Avenue, 4 mins; Close to M53, car park on site

Bristol (Avon)

(SWA) Map6 ST57

3D Gallery

Selling paintings, limited edition prints, sculpture, ceramics, turned wood, jewellery, tapestry. Framing service. Commissions arranged. [Sc,Pr,Ce,Wo,Je,Te]

Address: 13 Perry Road, Bristol BS1 5BG tel 0272 291 363
Contact: Andy Guck
Open: Mon-Sat 11-5.30, Wed 11-1.30
Policy: Approximately four exhibitions a year with regular exhibitors as well as work by new artists and makers introduced at exhibitions.
Access: [F]

Alistair Gill Gallery-Shop

Craft gallery set up in 1988. [Cr]

Address: 4 Christmas Steps, Bristol, Avon BS1 5BS tel 0272 221 204
Contact: Alistair Gill
Policy: It promotes high-quality work by contemporary designer-makers with textiles, jewellery, furniture and fine bookbinding as its specialities.

Sales: Almost all work is for sale; Commissions are encouraged

Arnolfini

An independent arts centre with a varied programme of exhibitions, cinema, performance, music, dance and video, with a café, bar and bookshop. [VA,Ph,Vi,LA]

Address: 16 Narrow Quay, Bristol, Avon BS1 4QA tel 0272 299191

Contact: Director Barry Barker

Open: Centre: Mon-Sat 10-11; Sun 12-10.30; Gallery: Mon-Sat 10-7.30, Sun 12-7

Policy: The gallery presents *'new and exciting developments in the visual arts in a local, national and international context and brings the visual arts to a new audience'*. An extensive education programme is run with the exhibition programme to *'contextualise and elucidate the exhibition'*. Conferences and other events are organised for the gallery and outside.

Sales: Work sold; Credit card; Credit scheme

The Space: The Downstairs Gallery has 67.5m linear hanging space and the Upstairs Gallery has 52m linear hanging space. Both galleries have spots and floods and direct fixing is used. Gallery plans available.

Exhibiting: [AW][EF] Send 15-20 slides together with CV and statement. Gallery covers exhibition costs. EPR supported. Commission is 33.3% or 25% depending on whether artist is represented by another gallery.

Access: [U][T][F] Close to city centre; BR Bristol Temple Meads 15 mins; Car park 2 mins

Arnolfini, Bristol

Bristol Craft Centre

The centre is run by a co-operative of makers working in the converted printing works and the gallery is located in the café. [Pa,Pr,Ph,Cr]

Address: 6 Leonard Lane, Bristol, Avon BS1 1EA tel 0272 297890

Contact: Co-ordinator Monica Poston

Open: Mon-Fri 10-6

Policy: The exhibition space is hired at £15 a month *'particularly for first-time exhibitors'*. A changing display of work from the workshops is also on display.

Sales: Work sold

The Space: Three display cabinets plus two display boards 4.6x1.96m and 6.11x1.96m.

Exhibiting: [AW] Applications to the Co-ordinator.The centre provides and mails a press release. Exhibitors must provide posters, handouts, insurance, labels, exhibition title *'back-up material'* and hanging. The centre reserves the right to *'vet the exhibition and publicity'*. A 20% commission is charged on sales.

Access: [X] Bus station 5 mins; BR Bristol Temple Meads 15 mins; Coach Station 10 mins

Bristol Guild Craft Gallery

Craft shop with regular temporary exhibitions. [Cr]

Address: 68/70 Park Street, Bristol BS1 5JX tel 25548

Sales: Work sold; Credit card

The Space: The exhibition space is on the second floor.

Bristol Museum & Art Gallery

A municipal museum and art gallery with permanent collections and occasional exhibitions by contemporary artists. [VA,Cr]

Address: Queen's Road, Bristol BS8 1RL tel 0272 299771

Contact: Director David Wilson

Open: Mon-Sat 10-5

Exhibiting: [AW] Considers any exhibition.

Croft Gallery

A commercial gallery with a large exhibition space and a framing and restoration workshop. [Pa,Pr,Dr]

Address: 26 Stokes Croft, Bristol, Avon BS1 3QD tel 0272 422213

Contact: R W Hart

Open: Mon-Sat 9.30-6

Policy: The two spaces are used to show a changing display of work and mixed exhibitions. The gallery aims *'to present a varied range of work in a variety of media from both established and up-and-coming artists'*. The work must be a *'commercially viable proposition'*.

Sales: Work sold; Credit card

The Space: A 12.75x6.75m gallery with screens, natural and fluorescent light. Gallery plans available.

Exhibiting: [AW] The gallery provides, publicity, preview, list of exhibits and a catalogue/card. The space can also be hired at £150 a week exclusive of promotion. A 40% commission is charged on sales.

Access: [X] City centre location

David Cross Gallery

Commercial gallery specialising in traditional British painting, drawing, landscape, marine, sporting subjects particularly those relating to Bristol and the South West.

Address: 3a Boyces Avenue, Bristol BS8 4AA tel 0272 732 614
Contact: Jo David
Open: Daily 9.30-6
Policy: Period and contemporary work shown. Also restoration studio and framing.
Sales: Work sold; Credit card
Exhibiting: **[AW]** Colour photographs and CV invited as first approach.
Access: Town centre half a mile

Eye Gallery

A commercial gallery and framing shop showing West Country artists in group and solo shows on a bi-monthly basis. [VA]

Address: 36 Frogmore Street, Bristol, Avon BS1 5NA tel 0272 221515
Contact: Nicholas Hankinson
Open: Mon-Fri 10-5.30, Sat 10-4.30
Policy: *'Work is sold to a widening circle of the local public with considerable expansion into the business community.'* Occasional talks are arranged with the exhibitions.
Sales: Work sold; Credit card; Credit scheme
The Space: The gallery has 80m linear hanging space 3m high with spot lighting, hanging rail and one show case available. Gallery plans available.
Exhibiting: **[AW]** Send slides or photographs with sizes. Insurance, publicity, preview, list of exhibits, catalogue/card provided by the gallery which takes 40% commission.
Access: **[F]**

Croft Gallery (Photo: Steve Tromans)

Frost & Reed

Commercial publishers showing work related to their publishing activities.

Address: Orchard Road, St George, Bristol BS5 7HS tel 0272 552 525
Contact: Director

Glevum Gallery Barge

Private gallery on a restored grain barge in Bristol City Docks. [VA,Ce]

Address: Merchants Quay, Bristol City Docks, Bristol BS1 4RN tel 227502
Contact: Owner Vincent Neave
Open: Tues-Sat 10.30-5, Sun 11.30-5
Policy: Specialises in work by contemporary artists, primarily marine and landscape, and showing eight to ten exhibitions a year.
Sales: Work sold; Credit card
The Space: The gallery is in the cargo hold of the barge and measures 20x5m. Direct fixing, lighting combination of natural and spotlights.
Exhibiting: **[AW]** Applications in writing and photographs of work to Vincent Neave. Gallery covers cost of insurance, publicity and mailing and half of preview. Commission is 33.3%.
Access: **[X]**

Guild Gallery

A space for hire from the Bristol Guild of Applied Art in their store and restaurant. [VA,Ph,Cr,Ar]

Address: 68 Park Street, Bristol BS1 5JX tel 0272 265548
Contact: Gallery Organiser John Stops
Open: Mon-Fri 9.30-5.30, Sat 9.30-5
Policy: The gallery shows a variety of work and is booked two years ahead.
Sales: Work sold
The Space: The gallery is 6x12m with work hung from battens on cup hooks. Natural and track lighting. Ample rostra for 3D display.
Exhibiting: **[AW]** For conditions and terms contact John Stops.
Access: **[X]** City centre location

Michael Stewart Fine Art

A commercial gallery specialising in the work of Sir William Russell Flint with occasional exhibitions of living British artists. [Pa]

Address: The Georgian House, Broad Street, Wrington, Bristol, Avon BS18 7LA tel 0934 863149
Contact: K S Gardner
Open: Mon-Fri 9-5
Sales: Work sold; Credit card
Access: **[F]**

Off-Centre Gallery

An artist-run commercial gallery specialising in contemporary prints from Britain and abroad. [Pa,Pr,Dr]

Address: 13 Cotswold Road, Windmill Hill, Bedminster,

Bristol, Avon BS3 4NX tel 0272 661782
Contact: Peter Ford or Christine Higgott
Open: Tues-Sat 11-6, Thurs, Fri 9; usually closed Feb, March
Policy: The gallery aims to *'give original printmaking the same status as painting and sculpture'* and to *'demonstrate the interest, versatility and variety of contemporary original printmaking'*. Several exhibitions mounted each year and some available to tour eg 'Prints with a Point', 'Painterly Prints', 'Art for Boardrooms'.
Sales: Work sold
The Space: Gallery one is 6x5m, and gallery two is 4x4m giving a total of 35m linear hanging space with spot lights and direct fixing.
Exhibiting: Open submission exhibitions are advertised in *Artists Newsletter* and elsewhere. Commission is 30%.
Access: [X] Buses 74,75,76,47,48,49,20,21 5 mins; BR Bristol Temple Meads 20 mins; On street parking

Pelter/Sands Gallery

A commercial gallery offering one of the best selections of paintings, drawings and sculpture in the West Country, ranging from the 18th century Dutch school to 20th century and contemporary British artists. [Pa,Dr,Sc]
Address: 43-45 Park Street, Bristol, Avon BS1 5NL
tel 0272 293 988
Contact: Rachel Fear, Chris Billing
Open: Tues-Sat 10-5.30; closed bank holidays
Policy: Temporary exhibitions include work by leading contemporary painters and sculptors. Large stock of 18th, 19th and 20th century paintings and watercolours.
Sales: Work sold
The Space: Two large gallery areas approximately 10x13m each.
Exhibiting: [AW] Applications in writing to Christopher Billing with slides or photographs and stamped addressed envelope for return.
Access: [S]

Off-Centre Gallery: 'Paper Chasing' by Peter Ford from the exhibition 'Art for Boardrooms'

Royal West of England Academy

A self-supporting society of artists with a permanent collection of painting and sculpture of elected members work, and a temporary exhibition programme. [VA]
Address: Queens Road, Clifton, Bristol, Avon BS8 1PX tel 0272 735129
Contact: Academy Secretary
Open: Daily 10-5.30
Policy: The programme aims to show *'works by distinguished artists, both members and others, and to encourage non-members to submit works for selection during the open exhibition'*.
Sales: Work sold
The Space: Natural lighting, spots during winter months.
Exhibiting: [AW] The academy's council considers requests to hire the galleries for exhibitions and provides mailing, and charges a 20% commission on sales.
Access: [L][F] Buses 8,9 from BR Bristol Temple Meads

Theatre Royal (Bristol Old Vic)

The oldest working theatre in England, Bristol Old Vic dates from 1766 and houses a studio theatre, The New Vic, dating from 1972 and within the theatre complex, Cooper's Gallery is 'available for exhibitions, functions and receptions'.
Address: King Street, Bristol BS1 4ED tel 0272 277 466
Contact: Dick Penny
Access: [U] except Buttery

Watershed Media Centre

A media centre with cinemas, video workshops, production facilities, darkrooms, restaurant, bar and conference facilities with exhibitions part of year in main gallery with other shows in the corridor gallery. [Ph]
Address: 1 Canons Road, Bristol, Avon BS1 5TX tel 0272 276444
Contact: Exhibition Organiser Peter Ride
Open: Daily 9am-10pm
Policy: The programme has an emphasis on *'contemporary photography with a commitment to work from the independent sector'*. The policy is to *'challenge the role of photography, raising issues about representation, reproduction and its inter-relation to other cultural practices'*. Major touring exhibition

programme.
Sales: Work sold
The Space: The corridor space is 40m linear, panels each 2.75m high. The gallery is 800 square metres, panels variable.
Exhibiting: [AW] insurance, transport, publicity, preview, and catalogue/card provided by the centre. A fee is paid *'where appropriate'* and the centre supports EPR. Work is sometimes commissioned on a co-sponsorship basis.
Access: [U][T][L] City centre location; BR Bristol Temple Meads 20 mins

Whole Baked Gallery

A gallery in a community café which is part of a community care project run by Community Care Volunteers. [VA,Ph,Sc]

Address: 7 Lawford Street, St Philips, Bristol B52 0DH tel 0272 552968 ext 147
Contact: Cafe Manager James McNeill
Open: Mon-Fri 9-6
Policy: *'Most of the exhibitions are by local unemployed artists. The aim of the gallery is to offer exhibition facilities and practise in mounting exhibitions to unemployed artists who are hoping to make a living through their artistic skills and need exposure'*. Work is also shown by *'community groups and people with disabilities'* and the gallery aims to have at least one thematic exhibition which focuses on issues or activities in the community. Sculpture is restricted to wall-based work only.
Sales: Work sold
The Space: The space is 18.5m linear with adjustable lighting.
Exhibiting: The gallery is able to provide publicity, list of exhibits and private view.
Access: [F][T] Buses 40-42,44/5,506/7,6,6a,7,36,38,530, 540,544,545,509,588 15 mins; Coach station 15 mins, BR Bristol Temple Meads 10 mins

Broadstairs (Kent)

(SEA) Map7 TR36

Broadstairs Library Gallery

Run by Kent County Libraries Department, this gallery exists primarily to show the work of artists based in East Kent. [VA,Ph,Cr]

Address: The Broadway, Broadstairs, Kent CT10 2BS tel 084 362 994
Contact: Group Librarian David Paynter
Open: Mon, Tues, Thurs 9.30-6, Wed, Sat 9.30-5, Fri 9.30-8
Policy: The gallery aims to promote the work of local artists working in a variety of media. Alongside these there are shows of museum and archive material from the department's extensive collection. An average of ten exhibitions, predominantly by living artists, are shown each year which run for between two to four weeks each. The exhibition space is occasionally used for films and small-scale music and theatre events.
Sales: Work sold
The Space: 12x6x3m high with 30m linear hanging space. Work is hung by rods and direct fixing, with fixed spot and fluorescent lighting. Two wall-mounted and three free-standing display cases available in foyer.
Exhibiting: [AW] Applications to Group Librarian a year in advance, enclosing slides or photographs and biography. Gallery finances insurance and list of exhibits. Support in principle for EPR. Commission 15%.
Access: [X] BR Broadstairs 2 mins; Public car park 1 min

Bromsgrove (Hereford & Worcester)

(WMA) Map4 SO97

Avoncroft Museum of Buildings

An open-air independent museum covering 15 acres. The museum features historical buildings rescued from demolition, and re-erected at Avoncroft. [Pr,Dr,Ph,Cr]

Address: Stoke Heath, Bromsgrove, Hereford & Worcester B60 4JR tel 0527 31886
Contact: Director M Thomas
Open: March-Nov 11-5.30; Closed Mon March,April,May, Sept,Oct,Nov; Closed Fri March,Nov
Policy: A larger exhibition space is being constructed to enable bigger and more varied exhibitions to be shown. The museum has a varied programme of events, attractions and educational activities. It currently features over 20 buildings covering seven centuries. Temporary exhibitions usually have an historical or architectural theme.
Exhibiting: [AW] Written applications should be made to the Curator, Simon Penn.
Access: [U][T] 2 miles south of Bromsgrove on the A38; Bus 144 from Birmingham & Worcester

Bruton (Somerset)

(SWA) Map6 ST63

Bruton Gallery

Bruton Gallery shows sculpture by Rodin, Bernard, Bourdelle and others as well as paintings, drawings and graphics by leading English, Scottish and French figurative artists of the 20th century. [VA]

Address: Bruton, Somerset BA10 tel 0749 812 205
Contact: Directors Michael and Sandra Le Marchant
Open: Mon-Sat 10-5.30
Policy: Also has a gallery in New York.

Buckden (Cambridgeshire)

(EA) Map5 TL27

L'Bidi Studio

Commercial art gallery linked to L'Bidi, St Ives (see separate entry). [VA,Ph,Cr]

Address: 81 High Street, Buckden, Huntingdon, Cambridgeshire PE18 9TA tel 0480 810545
Contact: Lindsay Beedie
Open: Mon-Sat 10-5.30; Closed Thurs also Sun 2-5
Policy: Programme of art and craft exhibitions lasting two to three weeks, both mixed and solo and a display of gallery artists between shows. Exhibiting contemporary

and representational watercolours, pastels, oils, sculpture, prints. Between exhibitions there is always a changing display of work.

Sales: Work sold; Credit card

The Space: 4.5x6x2.25 high. Natural light boosted by spots, rod hanging system.

Exhibiting: [AW] Telephone for an appointment. Gallery covers costs and work is mainly sold on consignment basis. Commission is 35.5%.

Access: [F] Shop **[X]** Gallery upstairs. Own parking, regular bus services from BR Huntingdon

Bungay (Suffolk)

(EA) Map5 TM79

Bookshop & Gallery

The gallery was founded in 1986 and is part of a business which includes a general bookshop and picture framing workshop. [Pa,Pr,Dr]

Address: 40 Earsham Street, Bungay, Suffolk NR35 1AQ tel 0986 5164

Contact: J Cook

Open: Mon-Fri 9-5.30 Sat 9-5

Policy: The gallery specialises in landscapes by local artists, predominantly in watercolour. In this way it is a showcase for artists with an East Anglian connection, catering both to local customers and tourists.

Sales: Work sold; Credit scheme; Credit card

The Space: Main hanging space comprises six screens each 0.91x1.83m and wall space 2.44x4.57m, with ceiling-mounted spotlights. Additional wall space available in side galleries. Access limited by staircase to first floor. Shop windows are used to supplement displays. The exhibition spaces are also used for book launch events.

Exhibiting: [AW] Personal visit by appointment preferred. Gallery covers insurance, publicity, list of exhibits and preview costs. Commission is 30% or 20% if work is framed by the gallery.

Access: [X] Public car park 2 mins; Bus stop 2 mins; On-road parking nearby

Burnley (Lancashire)

(NWA) Map3 SD83

Mid-Pennine Arts Association (Gallery Downstairs)

The Gallery Downstairs is part of the Mid-Pennine Arts Association which provides a professional programme of events and activities covering all aspects of the arts throughout East Lancashire. [VA,Ph,Cr,Ho,LA]

Address: Yorke Street, Burnley, Lancashire BB11 1HD tel 0282 21986

Contact: Exhibitions Organiser Sheenagh Mayo

Open: Mon-Fri 10-6, Sat 10-4, Sun 2-4

Policy: The association seeks to provide a varied programme of contemporary visual arts and craft exhibitions and to increase awareness and accessibility of work by professional artists and makers. Material is presented in such a way as to encourage an approach to the visual arts and craft through recreation and enjoyment. *'We seek to act as a catalyst for further activity and to provide an educational resource to the public and to schools within our area, in addition to encouraging and assisting in the advancement of the presentation, practice and study of fine art. Within these parameters we are always pleased to use the work of local artists and makers'.*

Sales: Work sold; Credit card

The Space: The gallery measures 14.5x10.5x3.5m offering 42-61m linear hanging space. Hanging is by mirror plates and lighting is by Concorde multi-track system with 60 lamps offering wall washes and spots. There is also thermostatic temperature control. The gallery also has two glass show cases programmed concurrently with the main exhibition. The exhibitions are always invigilated. Plans of the gallery are available.

Exhibiting: [AW][EF] Applications are welcome anytime and should include slides, biography and statement about the work. The gallery will pay for insurance, publicity, list of exhibits, preview costs, transport, mailing and catalogue. Gallery supports EPR. 20% commission taken on sales.

Access: [U][T] Town centre site; Bus, BR Burnley & car park 5 mins

Towneley Hall Art Gallery & Museum

The gallery is part of Towneley Hall, once the historic home of the Towneley family and now run by the Recreation and Leisure Department of Burnley Borough Council and set in 284 acres of parkland, housing collections of 18th and 19th Century English oil paintings and watercolours including paintings by Zoffany and Turner. [VA]

Address: Burnley, Lancashire BB12 3RQ tel 0282 24213

Contact: Curator J Susan Bourne

Open: Mon-Fri 10-5, Sun 12-5; Closed Sat

Policy: The temporary exhibition programme runs from Easter to September and includes work by contemporary regional artists and potters.

Sales: Work sold

The Space: One gallery has air-conditioning, all have UV filters and are lit by protected fluorescent tubes and spots. The galleries are on the upper floors, access is by stairs only. Gallery plans available.

Exhibiting: [AW][EF] Applications should be sent to the

Towneley Hall: 'Private Pathway' by Charles Hickson, oil on canvas, from the exhibition 'Lancashire South of the Sands'

Curator one year in advance and should include photographs or slides of work. The gallery pays for publicity, list of exhibits, mailing and catalogue. The gallery supports EPR and pays fees to artists.
Access: [U][X] Bus 10 mins; Car park in grounds

Wheatley Lane Library

A branch of Lancashire Libraries. [Pa,Ph]

Address: Wheatley Lane, Nr Burnley, Lancashire BB12 9QH tel 0282 693160
Contact: Mrs A Tallett
Open: Mon, Wed 2-4.30, 5-7
Policy: Twelve exhibitions have been held in the past year, six of which have been solo shows by contemporary artists. The library aims to display the work of local and other artists and to introduce that work to a wider audience.
The Space: Three boards 1.2x0.6m mounted on the lending library walls.
Exhibiting: [AW] Contact the District Librarian to apply for an exhibition.15% commission is charged.
Access: Car park

Burton Latimer (Northamptonshire)

(EMA) Map5 SP97

Burton Latimer Library

See Northamptonshire Libraries. [VA,Ph,Cr,Ar]

Address: High Street, Burton Latimer, Northamptonshire NN15 5RH
tel 053 672 3357
Contact: District Librarian Derrick Bond, Kettering Library, Sheep Street, Kettering, Northamptonshire tel 0536 512315
Open: Tues,Fri 10-1, 2-7; closed Mon, Sat
Sales: Work sold; Sales referred to exhibitor
The Space: Display area is 43.5 square metres with 14m linear hanging space on Scandon screens and 4m on walls. Track and natural light, tape-slide equipment available.
Exhibiting: [AW] District Librarian. Publicity and insurance provided, transport between libraries arranged for touring exhibitions. Commission is 10%.
Access: [F] Buses to Kettering; Car park at rear

Bury (Lancashire)

(NWA) Map3 SD83

Bury Metro Arts Association

A voluntary independent association, funded by Bury Metropolitan Council, which aids and encourages arts activity throughout the borough, with an arts centre at Derby Hall, which includes a performance space, box office, bar, gallery and craft display cabinets.

Address: Derby Hall, Market Street, Bury, Lancashire BL9 0BN tel 061 761 7107
Open: Daily 10-4; Closed Tues, Sun
Policy: Exhibitions generally run for one month, the programme is selected by a panel which meets three times a year and whose members are practising artists.
Sales: Work sold
The Space: The gallery has 31m linear hanging space and Concorde track lighting. Fixing is by mirror plates to chipboard. Five lockable display cabinets 1.6x3.35x1.6m deep are situated in the foyer area which have glass tops and fronts and interior lighting. Gallery plans available.
Exhibiting: [AW] The Association covers the costs of publicity, transport, insurance and preview costs. Submissions should be sent to the Visual Arts Panel along with up to ten slides, a brief biography and statement about the work. A commission of 20% is taken on sales.

Bury St Edmunds (Suffolk)

(EA) Map5 TL86

Bury St Edmunds Library

Exhibition space in public library, administered by Suffolk County Arts & Libraries Service Bury St Edmunds Area. [VA,Cr,Ph]

Address: Sergeants Walk, off St Andrews Street, Bury St Edmunds, Suffolk IP33 tel 0284 701611
Contact: Senior Information Librarian
Sales: Work sold; Sales referred to exhibitor
The Space: The space is 15 square metres.
Exhibiting: Programme booked for two years ahead; fee of 20% on all sales made from exhibition subject to a minimum charge of £17.50 payable in advance.

Bury St. Edmunds Art Gallery

Administered by a registered charity, it is situated on the first floor of a distinguished Georgian building in the middle of the town, with a mixed programme of temporary exhibitions and musical performances. [VA,Ph,Cr]

Address: Market Cross, Cornhill, Bury St Edmunds, Suffolk IP33 tel 0284 62081
Contact: Curator Sylvia Thomas, Manston Hall, Whepstead, Bury St Edmunds, Suffolk tel 0284 88229
Open: Tues-Sat 10.30-4.30
Policy: In a programme of some 14 exhibitions, each lasting up to 28 days, the gallery pursues a policy of integration of the visual and performing arts and thereby extending the significance of the current exhibition. Artists residencies, demonstrations and workshops supplement the gallery's profile.
Sales: Work sold
The Space: Linear hanging is 41.9m with a height of 2.4m.
Exhibiting: [AW] Gallery covers insurance, printing and mailing of publicity, list of exhibits, preview costs, 50% of transport, catalogue/card and part of artists' expenses. 25% commission is charged on sales.
Access: [U][L][T][F] Public car park 3 mins; BR 15 mins; Bus park 10 mins

Chimney Mill Galleries

Commercial gallery, also selling antique pine and country furniture. [VA]

Address: Chimney Mill, West Stow, Nr Bury St Edmunds, Suffolk IP28 6ER tel 028 484 234
Contact: Hilary Wenn
Open: Tues-Sun 11-5
Policy: Small number of three-week mixed exhibitions.
Sales: Work sold
The Space: Hallway 5x1m; 4 rooms: 8.5x4m; 5x4.5m; 5x2.5m; 6x6m. Hanging by nails in wall, strip lighting.
Exhibiting: Gallery covers exhibition costs and takes a commission of 30%.
Access: Rural area, no bus routes

St John's Street Gallery

Commercial art gallery founded in 1985, showing contemporary prints and watercolours between shows. [Pa,Pr,Dr]

Address: 26 St John's Street, Bury St Edmunds, Suffolk IP33 1SN tel 0284 69573
Contact: Director Paul Henly
Open: Tues-Sat 9.30-5.30
Policy: *'To provide access to a broad cross-section of contemporary art at reasonable prices.'* Three solo shows by living artists in 1987.
Sales: Work sold; Credit card
Exhibiting: [AW] By appointment. Gallery pays insurance and mailing of publicity. Hanging from picture rail, ceiling spots. Commission 33.3%.
Access: [S] BR, bus station and car park 5mins

Buxton (Derbyshire)

(NWA) Map5 SK07

Buxton Museum & Art Gallery

A municipal museum and art gallery run by Derbyshire County Council which has permanent collections of 19th and 20th Century watercolours and European prints. [VA]

Address: Terrace Road, Buxton, Derbyshire SK17 6DU tel 0298 4658
Contact: Curator
Open: Tues-Fri 9.30-5.30, Sat 9.30-5
Policy: Last year the gallery's programme included 14 exhibitions of living artists of which eight were solo shows. The policy is *'to show works from the permanent collection and temporary exhibitions with a great variety of media'.*
Sales: Work sold
The Space: The gallery measures 2.43x41.45m and has Concorde suspended track.
Exhibiting: [AW] Applications to be sent to Curator. The gallery will pay for insurance, printing of publicity, display, transport, mailing and catalogue. 15% commission is taken on sales.
Access: [U][F] BR Buxton 5 mins; Car park 1 min

David Russell

A small retail art shop with limited exhibition space. [VA]

Address: 10 Hall Bank, Buxton, Derbyshire SK17 6EW tel 0298 4510
Contact: David Russell
Open: Mon,Tues,Thurs,Fri 9-6, Wed 9-1, Sat 9-5
Policy: The exhibition programme specialises in showing the work of living artists from the region, particularly paintings and local pottery. The gallery provides a framing service and artists' materials are for sale.
Sales: Work sold
The Space: Linear hanging space is 8.12m, pictures are hung with cord and hooks and there is a mixture of natural and artificial lighting.
Exhibiting: [AW] Applications for solo shows only should be sent to David Russell. 25% commission is taken on sales.

Calshot (Hampshire)

(SA) Map7 SU40

Calshot Crafts Centre

Craftshop and gallery, exhibitions of craftwork, restaurant and nature trail. [Cr]

Address: Badminster Farm, Calshot, Hampshire SO4 tel 0703 898846
Open: Mon-Sun 10-5

Cambridge (Cambridgeshire)

(EA) Map5 TL45

Beldesign Art Gallery & Design Shop

A commercial gallery with connected craft shop. [Pa,Sc,Pr,Cr]

Address: 4 Silver Street, Cambridge CB3 9EL tel 0223 69622
Contact: Rebecca Wright
Open: Mon-Sat 10-6; Restricted opening bank holidays
Policy: *'To show the work of relatively-unknown painters, if possible below the age of 30. Somewhat anti-landscape and attracted by colour...general prices in the area of £200-300.'* Monthly exhibitions, mainly solo shows but some mixed. Permanent print collection.
Sales: Work sold; Credit card; Credit scheme
The Space: 6x4x3m high. Good natural light, white walls, spots. Cord hanging from picture rail. Maximum size picture 2x1.3m. Display cabinet for small fragile sculptures; showcases.
Exhibiting: [AW] Apply with slides and full CV to Rebecca Wright. Gallery pays all expenses except transport and artists' expenses, but expects £75 contribution. Gallery may be hired, fee negotiable. Commission 40% plus VAT.
Access: [S] 5mins Lion Yard car park

Broughton House Gallery

A commercial gallery. [VA]

Address: 98 King Street, Cambridge CB1 1LN tel 0223 314960
Contact: Owner Rosemary Davidson
Open: Tues-Sat 10.30-5.30; closed Jan & Feb
Policy: The gallery shows work by contemporary artists from many different countries, oils, watercolours, gouaches, acrylics, drawings, etchings and lithographs ranging in price from £25 to £500. There are nine to ten

monthly exhibitions a year. The setting is friendly and informal (children, babies and prams welcome) with a garden available for sitting and eventually to site sculpture.

Sales: Work sold

The Space: 30 square metres with 8 square metres hanging space. Hanging on battens, track floods and spots. Walled garden suitable for sculpture.

Exhibiting: [AW] Gallery pays for publicity, insurance and preview costs and takes a commission of 35%.

Access: [F] Multi-storey car parks 5mins; Meter parking outside

Cambridge Central Library

Public library in the centre of Cambridge with two exhibition spaces. [VA,Ph,Cr]

Address: 7 Lion Yard, Cambridge CB2 3QD tel 0223 65252 ext 203

Contact: Administrative Officer J W Franklin

Open: Mon-Sat 10-5

Policy: *'To provide on this easily accessible site a facility for artists of all types to try to exhibit their works for sale. We do not specialise.'* Around 300,000 people a year use the library. *'We try to keep a continuous programme of exhibitions in the exhibition room and exhibition area throughout the year.'*

Sales: Sales referred to exhibitor's steward

The Space: Exhibition room 13x7x8m with 27m linear hanging, wall-mounted track round perimeter, general lighting plus floodspots. Exhibition area 10x10x8m with 12m linear hanging space, wall mounted track round perimeter, general lighting plus daylight.

Exhibiting: [AW] To the Assistant Chief Librarian at any time. Booking forms are available from Library and hire charges are £82 for 7 days; £150 for 14 days, plus commission of 10% charged on sales.

Access: [U][T][F] Cambus routes 1,5; BR 25 mins(foot) 10 mins(bus); Car park 3 mins

Cambridge Darkroom

Contemporary photographic gallery with members' darkrooms, workshop and educational programme. [Ph,LA]

Broughton House Gallery (Photo: Nigel Luckhurst)

Address: Dale's Brewery, Gwydir Street, Cambridge CB1 2LJ tel 0223 350725

Contact: Director Mark Lumley

Open: Tues-Sat 12-6, Sun 2-5

Policy: It is *'devoted to the promotion of photography as the means of creative cultural practice, in particular the exploration of the boundaries and relationships between photography and other arts,'* it also accepts and produces major touring photographic shows.

Sales: Work sold

The Space: 12x12x3m high, plus approx 15m on screens. Blockboard walls and screens. Track lighting. Works 3x5m maximum size.

Exhibiting: [AW] To Director with ten workprints or slides plus CV and supporting material.

Access: [X] BR 5 mins; Car parking

Conservatory Gallery

Part of 'Business Arts' selling and hiring work directly to the public and to business. [VA,Ph,LA]

Address: 6 Hills Avenue, Cambridge CB1 4XA tel 0223 211311

Contact: Pamela Barrell

Open: Sat & 1st Sun of month 10-5 or by appointment

Policy: The gallery has a display of work for sale plus permanent sale collection, special mini-exhibitions and occasional larger ones.

Sales: Work sold; Credit scheme

The Space: Two rooms 6x3m, one 3x3m, corridor 10x1m, conservatory 12x3m garden for sculpture.

Exhibiting: [AW] Apply by letter. Hire fees by negotiation. The gallery insures work and takes a commission of 30%.

Access: [F] Bus 2mins; BR 15 mins; Ample car parking

Fitzwilliam Museum

Art gallery attached to university, founded 1816 with a wide permanent collection. [VA,Cr]

Address: Trumpington Street, Cambridge CB2 1RB tel 0223 332900

Contact: Director Professor A M Jaffé

Open: Tues-Sat. 10-5; Sun & bank holidays 2.15-5; closed 24 Dec-1Jan & Good Friday

Policy: The gallery aims to show as much as possible of the permanent collection to the public, it also shows Arts Council touring exhibitions and other temporary exhibitions.

Sales: Occasional selling exhibitions

The Space: 65 metres of hanging space, fluorescent and natural lighting, humidification controls.

Exhibiting: [AW] Write to the Director, programme normally arranged two to three years in advance.

Access: [U][T][L][F] Car park 10 mins; BR 20 mins

Gallery on the Cam

Commercial gallery situated on a barge on the river Cam. [VA,Ce,Te]

Address: Jesus Lock, Chesterton Road, Cambridge CB3 2AE tel 0223 316901

Contact: Philip Martin

Open: Tues-Sat 10-5 Sun 12-5; open bank holidays

Policy: *'A varied exhibition programme from the traditional mixed exhibitions at Christmas and in the summer to those held by small groups and individuals during the rest of the year.'*
Sales: Work sold
The Space: 26x4x2m high, 23m of hanging space. Hanging direct on to walls, which are hessian-covered chipboard. Considerable natural light plus spots. Not suitable for large work.
Exhibiting: **[AW]** Apply to Denise Collins, Gallery Administrator. Gallery meets all costs except transport, artist's expenses and display and takes a commission of 33.3%.
Access: **[X]** Bus 3 from city centre, BR 30 mins and car parks 15 mins; Some street parking

Heffer Gallery

A commercial gallery run by Heffers booksellers and stationers. [VA,Ph,Cr]

Address: Heffers Stationers, 19 Sidney Street, Cambridge CB2 3HL tel 0223 358241
Contact: Gallery Manager Christopher Witchall
Open: Mon-Sat 9-5.30
Policy: The gallery mounts solo and group exhibitions by mainly local and East Anglian artists working in a variety of media and contemporary styles. The exhibition programme runs from February to September and each run for two weeks with the exception of a two-month summer show.
Sales: Work sold; Credit card
The Space: 16x5.6x2.5m high. 40m linear hanging space with natural skylight lighting and hanging from picture rail.
Exhibiting: **[AW]** Apply with slides and CV or telephone to arrange an appointment. Programme planned a year in advance, the gallery finances printing and mailing of publicity, preview costs, catalogue and lists of exhibits and takes 33.3% commission.
Access: **[L]** City centre location, access to all transport

Kettle's Yard

The house, left to Cambridge University by Jim Ede, houses an excellent collection of British modernist art and craft. The gallery is a major focus for the arts in the region. [VA,Vi,LA]

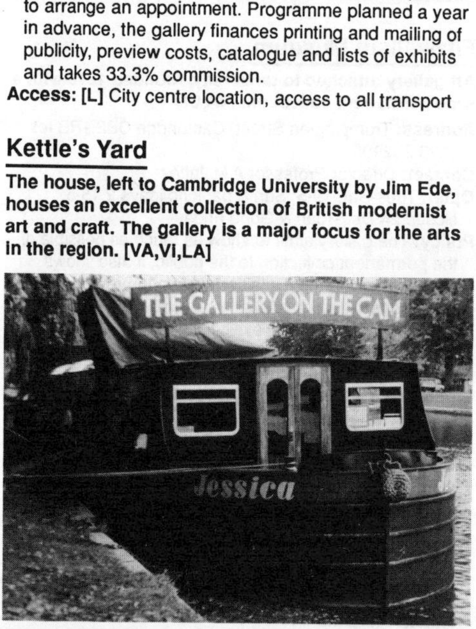

Gallery on the Cam

Address: Castle Street, Cambridge CB3 0AQ tel 0223 352124
Contact: Curator Hilary Gresty
Open: Tues-Sun 2-4 (collection); Tues, Wed, Fri, Sat 12.30-5.30, Thurs 12.30-7, Sun 2-5.30 (gallery)
Policy: Continuing exhibitions of the best in British and continental art. Most exhibitions are initiated or *'bought-in'* by the gallery. There is an artist in residence scheme which is nationally advertised. Runs extensive education programme. Bookshop with increasing range of magazines and catalogues.
Sales: Work sold
The Space: 180 square metres with100m linear hanging space, divisible into between two and four sections.
Exhibiting: **[AW]** Apply with slides and CV and return postage. Programmed up to two years in advance. Hanging is by direct fixing, spots plus natural light, environmental controls. The gallery meets all costs except framing and charges 25% commission.
Access: **[X]** Please call in advance. Close to city centre

Primavera

A well-established commercial art and craft gallery on the Crafts Council's selected list which shows two-week exhibitions of small-scale work in the gallery and changing displays from stock in the shop. [Pa,Sc,Ce,Gl,Wo,Je]

Address: 10 Kings Parade, Cambridge CB2 1SJ tel 0223 357708
Contact: Ronald Pile
Open: Mon-Sat 9.30-5.30
Policy: *'Primavera is essentially an outlet for first-rate British craftwork. Exhibitions offer both the gallery and the artist the opportunity to focus on particular media, approaches, explorations. Audiences generally already well-informed and interested.'*
Sales: Work sold; Credit card
The Space: Two rooms, both 4x6x2m high. Lighting 12v spots/floods. No natural light. Not suitable for large-scale work. Small garden patio space, and two glass cases with lighting.
Exhibiting: **[AW]** slides and photos must be sent in advance to the owner. Gallery pays the greater share of insurance, publicity, preview, display, mailing and catalogue. Commission negotiable.
Access: **[X]** Centre of town; Multi-storey car park 10 mins walk

Textile Studio

Shop selling natural fibre fabrics, textile crafts and clothes with temporary exhibitions. [Te]

Address: 3 Free School Lane, Cambridge CB3 3QA tel 0223 313583
Policy: Textile exhibitions, ancient and modern, foreign and domestic.
Sales: Work sold; Credit card

Trumpington Gallery

Commercial art gallery, also concerned with framing, restoration and conservation in a 14th century thatched building. [Pa,Pr,Dr]

Address: 52 High Street, Trumpington, Cambridge CB2 2LS tel 0223 841656
Contact: J Ball & J Miles
Open: Mon-Fri 10-6, Sat 10-1
Policy: Shows a mixture of 19th century and living artists, the latter mainly local and working in oils or watercolours.
Sales: Work sold; Credit scheme
The Space: 28m long, 2m high. Spotlights. Hessian covered chipboard walls.
Exhibiting: [AW]. Apply by telephone or in writing. Available on a hire or commission basis, exhibition costs negotiable. Pictures should *'not be too large'*. Commission negotiable.

Village College

School and community education centre. [Pa,Pr,Ph]
Address: Comberton, Cambridge CB3 7DU tel 022 026 2503
Contact: James Hall
Open: Mon-Fri 9.30-9.30 during term time
The Space: 11x8m with spots and 8x6.5m without spots.
Exhibiting: [AW] Two-dimensional work only, maximum size 2m in either direction. *'Nominal'* hire charge by negotiation, artist meets all costs. Commission is 10%.

Camelford (Cornwall)

(SWA) Map6 SX18

North Cornwall Museum & Gallery

A privately-owned award-winning museum with a permanent collection relating to North Cornwall and a temporary exhibition programme. [VA,Ph,Cr]
Address: The Clease, Camelford, Cornwall tel 0840 212954
Contact: Sally Holden
Open: Mon-Sat 10.30-5 April-end Sept
Sales: Work sold
The Space: The gallery is12.5x6.5x2.75m with fluorescent lighting.
Exhibiting: [AW] The museum provides a private view and charges 25% commission on sales.

Cannock (Staffordshire)

(WMA) Map4 SJ91

Cannock Library

A library space run by Staffordshire Libraries, Arts and Archives Department. [Pa,Pr,Dr,Ph,Cr]
Address: Manor Avenue, Cannock, Staffordshire WS11 1AA tel 054 35 2019/71114
Contact: Cannock Group Librarian Lynne Stanley
Open: Mon 9.30-7, Tues,Thurs, Fri 9-7, Wed, Sat 9-1
Policy: The exhibition programme is mostly local artists and societies, with the exhibitions changing monthly.
Sales: Work sold; Sales referred to exhibitor
The Space: 7.5x6.5m giving 20m linear hanging space with lighting by fluorescent, spots and natural light and direct fixing.
Exhibiting: [AW] *'Exhibitor is responsible for all exhibition expenses and insurance arrangements'.*
Access: [U][T][L] Town centre location close to public car parks

Canterbury (Kent)

(SEA) Map7 TR15

Canterbury College (Herbert Read Gallery)

This is primarily a teaching gallery showing exhibitions by contemporary artists. [VA]
Address: Canterbury College of Art, New Dover Road, Canterbury CT1 3AN tel 022 776 9371
Contact: Exhibitions Organiser
Open: Mon-Fri 10-5 during exhibitions
Policy: The gallery stages six public exhibitions a year and also initiates its own exhibitions and participates in the Canterbury Festival. There are also shows of student work.
The Space: A purpose-built exhibition space with natural and spot lighting.
Exhibiting: [AW]

Drew Gallery

A gallery mainly showing painting exhibitions by living artists but also dealing in other media with an annual summer show selected from degree shows in London and the South East. [VA,Cr,Je,Te]
Address: 16 Best Lane, Canterbury, Kent CT1 2JB tel 022 745 8759
Contact: Sandra Drew
Open: Mon-Wed 10-4, Fri-Sat 10-4
Policy: The gallery policy is to show an *'exciting well-balanced programme of exhibitions of contemporary art by local, national and international artists'*. Work is aimed at a domestic market and *'is of a scale and content in line with such a market'*. A high professional standard is maintained with work by younger artists encouraged and a large proportion of women artists are shown. Specific shows are accompanied by talks and educational projects. The gallery is also used for talks, slide shows and community meetings.
Sales: Work sold; Credit scheme; Credit card
The Space: Main gallery 18x14x13m high. Hall gallery, 27x4.5x13m high. Lighting by spots with hanging by rods and direct wall fixing. A glass display case is available. There is a small walled garden which can also be used.
Exhibiting: [AW] Applications with slides and CV to Sandra Drew. Gallery finances insurance, printing and mail-out of publicity and catalogue/card, list of exhibits and preview costs. There is a gallery hire fee and commission 33.3%.
Access: [S] Bus station 5 mins; BR Canterbury East 10 mins; BR Canterbury West 7mins; Public car park 1 min

Drew Gallery Projects

A branch of the Drew Gallery dealing with site-specific, out-of-gallery projects. [Sc,LA]
Address: 16 Best Lane, Canterbury, Kent CT1 2JB tel 022 745 8759

Contact: Sandra Drew
Policy: This new venture aims to promote sculpture, video and performance in public places and past projects have been combined with short residencies. The aim is to present the best and most exciting of what is evolving in this field. Sandra Drew wishes to promote *'a high level of communication between the artist and his/her public and to expose the arts to as wide a range of people as possible'*. Each project is accompanied by an educational programme, slide-shows, guided tours, workshops and open forum.
Sales: Work sold; Credit scheme; Credit card
The Space: Work is developed specifically for each site anywhere within the city of Canterbury provided that permission is given.
Exhibiting: **[EF]** Insurance, transport, printing and mail-out of publicity and preview costs are financed. All artists receive a fee and material allowance according to the available budget. Support in principle for EPR. Commission 33.3%.

Nevill Gallery

This commercial gallery deals mostly with figurative works by living artists. [Pa,Sc,Pr]
Address: 43 St Peters Street, Canterbury, Kent CT1 2BG tel 022 765 291
Contact: John Nevill, 8 Radnor Cliff, Sandgate, Folkestone, Kent CT20 2JN tel 0303 48403
Open: Mon-Sat 10-5
Policy: The gallery displays a limited number of exhibitions annually which usually show for two weeks. Alongside these there is a changing display of painting, sculpture and prints for sale.
Sales: Work sold; Credit card
The Space: Wall space is 30x3m high.
Exhibiting: **[AW]** Gallery finances preview costs, catalogue/card and mail-out of publicity and takes 33.3% commission.
Access: **[F]** Buses 5 mins; Public car park 5 mins

Royal Museum & Art Gallery

A local-authority run gallery mainly showing historical exhibitions but also occasionally exhibiting local artists. [Pa,Dr,Pr,Ph]
Address: High Street, Canterbury, Kent CT1 2JE tel 0227 452747
Contact: Curator
Open: Mon-Sat 10-5
Policy: The gallery's emphasis is on historical and travelling shows and those internally originated. An average of eight temporary exhibitions, each of between three and four weeks are shown a year, of which around a quarter are by living artists. An education programme is currently being researched. The permanent collection is of subjects related to Canterbury and area, and includes work by contemporary artists.
Sales: Work sold
The Space: 16x8m overall with rail hanging system and humidity, UV and light level controls, and high security.
Exhibiting: Usually by invitation. Commission 10%.
Access: **[X]** BR Canterbury 10 mins; Parking 10 mins

University of Kent (Graphics Gallery)

As a centre for the study of cartoons and caricature, this gallery specialises in exhibiting original cartoons, photographs and drawings. [VA,Ph]
Address: The Library, University of Kent, Canterbury, Kent CT2 7NU tel 022 776 4000 ext 3127
Contact: Research Fellow Liz Ottaway
Open: Term-time Mon-Fri 9-10, Sat 9-7, Sun 2-9. Otherwise Mon-Fri 9-7, Sat 9-5
Policy: The gallery has a policy of specialising in the graphic arts and has a collection of predominantly political 20th century cartoons. Exhibitions run for between six to eight weeks and mostly feature solo shows by living artists. The audience mainly comprises of students and academic staff. (See also Gulbenkian Theatre Foyer, University of Kent).
Sales: Sales referred to exhibitor
The Space: 12x3m with 30m linear hanging space with natural lighting and additional spots and fluorescent lighting; hanging is by rods and direct fixing. Gallery plans available.
Exhibiting: **[AW]** Applications one year in advance with examples of work. Gallery finances insurance and list of exhibits. Commission 20%.
Access: **[U][T][L]** Buses from Canterbury,Herne Bay and Whitstable; BR Canterbury West, Canterbury East some distance away; Visitors car park 10 mins

University of Kent (Gulbenkian Theatre Foyer)

This gallery functions alongside the theatre and runs a programme of small-scale exhibitions by living artists. [Pa,Pr,Ph,Dr]
Address: Gulbenkian Theatre, University of Kent, Canterbury, Kent CT2 7NZ tel 022 769 075
Contact: Njal A Morris
Open: During theatre performances
Policy: The gallery operates *'an open-door policy towards any artists who believes that their work deserves an audience'*. Exhibitions normally run for three weeks and are predominantly solo shows. The space is also used for meetings during conferences. (See also Graphics Gallery, University of Kent).
Sales: Work sold
The Space: Five 2x1m boards and five1x1m boards, the space cannot accommodate any work larger than these dimensions.
Exhibiting: **[AW]** Applications NA Morris. Gallery finances mail-out of publicity.
Access: **[F]** Buses from Canterbury, Herne Bay and Whitstable; BR Canterbury West, Canterbury East some distance away; Visitors car park 1 min

Carlisle (Cumbria)

(NA) Map3 NY35

Carlisle Museum & Art Gallery

Municipal art and craft gallery with a permanent collection of Pre-Raphaelites, local artists and Royal College artists 1930-1960. Also showing work by living artists, many from the region. [VA,Ph,Cr,LA]

Address: Castle Street, Carlisle, Cumbria CA3 8TP tel 0228 34781
Contact: Curator David Clarke
Open: Mon-Sat 9-5, open Sun July-Sep
Policy: As a large gallery in a vast rural county, the policy *'is to provide as wide and varied programme as possible. Young, less well-known and highly innovative artists are represented alongside established and traditional ones, to encourage the public to view new and less accessible work'.* As well as the immediate population shows are aimed at tourists especially during the summer and schools during the winter. Active programme of workshops, demonstrations, recitals and residencies.
Sales: Work sold
The Space: There are three galleries each giving about 34m linear hanging space and about 33 square metres. Gallery 1 and 3 have UV filtered skylight and spots; gallery 2 is artificially lit with provision for 40 lux. All galleries have direct fixing.
Exhibiting: **[AW]** Applications should be made at least a year and a half in advance and sent in writing with slides/photographs to the Exhibitions Organiser. The gallery provides insurance, publicity, list of exhibits, preview, transport, display and catalogue costs as well as artists' expenses. It supports EPR in principle and charges 20% commission.
Access: **[X]** BR Carlisle 15 mins; Bus station 10 mins; Car parks 5 mins

Gossipgate Garden Gallery

A commercial gallery run as a parallel business by 'countryside consultants' (architects and planners specialising in countryside projects) showing mixed exhibitions. [VA,Ph,Cr,LA]

Address: Treasury Court, 17 Fisher Street, Carlisle, Cumbria CA3 8RF tel 0228 21375
Contact: Sonia Kempsey, Gossipgate Gallery, The Butts, Alston, Cumbria CA9 3JU tel 0498 81806
Open: Mon-Sat 9-5
Policy: The aim is to promote the work of local artists and makers. Selection is limited to those from the north of England and the Borders. The gallery is looking for work of both quality and originality particularly by younger artists and makers needing to get their work known by a wider audience. (See also Gossipgate Gallery, Alston).
Sales: Work sold; Credit card
The Space: wallspace is 2.4x5m above craft display area plus 2.4x7.2m in coffee shop area. The craft display area is about 4 square metres.
Exhibiting: **[AW]** Telephone Sonia Kempsey to arrange an appointment. Gallery finances insurance, publicity, list of exhibits, preview, catalogue/card and charges 25% - 33.3% commission.
Access: **[F]** Bus & BR Carlisle 5 mins

Cartmel (Cumbria)

(NA) Map3 SD37

Anvil Gallery

A commercial gallery selling oils and watercolours 'mainly of conventional representational types'. [Pa,Pr]

Address: Cavendish Street, Cartmel, Near Grange-over-Sands, Cumbria LA11 6QU tel 044 854 362
Contact: W A R Denison
Open: Mon-Sat 10-4
Policy: The gallery shows contemporary work in a changing display. The gallery's clientele comes from a wide area and has been built up over many years.
Sales: Work sold
The Space: The gallery has 30m linear hanging space. Pictures are hung in groups on nylon line. Maximum size is half imperial.
Exhibiting: **[AW]** The gallery is always willing to see artists wanting to exhibit. The gallery covers insurance and charges 25% commission.
Access: **[F]** Buses from Grange-over-Sands, Kendal, Ulverston, Windermere; BR Grange-over-Sands 2.5 miles; Car park

Castle Eden (Co Durham)

(NA) Map3 NZ43

Castle Eden Gallery

A private gallery particularly suited to illustrative work though 'work is chosen for its excellence not type'. [VA,Ph,Cr]

Address: Castle Eden, Co Durham TS27 4SD tel 0429 836466
Contact: David Craske
Open: Mon-Fri 9-5
Sales: Work sold
The Space: The gallery is 46 square metres with 21 to 30m linear hanging, spots and natural light.
Exhibiting: **[AW]** Commission is 33.3% and the gallery covers insurance, publicity and preview. Cost of mailing, catalogue and transport are negotiable.

Chagford (Devon)

(SWA) Map6 SX78

Chagford Galleries

A craft shop with first-floor exhibition space, Chagford Galleries show solo and mixed exhibitions of paintings, prints and crafts. [VA,Cr]

Address: 20 The Square, Chagford, Devon TQ13 8AB tel 06473 3287
Contact: Partner Haldon R Hole, St Anthonys Close, Skaigh Lane, Belstone, Okehampton EX20 1RD
Open: Mon-Sat 10-1 & 2.30-5, Wed 10-1; open part-time in winter
Policy: regular exhibitions of local artists and ceramicists.
Sales: Work sold
The Space: Gallery is 6x4m.
Exhibiting: **[AW]**

Chelmsford (Essex)

(EA) Map7 TL70

Chelmsford & Essex Museum (Chelmsford Museum Service)

Municipal museum covering archaeology, social and local history, natural sciences, applied art and fine art, also regimental museum. [VA,Ce,Te,Gl]

Address: Oaklands Park, Moulsham Street, Chelmsford, Essex CM2 9AQ tel 0245 353066
Contact: Head of Museums Service Dr P R Andrew, Leisure Services Deptartment, Civic Centre, Chelmsford CM1 1JE
Open: Mon-Sat 10-5 Sun 2-5
Policy: The museum collects and displays work by post-war artists and works by Essex and East Anglian artists. At present the collection numbers some 600 works. There are plans to develop the service with the establishment of an art gallery.
Sales: Sales referred to exhibitor
The Space: Two separate rooms with linear hanging space of 27.7 and 21m and adjustable track lighting, hessian-covered blockboard with direct fixing, natural light available. Plans available. Lectures and meetings of local groups and societies are also held in the gallery space.
Exhibiting: [AW] Museum covers insurance, printing and mailing of publicity, list of exhibits, catalogue/card.
Access: [F] Ground floor, **[X]** First floor. Buses 152,154,155,350,356,42 mini-link and 44 from the bus or BR stations

Chelmsford Central Library Gallery

Gallery space within a library, available for hire by artists, as well as mounting its own occasional exhibitions. [VA,Cr]

Address: PO Box 882, County Hall, Market Road, Chelmsford CM1 1LH tel 0245 492758
Contact: Senior Librarian Robert Worcester
Open: Mon-Fri 9-7, Sat 9-5
Policy: To promote fine art within the local community by arranging a wide variety of exhibitions by both locally and nationally-renowned artists.
Sales: Work sold; Sales referred to exhibitor
The Space: The gallery is 68.35 square metres with a wall area 2.79 square metres and six display cases.
Exhibiting: [AW] Commission 20% on work sold.
Access: [F]

Essex Libraries

The headquarters for Essex libraries which co-ordinates and administers programmes of exhibitions within the county's libraries and although branch libraries are responsible for own programme, the county library acts as originator for occasional touring shows.

Address: County Library, Goldlay Gardens, Chelmsford CM2 0EW tel 0245 284981
Contact: Librarian (Promotion and Development) Connie Price
Policy: Essex Libraries has various galleries and exhibition spaces around the county which provide useful venues for both local and national exhibitions. A diverse range of exhibitions is hosted annually covering all areas of art, design, photography. See also entries for Witham, Wickford, Loughton, Saffron Walden, Harwich, Harlow, Grays, Chelmsford, South Woodham Ferrers, Southend on Sea, Colchester, Clacton on Sea, Brentwood and Basildon.
Sales: Work sold
The Space: Large exhibition areas at Southend, Chelmsford and Loughton. Medium size at Colchester and Witham. Varying amount of space at other libraries.
Exhibiting: [AW] Artists and makers welcome to apply to individual libraries or to Library Headquarters for initial guidance.

Cheltenham (Gloucestershire)

(SWA) Map4 SO92

Cheltenham Art Gallery and Museum

A municipal art gallery with historical and contemporary fine and applied arts collections, and a programme of temporary exhibitions run by Cheltenham Borough Council. [VA,Ph,Cr]

Address: Clarence Street, Cheltenham, Gloucestershire GL50 3JT tel 0242 237431
Contact: Director George Breeze
Open: Mon-Sat 10am-5.30pm; closed bank holidays
Policy: N.ew extension will be operational from Summer 1989. *'The aim will be to provide a varied programme of contemporary and historical exhibitions of art, craft, scientific and ethnological exhibitions with a strong*

Cheltenham Art Gallery & Museum: Plans for the new extension to be completed Spring 1989, with temporary exhibition space on ground floor.

potential for education'. It is also hoped to hold *'workshops and demonstrations with the possibility of artists/makers in residence'*. See also The Pittville Pump Room.
Sales: Work sold
The Space: is 8x6.4x2.4m giving 53m linear hanging space including screens.
Exhibiting: **[AW]** Apply to Jonathan Benington, Exhibition Officer. The gallery provides insurance, transport, mailing, list of exhibits, and preview. A 20% commission is charged on sales.
Access: **[L][F]** Town centre location, bus station and car parks 5 mins. BR Cheltenham 25 mins

College of St Paul & St Mary (Park Gallery)

A gallery in a college of higher education supported by South West Arts. [VA,Ph,Cr]
Address: The Park, Cheltenham, Gloucestershire 50 2RH tel 0242 513836
Contact: Exhibition Director Peter Lyons
Open: Mon-Fri 9-5
Policy: Six exhibitions a year are shown with the aim of exhibiting *'work of the highest professional quality from a wide range of arts and crafts'*.
Sales: Work sold
The Space: Two spaces are used one giving 30m linear hanging space and the other 17m linear hanging space. Both galleries have spots and natural light and direct fixing is used. Gallery plans available.
Exhibiting: **[AW]** Slides and CV required. The gallery provides insurance, publicity, preview, list of exhibits and catalogue/card. A 25% commission is charged on sales.
Access: South side of town centre off the A46; Bus station and BR Cheltenham Spa 10 mins

Courtyard Gallery

Commercial gallery showing contemporary jewellery, prints, glass and ceramics [Cr,Pr]
Address: Bath Terrace, Cheltenham, Gloucestershire GL50 2AL tel 0242 221711
Contact: Mr Jones
Open: Mon-Sat 9-5.30
Exhibiting: **[AW]** only sometimes

Ogle Fine Arts

The gallery runs a limited programme of exhibitions of contemporary British paintings and holds a large stock of limited edition prints. It supplies art for the working environment both to small firms and major companies throughout the UK. [Pa,Pr,Sc]
Address: 1 Wellington Square, Cheltenham, Gloucestershire GL50 4JU tel 0242 31011
Contact: Directors Douglas and Jenny Ogle
Open: Tues-Sat 10-2, at other times by appointment
Policy: The gallery relates to a wide range of painters, printmakers, sculptors whose work is included in presentations to businesses. These often take the form of in-house exhibitions from which work is selected for purchase. Advice and assistance given in forming collections and commissions negotiated. The gallery takes part in major UK contemporary art fairs.
Sales: Work sold
The Space: Ground floor exhibition space in two areas with 36m linear hanging space. Lower ground floor houses prints.
Exhibiting: **[AW]** Artists should contact the gallery in person. Gallery covers costs of insurance, publicity etc. Commission is 40%.
Access: **[S]** Town centre and parking 10 mins

Parade Gallery

A commercial gallery showing mainly solo shows of artists 'who have ability, originality and flair, definitely not choc box'. [Pa,Pr,Dr,Ph]
Address: 6 St James' Terrace, Suffolk Parade, Montpellier, Cheltenham, Gloucestershire GL50 2AA tel 0242 241897
Contact: Peter Kellow
Open: Tues-Sat 9-6.30
Policy: The gallery also offers a framing service.
Sales: Work sold
The Space: The gallery is 15 square metres giving 24m linear hanging space with hanging by screws/plates and rail and spots and natural light used. One showcase available.
Exhibiting: **[AW]** Insurance, publicity, preview, list of exhibits, catalogue/card and display provided by the gallery. A commission of 30% is charged on sales.
Access: **[S]** Bus stop 5 mins; car park 2 mins

Pittville Pump Room Museum

Run by Cheltenham Art Gallery & Museum, the Pump Room houses permanent collections of jewellery and costume, and a graphic display of Cheltenham's history. [Te,Je]
Address: Pittville Park, Cheltenham, Gloucestershire tel 0242 512740
Contact: Assistant Keeper Applied Art Helen Brown, Cheltenham Art Gallery & Museum, Clarence Street, Cheltenham GL50 3JT tel 0242 237431
Open: Tues-Sat 10.30-5 Nov-March; Tues-Sun 10.30-5 April-Oct; closed Good Friday and winter bank holidays; open Easter, Spring and August bank holidays
Policy: Temporary exhibitions are organised that relate to the permanent collections, and are usually costume, textiles and jewellery. *'These include contemporary and shows of an historical nature'*. The gallery also organises educational activities.
Sales: Work sold
The Space: The Oval Room Gallery is 8.95x9.85x4.85m giving 34.6m linear hanging space with screens with direct fixing and controlled lighting including a chandelier and spotlights.
Exhibiting: **[AW]** Apply to Helen Brown. The gallery provides insurance, publicity, preview, list of exhibits, catalogue/card and transport.
Access: **[X]** Bus 42 from bus station; BR Cheltenham 40 mins

Turtle Fine Art

A commercial gallery dealing in 19th and 20th century watercolours and oils with occasional exhibitions featuring contemporary artists on a commission basis. [Pa,Pr,Dr]

Address: 29-30 Suffolk Parade, Cheltenham, Gloucestershire GL50 2AE tel 0242 41646
Contact: Pat Field
Open: Mon-Sat 10-6.30
Sales: Work sold; Credit card
Exhibiting: [AW] Apply to Pat Field. Exhibitors must meet all exhibition costs.
Access: [F] On street parking

Yew Tree Gallery

A crafts and fine art gallery showing leading British artists and makers. [Pa,Cr]

Address: Green Lane, Little Witcombe, Nr Cheltenham, Gloucester GL3 4TX tel 0452 863516
Open: Tues-Sat 11-5.30, Sun 1.30-5.30
Policy: Previously at Ellastone, Derbyshire, the gallery is now in a 17th century farmhouse at the foot of Birdup Hill and shows an extensive programme of high-quality crafts and paintings.
Sales: Work sold
Exhibiting: [AW] The programme is by invitation and application.

Chester (Cheshire)

(NWA) Map4 SJ46

Ayling Porteous Gallery

A private gallery showing contemporary art with a permanent collection of work by previous exhibitors. [VA]

Address: 33 City Road, Chester, Cheshire CH1 3AE tel 0244 314556
Contact: Mick Ayling
Open: Daily 10-12.30 1.30-5; Closed Wed & Sun
Policy: Two or three new artists are invited to be included in the programme each year, usually ex-graduates who are shown alongside established artists from all parts of the country. Gallery policy is to sell work from exhibitions by attracting new and existing clients with work ranging from £50 upwards.
Sales: Work sold; Credit card; Credit scheme
The Space: Room 1 is 3.4x4.6x2.85m with 8m linear hanging space, Room 2 is 4.2x3.95x2.85m with 16.3m linear hanging space, Room 3 is 4.2x3.6x2.6m with 11.4m linear hanging space, Room 4 is 3.95x4.35x2.75m with 16.9m linear hanging space and Room is 5 3.9x6.1x2.75m with 16.9m linear hanging space plus the stairs and landing have 15m linear hanging space. Natural and artificial lighting. Maximum size of work 2x3.5m.
Exhibiting: The gallery will pay for insurance, printing of publicity, list of exhibits, preview costs, mailing and catalogue/card and takes 33.3% commission.
Access: [F] BR Chester 2 mins; Parking outside; Buses to BR

Bishops' Gallery

A gallery situated in a joint use school. 'We are committed to showing work of visiting artists, photographers and craftspeople and the work of pupils from the art, design and textiles departments.' [VA]

Address: Vaughans Lane, Great Boughton, Chester CH3 5XF tel 0244 313806
Contact: Head of Resources Keith Pilling, Mon,Thurs 9-7, Tues,Wed, Fri 9-4.30 term-time
Open: School hours term-time
Policy: The gallery exists for the benefit of the public and the school students. It aims to provide *'a service to artists in enabling them to exhibit without incurring cost and in providing the students with the opportunity of showing their work displayed alongside that of professional artists'.* The gallery generally shows seven exhibitions each year which run for approximately four weeks.
Sales: Work sold
The Space: The space measures 9.14x9.14x2.74m and 9.14x3.04m. plus the option of further small spaces in adjoining library.
Exhibiting: [AW] Applications to Keith Pilling to include photographs or examples of work. No commission charged. Gallery pays for insurance. Supports EPR. Some free advertisng and publicity. Exhibitors are invited to talk to 6 sixth forms and others about their work.
Access: [U] BR Chester 20 mins; Buses 4,5; Park and Ride 5 mins

Cheshire Libraries & Museums

The Arts Services touring exhibitions form part of the County Council's programme of organising arts activities in a variety of media. [Pa,Pr,Dr,Ph,Cr]

Address: Arts Services, 91 Hoole Road, Chester, Cheshire CH2 3NG tel 0244 320055
Contact: County Arts Officer Tom Andrewes
Policy: There are 55 branch libraries and main libraries in Cheshire, some with purpose-built exhibition areas. Five tours have been organised by Arts Services in the past year, they normally last for four months with the exhibition being displayed for one month in each venue, most of which are libraries. *'The purpose of Cheshire Arts Tours is to offer the public a wider range of imaginations by presenting to them the work of professional artists and makers from within the county and beyond. Most of the libraries are not ideal places to exhibit but the scheme does at least give the public - many of whom would not go into a gallery - opportunities to see samples of new techniques, and approaches to art which they would not otherwise have.'* Cheshire Libraries also take exhibitions from Merseyside Exhibitions and the North West Museums & Art Gallery Service. (See also Runcorn Library, Congleton Library).
Sales: Work sold
The Space: Variable.
Exhibiting: [AW] Applications along with a CV and slides or photographs should be submitted to Cheshire Arts Services. The service pays for insurance, publicity,

preview costs, transport, catalogue as well as display expenses. The practicalities of touring limit the size of works. 10% commission is taken.

Chester Library

The gallery situated in Chester Library is viewed as a 'trailer' for the future purpose-built gallery to be incorporated into the second half of the library. [Pa,Pr,Dr,Ph,Cr]

Address: Northgate Street, Chester, Cheshire CH1 2EF tel 0244 312935
Contact: Principal Librarian Graham Fisher
Open: Mon,Thurs 9.30-7 Tues,Wed, Fri 9.30-5, Sat 9.30-1
Policy: Chester Library participates in travelling exhibitions organised by Cheshire Libraries & Museums. These display work by professional artists from Cheshire and beyond, encompassing painting, drawing, prints, crafts and photography. *'The space is available for local amateurs but an attempt is made to seek out the imaginative.'* (See also Cheshire Libraries & Museums).
Sales: Sales referred to exhibitor
The Space: The main space is 8x2m high and lit by spotlights. In addition there are three double-sided hessian boards 1m x 2m and five exhibition cases.
Exhibiting: [AW] Artists interested in exhibiting in the library should apply to Graham Fisher but there is generally a waiting list. The gallery pays for insurance.
Access: [U][T] BR Chester 15 mins

Grosvenor Gallery

The gallery houses a permanent collection comprising of sporting scenes, portraits, silver, ceramics and local history as well as organising contemporary exhibitions. [VA,Ce]

Address: 27 Grosvenor Street, Chester, Cheshire CH1 2DD tel 0244 21616
Contact: Curator C N Moore
Open: Mon-Sat 10.30-5 Sun 2-5

Chesterfield (Derbyshire)

(EMA) Map5 SK37

Bowling Green Gallery

The gallery is part of a craft workshop and shop complex receiving grants from local authorities and East Midlands Arts. [VA,Ph,Cr]

Address: South Place, Chesterfield, Derbyshire S40 1SZ tel 0246 35237
Contact: Alan Wood, 72 Green Farm Close, Chesterfield, Derbyshire
Open: Mon-Sat 9.30-5.30
Policy: The gallery has an emphasis on showing high-quality touring exhibitions of various media. The gallery is also available for *'examples of local work'* through links with schools, colleges and societies.
Sales: Work sold
The Space: 25m linear wall space with movable screens and flexible lighting. Showcases can be obtained. Gallery plans available.
Exhibiting: [AW][EF] The gallery provides insurance, transport, printing and mailing. A 20% commission is charged on sales. Supports EPR.
Access: [X] Town centre location; Bus station and Chesterfield market 2 mins

Chesterfield College of Technology & Arts

A balcony area in the main art college building. [Pa,Pr,Ph]

Address: Sheffield Road, Chesterfield, Derbyshire S41 7LL tel 0246 31212
Contact: Exhibition Organiser Anthony Currell
Open: Mon-Fri 9.30-7.30, Sat 10.30-12 (mid Sept-May)
Policy: Solo and group exhibitions are shown mainly for a college audience.
The Space: The balcony area provides 50m linear hanging space using rods and hooks from a picture rail. Fluorescent lights are used, and the area is open on one side to studio space.
Exhibiting: [AW] Two-dimensional work only can be shown. Exhibitions are arranged by invitation or application to the exhibition organiser.
Access: [S] Town centre, bus station 5 mins; BR Chesterfield 15 mins

Peacock Heritage Centre

Housed in a 16th century building and run by Chesterfield Borough Council, the centre provides exhibition space, gift shop, information centre and audio-visual presentation of the history of Chesterfield. [VA,Cr]

Address: Low Pavement, Chesterfield, Derbyshire S40 1PB tel 0246 207778
Contact: Tourism Officer Mrs Wainwright
Open: Mon-Sat 12-5
Policy: The centre *'encourages exhibitions of local interest, or by local people'.*
Sales: Work sold
The Space: A 9x6m room with display stands and five partially-glazed lockable display cases with internal lighting.
Exhibiting: [AW] Apply in writing to the Tourism Officer. The centre provides insurance cover, a calendar of exhibitions, and charges 5% commission on sales. All other expenses are met by exhibitors.
Access: [X] Town centre location within easy reach of car parks, bus and BR Chesterfield

Chichester (W Sussex)

(SA) Map7 SU80

David Paul Gallery

Regular solo and mixed exhibitions of 20th century paintings, drawings and sculpture. [Pa,Sc]

Address: St. John's Street, Chichester, W Sussex PO19 tel 024 370 3077
Contact: Director
Open: 9.30-1 & 2.15-5; closed Thurs & Sun

Pallant House

An art and craft gallery with a varied programme of exhibitions and an expanding educational programme for primary and secondary schools. [VA,Ph,Cr]

Address: 9 North Pallant, Chichester, W Sussex PO19 1TJ tel 0243 774557
Contact: Curator David E Coke
Open: Tues-Sat 10-5.30
Policy: The exhibitions, which run for between six weeks and three months, *'cover as wide a range of temporary exhibitions as possible'*. The restored 1712 town house also houses permanent collections of 20th century art, 18th century furniture, porcelain and glass, and silhouettes. A charity with grants from the district council, it aims to attract all sections of the public. Gallery talks, workshops for schools and an artist in residence programme are also organised.
Sales: Sales referred to exhibitor
The Space: The Exhibition Gallery contains 32.6m linear hanging space and is 4.2m high, and the Garden Gallery 15m linear and 2.4m high, both are spotlit. Display cases are available.
Exhibiting: [AW] The gallery pays for insurance, printing and mailing of publicity, list of exhibits, display costs, private view and transport.
Access: [X] No bus route; Car parks nearby; BR Chichester 7 mins

West Sussex County Libraries

[Pa,Sc,Pr,Ph,Cr]

Address: Library Administration Centre, Tower Street, Chichester, W Sussex PO19 1QJ tel 0243 777 100
Contact: Mr R J Huse
Policy: Temporary exhibitions are held at the libraries at Bognor Regis, Burgess Hill, Chichester, Crawley, East Grinstead, Haywards Heath, Horsham, Lancing, Littlehampton, Petworth, Shoreham, West Wittering and Worthing.

Chippenham (Wiltshire)

(SA) Map6 ST97

Fox Talbot Museum of Photography

An art and craft gallery within a museum of photography. [Ph]

Address: Nr Chippenham, Wiltshire SN15 2LG tel 024 973 459
Contact: Curator Robert Lassam
Open: Daily 11-6 March-Nov 5
Policy: The museum, which honours the negative/positive photographic process invented by Fox Talbot, stages three two-month long exhibitions of photography a year during their eight-month opening period. It concentrates on 19th century photography with its permanent collection but also shows some contemporary work. Talks are given to schools, colleges and clubs. There is also a shop.
Sales: Sales referred to exhibitor; Credit card
The Space: A spotlit 2x18m display panel accommodating between thirty and forty 50x40cm framed prints. Spotlights and complete archival environmental controls. Gallery plans available.
Exhibiting: The Curator selects the subject for exhibitions and occasionally looks at new work. The gallery pays for insurance, private view, list of exhibits, publicity mail out and exhibition display.
Access: [F] Ground floor. Exit 17 on M4; Free car park; Trowbridge-Chippenham bus route

Chipping Norton (Oxfordshire)

(SA) Map7 SP32

Manor House Gallery

Gallery specialises in contemporary pastels and watercolours with a large stock of Cotswold artists. [Pa]

Address: West Street, Chipping Norton, Oxfordshire OX7 tel 0608 2620
Contact: Director Luigi Gennari
Open: Mon-Sat 9.30-5, Sun 10-5 (during exhibitions)
Policy: Occasional talks by artists are held and the gallery offers a framing service. A separate gallery in the Manor House runs an exhibition programme April-December.

Theatre (The)

A theatre gallery. [Pa,Pr,Ph,LA]

Address: 2 Spring Street, Chipping Norton, Oxfordshire OX7 5NL tel 0608 2349
Contact: Theatre Administrator Tamara Malcolm
Policy: The gallery promotes four exhibitions a year by local young professional artists. It is also available for hire.
Exhibiting: Help is given towards the cost of publicity, preview and catalogue. A commission is charged on sales.

Chorley (Lancashire)

(NWA) Map3 SD51

Chorley Central Library

A public library exhibition space. [Pa,Pr,Dr,Ph,Cr]

Address: Union Street, Chorley, Lancashire PR7 1EB tel 025 72 77222/3
Contact: District Librarian J D Farauhar
Open: Mon,Wed,Fri 10-7, Tues,Thurs 10-5, Sat 10-4
Policy: In the past year fourteen exhibitions have been mounted at the library, the great majority were concerned with displaying the work of contemporary artists and makers. *'The exhibition space was provided to give an outlet for local artists or makers, who may not aspire to a more formal and larger space'.*
Sales: Work sold
The Space: Two-dimensional items are displayed in a corridor gallery which has 12.2m linear space with hessian panelling, which is 2.6m high, and equipped with spot lighting. Two showcases are positioned in the foyer, which have glass shelving with internal lighting and measure 1.5x1.8x0.46m depth.
Exhibiting: [AW] Applications to be made to the District Librarian during office hours. The library charges 15%

commission on sales.
Access: [U][T][L][F]

Christchurch (Dorset)

(SA) Map7 SZ19

Red House Museum & Gardens

A municipal gallery, part of the Hampshire County Museums Service with temporary exhibitions gallery and permanent collections of costume, archaeology, natural and local history. [VA,Ph,Cr]

Address: Quay Road, Christchurch, Dorset BH23 1BU tel 0202 482860
Contact: Exhibitions Officer Jo Bailey, Hampshire County Museums Service, Chilcomb House, Chilcomb Lane, Winchester, Hampshire SO23 8RD tel 0962 846315
Open: Tues-Sat 10-5, Sun 2-5
Policy: This temporary exhibitions gallery is one of six galleries housed within museums throughout Hampshire. It receives six or seven touring exhibitions a year, about four of which include work by living artists or makers with a bias towards those living or working in or near Hampshire. It also holds two or three local exhibitions generated by local individuals or groups, such as camera clubs, art clubs and quilting groups. Exhibitions last five weeks and exhibiting artists are encouraged to give talks, demonstrations or workshops.
Sales: Work sold
The Space: The gallery is 10x5m with 30m of linear hanging space, direct fixing to the hessian covered walls and track spotlights, an Edmunds upright showcase 1.5x6m, a Marler-Hayley upright showcase 1.2x6m and an Octanorm upright showcase 1.2x6m. Gardens are available for outdoor displays.
Exhibiting: [AW] Applications in writing, accompanied by transparencies to Exhibitions Officer. The Museums Service pays for insurance, printing and mailing of publicity and transport. Commission is 20% plus VAT.
Access: [F] Temporary exhibitions gallery, [X] Some permanent galleries. Near town centre; Public car park 2 mins

Cirencester (Gloucestershire)

(SWA) Map7 SP00

Cirencester Workshops

The gallery is part of a contemporary craft centre run by a charitable trust, with a shop, workshops and coffee house. [Cr]

Address: Brewery Court, Cirencester, Gloucestershire GL7 1JH tel 0285 651566
Contact: Director Polly Clarke
Open: Mon-Sat 10-5.30
Policy: The gallery aims *'to show the best craftwork being produced by designer-makers within the United Kingdom; experimental and innovative designs are particularly welcome'*. A number of makers have workshops in the centre and the shop is on the Crafts Council selected list.
Sales: Work sold
The Space: The gallery is 12x6m with spots and fluorescent lights. Gallery plans available.
Exhibiting: [AW] Apply to the Director with slides and a CV. The centre provides insurance, publicity, preview, list of exhibits, catalogue/card and a 46% commission is charged on sales. EPR supported.
Access: [X] Disabled BR Swindon 15 mins drive; Car parking on site

Delahaye Gallery

A commercial gallery with an art shop and framing service. [VA,Ph]

Address: 24 Castle Street, Cirencester, Gloucestershire GL7 1QH tel 0285 654674
Contact: Jane Sampson
Open: Mon-Fri 9-5.30 (Thurs 9-1), Sat 9-5
Policy: *'We aim to provide a varied and stimulating programme of group, solo and thematic shows with a particular interest in up-and-coming artists. We look for qualities of individuality and creativity and our target audience is anyone who appreciates this.'*
Sales: Work sold
The Space: The main gallery is 5x5x3m giving 11m linear hanging space and the entrance hall has 13m linear hanging space. Work is hung on battens, and spots, floods and fluorescent lighting are used. One free-standing showcase.
Exhibiting: [AW] Applications at any time with slides and CV; please enclose a stamped addressed envelope for the return of slides. The gallery provides publicity and list of exhibits. A 20% commission is charged on sales.
Access: [X] Close to town centre

Niccol Centre

The centre runs classes for the 55 plus age group and also houses the Colt Theatre. [VA,Ph]

Address: Brewery Court, Cirencester, Gloucestershire L7 1SP tel 0285 67181
Contact: Exhibition Organiser Joe Macrae
Open: Mon-Fri 10-4, Sat 10-12 noon
Policy: The centre *'aims to exhibit a varied programme of a high standard'*.
Sales: Work sold
The Space: The Upper Gallery has 20m linear hanging space using picture hooks, the Middle Gallery has 16m linear hanging space using a picture rail, the Foyer Gallery has 4m linear hanging space and the Cafe 5m linear hanging space.
Exhibiting: [AW] The centre provides publicity, list of exhibits, private view and catalogue/card. A 33.3% commission is charged on sales.
Access: [U][T][X] Public car park

Clacton on Sea (Essex)

(EA) Map7 TM11

Clacton Library

Exhibition space in library available for hire. [VA,Cr]

Address: Station Road, Clacton on Sea, Essex CO15 1SF tel 0255 421207
Contact: Deputy Area Librarian Dianne Couch
Open: Mon, Wed, Fri 9-7, Tues 9-1, Thurs, Sat 9-5

Policy: See Essex Libraries.
Sales: Work sold; Sales referred to exhibitor
The Space: The floor area is 7.44 square metres with a wall area of 5.21 square metres and two display cases.
Exhibiting: [AW]
Access: [F]

Cleckheaton (W Yorkshire)

(YA) Map3 SE14

Red House Museum

Occasional complementary exhibitions are held in the museum with its collection of historic furniture and fittings. [Cr]

Address: Oxford Road, Gomersal, Cleckheaton, W Yorkshire BD19 tel 0484 513808
Contact: Keeper Stuart Davies, Kirklees Leisure Services, Red Doles Lane, Huddersfield, HD2 1YF tel 0484 513808
Open: Mon-Sat 10-5, Sun 1-5

Clifton Dykes (Cumbria)

(NA) Map3 NY52

Wetheriggs

A commercial gallery, part of a working pottery, with exhibitions and changing displays of 'mixed' work. [VA,Ph,Cr]

Address: Wetheriggs Pottery, Clifton Dykes, Penrith, Cumbria CA10 2DH tel 0768 62946
Contact: Dorothy Snell
Open: Mon-Sun 10-5; Weekends only Winter
Policy: Promotes selected artists and also runs classes in watercolour, photography, hooky rug and pottery with B&B.
Sales: Work sold; Credit card
The Space: One room 9.1x13.7 with picture rail and good lighting, two rooms with shop area, wall space in restaurant and sculpture garden. Gallery provides invigilation and lighting and takes *'a percentage'*. Supports the principle of EPR.
Exhibiting: [AW] Write to Dorothy Snell.
Access: [U][T] No public transport; BR Penrith 4 miles; Car park

Coalville (Leicestershire)

(EMA) Map5 SK41

Manor House

The manor house is run by Leicestershire Museums Service and occasionally holds exhibitions in the café. [Cr]

Address: Donington-le-Heath, Coalville, Leicestershire tel 0530 31259
Contact: Curator Jane May, Leicestershire Museums, Art Galleries Records Service, 90 New Walk, Leicester LE1 6TD tel 0533 554100
Open: Mon-Sat 10-5, Sun 2-5 Easter Sat-Sept; Mon-Fri 10-4.30, Sat 10.30-4 Oct-Good Fri
Access: [U][T] Car park

Cockermouth (Cumbria)

(NA) Map3 NY13

Castlegate House

Small commercial gallery in Georgian house. [Pa,Pr,Dr,Ph]

Address: Castlegate House, Cockermouth, Cumbria CA13 9HA tel 0900 822149
Contact: Director Chris Wadsworth
Open: Mon-Sat 10.30-4.30, Wed 10.30-7; closed Thurs
Policy: Runs solo and group exhibitions by established and young promising artists.
Sales: Work sold; Credit card; Credit scheme
The Space: Three rooms.
Exhibiting: [AW] Send slides and SAE.
Access: Car park at side

Colchester (Essex)

(EA) Map7 TM02

Adam Gallery

The gallery deals specifically in 19th and early 20th century watercolours and oils, with occasional exhibitions of contemporary work. [Pa,Pr]

Address: 7, East Street, Coggeshall, Colchester, Essex C06 1SH tel 0376 62803
Contact: PJ & PW Dye
Open: Mon-Sat 9-5.30 Sun 2-5.30
Policy: The gallery policy is based on the purchase, restoration and sale of works of art from 1800-1950. This is balanced by periodic shows of work by living artists within a reasonable price range. The gallery undertakes framing and conservation.
Sales: Work sold; Credit card
The Space: The gallery is 118 square metres, taking a maximum size of .75x1m.
Exhibiting: [AW] 33.3% commission. Gallery covers publicity printing and mailing, list of exhibits, catalogue/card and preview costs.
Access: [F] BR Kelvedon 3 miles; Public car park 2 mins

Chappel Galleries

A commercial gallery with a regular display of work by national artists and up to four temporary exhibitions a year. [Pa,Sc]

Address: 15 Colchester Road, Chappel, Colchester, Essex CO6 2DE tel 0206 240326
Contact: Edna Church
Open: Tues-Sun 10-6
Policy: Dealing only in professional artists the gallery sells 20th century work in the £400 plus range, and is looking to show more broadly contemporary work rather than just of a regional significance. The gallery offers framing and has a coffee room for patrons.
Sales: Work sold; Credit card
The Space: Five rooms with a total of 56m linear hanging. Sculpture garden currently being developed for spring 1989.
Exhibiting: [AW] Gallery available for hire. Gallery covers insurance and controls printing and mailing of

publicity, list of commission negotiable.
Access: [U] BR Chappel 10 mins; Eastern National route 88; Gallery car park for 20 vehicles

Colchester Arts Centre

Exhibition space within community arts centre based in a church. [VA,Cr,Ph]
Address: St Mary at the Walls, Church Street, Colchester, Essex CO1 1NF tel 0206 577301
Contact: Administrator Anita Pacione
Open: Mon-Sat 11-5 and most evenings
Policy: A gallery for the people which operates a non-selection policy which has featured local artists as well as national and international. Exhibitions run from one to four weeks. All media exhibited. There are two open art shows each year.
Sales: Work sold
The Space: The gallery is 13m long with hessian lined wooden walls which extend down both sides of the nave of the church. Daylight boosted by spots. Two display cases available.
Exhibiting: [AW] Write or call to book dates. Space is hired at £10 per artist per week and £5 for cabinets. Commission is 25%. Centre assists with publicity, display and private view.
Access: [U] Town centre site

Colchester Library

Exhibition space in library, available for hire. [VA,Cr]
Address: Trinity Square, Colchester, Essex CO1 1JB tel 0206 562243
Contact: Deputy Area Librarian: Colchester Hugh Weatherly
Open: Mon-Wed,Fri 9-7.30 Thurs,Sat 9-5
Sales: Work sold; sales referred to exhibitor
The Space: floor area: 13.39sqm; four display cases.
Exhibiting: [AW]
Access: [F][L]

Craftsman (The)

[VA,Cr]
Address: 22 Trinity Street, Colchester, Essex CO1 1JN tel 0206 47097
Contact: Mr Dalton
Open: Mon-Sat 9.30-5

Digby Gallery

Housed within Mercury Theatre complex, the gallery is an added facility for visitors to the theatre. [Pa,Pr,Dr,Ph]
Address: Mercury Theatre, Balkerne Gate, Colchester, Essex CO1 1PT tel 0206 577006
Contact: Hon Director Michael Chase, Lower Common Farmhouse, Chelsworth, Ipswich, Suffolk IP7 7HY tel 0449 740639
Open: Mon 10-5 Tues-Sat 10-end of last performance
Policy: The gallery enables artists to show their work free from the pressures of the market place. It is open to professional artists, and the programme consists of up to ten shows a year each timed to fit the current theatre production.
Sales: Work sold
Exhibiting: [AW] Gallery covers insurance and publicity printing, and takes 20% commission on sales.
Access: [L][S] Public car park 5 mins; Bus routes 5 mins; BR 20 mins

Essex University (University Gallery)

Located on the university campus, the gallery is closely connected with the Department of History of Art. [VA,Ph,Cr,LA]
Address: Essex University, Wivenhoe Park, Colchester, Essex CO4 3SQ tel 0206 87 2603/3002
Contact: Jim Latter
Open: Mon-Fri 11-5.30, closed Tues, Sat 12-4.30
Policy: A wide range of exhibitions covering all aspects of contemporary art, craft and design are shown and the gallery is also used extensively by the students on either the BA Art History course or MA Gallery Studies course. The programme fits with the university term, each show lasting for four weeks. The university has a permanent collection, mainly of 20th century paintings and prints. Workshops, readings and plays are also held in the space.
Sales: Work sold
The Space: 50m linear hanging space with a maximum height of 3.6m; track lighting; invigilation; alarm system and campus security guards. Three showcases one 0.76x1.82x1.21m, one 0.76x1.82x0.30m and one 0.76x1.82x1.82m.
Exhibiting: [AW] gallery covers: insurance, printing and mailing of publicity, list of exhibits, preview costs, display, transport, catalogue/card; variable commission on sales.
Access: [U][T][L] Bus 78

Minories Art Gallery

Independent gallery run by registered charity showing a continuous programme of exhibitions by both national and regional artists complemented by those that support the existing permanent collection. [VA,Ph,Cr]
Address: 74 High Street, Colchester, Essex CO1 1UE tel 0206 577067
Contact: Director Richard Stokes
Open: Tues-Sat 10.30-5, Sun 11-4, closed Mondays
Policy: The gallery operates a policy that combines both contemporary art and the heritage of the region. With the former it aims to exhibit new, innovative and/or experimental work from an international context, as well as devoting space to East Anglian artists within a programme of up to fourteen exhibitions in a year. As a focus for those with an interest in heritage, the gallery curates and exhibits its permanent collection [featuring regional works of art predominantly from the twentieth century] in a manner which enhances the building, itself a listed Georgian house built around a tudor dwelling. Supporting activities include talks and events related to specific exhibitions, events run by the Friends of the Minories. Art, craft and design shop for prints, publications and postcards. Licensed café and bar.
Sales: Credit scheme; Credit card

The Space: There are six exhibition spaces whose linear dimensions and height are 25x2.5m; 21x2m; 13x2.10; 12x2.10m; 21x2.5m; 16x2.10m. Works are hung on mirror plates. Lighting is tungsten halogen spotlight on track with dimmer controls. Each gallery has natural light which can be excluded. Works must be restricted to 2cwt and .95x2.10m. The external exhibition space is a walled garden of some third of an acre suitable for the display of sculpture. There are four showcases 70x60x95cm; two 130x60x60cm; three 90x80x30cm and four 110x60x10cm. Gallery plans are available for exhibitors.

Exhibiting: **[EF][AW]** The gallery covers the costs of: insurance, publicity, list of exhibits, preview costs, transport, mailing, and catalogue/card, as well as *'some'* artists' expenses.

Access: **[X]** NCP car park 1 min; Bus station 1 min; Local BR 5 mins; Mainline BR Colchester 20 mins

North Essex School of Art & Design Gallery

The gallery on the ground floor entrance of school of art and design which forms part of the Colchester Institute. [VA,Ph,Cr]

Address: Colchester Institute, Sheepen Road, Colchester, Essex CO3 3LL tel 0206 570271

Contact: Head of School of Art & Design Keith Albarn

Open: Mon-Fri 9.30-4.30 term-time only

Minories: Primary school pupils during 'For Sale' exhibition
(Photo: Sarah Mossop)

Policy: The gallery policy is to try and provide a professional venue for a wide range of exhibitions and events. These include solo shows by contemporary artists and designers, group shows, musical and theatre events, artworks on loan from foreign embassies as well as *'in-house'* displays of students' work.

Sales: Work sold

The Space: The overall space is 56 square metres with a total of 100m linear hanging space, white walls with overhead track spots. Plinths available for 3D work.

Exhibiting: **[AW]** Intending exhibitors should contact Ian Hay with relevant descriptions of their work or events plus a CV. Exhibitions run for a maximum of three weeks during the academic year.

Access: **[U][T]**

Prettygate Library

Exhibition space in public library, available for hire. [VA,Cr]

Address: Prettygate Road, Colchester, Essex CO3 4EQ tel 0206 563700

Contact: Librarian Dudley Diaper

Open: Mon 2-7, Tues,Thurs, Fri 9-7, Sat 9-5

Sales: Work sold; Sales referred to exhibitor

The Space: The floor area is 9.67 square metres.

Exhibiting: **[AW]**

Access: **[F]**

Colne (Lancashire)

(NWA) Map3 SD83

Barnoldswick Library

The library, which is a branch of Lancashire Libraries, houses a permanent collection of paintings and photographs concerned with the town's history and its surrounding area. [Pa,Dr,Ph,Cr]

Address: Fernlea Avenue, Barnoldswick, Colne, Lancashire BB8 5DW tel 0282 812147

Contact: District Librarian Mrs E Gregson

Open: Mon,Wed 9.30-7, Thurs & Fri 9.30-5, Sat 9.30-4

Policy: Exhibitions are usually shown for one month. The library aims to create *'a focal point in the town in which local artists and others, including schools, can show their work to a wider audience consisting mainly of library users'.*

The Space: Five boards are available, measuring 1.2x3.25m, 1.2x1.94m, 1.2x5.6m, 1.2x4.15m and 1.2x4.37m. Lighting is by spotlights. Overboards can be used when hanging heavier paintings and can be removed to exhibit drawings and photographs on hessian-covered boards when required. One showcase 1.5x1.5x0.3m is available in the foyer, the contents of which are visible outside as well as inside the building.

Exhibiting: **[AW]** Contact District Librarian in writing. 15% commission is charged.

Access: **[U][T][L]** Car park

Colne Library

A branch of Lancashire Libraries. [Pa,Dr,Ph,Cr]

Address: Market Street, Colne, Lancashire BB8 OHS tel 0282 865495/865045

Contact: Mrs C Bradley
Open: Mon,Wed 9.30-7, Tues 9.30-12, Thurs, Fri 9.30-5 Sat 9.30-4
Policy: Exhibitions held at the library mainly concentrate on displaying the work of contemporary artists and makers, shows usually last a month. The library occasionally arranges live craft demonstrations.
The Space: The wall space around the balcony measures 19.69x1m, with hessian-covered boards for exhibiting and spotlighting. Also available is a board 2.46x1.23m, suitable for drawing pins and staples only, plus a 2.7x1.58x5m glass-fronted case with removable shelves, situated in the foyer.
Exhibiting: [AW] Contact District Librarian. At present there is a three-year waiting list. 15% commission is taken on sales.
Access: [U][T][L] Bus station 2mins; Car park at rear

Congleton (Cheshire)

(NWA) Map4 SJ86

Congleton Library

A public library which is part of the Libraries and Museums Department of Cheshire County Council. [Pa,Sc,Dr,Ph,Cr]
Address: Market Square, Congleton, Cheshire CW12 1BU tel 0260 271141
Contact: Librarian in Charge Lesley Morgan
Open: Mon,Fri 9.30-8 Tues,Thurs 9.30-5.30 Sat 9-1 Wed closed
Policy: The exhibiting programme includes shows from the Cheshire Arts Tour Services and those generated by Cheshire County Council as well as local societies and individual artists. *'We aim at filling the area with changing and varied collections to interest and stimulate library users. Some displays give a lot of information on historical, topical or local issues. Art exhibitions also vary from the homely to the controversial, reflecting the ranges of tastes of the cross-section of ages who visit the building'.*
Sales: Sales referred to the exhibitor
The Space: The exhibition area is 12x6x3m high with two hessian-covered walls 6x2.4m and six panels 8.7x14.3m. Lighting by spotlights on suspended track.
Exhibiting: [AW][EF] Send CV and slides or photographs of work to the Librarian in Charge. The gallery pays for insurance and charges 10% commission plus VAT.
Access: [F] BR Congleton 15 mins walk; Nearby car park and buses

Corby (Northamptonshire)

(EMA) Map5 SP88

Corby Library

See also Northamptonshire Libraries. [VA,Ph,Cr]
Address: Chisholm House, 9 Queens Square, Corby, Northamptonshire NN17 1PZ tel 0536 203304
Contact: District Librarian Michael Sharman
Open: Mon,Tues,Thurs 9.30-8, Wed, Fri 9.30-5, Sat 9.30-4
Policy: Small art and/or craft displays arranged by East Midlands Arts (see separate entry), plus other similar displays by local artists, makers and local societies.
Sales: Work sold; Sales referred to exhibitor
The Space: Three 1.75x1.5m display boards, one crafts showcase with and one without video, 10m linear hanging space on Marler-Haley Big Screens.
Exhibiting: [AW] District Librarian. Publicity and insurance provided, transport between libraries arranged for touring exhibitions. Commission is 10%.
Access: [X] Town centre site; Bus station 5 mins

Corby Glen (Lincolnshire)

(LHA) Map5 SK92

Willoughby Memorial Trust Gallery

A gallery showing mainly the work of local artists and others. [VA,Ph,Cr]
Address: Moreley's Lane, Corby Glen, Nr Grantham, Lincolnshire tel 077 832 205
Contact: Hon Secretary P B Grimes, Estate Office, Grimsthorpe, Bourne, Lincolnshire PE10 0NB tel 0778 32 205
Open: Noon-5 during exhibitions
Policy: To enrich the life of those living in the area and to encourage others to visit. Approximately six exhibitions a year of painting and sculpture. Annual art competition and local schools exhibition.
Sales: Work sold
The Space: Two exhibition areas, plinths available.
Exhibiting: [AW]
Access: A151 Colstersworth to Bourne off A1

Coventry (W Midlands)

(WMA) Map5 SP37

Centre Crafts

A commercial gallery with two major exhibitions held in the Spring and Autumn. [Cr]
Address: 169 Spon Street, Coventry, W Midlands CV1 3BB tel 0203 27200
Contact: Mary O'Donovan
Open: Mon-Sat 9-5.30; closed bank holidays
Policy: The gallery aims *'to introduce the general public to small concentrations of artists and makers work at all times. We try to avoid fashionable work as our customers would not tolerate it. New work is of interest to them, and price is not as important if the work is good'.*
Sales: Work sold; Credit card; Credit scheme
The Space: A 6x3.5m space with display cases, fluorescent and spotlights and hanging by rail and direct fixing.
Exhibiting: Exhibitions are by invitation, but the centre is *'always pleased to see the work of new makers'.*
Access: [S] City centre location

Coventry Polytechnic (Lanchester Gallery)

A purpose-built gallery space within the polytechnic

with a reputation for showing promising new artists. [VA,Cr,Ph,LA]

Address: Coventry Polytechnic, Faculty of Art and Design, Gosford Street, Coventry, W Midlands CV1 5RZ tel 0203 838540

Contact: Peter McCarthy

Open: Mon-Fri 9-6, Sat 9-12

Policy: The gallery has a preference for solo exhibitions by young promising artists, designers, makers and photographers. Particular emphasis is placed on inviting local schools to the exhibitions and seminars are organised in conjunction with the exhibitions. A smaller gallery has a rolling programme of photography touring shows and solo photography shows.

Sales: Work sold

The Space: 15.4x4.5x3.5m with track lighting and direct fixing; the gallery is situated off the main entrance.

Exhibiting: [AW] Adverts are placed in art press for applications. Send CV, ten slides, press cuttings etc to Peter McCarthy. The gallery provides insurance, transport, publicity, catalogue, installation and preview. Exhibitors normally give a slide talk on their work.

Access: [U][T][L][F] City centre location; Bus station 3 mins; BR Coventry 15 mins

CRIS Community Arts

A community arts project working with groups and individuals to produce their own work using artists 'to assist in specialist art forms'. [Pr,Dr,Ph,Te]

Address: Koko Ltd, Unit 15, The Arches Industrial Estate, Spon End, Coventry, W Midlands CV1 3JQ tel 0203 77719

Contact: Linda Prue

Open: Mon-Fri 10-5.30; evenings and weekends by appointment

Policy: Special events, courses, workshops and exhibitions are held in community centres, schools, and other public venues in the Coventry area. Some exhibitions are held at Koko which is a community resource building situated fairly centrally in Coventry. This has exhibition and display space for photographic panels and posters. Art and photographic materials shop. CRIS has darkroom, layout and screen printing facilities.

Lanchester Gallery: Installation of sculpture by Paul Rodgers

The Space: The space at Koko is on both sides of corridors downstairs and upstairs totalling 66m linear hanging space.

Exhibiting: [AW] Assistance can be given for framing, and a fee is paid for sessional work.

Access: [U][T][L]

Herbert Art Gallery

A large municipal gallery within the Leisure Services department of Coventry City Council. [VA,Ph,LA]

Address: Jordan Well, Coventry, W Midlands CV1 5RW tel 0203 832387

Contact: Principal Keeper Patrick Day

Open: Mon-Sat 10-5.30, Sun 2-5

Policy: The gallery has a policy of showing work that is *'socially and politically relevant to Coventry'*. Promotion of younger artists is seen as a priority, but this takes place alongside a programme that includes historical exhibitions, touring shows, and displays from the permanent collection which contains examples of British watercolours, British figure drawing and local topography as well as contemporary art. The gallery organises a number of seminars, talks and practical workshops with the exhibitions.

Sales: Work sold

The Space: Three galleries are used for temporary exhibitions. Gallery four has 50m linear space, gallery

Herbert Art Gallery: 'Article 30, United Nations Declaration of Human Rights' by Robbin Harris

five 35m linear space and gallery six 45m linear space. Lighting is by spots and fluorescent tubes. Environmental controls available. Direct fixing or a picture rail used. Lift from loading bay is 2.5x2.5x2.5m approx, max weight two tons. Four large showcases are available.

Exhibiting: [AW][EF] Slides and CV to the Principal Keeper 24 months in advance of proposed showing dates. The gallery covers most exhibition costs, including transport, publicity and preview. Supports EPR.

Access: [U][T][L][F] Public car park 5 mins; Bus station 5 mins; BR Coventry 10 mins

Koko Ltd

A community resource space offering accommodation and facilities to community and voluntary groups or small businesses. [Ph,LA]

Address: Unit 15, The Arches Industrial Estate, Spon End, Coventry, W Midlands CV1 3JQ

Contact: Polly Dickenson

Open: Mon-Fri 9-10, Sat 9-5

Policy: The gallery space is situated in a main corridor and shows mostly local work. The centre has a non-racist, non-sexist policy that exhibitors must comply with. The programme is mostly *'information and issue-based'* exhibitions.

Sales: Sales referred to exhibitor

The Space: The corridor is fitted with 0.95m high panels providing 19m linear hanging space most suited to laminated exhibitions. Fluorescent lighting.

Exhibiting: [AW] Exhibitor responsible for all exhibition costs.

Access: [U][T][L] Car park; Buses 10,11,32,33,19,192 from city centre; BR Coventry 20 mins

Mead Gallery

A purpose-built gallery part of the Arts Centre complex which contains a concert hall, theatre, studio theatre, film theatre, music centre, conference room, bookshop and restaurant. [VA,Cr,Ph]

Address: The Arts Centre, The University of Warwick, Coventry, W Midlands CV4 7AL tel 0203 523523

Contact: Curator Katharine Eustace

Open: Mon-Fri 12-8, Sat 10-8, closed Sun (term-time only)

Policy: The large modern gallery shows a diverse range of contemporary and historical solo and group shows. Although a university gallery, its audience is drawn from a wide area, and associated workshops and talks are very popular. The exhibitions are always of a high standard of presentation and content. The university collection of largely 60s paintings and prints is housed at the centre, and the Rugby Collection of 20th century British painting is on permanent loan.

Sales: Work sold

The Space: 600 square metres of space can be used as one gallery or split into two or three galleries with a potential 300m linear hanging space using the screen system. Climatic controls, a flexible lighting system, three table-top showcases and glazed-roof sculpture court, complete the excellent facilities.

Exhibiting: The financial contribution to exhibitions varies from exhibition to exhibition.

Access: [U][T] Car parks on campus; Bus 12 from Coventry 35 mins

Museum of British Road Transport

A municipal museum showing a permanent collection of road transport.

Address: St Agnes Lane, Hales Street, Coventry, W Midlands CV1 1PN tel 0203 832425

Contact: Manager Barry Littlewood

Open: 10-5; Winter Fri-Sun 10-5

Policy: *'Largest municipally-owned transport collection in the world'.*

The Space: Board room 115 square metres and exhibition hall up to 1000 square metres suitable for stand alone exhibitions.

Exhibiting: [AW] Write to Manager.

Access: [U][T][L] Bus to Pool Meadow, BR Coventry

Cowes (Hampshire)

(SA) Map7 SZ49

Solent Gallery

A commercial gallery, one of two run by Harvey Bagnall (see Solent Gallery, Lymington) showing marine landscapes and wildlife paintings. [Pa,Pr]

Address: Ancasta Marina, Cowes, Isle of Wight PO31 tel 0893 294433

Contact: Owner Harvey Bagnall

Open: Mon-Sun 10.30-1 & 2-5.30, closed Wed [May-October]

Policy: The gallery's aim is to help artists by selling their work and it shows a range of work in oil, watercolour and gouache alongside original silkscreen and other

Mead Gallery: 'Relevation for the Hand' exhibition, 1987

limited-edition prints. The gallery shows *'the best in contemporary marine painting from around the UK to the thriving sailing community'.*

Sales: Work sold; Credit card; Credit scheme

Exhibiting: [AW] Telephone to arrange an appointment to show work or send slides or photographs. The gallery pays for insurance, publicity, list of exhibits and preview and catalogue and charges 40% commission including VAT.

Access: [U][T][F]

Crediton (Devon)

(SWA) Map6 SS80

Red House Arts Centre

A community-based arts centre with workshops, classes and community events planning an exhibition programme from January 1988. [VA,Cr,LA]

Address: St Lawrence Green, Crediton, Devon EX17 3LN tel 03632 4038

Contact: Paul & Daphne Cartwright

Open: Centre open all year for courses, gallery open Mon-Sat during school holidays

Policy: *'Our policy is to provide a mixture of exhibitions to appeal both to the local community and also a much wider, more radical, audience. Crediton is a lively country town with a strong arts community in a large catchment area 20 minutes from Exeter. We wish to exhibit new and exciting work from both established and new artists in either group or solo exhibitions and especially welcome shows by women or minority groups.'* As the space is used for art and drama classes during term-time, exhibitions will be programmed in the remaining weeks.

Sales: to be decided

The Space: 19 m linear hanging space in main gallery. A small courtyard is also available for sculpture.

Exhibiting: [AW] Applications in writing with slides. Financial terms are yet to be decided but *'we certainly intend to operate in a way favourable to arists'.*

Access: [U][T][F] Bus 377 Exeter-Crediton; BR Crediton 15 mins walk; Public car park 3 mins

Crowborough (E Sussex)

(SEA) Map7 TQ53

Green Lane Gallery

A gallery for Beacon School and the community with a varied programme of exhibitions which predominantly show the work of living artists. [Pa,Dr,Ph,Cr,LA]

Address: Beacon School, Green Lane, Crowborough, E Sussex TN6 2AS tel 089 265 3451

Contact: Tony Chisholm

Open: Mon-Fri 9-4 supervised. Sat 9.30-12 during term-time by arrangement with exhibitor

Policy: The gallery is placed on the school site at the heart of the community, and aims to provide a focal point for a wide range of audiences and exhibitions. There is a policy of making exhibitions accessible to as many people as possible and keeping costs, wherever possible, to a minimum. The gallery is anxious to involve exhibitors in seminars, workshops and residencies. Work displayed is used as a major learning resource by the school. The gallery is also keen to organise sitings of permanent or semi-permanent outdoor works.

Sales: Work sold

The Space: The gallery is 20x4x4m high with a movable screen system to suit exhibitors' needs and the spot lighting system runs the length of the gallery. Projection, slide, video and computer equipment are available if required. The gallery is also used for poetry readings. Gallery plans available.

Exhibiting: [AW] There is no hire fee for individual shows but a nominal charge for group shows. Gallery finances insurance, list of exhibits, mail-out of publicity (but not printing) and catalogue/card. Support in principle for EPR. Commission 10%.

Access: [X] BR Crowborough 25 mins; School car park 1 min

Darlington (Co Durham)

(NA) Map3 NZ21

Bernhardt Gallery

A private gallery showing watercolours, etchings, lithographs and screenprints. [Pa,Pr,Dr]

Address: 60 Coniscliffe Road, Darlington, Co Durham DL3 7RN tel 0325 56633

Contact: Margaret Reynolds

Open: Daily 9.30-5, Wed 9.30-1

Policy: The gallery shows work by professional and especially talented local artists, mounting periodic solo and group exhibitions.

Sales: Work sold

The Space: The gallery is 46 square metres with 22m linear hanging space and has spotlights. Hanging is by direct fixing.

Exhibiting: The gallery charges 33.3% commission.

Access: Car park nearby

Darlington Art Gallery

A municipal gallery with a permanent collection of local and regional 19th & 20th century paintings. [Pa,Pr,Ph]

Address: Crown Street, Darlington, Co Durham DL1 1ND tel 0325 462034

Contact: J S Mallam

Open: Mon-Fri 10-8, Sat 10-5.30; Closed bank holidays and preceding Sat

Policy: The gallery is hired out for exhibitions of work by living artists.

Sales: Work sold

The Space: The gallery is 17.4x8.8m with 44m linear hanging space. Hanging is on hessian-covered panels by rods or direct fixing with fluorescent and spot lighting.

Exhibiting: [AW] Gallery provides publicity, list of exhibits and charges 20% commission.

Access: [S] BR Darlington 15 mins; Bus station 10 mins; Car park 2 mins

Darlington Arts Centre

A multi-media arts centre run by the borough council with three exhibition spaces. [VA,Cr,LA]

Address: Vane Terrace, Darlington, Co Durham DL3 7AX tel 0325 483271

Contact: Exhibitions Officer Alison Lloyd

Open: Myles Meehan Gallery 10-8; Glass Corridor & Foyer Space 10am-10.30pm

Policy: The Myles Meehan Gallery shows contemporary work *'of a high standard and quality'* including Arts Council touring exhibitions. The Glass Corridor gallery, a busy thoroughfare, is used to show work by local artists and groups and photography exhibitions. The Foyer acts as an informal gallery *'where pictures are part of the background of eating and drinking'*. There is also a crafts display window. The programme balances touring exhibitions with those initiated by the gallery. There is a strong commitment to show the work of artists from the region. Workshops, talks, residencies and courses are also organised.

Sales: Work for sale; Credit scheme

The Space: Myles Meehan Gallery has 47m linear hanging space with direct fixing and spotlights. The Glass Corridor offers 24m linear hanging space with direct fixing and natural lighting. The exhibition spaces are also used for dance, art classes and recitals.

Exhibiting: [AW][EF] Send ten slides, proposal, CV and ability to undertake a workshop to the Exhibitions Officer. The gallery covers insurance, publicity, list of exhibits, artists' expenses and preview. Supports the principle of EPR.

Access: [F] BR Darlington 20 mins; Car park in immediate area

Dartford (Kent)

(SEA) Map7 TQ57

Gallery (The)

New gallery in the clock-tower of the shopping centre. [Pa,Cr]

Address: The Tower, Upper Street North, New Ash Green, Dartford, Kent DA3 8JR tel 0474 872 694

Contact: Lorna Fuller or Maxine Kennedy

Darlington Art Gallery

Policy: The Gallery aims to provide an outlet for work by local artists and makers. It plans to run monthly exhibitions, classes in various crafts and workshops for children.

Dartington (Devon)

(SWA) Map6 SX76

Dartington Cider Press Centre

A commercial gallery 'part of the craft shop stocking best quality local and British craftwork, mainstream work not avant garde, and appropriate price structure to mainstream sales'. [Sc,Cr]

Address: Shinners Bridge, Dartington, Devon TQ9 6TQ tel 0803 864171

Contact: Managing Director Roger Dalton

Open: Mon-Sat & some Suns in Summer 9.30-5.30; closed Christmas and New Year's Day

Policy: Special exhibitions arranged to relate to *'promotions in the centre eg Alternative Bouquets'*.

Sales: Work sold; Credit card

The Space: The gallery has 8x5m glass display cases along walls, with internal lighting and island displays on plinths.

Exhibiting: [AW] Apply to Roger Dalton. The centre provides insurance, publicity and mailing. A 30-40% commission is charged on sales.

Access: [U][T][F] X80 Torquay/Plymouth bus; Car parking

Dartmouth (Devon)

(SWA) Map6 SX85

Facets

A specialist gallery which has a good permanent collection of precious and non-precious jewellery, and holds temporary jewellery exhibitions. [Je]

Address: 14 Broadstone, Dartmouth, Devon TQ6 9NR tel 08043 3534

Contact: Norman Dilley

Open: Mon-Sat 9-5; closed Feb

Policy: Run by jewellers Norman and Jacqueline Dilley ensuring that *'the gallery maintains, commissions and*

Darlington Arts Centre: 'In the Form of Smoke', a performance by Jozepha Rogocki

shows jewellery designed and made to the highest standard. Over 50 designers and makers working in a variety of materials are shown and the collection ranges from £5-£500.

Sales: Work sold; Credit card

The Space: The gallery is divided into three sections where the work is displayed individually, either in internally lit wall or floor cabinets. There is a separate area which is normally used for exhibitions.

Exhibiting: [AW] Jewellery designers or makers should contact the gallery in writing with photographs of current work. The gallery covers all costs, insurance, private view, printing, publicity etc.

Higher Street Gallery

A Crafts Council selected gallery, its speciality is contemporary watercolours, it also shows ceramics, glass, textiles, wood, jewellery by leading British makers. [Pa,Cr,Pr]

Address: 1 Higher Street, Dartmouth, Devon TQ6 9RB tel 08043 3157

Contact: Ken Goodwin

Open: Mon-Sat 9.30-5, Wed 9.30-1

Policy: Specialises in contemporary watercolour paintings and recently introduced limited edition prints. Purchases and sells mixed crafts. The gallery puts on a maximum of four exhibitions a year.

Sales: Work sold; Credit card

The Space: Exhibitions are mounted within the sales area of the Gallery.

Exhibiting: [AW] Artists should contact the Gallery personally for details of exhibiting.

Access: [X] Public car park 5 mins

Simon Drew Gallery

A commercial gallery on the Crafts Council's selected list with a changing display of work and occasional exhibitions showing 'specific artists only and the work of different potters who produce work of a high standard'. [VA,Ce]

Address: 13 Foss Street, Dartmouth, Devon TQ6 9DR tel 08043 2832

Contact: Simon & Caroline Drew

Open: Mon-Sat 9-5; closed Wed pm Winter

Sales: Work sold; Credit card

The Space: The rooms used are 4.75x4.75m, 4.75x2.75m and 4.5x3m.

Exhibiting: Invited exhibitors are provided with insurance and preview and 33.3% commission is charged on sales.

Access: [S] Town centre location; Buses from BR Totnes

Datchet

(SA) Map7 SU97

Century Gallery

See Century Galleries, Henley-on-Thames.

Address: The Shop on the Green, Datchet SL tel 0753 681 2884

Open: Daily 10-5

Dawlish (Devon)

(SWA) Map6 SX97

Porch Galleries

A gallery, owned by Vogager Publications which publishes art cards, posters and books, which shows contemporary exhibitions throughout the year. [Pa,Sc,Pr,Ph,Cr]

Address: 2A Iddesleigh Terrace, Dawlish, Devon EX7 9HS tel 0626 867080

Contact: Director Dr A M Afifi

Open: Mon-Sat 10-5.30, limited opening Sun

Policy: The gallery was founded in 1988 through local demand and produces an exhibition every three weeks, showing a wide range of work. *'The policy is to exhibit good local work both amateur and professional and to bring in once a quarter from overseas or outside the area an artist unknown in our region.'* The gallery hosts meetings and events including writers' circles, theatre preview exhibitions and forums for other arts groups.

Sales: Work sold; Credit card; Credit scheme

The Space: The upper and lower galleries both have 22m linear hanging space with a maximum height of 4m. Lighting is direct and indirect with banks of spotlights and hanging is by nail, pegs and wire from ceiling hooks. There are also display tables and stands and a 2x2m window display. Gallery plans available.

Exhibiting: [AW] Send details and a reasonable number of photographs or slides. Gallery pays for insurance, publicity and mail out, catalogue and preview and takes between 20-25% commission. Supports EPR in principle.

Access: [X] Bus stations 1 min; Br Dawlish 2 mins; Car parks 2 mins

Vivian Gallery

A commercial textile gallery, opened in 1988, specialising in individually designed hand-made garments, jewellery and accessories. Also showing monthly exhibitions of small scale work. [Te,Je]

Address: 2 Queen Street, Dawlish, Devon EX7 9HB tel 0626 867254

Contact: Sarak Vivian

Open: Mon-Sat 9-6 plus some Sun afternoons and late evenings

Policy: Specialist gallery for garments, accessories and jellewery, one-off or very limited editions. *'Emphasis is on quality and value not avant garde extremes.'*

Sales: Work sold; Credit card; Commissions encouraged

The Space: Two rooms both combining garment rails and shelves with display, hanging and plinth areas. Good window frontage. Majority of space used for stock, the remainder for small monthly exhibitions.

Exhibiting: [AW] Widest possible range of work sought within the above policy from makers all over the country.

Access: [S] BR Dawlish & Buses 5 mins; Public car park 2 mins

Deal (Kent)

(SEA) Map7 TR35

Deal Library Gallery

Run by Kent County Libraries, this gallery shows a varied programme which centres on the work of living artists with particular connections to the area. [Pa,Pr,Dr,Ph,Cr]

Address: Broad Street, Deal, Kent CT14 6ER tel 030 437 2984

Contact: Group Librarian Paula Tempest

Open: Mon, Tues, Thurs 9.30-6, Wed 9.30-1, Fri 9.30-7, Sat 9.30-5

Policy: The gallery aims to promote the work of local living artists, showing work which would not otherwise be seen in the area. Exhibitions run for three to four weeks.

Sales: Work sold

The Space: 8x6x3m high with 21m linear hanging, the maximum hanging height is 2m. Lighting is by track-mounted spots.

Exhibiting: [AW] Apply to Group Librarian approximately 15 months in advance of desired showing dates. Enclose slides or photographs and biography. Gallery finances insurance, list of exhibits and mail-out of publicity. Support in principle for EPR. Commission 15%.

Access: [F] BR Deal 10 mins; Public car park 1 min

Debenham (Suffolk)

(EA) Map5 TM27

Debenham Gallery

Commercial gallery.

Address: 1 High Street, Debenham, Suffolk IP34 6QL tel 0728 860707

Dedham (Essex)

(EAA) Map7 TL03

Dedham Centre

An independent, commercial arts centre containing studios, gallery, pottery, restaurant and toy museum. [VA,Cr]

Address: High Street, Dedham, Colchester, Essex CO7 6AD tel 0206 322666

Contact: Jeremy Parkin

Open: Daily 10-5

Policy: The centre is housed in a converted chapel with three floors containing a variety of art and craft based activities. On the first and second floors are working craft areas, and studio space for artists: each ranging between 4.65 and 18.6 sqm. Of the twelve available spaces, three are reserved for artists, and rents range from £20 to £35 a week, with a winter reduction. A main hall is used for fairs, stalls, exhibitions, functions, courses, classes and community activities. Adjoining, in the smaller hall is a toy museum; a working pottery and a wholefood refreshment area completes the facilities.

Sales: Work sold

Exhibiting: Stalls and display areas can be rented on a daily basis, from £4.50 a weekday to £14 a weekend. Discounts are available for bookings over a week. The centre also sells work on an individual basis, charging 25% commission.

Delph (Lancashire)

(NWA) Map3 SD90

Artisan

A small craft gallery that opened in 1980 showing the owners work as well as that of other artists and makers. [VA,Cr,Ce]

Address: 3 King Street, Delph, Oldham, Lancashire OL3 5DL tel 045 774506

Contact: Anne Hamlett

Open: Wed, Thurs, Fri, Sat 10.30-5.30, Sun 2-5

Policy: The gallery shows six exhibitions a year each lasting about six weeks to two months. The policy is *'to promote good-quality crafts and paintings by living artists and makers. This is a tourist area so the summer season exhibition is targetted towards smaller sales and mixed exhibitions.'* The aim of the main exhibitions is to stimulate interest locally and throughout the Greater Manchester area. In addition to the exhibitions there may be a display which supplements the regular work. Anne Hamlett makes her own work at the back of the gallery and where people can *'see and discuss the process which goes into making the pieces'*. Workshops organised for the local education authorities.

Sales: Work sold; Credit card

The Space: In the small gallery hanging is by hooks and usually lit by track and spot. There is ample shelving and three display cases to display crafts. Paintings larger than 0.91x1.21 present a problem. Gallery plans are available.

Exhibiting: [AW] Applications should be sent to Anne Hamlett and should include a letter of introduction, CV, slides/photographs and selling prices. The gallery pays for insurance, list of exhibits. It takes 33.3% commission on sales.

Access: [S] Bus for Manchester, Oldham; Car park 2 mins

Denby Dale (N Yorkshire)

(YA) Map3 SE20

Gate, Studio & Gallery

Commercial gallery with regular changing exhibitions. [VA,Ce,Gl,Te]

Address: Springfield Mills, Norman Road, Denby Dale, Huddersfield, N Yorkshire HD8 8TH tel 0484 865429

Open: Tues-Fri 1.30-5.30, Sat 9.30-2 and by appointment

Policy: Specialises in work which has a *'spiritual'* quality.

Exhibiting: [AW]

Derby (Derbyshire)

(EMA) Map5 SK33

Art For All

An organisation promoting exhibitions in non-gallery venues in the Derby area as well as this exhibition space. Three venues are currently used (see under separate entries), Derby City Council House, Ilkeston Community Hospital and Derby City Hospital. [VA,Cr,Ph]

Address: Markeaton Park Craft Village, Derby DE3 3BG tel 0332 292920

Contact: Organiser Frank Walters

Open: Wed, Thurs, Fri 1-5, Sat, Sun and bank holidays 10-5

Policy: The organisation arranges regular touring programmes in various venues, loans exhibitions for touring and operates a picture loan scheme. The exhibition scheme hopes to increase the audience for the contemporary visual arts, increase understanding and enjoyment, and provide publicity and support for artists and makers working in the region. The sites used have been carefully selected, and equipped with blockboard-clad walls to provide a sympathetic environment for the exhibitions. The programme is wide-ranging with an emphasis on work from artists and makers in the region. The exhibitions are supported by East Midlands Arts, Derby City Council and Southern Derbyshire Health Authority.

Sales: Work sold

The Space: See individual entries.

Exhibiting: [AW][EF]. Slides and SAE to Frank Walters. Art For All provides insurance, transport, list of exhibits and installation if required. A 20% commission is charged on sales. Supports EPR.

Access: [U][T][F] Car park; Trent Bus 1,2,3,4 from Derby

Clock Yard Gallery

The gallery is situated in Pymms Champagne Bar, part of a redevelopment including specialist shops. [VA,Ph,Cr]

Address: 7 Clock Yard, Friargate, Derby DE4 tel 0332 32415

Contact: Jane Montague,

Open: Licensing hours

Policy: The gallery *'aims to encourage local artists and makers producing contemporary work'* and attract the *'attention of local people to the work'*.

Sales: Work sold

The Space: 12x3x4m giving 15m linear space with direct fixing and an *'excellent spotlighting system'*. Gallery plans are available.

Exhibiting: [AW] Some publicity is available.

Access: [U][T][F] Town centre 3 mins; BR Derby 10 mins

Derby Art Gallery

A municipal art gallery with permanent collections and three galleries for temporary exhibitions. [VA,Cr,Ph,De]

Address: The Strand, Derby DE1 1BS tel 0332 293111

Contact: Exhibitions Officer Sarah Kirby

Open: Tues-Sat 10-5

Policy: The gallery is beginning to *'establish itself as a venue for contemporary art and craft, as well as more traditional exhibitions'*. The exhibitions are drawn from a number of sources including national touring exhibitions and shows by established artists and makers in the region. A small crafts case in the shop holds a changing display of work for sale. The education department organises various activities alongside the exhibition programme.

Sales: Work sold

The Space: Gallery One is 8x20x4m giving 50m linear hanging space, Gallery Two is 8x16x4m giving 46m linear hanging space, Gallery Three is 6x8x4m giving 25m linear hanging space. Hanging is by direct fixing, track lighting is used, and lockable display cases are available. Gallery plans available.

Exhibiting: [AW] Send slides and CV to the Exhibitions Officer twelve months in advance. Applications particularly welcomed from professional artists and makers in the East Midlands. The gallery charges 20% commission and provides a poster, insurance, and mailing of publicity. One-way transport is usually provided.

Access: [U][T][L][F] City centre location close to car parks and buses; BR Derby 30 mins

Derby City Council House (Art For All)

See Art For All, Derby entry. [VA,Cr,Ph]

Address: Corporation Street, Derby DE1

Contact: Organiser Frank Walters, Markeaton Park Craft Village, Derby tel 0332 292920

Open: Mon-Fri 10-5

Sales: Work for display only

The Space: A 15m linear space in the Rates Hall with fluorescent and natural light, direct fixing and one wall-mounted showcase.

Exhibiting: See Art For All entry.

Access: [U][T] City centre location; Bus station & public car parks 2 mins

Derby City Hospital (Art For All)

See Art For All, Derby entry. [VA,Cr,Ph]

Address: Uttoxeter Road, Derby DE3 3NB

Contact: Organiser Frank Walters, Markeaton Park Craft Village, Derby tel 0332 292920

Open: Daily

Sales: Work sold

The Space: Corridor and waiting room area giving 30m linear hanging space with fluorescent and natural light, direct fixing and one free-standing showcase.

Exhibiting: See Art For All entry.

Access: [U][T] Car park; Trent Bus 15,16 from city centre

Derby Community Arts

A community arts centre supported by East Midlands Arts and Derby City and Derbyshire County Councils. [Ph]

Address: 31 Woods Lane, Derby DE3 3UA tel 0332 385602

Contact: Photography Worker Terry Morgan

Open: Mon-Fri 10-6
Policy: Most exhibitions are photographic and *'lean towards community photography and practice'.* Exhibitions are mainly for the centre users and other community groups in the area. Where possible, exhibition work is exchanged to keep costs down. Workshops are occasionally arranged with the exhibitions.
Sales: Sales referred to exhibitor
The Space: The centre has 33m linear hanging space with fluorescent lighting.
Exhibiting: [AW] Contact Terry Morgan. The centre provides insurance and mailing of publicity. EPR supported.
Access: [F] Close to the town centre; on street parking; BR Derby 20 mins

Derby Playhouse

The gallery is situated in the foyer of a theatre in a large shopping complex in the centre of Derby. [Pa,Pr,Dr]
Address: Eagle Centre, Derby DE1 2NF tel 0332 363271
Contact: Press and Information Officer
Open: 10-end of evening performance
Policy: The exhibition programme is mainly drawn from local and regional artists, and is selected to be *'appropriate to the sort of people attending the plays'.*
Sales: Work sold; Credit card
The Space: A 10m linear hanging space along a curved wall, equipped with hanging rods and artificial lighting. The foyer also has a popular café and the box office.
Exhibiting: [AW] Contact the Press and Information Officer to arrange an interview. Publicity and insurance provided by the theatre, artist responsible for hanging and transport. Sales co-ordinated by the box office.
Access: [U][T][L][X] Public car park and bus station 1 min, BR Derby 20 mins

Derbyshire College of Higher Education

A gallery space in the concourse of the art and design block of the college of higher education. [VA,Ph]
Address: Faculty of Art and Design, Derbyshire College of Higher Education, Kedleston Road, Derby DE3 1GB tel 0332 47181
Contact: Dean of Faculty Eric Glithero
Open: Mon-Fri 9.30-6
Policy: Although mainly used for exhibitions of students work, occasional temporary exhibitions are mounted or hired to broaden the scope of the gallery.
Sales: Work sold; Sales referred to exhibitor
The Space: A 13x2.5m corridor with suspended panels giving 50m of hanging space and spot lights.
Exhibiting: [EF] Costs *'by arrangement'.* Supports EPR.
Access: [F] Car park; 5 mins bus route to town centre; BR Derby 3 miles

Green Lane Gallery

A fully licensed gay bar and gallery. [Pa,Pr,Cr]
Address: 130 Green Lane, Derby DE1 1RY tel 0332 368652
Contact: Director Jeffery Tillett
Open: Mon-Sat 8.30pm-12 midnight; Sun 8.30pm-10.30pm; Fri & Sat 11-3
Policy: Exhibitions are shown in three rooms of a Georgian town house which also serves as a fully licensed gay bar. The exhibition programme is very varied, including local artists, European posters, and an annual Christmas show.
Sales: Work sold; Credit card
The Space: Domestic size.
Exhibiting: [AW] Apply in writing to the Director. The gallery provides insurance, publicity, mailing, and private view, A commission of 33.3% is charged on sales.
Access: [F] Close to city centre, car park adjacent

Ilkeston Community Hospital (Art For All)

See Art For All, Derby entry. [VA,Cr,Ph]
Address: Heanor Road, Ilkeston, Derbyshire DE7 8LN
Contact: Organiser Frank Walters, Markeaton Park Craft Village, Derby tel 0332 292920
Open: Daily
Sales: Work sold
The Space: Corridor and waiting room with 40m linear hanging space, fluorescent and natural light, direct fixing and two showcases on stands.
Exhibiting: See Art For All entry.
Access: [U][T] Car park; Bus 120 from Ilkeston

Metro Cinema Gallery

The Metro is the independent film theatre for Derby and Derbyshire supported by the British Film Institute, East Midlands Arts and Derby City and Derbyshire County Councils, housed in the premises of Derbyshire College of Higher Education. [Pa,Pr,Ph]
Address: Metro Cinema, Green Lane, Derby DE1 1SA tel 0332 40170
Contact: Laurie Hayward
Open: Daily 9-10, Mon 9-9
Policy: The programme is mostly photographic and complements the film programme. A mixture of *'historical and contemporary work of international, national and regional significance'* is shown within the context of an equal opportunities policy. Six major touring exhibitions and six exhibitions from local artists and young photographers are shown. Occasional photographic lectures and events are arranged.
Sales: Work sold
The Space: A specially equipped area with 50m linear space on 1.25m high panels with track lighting and direct fixing used.
Exhibiting: [AW][EF] The cinema provides insurance and publicity in the monthly brochure.
Access: [X] City centre location; BR Derby 10 mins

St Michael's Gallery

The gallery is run by Derby Cathedral, and forms part of the shop. [Pa,Sc,Ph,Cr]
Address: St Michael's House, Queen Street, Derby DE1 3DY tel 0332 41201
Contact: Arts Secretary Jean Flintham
Open: Mon-Sat 9.30-4.30

Policy: The monthly exhibitions are mostly solo. The gallery aims to encourage younger artists from the region and elsewhere, and show more established artists.
Sales: Work sold
The Space: 8.5x8m space giving 20m linear hanging space. Direct fixing and spots and natural light.
Exhibiting: [AW] The gallery supplies a list of exhibits, preview and mailing of publicity. Commission is 25% with a minimum charge of £75.
Access: [F] Derby city centre 5 mins

Workshop Gallery

A commercial gallery promoting Derbyshire artists, showing mainly 'landscapes, wild life studies, flower painting, and portrait studies in all media' and encouraging representational work. [VA]
Address: 22 Irongate, Derby DE1 3GP tel 0332 43178
Contact: John Grain
Open: Mon-Sat 9.30-5.30
Sales: Work sold; Sales referred to exhibitor
The Space: The gallery is 6x5x3m with spotlighting.
Exhibiting: [AW] Contact John Grain. The gallery provides insurance, publicity, preview and expenses. A commission of 25% is charged. EPR supported.
Access: [F] Close to the town centre

Desborough (Northamptonshire)

(EMA) Map5 SP88

Desborough Library

See Northamptonshire Libraries. [VA,Ph,Cr,Ar]
Address: High Street, Desborough, Northamptonshire NN14 2QS tel 0536 761085
Contact: District Librarian D Bond, Kettering Library, Sheep Street, Kettering NN16 0AN tel 0536 512315
Open: Tues-Fri 9.30-1,2-7; closed Mon,Sat
Sales: Work sold
The Space: The library has a purpose built gallery with track lighting and 13m x 1.2m high on Scandon screens around three walls. There is also a small case 1.2x1.2x0.3m side lit and tape slide equipment is available.
Exhibiting: [AW] District Librarian. Catalogues, publicity and insurance provided, transport between libraries arranged for touring exhibitions. Commission is 10%.
Access: [F] Buses from Kettering, Market Harborough; Close to A6

Desford (Leicestershire)

(EMA) Map5 SK40

Bosworth College Gallery

The gallery is part of a community college. [VA,Ph,Cr]
Address: The Bosworth College, Leicester Lane, Desford, Leicestershire LE9 9JL tel 04557 284112
Contact: Frank Cook
Open: Mon-Fri 10-3, evenings by arrangement
Policy: The gallery aims *'to encourage artists from all spheres of creative activity to exhibit their work in a venue other than a large town or city'.* See Leicestershire Education under Leicester.
Sales: Work sold
The Space: Gallery plans are available for exhibitors.
Exhibiting: [AW] Contact Frank Cook. A commission of 20% is charged on sales and artists and makers must hang their own exhibitions.
Access: Main bus route from Leicester to Market Bosworth

Dewsbury (W Yorkshire)

(YA) Map3 SE21

Dewsbury Exhibition Gallery

Occasional exhibitions are held in the gallery which is mainly concerned with the local history of the area. [Pa,Pr,Ph,Cr]
Address: Wellington Road, Dewsbury, W Yorkshire WF13
Contact: Keeper Robert Hall, Kirklees Leisure Services, Red Doles Lane, Huddersfield HD2 1YF tel 0484 513808 ext 216
Open: Mon-Fri 10-6, Sat 10-4
Access: [X] Parking close by

Dewsbury Museum

Exhibitions changing throughout the year in the museum which houses a collection of childhood and local history objects. [Pa,Cr]
Address: Crow Nest Park, Dewsbury, W Yorkshire WF13 2SF
Contact: Stuart Davies, Kirklees Leisure Services, Red Doles Lane, Huddersfield HD2 tel 0484 513808 ext 216
Access: [X]

Ditchling (East Sussex)

(SEA) Map7 TQ31

Craftsman Gallery

A crafts gallery and pottery workshop producing Jill Pryke's domestic thrown earthenware. [Cr]
Address: 8 High Street, Ditchling, E Sussex BN6 8TA tel 079 185 246
Contact: Owner Jill Pryke
Open: Mon-Sat 10-1 & 2-5, Wed 10-1; Closed Sun & bank holidays
Policy: A wide range of work by makers living and working in Sussex is shown in a changing display which includes batik, wall hangings, weaving, pottery, wood, engravings, jewellery, etchings and metalworking.
Sales: Work for sale
The Space: Hanging is by rail, with natural and spot lighting.
Exhibiting: [AW] The gallery invites Sussex-based makers to make an appointment for consideration. Commission charged is 33.3%.
Access: [X] BR Hassocks 2 miles

Doncaster (S Yorkshire)

(YA) Map3 SE50

Cusworth Hall Museum

A municipal museum with one room reserved for temporary exhibitions within a museum of South Yorkshire life. [Pa,Ph,Cr]

Address: Cusworth, Doncaster, S Yorkshire DN5 7TU tel 0302 782342
Contact: Curator Alison Morrish
Open: Mon-Thurs, Sat 11-5, Sun 1-5 (Feb-Oct); Mon-Thurs, Sat 11-4 (Dec-Jan)
Policy: The gallery exhibits work by local artists and makers which will *'Provide a varied programme covering as many different aspects as possible of local and social history and will appeal particularly to children, families and the non-specialist'*. Local artists are particularly encouraged. There are usually six exhibitions a year each lasting two months. In the past year, exhibitions have included a display by the local embroiderers' guild, a touch exhibition for the blind, and a watercolour and oil exhibition of local scenes by an artist living in the area. The gallery also arranges craft demonstrations and workshops relating to the collection and other activities inspired by the temporary exhibitions.
Sales: Work sold
The Space: The gallery has a total of 39m linear hanging space, in addition there are eight free-standing screens. The gallery is spot lit and the windows are treated with UV filters. Hanging is with mirror plates onto the walls. Showcases available for smaller three-dimensional work. The museum is surrounded by park land which may be used for one-day events or exhibitions.
Exhibiting: [AW] All applications are considered but exhibitions are usually at the invitation of the Curator. The gallery covers costs of insurance, printing of publicity, list of exhibits and mailing out of publicity and takes 15% commission.
Access: [S][X] Buses 212,274 from Doncaster North Bus Station & mini bus service; Car park adjacent

Doncaster Museum & Art Gallery

A municipal gallery with collections of European and British fine and applied art and changing temporary exhibitions. [Pa,Sc,Pr]

Address: Chequer Road, Doncaster, S Yorkshire DN1 2AE tel 0302 734287
Contact: Curator T Manby
Open: Mon-Sat 10-5, Sun 2-5, closed Fri
Policy: Monthly exhibitions are held of human history and culture, natural history, applied and decorative art and fine art subjects. The gallery also operates a school service and runs education programmes.
The Space: Exhibition gallery is 178 square metres.
Access: [U][T]

Metropolitan Institute of Higher Education (Church View Gallery)

A public gallery within the Art and Design Education department of Doncaster Metropolitan Institute of Higher Education showing visual arts and crafts with an emphasis on new work. [VA,Ph,Cr]

Address: Church View, Doncaster, S Yorkshire DN1 1RE tel 0302 22122 ext 276 and 247
Contact: Rob Ward
Open: Mon-Fri 9.15-5
Policy: The gallery is primarily an educational stimulus for students but also *'shows new work by artists and makers who have probably not exhibited before. As selling work is not a priority, commission on sales isn't charged... we are looking for strong, unusual work which will stimulate the students and the general public'*.
Sales: Sales referred to the exhibitor
The Space: The gallery is 11.5x9m and gallery plans are available.
Exhibiting: [AW] Artists and makers should send slides and information to Rob Ward. The gallery pays for insurance, printing and mailing of publicity.
Access: [L] BR Doncaster 5 mins

Dorking (Surrey)

(SEA) Map7 TQ14

Spectrum Gallery

Gallery founded in 1972. [VA,Ce,Gl]

Address: 268 High Street, Dorking, Surrey RH4 1QT tel 030 688 6088
Contact: Directors Denis or Sylvia Toomey
Open: Tues-Sat 9.15-5.30; closed Mon
Policy: Spectrum shows contemporary work in a variety of media and offers a framing and restoration service.
Sales: Work sold
Access: [F] Near town centre on A25; Bus stops near; BR Dorking 10 mins; Public car park opposite

Droitwich Spa (Hereford & Worcester)

(WMA) Map4 SO86

Droitwich Heritage Centre

A heritage centre run by Droitwich Town Council. [Pa,Ph,Pr]

Address: Heritage Way, Droitwich Spa, Hereford & Worcester WR9 8RF tel 0905 774312
Contact: Administrator Hamish Wood
Open: Summer 10-5, Winter 10-4
Policy: The centre *'has a policy of providing a continually changing programme of exhibitions dealing with a wide range of artistic media. Our aim is to encourage the public to view exhibitions and make more use of the centre'*. Talks, workshops and demonstrations are arranged depending on the exhibition. The programme is mainly general interest and mixed exhibitions.
Sales: Work sold
The Space: The space is 8x9.5m giving 35m linear of hanging space on Marler Hayley screens with track lighting.
Exhibiting: [AW] The exhibitor is responsible for all exhibition costs, including hire of space.
Access: [U][T][F] Town centre location; BR station nearby; Motorway links to M5 & M40

Dudley (W Midlands)

(WMA) Map4 SO99

Dudley Art Gallery

A municipal art gallery and museum with a permanent collection and temporary exhibition programme. [VA,Ph,Cr,Gl,LA]

Address: St James' Road, Dudley, W Midlands DY1 1HU tel 0384 456000 ext 5570

Contact: Curator Charles Hajdamach or Roger Dodsworth

Open: Mon-Sat 10-5

Policy: The exhibition programme features a number of contemporary exhibitions of regional and local artists/makers. A large open exhibition (Mid Art) is held annually for West Midlands artists. A collection of English glass from the 18th century to the present is held at Broadfield House.

Sales: Work sold

The Space: Two ground floor galleries of 12x8m and 12x6.5m and one first-floor gallery of 13x7.5m all with fluorescent and spot lighting.

Exhibiting: [AW] Contact the Curator. The gallery provides publicity, mailing and a list of exhibits.

Access: [F][X] Town centre location close to car parks and buses

Dulverton (Somerset)

(SWA) Map6 SS92

Exmoor Photographers Gallery

A commercial gallery opened in 1988 in Exmoor National Park which aims to provide space for independent photographers, established and talented newcomers. [Ph]

Address: 39 High Street, Dulverton, Somerset TA22 9DW tel 0398 23286

Contact: Curator Peter Hounslow

Open: Daily 9.30-5.30, phone to check

Policy: All aspects of photography are represented, though the gallery gives special emphasis to landscape work. Regular exhibitions plus a permanent stock of work from contributing photographers. There is also a cafe.

The Space: 90 square metres.

Exhibiting: [AW] Independent photographers are invited to sumbit work for possible exhibition. Gallery also available for hire.

Access: [F] Car or bus to Dulverton

Durham (Co Durham)

(NA) Map3 NZ24

DLI Museum & Art Gallery

The exhibition space is part of an arts centre run by Durham County Council Education Department which also houses the Durham Light Infantry regimental museum. [VA,Ph,Cr]

Address: Aykley Heads, Durham DH1 5TU tel 091 384 2214

Contact: Keeper-in-Charge Nerys Johnson

Open: Tues-Sat 10-5, Sun 2-5; Closed Mon except bank holidays

Policy: The aim is *'to put on a wide range of visual art exhibitions from all periods'* backed up by *'a lively education programme aimed at people with little or no experience of art'*. Contemporary exhibitions are either linked to other periods of art or are accompanied by creative workshops, talks etc. The print room houses small-scale exhibitions by North East artists.

Sales: Work sold

The Space: The Light Gallery is 20x9x2.7m giving 55m linear hanging space; the Dark Gallery is 15.5x9x2.7m giving 48m linear hanging space. Hanging is by rods or direct fixing. There are lighting tracks throughout with light level controls and air conditioning. Maximum size of paintings 2.4x1.8m, maximum weight of sculpture 2cwt. There are two Edmunds showcases.

Exhibiting: [AW] Write anytime enclosing slides/photographs to Nerys Johnson or Dennis Hardingham. The gallery finances insurance, publicity, list of exhibits, transport, catalogue and charges 15% commission.

Access: [U][T][L] BR Durham 10 mins; Bus station 10 mins; Car park

New Elvet Gallery

A commercial gallery. [Pa,Pr,Cr]

Address: 7 New Elvet, Durham DH1 3AQ tel 091 384 0081

Contact: Timandra Gustafson

Open: Mon-Sat 10-5

Policy: The gallery aims to display and sell a wide range of British contemporary crafts – jewellery, ceramics, glass, wood, textiles and limited edition prints.

Sales: Work sold; Credit card

The Space: The gallery is 6m square by 2.5m high with work displayed in glass cubes in the window; two lockable glass display cases and one lockable wall case. Work limited to smaller pieces.

Exhibiting: By invitation only. Gallery covers insurance, publicity, list of exhibits and charges 30% commission.

Access: [S] Buses to Durham City; Multi-storey and street parking

DLI Museum & Arts Centre: Installation of Tony Peart's exhibition

Oriental Museum

Run by the University of Durham as a museum of oriental art. [VA,Ph,Cr]

Address: Elvet Hill, Durham DH1 2TH tel 0385 66711
Contact: Keeper John Ruffle
Open: Mon-Fri 9.30-1 & 2.15-5, Sat 9.30-12 & 2.15-5; Closed Christmas & Easter
Policy: The museum has limited space for temporary exhibitions which are of two-dimensional work related to oriental culture. The programme is based on a major exhibition June-October with shorter exhibitions before and after Christmas.
The Space: The main space has 22.8m linear hanging space with spotlights and direct fixing to hessian-covered wall panels.
Exhibiting: [AW] Distribution of costs between gallery and artist varies and subject to discussion. Commission is 10%.
Access: [X] Some galleries

Saddler Gallery

A commercial gallery with a programme planned 'in an effort to meet public interest ranging from traditional landscape to non-objective abstract'. [Pa,Pr,Dr,Cr,Gl]

Address: 78 Saddler Street, Durham DH1 3NP tel 091 384 8541
Contact: Partner Pat Perkinton
Open: Mon-Sat 9.30-5; Closed Sun & bank holidays
Policy: The gallery's aim is to present a wide variety of styles in painting and printmaking reflecting the mood of 20th century art. There is also a framing workshop.
Sales: Work sold
Exhibiting: [AW] Apply during opening hours to Pat Parkinson or Geoff Osmond. Gallery covers insurance, artists contribute 50% to all preview costs and the gallery charges 33.3% commission.
Access: [X]

E Molesey (Surrey)

(SEA) Map7 TQ16

Art Enterprises

Art Enterprises aims to promote, exhibit and sell the work of practising artists and recent graduates by maintaining a slide register and providing marketing support to the artists. [VA]

Address: 135 Molesey Park Road, E Molesey, Hampton Court, Surrey KT8 0JX tel 01 979 6503
Contact: Jonathan Endfield
Open: By appointment
Policy: The company deals with a range of works from sculpture for buildings through to illustration work and portrait commissions. The company also organises exhibitions. Details of artists' works are sent to suitable clients.
Sales: Work sold
Exhibiting: [AW] Artists are welcome to send examples of their work. Commission is 30%.
Access: BR Hampton Court

Earby (Lancashire)

(NWA) Map3 SD94

Earby Library

A branch of Lancashire Libraries. [Pa,Dr,Ph]

Address: Water Street, Earby, Colne, Lancashire BB8 6RA tel 0282 843470
Contact: District Librarian Mrs A Brown
Open: Mon,Wed 10-12 1-7, Fri 10-12 1-5, Sat 10-12
Policy: Twelve exhibitions have been held during the past year, eight of which were solo shows. *'A focal point in the town in which local artists, and others (including schools), can show their work to a wider audience consisting mainly of library users'.*
The Space: Six boards mounted on the lending library walls measuring 0.6x2.46m, 0.6x1.3m, 0.6x3.4m, 0.6x3m, 0.6x2.76m and 0.6x2.46m.
Exhibiting: [AW] Contact the District Librarian. 15% commission is charged.
Access: [F] Bus Station 3 mins; Car park nearby

Eastbourne (E Sussex)

(SEA) Map7 TV69

Eastbourne College (Casson Gallery)

As part of an educational establishment, the gallery aims to show a wide variety of work dealing with contemporary issues as well as showing more traditional works. [VA]

Address: Eastbourne College, Old Wish Road,

New Elvet Gallery: A selection from the gallery. Large raku pot by Rudie Delanghe, teapot by Carl Gustafson, scent bottles by Chris Comins and Karlin Rushbrooke, wood bowl by Cecil Jordan, silk scarf by Jo Freeman

Eastbourne, E Sussex BN21 4JY tel 032 322 176
Contact: M J Owens tel 032 322 176
Open: Mon-Sat 9-6 during term-time
Policy: The gallery policy is to expose pupils to a wide range of visual arts works, and young artists are particularly promoted. Work is selected if it is thought to be *'a strong example'* of a particular genre of work. Artists are encouraged to hold slide shows and workshops for pupils.
Sales: Work sold
The Space: The gallery is 10x3.5x2.5m high, there is also a small upper gallery with 7.5m wall space for small works. Hanging is by rail that runs at a height of 1.5m around the gallery. Lighting is by track-mounted spots and plinths are available for sculpture. Gallery plans available.
Exhibiting: [AW] Apply in April to M J Owens enclosing slides and CV. Gallery finances insurance, list of exhibits and some preview costs. Commission 15%.
Access: [F] BR Eastbourne 5 mins

Eastbourne Library Gallery

Exhibition space in a busy central library. [Pa,Pr,Ph,Cr]

Address: Grove Road, Eastbourne, E Sussex BN21 4TL tel 032 322 834
Contact: Principal Librarian Neil Beck
Open: Mon-Fri 9.30-7, Sat 9.30-5, closed Wed
Policy: The gallery wishes to make available an exhibition area in which any local artists, individually or in groups, can display their work. Situated in the busy central library there is always a *'transient'* audience. Exhibitions are predominantly by solo and show for one month.
Sales: Sales referred to exhibitor
The Space: Display is on boards as follows; twelve 1x1m high, twelve 0.5x1m high, one 2x1m high and one 3x1.5m high. Boards are wall and *'island'* mounted.
Exhibiting: [AW] Apply to Principal Librarian with three or four samples of work. Gallery finances printing of publicity and list of exhibits. Commission 20%.
Access: [X] All town centre buses; BR Eastbourne 2 mins; Public car park 5 mins

Towner Art Gallery

This local authority gallery runs a wide ranging programme of exhibitions predominantly by living artists with thematic shows drawn from the gallery's large collection. [VA,Ph,Cr]

Address: High Street, Old Town, Eastbourne, E Sussex BN21 8BB tel 032 341 1688
Contact: Curator Penny Johnson
Open: Mon-Sat 10-5, Sun 2-5, closed Mon Nov-March
Policy: The gallery's policy is to run a lively and varied series of approximately 20 exhibitions a year which run for between six and eight weeks. Shows often have a theme devised by the gallery, the aim being to increase the visitors *'enjoyment, understanding and appreciation'* of both historical and contemporary work. Artist's talks and workshops are organised for solo shows, and guided tours are given for thematic exhibitions.
Sales: Work sold
The Space: Four galleries with 59m linear hanging space, one with 48m linear hanging space, upper galleries 90m linear hanging space. Hanging is by a mixture of mirror plates and hooks and chains. Lighting by spots and tubes.
Exhibiting: [AW][EF] Apply to Curator. Gallery finances insurance, printing and mail-out of publicity and catalogue/card, list of exhibits, transport and preview costs. Support in principle for EPR. Commission 10%-33.3%.
Access: [F] Buses from station; BR Eastbourne 15 mins

Eastleigh (Hampshire)

(SA) Map7 SU41

Eastleigh Museum

A museum run by Hampshire County Museums Service which houses a local history gallery, and runs a programme of smaller, locally generated exhibitions in addition to those described below. [VA,Ph,Cr]

Address: 25 High Street, Eastleigh, Hampshire SO5 5LF tel 0703 643026
Contact: Exhibitions Officer Jo Bailey, Hampshire County Museums Service, Chilcomb House, Chilcomb Lane, Winchester, Hampshire SO23 8RD tel 0962 846315
Open: Tues-Fri 10-5, Sat 10-4
Policy: This temporary exhibitions gallery is one of six galleries housed within museums throughout Hampshire. It receives six or seven touring exhibitions a year, about four of which include work by living artists or makers with a bias towards those living or working in or near Hampshire. It also holds two or three local exhibitions generated by local individuals or groups, such as camera clubs, art clubs and quilting groups. Exhibitions last five weeks and exhibiting artists are encouraged to give talks, demonstrations or workshops.
Sales: Work sold
The Space: The temporary exhibition gallery is 10.5x5.5m with 31.5m linear hanging space with direct fixing to hessian covered panels, spots on tracks. Display cases and gallery plans available.
Exhibiting: [AW] Applications in writing, accompanied by transparencies to Exhibitions Officer. The Museums Service pays for insurance, printing and mailing of publicity and transport. Commission is 20% plus VAT.
Access: [U][T] Town centre site; Public car park 5 mins

Eccles (Greater Manchester)

(NWA) Map3 SJ79

Monks Hall Museum

The museum runs a programme of exhibitions by contemporary artists. [VA]

Address: 42 Wellington Road, Eccles, Greater Manchester M30 0NP tel 061 789 4372
Open: Closed for a two-year period
The Space: Two areas of 18m square with direct fixing and a rail and fluorescent lighting.
Exhibiting: [AW] The gallery pays for publicity, mailing, catalogue and transport and takes 10% commission.
Access: [X] Parking

Egremont (Cumbria)

(WMA) Map3 NY01

Lowes Court Gallery

Grant-aided gallery run by charitable association showing work by artists living locally or with Cumbrian connections, which also operates as a tourist information centre. [VA,Ph,Cr,LA]

Address: 12 Main Street, Egremont, Cumbria CA22 2DW tel 0946 820693

Contact: Gallery Manager Jane Haywood

Open: Mon-Sat 10-1, 2-5; Closed Wed afternoons & Sun

Policy: The gallery organises monthly solo, two-person and group shows of contemporary art particularly by new and developing artists in all media and styles. Craft demonstrations related to exhibitions are organised.

Sales: Work sold

The Space: Main gallery is 5x4x3m and the back room 6x3x3m giving about 17m and 11m linear hanging space, there is also space in other rooms. There are spot and fluorescent lights, display cases and direct fixing. Maximum size of work 1.8m high.

Exhibiting: [AW][EF] Apply to Gallery Manager by telephone or letter. Exhibitions are fixed in November for the following year. The gallery covers the cost of insurance, publicity, list of exhibits, preview and charges 25% commission. Supports the principle of EPR.

Access: [F] Ground floor **[X]** Upstairs. Bus connections to Carlisle, Newcastle, BR Whitehaven and St Bees; Street parking; Car park 2 mins

Ellesmere (Shropshire)

(WMA) Map4 SJ33

Ellesmere College Arts Centre

An exhibition space in a college arts centre with a programme of music, dance, drama, poetry and workshops, as well as exhibitions. [VA,Ph,Cr]

Address: Ellesmere, Shropshire SY12 9AB tel 069 171 2828

Contact: Director Merriel Halsall-Williams, Daily 9-5, until 10pm on performance nights

Policy: The exhibition space is mainly used to show the work of local artists and makers.

Sales: Work sold

The Space: Space for approximately 55 works using hanging rods. Two small display cases available for small ceramics or sculpture.

Exhibiting: [AW] Contact the Director. A £40 hanging fee is charged, the centre provides publicity, list of exhibits and a preview.

Access: [U][T][S]

Elsham (Humberside)

(LHA) Map3 TA01

Wrawby Moor Art Gallery

Converted stable block owned and managed by the Elwes family as part of Elsham Country Park. [VA,Ph,Ho,Cr]

Address: Elsham Country Park, Estate Office, Elsham, Brigg, S Humberside DN20 0RA tel 0652 688698

Contact: Curator Gervese Elwes

Open: Easter-End Sep 11-5.30, Oct-Good Fri Sun only

Policy: General education, figurative art and national art profile. Displays change every six weeks between Easter and end of September. Craft shop and restaurant adjacent.

Sales: Work sold

The Space: 75m linear hanging space with an additional 75m on boards. Total floor area 250 square metres.

Exhibiting: Gallery covers costs of insurance, publicity, list of exhibits.Commission negotiable.

Access: [F] Car parking; M18 (junction 5) 1 mile, Humber Bridge 8 miles

Ely (Cambridgeshire)

(EA) Map5 TL58

Old Fire Engine House

[Pa,Pr]

Address: 25 St Mary's Green, Ely, Cambridgeshire CB7 4ER tel 0353 662582

Contact: Organiser Valerie Bent

Open: Mon-Fri 10.30-10.30, Sat 10.30-5.30, Sun 12.30-5.30

Policy: The gallery shows about ten monthly exhibitions a year.

Sales: Work sold

The Space: Two rooms each 5x3.5m.

Exhibiting: [AW] Examples of work to be submitted to gallery six to twelve months in advance. Gallery will share some costs of postage and private view and takes a commission of 33.3%.

Ewell (Surrey)

(SEA) Map7 TQ26

Bourne Hall

Large foyer area in a library and community centre. [VA]

Address: Spring Street, Ewell, Surrey KT17 tel 01 393 9573

Contact: Exhibitions Officer Janet Clemitson, Rainbow

Lowes Court Gallery

Centre, East Street, Epsom, Surrey KT17 1BN
Open: Mon, Wed, Thurs 10-5, Tues & Fri 10-8, Sat 10-5
Policy: The gallery shows a wide ranging programme of exhibitions including mid-scale touring shows.
The Space: Large foyer area in community centre.
Exhibiting: [AW] Commission 17%.

Exeter (Devon)

(SWA) Map6 SX99

Exeter and Devon Arts Centre

A gallery in the café 'specifically for artists in Exeter and Devon'. [Pa,Pr,Dr,Ph]

Address: Gandy Street, Exeter, Devon EX4 3LS tel 0392 219741
Contact: Programmer A Morley
Open: Daily 9-8 (Box office)
Policy: Monthly exhibitions, mainly from Exeter and West Country artists; paintings, photography - wall work only.
Sales: Work sold; Credit card
The Space: The gallery is 8x15m.
Exhibiting: [AW] Apply to the Programmer. The centre provides insurance, publicity, list of exhibits, and catalogue/card. 20% commission is charged on sales, and the centre supports EPR. Commission taken on sales.
Access: [U][T]

Exeter University (Library)

The gallery has two areas for exhibitions. [VA,Ph]

Address: University Library, Stocker Road, Exeter, Devon EX4 4PT tel 0392 263880
Contact: Sue Guy
Open: Daily 9-5.30; closed weekends during vacation
Policy: The foyer shows local artists and travelling exhibitions and The Wall exhibitions developing a theme.
Sales: Work sold sometimes
The Space: The foyer gallery is 11x2.75m plus the wall area of 6.5m linear hanging space.
Exhibiting: [AW] Artists are responsible for their own exhibition costs.
Access: [U][T][L][F] On the main university campus

Northcott Theatre

The 'leading repertory theatre in the South West' with exhibitions held in the upper foyer. [Pa,Dr,Ph]

Address: Stocker Road, Exeter, Devon EX4 4QB tel 0392 56182
Contact: House Manager Linda Webster
Open: Daily 10-6 (11pm during performances)
Policy: The theatre organises a *'varied programme of exhibitions of as high a standard as possible, and welcomes applications from both amateurs and professionals'.*
Sales: Work sold
The Space: Two walls each giving 6m linear hanging space plus 9.5m on the staircase.
Exhibiting: [AW] Apply three years in advance to the House Manager. The theatre provides insurance, publicity, limited mailing and a list of exhibits.
Access: [U][T][F] City Centre 10 mins

Royal Albert Memorial Museum

A municipal museum and art gallery with important collections of English paintings, ceramics, glass, Exeter silver and work by Devon artists with an active programme of temporary exhibitions. Also local and natural history and ethnology. [VA]

Address: Queen Street, Exeter, Devon EX4 3RX tel 0392 265 858
Contact: Exhibitions Officer Naomi Fabian
Open: Tues-Sat 10-5.30
Policy: Contemporay arts and crafts or any subject linked to permanent collection.
The Space: 80m linear hanging space with direct fixing, spots and fluorescent lights. Also two smaller spaces, one linked directly to main space (first floor) and one on ground floor.
Exhibiting: [AW] Applications to exhibit are sometimes accepted. Commission is 13% and the gallery covers the cost of insurance, publicity, mailing, private view and transport.
Access: [X]

Spacex Gallery

An independent gallery supported by South West Arts, Exeter City Council and Devon County Council with studios and an extensive contemporary exhibition programme. [VA,Ph,LA]

Address: 45 Preston Street, Exeter, Devon EX1 1DF tel 0392 431786
Contact: Director Robin Dobson
Open: Tues-Sat 10-5
Policy: The gallery aims to *'establish effective public access to a wide range of high-quality artwork by lesser-known as well as established, regional, national or international artists, and in particular those whose work is radical or experimental in the use of materials, developments or concepts'.*
Sales: Work sold; Credit scheme
The Space: Gallery A is 12x4.75x3.5m, the corridor space is 12x1.75x4.25m and Gallery B is 11.75x6.25x4.25m. Gallery plans available.

South Farnborough Galleries

Exhibiting: [AW][EF] Send slides, photos and CV in Oct/Nov. The gallery pays insurance, transport, publicity, preview, list of exhibits, catalogue/card and private view. Commission is 33.3%. EPR supported.
Access: [U][T] City centre location; BR Exeter 10 mins

Exmouth (Devon)

(SWA) Map6 SY08

Exmouth Rolle College Gallery

College gallery showing several exhibitions a year.

Address: Rolle College, Douglas Avenue, Exmouth EX8 2AT tel 0395 265 344
Contact: Howard Jones
Open: Mon-Fri 10-12.30 & 2-5, Sat 10-12.30
Policy: Local artists.
Exhibiting: [AW]

Falmouth (Cornwall)

(SWA) Map6 SW83

Falmouth Art Gallery

A municipal art gallery with a permanent collection and programme of temporary exhibitions covering a wide variety of subjects. [VA,Ph,Cr]

Address: Municipal Offices, Falmouth, Cornwall TR11 2RT tel 0326 313863
Contact: Curator Kate Dinn
Open: Mon-Fri 10-4.30
Policy: The programme includes historical, contemporary, solo, group and society exhibitions with the aim of providing *'opportunities for the residents and visitors to Falmouth to appreciate a wide range of good quality and/or interesting arts and crafts'.*
Sales: Work sold
The Space: Gallery One is 9x5.75x2.5m and gallery Two is 8x3.5x2.5m, both with a picture rail and fluorescent and spotlighting. Gallery plans available.
Exhibiting: [AW] Apply to the Curator. The gallery provides insurance, publicity, list of exhibits, and catalogue/card. A 20% commission is charged on sales for artists not participating in South West Arts Exhibition Payment Right, or 30% commission for artists participating in this scheme.
Access: [X] Town centre location close to car park and bus stop; BR Falmouth 20 mins

Farnborough (Hampshire)

(SA) Map7 SU85

South Farnborough Galleries

A commercial art and craft gallery which holds occasional exhibitions alongside a permanent display of over 150 pictures. [Pa,Pr]

Address: 153 Lynchford Road, Farnborough, Hampshire GU14 6HD tel 0252 549390
Contact: Proprietor Mr Bushnell
Open: Mon-Sat 10-5, closed Wed
Policy: *'We try to promote local and national artists whose work is representational and in the traditional mode'.* The exhibitions run from one to six weeks. Framing service available.
Sales: Work sold; Credit card; Credit scheme
The Space: There is a large exhibition space available to artists for hire. Artists exhibiting do not have to be working in representational or traditional styles.
Exhibiting: The space is hired out on negotiable terms. A commission of between 35% and 50% is charged.
Access: [F] BR North Camp 10 mins; Public car park 5 mins; Bus stop opposite gallery

Farnham (Surrey)

(SEA) Map7 SU84

Johnson Wax Kiln Gallery

This gallery is in an arts and community centre and exhibits 'the best of local amateur and professional artists, schools and art colleges'. [VA,Cr,Te,Fu]

Address: The Farnham Haltings, Bridge Square, Farnham, Surrey GU9 7QR tel 025 272 6234
Contact: Gallery Administrator Susan Bourke
Open: Mon-Fri 11.30-5.30, Sat 10-12 except first Sat of month when 10-4.30; closed Sun and bank holidays
Policy: The gallery is increasingly placing emphasis on its educational programme for schools and art colleges and encourages workshops, demonstrations and talks by those exhibiting. Particular interest is shown in the work of young artists and makers at the beginning of their careers, as well as traditional arts and crafts work.
Sales: Work sold; Credit card

Johnson Wax Kiln Gallery

The Space: 13x7x2.5m high, linear hanging space 35m. The gallery has a great sense of space created by the high timber lined kiln roof. Work is hung from rails, on white painted brick walls up to a height of 2.5 m. Natural roof light supplemented by fluorescent strips. Plinths and plate glass shelving available.

Exhibiting: [AW] Contact Gallery Administrator for application form. Gallery finances printing of publicity and catalogue/card and list of exhibits. There is a hire fee for the gallery. Commission 20%.

Access: [X] Buses 5 mins; BR Farnham 5 mins; Large car park available

New Ashgate Gallery

A commercial gallery on the Crafts Council's selected list showing a visual arts and crafts programme by living artists and makers, plus a craft gallery selling work from a changing display. [VA,Cr]

Address: Wagon Yard, Farnham, Surrey GU9 7JR tel 025 271 3208

Contact: Director Elfriede Windsor

Open: Tues-Sat 10-1.30, 2.30-5

Policy: The gallery is for professional artists and makers and amateur work is not accepted.

Sales: Work sold; Credit card; Credit scheme

The Space: 5x3.5m with hanging by rods, spot and natural lighting. Showcases available.

Exhibiting: [AW] Photographs/slides and biographical details (with SAE) to the Director. The gallery finances insurance and preview costs and charges the artist for private view cards. Commission 33.3%.

Access: [F] BR Farnham; Public car park 5 mins

Redgrave Theatre Gallery

Display areas in the theatre foyer and restaurant. [VA,Ph,Cr]

Address: Brightwells, Farnham, Surrey GU9 7SB tel 025 272 7000

Contact: Theatre Manager

Open: Mon 10-6, Tues-Sat 10-10.30, Sun 12-2

Policy: The theatre stages mainly small solo exhibitions aiming to provide space for *'up-and-coming artists, whilst providing an interesting diversion for the theatre-going public'*.

West Surrey College of Art & Design (James Hockey Gallery)

A purpose-built exhibition hall which is supplemented by an adjacent amenity area and display points throughout the college. [VA,Cr,De]

Address: West Surrey College of Art & Design, Falkner Road, Farnham, Surrey GU9 7DS tel 025 272 2441

Contact: Exhibitions Officer Ms D Peake

Open: Mon-Fri 11-5, Sat 10-12.30

Policy: The gallery shows a wide range of exhibitions of work by students, staff, individuals and groups of artists, as well as major retrospective shows. The work of designers, craftspeople and distant cultures is also shown. The cumulative effect of the programme is viewed as a teaching aid to students and as an accessible resource for other educational establishments and the public. Exhibitions normally run for three to four weeks.

The Space: The purpose-built exhibition space is 1500 square metres.

Access: [X]

Fenny Stratford (Buckinghamshire)

(BA) Map7 SP83

Fenny Lodge Gallery

A commercial gallery on the Crafts Council's selected list holding exhibitions in April/May and October/November. [Pa,Pr,Cr]

Address: Simpson Road, Fenny Startford, Bletchley, Milton Keynes, Buckinghamshire MK1 1D tel 0908 642207

Open: Mon-Fri 9-5, Sat 9-4

Policy: The gallery has a changing display of work supplemented by two large exhibitions of invited artists. The gallery specialises in *'British living artists, limited edition prints, ceramics, studio glass, designer jewellery and turned wood'*.

Sales: Work sold; Credit card; Credit scheme

The Space: 13.5 square metres of space with spotlights.

Access: [X] Car parking; Bus 6 from BR Bletchley; BR Fenny Stratford 25 mins

Fleetwood (Lancashire)

(NWA) Map3 SD34

Fleetwood Central Library

A branch of Lancashire Libraries, the exhibition space opened in May 1988. [VA]

Address: Fleetwood Central Library, North Abbot Street, Fleetwood, Lancashire FY7 6AJ tel 03917 78773

Contact: Librarian M Ramsbottom

Open: Closed Wednesday afternoons

Policy: *'It is hoped to show mostly the work of local contemporary artists. The programme will be for the benefit of local people and holiday visitors. Activities to accompany the exhibitions are planned to take place in the the future'.*

Sales: Work sold

The Space: Space 1 measures 10.97x8 m, Space 2 measures 8.22x1.52m. In addition there is a small area outside.

Exhibiting: Applications should be made in person with examples of work.

Access: [U][T][L] On bus and tram routes

Folkestone (Kent)

(SEA) Map7 TR23

Folkestone Museum & Art Gallery

Run by the libraries' department, the gallery shows a varied programme of exhibitions by artists and makers. [VA,Ph,Cr]

Address: Grace Hill, Folkestone, Kent CT20 1HD tel 030 385 0123

Contact: Group Librarian Mary Ward
Open: Mon-Fri 9-5.30, Wed 9-1, Sat 9-5
Policy: The gallery is an integral part of the Folkestone Library and the monthly changing programme of exhibitions aims to provide a cultural centre for the general public. Solo exhibitions are only be granted if the work shows *'a high standard of competence'*. Occasionally talks or residencies are organised. (See also Lady Sassoon Room, Folkestone Library).
Sales: Work sold
The Space: 13x9m with 53m linear hanging space and 411m square floor space with track-mounted spots. Work is mirror-plated to wall-mounted display panels and the area regularly patrolled by attendants.
Exhibiting: [AW] Apply one year in advance to Group Librarian. Gallery finances insurance, printing and mail-out of publicity and list of exhibits. Commission 15%.
Access: [X] BR Canterbury 12 mins; Public car park 2 mins

Lady Sassoon Room

Housed in Folkestone Museum and Art Gallery, the gallery shows national and regional touring shows as well as work by contemporary artists from the South East. [VA,Ph,Cr]
Address: Folkestone Library, Museum & Art Gallery, Grace Hill, Folkestone, Kent CT20 1HD tel 030 385 0123
Contact: Group Librarian Mary Ward
Open: Mon-Fri 9-5.30, Wed 9-1, Sat 9-5
Policy: The gallery shows a monthly changing programme of high-quality contemporary exhibitions which *'educate, inform and entertain'*. The intention is to promote the work of living artists through a programme designed to meet the needs and interests of residents and visitors to the area. Where possible, residencies, lectures and slide shows are organised. (See also Folkestone Museum & Art Gallery).
Sales: Work sold
The Space: 15x14x7m high with 53m linear hanging space, direct fixing to hanging surface with track-mounted spot lights and 3m maximum hanging height.
Exhibiting: [AW] Apply approximately 18 months in advance of desired showing dates, enclosing slides/photos and biography. The gallery finances insurance, list of exhibits, transport and catalogue/card. Commission 15%.
Access: [X] BR Folkestone 12 mins; Public car park 2 mins

Metropole Arts Centre

This gallery exhibits a wide selection of contemporary art, introducing new and established visual artists. [VA,Ph,Cr]
Address: The Leas, Folkestone, Kent CT20 2LS tel 0300 355 070
Contact: Artistic Director John Rice
Open: Mon-Sat 10-5, Sun 2.30-5
Policy: Gallery policy is to provide Kent with an opportunity to view high-quality art which would not be shown in museums or commercial galleries. The aim of the arts centre is to mount a wide range of arts activities and to be a stimulus for practising artists, and to offer the chance to show work in a suitable environment. Artists are encouraged to give talks about their work when exhibiting. A mixture of group and solo exhibitions normally run for five to six weeks.
Sales: Work sold
Exhibiting: [AW][EP] Gallery finances insurance, printing and mail-out of publicity and catalogue/card, list of exhibits, transport and preview costs. Support in principle for EPR. Commission 33.3%.
Access: [X] BR Folkestone 5 mins; Public car park 1 min

Foulridge (Lancashire)

(NWA) Map3 SD84

Foulridge Library

A branch of Lancashire Libraries. [Pa,Ph]
Address: Highfield Avenue, Foulridge, Colne, Lancashire BB8 7PB tel 0282 866908
Contact: District Librarian Mrs D Tillotson
Open: Mon-Fri 2-4.30, 5-7
Policy: Exhibitions generally last a month, the library aims to give artists and makers the opportunity to display work to a wider audience.
The Space: Three boards measuring 0.76m square are mounted on the walls of the lending library.
Exhibiting: No heavy items displayed and no nails to be used. Pictures must be hung within prescribed limits of the boards. 15% commission.
Access: [U][T] Car park at front

Freshwater (Isle of Wight)

(SA) Map7 SZ38

Freshwater Gallery

A gallery in a public library. [VA,Ph]
Address: Freshwater Library, School Green Road, Freshwater, Isle of Wight PO30 5TX tel 0983 752377
Contact: Deputy Director of Library Services M R Howley, Cultural Services HQ, Parkhurst Road, Newport, Isle of Wight tel 0983 822000
Open: Mon-Fri 9.30-6, Sat 9.30-4.30
Policy: The Cultural Services policy is to show work of quality from both professional and amateur artists, as well as to encourage and promote beginners of an acceptable exhibiting standard. Exhibitions run for one month.
Sales: Sales referred to exhibitor
The Space: The walls can take about 30 paintings of average size.
Exhibiting: [AW]Apply to the Director of Cultural Services. The library pays, on a discretionary basis, for printing and mailing of publicity, list of exhibits and transport.
Access: [X] Buses 7,7a,7c; Public car park 100 yds

Frodsham (Cheshire)

(NWA) Map4 SJ57

Castle Park Arts Centre

An arts centre gallery showing a range of temporary

exhibitions including amateur and professional work. [Pa,Pr,Dr,Ph,Cr]

Address: Off Fountain Lane, Frodsham, via Warrington, Cheshire WA6 6SE tel 0928 35832

Contact: Exhibitions Organiser Tricia Kerr, 11 Clifton Road, Runcorn, Cheshire WA7 4SX tel 09285 76676

Open: Tues,Sat 10-12.30 2-4.30 Sun 2-5

Policy: Of the annual programme of exhibitions, around a third are solo, a third two-person and the remainder group shows, including national competitions and work from local schools. Touring shows from the Arts Council are also shown. Exhibitions are often accompanied by workshops run by artists involving schools and the local community.

Sales: Work sold

The Space: The gallery has around 59m linear hanging space, with three galleries on two floors, of 9x5.5m, 10x6.8m and 10x6.8m. They cannot accommodate large sculpture. Two perspex-topped lockable display cases 1x1x.75m are available. Security. Gallery plans available. Outdoor spaces are available for sculpture.

Exhibiting: [AW] Applications to the Exhibitions Organiser. Programme is fixed at their annual meeting in October. Gallery pays for insurance, publicity and preview and takes 20% commission on sales.

Access: [U][T][L][F] Buses to Runcorn, Warrington, Northwich, Chester; BR Frodsham 10mins walk; Car parks 5 mins

Frome (Somerset)

(SWA) Map6 ST74

Black Swan Guild

An arts centre with a large first floor gallery showing work by local and nationally-known artists. [VA,Ph,Cr]

Address: 2 Bridge Street, Frome, Somerset BA11 1BB tel 0373 73980

Contact: Liz Rohan

Open: Tues-Sat 10-5 gallery, Mon-Sat 9.30-5.30 rest of centre

Policy: The centre provides a venue for artists and makers to show their work and to promote the arts in the area. Occasional lunch-time talks and evening or weekend events are arranged.

Sales: Work sold; Credit card

The Space: The gallery space is 13.2x4.5x2.65m.

Exhibiting: [AW] Insurance, publicity, list of exhibits, and a catalogue/card are provided. The centre charges a 30% commission on sales.

Access: [X] Bath/Bristol buses; BR Frome 15 mins

Merlin Theatre

A community arts centre supported by Somerset County Council with performances of music, dance, theatre and a programme of exhibitions in the foyer. [Pa,Pr,Dr,Ph]

Address: Bath Road, Frome, Somerset BA11 2HQ tel 0373 61360

Contact: Administrator Hilary Strong

Open: Mon-Fri 6-7, Sat 10-12 noon and during performances

Policy: The centre aims *'to show a varied selection of work'*, predominantly professional artists from the South West region with at least one nationally-renowned artist a year. As a community arts centre *'we aim to encourage local amateurs through mixed exhibitions two or three times a year. The programme is selected to complement the theatre activities.'*

Sales: Work sold; Credit card

The Space: A 6m wall 2m high plus two 2.5m boards. Spotlights.

Exhibiting: [AW][EF] Apply to the Administrator. The theatre provides insurance, publicity, list of exhibits and artists' expenses. A 20% commission is charged on sales.

Gainsborough (Lincolnshire)

(LHA) Map5 SK88

Richmond Park House

Municipal gallery in a Victorian house set in a park with playing field and children's play area, run jointly by Lincolnshire County Council and West Lindsey District Council. [Pa,Sc,Pr,Dr,Cr]

Address: Morton Terrace, Gainsborough, Lincolnshire DN21 tel 0427 2669

Contact: Assistant Keeper Jenny Vernon, Gainsborough Old Hall, Parnell Street, Gainsborough, Lincolnshire

Open: Daily 10-dusk

Policy: The policy for this gallery is currently under review as the house is undergoing major refurbishment.

Sales: Sales referred to exhibitor

The Space: Four small rooms approximately 5m square of space overall with strip lighting.

Exhibiting: [AW] To the Assistant Keeper. Gallery pays for printing and mailing of publicity, preview costs, transport, mailing of publicity and catalogue.

Access: [X] 1 mile from city centre; 1 mile from BR Gainsborough; 2 miles from BR Lea Road

Trinity Arts Centre

Arts and community centre incorporating 200 seat theatre & cinema, bar, workshop space, meeting rooms and gallery. [Pa,Pr,Ph]

Address: Trinity Street, Gainsborough, Lincolnshire DN21 2AL tel 0427 617242

Contact: Director Tim Harris

Open: Mon-Fri 10-5, Sat 10-12

Policy: The art centre presents a varied programme of twelve exhibitions a year in the visual media including local amateur and professional as well as touring professional artists aimed mainly at theatre users and casual visitors. Artists' talks are organised for school groups.

Sales: Work sold

The Space: The gallery is a rectangular room approximately 13x5m lit by a series of spotlights. Work is fixed to wall-mounted boards, crafts cannot at present be displayed.

Exhibiting: [AW] Application a year in advance to the Director. Venue pays for insurance, printing and mailing of publicity. The gallery supports EPR in principle.

Access: [U][T][F]

Garstang (Lancashire)

(NWA) Map3 SD52

Old Grammar School Arts Centre

A centre run by Garstang Arts Society, a group of art, craft, photographic and performing societies who collectively lease the centre from the Garstang Town Trust. [Pa,Dr,Ph,Cr,]

Address: Croston Road, Garstang, Lancashire PR3 tel 09952 6648

Contact: Exhibitions Organisers: Dorothy Bicknell, 15 Yewlands Drive, Garstang, Preston tel 09952 2628 or Marion Probyn, 95 Dorchester Road, Garstang, Preston tel 09952 3547

Open: Tues 10-12.30, 2-4, Thurs 10-4, Sat 10-12.30

Policy: The centre runs a programme of twelve changing exhibitions each year some of which are mixed and some solo shows. In addition to the main gallery, there is a smaller space where members' work is hung and changed each month. Local authority classes held.

Sales: Work sold

The Space: The main gallery is 9x4.50m with a maximum height for display of 1.8m and fluorescent lighting.

Exhibiting: Applications to exhibit should be made to the Exhibition Organisers. The centre pays towards insurance, printing of publicity and list of exhibits.

Access: [U][T][F]

Garton-on-the-Wolds (Humberside)

(LHA) Map3 SE95

Copernican Connection

A gallery on the Crafts Council's selected list which is situated beside the historic Norman Church of St. Michael's. [Cr]

Address: Church Farm, Garton-on-the-Wolds, Humberside YO25 0ET tel 0377 43988

Contact: Directors Brian & Mavis Walsh

Open: Tues-Sun 10-5 Summer, Wed-Sun 10-4 Winter; Other times by appointment

Policy: The gallery shows solo exhibitions by established makers.

Sales: Work sold

The Space: The upper gallery and long gallery now open.

Access: Off the A166 York-Driffield road

Gateshead (Tyne & Wear)

(NA) Map3 NZ26

Gateshead Central Library

Small gallery space within the central library and operated as part of the Libraries and Arts programme of arts activities. [Pa,Pr,Dr,Ph,Cr]

Address: Prince Consort Road, Gateshead, Tyne & Wear NE8 4LN tel 091 477 3478

Contact: General Arts Officer (Visual Arts)

Open: Mon,Tues,Thurs,Fri 9.30am-7.30pm, Wed 9.30-5, Sat 9.30-1

Policy: The gallery shows a changing programme of art, craft and photography, drawing work from artists in the region and from touring exhibitions. The library also operates a picture loan scheme.

Sales: Work sold

The Space: The gallery has 25.5m linear hanging space and is 2.4m high. There is track lighting with spots and floods, direct fixing, and a glazed showcase with fluorescent lighting. Other showcases and plinths available.

Exhibiting: [AW] Apply at any time of the year; booking is a year in advance. The library covers insurance, publicity and previews and in most cases transport. Commission is 20%.

Access: [U][T] Regular bus services to Gateshead/Newcastle, BR Newcastle and Metro

Shipley Art Gallery

A municipal gallery administered by Tyne & Wear Museums Service, housing a collection of Victorian and old master paintings, applied arts and contemporary crafts, and organising temporary exhibitions. [VA,Cr]

Address: Prince Consort Road, Gateshead, Tyne & Wear NE8 4JB tel 091 477 1495

Contact: Curator Andrew Greg

Open: Tues-Fri 10-5.30, Sat 10-4.30, Sun 2-5; bank holidays 10-5.30

Policy: The exhibition programme includes touring exhibitions, didactic exhibitions from the museum collection and work by local art societies, all backed by an active educational programme. The policy of

Gateshead Central Library: 'Vessels' by Sally Sedgwick, paper collage, 1988 (Photo: Richard Padwick)

concentrating on crafts is intended to *'promote a wide range of current media and techniques by exhibition, sales, demonstrations and workshops, and by creating a permanent collection'*.

Sales: Work sold

The Space: Two galleries, each 13.5x8.3m giving 37.7m linear hanging space which have direct fixing and track lighting with dimmers. Six showcases are available.

Exhibiting: [AW][EF] Makers may submit slides for possible mixed shows or selling displays - solo exhibitions are unlikely. The gallery provides insurance, publicity, list of exhibits, preview, display and transport. Supports the principle of EPR.

Access: [S] On many bus routes; BR 30mins; Car park 1 min

Gilberdyke (Humberside)

(LHA) Map3 SE82

South Farm Craft Gallery

A gallery, started in 1988, with a permanent display of ceramics by Jerry Harper and changing displays of contemporary work by other artists and makers. [Pa,Pr,Cr]

Address: Blacktoft, Gilberdyke, Goole, Humberside DN14 7XT tel 0430 441082

Contact: Jerry and Doreen Harper

Open: Wed-Sat 10-5, Sun 11-5, Wed-Sat 10-4, Sun 11-4 Jan-March, Closed Monday except bank holidays; Closed Jan-March

Policy: To promote and sell British art and craft with a local bias. As the gallery is situated in the heart of the country there is also a countryside and nature theme. Always looking for new and interesting ideas. Target audience among middle to high-income groups. Runs craft workshops for artists.

Sales: Work sold; Credit card

The Space: A ground floor gallery of 20 square metres, a first floor gallery of 40 square metres and a paved courtyard outside 20x9m.

Exhibiting: [AW] Artists and makers should send slides, CV and SAE to Doreen Harper. The hire charge and contribution to the costs of the exhibition are negotiable. The gallery takes 33.3% commission.

Access: [U][T] 2 miles from nearest bus or train at Gilberdyke; Car parking on site

Gillingham (Kent)

(SEA) Map7 TQ76

Gillingham Library Gallery

Run by Kent County Libraries, this gallery has a varied programme which features artists that have a particular relevance to the area. [VA,Ph,Cr]

Address: High Street, Gillingham, Kent ME7 1BG tel 063 428 1066

Contact: Group Librarian Stephen Robinson

Open: Mon, Tues, Thurs, Fri 9.30-7, Wed, Sat 9.30-1, 2-5

Policy: The gallery aims to promote the work of locally-based artists and to show exhibitions that may not otherwise be seen in the area. There are also touring shows and occasional museum archive exhibitions. Lectures and slide shows are organised when appropriate. Shows normally run for three to four weeks.

The Space: 9x6x6m with 25m linear hanging space, maximum hanging height 3m. Work is directly fixed to walls and lighting is by track-mounted spots.

Exhibiting: [AW] Apply to Group Librarian approximately 15 months in advance of desired showing dates enclosing slides or photographs and biography. Gallery finances insurance, list of exhibits and mail-out of publicity. Support in principle for EPR. Commission 15%.

Access: BR Gillingham 12 mins; Public car park 3 mins

Space Frame

Funded by Kent County Council, the gallery houses a regular programme of exhibitions by nationally-known, newly-emerging and local amateur artists and makers. [VA,Ph,Cr,LA]

Address: Gillingham Adult Education Centre, Green Street, Gillingham, Kent ME7 1XA tel 0634 56439

Contact: Tutor Organiser for Art Nicholette Goff

Open: Mon-Fri 9-4, 6-9

Policy: The aim of the gallery is to make available a space for work moving in new directions and to *'support innovative ideas in the arts'*. Artists are encouraged to give talks, demonstrations and workshops when possible. There is also a programme of regular lunch-time talks on arts and crafts.

Sales: Work sold

The Space: Gallery One 11x6x4.5m high with 18.5m linear hanging space and natural and fluorescent lighting. Gallery Two 10x2.5x4m high with 17m linear

Space Frame: 'Thatched Nun' by Nicholette Goff from 'Art Tutors Exhibition', conté drawing, 1988

hanging space and lighting by spots. Gallery three 6.5x2x3m high with 14m linear hanging space and lighting by flourescent tubes. The first gallery is a coffee bar for the centre with approximately 1500 students passing through weekly. Large sculptures cannot be accommodated. Gallery plans available.

Exhibiting: [AW] Applications with slides or photographs to Nicholette Goff. Gallery finances insurance list of exhibits and mail-out of publicity. Support in principle for EPR. Commission 20%.

Access: [X] BR Gillingham 2 mins; Public car park 2 mins

Glastonbury (Somerset)

(SWA) Map6 ST43

Somerset Rural Life Museum

The museum is run by the Somerset County Museums Service and offers a variety of permanent displays, temporary exhibitions, demonstrations, farming activities, music, dancing and special events. [VA,Ph,Cr]

Address: Abbey Farm, Chilkwell Street, Glastonbury, Somerset BA6 8DB tel 0458 32903

Contact: Keeper of Rural Life Mary Gryspeerdt

Open: Mon-Fri 10-5, Sat, Sun 2-6 Easter-Oct; 2.30-5 Nov-Easter

Policy: The temporary exhibition programme mainly contains work by West Country artists and makers in solo group shows. An active education programme encourages demonstrations and workshops by makers and artists. The museum aims *'to provide exhibitions of local interest, and to support local artists and makers.*

Sales: Work sold

The Space: The gallery uses hessian-covered wall panels giving 20m linear hanging space in a room 11x3.9m. A courtyard and display cases are available. Gallery plans available.

Exhibiting: [AW] Apply by letter initially. Insurance, publicity, preview, list of exhibits, catalogue/card, contribution to mailing are covered by the museum. A 20% commission is charged on sales.

Access: [U][T][F] Buses 163,376,378,677 10 mins to town hall

Gloucester (Gloucestershire)

(SWA) Map4 SO81

Gloucester City Museum & Art Gallery

A municipal art gallery and museum operated by Gloucester City Council with a permanent collection, displays of fine and applied arts and a programme of special exhibitions. [VA,Ph,Cr]

Address: Brunswick Road, Gloucester GL1 1HP tel 0452 24131

Contact: Director John Rhodes

Open: Mon-Sat 10-5

Policy: The gallery is one of five sites run by the council, and provides a *'varied programme of quality exhibitions on different themes in different media from different sources'*. The foyer gallery can be used for small solo shows at short notice.

Sales: Work sold

The Space: The Main Gallery is 9x12x3m with 42m linear hanging space, direct fixing on hessian-covered walls and fluorescent wall washers and spot lights used. The Foyer gallery is 4x4x3m with 10m linear hanging space available.

Exhibiting: [AW][EF] Applications from professional artists only (in groups if applying for the Main Gallery) The programme is booked 18-24 months in advance. Gallery provides insurance, publicity, transport and a list of exhibits. A 10% commission is charged on sales.

Access: [L][F] Bus station and BR Gloucester 10 mins

Godalming (Surrey)

(SEA) Map7 SU95

Godalming Museum

This newly opened gallery is run by the Godalming Museum Trust and aims to encourage the work of local or national organisations and individuals. [VA,Ph,Cr]

Address: 109a High Street, Godalming, Surrey GU7 1AQ tel 0483 42 6510

Contact: Chairman Museum Trust Cllr MM Gordon, Woodborough, Grosvenor Road, Godalming, Surrey GU7 1NZ tel 0483 42 7071

Open: Tues-Sat 10-5

Policy: The gallery hopes to become a focal point for the arts in Godalming. There is a small shop on the premises and the gallery is also used as a meeting room for various activities. Exhibitions are a mixture of group and solo shows and normally run for two to three weeks.

Sales: Work sold

The Space: 5x5x2m high with lighting by spots and humidity controls. Hanging is from picture rails, display stands and cases are available. There is also a garden space at the rear of the building.

Exhibiting: [AW] Contact the museum for application forms. The gallery is for hire at a fee of £10 per week for a minimum of two weeks. Commission 15%.

Access: [F][S] BR Godalming 2 mins; Public car park 2 mins

Thursley Textile Designs

An exhibition space running a programme of shows by relatively unknown as well as leading designers and makers. [Te]

Address: 1 Moushill Lane, Milford, Godalming, Surrey GU8 5BH tel 048 682 4769

Contact: Zoe O'Brien

Open: Mon-Sat 10-5.30

Policy: The premises also house a studio and shop making available a range of original textiles to a wide audience. Specialist exhibitions explore a variety of themes and techniques and there is also a permanent collection of handmade textiles from across the world Craft courses are run throughout the year and talks given to arranged visits from schools and colleges. All shows are by living designers and makers and normally run for one month.

Sales: Work sold; Credit card
The Space: Approximately 10m wall space with screens available.
Exhibiting: [AW] Apply to Zoe O'Brien. Gallery finances insurance, printing and mail-out of publicity and catalogue/card and list of exhibits. Commission 50%.
Access: [F] BR Milford 10 mins

Waverley Link Plus

Situated in the Waverley Borough Council offices, this gallery exhibits a cross-section of the arts, predominantly showing the work of living artists in solo shows. [VA,Ph,Cr]

Address: Waverley Borough Council, The Burys, Godalming, Surrey GU7 1HR tel 048 684 104 ext 394
Contact: Mary Morrison
Open: Mon-Sat 9-5.30; by appointment evenings
Policy: The gallery aims to show a wide variety of visual arts that will appeal to the many visitors and users of the building. The gallery can guarantee good coverage for exhibitors in the local paper and radio. Exhibitions are normally shown for two weeks.
Sales: Work sold; Sales referred to exhibitor
The Space: The gallery has 27m linear hanging space, there are also a number of reception and corridor areas available for use. A grassed area suitable for sculpture and near to the car park and river can also be used.
Exhibiting: [AW] Apply to Mary Morrison. The exhibition space is for hire. Gallery shares the costs of insurance, printing and mail-out of publicity and catalogue/card and list of exhibits. Commission 15%.
Access: [U][T][L] Buses to office complex; BR Godalming 4 mins; Public car park 2 mins

Goole (Humberside)

(LHA) Map3 SE72

Goole Library

Public library with first floor exhibition room, administered by Humberside Libraries & Arts. [VA]

Address: Market Square, Goole, Humberside DN14 5AA tel 0405 2187
Contact: Team Leader Margaret Carr

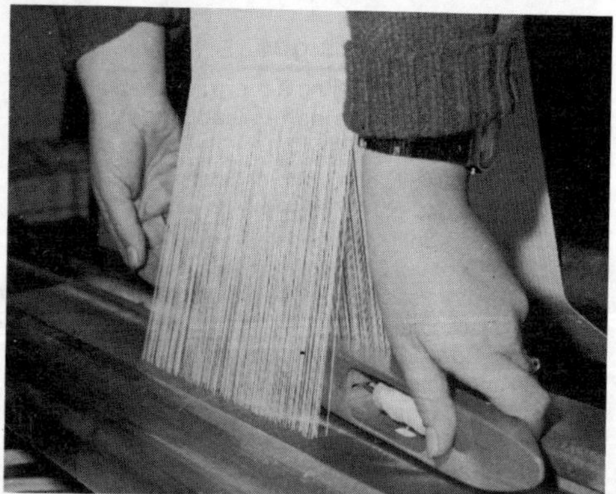

Thursley Textile Designs

The Space: Approximately 91 square metres with 33m linear space, direct fixing to walls, lit by spots, fluorescent tubes and natural daylight.
Exhibiting: [AW] Artists meet all expenses and the library takes 10% commission on sales.
Access: Access to first floor exhibition room difficult

Gosport (Hampshire)

(SA) Map7 SZ69

Gosport Museum

A local history museum supported by the borough council and showing a varied programme including local history and maritime projects and contemporary work. [Pa,Dr,Ph,Cr]

Address: Walpole Road, Gosport, Hampshire PO12 1LQ tel 0705 588035
Contact: Curator Denise Cutts
Open: Tues-Sat 9.30-4.30, Sun (May-Sept) 1-5
Policy: The exhibitions which run between four and six weeks, aim *'to provide a varied programme to suit all tastes and interests from scientific to crafts. For the art exhibitions, the policy is to support local artists and makers and sometimes to have joint exhibitions of contrasting work'*. The gallery can also be used for demonstrations and lectures though these are limited by lack of space.
Sales: Work sold
The Space: The gallery is 15.2x9.1m and has 30m linear hanging space and four custom-made showcases with environmental controls and spotlighting, and direct fixing to walls.
Exhibiting: [AW] Apply at any time to the Curator who keeps a record of all potential exhibitors. The gallery pays for printing and mailing of publicity, insurance, private view, catalogue or card and list of exhibits and charges 15% commission on sales.
Access: [F] Bus 2 mins; Free car park; Portsmouth ferry 10 mins

Grantham (Lincolnshire)

(LHA) Map5 SK93

Grantham Public Library

A new public library opened by Lincolnshire County Council Recreational Services in 1984 as part of a central shopping centre complex. [Pa,Pr,Dr,Ph,Cr]

Address: Isaac Newton Centre, St Peter's Hall, Grantham, Lincolnshire NG31 6PY tel 0476 591411
Contact: Assistant Area Librarian K J Hay
Open: Mon,Tues 9-6, Wed-Fri 9-7, Sat 9-1
Policy: The library mounts mainly small exhibitions of photography and paintings usually from artists local to the area. Each exhibition should be compatible with the cultural aims of the library.
Sales: Sales referred to exhibitor
The Space: 11x1.2m with wall-mounted hessian boards plus space for three-dimensional work lit by spotlights. There are two internally-lit wall-mounted glass cabinets 1.3x1.1x0.65m and a lockable glass cabinet 4.5x1.3x0.2m which can be fitted with glass shelves.

Exhibiting: [AW] Contact the Assistant Area Librarian. The library charges a hire fee of £10 a week to artists wishing to sell work.
Access: [L]

Museum & Art Gallery

A museum and gallery with a permanent collection including archaeology, natural history, and material relating to Sir Isaac Newton.
Address: St Peter's Hill, Grantham, Lincolnshire NG31 6PY tel 0476 68783
Contact: Curator Mr J F Smith, Stamford Museum, Broad Street, Stamford, Lincolnshire PE9 1PJ tel 0780 66317
Open: Mon-Sat 10-5, Sun 2-5 1 April - 30 Sept; Mon-Sat 10-12.30, 1.30-5 1 Oct - 31 March
The Space: 20m linear hanging space, 43m movable space.
Access: [U][T]

Grays (Essex)

(EA) Map7 TQ67

Grays Library

Exhibition space in library, available for hire. [VA,Cr]
Address: Orsett Road, Grays, Essex RM17 5DX tel 0375 383611
Contact: Deputy Area Librarian (Thurrock) Deborah Raddon
Open: Mon, Tues, Thurs, Fri 9-7.30, Wed, Sat 9-5
Sales: Work sold; Sales referred to exhibitor
The Space: A floor area of 6.70 square metres is available plus one display case.
Access: [L][F]

Thameside Theatre Foyer

Founded in 1971, the exhibition space has been formed out of a large ground floor foyer in a complex of theatre, library and local history museum administered by Thurrock Borough Council. [Pa,Pr,Dr,Ph]
Address: Orsett Road, Grays, Essex RM17 5DX tel 0375 382555
Contact: Assistant Leisure Manager Mark Allinson
Open: Mon-Sat 9-8
Policy: Policy allows the space to be booked for one-week periods for which non-commercial organisations are given free access, with a hire fee of £12.10 made to those *'making financial gain'*.
The Space: Area of 10x4m accommodating 10 Marler Haley *'big'* screens. Access is limited to opening 1.75x1.83m.
Exhibiting: Space available for bookings one year in advance.
Access: [U][T][L] Public car park behind

Great Eccleston (Lancashire)

(NWA) Map3 SD44

Handmade Art and Craft Gallery

A commercial gallery established in 1986 and situated in an old farm cottage dating back to 1745 set in a small village square. [VA,Cr]
Address: The Square, Great Eccleston, Nr Preston, Lancashire PR3 0ZB tel 0995 71207
Contact: Mr and Mrs A Cornforth
Open: Tues, Wed, Fri, Sat 9.30-5 October-Easter; Tues-Fri 9.30-5,Sat 10-5, Sun 11-6 Easter-October; Open bank holidays
Policy: The gallery mounts seven exhibitions a year each running for between one and two months. It has a variety of work on display by 60 selected makers and artists, amateur and professional demonstrations take place on selected Sundays and a framing service is available.
Sales: Work sold; Credit card
The Space: There are two spaces giving a total of 120m linear hanging space. Work is hung by hooks and the space is lit with spotlights. Paintings up to 1.82x1.21m can be accommodated but smaller work is preferred.
Exhibiting: [AW] Applications to exhibit should be sent to Mr and Mrs A Cornforth. The gallery pays for insurance, list of exhibits, mailing and catalogue. Publicity, preview and catalogue by arrangement. 30% commission is taken on sales.
Access: [F] Bus route from Preston, Blackpool and Lancaster; Car park nearby

Great Malvern (Hereford & Worcester)

(WMA) Map4 SO74

Malvern Art Gallery

A gallery space within the library run by Hereford and Worcester County Council which has a small collection of local scenes. [VA,Ph,Cr]
Address: Malvern Library, Graham Road, Great Malvern, Hereford & Worcester WR14 2HW tel 06845 61223
Contact: Librarian Keith Barber
Open: Mon,Thurs,Fri 9.30-5.30; Tues 9.30-8; Sat 9.30-4; closed bank holidays
Policy: Most exhibitions are from local and regional artists and makers, though occasional exhibitions are hired from the Area Museum Service and elsewhere. The gallery aims to show as wide a range of work as possible within the *'cash and physical limitations of the gallery'*.
Sales: Work sold
The Space: The two galleries provide 50m linear hanging space from a rail or direct fixing on mid-blue hessian boards. The windows have UV filters and the track lighting is adjustable. Daylight can be excluded from the lower gallery. A large showcase is available in the main library. Gallery plans available.
Exhibiting: [AW] Apply a year in advance to the librarian with slides or photographs. The gallery occasionally contributes to transport, insurance, publicity, and preview costs. Generally artists are expected to mount their own exhibitions.

Access: [U][T][X] Car park and bus stop nearby, BR Great Malvern 25 mins

Malvern Festival Theatre

A theatre based in the Winter Gardens Complex run by Malvern Hills District Council. [VA,Ph,Cr]

Address: Winter Gardens Complex, Grange Road, Great Malvern, Hereford & Worcester WR14 3HB tel 0684 892277

Contact: Vivian Cooke, The Studio, 1 Halas House, Holywell Road, Malvern Wells WR14 4LE tel 0684 574074

Open: Mon-Sat 10-5 and during performances

Policy: Three galleries spaces are used in the theatre to show a wide range of professional work from invited artists and makers. An annual festival exhibition is mounted, and provision made for showing work by local schools during the Christmas period.

Sales: Work sold; Credit card

The Space: The three spaces are the Foyer Gallery, the Stalls Gallery and the Circle Gallery. Each space can take ten to twelve works hung from a picture rail or screwed to the wall. Lighting is by spotlights in all galleries. A large showcase is available for craft exhibitions.

Exhibiting: [AW] Contact Vivian Cooke via the theatre box office. The theatre charges 15% commission on sales which goes to theatre funds. Insurance, publicity and mailing are provided.

Access: [X] Public car park adjacent; Malvern/Worcester bus route, BR Great Malvern 15 mins

Malvern Workshop

A non-profit making gallery which is part of a shop, café and studios. [VA,Cr]

Address: 90 Link Top, Great Malvern, Hereford & Worcester WR14 tel 06845 68993

Contact: Sandra Masterson, Birchwood Hall, Storridge, Nr Malvern WR13 53Z tel 088 64 203

Open: Wed-Sat 10-5, Sun 10.30-5

Policy: The gallery usually shows monthly solo exhibitions and the artists and makers selected are mainly based in the West Midlands. The exhibitions are selected to show new and stimulating work by younger artists and makers. The workshop provides a relaxed and friendly atmosphere for an area where there are few opportunities to see good-quality contemporary art and craft.

Sales: Work sold

The Space: The upstairs gallery, cafe and shop provides 25m linear hanging space, with spots and daylight. Downstairs 15m linear hanging space is provided with fluorescent and daylight. Direct fixing and picture rail used. An overall ceiling height of 2m restricts the showing of some work. All walls are painted white.

Exhibiting: [AW] Slides and CV required initially. The gallery contributes to publicity, printing, mailing, list of exhibits and preview costs. Commission of 25%. Gallery plans available. Supports EPR.

Access: [F] Upstairs, **[X]** downstairs. Bus stop 1 min Malvern and Worcester buses. BR Link Top 10 mins

Winter Gardens Complex

A leisure centre run by Malvern Hills District Council Tourism and Leisure Services Department which has a cinema, theatre, restaurant, swimming pool, information centre and pleasure garden with boating lake. [Pa,Ph]

Address: Winter Gardens, Grange Road, Great Malvern, Hereford & Worcester WR14 3HB tel 0684 892700

Contact: Wendy Townsend, Meadow Cottage, 14 Geraldine Road, Barnards Green, Malvern, Hereford & Worcester tel 0684 573638

Open: 10-5 all week, closed Suns in winter

Policy: The exhibitions are held in three separate galleries and normally run for six weeks. Local artists, mixed exhibitions and special exhibitions for the Malvern Festival in May and June are shown. The audience is mainly the local population and tourists.

Sales: Work sold

The Space: The exhibition areas are in the restaurant with 10m linear hanging space, the Pump Room with 7.5m linear hanging space and the stairs with 5m linear hanging space.

Exhibiting: The centre provides insurance, other costs are the responsibility of the artist.

Access: [U][T][L][X] Public car park adjacent, BR Great Malvern 15 mins; Malvern/Worcester bus route

Great Yarmouth (Norfolk)

(EA) Map5 TG50

Great Yarmouth Museums Galleries

Municipal gallery, part of Norfolk Museums Service. Permanent collection 19th & 20th century art. [VA,Ph,Cr]

Address: Central Library, Tolhouse Street, Great Yarmouth NR30 2SH tel 0493 858900

Contact: Museums Assistant Damian Eaton

Open: Mon-Sat 9.30-5.30, closed Sat 1-2; closed bank holidays and during re-hanging

Policy: *'To present a mix of exhibitions including local groups, individual artists, travelling shows, local schools and colleges'*. Annual winter open exhibition. Mainly mixed exhibitions of 3-4 weeks but also some two-week solo shows.

Sales: Sales referred to exhibitor

Malvern Workshops: Café

The Space: 1&2) 11x6.4x3.2m, 31 linear metres. 3) 8.3x6.3x3.2m high, 23m linear. 4) Mezzanine 10x7x3.8m high, 1.45m linear. Hanging by nails or screws into blockboard. Strip lighting with spot track, UV excluded. Six show cases. Size of work limited by door and lift dimensions & 1200lb weight limit.
Exhibiting: [AW] To Museums Assistant, 6-12 months in advance. Galleries for hire at fixed rates (£10-£30 week plus VAT). No commission.
Access: [L][F] Bus 5-10mins; BR 15mins; Own small car park

Hardies Gallery

Commercial gallery and framing shop. Generally changing display of work with two to three week long exhibitions each year mainly of paintings and prints. [VA]
Address: 205/6 High Street, Gorleston-on-Sea, Great Yarmouth, Norfolk NR31 6RR tel 0493 668003
Contact: Michael Wide
Open: Mon-Sat 10-6
Policy: Aims to *'stimulate interest in the visual arts through contemporary work'.*
Sales: Work sold; Credit card
The Space: Two rooms each 4.2x4x3.5m high, total 25m wall space.
Exhibiting: [AW] Write or phone. Gallery pays insurance on premises, printing, mailing of publicity and half preview costs. Commission 30%.
Access: [F] Bus Yarmouth-Lowestoft. BR Yarmouth 2 miles. Car park 1 minute

Grimsby (Humberside)

(LHA) Map3 TA21

Central Library

Public library funded by Humberside Leisure Services. [Pa,Sc,Pr,Dr,Cr]
Address: Town Hall Square, Grimsby, Humberside DN31 1HG tel 0472 240410
Contact: Entertainments Manager Alan Gregory
Open: Mon-Fri 10-8; Sat 9-4
Policy: There is at present no planned programme, but the library accepts *'any good local work'.*
Sales: Sales referred to exhibitors
The Space: 34.5x2m usable wall area with a floor area 15x9m. Work is secured to hanging rails. Gallery plan available.
Exhibiting: [AW] Contact the Entertainments Manager.
Access: [U][T][L] BR Grimsby 5 mins; Public car parks 1min

Grimsby College of Technology (Gallery One Hundred)

A gallery within a college showing occasional external work.
Address: Eleanor Road, Grimsby, S Humberside DN32 9DU tel 0472 361613
Contact: Director A Ludlum
Exhibiting: [AW] Donation welcomed from work sold. If the space is available it can be used.

Welholme Galleries

Municipal gallery converted from a redundant church, funded by Great Grimsby Borough Council. [Pa,Pr,Dr,Ph,Cr]
Address: Welholme Road, Grimsby, Humberside DN32 9LP tel 0472 242000
Contact: Curator Janet Tierney
Open: Tues-Sat 10-5
Policy: The gallery aims at providing a balanced mix of work by local amateur and professional artists and makers with Arts Council and other exhibitions of contemporary and earlier works. Exhibitions are aimed at a general rather than specialist audience.
Sales: Work sold
The Space: The gallery is a converted chapel with *'vast amounts of vertical space'* with screens, track lighting and UV filtered glass in the temporary exhibitions gallery and screens, fixed lighting and UV filtered glass in the main gallery. Plans available.
Exhibiting: [AW] to the Curator with CV and slides of work. Gallery pays for insurance, printing and mailing of publicity and catalogue and takes 10% commission on sales.
Access: [U][T][F]

Guildford (Surrey)

(SEA) Map7 SU95

Guildford Adult Education Institute (The Gallery)

Adult Education Centre showing various exhibitions.
Address: Sydenham Road, Guildford, Surrey GV1 3RX tel 048 360 978
Contact: J F Youngs

Guildford House Gallery

This local authority-run gallery regularly stages a variety of solo and group exhibitions. [VA,Ph,Cr]
Address: 155 High Street, Guildford, Surrey GU1 3AJ tel 048 3444741
Contact: Curator Miss I Rhodes
Open: Mon-Fri 10.30-4.50, Sat 10.30-4.15
Policy: The aim of the gallery is to arrange *'temporary and varied exhibitions and provide a meeting place for local cultural activities'.* Predominantly showing the work of living artists and makers, exhibitions run for three weeks. There is also a permanent collection of modern and traditional works.
Sales: Work sold
The Space: A variety of hanging spaces each 3m high are available in a total of six different rooms. Large sculptures cannot be accommodated. Glass display cases are available.
Exhibiting: [AW] Apply two years in advance to the Curator. Commission 20% and 25%.
Access: [F][S] BR Guildford 5 mins; Public car park 5 mins

Harvey Road Gallery

As part of the Guildford Adult Education Institute this gallery aims to provide a broad spectrum of varied exhibitions covering the fields of art, craft and design. [VA,Ph,Cr]

Address: Harvey Road, Guildford, Surrey GU1 3RX tel 048 360 978

Contact: Harvey Road Gallery Committee Malcolm Tite, Carol Orwin, Guildford Adult Education Institute, Sydenham Road, Guildford, Surrey

Open: Mon-Thurs 10-9, Fri 10-4.30, Sat 9.30-12.30

Policy: Gallery policy is to provide an exhibition facility for students of the Visual Arts Centre as well as showing a varied programme of exhibitions by groups and individuals working in a variety of media. The gallery caters for *'as wide an audience as possible'*. Predominantly showing the work of living artists, exhibitions normally run for three weeks. The exhibition space is also used as a classroom and teaching area and occasionally for meetings.

Sales: Work sold

The Space: 28x2.5m high with floor space of approximately 9x5m with flood and spot lighting. Showcases are available.

Exhibiting: [AW] Apply to Malcolm Tite or Carol Orwin. Gallery finances list of exhibits and charges a hire fee of £20 per week. Commission 20% (15% for students).

Access: [F] BR Guildford 20 mins; Public car park 3 mins

Jonleigh Gallery

The gallery specialises in exhibitions of 20th century artists and sculptors including Carel Weight, Peter Greenham and Ruskin Spear. [VA]

Address: The Street, Wonersh, Guildford, Surrey GU5 0PF tel 0483 893177

Contact: John Hudson-Lyons

Open: When closed, by appointment, including Sun

Policy: About four shows a year are held.

Exhibiting: Work is chosen by a selection committee.

Michael Stewart Fine Art

A commercial gallery specialising in the work of Sir William Russell Flint with occasional exhibitions of living British artists. [Pa]

Address: 61 Quarry Street, Guildford, Surrey tel 0483 504359

Contact: P S Shelley

Open: Tues-Sat 9-5

Access: [F]

University of Surrey (Library Gallery)

This university gallery runs a varied programme of visual arts, photography and crafts work by established artists. [VA,Ph,Cr]

Address: George Edwards Library, University of Surrey, Guildford, Surrey GU5 9EQ tel 048 350 9167

Contact: Arts Administrator Patricia Grayburn tel 048 350 9167

Open: Mon-Fri 10-5, Sat-Sun 2-5; closed bank holidays and weekends during vacations

Policy: Exhibiting the work of contemporary artists and housing touring shows, the gallery aims to appeal to university students and staff and the local community. Related talks are run with some exhibitions which normally show for three to four weeks. There is a permanent collection of works donated by artists or bought from the proceeds of exhibitions.

Sales: Work sold

The Space: Total of 23m linear hanging space. Hanging is by rods with over head lighting. Showcases are available. Electronic alarm and smoke-detector systems. Gallery plans available.

Exhibiting: [AW] Apply to Arts Administrator. Gallery finances insurance, printing and mail-out of publicity, list of exhibits and preview costs and charges a negotiable hire fee for exhibition spaces, terms on application. Support in principle for EPR. Commission 15%.

Access: [U][T][L][F] BR Guildford; Buses to university campus; Car parks on campus

Halesworth (Suffolk)

(EA) Map5 TM58

Halesworth Gallery

Non-commercial and non-profitmaking gallery showing contemporary work of the highest standard. [VA]

Address: Steeple End, Halesworth, Suffolk 1P19 tel 09867 3064/3384

Contact: Hon Secretary

Open: Mon-Sat 11-5, Sun 3-6, mid-May - mid-Sept

Halifax (W Yorkshire)

(YA) Map3 SE02

Dean Clough Contemporary Art Gallery

A commercial gallery established in 1986 within the Dean Clough Industrial Park in order to encourage sales of work by local artists and makers and provide a venue for the Dean Clough contemporary art collection. [VA,Ph,Cr,De,LA]

Address: Dean Clough Industrial Park, Halifax, W Yorkshire tel 0422 44555

Contact: Gallery Organiser Doug Binder,

Open: Mon-Fri 9-6, Sat 9-1

Policy: The gallery aims to exhibit works by lesser-known regional artists *'who might find some difficulty in finding a venue because of the nature of their work. The exhibitions are not meant to be selling shows although the works can be purchased'*. There are generally 13 exhibitions a year most of which are solo shows and each lasts for four weeks. The gallery attracts many people working in the immediate area who attend seminars, music concerts and visit the open studios attached to the gallery and visit the exhibitions.

Sales: Work sold; Credit card

The Space: The two galleries are 5x4.5x4m high and 4x6x2.5m high with 20 and 30 linear metres respectively. Neither room can accommodate heavy sculpture and are lit by spots. Gallery plans are available.

Exhibiting: [AW] Slides and CV should be sent to Doug

Binder. The gallery covers all exhibition costs except artist's expenses and framing and takes 20% commission.
Access: [L] BR Halifax 10 mins

Piece Hall Gallery

A municipal gallery which houses a collection of fine, decorative and ethnographic art with exhibitions of both contemporary and historical art and crafts. [VA,Ph,Cr,LA]

Address: The Piece Hall, Halifax, W Yorkshire HX1 1RE tel 0422 59031
Contact: Keeper of Exhibitions Barry Sheridan
Open: Mon-Sat 10-6
Policy: The emphasis is on showing high-quality work by professional artists and makers and concentrates on making contemporary art more accessible - often by putting it in historical context. The gallery is *'seen more than just an exhibition space and that it develops a broader role as a 'community resource'* providing a service of contacts, skills and advice which can respond to the needs and initiatives to facilitate a broad range of arts activities within the community'. There are on average eleven exhibitions a year each lasting between four and six weeks. Often the gallery organises a series of exhibitions which explore different aspects of one theme and there is a commitment to improving accessibility to the arts to sections of the community who may be alienated by particular social, economic or educational factors.
Sales: Work sold
The Space: The gallery has 63m linear hanging space in a long gallery divided by six bays and with windows along one side. The gallery is lit by spots and the windows have blinds and UV filters. Showcases available and a courtyard area is available for sculpture. Gallery plans are available.
Exhibiting: [AW][EF] Artists and makers should send slides and information to the Keeper. The gallery covers all exhibition costs except display and artists' expenses and takes 10% commission. Supports the principal of EPR.
Access: [U][L] BR Halifax 2 mins; Car park 2 mins

Throstle Nest Gallery

A commercial gallery specialising in the promotion of hand-crafted pieces. [Pa,Dr,Cr]

Address: Old Lindley, Holywell Green, Halifax, W Yorkshire HX4 9DF tel 0422 74388
Contact: Owner Pat Kaye
Open: Mon-Sun 10-5
Policy: The gallery *'aims to show high-quality crafts to a discerning public who wish to own objects made and produced by craftspeople. We try to stock a wide range of goods, both with type and price in mind, with the priority that anyone should be able to afford something which is craftmade'.* Half of the gallery is used for changing displays of work for sale, and around five exhibitions of between four and six weeks in length are shown a year. Demonstrations and occasional workshops are available for visitors.
Sales: Work sold
The Space: The galleries are 14x8x4m high and 5x8x4m high with a total of 17m linear hanging space. Two free-standing screens with 12m linear hanging space and six wall-mounted pegboard panels on stone walls provide extra space if needed. The galleries are spot lit. Gallery plans available.
Exhibiting: [AW] applications should be sent to Pat Kaye. The gallery pays for insurance, printing and mailing of publicity and takes 25% commission.
Access: [F] Off the main A643 to Rochdale road

Hamstall Ridware (Staffordshire)

(WMA) Map5 SK11

Ridware Arts Centre

A commercial arts centre in the Vale of the Trent with workshops, café, gallery, shop, gardens and animals. [VA,Cr]

Address: Hamstall Hall, Hamstall Ridware, Staffordshire WS15 3RS tel 088 922 351
Contact: Jennifer Hobbs
Open: Tues-Sun 10.30-5.30 March-Christmas; Sat,Sun 10.30-5 Christmas-March
Policy: A diverse programme of exhibitions and events *'to create interest, excitement and inspiration'.*
Sales: Work sold; Credit card
The Space: A converted barn of 40 square metres giving 25m linear hanging space. Direct fixing with spots and natural light.

Throstle Nest Gallery (Photo: Paul Barker)

Exhibiting: [AW] The centre charges 33.3% on sales and provides insurance, publicity, mailing, a list of exhibits and preview.

Access: [X] Off the A513 east of Rugeley

Harlow (Essex)

(EA) Map7 TL41

Harlow Library

Exhibition space in public library, available for hire. [Pa,Pr,Dr,Ph]

Address: The High, Harlow, Essex CM20 1HA tel 0279 413772

Contact: Deputy Area Librarian John Stradling

Open: Mon,Tues,Thurs, Fri 9-7.30, Wed, Sat 9-5

Policy: Artistic, literary, educational and local information exhibitions shown.

Sales: Work sold

The Space: The gallery has a floor area of 33.6 square metres.

Exhibiting: Commission of 20% on art and photographic work sold. Scale of charges for other exhibitors.

Access: [L][F]

Playhouse Gallery

The gallery is on the second floor of the Playhouse, a civic theatre serving Harlow and the surrounding area. [VA,Ph,Cr,LA]

Address: The Playhouse, The High, Harlow, Essex CM20 1LS tel 0279 24391

Contact: Exhibitions Co-ordinator Anthony Kinsey tel 0277 86255

Open: Mon-Sat 11-10

Policy: The gallery policy is to provide the local population and those from the eastern suburbs of London with an opportunity to experience a wide variety of original works of art and craft, in the main of a contemporary nature. Up to ten exhibitions a year, each lasting some three to four weeks, providing young or less well-known professional artists and makers the opportunity to show their work in a large, self-contained yet easily accessible space close to a regular flow of visitors. Workshops and talks in an educational context are regularly held.

Sales: Work sold; Credit card

The Space: The gallery is 4.27x10.98x14.03m.

Exhibiting: [AW] Gallery covers insurance, printing and some mailing of publicity, list of exhibits, transport, catalogue card, some artists' expenses. 20% commission on sales plus VAT.

Access: [U][T][L] BR Harlow 20 mins walk; Bus station 5 mins; Public car park adjacent

Harrogate (N Yorkshire)

(YA) Map3 SE35

Aquarius Gallery

Commercial shop and gallery. [Pa,Sc,Ce,Se]

Address: 1 Crown Place, Harrogate, N Yorkshire tel 503190

Open: Tues-Sat 10-5, closed 12.30-1.30

Godfrey and Twatt

A commercial gallery on the Crafts Council's selected list which, since its opening in 1985 has specialised in crafts and original prints. [Pr,Cr]

Address: 7 Westminster Arcade, Parliament Street, Harrogate, N Yorkshire HG1 2RN tel 0423 525300

Contact: Alex Twatt

Open: Mon-Sat 10-5.30

Policy: The gallery has changing displays and separate exhibitions which highlight the work of one particular artist or maker rather than group shows. There are generally four shows a year and a group exhibition at Christmas, each exhibition runs for four weeks.

Sales: Work sold; Credit card

The Space: There is one gallery of 8x3x3m high with shelving for three-dimensional works.

Exhibiting: Artists are invited to exhibit and the gallery covers the cost of insurance, printing of publicity, list of exhibits, preview costs, display, transport, mailing out of publicity, catalogue/card, takes 33.3% commission plus VAT. Supports the principle of EPR.

Access: [X] BR Harrogate 5 mins; Car park 1 min

Harrogate Art Gallery

Municipal gallery run by Harrogate Museums and Art Gallery Service which, as well as a permanent collection of oils and watercolours by leading British artists of the 19th to mid-20th centuries, has a regular programme of monthly temporary exhibitions. [VA,Ph,Cr]

Address: Library Buildings, Victoria Avenue, Harrogate, N Yorkshire HG1

Contact: Curator Pat Clegg, Royal Pump Room Museum, Royal Arcade, Harrogate HG1 2RY tel 0423 503 340

Open: Mon-Sat 10-5 during exhibitions

Policy: The programme provides a *'local platform for the arts from junior level onwards and includes exhibitions by district and regional professional artists'*. Some are solo shows and there are occasional large-scale exhibitions. When the gallery moves to a new site in the early 1990s, a new policy will be devised to suit the enhanced facility. See also Little Gallery, Courthouse Museum, Knaresborough.

Godfrey and Twatt Contemporary Crafts Gallery

Sales: Work sold
The Space: The gallery has UV protected lights and perspex-covered plinths of varying sizes. A steep flight of stairs limits the size of work that can be accommodated. Gallery plans are available.
Exhibiting: Gallery booked until 1990 after which policies are likely to change. 15% commission is charged on sales. The gallery meets the cost of insurance, publicity, preview, display, transport, mailing and catalogue.
Access: [X] BR 3 mins

Harrogate Leisure Centre (Conference Room)

Occasional exhibitions are mounted by members of the public within the leisure centre and conference centre. [VA,Ph,Cr]
Address: Hookstone Avenue, Harrogate, N Yorkshire HG2 8ER tel 0423 871269
Contact: Manager Mr Ledger
Open: Daily 10am-11pm
Access: [F]

Hartlepool (Cleveland)

(NA) Map3 NZ53

Gray Art Gallery & Museum

A municipal gallery housing a permanent collection of 19th century oils and watercolours, maritime scenes, work with local connections and having two galleries for a programme of exhibitions. [VA,Ph,Cr,Vi]
Address: Clarence Road, Hartlepool, Cleveland TS24 8BT tel 0492 266522 ext 259
Contact: Museums Officer Rachel Wilkins
Open: Mon-Sat 10-5.30, Sun 2-5
Policy: Exhibitions usually last six weeks and include local history, photography and sculpture by local artists, *'both contemporary and otherwise'*. Talks and demonstrations by artists are also organised.
Sales: Work sold; Credit scheme
The Space: Gallery 1 has 42m linear hanging space, and Gallery 2 has 23m. Hanging is by rods, lighting by track and daylight. There are three upright showcases. The galleries are also used by societies for evening meetings.
Exhibiting: [AW] Apply to E Law in the first instance. The gallery covers publicity, insurance, lists of exhibits and catalogue/card and charges 10% commission.
Access: [U][T] Ground floor; **[X]** First floor. Bus station 3 mins; BR Hartlepool 5 mins; Car park

Hartley Wintney (Hampshire)

(SA) Map7 SU75

Century Gallery

See Century Galleries, Henley-on-Thames.
Address: The High Street, Hartley Wintney, Hampshire RG27 tel 025126 2747
Contact: Manager Carolyn Patterson
Open: Daily 10-1 & 2-5

Harwich (Essex)

(EA) Map7 TM23

Harwich Library

Exhibition space in public library, available for hire. [VA,Cr]
Address: Upper Kingsway, Harwich, Essex CO12 3JT tel 0255 503499
Contact: Senior Library Assistant Margaret Macey
Open: Mon,Tues,Thurs, Fri 9-7, Sat 9-5
Policy: See Essex Libraries, Chelmsford
Sales: Work sold; Sales referred to exhibitor
The Space: The exhibition space is 6.51 square metres.
Access: [F]

Haslemere (Surrey)

(SEA) Map7 SU93

Haslemere Educational Museum

The museum houses collections of natural history, archaeology, local history and European arts and crafts and shows some temporary exhibitions. [VA,Ph,Cr]
Address: High Street, Haslemere, Surrey GU27 2LA tel 042 821 12
Contact: Curator Diana Smith
Open: Tues-Sat 10-5, Sun 2-5 April-Oct ; Tues-Sat 10-4 Nov-March
Policy: *'The aim of the museum is to forward and advance the study of science, literature and the fine arts.'* The museum was founded in 1888 and is a private society governed by trustees with a large active membership. The new curator is keen to encourage increased use of the exhibition space and to hold lectures and workshops in conjunction with exhibitions.
Sales: Work sold
The Space: Two rooms are available for hire 15x5m and 15x6m.
Exhibiting: [AW] Exhibitors are responsible for insurance, mounting and dismantling, surveillance and publicity. No commission charged. Contact the Curator for further information.
Access: [S] BR Haslemere 10 mins; Limited parking

Haslemere Educational Museum

Haslingden (Lancashire)

(NWA) Map3 SD72

Haslingden Library

A gallery within Haslingden Library which is a branch of Lancashire Libraries. [Pa,Pr,Dr,Ph,Cr]

Address: Higher Deardengate, Haslingden, Rossendale, Lancashire BB4 tel 0254 697003
Contact: Senior Librarian Victor Marcinkiewicz
Open: Mon-Thurs 9.30-5. Tues,Fri 9.30-7.30. Sat 9.30-4
Policy: Attempts are made to cater for all types of art and craft exhibitions. Lack of security and showcases present a problem in some instances. The gallery is also used for craft and drama workshops, public meetings and local society functions.
Sales: Work sold
The Space: The space measures 14x11x5m with hanging by hooks. Natural light is supplemented by flood lighting and spots.
Exhibiting: **[AW]** Applications to exhibit should be made by telephone, letter or a visit to the Senior Librarian. The gallery pays for publicity. 15% is taken on sales.
Access: **[U][T][X]** Bus stop 5 mins Bacup-Accrington route; Car park at rear

Hassocks (W Sussex)

(SEA) Map7 TQ31

Chichester House Gallery

A commercial art gallery. [Pa,Pr]

Address: High Street, Ditchling, Hassocks, W Sussex BN6 8SY tel 07918 4167
Contact: Directors Mr & Mrs John Hunter
Open: Tues, Thurs, Fri, Sat 11-1 & 2.30-5 and by appointment
Policy: The mixed exhibitions of painting and prints are normally shown from four to six weeks.
Sales: Work sold
Exhibiting: The gallery pays for printing and mailing of publicity, preview costs and a catalogue or card. A commission of 33.3% is charged on sales.

Mill Green Museum

Hastings (Sussex)

(SEA) Map7 TQ80

Hastings Museum & Art Gallery

This gallery runs a regular programme of exhibitions within the museum, with preference given to professional artists living in the area. [VA,Cr]

Address: Cambridge Road, Hastings, Sussex TN34 1ET tel 042 472 1202
Contact: Exhibitions Officer Lesley Cornish
Open: Mon-Sat 10-1 2-5, Sun 3-5
Policy: Gallery policy is to show *'good and varied work in a lively and balanced programme'*, sometimes reflecting aspects of the museum's varied collections. There are also historical and retrospective shows. About half of the exhibitions annually are by living artists and makers and are usually shown for four to five weeks. Educational activities related to exhibitions are organised for children and adults.
Sales: Work sold
The Space: 36m linear hanging space with no natural daylight. Gallery plans are available.
Exhibiting: **[AW]** Apply to Exhibitions Officer. Gallery finances insurance and printing and mail-out of publicity. Support in principle for EPR. Commission 15%.
Access: **[S]** Buses to town centre; BR Hastings 10 mins; Public car park 2 mins

Stables Theatre Gallery

This gallery mainly shows the work of professional artists with an occasional exhibition by *'good amateurs'* and is usually booked two years in advance. [Pa,Pr,Cr]

Address: High Street, Hastings, E Sussex TN34 3EY tel 042 442 3221
Contact: Hon. Secretary Mabel Stringfellow
Open: Mon-Sat 10.30-1, Sun 11-1
Sales: Work sold
The Space: 15x4.5m, hanging is by rods.
Exhibiting: **[AW]** Apply with slides or photographs of work. There is a hire fee of £20 per month. Commission 20% plus VAT.

Hatfield (Hertfordshire)

(EA) Map7 TL20

Mill Green Museum

Municipal art gallery and museum. [VA,Ph,Cr]

Address: Mill Green, Hatfield, Hertfordshire AL9 5PD tel 07072 71362
Contact: Curator Sue Kirby
Open: Tues-Fri 10-5, Sat, Sun, bank holidays 2-5
Policy: *'To provide a variety of temporary exhibitions on different themes with a local audience primarily in mind. Museum collections figure strongly but others are welcome, especially local craft workers.'*
Sales: Work sold
The Space: The gallery is 4.5x3.5x2m high with a linear hanging space of 10.5m, blinds at windows and environmental monitoring. Four showcases available plus garden and small summerhouse for outdoor exhibitions.
Exhibiting: [AW] Apply to the curator. Exhibitions lasts between six and eight weeks with craft demonstrations to tie in with exhibitions, plus special summer programme of demonstrations and events. Commission charged of 20%.
Access: [F] Hatfield BR 20mins, small car park, buses G32, WH2, WH7, WH8, WH17, WH18, 303,333, 341, 366

Havant (Hampshire)

(SA) Map7 SU70

Havant Museum

A municipal gallery run by the Hampshire County Museums Service which houses a permanent collection of fire-arms and holds temporary exhibitions. Local and natural history galleries opening 1989 and a local history. [VA,Ph,Cr]
Address: East Street, Havant, Hampshire PO9 1BS tel 0705 451155
Contact: Exhibitions Officer Jo Bailey, Hampshire County Museums Service, Chilcomb House, Chilcomb Lane, Winchester, Hampshire SO23 8RD tel 0962 846315
Open: Tues-Sat 10-5
Policy: This temporary exhibitions gallery is one of six galleries housed within museums throughout Hampshire. It receives six or seven touring exhibitions a year, about four of which include work by living artists or makers with a bias towards those living or working in or near Hampshire. It also holds two or three local exhibitions generated by local individuals or groups, such as camera clubs, art clubs and quilting groups. Exhibitions last five weeks and exhibiting artists are encouraged to give talks, demonstrations or workshops.
Sales: Work sold
The Space: The temporary exhibitions gallery is 8.3x5m giving about 25m linear hanging space on hessian-covered panels, with spots on tracks and no direct sunlight. Display cases and gallery plans available.
Exhibiting: [AW] Applications in writing, accompanied by transparencies, to Exhibitions Officer. The Museums Service pays for insurance, printing and mailing of publicity and transport. Commission is 20% plus VAT.
Access: [F] Temporary exhibitions gallery, **[X]** Some permanent galleries. Near town centre; BR Havant & car parks 7 mins; Limited free parking

Old Town Hall Arts Centre

A gallery due to open in 1989 within an arts centre which presents a range of arts activities. [VA,Ph,Te]
Address: Old Town Hall Arts Centre, East Street, Havant, Hampshire PO9 1BS tel 0705 472700
Contact: Director Paul Sadler
Open: Mon-Sat 10-11pm
Policy: The gallery will form part of the new extension due to open in February 1989 and policy is currently under review, although it will show painting, prints, drawing, photography, textiles and other wall-based or free-standing work by living artists.
Sales: Work sold; Credit card
The Space: The gallery will have two walls 8.7x2.85m, one 4.6x2.85m, one 2.1x2.85, one 2.5x2.85 and one 1.4x2.85m with multi-track lighting and direct fixing. Gallery plans available.
Exhibiting: [AW] Ask for an application form. The gallery will pay for insurance, publicity, preview, catalogue and artist's expenses and will take 25% commission. Supports EPR in principle.
Access: [U][T] Rail & bus stations 10 mins; Car park

Haworth (W Yorkshire)

(YA) Map3 SE03

Horse-Shoe Gallery

A commercial gallery specialising in good-quality paintings by nationally-known artists and a section devoted to Dales landscapes. [Pa]
Address: 72 Main Street, Haworth, W Yorkshire BD22 8DP tel 0535 43095/0274 613476
Contact: Eric Windsor
Open: Mon-Sun 10.30-5.30; Closed Mon in Winter
Policy: Over 250 works on display at any time within a continuous display.
Sales: Work sold
Access: [S]

Hebden Bridge (W Yorkshire)

(YA) Map3 SD92

South Bank Gallery

A commercial gallery with a permanent collection of arts and crafts integrated with changing exhibitions of contemporary work. [VA,Cr]
Address: Stubbing Wharf, Hebden Bridge, W Yorkshire HX7 6LU tel 0422 842070
Contact: Owner Valerie Tomlins
Open: Mon-Wed, Sat-Sun 12.30-5.30 Apr-June; Mon-Wed, Sat-Sun 12.30-7.30 July-Aug; Sept-March phone to confirm
Policy: Exhibitions are mixed-media, group shows and the gallery prefers to promote the work of lesser-known artists and makers as well as the more established. Eight exhibitions are shown a year and each lasting for eight weeks. The gallery has its own design studios and workshops producing ceramics and jewellery and activities relating to the exhibitions are organised within the gallery and occasionally in the local park where last year, they promoted two *'family events'* of Raku and kite

making.

Sales: Work sold; Credit card

The Space: There are two exhibition spaces with 54m and 24m linear hanging space, the maximum size painting that can be accommodated is 1.6x1.8m, and three-dimensional works are limited to 2.1x0.9m.

Exhibiting: **[AW]** Send slides to Valerie Tomlins, the gallery covers the cost of insurance, printing of publicity, list of exhibits, mailing out of publicity, preview costs are shared and the gallery takes 33.3% commission plus VAT.

Access: **[X]** BR Hebden Bridge 10 mins

Heckington (Lincolnshire)

(LHA) Map5 TF14

Pearoom Centre for Contemporary Crafts

The Pearoom Craft Centre houses twelve independent resident craftspeople, runs a craftshop for regional and national makers, a café-restaurant and a heritage exhibition gallery with the craft gallery opened in November 1988. [Cr]

Address: Station Yard, Hecklington, Lincolnshire NG34 9JJ tel 0529 60765

Contact: Director Elwee Iansen

Open: Mon-Sat 10-5.3, Sun 12-5.30 (May-October) Tues-Sat 10-5, Sun and bank holidays (November-April)

Policy: *'To provide a showcase for the makers, from Lincolnshire and Humberside especially, in which they can display their work, thereby increasing the public's awareness of their existence, the quality of their work and therefore their sales potential. Only work by living makers will be exhibited. Equally the gallery aims to be a resource centre for regional makers where they can see one another's work in an attempt to stimulate further the production of high-quality contemporary craftwork. A programme of educational activities is organised to support the exhibitions'.*

Sales: Work sold; Credit card

The Space: Main Gallery is 14.7x5.2m with hanging space of 30m and hanging by mirror plates or similar method, low-voltage track lighting and selection of good display units, some lockable. The Coffee Room Gallery is 14x5.3m with hanging space of 9.8m and hanging by wire from rail, low-voltage fixed spotlights. Gallery plans available.

Exhibiting: **[AW][EF]** Apply to the Director with slides and CV. Gallery pays for insurance, printing and mailing of publicity, preview costs, one-way transport, display mounting and catalogue. Commission on sales 27%. Gallery supports EPR in principle.

Access: **[U][T]** Ground floor only. **[X]** Galleries and restaurant. BR Heckington opposite; Own car park (22 cars); A17 3 mins; No bus connection

Hednesford (Staffordshire)

(WMA) Map5 SK01

Valley Heritage Centre

Heritage Centre run by Cannock Chase District Council with a museum, craft workshops, gallery, events area and collection of local social history objects. [VA,Cr]

Address: Valley Road, Hednesford, Staffordshire WS12 5QX tel 05438 77666

Contact: Curator Su Jeanes

Open: Opening May 1989

Policy: The exhibition programme will feature work from local, regional, and national sources. The displays will be historical or art-based and designed to *'stimulate visitors interest in what they might otherwise not get the chance to see'*. The craft workshops will produce work for sale and demonstrate crafts with local connections.

Sales: Sales referred to exhibitor

The Space: Room one is 12x8x2.5m with screens and fluorescent lights and room two is 4.5x3.5x2.5m with screens, fluorescent and natural light. Room three is 8x4.5x2.5m with screens, fluorescent and natural light.

Exhibiting: **[AW]** Applications should be made in writing to the Curator. The centre plans to offer insurance, printing, list of exhibits and preview costs. Commission on sales has yet to be finalised.

Access: **[U][T][F]** Car parks on site; Hednesford bus station 10 mins

Helmsley (N Yorkshire)

(YA) Map3 SE68

Look

A commercial gallery specialising in painting but also displaying some bronze sculpture and drawings with a permanent display of contemporary art. [Pa,Sc,Dr]

Address: 20 Castlegate, Helmsley, N Yorkshire YO6 5AB tel 0439 70545

Contact: Manager Nicholas Coombes

Open: Mon-Sat 10.30-5; Sun 2-5

Policy: The permanent collection changes at frequent intervals and runs concurrently with small individual exhibitions which tend to concentrate on fairly traditional themes and styles *'it is the express aim that all the work should be of a uniformly high standard and the dimensions suit domestic interiors and are reasonably priced'*.

Sales: Work sold; Credit card

The Space: Two downstairs galleries are 4.5x3x3m high and 4x4.5x3m high and one upstairs of 4.5x6x3m high, making a total of 62m linear hanging space. All have concealed fluorescent tubes and the galleries downstairs combine this light source with additional spots. The gallery favours *'domestic'* size paintings and will not accommodate work more than 1.5m square. In addition there are two showcases which can accommodate small displays of glass and sculpture.

Exhibiting: **[AW]** Applications are welcome any time and artists should phone or write for an appointment.

Access: **[F]** Staff entrance is available but disabled visitors are requested to ring the gallery prior to their visit. Car park 1 min

Sissons William Gallery

Occasional exhibitions are arranged in this commercial gallery now in its fifth year. [Pa,Pr,Cr]

Address: 23 Market Place, Helmsley, N Yorkshire YO6

5BJ tel 0439 71385
Contact: Mrs D Sissons
Open: Fri-Sat 10-6, Sun 2.30-6
Policy: *'We have mainly a rural theme, but are always delighted to see new artists and after several trips to the Staes feel we have one or two innovative ideas to exchange. Stock is constantly changing.'*
Sales: Work sold; Credit card
The Space: Two areas about 20x7m and other rooms on two floors.
Exhibiting: [AW] Artists should contact direct by prior appointment. Gallery covers cost of insurance, mailing, publicity and catalogue. Framing service at cost. Commission charged plus VAT.
Access: [X]

Helston (Cornwall)

(SWA) Map6 SW62

Cornwall Crafts Association at Trelowarren

Crafts shop and exhibitions housed in the Georgian stable-block of the beautiful Trelowarren estate with a licensed bistro and coffee bar. [Cr]
Address: Trelowarren, Mawgan-in-Meneage, Nr Helston, Cornwall TR12 6AF tel 032 622 567
Contact: Margaret Way
Open: Tues-Sun 11-5 from 7 April during exhibitions; closed Mon except bank holidays
Policy: See also Cornwall Crafts Association, Bodmin and Trelissick Gallery, Truro.

Hemel Hempstead (Hertfordshire)

(EA) Map7 TL00

Old Town Hall Arts Centre

An arts centre with a regular programme of theatre, film and cabaret events, the gallery is also used as a restaurant/brasserie. [VA,Ph]
Address: The Gallery, Old Town Hall Arts Centre, Hemel Hempstead, Hertfordshire HP1 3AE tel 0442 42827
Contact: Manager Michael Paton
Open: Mon-Sat 10-5 except bank holidays
Policy: *'To show the best available modern art that is suitable for a small-scale venue.'* A mixture of touring painting and photographic exhibitions with local artists and photographers.
Sales: Work sold
The Space: 35.5sq.m. exhibition area, 15.1m linear space, interrupted by doors/windows. Wall mounted work only. Plans available.
Exhibiting: [AW] By letter, requesting appointment. Gallery pays insurance and mailing of publicity and commission is 20%.
Access: [X] Local bus services; BR; nearby parking

Henley-in-Arden (Warwickshire)

(WMA) Map4 SP16

Gallery Upstairs

A workshop and shop with upstairs gallery in Elizabethan premises. [VA,Cr]
Address: Torquil Pottery, 81 High Street, Henley-in-Arden, Warwickshire B95 5AT tel 05642 2174
Contact: Reg Moon
Open: Mon-Sat 10-6
Policy: Mixed exhibitions showing the work of *'professional living artists and makers of a high standard'.*
Sales: Work sold; Credit card
The Space: A 5x16m room with spots and natural light.
Exhibiting: [AW] A commission of 15% is charged on sales.
Access: [X] Town centre location close to BR Henley and buses

Henley-on-Thames (Oxfordshire)

(WMA) Map7 SU78

Bohun Gallery

Commercial gallery founded in 1973 and holding ten exhibitions a year of work by contemporary artists and ten of leading contemporary ceramics. [Pa,Sc,Pr,Ce]
Address: 15 Reading Road, Henley-on-Thames, Oxfordshire RG9 1AB tel 0491 576 228
Contact: Director Patricia Spiers
Open: Mon-Sat 10-5.30; Closed Wed
Policy: The gallery stocks paintings and prints by past exhibitors including Elizabeth Frink, John Piper, David Hockney, Elizabeth Blackadder and Andre Bicat and other contemporary artists. It is *'interested to hear from professional figurative artists'.*
Sales: Work sold
The Space: 10x4m space with hanging from a rail with spots, fluorescent and natural light.
Exhibiting: The gallery meets the cost of insurance, publicity, mailing, catalogue and private view.

Century Galleries

A 'fine art consultancy service'. [Pa,Sc,Pr,Ce]
Address: Thames Side, Henley-on-Thames, Oxfordshire RG9 tel 0491 575 499
Contact: Director Michael Shemilt
Open: Daily 10-5
Policy: 30 exhibitions a year are shown, mostly by living *'nationally and internationally-known artists'* working in a wide range of styles and media. Work of about 100 artists is held in stock. Framing and restoration work is undertaken and a range of services offered to businesses including leasing and advice on office decoration etc. See entries for branches at Hartley Wintney and Datchet.
The Space: 33 square metres of exhibition space.

Hereford (Hereford & Worcester)

(WMA) Map4 SO54

Hatton Art Gallery

A purpose-built gallery in a city park to house the work of Brian Hatton, a Herefordshire artist killed in the First World War, but also showing some temporary exhibitions of contemporary work. [VA,Ph,Cr]

Address: Churchill Gardens Museum, Venns Lane, Hereford, Hereford & Worcester tel 0432 267409

Contact: Curator Anne Sandford

Open: Tues-Sun 2-5 Summer; Tues-Sat 2-5 Winter, open bank holidays

Policy: See Hereford City Museum and Art Gallery.

Sales: Work sold during temporary exhibitions

The Space: 15x7.5m with artificial light. Two wall mounted showcases. Gallery plans available.

Exhibiting: [AW] The gallery provides publicity, list of exhibits, catalogue/card, artists' expenses and help with hanging the exhibition. The gallery supports EPR. A 20% commission is charged on sales.

Access: [S] Situated outside the city centre on the A4103 Worcester road

Hereford City Museum & Art Gallery

A municipal art gallery and two branch museums, The Old House and Churchill Gardens. The art gallery has permanent displays of local history, nature etc and collections of fine art and a gallery space is devoted to temporary exhibitions. [VA,Ph,Cr]

Address: Broad Street, Hereford, Hereford & Worcester HR4 9AU tel 0432 268121 ext 207

Contact: Curator Anne Sandford

Open: Tues,Wed,Fri 10-6, Thurs,Sat10-5

Policy: *'The policy at the art gallery is to show a wide ranging selection of exhibitions from local and national sources and to reflect all areas of fine and applied art. We attempt to cater to all areas of society through exhibitions and ancillary workshops and lectures'.* Exhibitions normally last for three weeks with one third being solo shows, mostly artists from the area. Gallery plans available.

The Space: The gallery is 9.5x18m with a flexible screen system; direct fixing; showcases and spotlights

Exhibiting: [AW] The gallery provides publicity, list of exhibits, catalogue/card, artists expenses and help with hanging the exhibition. The gallery supports EPR. A 20% commission is charged on sales.

Access: [U][T][L] Situated opposite the Cathedral, above the library

Herefordshire College of Art and Design

The gallery is situated in the foyer of the college. [VA,Cr]

Address: Folly Lane, Hereford HR1 1LT tel 0432 273359

Contact: Lecturer in Charge of Printmaking Paul Scull

Open: Term-time during normal college hours

Policy: The programme of monthly exhibitions is a mixture of solo and touring shows, private collections and work from local schools and other art colleges. The audience is mainly college students and a large number of mature part-timers.

Sales: Sales referred to exhibitor

The Space: A 12x6.5m space giving 11m linear hanging space with 24 Click exhibition panels, three plinths, five hanging rails for textiles, and three large lockable glass cases. Spots and natural light.

Exhibiting: [AW] CV and slides, the gallery occasionally provides insurance.

Access: [U][T] City centre, bus and BR Hereford 15 mins; Bus to Whittern May

John McKellar

A commercial gallery specialising in contemporary jewellery which is on the Crafts Council's selected list. [Je]

Address: 23 Church Street, Hereford, Hereford & Worcester HR1 2LR tel 0432 354460

Contact: John McKellar

Open: Mon-Sat 9.30-5.30

Policy: The monthly exhibitions feature individual makers alongside a wide-ranging stock. The gallery is *'keen to promote jewellery on design content rather than materials value'.*

Sales: Work sold; Credit card

The Space: 9.5x4.5x3.5m with free-standing internally-lit display cases.

Exhibiting: [AW] The programme is organised a year in advance. The gallery provides insurance, publicity, mailing, list of exhibits, preview and catalogue/card. A commission of 45% is charged on sales.

Access: [S] Town centre location; Public car park 5 mins; BR Hereford 10 mins

John McKellar

Kemble Gallery

A non-profit making organisation showing the work of The Society of Craftsmen who pay an annual subscription. [VA,Cr]

Address: 29 Church Street, Hereford, Hereford & Worcester HR1 2LR tel 0432 266049
Contact: Christine Bulmer
Open: Mon-Sat 9.30am-5.30pm
Sales: Work sold; Credit card
The Space: Work larger than 2 metres square cannot be accommodated. A lockable glass display case is available.
Exhibiting: [AW] New members are assessed by a selection panel. A 37.5% commission is charged on sales.
Access: [F] Town centre location

Old Mayors Parlour Gallery

A private gallery available for hire for one or two-week exhibitions at £35 per week. [Pa,Pr,Dr,Ph,Cr]

Address: 23 Church Street, Hereford, Hereford & Worcester HR1 2LR
Contact: Christine Bulmer, Little Breinton, Hereford HR4 7PH
Open: To suit exhibitor
The Space: 5x6m space with good natural light and spot lights.
Exhibiting: [AW] Contact Christine Bulmer. Artist is responsible for all exhibition costs, hanging and invigilation.
Access: [X] City centre location

Hertford (Hertfordshire)

(EA) Map7 TL31

Corn Exchange

Multi-purpose hall available for hire administered by East Hertfordshire District Council. [VA]

Address: Fore Street, Hertford tel 0992 553109
Contact: Leisure Services Officer, Jack Graves or Bookings Clerk, Jill Muncer, East Herts District Council, The Castle, Hertford, SG14 1HR
Policy: Showing local art societies and occasional touring exhibitions. Annual Hertford Art Society Exhibition. No regular staffing.
The Space: Multi-purpose hall on first floor is 10x13m with natural light from roof, plus ancillary space 6.3x10 with artificial light. Hanging on battens around walls.
Exhibiting: [AW] Hire charges are £69 a day for non-commercial users with a 20% reduction for a week's hire and 40% for two weeks.
Access: [L] Town centre site; BR Hertford North, Hertford East short walk; Car park opposite

Hertford Museum

Independent museum with local collections of archeology, history, geology etc which also runs temporary exhibitions.

Address: 18 Bull Plain, Hertford SG14 1DT tel 0992 582686
Contact: Director Sarah Gray
Open: Tues-Sat 10-5
Policy: About eight changing exhibitions a year, including local interest and history produced in-house, small touring exhibitions and one or two a year by local artists and makers.
Sales: Work sold through museum shop
The Space: One gallery of 24 square metres with 11m linear hanging space supplemented with free-standing panels providing an additional 12m linear hanging space. Flexible track-mounted tungsten lights.
Exhibiting: [AW] Applications in writing to the Director. The Museum covers the cost of insurance, printing and publicity. Commission is 10%.
Access: [F] Town centre site; BR Hertford East 10 mins, BR Hertford North 20 mins; Public car park 2 mins

Hertfordshire Libraries

Most Hertfordshire Libraries have limited space for temporary exhibitions.

Address: County Hall, Hertford SQ13 8ES tel 0992 556606
Policy: Baldock Library, 8 Bell Row, Baldock, SG7 6AP tel 0462 893297; Berkhampstead Library, Kings Road, Berkhampstead HP4 3BD tel 0442 864545; Bishops Stortford Library, The Causeway, Bishops Stortford CM23 2EJ tel 0279 54946; Cheshunt Library, Turners Hill, Cheshunt, Waltham Cross EN8 8LB tel 0992 23582; Chorley Wood Library, Lower Road, Chorley Wood WD3 5LD tel 09278 2601; Croxley Green Library, Barton Way, Croxley Green WD3 3HB tel 0923 772119; Hitchin Library, Paynes Park, Hitchin SG5 1EW tel 0462 50133; Hoddesdon Library, 98A High Street, Hoddesdon EN11 8HD tel 0992 462296; Letchworth Central Library, Broadway, Letchworth SG6 3PF tel 0462 685646; North Watford Library, St Albans Road, Watford WD2 5RE tel 0923 225930; Oxley Library, Bridlington Road, South Oxley, Watford WD1 6AG tel 01 428 2868; Royston Library, Market Hill, Royston SG8 9JN tel 0763 43292; St Albans Central Library, The Maltings, St Albans AL1 3JQ tel 0727 60000; Stevenage Central Library, Southgate, Stevenage SG1 1HD 0438 369441; Ware Library, 87 High Street, Ware SG12 9AD tel 0920 2683; Welwyn Garden City Central Library, Campus West, Welwyn Garden City AL8 6AE tel 0707 332331.
The Space: Varying spaces from small display cases to separate exhibition rooms. Contact the Librarian for details.
Exhibiting: [AW] Contact the individual librarian.

Mill Bridge Rooms

A multi-purpose hall for community use, which can be booked for meetings, coffee mornings, sales of work, or for art and craft exhibitions. Self-catering facilities are available. [VA,Cr]

Address: Seed Warehouse, The Wash, Hertford SG14 tel 0992 587979
Contact: Museum Director Sarah Gray, Hertford Museum, 18 Bull Plain, Hertford, SG14 1DT tel 0992 582686
Open: Mon-Sat 9am-10pm

Policy: Bookings of the Mill Bridge Rooms are administered by the Hertford Museum (see separate entry) on a first-come, first served basis.
Sales: Referred to exhibitor
The Space: One 70 square metre space, with 23 linear metres of wall display boards and 6 metres of picture rail, flexible track mounted spots.
Exhibiting: **[AW]** Details of hire charges and equipment and booking forms available from the Museum Director to whom all applications should be made on standard forms. All exhibition costs are the responsibility of exhibitors.
Access: **[U][T]** Town centre site; BR Hertford East 15 mins, BR Hertford North 15 mins; Public car park 5 mins

Heswall (Merseyside)

(MA) Map4 SJ28

Dee Fine Arts

Commercial gallery and picture framing business with permanent display of contemporary paintings and prints, also around six changing exhibitions of similar work annually. [Pa,Pr,Dr]
Address: 182 Telegraph Road, Heswall, Merseyside L60 0AJ tel 051 342 6657
Contact: Gallery Directors John and Deirdre Waite
Open: Mon,Tues,Thurs-Sat 10-1,2.15-5; Weds 10-1
Policy: Temporary exhibition programme of work in watercolour, prints and local paintings with each exhibition usually lasting two weeks.
Sales: Work sold; Credit card
The Space: Upstairs space 8.6x3.7x2.5 with a linear space 17.2m with three fixed picture rails and tungsten halogen floods, fluorescents and natural light.
Exhibiting: **[AW]** Initial enquiries by telephone only to Deirdre Waite. Gallery hire costs £50 per week plus VAT. Gallery covers insurance, publicity and preview costs. Commission is 33.3%.
Access: **[X]** to upstairs gallery; **[S]** to main framing and permanent display on ground floor. Bus 72a Heswall centre; Parking difficult

Hexham (Northumberland)

(NA) Map3 NY96

Moothall Gallery

A small gallery, administered by the district council, which is part of a hall hired out for meetings, classes and social functions. [VA,Ph,Cr]
Address: Market Place, Hexham, Northumberland NE46 3NH tel 0434 604011
Contact: Sarah Wilson, Recreation & Amenities Department, Tynedale District Council, Prospect House, Hexham NE46 3NH
Open: Mon-Sat 10-4
Policy: The gallery is available for hire and shows are primarily by local groups, though there may be exhibitions from other groups and individuals during empty weeks or out of season.
Sales: Work sold
The Space: The space is 9x6m with hessian-covered screens 1.8m high. One internally-lit showcase.
Exhibiting: **[AW]** Hire fees are £12 a day, £60 a week for non-selling exhibitions; £21 a day, £105 a week for selling exhibitions. The hirer is responsible for all costs and invigilation except in the case of 'sponsored exhibitions' when the gallery charges 25% commission.
Access: **[S]** BR Hexham 10 mins; Car park 8 mins

Queens Hall Arts Centre

Gallery in a municipal arts centre which also houses theatre, darkroom and restaurant. [VA,Ph,Cr]
Address: Beaumont Street, Hexham, Northumberland NE46 3IS tel 0434 606787
Contact: Arts Assistant Dorothy Lathan
Open: Mon-Fri 10-5, Sat 10-12
Policy: Policy is to show work by local and national, amateur and professional artists and photographers.
Sales: Work sold; Credit card
The Space: Main gallery is 5x14x4m giving 27m linear hanging space lit by track spots. Studio one is 8x5x4m giving 20m linear hanging space lit by fluorescent lights. Small table-top showcases available. Weight limitations on floors. Spaces are also used for evening meetings except where delicate or floor-standing work is on show.
Exhibiting: **[AW]** Exhibitions are booked 12 months ahead, apply in writing with slides or photographs to Dorothy Lathan. The centre covers insurance, list of exhibits and publicity but charges £100 a month for the main gallery and £50 a month for studio one (or in both cases 30% commission, whichever is the greater).
Access: **[U][T][L]** Bus station 2 mins; BR Hexham 10 mins; Car park 10 mins

Hinckley (Leicestershire)

(EMA) Map5 SP49

Hinckley College of Further Education

A space in the college foyer showing small exhibitions of students' work and work from the County Collection. [Pa,Sc,Ph]
Address: London Road, Hinckley, Leicestershire LE10 1HQ tel 0455 251222
Contact: Head of Art & Design G Wilson,
Open: Mon-Fri 9-7
Exhibiting: **[AW]** Exhibitors are responsible for all costs and mounting the exhibition.
Access: **[U][T]**

Hitchin (Hertfordshire)

(EA) Map7 TL12

Hitchin Museum and Art Gallery

Municipal gallery and museum with large collection of watercolours by pupils of Lucas, Griggs and others. [VA,Ph,Ce,Te]
Address: Paynes Park, Hitchin, Hertfordshire SG5 1EQ tel 0462 34476
Contact: Alan Fleck
Open: Mon-Sat 10-5

Policy: *'To promote and encourage local artists in all media.'* Four-week mixed and solo exhibitions, mainly by living artists.
Sales: Work sold
The Space: 4.7x7m & 3.1x3.2m & 5.3x4.1m, a total space of 34.9 linear metres with hanging by hooks on battens. Extensive track lighting. Access door 0.84x2m; no weight limit. Eight desk cases available, space for outdoor sculpture.
Exhibiting: **[AW]** In writing or by telephone. Insurance, publicity, catalogue paid for by gallery which takes a commission of 23%.
Access: **[F]** BR Hitchin 20mins; Car park

Hoddesdon (Hertfordshire)

(EA) Map7 TL30

Lowewood Arts Centre

Address: High Street, Hoddesdon, Hertfordshire EN11 8BE tel 0992 465032
Contact: Hon General Secretary Mrs Winter, 1 Rodney Crescent, Hoddesdon, Herts EN11 9EW
Policy: To foster and encourage the arts in the Borough of Broxbourne.

Lowewood Museum

Local authority museum of local history.
Address: High Street, Hoddesdon, Hertfordshire EN11 8BE tel 0992 445596
Contact: Curator Elaine Sansom
Open: Wed & Sat 11-5; Parties Mon-Sat by appointment
Policy: Two rooms have permanent displays, a third has changing exhibitions of local and general interest.
The Space: Up to 30m linear hanging space, direct fixing, various display cases.
Access: **[X]** Car parking

Holmfirth (W Yorkshire)

(YA) Map3 SE10

Booth House Gallery

A commercial gallery set up in 1975 to deal in work by living artists and makers with a special emphasis on contemporary ceramics. [VA,Cr]
Address: 3 Booth House Lane, Holmfirth, W Yorkshire HD7 1QA tel 0484 685270
Contact: James and Liz Robison
Open: Sat-Sun 2-5, Mon-Fri telephone to confirm
Policy: The gallery contains the ceramic workshop and studio of Jim and Liz Robison who are *'pleased to show visitors around the workshops and kiln areas'*. Half of the gallery space is devoted to changing displays of pottery and stock by up to three other artists and makers and *'the gallery has regular exhibitions of work by leading artists and makers and a well-stocked shopping area selling domestic and other pottery, some by local and nationally known potters'*.
Sales: Work sold; Credit card; Credit scheme
The Space: The gallery is housed in a converted 19th century barn and has 18m linear hanging space ranging from 2.4m to 5.4m high. The gallery space is 24 square metres.
Exhibiting: **[AW]** Artists and makers are requested to send slides and information to Jim and Liz Robison. The gallery covers the cost of insurance, printing of publicity, preview costs, mailing out of publicity and the catalogue/card and takes 33.3% commission.
Access: **[F]** Bus route from Holmfirth to Holmbridge, Hinchliffe Mill 5 mins; Car park adjacent

Trevor Stubley Gallery

The gallery opened in 1988 in a converted weaver's cottage primarily to provide a showcase for paintings by Trevor Stubley. [VA,Ce]
Address: Greenfield Road, Holmfirth, W Yorkshire HD7 2XQ tel 0484 682026
Contact: Owners Trevor and Valerie Stubley
Open: Sun 10-5 Opening hours at other times are erratic, telephone call essential
Policy: The *'gallery exists primarily to exhibit and sell the work of the resident artist. The main subject matter ranges from landscapes in watercolour and gouache and larger oil works of Mediterranian countries'*. Works by other artists whose work is similar and of a sympathetic nature may be considered. The artist's studio is within the cottage and visitors may ask to see work in progress.
Sales: Work sold
The Space: The gallery has 30m linear hanging space and the height of the walls range from 2.5m to 3.5m. The gallery is lit by a mixture of natural and spot lights, with central heating and has some double glazing. No heavy sculpture or large works can be accommodated.
Exhibiting: Exhibitors are invited only and costs incurred by the artist are negotiable. The gallery takes 33.3% commission.
Access: **[F]** Situated on the main Trans-Pennine Barnsley-Manchester Road (A635); Car park outside galler;Bus stop Parkhead bus terminal *'One mile stiff walk up hill'*

Trevor Stubley Gallery: 'View from the Gallery' by Trevor Stubley

Holt (Norfolk)

(EA) Map5 TG03

Picturecraft of Holt

Commercial art gallery operating on a 'unique rental 'display bay' system'. [Pa,Dr,Ph]

Address: North Norfolk's Art Centre, 23 Lees Courtyard, Off Bull Street, Holt, Norfolk NR25 6HP tel 0263 713259
Contact: Principal Partner Michael Hill
Open: Mon-Sat 9-1 & 2-5; Closed Thurs 2-5
Policy: *'Nineteen artists exhibit each week in the display bays. Major solo shows are held during July-Sept. for one week each. The exhibition room holds local artists' exhibitions on a weekly basis.'* Regular demonstrations of calligraphy, oriental brushwork etc.
Sales: Work sold; Credit card (15% charge)
The Space: Series of display bays with pegboard backing ranging in width from 1.3-4m.
Exhibiting: [AW] Apply to the Assistant Manager. Available on a rental basis only. Prices range from £51 for a 1.3m wide bay off-season to £126 for a 3.5m bay high season for a fortnights rental.
Access: [F] Town centre; Car park

Picturecraft of Kelling

Commercial 'traditional' gallery, connected with the main gallery in Holt (3 miles away). [Pa,Pr,Dr,Ph,Cr]

Address: The Old Reading Room, Coast Road, Lower Kelling, Holt, Norfolk NR25 6EG tel 0263 70 528
Contact: Manager John Hill
Open: Mon-Sun 10-5, Closed Thurs
Policy: Continuous changing exhibition of work in a *'warm and homely atmosphere'*. See separate entry for Picturecraft of Holt.
Sales: Work sold; Credit card
The Space: Hanging by pegboard walls and centre display panels. Natural lighting with extra strip lights.
Exhibiting: [AW] Phone or write for an appointment. Works shown for between three to four weeks. Commission is 33.3%.
Access: [F] Car park

Picturecraft of Holt

Horsham (Sussex)

(SA) Map7 TQ13

Christ's Hospital Arts Centre

An arts complex in the grounds of Christ's Hospital school including a 500-seat theatre and a 180-seat Octagon. [Pa,Pr,Ph,Cr,LA]

Address: Christ's Hospital, Horsham, Sussex RH13 7LW tel 0403 52709
Contact: Box Office Manager
Open: 9.30-5.30 during school terms
Policy: It runs a programme of professional and school events throughout the school year and covering all the performing and visual arts.
Sales: Work for sale
The Space: Exhibitions are held in the foyer, staircases and passages connecting the complex to the Music School and classrooms. There is space for 20-40 paintings hung from rods and spotlit.
Exhibiting: The centre meets the cost of press publicity and takes 10 *commission or makes a hire charge.*
Access: [U][T] except Octagon. 2 miles Horsham centre; BR Horsham; BR Christ's Hospital, not Sun; Car park on site; Southdown bus, not Sun

Horsham Arts Centre Gallery

Arts centre with two exhibition spaces for contemporary exhibitions.

Address: Horsham Arts Centre, North Street, Horsham, E Sussex RH12 1RL tel 040 368 689
Contact: Visual Art Co-ordinator Diana Goodman
Open: Mon-Sat 10-7, Sun 2-7
Policy: *'We like to present every aspect of works of art.'*
Sales: Work sold
The Space: Ritz Foyer has 18m linear hanging space suitable for large paintings and the Capitol Foyer has five cabinets measuring 2x0.8m and eight 1.6x0.8m which can be used for smaller paintings, pottery, jewellery, etc.
Exhibiting: [AW] Commission is 20%.
Access: BR Horsham 5 mins

Picturecraft of Kelling

Hove (E Sussex)

(YA) Map7 TQ20

Hove Museum & Art Gallery

Municipal museum and art gallery housed in large Victorian villa. [VA,Cr,Ph]

Address: 19 New Church Road, Hove, E Sussex BN3 4AB tel 0273 779410
Contact: Curator J Boyden
Open: Tues-Fri 10-5, Sat 10-4.30, Sun 2-5 from March 89; closed bank holidays
Policy: The gallery programme includes historic and contemporary exhibitions of art, craft and photography. There is also an extensive collection of 19th and 20th century art. Predominantly exhibitions are group shows and last for between four to eight weeks.
The Space: The suite of four exhibition rooms on the ground floor are all of domestic rather than institutional, scale.
Exhibiting: Commission 33.3%.
Access: [U][T] ground floor only. Car park; BR Hove 1 hour from London Victoria

Huddersfield (W Yorkshire)

(YA) Map3 SE11

Bryam Galleries

Commercial gallery with occasional exhibitions organised in the shop section. [Pa,Pr,Cr]

Address: 5 Station Street, Huddersfield, W Yorkshire HD1 1LS tel 0484 25747
Contact: Proprietor D Hooley
Open: Mon-Sat 9.30-5, Wed 9.30-1
Policy: Original watercolours and oils by local and national artists in group and solo exhibitions.
Sales: Work sold
The Space: Gallery is 5x1.6m.
Exhibiting: Work bought outright and on sale or return basis.
Access: [F]

Huddersfield Art Gallery

A municipal gallery with a permanent collection of British fine art and a programme of temporary contemporary art exhibitions. [VA,Ph,Cr,LA]

Address: Princess Alexandra Walk, Huddersfield, W Yorkshire HD1 2SU tel 0484 513808 ext 216
Contact: Senior Curator Robert Hall
Open: Mon-Fri 10-6, Sat 10-4
Policy: The gallery *'presents the best of local, regional and national visual arts, with a bias towards contemporary work'.* Of the 15 exhibitions mounted each year half are solo shows. Touring exhibitions come in from other galleries and the Arts Council. Education workshops accompany the exhibitions and the spaces are also used for theatre, dance, poetry, music and performance events.
Sales: Work sold
The Space: Five galleries, two 9x5x2.65m high and others 6x3x2.65m high, 16x9x2.65m high and 23x9x2.65m high. Each have track and fluorescent lighting, carpeted floors and air conditioning and direct fixing to walls. Gallery plans are available.
Exhibiting: [AW][EF] Slides and information to be sent to the Senior Curator. The gallery covers all exhibition costs, takes 20% commission and supports the principal of EPR.
Access: [U][L][F] BR Huddersfield 10 mins; Bus station 5 mins

Huddersfield Sports Centre

The sports centre occasionally puts on exhibitions within the centre. [Pa,Sc,Cr,Dr,Ph]

Address: Southgate, Huddersfield, W Yorkshire DA1 1QX tel 0484 35231
Contact: Centre Manager Blackshaw
Open: Mon-Sat 9-10.30, Sun 9-5.30
Exhibiting: [AW] The centre accepts applications from individuals and groups wishing to use the space.
Access: [U]

Hull (Humberside)

(LHA) Map3 TA0928

Ferens Art Gallery

Municipal gallery funded by Hull City Council. [VA,Ph,Cr,Fi,Vi,LA]

Address: Queen Victoria Square, Hull, Humberside HU1 3RA tel 0482 222750
Contact: Senior Keeper Louise West
Open: Mon-Sat 10-5, Sun 1.30-4.30; closed Christmas Day, Boxing Day and Good Friday
Policy: *'To interest, animate, stimulate and educate the general public of all ages about art both old and new, local, national and international, through the permanent collections and a very lively and varied temporary exhibition programme which covers visual arts and crafts and architectural design. To enrich their lives and stimulate awareness of their own creativity'.* The Ferens has a very fine collection of 17th-19th century European Old Masters, with emphasis on Dutch and Flemish artists; 16th-20th century portraits; maritime paintings particularly 19th century school including John Ward;

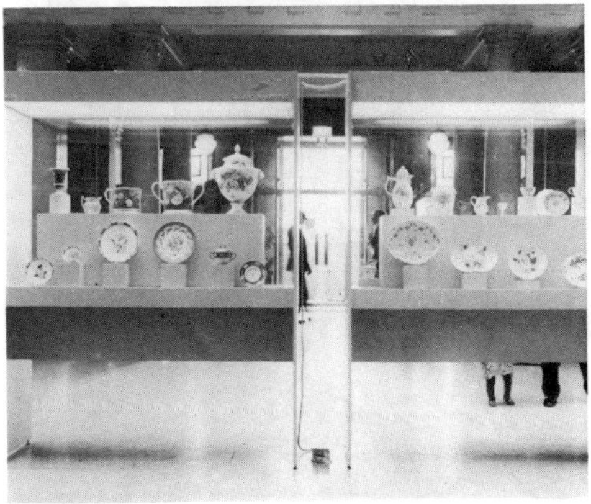

Ferens Art Gallery

19th and 20th century watercolours; 20th century art to present day; local topography.

The Space: Galleries 1-3 usually given over to permanent collection. A major new extension to the gallery will be started early 1989 which will give much improved facilities for contemporary exhibitions with the addition of an external sculpture court. Plans available.

Exhibiting: [AW][EF] To Senior Keeper with slides and CV. Gallery pays for insurance, printing and mailing of publicity, preview costs, transport, catalogue and artists' expenses and charges 10% commission plus VAT on sales. Supports EPR.

Access: [U][L] BR Hull 5 mins; Bus station 5 mins; Multi-storey car parks adjacent

Humberside College of Higher Education

Gallery based within the foyer of the Fine Art Department of Humberside College of Higher Education. [VA,Ph]

Address: Queens Gardens Fine Art Building Foyer, Hull, Humberside HU5 2AY tel 0482 25938 ext 235

Contact: Exhibitions Organiser

Policy: There is no formal exhibition policy. Current shows are selected by committee nine months in advance.

Sales: Work sold

The Space: 33m linear hanging space.

Exhibiting: Commission by agreement.

Posterngate Gallery

Municipal gallery associated with the Ferens Art Gallery funded by Hull City Council and Lincolnshire and Humberside Arts. [VA,Ph,Cr,]

Address: 6 Posterngate Gallery, Hull, Humberside HU1 2JN tel 0482 222745

Contact: Gallery Supervisor Deborah Dean

Open: Tues-Sat 10-5.30; closed Sun and Mon

Policy: *'To familiarise the general public with contemporary art, craft, and photography practises, across a wide range of media. An emphasis on* education, participation through workshops, talks and demonstrations. Increasing and developing programme of sales both through the exhibitions programme and the Ferens commissions register. Positive discrimination towards young unestablished artists particularly from the region'. Exhibitions change roughly once a month, and the main aims of the programme are quality and variety.

Posterngate Gallery

Sales: Work sold

The Space: Space approximately 13x6.5x2.75m with 38.75m linear hanging space. Gallery plans available.

Exhibiting: [AW][EF] Applications temporarily discontinued due to major building programme at parent gallery. Gallery pays for insurance, printing and mailing of publicity, preview costs, transport, catalogue and artists' expenses including fees for talks and workshops. EPR established 1988, currently £200 per solo show. Commission of 20% plus VAT on sales.

Access: [X] BR Hull 15 mins; Bus station 15 mins; Public car parks 5 mins

Posterngate Photography Workshop

Photographic gallery and workshop funded by Hull City Council, Lincolnshire and Humberside Arts and Humberside County Council. [Ph]

Address: 1st Floor, 6 Posterngate, Hull, Humberside HU1 2JN tel 0482 222745

Contact: Director Mick Fattorini

Open: Tues-Sat 10-5

Policy: The gallery shows a variety of photographic practices and issues to as wide a public as possible. It aims to attract *'non-gallery'* audiences through its education and outreach programme. Work exhibited includes professional and community based photography, work by women, ethnic photographers and people with disabilities.

Sales: Work sold

The Space: The gallery is 2x1.5m and 4.1x2.5m which cannot take works larger than 2.25x2.75m.

Exhibiting: [AW] Apply to the Director. Gallery pays for insurance, printing and mailing of publicity, preview costs and display costs. Exhibitors receive £80 for exhibiting and gallery supports EPR in principle.

Access: [X] BR Hull 15 mins; Bus station 15 mins; Public car parks 5 mins

Spring Street Theatre

Exhibition space in the theatre bar and reception run by the Education and Outreach Officer of Hull Truck Theatre Company. [Pa,Ph,LA]

Address: Spring Street, Hull, Humberside HU2 8RW tel 0482 224800

Contact: Exhibitions Organiser Jane Thomas

Open: Mon-Sat 12-2.30 and 6-10.30 (when theatre is open)

Policy: *'The exhibition space which specialises in black and white photography, displays the best professional photographic work we can afford, and to intersperse this with the work of amateurs who may never have exhibited before. Some painting exhibitions have been included recently. Performance and time-based work is shown in the main auditorium and studio theatre.'*

Sales: Work sold; Credit card
The Space: Hanging space 14.5m is with work hung by mirror plates if framed, map pins if encapsulated. Adjustable track lighting on display boards.
Exhibiting: [AW][EF] Applications to the Exhibitions Organiser. The gallery pays for insurance, preview costs, one-way transport and mailing of publicity. Exhibitors receive a fee for exhibiting and venue supports proposed plan for EPR. Commission on sales is 15%.
Access: [U][F] BR Hull 3 mins; Bus Station 3 mins; Four large car parks close by

University of Hull Art Collection

Situated on the campus of University of Hull. [VA]
Address: The Middleton Hall, University of Hull, Cottingham Road HU6 7RX tel 0482 465035
Contact: Hon Curator John Bernasconi
Open: Mon-Fri 2-4, Wed 12.30-4 (Term time only)
Policy: *'To provide a varied exhibition programme of interest to the University community and general public, with the emphasis on exhibitions of art historical significance and especially those relating to our special period of art in Britain 1890-1940'.* Permanent collection of British Art 1890-1940 and the Thompson Collection of Chinese ceramics.
Sales: Sales referred to exhibitors
The Space: Main gallery is 10.5x10m and the smaller gallery is 15x4m. The exhibition area has approximately 80m hanging space. Work hung is on rods. Lighting in first two spaces by spots and tubes and last has fluorescent tubes and daylight. Tubes fitted with UV filters.
Exhibiting: [AW] To Hon Curator. *'Opportunities for showing work by living artists very limited indeed'.* Gallery pays for insurance, printing and mailing of publicity and preview costs.
Access: [U] 103,104,105; Limited parking on campus

Hunstanton (Norfolk)

(EA) Map5 TF64

Ringstead Gallery

Commercial art gallery. [Pa]
Address: Ringstead, Hunstanton, Norfolk PE36 5JZ tel 048 525 316
Contact: D S Greer
Open: Mon-Sat 10-5
Policy: *'Continuous mixed exhibitions all year, with about six solo or theme exhibitions at intervals usually countryside, wildlife and sporting. Constantly seeking new paintings of quality in oils, watercolours or pastels.'*
Sales: Work sold
The Space: Two connecting galleries converted from old stable block, each 4x6m.
Exhibiting: [AW]
Access: [F]

Huntingdon (Cambridgeshire)

(EA) Map5 TL37

Angus Gallery

Part of the house of the owner, a freelance illustrator. [Pa,Pr,Ce]
Address: 15 East Street, St.Ives, Huntingdon, Cambridgeshire PE17 4PD tel 0480 300907
Contact: John Hutchinson
Open: Mon-Sat 10-12 & 2-5. Closed Thurs
Policy: *'A three year experiment to see if the existence of the gallery will provide an outlet for artists'* work.' Solo and theme exhibitions.
Sales: Work sold
The Space: *'Hanging space for around 50 paintings of 30 x 20.'*
Exhibiting: Hope to be able to accept artists *'in the near future'.* Commission 20%.
Access: [F] Car park 2 mins

Huyton (Merseyside)

(MA) Map3 SJ49

Knowsley Libraries

Several of Knowsley Libraries have exhibition space or display facilities. [VA,Cr]
Address: Knowsley Borough Council, Archway Road, Huyton, Merseyside L36 9US
Contact: Library Projects Officer Mike Fleming, Huyton Library, Derby Road, Huyton, Merseyside L36 9UJ tel 051 443 3744
Open: Various
Policy: A recently-established Arts Sub-Committee is revising arts provisions (see also entry for Kirkby Library).
Sales: Sales referred to exhibitor
The Space: Various.
Exhibiting: [AW] Contact Mike Fleming for details of library spaces.

Ightham (Kent)

(SEA) Map7 TQ55

Retigraphic/Pratt Contemporary Art

Gallery, print workshop and studio run by the Retigraphic Society - Contemporary Art Publishers. [VA]
Address: Ightham, Sevenoaks, Kent TN15 tel 073 288 2326
Open: Open by appointment Mon-Sun
Policy: As well as limited edition screen prints and etchings published by Retigraphic, paintings, drawings and sculpture are also on show.
Sales: Work sold

Ilkeston (Derbyshire)

(EMA) Map5 SK44

Erewash Museum

A museum of social history showing domestic and working life in the Erewash district, run by Erewash Borough Council. [Pa,Ph,Cr]

Address: High Street, Ilkeston, Derbyshire DE7 5JA tel 0602 440440 ext 331

Contact: Curator Rosemary Blake

Open: Thurs-Sat 10-4

Policy: The programme aims to reflect *'art, craft and project work being produced in the area'*. Most of the exhibitions are by local artists and makers, and local clubs, societies and community groups.

Sales: Work sold; Sales referred to exhibitor

The Space: 13m linear hanging space plus 8m linear hanging space of movable screens with spotlights and filtered daylight and hanging by direct fixing.

Exhibiting: [AW] Applications invited from local artists or exhibitions on local themes, contact the Curator. The gallery provides publicity and a list of exhibits. Commission is charged in the form of a donation to the museum.

Access: [F][X] Car parking at the museum; Bus from Ilkeston town centre

Bottle Kiln Gallery

A private gallery in a restored bottle kiln complex that includes a landscape garden service, café, and shop. [VA,Cr]

Address: High Lane East, West Hallam, Nr Ilkeston, Derbyshire DE7 6HP tel 0602 329442

Contact: Jennifer Turner

Open: Tues-Sun 10-5

Policy: The exhibitions in the gallery are mostly mixed or group exhibitions of East Midlands artists. Solo exhibitions are held in the café.

Sales: Work sold; Credit card

The Space: Gallery 35 square metres, Café 25 square metres, both with daylight and spots.

Exhibiting: [AW] Contact Celia Stone or Jenny Turner. Gallery provides insurance, printing, mailing, and list of exhibits.

Access: [U][F] Situated on the A609, Derby, Nottingham, Ilkeston buses

Ilkley (W Yorkshire)

(YA) Map3 SE44

Bradford & Ilkley Community College

An education institution which encourages artists and makers to provide work which demonstrates processes of working as well as the finished product. [VA,Ph,Cr]

Address: Ilkley Campus, Wells Road, Ilkley, W Yorkshire LS29 9RD tel 0943 609010

Contact: Ann Anderson

Open: Mon-Sat 9am-9pm

The Space: There are two spaces suitable in the library and the reception area.

Exhibiting: [AW] Applications in writing, the gallery takes 10% commission.

Hawksworth Gallery

Whilst there is no permanent exhibition space. Mary Sara acts as a free-lance exhibition organiser on behalf of her artists, taking their work to other venues in the North of England. [VA,Ph,Cr]

Address: 12 Weston Road, Ilkley, W Yorkshire LS29 8DW tel 0943 603165

Contact: Owner Mary Sara

Manor House Art Gallery & Museum

A municipal gallery with a collection of fine and decorative art, with an emphasis on the promotion of contemporary art from the region. [VA,Ph,Cr,LA]

Address: Castle Yard, Ilkley, W Yorkshire LS29 9DT tel 0943 600066

Contact: Keeper of Exhibitions Caroline Krzesinska, Cartwright Hall, Lister Park, Bradford tel 0274 493313

Open: Tues-Sun 10-5 (Oct-Mar); Tues-Sun 10-6 (Apr-Sept)

Policy: The policy is *'to involve the town of Ilkley and surrounding areas in a programme of mainstream contemporary art and craft, through exhibitions and accompanying lectures, residencies and workshops'*. The gallery particulary welcomes applications from young artists from the region although work from further afield is also considered. There are eight exhibitions a year most of which are of work by living artists and each exhibition lasts for six to eight weeks. The gallery especially favours two-person shows.

Sales: Work sold

The Space: There are two main exhibition spaces 4.8x6.6x2.4m high, with hanging by picture hooks over a rail and spots and general lights. Edmunds showcases are available for craft work. The difficult access and scale of galleries dictate small-scale works with a maximum length of 1.2m. There is a raised flagged courtyard to the front of the building 15x8m used for sculpture. Gallery plans are available.

Exhibiting: [AW][EF] Artists and makers should send slides to the Keeper of Exhibitions at Cartwright Hall. The gallery covers all exhibition costs and partial cost of the preview and display, the principle of EPR is supported and the gallery charges 20%-30% commission.

Access: [X] BR Ilkley 5 mins

Ipswich (Suffolk)

(EA) Map5 TM14

Area Library Service (Ipswich)

Co-ordinates activities and programmes for six exhibition spaces within libraries in the Ipswich area. [VA,Cr,Ph]

Address: Central Administration Unit, Suffolk County Arts & Libraries Service, St Andrew House, County Hall, Ipswich, Suffolk tel 04732 30000

.**Contact:** Area Service Manager (Ipswich) Diana

Bickerton, Ipswich Central Library, Northgate Street, Ipswich, Suffolk tel 0473 233411
Sales: Work sold; Sales referred to exhibitor
The Space: Hadleigh: 7.85x5.58m; Ipswich: small lockable glass cabinet in foyer; Woodbridge: lockable glass cabinet 1.83x1.22m in foyer, occasional use of 3.66m run using free-standing screens; Felixstowe: free-standing open exhibition case 1.22x0.61x1.52m, occasional use of 3.66m run using screens; Gainsborough (Ipswich): 3.05m run using free-standing screens; Chantry (Ipswich): 6.1m run using free-standing screens.
Exhibiting: Applications to Senior Library Assistant at each library. Artists pay fee of 20% of all sales made as a direct result of exhibition, subject to a minimum payment of £17.50 payable in advance.

Haste Gallery

The gallery is combined with an outlet for art materials and framing, and concentrates on showing artists with a regional significance, both historical and contemporary. [Pa,Pr,Dr]
Address: 3, Great Coleman Street, Ipswich, Suffolk IP4 2AD tel 0473 58429
Contact: J D Haste
Open: Mon-Sat 9-5
Policy: Exhibitions last for three to four weeks, and are complemented by a regularly changing display of work as well as a collection of oils and watercolours of East Anglia. Exhibitions are occasionally supported by demonstrations.
Sales: Work sold; Credit scheme; Credit card
The Space: Maximum size of work is 91cm in any direction.
Exhibiting: gallery covers: insurance, printing of publicity, list of exhibits, preview costs, display, mailing, catalogue, card and takes 36.5% commission on sales.
Access: [X] Public car parks nearby

John Russell Gallery

An art gallery specialising in the promotion of contemporary artists and their work. [Pa,Pr,Ph,Cr]
Address: Orwell Court, 13 Orwell Place, Ipswich, Suffolk IP4 1BD tel 0473 212051
Contact: Gallery Director Anthony R Coe
Open: Mon-Sat 9.30-5
Policy: The gallery shows 13 three-week exhibitions a year supported by a permanent collection of contemporary original prints. The gallery undertakes framing and conservation. The director gives talks on contemporary art to outside organisations.
Sales: Work sold
The Space: The gallery offers 133 square metres with 'correct' lighting and hanging rod system. 'Large' oils are restricted.
Exhibiting: [AW] Apply two years in advance. Gallery covers insurance, printing and mailing of publicity, preview costs, catalogue/card, and charges 33.3% commission. The gallery is available for hire at £75per week for three-week exhibitions.
Access: [F] BR Ipswich 20 mins; Public car park

Mill Gallery

The gallery is part of the owner's studio and shows a continuous display of his ceramics and paintings, prints and sculpture. [VA,Cr]
Address: Swilland, Ipswich, Suffolk IP6 9LW tel 0473 85460
Contact: Bernard Rooke
Open: Mon-Fri 9-6 Sat & bank holidays 11-5
Sales: Work sold; Credit card (Visa only)
Access: [F]

Wolsey Art Gallery, Christchurch Mansion

A municipal gallery with a broad programme that links contemporary artistic activity with a permanent collection of national importance. [VA]
Address: Ipswich Museums & Galleries, High Street, Ipswich, Suffolk IP1 3QH tel 0473 213761/2
Contact: Assistant Curator (Exhibitions) Rebecca Weaver
Open: Mon-Sat 10-5, Sun 2.30-4.30; closes at dusk in winter
Policy: Administered by Ipswich Borough Council the gallery's programme has included Arts Council exhibitions as well as those promoting both younger and less exposed artists, particularly those with a regional connection. The exhibition space is housed in a fine country house set in parkland in the middle of the town and houses an important collection of works by Constable and Gainsborough, as well as a comprehensive collection of twentieth century prints. Exhibitions are supported by a range of talks, schools workshops and artists residencies. Exhibitions last for six weeks and are selected to encourage understanding and interest of contemporary art.
The Space: The gallery is 21.78x8.41x3.30m; with 32m linear hanging space and overhead natural light supplemented by spotlights. Environmental controls to be installed in 1989. Maximum size of work is 3.26m diagonal.
Exhibiting: [AW] Gallery covers insurance and publicity printing, and charges 20% on sales.
Access: [S] BR 20 mins; Bus station 5 mins; Public car park 5 mins

Wolsey Art Gallery: Children's workshop run by Dale Devereaux Barker during the 10th Bradford Print Biennale

Ironbridge (Shropshire)

(WMA) Map4 SJ60

Old Shoe Shop Gallery

A shop with a changing display of craft work and an exhibition space. [Sc,Pr,Cr]

Address: High Street, Ironbridge, Shropshire TF8
Contact: Mrs Townend
Open: Thurs-Mon 10.30-5.30; Jan, Feb closed Thurs
Policy: The exhibitions feature *'top artists and makers work'* in an area not known to be *'craft minded'*. Occasional talks or workshops are promoted.
Sales: Work sold; Credit card
The Space: Several spaces on two floors are used for a display giving 54 square metres of space.
Exhibiting: [AW] Contact the gallery nine months before the date required. The gallery provides publicity, mailing, a list of exhibits and preview costs, and charges 33.3% commission on sales.
Access: [X] Situated in the town centre by the bridge

Irthlingborough (Northamptonshire)

(NA) Map5 SP97

Irthlingborough Library

See Northamptonshire Libraries. [VA,Ph,Cr]

Address: High Street, Irthlingborough, Northamptonshire NN8 tel 0933 650641
Contact: District Librarian Mike Davison, Higham Ferrers Library, Midland Road, Higham Ferrers, Northamptonshire tel 0933 314842
Open: Mon,Wed,Fri 10-12.30, 1.30-5, 5.30-7; closed Tues, Thurs, Sat
Sales: Work sold; Sales referred to exhibitor
The Space: The library has 4m linear hanging space plus 8m linear space on screens.
Exhibiting: [AW] District Librarian or Sue Gray. Publicity and insurance provided, transport between libraries arranged for touring exhibitions. Commission is 10%.
Access: [F]

Jarrow (Tyne & Wear)

(NA) Map3 NZ36

Bede Gallery

An independent gallery and local history museum with a permanent collection and a regular programme of contemporary art exhibitions. [VA,Ph]

Address: Springwell Park, Butchersbridge Road, Jarrow, Tyne & Wear NE32 5QA tel 091 489 1807
Contact: Gallery Director Vince Rea
Open: Tues-Fri 10-5, Sun 2-5
Policy: The gallery aims to provide *'the people of Jarrow with the opportunity to see new developments in the visual arts'*. The programme consists of established British and international artists, as well as *'young experimental artists'*. One way of achieving the gallery's main objective of *'maintaining close links with the local community'* is by providing an opportunity for North East artists with an outlet for their work and *'encouraging public appreciation of the visual arts'*. An art video library is available for viewing.
Sales: Work sold; Credit scheme
The Space: The gallery is 21.4x6x3m with strip and spot lights.
Exhibiting: [AW] Apply to Vince Rea.
Access: [X] Bus routes; Metro 20 mins, Street park

Bede Monastry Museum

A museum with a permanent collection on the life and times of the Venerable Bede also showing temporary exhibitions. [VA,Ph,Cr]

Address: Jarrow Hall, Church Bank, Jarrow, Tyne & Wear NE32 3DY tel 091 489 2106
Contact: Curator Susan A Mills
Open: Tues-Sat 10-5.30, Sun 2.30-5.30 April-Oct; Tues-Sat 11-4.30, Sun 2.30-5.30 Nov-March; open bank holidays
Policy: Exhibitions, which change every six weeks, may be on any subject though they have in the past covered local artists and makers, archaeology and aspects of social history.
Sales: Work sold
The Space: There are two temporary exhibition rooms, one 47 square metres with 15m linear hanging space, the other 37 square metres with 12m linear hanging space. There is also staircase which can be used for picture displays.
Exhibiting: [AW] New approaches and ideas from different artists are welcomed and non-local exhibitions encouraged. Prospective exhibitors should contact Susan Mills to arrange a meeting. If applying in writing send photographs of work. Museum covers cost of insurance, printing and mailing of publicity, etc. Museum charges 15% commission.
Access: Buses every 10 mins; Metro Jarrow 15 mins

Keele (Staffordshire)

(WMA) Map4 SJ84

Keele University Chancellor's Building Gallery

A purpose-built space in the Chancellors Building, supported by the university and grants from the Area Museum Service and West Midlands Arts. [VA,Ph,Cr]

Address: Keele University, Keele, Staffordshire ST5 5BG tel 0782 621111
Contact: Art Exhibitions Organiser A Drakakis-Smith, Art Exhibitions, Walter Moberley Hall, Keele University, Keele, Staffordshire ST5
Open: 9-9 364 days
Policy: *'The aim of Keele art exhibitions is to promote local talent and to show the current work of artists in the region and elsewhere'*. A *'varied programme of fine art, craft, sculpture, photography, as well as displaying informative/educational exhibitions of a more general nature'*.
Sales: Work sold
The Space: The Gallery has 27.5m linear space, with fluorescent, spots and daylight. The Concourse space

provides 17.5m linear space lit by spotlights. An outside courtyard can be used for sculpture. Gallery plans available.

Exhibiting: **[AW]** Slides and CV should be sent to the Exhibitions Organiser. The gallery provides insurance and printing of a poster, a commission of 10% is charged on sales.

Access: **[U][T]** Car park and buses to Keele on campus

Keighley (W Yorkshire)

(YA) Map3 SE04

Cliffe Castle

A municipal gallery with a permanent collection of Victorian fine and decorative art and an exhibition programme changing throughout the year. [VA,Ph,Cr]

Address: Spring Gardens, Keighley, W Yorkshire BD20 6LH tel 0274 664184

Contact: Keeper of Exhibitions Caroline Krzesinska, Cartwright Hall, Lister Park, Bradford tel 0274 493313

Open: Tues-Sun 10-6 (Apr-Sept); Tues-Sun 10-5 (Oct-Mar)

Policy: The gallery runs a lively programme of temporary exhibitions of ethnic and fine art material.

The Space: The exhibition space of 12x9m has 45m linear for paintings, hanging is by rods and the room has spot lights.

Exhibiting: **[AW]** Artists should write to the Keeper of Exhibitions at Cartwright Hall, the gallery covers the costs of insurance, publicity, catalogue/card and transport, and shares the preview costs. It charges from 20% to 30% commission.

Access: **[S]** BR Keighley; Buses Bradford/Keighley, Skipton/Keighley

Kendal (Cumbria)

(NA) Map3 SD59

Abbot Hall Art Gallery

A gallery, information and heritage centre run by an independent trust. [VA,Cr,LA]

Address: Kirkland, Kendal, Cumbria LA9 5AL tel 0539 22464

Contact: Director V Slowe

Open: Mon-Fri 10.30-5, Sun 2-5; Sat 10.30-5 Spring bank holiday - 31 Oct

Policy: The gallery houses a permanent collection of 18th century paintings, furniture and decorative art, contemporary paintings and craft, and local history. The temporary exhibitions consist of touring exhibitions and work in co-ordinated themes by local, regional and national artists. The gallery also organises lectures, craft workshops and study sessions and houses a well-stocked craft shop.

Sales: Work sold; Credit card; Credit scheme

The Space: The total space for temporary exhibitions amounts to 235 square metres, amounting to 91m linear hanging space most of which is 3m high some 15m length is 1.9m high. Lighting is by fluorescents with UV filters and hanging is by rods. Maximum painting size is 1.9m square. The galleries are also used for lectures and workshops.

Exhibiting: **[AW][EF]** Send slides or photographs, CV in the first instance to the Director. Gallery covers insurance, publicity, list of exhibits, previews, catalogue/cards and charges 30% commission. Supports the principle of EPR.

Access: **[S][L]** On several bus routes; BR Oxenholme 20 mins, BR Kendal 10 mins; Car park; Public car park 2 mins

Brewery Arts Centre (Photographic Gallery)

A multi-media arts centre with a gallery devoted to showing photography. [Ph]

Address: Highgate, Kendal, Cumbria LA9 4HE tel 0539 25133

Contact: Photography & Exhibition Organiser Hugh Greenland

Open: 9am-11pm

Policy: The policy is to show a wide range of photographic work, with a preference for Northern artists and concerns. A small budget restricts a desire to initiate shows, so most are from the national touring circuit. There are also darkrooms and a small archive. Workshops, lectures and evening classes are organised.

Sales: Sales referred to exhibitor

The Space: Room 1 is 11x6.2m, room 23.7x1.5m with free-hanging boards giving a total of 46m linear hanging space. There is daylight and lighting track with spots and floods. Gallery plans available.

Exhibiting: **[AW][EF]** The gallery covers insurance, publicity, one-way transport and occasionally helps with catalogue/card, artists' expenses and supply of frames. The gallery charges 15% commission. Exhibitions for touring are sometimes commissioned. Supports the principle of EPR.

Access: **[X]** Bus routes; BR Kendal 10 mins; Car park

Brewery Arts Centre: Photo workshop run by John Blakemore

Keswick (Cumbria)

(NA) Map3 NY22

Keswick Museum & Art Gallery

A private museum administered by the Fitz Park Trust (Charity) with galleries devoted mainly to literature and natural history but with space for temporary exhibitions. [VA,Cr]

Address: Fitz Park, Keswick, Cumbria CA12 4NF tel 076 87 73263
Contact: Curator N Grundy
Open: Mon-Sat 10-12.30, 2-5 April 1 - Oct 31
Policy: The intention is to give local artists and makers a forum in which their work can be viewed.
Sales: Sales referred to exhibitor
The Space: The space is 18.2m long by 2.4m high. There are also two cabinets 1.8x1.2x0.6m.
Exhibiting: **[AW]** Applications are considered in mid-November for the following year. Send a CV and, if possible, samples of work to the Curator. Exhibitors hang their work and have to cover costs. The gallery charges 15% commission.

Lakeland Guild Craft Gallery

Craft shop showing work by members and others, also showing occasional temporary exhibitions. [Cr]

Address: First Floor, Lakeland Sheepskin Centre, Keswick, Cumbria tel 076 87 74636
Open: Mon-Sat 10-5.30
Policy: At time of going to press policy changing, please phone for details.
Sales: Work sold
Access: **[X]**

Kettering (Northamptonshire)

(EMA) Map5 SP87

Alfred East Gallery

A purpose-built and refurbished art gallery with a permanent collection of work by Sir Alfred East RA and work from 1950-1975. [VA,Cr,Ph]

Address: Sheep Street, Kettering, Northamptonshire NN15 7QX tel 0536 410333
Contact: Head of Leisure Services Kettering Borough Council, Municipal Offices, Bowling Green Road, Kettering, Northamptonshire
Open: Mon-Sat 10-5; closed bank holidays
Policy: The gallery shows mainly work by contemporary artists and makers in its two exhibition spaces, as well as historical exhibitions based on the collection. Exhibitions include touring shows, local art societies, group and solo shows. The gallery provides a cultural centre in Kettering, promoting an interest in the arts and crafts. Exhibitors are mainly regional and local artists and makers. The gallery also hosts evening meetings, lectures and art classes.
Sales: Work sold
The Space: Large gallery 12x7x7m with fluorescent and filtered daylight giving 36.25m linear hanging space. Small gallery 8x7x7m with fluorescent and filtered daylight, giving 28.34m linear space. Corridor 10.5x3x3m with artificial light, giving 16.76m linear hanging space. Vertical and desk-type showcases if needed.
Exhibiting: **[AW]** apply to the Curator. The gallery contributes to most costs and charges 10% on sales.
Access: **[F]** Town centre location; Car parks 3 mins; BR Kettering 7 min; bus station 1 min

Kettering Library

See Northamptonshire Libraries. [VA,Ph,Cr,Ar]

Address: Sheep Street, Kettering, Northamptonshire NN16 0AN tel 0536 512315
Contact: District Librarian D Bond
Open: Mon-Wed 9.30-8, Thurs, Fri 9.30-5, Sat 9.30-4
Sales: Work sold
The Space: The library has 17m linear hanging space around the walls with two free-standing cabinets 1.3x1.3x0.6m and one wall cabinet 1.3x1.3x0.3m. Close circuit television security, slide tape equipment available.
Exhibiting: **[AW]** District Librarian. Catalogues, publicity and insurance provided, transport between libraries arranged for touring exhibitions. Commission is 10%.
Access: **[F]** Town centre location next to public car park; Bus station 5 min; BR Kettering 5 min

Pots and Prints

A commercial gallery, exhibition space and studio specialising in ceramics and contemporary prints. [Pa,Pr,Ce]

Address: 12 High Street, Brigstock, Kettering, Northamptonshire NN14 3HA tel 0536 73353
Contact: Jenny Dunbar
Open: Tues, Wed, Fri 10-5, closed 1-2; Thurs 10-1; Sat 10-2
Policy: The exhibitions are shown in a 17th century house, part of which was a bakehouse. There is a changing display of ceramics, produced on the premises, and prints. Exhibitions usually feature the work of one or two artists or makers and run for three weeks.
Sales: Work sold
The Space: The shop, landing and living rooms are used for exhibitions and provide 50 square metres. Track lighting and a picture rail used is for hanging.
Exhibiting: **[AW]** Contact Jenny or Tony Dunbar. The gallery provides insurance, publicity, list of exhibits and preview. A 25% commission is charged on sales.
Access: **[X]** Brigstock lies off the A6116 Corby to Thrapston road

Kings Lynn (Norfolk)

(EA) Map5 TF62

Bircham Gallery

A commercial gallery founded in 1988 in main tourist area adjoining Sandringham estate. [VA,Ph,Ce]

Address: Great Bircham, Nr King's Lynn, Norfolk PE31 6QW tel 048 523 604
Contact: Christopher & Deborah Harrison

Open: Mon-Sat 2-6
Policy: Continous changing exhibitions of contemporary East Anglian art. The programme includes solo, group and thematic exhibitions, whilst space is reserved for a stock of work by gallery artists. Outdoor sculpture garden opening 1989.
Sales: Work sold; Credit card
The Space: One room 3.8x3.4x2.35m high with 10.75m linear hanging space, and one 4.2x4.3x2.2m high with 14m linear. Third room 4x4.2x2.2m high with 12.7m linear hanging space. Hanging from rails, track spotlighting, fixed spots and natural light. Unsuitable for large indoor works.
Exhibiting: [AW] Write or telephone for an appointment. Gallery pays for publicity, insurance and private view. Commission is 33.3%.
Access: [S] Own car park

Fermoy Art Galleries

Part of an arts complex with theatre, coffee shop, restaurant and museum, the centre for a large rural area. [VA,Ph,Cr]
Address: The Fermoy Centre, 27 King Street, King's Lynn, Norfolk PE30 1HA tel 0553 774725
Contact: Gallery Administrator Brion Clinkingbeard
Open: 10-5 April-Sept, 11-4 Oct-March
Policy: A series of mainly contemporary art and craft exhibitions, both solo and mixed.
Sales: Work sold; Credit card
The Space: One space is 13x5m with 21 adjustable spots and 22 down lights and another 12x5m with 27 adjustable spots. Air conditioning. Five glass display cases for crafts in foyer area. Gallery plans available.
Exhibiting: [AW] Apply to Gallery Administrator. Gallery pays insurance and publicity costs; space for hire on variable terms. Commission charged of between 20% and 33.3%.
Access: [U][T][S] Close to town centre; Car park except on market days

Bircham Gallery

Lynn Museum

Museum and art gallery run by Norfolk Museums Service.
Address: Market Street, Kings Lynn, Norfolk PE30 1NL tel 0553 775001
Contact: Curator E M James
Open: Mon-Sat 10-5; Closed bank holidays
Access: [F]

Kingswinford (W Midlands)

(WMA) Map4 SO88

Broadfield House Glass Museum

A specialist museum run by Dudley Art Gallery exhibiting a collection of English glass from the 18th century to the present day with an emphasis on 19th century Stourbridge glass. [Gl]
Address: Compton Drive, Kingswinford, W Midlands DY6 9NS tel 0384 273011
Contact: Curator Charles Hajdamach or Roger Dodsworth (Keeper of Glass and Fine Art)
Open: Tues-Fri,Sun 2-5. Sat 10-5; open bank holidays 2-5
Policy: The gallery initiates and tours exhibitions of contemporary glass, and historical exhibitions. Large selection of studio, Scandinavian and Dartington glass for sale. Two glass-making studios at rear of museum.
Sales: Work sold
The Space: Nine rooms of Contact the Curator.
Access: [U][T] Ground floor only

Kirkby (Merseyside)

(MA) Map3 SJ49

Kirkby Library

Exhibition area in centre of Kirkby Library, features work by local artists and community groups often accompanied by talks, videos or workshops. [Pa,Dr,Ph,Cr]
Address: Newtown Gardens, Kirkby, Merseyside L32 2RR tel 051 443 4287
Contact: Branch Librarian John Cochrane
Open: Mon,Tues,Thurs 10-7, Fri 10-5, Sat 10-1,2-5
Policy: *'Our aim is to exhibit art and craft work by local people, particularly those from Kirkby itself who also form the target audience. The exhibitions are used to encourage people to join groups and activities, and to promote the area and its leisure facilities.'* They have also taken shows from Merseyside Exhibitions. (See also Knowsley Libraries).
Sales: Sales referred to exhibitor
The Space: Display gallery, pegboard with six 1.8x1.2m Marler Haley exhibition boards and stands suitable for picture hooks or velcro, not screws. Lockable glass display case 2.3x1.1m.
Exhibiting: [AW] Apply anytime in writing, by telephone or in person to the Branch Librarian. The Library does not charge hire or commission but does not offer any facilities other than the equipment detailed above.
Access: [S] In Kirkby Town Centre on buses from

Liverpool and close to BR Kirkby; Ample car parking 3mins

Kirkby Lonsdale (Cumbria)

(NA) Map3 SD67

Coach House Contemporary Art

A commercial gallery promoting contemporary work by a selection of established and emerging artists. [VA]

Address: 9 Main Street, Kirkby Lonsdale, via Carnforth, Lancashire LA6 2AQ tel 052 42 71142

Contact: Director Ian Higginbotham

Open: Mon-Sat 9.30-5

Policy: The gallery shows solo and group exhibitions and aims to gain the confidence of the art collector. It operates a framing service.

Sales: Work sold; Credit scheme; Credit card

The Space: The first floor gallery is 7.7x3.6x2.8m giving 15.8m linear hanging space. The second floor gallery is 6.6x4.8x2.1m giving 21.7m linear hanging space. There is good natural light plus track system with spots, hanging is by sliding rail. Gallery plans available.

Exhibiting: [AW] Apply by post to the Director enclosing large format photographs or slides with index list and a cross-reference number on the top right hand corner of the slide, and CV. The gallery covers insurance, publicity, list of exhibits, preview and charges 40% commission.

Access: Adjacent to A65 Leeds to Lakes route; 5 miles east of M6 junction 36

Kirkleatham (Cleveland)

(NA) Map3 NZ52

Kirkleatham Old Hall Museum & Pavilion

Restored Queen Anne building housing display of local life and history and also with occasional temporary exhibitions.

Address: Kirkleatham, Redcar, Cleveland TS10 5NW tel 0642 479500

Contact: Curator P S Philo

Open: Tues-Sun 9-5 April-Sept; Tues-Sun 10-4 Oct-March; closed Good Friday, Dec 23- Jan 2 (Mon except bank holidays)

Policy: Exhibitions of work of local artists, makers and also on local subjects or themes closely related to Langbaurgh Borough Council area.

Access: [U][T] Ground floor. Buses to Kirkleatham 281,262,263

Kirton in Lindsey (S Humberside)

(LHA) Map3 SK99

Huntcliff Secondary School

An exhibition space showing small-scale touring exhibitions. [VA,Ph,Cr]

Address: Redbourne Mere, Kirton in Lindsey, S Humberside DN21 4NN tel 0652 648276

Contact: Head of Art S Lucas

Knaresborough (N Yorkshire)

(YA) Map3 SE35

Courthouse Museum (Little Gallery)

Municipal local history museum run by Harrogate Museums & Art Gallery Service which programmes monthly temporary exhibitions in the Little Gallery. [VA,Ph,Cr]

Address: Castle Grounds, Knaresborough, N Yorkshire HG5

Contact: Pat Clegg Curator, Royal Pump Room Museum, Royal Parade, Harrogate HG1 2RY tel 0423 503 340

Open: Mon-Sat 10-5

Policy: Exhibitions have local or regional connections and include solo shows by professional artists. See also Harrogate Art Gallery.

Sales: Work sold

Exhibiting: [AW] Apply in writing to the Curator. 15% commission is charged on sales and the gallery covers costs of insurance, publicity, preview, display, transport, mailing and catalogue. Booked until 1990 after which there may be a policy change.

Goldsborough Gallery

A new commercial gallery exhibiting work by artists and makers from the region and nationwide. [VA,Ph,Cr,Ce]

Address: 4 York Place, Knaresborough, N Yorkshire HG5 0AA tel 0423 865109

Contact: Lois Pertee

Open: Mon-Sat 10.30-5

Policy: The aim of the gallery is to promote greater public awareness of contemporary art and craft which will be reinforced with the future involvement of local educational establishments. *'We feel that a high standard of work is essential and pricing must be realistic but we do not specialise in any particular style, medium or characteristic'.* During its first year, the exhibitions were connected to a geographical theme and thematic shows will continue but the central theme will change. Nine exhibitions are mounted a year, each lasting for five weeks and most are group shows. The gallery is now able to accommodate solo exhibitions in Gallery 2.

Sales: Work sold; Credit card

The Space: There are two galleries 9.5x4.5x2.7m high and 4.5x3.3x2.5m high giving a total of 26m hanging space. Both rooms have a mixture of spots, floods, fluorescent and natural light and there is a garden area 60m square with wall, grass and paved area which will be available to show some works. In addition there are four melamine showcases with shelves and glass doors for the display of small works. Gallery plans are available.

Exhibiting: [AW] Artists and makers should send slides and CV to Lois Pertee, the gallery covers insurance, printing and mailing of publicity, list of exhibits and takes 33.3% commission.

Access: [F][X] BR Knaresborough 10 mins; Bus station 2 mins; Car park 2 mins

the gallery and playhouse will be closed for refurbishment July 1989-May 1990 when it will open as the new 'West Yorkshire Playhouse'.

Sales: Work sold; Credit card

The Space: The gallery is divided into two identical halves, each including a craft display cabinet with 11m linear hanging space and an additional 3m hanging rail. The craft cases are 1.5x1.2x0.3m high with movable glass shelves. All the space is spot lit and alarmed. The maximum length of work that can be accommodated is 2m. Gallery plans are available.

Exhibiting: [AW] Artists and makers should send slides to the House Manager, the gallery covers the cost of insurance only and takes 20% commision.

Access: [U][T] BR Leeds 15 mins; Buses 28,56,57,93; Car park 5 mins

Leeds Polytechnic Gallery

A gallery run by staff and students of the polytechnic which mounts changing exhibitions throughout the term time. [VA,Ph,Cr,LA]

Address: Woodhouse Lane, Leeds, W Yorkshire LS1 3HQ

Contact: Exhibition Organiser

Open: Mon-Fri 9.30-5, Sat 9-12 (term-time only)

Policy: At time of going to press the administration and management of the gallery was under review. A re-organisation taking place April 1989.

Access: [U][T]

Pavilion Photography Centre

A space devoted to the promotion of photography by women, with darkroom facilities available to encourage access to the art form. [Ph]

Address: 235 Woodhouse Lane, Leeds, W Yorkshire LS2 3AP tel 0532 431749

Contact: Workers Michelle, Jackie, Jude

Open: Wed-Fri 10-4

Policy: To promote women's art work with a view to questioning the power relationships within our society. The Pavilion has a particular commitment to working with women of all races, ages, sexual orientation and abilities.

The Space: The space provides 30m linear hanging space.

Exhibiting: [AW]

Access: [U][T]

University Gallery Leeds

The gallery was opened in 1970 in order to show the university's permanent collection of British drawings, paintings and prints and to provide a space within the university for contemporary art exhibitions. [Pa,Pr,Dr,Ph,Cr]

Address: Parkinson Building, Leeds, W Yorkshire LS2 9JT tel 0532 332779

Contact: Keeper of University Art Collection Hilary Diaper

Open: Mon-Fri 10-5 (Term-time only)

Policy: A large amount of the space is now devoted to the display of the university's own collection through regular changing exhibitions. The gallery also mounts exhibitions from outside sources and it *'encourages local artists and makers to apply but less space will be available for contemporary art exhibitions'.* There are five exhibitions a year each lasting for a month.

Sales: Sales referred to exhibitor

The Space: There are three-interconnecting galleries one 8.7x8.2x2.2m high and two 5.9x8.2x2.5m high, hanging is by rod system or mirror plating and the gallery is spot lit. Work shown is limited in size by the doorways which are of 1.3x2m high and heavy works are difficult because of the stair access. There are two cases for three-dimensional objects.

Exhibiting: [AW][EF] Artists and makers should apply in writing to Hilary Diaper 18 months in advance. The gallery covers the costs of printing of publicity, list of exhibits, preview costs, mailing out publicity and catalogue/card. It supports the principle of EPR.

Access: [L] BR Leeds 15 mins; Bus routes 1,28,56,57,93; Car park 5 mins

Yorkshire Dance Centre

The centre provides 'community classes' open to the public, in all types of dance for people of all ages and all levels of ability and has an exhibition space. [VA,Ph]

Address: 3 St Peter's Buildings, St Peter's Square, Leeds, W Yorkshire LS9 8AH tel 0532 426066

Contact: Director Ruth Till

Open: Mon-Fri 9-10pm (term-time only), Mon-Fri 9-5, Sat & Sun 10-4

Policy: There is a small exhibition space within the centre which, for the past year, has been used for exhibitions by local artists. The criteria for the exhibitions is that they must all carry a *'dance theme'* - although the interpretation is left very wide. Over the past year, four mixed, group and one-person contemporary art exhibitions have been organised each lasting for two months. The contents of the exhibitions betray the dance specialisation and have included an exhibition of work by local artists, based on sketches done at the dance centre, a group exhibition of work by Leeds Polytechnic students, a photographic exhibition of a local mime artist and an exhibition of dance prints and cards. The space is also used for dancing and warming up and as a social venue.

Sales: Work sold

Exhibiting: [AW] Send slides and CV to Ruth Till and Alison Owen.

Access: [X] Access is being planned for the future BR Leeds 10 mins; Bus station 1 min; Car park 1 min

Yorkshire Post Newspaper Building (Foyer)

Occasional exhibitions in Yorkshire Post building. [VA,Ph,Cr]

Address: PO Box 168, Wellington Street, Leeds, W Yorkshire LS2 1RF tel 0532 432701 ext 514

Contact: Promotions and Publicity Assistant Paul Bolton

Open: Mon-Fri 9-5, Sat 9-12

Policy: *'Selection is by invitation only'.*

The Space: An area of 67 square metres on the ground floor of the building, windowed on three sides to a height of 12m. Exhibitions have to be free-stranding and must incorporate their own lighting.

Leek (Staffordshire)

(WMA) Map4 SJ95

Leek Art Gallery

A municipal art gallery run by Staffordshire Moorlands District Council, with a small permanent collection of local scenes. [Pa]

Address: Nicholson Institute, Stockwell Street, Leek, Staffordshire ST13 6HQ tel 0538 399181

Contact: Assistant Secretary G N Hyde, Moorlands House, Stockwell Street, Leek ST13 6HQ

Open: Tues,Wed,Fri 1-5, Sat 10-12 April-Sept, other times by appointment

Policy: The four exhibitions a year are usually group shows by local societies or the college of further education.

Sales: Sales referred to exhibitor

Exhibiting: [AW] Contact the Assistant Secretary. All exhibition costs are met by the artist, a 10% commission is charged on sales.

Access: [X] Bus 218 from Keele (Stoke-on-Trent); Public car park 5 mins walk

Leicester (Leicestershire)

(EMA) Map5 SK50

City Gallery

A gallery operated by Leicester City Council Recreation & Arts Department Community Arts Department. [VA,Ph,Cr]

Address: 90 Granby Street, Leicester LE1 6FB tel 0533 549922 ext 7345

Contact: Visual Arts Officer Rosie Kearton

Open: Tues - Fri 11-6, Sat 10-4

Policy: Opening April 1989 and replacing the Loseby Gallery, it will provide a platform for showing contemporary art and craft exhibitions with a total of 16 a year and an exhibition space for hire. Touring exhibitions will be initiated and there will be an education, workshops and residency programme.

Sales: Work sold

The Space: Gallery one is the permanent craft gallery with 112 square metres and 8m linear hanging space plus permanent showcases and controlled lighting. Gallery two has 560 square metres and 36.5 m linear hanging space. Gallery three upstairs has 130 square metres and 20m linear hanging space with a flexible hanging system and controlled lighting.

Exhibiting: [AW] Slides to the Visual Arts Officer. A minimum of 20% commission is charged on sales. The gallery meets the costs of promoted exhibitions. Hire of gallery three is £60 per week including 50 invitation cards and 25 poster blanks for over-printing.

Access: [F] to ground-floor galleries. Town centre location; BR Leicester 2 mins; Bus station 10 mins

City Gallery Touring Exhibitions

The touring service funded by the City Council and East Midlands Arts provides exhibitions for 16 non-gallery venues in Leicester. The venues are neighbourhood centres, hospitals and theatres. The exhibitions are usually small solo exhibitions and shown for up to two months in each venue. Local and regional artists and makers are sought to provide material for the exhibitions. [Pa,Pr,Dr,Ph]

Address: 90 Granby Street, Leicester LE1 6FB

Contact: Touring Exhibition Organiser

Open: Most venues open Mon-Fri 10-5

Policy: See City Gallery.

Sales: Sales referred to exhibitor

The Space: Various sizes and locations. Two craft showcases with video facility at two venues.

Exhibiting: [AW] Applications should be sent to the Touring Exhibition Organiser.

Craft Gallery

A commercial craft gallery and shop. [Cr]

Address: 54 London Road, Leicester LE2 0QD tel 0533 550773

Contact: Aldona Grodecka

Open: Mon-Sat 9-5

Policy: The gallery has a wide range of work by different makers and occasional exhibitions by individual makers. The changing display includes pottery, wood, jewellery and glass.

Sales: Work sold; Credit card

The Space: The centre of the shop is used for exhibitions. A display table 2x1m is used with spots and natural light.

Exhibiting: [AW] Contact Aldona Grodecka with slides and CV.

Access: [F] BR Leicester 2 mins; On street parking

East Midlands Shape

An independent organisation working with people who do not have access to the existing arts provision. [VA,Ph,Cr,LA]

Address: 27a Belvoir Street, Leicester LE1 6SL tel 0533 552933

Contact: Project Co-ordinator Steve Morris

Open: Various

Policy: *'Work is done in hospitals, prisons, day centres etc, in both visual arts and the performing arts'.* Exhibitions are organised alongside projects in various venues. Shape also organises an annual Prints for Hospitals competition drawing on the talents of fine art students from local colleges and polytechnics.

The Space: Various spaces used.

Exhibiting: For information on future projects contact Steve Morris.

Access: Belvoir Street is in the city centre; 5 mins bus station and BR Leicester

Gadsby Gallery

A commercial gallery founded in 1902. [VA]

Address: 22 Market Place, Leicester LE1 5GF tel 0533 22410/57792

Contact: Manager Michael Smith
Open: Mon-Sat 9-5
Policy: The Gadsby shows *'gallery and internationally-known artists', and work by local artists. Artists materials are on sale and there is a framing and restoration service.'*
Sales: Work sold

Groby Community College

Exhibition spaces in many of the community colleges are used by local and regional artists. Workshops, placements and residencies are organised. See Leicestershire Education Authority. [VA,Ph,Cr]

Address: Design Department, Groby Community College, Ratby Road, Groby, Leicester LE6 0GE tel 0533 879 921
Contact: Jon Whitten
Open: Mon-Thurs 9am-10pm, Fri 9-3.10
Policy: The majority of the exhibition space within the college is used for student work. There are occasional small exhibitions of work by local artists and a twice yearly arts and crafts fair. The college has an art collection on permanent display.
Sales: Work sold where appropriate
The Space: Four main areas of varying sizes.
Exhibiting: **[AW]** Write to Jon Whitten giving details of work. Commission and fees negotiable.
Access: **[U][T]** Buses from Leicester

Leicestershire Education Authority

Exhibition spaces in many of the community colleges are used by local and regional artists. Workshops, placements and residencies are organised. [VA,Ph,Cr]

Address: Education Department, Leicestershire County Council, County Hall, Glenfield, Leicester LE3 8RF tel 0533 317751
Contact: Arts Officer David Hughes
Policy: Exhibition facilities at Earl Shilton College, John Ellis College, Bosworth College, Groby Community College, Burleigh College, Rawlins College, Hindleys Community College, Moat Community College also at Coalville Community College, Countesthorpe Community College and Guthlaxton Community College. See separate entries for Groby Community College (Leicester) and Rawlins School & Community College (Quorn).
The Space: Various.
Exhibiting: For information contact the Head of Art at individual colleges or David Hughes at County Hall.

Leicester Polytechnic (Kimberlin Hall)

A purpose-built gallery run by Leicester Polytechnic situated in the library building. [VA,Cr,Ph,Ar,De,LA]

Address: Leicester Polytechnic, Mill Lane, Leicester LE1 9BH tel 0533 551551 ext 2684
Contact: Exhibition Organiser Daphne Jones
Open: Mon-Fri 10-5, Sat 10-1
Policy: A wide range of exhibitions for the student community and general public. The exhibitions are drawn from a number of regional and national sources, the majority of shows are group or mixed exhibitions.
Sales: Work sold; Sales referred to exhibitor
The Space: The gallery has an area of 265 square metres, giving 58.5m linear hanging space. Screens are available to provide extra wall space, and some showcases are available. Lighting is by floodlights. Gallery plans available.
Exhibiting: **[AW]** Slides and CV should be sent to the Exhibition Organiser. The gallery provides insurance, publicity, mailing, list of exhibits and preview. It occasionally provides transport. A commission of 25% is charged on sales.
Access: **[U][T][S]** 5 mins city centre buses and public car parks

Leicester Print Workshop

The print workshop is part of the Knighton Lane Artists Group and provides facilities and instruction for etching and relief printing. [Pr]

Address: 68 Knighton Lane, Leicester LE2 8BR tel 0533 830587
Contact: Sue Emsley
Open: Ring for details
Policy: Exhibitions are organised to show individual members' work, or mixed shows of members' work. Exhibitions are open to the public and a workshop or course is usually run along with the show.
Sales: Work sold; Sales referred to exhibitor
The Space: 12m linear showing space is available with good natural light.
Access: **[F][X]** Close to Leicestershire County Cricket ground

Leicester Royal Infirmary

An exhibition space in a major general hospital with a policy of purchasing and commissioning works of art. [Pa,Pr,Dr,Ph]

Address: Infirmary Square, Leicester LE1 5WW
Contact: David Wright, City Gallery Arts Trust, The Great Barn, Parklands, Great Linford, Milton Keynes, MK14 5DZ tel 0908 606791
Open: Daily 9-6
Policy: The programme is predominantly solo exhibitions, and is used to *'introduce the contemporary arts to a new audience through the organisation of exhibitions by professional regional artists in a major public building visited yearly by one million people'.*
Sales: Work sold
The Space: At time of going to press the space was being redeveloped, reopening 1989.
Exhibiting: **[AW]** Contact David Wright. Insurance, transport, list of exhibits, display and artists' expenses are provided.
Access: **[U][T][L]** City centre location close to bus station and BR Leicester

Leicestershire Libraries & Information Service

Display areas in libraries throughout the county, showing a wide range of work, usually by local artists and makers. [Pa,Pr,Dr,Ph,Cr,LA]

Address: Thames Tower, Navigation Street, Leicester

LE1 3TZ tel 0533 538921 ext 3532
Contact: Marketing Officer
Open: Various
Policy: The library and information service aims to provide a range of promotional and display work to publicise the service, the work of local community groups and artists work. Programmes of talks are occasionally tied in with a display, and some travelling displays are shown.
The Space: Most major libraries have 4x2m spaces available, some with special lighting.
Exhibiting: **[AW]** Applications should be made six months in advance to the Marketing Officer. The artist is responsible for exhibition costs.
Access: Various

Leicestershire Museum & Art Gallery

Leicestershire Museums and Records Service runs a number of specialist and regional museums and the Leicester Museum and Art Gallery has extensive collections of fine art, both historical and contemporary. [VA,Ph,Cr]

Address: 96 New Walk, Leicester LE1 6TD tel 0533 554100
Contact: Director P J Boylan
Open: Mon-Sat 10.30-5.30, Sun 2-5.30
Policy: Temporary exhibitions tend to be large researched shows of national significance and some large touring exhibitions from national museums and art galleries. Its programme includes multi-cultural events and educational activities.
The Space: 1140 square metres of space in seven galleries with environmental controls and high-level security.
Exhibiting: Exhibitions are arranged by invitation.
Access: **[U][T]** Located in the town centre close to the bus station and BR Leicester

Picture House

The specially-converted photography gallery is located within a teachers' resource centre where a collection of contemporary British photography is housed. [Ph]

Picture House: Tom Gilson presenting his work in the main gallery (Photo: Roger Bradley)

Address: 113 Princess Road East, Leicester LE1 7LA tel 0533 549083
Contact: Roger Bradley & Daiv Sizer
Open: Mon-Fri 9-5; some evenings during term-time
Policy: The gallery provides a major focal point for photography in the East Midlands. The exhibitions range from retrospectives of national figures to small exhibitions introducing the work of new young photographers. A range of educational activities and events are programmed alongside the exhibitions. Postcards are sold and a library of magazines and books is available to visitors. Darkrooms are used for practical workshops. No work of a sexist, racist or extreme political nature is shown.
Sales: Work sold
The Space: The main gallery provides 35m linear hanging space with direct fixing, fluorescent and natural light. The staircase gallery provides 8m linear hanging space with a hanging rail, fluorescent and natural light. Gallery plans available.
Exhibiting: **[AW][EF]** Applications should be sent to Roger or Daiv who present them to a monthly advisory group meeting. Personal callers are welcome by appointment. A commission of 10% is charged on sales. The gallery provides insurance, printing, publicity, transport, list of exhibits, and has a stock of frames for use in the gallery. Exhibition fee paid for main gallery exhibitions only.
Access: **[U][T][X]** Own car park; BR Leicester 5 mins

Vaughan College

A gallery housed in the University of Leicester department of Adult Education. [VA]

Address: St Nicholas Circle, Leicester LE1 4LB tel 0533 522454
Contact: Alan Caine
Open: Mon-Fri 9.30-9.30
Policy: The gallery concentrates on solo exhibitions that are *'Serious work with an individual stamp'*. All the exhibitions are professionally presented, and are *'work of quality and originality'*.
Sales: Work sold
The Space: Several spaces within the college totalling 50m with spot and fluorescent lights. Some display boards available.
Exhibiting: **[AW]** The exhibition committee meets two or three times a year. All costs are the responsibility of the artist. A 15% commission is charged on sales.
Access: **[F]** City centre location

Whiteman Gallery

A commercial gallery, opened October 1988, promoting 'quality works of art to companies, public bodies and collectors'. [VA,Ph]

Address: 12-14 Great Central Street, Leicester LE1 4JT tel 0533 559711
Contact: Duncan Whiteman, Magazine Business Centre, 11 Newarke Street, Leicester LE1 5SS
Open: Mon-Fri 10-5, Sat 11-4, Sun by appointment
Policy: The gallery promotes some 30 artists and carries a stock of prints and a slide library. It provides a full service including *'advice on purchase, special*

commissions, and on-site presentation'. The artists are professional, and at least five years out of college. Talks, seminars, lunches, business openings and other events are arranged.
Sales: Work sold; Credit card
The Space: First floor and second floor both 15x6.5m including storage and office space and very well lit.
Exhibiting: [AW] By letter or telephone to arrange an appointment. Insurance, publicity, preview, list of exhibits, catalogue/card provided by the gallery. Gallery can be hired at £150-£200 a week.
Access: [X] Close to city centre

Leigh (Greater Manchester)

(NWA) Map3 SJ69

Turnpike Gallery

The gallery runs a programme of temporary exhibitions including major touring shows and local exhibitions and also has a small collection of contemporary prints. See also Metropolitan Borough of Wigan. [VA]
Address: Leigh Library Centre, Civic Square, Leigh, Greater Manchester WN7 1EB tel 0942 679 407
Contact: Gallery Manager S O'Brien
Open: Mon-Fri 10-5.30, Wed 10-5, Sat 10-3
Sales: Work sold
The Space: The gallery is about 400 metres square with 70m linear hanging space, direct fixing and spots and fluorescent lights.
Exhibiting: [AW] 25% commission is charged and the gallery meets all exhibition expenses.

Leighton Buzzard (Bedfordshire)

(EA) Map7 SP92

Leighton Buzzard Library & Arts Centre

Public library and arts centre opened in 1979. A theatre, bar lounge and meeting rooms are on the top floor above the library, and the gallery is on ground and first floors. [VA,Ph,Cr]
Address: Lake Street, Leighton Buzzard, Bedfordshire LU7 8RX tel 0525 378310/371788
Contact: Arts Centre Manager Stuart Antrobus
Open: Mon 11-7, Tues-Fri 9.30-7, Sat 9-4
Policy: A programme of monthly exhibitions by local, regional and national artists, plus touring exhibitions. Associated workshops, talks, private views and residencies are occasionally arranged.
The Space: The library exhibition space is 42 square metres with 22m linear hanging space. Spots and fluorescents.
Exhibiting: [AW] Artists meet all expenses. Hanging charge on all 'saleable items', commission charged.
Access: [F]

Letchworth (Hertfordshire)

(EA) Map7 TL23

Letchworth Museum

Municipal museum and gallery. [VA,Ph,Cr]
Address: Broadway, Letchworth, Hertfordshire SG6 3PF tel 0462 685657
Contact: Curator Anna Mercer
Open: Mon-Sat 10-5; Closed bank holidays
Policy: *'Most of the work shown is by local artists, both amateur and professional, we interpret 'local'* very broadly and consider artists from outside the immediate area.' Exhibitions last between three and four weeks and there are occasional workshops for schools and the public.
Sales: Work sold
The Space: 12x6x2.5m high with linear hanging space of 32m. Hanging is by adjustable rods and hooks from rail. Adjustable track lighting. Some display cases, screens abd stands available.
Exhibiting: [AW] By letter to the Curator. EPR under consideration. Works need to be able to negotiate a flight of steps. Commission charged is 20% plus VAT.
Access: [X] Local buses; BR Letchworth 10mins; Car park 5mins; Car park for delivery of work

Lewes (E Sussex)

(SEA) Map7 TQ41

Craftwork

Small craft gallery situated in a crafts centre by West Street car park. [Cr,Pr]
Address: The Old Needlemakers, West Street, Lewes, E Sussex BN7 2NZ tel 027 347 5433
Contact: Owner Michael Pryke
Open: Mon-Sat 10-5; closed Sun & bank holidays
Policy: Craftwork aims to sell high quality work. Small items, especially in blown glass and wood are always in stock, also etchings and prints, candles and cards.
Sales: Work sold
The Space: Limited wall and display space.
Exhibiting: [AW] Write or ring for appointment.
Access: [S] Southdown buses; British Rail Lewes 10 mins walk

Leyburn (N Yorkshire)

(YA) Map3 SE19

Chandler Gallery

A commercial gallery with a permanent collection of prints and paintings. [Pa,Pr,Dr,Cr,Sc]
Address: 8 Commercial Square, Leyburn, N Yorkshire DL8 5BP tel 0969 23676
Contact: Owner Charles Chandler
Open: Mon-Sat 9-5, Wed 9-1 (April-Dec); Sun 11-4 (Jul-Sept)
Policy: There are two rooms, one houses a permanent display and the other has a regularly changing programme of five exhibitions a year, each lasting for three weeks. It is the intention of the organisers that the

majority of exhibitions in the future will be solo shows.
Sales: Work sold; Credit card; Credit scheme
The Space: The exhibition room of 2.9x5.9m has centre flood lighting. Paintings are hung by grooved battens and cup-hoods screwed into the frames or by picture hooks.
Exhibiting: [AW] Artists and makers should write sending slides or bring their work to the gallery. The gallery will cover the costs of insurance, printing of publicity, list of exhibits, preview costs, display (not framing) mailing out of publicity. The gallery takes 30% commission on works sold from the exhibition section and 25% on works from the permanent display.
Access: [X] Bus routes from Bedale, Richmond and Hawes; Car park 1 min

Old School Arts Workshop

An artist-run gallery with exhibitions changing every six weeks. [VA]
Address: Middleham, Leyburn, N Yorkshire DL8 4QC tel 0969 23056
Contact: Peter Hibbard
Open: Mon-Fri 10-5
Policy: The aim is to show *'the widest possible range of professional work in the visual arts'*, the gallery also functions as a residential study centre for sculpture and other visual arts.
The Space: A main exhibition space of 135m square with 19m linear hanging space with hanging by rail with spots and natural lighting.
Exhibiting: [AW] The gallery covers costs of insurance, mailing, catalogue and preview and shares the costs of transport and publicity. Commission is 25% on works sold.

Leyland (Lancashire)

(NWA) Map3 SD52

South Ribble Museum & Exhibition Centre

The Old Grammar School was restored by South Ribble Borough Council in 1977 and now houses an art gallery and the Borough's museum collection. [Pa,Pr,Dr,Ph,Cr]
Address: The Old Grammar School, Church Road, Leyland, Lancashire PR4 tel 0772 422041
Contact: Dr David Hunt
Open: Tues, Fri 10-4, Thurs 1-4, Sat 10-1
Policy: The gallery's policy is *'to provide a forum for local artists, especially amateurs, to enable them to display their work to a larger audience.'* The gallery is also used for local history and general interest displays.
Sales: Work sold; Credit card
The Space: The exhibition space, formerly a school room, has 50m linear hanging space and has flexible lighting and screen systems.
Exhibiting: [AW] Applications should be sent to the Custodian. The gallery pays towards printing and a list of exhibits. 20% Commission is taken on sales. The space is available for hire.
Access: [X] BR Leyland 15 mins; Town centre and bus stop 3 mins

Lichfield (Staffordshire)

(WMA) Map5 SK01

Greyfriars Gallery

A commercial gallery with an emphasis on living artists. [Pa,Pr]
Address: The Old Stables, Friars Alley, Lichfield, Staffordshire WS13 9PW tel 0543 250379
Contact: Brian & Mary Murray
Open: Tues-Sun 10-6
Policy: *'Aim to attract the 'discerning'* art buyer who will appreciate quality work both for pleasure and investment, but who perhaps cannot afford an *'old master'.'*
Sales: Work sold; Credit card; Credit scheme
The Space: Two rooms 9x5x3m high and 4x4x2m high with natural and track lighting with a patio garden area of about 80 square metres. Gallery plans available.
Exhibiting [AW] Contact Mary Murray. Gallery can be hired at £300 per week or agreed commission rate. Gallery covers insurance, printing of publicity, list of exhibits and preview. Commission is 33.3%.
Access: [F] BR Lichfield 5 mins; Bus station 5 mins; Car park adjacent

Lichfield Arts Centre

A small arts centre run by Lichfield District Arts Association for professional and amateur productions, events and exhibitions. [Pa,Pr,Dr,Ph]
Address: Bird Street, Lichfield, Staffordshire WS13 6PR tel 0543 262223
Contact: Kate Broom tel 0543 254068
Open: Mon-Fri 10.30-2.30,Sat 10.30-2.30
Policy: The exhibitions are drawn from local and regional sources. Usually half the exhibitions are of professional work and occasional workshops and events are arranged. The arts centre hopes to *'encourage higher standards by exhibiting work from outside the immediate area'* and increase public involvement and awareness of the visual arts.
Sales: Work sold
The Space: The gallery has 19m linear wall space and tungsten spotlights.
Exhibiting: [AW] Applications should be made to the Gallery Manager. The arts centre provides a preview and a list of exhibits.
Access: [S] Next to Minster Pond; BR Lichfield 10 mins; Public car park opposite

Lichfield Library Art Gallery

The gallery is housed upstairs from the library, and is administered by Staffordshire Libraries, Arts and Archives Department. [VA,Ph,Cr]
Address: Bird Street, Lichfield, Staffordshire WS13 6PN tel 0543 262177
Contact: Principal Area Librarian
Open: Mon,Tues,Thurs,Fri 10-6.30, Wed 10-5, Sat 9.30-1
Policy: Exhibitions are mostly from local sources, with special exhibitions during the Lichfield Festival.
Sales: Sales referred to exhibitor
The Space: Approximately 20m linear hanging space.

Exhibiting: [AW] Contact the Principal Area Librarian. The exhibitor is responsible for all exhibition costs.
Access: [X] Close to city centre and cathedral, bus station; BR Lichfield Town 15 mins

Lincoln (Lincolnshire)

(LHA) Map5 SK97

ARC Gallery

A commercial outlet, established in 1988, specialising in all areas of designer crafts. [Cr]

Address: 38/39 Bailgate, Lincoln LN1 3AP tel 0522 42717
Open: Tues-Sat 10-6, Sun 2-6
Policy: ARC Gallery sells and displays ceramics, glass, jewellery, knitware, leatherware and textiles by both regional and national makers.
Sales: Work sold; Credit card

Bishop Grosseteste College

A gallery in the college entrance showing about nine exhibitions are held a year changing monthly excepting April, July and August. [VA,Ph,Cr]

Address: Newport, Lincoln LN1 3DY tel 0522 27347
Contact: Head of the Art Centre
Open: Daily 9-9
The Space: Approximately 30m hanging space on hessian-covered Sundeala boards with ceiling-mounted track lighting.
Exhibiting: [AW] to the Head of Art Centre. Gallery pays for insurance, printing and mailing of publicity and may help with transport. Exhibitions are by invitation and application and *'we are pleased to receive applications from artists wishing to exhibit'*.

Branston Comprehensive School & Community College

The exhibition space is in the concert hall of the school which runs evening adult education classes and has an active Friends organisation. [VA,Ph,Cr,LA]

Address: Station Road, Branston, Lincoln, Lincolnshire LN4 1LH tel 0522 791 279
Contact: P. Hancocks
Open: 8.30-5 (school hours) & 7.30-9.30 (evening classes); Weekends 12-6
Policy: Weekend, one-week and one-month exhibitions of work by local artists, students and school pupils are held, mainly for the population of Branston and nearby villages. The school would like to develop the gallery space further, with the possibility of hiring it out.
Sales: Work sold.
The Space: The concert hall is 20x13m with 33m linear hanging space and 20 plywood screens. The Klemclip lighting system is plugged into the stage lighting controlled by a central light box. Gallery plans available.
Exhibiting: Apply in the first instance to the School Bursar. Insurance, publicity, list of exhibits, catalogue/card are provided by the gallery. Maximum dimensions of work: 2x1m. Commission is 15%.
Access: [F] Car parking on site; Bus stop 100m away

City School

A gallery founded in 1984 in a secondary school. [Pa,Ph]

Address: Skellingthorpe Road, Lincoln LN6 0EP tel 0522 683664
Contact: Headmaster P J Wilde
Open: Mon-Fri 9.30-6
Policy: The school has a special interest in photography and in exhibiting work by young people from overseas countries. The actual programme of around six exhibitions, mainly solo, is seen by 1000 pupils at school and by many visitors who attend the school for concerts, plays and dance productions.
Sales: Work sold
The Space: The two spaces are18x18m and 9x9m, with security system. Plans available.
Exhibiting: [AW] To the Headmaster at any time. Exhibition costs are negotiable.
Access: [F]

Edward King House

Large, light, airy first floor room, situated in the Old Palace, former residence of the Bishops of Lincoln.

Address: The Old Palace LN2 1PU tel 0522 27887
Contact: Warden Canon Rex Davis
Open: The house is open daily 8-10 but access to gallery is by arrangement
Policy: *'The gallery is open to artists in the process of establishing themselves who would like a lengthy (2-3 months) showing of their work in a secure and warm environment.'*
The Space: Gallery 6.3x15m with variable hanging space for 14 frames 1x0.8m.
Exhibiting: [AW] Artists should contact the Warden. Insurance, some printing costs covered. 20% commission.
Access: [X] BR Lincoln 10 mins; Car park; Next to Lincoln Cathedral

Harding House

The gallery forms part of Harding House Art Trust, a registered charity whose main aim is to provide studio space and promote arts particularly for young unestablished artists. [VA,Ph,LA]

Address: Steep Hill, Lincoln LN2 1LT tel 38456
Contact: Gallery Worker Martin Cairn
Policy: The gallery promotes regionally-based artists and makers, particularly young unestablished artists. *'There is no house style and decisions are made according to the quality of the work. Large work is welcome because of the height of the building. We see ourselves as providing an important alternative showing space in the region'.*
Sales: Work sold
The Space: 10x4.5x5m with approximately 20m wall hanging space and 13m hanging space on screens. Lighting by ten overhead spotlights and daylight with blackout facility plans available. The gallery is also used for readings, films and events.
Exhibiting: [AW][EF] Apply to Programme Committee by December each year with slides and or photographs and CV. Decisions are made after Christmas for the

programme twelve months ahead. The gallery pays for insurance, printing and mailing of publicity and catalogue. The gallery supports the principle of EPR.
Access: [S][X] BR Lincoln Central 10 mins; Public car parks 3 mins

LCAD Gallery

The gallery which predominantly shows contemporary art and craft, is part of Lincolnshire College of Art and Design. [Pa,Pr,Dr,Ph,Cr,De,LA]
Address: Lincolnshire College of Art & Design, Greestone Centre, Lindum Road, Lincoln LN2 1NP tel 0522 512912
Contact: Exhibitions Organiser Amanda Wadsley
Open: Mon-Fri 9-6. Closed Good Friday, Christmas Day and Boxing Day
Policy: The policy of this gallery is *'To encourage greater public awareness and understanding of the visual arts, craft and design through a broad range of temporary exhibitions with a bias towards work by contemporary artists, makers and designers. It has established a programme of exhibitions which are of interest to both the general public and the college, and actively promotes the work of both established and less well-known artists and makers, with regional, national and international reputations, with an emphasis on younger artists and makers'.* It is keen to broaden both the public's and college's enjoyment of the above through a lively prgramme of educational and interpretive events and to create an opportunity for direct contact and dialogue between artist and public. The gallery also reaches new audiences through outreach projects and touring of medium and small-scale exhibitions to exhibition centres and non-gallery venues. There is a permanent collection of contemporary paintings, prints, drawings, photographs, textiles and ceramics.
Sales: Work sold
The Space: The gallery is 14.5x7.5x2.5m with 85m of hanging space, spotlights, globe fittings and daylight. Work secured by mirror plates or similar to walls and panels.
Exhibiting: [AW][EF] To Exhibitions Organiser at the college with six slides or photographs and CV, plus statement about work or brief outline of proposed project. Exhibition programme meetings held twice each year. Gallery pays for insurance, printing and mailing of publicity, preview costs, display costs, transport, catalogue and artists' expenses. Gallery supports EPR in principle. Commission on sales 25%.
Access: [X] BR Lincoln Central 15 mins; Bus station 10 mins; Car park 2 mins walk

Lincolnshire County Council, Recreational Services, Libraries/Archives

Exhibition spaces at Lincoln, Stamford, Grantham, Boston, Spalding, Gainsborough and Sleaford libraries. See separate entry for Grantham Public Library.
Address: Brayford House, Lucy Tower Street, Lincoln LN1 1XN tel 0522 33541
Contact: Assistant Director R M Lyle
Open: Mon-Thurs 9-5 Fri 9-4.30
Exhibiting: [AW] Private exhibitors pay £10 per week hire fee, societies are exempt from this charge. Libraries will insure work for the latter but not for individuals.

Museum of Lincolnshire Life

Gallery houses displays of local history material and regular temporary exhibitions.
Address: The Old Barracks, Burton Road, Lincoln LN1 tel 0522 28448
Contact: Keeper of Social History Rodney Cousins
Open: Mon-Sat 10-5.30 Sun 2-5; Sun 10-5.30 May-September
Policy: 4-5 temporary exhibitions per year showing the widest range of Social History, mainly with local flavour, but from time to time will accept national or international material.
Sales: Work sold
The Space: Exhibition Gallery is 11x8m with natural 19th century brick finish, brick vaulted ceiling. Natural light can be excluded. Display boards and cases available. Security system.
Exhibiting: [AW] Applications to the Keeper. Commission agreed with Museum.
Access: [U][T]

Usher Gallery

Municipal gallery funded by Lincolnshire County Council. [VA,Ph,Cr,De,LA]
Address: Lindum Road LN2 1NN tel 0522 27980
Contact: Assistant Keeper/Exhibition Officer Judith Robinson/Amanda Wadsley
Open: Mon-Sat 10-5.30, Sun 2.30-5, closed Christmas Day, Boxing Day and Good Friday
Policy: The policy of the gallery is *'To encourage greater public awareness and understanding of the visual arts, crafts and design through a broad range of temporary exhibitions of an historical and contemporary nature and through the use of permanent collections and to actively promote the work of both established and less well-known artists with regional, national and international reputations. The gallery runs a lively programme of educational and interpretative events and reaches new audiences through outreach projects and the touring of large, medium and small-scale exhibitions.'* Permanent collection includes major works by Peter de Wint (1784-1849); topographical paintings of Lincolnshire; 19th century sculpture and 20th century paintings; James Ward Usher Bequest of clocks, watches, portrait miniatures, porcelain and silver; early English glass and Pinxton and Torksey porcelain.
Sales: Work sold
The Space: Three temporary exhibition galleries with 27m linear, 42m linear and 41m linear hanging space. Plans available. Work mirror-plated to walls or similar. Flexible track systems with spotlights plus skylights in one gallery. Controlled temperature and humidity in all galleries. UV filters and window blinds.
Exhibiting: [AW][EF] To Assistant Keeper with six slides or photographs, CV and brief statement of project, programme meetings are held quarterly. Gallery pays for insurance, printing and mailing of publicity, preview

costs, display costs, transport, catalogue and artists' expenses. Gallery supports EPR in principle. Commission on sales 25%.
Access: **[U][T][L]** 2 steps ramp available. BR Lincoln Central 15 mins; City bus station 10 mins; Public car park adjacent

Liverpool (Merseyside)

(MA) Map3 SJ39

Acorn Gallery

Independent artist-run gallery showing contemporary work, also has café, studio and shop spaces and produces quarterly Artspool magazine. [VA,Ph,Pr,Cr]

Address: Newington, Liverpool, Merseyside L1 4ED tel 051 709 5423
Contact: Janine Pinion
Open: Mon-Sat 10-5
Policy: The gallery shows monthly exhibitions of work by living artists, and also holds two open exhibitions which span July/August, December/January.
Sales: Work sold; Credit card; Credit scheme
The Space: Wall space 3m high 40m long with picture rail and spotlights. Floor space 10mx7m with plinths, 1mx2m covered cabinet and variety of display equipment.
Exhibiting: **[AW]** Slides and CV to Janine Pinion. Exhibition space hired. NAA recommended contracts used. Sponsorship and regional arts association support sought.
Access: **[X]** By prior arrangement City Centre buses 2 mins; BR Lime Street 4 mins; Merseyrail Underground Central Station 3 mins; parking at meters, St Georges Car park 5 mins

Bluecoat Display Centre

Non-profit making contemporary crafts gallery with permanent display and temporary exhibition programme. [Cr]

Address: Bluecoat Chambers, School Lane, Liverpool, Merseyside L1 3BX tel 051 709 4014
Contact: Director Maureen Bampton
Open: Tues-Sat 10.30-5.30
Policy: The Display Centre concentrates on showing and selling high-quality work by makers from all over Britain and is included on the Crafts Council's list of selected galleries. There are six temporary exhibitions a year, usually three weeks long, also occasional workshops and demonstrations.
Sales: Work sold; Credit card
The Space: 7x7mx10m high and two 1.3x1m display cases.
Exhibiting: **[AW]** Gallery pays preview, publicity, insurance and half transport costs.
Access: **[X]** City centre buses 5 mins; BR Lime Street 8 mins; Merseyrail Underground Central Station 5 mins; Car parks close by

Bluecoat Gallery

Part of Bluecoat Arts Centre, the gallery is publicly funded and presents a broad mix of monthly shows by living artists from Britain and abroad with a changing display of small work for sale in the cafe bar. [VA,Ph,Cr,Vi,LA]

Address: Bluecoat Chambers, School Lane, Liverpool, Merseyside L1 3BX tel 051 709 5689
Contact: Gallery Director Bryan Biggs
Open: Tues-Sat 10.30-5
Policy: *'The gallery's policy is to exhibit and otherwise promote, through workshops, residencies and site-specific projects, the work of artists both from the North West and from outside this area, thereby reflecting new developments within a broad area of contemporary visual arts activity.'* Regular evening classes, talks and other educational activities are run.
Sales: Work sold; Credit scheme
The Space: Four irregularly shaped interconnecting rooms. The main gallery area has 30m linear space, 74sqm floor space, carpeted floor, spotlights and natural light, others are 14m,16sqm; 17m, 32sqm; 18m, 31sqm, all with wooden floors, spotlights and some natural light. Display cases; four 1.3x0 .75x0.15m; two 0.75x1x1.75m. Gallery plans available. Also courtyard suitable for medium-sized sculpture, and interior and exterior performance areas.
Exhibiting: **[AW][EF]** To Gallery Director, twelve slides or photos plus CV, statement on work or exhibition proposal and SAE for return. All enquiries answered within two to three weeks. Gallery covers preview and publicity costs, transport, artists' expenses and display. Commission is 25%.
Access: **[S]** Building work to provide ramp access should be complete by 1989, disabled toilets and lift also planned. City centre buses 5 mins; BR Lime Street 6 mins; Merseyrail Underground Central Station 5 mins; Car parks close by

Bridewell Studios

A gallery space run by Art Space Merseyside Ltd. within their studio building near the city centre, showing work by both Bridewell-based artists and outsiders. [VA,Cr]

Address: Prescot Street, Liverpool L7 8UE tel 051 260 6333 or 263 6730
Contact: Director Susan Kam
Open: Mon-Sat by appointment only

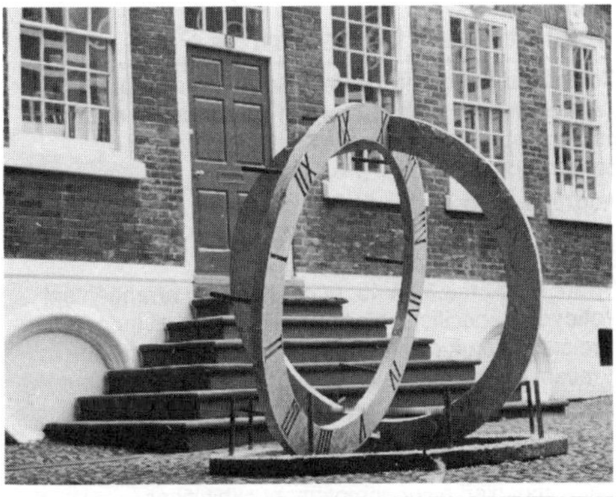

Bluecoat Gallery: '2nd Wave' by Andy Roberts

Policy: The gallery provides free exhibition space for artists within the studios, outsiders are charged a nominal fee, part of which goes towards publicity. The idea is to give young, unknown artists a chance to experience what organising an exhibition entails.
Sales: Sales referred to exhibitor
The Space: Linear hanging space 26m and floor area approximately 31square metres. Gallery plan can be drawn up on request.
Exhibiting: **[AW]** Apply with twelve slides of current work and type of work to be exhibited and CV; postage and packing must be included for return of slides. These are submitted to Bridewell general meetings for approval. Charge for space is £10, part of which covers listing in *Art around Merseyside* and *Look Alive*. Other publicity, costs and organisation are the responsibility of the artist. Supports EPR in principle.
Access: **[S]** Buses 9,10 stop opposite Royal Liverpool Hospital 1min; Small car park 3mins

Childwall Library

Branch library, with community room under construction, providing art, community, local history and educational exhibitions. [VA,Ph,Cr,LA]

Address: Childwall Road, Liverpool, Merseyside L15 6YB tel 051 722 3214
Contact: Librarian Ron Travis, Lister Drive Library, Green Lane, Liverpool, Merseyside, L13 7EB tel 051 220 9292
Open: Mon-Wed, Fri 9-9, Thurs, Sat 9-5
Policy: Aims to provide an interesting and varied programme of exhibitions relevant to the local community. Art groups and writers workshop meet in the library, readings and other events of local interest take place in the community room. (See also Liverpool Central Library).
Sales: Sales referred to exhibitor
The Space: Foyer and display area both 4.5x4.5x1.8m. Community room 9x6m. Screens available, no special lighting.
Exhibiting: **[AW]** Apply to Ron Travis at Lister Drive. Library provides publicity and help with display. Commission is 15%. Application form with list of conditions available.
Access: **[F]** Buses stop outside library, 79,78,H13,81,61,209; Car park alongside

Coach House, Calderstones Park

Converted coach house in a South Liverpool municipal park with exhibition space in the entrance hall showing temporary exhibitions of work by contemporary artists. [Pa,Ph,Pr,Dr]

Address: Mansion House, Calderstones Park, Liverpool, Merseyside L18 3JB tel 051 724 2371
Contact: Senior Ranger Kate Beecroft
Open: Mon-Fri 8.30-4.45; Other hours by arrangement
Policy: No specific exhibition policy, work on themes related to park environment welcomed. Majority of recent exhibitions have been by amateur artists but professionals are encouraged to apply. Educational courses and seminars are held in another part of the Mansion House complex, these are sometimes accompanied by or complement exhibitions.
Sales: Work sold
The Space: Wall-mounted and semi-detached hessian-covered screens, each 1x2.75m, tiled floor with natural and spot lighting. There is potential for outdoor sculpture in the park itself.
Exhibiting: **[AW]** to Kate Beecroft in writing or by telephone. Artist has to cover all costs including insurance and can organise a private view if they wish. Exhibition will be publicised in the park and through the council's information bulletin. If artists want extended show opening times, they will be asked to contribute towards overtime costs. Commission is 15% donated to Young Friends of the Park.
Access: **[U][T][F]** Buses 4,5,61,61a,68,72; Public car park 3 mins walk at park entrance

Crawford Arts Centre

Foyer and coffee bar area in a youth and community centre showing work produced at the centre. [VA,Ph,Cr]

Address: Mill Lane, Wavertree, Liverpool, Merseyside L15 8LQ tel 051 722 9091
Contact: Manager Fred Richings
Open: Mon-Fri 9.30-9, Sat 9.30-1, Sun 2-5
Policy: The centre mainly shows work produced by artists who run its workshops. The emphasis is on youth work and young people. In common with many other arts organisations using Community Programme Schemes, its nature will change after September 1988.
Sales: Work sold is not a priority
The Space: Variety of short wall spaces, screens and brick, in foyer and coffee bar area, large theatre room also sometimes available. Fluorescent lighting. Outdoor small field site suitable for *'robust'* sculpture.
Exhibiting: **[AW]** To Fred Richings in person or in writing if work is related to youth arts.
Access: **[U][T][F]** Buses 92,40,6; Car park on site; Close to end of M62

Davey Gallery

Commercial gallery above old-established picture framing business with two exhibition rooms, showing contemporary traditional paintings with a changing collection of work for sale as well as occasional temporary solo exhibitions. [Pa]

Address: 44 Duke Street, Liverpool, Merseyside L1 5AS tel 051 709 7560
Contact: Gallery Assistant Sheila Turner
Open: Mon-Sat 9-5
Policy: The emphasis is on traditional and figurative painting to show a good variety of work which will appeal to all tastes and pockets. Most work shown is by local artists and is of a professional standard. The audience is mainly drawn from framing customers, but selected mailings are done for previews for solo shows which usually last three weeks.
Sales: Work sold
The Space: Gallery One 6.5x6.5x2m linear hanging space 19m, spotlights, picture hooks. Gallery Two 7.8x3.6x2.7m, fluorescent lighting, picture hooks. Maximim height is 2.5m.
Exhibiting: **[AW]** To gallery in writing with slides and CV,

or telephone to arrange an appointment. Gallery hire is £40 per week, commission is 30%. Gallery insures work.
Access: [X] City centre Buses 5 mins; BR Lime Street 10 mins; Merseyrail Underground Central Station 7 mins; Car parks 5 mins; Parking meters

Edge Hill Library, Community Room

Community room used for meetings and activities which welcomes exhibitions that complement these and stimulate community involvement. [VA]

Address: Lodge Lane, Liverpool, Merseyside L8 0QH tel 051 709 5213
Contact: Senior Library Assistant Barbara Jackson
Open: Mon,Wed 1-9 Tues,Thurs-Sat 8.45-1, 2-5
Policy: Aims to foster and encourage art activity in the community and establish the library as an exhibition and display facility. (See also Liverpool Central Library).
The Space: Large room with fluorescent and natural light and central heating.
Exhibiting: [AW] Application form with list of conditions available.
Access: [U][F] Buses 26,27,47,126,127,147, 5,32,86,105,152,186,201

Great Georges Community Cultural Project, 'The Blackie'

Ground-floor exhibition space in large converted church building, run by Great Georges Community Cultural Project which organises and runs a daily programme of varied arts activities for the community. [VA,Ph,Cr,LA]

Address: Great Georges Street, Liverpool, Merseyside L1 5EW tel 051 709 5109
Contact: Bill Harpe,Wendy Harpe, Judy Bates, Sally Morris
Open: Mon-Sat 10 onwards, Sun 12 onwards
Policy: Shows work from The Blackie collection and regular exhibitions by other artists, with opportunities for both doing and viewing.
Sales: Work sold
The Space: Wall, screen and floor space.
Exhibiting: [AW] Apply to Duty Officer.
Access: [X] Buses 82c,21,20; Merseyrail Underground Central Station 12 mins; BR Lime Street Station 15 mins; Street parking

Hanover Galleries

Commercial gallery showing fortnightly exhibitions of local and national contemporary artists' work. [VA,Ph]

Address: 11-13 Hanover Street, Liverpool, Merseyside L1 3DN tel 051 709 3073
Contact: E Patricia Austin
Open: Tues-Sat 10.30-5
Policy: Also available for touring sponsored exhibitions.
Sales: Work sold
The Space: Gallery One, linear space 24.5m; Gallery Two, linear space 24m. Access to Gallery Two is by spiral staircase and therefore is not suitable for large sculpture. Track spots, natural light and movable hanging facilities in both galleries. Gallery is alarmed.
Exhibiting: [AW] Application details available from gallery reception, ten slides and CV are needed for initial application. Hire costs; Gallery One, £50 per week, £90 per fortnight; Gallery Two, £45 per week, £80 per fortnight. Gallery covers insurance up to £35,000, preview and publicity costs. Artist is expected to hang work. Commission is 15%.
Access: [S] to ground floor,[X] to first floor. City Centre buses 7 mins; BR Lime Street Station 10 mins; Merseyrail Underground Central Station 8 mins; Car parks and meters 2 mins

Harold House Jewish Youth & Community Centre

First-floor entrance area and ground-floor restaurant and bar areas in well-used Jewish community centre showing work related to centre activities as well as local artists and shows from Merseyside Exhibitions. [Pa,Pr,Ph,Dr,LA]

Address: Dunbabin Road, Liverpool, Merseyside L15 6XL tel 051 722 5671
Contact: Drama Worker Stanley Pettigrew
Open: Mon 10-5, Tues-Thurs 10-10, Sun 6.30-10
Policy: Will show almost anything of a professional standard, particularly work relating to young people.
Sales: Work sold
The Space: The upper area has a double picture rail at 1.5 and 2m height and approximately 5m linear space. The restaurant and bar have several small wall areas with and without single picture rail, longest run 2.5m, shortest 0.3m. Both spaces have natural and artificial light. Not suitable for large-scale or heavy work.
Exhibiting: [AW] to Stanley Pettigrew in writing. Centre will publicise shows in Jewish press and around local community. Artist is responsible for insurance, hanging and other costs. Nominal hire fee may be charged. Commission is 15%.
Access: [X] Buses 78 to Woolton Road, 78 to Childwall Fiveways; Street car parking only

Kensington Library, Community Room

A community facility available free of charge to any group or individual wanting to exhibit work of an artistic, educational or cultural nature. [VA,Ph,Cr]

Address: Kensington, Liverpool, Merseyside L7 2RJ tel 051 263 3742
Contact: Senior Library Assistant David Rennie
Open: Mon, Wed 1-9, Tues, Thurs-Sat 9-1, 2-5
Policy: Aims to foster and encourage art activity in the community and establish the library as an exhibition and display facility. Work exhibited includes living artists, women's and local history groups and schools. Occasionally other activities are put on alongside shows. (See also Liverpool Central Library).
Sales: Sales referred to exhibitor
The Space: A room 9x9x9m with 23m linear hanging space, fluorescent and natural light and central heating.
Exhibiting: [AW]
Access: [U][T][S] Buses 26,27,10a,104,9,9c,9d,10c, 139,143,210,218,320,401,402

Lister Drive Library

The library has purpose-built display cases in the foyer, and exhibition space in main library area which shows work by local artists and on community-related issues. [VA,Ph,Cr,LA]

Address: Green Lane, Liverpool, Merseyside L13 7EB tel 051 228 3004
Contact: Librarian Ron Travis
Open: Mon, Wed 1-9, Tues,Thurs-Sat 9-1,2-5
Policy: Aims to be showcase for local talent, and to stimulate local interest in and use of the library. Organises local history events, films, talks and writers workshops and readings and also takes exhibitions from Merseyside Exhibitions. (See also Liverpool Central Library).
Sales: Sales referred to exhibitor
The Space: Foyer lined with glass display cases, hardwood-backed not suitable for screws or nails, twelve 0.9x0.9x.45m. Display area in library 0.9x4.5m. Smaller items preferred.
Exhibiting: [AW] Apply to Ron Travis. Library will print publicity and help with display of work. Commission is 15%.
Access: [F] Buses from city centre; street parking only

Liverpool Central Library

Large city centre library with a permanent display of historical watercolours and drawings and a programme of temporary exhibitions of work by local artists and groups. [VA,Ph,Cr,LA]

Address: William Brown Street, Liverpool, Merseyside L3 8EW tel 051 207 2147
Contact: City Librarian, Neville Carrick BA FLA Barbara Higgins, exhibitions officer
Open: Mon-Fri 9-9 Sat 9-5; closed bank holidays
Policy: Work displayed subject to availability of space as display screens have to be used in various locations throughout the library. The library shows around 17 exhibitions a year, each for four weeks, all of which feature work by living artists and makers. Besides work by local artists and groups, the library also takes crafts shows from Merseyside Exhibitions. Liverpool City Libraries branches at Allerton, Childwall, Edge Hill, Everton, Fazakerley, Garston, Gillmoss, Great Homer Street, Kensington, Kirkdale, Knotty Ash, Larkhill, Lister Drive, Netherley, Norris Green, Speke, Spellow, Toxteth, Walton and Wavertree also show exhibitions, contact the City Librarian for more information.
Sales: Sales referred to exhibitor
The Space: Various sizes of screens and display cases, details on request.
Exhibiting [AW] Apply in writing to City Librarian or Exhibitions Officer at any time. Commission is 15%. Application forms with list of conditions available from central and branch libraries.
Access: [U][T][L][F] City centre buses few minutes walk; BR/Underground Lime Street 5 mins walk; Car park 5 mins walk

Liverpool University (Central Court Gallery)

Gallery re-opening in September 1988 after major re-building programme, showing contemporary work in all media, alongside a permanent collection of architectural paintings housed in the School of Architecture. [VA,Ph,Pr,De,Cr,LA]

Address: Liverpool University, School of Architecture, PO Box 147, Liverpool, Merseyside L69 3BX tel 051 794 2000 ext 2604
Contact: John Hardie
Open: Mon-Fri 9-5 (term-time); Closed June & July
Policy: *'Provides an open access environment for local artists together with an outlet for major architectural exhibits'.* Shows run three to four weeks. No restrictions on work exhibited, except where the university's rules would be broken. Lectures or slide shows organised when appropriate, space is also used for conferences.
Sales: Sales referred to exhibitor
The Space: Central Court: 76x3m, Golden Gallery: 38x3m, Entrance Hall: 40x4m, Coffee Bar space: 30x4m. Pinboards, spotlights, fluorescents and natural light. One glass display case 1x0.75m.
Exhibiting: Apply to John Hardie. No commission taken.
Access: [U][T][L][F] Frequent bus services; BR Lime Street 15 mins; Merseyrail Underground Central Station 15 mins; University car parks

Lyver & Boydell Gallery

Commercial gallery, established in 1851, specialising in oils, watercolours and prints for sale to collectors, mainly 19th and early 20th century work, some contemporary artists featured. [VA]

Address: 15 Castle Street, Liverpool, Merseyside L2 4SX tel 051 236 3256
Contact: Managing Director Mr Paul Breen
Open: Mon-Fri 10.30-5.30
Policy: The gallery has a tradition of holding a good selection of classical paintings and watercolours of the 19th century. This range is being developed to include better works of the early 20th century. A small selection of contemporary limited edition prints are carried.
Sales: Work sold
The Space: Display area is 111 square metres. Extensive wall display area with 13m window display.
Access: City centre location

Merseyside Exhibitions

Exhibition service touring contemporary visual art, photography and crafts to 'alternative' venues throughout the Merseyside region and its near neighbours. Also holds ARTDEX, a non-selective index of work by artists and makers. [VA,Ph,Cr,De,LA]

Address: Unit B61, Brunswick Enterprise Centre, Brunswick Business Park, Liverpool, Merseyside L3 4BD tel 051 708 7620
Contact: Director Rosemary Christmas
Open: Mon-Fri 9.30-5.30
Policy: Merseyside Exhibitions promotes the visual arts and crafts to the widest audience by taking work to venues not normally associated with exhibitions:

schools, libraries, shops, offices, community centres. We have a continually changing programme drawn from many sources including other visual arts organisations in the region as well as generating our own shows. Whenever possible we encourage venues to host workshops and generate activities to back up their exhibition booking.
Sales: Work sold; Credit card; Credit scheme
The Space: Merseyside Exhibitions has an index of around 150 venues in the region and averages around 150 exhibitions a year in over 70 of these venues. Exhibitions are designed to be flexible in nature and have a touring life of six to twelve months. MEX holds a stock of frames and operates van hire service for artists and arts organisations.
Exhibiting: **[AW]** Apply in first instance for inclusion on ARTDEX if living or working in the Merseyside region. If from elsewhere, apply in writing with slides, CV and exhibition proposal. All applications will be considered and replied to promptly. The touring aspect of the service and the small-scale nature of most venues necessarily means that heavy, large work is not suitable. Emphasis is placed on the educational aspect of exhibitions and contributors are asked to provide working drawings, samples, photographs and other back-up material besides finished pieces of work. We cover transport, insurance, publicity, framing and other display costs. Commission is 20%. Supports EPR and pays fees to makers.
Access: **[X]** To MEX office, all venues provide disabled access details for our index . To office bus 100 from Pier Head; Car Park on site

Museum of Labour History

Permanent exhibition of working class life on Merseyside from 1840 to present day, with programme of temporary exhibitions on related social themes. [VA,Ph,Cr]
Address: Islington, Liverpool, Merseyside L3 8EE tel 051 207 0001
Contact: Curator Loraine Knowles
Open: Mon-Sat 10-5, Sun 2-5
Policy: Temporary exhibition programme includes work by contemporary artists working on related issues, as well as touring historical exhibitions. A workshop, lecture and schools activity programme are run alongside shows.
Sales: Work sold
The Space: Exhibition space is in the entrance area of museum.
Access: **[U][T]** City Centre buses to Roe Street 3 mins; BR and Merseyrail Underground Lime Street station 3 mins; Car park 3 mins

Open Eye Gallery

A non-profit making photography gallery, with a programme of exhibitions, commissions, workshops and projects for the community and education sector. [Ph]
Address: 110-112 Bold Street, Liverpool, Merseyside L1 4JA tel 051 709 9460 ??
Contact: Gallery Co-ordinator John McDonald
Open: Tues-Sat 10-5.30
Policy: Particularly concerned with issue-based documentary photography. The gallery supports work by Merseyside photographers for communities on Merseyside, with an emphasis on multi-racial & multi-cultural work. All exhibitions are supported by workshops and projects which provide direct community involvement. Also holds a permanent collection of work produced on Merseyside. Open Eye Gallery moved to new premises in Bold Street in February 1989.
Sales: Sales referred to exhibitor; Credit card; Credit scheme
The Space: Ask for details.
Exhibiting: **[EF][AW]** Initial enquiries to John McDonald.
Access: **[F]**

Sudley Art Gallery

Permanent collection of fine arts, including work by Epstein, Frink, Turner and Wright of Derby. [VA,Ph,De]
Address: Mossley Hill Road, Liverpool, Merseyside L18 8BX tel 051 724 3245
Contact: Director Walker Art Gallery, William Brown Street, Liverpool L3 8EL tel 051 207 0001
Open: Mon-Sat 10-5, Sun 2-5
Policy: Temporary exhibitions have now been discontinued.
Access: Buses H25,82,80,20,21; Sudley Shuttle Bus on Sundays from outside Granada TV News Centre (Albert Dock near Tate Gallery Liverpool), free including guided tour of gallery, departs 2 and 3.30, returns 3.20 and 4.50

Tate Gallery Liverpool

Opened in May 1988 to house the national collection of modern art in a converted Grade I listed former dock warehouse; the gallery also has bookshop, reading room, video and tape libraries and education van. [VA,Ph,LA]
Address: Albert Dock, Liverpool, Merseyside L3 4BB tel 051 709 0507
Contact: Curator Richard Francis tel 051 709 3223
Open: Tues-Sun 11-7; Open bank holidays
Policy: *'Changing displays, nine months to three years,*

Tate Gallery Liverpool: Installation of 'Starlit Waters' exhibition

from the collection showing particular art movements or thematic developments. Temporary loan exhibitions of internationally recognised twentieth century artists', talks, workshops and other educational activities, including outreach, organised alongside these.'

Sales: Sales referred to exhibitor

The Space: Room Four 22x11x2.5m 60m linear; Room Five 10x11x2.5m 34m linear; Room Six 44x16x2.5m 120m linear. Fixings direct to wall, lighting flexible, fully air-conditioned. Access for work 0.4x7mx5m high; restricted floor loadings for sculpture. Gallery plans available.

Exhibiting: Supports EPR in principle, gallery normally covers all exhibiting costs.

Access: [U][T][L][F] Buses 222 to Albert Dock, other Pier Head routes 5 mins; Merseyrail Underground James Street 5 mins; BR Lime Street station 15 mins; Car park 5 mins

Unity Theatre

Café and auditorium space in community theatre which presents small-scale touring and independent productions. [Pa,Pr,Ph]

Address: Hope Place, Liverpool, Merseyside L1 9BG tel 051 709 4988

Contact: Director Graeme Phillips

Open: Performance times as advertised in local press, also open during daytime rehearsal and community group meetings

Policy: Work shown is related to performances or relevant theatre activities, eg Festival of Comedy. No regular programme of exhibitions at present.

Sales: Sales referred to exhibitor

The Space: Cafe, linear wall space only approx 15m; auditorium, two recessed alcoves 1x2.5m. Fluorescent lighting. Hanging rails in café area, suitable for small two-dimensional work only.

Exhibiting: [AW] To Director in writing with slides and CV. Hanging is artist's responsibility.

Access: [X] Buses to Philharmonic 72,73,80,86; BR and Merseyrail Underground 15 mins; Public car park behind Design Centre 3 mins

University of Liverpool (Senate House Exhibition Hall)

Exhibition hall in administrative building of Liverpool University, showing around five exhibitions during academic year of contemporary work. The university also holds a permanent collection of work dating from 1650 to present day. [VA,Ph,Cr]

Address: Abercromby Square, PO Box 147, Liverpool, Merseyside L69 3BX tel 051 794 2347

Contact: Curator Art Collections Janice Carpenter

Open: Mon-Fri 9-5

Policy: *'The permanent collections provide students and the general public with opportunities to enjoy and learn about the visual arts. The temporary exhibitions extend and enhance such opportunities.'* No particular specialisation, but best work available selected. Conducted tours and lectures organised on request.

Sales: Work sold

The Space: This venue wins the prize for providing the most detailed and relevant set of plans! The total linear space is 39.6m, all obstructions are detailed on plans. Hanging rods from rail 2.1m from floor, lights and natural light. Twenty-one Marler Haley screens and 18 stands, 1.8x1.2m. Five Varedplan cases 1.8x.6x.24m.

Exhibiting: [AW] To Curator, detailed information sheet available. University covers publicity, preview arrangements, insurance and hanging. Commission is 10%.

Access: [X] Buses 5,H21,79,76; BR Lime Street station and Merseyrail Undergound Central Station 10-15mins; Car parks on campus

Walker Art Gallery

One of seven government-funded museum institutions on Merseyside housing the most important provincial collection of Old Master paintings in England plus temporary exhibitions. [VA,Ph,Cr,LA]

Address: William Brown Street, Liverpool, Merseyside L3 8EL tel 051 207 0001

Contact: Head of Art Galleries Julian Treuherz

Open: Mon-Sat 10-5 Sun 2-5

Policy: As a new exhibition policy is being implemented from 1988. The gallery is likely to concentrate on exhibitions of non-contemporary art although such shows as the John Moores will continue. The space devoted to temporary exhibitions will be reduced, only one room being permanently devoted to this. Exhibitions normally run from four to six weeks, and the education department runs a full programme of exhibition-related activities.

Sales: Occasionally contemporary exhibits are for sale

The Space: 20.6x9.15x4.55m overall; no artificial lighting; daylight; fixed strip lighting at present, new halogen spots forthcoming. High and low cases 130cm long.

Exhibiting: Gallery originates exhibitions and takes touring exhibitions.

Access: [U][T][L][F] City Centre buses 3 mins; BR/Underground Lime Street 3 mins; St Georges car park 3 mins

London

(GLA)

5 Dryden Street Gallery

Gallery aiming to provide opportunities for lesser-known artists to show their work, run on a non-profit making basis. [VA]

Address: 5 Dryden Street, Covent Garden, London WC2E 9NW tel 01 240 2430

Contact: Katrina Johnson or Brian Howard-Heaton

Open: Mon-Fri 10-6

Policy: Exhibitions are organised on a self-help basis and change fortnightly. Wide variety of work shown, mostly small in size.

Sales: Work sold

The Space: One floor and staircase area plus some screens, total wall space about 11m.

Exhibiting: [AW] Forms can be obtained from the gallery, to be sent back with slides of work to the selection panel. Commission is 10%.

Access: Underground Covent Garden, Holborn

20th Century Gallery

Gallery showing Post-Impressionist and modern British arts and watercolours. [Pa]

Address: 821 Fulham Road, London SW6 tel 01 731 5888
Contact: Director
Open: Tues-Fri 10-6, Sat 10-1
Access: Bus 14; Underground Parsons Green

39 Steps Gallery

A commercial gallery which shows mainly two-dimensional work of an environmental nature, which promotes the work of younger artists. [VA]

Address: 273a Whitechapel Road, London E1 1BY tel 01 247 3588
Contact: Daniel Bird
Open: Mon-Fri 10.30-7, Sat 11-3; At other times by appointment
Policy: At present the gallery exhibits predominantly painting, but plans for the future include three dimensional work. Most of the work shown could be described as 'environmental'. The gallery is committed to showing and promoting the work of younger artists, and welcomes applications. A further aim is to widen an appreciation of contemporary art - *'It is no coincidence that the gallery was set up in East London at a time when extensive re-building is taking place, and people are moving into the area...'*. During the last twelve months the gallery has mounted 14 three-week exhibitions, the majority of which were solo shows. The gallery which is financed by the director and through sponsorship is also hired out for other purposes, for example for photo sessions.
Sales: Work sold
The Space: The gallery space is 8.3x4.4x2.6m, with good natural daylight and rail mounted spotlights. Hanging is by hook and wire to batten. Access is restricted to works of 2.5m maximum in any direction. Gallery plans are available.
Exhibiting: [AW] Applications are welcome at any time, although there may be considerable delay in replying. Slide applications should be sent to the Director, including return postage. The gallery covers the cost of publicity, catalogue, mailing, list of exhibits, preview and transport. The gallery takes 35% commission on sales of work. Supports EPR in principle.
Access: [X] Underground Whitechapel 10 secs

Actors' Institute Gallery

The gallery is run by and situated within the Actors' Institute and the gallery shows the work of younger artists in a variety of media. [VA]

Address: 137 Goswell Road, London EC1V 7ET tel 01 251 8178
Contact: Simon Lambert, Flat 10, 36 Dorset Square, London NW1 tel 01 720 5500
Open: Mon-Fri 10-5
Policy: It shows the work of *'up and coming and established artists who would not have the opportunity to show in the more established galleries'*. The gallery aims to introduce artists to commercial and private buyers. Work shown includes painting, sculpture, prints and drawings. Twelve month-long exhibitions are held each year, all are solo shows by living artists.
Sales: Sales referred to exhibitor
The Space: The gallery, which is an open-plan reception/coffee area with central seating has 15 m linear hanging space with 3m high walls.
Exhibiting: [AW] The gallery welcomes applications write or telephone Simon Lambert. A hire fee of £150 is charged, and a commission of 20% is taken on sales. The gallery covers the cost of the mailing of publicity and the private view.
Access: [L] Buses 4,277; Underground Angel, Barbican 5 mins

Actualities

A commercial gallery specialising in work which is often sculptural or photographic. [Sc,Ph]

Address: 152 Narrow Street, Limehouse, London E14 8BP tel 01 515 6036
Contact: Director Kay Roberts
Policy: The gallery invites proposals from artists working *'in an area loosely defined as architectural'*. Each project is site-specific in two ways: *'The work should have a direct relationship to the area surrounding Actualities'* and *'where possible the project should be in two parts, one work being based in the gallery, the second being situated outside the gallery space - in the community on which the project is based'*. *'Within the individual context of their work the artist will focus on the architectural and social flux at this time in the Docklands'*. In each case, work is made especially for the gallery. Proposals are collaborations with the gallery and ideas are discussed from an early stage.
Sales: Work sold
The Space: The gallery space is 8x4x2.5m, with 16m of hanging space. There are no limitations on fixing work and spotlights run the length of the space.
Exhibiting: [AW] Applications are welcome, contact the Director to discuss ideas at an early stage in the making of a proposal. The gallery covers the cost of insurance, publicity, mailing, list of exhibits, display and transport. Commission charged is negotiated with the artist.
Access: [F] Buses 5,15,40; Westferry (Docklands Light Railway) 2 mins

Adam Gallery

A commercial artist-run gallery showing new contemporary work, mostly solo shows, in any medium. [VA,Ph]

Address: 62 Walcot Square, London SE11 4TZ tel 01 582 1260
Contact: Adam Reynolds
Open: Variable according to exhibitor
Policy: Some work by gallery artists permanently available for viewing. Shows largely organised by exhibiting artist with some assistance from the gallery.
Sales: Work sold
The Space: One main space 3.6x4.3m with 13m linear hanging space, direct fixing and spots and daylight.

Exhibiting: [AW] Artist responsible for insurance and all specific costs. Commission is 25%.
Access: [X] Buses 3,109,159,196; BR Waterloo, Elephant & Castle, Lambeth North

Africa Centre Gallery

A gallery within an arts centre. [Pa,Pr,Ph,LA]
Address: 38 King Street, Covent Garden, London WC2E 8JT tel 01 836 1973
Contact: Keith Shiri
Open: Mon-Sat 10-5.30
Policy: An educational charity, the gallery holds regular exhibitions from Africa and the developing world and the centre also promotes plays, music, poetry and films as part of its policy of developing discussion and appreciation of African affairs.
The Space: The gallery is 17x10m and lit by spots and natural light with hanging is by rods.
Exhibiting: [AW] Applications are welcome and exhibitions are selected four times a year by an advisory panel. The gallery pays for insurance, publicity and mailing and takes 20% commission on sales.
Access: Buses 1,6,9,11,15,23,77,77a,176; Underground Covent Garden and Leicester Square

Al-Bizarre

Opened in February 1986, the gallery specialises in the influences of mythology, ethnic, spiritual, symbolic and folk art on contemporary art and crafts. [VA,Pa,Pr,Ph,Cr]
Address: 9 Jerdan Place, Fulham Broadway, London SW6 1BE tel 01 385 0278
Contact: Partner Natalia Kovacs
Open: Mon-Sat 10-6
Policy: Al-Bizarre aims to attract an interested but not necessarily converted audience, in the age range 25-50, to a wide range of art and crafts hoping to make the customer relaxed, able to browse through a mixture of paintings, tapestry, etchings, papier maché, jewellery and ceramics connected by the gallery's interest in root culture, pre-history, pagan and alternative religions.
Sales: Work sold; Credit card; Credit scheme
The Space: Two spaces 4.5x3x2.74m high and 3.6x2.4x1.9m high. Maximum limit on works 0.9m square.
Exhibiting: [AW] Artists interested in showing work should make an appointment to see Natalia Kovacs or send information and slides to the gallery which pays for insurance, printing and mailing of publicity, a list of exhibits and a preview and charges 33-50% commission on sales.
Access: [F][X] Buses 11,14,91,28,295; Underground Fulham Broadway 5 mins

Alba Fine Art

The gallery promotes contemporary art by some regular artists, introducing new artists through exhibitions. [Pa,Pr,Dr,Je,Ce]
Address: 3 Station Approach, Kew Gardens, Surrey TW9 3QB tel 01 948 2672
Contact: Wendy Fletcher or Christine Walker
Open: Tues-Sat 11-6 or by appointment
Policy: The gallery looks for promising graduates and other young artists producing mainly figurative or landscape work, certainly not too abstract, in the price range £150-£1,000, to sell to local residents.
Sales: Work sold; Credit card
Exhibiting: [AW] Artists are asked to telephone the gallery before submitting information and slides. The gallery covers insurance and 50% of the costs of publicity and preview. Commission on sales of 54%.
Access: [F] Underground Kew Gardens 1 min

Albemarle Gallery

A commercial gallery showing comtemporary paintings in monthly changing exhibitions. [VA]
Address: 18 Albemarle Street, London W1 tel 01 493 7968
Open: Mon-Fri 10-5.30, Sat 11-1
Access: Underground Green Park

Alexander Roussos Gallery

A commercial gallery which deals in and exhibits the work of established and younger artists on an 'international scale'. [VA,Ph]
Address: 22 Princes Street, London W1R 7RG tel 01 493 1480
Contact: Alexander Roussos, Katerina Gregos
Open: Tues-Fri 10-5, Sat 11-5; closed Sun & Mon
Policy: *'The direction of the gallery is centred around the promotion of internationally established artists, as well as young artists on an international scale.'* Artists are promoted within England as well as abroad. Work shown includes painting, sculpture, drawing, prints and photography. Seven one-person exhibitions lasting between four and six weeks are held a year. The gallery has a permanent collection of work by gallery artists.
Sales: Work sold; Credit scheme
The Space: The gallery is 280 square metres.
Exhibiting: [AW] *'The gallery reserves Saturday to view work by artists wishing to show work. No appointment needed'.* The gallery covers the costs of insurance, publicity, catalogue and card, mailing and the private view. Artists are usually paid a commission fee to produce work especially for exhibitions. 50% commission is taken on sales.
Access: [U][T][L] Bus routes; Underground Oxford Circus 1 min

Alpine Gallery

A gallery owned by the Alpine Club which is hired out to individuals and groups who administer and invigilate the exhibitions. Opening times vary according to the hirer. [Pa,Sc,Pr]
Address: 74 South Audley Street, London W1 tel 01 629 2280
Contact: Secretary Alpine Club tel 01 499 1542
Access: Buses 2b,6,7,8,12,15,16,16a,30,36,36a,73,74, 82,88; Underground Marble Arch

Amalgam Art

Gallery showing English arts and crafts, specialising in contemporary ceramics, prints and studio glass. [Cr,Pr]

Address: 3 Barnes High Street, London SW13 9LB tel 01 878 1279
Contact: T Boon & A Boon
Open: Tues-Sat 10-1.30, 2.30-6
Policy: To show fine and applied art by contemporary British artists on an equal status *'with an emphasis on quality at affordable prices, ie value for money'*.
Sales: Work sold
The Space: One floor 5x10m.
Exhibiting: **[AW]** to above, avoid November and December.
Access: Buses to Barnes Green; BR Barnes Bridge

Anderson O'Day Gallery

This commercial gallery on the Crafts Council's selected list which promotes the work of a selected group of artists usually in monthly solo shows that are exhibited alongside a selection of other gallery artists work. [VA]

Address: 255 Portobello Road, London W11 1LR tel 01 221 7592
Contact: Director Prue O'Day
Open: Tues-Sat 10-5
Policy: The aim of this gallery is to *'show the very best painters, sculptors, paperwork artists and printmakers who make up the new British art scene'*. Gallery policy is to *'encourage and nurture'* new talent and provide a forum for artists who have not had much exposure. The target audience includes art enthusiasts, patrons and established collectors as well as the general public. Artists are encouraged to give lectures to coincide with exhibitions.
Sales: Work sold; Credit card; Credit scheme
The Space: The approximate dimensions of the three galleries are 27x5x3m high in total.
Exhibiting: **[AW]** Apply with slides and SAE to Prue O'Day. After an initial appraisal is made, members of the selection panel may make studio visits to see original works. Arrangements for exhibiting costs and commission are *'confidential'*.
Access: Buses 7,15,27,28,31,52,295; Underground Ladbroke Grove 2 mins, Westbourne Grove, Notting Hill 10 mins

Angela Flowers Gallery

A commercial gallery showing the work of younger British artists. [VA,Ph]

Address: 11 Tottenham Mews, London W1P 9PJ tel 01 637 3089
Contact: Angela Flowers, Matthew Flowers
Open: Mon-Fri 10.30-6, Sat 10.30-12.30
Policy: In September 1988, the gallery opened a new branch called Flowers East at 199 Richmond Road, Hackney, London E8 tel 01 985 3333. This has 1500 square metres and the exhibition programme will include a permanent graphic gallery as well as showing more group exhibitions, aiming to complement the programme at Tottenham Mews.
The Space: The space is 5x3m with spot lighting.
Exhibiting: **[AW]** Applications are welcome. The gallery takes 50% commission and meets the cost of insurance, publicity, mailing, catalogue and private view.
Access: Buses 14,14a,24,29,73; Underground Goodge Street

Anima Gallery

Commercial gallery showing contemporary prints by British, American, Japanese and European artists.

Address: 132 Lots Road, London SW10 tel 01 352 7694
Contact: Director
Open: Mon-Fri 10-6
Policy: Abstract and figurative work for the architect, interior designer as well as the private collector.
Access: Buses 14,30,45,49,74; Underground South Kensington

Anna-Mei Chadwick

A gallery showing contemporary oil and watercolour paintings, prints and sculpture.

Address: 64 New Kings Road, London SW6 4LT tel 01 736 1928
Contact: Director Anna-Mei Chadwick
Open: Mon-Fri 10-6, Sat 10-5.30; Sun by appointment
Policy: The gallery specialises in affordable original works by living British artists. Throughout the year the gallery presents theme shows, mixed shows and solo exhibitions by both established and talented new artists.
Sales: Work sold; Credit card
The Space: Two galleries about 10x3m and a print room. South facing light, white walls, tungsten lighting.
Exhibiting: **[AW]** Artists seen by appointment.
Access: **[F]** Upper gallery **[X]** Lower gallery. Bus routes 14,22; Underground Parsons Green

Anne Berthoud Gallery

A commercial gallery dealing in and showing the work of living artists. [Pa,Pr]

Address: 10 Clifford Street (1st Floor), London W1X 1RB tel 01 437 1645
Contact: Anne Berthoud
Open: Mon-Fri 10-5, Sat 10-1
Policy: There are about eight exhibitions a year, alternating between solo shows of work by gallery artists and mixed shows which include the work of other artists. The style of work generally shown is *'borderline abstract/representational'*. The aim is to help younger, less well-known artists living and working in Britain.
Sales: Work sold
Exhibiting: The gallery takes between 30% and 50% commission and meets the cost of insurance, framing, publicity, mailing, catalogue and private view.
Access: Buses 3,6,7,8,9,12,13,14,14a,15,16a,19,22, 22b,25,38,53,73,88,113,135,137,159,176; Underground Piccadilly Circus, Oxford Circus, Grren Park

Annely Juda Fine Art

Gallery showing work by established twentieth century artists from Britain and abroad. [VA]

Address: 11 Tottenham Mews, off Tottenham Street, London W1 tel 01 637 5517/8/9
Contact: Director Annely Juda
Open: Mon-Fri 10-6, Sat 10-1 or by appointment
Sales: Work sold
The Space: Four rooms on three floors, each room 4x5m approx.
Exhibiting: **[AW]** from professional artists only, in 1986 they were fully committed until 1989.
Access: Bus routes Tottenham Court Road, Oxford Street; Underground Goodge Street

Anthony d'Offay

A commercial gallery showing and dealing in work by living artists in a variety of media. [VA]

Address: 9 & 23 Dering Street, London W1 tel 01 499 4100
Contact: Director Anthony d'Offay
Open: Mon-Fri 10-5.30, Sat 10-1
Policy: The programme of approximately eight exhibitions a year includes painting, drawing, sculpture and installation by British and international artists. Most shows are solo, lasting one month.
Sales: Work sold
Exhibiting: The gallery promotes a selected number of artists.
Access: Buses 3,6,7,8,12,13,15,16a,25,53,73,88,113, 135,137,159,176; Underground Oxford Circus and Green Park

Anthony Dawson

An artists' agent showing contemporary paintings, drawings and prints. [Pa,Dr,Pr]

Address: 41 Lilian Road, London SW13 9JF tel 01 748 1306
Contact: Director
Open: Mon-Sat 10-5
Access: Buses 60,118; BR Streatham Common

Anthony Reynolds Gallery

A gallery specialising in contemporary European and American artists.

Address: 37 Cowper Street, London EC2A 4AP tel 01 608 1516
Contact: Anthony Reynolds, Tues-Sun 11-6
Policy: The gallery shows changing exhibitions as well as performance and live art.
Access: Buses 5,43,55,76,141,214,243,263a,271; Underground Old Street

Applied Arts Showhouse

This showhouse promotes the work of over 400 contemporary artists-makers through a permanent collection of work and four small group exhibitions a year. It houses 5000 slide index through which clients commission one-off designs. [Cr]

Address: 109 Highbury Hill, Highbury, London N5 1TA tel 01 354 3073
Contact: Director, Sharon Plant or Curator, Polly Pollock
Open: Mon-Fri by appointment, some weekends and quarterly open house exhibitions
Policy: The aim of the showhouse is to promote the work of applied artists by attracting attention via the media and hence obtaining commissions from established and new clients. Clients include architects, interior designers and private collectors. In addition, photographers use the showhouse for promotional shoots to show the applied arts in a real environment. There is a permanent collection of furniture, ceramics and textiles. A garden is available to show works suitable for outdoor display and use.
Sales: Work sold
The Space: The gallery consists of nine large rooms in a private Victorian house.
Exhibiting: **[AW]** Apply with slides and CV to Sharon Plant. Occasionally a hire fee is charged. Gallery finances insurance, printing and mail-out of publicity, catalogue/card and preview costs. Commission 50% on direct sales, 33.3% on commissions.
Access: **[X]** Underground Arsenal 1 mins

Architectural Association

Gallery, in Association's office headquarters, showing frequent exhibitions of historical and contemporary architecture. [VA,Ar]

Address: 34 Bedford Square, London WC1 tel 01 636 0974
Contact: Assistant to Chairman Micky Hawkes
Open: Mon-Fri 10-7, Sat 10-1.30
Sales: Work sold
Access: Bus routes Tottenham Court Road; Underground Goodge Street, Russell Square

Argenta

A commercial gallery on the Crafts Council selected list showing jewellery by about 30 younger designers and makers which specialises in individual handmade jewellery. [Je]

Applied Arts Showhouse: Director Sharon Plant

Address: 82 Fulham Road, London SW3 tel 01 584 3119
Open: Mon-Sat 9.30-5.30
Sales: Work sold
Access: Underground South Kensington

Argile Gallery

Commercial gallery opened by Marie Saba in 1988. [Pa,Ce]

Address: 7 Blenheim Crescent, London W11 2EE tel 01 792 0888
Contact: Marie Saba
Open: Mon-Sat 10-6
Policy: The Argile specialises in contemporary British and international work by both established artists and new talents. Its Saturday Art Break brings together art collectors and selected up-and-coming artists invited to bring along their portfolios. The gallery plans monthly exhibitions, carries a permanent stock of ceramics and is building up a permanent collection of paintings.
Sales: Work sold; Credit card
The Space: There are about 121 square metres of wall space and maximum size of work acceptable is 2x3m. Ceramics are displayed in a glass covered courtyard.
Exhibiting: [AW] Artists should contact Marie Saba in person on Saturdays or slides may be sent by post, with SAE The gallery contributes to the cost of insurance, publicity, list of exhibits, catalogue or card, mailing out and preview. It charges a 40% commission.
Access: Underground Notting Hill and Ladbroke Grove

Art after Hours

'International Installations' take art exhibitions to a wide variety of unusual locations ranging from snack bars to empty warehouses'. [VA,LA]

Address: Limelight, 136 Shaftesbury Avenue, London WC2H tel 01 434 1761
Open: Tues,Fri,Sat 12-5, nightclub hours
Policy: Gallery artists are all young and British, some just out of college. The two protagonists of 'International Installations' are Sue Pocklington, consultant art buyer, and Roland Cowan, architect.
Sales: Work sold
Exhibiting: Contact agency in first instance.

Art for Offices

Comprehensive range of contemporary visual arts, photographs and prints for architects, interior designers, and the corporate sector. [VA,Ph,Te]

Address: 15 Dock Street, London E1 tel 01 481 1337
Contact: Directors Peter Harris & Andrew Hutchison
Open: 9.30-5.30 by appointment
Policy: Business offers full consultancy service for exhibitions and commissions to clients as outlined above using contemporary artists work.
Sales: Work sold
Exhibiting: [AW] Details from above, catalogues and information sent on request.
Access: Buses to Tower of London, Aldgate; BR Fenchurch Street; Underground Tower Hill, Aldgate, Aldgate East

Art Space Gallery

Architect-run gallery opened in 1987 to promote high quality contemporary art 'of its time'. [VA,Ph,Pr]

Address: 84 St Peters Street, Islington, London N1 tel 01 359 7002
Contact: Directors Michael & Oya Richardson
Open: Tues-Sat 2-7
Policy: Gallery has established its own list of artists including Stan Smith, Marisa Rueda and Robert Soden. Shows are held monthly by invitation, and are generally solo, including work from painters, sculptors, printmakers and photographers.
Sales: Work sold
Exhibiting: [AW] Gallery terms available on request. Apply in person or by sending photographs with work details to above.
Access: Buses 4,19,30,38,43,73,171,277,279; Underground Angel

Arts & Crafts Movement

Shop and gallery exhibiting high-quality work by contemporary makers, painters and photographers. [Cr,Pa,Pr]

Address: 11 West Hill, Wandsworth, London SW18 tel 01 870 9677
Open: Mon-Sun 10.30-6.30
Policy: The shop stocks a large variety of crafts including jewellery and hand-made cards. Regular exhibitions are held in the gallery of ceramics, textiles, paintings and prints.

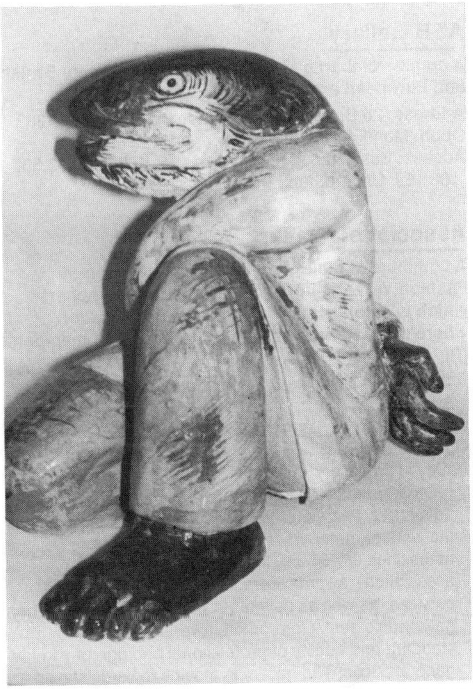

Arts & Crafts Movement: Ceramic sculpture by Pamela Leung

Sales: Work sold; Credit card
Exhibiting: **[AW]** Artists and makers are welcome to contact the gallery with a view to exhibiting their work. The gallery may also be hired.
Access: Buses 37,77a,170; Underground East Putney

Arts Theatre Gallery

The gallery, situated within, and run by the Arts/Unicorn Theatre, a charitable organisation for children, hired to young artists and showing work in a variety of two-dimensional media. [Pa,Pr,Dr]

Address: 6/7 Great Newport Street, London WC2H 7JB tel 01 379 3280
Contact: Dorothy Wooder
Open: Mon-Sat 10-10, Sun 10-4
Policy: The gallery aims to provide younger artists with *'a West End venue at reasonable rental'*. Work shown includes paintings, drawings and prints on a small scale. The gallery holds eleven solo exhibitions a year, these run for three to four weeks. All shows are the work of living artists, occasionally the work of children form local schools is shown.
Sales: Work sold
The Space: The exhibition space is part of the restaurant and foyer. Works are hung on display boards with a height of .80m. Gallery plans are available.
Exhibiting: **[AW]** Applications are welcome from artists, contact by telephone. The space is hired to artists and 30% commission is taken on sales.
Access: **[U][T]** Buses 1,24,29,176; BR Charing Cross; Underground Leicester Square

ASB Gallery

A commercial art gallery showing 20th century British and European artists.

Address: 28 Bruton Street, London W1 tel 01 491 1333
Open: Mon-Fri 10-5.30, Sat by appointment
Access: Buses 3,6,9,12,13,14,14a,15,19,22,22b,38,53, 88,159; Underground Piccadilly Circus

Association Gallery

A commercial gallery run by the Association of Fashion, Advertising and Editorial Photographers, which is a non-profit making trade organisation where the gallery mainly shows the work of members. [Ph]

Address: 9-10 Domingo Street, London EC1Y 0TA tel 01 608 1441/5
Contact: Gallery Administrator Valerie Lawton
Open: Mon-Fri 9.30-6
Policy: The gallery shows the work of professional photographers working in the areas of fashion, advertising and editorial. The main aims are to promote the work of members to advertising agencies, magazines etc. and to highlight the work of the association - awards, competitions, and associated services, as well as new members and assistants. The gallery also seeks to promote awareness of the standard and quality of professional photography to the general public. The gallery is moving towards showing more personal photographs and welcomes applications from photographers not represented by the association. 30 shows of approximately two weeks duration are held each year. These comprise solo, group, thematic and retrospective exhibitions. The gallery is financed by sponsorship and hire of the space to exhibitors.
Sales: Work sold; Sales referred to exhibitor
The Space: The gallery on the ground floor is 6x9x4.5m and this will be extended to include the basement in early 1989.
Exhibiting: **[AW]** Applications welcome from members. Contact the Gallery Administrator by phone, letter or personal call. The gallery charges a hire fee which relates to duration of exhibition.
Access: **[X]** Buses 4,5,55,243,277,279a; Underground Barbican 5 mins, Old Street 10 mins; Barbican car park 10 mins

Association of Illustrators Gallery

Gallery showcase for work by contemporary illustrators. [Dr,Pr]

Address: 1 Colville Place, off Charlotte Street, London W1P 1HN tel 01 636 4100
Contact: Gallery Administrator Caroline Beven
Open: Mon-Fri 10-5
Policy: Temporary exhibitions which change twice monthly, no permanent collection. Also shows work by Association's members.
Sales: Work sold
The Space: Space on two floors, approx 8x4.5m; hanging direct to walls; spots and natural light.
Exhibiting: **[AW]** From illustrators only, hire and other details available, discount for members.
Access: Bus routes Tottenham Court Road, Oxford Street; Underground Goodge Street

Athawes Art Gallery

A gallery run by the Acton Charities which makes its space available free to local artists. [VA]

Address: Rectory Road, Acton, London W3
Contact: Clerk 48 Perryn Road, London W3 7NA tel 01 743 3476
Exhibiting: **[AW]** Contact the clerk for details.

Austin/Desmond Fine Art

Commercial gallery. [Pa,Pr,Bo,Sc]

Address: Pied Bull Yard, 15A Bloomsbury Square, London WC1 tel 01 242 4443
Open: Mon-Fri 10.30-6.30, Sat 10.30-2.30
Policy: Modern and contemporary British artists, showing paintings, prints, books and sculpture.

B4 Studios

This is a photography co-operative with darkroom and exhibition facilities. [Ph]

Address: Westminster Square, Durham Street, London SE11 5JH tel 01 793 0487
Open: Tues-Sat 11-7
Policy: The studios also offer colour processing and run workshops.
Access: Underground/BR Vauxhall 3 mins

Bankside Gallery

Home of the Royal Society of Painters in Watercolours and the Royal Society of Painter/Etchers and Engravers, it holds open exhibitions and organises historical and loan exhibitions from Britain and abroad. [Pa,Pr]

Address: 48 Hopton Street, London SE1 9JH tel 01 928 7521

Contact: Director Michael Spender

Open: Tues 10-8, Wed-Sat 10-5, Sun 1-5

Policy: The gallery, which attracts a wide-ranging audience, aims to promote the art forms of watercolour and printmaking through a programme of 10 exhibitions a year, which include annual exhibitions by the Royal Society of Painters in Watercolours and the Royal Society of Painters/Etchers and Engravers, and by holding educational events such as lectures, slide shows, demonstrations and instruction days/courses. The gallery has charitable status and is financed by members' subscriptions and from sales commission.

Sales: Work sold; Credit card; Credit scheme

The Space: A large exhibition hall with 80m linear hanging space and museum standard security and lighting. Three showcases are available, suitable for small craft displays.

Exhibiting: [AW] Submissions to open shows are welcome, from watercolour painters for the summer exhibition, and from printmakers in all media for the annual spring exhibition. Substantial awards are given for outstanding works (details available from gallery). The gallery covers insurance, publicity, list of exhibits, preview costs, mailing of publicity and production of catalogues. Commission of 40% is taken on sales.

Access: [F] Buses 45,63,70,76,109,141,149,155; BR Waterloo 15 mins; Underground Blackfriars 8 mins, Waterloo 15 mins

Barbican Art Gallery

Municipal gallery run by the City of London Libraries and Art Galleries Department which holds major exhibitions of international significance and handles a large permanent collection. [VA,Ph,Cr]

Address: Barbican Centre, London EC2Y 8DS tel 01 588 5708

Contact: Director Libraries and Art Galleries, Melvin Barnes or Curator, John Hoole, Guildhall Library, Aldermanbury, London EC2P 2EJ

Open: Mon-Sat 10-18.45, Sun 12-17.45

Policy: The gallery specialises in major exhibitions of international significance, single artist retrospectives and thematic shows. Occasional shows by living artists are held. Six exhibitions are mounted a year each, lasting about two months. Exhibitions include painting, sculpture, prints, drawings, photography and crafts. The gallery holds a permanent collection of 3,000 paintings and sculptures, which is on loan thoughout London. The widest possible public is encouraged and a range of activities are organised by a full-time education officer.

Access: [U][T][L][F] Underground Barbican 10 mins, Moorgate 10 mins, St. Pauls 10 mins; Public car park on site

Barnet (Library Service)

Headquarters for the London Borough of Barnet's Library Service.

Address: Libraries Department, Administrative Offices, Ravensfield House, The Burroughs, Hendon, London NW4 4BE tel 01 202 5625

Contact: Arts Officer Joanne Hawley

Policy: See also entries for Totteridge Library, Hendon Library and North Finchley Library.

Basilisk Press

Houses largest collection of in-print private press books in United Kingdom, view by catalogue or appointment. [Pr]

Address: 10 Adamson Road, London NW3 3HR tel 01 722 2142

Open: By appointment

Sales: Work sold

Access: Underground Swiss Cottage; BR South Hampstead

Battersea Arts Centre

Gallery within an art centre. [VA,Ph,Cr,LA]

Address: Old Town Hall, Lavender Hill, London SW1 5TF tel 01 223 6557

Contact: Exhibitions Organiser Kathryn Standing

Open: Wed-Sun 12-8

Policy: Runs a monthly exhibition programme with an emphasis on commissioned, contemporary, innovative work in all media (installation/performance/film). The gallery is also interested in siting works outside the gallery area. Exhibitions are accompanied by slide talks and discussions by the artists, school and college visits and workshops are arranged.

Sales: Work sold; Credit card

The Space: Gallery one 7x7x4m high with 29m linear hanging space. Gallery two 7x5x3m high with 24m linear hanging space. Work is mounted on boards attached to walls. Track and tungsten spot lighting. Gallery plans available.

Exhibiting: [AW] Apply with proposal and slides to Exhibitions Organiser. Gallery finances insurance, printing and mail-out of publicity, catalogue/card, transport, display and artists costs and list of exhibits. Artists recieve a fee for exhibiting. Support in principle for EPR. Commission 20%.

Access: [U][T][L] Buses 19,37,39,45,49,77,77a, 156,170,249; BR Victoria, Waterloo 5 mins; Underground Clapham Common 25 mins

Battersea District Library

Library-run gallery with emphasis on local community and artists. [VA,Cr]

Address: 265 Lavender Hill, Battersea, London SW11 1JB tel 01 871 7380

Contact: Arts Officer for Battersea Charlie Catling

Open: Mon-Sat 10-5, closed Thurs

Policy: The policy is to encourage the practice and appreciation of the visual arts among local people. Variety is the essence of the programme with about twelve shows a year, a mixture of work by local residents, community groups plus an open exhibition for local artists each year.

Sales: Work sold

The Space: The space is most suitable for wall hung work with a hanging length of 30m, lighting by low power spots. Three museum style cabinets and one upright three-tiered glass cabinet.

Exhibiting: [AW] Applications from artists and groups in the Battersea area are welcome. Costs covered by the gallery are negotiable but the gallery takes a commission on sales of 15%.

Access: [X]

Battersea Park Library

A gallery space within a library showing contemporary art exhibitions. [VA]

Address: Battersea Park Road, London SW11 tel 01 871 7468

Contact: Librarian

Open: Mon-Wed 9.30-7, Fri, Sat 9.30-5; closed Thurs

Bedford Hill Gallery

Gallery showing quality work by unknown artists. [VA,Cr,LA]

Address: 50 Bedford Hill, Balham, London SW12 9RX tel 01 675 5446

Contact: Roy Woods

Open: Mon-Sat 10-7

Policy: *'The gallery operates an open policy'*. They are particularly interested in cross-cultural work. The exhibition space is also used for classes, art forums, cabaret and drama besides monthly group and solo temporary exhibitions.

Sales: Work sold

The Space: Work fixed directly to walls, spotlights.

Exhibiting: [AW] Apply to Roy Woods. Gallery covers insurance, publicity and transport. Commission is 30%.

Access: BR Balham

Belgrave Gallery

A commercial gallery specialising in British Post-Impressionists and modern painters.

Address: 22 Mason's Yard, Duke Street, London SW1 tel 01 930 0294

Contact: Director

Open: Mon-Fri 10-6

Access: Buses 9,14,19,22,38,509; Underground Piccadilly Circus and Green Park

Ben Uri Art Society

[Pa,Sc,Pr]

Address: 21 Dean Street, London W1V 6NE tel 01 437 2852

Contact: Curator Agi Katz

Open: Mon, Thurs 10-5; Closed Aug

Policy: A permanent collection of art by Jewish artists and exhibitions by Jewish artists or on Jewish themes.

Access: Buses 7,8,14,14a,19,22,22b,24,25,29,38,55, 73,134,176; Underground Tottenham Court Road

Benjamin Rhodes Gallery

Commercial gallery dealing in and showing work by young contemporary artists. [VA]

Address: 4 New Burlington Place, London W1X 1SB tel 01 434 1768/9

Contact: Benjamin Rhodes

Open: Mon-Fri 10-6, Sat 10.30-1.30

Policy: The gallery shows the work of young British and foreign artists in a variety of media - painting, drawing, sculpture and prints - through a programme of ten exhibitions a year. Most shows are solo with the occasional group exhibition of work by gallery artists.

Sales: Work sold; Credit scheme

Exhibiting: [AW] The gallery promotes a selected number of artists, but applications are welcome, send slides, a curriculum vitae and return postage to the directors.

Access: [S][X] Buses 9,10,14,19,22,38,73,88; Underground Green Park, Oxford Circus, Bond Street 5 mins

Bernard Jacobson

Contemporary print publishers and dealers holding regular temporary exhibitions. Gallery also at 50 West 57th Street, New York NY 100 19, USA. [Pr]

Address: 2a Cork Street, London W1 tel 01 439 8355/01 437 9140

Contact: Director

Open: Mon-Fri 10-6, Sat 10-1

Access: Buses 3,6,7,8,9,12,13,14,14a,15,16a,19,22, 22b,38,53,73,88,113,135,137,159,176; Underground Oxford Circus and Piccadilly Circus

Bethnal Green Library Hall

Exhibition space in a public library, see also Tower Hamlets Library Service.

Address: Cambridge Heath Road, London E2 0HL tel 01 980 3902/6274

Contact: Neighbourhood Librarian

Open: Mon,Tues,Thurs,Fri 9-8, Wed,Sat 9-5

Access: Buses 8,8a,106,253; Underground Bethnal Green

Bethnal Green Museum of Childhood

A branch of the Victoria & Albert Museum.

Address: Cambridge Heath Road, London E2 9PA tel 01 980 3204/4315

Contact: Anthony Burton

Open: Mon-Thurs & Sat 10-6, Sun 2.30-6; Closed Fri

Policy: The museum mounts historical exhibitions on themes relating to children. Five exhibitions are held a year each lasting four to six weeks and a permanent collection of toys, dolls, dolls' houses, puppets and children's dress is housed. A programme of children's workshops are held on Saturdays and activities are organised through the school holidays.

Access: Buses 8,8A,106,253; Underground Bethnal Green 5 mins; BR Cambridge Heath 10 mins; Limited parking at front of museum

Bezzaliel

A gallery which has revived the tradition of creating frames which can be appreciated as a work of art along with their contents. [Pa]

Address: 11-12 Halkin Arcade, Motcomb Street, London SW1 tel 01 737 6602
Contact: Lori Steinberg
Policy: The gallery's policy is to show artists from *'all spheres'*.

Bhownagree Gallery (Commonwealth Institute)

Gallery shows exhibitions of work by Commonwealth artists. [Pa,Cr,Te,Ph]

Address: Commonwealth Institute, Kensington High Street, London W8 6NQ tel 01 603 4535
Contact: Visual Arts Officer Indira Nandha,
Open: Mon-Sat 10-5, Sun 2-5
Policy: The emphasis is on paintings, crafts, photography and especially textiles. Six exhibitions are held a year and *'priority is given to artists whose work reflects their own cultural traditions and to those exhibitions with an integrated programme'*.
Sales: Work sold
The Space: One gallery, divided in two with a total of 33m linear hanging space.
Exhibiting: [AW] Applications to Indira Nandha for selection committee which meets twice a year. Gallery covers costs of printing and publicity. Artists covers framing, insurance and transport. Commission is 15%.
Access: Buses 9,27,28,31,33,49,73; Underground Kensington High Street

Birch & Conran Fine Art

Commercial gallery dealing in 20th century and contemporary art showing work by living artists in all media. [VA,Ph,Ce,LA]

Address: 40 Dean Street, Soho, London W1V 5AP tel 01 434 1246
Contact: James Birch, Paul Conran
Open: Mon-Fri 11-6; Sat by appointment
Policy: The gallery predominantly shows the work of living artists, both established and unknown, in a wide variety of media - painting, sculpture, photography, prints and ceramics and includes demonstrations and performance art. Approximately 23 exhibitions are held a year, mainly solo shows lasting between one and six weeks. Sales are made privately in Britain and abroad as well as to local galleries and museums.
Sales: Work sold; Credit scheme
The Space: The gallery has 85 square metres of exhibition space, with a large covered bookcase. Gallery plans are available.
Exhibiting: [AW] The gallery welcomes applications from artists and covers costs of insurance, publicity, mailing, catalogue, list of exhibits, preview, display and transport. Commission on sales varies. The space is occasionally hired out and terms vary.
Access: [F] Underground Piccadilly & Tottenham Court Road; Car park 2 mins

Bishopsgate Institute Gallery

The gallery is situated within and run by the Bishopsgate Foundation and Institute which is a charitable organisation. [Pa,Pr,Dr,Ph,Cr]

Address: Bishopsgate Institute, 230 Bishopsgate London EC2M 4QH tel 01 247 6844
Contact: Clerk to the Governors William Doyle
Open: Mon-Fri 9.30-5.30
Policy: The gallery runs a programme of 12 solo and mixed exhibitions a year each lasting one month. Work shown is by living artists in a variety of two-dimensional media and includes painting, prints, drawing, photography and needlework; work by *'the handicapped and disadvantaged is particularly encouraged'*. *'This is an open-access public building housing libraries, concert halls, meeting rooms etc., used intensively during the day by the local working population, with the aim of mixing art with general activities'*. The institute has a permanent collection of prints, maps and paintings mainly of the city of London.
Sales: Work sold
The Space: The space is *'a wide lined corridor'* on two levels, the upper gallery has 41.8m linear hanging space and the lower 21.5m linear space. There is a lobby of approximately 42sq m, and track lighting illuminates the space.
Exhibiting: [AW] write to the Clerk to the Governors.
Access: Buses 5,6,8,8a,9,11,22,22a,35,47,48,78,149; Underground Liverpool Street 5 mins; BR Liverpool Street 5 mins; Car park 5 mins

Black & White Gallery

A gallery specialising in black and white photographic originals and reproductions by masters and contemporary photographers. [Ph]

Address: 50-52 Monmouth Street, London WC2H 9DG tel 01 836 4109
Open: Mon-Sat 11-7

Black-Art Gallery - a Pan-African Artspace

Run by the Organisation for Black Arts Advancement and Learning Activities, the gallery is part of a community organisation, showing the work of artists of African Caribbean descent . There is also a small book and crafts shop which stocks a selection of Black Poetry, History & Art titles, as well as carving, jewellery, textiles and garments from East, West and Southern Africa. [VA,Ph,Cr,LA]

Address: OBAALA House, 225 Seven Sisters Road, Finsbury Park, Islington, London N4 2DA tel 01 263 1918
Contact: Director Shakka Dedi
Open: Tues-Fri 11-7, Sat 12-5
Policy: The Organisation for Black Arts Advancement and Learning Activities is a *'Pan-African community organisation'* which is committed to *'giving professional support to African-Caribbean artists'* and aims *'to reflect 360% of African Caribbean experience and aspirations'. 'In keeping with the African tradition of the unity of art forms, OBAALA draws no distinction between arts and*

crafts' and aims *'to bring about the desired unity between the arts and positive community development'.* The gallery encourages visitors to *'gain some insight into the work of living African-Caribbean artists and their creative expression and vision'.* It shows painting, sculpture, drawing, prints, photography, crafts and live art, with six exhibitions, each four to six weeks, a year mainly group or mixed, but the occasional solo show. The organisation also runs poetry, theatre, a shop, a summer arts school and an information resource. Performance events, music, drama, dance, 'the art of the spoken word' and discussion form important parts of the overall programme.

Sales: Sales referred to exhibitor

The Space: The gallery space is 13x6.5x3m with limited access through a 1x2.5m door.

Exhibiting: [AW] Applications are welcome from Black artists. Deadlines are advertised, usually April and October. The gallery finances insurance, publicity, catalogue, mailing, list of exhibits, preview, display, transport and artists' expenses. A commission is taken on sales from selected exhibitions.

Access: [F] Buses 4,19,29,230,236,253; Underground Finsbury Park 1 min; BR Finsbury Park 1 min

Blackfriars Photography Project

Display space available in the community centre. [Ph]

Address: Beormund Community Centre, 177 Abbey Street, London SE1 tel 01 237 9312

Contact: Project Worker Vivienne Reiss

Open: Mon-Fri 9-6

Policy: The photography project arranges exhibitions in the hall and foyer areas of work arising from their workshops and also from submissions by photographers.

The Space: The hall has four free-standing screens about 3.3x6.5m, with additional wall space in the foyer.

Exhibiting: [AW] Applications should go to the Project Workers and have to be approved by the community centre's management committee.

Access: [F] Downstairs. Buses 188,47,70,1,177; Underground London Bridge

Blackheath Gallery

Contemporary gallery showing oils, sculpture, watercolours and limited edition prints. [VA,Pr]

Address: 34a Tranquil Vale, London SE3 tel 01 852 1802

Contact: Director J Corless

Open: Mon-Wed,Fri,Sat 10-6

Sales: Work sold

Exhibiting: [AW] Applications welcomed from artists *'at home and abroad'.*

Access: BR Blackheath

Blackman Harvey Ltd

Large framing business with massive range of stock and some work on display. [VA,Pr]

Address: 11 Masons Avenue, Coleman Street, London EC2 tel 01 726 2502

Open: Mon-Fri 9.30-5

Policy: Also at 29 Earlham Street, London WC2 tel 01 836 1904, open Mon-Fri 9-6, Sat 10-4.

Access: Buses to Barbican; BR & Underground Moorgate

Blenheim Gallery

A commercial gallery showing changing exhibitions of contemporary paintings, prints and ceramics. [Pa,Pr,Ce]

Address: 3 Blenheim Crescent, London W11 tel 01 229 1341

Contact: Exhibition Organiser

Open: Tues-Sat 11-6

Access: Buses 7,15,52,52a; Underground Ladbroke Grove

Blond Fine Art

A private gallery showing 20th Century British painting, drawing, sculpture and graphics. [VA,Ce]

Address: Unit 10, Canal Side Studios, 2-4 Orsman Road, London W1 tel 01 437 1230

Contact: Director

Open: Mon-Fri 10-6, Sat 10-1; or by appointment

Access: Buses 3,6,7,8,12,13,15,16a,25,53,73, 88,113,135,137,159,176; Underground Oxford Circus

Bloomsbury Galleries I & II & Dixon Gallery

Three gallery spaces within the Institute of Education showing the work of living artists. [VA,Ph,Cr]

Address: Institute of Education, 20 Bedford Way, London WC1K 0AL tel 01 636 1500

Contact: Exhibition Organiser William Newland/Shirley Lackner

Open: Mon-Fri 9-8.30 (term-time); Mon-Fri 9-6 (vacations), Sat 9-12.30; Closed Sun

Policy: The institute aims to *'encourage young artists and makers through individual, group and college exhibitions to gain experience in mounting and publicising their work and to use the experience as a stepping stone for their careers', but also provides space for more-established artists. A varied programme of 27 shows a year, each lasting two weeks includes group, mixed and solo shows in a wide variety of media - painting, sculpture, drawing, prints, photography and crafts. Exhibitions relating to art education are included in the programme and shows from abroad 'complement the international activities of the Institute of Education'.* A permanent collection of 200 paintings, sculpture, prints and ceramics is housed.

Sales: Work sold

The Space: Bloomsbury I has 93m linear hanging space 2.5-3m in height, Bloomsbury II has 31m linear space 2.5m in height and Dixon Gallery has 62m linear space 2.5m in height. All are lit by a combination of natural and spot lighting. Hanging is from rails or by direct fixing to the wall and six showcases are available.

Exhibiting: [AW] Applications are welcome, send slides and details to the Exhibition Organiser. The space is hired out to exhibitors and the gallery covers costs of insurance, mailing, invitation cards to the preview to persons on the Institute's mailing list.

Access: [U][T][L][F] Buses 5,7,8,19,22,22b,25,38,55,68, X68,77,77a; Underground Russell Square 3 mins; Euston 5 mins; Goodge Street 5 mins; Warren Street 5 mins

Bloomsbury Theatre

A theatre foyer gallery showing two dimensional work by recent graduates and less established artists. [Pa,Pr,Dr,Ph]

Address: 15 Gordon Street, London WC1H 0RH tel 01 388 3363
Contact: Theatre Director Andy Arnold
Open: Evenings; at other times by appointment
Policy: The gallery, which is financed by the theatre, aims to show painting, prints and photography by recent graduates (especially from the Slade School of Art) and young artists who are unable to show in established galleries. Some exhibitions relate to the theatre programme, which includes opera, theatre, dance and music. Eight exhibitions of between four and six weeks were shown last year, including five solo shows.
Sales: Sales referred to exhibitor
The Space: A variety of wall spaces suitable for two-dimensional work are available, these are broken by theatre doors, bar, fire exits etc.
Exhibiting: [AW] Write or telephone the Theatre Director. Commission on sales is 10%.
Access: [S] Underground Euston, Euston Square

Book Works

Book Works deals solely with the work of artists using the book as their medium of expression and predominantly holds group shows by living artists and makers, in a variety of different venues. [Bo]

Address: Number 1 Arch, Green Dragon Court, Bedale Street, Borough Market, London SE1 9AH tel 01 407 1692
Contact: Jane Rolo
Open: By appointment
Policy: Apart from promoting the book form the gallery aims to bring together *'as many disparate elements of the field as possible'*. Writers, artists, printers and bookbinders are given the chance to exhibit and collaborate on projects. Occasionally workshops and discussions accompany exhibitions. Site works and site specific projects have been arranged locally. Book Works is presently seeking a more permanent exhibition space.
Sales: Work sold
The Space: At present Book Works has no permanent space. Exhibitions and events are organised for specific venues throughout the country and abroad. However the office is open for those wishing to look at work and discuss projects for artists to show us their work.
Exhibiting: [AW] Normally work is invited but artists may show work by appointment and discuss ideas for exhibitions. Gallery finances insurance, printing and mail-out of publicity, catalogue/card, list of exhibits, preview costs, display, transport and artists expenses. Commission 20-25%.
Access: [F] Buses to London Bridge; BR London Bridge 2 mins; Underground London Bridge 2 mins. Monument and Bank 5 mins

Boundary Gallery Ltd

Gallery showing monthly exhibitions of modern British masters and specialising in immigrant expressionist artists. [VA]

Address: 98 Boundary Road, St John's Wood, London NW8 0RH tel 01 624 1126
Contact: Director Agi Katz
Open: Tues-Sat 11-6
Policy: Shows work by established names like Bomberg, Epstein etc as well as contemporary and young artists like Ghisha Koenig, James MacDonald and Robert Speight.
Sales: Work sold
Access: Buses Swiss Cottage; BR South Hampstead, Kilburn High Road

Bow House Gallery

Commercial gallery, opened in 1988, dealing in and showing work by living artists. [Pa,Sc,Dr,Te]

Address: 35 Wood Street, Barnet, Hertfordshire EN5 4BE tel 01 440 4672
Contact: Pauline and John Brown
Open: Thurs-Sat 10-5, Sun 12-5; and by appointment
Policy: The gallery aims to *'present a wide range of work by professional artists - sculpture, painting, prints and textiles'* and provide *'affordable art for the home or work place', through a programme of six mixed exhibitions a year each lasting three weeks. A changing display of work by gallery artists can be seen by appointment between exhibitions. Demonstrations accompany some shows.*
Sales: Work sold; Credit card
The Space: The gallery of approximately 85 square metres has 37m linear hanging space lit by track and spot lights and hanging is by *'track and hanger'*. There are plinths, both built-in and temporary, for sculpture and a double-sided glass showcase 6x1x0.5m is available. A walled garden for sculpture is reached through the gallery.
Exhibiting: [AW] Applications are welcome, send slides or photographs. The gallery covers printing of publicity, mailing, list of exhibits and the preview and takes 40% commission plus VAT on sales.
Access: [X] Buses 26,84,107,263,307; Underground High Barnet 5 mins; Public car park 3 mins

Book Works: Xmas Show 1984

Bow Library

Exhibition space in a public library.

Address: Stafford Road, London E3
Contact: Neighbourhood Librarian
Open: Mon,Tues,Thurs,Fri 9-8, Wed 9-5, Sat 9-12.30 & 1.30-5
Policy: See also Tower Hamlets Library Service.
Access: Buses 8,8a,106

Brazilian Centre Gallery

Gallery showing exhibitions of Brazilian contemporary art, including painting, drawing, photography, print, sculpture and crafts. [VA,Cr]

Address: 15 Berkeley Street, London W1 tel 01 499 0877 ext 223
Contact: Cultural Commercial Sections Brazilian Embassy
Open: Mon-Fri 10-6
Policy: Exhibitions change monthly, appropriate shows are advertised in *Crafts* magazine.
Sales: Work sold
Access: Buses Piccadilly; Underground Green Park

British Library

The British Library has its own galleries for the display of books, manuscripts, maps, music, bindings and stamps from the library collection. Also has regular temporary exhibitions on specific topics related to the collections. [Bo,Ms]

Address: Great Russell Street, London WC1 tel 01 636 1544
Open: Mon-Sat 10-5, Sun 2.30-6
Access: Buses to Holborn; Underground Tottenham Court Road

British Museum

A national museum showing the works of mankind from prehistoric to comparatively recent times. Regular exhibitions in the Prints and Drawings Department.

Address: Great Russell Street, London WC1B 3DG tel 01 636 1555
Open: Mon-Sat 10-5, Sun 2.30-6
Access: [U][T][L][F] Buses 7,8,14,19,22,24,25,29,38,55, 68,73,77,77a,134; Underground Tottenham Court Road, Russell Square, Holborn

Brixton Tate Library

A public library showing temporary exhibitions of contemporary art. [VA]

Address: Brixton Oval, London SW2 tel 01 274 7451
Contact: Librarian
Open: Mon 9-7, Tues & Fri 9-6, Thurs 9-1, Sat 9.30-1; closed Thurs

Browse & Darby Limited

A commercial art gallery which specialises in 20th century British and French painting and sculpture. [Pa,Sc]

Address: 19 Cork Street, London W1 tel 01 734 7984
Contact: Director W Darby
Open: Mon-Fri 10-5.30, Sat 10.30-1
Policy: Exhibitions of contemporary English painting are also shown.
Access: Buses 3,6,9,12,13,14,14a,15,19,22,22b,38,53, 88,159,509; Underground Piccadilly Circus

Bruce Castle Museum

Collections of local and postal history and the museum of the Middlesex Regiment. [VA,Ph,Cr]

Address: Lordship Lane, Tottenham, London N17 8NU tel 01 808 8772
Contact: Curator
Open: Daily 1-5; Middlesex Regimental Museum Tues-Sat 1-5
Policy: Occasional temporary exhibitions are shown.
Access: Buses123,243; BR Bruce Grove

Brunel Gallery

This gallery predominantly exhibits the work of living artists and makers including students and teachers in monthly solo shows. [VA,Ph,Cr]

Address: Brunel University, Cleveland Road, Uxbridge, Middlesex UB8 3PH tel 0895 74000 ext 2052
Contact: Co-ordinator of Exhibitions & Design Alan Bennett
Open: Mon-Thurs 9-9, Oct-Easter; Fri-Sat 9.30-5, Sun 2-7, Mon-Fri 9-5, Easter-Sept; Closed Easter week
Policy: The gallery aims to provide a programme of exhibitions that will be of interest to both those who work in the university and the general public, with emphasis placed on *'accessible and interesting'* work. Gallery policy is to present a large proportion of shows displaying the work of *'committed and newly emerging artists that it believes deserve attention'*. Occasionally exhibition-related talks, workshops, demonstrations and concerts are organised.
Sales: Work sold
The Space: 14x14x3m high with 44m linear hanging space comprised of movable hessian-covered walls. Natural, fluorescent and spot lighting. Gallery plans available. The gallery space is occasionally used for other university activities.
Exhibiting: [AW] Apply with slides to the Co-ordinator of Exhibitions & Design. Gallery finances insurance, printing and mail-out of publicity, catalogue/card, list of exhibits, preview costs, display and transport costs. Commission 25%.
Access: [X] Buses 223,204,207 4 mins walk; BR West Drayton 30 mins walk; Underground Uxbridge 20 mins; Public car park 2 mins

Building Centre Gallery

Part of the Building Centre, the gallery provides an exhibition centre for the display of prints, drawings, products related to architecture and building.

[VA,Pa,Pr,Dr,Ph,Ar]

Address: 26 Store Street, London WC1E 7BT tel 01 637 1022
Contact: Events Services Manager Sheena Parsons
Open: Mon-Fri 9.30-5.15, Sat 10-1
Policy: The gallery mounts about eight month-long exhibitions a year on subjects loosely linked to the construction industry. The programme - of interest to a specialist and general audience - includes art based on architecture, art and design for buildings (ie architectural ironwork) and architectural artifacts.
Sales: Sales referred to exhibitor
The Space: Plans are available of the three interlocking galleries which can be used individually or as one large space. Details of the complex lighting and hanging systems are available on request.
Exhibiting: **[AW]** Applications welcomed but should be made in writing well in advance as the spaces are rapidly booked. Gallery £120 per day, £700 per week, Yerbury room £75 per day, Jubilee room £80 per day. The centre provides a list of exhibits and mails out publicity material. Commission on sales is 15%.
Access: **[U][T][L][F]** Underground Goodge Street 5 mins, Warren Street, Tottenham Court Road 8 mins; BR Euston 15 mins

Burgh House

Run by Burgh House Trust, a registered charity, as part of a community arts centre. [VA,Ph]

Address: New End Square, Hampstead, London NW3 1LT tel 01 431 0144
Contact: Administrator Pauline Pleasance
Open: Wed-Sun 12-5, bank holiday Mon 2-5; closed Christmas, New Year, Good Friday
Policy: A hire space which mainly shows work by living artists in a wide range of media - painting, sculpture, drawing, prints and photography, through a programme of approximately 20, two-week exhibitions a year, which are a combination of group and solo shows. The audience is wide ranging, the arts centre and facilities *'is open to all'* and visitors include people from the locality and all over London, as well as tourists from Britain and abroad. The trust also handles permanent and semi-permanent collections as well as mounting museum exhibitions and organising concerts, meetings and private functions.
Sales: Sales referred to exhibitor
The Space: A panelled room 5.5x5.5x2.5m with track and spot lighting. Hanging is from a picture rail only.
Exhibiting: **[AW]** Applications are welcome, write to the Administrator. The space is hired to artists at £200 for two weeks, no commission is taken on sales and artists are responsible for all organisation and expenses, A programme of events and a poster publicises all art centre activities.
Access: **[X]** Buses 24,46,168,268,C11; Underground Hampstead; BR Hampstead Heath

Cadogan Contemporary

A commercial gallery specialising in sporting and decorative painters. [Pa]

Address: 108 Draycott Avenue, London SW3 tel 01 581 5451
Contact: Director
Open: Mon-Fri 10-7
Policy: This gallery predominantly shows the work of young artists.
Access: Buses 11,19,22,219; Underground Sloane Square

Café Casbar

This gallery exhibiting predominantly prints, illustration and photography, aims to show solo exhibitions young talented artists that have not exhibited before. [Pa,Pr,Dr,Ph]

Address: 52 Earlham Street, Covent Garden, London WC2 tel 01 379 7768
Contact: Katie Law, Smith's of Covent Garden Limited, 28 Neal Street, Covent Garden, London, WC2 tel 01 836 6252
Open: Mon-Fri 9am-10.30pm, Sat 11-10.30, Sun 11-5.30
Policy: Artists are encouraged to play upon the café environment and use this as a theme for exhibitions, this also includes designing a menu cover and poster to be used for the duration of the show. The audience is drawn mainly from visitors to the café throughout the day and it is hoped that the prices of works would be kept reasonably low. Exhibitions usually last a month.
Sales: Work sold
The Space: Gallery approximately 2.5m high with 30m linear hanging space. Direct fixing with sunken spot lighting fitted with dimmer switches. The gallery cannot accommodate works larger than 1.5m square. Gallery plans available.
Exhibiting: Gallery finances insurance, printing and mail-out of publicity. Commission 30%.
Access: **[F]** BR Charing Cross 5 mins; Underground Leicester Square, Covent Garden 2 mins; Public car park 2 mins

Café Casbar

Café Gallery

The gallery is part of the Last Chance Centre, a local-authority funded community centre which runs art and sport-based classes for the local community. [Pa,Pr,Dr,Ph,Cr]

Address: The Last Chance Centre, 87 Masbro Road, London W14 0LR tel 01 748 3020 ext 3760, 01 603 1293

Contact: Martin Chesterman

Open: Mon-Fri 8.30-5, Sat 8.30-12noon

Policy: The gallery space is situated in the café which is the 'hub' of the community centre. Work shown is mainly two-dimensional, and recently the emphasis has been upon painting and photography, but drawings, prints, pottery, sculpture and jewellery are also shown. *'We aim to reflect the interests of the users of the centre, who include local building workers, employees of the BBC, people with disabilities and the local community in general. Over the last year ten month-long exhibitions have been held, being solo and group shows of work by living artists.'*

Sales: Work sold

The Space: Lighting is by spots. A double glass-framed showcase is available for small works.

Exhibiting: [AW] Applications are welcome, telephone or call personally. Commission of 10% is taken and frames are available for use by exhibitors. Gallery plans are also available.

Access: [U][T][L] Buses 9,12,27,28,33,49,73,88,105, 207,220,237,283,295; Underground Shepherds Bush, Hammersmith 10 mins

Café Gallery

Administered by Bermondsey Artists Group this gallery mainly shows solo exhibitions of members' work and work from local community groups but also stages open and invited exhibitions. [VA,Ph,Cr,LA]

Address: By the Pool, Southwark Park, Bermondsey, London SE16 tel 01 232 2170, 01 237 1230

Contact: Ron Henocq

Open: Summer 10-5, Winter 10-4

Policy: Gallery policy is to provide an alternative exhibition space for artists and other groups, and to encourage active involvement in the visual arts. Emphasis is placed on work that is relevant to the area. Shows normally run for three weeks.

Sales: Work sold; Credit card; Credit scheme

The Space: Main gallery 13x5.5x3.5m high. Kitchen gallery 5x3x3m high. Track-mounted tungsten and spot lighting. Gallery plans available.

Exhibiting: [AW] Gallery finances printing and mail-out of publicity and catalogue/card. Commission 25%.

Access: [F] Buses 1,47,70,108b,181,188; Underground Surrey Docks, Rotherhithe 2 mins; Thamesline Cherry Garden Pier

Cahill and Grebler Gallery

A commercial gallery showing contemporary work including sculpture and photographs from this country and elsewhere. [VA,Ph,Dr,LA]

Address: 65 Dalling Road, London W6 0JD tel 01 748 3742

Contact: Exhibition Organiser

Open: Mon-Sat 9-6

Policy: The gallery shows exhibitions and installations by UK and International artists in solo, group and theme shows, and for the next year, will operate solely as an exhibition space for hire.

Sales: Work sold; Credit card; Credit scheme

Exhibiting: [AW] The gallery is interested in seeing new work. Hire charge is per week, no commission charged. Gallery covers insurance and undertakes invigilation.

Access: [F] except basement Buses 226,9,73,27,10; Underground Hammersmith, Ravenscourt Park

Calvert Gallery

Gallery exhibiting graphic work. [Pr]

Address: 26 Pimlico Road, London SW1 tel 01 730 9347/8

Contact: Sarah Guinan

Open: Mon-Fri 10-6, Sat 11-4

Access: Buses 11,39; Underground Sloane Square

Camberwell Gallery

A gallery with a permanent stock of ceramics, glass, prints, sculpture, painting and crafts and changing exhibitions. [VA,Cr]

Address: 2 Grove Lane, London SE5 tel 01 703 8240

Open: Mon-Sat 12-7

Access: Buses 12,36,36a,171

Camberwell School of Art & Crafts

A gallery within an educational setting showing exhibitions of work from students as well as from other artists. [VA,Cr]

Address: The London Institute, Peckham Road, London SE5 tel 01 228 8949

Contact: Deputy Head Ms M Buck tel 01 703 0987 ext 160

Open: Mon- Fri 9.30-8

Sales: Work sold

Exhibiting: Commission is 25%.

Access: Buses 36,36A,36B from BR Victoria, 12,171 from BR Waterloo, 12 from BR Peckham Rye, 36,36a,36b from BR New Cross, New Cross Gate, 12,171 from BR Elephant & Castle; 36,36a,36b from Oval Underground

Camden Arts Centre

Contemporary arts centre showing all aspects of visual arts, photography and crafts. [VA,Ph,Cr]

Address: Arkwright Road, London NW3 6DG tel 01 435 2643 or 5224

Contact: Director Zuleika Dobson

Open: Mon-Fri 10.30-5.30, Sat, Sun 12-6

Policy: Four galleries with a bookshop and artshop. Educational workshops for schools and special groups relating to the exhibition programme. There is an art school run by CATMB and artist residencies.

Sales: Work sold

The Space: Four galleries, total linear space 119m. New gallery suitable for young and unestablished artists,

hanging by direct fixing, spotlights. Garden available for sculpture.
Exhibiting: [AW] Gallery covers insurance, publicity, mailing, transport and framing. Commission is 35%.
Access: [X] BR Finchley Road, Frognal; Underground Finchley Road, Hanpstead; Buses 82,13,113

Camden Institute

[VA,Cr,LA]

Address: 87 Holmes Road, London NW5 tel 01 267 1414
Contact: Charles Gebhard or Ashton Chadwick
The Space: A space of about 80 square metres with about 21.5m linear hanging space lit by spots, fluorescents and natural light. Hanging is from a rail.
Exhibiting: [AW] Apply to committee, commission is 10% and artists are responsible for all costs.
Access: Buses 27,134,135; Underground Kentish Town; BR Kentish Town

Camerawork

The gallery, part of a charitable organisation, shows and deals in photographic work by living artists, and is financed by public funds. [Ph]

Address: 121 Roman Road, Bethnal Green, London E2 0QN tel 01 980 6256
Contact: Anna Harding/Dawn Langley
Open: Tues-Fri 1-6, Sat 11-3
Policy: The gallery exhibits *'a broad range of photographic-based media including tape/slide, video, and photographic installation'* with an emphasis on *'work which addresses contemporary photographic and artistic debates as well as issues of social importance'.* Shows are predominantly the work of young British artists with some work from abroad. The programmme of nine exhibitions a year each lasting five weeks includes solo and *'theme based'* group shows, many are *'self-generated shows of new, often commissioned work'* and occasionally touring exhibitions are taken. The audience is wide ranging, local, national and international, and *'specialist audiences'* are targetted for particular exhibitions and events. A varied programme of talks and seminars is held in conjunction with shows, and the darkroom facilities are also used for practical courses and workshops in photography.
Sales: Work sold
The Space: The gallery with 30m linear hanging space, 3.7m high and an additional 8m of movable partitions has a large usable front window space as well as a back garden. Thorn lighting system is used and work is hung directly on white plasterboard walls. The gallery is alarmed and constantly invigilated. Gallery plans are available.
Exhibiting: [AW][EF] Applications are welcome. A monthly viewing date is held when artists can bring work/proposals, phone first for appointment. Exhibitors receive a fee and additional funding for production of work for some shows; the gallery supports EPR in principle. Insurance, printing of publicity, catalogue/card, list of exhibits, mailing, display and preview costs are covered and 30% commission is taken on sales.
Access: [U][T] Buses 8,8a,106,253; Underground Bethnal Green

Canada House Gallery

The gallery which is run by the Canadian High Commission and is situated within Canada House, shows work by Canadian artists. [VA,Ph,Cr,LA]

Address: Canada House, Trafalgar Square, London SW1 tel 01 629 9492 x 246
Contact: Visual Arts Officer Michael Regan
Open: Mon-Fri 11-5
Policy: The gallery holds exhibitions of contemporary Canadian art, including painting, sculpture, drawings, prints, crafts, photography and live art. The number and length of exhibitions is varied. The gallery also runs an education programme of talks, seminars and cultural events generated by the Cultural Affairs Department of Canada House. Many of these events relate to the exhibitions being held.
Sales: Work sold
The Space: Two galleries providing 222 square metres with 87m linear hanging space.
Exhibiting: [AW] Applications are welcome from Canadian artists only. The gallery finances insurance, publicity, catalogue and card, mailing, transport, private view and artists' costs.
Access: Disabled access by prior arrangement Underground Leicester Square, Piccadilly, Charing Cross

Carlile Gallery

A gallery showing a changing programme of contemporary visual arts including installation, painting and photography. [VA,Ph]

Address: 341 Goswell Road, London EC1 tel 01 837 1639
Contact: Director Barbara Carlile
Open: Tues-Sat 11-6
Access: Buses 4,19,30,38,43,73,153,171,171a,196, 214,263a,277,279,279a; Undergound Angel

Cartoon Gallery

This commercial gallery shows the work of established and up-and-coming cartoonists in a mixture of group and solo shows. [Dr,Pa,Pr]

Address: 83 Lambs Conduit Street, London WC1A 3NA tel 01 242 5335
Contact: Pat Huntley, Mel Calman
Open: Mon-Fri 10.30-5.30, Sat 11-2
Policy: The gallery aims to appeal to people that would not normally visit galleries and the *'atmosphere is informal'.* Many customers are young and buying for the first time. Graphic works (prints, watercolours and illustrations) are also shown. Exhibitions normally run for two to three weeks.
Sales: Work sold
Exhibiting: [AW] Apply with examples of work. There is a negotiable hire fee. Gallery finances printing and mail-out of publicity and preview costs. Commission 40%.
Access: [F] Buses 5,8,15,19,25,38; Underground Russell Square, Holborn 5 mins; Public car park 5 mins

Castlebar Gallery

Address: 17 Castlebar Road, Ealing, London W5 2DL tel 01 997 6060
Contact: Director
Open: Opening by appointment and on open days announced in the press
Policy: A private gallery holding mixed shows of contemporary work from time to time. Solo shows by arrangement.
Access: Buses 65,83,112,274,297; Underground Ealing Broadway; BR Ealing Broadway

Catto Gallery

A gallery specialising in 19th and 20th Century watercolours. [Pa]

Address: 100 Heath Street, Hampstead, London NW3 tel 01 435 6660
Open: Tues-Sat 10-6

CCA Galleries

A gallery which is 'Europe's leading publishers of lithographs, etchings, mezzotints and screenprints and which features the work of over 100 established and up-and-coming artists'. [Pa,Pr]

Address: 8 Dover Street, London W1X 3PJ tel 01 499 6701
Contact: Gallery Director Lynne Williams tel 01 499 6701
Open: Mon-Fri 9.30-5.30, Sat 10-4
Policy: It provides a varied exhibition programme of seven or eight solo or theme exhibitions a year which alternate with other exhibitions including the Summer and Christmas shows to make 14 exhibitions a year. Over 200 editions are commissioned a year by up to 80 artists to form the Collections. These *'offer a unique opportunity for artists to have their work brought before a wide audience'* and prints are sold world-wide by mail order from catalogues.
Access: Buses 9,14,19,22,25,38; Underground Green Park

Cecilia Colman Gallery

This commercial gallery, which is on the Crafts Council's selected list, exhibits the work of artists and makers and designers with a permanent collection shown alongside a changing display of work for sale. [Sc,Ce,Gl,Je,Te]

Address: 67 St John's Wood High Street, London NW8 7NL tel 01 722 0686
Contact: C. R. Colman
Open: Mon-Fri 10-5.30, Sat 2-5, Nov-Dec all day Sat
Policy: The gallery *'specialises in the finest British studio ceramics, blown and kiln formed glass, turned and carved wood, jewellery and textiles, and aims to bring together examples of new craft and design work by both established and emerging artists.'*
Sales: Work sold; Credit card
The Space: Gallery space 12x4m with open suspended shelving and lockable glazed display cabinets available.
Exhibiting: [AW] Apply to Cecilia Colman. Gallery finances insurance, printing and mail-out of publicity and preview costs. Commission 33.3%.
Access: [F] Underground St Johns Wood; Buses 13 46, 82,113

Centaur Gallery

Commercial gallery which deals in and shows the work of living artists as well as antiques. [VA]

Address: 82 Highgate High Street, Highgate Village, London N6 tel 01 340 0087
Contact: Dinah & Jan Wieliczko
Open: Mon-Fri 10-6
Policy: The gallery specialises in *'original, figurative, but non-academic work by lesser-known artists'*. The main aim is to promote artists' work by *'placing it in newly inspired collections often initiated by the gallery, we have a young and optimistic clientele, established over the years, which values our influence and advice'*. Painting, sculpture, prints and drawings, with a folk and ethnic bias are shown. Six month-long exhibitions are held each year, these are mainly mixed with some solo shows of work by living artists. A permanent collection of works by gallery artists is housed.
Sales: Work sold; Credit scheme
The Space: Extensive facilities available at Directors' discretion. There is a garden for the placing of sculpture.
Exhibiting: [AW] The gallery looks at the work of individual artists, and the policy is to promote a selected number of artists. 33.3% commission is taken on sales.
Access: [F] Buses 210,271; Underground Archway, Highgate 8 mins

Central School of Art & Design Gallery

This gallery primarily exhibits student work but also occasionally shows group exhibitions of work by

Cecilia Colman Gallery: stoneware vessel by Ben Arnup

other artists and design organisations. [VA,Ph,Cr,De,LA]

Address: Central School of Art and Design, Southampton Row, London WC1B 4AP tel 01 405 1825

Contact: Mike Oakley tel 01 404 5818

Open: Variable

Policy: The gallery's primary function is to display the work of current students. However exhibition proposals will be considered if the work to be shown is of the *'highest visual standard and will contribute by its presence to the education of students'*.

Sales: Sales referred to exhibitor

The Space: 20x8x6.5m with 36m linear hanging space. Limited access 2x1.5m. Gallery plans available.

Exhibiting: Exhibition space can be hired for up to four weeks at £600 a week.

Access: [X] Buses 19,38,68,507; Underground Holborn 2 mins; Public car park 3 mins

Central Space

The gallery, within an arts centre, is run by the Association for Cultural Advancement through Visual Art (ACAVA), an artists' charitable organisation. [VA,Ph,LA]

Address: 23-29 Faroe Road, London W14 0EL tel 01 603 3039

Contact: Duncan Smith, 6 Sinclair Road, London W14 0NH

Open: Mon-Sat 10-6

Policy: The gallery aims to show *'a wide range of innovative work in all media relevant to the artistic, cultural and social concerns of today'* through a programme of eleven, three-week exhibitions a year, including painting, sculpture, drawing, prints, photography and live art, with a particular emphasis on installation work. Most of the shows are solo, with the occasional two-person or mixed exhibition. ACAVA provides *'a context in which the question of relevance can be discussed by artists of different orientation and practise'* and attracts *'a diverse audience from local communities'* through a programme of workshops, festivals and cultural events which often relate to the work on show. Studios and facilities for artists are provided at the centre.

Sales: Work sold

The Space: The gallery with 44m linear hanging space is 3-4m high and lit by good daylight from a glass roof and overhead spots. Walls are white painted brick and hanging is by *'drilling, plugging and fixing'*. Gallery plans are available. The space is occasionally used for workshops and events related to exhibitions.

Exhibiting: [AW][EF] Applications are welcome, write to Duncan Smith including photographs of recent work and an outline of the exhibition proposal. The gallery supports EPR in principle and pays a fee for exhibiting. It covers printing of publicity, catalogue/card, mailing and list of exhibits and takes 30% commission on sales.

Access: [U][T][F] Buses 9,27,28,33,49,73,91; Underground Olympia 4 mins, Shepherds Bush 10 mins, Hammersmith 10 mins, Barons Court 10 mins

Centre 181 Gallery

A municipal gallery run by London Borough Hammersmith and Fulham, which shows a vast range of work and aims to represent artists of all cultural backgrounds resident within the borough. [VA,Ph,LA]

Address: 181 King Street, Hammersmith, London W6 tel 01 741 3696 ext 3532

Contact: Tim Eastop

Open: Mon-Fri 10-5

Policy: The gallery programme includes *'a range of artists from the various cultural backgrounds which make up significant proportions of the borough's population'. 'The gallery pursues an active policy of programming artists from the council's target groups, such as people with disabilities, women artists and ethnic minorities'* and aims to provide equal opportunities to each target group. The exhibition programme has included Caribbean crafts, Argentinian sculpture, Malaysian photographs, Asian textiles, live performance art and mainstream contemporary painting. Major aims are to facilitate access to contemporary art within the locality and to provide an exhibition service for local artists. Twelve month-long exhibitions are held a year, all by living artists and most solo shows. The gallery also runs a picture loan scheme of work by local established and up and coming painters, printmakers and photographers.

Sales: Work sold; Credit scheme

The Space: The space is 10x3x3.5m with approximately 20m linear hanging space available with lighting by spots and floods on track work is hung using mirror plates and self-tapping screws. The gallery can accommodate work up to 2.5x2.5m. Cases are available for small ceramics and jewellery. Occasional talks are held in the space.

Exhibiting: [AW] Applications are welcome from artists within the borough of Hammersmith and Fulham. Telephone or write for appointment with the Visual Arts Officer. Slides and examples of work will be looked at. Costs of insurance, printing of publicity, list of exhibits and mailing are covered. 50% of the private view costs are covered, and occasionally transport costs are met. The artist is asked to assist with the mailing. 20%

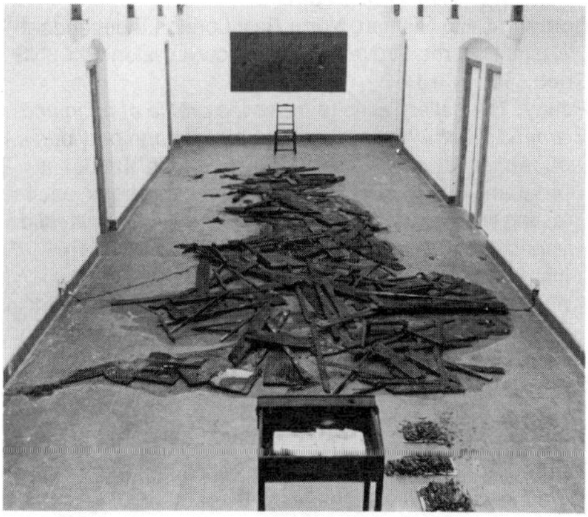

Central Space: 'Common Knowledge' an installation by Alison Marchant (Photo: FXP)

commission is taken on sales. Gallery plans are available. Supports EPR.
Access: [F] awaiting toilet facilities. Underground Hammersmith 8 mins, Ravenscourt 3 mins

Chalk Farm Gallery

A commercial gallery handling painting, sculpture and prints, with an extensive retail outlet for a wide range of cards. [Pa,Sc,Pr]

Address: 20 Chalk Farm Road, London NW1 8AG tel 01 267 3300
Contact: Su Ellen Shorter
Open: Mon-Sun 10-5.30
Policy: A busy, informal gallery which houses *'the largest selection of etchings and lithographs in Europe'* on two floors of the gallery. Exhibitions of original paintings are mounted on the upper floors. All work is for sale and customers are from *'all walks of life', 'most people leave having purchased something between £5 and £900'.* Visitors come from *'miles around'* to see the accompanying cardshop. The gallery also undertakes framing. The Twelve exhibitions a year on the first floor change every week to four weeks *'depending on popularity'.* All shows are of the work of living artists, some mixed and some solo.
Sales: Work sold; Credit card; Deposit scheme
The Space: The gallery has four floors; a basement 13x9m, the others 10x9m, with many alcoves and recesses. Work up to 2.8x3m can be accommodated. Three glass showcases are available.
Exhibiting: [AW] The gallery welcomes applications, contact Su Shorter. 40% commission is taken on sales and exhibition costs covered by gallery varies.
Access: [X] Buses 29,31,68; Underground Chalk Farm 5 mins, Camden 5 mins

Changing Room Gallery

Run by North East London Independent Arts, a 'local artists' pressure group and agency' and showing work by living artists. [VA,Ph,Cr,LA]

Address: Lloyd Park, Forest Road, Walthamstow, London E17 tel 01 521 7397
Contact: Clive Gillman, North East London Independant Arts, 6 Lucerne Grove, Walthamstow, London E17 3NS
Open: Sat, Sun 12-6
Policy: The gallery aims to *'raise the profile of art in and around Walthamstow, it acts as a focus and provides a showcase for artists in North East London'* through a programme of thirteen, mainly group exhibitions, each lasting two weeks. *'Many local organisations present a varied and balanced programme'* and work shown includes painting, sculpture, drawing, prints, photography, crafts and live art. The surrounding park is used in addition to the indoor space, and workshops in printing, sketching and mural painting are held.
Sales: Sales referred to exhibitors
The Space: The space is 7x10x4m with 24m linear hanging space.
Exhibiting: [AW] Applications are welcome from artists or groups with links with the area. Costs of printing and mailing of publicity are covered and the gallery supports EPR in principle.
Access: [F] Buses 34,69,123,212,275; Underground Walthamstow Central 15 mins; BR Walthamstow Central 15 mins; Car park 3 mins

Chantal-Scherrer Contemporary Art Gallery

Promotes contemporary artists through services to business and corporations. [VA,Ph]

Address: 31 York Mansions, Prince of Wales Drive, London SW11 tel 01 720 5810
Open: Mon-Fri 10-5, Sat by appointment
Policy: Mainly holds work in oil, acrylic, watercolour as well as sculpture, photography and limited edition prints. The gallery shows mixed and theme exhibitions and also sells direct to business and other corporations as well as working with designers and architects.

Chapman Gallery

A commercial gallery opened in 1987 specialising in British artists. [Pa,Sc,Dr]

Address: 31 Lower Richmond Road, Putney, London SW15 tel 01 785 4174
Contact: Keith Chapman
Open: Tues-Sat 11-6; Sun by appointment
Access: Buses 22,265; Underground Putney Bridge; BR Putney

Charles de Temple

Contemporary crafts gallery. [Cr]

Address: 52 Jermyn Street, London SW1 tel 01 499 3639
Contact: Director Charles de Temple
Open: Mon-Fri 11-5, Sat 10.30-12
Policy: Shows own work as well as regular programme of thematic, medium-based and one-person exhibitions of high standard crafts.
Sales: Work sold
The Space: Various spaces including window on to Piccadilly Arcade.
Exhibiting: [AW] must be of high standard.
Access: Buses to Piccadilly; Underground Green Park

Chats Palace

'Bar wall space' within a community centre. [Dr,Ph]

Address: 42/44 Brooksbys Walk, Homerton, London E9 tel 01 986 6714
Contact: Programme Organiser
Open: Tues-Sat 10
Policy: The gallery aims *'to exhibit the work of various groups from the ethnic and socially mixed local population, especially those with disabilities, women artists and photographers'* through a programme of six, two to three week, exhibitions. A varied programme of workshops are held, and work produced forms part of the exhibition programme. The space is within the bar/club, it is used as a meeting place and the gallery audience is predominantly centre visitors.
The Space: The space 45x1m is lit by the bar and spot lighting.
Exhibiting: [AW][EF] Applications are welcome, contact

the programme organiser. The gallery pays a commission fee to artists and covers the costs of printing of publicity and mailing. Supports EPR in principle.

Access: [U][T][F] Buses S2,22a,35,106,253,276; BR Homerton 5 mins

Cherry Orchard Vegetarian Restaurant

Restaurant space run by the Pure Land Co-operative, which is part of the London Buddhist Centre. [Pa,Pr,Dr,Ph]

Address: 241 Globe Road, London E2 0HU tel 01 980 6678

Contact: Joan Karmen, 43 Thomas Hollywood House, Approach Road, London E2 tel 01 981 3748

Open: Tues-Sat 12-10.30

Policy: The programme of nine, five to six week exhibitions includes a variety of small works in two dimensions - painting, prints, drawings and photography. The restaurant is of primary importance and *'work must not have violent, destructive or pornographic content'*. All work is by living artists and exhibitors are responsible for organisation with help from the restaurant representative. The audience is the restaurant customers who are *'youngish and live and work locally; teachers, social workers and local government workers predominate'*.

Sales: Sales referred to exhibitor

The Space: *'One large room and a small alcove which can hold 30 small works or twelve medium works'*. Hanging is by picture hooks from rail.

Exhibiting: **[AW]** Applications are welcome, send slides or telephone for an appointment with Joan Karmen.

Access: **[F]** Buses 8,8a,106,253; Underground Bethnal Green 5 mins

Chisenhale Dance Space

Primarily a dance space with foyer/coffee bar exhibition space. [Pa,Sc,Dr,Ph,Cr,LA]

Address: 64-84 Chisenhale Road, Bow, London E3 5QY tel 01 981 6617/980 8115

Contact: Nina Grahame, Amanda Leon

Open: Mon-Fri 10-5 (Varies)

Policy: A dance space specialising in *'new dance and movement-based work'*. Collaborations are organised with artists, the local community and Camerawork (see separate entry), and a small exhibition space is used to show work in a variety of media including painting, drawing, sculpture, photography, crafts and live art; *'we are interested in everything related to dance/movement and are open to suggestions'*. In the last year five exhibitions of work by living artists have been mounted and a varied programme of dance seminars, workshops, classes and performance showcases is held.

The Space: Foyer/coffee bar space with walls 3.5m high interrupted by *'obstacles, some movable'*.

Exhibiting: **[AW]** Applications welcome, apply to the Programming Committee. Publicity is provided through a quarterly newsletter.

Access: **[X]** Buses 8,8a,106,277; Underground Mile End, Bethnal Green both 10 mins; Local parking

Chisenhale Gallery

Independent gallery within Chisenhale Works artists' studios run by Art Place Trust Limited, a charity set up by artists to administer the building. [VA,Ph,LA]

Address: 64-84 Chisenhale Road, London E3 5EZ tel 01 981 4518

Contact: Director Emma Dexter

Open: Wed-Sat 1-6 during exhibitions, closed bank holidays

Policy: The gallery, situated in London's East End attracts visitors from all over London as well as from the immediate locality. The recent programme has included painting, sculpture, video, installation work and live art. Both solo and group shows are mounted. In future, the emphasis will be upon sculpture and large-scale installations or site specific work which utilises the large space offered. Shows will be of five to six weeks duration and six to eight shows will be organised per year. Discussions and artists' talks are sometimes held during exhibitions. Applications are welcome from locally based artists as well as those from outside London and abroad. Will also act as a London venue for contemporary art touring shows upon application.

Sales: Work sold

The Space: The gallery 19.8x11.5x4.5m high has 64m linear hanging space and is approximately 1000 square metres.The walls of brick and plasterboard, hanging by mirror plates and screws. The floor is concrete and there is a large off-street entrance with roller shutter door. The gallery is lit by tungsten halogen lighting on walls. Gallery plans are available to exhibitors.

Exhibiting: **[AW]** Applications are welcomed all year round, in the form of slides/photographs and written details sent to the Director, with SAE for return. Insurance, printing of publicity, list of exhibits, preview costs, transport and mailing out of publicity are covered wholly or partially by the gallery. Some production costs may be met. 25% commission is taken on sales. The gallery is available for hire for filming etc (not exhibitions), price on application.

Access: **[F]** Buses 8,8a,106,277; Underground Mile End 10 mins, Bethnal Green 15/20 mins; Free parking in Chisenhale Road

Chisenhale Gallery: 'The Consumption of Elements' an installation by S Trangmar and M Currah (Photo: Edward Woodman)

Chris Beetles Gallery

A gallery showing 19th and 20th century watercolours, drawings and illustrations. [Pa,Dr]

Address: 10 Ryder Street, London SW1 tel 01 839 7551/01 930 8586
Contact: Director
Open: Daily 10-5.30
Access: Buses 9,14,19,22,25,38,509; Underground Piccadilly Circus & Green Park

Christopher Hull Gallery

Independent gallery showing modern British and European painting and sculpture. [Pa,Sc]

Address: 17 Motcomb Street, London SW1 tel 01 235 0500
Contact: Christopher Hull
Policy: The gallery shows the work of *'younger artists of promise for the pleasure of all who visit'*. A revolving stock of works is kept. All work shown is by living artists. Twelve solo exhibitions of one month duration are held per year. The gallery is financed by commission taken on sales. A permanent stock is held and shown for Ayrton, Craxton, Minton, Sutherland, Vaughan and other post-war British artists.
Sales: Work sold; Credit scheme
The Space: Two large galleries are available.
Exhibiting: **[AW]** Applications are welcome and an artist is seen every day by appointment. Commission on sales is 25-40%.
Access: **[F]** Bus routes 19,22,137; Underground Sloan Square, Knightsbridge

Church Gallery

This gallery specialises in mainly solo exhibitions work that would not exist without the advent of 20th century technology. [VA,Ph]

Address: 34 Bryanston Street, Marble Arch, London W1 tel 01 281 3093
Contact: Claire Nelmes, 10 Windsor Road, London N7 6JG
Open: Tues-Sat 12-5.30
Policy: Gallery policy is to promote the work of artists that use modern technology including photography, computers, film and video. Work is aimed at both the traditional art establishment and a wider audience and exhibitions usually last a month.
Sales: Work sold; Credit scheme
The Space: Gallery one is 10x12x5m high and gallery two is 15x3x3m high. Gallery plans available.
Exhibiting: **[AW]** There is a hire fee of £200 per month. Gallery finances insurance, printing and mail-out of publicity and preview costs. Support in principle for EPR. Commission 30%.
Access: **[X]** Buses; Underground Marble Arch

Clapham Library

An exhibition space in a public library showing temporary visual arts exhibitions. [VA]

Address: Clapham Common North Side, London SW4 tel 01 622 4008
Open: Mon & Wed 11-8, Tues & Fri 9-6, Sat 2-5
Access: **[U][T][L]**

Coleridge

Gallery specialising in contemporary British glass. [Gl]

Address: 192 Piccadilly, London W1 tel 01 437 0106
Contact: Directors S & A Aaronson
Open: Mon-Fri 10-6.15, Sat 10-6
Policy: Shows comprehensive selection of British studio glass, with regular exhibitions throughout the year. See Coleridge also at 47B St George Street, Edinburgh.
Sales: Work sold
Access: Buses Piccadilly; Underground Green Park, Piccadilly Circus

Combined Harvest

This gallery promotes the work of 'artists and designers' in group and solo shows. [VA,Ph,LA]

Address: 128 Talbot Road (off Portobello Road), London NW11 1JA tel 01 221 4870
Contact: Barry Coles, Anthea Lahr
Open: Mon, Wed, Fri, Sat
Policy: Gallery policy is to exhibit the work of designers and visual artists in shows that have *'an interest beyond fine art - either in theme or performance'*. The gallery encourages events that complement exhibitions whenever possible.
Sales: Work sold; Credit scheme
The Space: 7x5x3m high with hanging by rail with track-mounted lighting. Shop window area and showcases also available.
Exhibiting: **[AW]** Applications with CV or visits to gallery welcomed. Gallery space for hire. Gallery finances insurance. Commission 33.3%.
Access: **[X]** Buses 28,31,52; Underground Ladbroke Grove, Notting Hill Gate 12 mins

Community Copyart

A photocopy workshop with a gallery showing work produced in that medium. [Pr]

Address: Culcross Buildings, Battlebridge Road, London NW1 tel 01 833 4417
Contact: Administrator
Open: Mon,Wed-Fri 10-6
Policy: The workshop is open for use for artists and the community and many of the exhibitions are accompanied by an educational workshop programme.
Access: **[F]** Buses 24,31,68,168; Underground Camden Town

Connaught Brown

A commercial gallery specialising in modern British, post impressionist and contemporary paintings, drawings and watercolours. [Pa,Dr,Sc]

Address: 2 Albermarle Street, London W1 tel 01 408 0632
Contact: Director Anthony Brown
Open: Mon-Fri 10-6, Sat 10-12.30
Policy: Four to five exhibitions per annum including at

least one contemporary exhibition. In between selection of work from gallery's stock.
Sales: Work sold
Access: **[F]** Buses 9,14,19,22,25,38,509; Underground Piccadilly Circus and Green Park

Contemporary Applied Arts

A gallery on the Crafts Council's selected list whose exhibition programme covers all areas of the applied arts in mainly group shows by selected artists and makers. [Cr]
Address: 43 Earlham Street, Covent Garden, London WC2H 9LD tel 01 836 6993
Contact: Director Tatjana Marsden
Open: Mon-Sat 10-5.30
Policy: As a membership association, gallery policy is to exhibit and sell members' works. The aim is to *'stimulate excellence in the crafts environment'* and to make the best contemporary craftwork available to the public and collectors. Alongside exhibitions there is a changing display of work for sale.
Sales: Work sold; Credit card
Exhibiting: **[AW]** Membership forms available on request. Membership is selected. Gallery finances insurance, printing and mail-out of publicity, catalogue/card, preview costs. Commission variable.
Access: **[S][X]** BR Charing Cross 10 mins; Underground Covent Garden 2 mins

Contemporary Textiles Gallery

This gallery, which is on the Crafts Council's selected list, stages a varied programme of exhibitions featuring a variety of textile works. There are four exhibitions a year showing the work of living artists and makers. [Cr,Te]
Address: 10 Golden Square, London W1R 3AF tel 01 439 9071
Contact: JE Harris
Open: Mon-Fri 10-6, Sat 11-5
Policy: The policy of the gallery is to promote and sell contemporary textile art and design, mainly for interiors. Clients are both private and corporate. There is also a changing display of work for sale.
Sales: Work sold; Credit card
The Space: Large gallery on two floors with track lighting and air conditioning.
Exhibiting: Gallery finances insurance, printing and mail-out of publicity, catalogue/card, list of exhibits, transport, display, and some artists' expenses. Commission variable.
Access: **[F]** Buses many; Underground Piccadilly Circus 2 mins

Conway Hall

Address: 25 Red Lion Square, London WC1R 4RL tel 01 242 8032/3
Contact: Exhibition Organiser G Austin
Open: 8.30-10.30pm
Access: **[F]** Buses 5,7,8,19,22,22b,25,38,55,68,77,77a, 168,171,188,196,501; Underground Holborn

Corporate Arts

Helps artists exhibit their work in the offices of private and public companies.
Address: 104 York Street, London W1
Contact: Sarah Hodson

Courtauld Institute Galleries

Galleries house several prestigious collections of fine art paintings and drawings including English watercolours, early Italian paintings and Impressionist work. [VA]
Address: Woburn Square, London WC1 tel 01 580 5015
Contact: Director Dennis Farr
Open: Mon-Sat 10-5, Sun 2-5
Access: Buses to Tottenham Court Road; Underground Russell Square, Goodge Street

Crafts Council Galleries

This gallery runs a varied programme of contemporary craftswork and historical exhibitions. [Cr]
Address: 12 Waterloo Place, Lower Regent Street, London SW1Y 4AU tel 01 930 4811
Contact: Ralph Turner
Open: Tues-Sat 10-5, Sun 2-5
Policy: Gallery policy is to *'present a changing programme of high-quality contemporary craftwork, supplemented by historical exhibitions in such a way as to encourage the understanding and appreciation of craft'.* All exhibition installations are professionally designed.
Sales: Work sold; Credit card; Credit scheme
The Space: Three exhibition spaces, gallery one 6x9m, galleries two and three 8x12m. Hanging is by direct fixing with natural and spot lighting.
Exhibiting: **[AW]** Applications are assessed by the Crafts Council Committee. Gallery meets all exhibition expenses. Will support EPR form April 1989.
Access: **[X]** Buses to Waterloo Place; BR/Underground Charing Cross 15 mins

Crafts Council Shop

Monthly exhibitions are arranged in the shop showcase, usually promoting the work of one maker with occasional group exhibitions based on a theme. [Cr]
Address: Victoria & Albert Museum, South Kensington, London SW7 2RL tel 01 589 5070
Contact: Shop Manager Clare Beck
Open: Mon-Sat 10-5.30, Sun 2.30-5.30
Policy: Work is selected from makers who are on the Crafts Council Index. The shop aims to show a wide variety of work by well established and lesser-known. The shop often arranges commissions and special orders to a customer's particular requirements and also provides a packing and postal service. Exhibitions are often linked with activities at the Crafts Council Gallery or events in the Victoria & Albert Museum.
Sales: Work sold; Credit card; Credit scheme
The Space: One secure display case 2x2x0.5m.
Exhibiting: Shop finances insurance, printing and mail-

out of publicity, catalogue/card, list of exhibits, preview costs, transport and artists' expenses. Commission charged is 100%.
Access: [U][T] Underground South Kensington 5 min

Craftsmen Potters Shop

This gallery, which is on the Crafts Council's selected list, shows mainly group exhibitions of ceramics of a domestic nature, with the emphasis on sculptural and figurative works. [Ce]

Address: William Blake House, 7 Marshall Street, London W1V 1FD tel 01 437 7605
Contact: Marta Donaghey
Open: Mon-Sat 10-5.30, Thurs 10-7
Policy: The aim of this outlet is to foster interest in studio ceramics and to share technical information with students, makers and collectors. Gallery policy is to promote the work of members of the Craftsmen Potters Association of Great Britain. Visitors include all levels of the general public, specialist collectors and overseas visitors. Talks, slide and film shows, workshop weekends and demonstrations are also organised.
Sales: Work sold; Credit card; Credit scheme
The Space: A gallery of 110 square metres with daylight and halogen lights. Stands and showcases available.
Exhibiting: Exhibitions are by invitation of the CPA Council. Gallery finances insurance, printing and mail-out of publicity, list of exhibits, preview and display costs. Support in principle for EPR. Commission 100% plus VAT.
Access: [S][X] Underground Oxford Circus, Piccadilly 5 mins

Crane Gallery

Commercial gallery dealing in Naive art 1750-1900, English and American paintings, quilts, weather-vanes, shopsigns and furniture, also contemporary artists whose work is amusing, witty and unusual. [Pa]

Crafts Council Shop at the V&A (Photo: Ed Barber)

Address: 171A Sloane Street, (First Floor), Knightsbridge, London SW1 tel 01 235 2464
Contact: Director Ian Burnell, Andras Kalman
Open: Mon-Fri 10-6, Sat 10-4

Crane Kalman Gallery

Gallery showing British and European 20th century paintings and sculpture and some contemporary artists. [VA]

Address: 178 Brompton Road, London SW3 tel 01 584 7566/3843
Contact: Director Andras Kalman
Open: Mon-Fri 10-6, Sat 10-4
Policy: The gallery shows Ben Nicholson, Graham Sutherland, Winifred Nicholson, Henry Moore, Lowry, Rusking Spear and others.
Sales: Work sold
Access: [S] Underground Knightsbridge or S Kensington

Crawshaw Gallery

Contemporary art gallery showing mainly paintings but also some sculptures. [VA,Ph]

Address: 180 Westbourne Grove W11 2RH tel 01 727 8649
Contact: Director JJ Wailes-Fairburn tel 01 727 8649
Policy: The gallery shows a range of contemporary work including thematic and solo exhibitions and has a policy of showing new artists as well as those who are well-established.
Sales: Work sold
The Space: White-walled split-level gallery with wooden stairs connecting to the office space on the top level where exhibitions continue. Grey carpet floor covering.
Exhibiting: [AW]
Access: [F] Bus routes 7,15,27,36

Creaser Gallery

A commercial gallery operating alongside Wareing and Wood Ltd specialist framers, promoting figurative and abstract art. [Pa,Pr,Dr]

Address: 316 Portobello Road, London W10 5RU tel 01 960 4928/3415
Contact: Owner Deborah Wood
Open: Tues-Sat 10.30-5.30
Policy: The gallery offers solo and group exhibitions to relatively unknown contemporary artists, and many artists are offered their first show on completing their training. Out of ten exhibitions mounted a year, three are group shows of which two may be open submissions on a theme.
Sales: Work sold; Credit card
The Space: Gallery 9x6x3.6m high with 25m hanging space. Concord track lighting and halogen 300 watt flood lights.
Exhibiting: [AW] Artists should send a CV and slides with SAE for the attention of Judith Groves, Director. The gallery covers insurance, printing and mailing of publicity, catalogue and preview costs.
Access: [F] Underground Ladbroke Grove 5 mins, Westbourne Park 10 mins; Buses 15,15a,52,52a,295

Croydon Central Library

This gallery space predominantly shows the work of local artists and societies in a mixture of group and solo shows. [Pa,Pr,Dr,Ph,Cr,LA]

Address: Mint Walk, Croydon, Surrey CR9 1ET tel 01 760 5400

Contact: Information Officer (Arts) Anna Knox, Central Library, Katharine Street, Croydon CR9 1ET tel 01 760 5400

Open: Mon 9-5, Tues-Fri 9-6, Sat 9-5

Policy: Gallery policy is to provide exhibition space free of charge for use by all local artists and cultural organisations. Occasionally the work of those living and working outside the area is also shown. Exhibitions are targetted towards local residents using the library facilities.

Sales: Sales referred to the exhibitor

The Space: Six free-standing display boards 1.5x1m each.

Exhibiting: [AW] Write or telephone for an application form. Commission 25%.

Access: [L] BR East Croydon 14 mins from London Bridge, 20 Mins from Victoria

Crucial

New painting and sculpture in changing mixed exhibitions. Contemporary art auctions run on first Saturday every month. [Pa,Sc]

Address: 204 Kensington Park Road, London W1 tel 01 229 1940

Contact: Director

Open: Mon-Sat 10-6

Access: Buses 52; Underground Notting Hill Gate

Crucial at Ravensdale

Gallery exhibits paintings and furniture, usually mixed shows lasting a month. [Pa,Sc,Fu]

Address: 34-35 Dean Street, London W1V 5AP tel 01 734 4686

Contact: Director, 204 Kensington Park Road, London W11 tel 01 229 1940

Open: Mon-Fri 9.30-5.30

Policy: Often gives first London show to young artists.

Sales: Work sold; Commission & design work undertaken

Exhibiting: [AW]

Access: Underground Tottenham Court Road

Crypt Gallery

The gallery is interested in works of a religious nature. [VA,Cr,LA]

Address: St Georges Church, Bloomsbury Way, London WC1A 2HR tel 01 405 3044

Contact: Rev Michael Day

Open: 12-7

Policy: Gallery policy is to offer young professional artists space to exhibit in central London. Exhibitions run for two weeks.

Sales: Sales referred to exhibitor

The Space: Area one 5x10m, area two 6x11m each with a hanging rail at 2m high, and natural and spot lighting. One showcase available. The church portico may also be used as an exhibition space.

Exhibiting: [AW] Apply to Michael Day. The exhibitions selection panel meets three or four times a year. Applicants are expected to organise and invigilate exhibitions. Commission 10%.

Access: Buses 7,8,19,22,25,38,55; Underground Holborn, Tottenham Court Road

Curwen Gallery

A gallery and print publishers showing monthly exhibitions of contemporary British art. [Pa,Pr]

Address: 4 Windmill Street, off Charlotte Street, London W1P 1HF tel 01 636 1459

Contact: Director Jane Hindley

Open: Mon-Fri 10-5.30, Sat 10.30-1

Policy: The gallery promotes contemporary artists working with a specific group as well as organising mixed exhibitions.

Access: Buses 14,14a,24,29,73; Underground Goodge Street

Dance Attic

A gallery at the entrance of large rehearsal studios in which a range of dance, theatrical and artistic activities takes place. [VA]

Address: 212/214 Putney Bridge Road, London SW15 tel 01 785 2055

Contact: Gallery Administrator Alexandra Crombie,

Crucial at Ravensdale: 'After the Fall of the Red Flag (in Blue)' by Mik Godley, oil on paper 100x70cm

Atwood House, Old Green Lane, Camberley, Surrey GU15 4LG tel 0276 23925 or at studios
Open: Mon-Sat 10-10, Sun 10-4
Policy: A changing programme of mainly solo two-week exhibitions is shown with the idea being *'to help artists'* and to fill the extra space with *'interesting pictures'* and *'original work'*.
Sales: Work sold
The Space: A long, wide gallery with around 23m linear hanging space with white walls, wooden floor and direct fixing which takes about 50 framed works. Gallery plans available.
Exhibiting: [AW] Contact the Administrator. Hire fee £35 a week, artist covers insurance, publicity and preview but no commission is taken on sales. Gallery is invigilated.
Access: Buses 220 to Putney Bridge Road, 17,74,30, 264,39,85,93,22 to Putney Bridge; Underground Putney Bridge

David Hicks

Features contemporary ceramics, textiles and wood. [Cr]
Address: 101 Jermyn Street, London SW1 tel 01 627 4400
Sales: Work sold
Access: Buses to Piccadilly; Underground Green Park, Piccadilly Circus

David Ker Fine Art

Commercial gallery dealing primarily in 19th and 20th century British artists showing some work by living artists. [Pa,Dr]
Address: 85 Bourne Street, London SW1W 8HF tel 01 730 8365
Contact: David Ker
Open: Mon-Fri 9.30-5.30
Policy: The gallery aims to *'provide affordable paintings, drawings and watercolours'* and holds nine exhibitions a year each lasting three weeks, these are predominantly mixed shows of figurative works with the occasional solo exhibition. It houses a permanent collection of 18th, 19th and 20th century British art and *'carries a sizeable stock of major paintings, particulary Scottish colourists, sporting artists and known and unknown English School artists'*.
Sales: Credit card; Credit scheme
Exhibiting: [AW] Figurative artists are welcome to apply. The gallery covers insurance, publicity, mailing, display, preview, transport and artists' expenses and takes 33.3% commission on sales.
Access: [X] Buses 11,19,22; Underground Sloan Square 2 mins

David Mellor

A kitchen and tableware shop placing special emphasis on products from small workshops, David Mellor cutlery and knives which is on the Crafts Council's selected list. [Cr]
Address: 26 James Street, Covent Garden, London WC2 tel 01 379 6947
Open: Mon-Fri 10-6.30, Sat 10-6
Sales: Work sold
Access: Underground Covent Garden

David Mellor

A kitchen and tableware shop selling equipment made by various makers, including pottery, woodware and baskets, and David Mellor cutlery which is on the Crafts Council's selected list. [C6]
Address: 4 Sloane Square, London SW1 tel 01 730 4259
Open: Mon-Sat 9.30-5.30
Sales: Work sold
Access: Underground Sloane Square

Design Centre

A venue for temporary exhibitions on a wide range of design issues.
Address: 28 Haymarket, London SW1Y 4SU tel 01 839 8000
Contact: Public Relations Dept
Open: Mon,Tues 10-6, Wed-Sat 10-8, Sun 10-1
Policy: The centre shows temporary exhibitions on important design issues intended to convince British industry that design is a key to commercial success, and aims to encourage the teaching of design and to increase the public's awareness of it. Exhibits range from product design/fashion/graphics and engineering design to ideas for the disabled. Also houses a design bookshop, Innovation Centre and Materials Information Centre. A centre for student work and advice on design education will be opened in 1989. Exhibits are not for sale but information on availability and manufacturers' details can be provided.
The Space: Approximately 1165 square metres and a further 1650 dedicated to the display of innovative new products and the work of young designers.
Exhibiting: Exhibits are researched to illustrate themes and designers and manufacturers should enquire about future exhibition plans from the press office ot exhibitions department.
Access: Bus routes 3,6,9,12,22b,53,159; Underground Piccadilly Circus

Desmond Page

A gallery dealing in a range of contemporary artists' work including Bill Woodrow, Anthony Gormley and Hamish Fulton. [VA]
Address: 28 Eldon Road, London W8 tel 01 937 0804
Contact: Director
Open: By appointment only
Access: Underground High Street Kensington

Diorama

The gallery is situated within the Diorama Community Arts Centre, which is a charitable, non-profit making organisation where work by local artists and others is shown. [VA,LA]
Address: 18 Park Square East, London NW1 tel 01 487 2896
Contact: Vicki Lewis

Open: Tues-Sun 12-6

Policy: The gallery aims to provide an exciting programme of contemporary art, showing the work of *'artists either working or resident in the locality, as well as other emerging artists.'* The centre organises talks, workshops and other events in conjunction with exhibitions, *'consequently making the arts relevant to the community'*. Exchange exhibitions with regional galleries are included in the programme. A wide variety of work is shown including painting, sculpture, prints, drawings and live art, all by living artists. Thirteen exhibitions of approximately three weeks duration are held per year. Mostly solo shows.

Sales: Work sold

The Space: The space is approximately 110m square, with walls 3m high. Gallery plans are available.

Exhibiting: [AW] Applications are welcomed, contact Vicki Lewis or Lynn Dennison. The costs of publicity, catalogue, card, poster, mailing, transport and private view are met by the gallery and 33.3% commission on sales is taken. The gallery supports EPR in principle.

Access: [U][T][L][F][S] Bus 30; Underground Great Portland Street 1 min, Regents Park 3 mins

Discreetly Bizzare Gallery

A gallery showing a range of contemporary work by established and younger artists in solo or group exhibitions. [VA]

Address: 166 New Cavendish Street, London W1 tel 01 631 3140

Contact: Director

Open: Tues-Sat 12-7

Dollisfield Gallery

Library space run by the Arts Office of the London Borough of Barnet showing the work of living artists. [Pa,Pr,Dr,Ph,Cr]

Address: Totteridge Library, Totteridge Lane, London N20 8DZ tel 01 202 1903

Contact: Arts Officer J Hawley, Ravensfield House, The Burroughs, Hendon, London NW4 4BE tel 01 202 5625

Open: Tues,Fri 10-1, 2-8, Wed 10-1, 2-5.30, Sat 10-1, 2-4

Policy: The programme of eight exhibitions a year are mainly the work of local artists in a variety of two-dimensional media - painting, drawing, photography, prints, crafts and textiles. The exhibitions run for three weeks each and are predominantly solo shows. Audiences are *'drawn mainly from North London and Hertfordshire'* and a programme of art lectures has recently been set up.

Sales: Work sold

The Space: The space is 6x5x3m and has *'ample natural light'* with hanging from picture rails and battens. *'One wall consists of a large bay window'*. Gallery plans are available.

Exhibiting: [AW] Applications welcome, contact the Arts Office. The space is hired out and costs covered by the gallery include insurance, printing, catalogue/card, list of exhibits and mailing. Commission of 15% is taken on sales.

Access: Bus 251; Underground Totteridge 5 mins

Dragonfly

A specialist glass gallery with a long-term display by a dozen artists. [Pa,Sc,Gl]

Address: 69 White Hart Lane, Barnes, London SW13 0PP tel 01 878 7892

Contact: Milena Oak

Open: Thurs,Fri,Sat 10-1, 2-5; and by appointment

Policy: The gallery concentrates on one-off and unusual glass pieces with the intention of interesting collectors, particularly from abroad. It also occasionally shows some painting and sculpture. A semi-permanent display of stained and blown glass is shown with a changing display of specialist and fine art work.

Sales: Work sold; Credit card

The Space: Main gallery 6.7x4.5, with 15m linear hanging space. Studio gallery 3.6x3.6, with 11m linear hanging space, both with spot lighting. Also a rear studio 3.6m square which can be used for exhibitions. Gallery plans are available.

Exhibiting: AW Applications should be made in writing with photographs. Suitable artists will be invited to bring work. The Gallery sometimes commissions painting on glass or blown glass but otherwise takes a commission on sales of 33.3%. It pays for mailing of publicity material and preview.

Access: [F] Bus 9; BR Barnes Bridge 5 mins; Street parking

Draycott Gallery

Commercial gallery dealing in and showing work by living artists. [VA,Cr]

Address: 163 Draycott Avenue, London SW3 3AJ tel 01 581 9905

Contact: Nick Soskin

Open: Mon-Sat 10-6, Sun and evenings by appointment

Policy: The gallery predominantly shows paintings and sculpture by living artists *'If we are interested in an artist, work will be included in a mixed show'* and *'work is handled on a sale or return basis'*. Mixed shows are held in July/August and the new year, with solo shows

Discreetly Bizzare Gallery: 'Cold Turkey' installation by Tim Head

for the remainder of the year. The audience includes collectors and those passing by the gallery.

Sales: Work sold; Credit card

The Space: The gallery is 9.5x5.5x3m with a 'window stage space' 3x3m.

Exhibiting: [AW] The gallery promotes a selected number of artists, but applications are welcome, send slides/photographs. Costs of insurance, printing and mailing of publicity, catalogue/card, list of exhibits, display and the preview are covered.

Access: [F] Buses C1,11,14,19,22,45,49,137,219; Underground South Kensington 3 mins, Sloane Square 10 mins

Drian Galleries

A gallery showing exhibitions of 'modern masters'.

Address: 7 Porchester Place, London W2 tel 01 723 9473

Contact: Director Halima Nalecz

Open: Mon-Fri 10-5, Sat 10-1

Access: Buses 6,7,8,15,16,16a,36,36a; Underground Marble Arch

Dulwich Picture Gallery

The first public art gallery in England, built by Sir John Soane, it houses a permanent collection of works by artists such as Rembrandt, Rubens, Claude, Poussin and Watteau. Occasional temporary exhibitions relating to an aspect of the permanent collection. [VA]

Address: College Road, London SE21 7AD tel 01 629 5234 Information line 01 693 8000

Contact: Director Giles Waterfield

Open: Tues-Sat 10-1, 2-5, Sun 2-5

Policy: Public guided tours Saturday and Sunday.

Access: BR West Dulwich (from Victoria), BR North Dulwich (London Bridge); Buses 3,12,37,78,176,185

Duncan Campbell Fine Art

A 'compact but very friendly' commercial gallery specialising in 20th century oils and watercolours and wood engraving. [Pa,Pr]

Address: 15 Thackeray Street, Kensington Square, London W8 5ET tel 01 937 8665

Contact: Duncan Stewart Campbell

Open: Tues-Fri 11-6, Sat 10-5

Policy: The gallery aims to promote talented artists whose work has been overlooked or who have not shown in London before. There are displays of work from private collections and about seven changing exhibitions a year, some solo shows, mainly by living artists. London agent for Rowland Hilder, Harry Weinberger, Jack Millar.

Sales: Work sold; Credit scheme

The Space: Lower gallery hanging length 9x2.8m high, upper gallery hanging length 8.8x1.8-2.8m high. Spot lighting on track and very large window to street.

Exhibiting: By invitation only. The gallery covers the costs of insurance printing and mailing of publicity, a list of exhibits, catalogue and preview. Commission on sales 35%.

Access: [F][X] Underground Kensington High Street 2 mins; Buses 9,52,73,27,28,31,33,49,52a; NCP car park 1 min

East West Restaurant

A restaurant which shows mainly small scale two-dimensional work. [Pa,Dr,Ph]

Address: 188 Old Street, London EC1V 9BP tel 01 608 0300

Contact: Manager J. Bienvenu

Open: Mon-Fri 11-10, Sat-Sun 11-3

Policy: The restaurant provides a space for artists to exhibit with a constant and changing audience. *'Our customers are very varied, from students to the very wealthy'*, they include *'media people, artists and office workers. Mainly a regular clientele.'* Twelve month-long exhibitions are held a year, all solo exhibitions of the work of living artists. Work shown includes painting, drawing and photography.

Sales: Sales referred to exhibitor

The Space: Linear hanging space is approximately 11m, broken by doors and windows. Maximum height of works is 1.8m. Lighting is by spot light.

Exhibiting: [AW] Applications welcome, contact the Manager.

Access: [X] Buses 5,55; Underground Old Street 1 min

Edward Totah

Contemporary gallery showing figurative and abstract art by artists from Britain and abroad. [VA]

Address: 13 Old Burlington Street, London W1 tel 01 734 0343

Contact: Director Edward Totah

Open: Mon 2-6, Tues-Fri 11-6, Sat 11-1

Policy: (Monthly) exhibitions of work by new and established names.

Sales: Work sold

The Space: Two galleries on two floors each 14x4m; variety of hanging methods; spotlights.

Exhibiting: [AW] Gallery covers insurance, mailing, publicity, catalogue and private view; cost of transport and artists travel shared. Commission varies.

Access: [X] Underground Piccadilly Circus

Edwin Pollard Gallery

Commercial gallery which deals in and shows the work of living professional artists. [Pa]

Address: 23 Church Road, Wimbledon Village, London SW19 5DQ tel 01 946 4114

Contact: Owner Edwin Pollard

Open: Wed-Sat 10-6

Policy: The gallery shows two-dimensional work of a *'representational or traditional manner'* and specialises in *'landscape, marine, still-life and the figure'*. The gallery has a changing display of works by a *'permanent stable'* of artists. Eight two-week exhibitions are held a year, featuring one, two or four artists.

Sales: Work sold; Credit scheme; Credit card

The Space: Maximum size of works shown is 1x1.3m. Gallery plans are available.

Exhibiting: [AW] Applications are welcomed, by

appointment. A negotiable hire fee is charged and the costs of printing, catalogue, card, mailing and the preview are covered by the gallery. A commission of 36.66% is taken on sales.

Access: **[U][T][F]** Buses 80,88,93; BR 10 mins; Underground 10 mins; Parking all round

Eileen Watson's Richmond Gallery

A gallery selling limited edition prints, watercolour, paintings, old engravings and antiquarian books.

Address: 63 Sheen Road, Richmond tel 01 940 9629
Contact: Eileen Watson
Open: Mon-Fri 9-6, Sat 10-3
Policy: The gallery also undertakes framing for the trade or individuals.
Access: Bus routes 33,37

Electrum Gallery

Contemporary jewellery gallery. [Je]

Address: 21 South Molton Street, London W1 tel 01 629 6325
Contact: Director Barbara Cartlidge
Open: Mon-Fri 10-6, Sat 10-1
Policy: Holds around ten exhibitions a year, shows over 45 different jewellers work in the gallery.
Sales: Work sold
Exhibiting: No applications from artists.
Access: Underground Bond Street

Endell Street Gallery

Brick-vaulted basement gallery in Covent Garden showing work by young professional artists and makers. [VA,Cr]

Address: Endell Street Place, 27-29 Endell Street, London WC2H 9BA tel 01 497 2934
Contact: Director Amanda Walbank
Open: Tues-Sat 11-6
Policy: To promote the work of professional young artists. Exhibitions change each month and include solo, dual and mixed shows. The programme is diverse, ranging from paintings, prints and sculpture to ceramics, glass and jewellery. The director is interested in encouraging talented handicapped artists.
Sales: Work sold
The Space: Main gallery is 12x7.5x2.5m, there is also a wide stairway for display work.
Exhibiting: **[AW]** Applications in writing to Amanda Walbank with SAE. The gallery covers the cost of insurance and splits the cost (50/50) of printing, publicity, list of exhibits, preview, mailing, catalogue/card with the artists. Commission is 50% but is negotiable.
Access: **[X]** BR Charing Cross 10 minsUnderground Covent Garden 1 min

Enfield Libraries

The London Borough of Enfield runs two galleries at Forty Hall and Palmers Green Library (see separate entries). It also runs exhibition spaces at four libraries. [Pa,Pr,Ph,Dr]

Address: Central Library, Cecil Road, Enfield EN2 6TW
Open: All listed libraries Tues,Thurs 9-8, Fri, Sat 9-5; Ridge Library also Mon 9-8
Policy: The libraries show exhibitions of work by local artists which usually run for one month and which are encouraged to travel to other libaries in the service. The libraries are: Ridge Avenue Library, Ridge Avenue, Winchmore Hill, London N21, tel 01 360 9662; De Bohun Library, Green Road, Southgate, London N14, tel 01 449 5425; Bowes Road Library, Bowes Road, New Southgate, London N11, tel 01 368 2085; Merryhills Library, Enfield Road, Enfield, Middlesex, tel 01 367 5250.
Sales: Work sold; Sales referred to exhibitor
The Space: Each library has limited exhibition space with hessian covered screens with a capacity for about 20 average sized paintings.
Exhibiting: **[AW]** Contact the librarian in charge of the library in the first instance. The Borough Librarian and Cultural Officer views examples of work. The Library covers insurance, some publicity and 30 catalogues. Commission is negotiable.

Europa Gallery

The headquarters for the London Borough of Sutton's Library Service.

Address: Central Library, St Nicholas Way, Sutton, Surrey SM1 1EA tel 01 661 5000
Contact: Marketing Manager Brian Turpin, Sutton Leisure, The Old Court House, Throwley Way, Sutton, Surrey SM1 4AF
Open: Tues-Sat 9.30-5.30
Policy: Suitable for arts, crafts and many commercial

Endell Street Gallery: 'Reflected Images' by Damon Bell

displays and promotions. See also entry for Sutton Arts Council.

Access: [F] BR Sutton

Everyman Cinema Foyer Gallery

A foyer space within 'the world's oldest repertory cinema' showing work by living artists. [Dr,Pr,Ph,Te]

Address: Everyman Cinema, Hollybush Vale, off Heath Street, Hampstead, London NW3 tel 01 435 1525/431 2240

Contact: Anna Turville, 9 Denning Road, London NW3 tel 01 794 5452

Open: Mon-Sun 2-10.30

Policy: The gallery aims to *'provide a showcase for young innovative artists'* and organises *'exhibitions in conjunction with the cinema's programme'* which attracts the attention of the large cinema-going public passing through the space. Approximately 14 three-week exhibitions a year which include drawings, prints, photography and textiles. All shows are solo and most are the work of *'young first-time exhibitors'*. The cinema also keeps a collection of posters dating back 50 years.

Sales: Sales referred to exhibitors

The Space: A foyer space which includes a small collection, limited to *'large poster-sized works'*.

Exhibiting: **[AW]** Applications are welcome through slides and SAE or personal visit with a portfolio. The space is hired to artists and 10% commission is taken on sales.

Access: **[X]** Buses 46,268,C11; Underground Hampstead Heath; BR Hampstead Heath

Fabian Carlsson Gallery

Commercial gallery exhibiting modern and contemporary work. [VA]

Address: 160 New Bond Street, London W1Y 0HR tel 01 409 0619

Contact: Fabian Carlsson, Clive Adams

Open: Mon-Fri 10-6, Sat 10-1

Policy: The gallery represents five younger British artists: Andy Goldsworthy, Hughie O'Donoghue, Michael Porter, Lance Smith and Vincent Woropay. It also exhibits emerging artists from abroad and deals in modern masters.

Sales: Work sold

The Space: 12x8x3m high with quartz halogen lighting.

Exhibiting: **[AW]** Apply with slides, CV and SAE. Gallery finances insurance, printing and mail-out of publicity, catalogue/card, list of exhibits, preview costs, display, transport and artists' expenses.

Access: **[F]** Underground Green Park, Oxford Circus, Bond Street

Fairhurst Gallery

A gallery stocking British oil and watercolour painting 1920-1988. [Pa]

Address: 291 New Kings Road, London SW6 tel 01 736 9132

Open: Mon-Fri 10-6, Sat 10.30-6

Fieldborne Galleries

A gallery showing about five exhibitions a year of contemporary British painters and sculptors. [VA]

Address: 63 Queens Grove, St John's Wood, London NW8 6ER tel 01 586 3600

Contact: Director Bernard & Victoria Stemfield

Open: Mon-Fri 10-5.30, Sat by appointment

Fifty One, West One

The gallery shows thematic exhibitions of small works. [VA,Ph]

Address: 51 Cleveland Street, London W1 tel 01 580 7285

Contact: Jon Hale

The Space: A space of about 5.5x3.5m with 20m linear. Maximum size of work 1.6x1.2m. Hanging is by direct fixing and lighting is by spots and natural light.

Exhibiting: **[AW]** Applications are welcome, a SAE ensures the return of slides/photographs. The gallery pays for insurance, mailing, private view and invitation cards and takes 30% commission.

Access: Buses C1,18,27,30,135,172; Underground Great Portland Street

Fine Art Associates

A gallery stocking a comprehensive stock of fine art from the 19th and 20th centuries.

Address: 229 Westbourne Grove, London W11 tel 01 229 6606

Contact: Director D Ewen

Open: Mon-Sat 9.30-6

Policy: The gallery sells to the trade and to individual collectors and shows mixed exhibitions of new stock.

Access: Buses 7,15,27,36

Fine Art Society

A gallery showing British arts 1850-1950. [VA]

Address: 148 New Bond Street, London W1Y 0JT tel 01 629 5116

Contact: Director

Open: Mon-Fri 9.30-5.30, Sat 10-1

Policy: Ten exhibitions a year of 19th and 20th century paintings, drawings, watercolours and sculpture and also decorative arts.

Access: Buses 25,509; Underground Bond Street

Fischer Fine Art

This commercial gallery exhibits the painting and sculpture by artists from the mid-20th century as well as contemporary work by established artists. [Pa,Sc,Dr,Cr]

Address: 30 King Street, St James', London SW1Y 6RJ tel 01 839 3942

Contact: Director Dr Wolfgang Fischer

Open: Mon-Fri 10-5.30, Sat 10-12.30 during exhibitions

Policy: The gallery aims to sell paintings and sculpture to museums, galleries and collectors. Solo exhibitions usually run for four to six weeks.

Sales: Work sold

Exhibiting: The gallery usually invites exhibitors but will see artists' work... Initially, applicants should telephone Jeffrey Solomons. Gallery finances insurance, printing and mail-out of publicity, catalogue/card, list of exhibits, preview costs and transport. Help is sometimes given with display but not for artists' expenses.
Access: [F] Buses 3 mins; Underground Piccadilly Circus, Green Park 5 mins

Flaxman Gallery

Commercial gallery showing and dealing in work by living artists. [Pa,Sc,Ph,LA]
Address: 3 Lever Street, London EC1V 3QU tel 01 253 9515
Contact: Directors Francesca Piovano, Edward Purkiss
Open: Tues-Sat 11-6; Closed Mon
Policy: The gallery aims to *'show interesting work from Britain and to stimulate an international discourse by presenting Czechoslovakian and Australian artists'* through a programme of ten exhibitions a year each lasting four to five weeks. A mixture of solo and group shows are mounted in a variety of media - painting, sculpture, photography and live art. Poetry readings are occasionally held.
Sales: Work sold; Credit scheme; Credit card
The Space: The space is approximately 17x12.3m and gallery plans are available.
Exhibiting: The gallery promotes a selected number of artists, it covers insurance, publicity, mailing and the preview and commission taken on sales varies.
Access: [F] Buses 4,5,55,243,279; Underground Angel, Barbican 7 mins

Footstool Restaurant Gallery

A changing exhibition programme in a restaurant.
Address: St John's Smiths Square, London SW1 tel 01 222 2168
Open: Mon-Fri 11.30-2.45, from 6 on concert nights & by appointment
Access: [S]

Forty Hall Museum

Built for Lord Mayor of London Sir Nicholas Raynton in 1629, Forty Hall houses 17th & 18th century furniture and pictures and local history displays and temporary exhibitions held within the gallery.
Address: Forty Hill, Enfield, London EN2 9HA tel 01 363 8196
Contact: Local History & Museums Officer J W Griffin, c/o Display Section, Southgate Town Hall, Green Lanes, Palmers Green, London N13 tel 01882 8841 ext 2723
Open: Tues-Sun 10-6; Tues-Sun 10-5 Oct-Easter
Policy: The policy is to stimulate local creative work and to show both amateur and professional work of quality as well as local art groups and societies. The exhibition gallery is used for large or travelling exhibitions and the Raynton Room for other exhibitions. Exhibitions normally last around four weeks.
Sales: Sales referred to exhibitor
The Space: The Raynton Room will take around 25-30 pictures.
Exhibiting: [AW] Apply to the Borough Librarian & Cultural Officer who wishes to see examples of work before agreements are made. Museum pays for insurance and 30 catalogues/price lists, and all other costs and arrangements are the responsiblity of the exhibitor. Commission is taken on sales although these are referred to exhibitors.
Access: [X] Ground floor only. Buses 231,191; BR Enfield Town & Enfield Chare; Parking

Foyles Gallery

Gallery in world-famous bookshop showing monthly exhibitions of contemporary arts and crafts. [VA,Cr]
Address: 119 Charing Cross Road, London WC2X 9FB tel 01 437 5660
Contact: Directors Christina Foyle & Ronald Batty
Open: Mon-Sat 10-6
Sales: Work sold
Access: BR & Underground Charing Cross

Framers Gallery

A commercial gallery showing monthly exhibitions by invited artists. [VA]
Address: 14 Fulham High Street, London SW6 tel 01 736 1916
Contact: Marjorie Green
Open: Mon, Wed-Fri 9-7, Tues, Sat 9-5
Sales: Work sold
The space: One large room.
Access: Underground Putney Bridge

Francis Graham-Dixon Gallery

Commercial gallery which deals in and shows the work of living artists and specialises in painting, drawing and sculpture, with the emphasis on abstraction. [Pa,Sc,Dr]
Address: 17-18 Great Sutton Street, London EC1V 0DN tel 01 250 1962
Contact: Director Francis Graham-Dixon
Open: Tues-Sun 11-6
Policy: The gallery *'exhibits and promotes a group of gallery artists, both within the UK and overseas, to a wide audience of collectors, both public and private, the business sector and the general public'*. The exhibition programme mainly consists of *'solo shows by established and emerging painters and sculptors. Selection of artists is based on quality of work as the primary consideration; commercial potential alone is not a factor'*. During the last twelve months ten one-month shows have been held and talks and seminars related to individual shows are planned.
Sales: Work sold; Credit scheme
The Space: The space is 15x7x2.8m, with 30m linear hanging space lit by halogen and low-voltage lighting. There is light industrial floor loading, and a 9m window frontage, with an additional window on the ground floor where work can be shown. The space is hired out for seminars and functions. Gallery plans are available.
Exhibiting: [AW] Applications are welcome, by appointment only and with prior letter or telephone call. A sample of work should be brought as well as

transparencies. The gallery shows a selected stable of artists only. The costs of insurance, publicity, card, mailing, transport and the preview are all covered by the gallery. The EPR is supported in principle.

Access: Buses 4,5,55,243,277,279,279a; Underground Barbican (Closed Sun) 4 mins, Farringdon 7 mins; Public car park in Great Sutton Street

Francis Kyle Gallery

A gallery promoting younger artists from British Isles. [VA]

Address: 9 Maddox Street, London W1 tel 01 499 6870
Contact: Director
Open: Mon-Fri 10-6, Sat 11-5
Policy: The gallery shows younger British artists and *'leading European and American artists'* and shows paintings, watercolours, drawings and limited edition prints.
Access: Buses 3,6,9,12,13,15,53,88,159; Underground Oxford Circus

Freuds

A commercial gallery in a fashionable café bar in central London. [Pa,Pr,Ph]

Address: 198 Shaftesbury Avenue, London WC2H 8JL tel 01 240 9933
Contact: Exhibitions Organiser Caroline Evans, 36 Great James Street, London WC1N 3HB tel 01 831 8641
Open: Mon-Sat 11am-11pm, Sun 5.30-10.30pm
Policy: A wide range of varied work by young artists. The gallery eschews *'restaurant art'* in favour of work which may be challenging, even difficult. Because of the nature of the space work must be capable of being hung on the wall. Exhibitions change monthly.
Sales: Work sold
Exhibiting: **[AW]** Apply in writing or telephone for further information. Commission charged.
Access: **[X]** Underground Tottenham Court Road 2 mins; Many buses

Fulham Gallery

London's only specialist contemporary watercolour gallery. [Pa,Sc,Cr]

Address: 41 Fulham Palace Road, London SW6 tel 01 736 9318
Contact: Jake Bell
Open: Mon-Fri 10-5.30; Evenings by appointment
Policy: Exhibitions are held quarterly and are shown alongside a changing display of stock.
Sales: Work sold
The Space: Three rooms totalling about 111 square metres.
Exhibiting: **[AW]**
Access: **[S]** Buses 74,220

Galerie 39

A commercial gallery specialising in contemporary Japanese fine art. [Pa,Pr]

Address: 96 George Street, London W1H 5RI tel 01 487 5038/9
Contact: Caroline Williams
Open: Mon-Fri 10-6
Policy: About four exhibitions a year are held. The gallery *'works closely with its office in Tokyo, and helps to select work by British artists to be shown in Japan'*.
The Space: An exhibition space of about 30 square metres.
Access: Buses 6,7,8,15,16,16a,36; Underground Marble Arch

Gallery 10

Gallery specialising in contemporary British art. [VA]

Address: 10 Grosvenor Street, London W1X 9FB tel 01 491 8103
Contact: Director Anne Marcou
Open: Mon-Fri 10-5.30, Sat 10-1
Policy: Regular exhibitions held throughout year.
Sales: Work sold
The Space: One floor.
Exhibiting: **[AW]** Applications welcome from *'professional artists'*.
Access: Underground Bond Street

Gallery 24

A gallery specialising in the best of unknown artists as well as those who are more established.

Address: 24 Powis Terrace, London W11 tel 01 229 4222
Contact: Director
Open: Tues-Sat 12-7
Access: Buses 7,52a

Gallery Kaleidoscope

A commercial gallery, established in 1977, promoting a comprehensive range of paintings and sculpture from the 18th century to the present day. [Pa,Sc,Pr]

Address: 64-66 Willesden Lane, London NW6 7SX tel 01 328 5833
Contact: Karl Barrie
Open: Mon-Sat 10-6
Policy: The gallery mounts about twelve two-week exhibitions a year, with a display of gallery stock in between. The gallery sells to collectors and local public looking for work for their homes in a medium-price range. It is always seeking new work and is very open-minded though realistic work does sell best.
Sales: Work sold; Credit card; Credit scheme
The Space: Two medium-size showrooms, work can't be very large.
Exhibiting: **[AW]** Artists should send information and slides. The gallery covers the costs of insurance, printing and mailing publicity, catalogue and preview and commission on sales is negotiable.
Access: Underground Kilburn or Willesden Green 5 mins; Easy parking

Gallery Lingard

A gallery specialising in showing watercolours and architectural drawings. [Pa,Dr]

Address: 50 Pall Mall, London SW1 tel 01 930 1645
Contact: Director

Open: Mon-Fri 10-5

Gallery on the Heath

Commercial gallery

Address: 14 Royal Parade, London SE3 tel 01 852 8220
Policy: Changing display of work by Greenwich artists. Framing service.

Gallery Seven

Gallery (formerly Ceramics 7 Gallery) with permanent collection on show by Ceramics 7 group members, also hosts temporary exhibitions of ceramics and paintings. [Ce,Pa]

Address: 7 Turnpin Lane, Greenwich, London SE10 9JA tel 01 858 2290
Contact: Ceramics 7 group
Open: Tues-Sun 11-5
Policy: Shows contemporary ceramic work, including jewellery, from makers in and outside London in monthly changing group shows.
Sales: Work sold
Access: BR Greenwich

Gallery Upstairs

This church gallery provides a new venue for 'adventurous' work. [VA,Ph,Cr]

Address: 197 Piccadilly, London W1V 9LF tel 01 734 4511
Contact: Arts Administrator Jacqueline Campbell
Open: Mon-Fri 9-5; Excluding church services
Policy: Gallery policy is is to offer the exhibition area to any artist who can *'best utilise the space'*. Exhibitions are usually solo shows of between four to five weeks.
Sales: Work sold
The Space: Alongside the gallery area there is a garden where sculpture may be exhibited. Church services are also held in part of the exhibition area. Gallery plans available.
Exhibiting: Flat rate charged, no commission.

Garden Gallery

Artist-run gallery specialising in contemporary paintings and prints, opposite main entrance to Kew Gardens. [VA,Cr,Pr]

Address: 3 Mortlake Terrace, Kew, Richmond, Surrey TW9 3DT tel 01 948 300
Contact: Proprietor Annie Holdway
Open: Mon, Tues, Thurs, Fri 10-4, Sat 1-4
Policy: Holds six to eight exhibitions a year, also includes sculpture and crafts in programme as well as the specialist areas. Has mixed thematic summer show and craft exhibition during November and December.
Sales: Work sold
The Space: Two rooms totalling 16.8m linear space; showcases available; hanging direct to walls; spotlights.
Exhibiting: [AW] Gallery covers insurance, catalogue and private view; publicity and mailing costs are shared. There is a hire charge for the space and commission is 10%.
Access: Buses Kew Gardens; BR Kew Bridge

Gayton Library

Library space run by London Borough of Harrow showing local amateur and professional artists. [VA,Ph,Cr]

Address: Gayton Road, Harrow, Middlesex HA1 2HL tel 01 427 6012/8986
Contact: Central Lending Librarian John Pennells
Open: Mon,Tues,Thurs 9-8, Fri 9-6, Sat 9-5; closed Wed
Policy: The gallery aims to *'promote the work of local artists and art and craft societies'* and *'to increase public awareness and generally raise the profile of art within the community through active participation'.* Twenty-seven exhibitions, both mixed and solo shows, each lasting two weeks, were held last year. The library also is the contact for exhibition spaces in the borough branch libraries. See also Harrow Library Service.
Sales: Sales refered to exhibitor
The Space: The exhibition space 11x6.5x10m has 8m hanging space with movable screens, 2.5x1m or 1x1m, and two freestanding display cabinets available. Hanging is by picture hooks. The space is occasionally used for library activities. Gallery plans are available.
Exhibiting: [AW] Applications are welcomed, write or telephone the Librarian. Commission on sales is 10% plus VAT and a booking fee of £15 is charged.
Access: [F] Bus routes to Harrow bus station; Underground Harrow-on-the-Hill

Geffrye Museum

This gallery stages long term exhibitions normally lasting for three to six months, with the emphasis placed on historical craftworks and occasional shows by contemporary makers. [Cr]

Address: Kingsland Road, London E2 8EA tel 01 739 9893
Contact: David Rodgers
Open: Tues-Sat 10-5, Sun 2-5; Closed between exhibitions
Policy: The museum aims to record and show the history of urban homes and home life. The emphasis is placed on furniture produced in East London and the aim is to make these works accessible to everyone. Talks and workshops are regularly organised for groups of adults and children.
Sales: Work sold; Credit card
The Space: 3m high with 30m linear hanging space with track-mounted spots and showcases available.
Exhibiting: [AW] Apply to David Rodgers. Gallery finances insurance, printing and mail-out of publicity, catalogue/card, preview, display and transport costs. Support in principle for EPR. Commission 33.3%.
Access: [S] Toilet adapted for disabled. Buses 22b,67, 149,243; Underground Old Street exit 2

Gill Dray Modern Pictures

A gallery showing British paintings and drawings from 1900 to present.

Address: Chenil Galleries, 181-183 King's Road, London SW3 tel 01 351 2921
Contact: Director
Open: Mon-Sat 10-6
Access: Buses 11,19,22,219

Gillian Jason Gallery

A gallery showing an extensive programme of modern and contemporary paintings, sculpture and drawings from Britain and Europe. [VA,Ph]

Address: 42 Inverness Street, London NW1 tel 01 267 4835
Contact: Gillian Jason
Open: Tues-Sat, 10.30-5.30
Policy: Six to eight solo exhibitions each year. Occasional theme shows.
The Space: Spaces of 8.5x5m and 8.5x4.5m with direct fixing and spots and natural light.
Exhibiting: [AW] Applications are welcome though the programme is planned far in advance. The gallery pays for insurance, publicity, mailing, catalogue and private view.
Access: [X] Buses 24,27,29,31,68,74,134,135,168, 214,253; Underground Camden Town

Gimpel Fils

This commercial gallery deals in the work of selected contemporary artists. [Pa,Sc,Dr]

Address: 30 Davies Street, London W1Y 1LG tel 01 493 2488
Contact: Directors Peter Gimpel, Rene Gimpel
Open: Mon-Fri 9.30-5.30, Sat 10-1
Policy: The gallery shows only the work of a selected number of artists, alongside a changing display of work for sale. There is an annual summer show.
Sales: Work sold; Credit scheme
The Space: 3m high with 28m linear hanging space. Track-mounted spot lighting.
Access: [F] Underground Bond Street 3 mins

Giray

A gallery established in 1988 showing 'important contemporary art by international artists, both established and unknown'. [VA]

Address: At time of going to press Giray was looking for new premises in central London.
Contact: Jezzar Giray
Policy: *'The gallery will continue to exhibit contemporary work both figurative painting and sculpture under its umbrella theme of mythologising. The gallery has defined mythmaking as the occupation with the traditional device of ordering data - both factual and fantastical - and in this way proscribes a certain 'world view'.* It shows both established and unknown artists and also encourages them to work in new media. Note: at the time of going to press Giray was closing at the Camberwell Church Street site to relocate in central London.
Sales: Work sold

Glasshouse

An artist-run workshop comprising hot and cold glass working facilities and displaying the work of the workshop members which is on the Crafts Council's selected list. [Gl]

Address: 65 Long Acre, Covent Garden, London WC2 tel 01 836 9785
Contact: Administrator Caroline Thomas
Open: Mon-Fri 10-5.30, Sat 11-4.30
Policy: The gallery shows two-week changing displays of work by workshop members. Each year there is an exhibition of new work and often an outside guest is invited to make work in the workshop and exhibit alongside the residents. The Glasshouse also undertakes commissions, restoration work and antique glass and allows the public to view the making of hot glass.
Sales: Work sold; Credit card
Exhibiting: Applications are not appropriate as exhibitions are from members or by invitation.
Access: [F] Underground Covent Garden 3 mins

Goethe-Institut

As part of the Cultural Institute this gallery specialises in exhibiting the work of 20th century German artists working in all media with approximately half the exhibitions by living artists. [VA,Sc]

Address: 50 Princes Gate, Exhibition Road, London SW7 2PH tel 01 581 3344
Open: Mon-Thurs 12-8, Fri 12-6, Sat 10-1 (telephone to confirm times)
Policy: The gallery seeks to present historical aspects of German art, particularly those artists or periods that are less familiar to British exhibition visitors. Also represented is the work of contemporary artists and current trends that have attracted attention in the Federal Republic of Germany. Occasionally lectures are organised to coincide with exhibitions.
The Space: 150 square metres with 50m linear hanging space. Lighting and humidity controls to suit all requirements. No large sculpture can be accommodated.
Access: [S] Underground South Kensington 5 mins

Goldsmiths' Gallery

This gallery stages a wide range of exhibitions both of a contemporary and historical nature. [VA,Ph,Cr,LA]

Address: Lewisham Way, New Cross, London SE14 6NW tel 01 692 7171 ext 2027
Contact: Curator Jill Sheridan
Open: Variable, Mon-Fri 12-7, Sat-Sun 12-5
Policy: The gallery aims at a varied programme of shows, mainly by living artists, that will satisfy the local community, the contemporary art audience and those who work and study at the University. There is also a permanent collection of visual art works. Seminars, lectures and tours directly related to exhibitions are regularly organised.
The Space: 19x7x4m high with 54m linear hanging space and track-mounted spot lighting. Gallery plans available. The space is also used for lectures, performances, recitals and readings.
Exhibiting: [AW] Apply to Goldsmiths Gallery at any time. Exhibition space usually available between July and August. Hire fee negotiable. Support in principle for EPR. Donation 10%.
Access: [S] Buses 21,36,36a/b,53,163,171,177a,212;

BR New Cross Gate 5 mins; Underground New Cross 5 mins

Gordon Gallery

Monthly exhibitions of figurative 20th century work. [Pa]

Address: Hampden House, 76 Durham Road, West Wimbledon, London SW20 0TL tel 01 946 9609
Contact: Director
Open: Mon-Wed, Fri 11-5.30, Sat 11-1, Closed Thurs
Access: Buses 156,157,164; BR Raynes Park

Grabowski Gallery II

Commercial gallery dealing in and showing the work of living artists. [Pa]

Address: 84 Sloan Avenue, London SW3 tel 01 589 4627
Contact: Wojtiek Grabowski
Open: Mon-Sat 11-11
Policy: The gallery is hired to artists and shows painting by *'young, unknown artists from Europe'* through a programme of five solo exhibitions each lasting two months. A wine bar is run on the premises.
Sales: Work sold
The Space: Two spaces, one 2.5m high with 23m linear hanging space and a bar, the other 3m high with 24m linear hanging space, both interrupted by doors and windows and a courtyard 4x9m. Gallery plans are available.
Exhibiting: [AW] Applications are welcome, send slides. The space is hired to artists at £1000 per week which includes *'our services'* and the gallery covers insurance, printing of publicity, mailing, catalogue/card, list of exhibits and the preview; 50% commission is taken on sales.
Access: [U] Buses 30,73; Underground South Kensington

Greenwich Citizens Gallery

A gallery run by the London Borough of Greenwich, with funding from Greater London Arts. [VA,Ph,CR,LA]

Address: 147 Powis Street, Woolwich, London SE18 tel 01 854 0055
Contact: Visual Arts Animateur Barbara Hunt tel 01 854 8888 ext 2313
Open: Tues-Sat 10-5
Policy: It operates a *'programming policy with the aim of targeting local people and priority groups who have historically been excluded from participating or representation in the visual arts and promotes artists who are normally discriminated against by mainstream white art institutions'*. The gallery wants to improve *'the relationship between artists and the community and has an active education policy to promote critical awareness of the visual arts and their relationship to social/political context'*. Policy statement available.
Sales: Work sold
The Space: The gallery is 11x13.41x3.66m with 30m linear hanging space and a variety of screens. Work is fixed directly to the walls using mirror plates and there is track lighting, air conditioning and humidifiers. Gallery plans available.
Exhibiting: [AW] The gallery covers insurance, publicity and mail out, preview, catalogue and transport and occasionally commissions work for exhibition. Commission is 20% and the gallery supports the principle of EPR.
Access: [U][T] Buses 37,53,54,75,96,99,122,177,178, 198,269,272,291; Underground & BR Woolwich Arsenal 5 mins; Car park 2 mins

Greenwich Printmakers Association

The association is a printmakers co-operative whose members staff and run the gallery. It mostly displays work by members. [Pr,Pa,Dr]

Address: 1a The Market, off College Approach, Greenwich, London SE10 tel 01 858 1569
Contact: Gallery Manager Annette Johnson
Open: Tues-Sun 10.30-5.30
Policy: There are four exhibitions a year. Work on show includes etching, lithography, screenprinting, relief prints, watercolours and drawings. The co-operative also mounts and tours travelling exhibitions in Britain and overseas.
Sales: Work sold; Credit card
Exhibiting: [AW] Work is selected by a changing committee of co-operative members. Applications for membership to membership secretary.
Access: [F] BR Greenwich 10 mins

Greenwich Theatre Art Gallery

This gallery mainly shows solo exhibitions by local artists, often those who are exhibiting for the first time. [Pa,Pr,Dr,Ph,Je,Te]

Address: Crooms Hill, Greenwich, London SE10 8ES tel 01 858 4447
Contact: Gallery Manager Debbie Williams
Open: Mon-Sat 10-6, and during performances
Policy: Gallery policy is to present a variety of work to the wide range of visitors to the theatre, often people not used to the gallery situation. The aim is to create a

Greenwich Theatre Art Gallery: From 'A Winters Journey' by William McClure Brown

relaxed and informal atmosphere so that *'potential customers are not made to feel uneasy about asking questions regarding the work and how to buy it'.*

Sales: Work sold; Credit card

The Space: The exhibition space is on two floors, 1.5m high with 24m linear hanging space. Hanging is by a flexible system of rods and hooks.

Exhibiting: [AW] Contact Debbie Williams for application form. Selection for the following year normally takes place in April. Gallery finances mail-out of publicity and list of exhibits. Commission 33.3%.

Access: [X] Buses 1,177,180,185,188; BR Greenwich 5 mins; Public car park 3 mins

Groucho Club

A private membership club which uses its reception rooms for exhibitions. [Pa,Pr,Dr,Ph]

Address: 45 Dean Street, London W1V 5AP tel 01 439 4685

Contact: Amanda White tel 01 221 0801

Open: Viewing by appointment or with a member only

Policy: It is the club's policy to exhibit work by young artists who are not represented by an agent or gallery. Exhibitions run for one month and although large mixed media paintings have dominated the programme there has also been a successful exhibition of fabrics. One of the club's restaurants is also used to display members' work for sale.

Sales: Work sold

The Space: Brasserie 9x9x2.4m high, exhibition room 9x12m with a continuous wall 1.2-1.8m in depth. Recessed directable spotlights plus wall lights in both spaces.

Exhibiting: Applications are welcome from members of the club or artists recommended by a member. The club gives the space free and does not take any commission on sales.

Access: [X] Underground Tottenham Court Road, Leicester Square, Piccadilly Circus 5 mins

Gunnersbury Park Museum

Museum with local history emphasis, has archaeological collection and six to eight temporary exhibitions a year of art, craft and photography. [VA,Cr]

Address: Gunnersbury Park, London W3 8LQ tel 01 992 1612

Contact: Curator J G Shelley

Open: Mon-Fri 1-5, Sat,Sun 2-5 March-Oct; Mon-Fri 1-4, Sat,Sun 2-4 Nov-Feb

Policy: To represent the people of Ealing and Hounslow and to support the equal opportunity policies of the London Boroughs of Ealing and Hounslow.

The Space: Exhibition space 10x5.5m. Hanging directly on walls, spots and natural light, screens and showcases available.

Exhibiting: [AW] Costs shared depending on type of exhibition. Commission on sales 15%.

Access: [F] Buses E3, (7 on Sun only); Underground Acton Town

Hackney Museum

Museum and gallery run by the London Borough of Hackney which collects and shows work based on the history of Hackney and the roots of its people. [VA,Ph,Cr]

Address: Central Hall, Mare Street, London E8 1HE tel 01 986 6914

Contact: Curator Christine Johnstone

Open: Tues-Fri 10-12.30, 1.30-5, Sat 1.30-5

Policy: The gallery *'concentrates on the lives of Hackney people through a programme of twelve exhibitions a year which include the work of artists who 'work, study or live in the borough'* as well as historical *'works and artifacts'.* Exhibitions in a variety of media run for four weeks, about half are solo shows and most are the work of living artists. *'All exhibitions must fit in with gallery policy'.* The target audience is *'the people of Hackney of every age and interest'.* The museum also holds a permanent collection.

Sales: Sales referred to exhibitor

The Space: A large flexible space 24.5x12.5x4.5m (not all space available at one time) with 55m linear hanging space, 30m free-standing screens 1m deep and fixed overhead lighting. Hanging is from rail or on screens and size of work is limited by a 1.5x2m door. Four Click quadrant showcases in a variety of sizes are available.

Exhibiting: [AW] Applications are welcomed from artists whose work is relevant to Hackney, write to the Curator. The gallery covers insurance, printing, publicity, catalogue/card, mailing and list of exhibits. Commission 10-25% is taken on sales.

Access: [U][T] Buses 22a,22b,30,35,38,55,106,236,253, 276,277; BR Hackney Central 5 mins

Hall Place

Hall Place is the administrative headquarters of Bexley Libraries and Museums Department, and presents a varied programme of visual arts and crafts exhibitions that are normally shown for three to six weeks. [VA,Ph,Cr]

Address: Bourne Road, Bexley, Kent DA5 1PQ tel 0322 526 574

Contact: Assistant Chief Librarian (Technical & Special Services) RJ Swindells

Open: GMT Mon-Sat 10-dusk, BST Mon-Sat 10-5, Sun and Bank holidays 2-6

Policy: Gallery policy is to provide a range of visual arts displays and exhibitions. Some exhibitions are targetted towards particular groups of children or schools but most are for the general public.

Sales: Work sold

The Space: 53m linear hanging space. Four display cases available. The space is also used for talks, promotions and art fairs. Gallery plans available.

Exhibiting: [AW] Exhibition space for hire, terms on application. Gallery may finance insurance, printing and mail-out of publicity, catalogue/card, list of exhibits, preview, display and transport costs. Commission 15% plus VAT.

Access: [F][X] BR Bexley 20 mins; Public car park 2 mins

Hamilton's Gallery

This commercial gallery specialises in vintage and contemporary photography (1920 to current) showing predominantly solo exhibitions. [Ph]

Address: 13 Carlos Place, London W1Y 5AG tel 01 499 9493/4
Contact: Director Andrew Cowan
Open: Mon-Fri 10-6, Sat 10-5
Policy: The gallery primarily aims to attract people interested in photography, as well as introducing and selling work to a wider audience.
Sales: Work sold; Credit card; Credit scheme
The Space: 1,219 square metres. Two display cases, 2x1m, available. Gallery plans available.
Exhibiting: **[AW]** Apply to Mark Slaski. Commission negotiable.
Access: **[X]** Buses 25,30,74,52; Underground Green Park, Bond Street 5 mins; Public car park 2 mins

Hardware Gallery

This commercial gallery gives priority to print shows by contemporary artists, and exhibitions normally run for four weeks. [VA]

Address: 277 Hornsey Road, Islington, London N7 6RZ tel 01 272 9651
Contact: Deirdre Kelly
Open: Mon-Fri 1-7, Sat 10-6
Policy: The gallery holds a broad spectrum of print works, Deirdre Kelly is herself a printmaker hence the motive for promoting this art form. Although most work is by London-based artists the gallery enjoys an excellent relationship with two Parisian studios. Work is sold to the general public as well as recognised collectors and dealers.
Sales: Work sold; Credit card; Credit scheme
The Space: 4x5x4m with 13m linear hanging space. Direct fixing to walls with spot lighting. Shop window frontage.
Exhibiting: **[AW]** Apply with slides and CV. Gallery finances insurance, printing and mail-out of publicity and list of exhibits. The exhibition space can be hired. Discount framing service available to exhibitors. Commission 33.3%.
Access: **[F]** Buses 14a; BR Finsbury Park 10 mins; Underground Finsbury Park 10 mins

Hardware Gallery: Director Deirdre Kelly during an exhibition by Liz Clifford

Harrow Library Service

The London Borough of Harrow runs small exhibition spaces in each branch library for details contact John Pennells, Central Lending Librarian.

Address: Headquarters, Civic Centre Library, PO box 4, Civic Centre, Harrow HA1 2UU tel 01 863 5611
Contact: Central Lending Librarian John Pennells, Gayton Library, Gayton Road, Harrow, Middlesex HA1 2HL tel 01 427 6012/8986
Policy: See also entry for Gayton Library, Harrow.

Harwood Gallery

A gallery specialising in contemporary limited editions, posters, original oils and watercolours. [Pa,Pr]

Address: (Elder and Blyth), 57A New King's Road, London SW6 tel 01 736 4274
Contact: Director
Open: Mon-Fri 10-5.30, Sat 10-5
Policy: The gallery also stocks cards and frames.
Access: Bus 22; Underground Parsons Green

Havering Library Service

A library gallery showing a diverse selection of temporary exhibitions including work by local artists.

Address: Central Library, St Edwards Way, Romford, Essex RM1 3AR tel 0708 46040/44297
Contact: Borough Librarian & Arts Officer D A Partridge
Open: Mon-Fri 9.30-8, Sat 9.30-5
Policy: The gallery holds fourteen exhibitions a year of painting, sculpture, print, drawing, photography, ceramics, textiles and wood.
Sales: Work usually for sale
The Space: One large exhibition room with a total of 131m square feet of hanging space on screens and walls. There are five free-standing screens each double sided 3.3m long x 1.6m high. Floor space is about 111 square metres. Spotlighting and controlled environment. Work limited to 3m high. Plans available.
Exhibiting: **[AW]** Artists are invited to exhibit but should apply to the Borough Librarian and Arts Officer. Commission is 10% plus VAT.
Access: **[L]** Public car park 8 mins

Hayward Gallery

This gallery stages large-scale exhibitions of established national and international artists. About half of the exhibitions annually are by contemporary artists with all shows running for two to three months. [VA,Ph,Ar,LA]

Address: South Bank Centre, London SE1 8XZ tel 01 928 3144 (Recorded information 01 261 0127)

Contact: Director, Hayward and Regional Exhibitions Joanna Drew, Exhibitions Department, South Bank Centre, Royal Festival Hall, London, SE1 8XX tel 01 921 0857

Open: Mon-Wed 10-8, Thurs-Sat 10-6, Sun 12-6

Policy: Gallery policy is to exhibit work of relevance to a contemporary audience and to support contemporary work in this country. Special lectures related to exhibitions and gallery tours are regularly organised.

Sales: Sales referred to exhibitor

The Space: Five interconnected galleries with 550 sq. metres of floor space and a flexible screen system. Three sculpture courts with a total area of 213 square metres. Exhibiting areas are also used for entertainment and educational purposes during exhibitions.

Exhibiting: Programme decisions are taken by the gallery director in consultation with an advisory group. Gallery finances all expenses. Exhibitors receive a fee for exhibiting. Support in principle for EPR.

Access: **[U]** access from car park via lift, **[L][F]**. Buses 1,4,68,70,76,149,168a,171,176,188,502,507; BR Waterloo; Underground Waterloo; Public car park

Heals Art Gallery

Shop showing work by contemporary makers including pottery, glass, china, toys, woodwork and cushions. [Cr]

Address: 196 Tottenham Court Road, London W1 tel 01 636 1666

Contact: Director

Open: Mon-Wed,Fri,Sat 9-5.30; Thurs 9.45-5.30

Policy: Holds eight exhibitions of contemporary work a year.

Sales: Work sold

Access: Buses to Tottenham Court Road; Underground Goodge Street

Heinz Gallery (RIBA)

Gallery showing work by contemporary and past architects, also visual art exhibitions on related themes. The gallery is part of the British Architectural Library Drawings Collection. [VA,Ar]

Address: 21 Portman Square, London W1H 9HF tel 01 580 5533 ext 4801

Contact: Exhibitions Officer Jane Preger

Open: Mon-Fri 11-5, Sat 10-1

Policy: Five exhibitions a year.

Exhibiting: Exhibitions programmed by invitation only.

Access: **[S]** Bus routes; Underground Marble Arch, Bond Street

Hendon Library

Public library within Barnet Library Service. [Pa,Pr,Dr,Ph]

Address: The Burroughs, Hendon, London NW4 4BQ tel 01 202 5625

Contact: Librarian-in-Charge, Special Services EA Holliday, Room 6, Ravensfield House, The Burroughs, Hendon, London NW4 4BE

Open: Mon-Thurs 9-8, Fri 9-5, Sat 9-4

Policy: The library aims to *'provide a venue for local artists, photographers and members of local art and photographic societies to show their work'*, it shows work by amateur and professional living artists in a variety of two-dimensional media - painting, drawing, prints and photography. The audience is mainly local residents and the space is used for library activities and hired out for meetings. See also Barnet Library Service.

Sales: Work sold; Sales referred to exhibitor

The Space: Linear hanging space of 19.5m is on hessian-covered panels lit by strip lights, work is hung on steel pins and the maximum size is 0.9x0.9m. Gallery plans are available.

Exhibiting: **[AW]** Applications welcome from local artists, contact the Librarian-in-Charge, Special Services. Commission is 15%.

Access: **[X]** Buses 113,143,183,186; Underground Hendon Central 10 mins, BR Hendon 15 mins

Heritage Centre (Kingston)

This municipal gallery runs a programme of exhibitions by local amateur and professional artists in both individual and group shows. [Pa,Pr,Ph]

Address: Wheatfield Way, Kingston upon Thames, Surrey KT5 8SW tel 01 546 5386

Contact: Barry R Eddison

Open: Mon-Sat 10-5; closed Sun and bank holidays

Policy: Normally exhibitions are by local artists or of local significance and the gallery predominantly shows the work of living artists. Most shows are solo and run for between two to four weeks.

Sales: Sales referred to exhibitor

The Space: Main gallery 18x1.5m high. Corridor gallery 12x4m high. Hanging in both spaces is on pegboard wall-mounted panels with a track lighting-system. Neither gallery can accommodate work larger than 2m square. Showcases are available. Gallery contains information desk and sales counter.

Exhibiting: **[AW]** Apply to Barry Eddison. Gallery finances insurance and printing and mail-out of publicity. There is a hire fee of £11.50 per day. Commission 10%.

Access: **[U][T]** Buses 65, 78, 213; BR Kingston; Public car park 2 mins

Heritage Centre (Spitalfields)

Temporary exhibitions and lectures are arranged in a unique Eastern European style synagogue, built in the 1880s in the backgarden of an 18th century Hugenot house. [Pa,Sc,Ph]

Address: 19 Princelet Street, Spitalfields, London E1 6QH tel 01 377 6901

Contact: Co-ordinator Dominic Dyson

Policy: The long-term aim is to establish a resource centre and museum for the study of immigration and the history of Spitalfields. Exhibitions are held in order to help fundraise. Local artists and community projects or artists working within the context of the centre's aims are encouraged to exhibit.
Exhibiting: [AW] Write to the Co-ordinator.
Access: [U][T] Underground Aldgate East

Higherwater Gallery

Commercial gallery, financed by the Red Indian Services Group, which primarily shows the work of artists living or working in London's East End. [VA,Ph]

Address: 82 Three Colt Street, Limehouse, London E14 8AP tel 01 538 3526
Contact: Gallery Administrator Eternity Futcher
Open: Tues, Thurs 11-7, Wed 10-2, Fri 10-6, Sat 1-5
Policy: *'The East End of London contains a high population of professional artists', 'The same area is becoming increasingly popular with the middle-class who set up home here to be closer to their places of work'.* The gallery aims to provide links between artists resident in the area and their *'new Docklands neighbours'.* All forms of visual art are considered for exhibition, including painting, sculpture, drawing, prints and photography. Five exhibitions, each lasting six to eight weeks, are held a year, all are mixed or group shows. The gallery is entirely funded by the Red Indian Services Group.
Sales: Work sold; Credit card; Credit scheme
The Space: The gallery space is approximately 10.5x3.5x3m, with *'one length composed of zig-zag design walls'*, and is lit by track lighting with movable fittings. There is a shop front with a window display area of 1.5x1x3m. Two-dimensional work is limited to 1.5x1.2m, maximum height of three-dimensional work is 0.8m.
Exhibiting: [AW] Applications are welcome from any artist living or working in East London, and who has degree-level training in art or has been exhibiting for some years. The costs of insurance, publicity, catalogue, card, mailing and the preview are covered by the gallery, and 38% commission is charged on sales. The exhibition space is occasionally hired out at £220 per week, which includes staffing and administration during the show. Commission taken is 20%.
Access: [U] Buses D1,5,15,40,106,277; Westferry Docklands Light Railway 2 mins

Holborn Library

An exhibition space in a public library. [VA]

Address: 32-38 Theobalds Road, London WC1 tel 01 405 2705
Contact: Librarian
Open: Mon, Thurs 9.30-8, Tues 9.30-6, Fri & Sat 9.30-5, closed Wed
Access: [F]

Holland Gallery

Commercial gallery showing and dealing in the work of living artists. [Pa,Sc,Dr]

Address: 129 Portland Road, London W11 4LW tel 01 727 7198
Contact: Renske Mann
Open: Tues-Sat 12-6
Policy: The gallery *'specialises in gifted but unknown contemporary artists working in oils, watercolour, pastels and charcoal with a bias towards the figurative and sculpture in bronze, stone, resin and terracotta'.* Approximately twelve exhibitions are held a year, a combination of solo and group shows each lasting two weeks. The gallery is *'in business to help artists'* and aims to provide *' contemporary original painting and sculpture at competitive prices to those with limited resources'.* The owners subsidise the gallery so that most of the income from sales *'goes into the artists' pocket and not on overheads'.*
Sales: Work sold; Credit scheme
The Space: There are two spaces, the hessian-walled ground floor gallery and white-walled basement are both lit by spotlights. There are shelves and a small courtyard suitable for sculpture, and the space is occasionally used for product launches.
Exhibiting: [AW] The gallery policy is to promote a selected number of artists but applications are welcome. Send slides, enclosing SAE or telephone for an appointment. Costs of printing, mailing, list of exhibits and public relations photographs are covered and commission of 30% is taken on sales.
Access: [F] Buses 12,88; Underground Holland Park 5 mins

Home Gallery

A gallery showing a changing programme of contemporary exhibitions within a fashion shop. [VA,Pr]

Address: 14 Ingestre Place, Nr Broadwick Street, London W1 tel 01 439 7620
Open: Mon-Sat 10-5
Access: Underground Piccadilly

Horizon Gallery

Run by the Indian Arts Council, a registered charity, showing work by Indian artists and other ethnic minorities. [VA,Ph,Cr,LA]

Address: 70 Marchmont Street, London WC1N 1AB tel 01 837 1431
Contact: Rakesh Mathur
Open: Mon 2-6, Tues-Fri 12-6, Sat 10-1
Policy: The gallery, which is part of an arts centre, promotes the work of leading Indian artists, Indian tribal art, *'ethnic minority painters'* and shows work with religious themes. Through a programme of 16, three and a half week exhibitions, it aims to *'ensure the continued vitality of established traditions, through the development of cross-cultural understanding in an increasingly inter-dependent world'* and target audiences are *' all those interested in something new and different'.* All work is by living artists working in a wide variety of media - painting, sculpture, drawing, prints, photography, crafts and live art, and the shows are a combination of group and solo exhibitions. The council has a permanent collection of work by gallery

artists.

Sales: Work sold

The Space: Two spaces 44x4.65x3.5m and 5x3m with a combination of daylight and good artificial lighting. Gallery plans are available and the spaces are also used for literary meetings, talks, lunches and cocktail parties.

Exhibiting: [AW] Applications are welcome and selection is by committee which meets every three months. Send a completed application form, slides, black and white photographs, CV and catalogues. The gallery covers insurance, catalogue/card, mailing of publicity and list of exhibits and takes 30% commission on sales. It supports EPR in principle.

Access: [U][T] Buses 68,77,77a,168,171; Underground Russell Square 3 mins; BR Euston and Kings Cross 7 mins; Car park 3 mins

Horniman Museum

A popular museum with ethnographical collections from all over the world special exhibitions held throughout the year. [VA,Cr]

Address: London Road, Forest Hill, London SE23 tel 01 699 1872/2339/4911

Contact: Director David Boston

Open: Mon-Sat 10.30-6, Sun 2-6 (except Christmas)

Policy: Also houses an important collection of musical instruments and organises lecture series and leisure activities for children and courses for adults.

Access: Buses; BR Forest Hill

Hounslow Library Centre Space

Library space run by the London Borough of Hounslow. [VA,Cr,Ph]

Address: 24 Treaty Centre, High Street, Hounslow TW3 1ES tel 01 570 0622

Contact: Head of Public Services Ian Morson

Open: Mon,Wed,Fri,Sat 9.30-5.30, Tues,Thurs 9.30-8

Policy: A new space, situated within an arts and library centre *'which is intended for general use and it is anticipated that there will be a lively and regular arts input'*. The potential audience is wide-ranging as *'the centre is situated in a shopping centre'* parts of which may also be used for exhibitions and a programme of workshops, seminars and *'culturally-related council exhibitions is planned'*.

Horizon Gallery: Warli, tribal art from West India

Sales: Sales referred to exhibitors

The Space: Two spaces, one 10x5m, the other with 6m linear hanging space, and an additional 30m linear hanging space is provided by free-standing screens. All areas are air conditioned and lit by spots.

Exhibiting: [AW] Applications welcome, write or telephone the Head of Public Services at least three months before projected date. Costs of printing of publicity and list of exhibits are covered and 10% commission is taken on sales.

Access: [U][T][L] Buses 81,98,116,117,120,202,203,222 223,232,237,257; Underground Hounslow Central 5 mins; BR Hounslow 10 mins; Car park in shopping centre

Hurlingham Gallery

A commercial gallery, for hire, dealing in and showing 19th, 20th century and contemporary art. [Pa,Sc,Pr]

Address: 297 New King's Road, Fulham, London SW6 tel 01 736 6911

Contact: Director Amos Levy

Open: Mon-Sat 10-7.30

Policy: The gallery is used by art dealers, out-of-town galleries, and living artists as well as mounting its own shows from *'time to time'*. A *'varied and exciting'* programme of seventeen shows of painting, sculpture and prints, lasting between one and six weeks are held a year. Most of these are mixed, with some solo shows.

Sales: Work sold; Credit scheme; Credit card

The Space: The gallery has two well-lit floors with a quantity of plinths and easels available. Gallery plans are available.

Exhibiting: [AW] Applications are welcome, examples of work must be made available, contact Amos Levy. Hire fee is £600 per week, 50% to be paid at time of booking.

Access: [U] Bus 22; Underground Putney Bridge 5 mins, Parsons Green 5 mins

Ice House

A small self-contained gallery with a programme of changing exhibitions. [VA,Cr,Ph]

Address: Holland Park, Kensington, London W8 tel 01 602 7345

Contact: Arts Officer Michael Goggin, Leighton House Museum, 12 Holland Park Road, London W14 8LZ tel 01 603 1123

Open: Mon-Sun 11-7

Policy: A programme of eight to ten exhibitions a year running from April to October, each generally running for two weeks.

Sales: Work sold

The Space: An unusual shaped space with hanging grid over the walls with good lighting.

Exhibiting: [AW] Contact the Arts Officer directly. The gallery is hired out to artists, no commission taken. Gallery undertakes listings and can distribute artists' leaflets locally.

Access: [F] Well situated for buses and underground

Imperial War Museum

The national museum covers all aspects of the two world wars and other conflicts involving Britain and the Commonwealth since 1914. Its art department holds the largest collection of war paintings and posters in this country and has a regular programme of changing exhibitions. [VA]

Address: Lambeth Road, London SE1 6HZ tel 01 735 8922
Contact: Director Dr A Borg
Open: Mon-Sat 10-5.50, Sun 2-5.50
Policy: The galleries are due to reopen in Spring 1989 after redevelopment work. Two new galleries will be used for the permanent display of paintings and drawings from the First and Second World Wars. The original galleries have been refurbished to form a suite of four large rooms. One of these will be the John Singer Sargent gallery; two will be used for temporary exhibitions and a smaller gallery will house temporary poster exhibitions on historical themes.
Access: [U][T][L] Underground Lambeth North or Elephant & Castle

Institute Francais (Galerie Matisse)

Gallery showing work by French artists. [VA,Ph]

Address: 17 Queensbury Place, London SW7 tel 01 589 6211
Open: Mon-Fri 10-6
The Space: Exhibition spaces of 11.7x5.5m and 12x8.5m lit by spots and natural light. Hanging is by rods and direct fixing, and show cases are available.

Institute of Contemporary Arts

This gallery and arts centre shows the work of living artists mainly in solo shows which are exhibited for eight weeks. [VA,Ph,Vi,LA]

Address: 12 Carlton House Terrace, London SW1 5AH tel 01 930 0493
Contact: Iona Blazwick
Open: Daily 12-11
Policy: The gallery programme ranges from major exhibitions to commissioned installations by established and newly emerging artists. Gallery policy is to show work that will confront the contemporary art scene and audience. Talks, seminars and workshops are organised to coincide with exhibitions. The Crafts Council also have a showcase in the building.
Sales: Work sold; Sales referred to exhibitor
The Space: Exhibition space is also used for performances and theatre events. Gallery plans available.
Exhibiting: [AW] Apply with slides to the Visual Arts Department. Gallery finances all expenses. Exhibitors may sometimes receive a fee for exhibiting. Support in principle for EPR. Commission 25% plus VAT.
Access: [U][T] Foyer, bookshop and cafe, **[X]** Otherwise - help available. Underground Piccadilly Circus 5 mins

Intaglio Printmaker

Gallery showing work by contemporary printmakers. [Pr]

Address: 323 Goswell Road, London EC1V tel 01 278 0641
Open: Mon-Fri 10-6, Sat 10-3
Policy: Also sells printmaking supplies and offers a framing service. Contemporary prints taken on consignment (sale/return) basis in all printmaking mediums including mono types.
Sales: Work sold
Access: Underground Angel

Interim Art

Gallery showing contemporary work including installations. [VA]

Address: 21 Beck Road, London E8 tel 01 254 9607
Contact: Director Maureen Paley
Open: Wed-Sun 1-6 and by appointment
Access: Buses 6,35,55,106,253; Underground Bethnal Green

Iraqi Cultural Centre

The gallery specialises in Arab arts, with emphasis on Iraqi art. [VA,Ph,Cr]

Address: 177-178 Tottenham Court Road, London W1P 9LF tel 01 637 9724
Contact: Director
Open: Mon-Sat 10-5
Policy: The gallery mounts six to eight exhibitions a year, contemporary and historical and including architecture and photography.
Access: Buses 14,14a,24,29,73,134; Underground Goodge Street

Island Arts Centre

An arts centre with two spaces for small exhibitions.

Address: Tiller Road, London E14 tel 01 98779 25
Contact: Co-ordinator Alison Kenny
Policy: Mainly work by local artists.
The Space: The exhibition spaces are on the walls of a room designed for performances.
Access: Bus 277; Docklands Light Railway

Islington Central Library Gallery

A library space run by the London Borough of Islington, showing work of local artists. [VA,Ph,Cr]

Address: London Borough of Islington Libraries Department, Central Library, 2 Fieldway Crescent, London N5 1PF tel 01 609 3051 ext 242
Contact: Special Services Librarian Bob Gray
Open: Mon-Thurs 9-8, Fri,Sat 9-5; Closed Sun
Policy: The gallery *'is available to anyone who lives, works or studies in the borough'*. The programme of 28 shows a year, each lasting two to three weeks, includes mixed and solo shows by living artists in a variety of media; *'exhibitions of interest to the local community, including local history material'* are also mounted. Twice a year the library runs 'Artmart', an exhibition of artworks available for loan or sale through the library.
Sales: Sales referred to exhibitor (except 'Artmart')
The Space: The gallery, on a mezzanine floor, is divided into two areas each with 16m linear hanging space, lit

by fluorescent tubes and spots. Two showcases are available. Gallery plans are available.

Exhibiting: [AW] Applications welcome from local artists, write to the Special Services Librarian. The library can help with publicity.

Access: [U][T][L] Buses 43,153,263a,271,279,279a, N92; BR/Underground Highbury and Islington 5 mins, Drayton Park 5 mins

Islington Factory Arts

A gallery within an arts centre housed in an old church. [VA,Cr]

Address: 2 Parkhurst Road, London N7 0SF tel 01 607 0561

Contact: Visual Arts Co-ordinator Phillippa Clayden, Denzil Forrester tel 01 607 0561

Open: Mon-Fri 11-6, Sat 2-6, Sun 11-5

Policy: The centre has two galleries, one showing photography, and the other a range of contemporary visual arts. Exhibitions change regularly and consist of group and solo shows. Artists are drawn mainly from London.

Sales: Work sold

The Space: The photography gallery is in the café area and accommodates around 30 framed works. The second gallery measures 10x12m.

Exhibiting: [AW] Submissions are invited. Ask for details of deadlines. The gallery takes 15% commission and distributes the artist's own publicity.

Access: [S] Buses 29,221,253,279; Underground Caledonian Road

Islington Library Service

Islington Library Service comprises the central library, ten branch libraries and a mobile library.

Address: Islington Central Library, 2 Fieldway Crescent, Islington, London N5 1PF tel 01 609 7331

Contact: Borough Librarian S N Marshall

The Space: Limited space available in most of the libraries for small displays. The Central Library has two areas on a mezzanine floor (see Islington Central Library).

Exhibiting: [AW] Write to the Special Services Librarian tel 01 609 3051 ext 242.

Islington Factory Arts, main gallery

J K Hill

This art and craft gallery holds occasional exhibitions, normally lasting two weeks and featuring the work of major British potters. [Ce]

Address: 151 Fulham Road, Chelsea, London SW3 6SN tel 01 584 7529

Contact: Janet Hill

Open: Mon-Sat 10.30-6.30

Policy: The gallery handles the work of over 150 potters, the aim being to stock and promote a wide range of ceramic styles and designs. Alongside exhibitions there is a changing display of work for sale. The gallery attracts people with a specialist interest in studio ceramics as well as more casual buyers.

Sales: Work sold; Credit card

The Space: Approximately 182 square metres.

Exhibiting: The gallery normally approaches potters that it wishes to represent. Gallery finances printing and mail-out of publicity, catalogue/card, list of exhibits and preview costs.

Access: [F] Buses 14,45,49; Underground South Kensington 5 mins

Jablonski Gallery

A converted eighteenth century artist's studio, the gallery specialises in contemporary figurative painting, sculpture and prints. [VA]

Address: 16 Woodstock Street, London W1R 1HE tel 01 629 4419

Contact: Director Jerzy Jablonski

Open: Mon-Fri 10-6, Sat 10.30-4

Policy: Changing exhibition programme includes short group exhibitions of work by young or unknown artists, as well as longer one or two-person exhibitions, of two to three weeks duration, of work by more established artists.

Sales: Work sold

The Space: Linear space 30.5m with picture rail, 65 square metres overall. Spotlights and good natural light.

Exhibiting: [AW] Send slides and CV to director. Gallery covers insurance, publicity, mailing and private view costs. Commission is 45%.

Access: Buses to Oxford Street, Piccadilly; Underground Bond Street

Janus Avivson Gallery

This commercial gallery and artists' agency deals in figurative work by young British and foreign artists, and shows predominantly solo shows exhibitions. [VA,Ph,Cr,Ce]

Address: 22c Camden Lock, Camden Town, London NW1 8AF tel 01 482 3091

Contact: Director Janus R Avivson, Avivson Artists' Agency, 150 Regent Street, London, W1R 5FA tel 0836 536007

Open: Wed-Sun 12-6

Policy: Gallery policy is to actively promote the work of young artists. Targeting a North London audience, as well as organising exchange shows with artists from the USA. In the future the gallery aims to adopt a more educational approach aimed at a younger audience. Seminars on the business side of art are also arranged

for artists.
Sales: Work sold; Sales referred to exhibitor; Credit card; Credit scheme
The Space: 82 square metres. The gallery cannot accommodate large-scale works. Exhibiting area is also used for quarterly seminars. Gallery plans available.
Exhibiting: [AW] Apply to Janus Avivson with slides, CV and SAE. Gallery finances insurance, printing and mail-out of publicity, list of exhibits, preview and display costs. Commission 25-50%.
Access: [F] Buses 24,31,168; Underground Camden Town 5 mins

Japanese Gallery

Commercial gallery run by the Awertheim Trading and Buying Agency Ltd, showing the work of Japanese woodcuts and prints, past and present. [Pr,Dr]
Address: 66D Kensington Church Street, London W8 4BY tel 01 229 2934
Contact: C D Wertheim
Open: Mon-Sat 10-6
Policy: The gallery programme of four, three-month exhibitions of Japanese woodcuts, with the occasional show of drawings or crafts, aims to provide original works starting at £5 to a varied audience. Most shows are mixed, with one solo show a year. The works on show are mainly those of the past, with some works by living artists. The gallery is happy to provide free authentification of Japanese works of art and lectures on Japanese prints can be arranged.
Sales: Work sold; Credit scheme; Credit card
The Space: The gallery space 5.5x4x3m has three walls and is lit by fluorescent strips and spots; hanging is by rods. A large pavement can provide an outdoor space.
Access: [F] Underground Kensington High Street 5 mins, Notting Hill Gate 5 mins

Japanese Gallery: 'Snowy Heron in the rain' by Gakusui

Jeanette Hayhurst Fine Glass

Gallery specialising in high-quality contemporary glass work. [Gl]
Address: 32a Kensington Church Street, London W8 tel 01 938 1539
Contact: Director Jeanette Hayhurst
Open: Mon-Fri 10.30-5, Sat 11-4
Policy: Recent shows have included work from Royal College of Art MA students, as well as solo and two-person shows by makers such as Keith Brocklehurst, David Pryterch, Jane Beebe and Anthony Stern. Shows last a fortnight. Permanent display of antique and contemporary glass for sale.
Sales: Work sold
Access: Underground High Street Kensington

John Cass School of Art Gallery

A foyer area in the faculty of art and design. [VA,Ph,Cr]
Address: City of London Polytechnic, Central House, 59-63 Whitechapel High Street, London E1 E1
Contact: Dean of Faculty Guy Beggs
Open: Mon-Fri 10-8.30
Policy: The gallery aims to provide a variety of types of exhibition by local artists and groups, by past and present students and by teaching staff. Exhibitions usually last three weeks and the arts faculty is keen to invite and select work of relevance to the students and to the local community.
Sales: Work sold
The Space: Two parallel walls each about 11.5m long with a hanging sytem and wall-mounted battening. Showcases available.
Exhibiting: [AW] Applications in writing to Julia Wilson or Nigel Maudsley in the Faculty of Art. No hire fee but exhibitors have to cover their own exhibiting costs.
Access: [U][T][L] Buses 5,10,15,22a,25,40,67,225,253; Underground Aldgate

JPL Fine Arts

A commercial gallery specialising in Impressionist and Post-Impressionist drawings, watercolours, pastels and paintings and 19th & 20th century French sculpture. [Pa,Sc,Dr]
Address: 26 Davies Street, London W1Y 1LH tel 01 493 2630
Contact: Director Christian Neffe
Open: Mon-Fri 10-5.30
Policy: Four exhibitions a year, three of which are on a particular artist, one a mixed show called 'Private View'

held late autumn. There is always a changing display of stock in the main gallery.

Sales: Work sold

Access: [F] Buses 6,7,8,12,13,15,16a,25,73,88,113, 135,137,159; Underground Bond Street

Judd Street Gallery

Commercial gallery which is mainly hired out to artists working in the traditional manner. [Pa,Pr,Dr,Ph,Cr]

Address: 99 Judd Street, London WC1H 9NE tel 01 388 1985

Contact: Alan Powers tel 01 387 3154

Open: Mon-Sat 12-7

Policy: The programme of 15 shows a year are *'one-person shows of artists not represented by other galleries ie young, based out of London or retired, with a tendency towards traditional and representational work'* in two-dimensional media. The gallery stages its own shows three or four times a year, including the owners work, and the work of artists of the 1920s and '30s. *'The domestic scale of the gallery also makes it suitable for crafts'.* Visitors and clients include known buyers as well as a local, passing trade.

Sales: Work sold; Sales referred to exhibitor

The Space: The three exhibition spaces 4x4x2.9m, 3x3x2.6m and 3x4.5x2m, with a total of 28m linear hanging space, are lit by movable spots on rails; hanging is by adjustable chains from a cornice rail and there is a showcase 1.5x.8x.1m. Size limitation is approximately 2m. Gallery plans are available.

Exhibiting: [AW] Applications are welcome to hire the space at £30 per day. Send slides and CV 12-18 months in advance. Commission taken on sales is up to 40% on own promotions, and the gallery supports EPR in principle.

Access: [S] BR Euston, St Pancras, Kings Cross 5 mins; Underground Euston, St Pancras, Kings Cross 5 mins, Russell Square 10 mins

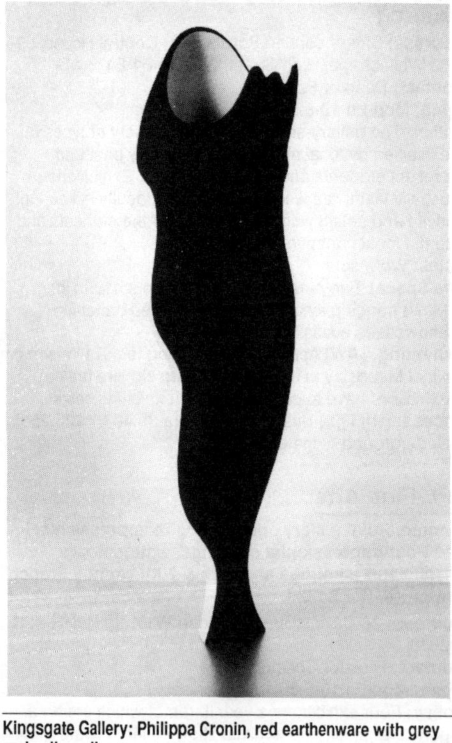

Kingsgate Gallery: Philippa Cronin, red earthenware with grey and yellow slip

Karsten Schubert

Commercial gallery showing contemporary art by living artists. [Pa,Sc,Dr]

Address: 85 Charlotte Street, London W1P 1LB tel 01 631 0031

Contact: Karsten Schubert

Open: Tues-Sat 10-6; closed Mon

Policy: The programme of international contemporary art includes the work of young and established artists from England, Europe and America whose work is *'conceptual/minimal orientated'.* The gallery promotes a selected number of artists. The ten shows a year are mainly solo and last three to six weeks.

Sales: Work sold

The Space: The gallery space is approximately 200 square metres.

Exhibiting: [AW] Send applications addressed to Karsten Schubert. *'We appreciate an information package containing photographic material and CV'.* The gallery covers costs of insurance, printing of publicity, catalogue/card, mailing, preview, transport, display and artists' expenses, and 50% commission is taken on sales.

Access: Underground Goodge Street & Warren Street

Kew Studio (Staircase Gallery)

A staircase exhibition area on two floors in a building used for educational projects, available for hire for solo or group exhibitions. [Pa,Pr,Ph]

Address: St Luke's House, Sandycombe Road, Kew Gardens, Richmond, Surrey TW10 tel 01 940 2791

Contact: Suzette Dodds

Open: Mon-Fri 10-12 noon

Policy: Two exhibitions a year organised by Suzette Dodds for members. Portfolio scheme for members.

Sales: Work sold

Exhibiting: [AW] Members pay £39 for six weeks for solo or group exhibitions, non-members £47.

King Street Galleries

A gallery showing 19th and 20th century British paintings and watercolours. [Pa]

Address: 17 King Street, St. James's, London SW1 tel 01 930 3993/9392

Contact: J Napier-Ford

Open: Mon-Fri 9.30-5.30, Sat 9.30-1

Access: Buses 3,6,9,12,13,14,14a,15,19,22,22b,38, 53,88,159; Underground Piccadilly Circus

Kingsgate Gallery

A gallery situated within large warehouse converted into artists workshops which shows fortnightly exhibitions of work by workshop members and others. [VA,Cr]

Address: 110-116 Kingsgate Road, London, NW6 tel 01 328 7878
Contact: Exhibition Organiser
Open: Mon-Sun 10-4
Sales: Work sold
The Space: Linear space 24.3m; 51sqm area; hanging by direct fixing to walls; spotlights and daylight.
Exhibiting: [AW] Artist is responsible for all costs. Weekly hire charge for space is £25-£50. Commission is 10%.
Access: BR Brondesbury; Underground West Hampstead

Knapp Gallery

Commercial gallery run and subsidised by Regent's College which is a registered charity. [VA,Ph,Cr]

Address: Regent's College, Inner Circle, Regent's Park, London NW1 4NS tel 01 487 7426
Contact: Eileen Jordan
Open: Mon-Sat 10-6; Closed bank holidays
Policy: The programme of nine exhibitions a year is predominantly of mixed shows of contemporary artists and makers working in a variety of media. Painters and printmakers *'have featured strongly in the programme'*, but sculpture, photography and crafts are shown as well as the occasional historical show; each exhibition runs for four or five weeks. The audience is wide ranging *'we encourage visitors from our international student body, staff on campus, the local community, visitors to the college and artists' friends and contacts'*, and the space *is used for poetry and prose readings, lectures, conference receptions and meetings.*
Sales: Work sold
The Space: The gallery is 13x8x2.4m with 45m of linear hanging space, and glass cases 1x1.5x.7m; gallery plans are available.
Exhibiting: [AW] Applications are welcome. Send slides or photographs, CV and SAE. The space is available for hire, at varied rates, to artists' groups who are required to share the costs of the private view and publicity, the gallery covers costs of insurance, and mailing; 20% commission is taken on sales.
Access: Buses 2b,13,18,27,30,74,159; Underground Baker Street 5 mins; parking within inner circle of Regent's Park after 11am

Knightsbridge Galleries

A private gallery specialising in contemporary watercolours of villages, landscapes, homes, gardens and animals by gallery artists. [Pa]

Address: 1st Floor, 35 Beauchamp Place, London SW3 1NU tel 01 584 8180
Contact: Nola Throssell
Open: Mon-Sat 10-6, Sun 11-6
Policy: *'The exhibitions cater for all tastes in paintings with works ranging from the exquisitely detailed to surrealism and abstraction.'* As well as exhibiting work in its own space exhibitions are also arranged at outside venues. English tea house within gallery.
Sales: Work sold; Credit card
The Space: 34 square metres of space in which all walls are available.
Exhibiting: [AW] Contact Nola Throssell. Mainly watercolours at Beauchamp Place, other media at other venues.
Access: Underground Knightsbridge; Harrods car park 5 mins

Knoedler

A gallery specialising in 20th century Masters and other contemporary work. [Pa]

Address: 22 Cork Street, London W1X 1HB tel 01 439 1096
Contact: Director J Kasmin
Open: Mon-Fri 10-5.30, Sat 10-1
Access: Buses 3,6,9,12,13,14,14a,15,19,22,22b,38, 53,88,159,509; Underground Piccadilly Circus

Krok'-ō-dīl

This commercial gallery predominantly shows contemporary work by London-based artists in a mixture of group and solo shows. [VA,Ph,Cr]

Address: 343 Goswell Road, The Angel, Islington, London EC1V 7JT tel 01 837 2416
Contact: Partners Michele Burke, Kenneth Prust
Open: Mon-Fri 10-6
Policy: To date the gallery has shown a variety of shows within the spectrum of fine art: painting, sculpture, ceramics, collage, textiles, jewellery and installations. Gallery policy is to keep costs to a minimum in order to give more people the opportunity to show and experiment. Target audiences are local residents as well as the wider London area and tourist market.
Sales: Sales referred to exhibitor
The Space: 8x5x3.5m high with 20m linear hanging space. Natural and track-mounted spot lighting. The gallery cannot accommodate work any larger than 3m in height. Fixed display cabinet available. Gallery plans and all other details available on request.
Exhibiting: [AW] Maximum of three participants per show. Contact gallery regarding availability. Hire fee is

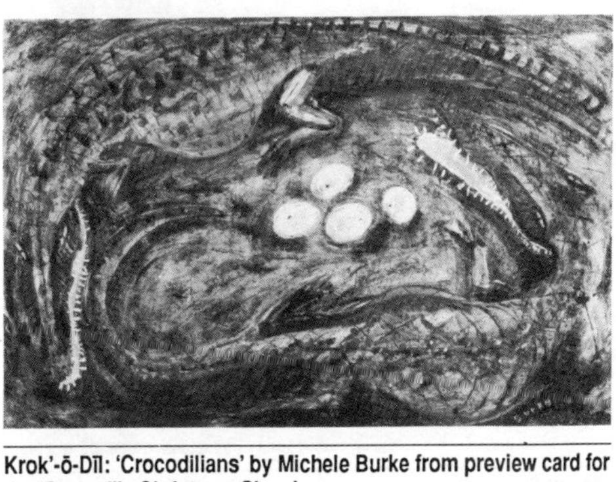

Krok'-ō-Dīl: 'Crocodilians' by Michele Burke from preview card for the 'Crocodile Christmas Show'

£200 per week plus VAT. Fee includes insurance, lighting, heating, no commission charged on sales.

Access: [F] Buses 4,19,30,38,43,73,153,171 171a,196,214,263a,277,279,279a; BR Kings Cross; Underground Angel directly opposite

Lamont Gallery

Commercial gallery showing and dealing in work by living artists in a variety of media. [VA]

Address: 65 Roman Road, Bethnal Green, London E2 0QN tel 01 981 6332

Contact: Director Andrew Lamont

Open: Tues-Sat 11-6 or by appointment

Policy: Situated at the heart of London's East End where the largest concentration of artists in Britain live and work, the gallery aims to attract new customers for contemporary art. This is achieved by keeping prices at a reasonable level and showing work in a variety of sizes and media. Mainly shows less-established artists and three-person shows are interspersed with solo shows. Work by women has proved particularly successful.

The Space: the gallery *'is situated in a converted Victorian hairdressing salon, with work exhibited on the ground level and in the basement reached by a period spiral staircase'*. Batten hanging and good lighting.

Exhibiting: [AW] Write to the Director with information, visual material and SAE or telephone for an appointment. Gallery charges a commission in exchange for exhibiting and promoting work.

Access: [X] Buses 8,8a,106, 253,277; Underground Bethnal Green

Lasson Gallery

A commercial gallery which lets the space to exhibitors for a hire fee. [VA,Ph,Cr,LA]

Address: 34 Duke Street, St James's, London SW1Y

Lamont Gallery

6DF tel 01 930 5950

Contact: Director

Open: Mon-Fri 10.30-5, Sat 11-1

Policy: Contemporary exhibitions are held throughout the year.

The Space: The gallery is lit by spots, hanging is by rods.

Access: Buses 3,6,9,12,13,14,14a,15,19,22,22b,38, 53,88,159,509; Underground Piccadilly Circus

Last Gallery

Gallery offering exhibition space to young and little-known artists. [VA]

Address: 157 Battersea Park Road, London SW8 4UB tel 01 627 0108

Contact: Wende Sylvester

Open: Tues-Fri 1-7, Sat 10-2, Sun 2.30-5

Policy: Galley seeks to enhance prospects for young aspiring artists, particularly those whose work may go *'against the grain'*.

Sales: Work sold

Access: BR Battersea

Lauderdale House (Upper Gallery)

Two galleries run by the Lauderdale House Society. [VA,Ph,Cr,LA]

Address: Waterlow Park, Highgate Hill, London N6 SHG tel 01 348 8716

Contact: Lesley Clyne

Open: Tues-Fri 11-4, Sat 1-5 dependent on private bookings, please check with the house, Sun 12-5

Policy: The galleries are hired to artists on a fixed fee basis for fortnightly or longer bookings.

The Space: The lower gallery is 15x5.8m and the upper gallery is 14x3m, both with hanging rods, spots and natural light.

Exhibiting: [AW] Applications are welcome and all expenses are the responsibility of the artist.

Access: [U][T] Lower gallery [X] Upper gallery. Tube Archway-Northern line; Buses 210,271,143,C11

Lefevre Gallery

A gallery specialising in 19th and 20th century European paintings and drawings. [Pa,Dr]

Address: 30 Bruton Street, London W1X 8JB tel 01 493 2107

Contact: Director

Open: Mon-Fri 10-5, Sat 10-12.30

Policy: Monthly exhibitions include British and European paintings and drawings and work by contemporary British artists.

Access: Buses 3,6,9,12,13,14,14a,15,19,2,22b,38,53, 88,159; Underground Piccadilly Circus

Leigh Gallery

A gallery on the Crafts Council's selected list specialising in studio pottery, glass, paintings and prints. [Pa,Pr,Ce,Gl]

Address: 17 Leigh Street, London WC1 tel 01 242 5177

Contact: Director Michael Ransom-Witt

Open: Mon-Fri 9.30-6, Sat 9.30-5

Policy: Around six exhibitions are held a year to accompany the regularly changing stock.
Access: [S] Buses 14,14a,17,18,30,45,46,63,73,77a, 214,22,259; Underground Kings Cross & Russell Square; BR Kings Cross

Leighton House Museum

A gallery and museum with a permanent collection of fine and decorative art from the 15th - 20th century and a programme of changing exhibitions. [VA,Ph,Cr,LA]
Address: 12 Holland Park Road, London W14 8LZ tel 01 602 3316
Contact: Curator Stephen Jones
Open: Mon-Fri 11-6, Sat 11-5; Closed bank holidays
Policy: A programme of eleven exhibitions held annually, each running for a minimum of two weeks. Solo exhibitions preferred.
Sales: Work sold
The Space: Two spaces available: a large purpose-built top-light gallery 10x8m with a smaller adjacent ancilliary gallery with display screens.
Exhibiting: [AW] Applications are welcome - contact the Curator. The gallery is hired out to artists, no commission is taken. The gallery can distribute leaflets locally.
Access: [X] Underground Kensington

Leinster Contemporary Art

A commercial gallery dealing in contemporary art. [VA]
Address: Suite 703, Business Design Centre, Upper Street, Islington, London N1 tel 01 288 6058
Open: Tues-Fri 11-6, Sat by appointment

Leinster Fine Art

A commercial gallery showing British and European painting. [Pa]
Address: Fourth Floor, 3 Clifford Street, London W1 tel 01 437 4534
Contact: Director
Open: Tues-Fri 11-6; Sat by appointment
Access: Buses 3,6,9,12,13,14,14a,15,19,22,22b,38, 53,88,159,509; Underground Piccadilly Circus

Lesley Craze

A commercial gallery on the Crafts Council's selected list which shows monthly exhibitions of contemporary crafts. [Cr]
Address: 5 Essex Road, London N1 tel 01 226 3200
Open: Wed-Sat 10-5
Sales: Work sold
Access: Underground Angel

Lewisham Visual Arts

The arts co-ordinating group for the London Borough of Lewisham which also has a shop front window gallery space next to theatre box office. [VA,Cr,Ph,Ho,Ar]
Address: Lewisham Theatre, Catford, London SE6 4TU tel 01 695 6000 ext 3497
Contact: Community Arts Team Jim Park
Policy: The free newsletter provides details of opportunities in Lewisham, including temporary or new exhibition space. Also offered is a publicity distribution service for artists and arts and community groups, who can also utilise the free equipment loan scheme. A small grant scheme is also available to artists offering sums up to £150.
Sales: Work sold
The Space: Two adjoining shop windows on High Street location, approximately 10 linear metres hanging space.
Exhibiting: [AW] Apply for written details to Jim Park.
Access: [F]

Liberty Retail

In-store gallery showing paintings and prints, also occasional craft, particularly textiles, shows. [VA,Cr]
Address: Regent Street, London W1 tel 01 734 1234
Open: Mon-Weds,Fri,Sat 9.30-6, Thurs 9.30-7
Access: Buses to Regent Street; Underground Oxford Circus

Light Fantastic (Gallery of Holography)

One of Britain's few holography galleries, showing lively and experimental work from Britain and all over the world. [Ho]
Address: 48 South Row, The Market, Covent Garden, London WC2 tel 01 836 6423
Contact: Peter Wood or Jane Sharratt
Open: Mon-Sat 10-7, Sun 12-6
Policy: Exhibitions change every four months, they also undertake commissions and have retail sales outlet. Admission charge.
Sales: Work sold
The Space: Gallery area 139 square metres.
Access: Buses to Covent Garden; Underground Covent Garden

Lewisham Visual Arts: display of holograms by Susan Gamble and Michael Wenyon (Photo: Jim Park)

Linda Blackstone Gallery

Commercial gallery showing and dealing in contemporary representational painting and sculpture. [Pa,Sc]

Address: The Old Slaughterhouse, Rear of 13 High Street, Pinner, Middlesex HA5 5QQ tel 01 868 5765
Contact: Linda Blackstone
Open: Wed-Sat 10-6
Policy: The gallery aims *'to bring fine art to the north western outlying districts of London'* through a programme of six, two-week exhibitions which include work by established and up-and-coming younger artists who specialise in landscape, marine and figurative themes - *'70% of gallery artists are members of RI, RSMA, ARBS, SBA, RMS and SWA'.* Two annual exhibitions are held, the Christmas show and an embroidery exhibition in January/February. Most exhibitions are mixed and a changing display of work for sale is held between shows. Lectures by artists and *'live demonstrations'* help to attract a wide ranging audience.
Sales: Work sold; Credit scheme; Credit card
The Space: Two gallery spaces, upstairs 7x4x2m, downstairs 7x5.5x2 and 2.5m have a combined linear hanging space of 23m and are lit by mini spot and flood lighting. Hanging is by rods and a showcase is available for minatures. Classical music is played and the space is occasionally used for charity exhibition evenings.
Exhibiting: The gallery covers publicity, catalogue/card, mailing, list of exhibits and the preview. Artists are asked to share the cost of glossy illustrated invitations and 36.66% commission plus VAT is taken on sales.
Access: [F][X] Underground Pinner; Own parking area; Public car park one min

Line Art Gallery

A commercial gallery, part of the international art magazine Art Line, showing usually solo exhibitions of contemporary work by sculptors, painters and printmakers from Britain and Abroad. [Pa,Pr,Dr,Ph]

Address: First Floor, 1-3 Garratt Lane, London SW18 tel 01 870 0427
Contact: Director Elizabeth Adeane
Open: By appointment Tues-Fri 11-6, Sat 11-4
Policy: A mixture of sponsored (ie Pirelli) shows and artists suggested by Art Line magazine. Interested in presenting regional artists in London.
Sales: Work sold
The Space: The first floor gallery has about 330 square metres of space with a ceiling height of 2.6m and is divided into two studios. The first floor gallery is carpeted and therefore unsuitable for *'structural alterations or messy floor works'.*
Exhibiting: [AW] Contact the gallery for details. Exhibitions are insured and the gallery provides 1500 -2000 mailing address labels, a fully-illustrated catalogue, invigilation and a display advertisement in *Art Line*. Send A5 SAE for illustrated brochure and details of charges. No commission charged.
Access: [X] Bus routes 44,220,280; Underground East Putney, Clapham Common 12mins; BR Clapham Junction 10mins, BR Wandsworth Town 4 mins

Lisson Gallery

Commercial gallery dealing in and showing work by living artists in a variety of media. [VA,Ph]

Address: 67 Lisson Street, London NW1 5DA tel 01 724 2739
Open: Mon-Fri 10-6, Sat 10-1
Policy: The gallery specialises in *'international avant-garde British sculpture'* and *'our interest is confined to contemporary art from 1965 to the present'.* It promotes British artists worldwide and represents foreign artists in Britain. A programme of ten exhibitions is held a year each lasting four to six weeks which includes painting, sculpture, drawing, prints and photography, most of these are solo exhibitions .
Sales: Work sold
The Space: The gallery is 255 square metres and has 100m linear hanging space. Gallery plans are available.
Exhibiting: [AW] The gallery promotes a selected number of artists but applications are welcome. Send transparencies or photographs to the Director. Insurance, printing of publicity, catalogue/card, mailing, display, preview, transport and artists costs are covered and 50% commission is taken on sales.
Access: [X] Buses 6,7,8,15,16,18,27,36; Underground Edgware Road 2 mins, Marylebone 5 mins; BR Marylebone NCP 1 min

Livesey Museum

Local history museum for the London Borough of Southwark. [VA,Cr]

Address: 682 Old Kent Road, London SE15 tel 01 639 5604
Contact: Keeper Janet Vitmayer
Open: Mon-Sat 10-5; closed between exhibitions
Policy: Has a changing programme of exhibitions which *'are intended to show a picture of the borough and beyond.'* Also provides talks, slide shows and educational or group visit facilities, besides normal museum facilities and services.
Access: Buses 141,177,53,21,78; BR Queens Road Peckham & South Bermondsey

Linda Blackstone Gallery: F Donald Blake 1988

Living Art

'Glass engraving and other presentation work for special occasions'. [Gl]

Address: 35 Kenway Road, London SW5 tel 01 370 2766
Open: Tues-Fri 1.30-6.30, Sat 9-1
Sales: Work sold
Access: Bus routes Earls Court; Underground Earls Court 1 min

Llewellyn Alexander (Fine Paintings)

A gallery specialising in 19th and 20th Century British and European paintings including oils and watercolours. [VA]

Address: 124-126 The Cut, Waterloo, London SE1 tel 01 620 1322
Open: Mon-Fri 10-7.30, Sat 2-7.30

Locus Gallery

Gallery specialising in sculpture, and in particular, work by Italian artists. [Sc,Cr]

Address: 116 Heath Street, Hampstead, London NW3 1DR tel 01 435 4005
Contact: Director Gudrun Fazzina
Open: Tues-Fri 10-5.30, Sat 10.30-5 & by appointment
Policy: Programme includes work in bronze, marble, terracotta and ceramics.
Sales: Work sold
The Space: Two floors approximately 5x13m.
Exhibiting: [AW] Applications will be *'considered'*.
Access: Buses to Hampstead; Underground Hampstead

Loggia

'Small private gallery' run by Free Painters and Sculptors, a limited company with charitable status. [VA]

Address: 15 Buckingham Gate, London SW1E 6LB tel 01 828 5963
Contact: Director Roy Rasmussen
Open: Mon-Fri 6-8, Sat & Sun 2-6
Policy: The gallery aims to *'further the education of the public in the understanding of the visual arts'* through a programme of fifteen exhibitions of members' work in a variety of media - painting, sculpture, drawings and prints. Most are solo shows with three group and three retrospectives a year each lasting three weeks. A bi-annual open exhibition, *'Trends'* is held and provincial shows are mounted from time to time. *'The gallery, which is run entirely by voluntary effort, aims to encourage young talented members as well as showing the work of those already established'*.
Sales: Work sold
The Space: A small patio is available for sculpture.
Exhibiting: The gallery is hired to exhibitors but covers the costs of catalogue/card, mailing and the preview. Commission of 25% is taken on sales.
Access: [S] Underground St James's Park 5 mins; BR Victoria 7 mins

Lombard Gallery

Regular exhibitions of contemporary work. [VA]

Address: 6 Westmorland Place, Bromley, Kent BR1 1DR tel 01 290 1392
Contact: Director
Open: Mon-Sat 9-5.30

London Contemporary Art

A gallery specialising in prints by contemporary British artists part of a three storey printing complex including etching, lithography, silkscreen and origination and design ateliers. [Pr]

Address: 132 Lots Road, Chelsea, London SW10 0RJ tel 01 352 3468
Contact: Marketing Manager Tracey Kehoe
Open: Mon-Fri 10-6, Sat 10-2
Policy: To promote the work of contemporary European artists, with a particular emphasis on prints and orginals by British artists. Bi-monthly exhibitions. The gallery has three sales people covering the North, Home Counties and South West and three corporate consultants.
Sales: Work sold
The Space: The gallery space is 31 square metres.
Access: Car parking at rear; Underground Earls Court; Hopper bus to Chelsea Harbour

London Ecology Centre

A gallery run by the London Ecology Centre Trust, and showing 'specifically ecological work'. [VA,Ph,Cr,LA]

Address: 45 Shelton Street, Covent Garden, London WC2H 9HJ tel 01 379 4324
Contact: Administrator Diana Cripps
Open: Mon-Sat 10-11pm
Policy: The gallery is used to promote *'awareness of ecology and nature conservation in London'* through a programme of 18, three-week shows. Work in a wide range of media is shown - painting, sculpture, drawing, prints, photography, crafts and live art - and all work is by living artists. *'An attractive, varied and balanced programme'* of work includes solo and group shows. The audience is wide ranging, mainly passers by, including tourists, and target audiences are those interested in *'art and ecology'*. The Trust aims to raise some income from sales of work and hires the space

London Contemporary Art: Directors Anthony Stancomb & Piers Johnstone with clients from Project Art & Art Contact

to artists. It also runs a programme of events relating to environmental issues.
Sales: Work sold
The Space: A gallery of 13x5x3.5m with a total of 36m linear hanging space lit by concealed track and spot lighting. Hanging is by direct fixing, and gallery plans are available.
Exhibiting: [AW] Telephone the Administrator before submitting a written application. The space is hired at £150 - 500 per week. The gallery covers mailing and printing of publicity and takes 20% commission on sales. It supports EPR in principle.
Access: [F][S] Buses 14,19,22,24,29; Underground Covent Garden 2 mins; NCP 5 mins; Bicycle rails nearby

London Film-makers Co-op

A cinema and performance space with exhibition area. [VA,LA]
Address: 42 Gloucester Avenue, Camden, London NW1 tel 01 586 4806/8516
Contact: Moira Sweeney
Open: Mon-Thurs 10-6, Fri & Sat 10-10
Policy: *'We specialise in screening avant-garde and experimental films which would otherwise rarely, if at all, get screened in this country'*. The programme of 18 showings a year includes *'triple screen films, slide and sound works, time-based media events, performance and installation work'*; small exhibitions of film makers' related visual art are held in the gallery which is *'an open space for artists to exhibit work and sell if possible'*. The cinema's *'unique policy is to screen little-known and established film-makers' work'*. Ten installations lasting up to one week, ten performances of one night and two exhibitions lasting one month are held each year and all work is by living film-makers. The cinema also holds 1500 artists' films in the distribution library and film-makers regularly discuss their work in conjunction with screening workshops. The cinema and equipment are available for hire.
Sales: Work sold
The Space: There are two hanging walls 4.5x6m and two 9x1.5m.
Exhibiting: [AW] Applications welcome in writing with detailed information regarding work to be shown. The gallery covers the costs of transport, mailing, catalogue/card and artists' expenses.
Access: Buses 24,29,31,68,74,134,137,253; Underground Camden Town, Chalk Farm

Louise Hallett Gallery

Commercial gallery dealing in and showing 20th century and contemporary art. [VA]
Address: 27 Junction Mews, Sale Place, London W2 1PN tel 01 724 9865
Contact: Louise Hallett
Open: Tues-Sat 11-7
Policy: The gallery specialises primarily in 20th century art of various media, mounting seven exhibitions a year lasting approximately seven weeks each. A combination of solo shows by gallery artists is augmented by mixed or theme shows. A large selection of 20th century work permanently in stock.
Sales: Work sold; Credit scheme; Credit card
The Space: A large and light space on ground and first floor, in a converted mission hall, with high ceilings and natural light.
Exhibiting: The gallery promotes a selected number of artists.
Access: [X] Buses 7,15,16,27,36; Underground Edgware Road

Lumley Cazalet

A gallery specialising in late 19th and 20th century original prints. [Pr]
Address: 24 Davies Street, London W1 tel 01 491 4767
Open: Mon-Fri 10-6

Lynne Stern Art Consultancy & Gallery

A gallery and consultancy which brings together business and private collectors with the work of contemporary artists. [VA]
Address: 15 Albemarle Street, London W1 tel 01 491 8905, 8906
Open: Mon-Fri 10-6, Sat 10-1
Policy: The gallery holds a large stock of work by established and some lesser-known emerging British artists. Specialises in artists in business and private collectors with purchasing and commissioning rather than operating as a purely retail gallery.
Sales: Works for sale
Access: [X] Underground: Green Park, Piccadilly

Lyric Theatre, Hammersmith

A theatre with exhibition space. [pa,Pr,Ph]
Address: King Street, Hammersmith, London W6 tel 01 741 0824
Contact: Christine Hanley
Open: Mon-Sat 10-11
Policy: Exhibitions hung in three foyer spaces.
The Space: Three foyer spaces with spots and daylight.
Exhibiting: The theatre covers insurance up to a limit, the artist is responsible for all other arrangements.
Access: Buses 27,91; Underground Hammersmith

Malcolm Innes Gallery

A gallery dealing with 19th and 20th century and contemporary Scottish landscapes, sporting and natural history pictures. [Pa]
Address: 172 Walton Street, London SW3 tel 01 584 0575/5559
Contact: Director
Open: Mon-Fri 9.30-6, Sat 10-1

Mall Galleries

Set of gallery rooms in imposing Georgian terrace which shows work by FBA member societies and individuals. [VA]
Address: Federation of British Artists [FBA], 17 Carlton House Terrace, London SW1Y 5BD tel 01 930 6844
Contact: Exhibitions Executive Anna Kindersley

Open: Daily 10-5 including most Sundays
Policy: The FBA is an umbrella organisation for many national art societies and groups who represent specialist interests including oil painters, watercolourists, marine artists, equestrian and wildlife artists and many others. The gallery's programme also includes work by other individual artists and groups, as well as the Hunting Group Prizes exhibition.
Sales: Work sold
Exhibiting: [AW]
Access: Buses to Trafalgar Square, Charing Cross; BR and Underground Charing Cross

Manor House Society

A gallery showing work by Jewish artists or work of Jewish interest within a multi-use centre. [VA,Cr]
Address: The Sternberg Centre for Judaism, 80 East End Road, London N3 2SY tel 01 346 2288
Contact: Visual Arts Director Kathryn Salomon
Open: Varies: Mon-Thurs 10-5, Sun 11-1, 3-5 or Mon-Thurs 10-5, Fri 10-1
Policy: The gallery's programme, which is predominantly work by living artists in month-long exhibitions, is varied and although some exhibitions are specialist, others attract the interest of a wide public.
Sales: Work sold
The Space: The exhibition space consists of 18th century panelled rooms in which pictures are hung from rods and hooks and lit by spots. Showcases can be available.
Exhibiting: [AW] Applications should be sent to the Visual Arts Director enclosing CV and slides. The gallery pays for insurance on site, publicity, card and list of exhibits and preview. It takes 25% commission on sales.
Access: [S][L][T] Buses 143,112,260,26,13; Underground Finchley Central

Manya Igel Fine Arts

A gallery dealing in 19th and 20th century British oils and watercolours. [Pa]
Address: 21-22 Peters Court, Porchester Road, London W2 tel 01 229 1669/8429
Contact: Director
Open: Mon-Fri 10-6; By appointment only
Access: Underground Royal Oak

Mario Flecha Gallery

A gallery showing contemporary work in changing exhibitions. [VA]
Address: 239 Liverpool Road, London N1 tel 01 607 5096
Open: Mon-Fri 2-7, Sat 11-1
Access: Underground Highbury

Mark Hancock Gallery

A commercial gallery dealing in fine and decorative English and continental 19th and 20th century oil paintings. [Pa]
Address: 184 Westbourne Grove, London W11 tel 01 229 7827
Contact: Director Mon-Fri 10-6, Sat 10-5
Sales: Work sold
Access: Buses 7,15,27; Underground Nottinghill Gate

Marlborough Fine Art

Founded in 1946, this commercial gallery shows selected old masters, Impressionist and 20th century fine arts. [VA]
Address: 6 Albemarle Street, London W1X 4BY tel 01 629 5161
Contact: Director
Open: Mon-Fri 10-5.30, Sat 10-12.30
Policy: Six to eight exhibitions a year of impressionist and 20th century paintings, drawings, watercolours and sculpture and master prints and photographers. The print gallery, Marlborough Graphics is at 39 Old Bond Street, London W1 tel 01 629 5161 and also holds regular exhibitions.
Access: Buses 3,6,9,12,13,14,14a,15,19,22,22b, 38,53,88,159; Underground Piccadilly Circus

Marlene Eleini Gallery

Commercial gallery dealing in 20th Century and contemporary art showing work by living artists. [VA,Ph]
Address: First Floor, 14 New Bond Street, London W1Y 9PF tel 01 408 0138
Contact: Director Marlene Eleini
Open: Mon-Fri 10-6, Sat by appointment
Policy: The gallery predominantly shows the work of living artists in a wide variety of media - painting, sculpture, drawing, prints and photography, *'mainly abstract and non-figurative work'*. Ten exhibitions are held a year, mainly solo shows lasting between four and six weeks. The gallery keeps a stock of works by *'classical German Expressionists, 20th Century masters and contemporary artists'*.
Sales: Work sold; Credit scheme
The Space: 21.5m linear hanging space 3m high has good natural light. The space restricts the size of work shown and gallery plans are available.
Exhibiting: [AW] The gallery promotes a selected number of artists but applications are welcome, contact the Assistant Director. It covers insurance, printing and mailing of publicity, list of exhibits, transport, preview and 50% of display costs and the commission taken varies.
Access: [X] Buses 3,6,7,8,9,12,13,14,14a,15,16a,19,22, 22b,25,38,53,73,88; Underground Green Park, Bond Street, Oxford Circus, Piccadilly; Car parks 2-10 mins

Marsham Street Gallery

A small commercial gallery showing contemporary art.
Address: 55 Marsham Street, London SW1 tel 01 222 3882
Exhibiting: [AW]

Mary Hayes Gallery

Contemporary visual arts gallery near Shepherds Bush. [VA]

Address: 68 Richmond Way, London W14 0AS tel 01 602 4354

Contact: Proprietor Mary Hayes

Open: Mon-Fri 12-7

Policy: *'To encourage the promotion of contemporary art, and to stimulate interest in new forms of creative expression....The purpose of the exhibitions is to break down the barriers that exist between the public and modern art.'*

Sales: Work sold

Exhibiting: [AW]

Access: Underground Shepherds Bush

Mary Ward Centre Gallery

A café space run and subsidised by the Mary Ward Centre, an adult education centre with charitable status. [VA,Ph,Cr]

Address: 42 Queen Square, London WC1N 3AQ tel 01 831 7711

Contact: Vice Principal Stephanie McKnight

Open: Mon-Sun 11-3, 4-9

Policy: The programme of five, five-week exhibitions held during term-time includes the work of professional artists as well as students working in a wide variety of media - painting, sculpture, drawing, photography, prints and crafts. Most are solo shows and all work must *'adhere to the non-sexist, non-racist principles of the equal opportunities policy'*. The audience is wide ranging and includes students, visitors to the centre and the public using the café facilities. In addition, an art workshop is held.

Sales: Work sold; Sales referred to exhibitor

The Space: The space of 12.5x6x3.5m is lit by spots on central runners. Work is limited to 2m maximum in any direction.

Exhibiting: [AW] Applications are welcome, contact the Vice Principal. The space is hired to exhibitors at £30 per exhibition.

Access: [U][T][S] Buses 5 mins; Underground 8 mins

Matt's Gallery

Independent gallery dealing in and showing work by living artists in a variety of media. [Pa,Sc,Dr,Ph,LA]

Address: 10 Martello Street, London Fields, London E8 tel 01 249 3799

Contact: Director Robin Klassnik

Open: Tmes vary

Policy: The gallery was set up *'in order to give British and international artists the opportunity to create a unique piece of work in direct response to the gallery space'*, artists *'work closely with the director in the making of each piece, often for a period of up to three months'*. The five exhibitions a year lasting two weeks each, are all solo shows and include work in a wide range of media - painting, sculpture, drawing, photography and live art. A regular programme of talks and seminars is also organised.

Sales: Work sold; Credit scheme

The Space: The gallery space is approximately 90 square metres.

Exhibiting: [EF] *'Artists should visit exhibitions and find out how the space operates before making applications'*. The gallery supports EPR in principle and pays artists a fee for exhibiting. Costs covered are agreed by negotiation and 25% commission is taken on sales.

Access: Buses 6,22,30,35,38,55,106,226,253,277; Underground Bethnal Green; BR London Fields (not Sundays)

Mayor Gallery

A privately-funded commercial art gallery. [Pa,Sc]

Address: 22a Cork Street, London W1X 1HB tel 01 734 3558

Contact: Directors James Mayor, Andrew Murray

Open: Mon-Fri 10-5.30, Sat 10-1

Policy: The programme, arranged by invitation, consists of mixed and solo exhibitions of 20th century British and American art. One annual exhibition is devoted to work from one of the country's public galleries.

Sales: Work sold

The Space: Two adjoining rooms, one 40 square metres, the other 25 square metres with track spot lighting.

Exhibiting: Exhibitions are by invitation.

Access: Buses 3,6,12,13,53,88,159; Underground Piccadilly Circus

Mayor Rowan Gallery

A contemporary art gallery with monthly changing exhibitions. [VA]

Address: 31a Bruton Place, London W1 tel 01 499 3011

Open: Mon-Fri 10-5.30, Sat 10-1

Medici Galleries

Regular exhibitions by contemporary British artists, plus prints and reproductions. Also at 26 Thurloe Street, South Kensington 01 589 1363. [Pa,Pr]

Address: 7 Grafton Street, London W1X 3LA tel 01 629 5675

Contact: Director

Matt's Gallery: 'Bureau de Change', an installation with £1000 loose change and security guard by Rose Finn-Kelcey
(Photo: Susan Omerod)

Open: Mon-Fri 9-5.30
Access: Buses 3,6,9,12,13,14,14a,15,19,22,22b,38, 53,88,159; Underground Piccadilly Circus

Mercury Gallery

A commercial gallery showing contemporary art and 20th century British, French and German art. [VA]

Address: 26 Cork Street, London W1X 1HB tel 01 734 7800
Contact: Director Gillian Raffles
Open: Mon-Fri 10-5.30, Sat 10-12.30
Policy: Ten exhibitions a year are held consisting of solo shows by gallery artists and two mixed of gallery artists and 20th century.
Sales: Work sold
The Space: Upper and lower galleries.
Access: **[F]** Upper gallery **[X]** Lower gallery. Buses 3,6,9,12,13,14,14a,15,19,22,22b,38,53,88,159; Underground Piccadilly Circus

Merrifield Studios

Gallery showing contemporary prints and paintings and also theatre designs. [Pa,Pr]

Address: 110 Heath Street, Hampstead, London NW3 tel 01 794 0343
Contact: Blackie Merrifield
Open: Wed-Sat 10-6, Sun 11-6
Access: Underground Hampstead (Existing Source)

Merton Library Service

The London Borough of Merton runs library spaces through the Library Department, Worsfield House, Chapel Orchard, Church Road, London CL4 3UE, contact Penny Parker.

Address: Crown House, London Road, Morden, Surrey SM4 5DX
Contact: Borough Librarian

Merz Contemporary Art

A commercial gallery, opened 1988, showing up-and-coming artists in a series of changing exhibitions. [VA,Pr,Cr]

Address: 62 Kenway Road, Earls Court, London SW5 0RD tel 01 244 6008
Contact: Directors Derek Ferguson, Dorothy Leiper
Open: Mon-Sat 10-7
Policy: Exhibits a broad range of work by up-and-coming as well as semi-established artists in group exhibitions lasting about five weeks each. *'The gallery aims at serious collectors of contemporary art as well as first time buyers ... could be loosely described as young professionals who are past the poster stage but can't afford Bond Street prices.'*
Sales: Work sold; Credit card
The Space: Gallery on two floors, the upstairs gallery is 7.6x4.5m with 17m linear hanging space, ceiling height is 3.1m. The Downstairs Gallery has a total of 25m linear hanging space.
Exhibiting: **[AW]** Willing to look at work at any time, apply by sending photographs or slides. The gallery covers insurance, publicity and list of exhibits. Commission is 38%. The owners are willing to consider hiring the gallery.
Access: **[F]** Upstairs gallery, **[X]** Downstairs gallery. Underground Earls Court 1 min

Michaelson & Orient

Commercial gallery on the Crafts Council's selected list dealing in and showing ceramics and textiles by living artists, formerly Anatol Orient. [Sc,Ce]

Address: 318 Portobello Road, London W10 5RU tel 01 969 4119
Contact: Anatol Orient & Maureen Michaelson
Open: Tues-Sat 10.30-5.30
Policy: The gallery, which aims to become Britain's premiere showcase for 20th century ceramic art, *'has made a convincing commitment to both artist potters and ceramic figurative sculptors'* and *'its development as regards looking at works in clay is reflected in the range and quality of works shown'*. Works by *'Britain's most innovative, as well as less-established artists'* are presented through a programme of ten exhibitions a year.
Sales: Work sold; Credit card
The Space: There are three spaces for exhibitions.
Exhibiting: **[AW]** Applications by postal submission of visuals only.
Access: **[X]** Buses 7,15,52,52a,195,31,27; Underground Ladbroke Grove & Westbourne Park

Millfield House Arts Centre

An exhibition space used as a coffee bar/lounge within an arts centre. [Pa,Pr,Dr,Ph,Cr]

Address: Silver Street, Edmonton, London N18 1PJ tel 01 803 6213/5283
Contact: Sarah Kessler
Open: Mon-Fri 9.30-10.30pm
Policy: A varied exhibition programme of twelve shows a year each lasting one month which include solo, mixed and theme shows in a wide variety of two-dimensional media - painting, drawing, photography, prints and crafts. Exhibitors are mainly local artists and the audience is made up of casual visitors and those

Mayor Gallery: 'American paintings with Chinese furniture', 1987

involved in, or visiting for, other activities being held at the centre. The centre offers drama and music events, workshops and classes, it has a rehearsal studio and hosts meetings. A 400-seat theatre and a library are due to open in December 1988.

Sales: Work sold

The Space: The wall space 10x1.5m is hessian-covered board and lit by overhead *'picture lights'; one upright glass cabinet is available.*

Exhibiting: [AW] Applications are welcome, contact Sarah Kessler, *'bookings are made up to two years in advance'*. The costs of insurance, printing, catalogue/card, list of exhibits and mailing are covered and 20% commission is taken on sales.

Access: [F] Buses 34,102,144; BR Silver Street 10 mins; Car park on site

Milne & Moller

A private gallery specialising in watercolour paintings from 1880-contemporary art. [Pa]

Address: 35 Colville Terrace, London W11 2BU tel 01 727 1679

Contact: Director Juliet Moller

Open: Sat 10-4 and by appointment

Policy: Regular solo and mixed exhibitions.

Access: Underground and buses nearby; Parking

MM Arts

'A roving gallery' run by an artists co-operative, which shows and deals in members' work. [VA]

Address: tel 01 735 9649

Contact: Agents Juliet Williams, 18 Cranworth Gardens, Oval, London SW9 0NS 01 735 9649. Oliver Bevan 130 Percy Road, London N12 9OL 01 740 8084

Open: Varies

Policy: *'A gallery without walls', it aims to exhibit work 'in house, office and work place - always matching the work to the venue'* and *' makes art more accessible to those who may not have the time or opportunity to visit galleries'.* In the last year work by the 15-18 members in a variety of media - painting, sculpture, drawing, prints - has been shown through a programme of eight exhibitions each lasting two to four weeks. All work is by living artists and solo and group shows are organised. MM Arts act as consultants and sell work direct to clients *'the general public, business, offices, restaurants, interior designers, architects etc'* as well as through the exhibition programme. Talks and educational activities are also held.

Sales: Work sold; Credit scheme; Credit card

The Space: *'Varies according to location/venue found by the agent'.*

Exhibiting: [AW] Applications welcome once a year according to turnover of members, send ten slides of recent work and a CV to Juliet Williams. Costs of insurance, printing of publicity, catalogue/card, mailing, list of exhibits and preview are covered, and 40% commission is taken on sales. A membership fee of £250 is payable.

Montpelier Studio

Gallery specialising in contemporary British art. [VA]

Address: 4 Montpelier Street, London, SW7 tel 01 584 0667

Contact: Director Bernice Sandelson

Open: Mon-Fri 10-5.30, Sat 10-1

Policy: Regular mixed exhibitions of twentieth century British painters and sculptors.

Sales: Work sold

The Space: Ground floor and basement spaces.

Exhibiting: [AW]

Access: Underground Knightsbridge

Moonshine Community Arts Workshop

A community arts workshop with space which can be used for exhibitions. [VA]

Address: 1090 Harrow Road, Kensal Green, London NW10 5QX tel 01 960 0055

Contact: Administrator Christine Brown

Open: Variable

Policy: The space is also used for video workshops, rehearsals and training.

The Space: The hall is 20x40m with a balcony around the sides.

Exhibiting: [AW] Artists can apply to mount, organise and fund their own exhibitions.

Access: [U] Bus 18; BR Underground Kensal Green

MM Arts: Shoe sculptures by Amanda Benson

Morley Gallery

This gallery shows a variety of exhibitions by individuals, organisations and community groups, including an annual students' show. [VA,Ph,Cr]

Address: 61 Westminster Bridge Road, London SE1 7HT tel 01 928 8501 ext 145
Contact: Director Adrian Bartlett/Susan Roach
Open: Mon-Fri 10-6
Policy: The gallery aims to provide a varied programme for students and public alike. There is no hire charge and it is felt that this policy enables the not-so-well-established artists to exhibit. Talks relating to exhibitions are organised with local schools when possible.
Sales: Work sold
The Space: The gallery comprises three interconnecting areas. Hanging is by rods with track-mounted spot and fluorescent lighting. Gallery plans available.
Exhibiting: [AW] Apply to Adrian Bartlett, work is selected by the gallery committee. Gallery finances insurance, mail-out of publicity and list of exhibits. Commission 35%.
Access: [F] Buses 12,53,171; BR Waterloo 10 min; Underground Lambeth North 3 mins

National Gallery

A national gallery of painting, European Art from 1200 - 1900. [Pa]

Address: Trafalgar Square, London WC2 5DN tel 01 839 3321 ext 252
Contact: Keeper Dr Allan Braham
Open: Mon-Sat 10-6, Sun 2-6
Policy: *'A specialist display space for the country's greatest collection of European paintings, and rarely, well nigh never, used for either contemporary exhibitions or exhibitions organised by people not employed by the gallery'*. The Sunley Room and Board Room are used for temporary shows. The content of shows is the *'result of discussion and collaboration between the Head of Exhibitions and the Director'*. Daily lectures and many educational events.
The Space: 46 gallery rooms, main level and lower level, gallery floor plans available.
Access: [U][T][L][F] Buses 1,3,6,9,11,12,13,15,22b, 24,29,53,77,77a,88,109,159,170,176,184,196; Charing Cross, Leicester Square, BR: Charing Cross

National Maritime Museum

The world's greatest maritime collections on the history of Britain and the sea including the Old Royal Observatory.

Address: Romney Road, Greenwich, London SE10 9NF
Contact: Head of Exhibitions D Cordingly
Open: Mon-Sat 10-5, Sun 2-5 Winter; Mon-Fri 10-6, Sun 2-6 Summer; Closed some bank holidays
Access: [F] Underground, Docklands Light Railway to Island Gardens; Boats from Westminster, Charing Cross & Tower piers; BR Charing Cross, Waterloo, London Bridge to Maze Hill

National Poetry Centre

Contemporary visual art gallery running programme of solo shows in media including drawing, photography, prints, graphics and sculpture. [VA,Cr]

Address: The Poetry Society, 21 Earls Court Square, London SW5 tel 01 373 7861
Contact: John Stathatos
Open: Mon-Fri 10-5
Sales: Work sold
Exhibiting: [AW]
Access: Buses and Underground to Earls Court

National Portrait Gallery

National gallery holding temporary exhibitions as well as a large permanent collection. [VA,Ph]

Address: St. Martin's Place, London WC2H 0HE tel 01 930 1552
Contact: Exhibitions Office
Open: Mon-Fri 10-5, Sat 10-6, Sun 2-6
Policy: The programme of eight, twelve-week exhibitions includes *'major international loan exhibitions and small solo shows'*, half of which are the work of living artists. The gallery also collects *'portraits of famous British men and women'*. The Education Department runs a continuous programme of lectures, talks, films and demonstrations.
The Space: There are three large exhibition areas 350 square metres, 230 square metres and 55 square metres with a combined linear hanging space of 135m.
Access: [X] Underground Charing Cross, Leicester Square; BR Charing Cross

Naturally British

Specialist craft outlet retailing cottage industries, including pottery, textiles, toys, jewellery, glass, clothes, firescreens and ceramic plaques. etc. [Cr]

Address: 13 New Row, London WC2N 4LF tel 01 240 0551
Contact: Managing Director Jon Blake
Open: Mon-Sat 10.30-6.30
Sales: Work sold
Access: Underground Leicester Square

National Portrait Gallery

New Academy Gallery/Business Art Galleries

A commercial gallery offering an art consultancy service to business. [VA]

Address: 34 Windmill Street, Off Charlotte Street, London W1P 1HH tel 01 323 4700
Contact: Martha Alleguen
Open: Mon-Fri 10-6, Sat 11-5
Policy: The gallery shows and deals in the work of living artists, both established and new, and holds the work of over 200 artists, mainly British, either on slide or in the gallery. The programme of twelve, one-month shows includes solo, group and theme exhibitions of work in a variety of media and styles - painting, sculpture, prints and textile work; the gallery aims to *'encourage both the private and corporate buyer and provide a strong stable of artists.'* It also arranges commissions.
Sales: Work sold; Credit card
The Space: The two galleries, downstairs with 37m linear space, upstairs with 12m, are 2.2m high and lit by movable spots on tracks. Works are limited to 2m in height and are hung on nails.
Exhibiting: [AW] *'Work may be brought to the gallery Tues-Fri before 11 and collected after 3'.* The gallery covers insurance, printing of publicity, catalogue/card, mailing and the preview, commission taken on sales varies. EPR supported in principle.
Access: [F] Underground Tottenham Court Road, Goodge Street 5 mins each

New Art Centre

A gallery showing 20th century European drawings and modern British masters. [Pa,Sc]

Address: 41 Sloane Street, London SW1X 9LU tel 01 235 5844

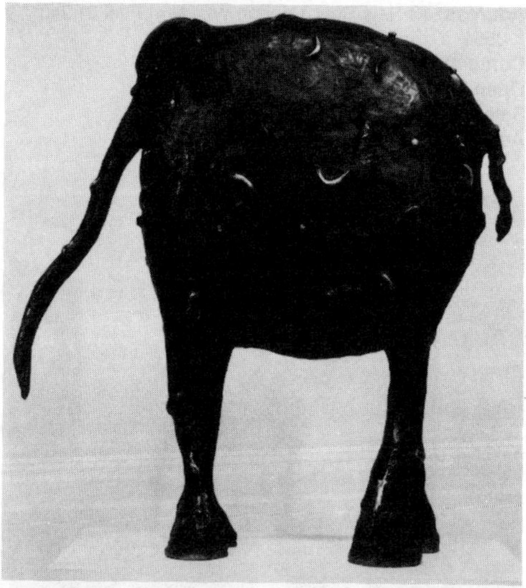

New Art Centre: 'Cosmic Elephant' by Sadiq, bronze, 23" high, 1988

Contact: Director
Open: Mon-Fri 10-6, Sat 11-3
Policy: Monthly exhibitions of 20th century work with sculpture shown in the Roche Court Sculpture Garden.
Sales: Work sold
The Space: Two galleries, street level and basement with day light and spot lighting.
Exhibiting: [AW] Write to the Director with information and visual material. Exhibitions for new artists are very limited.
Access: [F] Buses 9,14,19,22,30,52,52a,73,74,137; Underground Knightsbridge

New Gallery

A self-contained gallery adjacent to the library showing contemporary artists' work. [VA,Ph,Cr]

Address: Hornsey Library, Haringey Park, London N8 tel 01 348 3351
Contact: The Arts and Extensions Officer
Open: Mon-Fri 10-8, Sat 9-5
Sales: Work sold
Exhibiting: [AW] Applications welcome.

Newburgh Street Gallery

Commercial gallery dealing in 20th Century and contemporary art showing work by living artists'. [Pa,Sc,Dr]

Address: 9 Newburgh Street, London W1V 1LH tel 01 434 4455
Contact: T N Napier-Ford
Open: Mon-Fri 10-5.30
Policy: The gallery aims to *'provide a show place and sales opportunity for living artists of repute'* and shows mainly *'domestic-sized works by living British artists'* in a variety of media - painting, sculpture and drawing. Nine exhibitions are held a year, mainly solo shows lasting between two and three weeks. A changing display of work for sale is on show between exhibitions and *'customers are of all categories within the middle to upper income range'.*
Sales: Work sold; Credit scheme; Credit card
The Space: The space is 15x2.72x2.27m and hanging is on rods and chains from a picture rail. Gallery plans are available.
Exhibiting: [AW] Applications are welcome, contact the proprietor. The gallery is hired out at a negotiable rate. Costs of printing of publicity, catalogue/card, list of exhibits and the preview are covered by the gallery and 40% commission is taken on sales. Supports EPR in principle.
Access: [S] Buses 3,6,7,8,12,13,15,16a,25,53,73,88; Underground Oxford Circus

Newham Library Service

The department is responsible for Newham's Library Service.

Address: Leisure Services, Town Hall, East Ham, London E6 2RP
Contact: Director of Leisure Services 3-11 Nelson Street, London E6 tel 01 472 1430
Policy: The borough runs a number of library spaces,

and also has an Arts Council.

Nicola Jacobs Gallery

Private gallery, founded 1979, showing regular programme of contemporary British artists who are under contract to the gallery. [VA]

Address: 9 Cork Street, London W1X 1PD tel 01 839 3526
Contact: Nicola Jacobs
Open: Mon-Fri 10-5.30, Sat 10-1
Access: Underground Piccadilly Circus

Nigel Greenwood Gallery

Commercial gallery which deals and shows the work of selected artists. [VA]

Address: 4 New Burlington Street, London W1X 1FE tel 01 434 3795
Contact: Nigel Greenwood
Open: Mon-Fri 10-6, Sat 10-1.30, closed Sun
Policy: The gallery specialises in paintings and prints. The gallery incorporates Nigel Greenwood Books and stocks a wide range of catalogues, artists' books and monographs.
Sales: Work sold; Credit card; Credit scheme
Exhibiting: The gallery covers the cost of insurance.
Access: [S] Underground Oxford Circus, Piccadilly Circus

Night Gallery

As part of the Photographic School of London this commercial gallery only shows the work of foreign artists. [Ph]

Address: 52-54 Kenway Road, Earls Court, London SW5 0RA tel 01 370 3155
Contact: Paul Jenkins
Open: Mon-Fri 10-4

North Finchley Library

Public library within Barnet Library Service. [Pa,Pr,Dr,Ph]

Address: Ravensdale Avenue, London N12 9HP tel 01 445 4081
Contact: Librarian-in-Charge, Special Services E.A. Holliday, Room 6, Ravensfield House, The Burroughs, Hendon, London NW4 4BE tel 01 202 5625
Open: Tues-Thurs 9-8, Fri 9-5, Sat 9-4
Policy: The gallery aims to *'provide a venue for local artists, photographers and members of local societies to show their work'*. The programme of eight, four-week exhibitions of two-dimensional work by amateurs and professionals is a combination of mixed and solo shows. The audience is mainly local residents and the library operates a picture loan scheme of invited artists' work. See also Barnet Library Service
Sales: Work sold; Sales referred to exhibitors
The Space: The library has 28m linear hanging space, 1.5m in height, with hessian-covered soft board panels and angled, shaded strip lighting; work is hung on steel pins. Maximum size limit is 1.5m. Gallery plans are available. The space is used for meetings, lectures and other library activities.
Exhibiting: [AW] Applications welcome from local artists, contact the Librarian-in-Charge, Special Services. Commission of 15% is taken on sales.
Access: [X] Buses 13,17,26,82,125,221,260; Underground Woodside Park 10 mins

North Peckham Exhibition Gallery

This municipal gallery stages small photographic and painting exhibitions by local artists in a mixture of group and solo shows. [Pa,Pr,Dr,Ph,Cr]

Address: North Peckham Civic Centre, 600-608 Old Kent Road, London SE15 tel 01 639 2347
Contact: Branch Librarian
Open: Mon & Thurs 9.30-8, Tues, Fri, Sat 9.30-5
Policy: Gallery policy is to provide a space for local artists who are showing for the first time, the audience being those living in the North Peckham area who often have little access to original art.
Sales: Work sold
The Space: The space is a balcony area around three walls of the library, amounting to 10x9m. Gallery plans available.
Exhibiting: [AW] Apply to Branch Librarian. Gallery helps to finance display. Commission 5%.
Access: [U][T][L][F] Buses 21,53,70,78,141,177; Public car park 1 min

October Gallery

Commercial gallery dealing in and showing painting by living artists. [Pa]

Address: 24 Old Gloucester Street, London WC1N 3AL tel 01 242 7367
Contact: Corinna MacNeice
Open: Tues-Sat 12.30-4.30
Policy: The gallery predominantly shows the work of living artists and *'represents the work of artists from around the world'* and includes those from Europe, Asia, Africa, Middle East, the Americas, Japan and Australia, through a programme of ten, mainly solo, exhibitions a year each lasting between four and six weeks. It has a permanent collection of *'selected pieces by those artists the gallery represents'*.

Nigel Greenwood Gallery: Joel Fisher exhibition (Photo: Eileen Tweedy)

Sales: Work sold; Credit scheme; Credit card
The Space: The gallery is 5.5x13.5x3.5m and plans are available.
Exhibiting: [AW] Applications are welcome, send slides to the Director.
Access: [S] Buses 5,7,8,19,22,22b,25,38,55,68,77,77a; Underground Holborn and Russell Square 5 mins

Odette Gilbert Gallery

Commercial gallery dealing in and showing Modern British and contemporary artists'. [Pa,Sc,Dr]
Address: 5 Cork Street, London W1 tel 01 437 3175
Contact: Odette Gilbert
Open: Mon-Fri 9.30-6, Sat 10-1
Policy: The gallery specialises in Post-War British art and shows the work of living artists, predominantly figurative painting and drawing with some sculpture. It works with artists *'exclusively represented'* by the gallery through a programme of eight exhibitions a year each lasting one month, these are a mixture of solo and group shows.
Sales: Work sold
The Space: The space is 17x4.5m and gallery plans are available.
Exhibiting: [AW] The gallery promotes a selected number of artists but slide applications are welcome. Costs of insurance, publicity, mailing, list of exhibits, preview are covered.
Access: [F] Buses 9,14,19,22,25,38; Underground Piccadilly Circus, Green Park

Old Bull Arts Centre Gallery

An arts centre with charitable status running a wide range of activities and supported by London Borough of Barnet and Greater London Arts. [VA,Ce,Gl,Je]
Address: 68 High Street, Barnet, Hertfordshire EN5 5SJ tel 01 449 0048
Contact: Craftshop and Gallery Administrator Gary Edwards
Open: Mon-Sat 9.30-7.30
Policy: To show work from a wide variety of sources and media by young contemporary artists. Three-week exhibitions, of which approximately half are solo shows.
Sales: Work sold; Credit card
The Space: Two rooms, both 4m square.
Exhibiting: [AW][EF] Apply to Visual Arts Officer. Gallery pays for publicity. Artists' lectures welcomed.
Access: Tube High Barnet 5 mins; Car park 2 mins

Oliver Swann Galleries

Commercial gallery dealing in and showing two-dimensional work by living artists. [Pa]
Address: 117A-119 and 170 Walton Street, London SW3 tel 01 581 4229/01 584 8684
Contact: Oliver Swann, E Cruickshank
Open: Mon-Fri 10-6, Sat 11-3; At other times by appointment
Policy: The gallery shows a *'subjective choice of representational work in oils, watercolour and pastels; subject matter is wide ranging'* and aims *'to exhibit a growing number of artists with reputations amongst critics and collectors'*. Six exhibitions each lasting two to three weeks are held a year, most of these are solo shows, and the gallery houses both a permanent collection and a changing display of work by gallery artists.
Sales: Work sold; Credit card
Exhibiting: [AW] Applications are welcome, send slides with covering letter or make an appointment to visit. The gallery promotes a selected number of artists, occasionally hires out the space and sometimes pays artists a fee to produce work. Costs covered and commission taken on sales are by arrangement.
Access: Buses 14,30,74; Underground South Kensington 6 mins, Knightsbridge 10mins

Orangery (The)

A gallery with a programme of between six and eight exhibitions a year running from April to November. [VA,Cr,Ph]
Address: Holland Park, Kensington, London W8
Contact: Arts Officer Michael Goggin, Leighton House Museum, 12 Holland Park Road, London W14 8LZ tel 01603 1123
Open: Daily 11-7
Policy: Exhibitions generally last for two weeks.
Sales: Work sold
The Space: An attractive light, airy site in the heart of Holland Park. Screens and plinths available.
Exhibiting: [AW] Contact the Arts Officer. The gallery is hired to artists and the gallery undertakes press listings and can help with mounting shows and with distributing artists' leaflets. No commission taken on sales.
Access: [F][T][X]

The Orangery

Original Picture Shop

This commercial gallery normally stages two-week solo and theme shows. [Pa,Sc]

Address: 33 Mossop Street, London SW3 2RB tel 01 225 2696
Contact: Charlotte Lampard
Open: Tues-Fri 11-7, Sat 10-4
Policy: The shop exists to sell the work of young professional artists at reasonable prices. The gallery is informal and buyers are those who would *'feel intimidated by other galleries'.*
Sales: Work sold
Exhibiting: [AW] Apply to Charlotte Lampard. Gallery finances printing and mail-out of publicity and preview costs. Commission 40%.
Access: Underground Sloane Square, South Kensington 10 mins

Osbourne Studio Gallery

Commercial gallery dealing in and showing work by contemporary artists. [Pa,Sc,Pr]

Address: The Carriage Hall, 29 Floral Street, London WC2 tel 01 836 5040
Contact: Director Caroline Talbot-Ponsonby, Geoffrey Hughes
Open: Mon-Fri 10.30-6.30; and by appointment
Policy: The gallery specialises in work on a horse racing theme and shows the work of living artists, both established and those *'we feel are the respected artists of the future'.* The programme of seven shows, predominantly mixed, each lasting three to four weeks include painting, sculpture and prints; a summer sporting exhibition is mounted and the gallery organises exhibitions at outside venues. Clientele is mainly from the racing world, and a permanent collection of works on contemporary racing is housed.
Sales: Work sold; Credit card; Credit scheme
The Space: The gallery space measures 15.5x3m.
Access: [F] Underground Covent Garden 2 mins, Leicester Square 5 mins

Otis Gallery

The gallery 'whose premise is to provide exhibition space with a vision of bringing together contemporary and modern arts, in a variety of media'.

Address: C2R Metropolitan Wharf, Wapping Wall, London E1 tel 01 481 0691
Contact: Richard Brereton, Polly Horner, Gideon Ponte
Open: Wed-Sun 11-6
Policy: The gallery is located *'in the resurrected Dockland district of London'.* It is *'associated with the Barbara Braathen Gallery in New York City and the Abstraction Gallery in Los Angeles'* and aims to *'introduce English artists to American galleries as well as bringing American art to London'.*
The Space: The gallery with approximately 360 square metres of space *'overlooks the River Thames from the second floor of a converted Victorian warehouse'.*
Access: Bus 22a, Underground Wapping

Outlaws Club

This commercial gallery specialises in 'designer' jewellery and housewares with a changing display of work for sale. [Cr]

Address: 49 Endell Street, London WC2 tel 01 379 6940
Contact: Angela McLoughlin
Open: Mon-Fri 11-7, Sat 11-6
Policy: The gallery aims to provide the best selection of new work for the most competitive prices. Many items on show are exclusive.
Sales: Work sold; Credit card
The Space: One showing area with steel and glass display cabinets. Nothing larger than 0.5x0.5m can be accommodated.
Exhibiting: Gallery finances printing and mail-out of publicity and display costs.
Access: [F] Underground Tottenham Court Road, Covent Garden 3 mins

Palmers Green Library

Exhibition Space in a public library. [Pa,Pr,Ph]

Address: Broomfield Lane, Palmers Green, London N13 4EY tel 01 886 3728
Contact: Local History Museums Officer J W Griffiths, c/o Display Section, Southgate Town Hall, Green Lanes, Palmers Green, London N13 tel 01 8822 8841 ext 2723
Open: Mon,Tues,Thurs,Fri 9-8, Sat 9-5
Policy: Exhibitions of painting and other art forms, which run for around four weeks, include local individual artists, group and societies exhibitions and are by amateurs and professionals. See also Forty Hall Museum.
Sales: Work sold
The Space: Around 30-40 pictures may be hung.
Exhibiting: [AW] Applications to the Borough Librarian & Cultural Officer who wishes to see examples of work prior to an agreement. Gallery covers insurance and provides 30 catalogue/price lists with all other aspects of the exhibition being the responsibility of the exhibitor. Commission charged of 15% to individuals and 10% on societies.
Access: [X] BR Palmers Green

Park Walk Galleries

Gallery specialising in contemporary paintings, sculptures, etching and prints which also offers a specialist framing service. [VA]

Address: 20 Park Walk, London SW10 tel 01 351 0410
Contact: Director Samantha Metcalf
Open: Mon-Fri 10-6, Sat 11-4 or by appointment
Policy: See also Richard Allan Gallery.
Sales: Work sold
Access: Off Kings Road

Passmore Edwards Museum

A London Borough of Newham museum with collections of Essex archaeology, geology, local history and natural history.

Address: Romford Road, Stratford, London E15 4LZ tel 01 519 4296/01 534 2274
Contact: Curator

Open: Mon-Fri 10-5, Sat 10-1 & 2-5, bank holidays 2-5
Policy: Special exhibitions relate to the collections of the museum and the local area.
The Space: A small special exhibition area is available.
Exhibiting: [AW] The special exhibition programme is arranged by museum staff. Any artists with work that is connected with the local area should contact the Curator if they wish to be considered. A commission charged.
Access: [X] Bus routes 25,86,225; BR & Underground Stratford

Paton Gallery

A commercial gallery specialising in new British painting with international potential. [Pa]
Address: 2 Langley Court, Long Acre, Covent Garden, London WC2 tel 01 379 7854
Contact: Director Graham Paton
Open: Tues-Sat 11-6
Policy: The gallery mounts about nine exhibitions a year of new generation British painters with the emphasis on intelligence and painterly skill. It also shows a *'pick of the postgraduate talent'* each summer. It's market is international collectors, institutions and *'yuppies'*.
Sales: Work sold; Credit scheme
The Space: The gallery is on two floors and a mezzanine totalling 91 square m.
Exhibiting: By invitation only. The gallery covers the costs of insurance, printing and mailing of publicity, transport, artists' expenses, catalogue, list of exhibits and preview, and supports the principle of EPR. It takes a commission of 50%.
Access: Underground Covent Garden 2 mins

Paul Rice Gallery

Commercial gallery specialising in 20th century ceramics [Ce]
Address: 60 Blenheim Crescent, London W11 tel 01 229 8241
Contact: Paul and Shawn Rice
Exhibiting: Exhibitions by invitation only.
Access: Buses 15,52; Underground Ladbroke Grove

Pennybank Gallery

This gallery, part of the Clerkenwell Green Association for Craftsmen, encourages exhibitions by young makers in conjunction with better established artists and makers when possible, and predominantly shows two-week group shows.
Address: Pennybank Chambers, 33-35 St John's Square, London EC1M 4DS tel 01 250 0297
Contact: Gallery Director Margaret Barilone
Open: Decided by exhibitor
Policy: At present the gallery has no paid administrator, however if they can attract funding the gallery hopes to be engaged in more educational work. Lectures by craftspeople are also organised.
Sales: Work sold
The Space: 80 square metres, 6.5m high, with track-mounted lighting. A small courtyard is also available. The exhibition space is also used for meetings. Gallery plans available.
Exhibiting: [AW] Apply to Gallery Director. There is a negotiable hire fee of £50 per day.
Access: [T][L][F] Buses 5,22,55,63,143,243,277,279; Underground Farringdon 5 mins; Holborn Viaduct 15 mins; Public car park

Peoples Gallery

An 'alternative' community arts and crafts gallery, subsidised by public funds. [VA,Ph,Cr]
Address: 71-73 Prince of Wales Road, London NW5 3LT tel 01 267 0433
Contact: Administrator Margo Reid
Open: Tues-Fri 11-1, 2-5
Policy: The gallery aims to *'provide an outlet for those artists and makers who by virtue of their race, sex and class are denied opportunity to exhibit work and declare their statement as they wish'*. The programme of 17 exhibitions each lasting four to eight weeks includes a combination of mixed and solo shows in a wide variety of media - painting, sculpture, drawing, photography, prints and crafts. Work by black artists, those with disabilities and other minority groups have featured in the programme as well as work with a strong political theme. An annual *'Alternative Summer Exhibition'* is mounted and a small collection of sculpture and paintings is kept. A wide ranging audience from all sections of the community visit the gallery and a variety of classes and courses are held there.
Sales: Work sold
The Space: The gallery of approximately 50 square metres, is 3.5m high with spots and natural light and hanging by wall rails. The size of the gallery limits work to 2.5m in any direction. A small glass case is available for jewellery.
Exhibiting: [AW] Applications welcome, write or telephone for an appointment. The gallery covers printing of publicity, catalogue/card, mailing and preview costs and takes 25% commission on sales.
Access: [F] Buses 24,31,68,134; Underground Chalk Farm 5 mins; BR West Kentish Town min

Petersburg Press

Commercial gallery and publisher of limited edition prints and books. [VA]
Address: 59A Portobello Road, London W11 3DB tel 01 229 0105
Contact: Tamie Swett
Open: Mon-Fri 10-5.30
Policy: The gallery deals in and shows the work of a selected number of internationally-known artists working in a variety of media, and *'when pertinant, talks, lectures and events are organised for specific groups'*. Gallery also at 380 Latayelle Street, New York NY 10003, USA.
Sales: Work sold
Access: [U][F] Underground Notting Hill Gate

Photo Coop

A photo co-operative of professional photographers. The co-operative organises project groups on themes

or issues which generate work which is shown in libraries, galleries, cinemas and other community settings. [Ph]

Address: 61 Webbs Road, London SW11 tel 228 8949
Contact: Chris Boot

Photographers Gallery

A photographic gallery with charitable status dealing in and showing work by living artists. [Ph]

Address: 5 & 8 Great Newport Street, London WC2H 7HY tel 01 831 1772
Contact: Susan Davies
Open: Tues-Sat 11-7 and during opening events
Policy: The gallery aims *'to show current concerns within the contemporary independent photography sector both nationally and internationally'.* Work by well-known artists from Britain and abroad in a variety of photographic media from *'documentary to mixed-media installation'* is shown. The programme of 35 exhibitions a year includes solo, group and theme shows as well as specially commissioned work. *'Exhibitions provide a forum for debate and promote an understanding of photographic history within the context of the visual arts in general'.* The audience is wide ranging - students, amateur and professional photographers and the general public and the exhibitions in two spaces, are *'staggered to allow public viewing throughout the year'.* A collection of approximately 150 photographers' portfolios are for sale in the print room.
Sales: Work sold; Credit card
The Space: There are four spaces 15x5.5x4.5m, 12.5x2x3m, 10x10.5x3m and 10x4.5x3m with a combined linear hanging space of 112m. The Tom Hopkinson space is available for hire for parties, book launches and theatrical productions.
Exhibiting: **[AW]** *'Individual photographers are invited to submit work for the Portfolio Room exhibitions. Applications are welcome, 'the selection committee meets twice a year (March and October), and work is to be submitted by the end of the preceding month'.* Occasional commissions are offered and advertised through the press. Insurance, printing and mailing of publicity, display, transport and preview costs are covered and 40% commission is taken on sales.
Access: **[F]** Buses 1,24k,29,176; Underground Leicester Square 2 mins, Charing Cross 5 mins; BR Charing Cross 5 mins

Piccadilly Gallery

Monthly exhibitions of contemporary figurative work, symbolist and 20th century drawings and watercolours. [Pa]

Address: 16 Cork Street, London W1 tel 01 629 2875
Contact: Director
Open: Mon-Fri 10-5.30, Sat 10-12.30
Access: Buses 3,6,9,12,13,14,14a,15,53,88,259; Underground Piccadilly Circus

Piers Feetham

A gallery linked with a picture framers and restorers specialising in conservation framing. [VA]

Address: 475 Fulham Road, London SW6 1HL tel 01 381 5958
Contact: Director Piers Feetham
Open: Mon-Fri 10-1, 2-6
Policy: The gallery shows representational work by contemporary artists, many of them young.
Sales: Work sold
The Space: Approximately 20m linear hanging space arranged in two rooms. For reasons of space small work is preferred.
Exhibiting: **[AW]** Normally on a rental basis, details on application.
Access: Bus 14; Underground Fulham Broadway

Pimlico Arts & Media

Exhibition space for changing exhibitions. [VA]

Address: 1 Charlwood Street, London SW1 tel 01 630 6409
Contact: Administrator
Open: Mon-Fri 10-6
Access: **[U]**

Polish Cultural Institute

Gallery showing changing exhibitions of Polish art. [VA,Cr]

Address: 34 Portland Place, London W1 tel 01 636 6032
Contact: Director Henryk Zietek
Open: Mon-Wed,Fri 9-4, Thurs 9-8
Policy: Media shown includes paintings, graphics, photography, posters, tapestry and folk art.
Access: Bus routes; Underground Regents Park

Polska (Polish) YMCA

The Polish YMCA mainly organises its own activities which are necessarily of Polish nature.

Address: 46-47 Kensington Gardens Square, London W2
Policy: They are potentially interested in housing outside activities like exhibitions and film shows.
Access: Underground Royal Oak

Polytechnic of Central London (Marylebone Road Gallery)

Due to refurbishment and reorganisation the gallery is closed until 1989 when it will reopen with a new policy and programme. [Ph]

Address: Polytechnic of Central London, 35 Marylebone Road, London NW1 tel 01 580 2020 ext 335
Contact: Exhibition Consultant Richard Allen, 309 Regent Street, London W1R 8AL
Open: Mon-Fri 8-8
Access: Buses 18,27,172; Underground Baker Street

Polytechnic of Central London (Regent Street Gallery)

Due to refurbishment and reorganisation the gallery is closed until 1989 when it will have a new policy and programme. [VA,Ph]

Address: Polytechnic of Central London, 309 Regent

Street, London W1R 8AL tel 01 580 2020 ext 335
Contact: Exhibition Consultant, Cultural and Community Studies Richard Allen
Open: Mon-Fri 8.30-8.30
Sales: Work sold
Access: Buses Regent Street; Underground Oxford Circus

Pomeroy Purdy Gallery

Commercial gallery dealing in and showing work in a variety of media by living artists. [VA,Ph]

Address: Jacob Street Film Studios, Mill Street, London SE1 2BA tel 01 237 6062
Contact: Directors Richard Pomeroy, Jayne Purdy
Open: Tues-Fri 11-6.30, Sat 11-4
Policy: The gallery aims *'to exhibit the best of contemporary British art in all media, as well as work by well-known Australian artists'* through a programme of nine exhibitions a year each lasting four weeks. All work is by living artists and includes painting, sculpture, drawing, prints, photography and installation *' although work tends to centre on painting and photography and a cross-over between the two'*. The gallery is situated in Docklands and the audience comes from the surrounding area and the City, *'we also aim to attract serious art collectors and museum curators from Britain and abroad'*.
Sales: Work sold
The Space: A warehouse space 2.46m high with spot lighting. Work is hung directly on walls with mirror plates or wire. Gallery plans are available.
Exhibiting: [AW] Applications are welcome, send slides and CV to Richard Pomeroy. Insurance, printing of publicity, catalogue/card, mailing, list of exhibits, transport and private view are covered and 50% commission is taken on sales.
Access: [X] Bus 47; Underground London Bridge 15 mins, Tower Hill 10 mins; BR London Bridge; Local parking

Portal Gallery

Ten shows a year of British contemporary self-taught fantasy painters. [Pa]

Address: 16a Grafton Street, Bond Street, London W1X 3LF tel 01 629 3506/493 0706
Contact: Director Jess Wilder, Lionel Levy
Open: Mon-Fri 10-5.30, Sat 11-2
Access: Buses 3,6,9,12,13,14,14a,15,19,22,22b,38,53, 88,159; Underground Piccadilly Circus & Green Park

Portfolio Gallery

This commercial gallery specialises in exhibiting black and white photographs in a mixture of group and solo shows. [Ph]

Address: 345 Portobello Road, London W10 5SA tel 01 969 0453
Contact: Jayne Diggory, Gail Marcuson
Open: Tues-Sat 10.30-5.30
Policy: Gallery policy is to promote the original work mainly by young British photographers. Audiences include collectors, first-time buyers and *'all lovers of photography'*. The gallery plans to develop lectures and slide shows in the future.
Sales: Work sold; Credit card; Credit scheme
The Space: The gallery is 83 square metres.
Exhibiting: [AW] Apply to the gallery in writing or personally well in advance of proposed showing time.
Access: [F] Buses 15,52,52a; Underground Ladbroke Grove, Nottinghill, Westbourne Park

Posk Gallery

Run by the Polish Social and Cultural Association Limited. [VA,Ph,Cr]

Address: 238-246 King Street, London W6 0RF tel 01 741 1940
Contact: Janina Baranowska
Open: Mon-Sun 11-8
Policy: The gallery programme of 25, two-week exhibitions is predominantly the work of living artists in a variety of media - painting, sculpture, drawing, photography, prints and crafts. The shows are a mixture of solo and group exhibitions and the gallery has a permanent collection.
Sales: Work sold
The Space: The gallery which is 7.5x5.4x2.8m, has a total of 130m hanging space and has spotlights.
Exhibiting: [AW] Applications welcome, apply to Janina Baranowska. Commission of 15% is taken on sales.
Access: [X] Underground Ravenscourt 2 mins

Pride Gallery

A gallery specialising in British painting from the late 1950s with changing exhibitions.

Address: Radley Mews, 20 Stratford Road, London W8 6QD tel 01 938 4734
Open: Mon-Fri 10.30-7, Sat 10.30-2, Wed until 9
Access: Buses 31,74; Underground Earl's Court and High Street, Kensington

Pruskin Gallery

A gallery specialising in glass, bronze and ivory sculptures. [VA,Cr]

Address: 183 King's Road, London SW3 tel 01 352 9095
Contact: Director
Open: Tues-Sat 10-6 & by appointment
Policy: The gallery is also at 273 Kensington Church Street, London W8 Tel 01 937 1994 where it shows art nouveau, Deco furniture and sculpture and paintings.
Access: Buses 11,19,22,219

Pyramid Arts Development

An arts and multi-cultural organisation catering for the community.

Address: 10-16 Ashwin Street, Dalston, London E8 3EA tel 01 249 6026
Contact: Director Clive Roper
Policy: The centre provides facilities and courses in music, recording and literature and encourages educational development.
The Space: Space of around 330 square metres is currently available for exhibitions although, in the future,

this may change and exhibitions would then be mounted in other areas of the building.

Exhibiting: [AW] Contact Clive Roper. Artist responsible for organisation and all costs including insurance. A variable hire charge is made.

Access: [U] Buses 22,22a,22b,30,38,48,67,76,149, 243,243a,277; BR Dalston Junction

Raab Gallery

A contemporary art gallery with solo and group shows of expressionist painters from the 1960s onwards from Germany, Scotland, England, the Soviet Union and Italy.

Address: 29 Chapel Street, Belgrave Square, London SW1 tel 01 245 9521

Contact: Director

Open: Mon-Fri 10.30-7, Sat 11-5

Policy: The gallery holds about ten exhibitions a year, mainly of living artists. Those exhibitions are normally related to international art events on Expressionist and figurative works in museums or correspondent commercial galleries. One third of the exhibitions are normally for newly discovered young artists. A new gallery, RAAB Gallery Millbank, opened in February 1989 at 6 Vauxhall Road, Millbank, London (open Mon-Sat 10.30-6.30).

Sales: Work sold

Access: Buses 2b,25,36,36a,38,52,52a,82,500; Underground Hyde Park Corner

Railings Gallery

A gallery dealing in contemporary limited edition original prints and drawings by abstract and representational artists.

Address: 5 New Cavendish Street, London W1 tel 01 935 1114

Contact: Director Eric Sandes, Geihle Sander

Open: Mon-Sat 9-6.30

Rebecca Hossack Gallery

Commercial gallery showing and dealing in work by living artists in a variety of media. [VA,Ph]

Address: 35 Windmill Street, London W1 1HH tel 01 409 3599

Contact: Director Rebecca Hossack

Open: Mon-Sat 11-7

Policy: The gallery specialises in young British artists and Australian aboriginal art and aims *'to make contemporary fine art accessible to the public'*. Approximately twelve exhibitions are held a year, all solo shows lasting four weeks, these include painting, sculpture, drawing, photography and prints.

Sales: Work sold; Credit card; Credit scheme

The Space: The space approximately 160 square metres is lit by Erco Halogen lighting.

Exhibiting: [AW] The gallery promotes a selected number of artists but applications are welcome, write to Sabrina Crewe. Costs of insurance, printing, mailing, list of exhibits, preview and transport are covered and commission of 50% is taken on sales.

Access: [X] Buses 7,8,14,14a,19,22,22b,24,25,29,38, 55,73; Underground Goodge Street, Tottenham Court Road 5 mins

Redfern Gallery

A gallery specialising in 20th century paintings, sculpture, drawings and graphics. [VA]

Address: 20 Cork Street, London W1X 2HL tel 01 734 1732/0578

Contact: Directors

Open: Mon-Fri 10-5, Sat 10-12.30

Policy: The gallery shows monthly exhibitions of contemporary British and European artists.

Access: Buses 3,6,9,12,13,14,14a,15,19,22,22b,38, 53,88,159; Underground Piccadilly Circus, Green Park

Regatta

Limited edition print gallery, offering a wide range of contemporary printmakers' work. [Pr]

Address: 48 Hill Rise, Richmond, Surrey TW tel 01 940 9143

Contact: Nick Buchan & Gina Holland

Open: Mon-Sat 10.30-6, Sun 2-5.30

Policy: Gallery shows silkscreens, etchings, lithographs and blockprints by artists ranging from talented locals to established names and also offers a custom framing service.

Sales: Work sold

Exhibiting: [AW]

Access: BR Richmond

RIBA

Exhibition space is occasionally available in the Royal Institute of British Architects building for visual art and architecture exhibitions. [VA,Ar]

Address: 66 Portland Place, London W11 tel 01 636 3161

Contact: Bookings Officer Jeanette Donaldson

Policy: See also Heinz Gallery, London

Sales: Work sold

The Space: The gallery which is on the first floor, is also used for conferences and events. A sculpture court adjoins the gallery.

Richard Dickens Gallery

A gallery opened in 1988 aiming to show a range of work. [VA]

Address: 1 Burland Road, London SW11 6SA tel 01 223 8754

Contact: Richard Dickens

Open: Mon-Sat 10-5

Policy: Showing new work in a wide range of styles and media, also small sculpture.

Sales: Work sold

The Space: Approximately 35 square metres of floor space *'suitable for smaller works'* with 25m linear hanging space, 2.6m high.

Exhibiting: [AW] Applications welcome from *'professional'* artists for solo or shared exhibitions. Commission is 33.3%.

Access: [X] Buses 53,37,49; Underground Clapham South; BR Clapham Junction

Riverside Room

This small exhibition space seeks to promote a mixed programme of work in individual and group shows throughout the year. [Pa,Pr,Dr,Ph,Cr]

Address: Old Town Hall, Whittaker Avenue, Richmond TW9 1TP tel 01 940 9125

Contact: Arts Officer Vanessa Bone, London Borough of Richmond upon Thames, Libraries and Arts Department, The Cottage, Little Green, Richmond, Surrey, TW9 1QL tel 01 940 0031 ext 45

Open: Mon-Sat 10-5

Policy: The exhibitions' programme, which includes literature, memorabilia and architecture, is designed to cover a wide range of interests. Work on local themes or by local artists is favoured. However no art form or artist is excluded by any policy restrictions - the tastes of the gallery' visitors being *'certainly catholic'*.

Sales: Work sold

The Space: 8x10m with wall panels and hessian-covered free-standing screens, on which work is directly fixed. Natural and track-mounted spotlights. 2m maximum height for three-dimensional work. Gallery plans available. Exhibition space used for meetings, functions and as a café area.

Exhibiting: [AW] Apply to Vanessa Bone. There is a negotiable hire fee. Gallery finances insurance, printing and mail-out of publicity, list of exhibits and preview costs. Support in principle for EPR. Commission 20%.

Access: [U][L] Buses 27,33,37,65,90B,202,270,290; BR Richmond 5 mins; Underground Richmond 5 mins; Public car park Paradise Road 5 mins

Riverside Studios

Foyer exhibition area and gallery within arts centre. [VA,LA]

Address: Crisp Road, Hammersmith, London W6 tel 01 741 2251

Contact: Exhibition Organiser Greg Hilty

Open: Tues-Sun 12-8

Policy: Exhibitions range from contemporary painting and sculpture to historical work with performance art sometimes shown in theatre space. Foyer also has licensed bar and restaurant. Around 24 exhibitions annually.

Sales: Work sold

The Space: Foyer 10m linear hanging space, gallery 50m linear hanging space, brick and plaster walls, natural and artificial lighting, dark grey concrete floor.

Exhibiting: [AW]

Access: Underground Hammersmith

RONA Gallery

A gallery specialising in 20th century British naïve painters. [Pa]

Address: 1-2 Weighhouse Street, London W1 tel 01 491 3718/499 8830

Contact: Director Stanley Harries

Open: Mon-Sat 10.30-5.30

Policy: The gallery holds the Register of Naive and Popular Art (RONA) which is used to research exhibitions from the UK and elsewhere.

Access: Buses 6,7,8,12,13,15,16,25,73,88,113,135, 137,159,500,509; Underground Bond Street

Royal Academy of Arts

Oldest institution in Britain devoted to the fine arts, run by council of 80 academy members (painters,architects, engravers and sculptors). [VA]

Address: Piccadilly, London W1V 0DS tel 01 439 7438

Contact: Secretary

Open: Daily 10-6

Policy: *'It exists to encourage the widest possible participation in, and enjoyment of the visual arts'.* The academy hosts major international touring exhibitions, but also through competitive entry to its *'Summer Exhibition'* offers a unique exhibition opportunity to over 1000 participants each year.

Sales: Work sold

Exhibiting: Application details for 'Summer Exhibition' in arts press and the gallery usually in March.

Access: Buses 9,14,19,22,38; Underground Piccadilly and Green Park

Royal College of Art (Henry Moore Gallery, Gulbenkian Hall)

Exhibition area within major postgraduate education venue. [VA,Cr,De]

Address: Kensington Gore, London SW7 tel 01 584 5020

Contact: Exhibitions Organiser Ingrid Bleichroeder

Open: Mon-Fri 10-6

Policy: Shows work by staff and students from all departments within the college, with annual degree shows in mid-June and July with other college shows during the year. Also outside exhibitions.

Sales: Work sold

Access: Buses to Royal Albert Hall; Underground Knightsbridge, South Kensington

Royal Parade Gallery

This commercial gallery is the newest one in Blackheath and the only one dealing in original work. [VA,Ph,Ce]

Address: 9 Royal Parade, Blackheath, London SE3 0TL tel 01 463 9222

Contact: Director Alan Mitton

Open: Tues-Sat 10-6

Policy: The gallery aims to show only original works in either oil, watercolour, prints or ceramics by contemporary artists. In the main, the gallery will be given over to mixed exhibitions. However, there are periodic solo or group shows, on average every two months during the year.

Sales: Work sold; Credit card

The Space: 11x4x2m high with 33m linear hanging space. Hanging rod system plus hooks and lights are positioned to eliminate all reflections. Gallery plans available.

Exhibiting: [AW] Apply to Alan Mitton. Gallery finances insurance, with printing and mail-out of publicity, catalogue/card, list of exhibits, preview and display costs shared with artists. Commission 40% plus VAT.

Access: [F] BR Blackheath 5 mins

Runkel-Hue-Williams

Commercial gallery showing modern masters as well as contemporary work. [Pa,Sc,Dr]

Address: 6/8 Old Bond Street, London W1X 3TA tel 495 7017

Contact: Director Claus Runkel/Michael Hue-Williams

Open: Mon-Fri 10-5.30 and by appointment

exhibitions a year (with catalogues) with work by classical modern masters (mainly expressionists and surrealists) and well established international contemporary artists.

Sales: Work sold

Access: Buses 2,2b,10,11,16,24,25,29,36,36a,36b,38, 39,52,52a,70,76,82,185,500,507; Underground Victoria; BR Victoria

Saatchi Collection

Gallery housing a private collection of contemporary art by living artists. [Pa,Sc]

Address: 98A Boundary Road, London NW8 0RH tel 01 624 8299

Contact: Curator Julia Ernst

Open: Fri & Sat 12-6

Policy: The gallery *'only exhibits work from the collection'* and *'work is bought and shown in depth'*. A large number of works by relatively few artists make up the collection of painting and sculpture and up to three shows a year, each lasting four to eight months, are mounted.

Access: Bus 159; Underground Swiss Cottage, St John's Wood both 15-20 mins

Safari Studios

Opened in 1987, Safari Studios is an 'art and craft gallery and workshop producing, showing and selling jewellery, hand-printed fabrics, pottery and visual art'. [Pa,Je,Te,Ce,Ph]

Address: 115 St John Street, London EC1V 4QJ tel 01 250 1114

Contact: Sanaa Gateja, 44 Coniston Way, Blundell Street, London N7 9DD

Open: Tues-Fri 9.30-5

Policy: Founder Sanaa Gateja makes jewellery and creates paintings on Ugandan bark cloth. Resident artists are potter Jon Churchill and Joseph Olubo who specialises in hand-printed fabrics inspired by East African traditions. All three undertake commissions. There is also a programme of temporary exhibitions by contemporary artists and makers.

Sales: Work sold

The Space: 51 square metres.

Exhibiting: [AW] The gallery pays for insurance and mailing of publicity. 33.3% commission is charged on sales. Supports EPR.

Access: [F] Buses 4,5,55,279; Underground Farringdon 5 mins

Saga Scandinavian Art

'The only gallery in London showing contemporary works of art from the Nordic countries'. [VA,Cr]

Address: 3 Elystan Street, Chelsea, London SW3 3NT tel 01 584 5684

Open: Mon-Fri 10-5, Sat 10-1

Policy: New exhibitions every month of well-known artists from the Nordic Countries. Downstairs holds large stock of works by over 60 artists. Also *'consultants to offices for commissions and acquisitions of artwork'*.

Sales: Work sold

The Space: 66 square metres of exhibition space with large windows onto street.

Access: [U] Underground South Kensington or Sloane Square

St Martin in the Fields Gallery

A gallery in the crypt of St Martin in the Fields showing a wide range of contemporary work. [Pa,Pr,Ph,De,Te]

Address: Trafalgar Square, London WC2N 4JJ tel 01 839 8364/8367

Contact: Gallery Organiser Caroline Graham-Brown

Policy: The gallery, established in October 1988, aims to show art, textiles, graphic design and photography and to generate income to run the church, which has around 2000 visitors a day.

Sales: Work sold

The Space: There is around 600 square metres of hanging space.

Exhibiting: [AW] The gallery is let at £100 a week.

Access: [L] Charing Cross and Leicester Square Underground

St Thomas' Hospital

A hospital with a permanent exhibiting space showing contemporary two-dimensional work. [Pa,Dr,Pr]

Address: Lambeth Palace Road, London SE1 7EH tel 01 928 4506

Contact: Arts Co-ordinator Rosie Anne Pinney, Special Trustees, St Thomas' Hospital, London, SE1 7EH

Open: All the time

Policy: The aim of showing work in the hospital environment is to make art more accessible to those who may not normally visit galleries, and to provide visual interest and stimulation to patients. The hospital's collection of contemporary work is on display throughout the hospital and this lead to setting up a space to show month-long temporary exhibitions. Artists are also commissioned to do work for the hospital and to run workshops for patients.

Sales: Work sold; Sales referred to exhibitor

The Space: 2.5m high with 16m linear hanging space. Hanging is by rail with overhead fluorescent lighting. Work should be glazed. The exhibition space is a corridor in the hospital, there is also a central hall area that can be used for display.

Exhibiting: [AW] Apply to Rosie Anne Pinney with slides or examples of work. Commission is 15%.

Access: [U][T][L] Buses 12,53,88; BR Waterloo 5 mins;

Underground Waterloo, Westminster, Lambeth North 5 mins

Sally Hunter Fine Art

Commercial gallery showing and dealing in 20th century and contemporary painting. [Pa]

Address: 2 Motcomb Street, Belgrave Square, London SW1X 8JU tel 01 235 0934
Contact: Director Sally Hunter
Open: Mon-Fri 10-6, and by appointment
Policy: The gallery predominantly shows the work of living artists; paintings, drawings and watercolours by artists *'from the middle years of this century'*. Thirteen exhibitions are held a year, mainly solo shows lasting four weeks.
Sales: Work sold; Credit scheme
The Space: Works are limited to a maximum 2x1m.
Exhibiting: [AW] Applications are welcome, write to the Director enclosing slides. The gallery asks for a contribution towards publicity, mailing, catalogue/card, list of exhibits and preview costs, and takes 40% commission plus VAT on sales.
Access: [F] Buses C1,19,22,30,52,73,74,137 3 mins; Underground Hyde Park, Knightsbridge 5 mins; NCP car park 1 min

Sayat Nova Gallery

A commercial gallery dealing in and showing work by living artists in a variety of media. [VA,Ph,Cr,Te,Fu]

Address: 234 Archway, London N6 5AX tel 01 348 0991
Contact: Julie Brown
Open: Mon-Fri 9.30-5.30, Sat 9-5.45
Policy: The gallery aims *'to promote the work of the creative individual'* and *'provides a window to the public through which artists can show their skills'*. A programme of 14 exhibitions a year lasting one to two weeks includes watercolours, oils, prints, photography and *'constructions'*. Exhibitions are mainly solo and a changing display of sculpture, pottery, masks, textiles and furniture is on show.
Sales: Work sold
The Space: The space is 7.5x3.5x3m with a beamed ceiling and spot lights.
Exhibiting: [AW] Applications are welcome and 15-20% commission is taken on sales.
Access: [F][X] Buses 17,43,134,263; Underground Highgate 2 mins; Street parking

Seen Galleries Limited

A commercial gallery dealing in and showing the work of living artists. [VA]

Address: 8 Frederic Mews, off Kinnerton Street, London SW1X 8EQ tel 01 245 6131/2
Contact: Jeffrey Sion
Open: Mon-Fri 10-6, Sat 10-1
Policy: The gallery specialises in representational painting and prints and *'portable sculpture'*. Approximately two exhibitions lasting one month each are held a year and the gallery deals *'specifically with corporate clients, collectors and private buyers. Between shows a changing display of works for sale is mounted.*
Sales: Work sold; Credit card
Access: Underground Knightsbridge

Serpentine Gallery

An independent gallery primarily exhibiting contemporary paintings, drawings and sculpture in solo exhibitions. [Pa,Sc,Dr]

Address: Kensington Gardens, London W2 3XA tel 01 723 643/402 0343
Contact: Director Alister Warman
Open: Summer 10-6, Winter 10-dusk
Policy: The gallery attracts a large audience and exists as a showing space for contemporary art. The programme of exhibitions aims to continue a tradition of recognising the achievements of established British artists while reflecting new international developments and presenting work by younger artists. Talks relating to exhibitions are held at weekends. Workshops and school visits can be arranged by ringing Vivien Ashley.
The Space: Four gallery areas, two spaces at 13x7.5m, one at 10x6m and one at 10x10m. Gallery plans available.
Exhibiting: No applications can be accepted until mid 1990. Gallery finances all exhibition expenses.
Access: [U][T] Buses 9,12 52,10,88; Underground South Kensington, Lancaster Gate

Shaw Theatre Foyer

Theatre foyer space run and financed by the Libraries and Arts Department of the London Borough of Camden. [VA,Ph]

Address: 100 Euston Road, London NW1 2AJ tel 01 387 9887 x 5870
Contact: Visual Arts Officer Terry Bennett
Open: Mon,Thurs, Fri 9.30-8, Tues, Fri, Sat 9.30-5; Closed Wed
Policy: The gallery aims to *'demonstrate the underlying reasons for art being produced and to show the work of local artists within that context'* through a varied programme of 18 exhibitions, including theme shows, work making a social or political comment and children's art. Painting, sculpture, drawings, prints and photography are shown and regular talks, seminars, workshops, poetry readings and activities for children are held in the space. The gallery attracts a wide ranging audience including *'ethnic minorities, women, the elderly and the under 5s'*. A picture loan scheme is handled which *'represents English art over the past 25 years'*.
Sales: Work sold
The Space: The space has 39m of wall space with overhead spotlights and natural light as space looks out onto road; four show cases 2x1x0.3m.
Exhibiting: [AW] Group applications from local artists are preferred. Applications should be made to the Visual Arts Officer. Costs of insurance, printing of publicity, catalogue/card, mailing and list of exhibits are covered and 20% commissions is taken on sales. Supports EPR in principle.
Access: [U][T][L] Buses 14,47,72; Underground Euston, St Pancras, Kings Cross; BR Euston, Kings Cross

Sheila Harrison Gallery

A commercial gallery dealing in craft work. [Cr]

Address: 124 Jermyn Street, London SW1 tel 01 321 0366
Contact: Sheila Harrison
Open: Mon-Fri 10-6, Sat 10-4
Sales: Work sold; Credit card

Showroom (The)

An independent gallery dealing in and showing the work of living artists in a variety of media. [Pa,Sc,Dr,Ph,Vi,LA]

Address: 44 Bonner Road, Bethnal Green, London E2 9JS tel 01 980 6636
Contact: Director David Thorp
Open: Wed-Sun 1-6
Policy: The gallery specialises in non-commercial contemporary art *'principally from emerging artists as well as artists with established reputations'*. The gallery *'aims to show work that is innovative, experimental and excellent'* through a programme of exhibitions each lasting four to five weeks.
The Space: The two galleries 10x3-10x3-4.5m and 14x1-7x4m are lit by track lighting. Gallery plans are available.
Exhibiting: **[AW]** Applications welcome, send background information and slides to the Director. The costs of insurance, printing, catalogue/card, list of exhibits, mailing, preview, transport and artists' expenses are met and 30% commission is taken on sales. The gallery supports EPR in principle.
Access: **[F]** Buses 6, 35, 55, 106, 253, Underground Bethnal Green, BR Cambridge Heath, local parking

Sisterwrite Bookshop Gallery

A gallery within a bookshop showing issued-based contemporary work by women. [VA]

Address: 190 Upper Street, London N1 tel 01 226 9782
Contact: Administrator
Open: Mon-Sat 10-6, Thurs 10-7
Access: **[X]**

Sladmore Gallery

Commercial gallery dealing in 19th and 20th century sculpture and antiques and showing sculpture by living artists. [Sc]

Address: 32 Bruton Place, London W1X 7AA tel 01 499 0365
Contact: Edward Horswell
Open: Mon-Fri 10-6, Sat 10-1
Policy: The gallery specialises in *'fine antiques'* and animal sculpture, and promotes the work of two contemporary sculptors. The exhibition programme includes three shows each lasting three to four weeks and a changing selection of antiques. The gallery holds a permanent collection of 19th and early 20th century animal bronzes and aims to *'satisfy the requirements of an international clientele of discerning sculpture collectors'*.
Sales: Work sold
The Space: Glass display cabinets are available.
Access: **[U]** no toilet Underground Green Park 5 mins

Slaughterhouse Gallery

A contemporary art gallery providing a programme of exhibitions including visual arts, crafts and installations. [VA,Cr,LA]

Address: 63 Charterhouse Street, Smithfield, London EC1 tel 01 251 5888
Contact: Maggie Smith
Open: Mon-Sat 11-6
Policy: To show both established artists and to give students opportunities to exhibit. The vaulted basement is more suited to sculpture and installations.
Sales: Work sold
The Space: Three underground vaults with upper basement with available light.
Exhibiting: **[AW]** Space available for hire (discount rate for students).
Access: Situated centre Smithfield Meat Market; Underground Barbican, Farringdon

Sloan Street Gallery

Gallery shows painting, drawing, ceramics and sculpture by new or relatively unknown artists. [Pa,Dr,Sc,Ce]

Address: 158 Sloane Street, London SW1X 9BT tel 01 730 5835
Contact: Gordon or Danielle Allen
Open: Mon-Fri 10-5.30, Sat 10-2
Access: Buses 19,22,137; Underground Sloane Square

Small Mansion Arts Centre

Artist-run gallery within a studio group showing the work of living artists in all media. [VA,Ph,Cr]

Address: Gunnersbury Park, Popes Lane, London W3 8QL tel 01 993 8312

Slaughterhouse Gallery: The vaulted basement

Contact: Administrator

Open: Variable

Policy: *'A non-profit making space set in a Georgian mansion within a beautiful park'*. The gallery runs a varied programme of exhibitions including painting, sculpture, drawing, photography, prints, crafts and live art and aims to interest *'the local community as well as a wider arts public', it operates 'a non-sexist, non-racist policy'*. Ten exhibitions a year are mounted each lasting three to four weeks. The gallery runs weekly life drawing classes and a programme of workshops. Mainly group shows but the programme is dependent on level of funding raised from local authority and GLA.

Sales: Work sold

The Space: The gallery which is 6.5x11.5x4.5m and a foyer space 2.5x11.5x3m overlook the park and have natural light and spots. Gallery plans are available. The space is used for art-based conferences, lectures and workshops.

Exhibiting: [AW] The space is occasionally available for hire, write to the gallery. Costs of insurance, printing, card, mailing and preview are covered only for exhibitions promoted by the gallery and invigilation.

Access: [F] Bus E3; Underground Acton Town 5 mins

Smith's Galleries

Part of a large organisation, Smith's Galleries consist of three commercial galleries hired out on a weekly or daily basis. [VA,Cr,Te]

Address: 56 Earlham Street, Covent Garden, London WC2 tel 01 836 9701

Contact: Gallery Manager Katie Law, Smiths Head Office, 28 Neal Street, London WC2

Open: Mon-Sat 11-7

Policy: Whilst hiring out the spaces to applicants, Smiths tries to achieve a balance in the programme which includes subsidised college shows enabling students from outside the capital to have their work seen; a variety of art organisations including the Contemporary Arts Society Annual Art Market and the Association of Illustrators Annual Show; and commercial press/product launches and private parties. The galleries have an overall bias towards the fine and applied arts and to textiles.

Sales: Sales referred to exibitor

The Space: Smith's One, 33 Shelton Street 132 square metres x 2.2m high, linear hanging length 42m. Smith's Two, 54 Earlham Street 112 square metres x 2.2m high, linear hanging length 46m. Smith's Three, 33a Shelton Street 51 square metres x 2.2m high, linear hanging length 31m. Track lights in all galleries plus halogen lights in Smith's One, no fixed hanging system. Gallery plans available.

Exhibiting: [AW] Applications to hire any of the spaces should be made to the gallery office, 28 Neal Street. Hiring is confirmed six months in advance. Smith's mails out publicity material and takes a commission of 12.5%.

Access: [U][T] Underground Covent Garen 2 mins, Leicester Square 5 mins; public car park NCP St Martins Lane 5 mins

Soho Poly Theatre Gallery

A gallery space within a theatre. [VA]

Address: 16 Riding House Street, London W1 tel 01 636 9050

Contact: Administrator Annette Clancy

Open: Mon-Fri 2-8, Sat 4-8

Policy: The theatre is well-known for promoting new writers and performers and encourages the use of the gallery space in the same way. *'The theatre tries to thematically combine performance work and exhibitions and frequently produces seasons of new work.'*

Exhibiting: [AW] All costs have to be met by the artist although moral and physical help are plentiful. Commission is 15%.

Access: Underground Goodge Street & Oxford Circus

Solomon Gallery

A gallery showing contemporary art from Britain and Europe by established and up-and-coming artists.

Address: 10 Dover Street, London W1VA tel 01 499 4701/2

Contact: Director

Open: Mon-Fri 9.30-5.30; Sat by appointment

Access: Buses 3,6,9,12,13,14,14a,19,22,22b,38,53, 88,159,509; Underground Piccadilly Circus and Green Park

South Bank Craft Shop & Gallery

This commercial gallery on the Crafts Council's selected list specialises in the group shows of work of young contemporary applied artists. [Cr]

Address: Royal Festival Hall, London SE1 8XX tel 01 921 0839

Contact: Lisa Gee, Claire West

Open: Mon-Sun 12-8

Policy: Gallery policy is to show the wide range of applied arts currently produced by British artists. Target audiences are the visitors to the Royal Festival Hall as well as the more specialist applied arts audience. Artists are occasionally commissioned to produce works. Talks and workshops are organised by the South Bank Centre Education Department.

Sales: Work sold; Credit card

The Space: Display space in the main foyer of the Royal Festival Hall approximately 11 square metres.

Exhibiting: Gallery may finance insurance, printing and mail-out of publicity, catalogue/card, list of exhibits, preview and display costs. Support in principle for EPR. Commission 50%-100%.

Access: [U][T][L][F] BR Waterloo; Underground Waterloo, Embankment; Public car park

South London Art Gallery

A municipal gallery run by Arts Section of the London Borough of Southwark, with a permanent collection of 19th and 20th century prints, paintings and drawings. [VA,Pr]

Address: 65 Peckham Road, London SE5 8UH tel 01 703 6120

Contact: Keeper Kenneth Sharpe

Open: Tues-Sat 10-6, Sun 3-6 during exhibitions

Policy: Holds around ten exhibitions annually most of which are of work by living artists. Professional artists of all denominations are encouraged to exhibit. Commercial approach to services, such as a picture loan scheme, being developed to expand range of provisions available to the public.
Sales: Work sold
The Space: One main gallery 20x8m with a linear hanging space of 19m, direct fixing to walls, track lighting and daylight through glass roof. Two free-standing glass showcases about 1.6x.6x2m high. Gallery also used for performances, seminars and workshops. Gallery plans available. Limited hire of space available, terms open to negotiation.
Exhibiting: [AW] Apply in writing to the Senior Arts Officer, Southwark Arts, 186 Walworth Road, SE17 1JJ. Exhibition costs shared between gallery and artist. Commission is between 10% and 20%.
Access: [X] Buses 12,36,36a,36b,171; BR Elephant & Castle, New Cross, Peckham Rye; Underground Elephant & Castle, Oval

Southwark College Gallery

Situated in a shopping centre the gallery intends to perform a full educational role. [VA,Ph,Cr]
Address: Elephant & Castle Shopping Centre, London SE1 6TE
Contact: Gallery Administrator Lisa Pattenden, Southwark College, Albany Road, London SE5 0BN tel 01 928 9561 x 320 or 01 703 2936
Open: 9.30-4.30 five days a week (times published for each exhibition)
Policy: The gallery aims to offer its resources to the educational sector and practising artists and mounts about ten shows a year. School talks are given.
Sales: Sales referred to exhibitor
The Space: [AW] The space is 12x11m and lined on three sides with 2.4x1.2m white melamine boards. There is also adjustable screening the same size and the gallery has flat fluorescent lighting. Any work up to 2.4m high can be accommodated apart from very heavy sculpture.
Exhibiting: [AW] Applications should be made to the Gallery Administrator. The gallery covers mailing of publicity and charges 20% commission.
Access: [F] Underground Elephant & Castle 1 min; BR Elephant & Castle 1 min; Buses 171,12,68,35,40, 176,184,53,45,65,141,59,133,1

Southwell Brown Gallery

This gallery shows contemporary painting and sculpture. [Pa,Sc]
Address: 4 Friars Stile Road, Richmond, Surrey TW10 6NE tel 01 948 2776
Contact: W J Southwell Brown
Open: Wed-Sun 10-1, 2-6
Policy: Gallery policy is to show the work of *'artists of both the academic and avant-garde and also occasional exhibitions of modern and ancient paintings and sculpture of various nationalities. The common denominator harnessing these diverse groups is simply that each should be a first-class example of its kind'.*
Sales: Work sold
The Space: Space totals 335 square metres on two floors.
Exhibiting: [AW] Commission 33.3%.

Special Photographers Company

Commercial gallery dealing in and showing fine art photography. [Ph]
Address: 21 Kensington Park Road, London W11 2EV tel 01 221 3489
Contact: Catherine Turner
Open: Mon-Sun 9.30-6.30
Policy: The gallery promotes contemporary photography through a programme of ten, four-week, exhibitions, and aims to *'educate the public in appreciating photography as something of value.... We are trying to demystify the idea of an edition and lessen the fear of photography's reproducible nature'.* It specialises in *'manipulated and fine art photography'* by living artists, and shows *'collections of photographs which are very individual'.* A changing display of gallery photographs is held in the basement and the gallery acts as agent to a selected number of photographers.
Sales: Work sold; Credit card; Credit scheme
The Space: The gallery is approximately 110 square metres and *'doubles as an office Monday - Friday'.*
Exhibiting: [AW] Applications are welcome, send transparencies or press prints. The gallery is hired out and costs covered vary. 45% commission is taken on sales.
Access: Buses 7,15,28,31,52,52a 2 mins; Underground Ladbroke Grove 5 mins, Notting Hill Gate 10 mins

Spitalfields Workspace Gallery

Reception and boardroom area within a workspace which lets office and studio accommodation. [VA,Ph]
Address: 9 Heneage Street, Spitalfields, London E1 5LJ tel 01 377 9262
Contact: Manager Francoise Budd
Open: Mon-Fri 9.30-5.30
Policy: The gallery aims to *'promote contemporary artists (young and established)'* through a programme of 24 exhibitions a year each lasting two weeks and including a wide range of work - painting, sculpture, prints,

Special Photographers Company

drawings, and photography; architectural drawings and mobiles have also been shown. Exhibitions are solo shows organised on a self-help basis.
Sales: Work sold
The Space: The space is approximately 10x13m and sculpture is limited to small-scale.
Exhibiting: [AW] Applications are welcome, telephone for an appointment to show slides, photographs or actual work. Artists are responsible for all arrangements and meeting all costs; 15% commission is taken on sales.
Access: [X] Underground Aldgate East 6 mins, Liverpool Street 10 mins; BR Liverpool Street; NCP car park Whites Row off Commercial Street

Square Gallery

This gallery stages solo and group exhibitions by contemporary artists working in a variety of media and styles. [VA,Ph,Cr]
Address: 12 South Grove, Highgate Village, London N6 6BJ tel 01 340 4983
Contact: Director Harriet Green
Open: Tues-Fri 11-6, Sat 12-6
Policy: The gallery favours the work of young-up-and-coming artists and likes to show work by groups of artists working in different media, usually in exhibitions lasting two weeks. The audience is made up from local and surrounding individuals and business'.
Sales: Work sold; Credit scheme
The Space: 7.5x4x3m high with 17m linear hanging space.There is a hanging rail at 1.8m height with tungsten spot lighting. The gallery cannot accommodate large sculptures.
Exhibiting: [AW] Apply to Harriet Green with slides and CV for solo or group shows. There is a hire fee of £150 per week. Gallery provides invites, posters, mailing lists, invigilation, listings and framing. Discount to exhibitors. Commission 20%.
Access: [F] Underground Highgate or Archway; Buses 271,210,143

Stable Gallery

A gallery specialising in contemporary paintings and prints.
Address: 10 Bellevue Road, Wandsworth Common, London SW17 tel 01 767 4688

Square Gallery

Contact: Director
Open: Mon-Sat 9-5, Sun 11-4
Access: BR Wandsworth Common

Stanmore Library

Library space run and financed by the London Borough of Harrow. [Pa,Sc,Pr,Ph,Cr]
Address: 8 Stanmore Hill, Stanmore, HA7 3BQ tel 01 954 9955
Contact: Derek Knight
Open: Mon,Tues,Thurs 9-1 2-8, Fri 9-1, 2-6, Sat 9-5; Closed Wed
Policy: The gallery aims to *'promote the work of local artists and art and craft societies'* and to *'increase public awareness and generally raise the profile of art within the community through active participation'.* Twenty exhibitions, both mixed and solo shows, each lasting two weeks, were held last year. See also Harrow Library Service.
Sales: Sales referred to exhibitor
The Space: The space 10.5x3.5x3 has 37m of panels 1.2m high, with Igloo floodlights and hanging is by picture hooks. Two free-standing cases 1.5x.7x.3 and one wall-hung case 1.5x1.2x.3m are available and the library can supply plans of the space.
Exhibiting: [AW] Applications are welcome, contact Derek Knight. A booking fee of £15 is charged and 10% plus VAT commission is taken on sales.
Access: [F] Buses 142,209,251,340; Underground Stanmore 5 mins

Stephen Bartley Gallery

A gallery showing contemporary work in changing exhibitions and from gallery artists. [Pa,Sc]
Address: 62 Old Church Street, London SW3 tel 01 352 8686
Contact: Director
Open: Tues-Fri 11-6, Sat 10-4

Studio (The)

Commercial gallery dealing in 19th and 20th century watercolours and contemporary prints and watercolours showing work by living artists. [Pa,Pr]
Address: Porcelain and Pictures Limited, 1 Gastein Road, Fulham, London W6 8LT tel 01 385 7512
Contact: Edward & David Toms
Open: Mon-Sat 10-5
Policy: The gallery holds an *'on going exhibition of selected works by living artists, particularly those producing original, limited edition prints'.* Workshops are provided for picture framers and porcelain restorers and a programme of tuition and seminars are held on both subjects.
Sales: Work sold
The Space: Two walls on the ground floor and two in the cellar are each approximately 4.5x3m. Hanging is by *'Art Aid'* metal rods with multi-adjustable hooks. Works are limited in size to 1.5x1m and two bins, fixed boxes and a plan chest are available.
Exhibiting: A selected number of artists are promoted and 25% commission is taken on sales.

Access: [F] Underground Barons Court 5 mins; Parking in street

Studio Gallery

A small gallery space on the first floor of a shop. [Pa,Sc]

Address: 50 Caledonian Road, Kings Cross, London N1 9DP tel 01 837 9947
Contact: Deirdre Keetley
Open: As advertised and by invitation
Policy: Exhibitions of painting and sculpture in both contemporary and historical contexts by means of finished pieces of work and audio visual displays. The exhibition programme has expanded to include thematic exhibitions on local, fictional and topical subjects which incorporate works by young artists. The gallery aims to sell works through exhibitions and mail order.
Sales: Work sold
The Space: Track and natural lighting.
Access: Buses 14,14a,17,18,30,45,46,63,73,77a,214, 221,259; Underground Kings Cross; BR Kings Cross

Submarine Gallery

Contemporary art gallery opened in 1986. [VA,LA]

Address: 294 Pentonville Road, King's Cross, London N1 9NR tel 01 278 0230
Contact: Danuta Kuczys & Peter Lewis
Open: Mon-Sat 10-6
Sales: Work sold
Exhibiting: [AW]
Access: BR; Underground Kings Cross

Sue Rankin Gallery

Monthly exhibitions of paintings, watercolours and drawings by British artists. [Pa,Dr]

Address: 670 Fulham Road, London SW6 tel 01 736 4120
Contact: Director
Open: Tues-Fri 10-6, Sat 10-4, Sun by appointment
Sales: Work sold
Access: Bus 14; Underground Parsons Green

Sue Williams

This commercial gallery, which is on the Crafts Council's selected list, shows solo and group exhibitions in a combination of fine and applied arts, often the work of newly graduated students. [VA,Cr,Ce,Gl]

Address: 320 Portobello Road, London W10 5RU tel 01 960 6123
Contact: Director Sue Williams
Open: Tues-Sat 10-5.30
Policy: The gallery is dedicated to showing the work of young artists in a sympathetic environment and at affordable prices. It aims to help breakdown the barriers between fine art and craft by featuring a mixture of complementary objects in exhibitions. The gallery is also *'distinguished by its wholehearted commitment to selling the work on display'*.
Sales: Work sold; Credit card
The Space: Main gallery 8.5x5x3.5m high with 23m linear hanging space, work is directly fixed to walls. Shop area 3x2m. Plinths and shelving available. Gallery plans available.
Exhibiting: [AW] Apply by telephone to make appointment to show work, or send slides with SAE. Gallery finances insurance, printing and mail-out of publicity, catalogue/card, list of exhibits and preview costs. Support in principle for EPR. Commission 43%-50%.
Access: [F] Buses 7,15,27,28,31,52,295; Underground Ladbroke Grove 5 mins

Sutton College Gallery

A medium-sized intimate gallery in a college with all exhibits in lockable showcases. [VA,Ph,Cr]

Address: Sutton College of Liberal Arts, St Nicholas Way, Sutton, Surrey SM1 1EA tel 01 661 5060
Contact: Head of 3D Design Brian Starkey
Open: Mon-Fri 10-4 & 7-9, Sat 10-12 noon
Policy: To help young artists and makers who would find it difficult to show in London galleries. Leading artists and makers are invited to show at intervals (two or three a year). The gallery area is particularly suitable for ceramics, jewellery, prints and small sculptural items.
Sales: Work sold
The Space: The gallery space is 14x5.5m with 20 metres linear hanging space, ten show cases, direct fixing and spots and fluorescent lights.
Exhibiting: [AW] Commission is 25% and the gallery covers insurance, publicity, mailing, catalogue and private view.

Swiss Cottage Library Exhibition Hall

Exhibition Hall within a library run by the Libraries and Arts Department of the London Borough of Camden. [VA,Ph]

Address: 88 Avenue Road, London NW3 3HA tel 01 387 9887 ext 5870
Contact: Visual Arts Officer Terry Bennett/Paul Collett, Arts Section, St Pancras Library, 100 Euston Road, London NW1 2AJ
Open: Mon, Thurs 9.30-8,Tues, Fri, Sat 9.30-5; Closed Wed, Sun
Policy: The gallery aims to *'demonstrate the underlying reasons for art being produced and to show the work of local artists within that context'* through a varied programme of 18 exhibitions, including theme shows, work making a social or political comment and children's art. Painting, sculpture, drawings, prints and photography are shown and regular talks, seminars, workshops, poetry readings and activities for children are held in the space. The gallery attracts a wide ranging audience including *'ethnic minorities, women, the elderly and the under 5s'*. A picture loan scheme is handled which *'represents English art over the past 25 years'*.
Sales: Work sold
The Space: The gallery has 61m of wall space with daylight and overhead fluorescent tubes and four glazed 2x1x3m show cases. Gallery plans are available.

Exhibiting: **[AW]** Group applications from local artists are preferred and should be made to the Visual Arts Officer. The costs of insurance, printing of publicity, catalogue/card and list of exhibits are covered. Commission of 20% is taken on sales. Supports EPR in principle.
Access: **[U][T][L]** Buses 13,31,46,82,113,268,C11; Underground Swiss Cottage, Finchley Road

Tadema Gallery

Commercial gallery showing decorative art of the 20th century including modern British & Contintental paintings, sculpture & jewellery. [Pa,Sc,Je]

Address: 10 Charlton Place, Camden Passage, London N1 tel 01 359 1055
Open: Tues, Wed, Fri, Sat 10-5 or by appointment
Sales: Work sold
Access: Underground Angel

Talent Store Gallery

This gallery exhibits oils and watercolours to suit the more conventional tastes of its clientele. [Pa]

Address: 11 Eccleston Street, London SW1W 9LX tel 01 730 8117
Contact: Gallery Manager Rowena Haigh
Open: Mon-Fri 9.30-1, 2-5.30

Swiss Cottage Library: 'The Fruits of Apartheid is Oppression' by Geoff Staden

Policy: Gallery policy is to help young artists that have not previously exhibited to any great extent. The gallery aims to provide a start for these artists and to give them some experience of exhibiting. Each exhibition is shown for one month. The target audience is *'the ordinary person in the street'*.
Sales: Work sold
The Space: 5x10m with windows onto street.
Exhibiting: **[AW]** Apply with photographs of work to Gallery Manager. Gallery finances insurance, mail-out of publicity, catalogue/card and list of exhibits. Commission 33.3%.
Access: **[F]** BR Victoria 5 mins; Underground Victoria 5 mins

Tate Gallery

A national art gallery. [VA]

Address: Millbank, London SW1P 4RG tel 01 821 1313
Contact: Director Nicholas Serota
Open: Daily 10-6, Sun 2-6
Policy: The British collection of work from about 1500-1900, and the Modern collection of works by late 19th and 20th century British and foreign artists. The permanent collections are supplemented by regular temporary shows both retrospective and didactic ones, bookshop.
Access: Buses 2,2b,36,36a,36b,77a,88,185; Underground Pimlico

Thackeray Gallery

A privately-funded gallery with solo and mixed exhibitions. [Pa]

Address: 18 Thackeray Street, Kensington Square, London W8 5ET tel 01 937 5883
Contact: Priscilla Anderson
Open: Tues, Thurs, Fri 10-6, Sat 10-4, Wed 10-7; Closed Jan, Aug
Policy: The ground floor is usually used for solo exhibitions and the basement gallery usually holds mixed shows. Exhibitions normally run for three weeks. Only contemporary paintings and watercolours are exhibited.
Sales: Work sold
The Space: Ground floor and basement gallery.
Exhibiting: **[AW]** Artists should apply in writing, sending slides or photographs. Gallery heavily booked.
Access: **[X]** Buses 9,27,28,31,33,49,52,52a,73; Underground High Street Kensington

Thumb Gallery

A gallery specialising in paintings, drawings, watercolours and limited edition prints by contemporary British artists. [Pa,Dr]

Address: 38 Lexington Street, Soho, London W1R 3HR tel 01 439 7343
Contact: Director Jill George
Open: Mon-Fri 10-6, Sat 11-4
Policy: Monthly exhibition programme by invitation only and a permanent selection of prints and originals on display. The gallery arranges commissions for its artists.
The Space: A main exhibition room with 38m linear

space, with a further 18m available in the second gallery. Lighting is by spots and there is a specialist hanging system.

Exhibiting: Exhibition by invitation only. The gallery covers insurance and mailing and shares the cost of publicity.

Access: [X] Buses 3,6,7,8,12,13,14,14a,15,16a,19,22, 22b,24,25,38,55,73,88; Underground Oxford Circus and Tottenham Court Road

Todd Gallery

Commercial gallery dealing in and showing work by living artists. [Pa]

Address: 326 Portobello Road, London W10 tel 01 960 6209

Contact: Director Jenny Todd

Open: Tues-Sat 11-6

Policy: The gallery predominantly shows *'smaller paintings'* both abstract and figurative and *'gives preference to works of emotional immediacy rather then works of didactic intellectual formalism'*. The audience is wide ranging and a programme of twelve month-long exhibitions a year is held. These are mainly solo shows and all are the work of living artists. A stock of work by gallery artists is kept.

Sales: Work sold; Credit card

The Space: The two gallery spaces 9x3.5x3.5m and 5.5x2x2.5m have a combined linear hanging space of 25m. Gallery plans are available.

Exhibiting: [AW] Applications are welcome, send slides to the Director. The gallery covers insurance, publicity, catalogue/card, mailing, preview, transport and takes 50% commission on sales.

Access: [F] Buses 15,52; Underground Ladbroke Grove

Tom Allen Gallery

Gallery within a community arts centre with charitable status showing work by living artists. [VA,Ph,LA]

Address: Tom Allen Community Arts Centre, Grove Crescent Road, Stratford, London E15 1BJ tel 01 555 7289

Contact: Exhibitions Development Worker Clare Cumberlidge

Open: Mon-Fri 12-6; Closed bank holidays

Policy: The gallery is *'the only permanent exhibition space in the borough of Newham'* and aims to *'actively promote a positive development of the visual arts within the borough; both in terms of direct community involvement and in developing a clear comprehension of contemporary art and its concerns'*. The policy is *'implemented through a series of collaborative projects with established artists who are invited to introduce the public to their work through exhibitions and related workshops and seminars'*. The programme of ten, month-long exhibitions a year alternates solo shows with *'collaborative exhibitions between the artist and targetted sectors of the community'* and includes work in a wide range of media - painting, sculpture, drawing, prints, photography, installation, time-based media and live art, batik, rangoli etc.

Sales: Work sold; Sales referred to exhibitor

The Space: The space has 20.5m linear hanging space and additional foyer space of 6.75m, 4m high. Lighting is a combination of daylight, hallogen bulbs and tungsten track lighting and work is fixed directly to the walls. The foyer contains a bar and seating area and gallery plans are available.

Exhibiting: [AW] Applications are welcome, write to the Exhibitions Development Worker for policy guidelines; *'artists are then invited to submit proposals'* with slides or prints and SAE. Printing of publicity, catalogue/card, mailing, list of exhibits, transport and preview costs are covered and frames are available to artists. Artists are employed to run workshops and put together the collaborative shows. The gallery supports EPR in principle.

Access: [U][T] Buses S1,S2,86,108,238; Underground Stratford 3 mins, BR Stratford; Docklands Light Railway

Tower Hamlets Library Service

The department responsible for Tower Hamlets Library Service.

Policy: The borough runs exhibition spaces in a number of branch libraries. In common with other council functions the library services have been de-centralised into seven neighbourhoods. See separate entries for Bow Library (Bow Neighbourhood), Bethnal Green Library (Globe Town Neighbourhood), Lansbury Library (Poplar Neighbourhood) and Whitechapel Library (Bethnal Green Neighbourhood). The other three neighbourhoods are: Isle of Dogs Neighbourhood, Cubitt Town Library, Strattondale Street, London E14 9HG tel 01 987 3152; Stepney Neighbourhood, Sidney Street Library, Lindley Street, London E1 3AX tel 01 790 5616; Wapping Neighbourhood, Limehouse Library, 638 Commercial Road, London E14 7HS tel 01 987 3183.

Exhibiting: Contact the appropriate Neighbourhood Librarian.

Tricycle Theatre Gallery

A theatre showing solo exhibitions of contemporary art, reopening in Summer 1989. [Pa,Pr,Ph,Dr]

Address: 269 Kilburn High Road, London NW6 7JR tel 01 372 6611

Contact: Administrator Mary Lauder

Open: Mon-Sat 10am-11pm

Policy: Exhibitions change three-weekly, *'we try and encourage local artists, but exhibit work from all over England'*. Only two-dimensional work can be shown. Particularly encourages work from the Irish, Asian & Black communities.

Sales: Work sold

The Space: A space of 23m linear.

Exhibiting: Artists must do all their own publicity, hanging and arrange delivery of sold work and the gallery takes 15% commission. The theatre provides a brochure for each season.

Access: [U][T] Buses 8,16,16a,32; Underground Kilburn

Union Chapel

A large recently restored chapel which is still an active place for worship, with a range of community activities including exhibitions. [VA]

Address: Compton Terrace, Upper Street, London N1 tel 01 359 1433
Contact: Peter Walker
Policy: There is no selection committee and *'the artists themselves select the work and decide how and where to show it'*.
Sales: Work sold
Exhibiting: **[AW]** Ask for details. Commission is 10%.

Uxbridge Central Library

Public library. [VA,Ph,Cr]
Address: Central Library, 14-15 High Street, Uxbridge, Middlesex UB8 1JU tel 0895 50111 ext 2505
Contact: Library Manager R Mitchell
Open: Mon-Fri 9.30-8 Sat 9.30-5
Policy: *'We will consider for display any work without preconditions but retain overall control. Around 13,000 visitors per week.'* The monthly exhibitions are predominantly mixed ones.
Sales: Work sold
The Space: 27m linear by 2m high. 'Spacewall' hanging system, excellent natural light, ground floor position.
Exhibiting: **[AW]** Apply to Manager. The gallery prints publicity and takes 20% commission.
Access: **[U][T][L]** Underground Uxbridge 2mins. Buses 207, 223, 98 2mins

Vanessa Devereux Gallery

A gallery showing 20th century painting and sculpture and specialising in contemporary British painting. [VA]
Address: 11 Blenheim Crescent, London W11 tel 01 221 0606
Contact: Director Vanessa Devereux
Open: Mon-Fri 10-6, Sat 10-1
Access: Buses 7,15,27,28,31,52a

Vanneck Gallery

Commercial gallery dealing in and showing work by living artists in a variety of media. [VA,Ph,Cr]
Address: 22 Richmond Hill, Richmond, Surrey TW10 6QX tel 01 940 2035
Contact: Teresa Vanneck-Murray, The Doghouse, 29 Kennel Lane, Fetcham, Leatherhead, Surrey KT22 9PQ tel 0372 53572
Open: Mon-Sat 10.30-5.30, Sun 2-5.30
Policy: The gallery shows the work of *'up-and-coming artists'* in all media - painting, sculpture, drawing, prints, photography and crafts. Approximately ten exhibitions are held a year each lasting three weeks, most of these are solo shows and occasionally a group hires the space. The target audience is *'residents within a ten-mile radius'* and *'medium-sized pictures for the home'* are sold. Between shows the gallery displays antiques, antique paintings and prints.
Sales: Work sold; Credit card
The Space: The gallery is 15x4m, and has spot lights with hanging on *'batons for nails'*.
Exhibiting: **[AW]** Applications are welcome, send photographs/slides and CV to the Director's home address. The gallery offers insurance facilities and takes 30% commission on sales when no hire fee is charged.
Access: **[S]** Buses 27,33,37,71; Underground Richmond, BR Richmond

Victoria & Albert Museum

A major national and international museum with substantial collections of fine and decorative arts from the 14th to the 20th century. [VA,Cr,De]
Address: Cromwell Road, South Kensington, London SW7 2RL tel 01 938 8500
Contact: Relevant Curator or Exhibitions Department Michael Darby
Open: Mon-Sat 10-5.50, Sun 2.30-5.50
Policy: The museum mounts approximately 20 exhibitions a year, including about four solo shows, each for five to eight weeks. The programme aims to represent the collections over a period of time for both the specialist and general audience. There is a commitment to show the work of living artists and of 20th century artists and designers.
The Space: There are various galleries for changing exhibitions. Detailed information available from each department.
Exhibiting: **[AW]** Artists may approach individual curators where the museum is actively collecting in that area, ie not painting and sculpture. The museum is responsible for all the costs associated with an exhibition.
Access: **[U][T][L][S][X]** depends on gallery. Underground South Kensington 3 mins; Buses 30,74,14,49,45,C1

Victoria Miro

A commercial gallery showing and dealing the work of living artists. [VA,Ph]
Address: 21 Cork Street, London W1X 1HB tel 01 734 5082
Contact: David Gray
Open: Mon-Fri 10-6, Sat 11-4
Policy: *'An international gallery exhibiting the work of contemporary British and foreign artists'* working in a variety of media - painting, sculpture, drawing, photography and prints. Ten exhibitions are held a year, mainly solo shows lasting between four and six weeks.
Sales: Work sold
The Space: Two gallery spaces 7.4x6.2m and 3.7x3.4m are 3.3m in height. Gallery plans available.
Exhibiting: The gallery promotes a selected number of artists and the gallery covers insurance, publicity, mailing, preview, transport, display, artist's expenses and all other costs incurred. Commission taken on sales varies.
Access: **[S]** Buses 3,6,9,12,13,14,14a,15,19,22,22B,25, 38,53,88,159; Underground Green Park, Piccadilly Circus

Vortex Galleries

A gallery of contemporary art housed above a books shop and shop selling art cards, prints and frames. The gallery contains a cafe and doubles at night as a jazz bar. [VA]
Address: 139-141 Stoke Newington Church Street,

London N16 tel 01 254 6516
Contact: Irving Kinnersley
Policy: The gallery takes approximately twelve shows a year, generally by invitation although applications considered. Paintings generally shown, although some relief work considered.
The Space: One gallery of 100 square metres.
Exhibiting: **[AW]** Applications welcome, send slides, CV and SAE. Commission is 35%.
Access: Bus 73; BR Stoke Newington; Underground Manor House

Waddington Galleries

A private gallery showing 20th century painting and sculpture. [VA]
Address: 2,4,5,11,34 Cork Street, London W1 tel 01 439 6262, 437 8611
Contact: Director
Open: Mon-Fri 10-5.30, Sat 10-1, Thurs till 7
Policy: The gallery specialises in painting and sculpture, of the 20 British artists they exclusively represent and of the European and American artists they partially represent. One gallery is usually devoted to a mixed show of gallery stock, two are used for temporary shows and another for graphics.
The Space: Five galleries totalling about 650 square metres with spots and natural lighting and hanging by direct fixing, rods and rails.
Exhibiting: **[AW]** The galleries rarely show unknown work, but *'the directors are interested in seeing new work'* after first seeing slides and CV. The gallery covers all expenses and commission taken is variable.
Access: Buses 3,6,9,12,13,14,14a,15,19,22,22b,38,53, 88,159; Underground Piccadilly Circus

Warwick Arts Trust

The trust displays its own collection of contemporary painting and sculpture from April to October and for the rest of the year is available for hire. [VA]
Address: 33 Warwick Square, Pimlico, London SW1 12AQ tel 01 834 7856
Contact: House Manager Denis Conti
Open: Wed-Sun 10-5
Policy: The gallery concentrates on contemporary work, mainly abstract painting and sculpture by younger artists. The gallery can be hired for appropriate exhibitions between October and March. During November there is a selling show of work by young sculptors and painters.
Sales: Work sold
The Space: Plans are available for the three gallery spaces which are 7.3x3m, 8.8x3.6m and 3.9x4.2m.
Exhibiting: **[AW]** Applications to hire the spaces should be made to the Gallery Manager. The hirer is responsible for all the costs associated with the exhibition and there is a commission of 33.3%.
Access: **[S]** Underground Victoria and Pimlico 10 mins; Buses 2,2b,36,36b,185; BR Victoria 10 mins

Watermans Arts Centre

A multi-discipline arts centre comprising main and lower galleries, theatre, cinema, restaurant and bar. [VA,Vi,Ph,LA]
Address: 40 High Street, Brentford, Middlesex TW8 0DS tel 01 570 7728
Contact: Visual Arts Programmer Alison D MacLeod
Open: Mon-Fri 11-8, Sat 10-9, Sun 12-9
Policy: The main gallery exhibits new and innovative work covering all fine art media to a national and international standard. Site-specific projects are encouraged along with non-gallery sited work. The programme seeks to strike a balance between both young and established artists working within a contemporary context. There are an average of 9 exhibitions per year of approximately one month's duration. Exhibiting artists are also expected to participate in the community education programme, on a professional basis, by working with members of the community, the results of which form an on-going exhibition programme in the lower gallery space.
Sales: Work sold; Credit card
The Space: The main gallery measures 13.8x5.3m, with a linear hanging space of 83.5m. The space is versatile with a removable panel wall which, when retracted, exposes a continuous half-length window on to the river. There is therefore choice between natural and artificial light.
Exhibiting: **[AW][EF]** Artists should submit slides together with a brief, outlining their proposal and SAE. Watermans covers insurance, publicity and transport costs, including preview cards, posters, mailing etc. Some form of catalogue or documentation is produced. Specific project expenses may also be available.
Access: **[U][T][L][F]** Bus 65,237,267; Underground Gunnersbury, South Ealing; BR Kew Bridge

Westbourne Gallery

Commercial gallery dealing in and showing the work of living black artists. [VA]
Address: 453 Harrow Road, London W10 4RG tel 01 960 1867
Contact: Director S McNorthey
Open: Mon-Fri 10-6, Sat 10-3
Policy: The gallery aims to *'promote the range, quality and dimensions of contemporary Black Art to the widest possible audience'* which is *' an area often under-valued and under-projected'* through a programme of eleven exhibitions a year lasting two to four weeks. The exhibitions of painting, sculpture, drawings and prints are mainly solo shows by African, Asian, American and Caribbean artists including both the young and established. The gallery frequently *'finds itself acting as educators, consultant evaluers, exhibition organisers, artists'* agent or representative' and holds poetry readings, music performances and workshops in the space. A changing display of the work of gallery artists is on show, and a permanent collection of these artists' work is kept. The gallery is partly financed by Greater London Arts.
Sales: Work sold; Credit scheme; Credit card
The Space: The space of 7.5x3.5x4.5m has fluorescent tubes and mobile track lighting.
Exhibiting: **[AW]** *'Send a self-addressed envelope with a letter requesting the gallery's terms of exhibiting'.* Commission of 40% is taken on sales.

Access: **[F]** Buses 18,28,31,36,52 10 mins; Underground Westbourne Park

Westminster Boating Base

Recently opened, this gallery space intends to exhibit a wide variety of the visual arts. [VA,Ph,Cr]

Address: 136 Grosvenor Road, Dinorvic Wharf, London SW1V 3JY tel 01 821 7389

Contact: Director Robin Turner

Open: Daily 10-10

Policy: The gallery uses revenue from exhibitions to support the registered charitable work of the base.

Sales: Sales referred to exhibitor

The Space: Gallery one 10x7m, gallery two 11x4m both rooms with 40m linear hanging space. Outdoor terraces can also be used. The gallery is also used for lectures, business seminars, meetings and weddings.

Exhibiting: **[AW]** Apply to Robin Turner. Gallery is for hire at £250 per weekday, £350 at weekends. Hire fees are negotiable to charities.

Access: **[X]** Buses 2,22a,24,26; BR Victoria 15 mins; Underground Pimlico 2 mins

Westminster Library Service

The headquarters of the City of Westminster's Department of Leisure which includes the Library Service which has various exhibition spaces within 14 libraries.

Address: PO Box 240, Westminster City Hall, Victoria Street, London SW1E 6QP tel 01 798 2453

Contact: City Librarian P F Cox

Westside Gallery

This newly-opened commercial gallery shows work in a variety of media and styles. Exhibitions normally run for three weeks and there is a changing display of work for sale. [VA,Ph,Cr]

Address: 317 Upper Richmond Road West, East Sheen, London SW14 8QR tel 01 876 5315

Contact: Director Shelagh Gould

Open: Mon-Sat 9.30-5.30

Policy: To promote contemporary art.

Sales: Work sold; Credit card

The Space: Exhibition area approximately 13m, there is also a coffee bar and basement area. Gallery plans available.

Exhibiting: **[AW]** Apply in writing or in person to Shelagh Gould. Gallery finances insurance, printing of publicity, catalogue/card and preview costs. Commission 40%.

Access: **[F]** Buses 33, 37; BR Mortlake, Barnes 10 mins; Underground East Putney, Richmond and short bus ride

Whitechapel Art Gallery

The gallery, which is a registered charity, shows temporary exhibitions of modern and contemporary art. [VA,Ph,Cr,Fi,Vi,LA]

Address: 80-82 Whitechapel High Street, London E1 7QX tel 01 377 0107

Contact: Director Catherine Lampert

Open: Tues, Thurs-Sun 11-5, Wed 11-8

Policy: The gallery aims *'to increase people's awareness and enjoyment of modern and contemporary art'* through a programme which includes exhibitions by major artists, with smaller exhibitions of young British artists and exhibitions of *'particular interest to the local community'*. The gallery holds an annual open exhibition of local artists' work and organises small exhibitions in local venues. An extensive programme of events includes talks and lectures which relate to the exhibitions, workshops for local schools and community groups and an *'artists in schools'* scheme.

Sales: Work sold

The Space: Three gallery spaces 26x12x6m, 27x8x6m and 12x4x5m with a combined linear hanging space of 161m are lit by natural light, halogen spots and UV filtered fluorescent strips with automatically adjusting exterior louvered blinds. Environmental controls include air conditioning and temperature and humidity controls. Weight of work is limited to three tons in the two upper galleries. Gallery plans are available and the spaces are occasionally used for dance and performance events.

Exhibiting: **[AW]** Send slides, CV with a covering letter to Paul Bonaventura, Senior Exhibitions Co-ordinator. Costs of insurance, printing and mailing of publicity, catalogue/card, list of exhibits, preview, display and transport are covered and 10-20% commission is taken on sales. Few exhibitions are selected from applications.

Access: **[U][T][L][F]** Buses 10,25,225,253; Underground Aldgate East; Car park 5 mins

Whitechapel Library

Exhibition space in a public library.

Address: Whitechapel High Street, London E1 7QX tel 01 247 5272

Contact: Neighbourhood Librarian

Open: Mon,Tues,Thurs 9-8, Wed,Fri 9-6, Sat 9.30-12.30 & 1.30-5

Policy: See also Tower Hamlets Library Service.

Access: Buses 5,10,15,22a,25,40,67,78,225,253; Underground Aldgate East

William Morris Gallery

Alongside a permanent display of Pre-Raphaelite work, this gallery exhibits the work of contemporary artists and makers. [Pa]

Address: Lloyd Park, Forrest Road, Walthamstow, London E17 4PP tel 01 527 5544 ext 4390

Contact: Keeper Norah Gillow

Open: Tues-Sat 10-1, 2-5; First Sun in the month 10-12, 2-5; Closed Mon and bank holidays

Policy: The main aim of the gallery is to promote the work of William Morris and the Pre-Raphaelite movement. However the gallery is committed to staging at least one exhibition of contemporary work each year. The gallery favours local artists from the East End of London, although budgets for the forseeable future have been curtailed. Artists residencies, talks and workshops accompany exhibitions when possible.

Sales: Sales referred to exhibitor

The Space: 5x5x2.5m high with lighting by spots and a

comprehensive security system. Front lawn available for use. Showcases and gallery plans available.

Exhibiting: Artists should not make applications for the forseeable future.

Access: [S] Ramp for entrance **[X] First floor. Buses 34, 69, 97A, 123; BR Walthamstow Central 13 min; Underground Blackhorse Road; Public car park 1 min**

William Weston Gallery

A commercial gallery specialising in 19th, early 20th century and contemporary drawings, etchings and lithographs. [Pr]

Address: 7 Royal Arcade, Albemarle Street, London W1X 3HD tel 01 493 0722

Contact: Director

Open: Mon-Fri 10-6, Sat 10.30-1

Policy: Around five exhibitions a year are held.

Access: Buses 3,6,9,12,13,14,14a,15,19,22,22b,38,53, 88,159; Underground Piccadilly Circus

Wimbledon Library Exhibitions Room

Exhibition space created from old reference library, work being displayed on original shelving. [VA]

Address: Hill Road, Wimbledon, London SW19 tel 01 946 7432, 01 543 2222

Contact: P Parker

Open: Mon,Tues,Thurs,Fri 9-7, Wed,Sat 9-5

Sales: Work sold

The Space: Room 6x9m; fluorescent and natural light.

Exhibiting: [AW] Venue only contributes to the cost of publicity and there is a hire charge for the room.

Access: Buses 93,200; BR & Underground Wimbledon

Wine Gallery

A wine bar, restaurant and art gallery. [VA]

Address: 49 Hollywood Road, London SW10 tel 01 352 7572

Contact: Director

Policy: The gallery specialises in the promotion of local artists. Also at 232 Brompton Road, London SW3 tel 01 584 3493 and 294 Westbourne Grove, London W11 tel 01 299 1877.

Access: Buses 14,31

Wiseman Originals

This commercial gallery deals in contemporary limited edition original prints in group shows. [Pr]

Address: 34 West Square, London SE11 4SP tel 01 587 0747

Contact: Caroline Wiseman

Open: By appointment

Policy: The aim of the gallery is to enlarge the size of the market for contemporary art, and to reach *'the professional person with a disposable income'*. All works exhibited are of a varied and colourful nature, and works accepted should be *'appropriate to the style of the contemporary furnishings of our target group', or alternatively be suitable for offices. The gallery organises a series of exhibitions at London venues as* well as producing a mail-order catalogue.

Sales: Work sold

The Space: Exhibitions held at different venues.

Exhibiting: [AW] Apply in writing or by telephone to make an appointment. Gallery finances insurance, printing and mail-out of publicity, catalogue/card, preview, display and transport costs. Commission variable.

Access: [S]

Wood Green Central Library

An exhibition space in a library showing temporary exhibitions of contemporary art. [VA]

Address: High Road, London N22 6XD tel 01 888 1292

Contact: Area Librarian Richard Munro

Open: Mon-Thurs 9.30-8, Fri & Sat 9.30-5

Policy: Priority is given to work by local artists, and/or exhibitors of particular relevance to the local community.

The Space: This is a self-contained purpose-built gallery, about 16x8m within the library. There are also some smaller display areas.

Exhibiting: [AW] Contact Area Librarian.

Access: [L] Buses; Underground Wood Green; BR Alexandra Palace

Woodlands Art Gallery

This gallery exhibits a range of contemporary art work, mostly painting, tending towards 'new art' styles. [VA,Ph,Cr]

Address: 90 Mycenae Road, Blackheath, London SE3 7SE tel 01 858 4631

Contact: Exhibitions Organiser John C Bunston

Open: Mon-Fri 10-7.30, Sat 10-6, Sun 2-6; Closed Weds

Woodlands Art Gallery: 'Casting off the masks' by Elizabeth Lyons, oil on canvas, 42"x36", 1987

Policy: Most forms of art and craft are considered for exhibitions. Occasionally, groups are invited to exhibit by the selection committee.
Sales: Work sold
The Space: Four rooms approximately 5x6m, 6x10m, 7x8m and 5x8m, each room 3m high. Hanging is by adjustable rods with fluorescent lighting throughout. Gallery plans available.
Exhibiting: [AW] In the first instance, applicants should write to the gallery to get their name on file. They will then be contacted when selection meetings are due to take place and given a date to submit material for consideration. Gallery finances insurance, printing and mail-out of publicity, catalogue/card and list of exhibits. Commission 20% plus VAT.
Access: [S] Buses 53,54,75,108,286; BR Westcombe Park

Woolwich Pottery

Gallery in pottery workshops showing and selling work from Woolwich Pottery (stoneware and terra cotta), some photography included. [Ce,Ph]
Address: 2a Parry Place, London SE18 6AN tel 01 855 1871
Contact: Proprietor Philip Stanbridge
Open: Wed-Sat 10-5; closed Jan
Policy: *'If it's not good enough to take home and use it's not good enough for someone to pay money for.'*
Sales: Work sold
The Space: 4x3m display area and shelving.
Exhibiting: The display space can be hired at certain times of the year, price on application.
Access: [F] BR Woolwich Arsenal 2 mins

Woolwich Pottery: lidded jar, reduced stoneware with dry ash glaze, 140mm high

Wren Café Gallery

The gallery, part of St James Church, has a busy varied programme for an extensive passing audience in Piccadilly. [Pa,Pr,Dr,Ph,Cr]
Address: 35 Jermyn Street, London SW1Y 6DT tel 01 437 9419
Contact: Arts Administrator Jacqueline Campbell, 197 The Rectory, Piccadilly, London SW1Y tel 01 734 4511
Open: Mon-Sat 8-9, Sun 10-5
Policy: The gallery mounts about 13 exhibitions a year, all by living artists, ten of them solo shows. It is open to all artists whose work is wall mounted, from the enthusiastic amateur to students and professionals. The only firm rule is that the work should not put people off their lunch!
Sales: Work sold; Credit card
The Space: Large semi-conventional hanging space with mezzanine. Gallery plans are available.
Exhibiting: [AW] Artists should send information and slides to the Arts Administrator. The gallery can be hired at a charge of £150 for three weeks and the gallery pays for insurance, a list of exhibits and mailing of publicity. No commission charged.
Access: [F] Underground Piccadilly 3 mins; Buses 22,11,38

Wyllie Gallery

Commercial gallery dealing in and showing 19th and 20th Century and contemporary Marine paintings and prints. [Pa,Pr]
Address: 12 Needham Road, London W11 2RP tel 01 727 0606
Contact: John Wyllie
Open: Mon-Fri 9-6, Sat 10-2
Policy: The gallery specialises in the work of the Wyllie family from the 19th century onwards as well as showing the work of contemporary Marine Artists. It holds four mixed exhibitions a year of varying length, including an annual exhibition in November/ December; it also holds shows at Cowes, Bosham, Seaview and Bembridge.
The Space: The gallery has two floors and a garden, suitable for accommodating small works.
Exhibiting: Commission of 30% is taken on sales.
Access: [F] Underground 8 mins, Car park outside

Young Unknowns Gallery

Artist-run gallery, 'a unique showcase for art and design in any medium by artists of all ages.' [VA,Cr]
Address: 82 The Cut, London SE1 8LW tel 01 928 3415
Contact: Peter Sylveire & Maeve O'Brien
Open: Mon-Fri 12-7.30, Sat 10-3
Policy: *'To avoid personality cults and to establish common ground with the public, the gallery exhibits work in many themes, media and of a reasonable price range for any pocket.'* Gallery shows monthly exhibitions of featured artists and an on-going exhibition of unselected small works (A4U - Art for You].
Sales: Work sold
Exhibiting: [AW] Ideas for exhibitions always welcome. Commission is 33.3% featured artists and group shows, 25% Art for You submissions.

Access: BR & Underground Waterloo

Zamana Gallery

A cultural centre showing art and architecture of the third world. The chief sponsor is His Highness The Aga Khan. [Pa,Dr,Ph,Cr,LA]

Address: 1 Cromwell Gardens, London SW7 2SL tel 01 584 6612
Contact: Artistic Director Jane De'Athe
Open: Tues-Sat 10-5.30. Sun 12-5.30, Closed Mon
Policy: The gallery aims to *'improve understanding in the West of the arts and cultures of Asia and Africa, with an emphasis on the Islamic world'; it 'was conceived as a window through which can be viewed the rapidly changing cultures of the Third World'.* Each year four exhibitions are held lasting between eight and eleven weeks; shows include painting, drawing, photography, crafts and textiles. A programme of lectures and workshops relating to the shows are held, as well as musical evenings.
Sales: Work sold; Credit card at least one exhibition a year is a selling exhibition
The Space: The space 200x216.75m is air conditioned and has ceiling track lighting.
Exhibiting: [AW] Applications welcome, write to the Artistic Director.
Access: [U][T][L] Buses 14,30,45,49,74; Underground South Kensington

Zebra One Gallery

Regular exhibitions of contemporary work.

Address: Perrins Court, Hampstead, London NW3 tel 01 794 1281
Contact: Director
Open: Tues-Sat 10-6, Fri 10-7

Zella 9 Art Gallery

Gallery showing continuous mixed exhibitions of limited edition prints by British printmakers. [Pr]

Address: 2 Park Walk, London SW10 tel 01 351 0588
Contact: Director Mozella Gore
Open: Mon-Sun 10-9
Policy: Shows enormous variety of prints from major names to unknowns, from six pounds to five hundred pounds in price.
Sales: Work sold
Exhibiting: [AW] Work of professional nature can be submitted for sale, contact gallery for details.
Access: Off Kings Road

Long Buckby (Northamptonshire)

(EMA) Map5 SP66

Long Buckby Library

See Northamptonshire Libraries. [VA,Ph,Cr]

Address: Station Road, Long Buckby, Daventry, Northamptonshire NN6 7QB tel 0327 842796
Contact: District Librarian Ian Clarke, Daventry Library, North Street, Daventry, Northamptonshire tel 0327 703130
Open: Tues, Fri 10-1, 2-5, 5.30-7, Wed 2-5; closed Mon,Thurs,Sat
Sales: Work sold
The Space: The space has 3m linear hanging space on wall, plus 13m on screens. Track lighting, supervision from counter.
Exhibiting: [AW] District Librarian. Publicity and insurance provided, transport between libraries arranged for touring exhibitions. Commission is 10%.
Access: [F] BR Daventry 5 mins; Small car park

Long Eaton (Nottinghamshire)

(EMA) Map5 SK43

Chatsworth Centre

The home of Long Eaton District Arts Council promoting the visual arts, crafts and theatre. [Pa,Pr,Dr,Ph,Cr]

Address: West Gate, Long Eaton, Nottingham NG10 1EF tel 0602 729195
Contact: Director John Barker
Open: Mon-Sat 10-4
Policy: The small Studio Gallery is used to *'promote the work of local artists, photographers, and makers'* and is part of a theatre, community centre, art centre complex. Saturdays are used for demonstrations and sales of work.
Sales: Sales referred to exhibitor
The Space: The hanging space is 30x2m with two island displays and a showcase.
Exhibiting: [AW] Contact the Director. The centre provides insurance, publicity, mailing and a list of exhibits.
Access: [X] Car park on site

Loughborough (Leicestershire)

(EMA) Map5 SK51

East Midlands Exhibitions

A regional touring exhibition service run by East Midlands Arts aimed at non-gallery venues. [VA,Cr,Ph]

Address: Mountfields House, Forest Road, Loughborough LE11 3HU tel 0509 218292
Contact: Exhibition Co-ordinator
Policy: Small-scale exhibitions of work by regional artists and makers are produced for the extensive network of non-gallery venues in the East Midlands. The service works closely with the local authorities in providing high-quality, accessible exhibitions for new audiences, and training for venue staff. Craft exhibitions are usually accompanied by a professionally-made video of the maker, and venues are encouraged to arrange workshops or talks to accompany the exhibitions.
Sales: Work sold; Credit scheme
The Space: Various sizes and equipment available. All venues are selected for suitability. Specially-designed showcases and video cases used in conjunction with craft shows.
Exhibiting: Exhibitors are selected from the unrestricted Art Index held at East Midlands Arts. All costs in

mounting the exhibition are provided by the service. A commission of 15% is charged on sales. Fees for non-gallery tours are currently under review. Supports EPR.

Loughborough College of Art and Design

A foyer gallery in the entrance of the fine art department and the main foyer of the college. [VA,Ph,Cr]

Address: Radmoor, Loughborough, Leicestershire LE11 3BT tel 0509 261515
Contact: Pete Wheeler
Open: Mon-Fri 10-5
Policy: A wide range of exhibitions are shown primarily for *'educational reasons'* including exhibitions, thematic, solo and touring exhibitions.
Sales: Work sold
The Space: Main foyer 30m linear hanging space and fine art foyer 40m linear hanging space. Both areas are purpose-built with spot lighting.
Exhibiting: [AW] Contact Pete Wheeler. The college provides a poster, transport and list of exhibits.
Access: [F] Car park on site; 15 mins town centre; 25 mins BR Loughborough

Loughton (Essex)

(EA) Map7 TQ49

Loughton Library

Exhibition space in public library, available for hire. [VA,Cr]

Address: Traps Hill, Loughton, Essex IG10 1HD tel 01 502 0181/2
Contact: Daphne Powell
Open: Mon,Tues, Wed, Fri 9-7.30 Sat 9-5
Sales: Work sold; Sales referred to exhibitor
The Space: The floor area is 33.48 square metres and nine display cases are available.
Access: [L][F]

Lowestoft (Suffolk)

(EA) Map7 TM59

Area Library Service (Lowestoft)

Co-ordinates programmes in five libraries throughout North East Suffolk. [VA,Cr,Ph]

Address: Central Library, Clapham Road, Lowestoft, Suffolk NR32 1DR tel 0502 566325
Contact: Area Service Manager (Lowestoft), D Wallace. Lowestoft: Secretary's Office, Central Library, tel 0502 566325 ext 3301; Beccles and all other libraries: Acting Divisional Librarian, Beccles Library tel 0502 714073
Sales: Work sold; Sales referred to exhibitor
The Space: Aldeburgh: space available for up to three 1.83x1.83m free-standing screens; Beccles: seven double-sided hessian-covered screens 1.83x1.22m available; Framlingham: space for one 1.83x1.83m stand; Leiston: space for one 1.83x1.83m stand; Lowestoft: ground floor: space for 12 double-sided 1.83x1.22m hessian-covered screens, trestle tables for craft markets, small area for 1.83x1.83 stand: first floor: two lockable glass-fronted display cases 1.52m long each with three shelves, and one lockable 1.52x0.61m glass-topped display cabinet.
Exhibiting: Fee of 20% of all sales made from exhibition, subject to minimum payment of £20 payable in advance.

Lowestoft College School of Art & Design Gallery

The gallery operates within the Department of Art & Design in Lowestoft College, serving both college and local artistic needs. [VA,Ph,Cr,LA]

Address: Art Centre, Regent Road, Lowestoft, Suffolk NR32 tel 0502 83521 ext 281
Contact: Head of School of Art & Design Tony Collins tel ext 270
Open: Mon-Fri 10-4 Sat 10-12
Policy: The gallery services a local largely indigenous community in a seaside town situated at the most easterly point of the country: it is the only such facility in the area and aims to provide it with access to a broad range of visual arts practices, both popularist and challenging. Some exhibitions are supported by community arts workshops, talks and demonstrations. A total of twelve exhibitions a year, each lasting three weeks, are programmed.
Sales: Work sold; Credit card
The Space: The gallery is 2x32m with a floor area of 112 square metres; spot lighting on track; clip frames available. Gallery occasionally hired out for commercial exhibitions.
Exhibiting: [AW] Gallery covers: insurance, printing and mailing of publicity, list of exhibits, preview costs, display, transport, catalogue/card.
Access: [S] BR Lowestoft 5 mins, Bus station 2 mins; Public car parks 2 min;

Suffolk County Council Arts & Libraries

Co-ordinates activities within Suffolk Libraries, which are managed within three geographical areas. The Area Library Service for North East Suffolk, the Area Library Service for Ipswich and the Area Library Service for Bury St Edmunds, it also administers the SCILS gallery picture loan scheme. See also entries for Ipswich, Lowestoft, Bury St Edmunds, Sudbury, Newmarket and Stowmarket.

Address: Central Library, Clapham Road, Lowestoft, Suffolk NR32 1DR tel 0502 66325 ext 3300
Contact: Assistant Director, Arts & Libraries C Evans

Ludlow (Shropshire)

(WMA) Map4 SO57

Silk Top Hat Gallery

A private gallery featuring high-quality exhibitions and a changing display. [VA,Cr]

Address: 4 Quality Square, Ludlow, Shropshire SY8 1AR tel 0584 5363
Contact: Jill Howorth
Open: Mon-Sat 10-5, closed Thurs

Policy: The gallery *'shows work by selected artists using a changing programme of shows to promote particular artists or groups'*. The gallery also sells art materials, and runs a lively 'Friends' group with talks, trips, discounts on purchases and an extensive newsletter.
Sales: Work sold; Credit scheme
The Space: Three floors each 6x4.5m with a mixture of fluorescent, spots and natural light.
Exhibiting: [AW] Jill Howorth is *'always interested to see work of new artists and slides or photographs should be sent with a SAE. The gallery covers insurance, publicity, mailing, card, and preview. A commission of 33.3% is charged on sales. Supports EPR.*
Access: [X] Town centre location close to car park, BR Ludlow 5 mins

Luton (Bedfordshire)

(EA) Map7 TL02

033 Arts Centre

The gallery is used for installation and photography with two performance spaces used for 'live art' events. [Ph,LA]
Address: 33 Arts Centre, 33 Guildford Street, Luton, Bedfordshire LU1 2NQ tel 0582 419584
Contact: Exhibitions & Photography Co-ordinator Adam Geary
Open: Tues-Sat 12-6
Policy: To provide a supportive framework for artists working critically and experimentally in the areas of photography, installation and performance. Exhibiting artists will also be given the opportunity to install a site-specific work in the community. Such works will coincide with the exhibition and are regarded as being integral to exhibitions.
Sales: Sales referred to exhibitor
The Space: A gallery area overlooking town centre with good natural light and 80 square metres of hanging space, also ground floor performance space 5x10m with seating for 70 people.
Exhibiting: [AW][EF] Send proposals with documentation. All proposals should outline a specific work to be located in the community, together with ideas for workshops. Publicity, transport, expenses and insurance paid by gallery. The theatre and performance spaces can be hired (negotiable).
Access: [U][T] Town centre, rail, bus, car access

Barnfield College

Exhibition space in a college of further education.
Address: New Bedford Road, Luton, Bedfordshire LU3 2AX tel 0582 507531 ext 240
Contact: Head of School of Art & Design Mike Wrigglesworth
Open: Term-time only
Policy: Diverse selection of temporary exhibitions with around six a year.
Sales: By arrangement
The Space: A rectangular space around 10.5x4.5m which is due for refurbishment in 1989.
Exhibiting: Ask for details.
Access: [S] Two miles north of Luton centre on A6; BR Luton Midland Road

Luton Central Library

Exhibition space in a public library.
Address: Bridge Street, Luton, Bedfordshire LU1 2NG tel 0582 30161

Contact: Arts Librarian
Policy: Selection of the exhibition programme is from applications by groups or individuals, and exhibitions run for up to three weeks.
The Space: The second floor space has 40 square metres of hanging space with two lockable display cases, and the first floor space has 20 square metres shared with other library facilities. Both areas are spot lights.
Exhibiting: [AW] A small charge is made per item hung.

Luton Museum & Art Gallery

Municipal gallery and museum with a permanent collection of 18th and 19th century topographical artists. [Pa,Pr,Ph,Cr]
Address: Wardown Park, Luton, Bedfordshire LU2 7HA tel 0582 36941
Contact: Frank Hackett
Open: Mon-Sat 10-5 Sun 1-5
Policy: *'To maintain a changing exhibition of local and national artists'*. Monthly solo and group exhibitions plus two 'open' exhibitions a year. There is also a series of regular lectures.
Sales: Sales referred to exhibitor
The Space: 13x6x5m high with 38m linear, fluorescent lighting and filters on windows with blinds. Two display cases. Gallery plans available.
Exhibiting: [AW] In writing, or requesting forms for 'open' exhibitions. Gallery for hire £12, including insurance and publicity printing and mailing. No commission charged.
Access: [U][T] 1 miles north of town centre

Lutterworth (Leicestershire)

(EMA) Map5 SP58

Cedar House Craft Shop & Gallery

A commercial gallery opened in 1988 with a changing display of work and seasonal mixed exhibitions. [VA,Cr]
Address: Main Street, Peatling Pava, Nr Lutterworth, Leicestershire LE17 5QA tel 0533 478673
Contact: Jet Shackleton
Open: Thurs-Sun 12-8; Bank holidays and other times by arrangement
Policy: Solo or group exhibitions of three to four weeks duration are run alongside changing displays of contemporary crafts and fine art stocked by the gallery. Thematic exhibitions.
Sales: Work sold; Credit card
The Space: A variety of display cases and plinths with space for work including a courtyard. A further 60 square metres of wall space will be available Summer 1989. Lit by tungsten halogen spots. Gallery plans

Gallery plans available.
Exhibiting: [AW] Individuals and groups should apply to Jet Shackleton. The gallery provides publicity, preview, list of exhibits, catalogue/card. Commission is usually 33.3% or the gallery can be rented by negotiation.
Access: [F] Five miles M1 Junction 20

Lymington (Hampshire)

(SA) Map7 SZ39

Solent Gallery

A commercial gallery in Lymington, one of two owned by Harvey Bagnall (see Solent Gallery, Cowes) showing marine landscapes and wildlife paintings of particular appeal to the local yachting community. [Pa,Pr]

Address: 15 Gosport Street, Lymington, Hampshire SO41 9BG tel Owner
Contact: Harvey Bagnall
Open: Mon-Sat 9.30-5.30
Policy: The gallery intends to help artists by selling their work and shows a wide range of fine original paintings, mostly marine, wildlife and landscape paintings, with a selection of original silkscreen and limited edition prints.
Sales: Work sold; Credit card; Credit terms
The Space: The downstairs gallery is around 6.5x3x2.5m with 10m linear hanging space. The upstairs gallery is roughly the same size but a third gallery is only 2x2x2.5m with 5.4m linear hanging space and there is track spotlighting and hanging picture rails in all of them.
Exhibiting: [AW] Contact the owner to arrange to bring in examples of work or send photographs or slides. The gallery pays for insurance, printing and mailing of publicity, list of exhibits, preview costs and a catalogue or card and charges 40% commission including VAT.
Access: [U][T][F] BR Lymington station 5 mins; Buses to Southampton & Bournemouth; Car parks nearby

Cedar House Craft Shop & Gallery: Raku pot by Martin Shackleton, 4" high, 1988

Maidstone (Kent)

(SEA) Map7 TQ75

Maidstone Library Gallery

This gallery shows a broadly-based programme of exhibitions featuring national and regional touring shows as well as contemporary work by artists from London and the South East. [VA,Ph,Cr,LA]

Address: Saint Faiths Street, Maidstone, Kent ME14 1LH tel 0622 52344
Contact: Gallery Administrator David Young
Open: Mon-Fri 9.30-7, Sat 9.30-5
Policy: The gallery aims to show a balanced programme of works by locally-based artists, nationally-known artists, touring exhibitions and young unknowns. The space is suitable for most types of work and there is a growing schedule of talks, workshops and live events in the gallery. Exhibitions are geared towards meeting the needs and interests of the local community.
Sales: Work sold
The Space: 18x7x3m high with approximately 27m linear hanging space. Direct fixing by mirror plates to hessian-covered boards with natural lighting and track-mounted spots. There is also a sculpture court measuring 18x4m and an exhibition area in the foyer of the building for small-scale work, photography etc.
Exhibiting: [AW] Applications with slides or photographs to Exhibitions Organiser. Gallery finances insurance, printing and mail-out of publicity, list of exhibits and transport. Support in principle for EPR. Commission 15%.
Access: [X] Buses to town centre; BR Maidstone; Public car park 1 min

Maldon (Essex)

(EA) Map7 TL80

Oakwood Arts Centre

First-floor exhibition hall with pottery, framing, handicrafts and desk top publishing studios on ground floor and a café. [VA,Ph,Ce,Te]

Address: The Market Place, Maldon, Essex CM9 6UA tel 0621 56503
Contact: Administrator
Open: Mon-Sat 10-4
Policy: The exhibition hall is available for hire at the discretion of the centre, which will require to view a selection of the work to be exhibited. 3D work will be shown only in certain circumstances.
Sales: Work sold
The Space: 9.2x9.2m with 30.5m linear with hanging by

direct fixing and spotlighting.

Exhibiting: [AW] Exhibitions are held for weekends, weeks or months; no commission is taken and the gallery covers publicity and mailing.

Access: [X]

Malton (N Yorkshire)

(YA) Map3 SE77

Malton Library

A public library with a special display area reserved for art exhibitions. [VA,Ph,Cr]

Address: St. Michael's Street, Malton, N Yorkshire YO17 0LJ tel 0653 692714

Contact: Senior Library Assistant N Stubbs

Open: Mon-Fri 10-5, Sat 10-1, Tues & Fri 5-7, closed Thurs

Policy: The exhibitions area within the library displays work by local artists and also brings in small national touring exhibitions. There are five exhibitions shown a year and the library favours mixed media shows which last for one month.

Sales: Sales referred to exhibitor

The Space: There is one space 18x9x9m suitable for contemporary work.

Exhibiting: [AW] applications with slides should be sent to the Librarian.

Access: [F] BR Malton 4 mins; Bus station 4 mins

Manchester (Greater Manchester)

(NWA) Map3 SJ89

Castlefield Gallery

The gallery, a charitable organisation, was set up in 1984 by artists from the Manchester Artists Studio Association, to establish a venue in Manchester where contemporary art produced in Britain could be seen. [Pa,Sc,Pr,Dr]

Address: 5 Campfield Avenue Arcade, Off Deansgate, Manchester M3 4FN tel 061 832 8034

Contact: Gallery Organiser Celia Cross

Open: Tues-Sat 10-5, Sun 12-4.30; Closed Mon

Policy: The gallery is managed by a board of directors and the artistic policy is decided by a committee of artists from MASA with the day-to-day administration carried out by the Gallery Organiser. It aims to show the work of national and lesser-known artists but with particular emphasis on supporting regional artists. The exhibition programme aims to be of wide appeal and to reflect Britain's multi-cultural society, thereby including artists who work in a non-Western tradition. The gallery views education as playing a vital role and aims to organise events for all ages and social groups. The gallery also runs an 'Art Rack' of work for sale by local artists.

Sales: Work sold

The Space: The ground floor has 25m linear hanging space with lighting through two large windows and spots. The basement gallery has 20m linear hanging space and is lit by fluorescent and spot lighting. This space has a humidifer. Hanging is by mirror plating. Gallery plans are available.

Exhibiting: [AW] Send up to ten slides and CV to the Gallery Organiser. 30% commission on exhibitions and 15% Art Rack sales. The gallery will pay for insurance, transport, publicity, preview costs. Supports EPR.

Access: [S] ground floor, **[X]** basement. BR Deansgate 2 mins; Piccadilly and Victoria 20 mins; Bus station 15 mins; On numerous city centre bus routes; Car parking 2 mins

Colin Jellicoe Gallery

A private gallery which shows the work of Colin Jellicoe and 51 gallery artists who have work permanently in the gallery. [Pa,Pr,Dr,Sc,Ce]

Address: 82 Portland Street, Manchester, Greater Manchester M1 4QX tel 061 236 2716

Contact: Director Colin Jellicoe

Open: Mon-Fri 11-5, Sat 1-5

Policy: *'The gallery is not limited to specialist themes but over the years themes have emerged: landscape, townscape, traditional and modern figures and non-figurative work'.* The artists who have works permanently in the gallery are shown in mixed, group and solo shows. A new artist's work is first shown in mixed exhibitions before major ones are considered. Framing service available.

Sales: Work sold

The Space: The gallery is about 137 square metres and has 18.28m of linear hanging space with hanging by hooks and spotlights. Pictures should not exceed 1.82x1.82m.

Exhibiting: [AW] Applications are welcome anytime and should include SAE, slides or good colour photographs. If you wish to come in person make an appointment with Colin Jellicoe. Regular gallery artists pay a small hire fee and expenses if they arrange a show. Commission of 33.3% is taken on sales.

Access: [X] BR Piccadilly 5mins; Oxford Road 10mins; Victoria 10mins; Near many bus routes

Cornerhouse (Greater Manchester Film & Exhibition Centre

Cornerhouse is a visual arts centre comprising three art galleries, three cinemas, a bookshop, bar and café. [VA,Pr,Ph,Cr,De,LA]

Colin Jellicoe Gallery: On the left changing show by gallery artists, on the right paintings by Colin Jellicoe.

Address: 70 Oxford Street, Manchester M1 5NH tel 061 228 7621
Contact: Exhibitions Director Gerald Deslandes,
Open: Tues-Sun 12-8
Policy: The 1988 programme included 19 exhibitions, two of which have toured, 14 were organised by Cornerhouse whose policy is to make accessible and provide insight into all aspects of contemporary art and design for as wide an audience as possible. The programme includes thematic and issue-based shows as well as solo exhibitions. It has a lively education programme which is aimed at people of all ages.
Sales: Work sold; Credit scheme
The Space: Gallery 1 measures 12.19x7.62x2.74m. Gallery 215.84x7.62x2.74m and Gallery 3 20.72x7.62x4.87m with total linear hanging space of 45.57m, 42.26m and 54.48m respectively.
Exhibiting: [AW][EF] Applications from groups or individuals should be sent to the Exhibitions Director, and should include slides or photographs with CV and SAE. The gallery pays for insurance, printing, publicity display, private view, transport, mailing, catalogue and artist's expenses. Commission of 20% is charged on sales. Supports EPR. Cornerhouse is full committed to policies of equal opportunity.
Access: [U][T][L][F] BR Oxford Road Station 2 mins; Car park 2 mins; About 20 bus routes serving South Manchester pass Cornerhouse

Craft Centre

A commercial gallery within the Royal Exchange Theatre established in 1981, on the Crafts Council selected list and showing a wide range of contemporary crafts. [Cr]

Address: Royal Exchange Theatre, St Ann's Square, Manchester M2 7DM tel 061 833 9333
Contact: Manager Morag Shaw
Open: Mon,Tues,Thurs 11-7.30, Wed 11-2.30, Fri 11-8, Sat 11-4
Policy: *'The centre was established to promote the best of British crafts. We aim to give as broad a view of crafts as possible, giving our audience the opportunity to see groups of work that because of its style or price would not usually be purchased as stock. As well as staging exhibitions, of which there are six a year, there is a constant stock of ceramics, glass, textiles, wood and jewellery. We hope that there is always stock available for all ages and tastes. The centre recognises the importance of an education programme and since 1986 has organised events in schools, colleges and within community groups to help promote awareness and enjoyment of contempory crafts.'.*
Sales: Work sold; Credit card
The Space: Hanging space is limited and exhibitions are displayed in a set of free-standing shelves measuring 60x1.2m and front window display measuring 60x2.13m. Other display cases are also available.
Exhibiting: The centre pays for printing, publicity, list of exhibits and preview costs. 50%-77% commission is taken on sales.
Access: [U][T][L] BR Victoria and Piccadilly 15 mins; 20 bus routes pass outside; 5 car parks nearby

Crumpsall Library

A public gallery situated within a large recreational and educational complex. [Pa,Sc,Ph,LA]

Address: Abraham Moss Centre, Crescent Road, Crumpsall, Manchester M8 6UF tel 061 721 4555
Contact: Senior Librarian Paul Martin
Open: Closed Thurs
Policy: *'We welcome the exhibition of art and craft work on a no-cost basis, especially where the work is from local people. The library is particularly appropriate for exhibitions of students' work as it is situated centrally in North Manchester Community College. We would particularly welcome exhibitions that reflect the local multi-ethnic community.'*
Sales: Sales referred to exhibitor
The Space: Space adaptable depending on exhibition.
Exhibiting: [AW] Contact Paul Martin. The library pays for insurance and any other expenses are negotiable.
Access: [U][T][L][F] Large car park, BR nearby, frequent bus service

Fletcher Moss Art Gallery

A 19th century parsonage that contains local history displays and collections of locally-made furniture, glass and ceramics. [VA]

Address: The Old Parsonage, Wilmslow Road, Didsbury, Manchester M14 tel 061 236 9422
Open: Daily 10-6, Sun 2-6; Closed Tues Apr-Sept; Subject to alterations
Policy: Shows 20th century paintings from the collection and may show from 1989 photographic exhibitions.

Ginnel

A commercial art gallery established in 1977, generally shows twelve exhibitions a year, all of work by living artists, plus a changing display of work for sale. [Pa,Sc,Dr]

Address: Lloyd Street, Manchester, Greater Manchester M2 5ND tel 833 9037
Contact: Keith Mottershead
Open: Mon-Fri 9.30-5.30 or by appointment
Policy: The gallery moved to Manchester six years ago. *'The type of painting now sold is more broadly based with the emphasis being on quality of work rather than subject matter. Our aim is to show original works at prices acceptable to the general public and businesses of between £100 to £5000'.*
Sales: Work sold; Credit card; Credit scheme
The Space: The gallery is available for hire and is lit by spotlights.
Exhibiting: [AW] Applications to exhibit should be sent to J K or I S Mottershead. The gallery pays for printing of publicity, list of exhibits, preview costs, mailing and catalogue. 40% commission is charged on sales.
Access: BR Victoria 10 mins; Piccadilly 10 mins; Bus station 6 mins

Green Room

An important venue in the North West for the promotion and programming of live art events and performance. [LA]

Address: 54-56 Whitworth Street West, Manchester M1 5WW tel 061 236 1676

Policy: A venue for performing arts with an emphasis on new and innovative work including performance and live art. It also acts as a resource supporting and advising groups and individuals working in the field.

The Space: The venue, which is built into a railway arch, has a 170-seat auditorium, bar, cafe and also studio space for classes and workshops.

Exhibiting: [AW] Applications are welcome.

Hacienda Club

A city centre night club which shows a number of exhibitions and live art works as part of its programme. [Pa,Ph,De,LA]

Address: 11-13 Whitworth Street, Manchester M1 5WG tel 091 236 5051

Contact: Promotions Manager Paul Cons

Open: Wed-Sat 9pm-2am

Policy: The club responds to *'interesting ideas'* for exhibitions, installations and performances which are designed to work at night and in a night club situation. It also occasionally commissions temporary installations or sculptures.

Sales: Sales referred to exhibitor

The Space: The club is a large warehouse with theatre lighting and capacity for 1200 people.

Exhibiting: [AW] Contact Paul Cons. The club may contribute to the costs of exhibitions or performances and sometimes commissions the work. Technical assistance available.

Access: [S] City centre site; BR Manchester Piccadilly 10 mins

Horniman Bar, Library Theatre

Primarily a theatre with a small gallery in the bar area which is used to show the work of local artists during the theatre season of September to June. [Pa,Pr,Dr,Ph]

Address: St Peters Square, Manchester M2 5PD tel 061 228 3982

Contact: General Manager Deirdre Candlin

Open: 9am-10pm during performances, otherwise 9-5

Sales: Work sold

The Space: The gallery has 20m linear hanging space, with hooks and cord used to hang pictures and spot lighting.

Exhibiting: [AW] Applications should be made by telephone or in writing to the General Manager. The theatre pays for insurance and list of exhibits and takes 5% commission on sales.

Access: [L][F] BR Victoria and Piccadilly 10 mins; Bus station 5 mins; Car park 2 mins

Malcolm Bishop

Commercial gallery specialising in graphics. [Pr]

Address: 228-232 Wilmslow Road, Fallowfield, Manchester M14 tel 061 224 5433

Contact: Director Malcolm Bishop

Open: Mon-Sat 9-5.30, Wed 9-1

Policy: Changing display of work mainly of fine graphics from British and American artists.

Manchester City Art Galleries

A municipal gallery founded in 1823 and run by Manchester County Council with permanent collections of paintings, drawing and sculpture housed in Greek revival building and a diverse and dynamic range of exhibitions and programme of educational events in the gallery and in the community. [VA,LA]

Address: Moseley Street/Princess Street, Manchester M2 3JL tel 061 236 9422

Contact: Director Julian Spalding

Open: Mon-Sat 10-6, Sun 2-6

Policy: During the past twelve months, the gallery's programme included twelve exhibitions that showed the work of living artists. The programme is extremely varied ranging from automata to video art. It aims to cover all aspects of contemporary art, targetting as wide an audience as possible.

Sales: Work sold

The Space: The Athenaeum in Princess Street has 52 movable screens measuring 3.35x1.22m plus 5m wall space and approximately 98m hanging space. Full gallery lighting system and environmental controls. Maximum access 1x2.65.

Exhibiting: [AW] Applications should be sent to Howard Smith, Keeper of Exhibitions, City Art Gallery. No commission is taken.

Access: [L] on request **[X]** BR Victoria and Piccadilly 15 mins; Bus station 3 mins; Car park nearby

Manchester Polytechnic (Holden Gallery)

A gallery within the Art and Design Faculty of Manchester Polytechnic which runs at least ten exhibitions a year. [VA,Ph]

Address: Grosvenor Building, Manchester Polytechnic, Cavendish, All Saints, Manchester M15 6BR tel 061 228 6171 ext 2277

Contact: Mike Mason

Open: Mon-Fri 10-6 term time only

Policy: *'Our basic aim is to show work which relates to our academic programme which is wide ranging. We particularly support work of young or emerging artists in both fine art and craft work. The gallery has a collection of craftwork which is often on show, of particular note is the glassware which includes Tiffany and Whitefriars.*

Sales: Sales referred to exhibitor

The Space: 121.92m linear hanging space is available plus 20 show cases for craftwork. The maximum size painting that can be accommodated is 2.13m and for sculpture is 1.98 x 1.82m (larger if sectional).

Exhibiting: [AW][EF] Applications are welcome anytime from individuals or two joint exhibitors but not groups. The gallery pays for insurance, publicity, list of exhibits, display, transport, mailing and occasionally artists' expenses. Supports EPR.

Access: [X] BR Oxford Road 5 mins; Piccadilly 30 mins; Near bus route

Manchester Polytechnic (Righton Gallery)

The gallery is part of Manchester Polytechnic, administered by the Department of History of Art & Design but also used for exhibitions organised by different departments and by outside bodies. [VA]

Address: Department of History of Art & Design, Manchester Polytechnic, Righton Building, Cavendish Street, Manchester M15 6BG tel 061 228 6171 ext 2555

Contact: Head of Department D Donald

Open: Mon-Thurs 9-5.30, Fri 9-4.30

Policy: The gallery specialises in exhibitions which place art in a social, political or historical context and can be used in teaching. Of the eight exhibitions shown in the last twelve months, half were the work of living artists and designers and the faculty is a prime user. The target audience is the general public, particularly from the North West area and the very large staff and student population of the polytechnic and university. A more ambitious programme will be embarked upon now the security has been improved, and touring exhibitions from the Arts Council and other galleries can be taken. The polytechnic has a collection of works of design mainly 19th and 20th Century but not housed in this gallery.

Sales: Sales referred to exhibitor

The Space: Overall floor space is 290x150m and with screens, the linear hanging space is up to 540m. The space is available for hire and the fee is negotiable.

Exhibiting: [AW] Send applications to D Donald. Outside exhibitors must normally finance publicity, preview costs, lists of exhibits, display, mailing and catalogue. No commission is taken.

Access: [U][T][F] BR 20 mins; Car parks nearby; On main bus route to South Manchester

Portico Gallery

Portico gallery, established in 1965 and part of the Portico Library, a listed grade 2 building, shows an average of eleven exhibitions a year. [VA]

Address: 57 Mosley Street, entrance in Charlotte Street, Manchester, Greater Manchester M2 3HY tel 061 236 6785

Contact: Exhibitions Organiser

Open: Mon-Fri 9.30-4.30; occasional Thurs evening and Sat openings

Policy: Portico Library, founded in 1806 is a private subscription library, used as a lending library and club by members and for research by non-members. It also runs a literary prize and is used by organisations and small groups for meetings etc. The gallery aims to show a wide variety of painting, printmaking, photography, crafts and sculpture from established and not-so-established artists and makers working today. *'We have a Northern bias and show work which could be described as easily accessible to the general public'.* The gallery plans to hold one exhibition a year on 'Book Arts', ie book binding illustration or fine artists using methods associated with and about books. Artists give talks and demonstrations in conjunction with the exhibition programme.

Sales: Work sold

The Space: The gallery, situated in the centre of the library, measures 11.57x11.57m with an additional 40 panels in the form of 20 double-sided pairs of screens which can be arranged in various positions, also four cases which measure 1.01x44x36m. Fixing is by hooks and nails and there is some natural light which is supplemented by spot lighting. The gallery can accommodate pictures up to 1.45x87m.

Exhibiting: [AW] Applications should include six slides, relevant details and SAE to the Exhibitions Organiser. The gallery will pay for insurance, publicity, list of exhibits, preview costs, mailing and catalogue.

Access: [X] BR Piccadilly 5 mins; Victoria 20 mins; Bus stop 5 mins; Parking 3 mins

Portland Gallery

A private gallery showing regular exhibitions of art and ceramics. [VA]

Address: 120 Portland Street, Manchester M1 4PS tel 061 236 6153

Contact: Anton Gordon

Open: Daily 9.30-5.30, Sat 10-5

Royal Northern College of Music

[Pa,Sc,Cr,Ph]

Address: 124 Oxford Road, Manchester M13 9RD tel 061 273 6283 ext 280

Righton Gallery, Manchester Polytechnic

Portico Gallery

Contact: Exhibitions Organiser Philip Jones
Open: Daily 10-10
Policy: A programme of six-week exhibitions running September to July.
Exhibiting: Work is chosen by an exhibition committee.

Whitworth Art Gallery

A university gallery founded in 1889, which houses permanent collections consisting of fine and applied arts, including British drawings, old master prints, contemporary art, textiles and wallpaper. [VA,487079Cr]

Address: University of Manchester, Oxford Road, Manchester M15 6ER tel 061 273 4865
Contact: Exhibitions Officer J Tomlin
Open: Mon-Sat 10-5, Thurs 10-9
Policy: The gallery shows five or six exhibitions each year lasting for six to eight weeks. One exhibition each year is organised by the staff and students of the Art Gallery and Museum Studies course at the University of Manchester . The 'Whitworth Young Contemporaries', the national exhibition for art students, is held every other year. The programme is mixed with most exhibitions coming from the South Bank Centre and other galleries, although the gallery originates major exhibitions.
The Space: Two air-conditioned galleries are available each 24x9m with around 200m linear hanging space and hanging from central line and picture rail, hanging screens and spot and fluorescent lights. Exhibiting space for sculpture is also available in the grounds. Standard Edmunds upright and table cases available. Gallery plans available.
Exhibiting: [AW] The gallery welcomes applications by post with full supporting material. The gallery covers transport, insurance, publicity, preview and display costs, transport, catalogue and artists expenses.
Access: [L][F] Buses 40-45,157,191,P11,B5,B6; BR Oxford Road 20 mins; Car park

Mansfield (Nottinghamshire)

(EMA) Map5 SK56

Mansfield Community Arts Centre

A community arts centre largely funded by the county council. [VA,Ph]

Address: Leeming Street, Mansfield, Nottinghamshire NG18 1NG tel 0623 653309
Contact: Director Cliff Laycock
Open: Mon-Fri 9-5, Sat 9.30-12
Policy: The exhibitions are drawn from local and regional sources as well as the arts division of the county council. The centre provides local artists an opportunity to exhibit their work to all members of the community. Workshops by exhibiting artists are encouraged, and the centre runs art classes.
Sales: Sales referred to exhibitor
The Space: The foyer is used for exhibitions and provides 10m linear hanging space.
Exhibiting: [AW] Applications should be addressed to the Director. No commission is charged, and mounting the exhibition is the responsibility of the artist.
Access: [U][T] Town centre location close to bus routes and car parks

Mansfield Library

See Nottingham Libraries. [VA,Ph,Cr]

Address: Four Seasons Centre, Westgate, Mansfield, Nottinghamshire NG18 1NH tel 0623 27591
Contact: District Librarian
Sales: Work sold; Sales referred to exhibitor
The Space: About 15m linear hanging space.
Exhibiting: [AW] Contact the District Librarian.
Access: [F]

Mansfield Museum and Art Gallery

A municipal art gallery run by Mansfield District Council, with temporary exhibitions and natural and social history displays. [VA,Ph,Cr]

Address: Leeming Street, Mansfield, Nottinghamshire NG18 1NG tel 0623 663088
Contact: Curator Elizabeth Weston
Open: Mon-Sat 10-5; closed Sat 1-2
Policy: The exhibition programme includes a wide variety of exhibitions from local and regional artists and makers, and touring exhibitions from a variety of sources. The shop sells work by local artists and makers, and occasional workshops are arranged to accompany exhibitions.
Sales: Work sold
The Space: The gallery is 16x9m with track lighting and direct fixing. Four Edmunds showcases available.
Exhibiting: [AW] Write to the Curator with full details including costings. The gallery charges 15% commission on sales and provides insurance, publicity, display and occasionally a fee.
Access: [F] Town centre car parks and bus station 5 mins

West Nottinghamshire College

The gallery is housed in the Art and Design department of the college which offers full-time further education courses and other part-time courses. [Pa,Pr,Dr,Ph,Cr,De]

Address: Chesterfield Road South, Mansfield, Nottinghamshire NG18 5BH tel 0623 27191
Contact: Head of Art and Design Chris Craggs,
Open: Mon-Thurs 9-9, Fri 9-5
Policy: The wide-ranging programme features solo shows, touring exhibitions and student exhibitions.
Sales: Work sold; Sales referred to exhibitor
The Space: 175m linear of corridor space, unsuitable for large three-dimensional work, with direct fixing and good lighting. One large showcase is available. Gallery plans available.
Exhibiting: [AW] Contact the Head of Art and Design. The college provides insurance, publicity, mailing and preview. EPR supported.
Access: [F] Close to town centre; Car park 3 mins

March (Cambridgeshire)

(EA) Map5 TL49

March District Library

Exhibition space in a public library. [Pa,Ph,Cr]

Address: Gordon Avenue, March, Cambridgeshire PE15 8LT tel 035 42 53349
Contact: District Librarian John Stephens
Open: Mon & Fri 10-7 Wed-Thurs 10-6 Sat 9.30-5
Policy: Mainly local and amateur artists shown.
Sales: Work sold
The Space: The two portable stands are 2x3m.
Exhibiting: **[AW]** Apply to Librarian. Commission charged is 15%.
Access: **[U][T]**

Margate (Kent)

(SEA) Map7 TR37

Margate Library Gallery

The gallery has a broadly-based programme which features contemporary artists who have a particular relevance to the area, as well as national and regional touring shows. [VA,Ph,Cr]

Address: Central Library, Cecil Square, Margate, Kent CT9 1RE tel 084 322 3626
Contact: Group Librarian Hazel Halse
Open: Mon-Thurs 9.30-6, Fri 9.30-7, Sat 9.30-5
Policy: The gallery aims to provide a service to artists and to the general public in East Kent and to promote the work of living artists in the South East. Gallery policy is towards exhibitions that *'educate, inform and entertain'* and would not otherwise be seen in the area. The gallery's audience is drawn from a wide cross-section of residents and visitors to the area. Visual art and crafts predominate but the programme includes museum and archive exhibitions on occasions. Exhibitions normally show for three to four weeks.
Sales: Work sold
The Space: 16x12x2.5m high with 37m linear hanging space, and track-mounted spotlights with direct fixing to hanging surface. There is a weight limit of 600lbs. Gallery plans available.
Exhibiting: **[AW][EF]** Apply to Group Librarian approximately 15 months prior to desired showing dates. Gallery finances insurance, printing and mail-out of publicity and list of exhibits. Support in principle for EPR. Commission 15%.
Access: **[L][X]** BR Margate 10 mins; Public car park 3 mins

Market Harborough (Leicestershire)

(EMA) Map5 SP78

Frank Haynes Gallery

A commercial gallery showing work by artists and makers in the Leicestershire/Northamptonshire area. [VA,Ph,Cr]

Address: 50 Station Road, Great Bowden, Market Harborough, Leicestershire LE16 7HN tel 0858 64862
Contact: Frank Haynes
Open: Fri-Tues 2-5, Sun 10-5; closed July & Aug
Policy: The exhibitions usually feature the work of six artists and makers and last from one to two months. The work is high-quality and drawn from a number of sources, including young artists and makers. The workshops adjacent to the gallery are used for pottery and furniture making.
Sales: Work sold
The Space: Display is discussed with exhibitors.
Exhibiting: **[AW]** Contact Frank Haynes to arrange an appointment. A commission of 30% is charged on sales. Insurance and publicity is provided by the gallery.
Access: **[F]** Car parking, BR Market Harborough 20 mins

Harborough Museum

A 'social history museum for the Market Harborough area' run by Leicestershire Museums, Arts and Records Service. [Pr,Dr,Ph]

Address: Council Offices, Adam and Eve Street, Market Harborough, Leicestershire LE16 7LT tel 0858 32468
Contact: Keeper Steph Mastoris
Open: Mon-Sat 10-4.30, Sun 2-5
Policy: Exhibitions are mainly *'historical in content'*, though to *'attract other sectors of the public'* more contemporary exhibitions are planned. Occasional talks are arranged with the exhibitions.
The Space: A 5x4m gallery giving 11m linear hanging space in sections with direct fixing used and ceiling-mounted spot lights. Gallery plans available.
Exhibiting: Exhibitions by invitation. Exhibitors provided with insurance, printing, publicity, list of exhibits, preview, and catalogue/card.
Access: **[U][T][L]** Town centre location; Car parks 3 mins; BR Market Harborough 10 mins

Marlborough (Wiltshire)

(SA) Map7 SU16

Bajazzo Gallery

Commercial gallery. [Pa,Sc,Ce]

Address: 2 Silverless Street, Marlborough, Wiltshire SN8 1JQ tel 0672 52860
Contact: Director Karon Staniland
Open: Mon-Sat 10-1 & 2-4
Policy: Founded in 1972, the gallery shows paintings, sculpture and ceramics and runs courses in drawing and painting. Commissions are accepted for portraits in charcoal, pastel and oil.

Katharine House Gallery

Independent gallery housed in a timber-framed Tudor building. [Pa,Pr,Cr]

Address: The Parade, Marlborough, Wiltshire SN8 1NE tel 0672 54397
Contact: Michael Mitchell
Open: Wed-Sat 10-5, Sun 11-4
Policy: The gallery specialises in *'decorative non-functional ceramics, studio glass and contemporary wood engravings, though exhibitions frequently involve jewellery, furniture, textiles, paintings and prints'*. The

work of younger makers is regularly featured and it is *'an emphatic part of gallery policy that the public is given an opportunity to see these works'.* Exhibitions change monthly. A private press is attached to the gallery, producing editions of wood engravings and limited edition books.

Sales: 33% commission is charged

The Space: The gallery space is 58 square metres split into *'three distinct and irregular areas'*, with direct fixing to the walls and with spots and natural light.

Exhibiting: Exhibitions are arranged by invitation, though the gallery would consider applications. Gallery pays for insurance, publicity, mailing, catalogue and private view.

Marlborough Studio Art Gallery

Commercial gallery. [Pa,Cr]

Address: 4 Hughenden Yard, High Street, Marlborough, Wiltshire SN8 1LT tel 0672 54848

Contact: Proprietor Andy Le Poidevin

Open: Mon-Sat 10-1 & 2-5, Wed & Sun by appointment

Policy: Shows work by the owner and other local artists including Christopher Asheton Stones and Robert Hughes. All media including painting, pottery, wood turning and iron work are exhibited in a continuous display. Two selected exhibitions a year are held.

Exhibiting: [AW]

Mount House Gallery

A gallery under the auspicies of, but independent from, Marlborough College which holds exhibitions of education and cultural value to the college and the local community. [VA,Ph,Cr]

Address: Bridewell Street, Bath Road, Marlborough, Wiltshire tel 0672 55511 ext 291

Contact: Administrator Stephen Murfitt

Open: Tues-Sat 10-5, Sun 2-5

Policy: The gallery shows a wide variety of contemporary art, craft and design exhibitions with work very often sold though this is not the main purpose of the gallery. Exhibitions are normally shown for three weeks and seven are shown a year.

Sales: Work sold

The Space: The gallery has 19m of linear hanging space plus small spaces in window bays and lighting by spots. Gallery plans available.

Exhibiting: [AW] Applications should include slides or photographs in the first instance. The gallery pays for insurance only.

Access: [S] Buses 5&6 from Swindon to Salisbury via Marlborough

Matlock (Derbyshire)

(NA) Map5 SK36

Derbyshire Libraries

The public library service for Derbyshire. A 'more than just books' service for library users. [VA,Ph,Cr]

Address: County Library Headquarters, Smedley Street, Matlock, Derbyshire DE4 3AG tel 0629 580000 ext 6825

Contact: Director of Education

Open: Various

Policy: Predominantly exhibitions by local artists, with some hired-in exhibitions. The library service co-ordinates tours of some exhibitions, and local librarians book in their own programmes. Other events are programmed at the individual libraries.

Sales: Work sold

The Space: Sizes and facilities vary from separate gallery spaces to the use of screens in a reading area.

Exhibiting: [AW] Libraries are booked several months in advance. Contact the local library, or County Headquarters for touring exhibitions.

Middlesbrough (Cleveland)

(NA) Map3 NZ42

Artists in Middlesbrough

Artists' studio group also showing exhibitions. [VA,Ph,Cr]

Address: 1 Elliot Street, Off Corporation Road, Middlesbrough, Cleveland TS1 tel 0642 210756

The Space: The gallery is 7x3.5m giving 21m of linear hanging space.

Exhibiting: [AW]

Access: City centre site; BR Middlesbrough 5 mins; Bus station 5 mins

Captain Cook Birthplace Museum

Museum run by Middlesbrough Borough Council, illustrating the early life and voyages of Captain Cook.

Address: Stewart Park, Marton, Middlesbrough TS7 6AS tel 0642 311211

Contact: Hilary Wade tel 0642 813781

Open: Daily 10-6; 9-4 Winter

Policy: Twelve exhibitions a year of work by local artists, of local interest or on maritime subjects.

Sales: Work sold

The Space: Small display space 6x4.5m plus additional space on screens. Track lighting.

Exhibiting: The venue covers costs of insurance, publicity, and artists help towards preview costs. Commission 10%.

Cleveland College of Art & Design

A gallery in an art college setting. [VA,Ph,Cr,Vi,Fi,LA]

Address: Green Lane, Middlesbrough, Cleveland TS5 7RJ tel 0642 821441

Contact: Principal's Secretary

Open: Mon-Thurs 10-8, Fri 10-4.30 term-time

Policy: Varied exhibition programme covering design concepts and innovation as well as fine art and crafts. While the public are considered in terms of policy, the exhibition planning is also seen as relevant to the students of the college. Emphasis is placed on living artists and designers, with some historical shows.

The Space: The gallery has 72 square metres with 32.8m linear hanging space, direct fixing and spotlights.

Exhibiting: [AW] The gallery covers insurance and shares other costs and charges 20% commission. *'The college is not geared up to provide a major publicity*

drive for its exhibitions but can nevertheless provide a sympathetic ready-made audience for work and educational follow-up.'

Cleveland Crafts Centre

Crafts shop, gallery and workshops run by the Leisure Services of Cleveland County Council. [Cr]

Address: 37 Gilkes Street, Middlesbrough, Cleveland TS1 5EL tel 0642 226351
Contact: Craft Officer
Open: Tues-Sat 10-5; closed bank & statutory holidays
Policy: The gallery has a permanent collection studio ceramics and contemporary jewellery and runs a programme of temporary exhibitions. Education programme accompanies exhibitions.
Sales: Work sold
The Space: 166 square metres.
Exhibiting: **[AW]** Write enclosing slides to Crafts Officer. Gallery covers insurance, publicity, preview and display.
Access: **[U][T]** Gallery. On bus routes; BR Middlesbrough 15 mins

Cleveland Gallery

A gallery run by Cleveland County Museum Service, with a permanent collection of 17th-20th century decorative arts, antique maps, lace and contemporary drawings and prints and a regular programme of temporary exhibitions. [VA,Ph,Cr,Ho,LA]

Address: Victoria Road, Middlesbrough, Cleveland TS1 3QS tel 0642 225408
Contact: Exhibition Officer
Open: Tues-Sat 12-7; Closed bank holidays & Christmas
Policy: The gallery aims to show *'a varied programme from traditional paintings and drawings to less conventional art forms such as kites, robotics and t-shirt design, which we hope appeal to a varied audience of local residents, students and school children'*. Talks and workshops related to the exhibitions are organised.
Sales: Work sold
The Space: Gallery one has 50m linear hanging space and is 4m high; Gallery two has 20m linear hanging space and 2.8m high. Both are air-conditioned, lit by spots on track. Upright and desk cases available. Gallery plans available. Galleries are occasionally used for workshops.
Exhibiting: **[AW]** Submit slides and details to Exhibition Officer. The gallery covers all exhibiting costs and the commission is negotiable.
Access: **[F]** Bus station 15 mins; BR Middlesbrough 15 mins

Cleveland Libraries

Most Cleveland Libraries (covering Hartlepool, Middlesbrough, Stockton, Saltburn, Marske, Redcar, Billingham, Thornaby, Yarm) have limited space for temporary exhibitions and displays.

Address: Central Library, Victoria Square, Middlesbrough, Cleveland TS1 2AY tel 0642 248155
Exhibiting: **[AW]** Also contact Cleveland Arts, PO Box 12, Marton House, Borough Road, Middlesbrough, Cleveland TS4 2YP tel 0642 211347, for further details of library and other exhibition spaces in Cleveland.

Dorman Museum

Museum, run by Middlesbrough Borough Council, with collections of social, local, industrial and natural history with permanent displays of regional and Linthorpe Pottery. Also temporary exhibition programme.

Address: Linthorpe Road, Middlesbrough, Cleveland tel 0642 813781
Contact: Curator Hilary Wade
Open: Mon-Fri 10-6, Sat 10-5
Policy: Exhibitions of local interest or relate to the museum collections
Sales: Work sold
The Space: Gallery 20x10m, 200 square metres with 60m linear hanging space, with numerous display boards. Natural, spot and fluorescent lighting.
Exhibiting: **[AW]** Apply in writing or by phone. Gallery covers insurance, publicity and list of exhibits. Commission is 10%.

Middlesbrough Art Gallery

A municipal gallery with a temporary exhibition programme and a permanent collection of 16th-19th century British and foreign art and British 20th century art. [VA,Ph,Cr]

Address: 320 Linthorpe Road, Middlesbrough, Cleveland TS1 4AW tel 0642 247445
Contact: Assistant Curator, Fine Art
Open: Mon-Sat 10-6
Policy: Eight rooms are available for temporary exhibitions which consist of local, national and international solo and group shows covering a broad cross-section of styles. The gallery organises a picture loan scheme as well as talks by exhibitors, residencies and educational events linked to exhibitions.
Sales: Work sold
The Space: There is a total of 91m linear hanging space x 4.6m high in eight rooms each lit by tungsten-halogen movable spots. There are three display cases and an open-air sculpture court and gardens. Maximum size of work is 1.9m. The galleries are also used for the talks and workshops.
Exhibiting: **[AW][EF]** Send slides, CV and statement with covering letter to Vivienne Totty. The gallery covers all exhibition costs, pays an exhibition fees and commission fees for the production of work especially for exhibitions. Supports the principle of EPR.
Access: **[U]** Ground floor; **[X]** First floor Bus station 10 mins; BR Middlesbrough 10 mins

Ormesby Hall

National Trust property with room for temporary exhibitions.

Address: Ormesby, Middlesbrough, Cleveland tel 0642 324188
Contact: Janet Bridgman
Policy: Programme advised by Cleveland Arts.
Sales: Work sold

board. Two small tracks with spots.
Exhibiting: **[AW]** Some of the programme is arranged through Cleveland Arts but direct approaches also considered. Commission is 25%. Artists insure and hang their own work with help from staff.

Middleton (Greater Manchester)

(NWA) Map3 SD80

Langley Community School (80 Furrow Gallery)

Part of a community council which is community-controlled and within a school on a housing estate in Langley. [VA,Ce,Je,LA]

Address: Langley Community School, Windermere Road, Langley, Middleton, Greater Manchester tel 061 653 6661
Contact: Chairperson Bill Marn
Open: Mon-Fri 10-12, 1.30-3.30
Policy: *'We believe we are the only community art gallery in a school on a council estate. We aim to demystify art and make our gallery welcoming and accessible to working-class people. The gallery is run entirely by local volunteers. Our programme is as varied as possible to introduce as many media as possible to people in a non-threatening, non-elitist atmosphere'.* When possible, we arrange to have an artist in residence.
Sales: Work sold
Exhibiting: Applications to exhibit should be sent to Bryan Shaw. The gallery pays for insurance, publicity, lists of exhibits, preview costs, display, transport, mailing and catalogue. 10% commission is taken on sales.
Access: **[U][T][X]** pending **[L]**

Midhurst (W Sussex)

(SA) Map7 SU82

Tobycraft Gallery

A gallery showing pottery, glass, slate and wood with a permanent display of oil paintings, watercolours and Welsh tapestry which also holds spinning demonstrations. [Pa,Sc,Cr]

Address: Church Hill, Midhurst, W Sussex GU29 9NX tel 073 081 2688
Contact: J Reed or J Farguson
Open: Mon-Sat 10-5

Milford (Staffordshire)

(WMA) Map4 SJ92

Shugborough

A National Trust property administered and financed by Staffordshire County Council which houses the Staffordshire County Museum, the Park Farm and Country House (home of the Earl of Lichfield). The museum is housed in the servants quarters with original kitchens, laundry, butler's pantry and brew-house. [Pa,Sc,Pr,Ph,Cr]

Address: Shugborough, Milford, Nr Stafford, Staffordshire ST17 0XB tel 0889 881388
Contact: Promotions & Marketing Officer Elizabeth Machin
Open: Open daily from 11 Easter-Christmas; Open all year round to booked parties
Policy: Shugborough runs a programme of events alongside the permanent historical collections. The programme includes a tea exhibition in the Mansion House, craft fairs, class car shows etc.
The Space: Rooms in Mansion House reserved for exhibitions organised by Shugborough. Visitor information centre for temporary exhibitions related to a country estate.
Exhibiting: *'Specific exhibitions or exhibitions in keeping with a country estate'.*
Access: **[U][T]** ground floor all sites. Situated on the A513 Stafford to Lichfield Road

Milton Keynes (Buckinghamshire)

(BA) Map7 SP83

Barn (The)

The Courtyard Workshop is run by Milton Keynes Community Workshop Trust, an organisation which works 'with the public in crafts, visual arts and performance'. [Pa,Sc,Pr,Ph,Cr,LA]

Address: Courtyard Workshop, Parklands, Great Linford, Milton Keynes MK14 9DZ tel 0908 605432
Contact: Site Manager Mark Bell
Open: Daily 10-10; Closed 4-7
Policy: The one to two-week exhibitions are held four times a year and are used to *'promote primarily the work of young local artists and makers, and provide a viable contrast to major exhibitions elsewhere in the city'.* Regular visual arts courses are run independently of the exhibitions. The workshop is funded by the local arts association and regional arts association.
Sales: Work sold; Credit card; Credit scheme
The Space: The barn has 4.5x1.8x1.1m of space giving 11.3m linear hanging space. Work over 2.5x1.75m cannot be accommodated.
Exhibiting: **[AW]** Proposals should be sent to the Site

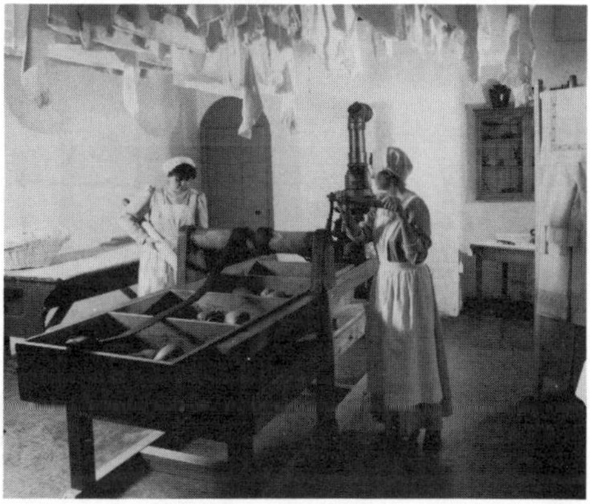

Shugborough: The laundry in the Museum

Manager. The workshop provides insurance, publicity, preview, list of exhibits. EPR supported.
Access: [U][T][F] Car park on site; Bus 7 from city centre

City Gallery Arts Trust

A visual arts agency, with charitable status organising commissions, residencies and sales of work for the public and private sector. [VA,Cr,Ph]

Address: The Great Barn, Parklands, Great Linford, Milton Keynes, Buckinghamshire MK14 5DZ tel 0908 606791
Contact: Director David Wright
Open: Mon-Fri 9-5.30
Policy: *'City Gallery organises exhibition programmes for some of its clients, mainly in public spaces'.* Last year 20 exhibitions were organised nearly half being solo shows.
Sales: Work sold
The Space: Various spaces used.
Exhibiting: [AW] Letter and slides to the Director. A commission of 33.3% is charged on sales. The gallery provides insurance, publicity, display, transport and expenses. Supports EPR.

Gallery In The Garden

A commercial gallery with separate premises within a popular garden centre. [VA,Cr]

Address: Frosts Garden Centre, Newport Road, Woburn Sands, Milton Keynes, Buckinghamshire MK17 8UE tel 0908 585047
Contact: Stevie Beckham
Open: Mon-Sun 10-4; closed Tues
Policy: *'The aim of this gallery is to provide display space mainly for local artists who produce a high standard of work'.* Two or three exhibitions a year are shown, together with weekend demonstrations.
Sales: Work sold; Credit card
The Space: 21m linear hanging space plus some screens and outdoor space. Hanging rail used, with spots and natural light from glass roof.
Exhibiting: [AW] Invited artists and selected exhibitions charged 30-40% on sales. Space also for hire at £5-£30 plus 20-30% commission depending on type and size of space. Information on dates, charges, and photographs available. The gallery provides most services, but artists and makers may be asked to contribute to the costs of the private view. Supports EPR.
Access: [F] Car park, BR Bletchley 3 min; Milton Keynes bus route

Gallery in the Garden

Milton Keynes Exhibition Gallery

Part of Buckinghamshire County Council Museum Service aiming to present 'the best in new contemporary art and craft alongside art history and local history exhibitions'. [VA,Ph,Cr]

Address: 555 Silbury Boulevard, Milton Keynes, Buckinghamshire MK9 3HL tel 0908 605536
Contact: Exhibition Officer Peter Laws
Open: Mon-Wed 9.30-6, Thurs-Fri 9.30-8, Sat 10-5
Policy: The monthly exhibition programme is two thirds contemporary work, concentrating on mixed exhibitions. An education programme of talks, films, visits and workshops is run in conjunction with the exhibition programme.
Sales: Work sold
The Space: 12x12x3.5m giving 45m linear hanging space with track lighting and environmental controls. Showcases and gallery plans are available.
Exhibiting: [AW] Contact the Exhibition Officer. The gallery provides insurance, transport, publicity, mailing, preview, list of exhibits, catalogue/card and expenses. A commission of 25% is charged on sales.
Access: [U][F] Free car park close by; Bus station 5 mins; BR Milton Keynes 15 mins

Stantonbury Gallery

A gallery in a secondary education complex which comprises a community centre, theatre and leisure centre, funded by the local authority. [VA,Ph]

Address: Stantonbury Campus, Milton Keynes, Buckinghamshire MK14 6BN tel 0908 220066
Contact: Arts Animateur Tony Francombe
Policy: The gallery encourages *'local artists by providing an exhibition space at no substantial cost to themselves'.* The gallery also shows work by professional artists from further afield to *'offer comparative work to the community'.* A programme of workshops are planned, and links with the educational and leisure programmes of the complex are encouraged.
Sales: Sales referred to exhibitor
The Space: 30m linear hanging by direct fixing. The gallery has natural and spot lighting.
Exhibiting: [AW] Enquiries should be addressed to Tony Francombe. The gallery provides insurance, and some publicity and mailing. EPR supported.
Access: [X] Car park; Frequent bus service from Milton Keynes bus station

Mirfield (W Yorkshire)

(YA) Map3 SE21

Eastthorpe Gallery

The gallery, part of Kirklees Art Space Society, provides an exhibition space for contemporary work,

especially print making as a complement to the print workshop facilities. [VA,Ph,Cr]

Address: Huddersfield Road, Mirfield, W Yorkshire WF14 8AT tel 0924 497646

Contact: Education Officer Daphne Alsop

Open: Mon-Sat 11-5

Policy: The aim is *'to promote the understanding and appreciation of the arts so that as many people as possible can have the opportunity to enjoy, develop and improve their knowledge and understanding through a full education programme and practical workshops. The emphasis is with audience participation which is made possible by the print and photography workshops, a full out-reach programme and the presence of artists' studios within the complex reinforcing the active roles of the gallery'.* There are nine exhibitions a year and a strong commitment towards group shows.

The Space: The gallery is 8x7x3m high with track, flood and individual spot lighting systems. Works are limited in size by the access door which is 1.2x1.8m high.

Exhibiting: [AW][EF] Artists and makers should send six to ten slides, CV and SAE to the Exhibitions Committee. The gallery covers all exhibition costs except artists' expenses and display, takes 30% commission and supports the principal of EPR.

Access: [U][S] BR Mirfield 5 mins; Car park 1 min

Morpeth (Northumberland)

(NA) Map3 NZ18

Cameo Gallery

A small exhibition space in a school. [VA,Ph]

Address: King Edward VI School, Morpeth, Northumberland NE34 8BT tel 0670 55415

Contact: Head of Creative Arts Faculty Wilf Rees

Open: Mon-Thurs 9.30-5 term-time

Sales: Work sold

The Space: There is 15m linear hanging space with additional space on screens. Hanging by rods and natural and spot.

Exhibiting: [AW] Exhibitions normally by invitation but would consider direct approach. Commission 20%

Eastthorpe Gallery: Workshop with Battyeford Middle School during the 'Work in Landscape' exhibition, 1988 (Photo: Jenny Hardman-Jones)

Chantry Silver

A silversmith workshop and shop also showing temporary exhibitions. [Pa,Dr]

Address: The Chantry Courtyard, Morpeth, Northumberland tel 0670 518817

Policy: Silver jewellery on display with small display of work by gallery artists.

Sales: Work sold

The Space: Small space in showroom for four works. Spot and fluorescent lights.

Exhibiting: [AW] Is prepared to take on new artists - arrange an appointment. Space can be rented. Commission 20%.

Nantwich (Cheshire)

(NWA) Map4 SJ65

Cotman Gallery

A commercial gallery housed in a 17th century listed building which specialises in work by the best British artists and makers. [Pa,Pr,Cr]

Address: 126 Hospital Street, Nantwich, Cheshire CW5 5RY tel 0270 624567

Contact: Dorothy Barley

Open: Thurs, Fri, Sat 10.30-1, 2-5

Policy: A changing display of watercolours, ceramics, etchings and wood is complemented by occasional exhibitions by gallery artists and makers.

Sales: Work sold; Credit card

The Space: The gallery has 45.72m linear hanging space, with hanging by direct fixing and lighting a combination of natural light and spots.

Exhibiting: [AW] Applications should be made to Dorothy Barley. The gallery shares costs for insurance, transport and mailing. 30% commission is taken on sales.

Access: Car park behind gallery 2 mins

Nelson (Lancashire)

(NWA) Map3 SD83

Barrowford Library

A branch of Lancashire Libraries. [Pa,Ph]

Address: Anne Street, Barrowford, Nelson, Lancashire BB9 8QH tel 0282 63038

Contact: District Librarian Mrs C Ashworth

Open: Mon, Wed, Fri 10-12, 1.30-5, 5.30-7; Sat 10-12

Policy: Twelve exhibitions have been held at the library in the past year. *'A focal point in the town in which local artists and others (including schools) can show their work to a wider audience of mainly library users'.*

The Space: The library has a number of display boards including one measuring 1.23x2.46m, three in the children's library measuring 1.6x1.46m,1.64x1.23m, 1.97x1.23m and an additional nine pegboards making a continuous row 1.46x0.71m.

Exhibiting: [AW] Contact the District Librarian. Pictures must be hung within the prescribed limits of the boards available.15% commission.

Access: [U] Bus service from Nelson to Higherford, Blacko or Barnoldswick; Street car parking

Brierfield Library

A branch of Lancashire Libraries. [Pa,Ph]

Address: Colne Road, Brierfield, Nelson, Lancashire BB9 5HW tel 0282 65816

Contact: Miss L Medley

Open: Mon 10-12 1-7, Tues 10-12 Wed,Thurs, Fri 10-12 1-5, Sat 10-12

Policy: Six one-person exhibitions have been held in the last year. *'A focal point in the town in which local artists and others (including schools) can show their work to a wider audience of mainly library users'.*

The Space: Six free-standing double-sided Marler Haley screens 1.5x1m are available in the lending library.

Exhibiting: [AW] Contact District Librarian. No heavy items, no nails to be used. 15% commission is taken.

Access: [X] Main-line bus routes between Burnley and Nelson; Car parking

Nelson Library

A branch of Lancashire Libraries, it has a permanent collection of paintings and photographs of the history of Nelson and the surrounding area. [Pa,Dr,Ph,Cr]

Address: Market Square, Nelson , Lancashire BB9 7LP tel 0282 692511

Contact: District Librarian Mrs S Byrne

Open: Mon,Wed,Fri 9.30-7; Tues,Thurs 9.30-5; Sat 9.30-4

Policy: The library aims to provide *'a focal point in the town in which local artists and others, including schools, can show their work to a wider audience'*. The month-long exhibitions sometimes include crafts demonstrations.

The Space: Displays can be mounted on the balcony on four boards measuring 1x2.46m and one board 1x1.24m. The Children's Library has three boards of 1.07x2.46m. In the Asian Library three boards of 1.07x2.46m, one board 1.07x1.24m. No heavy items, nails must not be used.

Exhibiting: [AW] Contact the District Librarian. 15% commission is charged.

Access: [U][L] BR Nelson and Buses 7 mins; Car park at rear

Pendle Photographic Gallery

The Pendle Photographic Gallery, part of Pendle Leisure Services, opened in February 1988 and is situated above the Tourist Information Centre. [Ph]

Address: 20 Scotland Road, Nelson, Lancs BB9 7UU tel 0282 67731 Ext 323

Contact: Gallery Organiser Jamie Woodley

Open: Mon-Sat 10-5,Tues 10-12, Sun 2-5

Policy: The gallery will show on average ten exhibitions a year, running four weeks each. *'It aims to serve East Lancashire specifically and will exhibit a continuous programme of solo and group shows both contemporary and historical, regional and national. Its prime aim is to highlight contemporary photographic practice.'* The gallery wishes to present photography in such a way as to encourage greater understanding of the medium through recreation and enjoyment and to make the exhibition programme available as an educational resource to the general public and educational establishments. They also aim to encourage and assist in advancing the presentation and practise of photography as an expressive medium.' A programme of joint educational events is organised with the Photography Department of Blackburn College and Nelson & Colne College.

Sales: Sales referred to exhibitor

The Space: The gallery has 36.57m linear hanging space plus centre screens with lighting by combination tracking (strip and spots) and daylight. The maximum size of frame that be accommodated is 2.13x1.82m.

Exhibiting: [AW][EF] The Gallery Organiser welcomes applications, either ring or write to make an appointment. The gallery pays for insurance, publicity, list of exhibits, preview costs, display, transport, mailing and artists expenses. Supports EPR. The gallery will pay a commission fee to produce work for exhibitions and 35% is taken on sales.

Access: [U][F] BR 2 mins; Bus stop 2 mins; Ample car parks nearby

Newbury (Berkshire)

(SA) Map7 SU46

Arts Workshop

First-floor exhibition space in an arts centre serving the local community. It mainly shows contemporary regional artists. There is also a large ground-floor space for special exhibitions, festivals etc. [Pa,Sc,Pr]

Address: Northcroft Lane, Newbury, Berkshire RG13 1BU tel 0635 47851

Contact: Richard Noyce

Open: Mon-Fri 10-4, Sat 10-1

Granary Exhibition Room (Newbury District Museum)

Self-contained exhibition space attached to Newbury District Museum. [VA,Cr,Ph]

Address: The Wharf, Newbury, Berkshire RG14 5AS

Contact: Assistant Curator Newbury District Museum, The Wharf, Newbury, Berkshire RG14 5AS tel 0635 30511

Open: Open during exhibitions

Policy: The room may be hired by artists and exhibitors.

Sales: Work sold

The Space: One gallery 15m long and a width of 4.75m widening to 5.3m.

Exhibiting: [AW] Hire details from the Assistant Curator.

Access: [F] Car parking

Newcastle-under-Lyme (Staffordshire)

(WMA) Map4 SJ84

Art Link

'Art Link which is funded by local authorities, charitable trusts and West Midlands Arts, promotes and encourages arts and creative activities for people with disabilities and special needs', throughout the West Midlands. [VA,Ph,Cr]

Address: 17a Hanover Street, Newcastle-under-Lyme, Staffordshire ST5 1HD tel 0782 614170
Contact: Co-ordinator Lee Corner
Open: Various
Policy: Art Link exhibitions are generally the result of workshop activities and projects and show the *'work of people with disabilities and special needs produced through their involvement with professional artists.'* The work of the professional artists is also included where appropriate. *'Art Link is committed to bringing to the attention of the wider public the skills, talents, and abilities of people designated "disabled"'.*
The Space: Various.

Borough Museum & Art Gallery

A museum and art gallery run by the Recreation and Amenities Department of the Borough Council. [Pa,Dr,Ph,Cr]
Address: Brampton Park, Newcastle-Under-Lyme, Staffordshire ST5 0QP tel 0782 619705
Contact: Curator Paul Bemrose
Open: Mon-Sat 9.30-6, closed 1-2; May-Sept Sun 2-5.30
Policy: The programme includes historical and contemporary exhibitions mainly reflecting work produced in the area or of relevance to the area. Workshops are sometimes organised in conjunction with the exhibitions.
The Space: The gallery has 40m linear wall space with an additional 20m linear available on display boards. Temporary wall-mounted show cases available for small craft works. Gallery plans available.
Exhibiting: [AW] Contact the Director of Recreation and Amenities, Civic Offices, Merrial Street, Newcastle-under-Lyme ST5 2AG. The gallery provides insurance and hanging the exhibition.
Access: [U][F] Close to town centre, car parks and buses

New Victoria Theatre

A foyer space in a new purpose-built theatre. [Pa,Pr,Dr,Ph]
Address: Eturia Road, Newcastle-under-Lyme, Staffordshire ST5 0JG tel 0782 717954
Contact: Front-of-House Manager Judy Bowker

Borough Museum & Art Gallery

Open: Mon-Sat 10-11 except non-performance days
Policy: The exhibition programme draws mainly on artists in the town and West Midlands region particularly those who would not normally have the opportunity of a large exhibition.
Sales: Work sold; Credit card
The Space: A curved wall opposite the cafe and bar area with 30m linear hanging space, hanging rail, spots and natural light.
Exhibiting: [AW] Contact the Front-of-House Manager. A 10% commission is charged on sales, and the theatre provides publicity, a list of exhibits, mailing and preview costs.
Access: [U][L][F] Own car park; Buses from town centre

Stoke & Newcastle Arts Project

An arts development agency that promotes an exchange of ideas, information, and skills, funded by local authorities and West Midlands Arts which occasionally organises temporary exhibitions. [Pa,Sc,Cr,LA]
Address: Unit 19, Barracks Workshops, Barracks Road, Newcastle-under-Lyme, Staffordshire ST5 1LG tel 0782 638775
Contact: Arts Worker
Open: Office hours when staffed
Policy: The programme *'has developed from project work with community groups'*, using exhibitions and artists to *'stimulate local participation in projects and promotions'*. Artists work alongside community groups to *'create new shared work'*. The agency provides information, training and a professional art service. Its work aims to show examples of equal opportunities in practise. Workshops are held as either a part of a project or as *'one-offs'* with neighbourhood groups and local education departments.
Sales: Sales referred to exhibitor
The Space: One multi-purpose space used with adjustable spots, fluorescent and natural lighting. The room is 12.2x5.2x3m with 22m linear space.
Exhibiting: The space can be hired. Artists and makers involved in projects are provided with publicity, mailing, preview and catalogue or card. Supports EPR.
Access: [X] Opposite Newcastle-Under-Lyme bus station; Public car park 3 mins; BR Stoke-On-Trent 3 miles

Newcastle-upon-Tyne (Tyne & Wear)

(NA) Map3 NZ26

Café Procopé

Cafe with active exhibition programme. [VA]
Address: 35 The Side, Quayside, Newcastle-upon-Tyne, Tyne & Wear NE1 tel 091 232 3848
Policy: Month long exhibitions.
Sales: Work sold
Exhibiting: [AW] Waiting list, no commission

Calouste Gulbenkian Gallery

The gallery is part of the Peoples Theatre. [VA,Ph,Cr,Fu,Fi,Vi,LA]

Address: People's Theatre, Stephenson Road, Heaton, Newcastle-upon-Tyne, Tyne & Wear NE6 5QF tel 091 265 5020
Contact: Chair Trevor Hopkins
Open: 6pm-10pm
Policy: *'Preference is given to showing the work of young local artists who would otherwise find an outlet in the area difficult, as well as group shows and exhibitions of craft and sculpture'.* There are also *'showcases for makers looking for an outlet to sell their work'* as well as a smaller and more intimate space in the theatre foyer used by amateur artists and first-time exhibitors. Exhibitions usually last two weeks.
Sales: Work sold
The Space: Main wall 20m x 5m high; two side walls each 5m long x 3m high plus six hanging boards 2x1.5m with spot and fluorescent lighting, direct fixing, one glass case. The space is occasionally used for performances and sales of craft work. Gallery plans available (also useful instructions for exhibitors).
Exhibiting: [AW] Apply to the Chair.
Access: [U][S] Gallery on two levels. On Bus routes, Car parking adjacent

Chameleon Gallery

A commercial gallery run with a picture framing business – Collier Framing – selling original work and reproduction prints by local and national artists. [Pa,Pr,Cr]
Address: Milburn House, Dean Street, Newcastle-upon-Tyne, Tyne & Wear NE1 1PQ tel 091 232 2819
Contact: Gallery Manager Clare Turner
Open: Mon-Fri 9-5.30, Thurs 9-7, Sat 9-5
Policy: The work in the gallery caters for a wide range of tastes: a varied and changing stock of work – including that of local artists – is shown alongside about six or seven temporary shows a year. Theme exhibitions featuring several artists are favoured to solo shows.
Sales: Work sold; Credit card
The Space: The hanging space is discontinuous totalling 12m by 3m high. Hanging is by direct fixing, lighting is by spots and there is a 1.5x.6m glass case.
Exhibiting: [AW] Apply to the Gallery Manager in writing or make an appointment. The gallery pays for insurance, publicity, list of exhibits, previews and charges 33.3% commission.
Access: [F] In city centre; BR Newcastle 5 mins; Meter parking outside

Gallery 7

Small commercial gallery. [VA,Cr,Ph]
Address: 7 Old Eldon Square, Newcastle-upon-Tyne, Tyne & Wear NE1 tel 091 261 5510
Contact: Bill Colwell
Policy: Exhibits contemporary work mainly in mixed exhibitions lasting between three to six weeks.
Sales: Work for sale
The Space: Expandable space, normally two rooms with four additional rooms in basement.
Exhibiting: [AW] Commission 30%. Artists insure work.
Access: City Centre site; Bus station 5 mins; BR Newcastle 10 mins; Metro 5 mins

Greys Gallery

A commercial gallery showing permanent exhibitions of work by local artists and two to three-week exhibitions by local and national artists. [VA,Cr]
Address: 77/79 High Street, Gosforth, Newcastle-upon-Tyne, Tyne & Wear NE3 4AA tel 091 284 8735
Contact: Gallery Administrator Jackie Evans
Open: Mon-Fri 10-5, Sat 10-1
Policy: The gallery is *'only interested in original work'* that is, paintings, ceramics, glass and jewellery'.
Sales: Work sold
The Space: First floor gallery.
Exhibiting: [AW] Gallery covers insurance and other costs are shared. The gallery's commission is 33.3%.
Access: [F]

Hatton Gallery

Gallery within the Fine Art Department of Newcastle University with temporary exhibitions and a permanent collection including the only remaining Merzbau of Kurt Schwitters. [VA,Ph]
Address: The University, Newcastle-upon-Tyne, Tyne & Wear NE1 7RU tel 091 232 8511 ext 2047
Contact: Exhibitions Director Dr John Milner
Open: Mon-Fri 10-.30, Sat 10-4.30 term-time only
Policy: Regular exhibitions of solo, group and thematic exhibitions in a large, well-lit gallery.
The Space: Five galleries with a total of 140m linear hanging space.
Exhibiting: [AW] Apply in writing to the Exhibitions Director enclosing visual material.
Access: [X] Assistance with wheelchairs by prior arrangement. City centre site; Buses 5 mins; BR Newcastle 10 mins

Laing Art Gallery

A local authority gallery, run by the Tyne & Wear Museum Service, with a permanent collection of British painting 18th century to present and British and European applied arts 17th century to present, and a temporary exhibition programme. [VA,LA]
Address: Higham Place, Newcastle-upon-Tyne, Tyne & Wear NE1 8AG tel 091 232 7734
Contact: Group Museums Officer (West) John Millard
Open: Tues-Fri 10-5.30, Sat 10-4.30, Sun 2.30-5.30
Policy: The exhibition programme, run in four galleries, attempts *'where possible to break down barriers between forms of production, and between contemporary and historical art'.* Many of the shows are the work of living artists and makers, last four weeks, and are solo, theme, mixed or group. Talks, seminars, workshops, demonstrations and other educational activities are organised by the Education Officer.
Sales: Work sold
The Space: Gallery one has 36m linear hanging space x 4.5m high; gallery two has 34m linear hanging space x 3.4m high; Gallery A has 40m linear hanging space x 8.8m high; Gallery B has 44m linear hanging space x 8.8m high. Lighting in each gallery is by spotlights on track.
Exhibiting: [AW][EF] Apply at any time with slides or photographs, CV, background information and/or

exhibition proposal, to Senior Art Exhibitions Officer. The gallery covers insurance, publicity, preview, transport, catalogue/card and charges 25%. Work is occasionally commissioned for exhibitions. Supports the principle of EPR.

Access: [U][L] City centre site; BR Newcastle 10 mins; Bus stations 10 mins, Metro 10 mins; Car park 1 min; Meter parking

Newcastle Arts Centre Craftshop

Arts centre with craft shop showing small exhibitions. [Cr]

Address: 67 Westgate Road, Newcastle-upon-Tyne, Tyne & Wear tel 091 261 5618

Contact: Mark Dobson

Open: Mon-Sat 9.30-5.30

Policy: Range of craft and wall-hanging work.

Sales: Work sold

Exhibiting: [AW] Send slides and CV. Work insured, no publicity but contribute to preview costs. Commission 33.3%

Access: [U] City centre site; BR Newcastle 5 mins; Metro 5 mins; Bus stations 5 & 10 mins; Car park 10 mins; Metre parking

Newcastle Arts Centre Frameshop

Frame shop which also shows temporary exhibitions. [VA]

Address: 69 Westgate Road, Newcastle-upon-Tyne, Tyne & Wear NE1 tel 091 261 0293

Contact: Mark Dobson

Open: Mon-Sat 9.30-5.30

Policy: Mixture of arranged exhibitions and space available for hire. Any work by living artists.

Sales: Work sold

The Space: Basement space with 370 square metres.

Exhibiting: [AW] Commission 33.3%. Gallery insures work. Internally arranged exhibitions no charge made for publicity, those hiring the space undertake their own publicity.

Access: [AW] City centre site; BR Newcastle 5 mins; Metro 5 mins; Bus station 5 & 10 mins; Car park 10 mins; Metre parking

Laing Art Gallery: Stephen Taylor Woodrow and children from Newcastle schools in a project organised by the gallery

Newcastle Central Library

Exhibition space off the entrance area to the library. [VA,Cr,Ph,LA]

Address: Princess Square, Newcastle-upon-Tyne, Tyne & Wear NE1 1MC tel 091 261 0691

Contact: Publicity Officer David Boyes

Open: Mon-Thurs 9-9, Fri-Sat 9-5

The Space: Space 13x6.5m with normal lighting, display case in foyer with spot lighting.

Exhibiting: [AW] Ask for application forms. Library insures up to £1000. No hire fee to amateurs but 20% commission; hire fees for professionals.

Newcastle Playhouse (New Playhouse Gallery)

An exhibition space within a theatre. [Pa,Sc,LA]

Address: Barras Bridge, Newcastle-upon-Tyne, Tyne & Wear NE1 7RH tel 091 261 0703

Contact: Director W Taylor

Open: Mon-Sat 9am-9pm; Closed Good Friday & Christmas Day

Policy: A varied series of exhibitions of painting and sculpture, some featuring one artist, some featuring several.

Sales: Work sold

The Space: Two spot-lit galleries each with 15.2x6m and some additional wall space on staircase. Also two alcoves in the main foyer.

Exhibiting: [AW]

Access: [U][T] City centre site, near Metro Haymarket and buses

Newcastle Polytechnic Gallery

A self-supporting gallery within Newcastle Polytechnic. [VA,Ph,Cr,LA]

Address: Library Building, Sandyford Road, Newcastle-upon-Tyne NE1 8ST tel 091 232 6003 ext 3224

Contact: Curator Mara-Helen Wood

Open: Mon-Fri 9-5

Policy: Shows a continuous programme of exhibitions of work by artists of national and international, as well as work by artists in the region. The gallery initiates touring exhibitions, thematic exhibitions, solo and group shows.

The Space: The gallery is 232 square metres with 76m linear hanging space, direct fixing, spots and flourescent lights.

Exhibiting: Mainly by invitation although applications from individuals and groups are also considered.

Newcastle University Long Gallery

Exhibition space in a long, wide corridor outside the Hatton Gallery within the Fine Art Department of the University. [Pa,Pr,Ph,Dr]

Address: Fine Art Department, The University, Barrass Bridge, Newcastle-upon-Tyne, Tyne & Wear NE1 tel 091 232 8511

Open: Mon-Fri 10-5.30, Sat 10-4.30

Northern Print

Printmakers workshop facilities for etching, relief, litho (stone and plate), silkscreen with editioning and co-publishing undertaken and small touring exhibitions and courses at all levels.

Address: 5 Charlotte Square, Newcastle-upon-Tyne, Tyne & Wear tel 091 232 7531

Contact: Director Frances Bugg

Open: Mon-Fri 10-6

Policy: Solo and mixed shows of members' work, past and present.

Projects UK

Sound and photographic activities and promoters of live art.

Address: 1 Black Swan Court, Westgate Road, Newcastle-upon-Tyne NE1 1SG tel 091 232 2410

Projects UK: Bow Gamelan Ensemble performing at the Laing Art Gallery as part of 'New Work Newcastle' a major festival of performance art organised by Projects UK (Photo: Steve Collins, Projects UK)

Contact: Jon Bewley or Simon Herbert

Policy: Commissions new time-based work and experimental forms. Operating nationally and internationally in conjunction with galleries and other arts organisations.

Exhibiting: [AW] Submissions in writing. There is no restrictions on context, format or location of projects.

Side Gallery

This grant-aided gallery is run by independent film-makers and specialises exclusively in documentary photography, 'showing the best from around the world, as well as commissioning work in the North East of England'. [Ph]

Address: 9 Side, Newcastle-upon-Tyne, Tyne & Wear NE1 3JE tel 091 232 2000

Contact: Pat McCarthy

Open: Tues-Sun 11-5

Policy: The gallery is interested in photographic practice which *'addresses social and political concerns'* with a specific commitment to work produced in the Northern region. There is also a 50-seater cinema used for talks, films and events related to exhibits. Specialist photography bookshop selling posters, postcards and publications with reference library.

The Space: Ground floor entrance has three walls 1.8, 1.8 & 3.6m long giving 7.3m linear hanging space. The first floor gallery has 48.6m linear hanging space and the top floor gallery has 15.2m linear hanging space. All galleries are 3.6m high. Lighting is by spots on tracks.

Exhibiting: [AW] Apply to the Exhibitions Organiser. Gallery covers insurance, publicity, display, transport and commissions for exhibitors.

Access: [S] Ground floor; **[X]** Upstairs. City centre site, BR Newcastle 10 mins; Bus station 10 mins; Metro 10 mins

Newmarket (Suffolk)

(EA) Map5 TL66

Bridge Street Gallery

Private gallery, Inuit sculptures, Modern British art and work by gallery artists and a continuous policy of month-long exhibitions by living artists. [Pa,Sc,Dr]

Address: Bridge Street, Moulton, Nr Newmarket, Suffolk CB8 8SP tel 0638 751769

Contact: Director Derick Halliwell

Open: Thurs-Sun 11-5

Policy: *'We aim to mount exhibitions of quality which would normally require a trip to London to see. Our target is clients with discerning taste and open minds.'*

Sales: Work sold; Credit card

The Space: One gallery is 7x5x3m high, second is 5x5x3m high, third is 8x3x2.5m high, all with overhead spots.

Exhibiting: [AW] Apply to Director. Commission charged is 33.3%.

Access: [U]

Newmarket Library

Exhibition space in three libraries administered by Suffolk County Arts & Libraries Service, Bury St Edmunds Area. See also entry for Lowestoft. [VA,Cr,Ph]

Address: The Rookery, Newmarket, Suffolk CB8 tel 0638 661216

Contact: Divisional Librarian

Sales: Work sold; Sales referred to exhibitor

The Space: Newmarket: 25 square metres; Mildenhall: 20 square metres and Brandon: 20 square metres.

Exhibiting: Booking period two months ahead, fee of 20% on all sales from exhibition subject to minimum charge of £17.50 payable in advance.

Newport (Isle of Wight)

(SA) Map7 SZ48

Isle of Wight Cultural Services Department

The department handling local authority galleries at Newport, Ryde and Freshwater Libraries and Ventnor. [VA,Ph,Cr]

Contact: Deputy Director of Cultural Services M R Howley, Cultural Services HQ, Parkhurst Road, Newport, Isle of Wight PO30 5TX tel 0983 522324/524541

Policy: Exhibitions change monthly and include all art forms. Prospective exhibits are viewed prior to confirmation of acceptance (see entries for Freshwater, Ryde, Newport and Ventnor).

Quay Arts Centre

A quayside arts centre in the centre of Newport that shows predominantly contemporary work of all kinds but also the occasional historical touring show. [VA,Ph,Cr]

Address: Sea Street, Newport, Isle of Wight PO30 5BD tel 0983 528825

Contact: Arts Administrator Ian Bilsborough

Open: Tues-Fri 11-5, Sat 11-4, Sun 2-5; closed Mon

Policy: *'The aims of the gallery are to introduce to the people of the Isle of Wight the best in contemporary art work and to aid in the educational processes in the country; to provide a space for historical exhibitions, dance and art related events and to enhance the cultural life of the community. Around 22 exhibitions a year are normally shown, each for around five weeks, and most are solo.*

Sales: Work sold

The Space: The main gallery is 19x8x2m with 50m linear hanging space. Both galleries have spotlights with dimmers and thermostatic heating. Gallery plans available.

Exhibiting: [AW] To Ian Bilsborough with a covering letter and slides or photographs which give a good indication of the work. The gallery pays for insurance, printing and mailing of publicity, list of exhibits, preview costs, transport, catalogue or card and artists' expenses. It supports the principle of EPR. Commission of 20% is charged.

Access: [X] Bus station 5 mins walk; Car part at Coppins Bridge

Seely Gallery

A gallery within a public library. [VA,Ph,Cr]

Address: Lord Louis Library, Newport, Isle of Wight PO30 1LL tel 0983 527655

Contact: Deputy Director of Cultural Services M R Howley, Cultural Services HQ, Parkhurst Road, Newport, Isle of Wight tel 0983 822000

Open: Mon, Tues, Wed, Fri 9-5.30, Thurs 9-7, Sat 9-5

Policy: The Cultural Services policy is to show work of quality from both professional and amateur artists, as well as to encourage and promote beginners of an acceptable exhibiting standard; this double objective being achieved by a selective offer of gallery venue. Seely Gallery is reserved, as far as practicable, for exhibitions of excellence. Exhibitions run for one month.

Sales: Sales referred to exhibitor

The Space: An octagonal first floor, narrow (3m width) gallery with 'well', giving 38m linear hanging space and fixing on rails and spotlights and electric roof ventilation. Gallery plans available.

Exhibiting: [AW] To the Director of Cultural Services. The library pays on a discretionary basis for printing and mailing of publicity, list of exhibits and transport.

Access: [X] Buses 1,1a,1b,1c,2,2a,3,5,5b,7,7a,8,9,16, 16b,16c,19,30,33,35,81,90,91; Public car park adjacent

Newton Abbot (Devon)

(SWA) Map6 SX87

Devon Guild of Craftsmen

A charitable organisation promoting the best of 'craftwork in the South West' with exhibitions, lectures, workshops and sales through a shop and café. [Sc,Pr,Cr]

Address: Riverside Mill, Bovey Tracey, Newton Abbot, Devon TQ13 9AE tel 0626 832223

Contact: Andy Christian

Open: Daily 10-5.30; closed Winter bank holidays

Policy: The guild runs a range of activities to promote the crafts including a library, collection, demonstrations, workshops and exhibitions. The exhibitions feature a wide range of work from regional, national and international makers as well as touring shows.

Sales: Work sold; Credit card

The Space: The downstairs showroom is 30x6m with spot lights, the upstairs gallery is 25x6m with fluorescent lights and the café is 9x5m with fluorescent lights. An outside courtyard area is also available. Cases for jewellery are available. Gallery plans available.

Exhibiting: [AW] The gallery pays for insurance, publicity, preview, list of exhibits, catalogue/card. The guild supports EPR. The commission varies between 25 and 40% depending on price.

Access: [F] Car park on site; BR Newton Abbott 5 miles

North Shields (Tyne & Wear)

(NA) Map3 NZ36

Vicarage Cottage Gallery

A commercial gallery showing temporary exhibitions of contemporary art and holding a changing stock of English and Scottish 20th and late 19th century artists. [VA]

Address: Preston Road, North Shields, Tyne & Wear NE29 9PJ tel 091 257 0935
Contact: George Lilly
Open: Sun 1-5, Thurs-Sat 10-5
Policy: Normally seven shows held a year in either solo or group exhibitions.
Sales: Work sold; Credit scheme
The Space: The gallery has two exhibition spaces and a subsidiary lobby area totalling 30m linear hanging space. A plan chest is available for unframed works on paper.
Exhibiting: [AW] Exhibition space can be hired, the gallery taking a small commission, otherwise commission is 33.3% with the gallery covering insurance and preview costs.
Access: [S] Bus 306 from Newcastle; Metro North Shields 1 mile; Car park

Vicarage Cottage Gallery

Wooden Doll

A place with people eating and drinking with temporary exhibitions. [VA,Ph]

Address: Hudson Street, North Shields, Tyne & Wear NE30 1JS tel 091 257 3747
Contact: Owner Pat Jones
Open: Mon-Sat 11-11pm, Sun 12-3, 7pm-10.30pm
Policy: Ten monthly exhibitions by professionals, amateurs and students with an open art exhibition July and August.
Sales: Work sold
The Space: Three connecting rooms, one being a balcony with a total of about 40 square metres. Hanging by rail with hooks.
Exhibiting: [AW]
Access: [F] Metro North Shields 2 mins

Northampton (Northamptonshire)

(EMA) Map5 SP76

Derngate Centre

A theatre, concert hall, conference centre and exhibition space with a wide programme in a centre purpose-built by Northampton Borough Council. [VA,Cr]

Address: 19/21 Guildhall Road, Northampton NN1 1DP tel 0604 26222
Contact: House Manager Paul Wheeler
Open: Daily 9-6 when theatre dark; 9am-11pm on performance days
Policy: The exhibition programme mainly uses local and regional artists, and work from local schools and colleges. Workshops and craft fairs are arranged. The restaurant and bar ensure day-time visitors.
Sales: Work sold; Credit card
The Space: Three spaces are used. Foyer has fifteen panels each 1.2x1.9m, with spot lighting and natural light, the circle has twelve panels 1.2x2.8m and the upper circle, a purpose-built gallery space, has 45m linear hanging space with natural and spot lighting. Hanging by picture hooks. Gallery plans available.
Exhibiting: [AW] Individuals or groups should contact the House Manager. Printing mailing and technical facilities are provided. A commission of 20% is charged on sales. Contracts are available.
Access: [][X] Situated in the town centre; Car park 1 min; Bus station 10 mins; BR Northampton 10 mins

Duston Library

See Northamptonshire Libraries. [VA,Ph,Cr]

Address: Pendle Road, Duston, Northamptonshire NN5 6DT tel 0604 585882
Contact: Librarian Tony Ward
Open: Mon 1-5, Tues 9.30-1, 2-5, Wed, Fri 9.30-1, 2-8, Sat 9.30-1; closed Thurs
Sales: Work sold
The Space: 6m wall space and a further 8m using screens.
Exhibiting: [AW] District Librarian. Publicity and insurance provided, transport between libraries arranged for touring exhibitions. Commission is 10%.

Access: [F] Public car park adjacent

Four Seasons Gallery

A commercial gallery specialising in paintings, prints and crafts with a special mixed exhibition occasionally held during the year. [Pa,Pr,Cr]

Address: 39 St Giles Street, Northampton NN1 1JF tel 0604 32287
Contact: George Hammerschmidt
Open: Mon-Fri 9.30-5.30, Sat 9.15-5
Policy: The gallery also undertakes framing.
Sales: Work sold; Credit card
The Space: The exhibition space is on the first floor above the craft shop. The space has sufficient room for *'50 medium-sized prints'*.
Exhibiting: Exhibition costs are shared between the gallery and artist.
Access: [X] Situated close to the town centre

Hibiscus

A commercial gallery selling work by established makers, and 'up and coming' newcomers. [Cr]

Address: 15 Bradshaw Street, Northampton NN1 2HL tel 0604 230652
Contact: Liz Nevison-Andrews
Open: Tues-Sat 10.30-5.30
Policy: The exhibitions are usually mixed shows with the emphasis on *'decorative and functional'*. The shop specialises in contemporary jewellery, ceramics, glass and wood.
Sales: Work sold; Credit card
The Space: The exhibition space has 25m linear wall space with track lighting.
Exhibiting: [AW] Slides should be sent to Liz Nevison-Andrews. The gallery charges 33.3% commission on sales, and covers insurance and preview costs.
Access: [X] Close to the Market Square; BR Northampton 10 mins

KUSCA Gallery

The gallery is housed in the school and community centre run by the education service and Kingsthorpe community association. [VA,Ph,Cr]

Address: Kingsthorpe Upper School, Boughton Green Road, Northampton NN2 7AF tel 0604 717479
Contact: Coordinator Gerald Porter
Open: Mon-Fri 9-9
Policy: The exhibition programme is a mixture of solo exhibitions from local and regional sources, and touring exhibitions from regional and national sources. When possible, workshops are arranged with the exhibitions. A large open courtyard (the Comquad) is available for sculpture exhibitions.
Sales: Work sold
The Space: 12x7x3.75m with hanging rail and direct fixing. Natural and spot lighting, with window blinds. Gallery plans available.
Exhibiting: [AW] Exhibition programme usually determined in May orJune for the following academic year. Slides should be sent to Gerald Porter. The gallery provides insurance, publicity, list of exhibits, preview and transport. A 15% commission is charged on sales. Supports EPR.
Access: [U][F] Situated on the North side of Northampton, A508 to Market Harborough, bus from town centre, BR Northampton 30 mins

Northampton College of Further Education

Exhibition space in the college library, with financial and publicity support from Northampton Arts Centre. [Ph]

Address: Booth Lane South, Northampton NN3 3RF tel 0604 403322 ext 246
Contact: BR McKee
Open: Normal college hours
Policy: The programme of photography exhibitions places *'emphasis on local artists, first exhibitions for students, commercial and industrial photography'*. Occasional touring exhibitions are booked, and future plans include workshops and links with Northampton Arts Centre's film programme.
Sales: Sales referred to exhibitor
The Space: There are 20 panels each 1x2m.
Exhibiting: [AW][EF] Applications in writing. The gallery provides publicity, mailing, and preview. EPR supported.
Access: [U][L] Parking at the college; Bus 45 from city centre

Northampton Local Education Authority

'Many of our schools and education establishments are able to provide display space for a wide variety of two and three-dimensional art works.' [VA,Ph,Cr]

Address: Design Education Centre, Nene College, Park Campus, Boughton Green Road, Northampton NN2 7AL tel 0604 715000 ext 272
Contact: Advisory Teacher for Art & Design Ian Middleton
Policy: *'Our policy is to enhance and encourage the work of children and adults in the area by working alongside artists and makers through residencies and by displaying work together as a mutual source of reference, enrichment and stimulus.*
Sales: Work sold sometimes
The Space: Display screens and lighting are available from the education authority for use in schools.
Exhibiting: [AW] Artists and exhibitors are welcome to contact the Design Education Centre to discuss the opportunities and potential of this initiative.

Northamptonshire Libraries

The libraries show a variety of work from the region and elsewhere. Touring exhibitions are arranged by the Arts and Libraries group. [VA,Ph,Cr,Ar]

Address: Libraries Department, Northamptonshire County Council, 27 Guildhall Road, Northampton NN1 1DE tel 0604 202621
Contact: Arts Officer Lesley Haggar or, Dr D R Bond, Kettering Library tel 0536 512315
Open: See entries for individual libraries
Policy: There are a number of libraries that show exhibitions *'to encourage and support work in the visual*

arts and crafts by giving artists and makers the opportunity to show and sell their work in an informal and sympathetic environment'. The service is highly-developed with a network of library spaces that co-operate in touring exhibitions and arranging extra activities. The staff are aware of the needs of artists and makers and aim to provide a professional service. A few libraries have special showcases for small touring craft exhibitions, provided by regional services, coupled with video facilities and display screens to provide more information. The spaces are also available to individuals and groups for their own exhibitions. Standards of presentation and content are as high as possible, with an emphasis on making the work as accessible as possible for the library users.'

Sales: Work sold; Sales referred to exhibitor

The Space: Most libraries have wall space and screens suitable for art work and track lighting. Newly refurbished libraries have been equipped with separate gallery space. Wall panels are hessian-covered. See also individual entries for Brackley, Burton Latimer, Corby, Desborough, Duston, Irthlingborough, Kettering, Long Buckby, Raunds, Rothwell, Towcester, Wellingborough, and Weston Favell. A new library gallery will open in Daventry in Spring 1989.

Exhibiting: [AW] Contact the District Librarian or Lesley Haggar, Arts and Libraries Group, Northamptonshire Libraries. The libraries provide insurance, publicity and transport between libraries for touring exhibitions. A 10% commission is charged on sales.

Access: [F] Normally libraries are situated in town centres

University Centre Northampton

The gallery is housed in the Department of Adult Education of the University of Leicester which caters for day and evening classes. [Pa,Dr,Ph]

Address: Barrack Road, Northampton NN2 6AF tel 0604 30084

Contact: Alan Caine

Open: Mon-Fri 9-9.30

Policy: The *'policy is to provide space for local and non-local artists to display their work'.*

Sales: Work sold

The Space: A 12x4.5m space, with spot lights and hanging rail. The room is part of the Common Room.

Exhibiting: Hanging, publicity and insurance are the exhibitor's responsibility, no hire charge, commission 15%.

Access: [U][F] Parking in surrounding streets; BR Northampton 20 mins

Weston Favell Library

See Northamptonshire Libraries. [VA,Ph,Cr]

Address: Weston Favell Centre, Northampton NN3 4JZ tel 0604 413327/8

Contact: Librarian Miss Ellice-Jones

Open: Mon,Tues,Thurs, Fri 10-8, Sat 9-4; closed Wed

Sales: Work sold: Sales referred to exhibitor

The Space: The space has 6m linear hanging space.

Exhibiting: [AW] Librarian. Publicity, insurance provided, as well as transport between libraries for touring exhibitions. Commission is 10%.

Access: [F] ramp **[L]**. Buses frequent services to town centre. Car park on ground floor

Northwich (Cheshire)

(NWA) Map4 SJ67

Weaver Gallery

A commercial art gallery opened in 1970 that specialises in selling contemporary painting. [VA]

Address: 12 High Street, Weaverham, Northwich, Cheshire CW8 3HB tel 0606 853585

Contact: Brian Bailey

Open: Mon-Sat 9.30-5

Policy: The gallery aims to present good contemporary art for collectors and buyers who value original work. During the last twelve months the gallery has shown seven solo exhibitions each lasting three weeks. In addition, the gallery has changing displays of work for sale.

Sales: Work sold; Credit card

The Space: The four galleries have wall space measuring 15x2.50m, 15x2.50m, 18x2.50m and 20x2.50m and have fluorescent lighting and spot lights.

Exhibiting: [AW] Applications to Brian Bailey should include a letter and slides. Work measuring more than 1.50x1m is not accepted. The gallery hire charges are negotiable. It pays towards insurance, publicity, preview costs, mailing and catalogue and takes 33.3% commission. Exhibiting artists get special discounts for framing.

Access: [F] Gallery car park

Norwich (Norfolk)

(EA) Map5 TG20

Advice Arcade Gallery

An advice centre, utilising first floor space as an art gallery, housed in a listed building in the city centre. [VA]

Address: Advice Arcade, 4 Guildhall Hill, Norwich, Norfolk NR2 1JH tel 0603 665755

Contact: Advice Arcade Manager Liz Edwards

Open: Mon-Fri 10-5

Policy: *'The city council has a policy of displaying works of art in its public buildings to encourage an appreciation of art as a part of everyday life. The gallery aims to offer local artists an opportunity to show larger works not normally accepted by commercial galleries.'* Quarterly mixed exhibitions plus *'special events'*.

Sales: Work sold

The Space: Linear hanging space of around 55m on hessian-covered wall boards 2.5x1.2m, mirror plates to be pre-fixed by artist. Overhead picture lighting.

Exhibiting: [AW] Apply to Pat Jourdan, 5 Onley Street, Norwich, telephone 0603 611387. Hanging fee £3 per picture to cover publicity and private view. Commission charged is 20%.

Access: [X] Car park 2mins, BR 15mins

Assembly House

Arts centre and meeting place, including cinema and cafeteria in Georgian building which is administered by an arts trust with charitable status. [VA,Ph,Cr]

Address: Theatre Street, Norwich, Norfolk NR2 1RG tel 0603 626402
Contact: Manager Bernard Ducker
Open: Mon-Sat 10-6
Policy: Exhibitors are selected *'to encourage the general public to use the building and add interest for visitors.'* The gallery shows almost entirely living artists.
Sales: Sales referred to exhibitor
The Space: One gallery is 7x6.5x4m high with a wall length 25.6m, the other is 8x6.5x4m high with a wall length 28.6m. Lighting is by revolving spots. Door width 1.25m. The open green to front of building has been used in the past for large sculpture.
Exhibiting: [AW] Submit applications in April in writing for allocations made at the beginning of May. Week-long exhibitions. Hire fee payable and commission is10%.
Access: [U][F] City centre site; Car park

Cinema City

Regional film theatre showing independent and alternative films with associated media and adult education activities. [VA,Ph]

Address: St Andrew's Street, Norwich, Norfolk NR2 4AD tel 0603 622047
Contact: Theatre Controller Kingsley Canham
Open: Mon-Sat 7-11, Sun 7-10 (pm)
Policy: *'A space for local artists and students to exhibit and sell their work in a non-commercial, non-competitive environment.'* Mixed and solo exhibitions of between one and two weeks.
Sales: Sales referred to exhibitor
The Space: The bar area has six boards 2mx1m high and one 4mx1m high with two lights fixed to each board.
Exhibiting: [AW] To Theatre Controller. Hire charge is £5 a week. No sculpture or work can be hung on the building's walls. Commission charged is 10%.
Access: [X] City centre site; Close to large car parks

Conroy-Foley Designer Craft

Specialist crafts outlet. [VA,Cr]

Address: 6 Merchant's Court, St.George's Street, Norwich, Norfolk NR2 tel 0603 630338
Contact: Jane Foley
Open: Mon-Sat 9.30-5.30
Policy: Work sold on consignment. High-quality crafts and fine art, no solo exhibitions.
Sales: Work sold
The Space: The gallery is 8x7x4m.
Exhibiting: [AW]

Contact Gallery

Artists' collective gallery which is partly funded by city council and RAA. [VA,Ph,Cr]

Address: 56 St Benedict's Street, Norwich, Norfolk NR2 4AR tel 0603 760219
Contact: Committee
Open: Mon-Sat 11-6
Policy: *'To advance public knowledge and appreciation of contemporary art'* by making contact with as much of the population as possible. The gallery concentrates on living artists from East Anglia, but this is not exclusive.
Sales: Work sold
The Space: Two rooms 3.5m high and 25m linear space with hanging on wooden battens fixed to walls.
Exhibiting: [AW] In writing with slides etc. Gallery pays for publicity and preview costs. The gallery liaises with artist to obtain sponsorship. Commission charged is 20%.
Access: [X] City centre; Car park 3mins

Crome Gallery

Frame shop with gallery in rear. [Pa,Pr]

Address: 34 Elm Hill, Norwich, Norfolk NR3 1HG tel 0603 622827 & 614781
Policy: Continuing exhibition of work sold on consignment.
Sales: Work sold; Credit card
The Space: The gallery is 4x4x3m high.
Exhibiting: [AW]
Access: [S]

Glasshouse Gallery

Commercial gallery specialising in watercolours, oils and etchings, mainly East Anglian scenes. Some week-long individual exhibitions but a mainly changing display of work. [Pa,Pr]

Address: 11 Wensum Street, Elm Hill, Norwich, Norfolk NR3 1LA tel 0603 615200
Contact: D Pegram
Open: Mon-Sat 10-5
Policy: Modern-style etchings, silkscreen, watercolours and oils by living artists, predominantly representational work.
Sales: Work sold; Credit scheme; Credit card
The Space: Gallery 1 is 8x4x3m high with 16m wall display, Gallery 2 is 10x5x10m high, 20m wall display and Gallery 3 is 10x6x3m high.
Exhibiting: [AW] In writing to the gallery. Gallery pays for insurance, printing, preview, display, mailing and catalogue. The space is hired by negotiation and

Contact Gallery: glass figures by David Reekie, left 'Waiting Man No2'. right 'Waiting Man No1', each about 35cm high, 1988

commission charged is 40%.
Access: [F] City centre, close to cathedral

Maddermarket Theatre

A purpose-built theatre with exhibition space. [VA,Cr]
Address: St John's Alley, Norwich, Norfolk tel 0603 626560
Contact: Administrator Nick Mowat
Open: Mon-Sat 10-5 and during performances
Policy: Show artistic work of an acceptable quality. Both mixed and solo exhibitions.
Sales: Work sold
The Space: The theatre foyer and bar is a very large irregular space of nearly 50m linear. Some space for sculpture in courtyards.
Exhibiting: [AW] Hire fee plus commission is charged and the artist pays all expenses, gallery will staff private view and organise wine.
Access: [X] Close city centre; Ample car parking

Mandells Gallery

Commercial art gallery founded in 1966. [VA]
Address: Elm Hill, Norwich, Norfolk NR3 tel 0603 626892 & 629150
Contact: Mr Allen
Open: Mon-Sat 9-5.30, Sun by appointment
Policy: The gallery specialises in twentieth century and contemporary representational art. Some solo exhibitions, mainly by *'gallery artists'*.
Sales: Work sold
The Space: The three large rooms are 5x5m, 5x8m, and 8x10m.
Access: [S] Close city centre, adjoining public car park

Norfolk County Council Libraries & Information Service

Selected public libraries in Norfolk. [VA]
Address: County Hall, Martineau Lane, Norwich, Norfolk NR1 2DH tel 0603 611122 ext 5363
Contact: Arts Officer Diana Treacher
Open: Various
Policy: *'Display art and craft work by living Norfolk artists in order to stimulate interest in, and income for, these artists.'*
Sales: Work sold
The Space: Various. *'There are 45 libraries in Norfolk, all of which will have gallery space in time.'*
Exhibiting: [AW] Apply to Arts Officer.

Norwich Arts Centre

Part of general arts centre with a gallery in the restaurant area. [Ph,Cr]
Address: St Benedicts Street, Norwich, Norfolk NR2 4PG tel 0603 660352
Contact: Exhibitions Organiser Sue Monypenny
Open: Mon-Sun 10-6 and evenings Mon-Sat
Policy: The gallery specialises in photography, including monthly touring and local shows, and workshops etc. There is a darkroom for hire and exhibitors are requested to give talks.
Sales: Work sold
The Space: Large main area with staircase and mezzanine floor, with showcases for craft work.
Exhibiting: [AW] Apply with details and slides. Photographs exhibited must be glazed. Division of exhibition costs is negotiable and the commission on crafts sales is 20%.
Access: [U] Close town centre; Street parking

Norwich Castle Museum

Municipal Gallery run by Norfolk County Council as the centre of their museums service which specialises in large-scale touring exhibitions with some use by local societies. [VA,Ph,Cr]
Address: Norwich Castle Museum, Norwich, Norfolk NR1 3JU tel 0603 611277 ext 21
Contact: Director Francis Cheetham
Open: Mon-Sat 10-5, Sun 2-5; closed Christmas, New Year and Good Friday
Policy: *'To make museums more accessible to the general public, with an emphasis on educational and children's events.'* Strong permanent collection of Norwich School painters, archaeology, natural history, social history etc. Exhibitions fall into three categories: national touring exhibitions, those from local societies, and those generated by the museum.
The Space: Two temporary exhibition galleries, each 20x8x3m high. Fluorescent wall lighting and tracks. The gallery is indemnified for insurance cover.
Exhibiting: The gallery covers insurance, publicity and preview costs.
Access: [U][T][L][F] City Centre; 10 mins BR Norwich

Norwich School of Art Gallery

Attached to Norwich School of Art, with full public access, the gallery shows college department exhibitions for one term, the other two terms are devoted to exhibitions the gallery initiates and tours, and exhibitions organised by other bodies. [VA]
Address: Norwich School of Art, St George's Street, Norwich, Norfolk NR3 1BB tel 0603 610561 ext 62
Contact: Curator Lynda Checketts
Open: Mon-Sat 10-5
Policy: The gallery prefers mixed shows, believing that solo shows can be detrimental. *'We are particularly interested in exhibitions on aspects of art and design education. The practice of art and design is the cornerstone of our programme. We like to initiate the majority of exhibitions and have extensive experience of touring locally and nationally. We take on researched exhibitions and projects with other curators. The gallery is also works with young artists in the region.*
Sales: Work sold
The Space: 6.7x11.7x3m high, plus 15 screens 1.3x2.6m high. There are two glass cases 1.3x0.6x1.5m high. Also a foyer area. Redevelopment to a riverside frontage planned for 1989/90 will increase space by 25%.
Exhibiting: [EF][AW] Send slides to the Curator. Slides are viewed by the Gallery Management Committee at programme meetings held once a term. Gallery meets all expenses and takes a commission of 25%.

Access: [F] City centre; local car park; BR Norwich ten minutes walk

Sainsbury Centre for the Visual Arts

The centre was built to provide galleries for the Robert and Lisa Sainsbury Collection and also has a special exhibition area. [VA,Ph,Cr]

Address: University of East Anglia, Norwich, Norfolk NR4 7TJ tel 0603 56161
Contact: Keeper Derek Gillman tel 0603 592466
Open: Tues-Sun 12-5
Policy: The centre puts on three special exhibitions a year, each running for between two and three months. Of these, at least one concentrates on modern Western art and one on non-Western art and exhibitions generally have some relationship to the collection which is of Western and African art as well as work from the Pacific and Americas and antiquities from Asia, Egypt and the ancient Mediterranean.
The Space: The galleries are 400 square metres.
Exhibiting: Exhibitions by invitation only.
Access: [U][T][L] Buses 526,527 from city centre, Castle Meadow or Surrey Street bus station; City Line minibus 4,5; on B1108; Parking on campus

St Gregory's Arts Centre

Run by a charitable trust as a community arts centre for local musicians and artists, but also open to professionals. [VA,Ph,CR]

Address: St Gregory's Arts Centre, Pottergate, Norwich, Norfolk NR2 tel 0603 628777
Contact: The Administrator Frances Hardy, St.Gregory's Office, 15 Pottergate, Norwich NR2 1DS
Open: Mon-Sat 10-4
Policy: *'To encourage local amateur artists, young professionals or recent college graduates looking for a first exhibition'* but the gallery also welcomes more experienced exhibitors. Exhibitions last between one and two weeks.
Sales: Sales referred to exhibitor
The Space: A redundant church with solid permanent plywood panels and 12m total length. Fixing is direct into boards. There is natural light plus spots on central pillars. Free-standing works must be easily movable to accommodate evening concerts and there is no fixing to church fabric. Plans available.
Exhibiting: [AW] Space for hire at £60-£65 a week. Apply with as much detail as possible, decisions are made by an events committee. The gallery prints the publicity.
Access: [F] City centre; Large car parks close by

Nottingham (Nottinghamshire)

(EMA) Map5 SK54

Arnold Library

See Nottingham Libraries. [VA,Ph,Cr]

Address: Front Street, Arnold, Nottingham NG5 7EE tel 0602 202247
Contact: District Librarian
Sales: Work sold; Sales referred to exhibitor
The Space: About 12m linear hanging space.
Exhibiting: [AW] Contact the District Librarian.
Access: [U]

Beeston Library

[VA,Ph,Cr]

Address: Foster Avenue, Beeston, Nottingham NG9 1AE tel 0602 255168
Contact: District Librarian
Policy: See Nottingham Libraries.
Sales: Work sold; Sales referred to exhibitor
The Space: Approx 18m linear hanging space.
Exhibiting: [AW] Contact the District Librarian.
Access: [F]

Bingham Library

See Nottingham Libraries. [VA,Ph,Cr]

Address: Eaton Place, Bingham, Nottingham NG13 8BE
Contact: District Librarian
Sales: Work sold; Sales referred to exhibitor
The Space: About 15m linear hanging space.
Exhibiting: [AW] Contact the District Librarian.
Access: [F]

Focal Point

An independent photography gallery partly funded by East Midlands Arts founded in 1987. [Ph]

Address: 10 Commerce Square, Lace Market, Nottingham NG1 1HS tel 0602 588876
Contact: Alec Leggat
Open: Tues-Sat 12-6
Policy: The programme shows mostly photographers in the East Midlands. Workshop sessions, talks and discussions are organised where appropriate.
Sales: Work sold
The Space: 30m linear hanging space with track lighting and daylight and direct fixing. Gallery plans available.
Exhibiting: [AW] Contact any Focal Point worker. The gallery provides a full exhibition service, *'though a fee is*

Focal Point

not always available'. Supports EPR.
Access: [X] Car parking close by; Bus station and BR Nottingham 5 mins

Focus Gallery

A commercial gallery with a changing display of work for sale and a framing service. [VA,Cr]

Address: 108 Derby Road, Nottingham NG1 5FB tel 0602 417913
Contact: Director Norman Rowland
Open: Mon-Sat 9.30-5.30
Policy: A continuous display of British crafts and prints for immediate sale.
Sales: Work sold; Credit card
The Space: Two spaces each 5x10m with direct fixing, spots and fluorescent lights.
Access: [X] City centre 5 mins

Meadows Community Arts

A community arts project offering a variety of activities and projects including the visual arts. [VA,Ph]

Address: Queens Walk Centre, The Meadows, Nottingham NG2 2DF
Contact: Stephen Gregory

Castle Museum & Art Gallery: 'Final preparation for the bride at a Hindu wedding' by Tim Smith, Bradford Heritage Recording Unit, 1987

Nottingham Castle Museum & Art Gallery

A municipal museum and art gallery originating a 'broad mixture of historical and contemporary exhibitions in a variety of media'. [VA,Cr,Ph,LA]

Address: The Castle, Nottingham G1 6EL tel 0602 483504
Contact: Exhibitions Officer Jane Bevan
Open: 10-5.45 April-Sept; 10-4.45 Oct-March
Policy: Temporary exhibition spaces are used to show two or three major historical exhibitions a year with a lively programme that *'aims to engage the castle's large audience (500,000 visitors a year) with contemporary art work'*. The programme includes solo and thematic group shows, including performance and installation work. *'There is a commitment to working outside the gallery and to making maximum use of the castle's unique architectural and landscape features'*. Artists and makers with international and national reputations are shown as well as *'Artists'* Showcase' exhibitions of artists and makers from the East Midlands in a space devoted to promoting and selling their work. The museum shop is recognised by the Crafts Council and features a changing display of work for sale, as well as special exhibitions. An education programme runs alongside the exhibition programme, and there is a commitment to artists' workshops for schools and adults, as well as talks, lectures, guided tours and video and tape/slide presentations. Concerts, poetry, drama and dance are also promoted.
Sales: Work sold; Credit card; Credit scheme
The Space: Gallery A has 40m linear hanging space and Gallery B has 56m linear hanging space, both with additional screens, adjustable lighting and controlled environment. The Artists' Showcase space provides 60m linear and purpose-built lockable display cases. Display cases are also available for use in galleries A & B. The castle grounds are used for sculpture exhibitions and occasional events. Gallery plans available.
Exhibiting: **[AW]** Main galleries are not available for solo shows not initiated by the gallery staff. Applications and proposals for thematic or group shows are welcomed. Applications for solo shows from artists and makers in the East Midlands are welcomed for the Artists' Showcase programme. The gallery provides insurance, transport, publicity, a list of exhibits and preview.
Access: [U][T][L] City centre location; Bus to Maid Marion Way or Castle Boulevard; BR Nottingham 10 mins; Standard Hill car park 5 mins

Nottingham City Artists

An independent studio complex established in 1986. [VA]

Address: 42 Canal Street, Nottingham NG1 7EH tel 0602 587472
Contact: Chris Campbell
Open: By appointment
Policy: Educational activities, including occasional exhibitions are held in part of the building. The space is mainly used by studio members, but is available to other artists for invited private audiences in negotiation with Nottingham City Artists.
Sales: Work sold: Sales referred to exhibitor

The Space: The gallery/education space is located on the ground floor at the front of the building. Large picture window to street. Two rooms with floor area of 44 square metres.
Exhibiting: The space is available for rent.
Access: City centre location; Broadmarsh public car park 2 mins; BR Nottingham 5 mins

Nottingham Community Arts Centre

A community arts centre funded by East Midlands Arts, Nottingham City and Nottinghamshire County Councils. Which runs courses and provides facilities for textiles, photography, video and printing. [Pa,Pr,Dr,Ph,Cr(textiles)]

Address: 39 Gregory Boulevard, Hyson Green, Nottingham NG7 6BE tel 0602 782463
Contact: Diane Bailey, Janet Vernon
Open: Tues,Wed,Fri 9.30-5
Policy: The centre aims to show twelve exhibitions in three seasons (Spring, Summer, Autumn) comprising *'small-scale touring exhibitions, local artists, and work produced in the centre'*. The exhibitions concentrate on *'local anti-sexist, anti-racist and issue-based work', particularly work which presents a 'positive images of oppressed groups'*. Workshops are arranged with exhibitions.
Sales: Sales referred to exhibitors
The Space: A 6x8m space with natural lighting and direct fixing is used. The space is unsuitable for three-dimensional work.
Exhibiting: [AW] The centre provides insurance, transport, publicity, mailing, display and artists expenses. A fee is paid in conjunction with workshops. EPR supported.
Access: [F][X] On street parking; Buses 81,82,85 95 to Hyson Green/Radford Road; BR Nottingham 20 mins, with buses 85,95 bus from station

Nottingham Libraries

Nottinghamshire County Council Leisure Services department runs the library service with over 40 libraries with exhibition spaces. [VA,Ph,Cr]

Address: Trent Bridge House, Fox Road, West Bridgeford, Nottingham NG2 6BJ tel 0602 824218
Contact: Exhibitions Officer Barry Prothero
Open: Normal library hours
Policy: A wide ranging and comprehensive touring exhibition service showing work by professional artists and makers from the region. Exhibitions are normally shown for four weeks and half the exhibitions are solo shows. Other exhibitions are thematic, historical, or commissioned exhibitions. An extensive workshop and education programme aimed at local schools and library users runs alongside the exhibition programmes. Each exhibition is usually toured to eight venues. A programme is published covering all the exhibitions. Libraries with the best facilities and separate exhibition areas are listed separately. See Arnold, Beeston, Bingham, Mansfield and West Bridgford.
Sales: Work sold; Sales referred to exhibitor
The Space: Spaces vary from 6m linear hanging space to purpose-built exhibition spaces with 35m linear hanging space. Showcases are available in some libraries. Where possible direct fixing is used. Large or heavy work that is difficult to transport cannot be shown.
Exhibiting: [AW] Artists and makers in Nottinghamshire should contact the Exhibitions Officer. The library service provides insurance, publicity and transport.
Access: Most spaces have disabled access

Nottingham Playhouse

The gallery space is in the foyer of the theatre. [VA,Ph,Cr,LA]

Address: Wellington Circus, Nottingham NG1 5AF tel 0602 474361
Contact: Theatre Manager Christabel King
Open: 10-10 (theatre is opening times)
Policy: A wide variety of shows are staged, with half of them being solo exhibitions. The programme includes local and regional artists as well as national touring exhibitions. The theatre is planning to make showcases available to makers for selling crafts.
Sales: Work sold; Credit card
The Space: Eight large double-sided screens give 18m linear hanging space with natural, spots and fluorescent light.
Exhibiting: [AW] Exhibitors must hang their own shows and a commission of 25% is charged on sales.
Access: [U][T][L][F] Close to city centre car parks; Bus station and BR Nottingham 10 mins

Nottingham University Art Gallery

The gallery is part of the Department of Art History and shows major exhibitions of historical work, as well as recent developments in art. [VA,Ph]

Address: Portland Building, University Park, Nottingham NG7 2RD tel 0602 484848 ext 2253
Contact: Curator Joanne Wright
Open: Mon-Fri 10-7, Sat 11-5 (term-time)
Policy: Exhibitions are shown during the academic year (Oct-June) and usually last four weeks. Exhibitions range from those organised by the art history department to touring shows and exhibitions with *'inter-disciplinary appeal'*. Occasional concerts are staged in the gallery as appropriate to the exhibition.
The Space: The main gallery is 15x7.5x4m giving 35m linear hanging space, the small gallery is 10x4.25.2.5m giving 24m linear hanging space. Both galleries have humidity and lighting controls in compliance with national standards. Security and smoke alarms are also used. Gallery plans available.
Exhibiting: [AW] The gallery is heavily booked in advance. Applications should be made to the Curator. The gallery covers all exhibition costs.
Access: [U][T][L][F] Parking on campus; Buses 12 & 13 from town centre

Patchings Farm Art Centre

An independent arts centre which opened in July 1988. The centre is housed in renovated farm buildings and comprising gallery, pottery workshop, studio, restaurant, art materials shop, framing service and farming exhibition. [Pa,Dr,Pr,Ph]

Address: Oxton Road; Nr Calverton, Nottingham NG14 6NU tel 0602 653479
Contact: Co-Proprietor Ms E Wood
Open: Daily 9am-10pm
Policy: The centre aims *'to be an accessible outlet for artists of all ages'* and *'to stimulate interest and understanding of the artists'* work exhibited and encourage public participation in the field of art'. Workshops, talks and classes are arranged throughout the year.
Sales: Work sold; Credit card
The Space: 51m linear hanging space.
Exhibiting: **[AW]** In writing to Ms E Wood. The centre provides printing, mailing, a list of exhibits and preview. 10% commission charged on sales.
Access: **[U][T][X]** Car park on site, Main Nottingham/Calverton bus route

Project Pehchan

An arts and community project funded by Nottingham County Council with some project funding from East Midlands Arts. It has established an Arts Unit to promote asian arts within the City. [VA,Ph,Cr]
Address: Sneinton Youth & Community Centre, Beaumont Street, Nottingham NG2 4PY tel 0602 410104
Contact: Team Leader S N Khan
Open: Mon-Fri 9.30am-10pm, Sun 12-6
Policy: The project organises events and exhibitions for the local Asian community, particularly for young people. Can exhibit photographs, crafts and painting.
The Space: The Centre has a large hall, a lounge and committee room.
Access: **[F]**

Queens Medical Centre

A major general hospital with a fine art collection and occasional exhibitions. [VA]
Address: University Hospital,Clifton Boulevard, Nottingham NG7 2UH
Contact: Fiona Brightman

Trent Polytechnic (Bonington Gallery)

A large well-equipped gallery in the polytechnic showing a wide range of exhibitions. [VA,Cr,Ph,LA]

Patchings Farm Art Centre

Address: Fine Art Department, Trent Polytechnic, Dryden Street, Nottingham NG1 4FX tel 0602 418248 ext 2102
Contact: Gallery Organiser
Open: Mon-Fri 9-8
Policy: The gallery is used for major art exhibitions as well as fashion shows and promotional events. Most exhibitions are solo or two-person shows of artists and makers in the region. The adjoining lecture theatre makes it possible to hold seminars and talks in conjunction with the shows.
Sales: Sales referred to exhibitor
The Space: A 165 square metre space giving 26.5m linear hanging space. Track and natural light.
Exhibiting: A booking requisition is available from the Gallery Organiser. The gallery provides insurance, publicity, transport, list of exhibits, and preview.
Access: **[F][S]** 10 mins city centre; BR Nottingham 15 mins

West Bridgford Library

See Nottingham Libraries. [VA,Ph,Cr]
Address: Bridgford Road, West Bridgford, Nottingham NG2 6AT tel 0602 816506
Contact: District Librarian
Sales: Work sold; Sales referred to exhibitor
The Space: Approx 14m linear hanging space plus a small courtyard for outdoor sculpture.
Exhibiting: **[AW]** Contact the District Librarian.
Access: **[F]**

Nuneaton (Warwickshire)

(WMA) Map5 SP39

Nuneaton Museum & Art Gallery

A municipal art gallery run by the Leisure and Recreation Department of Nuneaton and Bedworth Borough Council with permanent collections of fine and decorative art, local history, geology and George Eliot personalia. [VA,Ph,Cr]
Address: Riversley Park, Nuneaton, Warwickshire CV11 5TU tel 0203 376473
Contact: Museum Curator Ann Robson
Open: Mon-Fri 12-7, Sat, Sun 10-7; closes at 5 in Winter
Policy: The aim of the exhibition programme is to *'promote as wide a variety of work as possible'*. The majority of exhibitions are by local amateur artists or societies, however *'artists from throughout the country are welcome to apply'*. Occasional demonstrations and talks are arranged.
Sales: Work sold
The Space: Two galleries both with 35m hanging space with fluorescent and daylight and hanging by a hook system. Metal or wood-framed display cases are available.
Exhibiting: **[AW]** Contact the Curator 18 months in advance. Insurance, printing and mailing provided. A commission of 10% is charged on sales.
Access: **[F]** On the Coventry/Nuneaton bus route; Public car park 5 mins; BR Nuneaton 15 mins

Oakham (Leicestershire)

(EMA) Map5 SK80

Rutland County Museum

The museum is run by Leicestershire Museums, Art Galleries and Records Service and temporary exhibitions alternate with permanent displays, mainly of rural life material, housed in a late 18th century riding school. [VA,Cr,Ph]

Address: Catmos Street, Oakham, Leicestershire LE15 6HW tel 0572 3654
Contact: Keeper T Clough
Open: Tues-Sat 10-5, closed 1-2; Sun April-Oct 2-5
Policy: A variable exhibition space is used for exhibitions of interest to the local community, and exhibitions drawn from the permanent collection.
Sales: Work sold
Exhibiting: [AW] Informal enquiries to the keeper. Commission is 20% with the museum providing insurance and sharing other costs *'by agreement'*.
Access: [F] Town Centre

Ockley (Surrey)

(SEA) Map7 TQ14

Hannah Peschar Gallery

In a programme running from May to October, this outdoor sculpture garden, which is on the Crafts Council's selected list, specialises in showing sculpture and large-scale ceramic pots and urns. [Sc,Cr]

Address: Black and White Cottage, Standon Lane, Ockley, Surrey RH5 5QR tel 030679 269
Contact: Hannah Peschar
Open: Fri & Sat 11-6, Sun 2-5 May-Oct; at other times by appointment
Policy: Hannah Peschar's aim is *'to show how well original work can look outdoors'*. In spite of the large size of the garden a sense of intimacy is maintained to show *'that the work can easily add to the aesthetic value of an urban garden or balcony'*. A selection of mainly British artists are promoted with the visitor given a wide range of choice in terms of style, size and materials. There are guided tours for visitors and lectures organised for students.
Sales: Work sold; Credit scheme
The Space: Two acres of grass, woodland, walks and ponds. Work needing heavy transport and lifting equipment is a problem as *'the garden is very delicate'*. The garden is also used for organised picnics for groups.
Exhibiting: [AW] Apply to Hannah Peschar. Gallery finances printing and mail-out of publicity and catalogue/card, list of exhibits, preview costs and display.
Access: [U] By car on A29

Hannah Peschar Gallery: for outdoor sculpture & garden art (Photo: Ron Sutherland)

Oldham (Lancashire)

(NWA) Map3 SD90

Grange Arts Centre

A centre holding exhibitions in the foyer and performance areas. [VA,Cr]

Address: Rochdale Road, Oldham, Lancashire OL9 6EA tel 061 624 8012
Open: Mon-Sat 9-11pm

Oldham Art Gallery

A municipal art gallery run by Oldham Metropolitan Borough with collections of 19th and 20th century art and a temporary exhibition programme. [VA]

Address: Union Street, Oldham, Greater Manchester OL1 1DN tel 061 678 4651
Contact: Principal Museum Officer Aileen B McEvoy
Open: Mon,Wed,Thurs,Fri 10-5, Tues 10-1, Sat 10-4
Policy: The gallery is committed to supporting living artists, promoting art and photography, exhibiting its collections and increasing public awareness and appreciation of art in general. During the last twelve months, the gallery has had 26 exhibitions which have shown the work of living artists, six of which were solo shows. Educational activities are arranged for some exhibitions.
Sales: Work sold; Sales referred to exhibitor
The Space: Gallery one has 43.58m linear hanging space, gallery two has 44.50m linear hanging space,

Oldham Art Gallery: 'Built In' by Val Murray during her residency at the gallery in 1987 (Photo: Peter Fox)

gallery three has 21.28m linear hanging space gallery four has 27.84m linear hanging space, gallery five has 30.48m linear hanging space, gallery six has 32.30m linear hanging space and gallery seven 24.68m linear hanging space. Works are mirror-plated to the walls and lit by natural and track light.

Exhibiting: [AW][EF] A leaflet is available from the gallery on how to apply. The gallery helps to finance insurance, printing and publicity, list of exhibits, preview costs, display, transport, mailing, catalogue, and the artist's expenses and takes 10% commission. Supports EPR and, once a year, the gallery commissions a work for the permanent collection.

Access: [L][F] BR 5 mins; Bus station 5 mins; Car park at rear

Ollerton (Nottinghamshire)

(EMA) Map5 SK66

Rufford Craft Centre & Sculpture Park

A gallery, craft centre and country park run by Nottinghamshire County Council Leisure Services Department with a permanent sculpture collection and programme of exhibitions, events and activities. [VA,Cr]

Address: Rufford Country Park, Nr Ollerton, Newark, Nottinghamshire NG22 9DF tel 0623 822944

Contact: Interpretation/Craft Officer Peter Dworok

Open: Mon-Sun 11am-5pm; limited opening Jan & Feb

Policy: Using three galleries and outdoor spaces exhibitions by nationally known as well as regional artists are shown together with a strong education programme of residencies, workshops and demonstrations. The gallery aims to provide *'an interesting and varied programme with a maximum amount of information...to enhance the visitors' enjoyment of the facilities at Rufford'.* 20 exhibitions are organised each year including eight major craft exhibitions, and three major outdoor sculpture shows. They also aim *'to provide a showing space for artists and makers from ethnic minority groups'.*

Sales: Work sold; Credit card

Rufford Craft Centre: Work by Jane McKeating in the exhibition 'Stitches and Threads' an embroidery exhibition shown in 1986

The Space: Main Gallery 60x15m, Sideshow Gallery 50m linear hanging space, Fringe Gallery 21m linear hanging space. Direct fixing and artificial and daylight used. Each exhibition is specifically designed for the exhibits. Outdoor sculpture showing areas around the main craft centre building.

Exhibiting: [AW] All costs except artists'/makers' expenses met by the gallery. A selection of slides or photographs and a CV are normally required as an application to exhibit. Applications should be addressed to the Interpretation/Craft Officer. Commission charged is between 10-33.3%.

Access: [U][T] Situated on the A614 two miles south of Ollerton

Ombersley (Hereford & Worcester)

(WMA) Map4 SO86

Ombersley Gallery

A private gallery with galleries and a tea room. [Pa,Sc,Cr]

Address: Church Terrace, Ombersley, Hereford & Worcester WR9 0EP tel 0905 620655

Contact: Carole Dalzell

Open: Tues-Sat 10-5

Policy: *'The aim of the Gallery is to appeal to collectors and visitors with a selection of the finest work'.* Mixed and solo exhibitions are mounted, and there is always a changing display of work for sale.

Sales: Work sold; Credit card; Credit scheme

The Space: Gallery 1 is 55 square metres, Gallery 2 is 16 square metres, Gallery 3 is 10 square metres. Spot lights and hessian-covered walls. A large lockable case is available for jewellery.

Exhibiting: [AW] The gallery provides insurance, printing, mailing and private view. Commission is 55%.

Access: [F][S] Free parking in village; Worcester-Kidderminster bus; BR Droitwich Spa

Ormskirk (Lancashire)

(MA) Map3 SD40

Edge Hill College of Higher Education (The Cave)

A gallery in the foyer of the main college entrance which serves the college community of two thousand students, visitors and the local community and shows a varied programme of small to medium-scale work by living artists. [VA,Pr,Ph,Cr]

Address: St Helens Road, Ormskirk, Lancashire L39 4QP tel 0695 75171 ext 220/291

Contact: Head of Art Department/Art Technician Tom Titherington/Joan Steele

Open: Mon-Fri 9-5

Policy: Temporary exhibition programme open to any artist whose work is considered to be of sufficient interest to a wide audience, ranging from those with specialist knowledge to members of the general public. The colleges' permanent collection is shown around the campus.

Sales: Work sold
The Space: Four glass-fronted showcases, two 1.8x0.9x0.6, two 1.8x0.6x0.6. Ten 2.4x1.2m movable Marler Haley screens and poles, with work limited to these sizes. Light track and spotlights. Enclosed lawn for sculpture.
Exhibiting: **[AW]** Contact Head of Department or Art Technician. College only provides list of exhibits. Commission is 10%. Supports EPR in principle.
Access: **[U][T]** Ormskirk town centre bus and BR 10 mins; Ample car parking on campus

Oswestry (Shropshire)

(WMA) Map4 SJ22

Chapel Art Centre

A commercial gallery in a converted chapel showing monthly exhibitions of 'contemporary, local professional artists', framing, restoration and artists materials sold. [Pa,Pr,Dr]

Address: Plough Bank, Oswestry, Shropshire SY10 tel 0691 656870
Contact: D Williams
Open: Mon-Wed,Fri,Sat 9-5
Sales: Work sold; Sales referred to exhibitor
The Space: 11x4x10m with spotlights and natural light.
Exhibiting: **[AW]** Gallery provides insurance, printing, mailing, list of exhibits and catalogue/card. Preview costs are shared. A 25% commission is charged on sales.
Access: **[S]** Car park 1 min; Bus station 2 mins; BR Oswestry 40 mins

Oundle (Northamptonshire)

(EMA) Map5 TL08

Yarrow Gallery

Gallery within a school aimed mainly at the school community. [VA,Ph,Cr]

Address: Oundle School, Oundle, Northamptonshire PE8 tel 0832 74034
Contact: Head of Art
Open: Mon-Sat 10.30-5, closed 1-2.30; Sun 11-1
Policy: Six exhibitions are held annually, and one or two local exhibitions are arranged.
Sales: Work sold
The Space: 50m linear hanging space on screens and walls with direct fixing, track lights and spots.
Exhibiting: The programme is booked two years ahead. The gallery charges 10% commission on sales.

Oxford (Oxfordshire)

(SA) Map7 SP50

Ashmolean Museum (McAlpine Gallery)

A university museum with a major collection of European and Oriental art with Departments of Western Art, Oriental Art, Antiquities and a coin room; the McAlpine Gallery shows occasional temporary exhibitions some of which are of contemporary art. [VA]

Address: Beaumont Street, Oxford OX1 2PH tel 0865 278041
Contact: Keeper of Western Art Nicholas Penny
Open: Weekdays 10-4, Sun 2-4; closed Mon
Policy: *'The museum mounts loan exhibitions appropriate to the museum, often directly related to their own holdings. At least one exhibition a year is devoted to the work of a living artist or artists'* and there are one or two exhibitions of twentieth century art. Exhibitions are normally shown for two months. Also a small exhibition gallery in the Department of Eastern Art.
Sales: Sales referred to exhibitor
The Space: The gallery is 3.3m high with a hanging height of 2.8m. There are a number of Edmunds desktop cases available.
Exhibiting: There is no provision for applications and the gallery will occasionally pay for insurance, printing and mailing of publicity and transport. They will rarely pay for a catalogue or card but will usually pay for a list of exhibits and preview costs.
Acdess: **[L][X]** Town centre site; BR Oxford 10 mins walk; Coach terminal nearby

Christ Church Picture Gallery

A private gallery existing primarily to exhibit the college's collection of old master paintings and drawings, including works by Raphael, Michelangelo, Da Vinci, Tintoretto, Van Dyck. Changing displays in the print room are selected from over 2000 old master drawings and prints. Special temporary exhibitions are also held. [Pa,Pr]

Address: Christ Church, Oxford OX1 1DP tel 0865 276172
Contact: Curator
Open: Mon-Sat 10.30-1 & 2-4.30, Sun 2-4.30; Open to 5.30 Easter - Sept
Policy: Applications to exhibit are accepted *'where the exhibition has some particular relevance to the college, the collection, Oxford, etc'.*
Exhibiting: Showcases are available; publicity and private view costs are shared.
Access: **[X]** No parking

Computer Corridor

A corridor exhibition space within the Polytechnic. [Pa,Pr,Dr,Ph,Cr]

Address: Oxford Polytechnic, Headington, Oxford OX3 0BP tel 0865 819460
Contact: Head of Visual Arts Tony Evora
Open: Mon-Fri 9-9pm
Policy: A wide range of exhibitions, seen by students, staff and the public, is shown ranging from graphics and illustration to avant-garde in print. Local artists show during the Oxfordshire Artweek and at other times of the year as well as exhibitions from abroad, the school of architecture and artists in residence. The exhibitions are shown for three weeks on average. The Polytechnic has a permanent collection of work bought from final-year students.
The Space: The exhibition space is 35x2x2.7m and will take around 45 flat A2-sized works.
Exhibiting: **[AW]** Apply by post or telephone to the Head

of Visual Arts, Music & Publishing Department. The gallery pays for insurance, list of exhibits, mailing of publicity, preview refreshments and occasionally transport.

Access: [U] Bus stop to city centre

Museum of Modern Art

The Museum of Modern Art has an international reputation for innovative exhibitions of recent modern art which contribute to the current debate on the history, function and future role of the visual arts. [VA,Ph,Ar,LA]

Address: 30 Pembroke Street, Oxford OX1 1BP tel 0865 722733

Contact: Director David Elliott,

Open: Tues-Sat 10-6, Sun 2-6; closed Mon

Policy: *'The museum is actively engaged in creating a larger and more heterogenous audience for contemporary art, playing a leading part in framing new viewpoints which counteract ethnocentricity and in presenting new work which has not been previously seen or valued. There is a strong educational programme which comes from the education department and this, together with the community programme, fosters an approach to culture that non-competitive and emphasises the enjoyment and fulfillment of the participants. An active programme of talks, seminars and workshops is also undertaken. Café on the lower floor, bookshop at street level.*

Sales: Work sold

The Space: The museum has security and environmental control to international museum standards. Gallery plans available.

Exhibiting: [AW] Applications should be sent to the Director, with CV and exhibition proposal plus slides or photographs of work and SAE for return of material. The museum finances all costs and supports EPR. A 30% commission is charged on sales.

Access: [L] Town centre site; BR Oxford 10 mins; Coach station 2 mins; City centre car parking

Museum of Oxford

A municipal gallery with a permanent collection of local history and topography of Oxford and Oxfordshire and also showing temporary exhibitions on local history, archaeology and by local artists. [VA,Ph,Cr]

Address: St Aldates, Oxford OX1 1DZ tel 0865 815539

Contact: Curator Nancy Hood

Open: Tues-Sat 10-5

Policy: *'We like to vary the temporary exhibition programme exhibitions which relates usually to the city and county collections with work by local groups of artists and other societies etc. Not all exhibitions need be local but these would be limited to a few times a year'.*

Sales: Work sold

The Space: The gallery has 14m linear hanging space and built-in showcases and track and daylight, and another 16m linear hanging space with curtained windows and track lighting. Gallery plans available.

Exhibiting: [AW] Apply to the Curator well in advance of the programme which is published through leaflets in April and October for the March and August deadlines. The exhibition space is hired out on *'reasonable and negotiable'* terms and the gallery supports EPR. Commission charged is 10%.

Access: [S] Central Oxford. BR Oxford 5 mins; On all bus routes

Oxford Gallery

A commercial art and craft gallery founded in 1968, with shop front facade in the centre of Oxford's High Street. [Pa,Pr,Dr,Cr]

Address: 23 High Street, Oxford OX1 4AH tel 0865 242731

Contact: Valerie Stewart

Open: Mon-Sat 10-5; closed bank holidays

Policy: The gallery shows fine and applied arts on an equal basis and exhibits the work of established figures alongside that of newer talents. It has a reputation for its collection of international limited edition prints, ceramics and jewellery. One exhibition a year is by selected graduate students. Of the annual programme of ten exhibitions, each of which last four and a half weeks, five are solo.

Sales: Work sold; Credit scheme; Credit card

The Space: Gallery plans available for the ground floor and basement gallery, each being approximately 8.5x4.8m. Lockable, alarmed showcases are available.

Exhibiting: [AW] Submit slides with CV and SAE and return postage in the first instance. If the gallery is interested, applicants are asked to bring examples. The gallery pays for insurance, printing of publicity, list of exhibits and a catalogue or card and charges between 46-50% on sales.

Access: [F] Ground floor gallery, **[X]** Lower gallery. BR Oxford 12-15 mins walk; Bus station 10 mins; Car park 5 mins

Photography Workshop

Gallery area is an integral part of the workshop which houses extensive darkrooms and studio for hire. [Ph]

Address: 103/104 St Mary's Road, Cowley, Oxford, Oxfordshire OX4 1QD tel 0865 246 027

Contact: Keith Barnes

Oxford Gallery: Alan Caiger Smith (Photo: D Elliott)

Open: Mon-Sat 10-10

Policy: The exhibition space is to provide *'interest and attract photographers and artists using the workshop. We do not exhibit primarily to sell work, but to further visual awareness'.*

The Space: 13m linear space with direct fixing, spots and natural light.

Exhibiting: [AW] Artist meets all exhibition expenses. 20% commission charged on sales.

Stables Gallery

A small art gallery within Oxford University's medical college showing visual arts and crafts. [VA,Ph,Cr]

Address: Green College, Woodstock Road, Oxford OX2 6HG tel 0865 274770

Contact: College Secretary Diane Price tel 0865 274781

Open: 10-6

Policy: To provide a facility for amateur and professional artists, particularly those showing for the first time. Most exhibitors are local and the exhibitions run for two weeks. *'The gallery is off the main tourist route and slightly out of the centre of town and therefore has small audiences'.*

Sales: Sales referred to exhibitor

The Space: The gallery comprises a curved brick wall with hanging rods and track lighting.

Exhibiting: [AW] Artists should contact the College Secretary. The gallery is generally booked a year in advance.

Access [F] City centre 10 mins walk; Frequent buses

Padiham (Lancashire)

(NWA) Map3 SD73

Coach House Gallery

The gallery is within a National Trust property operated by the Gawthorpe Foundation and Gawthorpe Enterprises Ltd. [Pa,Pr,Cr,Te]

Address: Gawthorpe Hall, Padiham, Burnley, Lancashire BB12 8UA tel 0282 78511

Contact: Director Roger Dyson

Open: Mon-Fri 10-12.30, 2-5, Sat-Sun 2-5 March-Dec

Policy: The hall houses the Rachel Kay-Shuttleworth collections of embroidery, lace and costume and consequently the exhibition programme reflects this by emphasising contemporary textiles. The aim of the gallery is to make available to general visitors and students work by contemporary professional makers of high standard and also to present and market work by recent graduates and to encourage people through its exhibitions, demonstrations and lectures to become creative and achieve greater understanding of the arts. The Education Officer organises a regular programme of craft courses. Craft shop with regular changing stock.

Coach House Gallery, Gawthorpe Hall

Sales: Work sold; Credit card

The Space: The upper gallery has 12.49m linear hanging space with spots and natural light and hanging by hooks. Gallery plans available.

Exhibiting: Applications should be sent to the Director.

Access: [U][T][F] Main bus routes 10 mins; Car park 2 mins

Par (Cornwall)

(SWA) Map6 SX05

Mid-Cornwall Galleries

A commercial gallery with a café showing mixed exhibitions featuring 'a large proportion of work from South West people'. [VA,Cr]

Address: Biscovey, Par, Cornwall PL24 2EG tel 0726 812131

Contact: Mrs Gould

Open: Mon-Fri 10-5

Policy: The exhibitions feature artists' and makers' group shows of three to twelve people. The gallery aims *'to sell high-quality painting, prints etc with high-quality craft work'.*

Sales: Work sold; Credit card

The Space: The gallery is in a converted school with 550 square metres of space, track lighting and four 1.25x1.25m showcases. Gallery plans available.

Exhibiting: [AW] Apply with slides. The gallery provides insurance, publicity, preview, list of exhibits, catalogue/card.

Access: [S] On the A390; Buses and BR St Austell 3 miles

Penrith (Cumbria)

(NA) Map3 NY53

Penrith Museum

A municipal museum showing local history with a proposed space for temporary exhibitions. [VA,Cr,Ph]

Address: Robinson's School, Middlegate, Penrith, Cumbria CA11 7PT tel 0768 64671

Contact: Curator Judith Clarke, From Summer 1989 Mon-Sat 10-5; Sun 1-6 April - Oct

Open: Mon-Sat 10-5 April-Oct; Mon,Tues,Thurs 10-5 Nov-March

Policy: A new exhibition space planned to open in Summer 1989 will be used to show a diverse selection of temporary exhibitions, including work by local artists and makers, as well as local social history.

Exhibiting: [AW] Applications welcome after Summer 1989.

Access: BR Penrith; Car parks close by

Penzance (Cornwall)

(SWA) Map6 SW43

Bread Street Gallery

A gallery extablished in 1988 showing work by both newcomers and established artists. [VA,Cr]

Address: Bread Street, Penzance, Cornwall TR18 2EQ

Contact: Director Melissa Hardie, The Old Post Office, Newmill, Penzance, Cornwall TR20 4XN tel 0736 60549

Open: Variable

Policy: The gallery *'is a warm, dry and empty building of character, small and intimate as well as spacious enough to accommodate an exhibition mounted by one or two artists of alternatively a group, mixed media show'*. It offers short-term space to unknown as well as well-known artists in a thriving arts community.

Sales: Work sold

The Space: The space can be screened and built-in shelving and tables are available. Three small, inter-connecting rooms lending themselves to many different treatments. General and spot light.

Exhibiting: [AW] Applications are welcome. Artists set their own opening time and share invigilation. Publicity is the artists responsibility although the gallery can help with secretarial services and a mailing list of interested people in Cornwall. Weekly rental charge plus 10% commission.

Access: City centre 3 mins; BR Penzance 3 mins; Public car park 3 mins

Jamieson Library

A gallery within a specialist library. [VA,Cr]

Address: The Hive, The Old Post Office, Hewmill, Penzance, Cornwall TR20 4XN tel 0736 60549

Contact: Directors Melissa Hardie, Philip Budden

Open: Varies - by arrangement

Policy: The library is a study collection on books, and art objects on the subject of women, with over 10,000 books and items held. The gallery shows visual art and craft work by women artists in two-week exhibitions. The library is also the base for Palten Press and Deborah Books.

Sales: Work sold

The Space: Library shelves are screened to provide white, clear walls for hanging. Mobile display tables and spot lighting.

Exhibiting: [AW] Applications from Women artists welcome. Only two-three exhibitions scheduled a year. Library handles publicity, printing and preview costs. Commission is 20%.

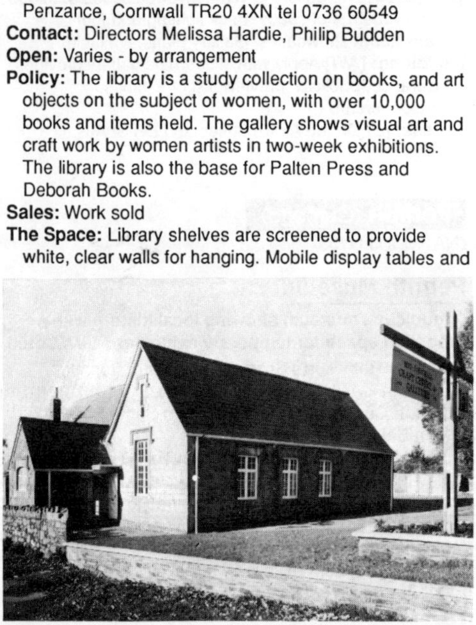

Mid-Cornwall Arts Centre See previous page

Newlyn Orion Galleries

A gallery showing an extensive programme contemporary visual art. [VA,Cr]

Address: Newlyn Art Gallery, Penzance, Cornwall TR20 5PZ tel 0736 63715

Contact: Director John Halkes

Open: Mon-Sat 10-5, 10-6 July & August

Policy: The programme includes painting, ceramics, photography, sculpture and other crafts. The gallery shop sells books, catalogues and cards. There is an extensive education programme and outreach to special needs groups. Major national touring and solo exhibitions mounted.

Sales: Work sold

The Space: The four galleries have 41m, 18m, 13m and 25m linear hanging space with direct fixing and spotlights, fluorescent and daylight. Showcases are available.

Exhibiting: Exhibitions are by invitation only and the gallery covers all expenses.

Trelissick Gallery (Cornwall Crafts Association)

A new gallery showing and selling work by members of the Cornwall Crafts Association. [VA,Cr]

Address: Trelissick Gardens, King Harry Ferry, Truro, Cornwall tel 0872 862423

Contact: Gunni Crowther

Open: Mon-Sat 11-6, Sun 1-5 March-Dec

Policy: See also details on the two other Cornwall Crafts Association's galleries at Bodmin and Helston.

Sales: Work sold

The Space: A two story gallery shared with Newlyn Orion Galleries. Each gallery has about 38m linear hanging space.

Access: [S] Ground floor

Trelissick Gallery (Newlyn Orion Galleries)

A gallery showing an extensive programme contemporary visual art. [VA,Cr]

Address: Trelissick Gardens, King Harry Ferry, Truro, Cornwall

Contact: Director John Halkes, Newlyn Orion Galleries, Penzance, Cornwall tel 0736 63715

Open: Mon-Sat 11-6, Sun 1-5

Policy: The programme includes painting, ceramics, photography, sculpture and other crafts. The programme uses thematic and group exhibitions to explore current art practice in the South West region.

Sales: Work sold

The Space: A two story gallery shared with Cornwall Crafts Association. Each gallery has about 38m linear hanging space.

Exhibiting: Exhibitions are by invitation only.

Wolf At The Door

A commercial gallery showing contemporary work 'as interesting as possible as well as being a high-standard. [VA,Ph,Cr]

Address: Bread Street, Penzance, Cornwall TR18 6EQ tel 0736 60573
Contact: Lu Simmons
Open: Mon-Fri 10-5, Sat 10-4; closed Wed, Sun
Policy: *'Work from known and unknown artists'* is shown in two galleries. The upper gallery has solo exhibitions and the lower gallery has mixed exhibitions. *'New lively exciting work preferred'*. The gallery also arranges talks and workshops.
Sales: Work sold; Credit card; Credit scheme
The Space: Two spaces each 6.5x7.7x2.25m with spots and natural light and direct fixing. Show cases for jewellery. Gallery plans available.
Exhibiting: [AW] Apply with slides, CV and SAE. Insurance, publicity, preview, list of exhibits, catalogue/card provided by the gallery. EPR supported.
Access: [S] BR Penzance 5 mins; Car park 2 mins

Peterborough (Cambridgeshire)

(EA) Map5 TL19

Bretton Library

Public library with exhibition space.

Address: The Cresset, Bretton Centre, Peterborough, Cambridgeshire PE3 8DX tel 0733 265705
Contact: Librarian Evone Cross
Open: Tues-Wed 10-6, Thurs-Fri 10-8, Sat 9.30-5
Policy: Exhibitions range from *'fine art, scholastic themes and social issues to publicity campaigns, sometimes self-generated, sometimes sought, but usually through approaches by potential exhibitors'.*
The Space: Two spaces, one a *'shop window'* to the shopping centre 6x3x1.5m high, mainly mounted on screens, the other a room 6x4m, with 8.5m linear plus screens.
Exhibiting: [AW] Financial responsibility *'varies'*. Commission charged is 10%.

David Holmes Gallery

Compact gallery run by a practising artist which specialises in British painting of a topographical and neo-romantic nature from 1720-1988. [VA]

Address: The Stable Block, Thorpe Hall, Thorpe Road, Peterborough, Cambridgeshire PE3 6JE
Contact: David Holmes, 12 Eastfield Road, Peterborough, Cambridgeshire PE1 4AN
Open: Wed-Sun 1-5
Policy: Showing work of a topographical nature that has a specific reference to East Anglia, this small gallery reflects in its programme the particular interests of the artist/director, whose other passion is for neo-romantic work. An average of six exhibitions a year each lasting six to eight weeks are mounted in a space that also functions as the owner's studio.
Sales: Work sold; Credit scheme
The Space: The gallery is 5x3.5m with spotlighting. The maximum size of work which can be accommodated is 0.91x1.22m.
Exhibiting: The gallery aims to establish a stable of artists, from whom work would be bought by the gallery for specific exhibitions, as well as commissioning particular work. Gallery covers printing and mailing of publicity and a list of exhibits.
Access: [X] BR Peterborough 15 min; Buses 14-16 to Longthorpe

Orton District Library

Exhibition space in a public library. [VA,Ph,Cr]

Address: Bushfield, Orton Goldhay, Peterborough, Cambridgeshire PE2 0RQ tel 0733 234448
Contact: District Librarian Martin Stone
Open: Tues 10-6, Wed, Fri 10-8, Thurs 10-5, Sat 9.30-5
Policy: No specific bias, but the library tends to encourage the local community.
The Space: Three display windows with spots and hessian display panels and *'plenty of space within the library itself.... It is difficult to fill the space available'.*
Exhibiting: [AW]
Access: [F]

Wolf at the Door

David Holmes Gallery: 'Lihou Island' by Rigby Graham, oil, 1978

Peterborough England

Peterborough Arts Centre (Lady Lodge)

Arts centre with three gallery spaces, performance area, craft studios and media workshop. [VA,Ph,Cr,Vi,Ho]

Address: Orton Goldhay, Peterborough, Cambridgeshire PE2 0JQ tel 0733 237703
Contact: Director Christine Redington
Open: Mon-Sat 9-5.30
Policy: The gallery spaces enable a diverse programme of temporary exhibitions. The emphasis is on work by local and regional artists and photographers and touring exhibitions. Where possible the centre presents weekends workshop linked to the exhibition on shows. Exhibitions also accompanied by workshops and lectures.
The Space: Three exhibition spaces, one suitable for large-scale work, all with natural and artificial light.
Exhibiting: [AW] Applications to the Director. The gallery covers cost of insurance, display and transport, publicity and posters if required. Commission is 25%.

Peterborough Museum & Art Gallery

Municipal gallery and museum supported by Peterborough City Council. [VA,Ph,Cr,LA]

Address: Priestgate, Peterborough, Cambridgeshire PE1 1LF tel 0733 43329
Contact: Assistant Curator, Exhibitions and Fine Art
Open: May-Sept. Tues-Sat 10-5; Oct-April Tues-Fri 12-5, Sat 10-5
Policy: *'To show in the programme a broad selection of exhibitions from arts, crafts, photography etc. To strengthen the links between practitioner and public by creating opportunities for interaction.'* The Annual *'Pacesetters'* exhibition is chosen from national submission. The four to five week exhibitions are mainly mixed but also some solo. Educational activities are encouraged.
Sales: Work sold
The Space: One gallery 15x7x3m high, with 52m linear, one 7x7x3m high, with 25m linear, and a third 15x7x3m high, with 44m linear. All with track and spot lighting and blinds over skylights. Three show cases 2.5x0.25x2m, 1x1x2m, 1.6x1x2m.
Exhibiting: [AW][EF] Most exhibitions are initiated by the Curator. The gallery pays for everything except display and charges commission of 10%. (25% for craft case shows).
Access: [F] All transport within 5 mins walk

Werrington Public Library

Exhibition in a Public library. [VA.Ph,Cr]

Address: Staniland Way, Werrington, Peterborough, Cambridgeshire PE4 6JT tel 0733 76666
Contact: Sub-Librarian Peter Aldridge
Open: Tues-Wed 10-5.30, Thurs-Fri 10-7, Sat 9.30-5
Policy: Cambridgeshire County Council policy.
The Space: One room 9x9m, two glass-fronted cases 4x2m, plus other space in the library used for free-standing and wall-mounted displays.
Exhibiting: [AW] Commission 10%.
Access: [U][T] Public car park 2 mins

Plymouth (Devon)

(SWA) Map6 SX45

Barbican Theatre Gallery

A theatre-in-education project which encourages artists under 25 and professional contemporary work. [Pa,Dr,Pr]

Address: Castle Street, Plymouth, Devon PL1 2NJ tel 0752 267131
Contact: Theatre Administrator Margaret Jones
Open: Mon-Fri 10am-10pm, Sat 6-10pm
Sales: Work sold; Sales referred to exhibitor
The Space: Approximately 23m linear hanging space.
Exhibiting: [AW] Exhibitors must meet all exhibition costs.
Access: [X] City centre 10 mins; Bus station 10 mins; BR Plymouth 20 mins

Plymouth Arts Centre

An independent arts centre funded by South West Arts, Plymouth City Council and Devon County Council with three galleries, cinema, film and video production workshop and an extensive education programme. [VA,Ph,Pr,Vi,LA]

Address: 38 Looe Street, Plymouth, Devon PL4 0EB tel 0752 660060
Contact: Visual Arts Co-ordinator Rosemary Greenlees
Open: Mon 10-5, Tues-Sat 10-8, Sun 5-8
Policy: The programme includes a *'very broad range of exhibitions by local and nationally-known artists, including touring exhibitions, solo and thematic group shows'*. The exhibitions programme provides an opportunity to see work produced outside the area as well as support for artists working in the region.
Sales: Work sold; Credit card
The Space: Gallery One is 13.5x5x2.7m giving 31m linear hanging space, Gallery Two is 11x4.3x2.6m giving 19.5m linear hanging space and Gallery Three is 6.6x6x2.2m giving 13.7m linear hanging space. Track lighting and some natural light in Gallery Three. Gallery plans available.
Exhibiting: [AW][EF] Insurance, transport, publicity, preview, list of exhibits, catalogue/card and display. Commission is 33.3%. EPR supported.
Access: [S][X] Opposite main bus station; Car park 5 mins; BR Plymouth 15 mins

Plymouth City Museum & Art Gallery

A municipal museum and art gallery with permanent collections and a regular programme of exhibitions. Substantial education and interpretation activities. [VA,Ph,Cr,Vi,Ar,LA]

Address: Drake Circus, Plymouth, Devon PL4 8AJ tel 0752 668 000 ext 4382
Contact: Exhibition Officer Sarah Shalgosky,
Open: Tues-Sat 10-5.30, Sun 2-5; closed Mon except bank holidays
Policy: The programme of temporary exhibitions features 10-12 shows a year. We aim to present a broad range of visual culture including historical exhibitions and work by contemporary artists in all media and from different

cultures. Proposals for thematic exhibitions are particularly welcome. The outreach policy encourages proposals for site specific work in the community.

Sales: Work sold

The Space: One large gallery 244m square (59 linear metres). Fluorescent lighting plus spotlights. Direct fixing, VHS monitor available. Smaller gallery spaces sometimes available. Gallery plans on request.

Exhibiting: [AW][EF] Applications to exhibition officer with CV, exhibition proposal and visual material. The museum covers costs of insurance, printing and publicity, display, transport. Exhibition payment right where applicable.

Access: [F] rear of building **[L]** BR Plymouth 5 mins; Bus to Drake Circus; City centre 5 mins

Plymouth Theatre Royal

The theatre uses the foyer as a gallery to show 'the work of regional, national and international artists and photographers of the highest standard'. [VA,Cr]

Address: Royal Parade, Plymouth, Devon PL1 2TR tel 0752 668282

Contact: Projects Co-ordinator Angela Lanyon

Open: Mon-Sat 10-10

Policy: The programme is mostly solo exhibitions of artists *'living and working in the West Country, Devon and Cornwall'*. The work is *'small to medium between £25 and £200 with an emphasis on the easily accessible'*.

Sales: Work sold; Credit card

The Space: Five hessian-covered boards each 1.2x1.6m giving a hanging length of 6m. One large showcase for craft exhibitions with five adjustable shelves each 0.95x0.55m.

Exhibiting: [AW] Applications are invited from Devon and Cornwall artists and makers. The theatre provides insurance, list of exhibits, and mailing of publicity.

Access: [U][T][L][F] Town centre location; BR Plymouth 10 mins

Pocklington (Humberside)

(LHA) Map3 SE84

Wilton House Gallery

A commercial gallery on the Crafts Council's selected list specialising in ceramics and glass made by the country's leading makers. The gallery also displays a constantly changing exhibition of ancient art and antiquities. [Ce]

Address: 95 Market Street, Pocklington, Humberside YO4 2AE tel 0759 304858

Contact: John Moor

Open: Mon, Tues,Thurs, Fri 10-4.30, Sat 10-12.30 & by appointment

Policy: The gallery aims to promote and encourage a better understanding by the public of the hand-crafted object by mounting continuous exhibitions of the finest ceramic work, *'the emphasis is always on quality for both traditional and designer made work, both functional and decorative pieces by makers past and living'*.**Sales:** Work sold; Credit card; Credit scheme

The Space: The gallery is on two floors giving approximately 111 square metres of display space.

Exhibiting: [AW] Makers should send slides and information to John Moor. The gallery covers the cost of insurance, printing of publicity, list of exhibits, preview costs, mailing out of publicity and the catalogue/card and takes 40% commission.

Access: [S]

Portsmouth (Hampshire)

(SA) Map7 SU60

Aspex Gallery

A large exhibition and studio complex housed in a converted 19th century church and set up by artists. [VA,Ph,Cr,LA]

Address: 27 Brougham Road, Portsmouth PO5 4PA tel 0705 812121

Contact: Director Les Buckingham

Open: Tues-Thurs 11-6, Fri & Sat 11-5, Sun 2-6, closed Mon

Policy: The gallery, managed independently but in co-operation with the studio group, shows new work by living artists and runs an active educational programme in association with local communities. Exhibitions run for four to six weeks, with more than a third being solo shows.

Sales: Work sold

The Space: The gallery is 762 square metres with 42.6m linear hanging space, with the possibility of extra screens. Walls are 3m high, with track lighting to 4.2m. It is difficult to show large sculpture.

Exhibiting: [AW][EF] Applications should be sent to the Director with slides, CV and a statement at any time. The gallery pays for insurance, printing and mailing of publicity, lists of exhibits, preview costs, transport, a catalogue/card and some expenses by agreement. A commission of 10% is charged on sales and EPR is supported.

Access [X] Bus 17,18 within 5 mins walk; BR Portsmouth and public car parks 5-10 mins walk

Aspex Gallery: 'The Cenotaph Project: Class of Rulers' by Stuart Brisley & Maya Balcioglu, 1988 (Photo: John McPherson)

City Museum & Art Gallery

A municipal museum with a permanent collection of fine and decorative art from the 15th century to the present day with a specialist crafts gallery and shop showing work by contemporary British makers. [VA,Dr,Cr]

Address: Museum Road, Old Portsmouth, Hampshire PO1 2LJ tel 0705 827261

Contact: Keeper of Art Rosalinda MC Hardiman

Open: Daily 10.30-5.30 (closed four days over Christmas)

Policy: The gallery has been reducing the small exhibitions of contemporary work following the opening of Aspex and now concentrates more on in-house exhibitions. The crafts gallery will continue to show contemporary crafts, including some touring shows. Recent exhibitions include a major exhibition on the local aircraft industry. Exhibitions run for between one and six months.

Sales: Work sold; Credit card

The Space: The museum has full environmental controls and full security. The Arts Council Gallery has 58.5m linear hanging space and the Crafts Gallery is 18x6x2.4m, both with direct fixing to walls. The gallery can not show work more than 2.13m high, show cases available. The grounds are available for sturdy installations and sculpture. Gallery plans available.

Exhibiting: [AW] Applications accepted throughout the year addressed to the Art Department, decisions made by all the Exhibition Committee. The museum pays for insurance, some printing of publicity, list of exhibits, mailing of publicity and sometimes a catalogue or card. Transport is in-house as is the hanging. The museum supports EPR. A commission charged is 15-50%.

Access: [U][T][S] Car park; BR Portsmouth Harbour 5 mins

Portsmouth City Museum and Art Gallery: 'Crafts Across Portsmouth' showing wood bowls by Jim Partridge and window grilles commissioned from Peter Parkinson, blacksmith from north Hampshire.

Screenworks Gallery

A photography gallery housed at a community arts centre. [Ph]

Address: The Hornpipe, 143 Kingston Road, Portsmouth PO2 7EB tel 0705 861851

Contact: Chris Cheshire & Michael Craven

Policy: The gallery aims to show the broadest spectrum of photography - from work of national importance to community-based photography. Facilities include an education programme with video, film and photography workshops and a photographers' slide library is planned.

Prescot (Merseyside)

(MA) Map3 SJ49

Prescot Museum

The museum specialises in the history of horology in South West Lancashire, and runs a programme of temporary exhibitions from local or national touring sources as well as initiating horological exhibitions. [VA,Cr]

Address: 34 Church Street, Prescot, Merseyside L34 3LA tel 051 430 7787

Contact: Curator R J Griffiths

Open: Tues-Sat 10-5 Sun 2-5; closed Mon; open bank holidays

Policy: The museum concentrates on horology and local history. It also runs a programme of activities related to these, particularly for children. Few of its temporary exhibitions are by living artists.

Sales: Work sold

The Space: Space 11.25x4x2.5m high with Concord Lytespan ceiling tracks and daylight can be excluded. Gallery plans available.

Exhibiting: [AW] Apply to Curator. Museum covers insurance, printing, publicity, preview, transport and display. Commission varies from 10 to 25%.

Access: [S] Ground floor only. Buses to Prescot from Liverpool, St Helens, Wigan and Manchester; BR Prescot (weekdays only) 10m mins; Free car parking on High Street and Eccleston Street

Prestbury (Cheshire)

(NWA) Map4 SJ87

Artizana

Opened in 1984, the gallery holds four exhibitions each year and is on the Craft Council's list of selected galleries. [Pa,Sc,Cr]

Address: The Village, Prestbury, Cheshire SK10 4DG tel 0625 827582

Contact: Owner Ramez Ghazoul

Open: Mon-Sat 10.30-6, Sun 2-6

Policy: The gallery has collections of glass, ceramics, jewellery, embroidery and wood which are on permanent display. It aims *'to provide a widely varied and ever-changing representation of the very best in contemporary British crafts that appeals to a wide cross-section of people. Particular emphasis is placed on supporting Northern makers and providing opportunities for the young and upcoming to exhibit their work'.* Occasional lectures and demonstrations take place. The target audience includes architects, collectors, interior designers, professionals and interested members of the public.

Sales: Work sold

The Space: The gallery is 15x5x3m with a total of 30m linear hanging space.

Exhibiting: [AW] Applications to exhibit should be sent to the gallery twelve to eighteen months in advance. It pays towards insurance, publicity, list of exhibits, preview, transport, mailing and catalogue. 40-50% commission is taken. Supports EPR.

Access: [F] BR Prestbury 10 mins; Public car park 1 min

Preston (Lancashire)

(NWA) Map3 SD52

Beacon Fell Craft Gallery

A commercial craft gallery founded in 1985 which organises two major exhibitions a year, with smaller changing exhibitions and displays, mainly of paintings and craftwork from the North West. [VA,Cr]

Address: Middle Lickhurst, Beacon Fell Country Park, Goosnargh, Preston, Lancashire PR3 2ER tel 0995 40658

Contact: Owner Margaret Ashworth

Open: Tues-Fri 1-5, Sat-Sun 10.30-5.30 Easter-Dec; Sun only 10.30-5.30 Jan-Easter

Policy: *'The gallery is committed to supporting and encouraging North West artists and makers. We believe our personal approach enables us to demonstrate the unique qualities achieved where skill and soul are combined in producing the work that's on exhibition'.* The major exhibitions last between two and three months. The gallery likes to give amateurs the opportunity to exhibit alongside professionals and to provide the public with the opportunity to see a rich diversity of work which is also varied in price. During most Sundays in the summer, demonstrations are arranged.

Sales: Work sold; Credit card

The Space: Double height main gallery 9x4.5m with 7x3.5m mezzanine, demonstration and display workshop with 7x5m work space. External closed courtyard available for sculpture.

Exhibiting: [AW] Applications should be sent to Andrew Ashworth. The gallery pays for insurance, publicity, preview costs, mailing and catalogue. 25% commission is taken on art work less than £100 and 20% is taken on work over £100, commission on all craftwork is 33.3%.

Access: [F] Parking near gallery

County & Regimental Museum

The museum was recently founded in May 1988 and aims to provide a wide variety of fine arts and crafts exhibitions, as well as exhibitions on social history and military themes. [VA]

Address: Stanley Street, Preston, Lancashire PR1 4YP tel 0772 264075

Contact: County Museums Officer J D Blundell

Open: Mon-Sat 10-5; Closed Thurs, Sun & bank holidays

Policy: *'The arts and crafts exhibitions in the museum must have a relevance to the whole county, as opposed to just the locality of Preston'.*

Sales: Work sold

The Space: The small gallery measures 8.2x6x4.6m, and the larger gallery measures 6x22x2.8m.

Exhibiting: [AW] Contact Caroline Simon, Museum Headquarters, Stanley Street, Preston. The museum assists with printing of publicity, preview and display costs, transport and catalogues. 15% commission is charged on sales.

Access: [F] Bus Station 5 mins walk; BR Preston 15-20 mins walk

Dallas Inman Gallery

A gallery promoting and selling work by Northern artists and makers and also showing Victorian paintings. [VA,Cr]

Address: 36 Friargate, Preston, Lancashire PR1 2AT tel 0772 59670

Contact: Dallas Inman

Open: Tues, Wed, Fri, Sat 10-5

Policy: A programme of solo exhibitions is shown.

Harris Museum & Art Gallery

A municipal museum and art gallery run by Preston Borough Council with permanent collections of fine and decorative arts and a varied exhibition programme. [VA,LA]

Address: Market Square, Preston, Lancashire PR1 2PP tel 0772 58248

Contact: Museum & Art Officer Vivienne Bennett

Open: Mon-Sat 10-5; closed bank holidays

Policy: *'The Harris exhibition policy is to increase awareness, understanding and enjoyment of contemporary art amongst the local and regional public. Exhibitions aim to highlight a broad range of contemporary art practice and to present it in an interesting, varied and accessible way. There is an active policy to promote artists'* work which is part of, or influenced by non-Western cultures throughout the programme of shows and events. An on-going concern is to increase disabled and disadvantaged peoples' access to, and involvement in all activities. There are regular educational activities for schools, play schemes, the general public and special needs groups.

Sales: Work sold

The Space: Gallery one is 8.8x9.1x3.3m with 32.7m linear hanging space, Gallery two is 16.7x9x3.3m with 42.7m linear hanging space and gallery three is 8.9x9.1x3.3 with 32.3m linear hanging space. There is natural light and a flexible track system with tungsten and spots. Fixing is by mirror plates. The galleries are situated on the second floor with access for exhibits via a passenger lift which limits the weight and size of work.

Exhibiting: [AW][EF] Ten slides plus relevant information should be sent to Emma Anderson, Exhibition Officer. Slides may be sent anytime and will be returned within four weeks. The gallery covers the cost of insurance, publicity, display, transport, preview, mailing and expenses where appropriate. Artists receive a commission fee to produce work especially for exhibitions. 10% commission is taken on sales. Supports EPR.

Access: [L][F] BR Preston 15 mins; Bus station 3 mins; Car park 5 mins

Lancashire Libraries

The library service for Lancashire.

Address: Libraries Headquarters, Lancashire County Council, 143 Corporation Street, Preston, Lancashire PR1 8RH tel 0772 54868

Contact: Assistant County Librarian R Wand

Policy: Most of Lancashire libraries have exhibition provision. See also separate entries for Wheatley Lane, Burnley, Chorley Central Library and Barnoldswick Library, Colne.

Exhibiting: [AW] Contact individual branch librarians.

Lancashire Polytechnic (Faculty of Arts)

An exhibition space within the Faculty of Arts of Lancashire Polytechnic. [VA,Ph]

Address: Victoria Building, Lancashire Polytechnic, Preston, Lancashire PR1 2TQ tel 0772 22141

Contact: Exhibitions Organiser Nigel Lewis

Open: Mon-Thurs 9-5, Fri 9-4

Policy: The space within the Faculty of Arts is intended to be used by polytechnic staff as well as outside artists to exhibit their work and showing a wide variety of media. The space is occasionally used for open days, plays and career conventions. The gallery works closely with the St Peters Arts Centre.

Sales: Sales referred to exhibitor

The Space: The ground-floor and mezzanine floor exhibition spaces have 29.87m linear hanging space. Gallery plans are available.

Exhibiting: [AW] Write or telephone Nigel Lewis to be considered for an exhibition. Costs of publicity, list of exhibits, preview costs, display, transport and mailing are paid by the faculty.

Access: [U][T][L][F] BR Preston 10 mins; Bus stop 1 min; two car parks nearby

Samlesbury Hall

An art and craft gallery which has 105 exhibitions a year varying in length from one to three weeks alongside continuing displays of art work. [VA]

Address: Preston New Road, Samlesbury, Preston, Lancashire PR5 OUP tel 0254 81 2229

Contact: Arthur Bickerstaffe

Open: 11.30-4 Winter; 11.30-5 Summer

Policy: Admission is adults £2 and children 80p. The hall also has a tea-room.

Sales: Work sold

The Space: Approximately 444 square metres floor display area with 55m linear hanging space.

Exhibiting: The hall pays insurance, printing of publicity and catalogues. Commission is 20%.

Access: [X] Ribble bus 150 Blackburn to Preston; parking for 80 vehicles

Vernon Gallery

The Vernon Gallery, a non-commercial gallery owned and run by Building Design Partnership, a multi-disciplinary design practice, holds eleven contemporary exhibitions a year. [VA]

Address: Vernon Street, Moor Lane, Preston, Lancashire PR1 3PQ tel 0772 59383

Contact: Building Design Partnership Arts Society Committee

Open: Mon-Fri 9-5.30

Policy: *'The gallery has a policy of exhibiting artists work we consider to be innovative, or of a quality and type which may not normally be selected for commercial galleries. We occasionally exhibit work of local colleges and schools to bring their activities to the attention of a wider public. Although there is no education programme at present it is hoped to arrange talks and demonstrations by the exhibitors in the future.'*

Sales: Sales referred to exhibitor

The Space: The gallery has 25m linear hanging space and 21 hessian-covered screens measuring 1m wide, to create a flexible arrangement. Hanging is by a silent/gliss rail with cord on the walls and screens from a fixed height of approximately 2.5m and spotlights. The gallery can accommodate works up to 2.5x3m and is used as a buffet area during concerts and private functions. Gallery plans available.

Exhibiting: [AW] Applications should be sent to Anne McVittie, Secretary of BDP Arts Society. The gallery will pay for publicity, mailing and, on occasions, a list of exhibits and catalogue. It will also pay for all costs of the private view except wine.

Access: BR Preston 10 mins

Quorn (Leicestershire)

(EMA) Map5 SK51

Rawlins School & Community College

Exhibition spaces in many of the Leicestershire community colleges are used by local and regional artists, with workshops, placements and residencies organised. [VA,Ph,Cr]

Address: Quorn, Loughborough, Leicestershire LE12 8DY tel 0509 412406

Contact: Vice-Principal (Community) Jackie Edwards

Open: Mon-Fri 9am-10pm

Policy: Rawlins Arts Centre mounts its own exhibitions at intervals throughout the year and favours local artists or work which is of particular interest to the community. See also Leicestershire Education Authority.

Sales: Work sold; Credit card

The Space: The exhibition space is in the bar and library areas. Hanging is on screens or picture rail. Glass display case available.

Exhibiting: **[AW]** Write to Vice-Principal (Community). Gallery covers cost of printing and publicity but not insurance.
Access: **[F]** College on A6 11 miles north of Leicester 2 miles south of Loughborough; Car parking

Ramsgate (Kent)

(SEA) Map7 TR36

Addington Street Studio & Gallery

A commercial gallery attached to Pat Castle's studio and living space. [VA,Ph,Cr]

Address: 49 Addington Street, Ramsgate, Kent CT11 9JJ tel 084 359 7405
Contact: Pat Castle tel 01 800 3410
Open: During exhibitions 10-1, 2.30-5; and by appointment
Policy: This gallery shows the owner's work in a permanent display alongside a programme of mixed and solo exhibitions. The gallery also hosts poetry readings, meetings and other small-scale events and takes an active part in local community activities such as theatre workshops and street fairs.
Sales: Work sold
The Space: Upper and lower galleries, each 4x6x2m high with approximately 12m linear hanging space. Locking cabinet available. For space reasons, only small-scale sculpture can be shown.
Exhibiting: **[AW]** Apply to Pat Castle. Gallery helps to finance insurance, printing and mailing of publicity, list of exhibits, preview costs, catalogue/card. Commission 33.3%.
Access: All buses to town centre; BR Ramsgate; Public car park 5 mins

Ramsgate Library Gallery

This gallery runs a varied high-quality programme concentrating on the best of contemporary art, but also occasionally stages historical shows. [VA,Ph,Cr]

Address: Guildford Lawn, Ramsgate, Kent CT11 9AY tel 084 359 3532
Contact: Arts and Exhibitions Officer John Brazier
Open: Mon-Wed 9.30-6, Thurs, Sat 9.30-5, Fri 9.30-8
Policy: The gallery aims to show a continuous programme of exhibitions covering all aspects of the visual arts together with a related programme of special events. Exhibitions are intended to provide an informative and entertaining educational programme that will appeal to local residents and visitors alike. Artists' workshops and residencies are arranged where appropriate. Predominantly showing the work of living artists, exhibitions normally run for four to five weeks, about half of which are solo shows.
Sales: Work sold
The Space: 14x13x6m high with 53m linear hanging space and a maximum of 3m hanging height. Fixing is direct to hanging surface with track-mounted spot lights and humidity and temperature controls. Gallery plans available.
Exhibiting: **[AW][EF]** Apply with slides or photographs to the Exhibitions Officer approximately 18 months in advance. Gallery finances insurance, printing and mail-out of publicity and catalogue/card, list of exhibits and transport. Exhibition commissions are offered where appropriate. Support in principle for EPR. Commission 20%.
Access: **[X]** BR station 10 mins; Public car park 3 min

Raunds (Northamptonshire)

(EMA) Map5 SP97

Raunds Library

See Northamptonshire Libraries. [VA,Ph,Cr]

Address: High Street, Raunds, Wellingborough, Northamptonshire NN9 6HT tel 0933 623671
Contact: District Librarian Mike Davison or Sue Gray, Higham Ferrers Library, Midland Road, Higham Ferrers, Northamptonshire tel 0933 314842
Sales: Work sold
The Space: The library has12m linear hanging space on walls.
Exhibiting: **[AW]** District Librarian or Sue Gray. Publicity and insurance provided. Transport between libraries arranged for touring exhibitions. Commission is 10%.
Access: **[F]**

Rawtenstall (Lancashire)

(NWA) Map3 SD82

Rawtenstall Library

A branch library run by Lancashire Libraries. [Pa,Pr,Ph]

Address: Haslingden Road, Rawtenstall, Rossendale, Lancashire BB4 6QU tel 0706 227911
Contact: District Librarian J D Mclaney
Policy: *'To provide exhibition space for paintings, prints and photographs for single artists, group shows or art societies'.*
Sales: Work sold
The Space: The area measures 10x7.50x7m giving 15m linear hanging space lit by tungsten spots and fluorescent tubes.
Exhibiting: **[AW]** Applications are welcome any time by letter, telephone or in person to the District Librarian.
Access: **[X]**

Harris Museum: artist Keith Khan discussing carnival masks with pupils from Wellfield High School, Leyland

Rossendale Museum

A municipal gallery mainly showing the work of local artists. [Pa,Cr]

Address: Whitaker Park, Rawtenstall, Rossendale, Lancashire BB4 6RE tel 0706 217777
Contact: Curator S Cruise
Open: Mon-Fri 1-5, Sat 10-12, 1-5, Sun 1-5; Apr-Oct, Sun 1-4, Nov-March
Policy: *'Our exhibitions are largely aimed at local people, hence the proliferation of local art and craft exhibitions. However, we also aim to attract a wider audience with a variety of other exhibitions but these usually keep to subjects which fall within the museum's collecting policy'.* There are occasional educational activities.
Sales: Work sold
The Space: The second floor gallery has 27.43m linear hanging space and seven display cases. As access is via a steep staircase, size and weight of exhibits is limited. Gallery plans are available.
Exhibiting: [AW] Written applications should be sent to the Curator. The gallery pays for list of exhibits and 10% commission is taken on sales.
Access: [X] Bus 4 between Bacup and Accrington; Limited parking within the park

Rayleigh (Essex)

(EA) Map7 TQ89

Rayleigh Library

Exhibition space in public library, available for hire. [VA,Cr]

Address: 132/4 High Street, Rayleigh, Essex SS6 7BX tel 0268 775830
Contact: Deputy Area Librarian Pat Henbest
Open: Mon,Tues,Thurs, Fri 9-7.30, Wed 9-1, Sat 9-5
Policy: See also entry for Essex Libraries, Chelsmford.
Sales: Work sold; Sales referred to exhibitor
The Space: The exhibition space is 50.2 square metres.
Access: [F]

Reading (Berkshire)

(SA) Map7 SU77

Hexagon

A gallery in the lower foyer of the theatre. [Pa,Pr,Dr,Ph]

Address: Queens Walk, Reading, Berkshire RG1 7UA tel 0734 390390
Contact: Director M Eakin
Open: Foyers normally open Mon-Sat 10am-10pm
Policy and Programme: The policy is to present exhibitions by local and other artists and photographers. Anything is considered, although no budget is available to buy in expensive exhibitions. The target audience is more a cross-section of people who use the space to eat, drink and attend performances as well as those coming in specially for the exhibition. The exhibitions run for three to four weeks, with fourteen a year and over a quarter of a million people pass through the doors each year.
Sales: Work sold: Credit card
The Space: The exhibition area has 45m linear hanging space.
Exhibiting [AW] Send with slides of photographic prints and CV to the House Manager, Mr S Hollingbery. The gallery pays for insurance, an entry in the theatre's diary of events, list of exhibits £25 a week. A commission of 20% is charged on sales.
Access: [U][L][F] Public car park adjacent, Reading 10 mins; Town centre bus routes

Rickmansworth (Hertfordshire)

(EA) Map7 TQ09

Watersmeet Centre

Foyer space in multi-purpose arts centre.

Address: High Street, Rickmansworth, Hertfordshire WD3 1HJ tel 0923 771542
Contact: Entertainments & Catering Manager John Welham
The Space: Two spaces in bar and foyer area.
Access: [F] London 28 mins BR & Metroplitan Line; Easy access to motorways; Free parking in town

Ripley (N Yorkshire)

(YA) Map3 SE26

Chantry House Gallery

A commercial gallery established in 1980 specialising in painting and prints by comtemporary artists. [Pa,Pr]

Address: Chantry House, Ripley, N Yorkshire HG3 3AY tel 0423 770141
Contact: Audrey Atkinson
Open: Tues-Sat 10.30-5, Sun 2-5.30; Closed Christmas - Easter
Policy: The gallery is particularly interested in showing scenes of the Yorkshire Dales, Lake District scenes, farm animals and characters, boating scenes and overseas landscapes in oils, watercolours, pastels and prints and is keen to show a varied display of work. There is a changing display of work, with the one temporary exhibition being held annually at the begining of the season.
Sales: Work sold; Credit card
The Space: There is one main gallery of 15x7.5x6m high.
Exhibiting: [AW] Artists should make an appointment at the gallery with Audrey Atkinson. Commission taken by the gallery is negotiable.
Access: [F] Buses to Rippon-Harrogate; Car park 1 min

Rochdale (Lancashire)

(NWA) Map3 SD81

Rochdale Art Gallery

The gallery has a permanent collection incorporating a wide range of work donated by local 19th century industrialists and a temporary programme of art in a social context. [VA]

Address: Esplanade, Rochdale, Lancashire OL16 1AH tel 0706 342154

Contact: Arts & Exhibitions Officer or Assistant Arts & Exhibitions Officer Jill Morgan, Sarah Edge, Lubiana Himid

Open: Mon-Fri 10-5, Wed 10-1, Sat 10-4

Policy: *'The gallery has an agreed policy based on the council's manifesto policy for the arts, copies of which are available on request. The policy aims to present contemporary and historical art in a social context, to increase the accessibility of art, to encourage local communities to participate in art, to take positive action to represent the art and history of Black people, of women and of lesbian and gay artists, and to improve access to and representation of art by and for people with disabilities.'* The gallery also initiates community arts projects and workshops. Free creche facilities.

Sales: Work sold

The Space: The galleries are 20x9m, 17.5x9m and two spaces measuring 9x9m, all with hanging height of 5m. The walls consist of blockboard with artex finish with hanging by screws or fixings and rail. UV filtered lighting, track lighting with lux controls in all galleries and natural lighting. The gallery sometimes has display space in local parks and other public areas. Gallery plans available.

Exhibiting: [AW][EF] Exhibition applications should be made to the exhibitions team at Rochdale Gallery. The gallery pays for insurance, publicity, preview and display costs, transport and catalogue card and artists' expenses. Artists are sometime paid commissions to produce new work and receive a fee for exhibiting. 10% commission taken. The gallery supports EPR.

Access: [X] Bus Station 5 mins; BR Rochdale 15mins; Free parking

Rochester (Kent)

(SEA) Map7 TQ89

Langley Galleries

This art and craft gallery deals in work by living artists with a changing display of 19th and 20th century oils and watercolours. [Pa,Pr]

Address: 153 High Street, Rochester, Kent ME1 1EL tel 063 481 1802

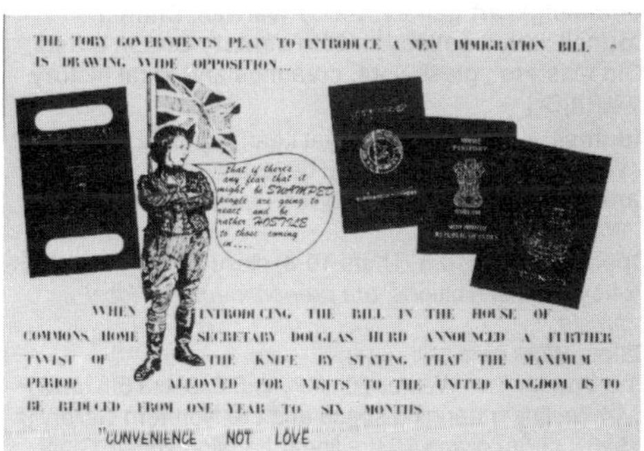

Rochdale Art Gallery: by Chila Kumari Burman from the exhibition 'The Medium and the Message'

Contact: Proprietor Kenneth J Cook

Open: Mon-Sat 9-5.30

Access: [F] BR Rochester 3 mins; Public car park 2 mins

Medway Gallery

This gallery runs a varied programme of exhibitions by individuals and groups, and also features touring exhibitions. [VA,Ph,Cr]

Address: Medway Adult Education Centre, Eastgate, Rochester, Kent ME1 1EW tel 063 445 359

Contact: Head of Art Gary Bassett

Open: Mon-Fri 9-4, 6-8.30 (term-time)

Policy: The gallery offers space to both established and aspiring artists and will discuss the possibility of exhibiting any art form. Exhibitions are aimed at students and the local community. Occasional talks, demonstrations and appreciation courses are arranged. Predominantly showing the work of living artists/makers, exhibitions normally run for three to four weeks.

Sales: Work sold

The Space: Main gallery is 13x10x5m high with 30m linear hanging space. Work is hung by mirror plates or hooks with directional spot lighting. Secondary gallery 12x10x5m high with 30m linear hanging space. Natural and fluorescent lighting. There is also a corridor space available 10x2x5m high. Exhibition space may also be used as a coffee room and for special lectures. Display cases and gallery plans available.

Exhibiting: [AW] Apply to Gary Bassett. The gallery finances insurance, printing and mail-out of publicity, list of exhibits and preview costs where applicable. There is a negotiable hire fee. Commission 10-20%.

Access: Buses from Chatham and Maidstone; BR Rochester 5 mins; Public car park 2 mins

Rothbury (Northumberland)

(NA) Map2 NU00

Coquetdale Gallery

Private gallery selling work from changing exhibitions with two rooms permanently for artists who become members. [VA,Ph,Cr]

Address: Church House, Rothbury, Northumberland NE65 7EH

Contact: Custodian Christine Cole, Melrose House, Snitter, Thropton, Morpeth, Northumberland NE65 7EH

Open: Tues-Sun 10.30-4 Easter-Oct

Policy: Most visitors are tourists, and work is mainly of *'styles that have wide appeal'*. The gallery's charitable object is to promote art and to provide an opportunity for the display of visual arts and rural crafts.

Sales: Work sold

The Space: One gallery has 10m and the other 9m linear hanging space with hanging rods and fluorescent lighting.

Exhibiting: [AW] Contact the Custodian in person or by writing with examples of work. Gallery covers insurance, publicity, list of exhibits, catalogue/card and charges 25% commission.

Access: [S] Bus 516 Newcastle - Thropton; Car park 3 mins; Street parking

Rotherham (S Yorkshire)

(YA) Map3 SK49

Brian O'Malley Cental Library & Arts Centre

An arts centre which includes a gallery, workshops and studios and other community resources. [VA,Cr]

Address: Walker Place, Rotherham, S Yorkshire S65 1JH tel 0709 382121 ext 3628

Contact: M Densley

Policy: The gallery stages about ten exhibitions a year which *'reflect the culture of the locality and region', some of which are bought in. The centre hopes to encourage local talent by mounting exhibitions by regional artists and societies,and the staff and students of local colleges and schools stage frequent exhibitions.*

The Space: The gallery covers 200m square with 150m linear hanging space that can be sub-divided by screens according to need. Natural light is excluded and all areas have controllable lighting.

Exhibiting: [AW] Artists and makers should apply to M Densley. The gallery covers the cost of insurance, publicity, mailing and catalogue costs and charges 15% commission.

Access: [U][T] Public car park at rear; Bus routes close by; BR Rotherham central

Rotherham College of Arts & Technology (Gallery)

Exhibitions are held in the foyer of the main college building. [VA,Cr,Ph]

Address: Eastwood Lane, Rotherham, S Yorkshire S65 1EG tel 0709 362111 ext 2762

Contact: Mr A J Hodgson

Open: Mon-Fri 9-9 Exhibitions run from September to June during the academic year

Policy: Exhibitions usually run for two weeks and student exhibitions are a priority but artists from outside the college are occasionally shown.

The Space: The space is 11.4x9m and also has display screens as needed.

Exhibiting: [AW] Potential exhibitors are requested to make early enquiries and arrangements for booking the space and artists must transport and hang their own work though help with hanging can be given.

Access: [U][T]

Rothwell (Northamptonshire)

(EMA) Map5 SP88

Rothwell Library

See Northamptonshire Libraries. [VA,Ph,Cr,Ar]

Address: Market Hill, Rothwell, Kettering, Northamptonshire NN1 tel 0536 711850

Contact: District Librarian D Bond, Kettering Library, Sheep Street, Kettering NN16 0AN tel 0536 512315

Open: Mon,Tues,Wed,Fri 10-1, 2-7; closed Thurs & Sat

Sales: Work sold

The Space: A purpose-built gallery space of 10m linear with an extra 20m on screens and a built-in showcase 1.2x1.2x0.3m and a 3m long foyer showcase. The gallery is 44 square metres with track lighting and UV filtered daylight. All areas supervised from library counter. The gallery can be used independently from the library for workshops, lectures etc.

Exhibiting: [AW] District Librarian. Foyer case can be booked independently. Catalogues, publicity and insurance provided, transport between libraries arranged for touring exhibitions. Commission is 10%.

Access: [U][T] Town centre site; Buses from Kettering or Market Harborough; Car park close

Grange

This municipal gallery aims to show the work of as many locally-based artists as possible. [VA]

Address: The Green, Rottingdean, Brighton, E Sussex BN2 7HA tel 027 301004

Contact: Exhibitions Officer John Filkin, Brighton Museum and Art Gallery, Brighton, East Sussex, BN1 1UE tel 027 360 3005

Open: Mon,Thurs,Sat 10-5, Tues, Fri 10-1, 2-5; Sun 2-5, closed Wed

Policy: Gallery policy is to *'support, show and sell the work of local artists'*, with the emphasis on showing works in a variety of media. Exhibitions are normally solo and run for four weeks.

Sales: Work sold

The Space: 18x4.5x3.5m high with 45m linear hanging space. There is a chain hanging system. Steps and doors limit the size and weight of work that can be accommodated. Display cases and gallery plans are available.

Exhibiting: [AW] Apply to John Filkin. Gallery finances insurance, printing and mail-out of publicity and catalogue, list of exhibits and transport. Hire fee is charged. Support in principle for EPR. Commission 33.3%.

Access: [X] Buses 2, 27 from Brighton; Public car park 2 mins

Royal Leamington Spa (Warwickshire)

(WMA) Map5 SP36

Leamington Art Gallery & Museum

A municipal art gallery run by Warwick District Council with a collection 20th century British artists, 'Old Masters', glassware, ceramics and local history. [VA,Ph,Cr]

Address: Avenue Road, Royal Leamington Spa, Warwickshire CV31 3PP tel 0926 26559

Contact: Museum and Exhibitions Manager Jeffery Watkin

Open: Mon-Sat 10-5, Thurs 10-8, closed 1-2

Policy: The exhibitions *'are predominantly by local artists'.*

Sales: Work sold

The Space: The Western Gallery is 5.6x6.4x3.5m giving 14.2m linear hanging space and the Northern Gallery is 9x6.4x3.5m giving 26.8m linear hanging space. Glass showcases and gallery plans are available.

Exhibiting: [AW] Applications one year in advance to the Museum and Exhibitions Manager. The gallery provides

publicity and mailing and charges 10% plus VAT on sales.
Access: [F] Car park 8 mins; Bus and BR Leamington 5 mins

Mid-Warwickshire College of Further Education, Art and Design Block

Monthly shows are held in the entrance hall of the art department. [VA,Ph,Cr,LA]

Address: Warwick New Road, Royal Leamington Spa, Warwickshire CV32 5JE tel 0926 311711 ext 259/287
Contact: Exhibition Organiser John Herbert
Open: Mon-Thurs 9-9, Fri 9-4.30
Policy: A wide variety of exhibitions are shown, focusing on the work of younger artists and makers. The exhibitions *'challenge and stimulate'* the student community.
Sales: Work sold
The Space: A 13x8x3.5m high space equipped with track lighting giving 20m of hanging space.
Exhibiting: Printing and mailing of publicity is provided, artists/makers should apply with slides and CV. The gallery takes 10% commission on sales.
Access: [S] Car park on site; Main bus route from town; BR Leamington Spa 15 mins

Royal Spa Centre

A multi-purpose entertainment and leisure complex funded and administered by Warwick District Council. [Pa,Pr,Dr]

Address: Newbold Terrace, Royal Leamington Spa, Warwickshire CV32 4HN tel 0926 34418
Contact: General Manager & Licensee Peter F Cresswell
Open: Mon-Sat 10-5
Policy: The exhibition programme has been *'exclusively work by local artists'*. The centre has a large and wide audience, and exhibitions have ranged from *'experienced artists to beginners'*.
Sales: Work sold; Credit card
The Space: Ground floor space 10.2x2.8m, Balcony 42.6x2.6m both with hanging by chain and rail.
Exhibiting: [AW] The centre provides publicity and a list of exhibits. A commission of 10% + VAT is charged on sales.
Access: [U][T] Ground floor only. Public car parks close by; BR Leamington Spa 10 mins

Royston (Hertfordshire)

(EA) Map7 TL34

Royston Museum

Municipal gallery and museum with temporary exhibitions every four to five weeks.

Address: Lower King Street, Royston, Hertfordshire SG8 5AL tel 0763 42587
Contact: The Curator Emma Bond
Open: Wed & Sat 10-5 or by appointment
The Space: One room 3.6x6m, spot lighting, direct hanging.
Access: Access to ground floor only

Rugby (Warwickshire)

(WMA) Map5 SP57

Art Gallery & Museum

The existing Rugby Library Gallery is (hopefully) being replaced by a new building and the present gallery is booked to 1990. [Pc,Pr,Dr]

Address: St Matthew's Street, Rugby, Warwickshire CV21 3BZ tel 0788 542687
Contact: Area Librarian Kevin Smith
Open: Mon, Tues, Thurs, Fri 9.30-8, Wed 9.30-5, Sat 9.30-4
Policy: The gallery displays the work of local art groups, with occasional travelling exhibitions produced by the Area Museum Service. Work should start on new premises early in 1991.
Sales: Work sold
The Space: 95 square metres with 37m wall space.
Exhibiting: [AW] Contact Area Librarian. 10% commission on sales.
Access: [X]

Leamington Hastings Galleries

A commercial gallery founded in 1988. [Cr]

Address: Leamington Hastings, Rugby, Warwickshire CV23 8DY tel 0926 632754
Contact: G C MacFarquhar
Open: Wed-Sun 2-6
Policy: The gallery shows contemporary British craft work in all media. Exhibitions feature a particular craft or the work of one maker.
Sales: Work sold; Credit card
The Space: 30 square metres with track lighting. Gallery plans available.
Exhibiting: [AW] Contact G C or P A MacFarquhar by telephone or letter. Printing, mailing and preview provided by the gallery. Commission of 33.3% charged on sales.
Access: [X] A426 from Rugby and A423 from Coventry

Runcorn (Cheshire)

(MA) Map4 SJ58

Norton Priory Museum

Museum showing permanent collection on the life and work of Norton Priory 1134-1921, with programme of temporary exhibitions on related themes with a sculpture trail in the grounds and an annual outdoor sculpture workshop programme. [VA,Ph,Cr]

Address: Warrington Road, Runcorn, Cheshire WA7 1RE tel 09285 69895
Contact: Museum Director Margaret Warhurst
Open: Mon-Fri 12-5, Sat, Sun & bank holidays 12-6, March-Oct; Mon-Sun 12-4 Nov-Feb
Policy: Exhibitions are organised on themes related to the priory, eg sculpture, tile-making, pottery etc. The main exhibition each year relates to the outdoor sculpture workshops which provide an opportunity to work alongside a professional artist. The sculpture trail is of work created by visitors during the sculpture workshops.

Local amateur artists and groups are encouraged to exhibit in the winter months as part of the service to the community and to encourage local people to make regular use of the facilities. Workshops and demonstrations are organised alongside temporary exhibitions.

Sales: Work sold

The Space: A 16 acre outdoor site and a flexible indoor area 8.9x3.3x3m, with fixed and movable screens, spotlights and UV screening. Limitations to normal door size. Three display cases 8x1.7x.55m with up to five shelves, two cases 85x0.8x0.55m two shelves, six cases 1.2x1.8m and three 2x1.2m.

Exhibiting: **[AW]** Informal approach to Director at any time, formal agreement necessary before end of June for exhibition in following year. Museum covers insurance and publicity, and has some frames available. Commission is 15%.

Access: **[U][T][F]** Half mile walk from nearest bus stop; BR Runcorn and Runcorn East beyond normal walking distance; Free car park

Runcorn Shopping City Library

Large public library on several floors which houses a wide range of exhibitions and displays, many from local people, both amateur and professional, and occasionally from elsewhere. [VA,Ph,Cr,LA]

Address: Runcorn Shopping City, Runcorn, Cheshire WA7 2PF tel 09285 715351

Contact: Library Exhibition Dept Sue Benson

Open: Mon-Wed 9.30-6, Thurs-Fri 9.30-8, Sat 9.30-1

Policy: *'As a learning centre, the library aims to broaden people's experience and awareness of different art and craft forms,'* to stimulate and to encourage regular visits and the use of other library facilities. There is no specific exhibition policy, but the library will look carefully at exhibitions on contentious issues as these are often thought by the public to reflect library views.

Sales: Work sold; sales referred to exhibitor

The Space: The main exhibition space on Level 3 has 35m linear hanging space and a movable spotlight system with tracking. The space on Level 4 is suitable for free-standing cases and houses four 0.5x0.5x0.5m locking cases and two 3.5x1.5x.9m wall-mounted cases. Gallery plans available.

Exhibiting: **[AW][EF]** Apply in writing to Display Officer at the Library. The exhibition programme is organised twelve months ahead. Library covers insurance, and will hang work if artist wants. Commission is 10%.

Access: **[U][T][L][F]** need to approach library through shopping malls which are accessible by car through car parks. Buses New Town Circular, T7,T7X,T8,T8X; BR Runcorn 20 mins bus ride; Public car park 3mins

Ryde (Isle of Wight)

(SA) Map7 SZ59

Ryde Library Gallery

A gallery within a public library. [VA,Ph,Cr]

Address: George Street, Ryde, Isle of Wight PO33 2JE tel 0983 62170

Contact: Deputy Director of Cultural Services M R Howley, Cultural Services HQ, Parkhurst Road, Newport, Isle of Wight tel 0983 822000

Open: Mon & Wed 9.30-6, Thurs & Sat 9.30-5, Fri 9.30-7

Policy: The Cultural Services policy is to show work of quality from both professional and amateur artists, as well as to encourage and promote beginners of an acceptable exhibiting standard; this double objective being achieved by a selective offer of gallery venue. All exhibitions run for one month.

Sales: Sales referred to exhibitor

The Space: A first floor, narrow gallery (its widest point being 3m) surrounding a *'well'* overlooking the lending library with a 50m linear space, 2.4 height. Pendant light fittings hang over the well area.

Exhibiting: **[AW]** To the Director of Cultural Services. The library pays on a discretionary basis for printing and mailing of publicity, list of exhibits and transport. No commission is charged.

Access: **[X]** Buses 8 & 6; Public car parks 2 mins; Public car parking adjacent

Rye (Sussex)

(SEA) Map7 TQ92

Kurrein Gallery

This commercial gallery deals in the work of living artists alongside a changing display of work for sale. [Pa,Pr,Cr,Je,Gl]

Address: 7 Lion Street, Rye, Sussex TN31 7LB tel 079 722 3383

Contact: Fred and Ella Kurrein

Open: Wed-Sat 10-5

Policy: Gallery policy is to display the best of contemporary British craft and prints by trained artists. The accent is on *'British art of the highest standard'*. Work is mostly bought in by the gallery.

Sales: Work sold; Credit card

The Space: Maximum wall area of 1.5x1m. Lockable display cases are available for jewellery.

Access: **[F]** Bus Station Rye 5 mins; BR Rye 5 mins; Public car park 5 mins

Rye Art Gallery (Easton Rooms)

This gallery exhibits a broad spectrum of contemporary visual arts and crafts, with an emphasis on the 'high quality of items displayed'. [VA,Ph,Cr]

Address: 107 High Street, Rye, Sussex TN31 7JE tel 079 722 2433

Contact: Manager Eric Money

Open: Mon-Sat 10.30-1, 2-5, Sun 2.30-5

Policy: The main aim of the gallery is to exhibit work by the best artists and makers living in the South. In conjunction with the monthly exhibitions, all featuring the work of living artists, there is a continuous selection of paintings, prints and crafts on display and for sale. The gallery also organises talks, outings and films for the 'Friends of Rye Art Galleries'.

Sales: Work sold; Credit scheme; Credit card

The Space: The height of the gallery is 2m with 50m of linear hanging space. Lighting is by spots. There is a small craft gallery equipped for the display of pottery, jewellery and other crafts and a paved courtyard area that can be used. Gallery plans are available.

Exhibiting: **[AW]** The gallery committee selects exhibitions every three months. Gallery finances insurance, printing and mail-out of publicity and preview costs. Commission 37%.

Access: **[X]** BR Rye 3 mins

Rye Art Gallery (Stormont Studio)

This part of the Rye Art Gallery is predominantly concerned with exhibiting work which is of cultural interest and historical importance. [VA,Ph,Cr]

Address: Ockman Lane, East Street, Rye, Sussex TN31 7JE tel 079 722 3218

Contact: Manager Eric Money

Open: Mon-Sat 10.30-1, 2-5, Sun 2.30-5

Policy: A registered charity, this gallery was originally set up to promote the *'understanding and appreciation of the fine arts, now interpreted in the widest sense'*. The gallery is seen in general terms as having an educational function with talks and slide shows regularly held by the 'Friends of Rye Art Galleries' in the exhibiting area. There are nine shows a year, one of which focuses on the permanent collection which includes Edward Burra, Duncan Grant, Ivon Hitchens. About five shows a year are by living artists and makers, with exhibitions lasting for four to six weeks. Exhibitions are aimed at a wide audience in the hope of introducing the arts to those unused to gallery activities and to *'remove all intimidation'*. (See also Easton Rooms, Rye Art Gallery).

Sales: Work sold in some shows

The Space: The height of the gallery is 2m with 65m linear hanging space. All lighting is fitted with a dimmer system. There is a paved courtyard area which can be used and lockable showcases are available. The exhibition space is also used for life classes and writers' workshops.

Exhibiting: Gallery finances insurance, printing and mail-out of publicity and catalogue/card, preview costs and transport.

Access: **[U][T][F]** BR Rye 3 mins

Saddleworth (Lancashire)

(NWA) Map3 SD90

John McCombs Gallery

A commercial gallery showing traditionally-based paintings in a popular tourist area which is part of a craft centre where local crafts are sold. [VA,Cr]

Address: Saddleworth Crafts, 12 King Street, Delph, Saddleworth, Near Oldham, Lancashire OL3 5DQ Tel 04577 4705

Contact: John McCombs

Open: Mon-Sat 10-5. Sun 2-5

Policy: Most of the work on show during any of the five exhibitions that take place annually tends to be one or more of the seven gallery artists. In addition to exhibitions, there is a changing display of work for sale which specialises in showing,'Delph the people and the place' by the resident artist John McCombs. Educational activities include painting workshops and group visits from schools in the area. Gallery artists undertake commissions.

Sales: Work sold

The Space: The gallery is 4.26x3.65m with 2.43m depth of wall display and works are lit by spot lights. The gallery is approached up a stairway so it is impossible to accommodate very large paintings or heavy sculpture.

Exhibiting: The gallery prefers to invite artists to exhibit. It pays preview costs, otherwise artists and the gallery share expenses. 20% commission is taken on sales.

Access: **[X]** Buses 183, 184 from Manchester via Oldham, 355 from Ashton under Lyne

Saffron Walden (Essex)

(EA) Map7 TL53

Exchange Gallery, Saffron Walden Library & Arts Centre

The gallery is in a part of the lending library which is a public access area and attracts a wide range of interest. [Pr,Pa,Dr,Ph,Cr]

Address: 2 King Street, Saffron Walden, Essex CB10 1ES tel 0799 23178

Contact: Area Librarian & Arts Director John Shaw-Ridler

Open: Mon,Tues,Thurs, Fri 9-7, Sat 9-5

Policy: The gallery shows work by working artists mainly from East Anglia and London but also occasionally from further afield. It holds 17 exhibitions a year, lasting three weeks each. The gallery exhibits mainly paintings, prints, drawings and photographs although there are limited facilities for small ceramic and glass objects and jewellery, sculpture is not possible.

Sales: Work sold; All work exhibited should be for sale; NFS exhibits by negotiation

The Space: The gallery, on a mezzanine floor, is 67.8 square metres with exhibition panels. Hanging is either direct or by picture cord and lighting is by spots.

Exhibiting: **[AW]** Write to the Arts Director with information and visual information. The programme is often booked two years ahead. The gallery pays for insurance, some printing and publicity, mailing and the exhibitor is responsible for list of exhibits, pre-view and any transport. Commission is 20%.

Access: **[F][L]** BR Audley End then bus, taxi to Saffron Walden 2 miles; Public car park 2 mins

Fry Art Gallery

The gallery houses a collection based on the artistic community in Great Bardfield before and after the second world war, together with temporary exhibitions that demonstrate the continuing artistic traditions in the north west of Essex. [VA]

Address: Bridge End Gardens, Castle Street, Saffron Walden, Essex CB10 1BD

Contact: Fry Art Gallery Society

Open: Sat, Sun, bank holidays, 2.45-5.30 Easter-Oct**Policy:** The gallery is a registered charity, and is not concerned with sales, although an annual two-day picture sale is held for invited artists each November.

Access: **[S]** Public car park nearby; BR Audley End 2 miles

Saffron Walden Museum

Permanent collections of archaeology, natural history, geology, local history, ceramics, glass, costume with temporary exhibitions. [VA]

Address: Museum Street, Saffron Walden, Essex CM10 1LJ tel 0799 22494
Contact: Assistant Curator Sheila Jordain
Open: Mon-Sat 11-5; Mon-Sat 11-4 (Oct-March)
Policy: Occasional temporary exhibitions, may be two or three a year.

St Albans (Hertfordshire)

(EA) Map7 TL10

Holywell Gallery

A commercial gallery showing monthly exhibitions of contemporary figurative paintings as well as pottery and sculpture. [VA,Ph,Cr]

Address: 60 Holywell Hill, St Albans, Hertfordshire AL1 1RN tel 0727 55407
Contact: Claire Brown & Suzanne Chapman
Open: Tues-Sat 10-5
Policy: The gallery also sells antiques.
Sales: Work sold
The Space: The gallery is 5x6m with direct fixing to walls, picture rail and spots with fluorescent tube lights and daylight.
Exhibiting: [AW] We welcome artists to exhibit. Gallery pays for insurance, publicity and mail out, catalogue and private view and charges a hire fee. Commission is 40%.

Margaret Harvey Gallery

Gallery within a college of art and design. [VA,Ph,Cr,Ce]

Address: Hertfordshire College of Art and Design, 7 Hatfield Road, St Albans, Hertfordshire AL1 3RS tel 0727 64414
Contact: Exhibitions Officer Janis Jefferies
Open: Mon-Fri 10-5 Sat 11-4; closed bank holidays
Policy: *'To show mainly contemporary art and design work of a professional standard. It will be developing an education programme to complement the exhibitions.'* A mixture of touring, local, student and professional exhibitions of about two weeks each. *'Further development is anticipated following the appointment of an Exhibitions Officer'.*
Sales: Work sold
The Space: Purpose built glass-walled area 10x6x3m high with wall hanging space supplemented by screens. Corridor space is also available. Solid floor, adequate mobile spots. Security locked glass-fronted cabinet 2x2.6m. Lawns to front and rear suitable for sculpture.
Exhibiting: [AW] To Exhibitions Officer. Gallery pays transport, insurance, private view, and publicity mailing and takes a commission of 20%.
Access: [U][T][F] BR 12mins, adjacent car parking. Close M1 & M25 motorway junctions

St Albans Central Library

Public Library in busy shopping complex, next door to Maltings Arts Centre. [Pa,Ph]

Address: The Maltings, St Albans, Hertfordshire AL1 3JG tel 0727 60000
Contact: Librarian Mrs H Adams
Open: Mon,Tues,Wed,Fri 9.30-7.30, Thurs,Sat 9.30-1
Policy: Touring exhibitions and local artists work shown.
Sales: Work sold
The Space: Seven 2.9x2.4m velgrip covered panels with picture rail along the top and a picture rail on an opposite brick wall. Plinths available.
Exhibiting: Commission charged by arrangement.
Access: [F] BR St Albans; Multi-storey car park adjacent

St Helens (Merseyside)

(MA) Map3 SJ59

Citadel Arts Centre

Community theatre building with emphasis on young people, exhibition spaces in café area and first floor rehearsal and exhibition room opening in September 1988. [VA,LA]

Address: Waterloo Street, St Helens, Merseyside WA10 1PX tel 0744 35436
Contact: Exhibitions Co-ordinator Lorraine Fleming
Open: Mon-Sat 10-6
Policy: *'The Citadel is an arts resource for young people in St Helens and in this capacity should be a major contribution to the cultural life of the town. Our primary purpose is to enable young people to devise and invent new forms of leisure and self-expression, and give them a positive and satisfying range of activities that are easily accessible. It promotes performing and visual arts activities and operates a thorough non-sexist, non-racist, non-commercial policy.'* There will be a programme of workshops and related educational activities alongside the exhibition programme.
Sales: Work sold
The Space: Ground floor café has linear space of 13m interrupted by five buttresses. First floor rehearsal/exhibition room has linear space of 26m

Citadel Arts Centre

interrupted by ten buttresses. Some exhibition screens available. Two-dimensional wall-based work preferred.

Exhibiting: [AW] To Lorraine Fleming in person or in writing. The costs for hire of exhibition space vary but the maximum is £75. Centre covers insurance up to £1000, list of exhibits, display and publicity mail out. Commission is 10%.

Access: [U][T] All St Helens Town Centre buses; BR St Helens Central station 5 mins; Public car park 2 mins

Community Arts St Helens (CASH)

St Helens Borough Council is reorganising its arts policy and aims to bring art into the community through organisations like CASH. [VA,Cr]

Address: The Citadel, Waterloo Street, St Helens WA10 1PX tel 0744 35436

Contact: Andy Cave

Policy: CASH is interested to hear from artists wanting to exhibit in libraries and schools and who want to be artists in residence in schools in St Helens.

Pilkington Glass Museum

Part of the Pilkington Glass Works, the gallery houses a permanent exhibition on the history of glass, its current uses and the glassmaking process, also has around six month-long temporary exhibitions annually. [VA,Ph,Cr]

Address: Prescot Road, St Helens, Merseyside WA10 3TT tel 0744 28882 ext 2499

Contact: Curator Ian Burgoyne

Open: Mon-Fri 10-5 Sat; Sun and bank holidays 2-4.30

Policy: Presents temporary exhibitions of historical and contemporary work on glass-related themes, as well as other crafts and paintings. These come from North West Museum and Art Gallery Service and are also initiated by local artists, groups and the museum itself.

Sales: Work sold

The Space: Large lecture room with around 20m wall space for paintings, also wall-mounted display cases. Track lighting with down and up lights in cases. Also six movable glass cases of various sizes and types.

Exhibiting: [AW] Apply to Curator by telephone or in writing in first instance for further details. No commission charged.

Access: [S][L][T]. Buses from Liverpool pass in front; Car park on site

Pilkington Glass Museum

St Helens Museum & Art Gallery

The gallery has a permanent collection of Fine and Decorative Art of 19th and 20th century, with a programme of monthly exhibitions, some by contemporary artists. [VA,Ph,Cr]

Address: College Street, St Helens, Merseyside WA10 1TW tel 0744 24061 ext 2961

Contact: Museum Officer Tom Craig

Open: Mon-Fri 10-5 Sat 10-1

Policy: The stated policy is *'to present the heritage and material culture of St Helens, and bring other arts and media into the borough.'* The museum provides a varied programme covering a wide range of arts and media. Leisure courses are held in the temporary exhibition space.

Sales: Work sold

The Space: The room for temporary exhibitions is 10.5x7.6x2.5m high with 35m linear hanging space. Lighting is Thorn-EMI track system with individual spotlights, integrated ceiling downlights. The room is air-conditioned for temperature and humidity. There are five Edmonds glass display cases each 2.5x.75x3.2m.

Exhibiting: Gallery covers insurance and some publicity costs.

Access: [U][T][F] BR St Helens Central station 10 mins; Public car parks 1min

St Ives (Cambridgeshire)

(EA) Map7 TL37

L'Bidi Studio

Commercial art gallery, linked to L'Bidi Studio in Buckden, Huntingdon. [VA,Ph,Cr]

Address: 40 The Broadway, St Ives, Cambridgeshire PE17 4BN tel 0480 66886

Contact: Lindsay Beedie, 81 High Street, Buckden, Huntingdon, Cambridgeshire PE18 9TA tel 0480 810 545

Open: Mon-Sat 10-5.30; closed Thurs; Also open Sun 2-5 May-Aug

Policy: *'The exhibition and sale of good quality watercolours, pastels, oil paintings, sculpture, prints and hand made craft items.'* Exhibitions 2-3 weeks, both group and solo. Work mainly contemporary and representational. Between exhibitions there is a changing display of work.

Sales: Work sold; Credit card

The Space: 13x5.5x2m high plus adjoining space 5x5.5x2m high. Natural light with rod hanging system.

Exhibiting: [AW] Telephone Lindsay Beedie for an appointment. Commission 35%.

Access: [F] Shop, [X] Gallery upstairs; Adjacent car parking. Buses from BR (Huntingdon)

St Ives (Cornwall)

(EA) Map6 SW54

New Craftsman

A Crafts Council selected gallery showing pottery, weaving, jewellery etc by leading English makers. It also shows paintings, prints and sculpture. [VA,Cr]

Address: 24 Fore Street, St Ives, Cornwall TR26 1HE tel 0736 795 652

Contact: Janet Leach/Mary Redgrave

Open: Mon-Sat 10-6, Sun 2-6 Summer; Mon-Sat 10-5 Winter

Policy: The gallery shows paintings, prints and sculpture from artists living and working in Cornwall. Crafts are shown from all over the country.

Sales: Work sold; Credit card

Exhibiting: No solo shows mounted.

Access: [F][X] ground floor

Penwith Galleries

A gallery run by Penwith Society of Arts with artists' studios, print workshop and shop. [VA,Cr,Ce,Je]

Address: Back Road West, St Ives, Cornwall TR26 1NL tel 0736 795579

Contact: Curator Kathleen Watkins

Open: Tues-Sat 10-5; closed 1-2.30

Policy: The gallery shows a variety of solo and mixed exhibitions of fine art and craft work aiming to further *'the arts in Cornwall'*.

Sales: Work sold; Credit card; Credit scheme

Access: [S]

Salt House Gallery

The gallery holds seven solo exhibitions a year as well as a continuous changing display and aims to encourage unknown as well as established artists. [VA,Ph,Cr]

Address: Norway Square, St Ives, Cornwall TR26 1NB tel 0736 795 003

Contact: Director R S Devereux

Open: 10.30-5

The Space: There are two spaces of 32 square metres and one of 66 square metres on two floors.

Exhibiting: [AW] The programme is planned two years ahead.

Wills Lane Gallery

The Wills Lane is a small private gallery founded in 1968 with a continuous programme of mixed and solo shows of mainly abstract work by contemporary British artists including Hepworth, Hilton and Nicholson and also showing work by young artists. [Pa,Sc,Pr]

Address: Wills Lane, St Ives, Cornwall tel 0736 795 723/795 240

Contact: Director Henry Gilbert

Open: Daily 10-4

St Leonards on Sea (E Sussex)

(SEA) Map7 TQ80

Photogallery

This gallery specialises in photography, mostly contemporary, some historical. [Ph]

Address: 2 Shepherd Street, St Leonards on Sea, E Sussex TN38 0ET tel 042 444 0140

Contact: Administrator Morris Newcombe or Lesley Cornish

Open: Wed-Sat 11-6

Policy: The programme aims to cover the whole spectrum of photography. Exhibitions, which are a mixture of group and solo shows, normally run for one month. The gallery tends to favour artists living and working in the South East. Travelling exhibitions, an educational programme and lectures are also organised.

Sales: Work sold

The Space: 12x8m hanging is by rods with spotlighting.

Exhibiting: [AW] Gallery covers insurance, framing, publicity, mail-out, catalogue and 50% of preview costs. Commission 33.3%.

Salford (Greater Manchester)

(NWA) Map3 SJ79

City of Salford Cultural Services

Cultural services for Salford managing exhibition spaces in galleries, museums and libraries. [VA,Cr,Fi,Vi]

Address: City of Salford, Joule House, Acton Square, Salford, Greater Manchester M5 4NY tel 061 736 9448

Contact: Cultural Services Manager Royston Futter

Open: Various basically Mon-Fri 10-4.45, Sun 2-5

Policy: Salford runs the Lowry Centre with four galleries, Viewpoint photographic gallery (see separate entry), Mining Museum and many libraries with exhibition spaces. The Lowry Centre collects and displays Victorian and 20th century paintings and the work of L S Lowry, the Mining Museum mining art. Opportunities exist for the exhibition of any art form within the service.

The Space: The Lowry Centre: 4 galleries of 500 square metres each; Viewpoint 1 gallery of 500 square metres; Mining Museum 1 gallery of 200 square metres; with approximately 500 square metres of space in various libraries.

Exhibiting: [AW] For details contact the Cultural Services Manager.

Access: [U][T] Free parking at all galleries

Salford Museum & Art Gallery

Salford Museum and Art Gallery is run by Salford Cultural Services which controls libraries, museums and art galleries, art centres and community art schemes. [VA]

Address: Peel Park, Salford, Greater Manchester M5 4WU tel 061 736 2649

Contact: Principal Museum Officer Mike Leber

Open: Mon-Fri 10-4.45, Sun 2-5

Policy: The gallery generally shows 20 exhibitions each year, of these approximately 60% predominantly show the work of living artists. It aims to show as broad a selection of work as possible with the temporary exhibition programme of hired exhibitions, self-initiated and thematic shows supplemented by exhibitions from the collection. The gallery holds solo shows of professional local and regional artists and art associations and promotes the work of less-established artists from the area. The educational programme includes lectures, workshops and audio visual displays. Its collections include Victorian paintings and work by LS Lowry.

Sales: Work sold

The Space: The South Gallery has 63.39m linear hanging space, the Café Gallery has 39.31m linear hanging space and the landing 21.94m linear hanging space. All have humidifiers and strip lights and there are plans to install a track system with spots. Gallery plans are available.

Exhibiting: [AW] Applications should be sent to the Exhibitions Organiser. The gallery finances insurance, publicity, list of exhibits, mailing and catalogue and takes 20% commission on sales.

Access: [U][T][L] BR Salford 5 mins; Car park at the gallery; Manchester city centre 10 mins by bus

Viewpoint Photography Gallery

The only major photographic gallery in Greater Manchester, it opened in 1987 and is one of the galleries operated by Salford Cultural Services. [Ph]

Address: The Old Fire Station, The Cresent, Salford M5 4NZ tel 061 737 1040

Contact: Keeper of Photography Neil Wilkie

Open: Tues-Fri 10-5, Sun 2-5

Policy: The gallery shows a wide range of exhibitions including major national and international shows, thematic exhibitions which use archival material and work of regionally-based photographers. It aims to attract a very broad audience locally and nationally. The gallery runs an education service linked to the exhibition programme.

Sales: Work sold

The Space: Exhibition Hall measures 10.6x21m plus an additional 18 double-sided screens 1.4m wide operating on a track system. The layout and lighting are very flexible.

Exhibiting: [AW][EF] Applications should be sent to Neil Wilkie. The gallery pays costs for insurance, printing of publicity, list of exhibits, preview costs, display, transport, mailing and catalogue. Photographers receive a fee if commissioned to produce work for a specific exhibition. 10% commission taken on sale of work.

Access: [U][T] BR Salford Cresent 3 mins; Situated on bus route to central Manchester; Acton Square car park nearby

Viewpoint Photography Gallery

Salisbury (Wiltshire)

(SA) Map7 SU12

Bill Toop Gallery

A commercial art and craft gallery founded in 1976 with a permanent display of the owners' watercolour work. [Pa,Pr,Cr]

Address: 21 New Street, Salisbury, Wiltshire SP1 1PH tel 0722 20916

Contact: Bill and Elizabeth Toop, 2 The Crescent, Hill View Road, Salisbury, Wiltshire

Open: Mon,Tues,Thurs,Fri 10-2, 2.30-5.30, Sat 10.30-5.30, closed Wed and Sun

Policy: The policy is to provide a showcase for the owners' work and also to show the work of established printmakers and a low-cost range of ceramics by a range of British makers. Cards and prints also sold. Framing service.

Sales: Work sold; Credit scheme

The Space: Gallery plus two showcases for craft jewellery.

Exhibiting: Commission of 40% is charged on sales.

Access: [F] Close to city centre buses; BR Salisbury 7 min; Multi-storey car park near

Courcoux & Courcoux

A Crafts Council selected gallery. [Ce,Sc,Pa,Gl]

Address: 90-92 Crane Street, Salisbury, Wiltshire SP1 2QD tel 0722 33347

Open: Mon-Sat 10-5

Policy: Shows work by leading potters such as Coper,

Bill Toop Gallery: Work by Bill Toop

Rie, Leach, Hamada, Odundo, Henderson and Roberts as well as contemporary sculptors and painters. The garden houses a cold glass studio.

Playhouse Gallery

An art gallery within the foyer and bar area of a theatre. [Pa,Pr,Ph]

Address: Salisbury Playhouse, Malthouse Lane, Salisbury, Wiltshire SP2 7RA tel 0722 20117

Contact: Gallery Co-ordinator Nancy Strike

Open: Mon-Sat from 10.15

Policy: To present a wide range of locally-based as well as internationally and nationally-known artists as a means of enhancing the theatre's front of house area, and providing another art form as part of our service to the community. The mostly solo exhibitions are shown for four weeks each.

Sales: Work sold; Credit card

The Space: The hanging space includes two long galleries, forming part of the theatre foyer, as well as wall space in the theatre bar. All areas have good natural lighting and are lit at night with focus spot lights. Further details on request.

Exhibiting: [AW] Applications to go to the Selection Committee. The gallery pays for insurance, printing and mailing of publicity, list of exhibits, preview costs and transport. Commission on sales is 33.3%.

Access: [U][T][L]

Salisbury Arts Centre

An arts centre for performance and visual arts with arts and craft workshops. [VA,Ph,Cr]

Address: Bedwin Street, Salisbury, Wiltshire SP1 3UT tel 0722 21744

Contact: Director J C Struthers

Open: Tues-Sat 10-6

Policy: The exhibition policy is to show contemporary fine art with an emphasis towards young painters and occasionally exhibitions of crafts, sculpture and photography. The exhibitions run for four weeks.

Sales: Work sold; Credit card

The Space: One gallery is 14x4.5x3m with 28m linear hanging space and track lighting; the other is 9.5x4x3m with 16m linear hanging space and wallmounted spots. Gallery plans are available.

Exhibiting: [AW] At any time to the Director. The Gallery pays for insurance, printing and mailing of publicity, and a list of exhibits. Commission on sales is charged at 25%. It supports EPR.

Access: [U][T][F] BR 10 mins; Public car parks 1 min

Salisbury Library (Main, Young & Creasey Galleries)

A large municipal public library with three galleries, situated on the first floor of the building, one of which is reserved for the Creasey collection of contemporary art. [VA,Ph,Cr,Ho]

Address: Salisbury Library, Market Place, Salisbury, Wiltshire SP1 1BL tel 0722 24145

Contact: Monte Little

Open: Mon 10-7, Tues 9.30-7, Wed 10-7, Thurs 10-5, Fri 10-7, Sat 9.30-5; closed bank holidays. Creasey Collection is open Mon,Tues & Fri 2.30-5.30, Wed 2.30-7 and by arrangement

Policy: The galleries are seen as an extension to the cultural and recreational services offered by this large city library. National, regional and local talent is shown and the programme includes many first-time exhibitions. The object is to encourage the widest possible appreciation of the artist without elitist tendencies and without pre conceived boundaries on the type of work that may be shown. The exhibitions run for three to four weeks. The Creasey collection includes work by final-year students from local art colleges. The galleries are also used for meetings by clubs, societies and cultural groups outside exhibition hours.

Sales: Sales referred to exhibitors

The Space: The main gallery is 14.3x6.9x2.6m with a 34.6m linear hanging space and the Young Gallery and Creasey Gallery 6.5x6.4x2.6m with a 14.9m linear hanging space. All galleries have Concord track lighting and the latter has environmental control and security systems. Hanging is by a rod and hook system and there are four 'Click' showcases.

Exhibiting: [AW] Applications in writing with a CV to Monte Little. Hire charges and commission on request.

Access: [U][T][L][S] Central to car parks, buses and trains

Sandwich (Kent)

(SEA) Map7 TR35

James Atkinson Gallery

Private gallery. [Pa,Sc,Pr]

Address: 38 King Street, Sandwich, Kent CT13 9BL tel 030 461 7216

Contact: James Atkinson

Open: Mon-Sat 10-12.30 & 2.15-5 or by appointment; Closed Wed

Policy: It specialises in 19th century paintings and watercolours and modern marine paintings and also shows *'a varied selection'* of work by contemporary artists. Restoration, cleaning and framing are undertaken.

Sales: Work sold

Exhibiting: Terms are negotiable, either on a commission basis or rental. *'Both to include free advisory service on all aspects of exhibiting, advertising, marketing, etc.'*

Sawbridgeworth (Hertfordshire)

(EA) Map7 TL41

Gowan Gallery

Commercial art gallery, originally an 18th century shop. [VA,Ce,Je,Gl,Wo]

Address: 3 Bell Street, Sawbridgeworth, Hertfordshire CM21 9AR tel 0279 600004

Contact: Joanne Gowan

Open: Tues-Sat 10-6

Policy: Continuous collection of arts including glass, wood, fine art, sculpture, prints and jewellery is also designed and made at the gallery. Two special exhibitions each year when one artist or maker is

promoted.
Sales: Work sold; Credit card
The Space: Small gallery area approximately 44 square metres. There are a number of old wooden display cases with glass shelves, and tungsten and halogen spots.
Exhibiting: [AW] Artists should contact the gallery by telephone to make an appointment. It covers the cost of publicity, insurance, preview and list of exhibits. Commission is negotiable.
Access: [F] Free public car park nearby

Scarborough (N Yorkshire)

(YA) Map3 TA08

Scarborough Art Gallery

A municipal gallery which houses a collection of Victorian art and has a changing exhibition programme of contemporary art. [VA,Ph,Cr]
Address: The Crescent, Scarborough, N Yorkshire YO11 2PW tel 0723 374753
Contact: Curator Josie Montgomery
Open: Mon-Sat 10-1, 2-5; Sun 2-5 Summer only
Policy: The contemporary art programme aims to *'cover most sections of the visual arts with no particular specialisation although painting tends to dominate'*. The gallery hosts an annual open for local artists and a Yorkshire artists biennial for artists living and working in the region. The gallery benefits from the tourist trade. There are eleven exhibitions a year each lasting four weeks and the gallery mounts both solo and group shows.
Sales: Work sold
The Space: The three galleries on the first floor which are used for temporary exhibitions are 7x4m, 6x4m and 9x5m and a balcony area which allows for paintings to be hung along the 12m linear of hanging space giving a total floor area of 37m square and 60 linear meters. Hanging is with mirror plates into the walls. There is a patio area outside for sculpture and the gallery has twelve wooden showcases with individual lighting system, six wall showcases with shelves and a new lighting system and blinds to exclude daylight. Gallery plans are available.
Exhibiting: [AW] Artists and makers should write, sending slides to Josie Montgomery. The gallery covers all exhibition costs except artists expenses, takes 11% commission and supports EPR.
Access: [F] ground floor only BR Scarborough 5 mins; Bus station 5 mins

Workshop Gallery

The gallery is maintained and run by members of Crescent Arts Workshop as a public gallery showing a wide range of media and other art-based events. [VA,Ph,Cr,LA]
Address: Crescent Arts Workshop, The Crescent, Scarborough, N Yorkshire YO11 2PW tel 0723 351461
Contact: Exhibition Organiser
Open: Tues-Sat 10-1,2-5
Policy: The gallery aims to provide artists, local or national, a venue in which to show their work. No particular syle if favoured by the selectors but exhibitions tend to be solo although the gallery does welcome applications from groups and societies. The main criteria is that artists have to met before exhibiting is that they have not exhibited elsewhere in the region in the past year other than *'open shows'*. Generally sculpture is not shown in the gallery because of space limitation but oudoor work can be shown in the grounds of the adjacent park but this is at the owner's risk. There is a full education programme supporting the exhibitions as well as occasional talks and lectures.
Sales: Work sold
The Space: The main gallery is 5x9x2.4m high and decorated between each show. It has lights which can be directed. The corridor gallery is 3x1.5x2.4m high and suitable for smaller work. Large sculptures are shown in the workshop yard which is 7.6x18m and partly covered and also in a large 'sculpture park' area of 1.5 acres. Gallery plans are available.
Exhibiting: [AW][EF] During August the exhibitions for the following year are selected and artists and makers are advised to send slides and an application form before then. The gallery covers insurance, printing of publicity, list of exhibits, preview costs, mailing out of publicity, catalogue/card and takes 25% commission. It supports the principle of EPR .
Access: [X] BR Scarborough 5 mins; Bus station 5 mins; Car park 1 min

Scunthorpe (South Humberside)

(LHA) Map3 SE81

Normanby Hall Country Park

350 acre country park with woodland, formal gardens and deer park. Craft and coutryside centre, farming museum, Regency mansion, golf club, horse riding. [Sc]
Address: Normanby, Scunthorpe, Humberside DN15 9HU tel 0724 720588/720215
Contact: Exhibition Organiser Vivienne Totty, Museum and Art Gallery, Oswald Road, Scunthorpe DN15 7BD tel 0724 843533
Open: Dawn - dusk all year
Policy: Although there is no firm policy at present

Workshop Gallery: 'Denis the Menace' Crescent Arts Workshop's beach work celebrating the centenary of the Beano (Photo: Scarborough & District Newspapers Ltd)

pending the appointment of an exhibitions organiser, it is hoped to develop a sculpture park at Normanby with either additional permanent acquisitions and/or temporary shows.

The Space: Formal gardens and woodland surrounding the hall.

Exhibiting: [AW] Applications to Exhibition Organiser.

Access: [U][T] 4 miles north of Scunthorpe on B1430 to Burton Stather; Car park in park off Thealby Lane

Scunthorpe Central Library

A public library administered by Humberside Leisure Services with two exhibition spaces.

Address: Carlton Street, Scunthorpe, S Humberside DN15 6TX tel 0724 860161

Contact: Group Librarian David Bell

Open: Mon-Fri 10-5, Sat 9.30-4

The Space: The ground floor has a purpose-built 3m high exhibition area with picture rail and hangers provided, 16m wall space plus free-standing screens and display cabinets. The first floor takes approximately 40 pictures on fixed wall hooks and has 18m linear wall space 2m high. Both areas are lit by a mixture of strip lights and track-mounted spots. Plans available.

Exhibiting: [AW]

Scunthorpe Museum and Art Gallery

Municipal gallery run by Scunthorpe Borough Council. Regional museum for South Humberside (local history, archaeology and natural science) with two temporary exhibition galleries. [VA,Ph,Cr]

Address: Oswald Road, Scunthorpe, Humberside DN15 7BD tel 0724 843533

Contact: Exhibition Organiser Vivienne Totty

Open: Mon-Sat 10-5, Sun 2-5

Policy: Policy currently under review pending appointment of Exhibition Organiser (funded by LHA). Permanent collection of prints and drawings by regional artists depicting local scenes.

Sales: Work sold

The Space: Gallery 1 is 15x6x3.5m with 35m hanging length, work fixed to blockboard walls, lit by fluorescent strips and track-mounted spots. Gallery 2 is 12x6x3.5m with 25m hanging length, work fixed by mirror plates to 1.25m deep wall-mounted blockboard panels, lit by track-mounted spots. Gallery 3 is 1.75x3x3.5m with 6.5m hanging length, work fixed by mirror plates to wall-mounted panels as in gallery 2, lit by fluorescent strips and track-mounted spots. Plans available.

Exhibiting: [AW] [EF] Application form available from Exhibitions Organiser which should be submitted at least one year in advance of proposed exhibition. Gallery pays for insurance, printing and mailing of publicity, preview costs and catalogue. Gallery supports EPR in principle and charges 20% commission on sales.

Access: [X] BR Scunthorpe 5 mins; on main bus routes (bus stop outside museum); Car park for visitors to rear of museum

Thomas Sumpter Comprehensive School

A comprehensive school showing exhibitions as an educational resource with 1150, 11-16 year old pupils. [Pa,Pr,Dr,Ph,Cr]

Address: Chandos Road, Scunthorpe, Humberside DN17 1HA tel 0724 868666

Contact: Headmaster B Parkington

Open: During school hours

Policy: As the primary aim is to use exhibitions as an educational resource, wherever possible, the programme includes workshops by exhibiting artists, sometimes combined with creative writing workshops. Members of the public are most welcome to view the five annual exhibitions which comprise one textiles, two photography and of two prints, drawings and paintings.

Sales: Sales referred to exhibitors

The Space: 37.5m hanging space on 1.25m deep Sundeala board panels situated along main building ground floor corridor.

Exhibiting: [AW][EF] Apply to the school office. School pays for insurance, display costs, transport and artists' expenses.

Access: [F] Car park on campus; 20 mins walk town centre

Settle (N Yorkshire)

(YA) Map3 SD86

Linton Court Gallery

A commercial gallery established in 1980 specialising in contemporary art exhibitions with a permanent collection of watercolours, prints and ceramics. [VA,Sc,Cr]

Address: Duke Street, Settle, N Yorkshire BD27 tel 07292 2695

Contact: Ann Carr

Open: Tues-Fri 11-5, Sun 2-5 (Apr-Oct); Sat 11-4, Sun 2-4 (Oct-March)

Policy: From April to October the gallery mounts regular monthly exhibitions with a policy *'to have a variety of styles of painting, so that each month the public can expect something different. The gallery gives first showings to young and promising artists as well as the more established'.* During the winter months the exhibitions concentrate on work by the 'gallery artists', local art groups and photographic exhibitions.

Sales: Work sold; Credit card

The Space: The gallery is in a converted hay loft and benefits from a high-walled room, gallery plans are available.

Exhibiting: [AW] Artists should write, with slides, to Ann Carr. The gallery covers the cost of insurance, printing of publicity, list of exhibits, preview costs, mailing out of publicity and catalogue, the gallery takes 33.3% commission.

Access: [X] BR Settle 5 mins; Car park 5 mins

Sevenoaks (Kent)

(SEA) Map7 TQ55

Pegasus Gallery

This commercial gallery deals with the work of living artists. [Pr,Cr,Gl]

Address: 67b London Road, Sevenoaks, Kent TN13 1AU tel 073 245 0947
Contact: David Sharp, 84 Glentrammon Road, Orpington, Kent, BR6 6DG tel 068 955 320
Open: Mon-Sat 9.30-5.30, Wed 9.30-1
Policy: Specialising in all forms of printmaking, this gallery concentrates on a changing display of work by contemporary artists *'for the decoration of homes and offices'*.
Sales: Work sold; Credit card
Access: **[F]** BR Sevenoaks 10 mins; Public car park 2 mins

Sevenoaks Library Gallery

This gallery runs a regular programme of exhibitions featuring local artists as well as occasional museum and archive exhibitions and travelling exhibitions. [VA,Ph,Cr]

Address: Buckhurst Lane, Sevenoaks, Kent TN13 1LQ tel 0732 453118
Contact: Group Librarian Peter Swan
Open: Mon-Wed, Fri 9.30-5.30, Thurs 9.30-7, Sat 9-5
Policy: The gallery aims to promote the work of artists with a particular relevance to the area, and to show exhibitions which would not otherwise be seen in the area. National and regional touring shows are also exhibited. The majority of shows are solo and normally run for four weeks. Artists, lectures and slide-shows are also arranged where appropriate.
Sales: Work sold
The Space: 7x3x2.5m high with 25m linear hanging space. Direct fixing to walls with track-mounted spotlights. Maximum hanging height 2.5m. Occasionally the space is used for meetings.
Exhibiting: **[AW]** Apply to Group Librarian with slides or photographs approximately 15 months in advance. Gallery finances insurance, list of exhibits and mail-out of publicity. Support in principle for EPR. Commission 15%. At time of going to press, booked until end of 1991.
Access: **[L][X]** BR Sevenoaks 12 mins; Public car park 2 mins

Shebbear (Devon)

(SWA) Map6 SS40

Shebbear College (Little Gallery)

The gallery shows work by makers and figurative artists. The gallery also functions as an additional publicity outlet for any other gallery which may wish to use the opportunity.

Address: Shebbear, North Devon EX20 5JH tel 040928 228/570
Contact: Stephen Foster
Open: Mon-Sat 10-, Sun by telephone appointment
Policy: A community link, encouraging support for artists and makers amongst the North Devon rural communities. Displays are arranged to coincide with major college functions to ensure a good audience for exhibitors.
Sales: Work sold
The Space: The gallery measures 25x2.5m with five fixed wall panels and has day and artificial light. Glass cabinets and four free-standing double-sided panels (1.3x1.5m) also available.
Exhibiting: **[AW]** It provides all publicity but not insurance and no commission is charged. Some artists and makers accept opportunities to undertake *'day residencies'*.
Access: Car park

Sheffield (S Yorkshire)

(YA) Map3 SK38

Bishops' House

A municipal museum in a timber-framed Tudor house featuring a continuous programme of temporary exhibitions. [Pa,Cr]

Address: Meersbrook Park, Norton Lees Lane, Sheffield, S Yorkshire S8 9BE tel 0742 557701
Contact: Keeper, Social & Labour History David Bostwick, Sheffield City Museums, Weston Park, Sheffield S10 2TP tel 0742 768588
Open: Wed-Sat 10-5, Sun 11-5
Policy: Much of the exhibition space is reserved for objects and paintings from the museum's reserve collections but work by local makers and pictures by local topographical artists are shown occasionally.
The Space: There are three main exhibition areas, with adjustable track lighting, constant temperature and humidity levels, air filtering and ultra-violet light screening. Each area has fixed wall display panels, together with adjustable free-standing display screens and movable glass-topped showcases.
Exhibiting: **[AW]**
Access: **[X]**

Crucible Theatre (Crucible Gallery)

Exhibitions are held throughout the year in the foyer area of the theatre. [Pa,Pr,Ph]

Address: Norfolk Street, Sheffield, S Yorkshire S1 1DA tel 0742 760621
Contact: Nicholas Horsey
Policy: Four-week exhibitions which, if possible, tie in with the stage production eg a portfolio of photographs of present day farmworkers to coincide with a production of 'Cider With Rosie'.
Sales: Work sold
The Space: 100 linear feet (with 1.3m drop) over six exhibition boards. The theatre has 50 exhibition frames for photographs or smaller graphic work.
Exhibiting: **[AW]** Photographers, artists with a body of work to show should contact the above. 15% commission.
Access: **[U][T]** Main bus routes; BR Sheffield Victoria; Car park close

Five Arches Community Centre

Community resources centre and café with space for exhibitions. [VA,Ph,Cr]

Address: Penrith Road, Sheffield, S Yorkshire tel 0742 323397

Contact: Caroline Tyrer

Policy: Shows work by local community.

Access: [U][T]

Graves Art Gallery

A municipal gallery with responsibility for the care and display of a collection of European art and a changing exhibition programme of both contemporary and historical art. [VA,Ph,Cr,LA]

Address: Surrey Street, Sheffield, S Yorkshire S1 1XZ tel 0742 734781

Contact: Deputy Director of Arts David Alston

Open: Mon-Sat 10-6

Policy: The gallery has a commitment to mounting a broad range of exhibitions of contemporary and historical art for *'a large city public and to provide a service centred on the visual arts for those who live, work and are educated in Sheffield'*. Exhibitions being planned include the inauguration of an annual show of less established artists whose work has not been widely shown. There are 24 exhibitions organised a year which are divided equally between displays using the permanent collection and exhibitions hired or originated by the gallery of predominantly living artists and makers work, each exhibition lasts for between four and six weeks and is complemented by a continuous education programme.

Sales: Work sold

The Space: All galleries are top-lit and have a mixture of spots and floods. One gallery has total controlled lighting for delicate works on paper and all galleries have portable humidifers for full environmental control and a dado which prevents work being hung at floor level. Gallery plans are available.

Exhibiting: **[AW][EF]** Artists and makers should send slides and statement to the Assistant Keeper Anne Goodchild, the gallery covers all exhibition costs but the provision of catalogue and preview will vary from exhibition to exhibition.

Access: **[L]** BR Sheffield 5 mins; Bus station 5 mins; Car park 5 mins

Mappin Art Gallery

A municipal gallery with a permanent collection of European and American art and regular exhibitions of contemporary art. [VA,Ph,Cr,LA]

Address: Weston Park, Sheffield, S Yorkshire S10 2YP tel 0742 726281 & 754091

Contact: Keeper Mike Tooby

Open: Tues-Sat 10-5, Sun 2-5

Policy: The gallery initiates its own solo, group and *'community-based'* exhibitions which are *'group, thematic, historical, mixed or didactic'* as well as hiring in exhibitions from other venues. The gallery hosts the annual 'Open Art' exhibition and has a space reserved for Sheffield-based artists and makers. There is a full education programme which complements the exhibitions and Mappin Art Workshops run an adult education programme. There are 30 exhibitions a year, 20 of which will be of work by living artists either in group or solo shows and each exhibition lasts for one to two months. Run in collaboration with other Sheffield City Art Galleries.

Sales: Sales referred to the exhibitor

The Space: Four galleries each with 60m linear hanging space and one space with12m linear hanging space giving a total of 1702 square metres. The coffee area is also based for two-dimensional works. Gallery plans are available on request.

Exhibiting: **[AW][EF]** Applications with slides in writing to the Keeper, the gallery covers all exhibition costs and occasionally commissions works and pays a negotiated fee. The gallery supports the principle of EPR.

Access: **[U][T][L][F]** Buses 5,6,8,51,52,60,95

Millhouse Gallery

A commercial gallery specialising in promoting contemporary crafts and which has recently began to organise craft exhibitions. [Cr]

Address: 263 Manchester Road, Millhouse Green, Sheffield, S Yorkshire S30 6NP tel 0226 765 105

Contact: Jenny Kellington

Open: 10-6 Tues-Sat

Policy: The aim of the gallery is to have *'a continuous display of craft work for sale and two or three craft exhibitions a year where the exhibition space, it is hoped, will be offered free to makers'*. The exhibitions are intended to be group mixed-media shows which last for one month.

Sales: Work sold

The Space: There is one large gallery 8x5m with spot lights, two overhead lights and large windows providing natural light. Fixed shelving for three-dimensional work is combined with furniture for displaying work. The gallery is on the first floor which restricts the size and weight of objects to *'domestic'*.

Exhibiting: **[AW]** Makers should send slides to the gallery. It is hoped to offer the space free and that the gallery will make contributions towards the costs of advertising and cover the costs of mailing out of publicity and preview costs and take 25% commission.

Access: **[X]** Bus route main Barnsley to Huddersfield line; Car park 1 min

Mappin Art Gallery: Rosie Leventon installation

Myrtle Springs Centre & Starworks

The gallery is within part of a campus which includes a school, youth centre, adult education centre and swimming pool. [VA,Cr]

Address: East Bank Road, Sheffield, S Yorkshire S2 2AL tel 0742 392635, 441475

Contact: Arts Co-ordinator Deborah Egan, 53 Crescent Road, Nether Edge, Sheffield S7 1HN

Open: Mon 9.30-9.30pm

Policy: Set up to respond to the needs of the East Sheffield community, arranges activities in a number of venues ranging from working men's clubs to unused school classrooms. Exhibitions are staged in a hexagonal room also used for concerts. Shows are held every three to four weeks.

Sales: Work sold

Exhibiting: No commission charged.

Ruskin Gallery (Ruskin Craft Gallery)

A municipal gallery opened in 1985 in order to care, maintain and display the collection of the Guild of St George artifacts which show the varied interests of John Ruskin and the Ruskin Craft Gallery, established in 1988, displaying regular changing exhibitions which occasionally illuminate the permanent collection and provide a space for contemporary craft work. [Pa,Pr,Dr,Ph,Cr]

Address: 101 Norfolk Street, Sheffield, S Yorkshire S1 2JE tel 0742 735299

Contact: Keeper Janet Barnes

Open: Mon-Fri 10-6, Sat 10-5

Policy: The gallery shows some work by living artist in order to draw attention to the permanent collection of manuscripts, prints and other objects which were of interest to John Ruskin, *'this gives a broad base of media and the contemporary art exhibitions are showing ideas which Ruskin favoured continuing today'*. All six exhibitions a year are originated by the gallery and each show lasts two months. It is planned that one exhibition a year will be by contemporary makers. Last year there was an exhibition of contemporary calligraphy chosen because it reflected Ruskin's own interest in the subject and brought the theme up to date. Workshops and demonstrations are linked to the exhibitions wherever possible. The Ruskin Craft Gallery exhibits contemporary crafts of a wide spectrum.

Sales: Work sold

The Space: The main exhibition area is on the mezzanine floor with controlled lighting, show cases and limited wall space. The Ruskin Craft Gallery exhibits work on open display with some locked display cases.

Exhibiting: [AW] Applications for the craft gallery must be sent to the Keeper, the gallery covers the cost of insurance, printing of publicity, list of exhibitions, preview costs, display, transport, mailing out of publicity, catalogue and artists expenses which are negotiable and do not always apply. The gallery occasionally pays a fee, is supportive of the principle of EPR and takes a commission which is negotiable.

Access: [U][T][S][X] BR Sheffield 10 min; Car park 2 min

Sheffield City Polytechnic (Polytechnic Gallery)

A public gallery within the polytechnic which provides a showcase for students' work and annual degree shows. [VA,Ph,Cr,LA]

Address: Psalter Lane, Sheffield, S Yorkshire S11 8UZ tel 0742 556101

Contact: John Kirby

Open: Mon-Fri 9-5 term-time only

Policy: Whilst providing the students and public with a showcase for polytechnic students, the gallery also aims to *'show work by artists which promotes discussion and debate and continues to provide a forum for contemporary art within the confines of the college'*. The exhibitions last for two to four weeks and the artists are invited to talk about the work on show.

Sales: Work sold

The Space: There are two galleries one with 30m linear hanging space and the main space with 52m linear hanging space. There are a variety of showcases available in different sizes.

Exhibiting: [AW] Artists and makers should send slides to the Gallery Committee at the polytechnic. The gallery covers the cost of insurance, printing of publicity, display, transport, mailing out of publicity and artists' expenses. Supports the principle of EPR.

Access: [U][T] Bus route 3; Car park 1 min

Touring Exhibitions Service

A touring exhibition service to fifteen community venues in Sheffield. [VA,Cr]

Address: c/o Ruskin Gallery, 101 Norfolk Street, Sheffield S1 2JE tel 0742 734791

Contact: Sally Goldsmith

Policy: The exhibitions service shows mainly paintings, prints, drawings and crafts in month-long exhibitions held in further education establishments, community centres and some secondary schools. Educational activities - talks and workshops etc - are often organised and fee-paid for artists.

Sales: Work sold; Sales referred to exhibitor

The Space: Most exhibition spaces are small-foyers, coffee bars etc and usually have hessian-covered chipboard on the walls to make hanging by mirror plates possible.

Exhibiting: [AW][EF] If the exhibition is not toured by the service, artists can approach most venues directly, and a directory of local spaces will be available early 1989 to include contacts, access, types of exhibitions taken. Contact Sally Goldsmith for more information.

University of Sheffield (Library Exhibition Area)

The exhibition area within the library is principally used by the University's Fine Art Society for art exhibitions and to display the library's rare books or special collections. [Pa,Pr,Dr,Ph]

Address: Main Library, Western Park, Sheffield, S Yorkshire S10 2TN tel 0742 768555

Contact: Sub Librarian (Reader Services) Christine Stockton

Open: Mon-Thurs 9-9.30, Fri 9-5, Sat 9-1 term; Mon-Fri 9-5, Sat 9-12.30 vacation

Policy: The art exhibition programme is mainly organised by the society, giving its members an opportunity to display and sell work in an annual members' exhibition, although other shows of mainly local artists work is shown and the gallery aims to bring contemporary work on to the campus in exhibitions, running throughout the term, which last for two weeks each. Book displays are arranged by library staff.

Sales: Work sold

The Space: The gallery has 13.7m linear hanging space and additional screens which will take up to 45 paintings. Showcases are also available on request.

Exhibiting: [AW] Applications should be sent to Dr Teale, Physics or Dr Harper, Architecture, who *'would like more artists to approach us with an exhibition proposal'*. The gallery pays for transport (within reason), printing and mail out of publicity and lists of exhibits and takes 20% commission.

Access: [U][T] BR Sheffield 20 mins; Buses 50,51,52,60,95; Car park restricted during the day in term-time, evening parking available

Untitled Gallery

A photographic resource centre comprising galleries, darkrooms, workshops, library, materials shop and café. [Pr,Ph,LA]

Address: Brown Street, Sheffield, S Yorkshire S1 2BS tel 0742 725947

Contact: Manager Matthew Conduit

Open: Tues-Sat 10-5.30

Policy: The gallery aims to promote the *'diversity of contemporary photographic practice, especially those areas which foster an investigative and critical view of the medium in all its uses, through exhibition, education programmes and publications'*. The gallery encourages a *'regional view'* by mounting exhibitions which deal with the region's history, industries, geography, politics, culture and people whilst providing resources for photographers on the premisies. The emphasis is on the promotion of new work by younger artists and on the encouragement of local photographers. There are about ten exhibitions a year each lasting for four to six weeks, three of these may be solo exhibitions and most are of work by contemporary artists. Education programme of lectures, workshops and evening classes.

Untitled Gallery: 'Family - My History - My-Self' from the series 'Awakening' by Gina Glover, Photo Co-Op London

Sales: Work sold

The Space: There are two exhibition areas and additional wall space in the library and coffee area giving a total of 182m linear hanging space. In addition a roof garden is a possible sculpture site.

Exhibiting: [AW][EF] Photographers should contact Matthew Conduit in writing. The gallery covers all exhibition costs and occasionally commissions work especially for exhibitions and supports the principle of EPR and takes 25-30% commission. The exhibition space can be hired for other events for a negotiable fee.

Access: [U][T][F] BR Sheffield 2 mins; Bus station 1 mins; Car park 1 min

Walkley Centre Gallery

Based in a busy community education centre, itself a part of Loxley Tertiary College. [VA,Ph,Cr]

Address: South Road, Sheffield, S Yorkshire S6 3TA tel 0742 330360

Contact: Caroline Irving

Open: Mon-Fri 9-4, Mon & Wed 7-9

Policy: *'The gallery aims to show a rich mixture of exhibitions to inspire, stimulate and inform our public. We encourage short residencies, visits and talks by artists (unpaid unfortunately). We use the exhibitions as a basis for educational projects and do follow up work whenever possible.'*

Sales: Work sometimes for sale

The Space: An area of 40m square giving a total of 18m linear space for hanging two-dimensional work which has a mixture of natural and artificial light. *'The gallery is in chronic need of repair and refitting or resiting within the centre. We hope to do this soon.'*

Exhibiting: [AW] Commission is 10% and the artist meets the cost of mailing, insurance, transport and publicity and preview costs are shared.

Access: [X] Frontoing onto main shopping street; Bus 95

Yorkshire Art Space Society (Matilda Gallery)

Yorkshire Art Space Society, a charitable trust established in order to provide affordable studio and workshop space for artists and makers houses a gallery which promotes work both by the group and by other artists and makers. [VA,Ph,Cr,LA]

Address: Sydney Works, 111 Matilda Street, Sheffield, S Yorkshire S1 4QF tel 0742 761769 and 761869

Contact: Exhibitions Organiser

Open: Mon-Fri 10-4

Policy: The gallery aims to mount exhibitions which illustrate the broad spectrum of production practices currently being employed and encourage active participation and understanding through educational activities, workshops and events related to the work on show. The *'audience is as diverse as the community we are situated in and the group is actively involving schools, unemployed groups and people with disabilities in the events'*. There is one exhibition every month and the gallery favours group shows.

Sales: Work sold; Credit scheme

The Space: There are two galleries both lit by spots and fluorescent strip lighting, in addition there are five plinths available and one individually-lit showcase for three-dimensional work.

Exhibiting: [AW] Artists and makers should send slides and exhibition proposal to the Exhibition Organiser. The gallery covers the costs of insurance, printing of publicity, list of exhibits, preview costs, mailing out of publicity and catalogue/card and takes 20% commission. The exhibition space can be hired for £80 a month to non-YASS members which includes publicity, insurance and a preview. Supports the principle of EPR.

Access: [U][T] Ground floor gallery only. BR Sheffield 7 mins

Sherborne (Dorset)

(SWA) Map6 ST61

Melbury Gallery

The gallery holds regular exhibitions in addition to its permanent display of high-quality work by leading artists and makers usually from the South West. [VA,Cr]

Address: 93 Cheap Street, Sherborne, Dorset DT9 3LS tel 0935 814 027

Contact: Director

Policy: A wide variety of work is on offer, from sculpture to etchings, jewellery, clothes and blown glass. Its resident stained glass artist undertakes commissions and repairs.

Shrewsbury (Shropshire)

(NWA) Map4 SJ41

Gateway

An education and arts centre housing the Shropshire community education service, Shrewsbury and District Arts Association and courses for Birmingham University Extra Mural Department. [VA,Cr,Ph]

Address: Education and Arts Centre, Chester Street, Shrewsbury, Shropshire SY1 1NB tel 0743 55159

Contact: Exhibitions Organiser Elizabeth Perkins

Open: Mon-Fri 10-10, Sat 10-4

Policy: A purpose-built art and education centre offering a wide variety of courses, performances and exhibitions. The exhibitions are mostly of local artists and makers with an annual open exhibition. Gallery talks, demonstrations and courses are organised alongside the exhibition programme. The foyer and riverside café are also equipped for exhibitions.

Sales: Work sold

The Space: The gallery is 7x5.5m with adjustable spots. Extra screens can be provided. Various display cases are available and direct fixing or hanging rods can be used. The corridor outside the gallery can also be used as an extension to the main space. Walls are covered in beige hessian. The cafe provides 20m linear hanging space on hessian-covered boards. The foyer is primarily used for small exhibitions in display cases. Gallery plans available.

Exhibiting: [AW] Application forms are available six to twelve months in advance from the Exhibition Organiser. A commission of 20% is charged on sales and the gallery provides insurance, publicity, printing, list of exhibits and display.

Access: [U][L][F] BR Shrewsbury, bus station and car parks 2 mins

Rowley's House Museum

A museum run by Shrewsbury Museum Service and mainly devoted to museum exhibitions 'and available perhaps one month a year to living artists'. [VA,Cr]

Address: Barker Street, Shrewsbury, Shropshire SY1 1QT tel 0743 61196

Contact: Curator Vivien Bellamy

Access: Town centre next to bus station

Shropshire Libraries

A network of exhibition and display facilities in 33 branch libraries throughout Shropshire. [VA,Ph,Cr]

Address: Shropshire Libraries Headquarters, Column House, 7 London Road, Shrewsbury, Shropshire SY2 6NW tel 0743 253666

Contact: Chief Librarian C R Field

Open: Various

Policy: The library service encourages *'artists to use our premises, and especially those who have never exhibited before'. 'Over 50% of the population of Shropshire voluntarily visit our libraries. There is a great potential for artists to have their work seen'.*

Sales: Sales referred to exhibitor

The Space: Various.

Exhibiting: [AW] Contact Library Headquarters. The library service provides insurance, publicity and a list of exhibits. A 10% commission is charged on sales.

Tower Gallery, St Julian's Craft Centre for Shropshire

The gallery is converted from a 12th century tower with studios open to the public as part of the premises, also a vegetarian restaurant. [VA,Cr]

Address: St Julian's Church Shrewsbury, Shropshire SY1 1UH tel 0743 53516

Contact: Proprietor Andrew Wright

Open: Mon-Wed, Fri, Sat 10-5

Policy: To exhibit local work of quality and saleability. Each exhibitor is offered a fortnight's exhibition. Customers have shown a preference for local views, embroidered pictures and for commissioning pet portraits.

Sales: Work sold

The Space: Three 2.5x1.5m boards and artificial lighting.

Exhibiting: [AW] Exhibitors should apply in person bringing examples of their work. A charge of £5 per week is made for the use of the space and 10% commission is charged if commission exceeds the basic charge. All expenses are the responsibility of the artist or maker. Gallery booked at least a year ahead.

Access: [S] Town centre site

Silverdale (Lancashire)

(NWA) Map3 SD47

Wolf House Gallery

A commercial gallery situated in an old Georgian farmhouse in the countryside which organises workshops and practical art courses as well as exhibitions. [VA,Cr]

Address: Gibraltar, Silverdale, Carnforth, Lancashire LA5 OTX tel 0524 701405

Contact: Edward or Denise Dowbiggin

Open: Tues-Sun 10.30-1, 2-5.30 Summer; Tues-Fri 2-5 Sat, Sun 10.30-5.30 Spring; Tues-Fri 2-5.30, Sat-Sun 10.30 Autumn; Sat-Sun 10.30-5.30 Winter; Closed Mon, open bank holidays

Policy: Holds a variety of mixed exhibitions. *'Our range is now so extensive and we are approached by so many potential exhibitors that new work has to fill an existing gap.'*

Sales: Work sold; Credit card; Credit scheme

Exhibiting: [AW] Telephone to make an appointment and preferably to look around the gallery beforehand. Gallery pays for printing of publicity, preview costs, mailing, and catalogue. It takes commission of 25% plus VAT.

Access: [X] Individual wheelchairs welcome BR Silverdale 25 mins; Bus 15 mins; Car park

Skelmersdale (Lancashire)

(NWA) Map3 SD40

Library Arts Centre

Purpose-built gallery and performance space below Skelmersdale Central Library, serving the local community and whole of West Lancashire and showing temporary exhibitions only, ranging from social history to Arts Council touring, as well as contemporary artists' work. [VA,Cr,LA]

Address: Central Library, Southway, Skelmersdale, Lancashire WN8 6NL tel 0695 20312

Contact: Arts Co-ordinator Eddie Ohren

Open: Tues-Fri 1-5, Sat 10-1, 2-4

Policy: The centre aims to show a varied and interesting exhibition programme covering all aspects of the visual and performing arts. Lectures, workshops and demonstrations are organised alongside exhibitions. A wide range of community groups use the centre.

Sales: Work sold

The Space: Walls and screens used are in a space with movable seating and adaptable floor space and a platform for performances. Size of work limited to 2.4m high. Display cases. Three display cases 1.6x1x0.6m, four display cases 0.7x0.7x0.7m and two of 1.6x0.6x0.2m. The exhibition area is also used for performances and community activities.

Exhibiting: [AW] Apply to Arts Co-ordinator at any time in writing with CV and slides or photographs of work to be exhibited. Centre covers insurance, publicity, preview costs and transport. Commission is 15%. Supports EPR in principle.

Access: [U][L][F] Local bus routes near; Parking adjacent

St Thomas the Apostle RC High School

Foyer and corridors of school which are used for visual arts and crafts displays by artists from the region. [Pa,Pr,Dr,Ph,Te,Ce,Je]

Address: Glenburn Road, Skelmersdale, Lancashire WN8 6JW tel 0695 25635

Contact: Head of Design Faculty Roger O'Connor

Open: Mon-Fri 8.45-3.30 other hours by arrangement

Policy: The school aims to bring visual arts and crafts to the young people of Skelmersdale and to be used as a resource by local educational establishments and the local community.

Sales: Sales referred to exhibitor

The Space: Foyer area 20x20x10m, corridor 30x4x3m with hanging by picture hooks and spots, electric and natural lights. Display cases 1.8x1x1m lit, 1x1.8x0.6 unlit with shelves.

Exhibiting: [AW] Apply to Head of Faculty of Design, hire of space and commission fees negotiable.

Access: [X] Near to bus routes; Ample car parking on school site

Slough (Berkshire)

(SA) Map7 SU97

Slough Museum

An independent local history museum showing temporary exhibitions covering a variety of aspects of the history of Slough with a permanent collection of objects and photographs relating to this. [Ph]

Address: 23 Bath Road, Slough, Berkshire SL6 5AN tel 0753 26422

Contact: Curator Miss I M Phoenix

Open: Wed-Fri 12-4, Sat & Sun 2-5

Policy: The aims of the Slough Museum are to foster public understanding.and enjoyment of the environment with specific regard to the town of Slough, to encourage an appreciation of local history and to strengthen local roots. School visits and talks to local societies are arranged.

The Space: Gallery plans available.

Exhibiting: [AW] Contact the Curator.

Access: [U] BR Slough 15 mins walk; bus stop 50 yards; limited free parking

Snape (N Yorkshire)

(YA) Map3 SE28

Thornton Gallery

A commercial gallery specialising in shows of North country artists and mainly nineteenth and early twentieth century paintings. [Pa]

Policy: An annual exhibition in December is dedicated to paintings and drawings by Yorkshire artists.

Solihull (W Midlands)

(WMA) Map4 SP17

Solihull Central Library

A purpose-built exhibition space in the foyer of the library. [VA,Ph,Cr]

Address: Homer Road, Solihull, W Midllands B91 3RG tel 021 704 6965
Contact: Chief Librarian & Arts Officer J W Lendon
Open: Mon & Tues 9.30-5.30, Thurs & Fri 9.30-8, Sat 9.30-5
Policy: A wide range of exhibitions are shown, mostly from local sources and artists.
The Space: 6x12m space with showcases, direct fixing and spotlighting.
Exhibiting: [AW] Commission is 15% and the artist pays a hire fee and meets all exhibition expenses.
Access: [U] Located in the town centre

South Woodham Ferrers (Essex)

(EA) Map7 TQ89

South Woodham Ferrers Library

Exhibition space in public library, available for hire. [VA,Cr]

Address: Trinity Square, South Woodham Ferrers, Essex CM3 5JU tel 0245 329555
Contact: Librarian Marilyn Slator
Open: Tues,Thurs 9-7, Fri, Sat 9-5
Sales: Work sold; Sales referred to exhibitor
The Space: The floor area is 51.34 square metres.
Access: [F]

Southampton (Hampshire)

(SA) Map7 SU41

First Gallery

A self-financing, private exhibition space in the owner's own house with permanent display of pots, pictures and sculptures and part of the house transformed for exhibitions plus small patio and lawn for outside exhibits. [VA,Ph,Cr]

Address: 1 Burnham Chase, Bitterne, Southampton, Hampshire SO2 5DG tel 0703 462723
Contact: Margery Clarke
Open: By appointment, 2-8 during exhibition
Policy: *'The gallery's policy is to emphasise in a welcoming way that art is part of every-day life around us. We deliberately remain very small, pleasant and yet professional, and extend by initiating touring exhibitions or joint ventures. Our target is anyone interested in looking or buying and our aim is positively to make life more interesting for them. We aim to encourage and make opportunities for both viewers and exhibitors'.*
Sales: Work sold
The Space: Space set aside in the owner's home.
Exhibiting: *'Always interested but we are very restricted'.* To apply, telephone Margery Clarke. Gallery pays towards printing and mailing of publicity, list of exhibits and preview costs and takes 33.3% commission.
Access: [S] Bus 24 from Southampton; Parking outside

Gantry

A community arts centre showing film, theatre, jazz and visual arts with workshops in all activities. [VA,Ph]

Address: Off Blechynden Terrace, Southampton, Hampshire SO1 0GW tel 0703 229319
Contact: Exhibitions Committee
Open: Mon-Fri 10-4, Sat 11-2 and evening performances
Policy: *'Provides an exhibition space where locally-based artists and those from elsewhere can exhibit and sell their work, the aim being to heighten local awareness of artists and their work. We wish to appeal to a wide audience and show works in many media and to encourage participation from all cultures in the community. We also arrange accompanying activities and would like to show more artists'* work from other regions.' Exhibitions run for four weeks.
Sales: Work sold; Credit card
The Space: The space is 11x5x2.5m (rising to 3.5m) with 25m linear hanging space and track spotlights. Gallery plans available.
Exhibiting: [AW] Artists and groups should send photographs of work and accompanying information to the Exhibitions Committee. The gallery pays for insurance, printing and mailing of publicity, list of exhibits, preview costs and a card. Commission is 15%. Supports EPR.
Access: [U] BR Southampton Station 2 mins walk; Public car parks 2 mins; Close to bus routes

John Hansard Gallery

A gallery set on the campus of Southampton University and holding major exhibitions and touring exhibitions which include installation and issue-based work. [VA,Ph,Cr,LA]

Address: The University, Highfield, Southampton, Hampshire SO9 5NH tel 0703 559122 ext 2158
Contact: Exhibition Organiser Isobel Johnston
Open: Mon-Sat 10-6
Policy: The gallery seeks exhibitions that stimulate debate around wider social issues, often working with other university departments. There is an emphasis on challenging new work and a special interest in site-specific or installation-based work. Series of talks or seminars putting the exhibitions into a wider context are an important part of the gallery programme. Around seven exhibitions are held a year, each running for six weeks. Gallery shop sells catalogues, magazines, posters and cards.
Sales: Work sold
The Space: Gallery space of 1127 square metres with 69.49m linear hanging space which can be extended to 106m if needed. Direct fixing and spotlighting. Gallery plans available.
Exhibiting: [AW] Applications are considered at any time. The gallery pays for insurance, printing and mailing of publicity, list of exhibits, preview costs, display costs, transport catalogue/card and artists' expenses. Artists sometimes receive a commission fee. Commission on sales is 25% plus VAT.

Access: [U][T][F] Bus 10 from town centre; University car parks near

Lords Hill Library

A branch library, within the Southampton division of the Hampshire County Libraries, which shows work by local artists and book-related displays and group exhibitions. [Pa,Ph,Cr]

Address: District Centre, Lords Hill, Southampton, Hampshire SO1 8HY tel 0703 732845
Contact: Senior Librarian I M Lawrence
Open: Tues-Fri 10-7, Sat 10-4
Policy: The library has shown displays by local architectural award winners, craft displays and photographic exhibitions as well as a permanent but changing display from Southampton Art Society. *'Clearly we have responsibilities to provide facilities for local artists but would welcome work by people from other areas but we do not have any funds for transport etc'.* Exhibitions run for one month.
Sales: Sales referred to exhibitors
The Space: A main wall with 9m linear hanging space and two side walls with 3m linear hanging space, all 2.5m high and in hessian-covered Sundeala board. Track spotlighting and blinds to exclude daylight.
Exhibiting: [AW] Applications should be sent to the Senior Librarian six months in advance. Commission of 10% on sales.
Access: [U][T] Numerous buses from town centre; Large car park adjacent

Southampton Art Gallery

Municipal art gallery with a permanent collection of historical and contemporary art and an exhibition programme which complements the collection. [VA,Cr]

Address: Civic Centre, Southampton SO9 4XF tel 0703 223855 ext 769
Contact: Keeper of Art
Open: Tues-Sun
Policy: The main policy is to bring good-quality work into the rgion rather than to show local artists although there is usually one or two slots in the programme for local work. There is a strong emphasis on educational activities.
The Space: There are two galleries, the larger has 440m linear hanging space which is used for group and thematic shows, the smaller has 24m linear hanging space and is usually used for solo exhibitions.
Exhibiting: [AW] Group exhibitions are normally initiated by the gallery but applications for solo exhibitions are invited.

Southend-on-Sea (Essex)

(EA) Map7 TQ88

Mostly Photographic Gallery & Workshop

Two spaces showing mainly photography, with some painting and printmaking. [Pa,Pr,Ph]

Address: 10/11 Market Place, off Alexandra Street, Southend-on-Sea, Essex SS1 1DA tel 0702 352784
Contact: J MacDonald
Open: Mon-Sat 9.30-5
The Space: The galleries are both 9.15x5.49m.
Exhibiting: [AW]

Southend-on-Sea Library

Four galleries in the central library, available for hire. [VA,Cr]

Address: Central Library, Victoria Avenue, Southend-on-Sea, Essex SS2 6EX tel 0702 612621
Contact: Arts Librarian Mark Tunes
Open: Mon-Fri 9-7, Sat 9-5
Sales: Work sold; Sales referred to exhibitor
The Space: Total floor area is 317.22 square metres with four display cases.
Access: [L]

Southport (Merseyside)

(MA) Map3 SD31

Atkinson Art Gallery

'The gallery is the principle forum for the visual arts in Sefton, with regularly changing displays from its permanent collection and a busy programme of temporary exhibitions.' [VA,Cr,LA]

Address: Lord Street, Southport, Merseyside PR8 1DH tel 0704 33133 ext 2111
Contact: Keeper of Fine Art Stephen Forshaw
Open: Mon-Wed, Fri 10-5, Thurs, Sat 10-1; closed Sun
Policy: *'The gallery aims to provide visitors with an insight into a wide range of artistic practice, embracing past and present, tradition and experimentation.'* It has a permanent collection from 18th, 19th and 20th centuries and is building up its range of contemporary work. A picture hire scheme is operated to ensure that items from the collection are used and enjoyed by people in their own homes. The gallery runs two temporary exhibitions almost every month and the great majority of these feature the work of living artists. It also hosts slide and film shows, talks, lectures and workshops, and has rooms available for hire with 50% reduction for cultural activities.
Sales: Work sold
The Space: The gallery is currently being re-developed, but work is fixed by mirror plates and screws. Lighting is UV protected strip lighting, light track with directional spots, and daylight controlled by electronic venetian blind system. Seven display cases of various sizes available. First floor gallery is unsuitable for very heavy sculpture. Gallery plans available.
Exhibiting: [AW] Apply to Keeper in writing with CV and slides or photographs. The gallery covers insurance, publicity and preview costs. Commission is 20%.
Access: [X] Town centre site; BR and Merseyrail station 5 mins; Car parks 5 mins

Birkdale Branch Library

A busy branch library with 25,000 regular users, showing mainly amateur work and occasional touring exhibitions. [VA,Ph,Cr]

Address: 244-246 Liverpool Road, Southport,

Merseyside PR8 4PD tel 0704 67380
Contact: Branch Librarian Miss D R Draper
Open: Mon Tues 10-5, Wed,Fri 10-8, Thurs,Sat 10-1; Closed 1-2 every day
Policy: Averages ten exhibitions a year, all by living artists. (See also Sefton Libraries).
Sales: Sales referred to exhibitor
The Space: Wall space and fluorescent lighting suitable for hanging paintings. Two glass display cases 1.7x2.5x0.75m with plinths but no shelves also available.
Exhibiting: [AW] Apply to Branch Librarian. Library insures work.
Access: [U][T] 15 mins bus from Southport; BR Birkdale 15 mins; Public car park adjacent

Sefton Libraries

Sefton's branch libraries have varying amounts of exhibition and display facilities. [VA,Cr]
Address: Sefton Metropolitan Borough Council, 9 Eastbank Street, Southport, Merseyside PR8 tel 0704 33133 ext 2115
Contact: Libraries & Arts Officer Roy Marston
Open: Various
Policy: (See also Birkdale Branch Library).
Sales: Sales referred to exhibitor
The Space: Various.
Exhibiting: For further information and applications to exhibit contact Roy Marston, Libraries & Arts Officer or Steven Forshaw, Keeper of Fine Art, Atkinson Art Gallery, Lord Street, Southport, Merseyside PR8 1DH.

Southwold (Suffolk)

(EA) Map5 TM67

Great Eastern Craft Co-operative

The gallery is run by a co-operative of ten makers as an outlet for their own work with a limited number of non-members also supplying the gallery. [Cr]
Address: 10 Market Place, Southwold, Suffolk IP18 6EE
Contact: Secretary Peter Mulley, Oak Tree Design Workshop, Cratfield Road, Huntingfield, Halesworth, Suffolk IP19 0QB tel 098683 516
Open: Tues-Sun 10-5; Sat-Sun 10-5 January-March
Sales: Work sold
The Space: The gallery is13x7x2.4m.
Exhibiting: Commission on sales for non-members 33.3%.
Access: [F]

Portland Studio

[Pa,Pr]
Address: Portland House, High Street, Southwold, Suffolk IP18 6AB tel 0502 723652
Contact: Melanie Strank
Open: Daily 9-1 2-5.30 June-Oct
Policy: Specialises in the sale of original prints, although exhibitions of paintings, drawings and sculpture are staged. Gallery supplies art to offices.
Sales: Work sold
The Space: 10x5m irregular hanging space with spot lighting and good window display area.
Exhibiting: [AW] Write to gallery with information and visual material - or arrange an appointment. Commission 40%. Space may be hired for individual exhibitions.
Access: [X]

Spalding (Lincolnshire)

(LHA) Map5 TF22

Ayscoughfee Hall

New museum and gardens, opened 1987, with permanent displays on land reclamation, agriculture, horticulture and social history.
Address: Church Gate, Spalding, Lincolnshire PE11 2RA tel 0775 5468
Contact: Museum and Tourism Officer Susanna Davis
Open: Mon-Thurs 10-5, Fri 10-2.30; plus Sat 10-5, Sun & bank holiday Mon 11-5 April-end Oct
Policy: To collect and conserve materials relating to South Holland and to present displays on the history of the area as well as provide a gallery for temporary exhibitions which consist of work by local artists and photographers, and travelling exhibitions from Arts Council, East Midlands Area Museum Service, Lincolnshire County Council and South Holland Museum Service.
Exhibiting: [AW]
Access: [U][T] Ground floor. Public car park 2 mins

Stafford (Staffordshire)

(WMA) Map4 SJ92

Stafford Art Gallery

A municipal gallery exclusively showing temporary exhibitions with an 'impressive craft shop', selected for quality by the Crafts Council. [VA,Ph,Cr]
Address: The Green, Lichfield Road, Stafford ST17 4BJ tel 0785 57303
Contact: Arts Promotion Officer John Rhodes
Open: Tues-Fri 10-5, Sat 10-4
Policy: The exhibition programme shows a wide variety

Atkinson Art Gallery: 'Whither Goest Thou' by John Bellany

of work from regional and national sources. The gallery concentrates on high-quality craft work from established makers and new makers.

Sales: Work sold; Credit card

The Space: The gallery is 15x8m with track lighting and direct fixing. The shop area is also used for exhibitions and is equipped with open display areas, cases for jewellery and track lighting.

Exhibiting: [AW] Contact John Rhodes. The gallery provides, insurance, transport, publicity, mailing, list of exhibits, card and preview.

Access: [U][T] Located in the town centre; BR Stafford 10 mins

Stalybridge (Lancashire)

(NWA) Map3 SJ99

Astley Cheetham Art Gallery

The gallery houses the Cheetham Collection which includes a diverse selection of paintings ranging from 14th century Italian art up to Burne-Jones and also organises contemporary arts, crafts and photography exhibitions. [VA]

Address: Trinity Street, Stalybridge, Lancashire SK15 2BN tel 061 338 2708/3831

Contact: Museums Officer

Open: Mon-Fri 1-7.30, Sun 9-4; Closed Sat,Thurs

Policy: About ten exhibitions of work by contemporary artists and schools organised a year.

The Space: Gallery 15x8m.

Exhibiting: [AW] Commission 10%.

Stamford (Lincolnshire)

(EA) Map7 TF00

Stamford Arts Centre (Wilfred Wood Art Gallery)

Part of Stamford Theatre and Arts Centre. [VA,Ph]

Address: 27 St Mary's Street, Stamford, Lincolnshire PE9 2BN tel 0780 63203

Contact: Director Celia Frisby

Open: Tues-Sat 11-5

Policy: The gallery is mainly concerned with promoting contemporary art, from selected artists all over the country, but in line with general centre policy, a small amount of exhibition time is devoted to local artists. Last year, of the 14 exhibitions, seven were solo. A sculpture garden may be established in the future.

Sales: Work sold

The Space: The gallery is 18x4.5m with work mirror-plated to walls. Area at present lit by fluorescent tubes with skylights and French windows. Plan available.

Exhibiting: [AW] Artists requested to submit 10 slides plus CV in August for annual selection committee in September. Annual Open Exhibition in June/July advertised in April. Gallery pays for insurance, printing and mailing of publicity and catalogue. Supports EPR in principle. 20% commission on sales.

Access: [U][T][S] ramp available. BR Stamford 10 mins; Bus station 10 mins; Wharf Road Car Park 2 mins

Torkington Gallery

Torkington Gallery

A commercial art and craft gallery which opened in 1988. [VA,Cr]

Address: 38 St Peters Street, Stamford, Lincolnshire PE9 2PF tel 0780 62281

Contact: Directors Will & Christine Illsley

Open: Mon-Sat 10-1 & 2-5

Policy: Situated in a Georgian town house, the gallery shows a selection of work by the owners and aims to promote a range of contemporary work from both within and outside the region through a combination of regularly changing displays of work, and four exhibitions each year - these are group shows on a specific theme. There are occasionally solo and two-person shows. The range of work primarily covers paintings, prints (etchings and lithographs), ceramics and textiles with an emphasis on hand-painted silks.

Sales: Work sold; Credit card

The Space: The gallery is 12x5x2.75m with up to 23m linear hanging space. Work is hung by pin and cord and lighting is low-voltage tungsten halogen.

Exhibiting: [AW] To Will and Christine Illsley in writing with slides or photos of recent work. Applications can be submitted throughout the year. The gallery pays for insurance, printing and mailing of publicity and takes 33.3% commission on sales.

Access: [S] BR Stamford 5 mins; Public car park 3 mins

Stevenage (Hertfordshire)

(EA) Map7 TL22

Stevenage Leisure Centre

Housed in municipal leisure centre with sports facilities and theatre. There is a large exhibition space and two smaller areas. [VA,Ph,Cr]

Address: Stevenage Leisure Centre, Lytton Way, Stevenage, Hertfordshire SG1 1LZ tel 0438 317956 ext 39

Contact: Arts & Crafts Officer Jackie Dyason

Open: Mon-Sun 10-9

Policy: The gallery is decreasing the number of touring shows in favour of individual exhibitors not necessarily local. Some exhibitions to reflect the centre's education programme.

Sales: Work sold
The Space: The main area is 11x9x3m high with screens 10x2m high, also two smaller areas. Suspended grid track lights and hanging by mirror plates.
Exhibiting: [AW][EF] Apply with slides to Arts and Crafts officer. Gallery pays all costs except for framing and artist's expenses. Commission charged is 20%.
Access: [U][T][L] Bus station 2 mins; BR Stevenage 2mins; Car parks

Stevenage Museum

Local authority museum, funded by Stevenage Borough Council. [VA,Ph,Cr]
Address: St George's Way, Stevenage, Hertfordshire SG1 1XX tel 0438 354292
Contact: Designer/Exhibitions Officer Geoff Wingate
Open: Mon-Sat 10-5
Policy: *'We only intend to exhibit the work of local artists in our small exhibition area or nationally-known artists in our larger area. This policy is presently under review.'*
Sales: Work sold
The Space: The large area is 7x6x2.5m high with 25m linear space and the small area is 5x2.5x2.5m high. Work is screwed to softboard panels, and there are display cases for three dimensional work plus some open display possible. The spotlights have dimmers. Plans available.

Stevenage Leisure Centre: lead mask by Bernard Morot-Gaudry from Stevenage's twin town Autun, France

Exhibiting: [AW] Local artists welcome to apply. The gallery pays for insurance and publicity costs and charges a commission of 20%.
Access: [U][T][F] BR and bus station 5 mins; Car park 2 mins

Stockport (Greater Manchester)

(NWA) Map4 SJ88

Stockport Art Gallery

A local authority gallery showing visual arts and crafts. [VA,Cr]
Address: Memorial Building, Wellington Road South, Stockport, Greater Manchester SK3 8AB tel 061 474 4453
Contact: Visual Arts Outreach Officer, Exhibitions Officer Mike Bloom, Andy Firth tel 061 474 4454
Open: Mon-Fri 11-5, Sat 10-5
Policy: Aims to present the visual arts in an exciting and approachable way and to provide opportunities for the public to participate through demonstrations, workshops, activities and lectures. The Artlink loan and purchase scheme is operated for contemporary art and crafts and the gallery also has a small permanent collection of 19th and 20th century British painting.
Sales: Work sold
The Space: Two galleries with a total of 65m linear space with screens also available.
Exhibiting: [AW] Write to Exhibitions Officer with visual material. The gallery covers the cost of insurance, printing, publicity and mailing.
Access [F] Lower galleries. BR Stockport 5 mins; Bus station 10 mins

Stockton-on-Tees (Cleveland)

(NA) Map3 NZ41

Dovecot Arts Centre

Small gallery in the reception area of a theatre-based arts centre. [Pa,Ph,Cr,LA]
Address: Dovecot Street, Stockton-on-Tees, Cleveland

Stockport Museum & Art Gallery: Arts Council touring exhibition

TS19 1LL tel 0642 611625
Contact: Director Frank Wilson
Policy: Changing exhibitions of work by local and regional artists.
Sales: Work sold
The Space: Exhibition area is 64 square metres with 35m linear hanging space. Lighting by spots and daylight. Showcases are available.
Exhibiting: **[AW]**

Stoke-on-Trent (Staffordshire)

(WMA) Map4 SJ84

Burslem Recreation Centre

A recreation centre run by the Parks and Recreation Department. with provision for local artists to display works for sale. [VA]
Address: Market Place, Burslem, Stoke-on-Trent ST6 3DS tel 0782 813363
Contact: Centre Manager Vernon Elkin

City Museum & Art Gallery

A large municipal art gallery with a permanent collection, temporary exhibitions and education programme. [VA,Ph,Cr]
Address: Bethesda Street, Hanley, Stoke-on-Trent ST1 3DE tel 0782 202173
Contact: Keeper of Fine Art Jennifer Rennie
Open: Mon-Sat 10.30-5, Sun 2-5
Policy: The temporary exhibition programme shows work of national quality. Exhibitions are originated by the gallery staff, or are touring exhibitions from national sources. The fine art department holds an artists slide register for the area.
Sales: Work sold
The Space: Two adjoining spaces with 230m linear hanging space plus a sculpture court which can be used for installations. Hanging is by direct fixing and rods, lighting is by spots.
Exhibiting: **[AW]** The programme is by invitation and application. The gallery takes 10% commission and covers all exhibition costs except framing and private view.
Access: **[U][T][L]** City centre location

Flaxman Gallery

A purpose-built gallery space in the Faculty of Art and Design run by the Polytechnic. [VA,Ph,Cr]
Address: Staffordshire Polytechnic, College Road, Stoke-on-Trent, Staffordshire ST4 2DE tel 0782 744531 ext 3349
Contact: J G Skinner
Open: Mon-Fri 9.30-5.30, Tues,Thurs Fri,Sat 6pm-8pm
Policy: A wide range of exhibitions, mainly promoting the work of *'living artists, graduates and exhibitions which reflect the work of the faculty'.* (Fine Art, Design, History of Art and Design).
Sales: Work sold; Sales referred to exhibitor
The Space: A 13x7x2.75m space with spots, and natural light and direct fixing. Gallery plans available.
Exhibiting: **[AW]** Written applications to Susan Leeks, Art & Design Faculty Office, Flaxman Building, Staffordshire Polytechnic. The gallery provides insurance, publicity, transport, mailing, and preview.
Access: **[F]** Car park; Buses from city centre; BR Stoke-On-Trent 2 mins

Lee Hunt

A commercial gallery run in a private house. [VA,Ph,Cr]
Address: 58 Sackville Street, Stoke-on-Trent ST4 6HX tel 0782 627304
Contact: Lee Hunt
Open: By appointment
Policy: The gallery promotes artists work through month-long exhibitions.
Sales: Work sold
The Space: Small work can be displayed in this Victorian town house and screens and spot lights are used. The small patio and garden is used for small-scale sculpture exhibitions.
Exhibiting: **[AW]** Send slides and CV. Commission is 33.3%.
Access: **[X]** Close to BR Etruria and on bus route Newcastle to Hanley

Lowen Gallery

A 'self-financing' commercial gallery on the Crafts Council's selected list showing high-quality contemporary fine art and craft work. [Pa,Pr,Dr,Cr]
Address: 471 Hartshill Road, Hartshill, Stoke-on-Trent, Staffordshire ST4 6AA tel 0782 623762
Contact: Claire Lowen
Open: Mon-Sat 10-5, closed Thurs
Policy: Exhibitions are booked up to twelve months in advance, and are usually thematic. Exhibitors are usually from *'outside the local area', up-and-coming artists and makers and established makers. The gallery also has a changing display of work for sale, and runs a craft showcase at the New Vic Theatre.*
Sales: Work sold
The Space: The ground floor and first floor galleries are both 4x8m with spots and natural lighting. Showcases are 1.9x0.75x0.75m. Gallery plans available.
Exhibiting: **[AW]** In writing to Claire Lowen. Gallery provides insurance, publicity, list of exhibits, mailing, catalogue/card and preview.
Access: **[F][X]** On street parking; BR Stoke-on-Trent 25 mins

Stonham Aspal (Suffolk)

(EA) Map5 TM28

Caldecott Gallery

Private commercial gallery as part of framing business. [VA]
Address: The Stables, Lewis Farm, Stonham Aspal, Suffolk IP14 6AU tel 047339 895
Contact: Malcolm Banks
Open: Mon-Sat 9-5
Policy: The gallery is hired to exhibitors.
Sales: Work sold

The Space: The gallery is 6.1x3.6m.

Stowmarket (Suffolk)

(EA) Map5 TM26

Museum of East Anglian Life

A 30 acre open air independent museum in the course of developing a facility for the exhibiting of contemporary art and craft. [VA,Cr]

Address: Stowmarket, Suffolk IP14 1DL tel 0449 612229
Contact: Curator Lesley Colsell
Open: Mon-Sat 11-5, Sun 12-5; Sun 12-6 June, July, August
Policy: To show contemporary work by East Anglian artists reflecting the historical collections and craft workshops within the Museum. Three or four exhibitions organised a year.
Sales: Work sold
The Space: Modern gallery on first floor of the museums new shop and entrance building.
Exhibiting: **[AW]** Artists who work or who have worked in East Anglia are welcome to apply.
Access: **[X]** Town centre 2 mins; Bus & BR Stowmarket 5 mins

Stowmarket Library

Exhibition space in a library. [VA,Cr,Ph]

Address: Milton Road, Stowmarket, Suffolk IP14 tel 0449 96613143
Contact: Acting Divisional Librarian
Policy: There are three libraries in the Bury St Edmunds area of Suffolk County Arts and Libraries Service. They are at Stowmarket, Needham Market and Emswell.
Sales: Work sold; Sales referred to exhibitor
The Space: Stowmarket: 15 square metres; Needham Market: 4 square metres and Elmswell: 4 square metres.
Exhibiting: Contact Stowmarket Library for details. Six months booking period, fee of 20% on all sales from exhibition subject to minimum charge of £17.50 payable in advance.

Stratford-upon-Avon (Warwickshire)

(WMA) Map5 SP25

Peter Dingley Gallery

A private gallery on the Crafts Council's selected list with exhibitions and a changing display of work by leading makers. [Cr]

Address: 8 Chapel Street, Stratford-upon-Avon, Warwickshire CV37 3EP tel 0789 205001
Contact: Peter Dingley
Open: Mon-Sat 9.30-1.30, 2.30-5.30, closed Thurs pm
Policy: The gallery has two solo and two thematic exhibitions a year, as well as a changing display of work by well-known makers and new-comers.
Sales: Work sold
The Space: Two galleries each 16 square metres and a shop area of the same size.
Exhibiting: The gallery provides insurance, publicity, list of exhibits, preview transport and display costs.
Access: **[F]** Town centre location; Public car park, buses 3 mins

RSC Collection

A permanent collection of work relating to the theatre and temporary exhibitions. [Pa,Sc,LA]

Address: Royal Shakespeare Theatre, Waterside, Stratford-upon-Avon, Warwickshire CV37 6BB tel 0789 296655
Contact: Brian Glover
Open: Mon-Sat 9.15-8; Sun 12-5; Nov-March 11-4
Policy: The theatre has artist in residence programmes and the resulting work is shown in the gallery.
Sales: Work sold; Credit card
The Space: Three spaces are used, ground floor 8x4.5x4.5m, first floor main room 12x6x6m and a small room 8x4.5x4.5m.
Exhibiting: **[AW]** Applications for the artist in residence programme should be made to Brian Glover.
Access: **[U][T]** Theatre well signposted

Street (Somerset)

(SWA) Map6 ST43

Crispin Hall Crafts Centre

[VA,Cr]

Address: Crispin Street, Street, Somerset BA16 0HP tel 0458 45172
Open: Mon-Fri 1.30-4.30, Sat 10.30-4.30
Policy: *'A centre serving the local community and showing the best fine art and craft available.'*

Strood (Kent)

(SEA) Map7 TQ76

Richmond House Studio

This is a newly-established mobile gallery dealing with the sale or rent of paintings, prints and photography. [Pa,Pr,Ph]

Address: Richmond House, 13 Weston Road, Strood, Rochester, Kent ME2 3EZ tel 063 471 7236
Policy: The policy of this new venture is to offer fine quality work for sale. Work may be bought outright or rented on a monthly or three-monthly basis with the display being changed as required. A framing and portrait service (working from photographs) is also available. Commissions are accepted from firms or companies wanting paintings on any subject to be given as presentations or prizes. A photo-glazing service is also available.
Sales: Work sold

Strood Library (Exhibition Hall)

This exhibition hall is open to the work of talented amateurs as well as professionals and encourages work in all media. [VA,Ph,Cr]

Address: Strood Library, 32 Bryant Road, Strood, Kent

ME2 3EP tel 063 471 8161
Contact: Group Librarian Jill Ayers
Open: Mon-Weds, Fri 9.30-7, Sat 9.30-5
Policy: The gallery programme is intended to promote the work of living artists from the area as well as featuring national and regional touring shows. Predominantly exhibiting one-person shows which last for three to four weeks, artists are encouraged to give demonstrations and talks to complement their exhibitions.
Sales: Work sold
The Space: 15x14x6m high with 42m linear hanging space; direct fixing to 20m wallspace with 22m of free-standing screens hanging system and fluorescent lighting. Maximum hanging height 1.5m. Showcases are available.
Exhibiting: [AW] Apply to Group Librarian with slides or photographs 15 months in advance. Gallery finances insurance, mail-out of publicity and list of exhibits. Support in principle for EPR. Commission 15%.
Access: [U][T][S] BR Strood 15 mins; Public car park 1 min

Sudbury (Suffolk)

(EA) Map7 TL84

Clare Gallery

A commercial gallery that caters for local residents and tourists in East Anglia, it shows oils, watercolours and pastels mainly by regional artists. [Pa,Sc]
Address: 8, High Street, Clare, Sudbury, Suffolk C010 8NY tel 0787 277825
Contact: Jill Kaye
Open: Mon-Sun 10.15-1 2.15-5; closed Wed
Policy: The gallery sells contemporary and historical work.
Sales: Work sold
The Space: The gallery is 7.9x5.1m with spotlighting.
Exhibiting: [AW] Gallery covers publicity printing and mailing, list of exhibits, preview costs and charges 33.3% commission on sales.
Access: [F] BR Sudbury 8 miles

Gainsborough's House

The gallery is the birthplace of Thomas Gainsborough and Georgian townhouse with rooms that display the permanent collection and temporary exhibitions; a walled garden and print workshop complement the unique development. [VA,Ph,Cr]
Address: Sudbury, Suffolk CO10 6EU tel 0787 72958
Contact: Curator Hugh Belsey
Open: Tues-Sat 10-5, Sun & bank holidays 2-5; closed Mon, Good Friday, between Christmas and New Year, and at 4 between 1 Oct and Easter
Policy: The gallery shows up to ten exhibitions a year, each lasting up to six weeks, and predominantly of work by living artists. These are selected to complement and extend the permanent collection of the work of Thomas Gainsborough and his close associates. The new Craft gallery encourages a commitment to the continuous display of crafts, and the print workshop similarly to at least one showing of prints a year. Supporting activities are arranged for specific shows, and the print workshop runs courses for the local adult education authority and several four-day summer workshops.
Sales: Work sold; Credit card
The Space: 22.85m linear hanging space in temporary display spaces, with spot lighting dimmer controlled and humidifier monitored by thermohydrograph. Craft gallery also has 22.85 linear hanging space, and dimmer controlled spot lighting. Limitations on access for works larger than 2.23x0.96m. Garden can accommodate larger pieces of sculpture. Gallery is used for meetings and lectures outside opening hours.
Exhibiting: [AW][EF] The exhibition sub-committee meets two or three times a year. Gallery covers insurance, printing and mailing of publicity, list of exhibits, preview costs, transport and catalogue/card. Gallery takes 30% commission on sales plus VAT.
Access: [F] BR Sudbury 10 mins; Buses from Ipswich, Bury St Edmunds and Colchester; Public car parks 10mins

Museum of Childhood

The hall is owned by the National Trust and the Museum is run by Derbyshire Museums Service. [Pa,Sc,Ph,Cr]
Address: Sudbury Hall, Sudbury, Derbyshire DE6 5HT tel 0283 78 305
Contact: Curator Natalia Wieczorek
Open: Wed-Sun 1-5.30 including bank holidays April-Oct
Policy: The museum runs a programme of events and education activities in conjunction with a temporary exhibition and large collection of 19th & 20th century toys. Exhibitions are usually thematic and related to children. The Sudbury pots collection of 20th century studio ceramics which is in the museum also has a study centre for the use of students, researchers and groups where the reserve collection may be seen. Prior booking is essential to see this fine collection.
The Space: The temporary exhibition space is 11x6m with wall-mounted track and high-level fixed floods.
Exhibiting: Artists are invited to exhibit.
Access: [U][T][F] Situated on the A50 by the junction with the A515, 13 miles west of Derby; Bus 401 Stevensons' from Uttoxeter or Burton-on-Trent

Quay Gallery

Multi-purpose leisure arts centre, home of Sudbury Dramatic Society and other drama, music, art and craft societies, of which the gallery is one facility. [Pa,Pr,Dr,Ph]
Address: Quay Lane, Sudbury, Suffolk CO10 6AN tel 0787 74745
Contact: Gallery Co-ordinator Peter D Johnson
Open: Mon-Sun 10-10.30pm
Policy: The gallery operates as a commercial space, showing mainly solo shows, each lasting four weeks. Visitors to the exhibitions are encouraged to purchase as well as appreciate. Local amateur and professional artists are involved through submission to the annual open summer exhibition.
Sales: Work sold; Credit card
The Space: Exhibiting space includes walls of foyer,

staircases, bar and restaurant of the centre.
Exhibiting: **[AW]** Artists should contact the gallery by letter. Gallery covers insurance, and other costs are by arrangement.
Access: BR Sudbury 5 mins

Sudbury Library

Exhibition spaces in five libraries administered by Suffolk County Arts & Libraries Service, Bury St Edmunds Area, see also entry for Lowestoft. [VA,Cr,Ph]

Address: Market Hill, Sudbury, Suffolk CO10 tel 0787 72092
Contact: Acting Divisional Librarian
Sales: Work sold; Sales referred to exhibitor
The Space: Sudbury: 15 square metres; Haverhill: 10 square metres; Clare: 4 square metres; Glemsford: 4 square metres and Kedington: 4 square metres.
Exhibiting: Sudbury booked for one year ahead, remainder six months, fee of 20% on all sales from exhibition subject to minimum charge of £17.50 payable in advance.

Sunderland (Tyne & Wear)

(NA) Map3 NZ35

Northern Centre for Contemporary Art

A grant-aided gallery showing contemporary art. [VA,Ph,Cr,LA]

Address: 17 Grange Terrace, Stockton Road, Sunderland, Tyne & Wear SR2 7DF tel 091 514 1214
Contact: Director Tony Knipe
Open: Tues-Fri 10-6, Sat 10-4
Policy: The gallery *'offers the people of Sunderland and the region the opportunity of seeing a range of high-quality exhibitions'*. It also runs a picture loan scheme, educational workshops and has a licensed restaurant.
Sales: Work sold; Credit scheme; Credit card
The Space: Gallery one and two are 110 square metres with 40m linear hanging space; Gallery three is 60 square metres with 32m linear; Gallery four and the reception gallery (craft galleries) are 55 square metres with 26m linear. Glass-topped plinths available.
Exhibiting: **[AW][EF]** Gallery covers all exhibition costs and charges 30% commission. Supports the principle of EPR.
Access: **[X]** Bus station 2 mins; BR Sunderland 8 mins

Sunderland Museum & Art Gallery

A municipal museum and art gallery run by Tyne & Wear Museums Service. [VA,Ph,Cr]

Address: Borough Road, Sunderland, Tyne & Wear SR1 1PP tel 091 514 1235
Contact: Group Museums Officer (East) Neil Sinclair
Open: Tues-Fri 10-5.30, Sat 10-4, Sun 2-5
Policy: The gallery presents a varied programme of temporary exhibitions covering a wide range of subjects including contemporary art and applied art. It also runs a programme of talks, workshops, demonstrations, etc.
Sales: Work sold
The Space: The temporary exhibition gallery is 19.2x10x4.3m giving 58m linear hanging space, with more hanging space available on screens. There is direct fixing, track lighting and humidifier. Upright and desk cases available. The gallery is also used for educational activities, demonstrations and occasionally for lectures and meetings.
Exhibiting: **[AW][EF]** Gallery covers insurance, publicity, list of exhibits, previews, display and catalogue/card and charges 25% commission. Supports the principle of EPR.
Access: **[U][T][L]** Town centre site; BR Sunderland 5 mins; Car parks & buses 5 mins

Sunderland Art Gallery: 'Noah's Ark' by Chris Sell, Woodcut, 1988, from a Sunderland Artists' Group exhibition

Sunderland Polytechnic (Reg Vardy Foundation)

Run by the Polytechnic and formerly known as the Backhouse Gallery. [VA,Cr]

Address: School of Art & Design, Backhouse Park, Ryhope Road, Sunderland SE2 7EE tel 091 514 1211, 515 2128
Contact: Stephen McNulty, Mandy Wright
Open: Mon-Fri 10-5
Policy: The policy is to promote a selected number of artists and a collection of contemporary prints and a sculpture park are planned. Space also used for lectures, seminars etc.
The Space: Two galleries both with about 33m linear hanging space.
Exhibiting: [AW] Address applications to Stephen McNulty at least one academic year in advance. The gallery covers insurance, publicity, list of exhibits, preview, display, catalogue/card and takes 25% commission. Supports the principle of EPR.
Access: [S] BR Sunderland 15 mins; Bus station 15 mins

Sunninghill (Berkshire)

(SA) Map7 SU96

Austin/Desmond Fine Art Ltd

Commercial gallery. [Pa,Pr,Bo]

Address: 3 High Street, Sunninghill, Ascot, Berkshire SL5 9NQ tel 0990 291 201
Open: Mon-Fri 10-5.30, Sat 10-1
Policy: Modern British and contemporary paintings by British artists, books and prints.

Sutton Coldfield (Warwickshire)

(WMA) Map4 SP19

Sutton Coldfield Town Hall

The town hall has two rooms available for exhibitions. The Bedford Suite is suitable for small exhibitions, and the Vesey suite for larger exhibitions. [VA,Cr,Ph]

Address: Upper Clifton Road, Sutton Coldfield, Warwickshire B73 6AB tel 021 355 8990
Contact: Alison Stanley
Open: By arrangement
Exhibiting: [AW] Contact Alison Stanley. Hire charges available on request.
Access: [F] Town centre site close to car parks and buses

Swainby (N Yorkshire)

(YA) Map3 NZ40

Swainby Galleries

A commercial gallery. [Pa,Ph,Cr,Dr,Ce]

Address: 58 High Street, Swainby, Northallerton, N Yorkshire DL6 tel 0642 701 031
Contact: Lionel and Elizabeth Smith
Open: Wed-Sun 11-5
Sales: Work sold
The Space: A space with 9m linear hanging space and mixed lighting.
Exhibiting: [AW] The gallery takes 30% commission and meets the cost of insurance and publicity.

Swindon (Wiltshire)

(SA) Map7 SU18

Media Arts Lab

A local authority multi-media arts centre with facilities for making or watching film, video, photography and sound. [LA]

Address: Town Hall Studios, Regent Circus, Swindon, Wiltshire SN1 1QF tel 0793 2616 ext 3140
Contact: Martin Parry
Open: Mon-Fri 9-5
Policy: Occasional one-night multi-media events or film and video screenings and other live art. *'A lively media-centre for all from the novice to the experienced - where you can make, watch, enjoy or criticise the products of film, video, photography or sound'.* There is a strong educational and workshop programme of activities.
Sales: Credit card
The Space: Small theatre space.
Exhibiting: Terms and conditions are negotiable.
Access: [L] BR Swindon; Various buses near

Public Arts - Swindon

Local-authority, arts centres showing a range of exhibitions. [VA,Ph,Cr,LA]

Address: Joliffe Studio, Wyvern Theatre, Theatre Square, Swindon, Wiltshire SN1 1QR tel 0793 26161 ext 3149
Contact: Alistair Snow
Open: 10-4 and during evening performances
Policy: Exhibitions are normally shown for four to six weeks in four exhibition spaces, and of 30 exhibitions last year, 17 were solo. Exhibitions and public events are also organised in parks and hospitals in the town centre.
Sales: Work sold
Exhibiting: [AW][EF] Applications are welcome from individuals with slides, CV and supporting information. The centre pays for insurance, printing and mailing of publicity, list of exhibits, preview costs, transport, catalogue or card, and the artists' expenses. A 15% commission is charged on sales. Supports EPR.
Access: [U][T][L]

Swinton (Greater Manchester)

(NWA) Map3 SD70

Memorial Art Gallery

A purpose-built gallery in the central library which is run by the City of Salford. [VA,Cr]

Address: Central Library, Chorley Road, Swinton, Greater Manchester M27 2AF
The Space: The gallery is 400 square metres with hanging by screws and rails and with fluorescent lighting.

Exhibiting: [AW] Applications are welcome, the costs of publicity are covered and 10% commission is charged on sales.

Tamworth (Staffordshire)

(WMA) Map5 SK20

Central Library

An exhibition space used as a focal point for the town's cultural activities. [VA,Cr,Ph]

Address: Corporation Street, Tamworth, Staffordshire B79 7DN tel 0827 52244
Contact: Principal Area Librarian G Dillon
Open: Mon,Tues,Thurs,Fri 9-6, Wed,Sat 9-1
Policy: Exhibitions of local interest, or by local artists or makers are shown. The gallery space is being used to emphasise the library as a cultural focal point for Tamworth.
Sales: Work sold
The Space: A 10x3m space with fluorescent, spots and natural light. Direct fixing.Three table-top and two upright showcases available.
Exhibiting: Applications from local artists and makers are given priority. The space is booked one year ahead and 15% commission is charged on sales. The exhibitor is responsible for all costs.
Access: [U][T][F][L] Located in the town centre

Taunton (Somerset)

(SWA) Map6 ST22

Makers

A makers' co-operative with twelve members whose work is shown in the gallery. [Pr,Cr]

Address: 7A Bath Place, Taunton, Somerset TA1 4ER tel 0823 251121
Contact: Secretary Pippa Beltham, T&S Workshop, Langport, Somerset TA10 9PQ
Open: Mon-Sat 9-5.30
Sales: Work sold; Credit card
The Space: Two spaces, one 6x3.5m and one 3.75x3.5m.
Exhibiting: [AW] Insurance, publicity, and catalogue/card are provided by the gallery. A commission of 15% is charged on sales.
Access: [F] Taunton town centre

Teignmouth (Devon)

(SWA) Map6 SX97

Church House Gallery & Ceramic Workshop

Gallery established in 1988 specialising in ceramics, wood, glass and fine art. [VA,Ce,Gl,Wo]

Address: 1 Exeter Street, St James's Precinct, Teignmouth, Devon TQ14 8JJ tel 062 674 152
Contact: Dil and Wendy Yardley, Tues,Wed,Fri,Sat 10-5, Thurs 10-1
Policy: The gallery aims to promote high-quality ceramics, crafts and fine art. Stocks stoneware, porcelain, terra cota, ceramics thrown, cast and hand-built in the gallery studios.
Sales: Work sold
Exhibiting: [AW] Artists and makers are welcome to apply for information regarding exhibitions. Commission is 25%.
Access: [S] BR Teignmouth 5 mins; Public car parking

Telford (Shropshire)

(WMA) Map4 SJ60

Elton Gallery

Part of the Ironbridge Gorge Museum Trust, the gallery shows work 'tracing the art of the industrial revolution'. Exhibitions are generally thematic, 'interpreting social, industrial and art history'. [Pr,Dr]

Address: Ironbridge Gorge Museum, Coalbrookedale, Telford, Shropshire TF8 7DG tel 0952 452751
Contact: Curator of Art David de Haan
Open: Mon-Fri 10-5, Sat Sun 10-6 Summer; daily 10-5 Winter
Access: [U][T] Car park

Tetbury (Gloucestershire)

(SWA) Map6 ST89

Gumstool Gallery

A private gallery managed by artists with 'continuous mixed exhibitions introducing new work monthly'. [VA,Ce]

Address: Tetbury, Gloucestershire GL8 8DG tel 0666 53710
Contact: Pamela Cox
Open: Mon-Sat 10-5.30, Thurs 10-1, Sun by appointment
Policy: The gallery is part of a 17th century house also housing studios and workshops. Three special exhibitions are arranged each year, including one exhibition sponsored for charity. A wide range of work is shown including abstract, figurative and topographical in varied media.
Sales: Work sold; Credit scheme
The Space: Two rooms are used giving 25m linear space plus a courtyard. Fluorescent, spots and natural lighting. Gallery plans available. Shelves and stands available for ceramics and sculpture.
Exhibiting: [AW] Applications to exhibit are welcome via studio visits and interviews by appointment. The gallery provides insurance, publicity, preview, list of exhibits and catalogue/card. Commission is 33.3%.
Access: [U][T][F] Car parking

Thames Ditton (Surrey)

(SEA) Map7 TQ16

Fraser Carver Gallery

This commercial gallery stages group and theme painting exhibitions, between which general mixed shows of gallery artists are shown. [Pa]

Address: 1 High Street, Thames Ditton, Surrey KT7 0SD

tel 01 398 7860
Contact: Roderick Baxter
Open: Tues-Sat 10-5.30
Policy: The gallery presents continually changing exhibitions by professional artists working in a traditional and representational manner. The gallery represents artists well established in their field and also up-and-coming artists that it is felt *'will sustain a lasting appreciation'*. The gallery is *'pleased to advise on the investment potential of our artists, and to set up portfolios for collectors interested in specific subjects'*.
Sales: Work sold; Credit scheme; Credit card
The Space: One gallery is 5x3.5x3m high, another 5x2x3m high, and two each 5x6x2.5m high giving a total of 43m linear hanging space on rails with spot lighting.
Exhibiting: [AW] Send slides or photographs, or artists may contact Roderick Baxter to arrange a time to visit the gallery with a selection of work. Gallery finances printing and mail-out of publicity and catalogue/card and preview costs.
Access: [S] BR Thames Ditton 2 mins; Public car park 2 mins

Thornbury (Avon)

(SWA) Map6 ST69

Patricia Wells Gallery

A commercial gallery showing four promotional exhibitions a year, with a permanent stock of the work of over 200 artists. [VA]

Address: Morton House, Lower Morton, Thornbury, Avon BS12 1RA tel 0454 412288
Contact: Patricia Wells
Open: During exhibitions 11-1, 2-5
Policy: The gallery specialises in *'the promotion and sale of the work of selected professional artists'*.
Sales: Work sold; Credit card; Credit scheme
The Space: The three galleries are 22x8m, 22x2.75m and 9x5.5m with spots, fluorescents and natural light. There is a garden for large sculpture. Gallery plans available.
Exhibiting: [AW] Contact Patricia Wells.
Access: [F] Junction 14 on the M5

Thornton (W Yorkshire)

(YA) Map3 SE13

South Square Gallery

An art gallery within a complex of artists' studios. [Pa,Pr,Dr,Ph,Cr,Ce]

Address: South Square, Thornton, W Yorkshire BD1 33LD tel 0274 834398
Contact: Tony Sharp
Open: Mon-Sat 11-5, Sun 2-4
Policy: The gallery mixes work by artists living in the region with work by artists and makers from outside Britain, in the past the gallery has exhibited African prints and crafts together with British produced work and this is an area the organisers wish to pursue. There are ten exhibitions mounted a year each lasting for one month, the majority are group shows by living artists and makers.
Sales: Work sold
The Space: The gallery has 60m linear hanging spaces with suspended mobile spot lighting, walls are stone and accommodate heavy work. Gallery plans are available.
Exhibiting: [AW] Artists and makers should send slides or photographs to Tony Sharp, the gallery covers, list of exhibits, preview costs and catalogue/card and takes 33.3% commission.
Access: [L] Bus route from Bradford; Car park 1 min

Tonbridge (Kent)

(SEA) Map7 TQ54

Angel Centre

This commercial gallery deals with the work of living artists in a variety of media, mostly in group shows. [Pa,Pr,Dr,Ph,Cr,LA]

Address: Angel Lane, Tonbridge, Kent TN9 1SF tel 073 235 9588
Contact: Manager BK Nichol
Open: Mon-Sun 9-11
Policy: As part of a sports and leisure centre, the gallery

Gumstool Gallery see previous page

space is available for any form of exhibition or display. Policy is *'to ensure a balanced programme based on demand'*. Talks and slide-shows are arranged occasionally when applicable to the event. Apart from the annual art exhibition, most shows last for two or three days only.

Sales: Sales referred to exhibitor

The Space: Jim May Hall 25x33m. Medway Hall 13x16m. Both spaces have natural and fluorescent lighting with additional theatre lighting available. There is also a foyer and an outdoor space 9x15m available for use. Gallery plans are available. Exhibitions spaces are also used for many sports and leisure events.

Exhibiting: [AW] Apply to the Manager. There is a negotiable hire fee for each space.

Access: [U][T][L][F][X] BR Tonbridge 5 mins; Public car park 2 mins

Tonbridge Library Gallery

Shows are primarily the work of locally-based artists, but touring exhibitions are also shown. [Pa,Pr,Dr,Ph,Cr]

Address: Avebury Avenue, Tonbridge, Kent TN9 1TG tel 073 235 2754

Contact: Group Librarian Janice Douglas

Open: Mon,Tues,Thurs 9.30-7, Wed,Fri 9.30-6, Sat 9.30-5

Policy: As part of the Kent County Libraries service the gallery programme is intended to promote the work of living artists working in the area and to show exhibitions which would not otherwise be seen in the area.

Sales: Work sold

The Space: The exhibition areas are 11x4x2.5m high and 11x11x2.5m high, and in each, hanging is by rods with spot lighting. Two display cases are available.

Exhibiting: [AW] Apply to Group Librarian with slides or photographs approximately 15 months in advance of desired showing dates. Gallery finances insurance, list of exhibits and mail-out of publicity. Support in principal for EPR. Commission 15%.

Access: [U][T] BR Tonbridge 5 mins; Public car park 5 mins

Torquay (Devon)

(SWA) Map6 SX96

Torre Abbey

A stately home owned by Torbay Borough Council with a permanent gallery, museum, furnished period rooms, monastic ruins, chapel and extensive gardens. [Pa,Sc,Cr]

Address: The Kings Drive, Torquay, Devon TQ2 5JX tel 0803 293593

Contact: Senior Curator Mr Retallick

Open: Daily 10-5; closed Nov-March

Policy: The *'majority of exhibitions are those organised by local art and/or craft societies'*. Some touring exhibitions are shown from the Area Museums Council and other institutions.

Sales: Sales referred to exhibitor

The Space: Main Gallery on the second floor is 30x8x2.5m giving 50m linear hanging space plus extra space on screens. The small gallery is 5x4.75x2.5m giving 15m linear hanging space. Grounds sometimes used for *'certain types of show'*. Gallery plans available.

Exhibiting: [AW] Apply to the Curator *'preferably groups, solo shows are only held if no sales are allowed'*.

Access: [X] Car park 5 mins; BR Torquay 8 mins

Torrington (Devon)

(SWA) Map6 SS41

Plough Theatre

A gallery space in the foyer of a theatre in a converted pub. [VA,Ph,Cr]

Address: The Plough, Fore Street, Great Torrington, Devon EX38 8HQ tel 0805 22552

Contact: Theatre Director Jenny Neesham

Open: Tues-Sat 10-5 and 6.30-9

Policy: The monthly programme is predominantly work by local artists.

Sales: Work sold

The Space: The gallery has 16m linear hanging space with *'basic lighting', though improvements are 'scheduled'*.

Exhibiting: [AW] Apply to the Director. The theatre provides insurance, transport, preview, list of exhibits, and artists' expenses. Preview costs split equally between theatre and exhibitor. A commission of 25% is charged on sales.

Access: [U][T] Town centre location; BR Barnstable

Totnes (Devon)

(SWA) Map6 SX86

88

88 is a craft shop with a small gallery holding occasional exhibitions. [Pa,Sc,Pr,Cr]

Address: 88 High Street, Totnes, Devon TQ9 5SN tel 0803 864 207

Contact: Gillian White

Sales: Work sold

The Space: The gallery is about 6x4m. Walls are rough stone or white painted with a large stone recess in one wall and there is a flag floor. Lighting is by spots.

Gothic House: 'Repairing Richmond Lock' by Bernard Batchelor
see next page

Exhibiting: [AW] The gallery charges 30% commission and pays for insurance, publicity, mailing, catalogue and private view.

Gothic House

A private gallery dealing in 'watercolour masters' only. [Pa]

Address: Bank Lane, Fore Street, Totnes, Devon tel 0803 864219
Contact: Beverley James Pyke
Open: Mon-Sat 10-6; closed 1pm-2.30; closed Wed in Winter and Tues in Summer
Policy: Fine modern work only.
Sales: Work sold
Access: BR Totnes 10 mins

Marshall Arts Gallery

A small commercial gallery specialising in individual works by West-Country artists and makers. [VA,Cr]

Address: 3 Warland, The Plains, Totnes, Devon TQ9 5EL tel 0803 863533
Open: Mon-Sat 10-1, 2-5; closed Sat & Thurs afternoon; closed Mon & Thurs Winter

Towcester (Northamptonshire)

(EMA) Map5 SP65

Blakesley Gallery

A private gallery in a converted 400-year old barn. [Pa,Pr,Dr,Cr]

Address: The Green, Blakesley, Towcester, Northamptonshire NN12 8RD tel 0327 860274
Contact: Proprietor Ann Purser
Open: Wed-Sun 10-5
Policy: The gallery shows high-quality work by artists from all over the country. *'Figurative painting, predominantly watercolour landscapes'* are shown with *'High-quality ceramics, glass and jewellery'.*
Sales: Work sold; Credit card
The Space: Fluorescent and spot lights used in conjunction with direct fixing.
Exhibiting: [AW] The gallery provides insurance, publicity, preview, transport and mailing, and a 33.3% commission is charged on sales.
Access: [U][T][F] Close to A5 and B4525 west of Towcester

Towcester Library

See Northamptonshire Libraries. [VA,Ph,Cr,Ar]

Address: Richmond Road, Towcester, Northamptonshire NN12 7EX tel 0327 50794
Contact: District Librarian Miss Hudson, Brackley Library, Manor Road, Brackley, Northamptonshire tel 0280 703455
Open: Mon,Wed,Thurs,Fri 10-1, 2-5, 5.30-7, Sat 9.30-12.30; closed Tues
Sales: Work sold
The Space: The gallery has 20m linear hanging space on wall display boards, three lockable display cases, track lighting and natural light. A meeting room is available for workshops and talks. The library is a newly converted school building with an exhibition area of 74 square metres within library secure area.
Exhibiting: [AW] District Librarian. Publicity and insurance provided, transport between libraries arranged for touring exhibitions. Commission is 10%.
Access: [F] Buses from Northampton, Banbury; Car park; Close to A5

Trawden (Lancashire)

(NWA) Map3 SD93

Trawden Library

A branch of Lancashire libraries. [Pa,Pr,Ph]

Address: Colne Road, Trawden, Colne, Lancashire BB8 8RU tel 0282 866806
Contact: Branch Librarian Mrs D Richards
Open: Tues,Fri 2-4.30 5-7
Policy: Twelve exhibitions a year usually lasting a month.
The Space: Seven boards 0.76x0.76m, one board 1.38x0.76m.
Exhibiting: [AW] No heavy items; no nails to be used. Pictures must hang within the prescribed limits of the boards. 15% commission. Contact District Librarian in writing.
Access: [U][T]

Truro (Cornwall)

(SWA) Map6 SW84

County Museum & Art Gallery

An independent museum and art gallery run by the Royal Institution of Cornwall, a learned society and charitable trust. [VA,Ph,Cr]

Address: River Street, Truro, Cornwall TR1 2SJ tel 0872 72205
Contact: Director Caroline Dudley
Open: Mon-Sat 9-5
Policy: A display of the permanent collection of mostly Cornish artists plus temporary exhibitions mainly art, some craft especially needlework and embroidery'. One or two exhibitions a year.
Sales: Work sold
The Space: Gallery One 18x9x3.75m; Gallery Two 12.5x9x3.75m with direct fixing and lighting by fluorescents and tungsten floods.
Exhibiting: [AW] Twelve months in advance. The museum provides insurance, mailing and preview, list of exhibits. Gallery takes 33.3% commission.
Access: Car park 5 mins; BR Truro 10 mins

Tunbridge Wells (Kent)

(SEA) Map7 TQ53

Clare Gallery

A private gallery. [Pa,Sc]

Address: 21 High Street, Tunbridge Wells, Kent TN1 1UT tel 089 238 717
Contact: M Ettinger
Open: Mon-Sat 8-5.30

Sales: Work sold
The Space: Gallery is 182 square metres with direct fixing and spots, fluorescent and natural light.
Exhibiting: **[AW]** A hire fee is charged and 5% commission taken. The gallery pays for insurance and framing *'by arrangement'* and all other expenses are the responsibility of the artists.

Frankham Gallery

Commercial art gallery.
Address: 4 Nevill Street, Tunbridge Wells, Kent TN2 5SA tel 089 229 244
Contact: Mr Michael Wells
Open: Mon-Sat 10-1, 2-5

Hang Ups

This commercial gallery deals exclusively in prints, both framed and unframed, with an increasing range of limited editions, offering 'a wide choice in unfussy surroundings'. [Pr]
Address: 19-21 Mount Pleasant, Tunbridge Wells, Kent TN1 1NT tel 089 226 533
Contact: Mike Blacker
Open: Mon-Fri 10-5.30
Access: **[F]** BR Tunbridge Wells 1 min; Car park 1 min

Pine Gallery

A commercial gallery showing contemporary work in solo and two-person exhibitions. [VA]
Address: 18 Goods Station Road, Tunbridge Wells, Kent TN tel 089 237 604
Open: Mon-Sat 9-5
Access: BR Tunbridge Wells 15mins

Trinity Gallery

An arts centre gallery exhibiting group and individual shows on a regular basis. [VA,Cr,LA]
Address: Trinity Arts Centre, Church Road, Tunbridge Wells, Kent TN1 1JP tel 089 244 699
Contact: Gallery Organiser Adrienne Blake
Open: Mon-Sat 10-2.30; also open one hour before performances
Policy: This is an independent gallery with no commercial pressures and is therefore free to present the work of *'the young, the unknown and the avant-garde'* Sometimes the work may provide totally new experiences and at other times may *'reinforce the familiar in a different guise'*. The gallery hopes to *'extend the boundaries of art and if on occasions controversy ensues, we also hope that our supporters will find this stimulating and rewarding'*.
Sales: Work sold
The Space: 9x2.5x3.5m high with hanging by rods. An emergency exit must be kept clear of free-standing objects. Gallery plans are available.
Exhibiting: **[AW]** Applications with slides to Gallery Organiser to arrive the first week in any month. Gallery finances printing and mail-out of publicity and catalogue/card. There is a hire fee of £20 per week. Commission 20%.
Access: **[U][T][F]** BR Tunbridge Wells 4 mins; Public car park 4 mins

Tunbridge Wells Museum & Art Gallery

This municipal gallery shows the work of living artists as well as touring shows. [VA,Ph,Cr]
Address: Civic Centre, Mount Pleasant Road, Tunbridge Wells, Kent TN1 1NS tel 089 226 121
Contact: Museum Curator Dr M L J Rowlands
Open: Mon-Fri 10-5.30, Sat 9.30-5; closed bank holidays
Policy: Gallery policy is to stage a varied programme, which includes exhibitions from the gallery's permanent collection, touring shows and the work of local societies and individuals. There is an annual art and craft exhibition organised by the Recreation and Leisure Service and all exhibitions are designed to appeal to residents in the local area.
Sales: Sales referred to exhibitor
The Space: The gallery is 12.5x13.5x7m. Hanging is by rods with track-mounted floodlights with dimmers. Gallery plans are available.
Exhibiting: Apply to Museum Curator for regulations and conditions of hire. Gallery finances insurance. Commission 20%.
Access: **[X]** BR Tunbridge Wells 2 mins; Public car park 2 mins

Tynemouth (Tyne & Wear)

(NA) Map3 NZ36

Holly House Gallery

A commercial craft and print gallery which is on the Crafts Council's selected list. [Pa,Pr,Cr]
Address: 14 Front Street, Tynemouth, N Shields, Tyne & Wear NE30 4DX tel 091 259 2753
Contact: Timandra Gustafson
Open: Mon-Sat 10-5
Policy: The gallery's policy is display and sell *'the best of British craft'* - ceramics, glass, wood, jewellery, textiles and limited edition prints. The aim is to make available work that would not otherwise be seen by people of the area.
Sales: Work sold; Credit scheme; Credit card
The Space: The display space is 6m square x 3.6m high. Most work is exhibited on plinths, with two lockable glass cases for jewellery and a lockable wall case. Work is limited to 1.2m square and large and heavy objects can not be accommodated.
Exhibiting: Exhibition is by invitation only. Gallery covers the cost of insurance, publicity, list of exhibits and catalogue card and charges 30% commission.
Access: **[X]** Metro Tynemouth 2 mins; Bus routes; Street parking

Uckfield (E Sussex)

(SEA) Map7 TQ42

Ashdown Gallery

This commercial gallery which is on the Crafts Council's selected list, stages theme exhibitions by well-known artists and makers and also shows work

by selected graduates from art and design schools in the South East in the summer. [Pa,Pr,Cr]

Address: 70 Newtown High Street, Uckfield, E Sussex TN22 5DE tel 0825 67180

Contact: Margaret Skeates

Open: Tues-Sat 10-5; closed Jan

Policy: Gallery policy is to promote the work of established craftspeople and to introduce the work of newly-qualified artists and makers to as wide a public as possible. Strong emphasis is placed on the design content of work and the skills shown in its fabrication. There is a changing display of work for sale in addition to exhibitions. The gallery hosts only group exhibitions which last for three to four weeks.

Sales: Work sold; Credit card

The Space: The three gallery spaces are 4.5x4x3m high, 4.5x3.5x2m high and 8.5x2.5x2m high, each being lit by track-mounted spots, floods and halogen lights. There are special display fittings for jewellery, and lockable display cases are available.

Exhibiting: [AW] Apply to Margaret Skeates. Gallery finances insurance, printing and mail-out of publicity and preview costs.

Access: [F] BR Uckfield 3 mins; Public car park 1 min

Uley (Gloucestershire)

(SWA) Map6 ST79

Prema Arts Centre

A rural arts centre based in a converted chapel with a programme of classes, workshops, theatre, dance, music, and exhibitions. [Pa,Pr,Dr,Ph]

Address: South Street, Uley, Gloucestershire GL11 5SS tel 0453 860703

Contact: Andrew Wood

Open: Daily 10-6

Policy: The centre has a programme of predominantly solo exhibitions of *'living, working, innovative artists'* which are *'invariably of a very high-standard.'*

Sales: Work sold

The Space: A 13x10m space giving 45m linear hanging space. Gallery plans available.

Exhibiting: [AW] Contact Andrew Wood. The centre provides insurance, publicity, mailing and list of exhibits.

Access: [X] Car park on site

Prema Arts Centre: work by Shafique Uddin, artist in residence at a local primary school (Photo: John Webb)

Ulverston (Cumbria)

(NA) Map3 SD27

Renaissance Centre

An area arts association with 'a very limited amount of display space' in the coffee-shop. [Pa,Pr,Ph,Cr]

Address: Fountain Street, Ulverston, Cumbria LA12 7EQ tel 0229 52299

Contact: Christine Denmead

Open: Mon-Sat 10-4.30

Policy: The centre's main brief is in the performing arts, *'but we also do what we can, given very limited resources, to include the plastic arts in our work.'* There is one exhibition a month.

Sales: Work sold

The Space: A couple of short walls in the coffee shop with spotlighting and hanging on nylon line.

Exhibiting: [AW] The programme is by invitation and application, the gallery takes 10% commission and does not meet exhibition expenses.

Uppermill (Lancashire)

(NWA) Map3 SD90

Saddleworth Museum & Art Gallery

A museum and art gallery which shows seven exhibitions a year all of living artists' work. [VA]

Address: High Street, Uppermill, Oldham, Lancashire OL3 6HS tel 04577 4093

Contact: Curator

Open: Open daily

Policy: Exhibitions mainly of the work of local and regional artists, also photography. About seven art exhibitions a year. Museum and travelling exhibitions on various subjects are also put on in the gallery.

Sales: Work sold

The Space: A triangular gallery in a fine setting overlooking the Huddersfield Canal. About 15m along the longest side. Fluorescent and spot lighting.

Exhibiting: Applications should be sent to the Curator.

Access: [U][T] BR Greenfield 10 mins; On bus route to Oldham and Manchester

Uppingham (Leicestershire)

(EMA) Map5 SP89

Goldmark Gallery

A commercial gallery opened in 1987 and specialising in high-quality work from regional and national sources. [VA]

Address: Orange Street, Uppingham, Rutland, Leicestershire LE15 9SQ tel 0572 822650

Contact: Mike Goldmark

Open: Mon-Sat 9.30-5.30

Policy: the Gallery specialises in 19th and 20th century British art including work by Ayton and Sutherland.

Sales: Work sold

The Space: The gallery is around 660 square metres.

Ventnor (Isle of Wight)

(SA) Map7 SZ57

Ventnor Library

A library exhibition area with spaces above and between shelving for hanging pictures. [VA,Ph,Cr]

Address: High Street, Ventnor, Isle of Wight PO38 1LZ tel 0983 852039

Contact: Deputy Director of Cultural Services M R Howley, Cultural Services HQ, Parkhurst Road, Newport, Isle of Wight PO30 5TX tel 0983 822000

Open: Mon-Thurs 9.30-6, Sat 9.30-4.30

Policy: The Cultural Services' policy is to show work of quality from both professional and amateur artists as well as to encourage and promote beginners of an acceptable exhibiting standard. The majority of exhibitions come from groups. Exhibitions normally run for one month though an extension is often agreed if there is no following bookings.

Sales: Sales referred to exhibitor

The Space: The walls and foyer can take, say 70 paintings of average size.

Exhibiting: Applications to the Director of Cultural Services, Parkhurst Road, Newport, Isle of Wight PO30 5TX. The library pays for printing and mailing of publicity and transport. Gallery plans available.

Access: [U][T] Buses 16,16a,16b,16c,45,46; Public car park 2 mins

Wakefield (W Yorkshire)

(YA) Map3 SE32

Arts Centre (Wakefield District College)

Exhibitions held throughout the year. [VA,Ph,Cr]

Address: Margaret Street, Wakefield, W Yorkshire WF1 2DH tel 0924 370501 ext 234

Contact: Exhibitions Officer Pete Morton

Open: Mon-Thurs 9-9, Fri 9-4

Policy: Mainly showing young and up-coming artists but also making room for established artists.

Sales: Work sold

The Space: Four gallery spaces with track lighting, display cases available. Limited space for sculpture, maximum size work 2.6m in height.

Exhibiting: [AW] Contact Exhibitions Officer.

Access: [U][T]

Marie Jordan Gallery

A commercial gallery on the Crafts Council's selected list specialising in domestic-scale works for sale to the discerning customer. [VA,Cr]

Address: 659 Barnsley Road, Wakefield, W Yorkshire WF2 6HJ tel 0924 255419

Contact: Marie Jordan

Open: Thurs,Fri,Sat,Sun 10-6

Policy: The gallery has changing displays of work for sale and four exhibitions a year, it aims to introduce and promote at least one new artist or maker to the gallery each month. All work is British and contemporary with the accent on quality, prices vary but range from £10 - £1000. Exhibitions last for four to six weeks and the gallery favours solo promotions or group shows.

Sales: Work sold; Credit card; Credit scheme

The Space: Gallery is 16.5x3.6m with a ceiling height of 3.3m rising to 5m. Upright showcases available.

Exhibiting: [AW] Artists and makers should contact Marie Jordan in the first instance with slides and information and visits are then arranged by appointment. The gallery covers the costs of insurance, printing of publicity, preview costs, display, mailing out of publicity and catalogue/card and takes 40% commission plus VAT.

Access: [S][X] On A61, Car park I min

Wakefield Art Gallery (Elizabethan Exhibition Gallery)

A municipal temporary exhibitions gallery run under the auspicies of Wakefield Art Gallery which houses a permanent collection of fine and decorative art and organises ten exhibitions a year of contemporary art. [VA,Cr]

Address: Wentworth Terrace, Wakefield, W Yorkshire WF1 3QW tel 0924 370211 ext 8031

Contact: Exhibition Officer

Open: Mon-Sat 10.30-5; Sun 2.30-5.30

Sales: Sales referred to exhibitor

The Space: The gallery is 18x6m with a total of 39m linear hanging space, with movable screens giving a further 48m linear hanging space although as these screens cannot be moved from the gallery they reduce the usable floor space. A first-floor balcony is also used for small displays. There is direct fixing, with spot and natural light.

Exhibiting: [AW] Artists and makers should contact the Exhibitions Officer.

Yorkshire Sculpture Park

An independent charitable trust established in 1977 in order to pioneer the enjoyment and understanding of contemporary sculpture in an outdoor setting with a permanent collection of modern sculpture and continuous changing exhibitions. [Sc,LA]

Address: Bretton Hall, West Bretton, Wakefield, W Yorkshire WF4 4LG tel 0924 830579 (Administration); 830302 (information)

Contact: Administrator Angela de Courcy Bower

Open: Mon-Sun 10-4 (Winter); Mon-Sun 10-6 (Summer)

Policy: Through a programme of temporary exhibitions and a collection of sculpture, the Park aims to show a variety of approaches, media and techniques to a wide audience. Education work along with public participation in sculpture workshops, demonstrations, and some artist residencies are an important aspect of the Park's activities in de-mystifying the process of making sculpture. There are several open-air exhibitions a year lasting about three months. Exhibitions reflect national and international developments and are a mixture of group, thematic and solo shows. The Park also acts as a consultant on public arts and holds a slide index on sculptors.

The Space: At present there is one major outdoor site of 100 acres.

Exhibiting: **[AW][EF]** Exhibitors are usually invited but the park is always interested to learn of new work. There is an index to which sculptors may submit slides. CV and slides should be sent to the Administrator. The gallery covers all exhibition costs and supports the principle of EPR.
Access: **[U][T]** Buses from Leeds, Wakefield, Holmfirth and Barnsley; Car park

Wallingford (Oxfordshire)

(SA) Map7 SU68

Julius Gottlieb Gallery

A purpose-built gallery situated on the campus of a large Jewish Public School. [VA,Cr]

Address: Carmel College, Mongewell Park, Wallingford, Oxfordshire tel 0491 34739/37505
Contact: Exhibition Director Rob Campbell
Open: Sun-Fri 10-4; closed Sat
Policy: *'We aim to produce an educational resource as we are on a school campus and also show work of interest to the general public. We would like more people to know of and use the gallery and want to encourage living artists and makers to present a broad spectrum of work'.*
Sales: Work sold
The Space: The space (on curved wall) is 40x2.5m with track spotlights and the gallery is built in a pyramid shape, and the space is on three levels. There is a large brick paved area outside.
Exhibiting: **[AW]** The Exhibitions Director with slides and written information. The gallery pays for insurance, printing and mailing of publicity, list of exhibits, preview costs, transport and a card. A commission of 30% is charged on sales.
Access: **[U][T]** Free car park

Wallsend (Tyne & Wear)

(NA) Map3 NZ26

Buddle Arts Centre

A gallery within an arts centre which has theatre space, workshops, darkroom, photographic, sound & film equipment which may be hired. [VA,Ph,Cr,LA]

Address: 258b Station Road, Wallsend, Tyne & Wear NE28 8RH tel 091 262 4276
Contact: Manager Mr G A Perkins
Open: Tues-Fri 10-9, Sat 10-1, 2-5, 6-9
Policy: Varied programme of twelve exhibitions a year with large photographic content showing local artists, group and touring shows. Some photographic exhibitions originated and available for hire. During school holidays childrens work is displayed and an annual open selling exhibition is organised in November and December. The arts centre holds regular art and craft workshops.
Sales: Work sold
The Space: The exhibition space is 130 square metres with 42.6m linear hanging space.
Exhibiting: **[AW]** The programme is by invitation and application. The space is available for hire.
Access: **[U][T]** Metro Wallsend; Car park in nearby shopping centre

Wallsend Heritage Centre

Run by the local authority this is mainly a local history and archaeology centre, though they do provide a 'showcase' for local artists and for the museum service's art collection.

Address: 2 Buddle Street, Wallsend, Tyne & Wear NE28 6EH tel 091 262 0012
Contact: Curator Richard Ellam
Open: Tues-Fri 10-5.30, Sat 10-4.30, Sun 1-5
Policy: Regularly organises educational activities.
Sales: Work sold
The Space: The gallery, on the first floor, is 9.1x4.5x3m giving 15m linear hanging space with another 25m hanging space on screens. There is direct fixing, daylight, one upright and three desk cases.
Exhibiting: **[AW]** Apply in writing to the Curator. The programme is fixed in August for the following year. The gallery covers insurance, publicity, list of exhibits, preview and charges 25% commission.
Access: **[U][T]** Ground floor **[X]** Upstairs. Metro Wallsend 2 mins; Bus station 2 mins; Car park adjacent

Walsall (W Midlands)

(WMA) Map4 SP09

Walsall Museum & Art Gallery

A municipal museum and art gallery run by Walsall Metropolitan Borough Council housing the Garman-Ryan collection and EM Flint temporary exhibition galleries. [VA,Ph,Cr]

Address: Lichfield Street, Walsall, W Midlands WS1 1TR tel 0922 650000 ext 3124
Contact: Keeper of Fine Art Jo Digger
Open: Mon-Fri 10-6; Sat 10-4.45; closed Sun and bank holidays
Policy: The programme features exhibitions of West Midlands artists and makers, local history, social history and touring exhibitions. An education programme of talks, lectures and workshops is run alongside the exhibition programme.
Sales: Work sold; Sales referred to exhibitor
The Space: Two galleries are used for temporary exhibitions, Gallery One provides 70m linear hanging space including screens and Gallery Two has 22m linear hanging space. Adjustable flood and spotlights are used, and hanging is by direct fixing. Twelve hexagonal showcases 1x1m are available.
Exhibiting: **[AW]** Slides or photographs to the Keeper. The gallery provides one-way transport, insurance publicity, and a list of exhibits. A catalogue/card is occasionally available. Supports EPR.
Access: **[L]** Town centre location site; Car park; Bus station and BR Walsall

Waltham Abbey (Essex)

(EA) Map7 TL30

Epping Forest District Museum

Municipal museum showing temporary exhibitions on a range of subjects from historical (local social history) to fine and decorative arts. [VA,Cr,Ph]

Address: 39-41 Sun Street, Waltham Abbey, Essex EN9 1EL tel 0992 716882
Contact: Museum Officer Kate Carver
Open: Fri-Mon 2-5, Tues 12-5
Policy: Runs a county-wide annual open exhibition, Artists in Essex.
Sales: Work sold from temporary exhibitions
The Space: New gallery on first floor, 77 square feet with about 22m linear hanging space and a smaller gallery of 27 square metres and 8m linear hanging space.
Exhibiting: [AW] Programme booked up 18 months to two years ahead but occasional vacancies do occur within that period.
Access: [F] Ground floor BR Waltham Cross; Bus 250 Waltham Cross to Loughton

Ware (Hertfordshire)

(EA) Map7 TL31

Trading Places

A commercial gallery showing modern and contemporary art. [VA,Cr]

Address: 11 New Road, Ware, Hertfordshire SG12 7BS tel 0920 69620
Contact: Kaleem Siddiki & Julia Skinner
Sales: Work sold
The Space: Three floors and 333 square metres.

Wareham (Dorset)

(SWA) Map6 SY98

Trinity Art Gallery

A commercial gallery with an 'ever changing exhibition of paintings and sculpture.... We encourage unknown artists along with known artists'. [Pa,Sc,Cr]

Address: 32A South Street, Wareham, Dorset BH20 4LU tel 0935 6541
Contact: Douglas Chaffey
Open: 10-5.30; closed Wed
Sales: Work sold
The Space: A converted church with room for 600 paintings hung on peg board screens. Concealed strip lighting used, some showcases available.
Exhibiting: [AW] Apply to the gallery with slides. The gallery provides insurance, publicity and mailing. A 25% commission is charged on sales.
Access: [S]

Warminster (Wiltshire)

(SA) Map6 ST84

Athenaeum

An arts centre with theatre and cinema with a coffee bar gallery. [Pa,Pr,Dr,Ph]

Address: High Street, Warminster, Wiltshire BA12 9AE tel 0985 218519
Contact: Director Shona Powell
Open: Mon-Fri 10-2, Sat 10-12.30
Policy: The gallery aims to *'encourage participation in, and enjoyment of, as a wide a range of arts actvities as possible by as wide a group of ages and abilities and to present a varied selection of art work - photography, paintings, drawings etc - by both professional and amateur artists, in an informal setting. We hope to encourage both the casual visitor to the coffee lounge and the theatre-goer to have the time to look at and enjoy the work on the walls'.*
Sales: Work sold
The Space: Approximately 24m linear hanging space with fixings by mirror plates directly to wall.
Exhibiting [AW] Apply to the Director at any time. The gallery pays for insurance and printing of publicity and takes 10% commission.
Access [S] BR Warminster 10 mins; Car park 2 mins

Warrington (Cheshire)

(WMA) Map4 SJ68

Warrington Museum and Art Gallery

A municipal museum and art gallery founded in 1848 with collections of 18th and 19th century fine art with a temporary exhibitions programme. [Pa,Pr,Dr,Ph,Cr]

Address: Bold Street, Warrington, Cheshire WA1 1JG tel 0925 30550/444400
Contact: Curator Alan Leigh
Open: Mon-Fri 10-5.30, Sat 10-5; Closed Sun and bank holidays
Policy: The aim of the gallery is to provide a varied programme of exhibitions which will have both national and regional appeal. The programme includes a combination of historic and contemporary material to stimulate an interest in art of both the past and present. Within the limitations of the building, all visual art forms are encouraged though solo shows are restricted to professional artists. A fundamental aim of the gallery is to promote public involvement with exhibitions through activities organised by the education department.
Sales: Work sold
The Space: The three temporary exhibition spaces include a gallery which measures 21.2x8.51x4m with 40.4m linear hanging space, and a small gallery which measures 15x4.5x3m with 30m linear hanging space and the exhibition room which measures 9x2.9x3m with 18m linear hanging space. The galleries are on the first floor and access for exhibits is via the lift which can accommodate weights up to 30 cwt and items measuring no more than 1.9x1.2m.
Exhibiting: [AW][EF] Applications to exhibit should be sent to CE Gray, Keeper of Art and should include previous press releases and photographs of work. The

gallery finances, insurance, publicity and mailing. Commission of 10% is taken on sales. Supports EPR.
Access: [L] BR Bank Quay and Central 6 mins; Bus Station 5 mins; Mersey Street car park 5 mins

Warwick (Warwickshire)

(WMA) Map5 SP26

Church Street Gallery

A private gallery showing mixed exhibitions of a wide range of work. [VA,Ph]

Address: 5 Church Street, Warwick CV34 4AB tel 0926 491071
Contact: TG Jones
Open: Wed-Sat 9.30-4.30
Policy: The gallery tries to *'work closely with all our artists with respect to their particular requirements'.* Four seasonal exhibitions are mounted, and the gallery has a changing display of work for sale, and provides a framing service.
Sales: Work sold; Credit card
The Space: Gallery one has 12m linear hanging space, gallery two has 13m linear hanging space.
Exhibiting: [AW] Slides or photographs should be sent to the Manager. The gallery charges 33.3% commission on sales and provides insurance, printing, mailing, a list of exhibits and private view.
Access: [F] Town centre location; Market Square buses 1 min; BR Warwick 5 mins

Warrington Museum: Philip Cox working on a figure for 'The Tales of Robin Hood' from his exhibition 'Paper People'

Warwickshire Libraries

The library service has a number of display areas normally used by local artists and societies and occasional special exhibitions are mounted and toured. [VA,Ph,Cr]

Address: County Library Headquarters, Barrack Street, Warwick CV34 4TH tel 0926 410 410
Contact: David Shenton
Open: Various
Sales: Sales referred to exhibitor
The Space: Various.
Exhibiting: [AW] Contact the Library Headquarters or local librarian. Exhibitors meet all exhibition costs.

Warwickshire Museum

A recently refurbished museum run by Warwickshire County Council. [VA,Cr,Ph]

Address: Market Place, Warwick CV34 4SA tel 0926 410410 ext 2329,2500
Contact: County Museum Curator Dr WC Allan
Open: Mon-Sat 10-5.30; May-Sept Sun 2.30-5
Policy: The programme is mostly devoted to exhibitions and permanent displays of local and county history. A few temporary exhibitions are shown usually of regionally-based artists or groups. An associated gallery at Rugby library shows more exhibitions of local groups and artists.
Sales: Work occasionally for sale
The Space: A space of 50 square metres with spot and flood lighting.
Exhibiting: [AW] Contact the County Museum Curator.
Access: [F] Town centre location

Washington (Tyne & Wear)

(NA) Map3 NZ35

Washington Arts Centre

Municiple arts centre with two spaces for temporary exhibitions. [VA,Ph,Cr,LA]

Address: Biddick Farm, Fatfield, Washington, Tyne & Wear NE38 8AB tel 091 41 66440
Contact: Programme Officer Adam Sutherland
Open: Tue-Sat 10-5
Policy: The policy is to show the work of local artists and work reflecting local culture, as well as *'quality art and craft from around the globe'.* Exhibitions are often integrated with the other arts activities: music, dance, theatre etc.
Sales: Work sold
The Space: Main gallery is 21.3x42.5m x 2.7m high; the Granary Bar has 1.8x1.2m panel and 3.6x2.7m wall space. Hanging by mirror plates. Outside temporary spaces in courtyard and field.
Exhibiting: [AW] Apply in writing to Adam Sutherland. The centre *'can contribute only a little towards some of the costs of insurance, publicity, list of exhibits, previews and transport'* and charges 33.3% commission.
Access: [U] Buses 179,194,C38,777 & Minilink 186,173

Watford (Hertfordshire)

(EA) Map7 TQ19

Watford Central Library

Public library. Variable programme, most art forms including paintings, drawings, prints, photographs, sculpture and ceramics. [Pa]

Address: Hempstead Road, Watford, Hertfordshire WD1 3EU tel 0923 226230

Contact: Librarian Mr S R Moore

Open: Mon,Tues,Thurs, Fri 9.30-8pm; Wed,Sat 9.30-1; closed Sun

Policy: To support, promote local artists and groups. Major annual exhibition, Watford & District Local Artists Exhibition held every July to August. Will also book artists from outside local area.

Sales: Work sold handled by library or referred to exhibitor

The Space: Large space.

Exhibiting: Contact the Librarian. 20% commission charged on sales handled by library and 5% on referred sales.

Access: [X] Gallery on first floor. Small car park at rear

Wednesbury (W Midlands)

(WMA) Map4 SP09

Wednesbury Museum & Art Gallery

A municipal museum and art gallery with a permanent collection and temporary exhibition programme of local and regional artists. [VA,Cr]

Address: Holyhead Road, Wednesbury, W Midlands WS10 7DF tel 021 556 0683

Contact: Martin Senior

Policy: Showing a wide variety of work including touring exhibitions from Ikon Gallery and Arts Council and work by local artists.

The Space: Gallery 16x6m

Exhibiting: [AW] Preference for craft work which is more in line with audience.

Access: [X]

Wellingborough (Northamptonshire)

(EMA) Map5 SP86

Arts Barn

A music, art and drama centre with a programme of concerts, exhibitions, classes, workshops, and rooms used by groups and societies. [VA,Ph,LA]

Address: Market Square, Wellingborough, Northamptonshire NN8 1AR tel 0933 79059

Contact: K Tompkins

Open: Mon-Sat 10-3; closed Thurs

Policy: The exhibition programme aims to *'give established and new artists a showcase for their work'*. The Barn varies the programme to appeal to a *'wide range of tastes as well as undertaking to sell the work'*.

Sales: Work sold

The Space: 9x4x2.15m giving 33m linear hanging space where work is hung directly on *'stone and brick walls'*, using adjustable spotlights.

Exhibiting: [AW] Apply in writing. Insurance, mailing and a card are provided by the gallery and a commission of 25% is charged on sales.

Access: [F] 2 mins from central bus stop; Town centre parking 5 mins

Gallery (The)

A private gallery that also hires the gallery space. [VA,Cr]

Address: 108 Midland Road, Wellingborough, Northamptonshire NN8 1NB tel 0933 229321

Contact: John Black

Open: Tues-Sat 9-5

Sales: Work sold

The Space: Three spaces on two floors with a basement studio/workshop area.

Exhibiting: [AW] The gallery provides a private view and musical evening once a month and charges 20% commission on sales.

Wellingborough Library

See Northamptonshire Libraries. [VA,Ph,C,Ar]

Address: Pebble Lane, Wellingborough, Northamptonshire NN8 1AS tel 0933 225365

Contact: District Librarian Michael Davison or Julie Wilson

Open: Mon-Thurs 10-6, Fri 9.30-8, Sat 9.30-4

Policy: Workshops and demonstrations arranged.

Sales: Work sold

The Space: The library has 12m linear screen space plus one craft showcase with display boards and video. The display area is 32 square metres with track lighting.

Exhibiting: [AW] District Librarian. Publicity, insurance provided, as well as transport between libraries for touring exhibitions. Commission is 10%.

Access: [L] Buses from Northampton, Kettering, Milton Keynes; BR Wellingborough 15 mins; Car park

Wells (Somerset)

(SWA) Map6 ST54

Sirota Gallery

A commercial gallery showing 'mixed shows interspersed with five solo shows a year'. [VA,Cr]

Address: 23 Sadler Street, Wells, Somerset BA5 2RR tel 0749 74553

Contact: B & J Sirota

Open: Daily 10-5; half day Wed

Policy: The gallery aims to *'exhibit work of a very high standard. We show artists who perhaps already have their work with London galleries and are well-established on the ladder. However we are always willing to look at and show new painters. Completely abstract work is avoided at the moment.'*

Sales: Work sold; Credit card; Credit scheme

The Space. The gallery has 25m linear with spotlights.

Exhibiting: [AW] Apply with slides and a CV. The gallery provides publicity and catalogue/card.

Access: [F] Town centre location

West Bretton (W Yorkshire)

(YA) Map3 SE41

Bretton Hall College (Gallery)

Gallery within one of the North's leading colleges of arts and education. [VA,Cr]

Address: West Bretton, Nr Wakefield, W Yorkshire WF4 4LG tel 092 485 261
Contact: David Hill
Open: Mon-Fri 9-5, Sat 10-4
Policy: Changing exhibitions of established and younger artists and designers with between six and nine shows of between five and six weeks a year during term-time. Programme usually includes one Bretton graduate a year. Shorter shows co-incide with festivals and conferences at the college.
Sales: Work sold
The Space: A space of 10x9m with 27m linear hanging space with spot lights and natural light.
Exhibiting: [AW] Artists meet the cost of publicity. The college covers insurance and takes 15% commission on sales.
Access: [S]

West Wycombe (Buckinghamshire)

(BA) Map7 SU89

Black Boy Gallery

A commercial gallery with a regular exhibition programme and over half the shows being solo exhibitions. [VA,Ph,Cr,Ce,Gl,LA]

Address: 14 High Street, West Wycombe, Buckinghamshire HP14 3AE
Contact: Andrew Hale
Open: Mon-Sat 9.30-5.30
Sales: Work sold; Credit card
Exhibiting: [AW] Contact Andrew Hale in writing, 40% commission charged on sales.
Access: [F] Town centre location

Westcliff-on-Sea (Essex)

(EA) Map7 TQ88

Beecroft Art Gallery

A municipal gallery, run by Southend on Sea Borough Council, it operates a broad programme of some 20 shows a year together with work from the permanent collection. [VA,Ph,Cr]

Address: Station Road, Westcliff-on-Sea, Essex SS0 7RA tel 0702 347418
Contact: Keeper of Art C F Leming
Open: Mon-Thurs, Sat 9.30-5.30, Fri 9.30-5
Policy: To function as a focus for the display and encouragement of the visual arts within Essex in general and South East Essex in particular; to acquire, preserve and display evidence of contemporary British art with special reference to the county of Essex and to make available for public hire or loan a range of low-value original works or reproductions. Temporary exhibitions range from solo shows to groups from within and outside the region, the Annual Open Exhibition, and schools exhibition. The gallery is used by a number of local art groups, friends of the gallery, and local organisations. Occasional lectures by artists are also arranged.
Sales: Work sold
The Space: Up to eight galleries available each with a combination of track spot lighting and natural light which can be controlled to varying degrees. Hanging is by hooks and chains from picture rails. Thermostatically controlled heaters, humidifiers and fans. Maximim dimension of work is 2.44m.
Exhibiting: [AW] Write to Keeper of Art. Works are commissioned and purchased for the permanent collection. Gallery covers insurance, printing and mailing of publicity, list of exhibits, sometimes transport and catalogue. Commission on sales of 20%.
Access: [F][X] BR Westcliff on Sea 5 mins; Bus 24

Whitby (N Yorkshire)

(YA) Map3 NZ81

Pannett Art Gallery

A municipal gallery with a permanent collection of English watercolours and oil paintings which holds summer temporary exhibitions. [VA,Cr]

Address: Pannett Park, Whitby, N Yorkshire YO21 1RE tel 0974 602908
Contact: Curator

Whitehaven (Cumbria)

(NA) Map3 NX91

Whitehaven Museum & Art Gallery

A museum run by Copeland Borough Council with a programme of temporary exhibitions. [VA,Ph,Cr]

Address: Civic Hall, Lowther Street, Whitehaven, Cumbria CA28 7SH tel 0946 3111 ext307
Contact: Curator
Open: Mon-Fri 9-5, Sat 10-4
Policy: To provide a programme of free admission exhibitions throughout the year at approximately monthly intervals, on a wide range of topics including solo and group art, sculpture, craft, photography, local history, etc.
The Space: The exhibition space is 100 square metres and hanging is by wires. There are spotlights, screens and showcases. The space is also used for lectures and meetings.
Exhibiting: [AW] The programme is by invitation and from application by individuals and groups. The gallery covers insurance, mailing, transport and artist's travel expenses and shares the cost of publicity. Previews are funded by the exhibitor.
Access: [U][T]

Whitstable (Kent)

(SEA) Map7 TR16

Harbour Gallery

This commercial gallery houses a changing display of work by 40 designer/makers, specialising in small-scale ceramics and glass. [Cr,Je,Ce,Gl,]

Address: 39 Harbour Street, Whitstable, Kent CT5 1AH tel 022 726 4842

Contact: Proprietor Ruth Lyne

Open: Mon-Sat 9.30-5.30

Policy: The policy of the gallery is to bring a selection of high-quality designer crafts to the people of Kent. Most work is *'domestic scale'* due to the limitations of the display area.

Sales: Work sold; Credit card

The Space: 3x6m with lighting by spots. Work is exhibited on shelving and wall display units, there is no space for hanging work. The gallery has a large shop window frontage. Table-top and wall mounted display cases are available.

Exhibiting: [AW] Apply to Ruth Lyne with photographs and price of work. Gallery finances insurance and postage of purchased work when necessary. Commission 40%.

Access: [U][T][F] Bus routes from town centre; Public car park 1 min

Wickford (Essex)

(EA) Map7 TQ79

Wickford Library

Exhibition space in public gallery, available for hire. [VA,Cr]

Address: Market Road, Wickford, Essex SS12 OAG tel 0268 732354

Contact: Librarian Chris Booty

Open: Mon,Tues,Thurs,Fri: 9-7, Sat 9-5

Policy: Exhibitions of an educational or cultural nature, arts and craft exhibitions with or without the sale of work, exhibitions nominated by other bodies including industrial and commercial organisations.

Sales: Work sold

The Space: floor area: 27.9 square metres; one showcase.

Exhibiting: [AW] Applications direct to library. Charges according to nature of exhibition. Exhibitor normally arranges own insurance. Publicity material and press releases can be arranged if required.

Access: [F] BR Wickford 2 mins; Car park 2 mins

Wigan (Lancashire)

(NWA) Map3 SD50

Drumcroon Education Art Centre

A gallery and visual arts resource for Wigan's young people. Funded chiefly by the education Department of the Metropolitan Borough of Wigan. [VA,Cr]

Address: 2 Parsons Walk, Wigan, Lancashire WN1 1RS tel 0942 321840/33303

Contact: Gallery Education Officer Keith Walker

Open: Mon-Fri 9-5, Sat 10-1

Policy: To give all Wigan's young people, irrespective of age, their teachers and the local community access to the range, breadth and variety of the visual arts through the main focus of contemporary makers, taking into account such issues as those of race, gender and special needs. To give further insight and understanding, the centre provides its visitors with opportunities to engage in related practical activities. It also attempts to place each exhibition into a contextual framework by demonstrating process through resident artists and makers, and through the use of secondary source material which has the potential to range across time, place and cultures.

The Space: A main gallery, a small gallery and entrance area provide sufficient space for the display of a large body of work. Work is also displayed in the coffee lounge and conference room. All these areas are lit by spots and natural light. Gallery plan available.

Exhibiting: [AW][EF] 25% commission.

Access: [F]

Metropolitan Borough of Wigan

Exhibition space is available in the following buildings in the Wigan area: Golborne Library, Tanners Lane, Golborne, Nr Warrington; Shevington Library, Gathurst Lane, Shevington, Nr Wigan WN6 8HA; Standish Library, Cross Street, Standish, Nr Wigan WN6 0HQ. See also entries for Turnpike Gallery, Leigh and Powell Gallery, Wigan.

Address: Departmemt of Leisure, Station Road, Wigan, Greater Manchester WN1 1SZ tel 0942 827627

Contact: Director of Leisure

Powell Gallery

Opened in 1987, the Powell Gallery is sited in a children's library run by Wigan's Department of Leisure.

Address: The Wiend Centre, The Wiend, Millgate, Wigan WN1 1PF tel 0942 828 100

Contact: Children's Librarian Deirdre Patterson

Open: Mon-Fri 10-5.30, Sat 10.30-5

Drumcroon Education Art Centre: Michael Rothenstein in residence at Drumcroon during the 1987 print extravaganza
(Photo: Duncan Baxter, Sunday Times)

Policy: Its exhibitions have been largely heritage-based accompanied by drama-based interpretation for children. A range of activities for children also takes place at the library. Exhibitions *'should preferably be aimed at children and with an emphasis on science and technology, though other material is acceptable'.*
Sales: Sales referred to exhibitors
The Space: There are up to 15 free-standing double-sided panels 2.5x1m in size. There is background lighting and out-of-hours security control. Top-lit lockable showcases are available up to 10x1x1m.
Exhibiting: [AW] Size of work is limited by an entry gate opening to a width of less than 1m. Hire of the space and commission on sales are negotiable.
Access: [U][L] Town centre; BR Wallgate 10mins; BR North Western 10mins

Wimborne Minster (Dorset)

(SWA) Map7 SZ09

Dorset Craft Guild Walford Mill Craft Centre

Craft centre catering for all craft activities including craftshop and exhibitions. [Cr]
Address: Stone Lane, Wimborne Minster, Dorset BH21 1NL tel 841400
Contact: Publicity Officer Philip Goulden
Open: Daily 10-5 except Christmas, Boxing & New Years day
Policy: A diverse selection of exhibitions, generally to promote high standards in craft work.
Sales: Work sold; Credit card
The Space: The gallery is 12x6x2.5 with a pitched roof; spotlights on twin tracks. Vertical and horizontal screens, display boxes and cabinets available. Gallery plans available.
Exhibiting: [AW] Apply to the Co-ordinator.
Access: [U][T] 1/4 mile north of Wimborne centre; Free car park

Winchester (Hampshire)

(SA) Map7 SU42

The Guildhall

A municipal gallery, part of Winchester City Museum Services, with a collection of mainly 19th century watercolours of topographical interest together with prints, oils and etchings of local Hampshire themes and a monthly changing exhibition programme both contemporary and traditional. [VA,Cr,LA]
Address: The Broadway, Winchester, Hampshire SO23 9LJ tel 0962 840222 ext 2296
Contact: Keeper of Exhibitions Christopher Wardman Bradbury, Hyde Historic Resources Centre, 75 Hyde Street, Winchester SO23 7DW tel 0962 64639
Open: Tues-Sat 10-5, Sun & Mon 2-5 (summer); Tues-Sat 10-5, Sun 2-5 (winter)
Policy: to provide an exhibition area for artists, professional and amateur, and groups in a lively and varied programme of exhibitions both traditional and contemporary. There is an annual exhibition by the local art club plus exhibitions by the local photographic society and craft guilds plus exhibitions of students' and childrens' work. The Guildhall also runs workshops and an educational programme for local schools and musical evenings to encourage interaction between school, painters and musicians.
Sales: Work sold
The Space: The gallery is 16x12x4.5m with screens with hessian-covered blockboard walls, track lighting with spot lights. Gallery plans available.
Exhibiting: [AW] Contact Hyde Historic Resources Centre. The gallery pays for insurance, printing and mailing of publicity, list of exhibits, catalogue or cards and places an advertisement in the local paper and charges 20% commission on sales.
Access: [U][T][L][F] BR Winchester 10 mins; Bus station opposite; Car parks 2 mins

Winchester Gallery

A gallery within Winchester School of Art drawing its audience from the college as well as outside. [Pa,Sc,Pr,Dr,Ph,Cr]
Address: Park Avenue, Winchester, Hampshire SO23 8DL tel 0962 842500
Contact: Director John Gillett
Open: Mon-Thurs 10-5, Fri 10-4.30; term-time Sat 9-12
Policy: The programme *'aims to complement and contrast with course content within school and to raise debate and establish gallery identity'.*
Sales: Work sold
The Space: The two connecting galleries have 50m linear hanging space and 40m linear hanging space.
Exhibiting: [AW][EF] Send slides and information to the Director. The gallery pays for insurance, printing and mailing of publicity, list of exhibits, preview costs, transport, catalogue/card and the artists' expenses. The gallery occasionally commissions work related to special projects or residencies. A commission of 15% is charged on sales. Supports EPR. Gallery plans available.
Access: [F][L] Car park; Winchester 10 mins; BR Waterloo 55 mins

Winchester Gallery: paintings by Clyde Hopkins

Windsor (Berkshire)

(NWA) Map7 SU97

Windsor Community Arts Centre, Old Court Gallery

Gallery is an integral part of a community arts centre. [VA,Ph,Cr]

Address: Windsor Community Arts Centre, St Leonard's Road, Windsor, Berkshire SL4 3DB tel 0753 85942
Contact: Co-ordinator Jenny Joyce
Open: Mon-Sun times vary
Policy: Its policy is to present a varied and balanced programme of work by professional and amateur artists, responding to the enthusiasms of arts centre members and related to activities taking place there. It caters for all age groups and is run by a committee. Exhibitions run for two to three weeks.
Sales: Work sold; Credit card
The Space: Gallery space available is 3x15m in addition to staircase space, 4x6.5m linear hanging space in the bar area and a 3x2x.5m showcase.
Exhibiting: The gallery pays for mailing out of publicity and charges 20% commission on sales.
Access: [X] BR 15 mins; Car park on site

Winsford (Cheshire)

(NWA) Map4 SJ66

Cheshire Visual Arts Centre

Chesire Visual Arts Centre is run by Cheshire Education Department and opened in 1987 and runs four main exhibitions lasting three months each a year. [VA,Cr,Te,LA]

Address: Woodford Lodge, Woodford Lane, Winsford, Cheshire CW7 4EH tel 0606 557328
Contact: Senior Art Advisor David Firmstone, County Hall, Education Department, Chester, Cheshire tel 0244 603350
Open: Mon-Fri 9-4.30
Policy: *'The centre is, in the first instance for teachers and pupils to develop work related to the critical studies element of GCSE and also to introduce students to professional works of art, and develop curriculum themes through the visual arts in schools'.* In addition to the main programme there are small frequently-changing exhibitions. The centre's collections include painting, textiles, sculpture and ceramics. It welcomes visits from members of the public.
Sales: Work sold
The Space: The gallery is an open space 18x17m with 9m high walls and cladding up to 4m. A system of movable wall units is available giving up to 170m extra hanging space. Lighting is by sodium ceiling lights and spot lights. Size limit is 2.43x1.82m.
Exhibiting: [AW] Applications to exhibit should be sent to David Firmstone, Senior Art Advisor, County Hall, Chester. The centre finances insurance, publicity, list of exhibits, preview costs, transport, mailing and catalogue. Artists may be paid a commission fee to produce work especially for exhibitions.
Access: [U][T][L] Buses from Chester and Northwich

Wirksworth (Derbyshire)

(EMA) Map5 SK25

Gallery (The)

A private gallery showing work by artists, sculptors, potters, glassmakers and printmakers. [VA,Cr]

Address: 4 West End, Wirksworth, Derbyshire DE4 4EG tel 062 982 3557
Contact: Marguerite or Michael Howard
Open: Thurs-Sat 10.30-5 April-Dec
Policy: Two major mixed Art Exhibitions a year plus artist and maker of the month exhibition.
Sales: Work sold
Exhibiting: [AW] Exhibitions are by invitation and application sent to Marguerite or Michael Howard.
Access: [S] Car park 1 min

Witham (Essex)

(EA) Map7 TL81

Witham Library

Exhibition space in public library, available for hire. [VA,Cr]

Address: 18 Newland Street, Witham, Essex CM8 2AQ tel 0376 519625
Contact: Deputy Area Librarian Sue Oliver
Open: Mon,Tues,Thurs,Fri 9-7, Sat 9-5
Sales: Work sold; Sales referred to exhibitor
The Space: The exhibition space is 27.90 square metres with three showcases.
Access: [L][F]

Wolverhampton (W Midlands)

(WMA) Map4 SO99

Eagle Works

An independent group studio with a gallery space offering an immediate and inexpensive venue to artists wishing to show their work. [VA,Ph]

Address: Alexandra Street, Wolverhampton, W Midlands

Eagle Works: Wolverhampton Artists Group

WV3 0TE tel 0902 25958
Contact: Gallery Organiser
Open: Mon-Sat 10-5
Policy: *'The gallery exists to promote exciting new work in all areas of fine art, and to bring it to the notice of as wide a public as possible. This includes the local press, art organisations, schools, colleges, gallery curators, and the local public'.* The gallery is also used for public workshops.
Sales: Work sold
The Space: The gallery is 11x3.5x2.5m giving 20m linear hanging space with direct fixing, spots and fluorescent lights.
Exhibiting: **[AW][EF]** Slides should be sent to the Gallery Organiser. Supports EPR. Commission is 15%. Gallery plan and contract available, send SAE.
Access: **[X]** On street parking; BR Wolverhampton 10 mins

Wolverhampton Museum & Art Gallery

A municipal art gallery and museum operated by Wolverhampton Borough Council Leisure Services Department which also houses the Light House media centre. [VA,Ph,Cr,LA]
Address: Lichfield Street, Wolverhampton, W Midlands WV1 1DU tel 0902 312032
Contact: Keeper of Fine Art Brendan Flynn
Open: Mon-Sat 10-6
Policy: The permanent collection contains British painting from the 18th and 19th centuries and a 20th century collection of American Pop, Photo-realism and contemporary painting and sculpture. The temporary exhibition programme *'is often of national, not just local, significance'.* The majority of exhibitions are solo shows. The gallery attempts *'to exhibit lively and challenging shows of contemporary art alongside our permanent displays of historical paintings. The town has a multi-racial community, and the policy reflects this by including shows likely to interest minority audiences as well as a broad section of the community'.*The gallery has an extensive education programme including talks, seminars, residencies and lectures.

Wolverhampton Art Gallery: Tara Babel, Jeremy Welsh and Richard Layzell live artists at Wolverhampton, 1988

Sales: Work sold; Sales referred to exhibitor
The Space: Four galleries are used for temporary exhibitions, all of which have environmental controls and track lighting. Gallery One has 36.5m linear hanging space, Gallery Two has 40m linear hanging space, Gallery Three has 24.4m linear hanging space, and Gallery Four has 55m linear hanging space. The gallery has a number of upright Edmunds cases with interior lighting. Gallery plans available.
Exhibiting: **[AW][EF]** Slides, CV and a SAE should be sent to the Fine Art Department. The programme is planned two years ahead. The gallery provides all exhibition costs except private view. No commission is charged on sales.
Access: **[U][T][L]** City centre location; Public car park and BR Wolverhampton 5 mins

Wolverhampton Polytechnic

A foyer space and a purpose-built gallery in the fine art department showing a wide range of exhibitions from regional sources, staff and students. [VA,Ph,Ce,Fi,Vi,LA]
Address: Faculty of Art and Design, Molineux Street, Wolverhampton, W Midlands WV1 1DT tel 0902 29911
Contact: Head of Fine Art Knighton Koskins
Open: Mon-Fri 10-5
Policy: Open selection, showing painting, sculpture, graphics, ceramics, film, video, live art.
Exhibiting: **[AW][EF]**
Access: **[U][T][L][F]**

Woodbridge (Suffolk)

(EA) Map5 TM67

Deben Gallery

Private gallery promoting the work of young East Anglian artists. [VA]
Address: 26 Market Hill, Woodbridge, Suffolk IP12 4LU tel 03943 3216
Contact: Mrs Walpole
Open: Mon-Sat 9.30-1, 2-5; closed Wed

Denis Taplin Gallery

Commercial gallery for invited artists only in mixed shows with occasional solo exhibitions. [VA,Cr]
Address: 68 Thoroughfare, Woodbridge, Suffolk IP12 1AL tel 03943 6603
Contact: Denis Taplin
Open: Mon-Sat 9.30-5.30; closed Wed pm
Policy: *'The gallery shows work by living artists, the pictures are 'painterly' rather than 'graphic'. Sculpture and free blown glass and ceramics are also shown. A constantly changing mixture.'*
Sales: Work sold
The Space: 30m linear hanging space with hanging from a rail and spotlighting.
Exhibiting: Gallery covers insurance, some expenses are charged for solo exhibitions. Commission is 36%.
Access: **[F]** Public car park 4 mins

Fraser Gallery

A commercial gallery dealing in limited edition prints and antique maps, with framing and restoration service. [Pr]

Address: 62a New Street, Woodbridge, Suffolk IP12 1DX tel 03943 7535
Contact: Rosemary Fraser
Open: Mon-Sat 10-5
Policy: Ever changing display and three special exhibitions a year of solo or two person shows. Paintings, gouache, watercolours shown by local and other artists.
Sales: Work sold
The Space: Gallery about 6.5x16m with hanging rails fixed to wall with groove.
Exhibiting: [AW] Artists should contact gallery to make an appointment. Commission is 33.3%.
Access: [F] Part of gallery. Street parking; BR Woodbridge

Woodstock (Oxfordshire)

(SA) Map7 SP41

Jonathan Poole Gallery

The gallery specialises in contemporary sculpture, paintings and drawings. [VA,Ce]

Address: 2 Market Place, Woodstock, Oxon OX7 1YA N1 tel 0993 813381
Contact: Jonathan Poole, Julia Griffith
Open: Mon-Sat 10-6, Sun by appointment
Policy: It organises about eight solo exhibitions plus mixed shows by gallery artists in both London and Woodstock. The gallery now specialises in contemporary sculpture and drawings. There is also a selection of oils and watercolours by selected group artists. Jonathan Poole is also the exclusive UK representative for the John Lennon Estate.

Oxfordshire County Museum Service

There are exhibition galleries at Woodstock, Oxford and Banbury, smaller areas at Wantage and Abingdon, and small areas in the coffee bars at Oxford and Banbury. [VA,Ph,Cr]

Address: Oxfordshire County Museum, Fletcher's House, Woodstock, Oxfordshire OX7 1SP tel 0993 811 456
Contact: Director of Museum Services J A Bateman
Open: Mon-Fri 10-5, Sat 10-6, Sun 2-6 May-Sept; Tues-Fri 10-4, Sat 10-5, Sun 2-5 Oct-April
Policy: Exhibitions are *'usually, but not essentially, devoted to the work of local artists'.*
The Space: There are about 50-60 square metres at Woodstock, Oxford and Banbury.
Exhibiting: [AW] All space is available for hire. Selection is by an exhibitions committee, usually from applications. The artist's or maker's work is normally inspected before an exhibition is given.

Worcester (Hereford & Worcester)

(WMA) Map4 SO85

City Museum & Art Gallery

The art gallery is part of the municipal museum. It has a strong contemporary art programme and an historical collection and collection of contemporary prints. [VA,Ph,Cr,LA]

Address: Foregate Street, Worcester, Hereford & Worcester WR1 1DT tel 0905 25371
Contact: Art and Exhibitions Officer Sheila McGregor
Open: Mon-Wed & Fri 9.30-6; Sat 9.30-5
Policy: The programme includes work from local, regional, and national sources, and embraces a wide variety of media including video and installations. Exhibitions are usually accompanied by educational events. The gallery is embarking on a programme to *'target specific sections of the community'* and to increase the number of craft exhibitions.
Sales: Work sold
The Space: Three galleries are used, each with natural, fluorescent and spot lighting. The walls are hessian-covered and direct fixing is used. Gallery One has 140 square metres and 18.3m linear hanging space. Gallery Two 303 square metres with 32m linear space. Gallery Three has 140 square metres with 22.2m linear space. Gallery plans available showing all obstructions and facilities.
Exhibiting: [AW] Applications, including slides and CV should be made to Sheila McGregor. The gallery provides insurance, publicity, mailing, transport, list of exhibits, catalogue or card and preview. Supports EPR.
Access: [X] Situated in the city centre close to public car parks; Bus station 10 mins; BR Worcester Foregate Street 2 mins

Framed

A commercial gallery and framers showing a variety of work from local, regional and national sources. [VA]

Address: 46 Friar Street, Worcester, Hereford & Worcester WR1 2NA tel 0905 28836
Contact: Partner David Birtwhistle
Open: Tues-Sat 10.30-4.30
Policy: A general collection is displayed alongside a series of special exhibitions (average ten a year).
Sales: Work sold; Credit card
The Space: 60m linear hanging space in five rooms of a half-timbered building. Hanging rail and a mixture of filtered natural light, fluorescent and spot lights. The galleries are domestic in scale and rather informal.
Exhibiting: [AW] Exhibitions are offered to artists already showing work in the gallery. Artists wishing to be considered for exhibiting in the general collection should submit work by appointment (not Saturdays). The gallery contributes towards publicity, mailing and preview costs, and charges 35% commission on sales. Insurance is provided.
Access: [F] Cathedral multi-storey car park 1 min; Bus station 10 mins; BR Worcester Foregate Street 10 mins

Swan Theatre

A gallery in the restaurant and the back of the auditorium in the Swan Theatre. [Pa,Dr]

Address: The Moors, Worcester, Hereford & Worcester WR1 3EF tel 0905 620624

Contact: Hon Secretary Worcester Society of Artists Sheila Sadler

Open: Theatre opening times

Policy: The monthly exhibitions are organised by the Worcester Society of Artists and are mostly shows of local artists work.

Sales: Work sold

The Space: A total of 25m linear hanging space is available using hanging rods and spotlighting.

Exhibiting: **[AW]** Contact the Hon Secretary Worcester Society of Artists. A commission of 15% is charged on sales, and insurance and printing of publicity is provided.

Access: **[U][T][X]** Situated in the town centre

Worcester Arts Workshop Gallery

A community arts centre specialising in performing and visual arts, with an extensive programme of events, performances, exhibitions and classes funded by the city council and West Midlands Arts. [VA,Ph,Cr]

Address: 21 Sansome Street, Worcester WR1 IUH tel 0905 21095

Contact: Director Jessica Harris

Open: Mon-Fri 10-5, Sat 10-1 (term-time)

Policy: Two exhibitions are shown each term, one of which is from the local community and the other regional or national. A wide range of art classes are held at the arts workshop and events and workshops are programmed alongside the exhibitions.

Sales: Work sold

The Space: Seven panels in the café and bar are used giving 10m linear hanging space. Gallery plans available.

Exhibiting: **[AW][EF]** Contact the Centre Manager. The workshop provides insurance, printing and mailing of publicity and artists expenses. Supports the principle of EPR.

Access: **[U][T][F]** Close to city centre; Angel Place bus station 5 mins; BR Worcester Foregate Street 2 mins

Terrace Gallery

Workington (Cumbria)

(NA) Map3 NX92

Carnegie Theatre & Arts Centre

The gallery is part of an arts centre and host touring exhibitions of photography as well as mounting selling shows of local painting. 'It is hoped that graphics, drawing and print will be exhibited in the future.' [Pa,Ph,Pr,Dr,LA]

Address: Finkle Street, Workington, Cumbria CA14 2BD tel 0900 2122

Contact: T Y Slinger

Open: Mon-Sat 9-5

Policy: The centre is well used by elderly and disabled groups and is particularly interested in exhibitions which may promote a wider understanding of the problems associated with various disabilities.

The Space: There are six heavy-duty, double-sided mobile screens each being 3m x 2.1m high and giving 8.5m linear hanging wall space, with track lighting.

Exhibiting: **[AW]** Apply to the Assistant Manager. The gallery covers display and transport and charges 10% commission. Supports the principle of EPR.

Access: **[F]** BR Workington 10 mins; Bus station 1 min; Town centre car parks 2 mins

Worthing (West Sussex)

(SA) Map7 TQ10

Terrace Gallery

A town centre commercial art and craft gallery in a Regency building showing contemporary art and craft by professional artists and makers. [VA,Cr]

Address: 7 Liverpool Terrace, Worthing, W Sussex BN11 1TA tel 0903 212926

Contact: Director Margrit Avon

Open: Tues-Fri 10.30-4.30, Sat 10.30-1; closed Jan & Aug

Policy: The gallery, which is on the Crafts Council selected list, aims to *'bring to the attention of the public the best in contemporary art and craft, showing only work by professional artists nationally and often internationally, as well as those just beginning to make their mark. The emphasis is always on quality as well as exciting new ideas with the work on show well-displayed in pleasant surroundings. We encourage the public to come in and browse in order to widen our audience and make people feel it can be an enjoyable experience to visit a contemporary art gallery'.* The exhibition programme is of mixed shows including painting, ceramics, studio glass and sculpture.

Sales: Work sold

The Space: The floor area is 164 square metres, the wall space can accommodate 50 paintings plus a shelf space of around 19.8 square metres. Plinths and boxes are provided and there is a private courtyard for sculpture.

Exhibiting: **[AW]** Initially send slides or photographs of work or show work by appointment to the Director. Exhibitions are arranged about a year in advance. The gallery pays for insurance, publicity and a list of exhibits and takes 33.3% commission.

Access: [S] Town centre; Near bus and train; Car parking

Yeovil (Somerset)

(SWA) Map6 ST51

Rimpton House Gallery

A private gallery that 'aims to show high quality work by professional living artists in most media, in the warm and friendly atmosphere of our Somerset manor house'. [VA,Ce,Gl]

Address: Rimpton House, Rimpton, Yeovil, Somerset BA22 8AS tel 0935 851108

Contact: Bernard & Christian Stawt

Open: Daily 10.30-5.30 (during exhibitions) By telephone appointment in between

Policy: *'Our policy is to bring high-quality art to an area lacking in outlets for work of London standards. We hold three or four major exhibitions each year and include ceramics and sculpture.*

Sales: Work sold; Sales referred to exhibitor

The Space: Five rooms are used for hanging work from picture rails giving 100m linear of showing space with spots, fluorescent and natural light. Terrace and grassed area can be used for sculpture. Also good many surfaces for the display of ceramics.

Exhibiting: [AW] Apply with slides. The gallery pays for insurance, publicity, preview, list of exhibits and a catalogue/card. A 33.3% commission is charged on sales.

Access: [U][T]

York (Yorkshire)

(YA) Map3 SE65

Bar Convent Museum

A museum of Christianity where all exhibitions are either on that theme or related to the history of the convent. [VA,Ph,Cr]

Address: 17 Blossom Street, York, Yorkshire YO2 2AH tel 0904 643238

Contact: Curator Peter Walton

Open: Mon-Sat 10-5, Sun 2-5

Policy: The gallery aims to *'present a wide range of Christian art and ideas to an audience which is presently mainly adult Christians, although the museum hopes to widen its audience.'* Of the last year's twelve exhibitions, six were by living artists. Exhibitions are usually accompanied by a talk.

Sales : Work sold; Credit card

The Space: The gallery with high security is 13x6x4m with 38m linear hanging space and a flexible screen system, with direct fixing, spotlights and daylight which ca n be excluded. It has air conditioning and three secure glass cases, 2x1.25x0.75m, 2x,75x0.75m and 1x1.25x1.25m, are available. Space is also available in the corridors, staircases and in the garden which is 400 square metres. Gallery plans available.

Exhibiting: [AW] Applications to the Curator. The gallery pays for insurance, publicity and mail out, catalogue, preview, display and artist's expenses, Commission is 15%. Supports the principle of EPR.

Access: [L][F][S] Buses stop outside; BR York 3 mins; Car park 1 min

Burton Stone Community Centre

A community centre providing a wide range of art and sport activities and catering for the educational and social needs of a wide section of the community. [Pr,Dr,Ph,LA]

Address: Evelyn Crescent, York, N Yorkshire YO3 6DR tel 0904 645816

Contact: Manager Bryn Jones

Open: Mon-Sat 9-10; Sun 10-6

Policy: As a new facility, the centre aims to put on activities and exhibitions which will appeal to the immediate audience within a large council estate and will be of general interest to the wider catchment area in the city. The centre *'is looking to encourage community and fringe artists to bring their work to display at the centre and to run workshops and are particularly interested to see artists whose work will be of particular relevance to the centre's community. Since its opening in 1986 focus has been on the workshops and community art aspects including community art events, fashion and drawing displays, photographic and print demonstrations. There have not been any solo shows and the exhibitions last from 'one day to one year'.* The educational programme is continually developing and will increase with future exhibitions.

The Space: There is not gallery as such, but five rooms are available for two-dimensional work one 9x7m, two 6x6m, an activity room 12x17 and a gymnasium of 17x10m. These spaces are also used for education activities, sport and social use.

Exhibiting: [AW] Artists should contact the Manager.

Access: [U][T][L]

Grape Lane Gallery

A commercial gallery which has specialised in selling and displaying paintings, limited edition prints, sculpture and ceramics to the discerning public. [VA,Cr]

Address: 17 Grape Lane, York, N Yorkshire YO1 2HU tel 0904 643815

Bar Convent Museum: 'Salvation Army, Beach Service, Scarborough' from the exhibition 'Faith' by Ross Williams

Contact: Owner G O Worsley
Open: Mon-Sat 10-5.30
Policy: The gallery aims *'to show the best contemporary art from new and established artists within the region and beyond to a wide audience'*. There is no general style of work shown but work has to be fairly small-scale and *'although we like to think that we are fairly adventurous we do not think that 'way-out' work would sell here'*. About ten monthly shows most of which are solo exhibitions.
Sales: Work sold; Credit card; Credit scheme
The Space: There are three galleries 5x2x2.5m high, 6x6x2.5m high and 5x7x2.5m high giving a total of 37m linear hanging space and an extensive spot lighting system supported by natural light. Gallery plans are available.
Exhibiting: **[AW]** *'We always welcome applications from artists wishing to exhibit with us'*. Artists and makers should send slides and information to the gallery which covers the costs of insurance, printing of publicity, list of exhibits, preview costs, transport, mailing out of publicity and the catalogue and takes 40% commission.
Access: **[F]** BR York 10 mins; Bus station 5 mins; Car park 5 mins

Impressions Gallery of Photography

An independent photographic gallery founded in 1972 in order to provide a platform for photographers and space to exhibit their work. Also shop and darkrooms. [Ph,Vi]

Address: 17 Colliergate, York, N Yorkshire YO1 2BN tel 0904 654724
Contact: Director Paul Wombell
Open: Mon-Sat 10.30-5.30
Policy: *'The gallery exhibits innovative, challenging and creative photographic work which questions the dominant forms of photographic representation and practice. The gallery recognises the diverse range of photographic practices in our culture and creates access to the critical and practical skills and the creative possibilities of the photographic process'*. The gallery favours groups and thematic exhibitions and has eight exhibitions a year each lasting six weeks. Occasionally, photographers are approached to produce work especially for exhibition. Outreach and educational work is an important part of the programme and all the exhibitions have talks and workshops integrated within them. Basic introduction courses on photography are also held in the connecting workshops. Impressions is moving to 29 Castlegate, York in 1991/92.
Sales: Work sold
The Space: There are three spaces within the gallery, 5x5x2.5m high, 5x6x2.5m high and 5x5x2.5m high giving a total of 45m linear hanging space with spot and strip lighting. Daylight can be excluded. Gallery plans are available for exhibitors.
Exhibiting: **[AW][EF]** Photographers should contact the Director. The gallery covers most exhibition costs and supports the principle of EPR.
Access: **[X]** BR York 10 mins; car park 5 mins

Impressions Gallery

Priory Street Sports & Community Centre

Monthly exhibitions in the centre's café area. [Pa,Pr,Ph,Cr]

Address: 15 Priory Street YO1 1ET tel 0904 39968
Contact: Manager Alex Brown
Access: **[U][T]**

Stonegate Gallery

A commercial art gallery specialising in contemporary painting. [Pa,Dr]

Address: 52A Stonegate, York, N Yorkshire YO1 2AS tel 0904 35141
Contact: Owner Alan Hitchcock
Open: Tues-Sat 10.30-5 April-Oct and Christmas
Policy: The gallery shows work by both *'local and national artists, the choice of work is very much a personal one since I will only show work which I like. Whilst saleability is a consideration, it is not the prime reason for selection and the fairly conventional tastes of York does not prevent the showing of work which is unusual or by young unestablished artists providing that it is well executed and presented'*. There are ten exhibitions a year and the gallery mounts solo and group shows, each exhibition lasts for three weeks.
Sales: Work sold; Credit scheme
The Space: The gallery has 30m linear hanging space in a room 2m high with hanging from a rail, and track lighting. Gallery plans are available.
Exhibiting: **[AW]** Artists should write to Alan Hitchcock. The gallery covers insurance, printing of publicity, list of exhibits, preview costs, mailing out of publicity and catalogue and takes 34.5% commission.
Access: **[F]** Bootham car park 5 mins

Theatre Royal

Small exhibitions are held in the foyer area of the theatre throughout the year. [Pa,Pr,Ph]

Address: St Leonard's Place, York, N Yorkshire YO1 2HD tel 0904 658162
Contact: House Manager Ros Brickstock
Open: Mon-Sat 10-7.30
Policy: Exhibitions of work by local artists. Exhibitions change each month.
Sales: Work sold

The Space: One long corridor.
Exhibiting: [AW] Contact House Manager in person, by phone or by post.
Access: [U][T] City centre site; BR York 10 mins; Public car park 10 mins

University of York (Kings Manor Gallery)

This recently opened gallery within the university provides a city-centre venue for local artists to exhibit their work as well as hosting national collections. [VA,Ph,Cr]

Address: Exhibition Square, York, N Yorkshire YO1 2EP tel 0904 432464
Contact: Events and Exhibitions Manager Michael Powell
Open: Mon-Sun 10-4
Policy: The gallery aims to *'provide a professional venue for the display of works of art within the city centre and promote the artistic commitment of the university's Visual Arts Society by encouraging local artists through university generated shows'*. Solo and group shows are being planned for the future which will last for one month each and will be accompanied by an education programme.
Sales: Work sold
The Space: There is one space of 12x5x3m high giving 34m linear hanging space with a *'lifespan track system'* and humidity control. Access for large works is restricted and there are areas adjacent to the gallery for outdoor sculptures. Gallery plans are available.
Exhibiting: [AW] Artists and makers should send sides to Mike Powell. The gallery will cover all exhibition costs and takes 20% commission.
Access: [S][X] Bus routes to university; Car park 5 mins

York Art's Centre

An established venue for theatre, dance, music and visual arts.

Address: Micklegate, York YO1 1JG tel 0904 627129
Contact: Programmer Andy Buchanan
Policy: The area reserved for exhibition is in the foyer and the café/bar area which shows work which ties in with other aspects of the centre's programme and gives space for local artists. It also *'encourages those whose work is socially and politically aware'*.
The Space: The area has space of 14m linear meters hanging space with hessian-covered boards providing room for works to be hung by direct fixing with spotlights and also small glass fronted display cabinet.
Exhibiting: [AW] gallery meets publicity, mailing and catalogue costs, transport is negotiable.
Access: [U][T] Car Park, Rougier Street

York Central Library

Space available to local groups and organisations who wish to put on exhibitions. [VA,Ph,Cr]

Address: Museum Street, York, N Yorkshire YO1 2DS tel 0904 655631
Contact: Area Librarian Jane Lockwood
Open: Mon-Wed, Fri 9-8, Thurs 9-5.30, Sat 9-4
Policy: Space available free of charge to local groups and organisations wishing to publicise and promote their activities or services.
The Space: Display boards and wooden framed display cases.
Exhibiting: [AW] Applications in writing. Items exhibited at owner's risk.
Access: [F]

York City Art Gallery

A municipal gallery with responsibility for the care, maintenence and display of the permanent collection of European Old Masters from c 1350 and British art spanning five hundred years. The two temporary exhibition spaces within the gallery are available for contemporary art and craft as well as for historical exhibitions. [VA,Cr,LA]

Address: Exhibition Square, York, N Yorkshire YO1 2EW tel 0904 623839
Contact: Exhibitions Officer Helena Moore
Open: Mon-Sat 10-5, Sun 2.30-5
Policy: The gallery aims to complement the permanent displays by exhibitions and an events programme which is *'wide ranging and varied in order to cater for as many visitors as possible with their different tastes and interests. Quality and variety are key features of the programme and education and information are principal concerns'*. Between nine and ten exhibitions are held each year, but only about half are devoted to living artists and the Gallery favours, but not exclusively, group shows. Lectures, demonstrations and workshops are regarded as important elements within the programme and the gallery has organised artists' residencies.
Sales: Work sold
The Space: There is one main exhibition gallery 20x7x3m high giving 62m linear hanging space. Movable screens provide an extra 33m linear and *'allows considerable variety in appearance'* breaking the room up into sections'. The walls are normally beige and the skirting boards and wall above the hanging area is chocolate brown. There is a flecked brown carpet, no natural light. There is no lift to the first floor so works of great size and weight are avoided. Works can also be displayed in the entrance hall which has 11m hanging space plus extra screens. There are four perspex display cases. Gallery plans are available.
Exhibiting: [AW] Artists and makers should send slides and information to the gallery. The programme is usually planned one year in advance and the gallery covers all exhibition costs, takes 10% commission and supports the principle of EPR.
Access: [U][T][F][L] BR York 15 mins; Car park 5 mins

Yorkshire Museum

A local authority museum with responsibility for the care, maintenance and display of the permanent collection with a temporary exhibition space. [VA]

Address: Museum Gardens, York, N Yorkshire YO1 2DR tel 0904 629745
Contact: Curator Brian J Hayton
Open: Mon-Sat 10-5; Sun 1-5
Policy: Exhibitions are selected to *'fit in with the subjects that are in the permanent collections of archaeology,*

geology, natural history and applied arts'.

The Space: The space is 67m square which may be enlarged to double the size under special circumstances.

Access: [U][T]

Yoxford (Suffolk)

(EA) Map5 TM36

Yoxford Gallery

The gallery functions as a commercial gallery for five months, and a community facility for the remainder of the year. [VA,Ph]

Address: Yoxford, Suffolk IP17 3EP tel 072877 327

Contact: Vera Delf, Deborah Ardizzone

Open: Tues-Sat 11-5, Sun 2.30-5, open bank holidays, June-Oct

Policy: The gallery pursues a wide-ranging policy of introducing new and unknown artists to a summer season of tourists: it is set in a large wild garden, and the shows often reflect this. Three mixed exhibitions cover this responsibility, and there is a second space which is available for local artists to rent. A small permanent collection of works by Becker, Ardizzone and Bawden complements the temporary exhibitions. The spaces are also used by local organisations and pressure groups for meetings and exhibitions, as well as films by local filmmakers.

Sales: Work sold

The Space: Gallery 1 is 7.5x4.25x2.5m with 16m linear hanging space. Gallery 2 is 3x4.25x2.5m with 11.5m linear hanging space. Both have spotlights and natural light, with picture rails at two levels for hanging works. Courtyard and garden suitable for the display of sculpture.

Exhibiting: **[AW]** Gallery 2 available for hire: £50 per week. Gallery covers insurance, publicity printing and mailing, list of exhibits, preview costs and catalogue/card. Commission on sales is 40%.

Access: **[S]** BR Darsham 20 mins; Parking outside gallery

Right: Kenny Gallery, Galway (Photo: Tadhg Keady)

IRELAND

Athlone (Co Westmeath)

(ACE) Map8 N04

Dolan Moore Gallery

A commercial gallery specialising in contemporary Irish art. [VA]

Address: 33 Church Street, Athlone, Co Westmeath tel 0902 78507
Contact: Director Patrick Dolan, Amy Moore
Open: Mon-Sat 9-6
Policy: The gallery promotes and exhibits a number of Irish artists working in painting, sculpture etc. Eight shows are organised a year, mainly by individual contemporary artists; in between these four to six week exhibitions, the gallery organises two week exhibitions of its gallery artists. Its main aim is to *'promote an awareness of contemporary art produced in Ireland and abroad in the Midland area'*. The gallery hopes to initiate a series of performance works and seminars in the near future.
Sales: Work sold; Credit scheme; Credit card
The Space: Gallery 1 is 8x6x3m high and Gallery 2 is 5x7x3m high with a linear hanging space of 25 and 18m respectively. Two stairways and a hallway are also available for exhibition. Hanging of work is by rods and is lit by a mixture of spots and natural light. Gallery plans available.
Exhibiting: [AW] Artists should submit CV and documentation of work. The gallery covers all exhibition costs including artists' expenses and charges 33.3% commission on all work sold.
Access: [X] Bus 10 mins; Train 10 mins; Car park 3 mins

Ballinamore (Co Leitrim)

(ACE) Map8 H11

Leitrim County Library

Servicing nine branch libraries, contact the Librarian for details. [VA]

Address: Ballinamore, Co Leitrim tel 078 44012/44424
Contact: Librarian Sean O Suilleabhain
Open: Mon-Fri 10-6
Policy: Small occasional exhibitions in three branch libraries.
Sales: Sales arranged
The Space: There is on average space for 30 works at each venue.
Exhibiting: [AW] Applications welcome, no fees charged except insurance where appropriate.
Access: [F]

Ballycasey (Co Clare)

(ACE) Map9 R36

Ballycasey House Gallery

A private gallery assisted by (FADCO) Shannon Free Airport Development Company rent assisted scheme. [VA,Ph,Cr]

Address: Ballycasey, Shannon, Co Clare tel 061 364513
Contact: Director Catrina O'Connor
Policy: The gallery aims to support artists living and working in the mid-west region by organising a combination of solo and group exhibitions. Each year the gallery hosts a *'new generation'* show for recent art college graduates.
Sales: Work sold
The Space: The gallery, consisting in total of 270x270m is situated in an 18th century farm house with large light windows, and consists of two main ground floor spaces adjacent to the hall/reception area which is also used as an exhibition area.
Exhibiting: [AW] 33.3% commission is charged on work sold.
Access: Shannon airport 10 mins

Bantry (Co Cork)

(ACE) Map9 W04

O Riada Gallery

A commercial gallery established in 1987 and specialising in fine art and crafts. [Pa,Pr,Dr,Cr]

Address: Bantry, Co Cork tel 027 51233
Contact: Directors
Open: Mon-Sat 10-5
Policy: The gallery aims *'to explore the relationship between fine art and craftwork by stressing the "objet d'art" side of the latter'*. It sees its audience as the townspeople of Bantry and visitors of which the directors prefer *'the Mercedes-driving Germans rather than Americans in coaches'*. Most exhibitions, of which eight are organised a year, are group thematic shows combining artists and craftworkers. A separate section of the gallery is devoted to a changing display of craft.
Sales: Work sold; Credit card
The Space: The gallery is 7.31x6.4x2.75m high and the work is lit by a combination of natural light and spots.
Exhibiting: [AW] The gallery covers an exhibition list, publicity mailing, transport and display costs, and supports in principle EPR. Commission on work sold varies.
Access: [U][T] Car park 3 mins

Bunratty (Co Clare)

(ACE) Map9 R46

Timestone Gallery

A private gallery showing the work of young unestablished Irish artists and various local craft exhibitions. [VA,Cr]

Address: Bunratty, Co Clare tel 061 364688
Contact: Exhibition Organiser Maria Hannan

Carlow (Co Carlow)

(ACE) Map9 S77

Carlow County Library

Servicing three branch libraries, contact the Librarian for details. [VA]

Address: Dublin Street, Carlow tel 0503 31126
Contact: Librarian Tom King

Castlebar (Co Mayo)

(ACE) Map8 M19

Mayo County Library

Servicing twelve branch libraries, contact the Librarian for details. [VA]

Address: Mountain View, Castlebar, Co Mayo tel 094 21342
Contact: Librarian Patrick McMahon
Exhibiting: [AW]
Access: [U][T]

Castleisland (Co Kerry)

(ACE) Map9 R00

Ivyleaf Arts Centre

The arts centre is run by Island Players Drama Group and exhibitions of local amateur artists are held to coincide with evening drama productions. [VA,Ph]

Address: Old Church Lane, Castleisland, Co Kerry tel 066 41135
Contact: Jerome Stack
Open: Mon-Sat 8-10
Policy: The centre's exhibitions complement the drama events, with the main aim of promoting local interest in the visual arts. As the centre caters for a specific audience, local photography plays a large part in the small exhibition programme. Exhibitions which last one week take place approximately six times a year, and have mainly so far been by amateur artists.
Sales: Sales referred to exhibitor
The Space: The upstairs gallery has 10m linear hanging space and the downstairs main hall has 13m linear hanging space.
Exhibiting: [AW] Although the programme has only included amateur artists in the past, space can be hired for exhibitions. The gallery covers insurance costs.
Access: Public car park 2 mins

Cavan (Co Cavan)

(ACE) Map8 H40

Cavan County Library

Servicing thirteen branch libraries, contact the Librarian for details. [VA]

Address: Farnham Street, Cavan tel 049 31799
Contact: Librarian Gerard Maher

Clones (Co Monaghan)

(ACE) Map8 H52

Monaghan County Library

Servicing seven branch libraries, contact the Librarian for details. [VA]

Address: The Diamond, Clones, Monaghan tel 047 51143
Contact: Librarian John Graham

Clonmel (Co Tipperary)

(ACE) Map9 S22

Tipperary (SR) County Museum

The museum funded by the local authority, houses a collection of modern Irish painting and sculpture. [VA,Ph,Cr]

Address: Parnell Street, Clonmel, Co Tipperary, Ireland tel 052 21399 x349
Contact: Curator P Holland
Open: Tues-Sat 10-5; closed 1-2
Policy: The museum aims to present a regular programme of touring exhibitions as well as generating exhibitions from local artists within the county.
Sales: Work sold; sales referred to exhibitor
The Space: The display gallery, being renovated at time of going to press, will be 11.8x6.8m with a hanging height of about 2m and a length of 20m. There will be a spotlight system and UV and humidity controls.
Exhibiting: [AW] All exhibition costs negotiable.
Access: [X] Town centre location; Public car park 3 mins

Cork (Co Cork)

(ACE) Map9 W67

Cork City Library

Servicing six branch libraries, contact the Librarian for details. [VA]

Address: Grand Parade, Cork tel 0002 277110
Contact: Librarian Hanna O'Sullivan

Cork County Library

Servicing 30 branch libraries, contact the Librarian for details. [VA]

Address: Farranlea Road tel 0002 546499/546591
Contact: Librarian Ruth Flanagan
Policy: The library generally hosts exhibitions by local artists in group shows and has housed national touring exhibitions.
The Space: Space and opening times vary according to the venue.

Crawford Municipal Art Gallery

The Crawford Muncipal Art Gallery is Cork's major art gallery administered by the VEC, who also administer the Crawford College of Art, the School of Music and other technical schools. [VA,Ph,Cr,LA]

Address: Emmet Place, Cork tel 021 273377
Contact: Curator Peter Murray
Open: Mon-Sat 10-5
Policy: The gallery aims to help artists in Ireland and especially in the Cork area to exhibit their work in exhibitions of a high standard. The gallery originates several exhibitions a year in continuing programmes designed to promote Irish art and occasionally tours originated exhibitions of Irish art abroad as well as bringing in work by international artists. On average two temporary exhibitions are organised a month; either large group shows of contemporary art or solo

shows of Irish art over the last century. The gallery hosts shows organised by other galleries, both in Ireland and abroad and roughly half of its resources are devoted to art of previous generations, and half to contemporary art. There is a large bi-annual exhibition of sculpture and drawing (SADE). Exhibitions include the work of prominent British and Irish artists and a range of international thematic shows. The permanent collection includes 18th - 20th century Irish and British paintings and sculpture and 30 casts of classical and neo-classical sculptures. The gallery is used for seminars and workshops and houses an art education workshop run by the Teacher's Centre within the gallery.

Sales: Selling is not a priority in the gallery's programme

The Space: The gallery has sculpture galleries downstairs used for temporary exhibitions with approximately 66m linear space with a height of 10m. On the third floor, four rooms are used alternatively for the gallery's modern collection and temporary exhibitions; each room averages 8x8m. Lighting is a mixture of fluorescent and tungsten with very large studio windows in all galleries except the watercolour room, which is lit by adjustable spots.

Exhibiting: **[AW]** Artists should submit CV and documentation, ideally one year in advance. However because of the range of galleries, the Crawford can be flexible in accommodating exhibitions at shorter notice, and this may be done if the exhibition is a significant asset to the gallery's programme. Solo unsolicited applications are less welcome than group applications. The gallery covers insurance, some publicity and preview costs. 20%-40% commission is charged on work sold. Gallery plans available.

Access: **[L][S][X]** Situated beside the Opera House in the centre of Cork

La Galerie

The gallery shows small-scale figurative artists from Ireland and Britain. [Pa,Dr,Pr]

Address: 32 Grand Parade, Cork tel 021 277376

Contact: Owners D O'Mahony & F O'Mahony

Open: Mon-Sat 9-5.30; closed 1.30-2.30

Crawford Municipal Art Gallery: SADE exhibition 1987

Policy: The gallery sees the work that it exhibits as of *'a conservative rather than an avant garde nature'* and therefore having a *'fairly wide appeal'*. A framing service is offered.

Sales: Work sold; Credit card

Exhibiting: **[AW]** Artists are asked to submit samples of work. 33.3% commission is charged on work sold.

Access: **[U][T]** City centre buses

Lavitts Quay Gallery

The gallery is run by the Cork Arts Society, founded in 1963 to create an awareness and appreciation of the visual arts, mainly through exhibitions, but also lectures and demonstrations. [VA,Ph,Cr]

Address: 16 Lavitts Quay, Quay, Cork tel 021 277749

Contact: Administrator Charlo Quain

Open: Tues-Sat 10.30-6; closed 2-3

Policy: The gallery aims to promote a wide range of artists' work including photography, weaving, sculpture and painting. Emphasis is placed on exhibiting *'reasonably-priced'* works to encourage public sales. The gallery shows approximately 20 exhibitions a year by living artists and has a continual display of work by established and professional artists.

Sales: Work sold; Credit scheme

The Space: The three galleries are 3x3x3m high and 6x4.5x3.5m high and 6x4x3.5m high and lit by spots and flood lights. The work is hung on rods. Gallery plans available.

Exhibiting: **[AW]** Artists should submit slides of six works initially but original work is requested. Space can be hired for £150 per fortnight; the gallery covers no exhibiting costs and charges 15% commission on main gallery sales and 33.3% in other spaces. The gallery supports the principle of EPR.

Access: **[X]** Public transport within 3 mins of the gallery

Triskel Arts Centre

The gallery is part of an arts centre which moved to spacious premises in early 1988, and shows a wide range of contemporary art including painting, sculpture, photography, installation and performance work. [VA,Ph,Cr,LA]

Address: Tobin Street, off South Main Street, Cork, Ireland tel 021 272022

Contact: Robbie McDonald

Open: Mon 11-3, Tues, Fri 11-6, Thurs 11-7, Sat 11-5

Policy: The arts centre not only presents a regular programme of contemporary two- and three-dimensional Irish art, but actively promotes all kinds of music, poetry, theatre, film and live art. Twelve exhibitions are organised a year, each lasting three to four weeks, with the majority of exhibitions devoted to individual living artists. A smaller gallery, the Atrium Gallery which adjoins the main gallery, although previously used to accommodate exhibits from the current major exhibition, has recently become available for smaller shows. The gallery also runs a regular programme of workshops, school visits and lectures.

Sales: Work sold

The Space: The main gallery offers 304 square metres for painting and sculpture shows and the Atrium gallery complements this with 182x182m. The centre also houses a 100-seat auditorium, equipped with LX board with six spots and inhouse PA system. There is an optional stage platform and the auditorium is equipped for cinema (16mm). The adjoining public park is available for outdoor work.

Exhibiting: [AW] Artists should submit a portfolio including a minimum of six slides. The gallery covers all exhibition expenses except transport, mounting costs and artists' expenses, although artists in residence are employed on a Social Employment Scheme. 25% commission is charged on sale of works.

Access: [U][T] All bus routes; Bus stop 2 mins; Public car park 4 mins

University College Cork (Boole Library)

The library is situated in University College Cork and the exhibition programme is run by the Visual Arts Committee. [VA,Ph,Cr,LA]

Address: University College Cork, Cork tel 021 276871 ext2760

Contact: Visual Arts Co-ordinator Johnny Hanrahan

Open: Mon-Fri 10-5

Policy: The library exhibits a wide variety of contemporary Irish art and is particularly keen to support Cork artists. Eight exhibitions, predominantly group shows, are organised a year, and the committee often purchases work from each exhibition to add to its permanent collection of Irish paintings and sculpture. Talks accompany a number of exhibitions.

Sales: Work sold; Credit card

The Space: The library has a 22m linear hanging space with an open area for sculpture. Gallery plans available.

Exhibiting: [AW] The Visual Arts Committee covers most exhibition costs by arrangement with exhibitors. Commission is 5%.

Access: [U][T][L][F] Cork City centre

Droichead Nua (Co Kildare)

(ACE) Map9 N81

Kildare County Library

Servicing seventeen branch libraries, contact the Librarian for details. [VA]

Address: Athgarvan Street, Droichead Nua, Co Kildare tel 045 31486/31109

Contact: Librarian Donal O'Gorman

Open: Library hours

Dublin (Co Dublin)

(ACE) Map8 O13

Arnotts Gallery

Arnotts is a large department store in the heart of Dublin, running an exhibition programme on the top floor of its building. [Pr,Dr,Ph,Cr]

Address: Henry Street, Dublin 1 tel 01 721111

Contact: Sales & Marketing Manager Bill Kelly

Open: Mon-Sat 9-5.30

Policy: The gallery aims to show a very broad range of art-related activities including; patchwork and embroidery, crafts, prints, watercolours etc. The space houses the annual Arnotts National Portrait Exhibition and the Irish Crafts Fair. The gallery sees its main purpose as entertaining *'the public who would not usually visit galleries as they are located usually in side streets and obscure places'*. Lunchtime concerts, knitting demonstrations, classes, workshops and lectures are organised on a regular basis. 20 exhibitions, mainly group thematic shows lasting two-and-a-half weeks are presented each year.

Sales: Sales referred to exhibitor; Credit scheme; Credit card

The Space: The gallery is approximately 900 square metres with wooden walls for convenient hanging of works; work is lit by floods. Gallery plans available.

Exhibiting: [AW] The gallery covers most exhibition costs except catalogue, transport and artists' expenses. No commission is charged on work sold.

Access: [L] All bus and train routes

Bank of Ireland Exhibition Centre

The exhibition centre is the Bank of Ireland's major space in Ireland specialising in contemporary Irish art. [VA,Ph,Cr,LA]

Address: Head Office, Lower Baggot Street, Dublin 2 tel 01 615933 ext 2265

Contact: Barry O'Kelly

Open: Mon-Fri 10-5

Policy: The bank has an extensive collection of contemporary Irish art from 1972 to the present which is on show in the exhibition centre throughout the year. Applications from groups and organisations working in a diverse range of media are accepted and those selected shown on a regular basis; these shows are accompanied by a varied programme of talks, seminars and other educational activities. The bank's forecourt displays a permanent sculpture.

Sales: Work sold; Sales referred to exhibitor

The Space: The galleries are 250 square metres and 150 square metres and the bank has a wide range of exhibition equipment to facilitate hanging of shows. Gallery plans and a comprehensive list of equipment are available.

Exhibiting: [AW] From groups and organisations. The exhibitor must cover all costs and no commission is charged on work sold.

Access: [L][X] City centre location

Crafts Council of Ireland (Crafts Council Gallery)

The gallery founded in 1988 and run by the Crafts Council of Ireland has been established as a showcase for Irish craft and acts as an information centre and crafts promotional agency. [Cr]

Address: Powerscourt Townhouse, South William Street, Dublin 2 tel 01 797383/797368

Contact: Administrator Margaret McAnallen

Open: Tues-Sat 10-6

Policy: The gallery aims to provide a platform for the best of Irish craftwork and *'to promote work of the highest standard to the general public with a view to changing*

the perception of what craft is'. The gallery hopes to show work from other countries to increase the awareness of the medium of craft and the standards of design and craft skills. The Crafts Council organises a series of talks, seminars and workshops and has a permanent collection of contemporary ceramics.

Sales: Work sold; Credit scheme; Credit card

The Space: The gallery is 250 square metres.

Exhibiting: [AW] Artists should submit documentation of works. The gallery covers insurance, preview, publicity and display costs for exhibitions. 30% commission is charged on special exhibitions only.

Access: [X] All city centre bus and DART routes; Car park 1 min

Douglas Hyde Gallery

A large independent gallery catering for major exhibitions of contemporary Irish and international art. [VA,Ph,LA]

Address: Trinity College, Dublin 2 tel 01 772941

Contact: Director Patrick T Murphy

Open: Mon-Fri 11-6, Thurs 11-7, Sat 11-5

Policy: The gallery presents eight major exhibitions a year, of which five are self-curated, combining new work by Irish artists and shows by prominent international artists. Exhibitions are accompanied by substantial catalogues and monographs and a programme of seminars, talks and panel discussions relating to specific shows or issues of critical debate are organised on a regular basis.

Sales: Sales referred to exhibitor or designated agent

The Space: The gallery is 100 square metres and work is hung directly on the walls and lit by halogen and spots. Gallery plans available.

Exhibiting: Exhibitions by invitation. The gallery covers all exhibition costs and artists' expenses are negotiable. The gallery supports the principle of EPR.

Access: [U][T][L] Group wheelchair access by arrangement. City centre location; Public car park 2 mins

Dublin Corporation Community & Youth Information Centre

The centre is used by a range of community and youth organisations who organise regular information displays. [VA,Ph,Cr]

Address: Sackville House, Sackville Place, Dublin 1 tel 01 786844

Contact: Librarian

Open: Mon-Wed 9.30-6, Thurs-Sat 9.30-5

Policy: The centre has a small exhibition area which is available to community groups, individuals and youth groups in the Dublin area. Twelve exhibitions are organised a year but these are all group presentations. Talks related to the centre's own information displays are given on a regular basis.

Exhibiting: [AW] The centre welcomes applications from community and youth groups and to a lesser extent individuals. No commission.

Access: [U][T] The centre is served by all city centre buses; Car park 3 mins

Dublin Public Libraries

Dublin Public Libraries is the administrative headquarters of some 50 service points in Dublin city centre and county including 35 branch libraries and special services. [VA,Ph,Cr,LA]

Address: Cumberland House, Fenian Street, Dublin 2 tel 01 619000

Contact: Librarian Deirdre Ellis-King

Policy: The policy is to provide venues for community arts in the broadest sense, eg drama, art lectures, picture loan and literature. The programmes are aimed at both school children and also adult readers (who include illiterate, unemployed, senior citizens and specific target groups such as parents, mothers etc.) Exhibitions have included work by local artists, photographers etc. and the libraries run regular lectures, talks and workshops to complement the ongoing exhibition programme.

Sales: Sales referred to exhibitor

The Space: Details from each local branch librarian, contact the above address for lists of branch libraries.

Exhibiting: [AW] The libraries do not cover any exhibition costs although they may collect work in certain circumstances.

Gallery of Photography

A gallery dealing exclusively in photography. [Ph]

Address: 37-39 Wellington Quay, Dublin 2 tel 01 714654

Contact: Director John Osman

Open: Mon-Sun 11-6

Policy: The gallery sees its main aim as promoting photography as an art form and organises one exhibition a month of a mixture of 19th and 20th century Irish and International photographers. It has a permanent collection of 19th century photographers of Irish interest.

Sales: Work sold; Credit scheme; Credit card

The Space: Three galleries 15x6x4m high, 10x6x4m high and 9x7x4m high with linear hanging space of 20, 15 and 15m respectively. Gallery plans available.

Exhibiting: [AW] The gallery covers all exhibition costs except artists' expenses and charges 40% commission on all work sold.

Access: [U][T][F] City centre 1 min

Douglas Hyde Gallery: 'Blind' by Dorothy Cross, 1988

Grafton Gallery

A commercial gallery specialising in the work of contemporary Irish artists. [VA]

Address: 3 Anne's Lane, South Anne Street, Dublin 2 tel 01 791835
Contact: Director Ciaran MacGonigal
Open: Mon-Fri 10-5.30, Sat 10-1
Sales: Work sold
Exhibiting: **[AW]**

Graphic Studio Dublin

Graphic Studio is the only gallery in Ireland dealing exclusively in prints by contemporary Irish artists, and acts as a showcase for its parent organisations in Dublin, Black Church Print Studio and Graphic Studio Dublin. [Pr]

Address: 8a Cope Street, Dublin 2
Contact: Administrator Jane Powers
Open: Mon-Sat 10.30-6
Policy: The gallery aims to promote the medium of print by organising group and solo exhibitions of emerging and established Irish artists and artists of international repute. Throughout the year the gallery exhibits a changing display of Irish etchings, lithographs, screenprints and woodblock prints etc. As well as catering for the traditional gallery clientele the gallery attracts tourists, educational groups and people with limited income whose budgets are ideally suited to purchasing a print. Graphic Studio also houses a permanent collection of contemporary Irish graphics.

Graphic Studio Dublin: 'Party Child' by Carmel Benson, drypoint

Sales: Work sold; Credit scheme; Credit card
The Space: The gallery is 133 square metres.
Exhibiting: **[AW]** All exhibition costs are negotiable and 33.3% plus VAT is charged on work sold.
Access: **[S]** Lower floor **[X]** Upper floor. Buses 3 mins; CIE Station 10 mins

Hendriks Gallery

A commercial gallery representing a number of contemporary Irish artists. [VA,Ph]

Address: 119 St. Stephen's Green, Dublin 2 tel 01 756062
Contact: Director Blaithin De Sachy
Sales: Work sold
Exhibiting: **[AW]**
Access: **[X]** City centre location; Public car park 5 mins

Hugh Lane Municipal Gallery of Modern Art

The municipal gallery is run by Dublin Corporation and displays its permanent collection of various 19th and 20th Century paintings and watercolours from Irish, British and international sources. [VA]

Address: Charlemont House, Parnell Square, Dublin tel 01 741903
Contact: Curator Ethna Waldron
Open: Tues-Sat 9.30-6, Sun 11-5
Policy: A small number of contemporary Irish and international exhibitions are originated each year: externally curated shows are also exhibited from time to time. The gallery also runs a lecture programme or concert each Sunday during the year. Also gallery shop.
Access: **[L][S]** Buses 3,10,11,11a,12,13,13a,14,16, 16a,19,19a,22,22a,36; CIE Connolly Station 10 mins

Kerlin Gallery

A new commercial gallery representing contemporary Irish art at home and abroad. [VA,Ph,LA]

Address: 38 Dawson Street, Dublin 2 tel 01 779179
Contact: Director John Kennedy
Open: Mon-Fri 10-6, Sat 11-5
Policy: The gallery aims to *'promote the growth and development of contemporary Irish art at home and abroad'*. It represents a number of artists mainly from Northern Ireland, and as well as organising regular exhibitions of their work shows the work of other Irish, British and occasionally international artists.
Sales: Work sold; Credit scheme; Credit card
The Space: The gallery is 600 square metres and work is hung from rails and lit by wall washers. Gallery plans available.
Exhibiting: **[AW]** The gallery cover exhibition publicity and preview costs. 45% (including VAT) commission is charged on work sold.
Access: City centre; Public car park 2 mins

Kilmainham Gaol & Museum

Kilmainham Gaol and Museum is part of Parks and Monuments Service of the Office of Public Works, custodian of the Nation's Natural and Physical

Heritage; originally a gaol in 1796 it was converted into a national museum in 1966. [VA,Dr]

Address: Inchicore Road, Kilmainham, Dublin, Ireland 8 tel 01 535984

Contact: Patrick Cooke, John Toolan

Open: Mon-Fri 10-4.30 by appointment, Wed & Sat 2-6 Oct-May; Daily 11-6 June - Sept

Policy: The museum's policy is to devise an exhibition and display programme which reflects aspects of the historical period 1796-1929. There is a permanent exhibition of historical artifacts of the prison itself between 1796-1924. The gaol houses a permanent collection of historical painting/portraits. Lectures and talks are organised on an occasional basis.

Exhibiting: [AW] Depending on suitability. Exhibition costs and commission to be negotiated.

Access: [X] Bus 79 from O'Connell Street or 51,51A,51B,23

Marlay Park Craft Centre

A craft centre showing a range of local craftwork and occasionally painting and sculpture. [VA,Cr]

Address: Marlay Park, Rathfarnham, Dublin 16 tel 01 942083

Contact: Organiser M Meddings, F Desmond

Open: Winter 10-5; Summer 10-9

Policy: The courtyard and park are administered by Dublin City Council and the workshops are run individually. Diaplay areas are attached to the wood, ceramics, glass, weaving, copperwork and artists' workshops. The park is used for the display of work and it has been used to stage 'The Independent Sculptors exhibition'.

Sales: Work sold; Credit card

Exhibiting: [AW]

Access: [U][T][F][S] Bus 48A,16,47B; Public car park 2 mins

National Gallery of Ireland

A state-funded national gallery with a permanent collection of old masters and other well-known deceased artists featuring painting, drawing and prints which also houses a small collection of period sculpture and a major collection of Irish art. [VA]

Address: Merrion Square West, Dublin 2 tel 01 615133

Contact: Education Officer Marie Bourke

Open: Mon-Sat 10-6, Thurs 10-9, Sun 2-5

Policy: The gallery organises regular exhibitions of its wide collection and presents a range of touring and travelling shows by the work of deceased artists. A lecture theatre hosts seminars and an education programme offering training courses for teachers. Substantial catalogues and related publications accompany many of the exhibitions.

Exhibiting: Exhibitions of contemporary art are not a function of the gallery.

Access: [L][S] Buses 6,7,8,45; DART Pearse Station 6 mins; Public car park 6 mins

National Museum Exhibition Centre (National Museum)

The centre is administered by the National Museum, and provides a showcase for temporary exhibitions organised by the museum.

Address: 7-9 Merrion Row, Dublin 2 tel 01 618811

Contact: Director

Open: Tues-Sat 10-5, Sun 2-5

Policy: The centre organises a number of exhibitions each year which usually include objects which complement the permanent collection. Of the three shows organised last year material included archaeological illustrations and folk life. Series of talks or individual lectures are organised on a regular basis.

Sales: Sales referred to exhibitor

The Space: The exhibition space is 20x13x3.3m high and work is usually displayed on free-standing boards and lit by spots. Gallery plans available.

Access: [U][T] Buses 10,11,13,14,15; Public car park 5 mins

National Museum of Ireland

The National Museum, founded in 1877, organises exhibitions of decorative arts and archaeology that complement its permanent collection. [Cr]

Address: Kildare Street, Dublin 2 tel 01 618811

Contact: Director

Open: Tues-Sat 10-5, Sun 2-5

Policy: The museum collects, conserves, displays and interprets objects illustrative of the National Heritage, both artistic and natural. Temporary exhibitions are displayed at the National Museum Exhibition Centre, 7-9 Merrion Row, Dublin 2.

Oliver Dowling Gallery

A commercial gallery representing a number of contemporary Irish artists. [VA,Ph]

Address: 19 Kildare Street, Dublin 2 tel 01 766573

Contact: Oliver Dowling

Open: Mon-Fri 10-5.30, Sat 10-1

Policy: The gallery promotes a body of artists attached to the gallery whose work could be described generally as minimal or conceptual. Work by international artists also complements the gallery's programme. Ten exhibitions of contemporary art, predominantly solo shows lasting three weeks, are organised each year.

Sales: Work sold

The Space: The gallery is 120x120m with 25m linear hanging space. Works are hung by nails and lit by spots and natural light. Gallery plans available.

Exhibiting: [AW] From individual artists. The gallery covers all exhibition costs. 33.3 % commission is charged on work sold.

Access: [X] Most city centre buses

Oriel Gallery 13

A commercial gallery specialising in 19th and 20th century Irish painting. [Pa,Sc,Dr]

Address: 17 Clare Street, Dublin 2 tel 01 763410

Contact: Oliver Nulty

Open: Mon-Fri 10-5.30, Sat 10-1

Policy: The gallery sees its aim as generally promoting Irish painting. Six exhibitions, half of which are by living artists, and lasting two weeks are organised each year.

Sales: Work sold; Credit scheme; Credit card

The Space: A Georgian house with five exhibition spaces.

Exhibiting: [AW] The gallery covers insurance and some publicity costs for exhibitions and charges 35% commission on work sold.

Access: [U][T] Bus 6,78,48,62,44; DART 5 mins

Peacock Foyer Gallery

The gallery is based in the foyer of the Peacock Theatre and specialises in showing the work of unestablished artists. [Pa,Pr,Dr,Ph]

Address: Lower Abbey Street, Dublin tel 01 787664

Contact: Gallery Administrator Anne McMonagle

Open: Mon-Fri 10.30-10.30; closed 3.30-7.15; Sat 7.15-10.30

Policy: The gallery usually exhibits the work of students recently graduated from art college or provides the first exhibition for semi-professional artists.

Sales: Work sold

The Space: The foyer is divided into two spaces of 3x10x4m high and 5x7x4m high. Work is hung from rods and lit by spots. Gallery plans available.

Exhibiting: [AW] There is a small start-up fee and a commission of 25%.

Access: [X] CIE Connolly Station 1 min; DART 5 mins; Public car park 1 min

Pearse Museum

The Pearse Museum is run by the National Parks and Monuments Service, the state body responsible for the care, conservation and development of protected natural habitats and historical monuments. [Sc]

Address: St. Enda's Park, Rathfarnham, Dublin, Ireland 16 tel 01 934208

Contact: Curator Pat Cooke

Open: Mon-Sun 10-3.30/4.30/5.30/6 (depending on month of year); closed 12.30-2

Policy: The museum aims primarily to present the life and philosophy of Partick Pearse through a combination of exhibition, audio-visual show and literature in an objective historical light. The main exhibition, drawn from the permanent collection, focuses on the life and educational ideals of Patrick Pearse. Recently the museum opened a new exhibition room geared towards temporary exhibitions, and in the summer of 1988, the Sculptor's Society of Ireland staged an indoor-outdoor exhibition making use of the museum and the surrounding parkland. The museum also houses a body of sculpture by Pearse's brother, William.

Exhibiting: [AW] Transport costs are negotiable.

Access: [U][T] Except first floor. Bus 5 mins; Car park 5 mins

Project Arts Centre

A combined arts centre offering visual art, theatre, dance, contemporary music, poetry, an Gaeilge and other events. [VA,Ph,Cr,LA]

Address: 39 East Essex Street, Dublin 2 tel 01 712321

Contact: Director Tim O'Neill

Open: Mon-Fri 11.30-11, Sat 2-11

Policy: The gallery specialises in *'young/emerging/ unfunded artists or established artists seeking new directions in their work'*. The programme reflects mainly contemporary Irish artists at present as a result of limited funding. All exhibitions are by living artists and last three weeks of which the majority are solo shows; workshops and discussions about artists' work takes place as required.

Sales: Work sold

The Space: The gallery, a converted printing works with a glass A-frame roof is 9x11x4m high. Work is hung by screws and lit by spots. Gallery plans available.

Exhibiting: [AW] Artists should submit no more than twelve slides and a CV. The gallery covers insurance and publicity costs and supports in principle EPR. Commission on work sold is 30%.

Access: [U][T][F] All city centre buses to Dame Street; DART Tara Street Station 10 mins; Car parking on street available

Royal Hospital Kilmainham

The Royal Hospital Kilmainham is a National Centre for the Arts, and a major banqueting centre for state protocol and commercial functions. [VA,Ph,Cr,Vi,Ar,LA]

Address: Dublin 8 tel 01 718666

Contact: Exhibitions Officer Ruairi o Cuiv

Open: Tues-Sat 2-5, Sun 12-5

Policy: The Royal Hospital aims to host a wide range of exhibitions, most of which are curated by outside agencies. The four galleries in the building have accommodated major exhibitions of contemporary Irish art as well as craft, photography and historical painting. The hospital recently hosted the Chinese exhibition, The Emperors and the George Costakis Collection of Russian Avant-Garde Art. Along with the exhibition programme are organised many concerts, lectures, outdoor theatre and jazz events. A permanent collection, the Madden Arnholz Bequest of 1200 prints (1500-1923) is housed on the premises.

Sales: Work sold; Credit card

The Space: The East Gallery is 65x9.5x4m high, the South Gallery (on the first floor) is 65x9.5x4m high and the South gallery (on the ground floor) is 30x5.5x4m high and the Europa Nostra is 12.6x5.4x4m high; offering 200, 200, 61.5 and 20m linear hanging space respectively. Work is lit by spots. Gallery plans available.

Exhibiting: [AW] The gallery only covers the mailing out of publicity, charges 30% commission on work sold and supports in principle EPR.

Access: [U][T][L] Buses 24,51,63,69,78,79; DART Feeder Bus 90; Car park on site

Royal Institute of the Architects of Ireland

A commercial gallery run by the Royal Institute of the Architects of Ireland. [Ar]

Address: 8 Merrion Square, Dublin 2

tel 01 764309/761703

Contact: General Secretary John Graby

Open: Mon-Fri 9.30-5.30

Policy: The gallery runs a small number of architectural and building-related exhibitions each year, each lasting about two weeks. The Awards Gallery contains a permanent collection of RIAI award-winning buildings and the RIAI runs many education courses, talks, lectures etc, all of which are architecturally related. Bookshop with largest stock of architectural titles in Ireland.

The Space: Room 1 is 6.5x9x3m high and Room 2 is 8x5.8x3m high. Exhibitions are free-standing and cannot be hung on the walls.

Exhibiting: [AW] The institute only covers insurance, and the rooms are available for hire at Room 1 full day Ir£170.00, evening Ir£100.00, Room 2 full day Ir£250.00, evening Ir£150.

Access: [X] Buses 7,7a,8,46a,6,6a,54; DART 2 mins

Solomon Gallery

A commercial gallery founded in 1981 specialising in contemporary painting and sculpture and craftwork by Irish artists from home and abroad. [VA,Cr]

Address: Powerscourt Centre, South William Street, Dublin 2 tel 01 794237

Contact: Suzanne MacDougald

Open: Mon-Sat 10-5.30

Policy: The gallery exhibits, promotes and sells painting, sculpture and crafts by contemporary Irish artists with a particular emphasis on studio glass. Twelve exhibitions are organised a year, mainly the work of individual living artists. The gallery holds lectures in Irish painting and sculpture and international studio glass, although it sees its target audience as private and commercial.

Sales: Work sold; Credit card (on craft only)

The Space: The two galleries are 14x7x5m high, and 5x4x5m high, and lit by spot lights. Work is hung on rods. Gallery plans available.

Exhibiting: [AW] Artists should submit CV and documentation of work. Some craft work is commissioned, especially studio glass and wood. The gallery pays for insurance and publicity costs; catalogue costs are shared with the artists, commission on work is 40% excluding VAT.

Access: [X] Bus/trains all routes 5-10 mins; Public car park 3 mins

Taylor Galleries

A commercial gallery showing a broad range of mainly established contemporary Irish artists. [VA]

Address: 6 Dawson Street, Dublin 2 tel 01 776089

Contact: Director John Taylor

Open: Mon-Fri 10-5.30, Sat 11-1

Policy: The gallery deals in early to mid 20th century and contemporary Irish art. A wide range of contemporary styles are shown. Exhibitions are held every three weeks, mainly of work by gallery artists. There is a changing display of gallery stock.

Sales: Work sold; Credit scheme

The Space: The gallery consists of two rooms 7x6x3m high and 7.5x3.5x3m high. Work is lit by natural and spot lights. Gallery plans available.

Exhibiting: [AW] The gallery covers insurance, preview, display and some publicity costs, and charges 33.3% commission on work sold.

Access: [X] Buses 7,8,46A,64A,15A,15B,84; DART 10 mins; Public car park 3 mins

Temple Bar Gallery & Studios

Temple Bar is a co-operative venture with 32 studios for artists and a gallery showing contemporary Irish art. [VA,Ph,Cr]

Address: 4-8 Temple Bar, Dublin 2 tel 01 710073

Contact: Administrator Clair Stanbridge

Open: Mon-Fri 11.30-6, Sat-Sun 12-4

Policy: The gallery aims to show work by new and established artists, in group, two-person or solo shows. Many exhibitions are by recently graduated students working in painting, sculpture and photography. The gallery sees its target audience as *'students, the "ordinary person in the street", buyers and other interested groups'* and runs a series of lunchtime lectures for all exhibitions as well as a monthly debate on a specific art topic. Exhibitions last for approximately three weeks, and of the 22 shows organised each year the majority are by living artists.

Sales: Sales referred to exhibitor; Credit scheme

The Space: The gallery is 12x7x4m high with spot lighting. Gallery plans available.

Exhibiting: [AW] Artists should submit slides of recent work. The gallery only covers publicity printing costs, and although no commission is charged on work sold, exhibitors pay for the hire of space. The gallery supports in principle EPR.

Access: [U][T] All bus routes to Fleet Street and Aston Quay; DART Tara Street Station

Tom Caldwell Galleries

A commercial gallery founded in 1974, which acts as agent for a small body of artists. [Pa,Sc,Dr]

Address: 31 Upper Fitzwilliam Street, Dublin 2 tel 01 688629

Contact: Owner Tom Caldwell

Open: Tues-Fri 11-5, Sat 11-1

Policy: The gallery promotes a number of contemporary Irish artists and shows on average eight exhibitions a year; two of those exhibitions are usually the work of young emerging artists.

Sales: Work sold; Credit scheme; Credit card

The Space: The gallery is 15x7x3m high with a linear hanging space of 40m. Work is hung from rods and lit by spots.

Exhibiting: The gallery covers all costs except artists' expenses. 40% commission is charged on work sold.

Dun Laoghaire (Co Dublin)

(ACE) Map8 022

Dun Laoghaire Public Library

Servicing four branch libraries, contact the Librarian for details. [VA]

Address: Lower George's Street, Dun Laoghaire, Co

Dublin tel 01 801254/801147
Contact: Librarian Muiris O Raghaill

Dundalk (Co Louth)

(ACE) Map8 J00

Louth County Library HQ

Servicing three branch libraries, contact the Librarian for details. [VA]

Address: Chapel Street, Dundalk, Co Louth tel 042 35457
Contact: Librarian Ann Ward

Ennis (Co Clare)

(ACE) Map9 R37

Clare County Library HQ

Servicing fourteen branch libraries, contact the Librarian for details. See also Ennistymon Branch Library and Sean Lemas Library, Shannon. [VA]

Address: Mill Road, Ennis, Co Clare, Ireland tel 065 21616
Contact: County Librarian Noel Crowley
Open: Varies at each branch but generally 11-5.30 Mon-Fri opening till 8 two nights a week
Policy: Exhibition space for local artists, touring exhibitions are also excepted which have an artistic or historical element.
Sales: Sales referred to exhibitor
The Space: 30-50 square metres of wall space.
Exhibiting: [AW] Write to County Librarian with details of exhibition. Opening, hanging is the responsibility of the exhibitor with help of library staff. No commission charged.
Access: [U][T]

Ennistymon (Co Clare)

(ACE) Map9 R18

Ennistymon Branch Library

A Clare County library displaying mainly photography, community arts and schools' work. [Pa,Ph,LA]

Address: Ennistymon, Co Clare tel 065 71245
Contact: Senior Library Assistant Anthony Edwards
Open: Mon-Fri 11-8.30; closed 1-3,5.30-7
Policy: The library runs four or five exhibitions a year to provide the local community with a visual, educational information service. The library also houses the Lawrence Collection - photographs from North Clare (c. 1900) from the National Library.
Sales: Work sold; Credit card
The Space: The library has 55 square metres of wall space for exhibition purposes. Work is hung from rails.
Exhibiting: [AW] The library covers some display and publicity mailing costs and does not charge commission on work sold.
Access: [F] Town centre 2 mins

Fermoy (Co Cork)

(ACE) Map8 W89

Fermoy Art Gallery

A commercial gallery founded in 1987 showing figurative work by local artists. [VA,Ph,Cr]

Address: 2 Pearse Street, Fermoy, Co Cork tel 025 32345
Contact: Proprietor Myles Gallagher
Open: Mon-Sat 10-9, Sun 12-8
Policy: The gallery aims to *'support artists whose income is derived solely from their art'* and is particularly keen to involve children in an appreciation of the visual arts. A number of demonstrations, poetry readings and classes in visual awareness are organised on a regular basis. Of the two spaces available for exhibition, one is devoted to a changing display of landscape, portrait and still life works, etc. and the other caters for four group exhibitions a year lasting two to four weeks.
Sales: Work sold
The Space: Gallery 1 is 5x5x2m high and Gallery 2 is 6x4x2m with linear hanging space of 15 and 16m respectively. Works are screwed to the wall and lit by spots.
Exhibiting: [AW] Artists should submit slides of work. The gallery covers insurance, publicity and preview costs and charges 25% commission on work sold or a hire fee + 10% commission.
Access: [X] Car park outside gallery

Foynes (Co Limerick)

(ACE) Map9 R25

Foynes Branch Library

A library run by Limerick County Library providing a varied programme of exhibitions by local groups and professional artists. [VA,Ph,Cr,LA]

Address: Main Street, Foynes, Co Limerick tel 069 65365
Contact: Branch Librarian Irene Kelly

Fermoy Art Gallery: Gallery 2

Open: Tues,Thurs 10-5.30; closed 12.30-2; Wed,Fri 6-8.30; Sat 5-7

Policy: The library combines exhibitions of work by contemporary Irish artists with historical and documentary displays of local interest. A collection of woodcuts depicting the history of Foynes by students from Limerick College of Art & Design is to be created for permanent display. Artists give talks to students and school groups about their work on exhibition.

Sales: Sales referred to exhibitor

The Space: The exhibition space is 15x6x3m high with linear hanging space of 15m. Work is hung by hooks and lit by spots.

Exhibiting: [AW] The library only covers insurance but charges no commission on work sold.

Access: [U][T][L]

Galway (Co Galway)

(ACE) Map9 M32

Galway County Library HQ

Servicing 26 branch libraries, contact the Librarian for details. [VA]

Address: Island House, Cathedral Square, Co Galway tel 091 62471

Contact: Librarian Thomas Sharkey

Kenny's Gallery

The gallery is run by Kenny's Bookshop, a 48-year-old establishment dealing in antiquarian books, maps and prints. [Pa,Sc,Pr,Ph]

Address: Middle Street, Galway, Ireland tel 091 62739

Contact: Tom Kenny

Open: Mon-Sat 9-6

Policy: The gallery promotes and sells the work of a range of figurative artists working in landscape, portraiture etc. Exhibitions organised twelve times a year are the work of living artists and last three weeks. The gallery's target audience is largely the Galway area and the West of Ireland although tourists regularly visit and purchase works. A number of school trips are organised for groups wishing to learn more about the gallery and its exhibiting artists. A small yard is available for sculpture.

Kennys: The sculpture yard (Photo: Tadhg Keady)

Sales: Work sold; Sales referred to exhibitor; Credit scheme; Credit card

The Space: The gallery is 3m high and has a linear hanging space of 40m. Work hangs on wooden rails and is lit by spots and fluorescent lighting.

Exhibiting: [AW] Artists should submit actual work or documentation. The gallery covers insurance and publicity costs and charges 40% commission on work sold.

Access: [F] All bus routes; Car park 2 mins

Nun's Island Arts Centre

An independent arts centre based in a refurbished church. [VA,Ph,Cr]

Address: Nun's Island, Galway tel 0009 65886

Contact: Administrator Elizabeth MacAvoy

Open: Mon-Sat 11-5.30

Policy: The centre aims to *'promote a broad spectrum of arts activity and secure housing and facilities for arts in Galway'*. One exhibition is organised each month and shows are a combination of contemporary Irish art drawn either from Arts Council Eire touring shows or individual applications; the centre is also keen to support artists working specifically in the west of Ireland. A complementary programme of talks, seminars and workshops continue throughout the year.

Sales: Work sold

The Space: The gallery is 8x17x7m high and work is hung directly on the walls and lit by tungsten and daylight. Gallery plans available.

Exhibiting: [AW] All exhibition costs are incurred by the artist except when subsidised by the Arts Council Eire. 20% commission is charged on work sold and the centre supports the principle of EPR.

Access: [F] Town centre location; Public car park 1 min

Spanish Arch Gallery

A private gallery subsidised by the owners who exhibit a number of contemporary Irish artists with an adjoining etching print studio. [VA]

Address: Long Walk, Galway

Contact: Administrator Pamela Chater or Leonie King,, Oranmore, Co Galway tel 091 94256 (after 5)

Open: Summer Mon-Sat 11-5, Winter Wed-Sat 11-5

Policy: The gallery *'acts as a forum for the less commercial artists working in a fine art (non-craft) context from both Galway and further afield'*. The gallery is closed between January and May and during the other months of the year organises five exhibitions of living artists in group and individual shows. The gallery benefits from the local art festival which brings in large numbers of visitors to the area.

Sales: Work sold; Sales referred to exhibitor; Credit scheme; Credit card

The Space: The gallery is 7x4x4m high. Gallery plans available.

Exhibiting: [AW] The gallery covers all exhibiting costs and charges 33.3% commission on work sold.

Access: [F] Centre of Galway

Stone Art Gallery

A commercial gallery specialising in contemporary Irish art and stonecraft. [VA,Cr]

Address: Spiddal, Co Galway tel 091 83355
Contact: Director Jesus Modia
Open: Mon-Fri 9-6, Sat-Sun 1-6
Policy: The gallery organises approximately six exhibitions a year of contemporary sculpture and painting. Exhibitions lasts for two or three weeks and are usually solo exhibitions of established contemporary Irish artists, especially those working in stonecraft. Adjacent grounds are available for outdoor work.
Sales: Work sold; Credit card
The Space: The gallery is approximately 50x50m and is lit with spots and fluorescent lights.
Exhibiting: [AW] The gallery provides insurance cover and publicity costs for exhibitions and charges 25% commission on work sold.
Access: [F] Twelve miles from Galway on main Connemara bus routes

Gortin (Co Tyrone)

(ACE) Map8 H48

Sperrin Heritage Centre

The purpose-built heritage centre runs a cultural programme reflecting the local environment and natural resources and houses a craft shop and tea shop. [VA,Cr]

Address: 247 Glenelly Road, Cranagh, Gortin, Co Tyron BT79 8LS tel 06026 48142/3
Contact: Administrator Nuala Morris
Open: Mon-Fri 11-6; Sat 11.30-6; Sun 2-7 Summer; Mon-Sat 11-5, Sun 1-6 Winter
Policy: The centre runs a mixed programme of exhibitions which relate directly to the Sperrin area and regularly displays various Arts Council of Northern Ireland touring exhibitions.
Sales: Work sold
The Space: The gallery is 5x10.5x3m high. Work is hung on walls and lit with spots.
Exhibiting: [AW] The centre welcomes applications from artists of various medium. The centre covers insurance costs. Commission is 15%.
Access: [U][T][F] Public car park on site

Greystones (Co Wicklow)

(ACE) Map8 O21

Wicklow County Library

Servicing 14 branch libraries, contact the Librarian for details. [VA]

Address: Wicklow County Library, Greystones, Co Wicklow tel 01 874387
Contact: Librarian Joseph Hayes

Kilcock (Co Kildare)

(ACE) Map9 N83

Kilcock Art Gallery

A commercial gallery showing the work of Irish artists. [VA]

Address: School Street, Kilcock, Co Kildare tel 01 287619
Contact: Director Breda Smith

Kilkenny (Co Kilkenny)

(ACE) Map9 S55

Butler Gallery

The gallery, run by Kilkenny Art Gallery Society, is situated in the servants' quarters of Kilkenny Castle which was refurbished in 1976 as a gallery by the Office of Public Works. [VA,Ph,Cr]

Address: Kilkenny Castle, Kilkenny tel 056 27127/27129
Contact: Honorary Secretary Susan Butler
Open: Summer: Mon-Sun 10-7; Tues-Sun 10.30-5.15; closed 12.45-2 Winter
Policy: The gallery originates a small number of exhibitions a year by leading contemporary Irish and British artists and accompanies these shows with a range of artists' talks and seminars. The castle houses a permanent collection of Irish art from 1900 to the present; videos on art and artists provide an ongoing programme, supplementing the temporary exhibitions.
Sales: Work sold
The Space: The gallery consists of five interconnected rooms with two corridors for print and photographic work. Gallery plans available. Work is hung directly on the walls and lit by spots and floods.
Exhibiting: [AW] The gallery covers all exhibition costs and charges between 15 and 20% commission. The gallery supports in principle EPR.
Access: [X] CIE Kilkenny Station 10 mins; Public car park outside castle

Kilkenny County Library HQ

Servicing four branch libraries, contact the Librarian for details. [VA]

Address: 6 John's Quay, Kilkenny tel 056 22021/22606
Contact: Librarian James Fogarty
Open: Library hours

Killarney (Co Kerry)

(ACE) Map9 V99

Frank Lewis Gallery

A commercial gallery exhibiting a wide range of paintings from traditional and figurative to impressionist and abstract paintings as well as photographs and sculpture. [Pa,Sc,Ph,Cr]

Address: 6 Bridewell, Killarney, Co Kerry, Ireland tel 064 31108
Contact: Frank Lewis
Open: Mon-Sat 10-6

Policy: The gallery shows and sells the work of leading and emerging artists most of whom are living in South West Ireland. About half of the gallery work is sold to the large number of visitors who come from Killarney area and about half to people who live in the region.
Sales: Work sold; Credit card
The Space: Gallery plans available. Gallery 1 is 6x5x2.5m high and Gallery 2 is 4x3x2.5m high. Hanging of works is by rods and lit by spots.
Exhibiting: **[AW]** Gallery owner makes studio visits twice a year. The gallery covers exhibition publicity costs and charges 35% commission on work sold.
Access: **[U][T]**

Letterkenny (Co Donegal)

(ACE) Map8 C11

Donegal County Library HQ

Servicing 17 branch libraries and the County Museum and Lifford Courthouse, contact the Librarian for details. [VA]
Address: High Road, Letterkenny, Co Donegal tel 074 21968
Contact: Librarian Liam Ronayne
Policy: Showing Donegal and Irish artists with touring exhibitions from the Arts Council and other national institutions.
Exhibiting: **[AW]** Contact the Arts Organiser at the above address.

Frank Lewis Gallery

Donegal County Museum

Run by Donegal County Council, this provides the main museum service in the Donegal region. [Pa,Ph,Cr]
Address: High Road, Letterkenny, Co Donegal tel 074 21968
Contact: Curator Paula Harvey
Open: Tues-Fri 11-5, Sat 1-5
Policy: The primary aims of the museum are to collect, document, preserve, exhibit and interpret the material evidence and associated information of the archaeology, history, folklife, social and natural history and geology of the county and its environs. As part of its overall programme, the museum hosts a series of visual arts and crafts exhibitions mainly drawn from Arts Council Eire and museum touring programmes. A permanent collection of archaeology, local history and arts and crafts relating to the area are housed in the building and an extensive education programme offering illustrated talks and workshops. complements all aspects of the museum's work.
Sales: Sales referred to exhibitor
The Space: The exhibition space is 40x30x2.5m high and work is displayed in hanging frames and lit by spots and fluorescent lighting.
Exhibiting: **[AW]**
Access: **[X]** Town centre 2 mins

Glebe Gallery

The gallery forms part of the bequest to the nation by Derek Hill of his house, St Columb's and art collection and surrounding gardens, the estate administered by the National Parks Service of the Office of Public Works. [VA,Ph,Cr]
Address: Church Hill, Letterkenny, Co Donegal tel 074 37071
Contact: Curator
Open: Tues-Sat 11-6.30, Sun 1-6.30 Easter week, June-Sept
Policy: The gallery's purpose is primarily to display the Derek Hill Collection, (British, Irish and European works from 1850 to the present) however as a major gallery in the North West they are building a collection of Donegal-related works, whether paintings, sculpture, tapestry or quilts. The gallery will on occasion organise exhibitions which complement the permanent collection and the surrounding environs, and the space is used for lectures and receptions.
Sales: Work sold; Sales referred to exhibitor
The Space: The ground floor space is 30x4x2.5m high and the first floor space 30x4x2m high with linear hanging space of 25 and 28m respectively. Work is lit by spots and hung from picture rails. A range of wall-mounted and floor-standing cases are available and the gardens and grounds can accommodate outside sculpture.
Exhibiting: **[AW]** Artists should submit photographs of work between October and March. Apply to gallery for exhibiting details.
Access: **[F][X]** Access by private transport only

Limerick (Co Limerick)

(ACE) Map9 R55

Belltable Arts Centre

The arts centre runs a visual arts programme as a complement to its theatre productions. [VA,Ph,Cr]

Address: 69 O'Connell Street, Limerick tel 061 319866
Contact: Administrator Emer McNamara
Open: Mon-Sat 9.30-10.30
Policy: The centre organises a diverse range of exhibitions a year including Arts Council Eire touring shows, group and individual shows by local artists and travelling shows from further afield. An education programme with workshops is organised in conjunction with specific exhibitions.
Sales: Work sold; Credit scheme; credit card
The Space: The gallery of 616 square metres is divided between the foyer area and the coffee bar. A stairwell is also sometimes used as a further exhibition area.
Exhibiting: [AW] The gallery covers some exhibition preview costs and insurance and charges 25% commission on work sold.
Access: [U][T] Trains and buses 5 mins; Public car park 10 mins

Limerick City Gallery of Art

A city gallery with a permanent collection of period and contemporary art. [VA,Ph]

Address: Pery Square, Limerick tel 061 310633
Contact: Director/Curator Paul M O'Reilly
Open: Mon-Fri 10-6, Thurs 10-7, Sat 10-1; closed 1-2
Policy: The gallery receives a broad range of touring exhibitions, both local and national, and is a venue for a number of major Irish open competition exhibitions (EVA, Independents, Oireachtas). Future plans are to initiate exhibitions by prominent international artists, as well as accommodating large touring shows by artists working outside Ireland.
Sales: Work sold
The Space: The gallery consists of ten spaces over two floors, leading in a cluster arrangement off a centre space. The total exhibition is 1000 square metres.
Access: [X] Town centre 10 mins; Parking outside gallery

Limerick City Library

Servicing two branch libraries, contact the Librarian for details. [VA]

Address: The Granary, Michael Street, Co Limerick tel 061 314668
Contact: Librarian Maurice Flynn

Limerick County Library HQ

Servicing 23 branch libraries, contact the Librarian for details. See also Foynes Branch Library and Newcastle West Library. [VA]

Address: 58 O'Connell Street, Co Limerick tel 061 318692/318477
Contact: Librarian Roisin De Nais
Open: Library hours

Riverrun Gallery

Commercial gallery opened in 1987 to promote the work of contemporary Irish artists; the building also houses a poster shop and restaurant. [VA]

Address: Honan's Quay, Limerick, Ireland tel 061 40277
Contact: Director Brid Dukes
Open: Mon-Sat 10-5.30
Policy: the gallery aims to promote and sell two and three-dimensional contemporary Irish art to public institutions, companies and the general public. A number of individual artists are represented by the gallery who seek to promote their work and other artists work in Europe and USA. Last year's programme incorporated individual and group exhibitions by living artists, with each exhibition running for approximtely four weeks.
Sales: Work sold; Credit scheme
The Space: The gallery is 21x6x3m high with 53m of linear hanging space. Gallery plans available.
Exhibiting: [AW] Artists should submit CV and documentation of work. The gallery covers insurance costs, preview and all publicity expenses. It supports the principle of EPR.
Access: [X] CIE Limerick Station 10 mins; Public car park and taxi rank opposite gallery

Lismore (Co Waterford)

(ACE) Map9 X09

Waterford County Library

Servicing ten branch libraries, contact the Librarian for details. [VA]

Address: Waterford County Library, Lismore, Co Waterford tel 058 54128
Contact: Librarian Donal Brady
Open: Library hours

Longford (Co Longford)

(ACE) Map8 N17

Carroll Gallery

A commercial gallery exhibiting contemporary Irish art. [Pa,Sc,Pr]

Address: Keon's Terrace, Longford tel 043 41148
Contact: Terry Carroll
Open: Mon-Fri 10-5, Sat 11-5
Policy: The gallery aims to *'sell and show good contemporary Irish art to the general public'*. It shows a range of group and individual artists' work in exhibitions lasting three weeks, and has a permanent collection of its gallery artists.
Sales: Work sold; Credit scheme; Credit card
The Space: The gallery is 10x6x3.5m high; adjacent to the gallery is an outdoor sculpture area of 6x6m.
Exhibiting: The gallery covers some publicity and preview costs; 33.3% commission is charged on work sold.
Access: [S]

Longford County Library HQ

Servicing five branch libraries, contact the Librarian for details. [VA]

Address: Annaly Carpark, Longford tel 043 41124/41125
Contact: Librarian Mary Morrissey
Open: Mon, Wed 10-1, 2-8.30, Tues, Thurs 10-1, 2-5.30, Fri 10-1,2-5
Policy: Exhibits library material and displays arranged by local community groups and artists.
The Space: Exhibition area is 16 square metres with wall-mounted display facilities, glass cases, special lighting and exhibition stands.
Exhibiting: [AW] Apply in writing to County Librarian.
Access: [U][T][L]

Monaghan (Co Monaghan)

(ACE) Map8 H63

Monaghan County Museum

The museum, with permanent collections on archaeology, history and lace, is run by Monaghan County Council and organises a regular programme of exhibitions. [VA,Ph,Cr]

Address: 1-2 Hill Street, Monaghan tel 047 82928
Contact: Curator Aidan Walsh
Open: Tues-Sat 11-5, closed 1-2
Policy: The museum sees its aim as *'providing a display space for the exhibition of the work of local artists, touring shows and its own permanent collection of 18th, 19th and 20th century local interest paintings'*. Nine exhibitions, mainly group shows, each lasting two to three weeks, are organised a year.
Sales: Work sold
The Space: The gallery is 7.8x15x3.5m high with 35m linear hanging space. Gallery plans available. A small sculpture court 2x2m is adjacent to the main building.
Exhibiting: [AW] Exhibition finance negotiable. Commission 25%.
Access: [U][T][F] No buses; Car park 2 mins

Mullingar (Co Westmeath)

(ACE) Map8 N45

Jill Whyte Gallery

A private gallery showing the work of Midlands and Irish artists. [VA,Cr]

Address: Castle Street, Mullingar, Co Westmeath tel 044 48662
Contact: Exhibition Organiser
Sales: Work sold
The Space: The gallery is approximately 17x17m.
Exhibiting: [AW]

Mullingar County Library HQ

Servicing eight branch libraries, contact the Librarian for details. [VA]

Address: Dublin Road, Mullingar, Co Westmeath tel 044 40781/2/3
Contact: Librarian Marian Keaney

Navan (Co Meath)

(ACE) Map7 SU18

Meath County Library

Servicing 13 branch libraries, contact the Librarian for details. [VA]

Address: Railway Street, Navan, Co Meath tel 046 21451/21134
Contact: Librarian Liam Smith

Newcastle West (Co Limerick)

(ACE) Map9 R23

Newcastle West Library

The library comes under the auspices of Limerick County Library and through its exhibitions programme caters for a wide section of the public. [VA,Ph,Cr,LA]

Address: Newcastle West, co Limerick tel 069 62273
Contact: Librarian Aileen Dillane
Open: Mon,Sat 10.30-5; closed 12.45-2.15; Tues,Fri 10.30-8; Weds,Thurs 10.30-5
Policy: The library aims to *'create an awareness of the arts in the local community by running a varied programme of community and artist-based exhibitions. A number of historical exhibitions displaying documents and photographs also complement the programme and discussions and talks take place on a regular basis'*.
Sales: Sales referred to exhibitor
The Space: The exhibition space is 7.2x6x2.7m high with a 17.35m linear hanging space. Work is hung from picture rails or hooks and is lit mainly by natural light.
Exhibiting: [AW] The library covers insurance and some exhibition publicity costs as well as occasionally paying for transport. No commission is charged on work sold. The library supports in principle EPR.
Access: [U][T][F] Main route from Limerick-Killarney

Portlaoise (Co Laois)

(ACE) Map9 S49

Laois County Library

Servicing seven branch libraries, contact the Librarian for details. [VA]

Address: County Hall, James Fintan Lalor Avenue, Portlaoise, Co Laois tel 0502 22044
Contact: Librarian E Phelan

Roscommon (Co Roscommon)

(ACE) Map8 M86

Roscommon County Library

Servicing seven branch libraries, contact the Librarian for details. [VA]

Address: Abbey Street, Roscommon tel 0903 26100
Contact: Librarian Helen Kilcline

Roscrea (Co Tipperary)

(ACE) Map9 S18

Damer House, Roscrea

The Roscrea Heritage Centre is a charitable trust whose aims are to develop the Castle complex and Damer House as a cultural/heritage centre. [Pa,Sc,Pr]

Address: Damer House, Roscrea, Co Tipperary, Ireland tel 0505 21850
Contact: Administrator William Hayes
Open: Summer season 10-5, Sun 2-5; and by appointment
Policy: The centre mounts exhibitions which provide information and entertainment for passing visitors and local schools. Occasionally exhibitions of the work of living artists are organised, however there are regular displays of local interest, artefacts and environmental exhibitions. The centre shows on average four exhibitions a year during the summer months, and has a permanent collection of material relating to manastic life and activity in the 6th-9th centuries, and to Irish farm life in the late 19th and early 20th centuries. Seminars and talks are organised on an irregular basis but are not specifically related to an exhibition on view.
Sales: Work sold
The Space: The White Room is 6.5x6.5m; the Blue Room is 5.5x7.5m; the Green Room is 5.5x6.5m; the Kelly Collection Room is 6x5.5m; the Environmental Survey Room is 5.5x4.5m and the top floor exhibition space is 10x12.5m. The Annex comprises the Environmental Survey Project Room of 4.5x4.5m; the Monastic Midlands Room of 9x9m and the Annex of 12x9m.
Exhibiting: [AW] The centre does not cover any exhibition costs and charges 15% commission on work sold. Gallery plans available.
Access: [X] Trains from Dublin 1 hour and Limerick 1 hour

Rosscarbery (Co Cork)

(ACE) Map9 W23

Angela Flowers (Ireland) Inc

Commercial gallery specialising in contemporary British and Irish art, showing one three-week exhibition a year during August. [VA,Ph]

Address: Downeen, Rosscarbery, Co Cork tel 023 48158
Contact: Angela Flowers, 11 Tottenham Mews, London W1P 9PJ tel 01 637 3089
Open: August only, Mon-Sun 11-7
Policy: To bring the work of living artists to West Cork in order to increase local interest in art and further afield and *'to show visitors from abroad the beauties of west Cork'*. The gallery has a permanent collection of contemporary British and Irish art.
Sales: Work sold
The Space: The gallery is 13x5x2.5m high with 20 linear metres of hanging space. The gallery also has access to four half-acre fields for outdoor works.
Exhibiting: Exhibitions are selected by the gallery. The gallery covers all costs of exhibition promotion, hanging and display except artists' expenses; commission on sales is 40%.
Access: [F]

Shannon (Co Clare)

(ACE) Map9 R36

Sean Lemass Library

The library is run by Clare County Libraries with exhibitions forming an important part of its activities. [VA,Ph,Cr]

Address: Town Centre, Shannon, Co Clare tel 061 364266
Contact: The Librarian
Open: Mon-Fri 11-5.30; Tues, Fri 11-8
Policy: The library's exhibition programme includes arts and crafts as well as scientific, historical and industrial displays. One exhibition is organised each month and is accompanied by various talks, lectures or demonstrations.
Sales: Sales referred to exhibitor
The Space: The entrance foyer to the library provides two hanging spaces of modular design 6.7x1.5m high and 3.6x1.8m high.
Exhibiting: [AW] The library covers exhibition publicity costs and does not charge commission on work sold.
Access: [U][T][F] Adjacent to local bus services; Car park 1 min

Skibbereen (Co Cork)

(ACE) Map9 W13

West Cork Arts Centre

The centre runs a regular programme of exhibitions as well as providing a wide range of music, dancing, crafts and creative writing classes and workshops. [VA,Ph,Cr]

Address: North Street, Skibbereen, Co Cork tel 028 22090
Contact: Secretary
Open: Mon-Sat 12.30-5
Policy: The gallery primarily promotes the work of artists living in County Cork, however it also hosts a number of Arts Council Eire touring exhibitions. Of the 15 exhibitions they hold each year, most focus on the traditional media of printmaking, watercolour and landscape painting; shows which last for three weeks are a mixture of solo and group presentations.
Sales: Work sold; Credit scheme; Credit card
The Space: Gallery 1 has 50 square metres, Gallery 2 has 75 square metres and Gallery 3 30 square metres with linear hanging space of 27, 31 and 20 m respectively. Gallery plans available.
Exhibiting: [AW] The gallery covers insurance, preview costs and some publicity expenses. 33.3% commission is charged on work sold. The gallery supports in principle EPR.
Access: [F] Buses from Cork daily; Car park opposite centre

Sligo (Co Sligo)

(ACE) Map8 G63

Sligo County Library

Servicing four branch libraries, contact the Librarian for details. [VA]

Address: The Courthouse, Sligo, Ireland tel 071 42212
Contact: Librarian John McTernan

Thurles (Co Tipperary)

(ACE) Map9 S15

Bank of Ireland

A gallery administered by the Bank of Ireland. [Pa,Pr,Dr,Ph]

Address: Liberty Square, Thurles, Co Tipperary tel 0504 21511
Contact: Assistant Manager Liam Lyons
Open: Mon 10-5, Tues-Fri 10-3; closed 12.30-1.30
Policy: The bank uses an office space to show the work of a range of Irish artists. Local art groups and schools visit the bank after hours to view and discuss the work on display. Of the eight exhibitions organised a year, each lasting a month, 40% are by individual artists and the rest group shows.
Sales: Work sold; Credit card
The Space: The office is 3m high and offers a linear hanging space of 33m; a counter area also provides 10x3.5m of hanging space. Work is hung from rails. Gallery plans available.
Exhibiting: [AW] The bank covers insurance and list of exhibits. No commission is charged on work sold.
Access: [S] Car Park on site

Tipperary Joint Libraries Committee

Servicing 17 branch libraries, contact the Librarian for details. [VA]

Address: County Library, Castle Avenue, Thurles, Co Tipperary tel 0504 21102/21555
Contact: Librarian Donal Brady

Tralee (Co Kerry)

(ACE) Map9 Q81

Kerry County Library HQ

Servicing nine branch libraries, contact the Librarian for details. [VA]

Address: Moyderwell, Tralee, Co Kerry tel 066 21200
Contact: Librarian Kathleen Browne

Siamsa Tire Theatre

A limited company, Siamsa Tire National Folk Theatre presents exhibitions regularly in its foyer space. [VA,Ph,Cr]

Address: Godfrey Place, Tralee, Co Kerry tel 066 23055
Contact: Manager Martin Whelan
Open: Mon-Sat 10-6
Policy: The theatre aims to reflect traditional culture both inside and outside Kerry by accommodating a range of exhibitions which include Arts Council Eire group and individual touring shows, local art groups and individual artists working in the Kerry region. Almost 20 exhibitions are organised a year and can last from one to four weeks.
Sales: Work sold; Credit card
The Space: The foyer is 16x12x3m high. Work is hung from a rail and lit by floods. Gallery plans available.
Exhibiting: [AW] The theatre does not cover any exhibition expenses and as a rental charge is levied, no commission is charged on work sold.
Access: [S] Town centre location; Public car park 1 min

Tuam (Co Galway)

(ACE) Map9 M32

Tuam Theatre Guild & Arts Centre

The centre functions mainly as a theatre but it holds four or five exhibitions a year in the exhibition space. [VA]

Address: 5 St. Jarlath's, Bishop Street, Tuam, Co Galway tel 093 24386
Contact: Exhibition Organiser Jarlath Canney

Tullamore (Co Offaly)

(ACE) Map9 N32

Offaly County Library

Servicing nine branch libraries, contact the Librarian for details. [VA]

Address: O'Connor Square, Tullamore, Co Offaly tel 0506 21113/21419
Contact: Librarian Ann Coughlan
Open: Library Hours

Waterford (Co Waterford)

(ACE) Map9 S61

Garter Lane Arts Centre

The arts centre runs a regular programme of contemporary Irish art as well as organising smaller shows of local interest, mainly print and photography. Classes in poetry, drama and dance also feature in the centre's programme. [VA,Ph,LA]

Address: 5 O'Connell Street, Waterford tel 051 55038/77153
Contact: Administrator Bridget Ryan
Open: Tues-Thurs 10-6, Fri-Sat 10-9
Policy: The centre aims to provide a broad-based programme of exhibitions and events, utilising its main gallery for emerging and established contemporary Irish artists, and its side gallery for show of local appeal. 22 exhibitions are mounted each year, all the work of living artists and half are solo exhibitions; main gallery shows last for two weeks and side gallery shows for three to four weeks. Slide shows, films and talks accompany many of the exhibitions and the centre houses the Waterford Civic Collection of works from 1900 to the present.

Sales: Work sold

The Space: The main gallery is 9x7x4m high and the side gallery is 8x8x4m high. A new space of 110 square metres will also become available for a permanent sculpture exhibition in the near future. In the past a small back garden has been used for three-dimensional displays. 16 display cases and 16 plinths are also available for display. Gallery plans available.

Exhibiting: [AW] Artists should submit CV and documentation. The centre covers publicity costs of exhibitions and charges 25% commission on work sold.

Access: [S][X] Walking distance from city centre 10 mins

Waterford Municipal Library

Servicing three branch libraries, contact the Librarian for details. [VA]

Address: Lady Lane, Waterford tel 051 73506
Contact: Librarian Patricia Fanning
Open: Library hours

Wexford (Co Wexford)

(ACE) Map9 T02

Wexford Arts Centre

The arts centre presents a multi-faceted programme of visual arts and crafts. [VA,Ph,Cr]

Address: Cornmarket, Wexford tel 053 23764/24544
Contact: Artistic Director Patrick Sutton
Open: Mon-Sat 10-6

Policy: The centre runs a regular programme of touring shows and encourages artists in the local community by staging group and solo exhibitions. Also housed in the premises is a darkroom which is used regularly by local groups and occasionally by visiting artists.

Sales: Works for sale

The Space: The centre has three spaces available for exhibitions: the Pillar Room, a large accessible ground floor gallery and two upstairs spaces, a large 'ballroom' and smaller 'supper room'. A coffee bar also provides supplementary hanging space.

Exhibiting: [AW] The gallery covers publicity costs for exhibitions but not artist's expenses. 25% commission is charged on work sold.

Access: Disabled access being developed. Town centre location; Public car park outside centre

Garter Lane Arts Centre: during the second phase of renovation

Wexford County Library

Servicing five branch libraries, contact the Librarian for details. [VA]

Address: Abbey Street, Wexford tel 053 22211
Contact: Librarian Catherine O'Rourke
Open: Library hours
Access:

Right: Lurgan College of Further Education (Corridor Gallery), Lurgan. Sculpture by Tom Bevan from the exhibition 'The New North', 1988 (Photo: Tony Corey)

N IRELAND

Antrim (Co Antrim)

(ACNI) Map8 J18

Clotworthy House Arts Centre

An arts centre run by Antrim Borough Council which organises exhibitions along with theatre, music and various community events. [VA,Ph,Cr]

Address: Randalstown Road, Co Antrim tel 08494 67531
Contact: Community Arts Officer Nick Livingston
Open: Mon-Fri 9.30-9.30
Policy: The gallery is closed pending repairs and refurbishment and is likely to remain so during 1989. Provision has, however, been made to house temporary exhibitions are other public locations. *'We are committed to the principle of providing a varied experience of the visual arts and making arts accessible to the widest possible public. The gallery takes Arts Council touring exhibitions and organises lectures, talks and demonstrations for schools and others.*
Sales: Work sold
The Space: The main gallery is 7x4.5x3m high, the minor gallery(A) is 4.3x3.5x3m high and the minor gallery(B) is 4.3x3.5x3m high with a linear hanging space of 16, 8 and 9.3m respectively. Hanging is by rods and lit by spots. Display units, and screens are available. Gallery plans available.
Exhibiting: [AW] The gallery welcomes enquiries from artists for its exhibitions in other public locations. The gallery covers all exhibitions costs except transport and artists' expenses. No commission is charged on work sold.
Access: [U][T] Bus station 8 mins; NIR Antrim station 8 min

Armagh (Co Armagh)

(ACNI) Map8 H84

Armagh County Museum

The museum is a regional branch of the Ulster Museum funded by the Department of Education through the Ulster Museums Trust. [VA,Ph,Cr]

Address: The Mall East, Armagh, Armagh BT61 9BE tel 0861 523070
Contact: D Weatherup
Open: Mon-Sat 10-1, 2-5
Policy: It runs a varied programme drawing on many Arts Council of Northern Ireland touring exhibitions, occasionally solo shows complement the mixed media presentations. Shows last for approximately two weeks and are organised eight times a year. A permanent collection of local portraits, topographical paintings and drawings are housed in the building.
Sales: Work sold
The Space: Gallery 1 is 8x6x3m high and Gallery 2 is 11x8x3m high.
Exhibiting: The museum covers publicity and exhibition preview costs. No commission is charged on work sold.
Access: [X] Bus Belfast/Armagh; CIE Dublin/Armagh; Car park on site

Southern Education and Library Board

SELB is the administrative centre for all branch libraries in its jurisdiction. (See also Brownlow Branch Library, Craigavon). Contact the Chief Librarian for details of branch libraries. [VA]

Address: SELB Library HQ, 1 Markethill Road, Armagh BT60 1NR tel 0861 525353
Contact: Chief Librarian W Carson
Open: Library hours
The Space: Details from each local branch librarian.

Ballymena (Co Antrim)

(ACNI) Map8 D10

North Eastern Education & Library Board

NEELB is the administrative centre for all branch libraries in its jurisdiction. Contact the Chief Librarian for details of branch libraries in Antrim, Ballymena, Ballymoney, Carrickfergus, Coleraine, Larne, Maghera, Magherafelt, Newtownabbey, Portrush, Portstewart, Whitehead and smaller towns and villages. [VA]

Address: NEELB Library Service, Area Library, Demesne Avenue, Ballymena, Co Antrim BT43 7BG tel 0266 41531/2/3
Contact: Chief Librarian
Open: Library hours
Policy: To display a wide range of arts, crafts and other objects, often accompanied by books from library stock.
The Space: Details from each local branch librarian.
Exhibiting: [AW] Contact Chief Librarian.
Access: Varies

Ballynahinch (Co Down)

(ACNI) Map8 J35

South Eastern Education & Library Board

South Eastern Education and Library Board is the administrative headquarters of all branch libraries in its jurisdiction. [VA]

Address: Library Headquarters, Ballynahinch, Co Down BT24 8DH tel 0238 562639
Contact: Chief Librarian
Policy: It is the policy of the service to encourage local individuals and groups to take an active interest in bringing the visual arts to the attention of the community. Exhibition space is available at Ballynahinch, Bangor, Carryduff, Castlewellan, Cregagh, Donaghadee, Downpatrick, Dundonald, Newcastle, Newtownards, Saintfield and Tullycarnet for staging temporary exhibitions. Individual artists (amateur and semi-professional) local arts societies and groups, camera clubs, craft groups or anyone interested in using the space is welcome.
Exhibiting: [AW] No fee is charged for the use of the accommodation but the exhibitor is responsible for staffing any exhibition and for handling any sale transactions. Anyone interested should contact the local librarian.

Belfast (Co Antrim)

(ACNI) Map8 J37

Art Advice

Art Advice are contemporary European art consultants and represent a number of artists in Ireland and USA. [VA,Ph,Cr]

Address: 136 Great Victoria Street, Belfast, Co Antrim BT2 7BG tel 0232 324726
Contact: Elaine Hogg
Open: Mon-Fri 10-5
Policy: The gallery provides an art collection consultancy service aimed at specialist trade interests ie architects, interior designers, corporate and public collectors, investment, houses etc. The gallery also represents a limited group of contemporary artists living and working in Ireland whose work is shown both in the gallery in Belfast and its counterpart in New York.
Sales: Work sold; Credit scheme
The Space: The gallery downstairs is 3x2.5x2m high and upstairs is 4x2.5x2m high with linear hanging space of 8 and 12m respectively. Work is lit by spots. Gallery plans available.
Exhibiting: [AW] Artists should submit CV and documentation of work. The gallery covers all exhibition costs except artists' expenses and charges 15% commission on work sold. Supports the principle of EPR.
Access: [X] All city centre buses 5 mins; NIR Botanic Station 5 mins; Car parks 5 mins

Arts Council Gallery

A public gallery run by the Arts Council of Northern Ireland promoting both Irish and occasionally international art, as well as catering for exhibitions originated outside the country. The gallery has a fine art bookshop, video viewing area and coffee bar. [VA,Ph,Cr,LA]

Address: Bedford House, Bedford Street, Belfast, Co Antrim BT2 tel 0232 321402
Contact: Gallery Manager Noirin McKinney
Open: Tues-Sat 10-6
Policy: The gallery aims to provide a platform for artists based in Northern Ireland as well as exhibiting a range of touring shows curated by other galleries and exhibition spaces. Exhibitions take the form of solo, two-person or group shows with the downstairs exhibition area being given over to the display of larger sculptural or printed works. A permanent collection of contemporary Irish painters is held at the Arts Council of Northern Ireland's headquarters.
Sales: Work sold
The Space: The gallery consists of two spaces with the ground floor and the first floor area providing 35 and 25m of linear hanging space respectively. Gallery plans available.
Exhibiting: [AW] The gallery covers all exhibition costs and provides artists' expenses.
Access: [U][T] City Centre location; Public car park 3 mins

Belfast Public Libraries

Belfast Public Libraries is the administrative centre for all branch libraries in Belfast. Contact the Chief Librarian for details of branch libraries. [VA]

Address: Belfast Central Library, Royal Avenue, Belfast, Co Antrim BT1 1EA tel 0232 243233
Contact: Chief Librarian J Montgomery
Open: Library Hours
The Space: Details from each local branch librarian.

Bell Gallery

A commercial gallery showing a range of work from 19th century to contemporary work of Irish artists. [VA]

Address: 13 Adelaide Park, Belfast, Co Antrim BT9 6FX tel 0232 662998
Contact: Director Nelson Bell
Sales: Work sold
The Space: The gallery occupies two front rooms in a large detached Georgian house.
Exhibiting: [AW]
Access: [S] Bus 59; NIR Adelaide Station 2 mins; Car parking outside gallery

Cavehill Gallery

A commercial gallery run from the home of the owners, mainly specialising in contemporary Irish artists. [VA]

Address: 18 Old Cavehill Road, Belfast, Co Antrim BT15 5GT tel 0232 776784
Contact: Catherine & Joe McWilliams
Open: Mon-Sat 1-6
Policy: The gallery, situated off the gallery circuit in North Belfast, hopes to encourage mid-career artists who are under-exposed as well as a small number of younger artists. Of the eight exhibitions shown a year, all are solo shows, with the exception of a *'Summer mixed show'*. Exhibitions which last for two and a half weeks tend towards the *'figurative with abstract expressionist qualities'*.
Sales: Work sold; Credit scheme
The Space: The gallery is 4x6x4m high with linear hanging space of 32m. Work is hung from picture rails and lit by spots. Limitation on works exhibited 2x2m. A large garden may be used for sculpture exhibitions in the future.
Exhibiting: [AW] Artists should submit CV and documentation of work including recent catalogues during July and August. The gallery covers insurance, publicity and preview costs. 33.3% commission is charged on work sold.
Access: [S] Antrim Road buses; Car park available on street

Fenderesky Art Gallery

An independent gallery founded in 1983 and specialising in contemporary Irish art. [VA,Ph]

Address: 4 Malone Road, Belfast, Co Antrim BT9 tel 0232 681577
Contact: Jamshid Mirfenderesky
Open: Tues-Sat 12-6

Policy: The gallery aims to *'promote the art of the new generation of Irish artists and to bring to the attention of a wider public the nuances and the achievements of contemporary visual art in Ireland'*. Exhibitions are accompanied by regular lectures by artists, critics and historians on issues related to contemporary art in Ireland and worldwide.
Sales: Work sold; Credit scheme
The Space: The gallery is made up of three rooms giving a linear hanging space of 40m.
Exhibiting: The gallery covers insurance, preview and publicity costs of exhibitions and charges 40% commission on work sold.
Access: [S] Buses 59,69,71,72; NIR Botanic Station 10 mins; Parking space 5 mins

Magee Gallery

The gallery is part of John Magee Limited, fine art dealers and gift specialists, and is a commercial gallery specialising in traditional landscape and still life paintings and watercolours. [VA]
Address: 455/457 Ormeau Road, Belfast, Co Antrim BT7 3GQ tel 0232 693830
Contact: Managing Director R R Miller
Open: Mon-Sat 9-5
Policy: Throughout the year the gallery exhibits a changing display of work, mainly by artists producing representational work. Exhibitions of the work of individual artists are organised four times a year and last approximately two weeks. The gallery offers a framing and restoration service and sells limited edition prints.
Sales: Work sold; Sales referred to exhibitor; Credit card; Credit scheme
The Space: The exhibition area is 14x5x3m high with 22m linear hanging space.
Exhibiting: [AW] The gallery covers exhibition presentation costs except framing, mounting , transport and artists' expenses.
Access: [X]

Fendereskey Art Gallery

Octagon Gallery

The gallery, funded by the Arts Council of Northern Ireland shows predominantly contemporary Irish art. [VA,Ph,LA]
Address: Orpheus Building, York Street, Belfast, Co Antrim BT15 1AA tel 0232 246259
Contact: Exhibitions Director Liam Kelly
Open: Tues-Fri 11-5
Policy: The gallery exhibits contemporary Irish and international art including traditional forms and performance and installational work with an emphasis on community-related projects. Lectures and artists' talks are organised periodically.
Sales: Work sold
The Space: The gallery is 7x10x4m high with a linear hanging space of 30 metres. Work is hung directly on the walls and lit by spots. Gallery plans available.
Exhibiting: [AW] As budget permits the gallery usually tries to cover publicity, transport, catalogue and reception costs. Commission is 33.3%.
Access: [F][U][T] Buses 10,61,64; NIR York Street 15 mins; Car Park 2 mins

On The Wall Gallery

A commercial gallery run by the Kerlin Gallery in Dublin, specialising in promoting a small body of both younger and established contemporary artists living in Northern Ireland. [VA,Ph,Cr]
Address: 99 Botanic Avenue, Belfast, Co Antrim BT7 1JN tel 0232 231222
Contact: Director David Fitzgerald
Open: Mon-Sat 10-6
Policy: It presents regular exhibitions of its gallery artists, as well as providing a forum for many unestablished younger artists. Ceramics exhibitions are a regular feature of their exhibition programme and the gallery sells a range of contemporary ceramics and design artefacts. Roughly twelve exhibitions, mainly by living artists in solo shows, are organised a year and last approximately three weeks.
Sales: Work sold; Credit scheme; Credit card
The Space: One gallery of 25m of linear hanging space. The gallery has low-voltage lighting and hanging is by a mixture of rods and screws.
Exhibiting: [AW]
Access: [F] Full bus service; NIR Botanic station 1 min; City centre 10 mins

Tom Caldwell Galleries

A commercial gallery founded in 1974, which acts as agent for a small body of artists. [VA,Ce,Je]
Address: 52 Bradbury Place, Belfast, Co Antrim BT7 1RT tel 0232 323226
Contact: Tom Caldwell
Open: Mon-Fri 11-5, Sat 11-1
Policy: The gallery promotes a number of contemporary Irish artists and shows on average eight exhibitions a year; two of which are usually the work of young emerging artists.
Sales: Work sold; Credit scheme; Credit card
The Space: The gallery is 15x7x3m high with a linear hanging space of 40m. Work is hung from rods and lit

by spots.

Exhibiting: The gallery covers all costs except artists' expenses. 40% commission is charged on work sold.

Access: [X]

Ulster Museum

Northern Ireland's premier museum which has a well-equipped space for temporary exhibitions organises a programme of contemporary Irish and international art as well as curating a number of exhibitions by deceased Irish artists. [VA,Ph,Cr]

Address: Botanic Gardens, Belfast, Co Antrim tel 0232 668251

Contact: Director of Art Ted Hickey

Open: Mon-Fri 10-5, Sat 1-5, Sun 2-5

Policy: The museum does not accept applications from individual artists.

Access: [U][T] Buses 69; NIR Botanic Station 5 mins; Public car park 15 mins

Coleraine (Co Londonderry)

(ACNI) Map8 C83

University of Ulster (Riverside Gallery)

A university-run gallery situated in the main foyer of the Riverside Theatre, University of Ulster. [Pa,Pr,Dr,Ph]

Address: Riverside Theatre, Coleraine, Co Londonderry BT52 1SA tel 0265 44141 ext 4430

Contact: University Arts Administrator Jeremy Lewis

Open: Mon-Sat 10.30-10 (except when theatre is closed)

Policy: The gallery specialises in first exhibitions by young graduates, and targets its publicity at schools and students. There is a captive audience for exhibitions in so far as theatre patrons have to pass the work on display. The gallery organises a mixture of eight group and solo exhibitions a year, each lasting one month. Two major lectures take place a year over the University's four campuses on art and art-related topics and are open to the public and free of charge.

Sales: Work sold

The Space: The foyer has a total linear hanging space of 36m. Gallery plans available.

Exhibiting: [AW] The gallery covers all exhibition costs except display and artists' expenses. 15% commission is charged on work sold.

Access: [U][T][L][F] Regular bus and train services; Car park on site

Craigavon (Co Armagh)

(ACNI) Map8 J05

Brownlow Branch Library (Brownlow Library Gallery)

A library run by Southern Education and Library Board offering exhibition space to a wide variety of users. [VA,Ph,Cr]

Address: Brownlow Road, Craigavon, Co Armagh BT65 5DL tel 0762 341946

Contact: Librarian Aideen D'Arcy

Open: Mon,Wed,Fri 10-5.30, Tues,Thurs 10-8, Sat 10-5

Policy: The library aims to display arts and crafts from as wide a spectrum of artists, amateur and professional, as possible and is keen to encourage schools and children and local people who may not have had their work shown before; a particular *'standard'* of work is not insisted upon. School projects and publicity displays from charities and voluntary organisations also go to make up the programme.

Sales: Sales referred to exhibitor

The Space: The library has 30.5m linear hanging space available for exhibitions which are mounted on hessian-covered walls. Work is lit by strip and spot lighting; free-standing boards are also available.

Exhibiting: [AW] The library covers limited insurance and provides a list of exhibits.

Access: Bus stops outside library; Car park on site

Pinebank House Arts Centre (Peacock Gallery)

A gallery within Pinebank House Arts Centre complex run by Craigavon District Council running a regular programme of exhibitions mainly by young artists from Northern Ireland. [VA,Ph,Cr]

Address: Tullygally Road, Craigavon, Co Armagh BT65 5BY tel 0762 41033/41082

Contact: Art Development Officer Rosaleen McMullan tel 0762 41618

Open: Mon-Fri 10-5

Policy: The gallery presents a wide variety of contemporary sculpture, painting and mixed-media exhibitions especially by artists recently graduated from art college. Regular lectures and seminars are held in conjunction with exhibitions and group visits are arranged, if possible with the artist in attendance. A large courtyard is adjacent to the gallery and can be used for outdoor sculptural works. The gallery is sometimes used for public meetings. Twelve exhibitions by living artists are held each year.

Sales: Work sold

The Space: The gallery is 30x6x3m high with track lighting and a rail system for hanging. Gallery plans available.

Exhibiting: [AW] The gallery covers insurance and some publicity costs. No commission is charged on work sold.

Access: [U][T] Brownlow bus from Lurgan centre; Bus stop from train 5 mins; Car park on site

Derry (Co Londonderry)

(ACNI) Map8 C41

Foyle Arts Centre

The centre, funded by Derry City council with elements of the programme funded by Orchard Gallery, runs a varied programme of visual arts, music and performance based work. [VA,Ph,Cr,LA]

Address: Lawrence Hill, Derry, Co Londonderry BT48 7NJ tel 0504 260978

Contact: Organiser Declan McGonagle

Open: Tues-Sat 11-6

Policy: The centre is a multi-purpose venue, accommodating studio, workshop, residency, rehearsal,

seminar, conference and performance space. The centre also provides an administrative base for a number of professional and voluntary groups in the City as well as a series of neighbourhood projects linked to the city council community services programme. A range of contemporary visual art exhibitions, programmed by the Orchard Gallery, are organised at Foyle throughout the year.
Sales: Work sold
The Space: The centre is a renovated 19th century school building. Gallery plans available.
Exhibiting: [AW]

Gordon Gallery

A commercial gallery specialising mainly in established Irish painters and sculptors. [Pa,Sc]
Address: 36 Ferryquay Street, Derry, Co Londonderry BT48 6JB tel 0504 266261
Contact: Director Nat Gordon
Open: Mon-Fri,Wed 11-5.30, Thurs,Sat 11-1
Policy: The gallery organises twelve exhibitions a year usually by invitation. Occasionally work by English and European artists is shown and younger artists' work can be seen in annual Christmas and summer group shows.
Sales: Work sold
The Space: The gallery consists of two linked second floor spaces with a total area of 15x4m and 7x5m with a linear hanging space of 62m.
Exhibiting: 40% commission is charged on work sold.
Access: City Centre location

Orchard Gallery: 'Targets' a series of life size cut-out figures by Siteworks, a group of four artists involved in public art projects

Orchard Gallery

A major public gallery subsidised by the Arts Council of Northern Ireland and Derry City Council showing an ambitious programme of contemporary exhibitions from Ireland and abroad, including performance, film, installations and video. [VA,Ph,Cr,LA]
Address: Orchard Street, Derry, N Ireland BT48 6EG tel 0504 269675
Contact: Organiser Declan McGonagle
Open: Tues-Sat 10-6
Policy: The gallery runs a continuous programme of temporary exhibitions reflecting current activity in art, internationally, nationally, regionally and locally; mainly contemporary with occasional historical/retrospective exhibitions. The gallery collaborates regularly with other galleries to instigate major shows and throughout the year organises a varied programme of public art projects. Almost all exhibitions are accompanied by substantial publications and a variety of printed matter. A full programme of talks, discussions, seminars, films and events are organised around exhibitions and are determined in detail by the nature of each artist's work.
Sales: Work sold
The Space: The main gallery is 16x8x3.3m high and the side gallery of 4x4x3.3m high with linear hanging space of 48m and 12m respectively. Work is hung directly on the walls and lit by spots. Gallery plans available.
Exhibiting: [AW][AE] The gallery covers all exhibition costs and charges 15% commission on work sold. It supports the principle of EPR.
Access: [S] Bus station 2 mins; NIR Londonderry station 15 mins; Public car park 1 min

Enniskillen (Co Fermanagh)

(ACNI) Map8 H24

Ardhowen, The Theatre by the Lakes

Ardhowen is a regional theatre space with a restaurant and bar, running a continuous programme of photographic exhibitions. [Ph]
Address: Dublin Road, Enniskillen, Co Fermanagh tel 0365 23233
Contact: Manager & Artistic Director Eamonn Bradley
Open: Mon-Sat 11-4.30
Sales: Work sold
The Space: The exhibition space, based in the theatre foyer, is 25x12x2.5m high.
Access: [U][T] Buses 15 mins; Public car park on site

Fermanagh County Museum

The museum is run by Fermanagh District Council specialising in museological exhibitions. [Ph,Cr]
Address: Castle Barracks, Enniskillen, Co Fermanagh tel 0365 25050
Contact: Curator H Lanigan Wood
Open: Mon-Fri 10-5; closed 1-2; Sat (May-Sept) 2-5; Sun (Jul-Aug) 2-5
Policy: The museum aims to provide a wide range of social history, craft and local photography exhibitions. Exhibitions which last six weeks are organised six times a year, and accompanied by talks and lectures,

demonstrations and craft displays for school groups and the general public; a permanent collection of local history and archaeology is housed in the museum.
Sales: Work sold
The Space: The gallery is 6x13m and work is lit by low-voltage lighting.
Access: [X] Car park 1 min

Hillsborough (Co Down)

(ACNI) Map8 J25

Shambles Gallery

A commercial gallery which occupies part of a larger complex, the Hillsborough Arts Centre and specialises in showing the work of contemporary Irish painters and sculptors. [Pa,Sc]

Address: Inns Court Park Lane, Dromore Road, Hillsborough, Co Down tel 0846 682946
Contact: Administrator Sheila Flanagan
Open: Tues-Sat 10-5
Policy: The gallery with a stable of contemporary Irish artists organises three to four exhibitions a year and aims eventually to specialise in contemporary Irish sculpture. During the year poetry readings and musical events complement the programme. The gallery also houses a small collection of painting and sculpture which can be seen by appointment outside gallery opening hours.
Sales: Work sold; Credit scheme; Credit card
The Space: The gallery, originally two farm labourers' cottages, is approximately 333 square metres. Gallery plans available.
Exhibiting: [AW] The gallery covers publicity and preview costs.
Access: [U][T] Ulsterbus 38 3 mins; Public car park 8 mins

Lisburn (Co Antrim)

(ACNI) Map8 J26

Harmony Hill Arts Centre

The arts centre is run and funded by the local council and as well as running a regular programme of exhibitions, it organises workshops and adult classes etc. [VA,Ph,Cr]

Address: 54 Harmony Hill, Lisburn, Co Antrim BT27 4EF tel 08462 78219
Contact: Arts Organiser Chris Bailey
Open: Mon-Fri 9-10, Sat 10-1
Policy: The arts centre presents a range of local amateur group exhibitions and individual shows of contemporary art, as well as accommodating provincial touring exhibitions. Exhibitions last two weeks and over the last year, 22 exhibitions by living artists were organised. The centre is situated in extensive grounds which can be made available for outdoor works.
Sales: Work sold
The Space: The space is 6.25x4.5x3.5m high and an adjacent room 3.5x3.5x3.5m high is also available. Work is lit by spots. Other rooms and areas also used for exhibition purposes where appropriate. Gallery plans available.
Exhibiting: [AW] The centre covers most exhibition costs but does not cover transport or artists' expenses. 10% commission is charged on work sold. The centre supports in principle EPR.
Access: [U] Bus Belfast 5 mins; NIR Lambeg Station 10 mins; Car park on site

Lurgan (Co Armagh)

(ACNI) Map8 J05

Lurgan College of Further Education (Corridor Gallery)

The gallery is run by the Creative Arts Department of Lurgan College of Further Education and draws its name from its location in the entrance foyer. [VA,Ph,Cr,LA]

Address: Lurgan College of Further Education, Kitchen Hill, Lurgan, Co Armagh BT66 6AZ tel 0762 326135
Contact: Gallery Director Dan Bruijel
Open: Mon-Fri 9-5
Policy: The gallery, established in 1984, originally provided a platform for local and visiting photographers, but over the years has expanded its programme to include a very diverse range of mixed-media, painting, and sculpture exhibitions. All its exhibitions feature the work of living artists, and in the sixteen shows it organises each year it has been particularly supportive of the talent emerging in its local constituency. As well as building up a collection of contemporary art, the gallery organises regular lectures and seminars, conducted by exhibiting artists, critics, gallery directors, etc. Grounds around the college are available for outdoor work.
The Space: The gallery space, 21x9m is lit by both natural light and spots. 16 glass and wooden showcases are available. Gallery plans available.
Exhibiting: [AW] The gallery covers all exhibition costs, except framing or mounting of works and artists' exhibition expenses.
Access: [U][L] Trains 5 mins; Car park on site

Lurgan College of Further Education: 'Battle Lines' from the Craigavon series by Brendan Kelly, artist in residence at the Brownlow Rescource Centre

Newcastle (Co Down)

(ACNI) Map8 J33

Newcastle Centre

The centre, run by Down District Council, is part of the local leisure centre with a foyer exhibition area. [VA,Ph,Cr]

Address: Central Promenade, Newcastle, Co Down tel 03967 22222

Contact: Arts Officer Belinda Loftus, Down District Council, 24 St Nangford Road, Downpatrick BT30 6SR tel 0396 614331 ext 255

Open: Mon-Sat 10-10, Sun 2-6

Policy: The centre aims to bring a wide range of contemporary visual arts to the area, prinicipally for local viewers, but also for those outside the district. One exhibition/visual arts event is mounted a month, using the Newcastle Centre, Down Leisure Centre and local libraries etc. These events feature work *'by professional and amateur, traditional and avant garde, student and established artists from the district, the rest of Ireland and elsewhere'*. Talks, workshops and discussions are organised on a regular basis and the council has a small collection of paintings and prints by artists from the district.

Sales: Sales referred to exhibitor

The Space: The exhibition space is 7x7x3m high with a 9m linear hanging space. Screens are also available for hanging work.

Exhibiting: [AW] Artists should submit CV and a minimum of six and a maximum of twelve slides of recent work. The centre covers insurance and exhibition presentation costs with display, transport, catalogue and artists' expenses discretionary.

Access: [U][F] Buses from Belfast and Newry; Public car park on site

Newry (Co Down)

(ACNI) Map8 J02

Newry & Mourne Arts Centre

The centre, run by Newry and Mourne District Council, organises a regular programme of exhibitions as well as theatre, drama, music and dance events. [VA,Ph,Cr]

Address: 1A Bank Parade, Newry, Co Down tel 0693 61244

Contact: Arts Director John Keyes

Open: Mon-Sat 11-10.30; closed 4-7.30

Policy: The centre which has three galleries catering for local amateur artists, young professional artists and established artists, aims to provide the public of Newry with a cross-section of visual art activity. The foyer gallery shows local Arts Society members' work i.e. landscape and still lives etc.; the Museum gallery caters for young unrecognised artists or exhibitions of local topical interest; and the Carrol Gallery promotes the work of contemporary Irish and occasionally European artists. A craft shop is housed in the building and the centre has a permanent collection of contemporary art and local and historical interest artefacts.

Sales: Work sold

The Space: Gallery plans available.

Exhibiting: [AW] The centre covers all exhibitions costs except framing and mounting. 10% commission is charged on work sold in the Carroll Gallery and the other two galleries are hired on a daily basis.

Access: [U][L][F] Town centre location

Newtownards (Co Down)

(ACNI) Map8 J47

Ards Arts Centre

The arts centre is run by the local authority through an arts sub-committee which is responsible for on and off-site arts promotions of the council. [VA,Ph,Cr]

Address: Town Hall, Conway Square, Newtownards, Co Down BT23 4DD tel 0247 810803

Contact: Arts Officer Maureen Armstrong

Open: Mon-Fri 9-5

Policy: The gallery aims to widen the appeal of arts and crafts amongst the local community. Exhibitions are mostly drawn from professional and semi-professional artists within the area and take place approximately sixteen times a year. Art classes are run on a regular basis for schools and members of the public.

Sales: Work sold

The Space: Two galleries 26x26m and 19x19m with a total linear hanging space of 28.5m. Work is hung from brass hooks and lit by a combination of daylight and fluorescent overhead lighting.

Exhibiting: [AW] Artists should make applications one year in advance of proposed exhibition. The gallery covers insurance and a proportion of publicity and charges no commission on work sold.

Access: [F] Bus 10 mins (to Belfast); Car park 10 mins

Omagh (Co Tyrone)

(ACNI) Map8 H47

Western Education & Library Board

WELB is the administrative centre for all branch libraries in its jurisdiction. Contact the Chief Librarian for details of branch libraries. [VA]

Address: WELB Library Service, 41 Dublin Road, Omagh, Co Tyrone BT78 1HG tel 0662 44821

Contact: Chief Librarian Russell Farrow

Open: Library hours

The Space: Details from each local branch librarian.

Portadown (Co Armagh)

(ACNI) Map8 J05

Roy Edwards Fine Arts

A commercial gallery specialising in traditional Irish landscape painting. [Pa]

Address: Mahon Road, Portadown, Co Armagh BT62 3EH tel 0762 339116

Contact: Directors Roy Woolsey and Edward Cassidy

Open: Mon-Fri 9-5.30; closed 1-2

Policy: The gallery shows a continuous display of oils

and watercolours by Irish landscape artists which are purchased from the artist outright. Occasionally solo exhibitions lasting three to four weeks are organised in conjunction with the continuous programme. The gallery's main outlet is to private houses and presentation gifts etc.
Sales: Work sold
Exhibiting: All paintings selected for exhibition are purchased from the artist and therefore there is no commission charged.
Access: **[F]** Bus Portadown/Newry; Car park on site

Portrush (Co Antrim)

(ACNI) Map8 C84

Portrush Gallery

A commercial gallery specialising in mainly marine and landscape figurative painting. [Pa]
Address: 93-95 Main Street, Portrush, Co Antrim tel 0265 823739
Contact: Gabrielle Orok
Open: Mon-Sat 10-6; closed Wed
Policy: The gallery runs a continuous display of works by local artists and is keen to encourage younger artists. It sees its target audience as the general public and tourists.
Sales: Work sold; Credit scheme
The Space: The gallery is made up of three rooms 7.5x6x2.75m high, 3x3x2.75m high and 6x3x2,3m high with linear hanging space of 21, 10 and 15m respectively. Works are hung by cords and lit by a combination of fluorescent, tungsten and natural light.
Exhibiting: **[AW]** The gallery covers no exhibition costs and charges 25% commission on work sold.
Access: **[F]** Bus 5 mins; NIR Portrush station 5 mins; Car park 3 mins

Portstewart (Co Londonderry)

(ACNI) Map8 C83

Flowerfield Arts Centre (Flowerfield Gallery)

Part of the Flowerfield Arts Centre, the gallery occupies two spaces and shows mainly young artists from Northern Ireland. [VA,Ph,Cr]
Address: 185 Coleraine Road, Portstewart, Co Londonderry BT55 7HU tel 0265 833959
Contact: Centre Organiser Cara MacMahon
Open: Mon-Fri 10-5, Sat 10-2
Policy: The gallery aims to offer a platform to younger artists and local non-professional artists to provide experience of exhibiting and increasing the artists' profile in Northern Ireland. As it caters for a local audience and tourists, it encourages local amateur artists to take part in small group exhibitions. As well as presenting painting and sculpture, the gallery shows a wide range of textiles, photographs, lace and weaving and also Arts Council of Northern Ireland touring exhibitions. Twelve month-long shows are organised a year. The gallery has a permanent collection of contemporary prints and the centre runs classes and courses in the arts.**Sales:** Work sold; Credit scheme
The Space: The three galleries are 11x5x3.3m high and 6.5x6x3.3m high and 5x4x3.3m high and lit with spot lights and/or natural light. The linear hanging space is 21 and 11m respectively. Works are hung by rods and there are twelve plinths of various sizes. Gallery plans available.
Exhibiting: **[AW]** All artists welcome to submit applications. The gallery covers all costs except framing and mounting of works, transportation and artists' expenses. 20% commission is charged on sales.
Access: **[F]** Buses Coleraine/Portstewart 140; Car park on site

Warrenpoint (Co Down)

(ACNI) Map8 J11

Narrow Water Gallery

A new private gallery specialising in contemporary Irish, British and international art. [VA,Ph,Cr]
Address: Narrow Water Castle, Warrenpoint, Co Down BT34 3LE tel 06937 73940
Contact: Director Maeve Hall
Open: Tues-Sat 2-6, Wed 2-8
Policy: The gallery aims to promote contemporary mainstream art in a rural context as well as providing a platform for local artists in Down district. Artist in residence schemes and painting weekends are planned for the future as well as schools visits and evening classes.
Sales: Work sold
The Space: The gallery consists of 660x660m spread across two large rooms situated in the Narrow Water Castle. Work is hung directly on the walls and lit by halogen spots. Gallery plans available.
Exhibiting: **[AW]** The gallery covers all exhibition costs except artists' expenses and charges 40% commission on work sold. The gallery supports in principle EPR.
Access: **[X]** Although arrangements can be made for group disabled visits. Bus Newry-Warrenpoint 1 min; Public car park on site

Right: Gatehouse Gallery, Glasgow. Gallery entrance

SCOTLAND

Aberdeen (Grampian Region)

(SAC) Map1 NJ90

Aberdeen Art Gallery & Museums

A municipal gallery founded in 1884, run by City of Aberdeen District Council with a temporary programme and a permanent collection covering all aspects of the visual arts. [VA,Ph,Cr,Fi,Vi,Ar,LA]

Address: Schoolhill, Aberdeen AB9 1FQ tel 0224 646333
Contact: Director Ian McKenzie Smith
Open: Mon-Sat 10-5, Sun 2-5, Thurs 10-8
Policy: The gallery's aim is to *'stimulate and maintain the public's interest in the arts through a vigorous programme of acquisition, conservation, research, interpretation and exhibition, along with related events based on material available from local, Scottish and international sources.'* Many temporary exhibitions came through other organisations (like the Arts Council and the Scottish Museums Council). Of the 84 exhibitions the gallery showed in 1988 at least 44 included work by living artists and ten were solo shows. The permanent collection contains work from the 18th, 19th and 20th centuries with an emphasis on contemporary fine and applied art. There is an artist and craftworker in residence programme. Workshops, children's activities and talks are held. In addition, the gallery runs a programme which includes world cinema, dance, literature, drama and music.
Sales: Work sold; Credit card
The Space: The three rooms for the temporary exhibitions programme have a total linear hanging space of 132.26m. There is a lighting track and de-humidifiers in all three rooms. Edmonds cases are available for display. Gallery plans are available.
Exhibiting: [AW] Artists should contact the Director at least 18 months in advance. The gallery normally covers most exhibition costs. Minimum commission is 25%.
Access: [U][T][L] Bus & BR Aberdeen stations 10 mins; Parking 250m; Aberdeen Airport & Heliport 25 mins

Aberdeen Arts Centre Gallery

A gallery within an arts centre with a particular emphasis on theatre. [VA,Ph,Cr]

Address: 33 King Street, Aberdeen AB2 3AA tel 0224 635208
Contact: Administrator Arthur Deans
Open: Mon-Sat 10-5
Policy: The gallery provides space for local artists as well as mounting occasional touring exhibitions. Of the 15 exhibitions a year, about nine are solo shows. All work is by living artists. The gallery also has a collection of prints by local artists.
Sales: Work sold
The Space: Main gallery (6x8x3m high) has 25m linear hanging space. The corridor has 25m linear hanging space and the secondary room 17m linear. Hanging is by rods with sliding hooks, and there are spot lights and tungston bulbs. The gallery also has a glass case on legs.
Exhibiting: [AW] Contact the Administrator in writing or by phone. Commission 20% on work sold.
Access: [U][T][L][F] City centre

Grays School of Art

Exhibition space within Aberdeen's art college. [VA,LA]

Address: Garthdee, Aberdeen AB9 2OB tel 0224 313247
Contact: Prof Eric Spiller
Policy: The college shows a programme of temporary exhibitions of fine art and design, mainly for the benefit of students. However, larger exhibitions with the public in mind are occasionally held.

Peacock/Artspace

Peacock Printmakers and Artspace merged in 1986 into an organisation which includes printmaking facilities and a gallery specialising in contemporary art. [VA,Ph]

Address: 21 Castle Street, Aberdeen AB1 1AJ tel 0224 639539
Contact: Director Arthur Watson
Open: Mon-Sat 9.30-5.30
Policy: The exhibition programme includes work of national and international importance. The Peacock Gallery shows mainly prints, photographs and work by North East artists. Artspace shows larger group and solo shows by contemporary painters. Touring exhibitions from other major galleries in Scotland are also shown. Of the 30 exhibitions a year, 70% are solo shows and each exhibition is shown for three to four weeks. The gallery aims to show exhibitions which cater for both public and artists in the area. An education officer has increased the number of workshops and classes for the community and schools. Talks are held regularly.
Sales: Work sold
The Space: There are three galleries. Gallery one has 45-60m linear hanging space, Gallery two 23m linear, Peacock Gallery 15m linear. Hanging in all galleries is by rods and direct fixing. There is halogen lighting and spots.
Exhibiting: [AW] Artists should write with details to the Exhibitions Officer. The gallery covers cost of insurance, printing and mailing of publicity, list of exhibits, preview and display. Commission 33.3% on work sold.
Access: [U][T][F] Car Park 2 mins; BR Aberdeen 10 mins

Alloa (Central Region)

(SAC) Map2 NS89

Alloa Museum

A small local museum which shows occasional temporary exhibitions.

Address: 15 Mar Street, Alloa, Clackmannanshire FK10 1HT tel 0259 722160
Open: Mon,Wed,Thurs,Fri 10.30-6, Tues 10.30-4, Sat 9.30-12
Access: Next to District Library

Arbroath (Tayside Region)

(SAC) Map2 NO64

Arbroath Art Gallery

An art gallery specialising in local work with a large collection of paintings by JW Herald. [Pa,Cr]

Address: Public Library, Hill Terrace, Arbroath DD11 1AH tel 72248

Contact: Montrose Museum & Art Gallery, Panmure Place, Montrose DD10 8HE tel 0674 73232

Open: Mon-Fri 9.30-6, Sat 9.30-5

Policy: Annual programme of around ten temporary exhibitions mostly solo exhibitions by local artists and makers. Occasional group and society exhibitions.

Exhibiting: Gallery available for hire.

Access: Town centre site

Ayr (Strathclyde Region)

(SAC) Map2 NS32

Maclaurin Art Gallery & Rozelle House

A municipal gallery set in a country park run by Kyle and Carrick District Council. [VA,Ph,Ce,Je,LA]

Address: Monument Road, Ayr, Ayrshire KA7 4NQ tel 0292 45447/43708

Contact: Curator Mike Bailey

Open: Mon-Sat 11-5; Sun 2-5 April-Oct

Policy: The gallery aims to promote contemporary art through national touring exhibitions as well as developing their own collection of contemporary art which includes work by Henry Moore and Bridget Riley. It also provides the opportunity for local community groups and young artists and makers (professional and amateur) to show in a professional gallery at low cost within a wide range of exhibitions. Talks and workshops are held occasionally and there is a regular programme of art videos. The gallery holds 50 exhibitions a year, 80% of which are by living artists and 20% solo shows.

Sales: Work sold

The Space: The five rooms for temporary exhibitions in the Maclaurin Art Gallery have 21, 21, 33, 30 and 28 linear metres hanging space, and a selection of showcases is available. There is a courtyard area. Rozelle House's two exhibition rooms are occasionally offered to artists but are mostly used for local displays and the permanent collection. Linear hanging space is 30.3 and 25.7 metres respectively. Access is restricted to canvasses 220cm and crates 170x40cm.

Exhibiting: [AW] Artists and makers are invited to apply to the Curator at any time. The gallery covers cost of insurance, list of exhibits and mailing out of publicity. Commission 20% on work sold. EPR would be supported.

Access: [F] On bus route from Ayr town centre; Parking within Rozelle Park; BR Ayr 20 mins

Broughton (Borders Region)

(SAC) Map2 NT13

Broughton Gallery

A private commercial gallery in a rural setting. [VA,Ph,Cr]

Address: Broughton, Nr Biggar, Lanarkshire ML12 6HJ tel 08994 234

Contact: Director Graham Buchanan-Dunlop

Open: Daily 10.30-6; Closed Wed April-Sept & mid-Nov to mid-Dec

Policy: The gallery promotes the work of both established and lesser- known British artists and makers, generally favouring a figurative style. Seven exhibitions a year are held, all the work of living artists and including four solo shows. Visitors to the gallery include residents of Edinburgh and Glasgow and tourists from England and abroad. Occasional concerts are mounted.

Sales: Work sold

The Space: A total of 42m linear hanging space in three spaces - main gallery, corridor and hall. Ceiling height 4 metres throughout. Track lighting, hanging from rails.

Exhibiting: [AW] Individual artists are invited to write with photographs at any time. The gallery covers most of the cost of insurance, printing and mailing of publicity, list of exhibits, preview and catalogue/card. Commission 33.3% on work sold.

Access: [S] Infrequent bus service to Broughton; Parking at gallery

Buckie (Grampian Region)

(SAC) Map1 NJ46

Buckie Maritime Museum & Peter Anson Gallery

A local museum with an adjoining gallery with a small permanent collection. [Pa,Ph]

Address: Townhouse West, Cluny Place, Buckie, Moray AB5 1HB tel 0542 32121

Contact: District Curator Ian Morrison, Falconer Museum, Tolbooth Street, Forres, Moray IV36 OPH tel 0309 73701

Open: Mon-Fri 10-8, Sat 10-12

Broughton Gallery (Photo: Colin Baxter)

Policy: Temporary exhibitions are held.
The Space: One gallery 6.5x5.4m.
Exhibiting: **[AW]** Write to the District Curator with full information and proposals.
Access: **[F]** Town centre; Car park

Carnoustie (Tayside Region)

(SAC) Map2 NO53

Carnoustie Public Library

A varied programme of fine art exhibitions in a first floor gallery. [Pa]

Address: High Street, Carnoustie, Tayside DD7 tel 0241 59620
Contact: Librarian

Castle Douglas (Dumfries & Galloway)

(SAC) Map2 NX73

Castle Douglas Art Gallery

A gallery which houses the permanent collection of paintings by Ethel Bristowe. [Pa]

Address: Market Street, Castle Douglas DG7 1BE tel 0557 30291
Contact: Director of Administration Council Offices, Kirkcudbright DG6 4JG
Open: Gallery locked - key can be obtained during office hours from District Council Offices, St Andrew Street, Castle Douglas
Policy: Temporary exhibitions of local artists are held.
Access: Town centre

Cleland (Strathclyde Region)

(SAC) Map2 NS75

Cleland Arts Schoolhouse

An Urban-Aid funded project set up to stimulate participation in the visual and performing arts.

Address: 24 Main Street, Cleland, Lanarkshire ML1 5QN tel 0698 861740
Contact: Project Leader Gordon Swinton
Open: Mon-Fri 9-4.45, 5.30-9.30
Policy: The schoolhouse is a new project with an educational priority. *'We offer classes and activities throughout the year for children, youth and adults.'* Exhibitions are held within this community learning context. The arts centre is funded in part by Strathclyde Regional Council and the Scottish Office Urban Renewal Unit.
Sales: Work sold
The Space: The gallery is 6x4x3m high with low-voltage track lighting and hanging by hooks and wire. A garden to the front of the schoolhouse can be used for sculpture.
Exhibiting: **[AW]** The exhibition space is also for hire. The gallery covers cost of insurance, printing of publicity and list of exhibits. Commission 15% on work sold.
Access: **[U][T]** BR Cleland 10 mins; Bus routes from Wishaw 44.92.93.248

Cumnock (Strathclyde Region)

(SAC) Map2 NS51

Baird Institute Museum

A municipal museum and gallery run by Cumnock and Doon Valley District Council. [Pa,Ph,Cr]

Address: Lugar Street, Cumnock, Ayrshire KA18 1AD tel 0290 22111
Contact: Curator John Laurenson, Cumnock & Doon Valley District Library H.Q., Council Offices, Lugar, Ayrshire, KA18 3JQ
Open: Fri 9.30-1, 1.30-4, Sat 11-1
Policy: Aiming to promote local arts and crafts in the area, the gallery mainly shows work by the local art group and the local camera club once a year. The rest of the exhibition programme tends to relate to museum subjects. Each exhibition lasts two months.
Sales: Work sold; Sales referred to exhibitor
The Space: The exhibition area has room for about 100 average-sized paintings and drawings. Lighting has UV exclusion film.
Exhibiting: **[AW]** Write to the Curator at the Cumnock & Doon Valley District Library.
Access: **[X]**

Dalkeith (Lothian Region)

(SAC) Map2 NT36

Dalkeith Arts Centre

A gallery run by the Dalkeith Arts Guild. [VA,Cr]

Address: White Hart Street, Dalkeith EH22 1AE tel 031 663 6986
Contact: District Librarian B D Osborne, Midlothian District Libraries, 7 Station Road, Roslin EH25 9PF tel 031 440 2210
Policy: As well as a temporary exhibition programme, the centre also holds concerts, public and private meetings and library events.
Sales: Work sold
The Space: There are 26.5m linear hanging space in a room 15.5x7.3x3m high with picture rails for hanging, spotlights and general overhead lighting and natural light on one wall.
Exhibiting: Write to the Dalkeith Arts Guild at the centre for details of applying.
Access: **[U][T]**

Dumbarton (Strathclyde Region)

(SAC) Map2 NS47

Dumbarton Public Library

Exhibition space within Dumbarton Public Library. [Pa,Ph]

Address: Strathleven Place, Dumbarton G82 1BD tel 0389 63129
Contact: Assistant Director of Civic Amenities Michael Taylor, Library HQ, Levenford House, Helenslee Road, Dumbarton, G82 4AJ tel 0389 65100
Open: Mon,Tues,Thurs 10-8, Wed,Fri,Sat 10-5
Policy: The museum room exhibits mainly thematic

presentations relating to the history of the area. The balcony exhibits work by local artists and art clubs. Small touring exhibitions are hired in. There are about ten balcony exhibitions a year. Talks and meetings are also held in the balcony.

Sales: Sales referred to exhibitor

The Space: About 20m linear hanging space with parallel wooden hanging ribs. No work over 2 metres wide and 1 metre high.

Exhibiting: **[AW]** Write to the Assistant Director at least six months in advance. The gallery covers cost of insurance, printing of publicity and list of exhibits.

Access: **[U][T][L][X]** for balcony only Local buses stop 100 yards away; BR Dumbarton Central 200 yards; Car park adjacent

Dumfries (Dumfries & Galloway Region)

() Map2 NX97

Bryden Gallery

A commercial gallery specialising in Scottish landscape painting with changing displays and temporary exhibitions. [VA,Ce,Je]

Address: 11 Galloway Street, Dumfries, Dumfries & Galloway DG2 7TL tel 0387 67337

Contact: Hugh Bryden

Open: Mon-Wed, Fri,Sat 10-5

Policy: Displays work by local artists, 19th and 20th century paintings of South West Scotland and original artists' prints ranging from 19th century to present day. About three exhibitions a year lasting two weeks of work by living artists.

Sales: Work sold

The Space: 19m linear hanging space with direct fixing, spotlights on track. Two small jewellery cases. Gallery plans available.

Exhibiting: **[AW]** Exhibitions are by invitation and application. Gallery covers insurance, publicity and list of exhibits. Commission is 25%. Supports the principle of EPR.

Access: **[F]** BR Dumfries 5 mins; Bus station 2 mins; Car park close

Bryden Gallery

Gracefield - The Arts Centre for South West Scotland

A municipal arts centre run by Dumfries and Galloway Regional Council showing temporary exhibitions of contemporary art. [VA,Ph,Cr,LA]

Address: 28 Edinburgh Road, Dumfries DG1 1JQ tel 0387 62084

Contact: Dumfries & Galloway Arts Officer John Stewart-Young

Open: Daily 12-5 Winter; Mon-Sat 10-5, Sun 12-5 Summer

Policy: In the past, work of a traditional nature has been shown in the five galleries, but with the opening of new studios the scope of the programme has been widened to include all forms of contemporary art including performance. *'The gallery aims to show the best work being made both in the region and nationally through a lively programme of exhibitions.'* The permanent collection (mostly Scottish School - Glasgow Boys etc.) is shown at regular intervals. With the emphasis on a younger audience, the studios also accommodate many local community arts groups. Workshops and lectures with visiting artists and photographers are held on a regular basis.

Sales: Work sold

The Space: There are five galleries, the largest 10.9x3.6m, with track lighting and hanging rods. There are also four new studios and a large exhibition hall is 15.15x9m for exhibiting with track lighting and screens.

Exhibiting: **[AW]** Artists are advised to send a letter with slides in September. The gallery covers cost of insurance, list of exhibits and mailing of publicity. Commission 20% on work sold.

Access: **[U][T]** Arts centre car park; Town centre 10 mins

Robert Burns Centre

A municipal museum/gallery run by Nithsdale District Council. [Pa,Pr,Dr,Ph]

Address: Mill Road, Dumfries DG2 7BE tel 0387 64808

Contact: Curator David Lockwood, Dumfries Museum, The Observatory, Dumfries DG2 7SW tel 0387 53374

Gracefield Arts Centre: paper person looking at the Inverclyde Biennial, 1988

Open: Mon-Sat 10-8, Sun 2-5 April-Sept; Tues-Sat 10-1, 2-5 Oct-March
Policy: The museum's main function is to tell the story of Robert Burns, Scotland's most famous poet. There are, however, six temporary exhibitions held a year, usually showing the work of local artists, of which about two are solo shows. The centre includes an audio-visual theatre, exhibition area, shop and café.
Sales: Sales referred to exhibitor
The Space: The wall space amounts to about 60m linear, frequently interrupted by windows and therefore not suitable for large works. The hanging hook and rail system must be used by exhibitors.
Exhibiting: [AW] Artists should write for an application form from the Director at Dumfries Museum. The space is booked rather than work selected. No hire fee is charged, but no costs are covered by gallery.
Access: [U][T][L] BR Dumfries 20 mins; Bus station 5 mins

Dunblane (Central Region)

(SAC) Map2 NN70

Cornerstone Gallery

A small commercial gallery in a 400-year old building. [Pa]
Address: Cathedral Square, Dunblane, Perthshire FK10 OLH tel 0786 823696
Contact: Mr & Mrs Flockhart
Open: Mon-Sat 9.30-12.30, 1-5
Policy: Only professional living artists shown. A wide range of work shown - landscape to abstract, watercolour to oil. Of the 13 exhibitions shown each year, nine are solo shows.
Sales: Work sold
The Space: One room with 26m linear hanging space and natural and overhead lighting. Painting size maximum 1x1m.
Exhibiting: [AW] Contact the gallery. Commission and hire of the gallery is negotiable.
Access: [X]

Dundee (Tayside Region)

(SAC) Map2 NO43

Bonar Hall

[Ph]
Address: The University of Dundee, Park Place, Dundee DD1 4HN tel 0382 29450
Contact: Director John Cassels
Open: Open as advertised
Policy: A regular programme of photography exhibitions.

Duncan of Jordanstone College

Three gallery spaces within Dundee's college of art. [VA,Ph,Cr,Ar,LA]
Address: Perth Road, Dundee, Angus DD1 4HT tel 0382 23261
Contact: Exhibitions Organiser Peter Esgate
Open: Francis Cooper Gallery Mon-Fri 10-4; Angela Bradshaw Gallery Mon-Thurs 9.30-8.30, Fri 9.30-5; Level 5 Artspace Mon-Fri 9-9, Sat 9-4
Policy: The galleries aim to promote contemporary art in all its aspects and media and at the same time complement the teaching syllabus.
Sales: Sales referred to exhibitor
The Space: The Francis Cooper Gallery is 17x9x3.5m, the Angela Bradshaw Gallery is 8x6.5x2.3m, Level 5 is 30x12x3.5m. Approximately 42m linear hanging space in total. Hanging systems include hooks, picture rods and mirror plates.
Exhibiting: [AW] Artists are asked to apply in writing to the Exhibitions Organiser. The college cover all exhibition costs within agreed limits and exhibitors occasionally receive a fee. The EPR would be supported.
Access: [U][T][L][F] BR Dundee15 mins; Bus stops outside college; City centre 10 mins

Dundee Arts Centre

The centre has no purpose-built exhibition space but can adapt the main hall, cafe and corridors for occasional use. [Pa]
Address: St Mary Place, Dundee DD1 5RB tel 0382 201035
Contact: Senior Community Education Worker George Docherty
Open: Mon-Fri 9.30-7.30, Sat 9.30-12.30
Policy: Works relevant to the community are favoured.
Exhibiting: There is a total of 90m linear hanging space in a gallery, corridor and café.
Access: 1 mile city centre off Lochee Road; Car park

Dundee Central Library

The Central Library with main exhibition area and a foyer for larger exhibitions.
Address: The Wellgate, Dundee, Tayside DD1 1DB tel 0382 23141 ext 4335
Contact: Principal Librarian Moira Methven
Open: Mon-Fri 9.30-9pm, Sat 9.30-5
Policy: The exhibition area is available free of charge to non-profit making organisations. The Libraries Department is responsible for the management of the area including the monitoring of the nature and standard of the exhibits.
The Space: The main exhibition area is about 72 square metres an additional space 25x4m is available for larger exhibitions in the Upper Foyer and is suitable for exhibition boards (16, 1.3x1m Marler Haley boards) arranged in row.
Access: [L] from shopping mall and multi-storey car park Situated in shopping mall; Car park adjacent

Dundee Rep Gallery

A gallery in the foyer of Dundee Repetory Theatre. [VA,Ph,Cr]
Address: Tay Square, Dundee DD1 1PB tel 0382 27684
Contact: House Manager Ann Pledger
Open: Mon-Sat 10-10
Policy: The policy is to show a diverse range of contemporary work by artists in the Dundee area in this

multi-purpose space. The gallery's activities are funded by commission on work sold.

Sales: Work sold

The Space: 18m linear hanging space in the foyer, plus other wall spaces when available.

Exhibiting: [AW] Gallery covers cost of insurance and list of exhibits. Commission 25% on work sold.

Access: [U][T] BR Dundee 5 mins; Public car park 2 mins

McManus Galleries

A muncipal gallery and museum with a permanent collection and a programme of temporary exhibitions run by City of Dundee District Council. [VA,Ph,Cr,LA]

Address: Dundee Art Galleries & Museums, McManus Galleries, Albert Square, Dundee DD1 1DA tel 0382 23141

Contact: Curator Adam Ritchie

Open: 10-5 Mon-Sat

Policy: The exhibition programme includes touring shows from other organisations and shows initiated in-house. The latter includes those developing themes suggested by the permanent collection which is weighted towards 19th and 20th century Scottish art. Temporary exhibitions range from historic themes to contemporary art, though there is an emphasis on Scottish art. Of the 15 exhibitions shown a year, nine are by living artists and five are solo shows. Each exhibition is shown for four to six weeks. The education department runs workshops, talks and schools events.

Sales: Work sometimes for sale

The Space: Gallery 5 has 20.7m linear hanging space, Gallery 7 has 54.9m linear hanging space, Gallery 8 has 48.8m linear hanging space and Gallery 9 has 29.9m linear hanging space. The hanging system is by hooks into horizontal steel wallbars and the lighting a mixture of daylight and track lighting with Par 38 and wall floods. Heating is thermostatically controlled with portable humidification units. The gallery has standard upright and desk Edmonds cases.

Exhibiting: [AW] Artists should contact the Keeper of Art in writing with details of proposal at least 18 months in advance of proposed date. Commissions have been rare in the past but the gallery is considering commissioning installation work for future exhibitions. Costs covered depends on the type of exhibition. Commission 15% on work sold.

Access: [U][T][L][F] BR Dundee 10 mins; Car parks 2 and 5 mins

Roseangle Gallery

A gallery owned and run by the Dundee Art Society with a permanent collection of former members' work from the past 100 years and which holds regular temporary exhibitions. [VA,Cr]

Address: 17 Roseangle, Dundee DD1 4LP tel 0382 22429

Contact: Exhibitions Convener Margaret McIntyre, Bridge House, 9 Beechwood Terrace, Dundee

Open: Daily 11-5 during exhibitions

Policy: The gallery, to which the audience is mostly local, shows work mainly by members of the Dundee Art Society, but occasionaly there are shows of work by students from Dundee College of Art. At least three solo shows by artists who aren't necessarily members are shown a year. Also three group exhibitions of members' work, professional and amateur. A series of lectures and social events is run throughout the winter months.

Sales: Work sold

The Space: The main gallery is 15.8x4.5x3m high, the side gallery is 3.9x4.8x2.5m high and an entrance gallery is 4.8x3.4x2.5m high, with a linear hanging space of 35.3m, 15.1m, 11.3m respectively. All work must go through a standard door and weigh no more than a piano.

Exhibiting: [AW] Applications with details of work, slides or photographs and a short CV should be sent to the Exhibitions Convener's address. The gallery is run on a hire system and is available at £40 per week (including heat and light) plus 20% commission on work sold. This does not include preview, publicity or invigilation costs which are dealt with on an individual basis.

Access: [S] BR Dundee 10 mins; Any Perth Road bus; Art college & University 3 mins

Seagate Gallery

A new gallery for contemporary art and printmakers' workshop founded in 1986 by the Dundee Printmakers' Workshop. [VA]

Address: 36-40 Seagate, Dundee DD1 2EJ tel 0382 26331

Contact: Keith Fraser

Open: Mon-Sat 10-5.30

Policy: The emphasis to date has been on the work of younger, lesser-known artists. Approximately 13 exhibitions, of which nine are solo, are shown each year. Each exhibition is complemented by an educational workshop which the artist is encouraged to lead. There are extensive print workshop facilities (etching, screenprinting, lithography, relief etc.) adjoining the gallery. Recently, the gallery has been used as a dance space and most private views are accompanied by music by local bands. Funding is gleaned from a variety of sources including income from framing, graphics, materials and art-related goods, commissions and grants from the Scottish Arts Council.

Sales: Work sold

The Space: It is possible to cope with most work in this large space. Plans are available.

Exhibiting: [AW] Submissions should be made to Keith Fraser or Bob McGilvray at any time and should include CV, at least twelve good-quality slides, previous catalogues, etc. The gallery covers cost of insurance, printing and mailing of publicity, list of exhibits, transport and occasionally framing. Commission 30% on work sold.

Access: [U][T] BR Dundee 10 mins; Bus station 2 mins; Car park 2 mins

Dunkeld (Tayside)

(SAC) Map2 NO04

Atholl Gallery

A private gallery opened in 1987. [VA,Cr]

Address: 6 Atholl Street, Dunkeld, Perthshire PH8 OAR

tel 03502 8855
Contact: Dr Antony Pleasance 0738 88244, 5 New Cottages, Glenalmond, Perth PH1 3RY
Open: Mon-Sat 11-5
Policy: Mainstream contemporary Scottish art shown in about ten exhibitions a year. Both group and solo shows are run from three to four weeks long. While the main gallery is used for temporary exhibitions, there is always a permanent display of Scottish paintings and crafts in two other rooms.
Sales: Work sold; Credit card
The Space: The main gallery is 110 square metres with 30 lamps and a hook system. There is a limit of 3m on size of paintings. Locked jewellery cases and glass shelving for crafts are available.
Exhibiting: [AW] Artists are invited to visit the gallery to discuss exhibitions or to write or phone with details. All artists must be resident in Scotland, be Scottish or deal in Scottish subjects. The gallery covers cost of insurance, printing and mailing of publicity, list of exhibits, preview and catalogue/card. Commission 40% on work sold.
Access: [S] Buses and car park 1 min

Dunvegan (Highland Region)

(SAC) Map1 NG24

Orbost Gallery

A commercial visual arts gallery set up in 1977. [VA]
Address: Dunvegan, Isle of Skye IV55 82B tel 047 022 207
Contact: Dr David Roberts
Open: Daily 10-6 Tourist season; Sat 10-6 or by appointment out of season
Policy: *'We sell pictures to make a living and to enable other artists to do so.'* Work shown is mostly traditional or representational. Wood engravings are made in the gallery on an early 19th century Columbian press. About eight to ten artists a year exhibit.
Sales: Work sold; Credit card
The Space: 30m linear hanging space available. Work should be no more than 1.8m square. Sculpture should be no larger than 2m high and 1m wide.
Exhibiting: [AW] Individuals are invited to write to the gallery which covers cost of insurance, printing of publicity and display. Commission of 25% on work sold.
Access: [U][T] Walk of 3 miles from Dunvegan or Portree

Edinburgh (Lothian Region)

(SAC) Map2 NT27

369 Gallery

Founded by Andrew Brown in 1978, the gallery moved in 1985 to its present large premises. [Pa]
Address: 233 Cowgate, Edinburgh EH1 1NQ tel 031 225 3013
Contact: Director Andrew Brown
Open: Mon-Sat 10.30-5.30
Policy: On three floors, 369 consists of three large galleries, an education room and recently-renovated artists studios. Exhibitions showing the work of contemporary artists living in Scotland change every month. A lively education programme of life-drawing and painting classes attracts a wide age group. The second floor is occupied by seven Scottish painters. 369 shows gallery artists internationally. The Gilded Balloon Theatre is also part of 369's operations and regular cabaret and performances are shown there.
Sales: Work sold; Credit scheme
The Space: The galleries are on three floors; gravity rod hanging system; no work over 2.1m.
Exhibiting: *'We usually invite artists/groups to exhibit and only rarely accept applications.'* Artists wishing to exhibit should contact the Director. The gallery covers cost of insurance, list of exhibits, printing and mailing of publicity and catalogue/card. Commission 40% on work sold.
Access: [U][T] Ground floor gallery **[X]** Upper floors. BR 10 mins; Parking limited

Assembly Rooms

A large multi-purpose building run by Edinburgh District Council, Department of Recreation. [VA,Ph,Cr,LA]
Address: 54 George Street, Edinburgh EH2 2LR tel 031 225 3614
Contact: Events Organiser Kate Craik
Open: The Assembly Rooms will be closed from October 1988 to July 1989 for major upgrading
Policy: The Assembly Rooms runs exhibitions in the foyer to coincide with major events and also hires out space. It is hoped that after renovation, there will be a more sophisticated exhibition system and policy.
The Space: Foyer exhibitions are normally hung from movable boards. Larger-scale exhibitions in rooms upstairs are normally arranged by people who hire the building and bring their own display systems.
Exhibiting: [AW] Write to Kate Craik in the first instance. A meeting can then be arranged to discuss possibilities. Note the closure from October mentioned above. There are five rooms available for hire - contact Kate Craik for details.
Access: [U][T][L] BR Waverley 5 mins; Bus station 5 mins; Street parking

Backroom Gallery

A gallery showing contemporary work. [VA,Cr]
Address: Underneath the Arches, 42 London Street, Edinburgh EH tel 031 556 8329
Contact: Michael Durnan
Open: Mon-Sat 10.30-5.30
Policy: The gallery shows first-time and established exhibitors.
Sales: Work sold
The Space: The gallery is around 5x5m, plus an additional 2m linear hanging space, with spotlighting.
Exhibiting: [AW] Applications are welcome.

Carlyle's Gallery

A new commercial gallery/tearoom. [Pa,Pr]
Address: North Bridge, Edinburgh EH1 1SO tel 557 5068
Contact: A Wilson

Open: Mon-Sat 10-6

Policy: Carlyle's deals in Scottish painting from the 18th century to contemporary decorative work as well as representing young Scottish painters.

Sales: Work sold; Credit card; Credit scheme

The Space: Main gallery is 28x8x3m and a complex space is available upstairs. Maximum size of works 2.5x2m.

Exhibiting: [AW] Hiring is negotiated with each client. The gallery covers cost of insurance, printing of publicity, list of exhibits and catalogue. Commission 33.3% on work sold.

Access: [U][T] Public car park 2 mins

City of Edinburgh Art Centre

The City Art Centre is part of the Museum and Galleries division of the Recreation Department of Edinburgh District Council. [VA,Ph,Cr]

Address: 2 Market Street, Edinburgh EH1 1DE tel 031 225 2424 Ex 6650

Contact: Keeper of Fine Art Collections Ian O'Riordan

Open: Mon-Sat 10-6 (June-Sept); Mon-Sat 10-5 (Oct-May) ; During Edinburgh Festival also Sun 2-5

Policy: As well as mounting major international loan exhibitions like *'Gold of the Pharaohs', the art centre has a varied temporary exhibition programme which has included contemporary jewellery, American abstract art, art college degree shows and solo shows by Scottish artists with a policy aimed at attracting both international and local audiences. The city's permanent collection of art, both contemporary and historic, is shown in regular, selected exhibitions throughout the year. The gallery has an on going acquisitions policy to add to that collection. Artists must be either Scottish or have worked in Scotland (preferably Edinburgh) to qualify for purchase. Particular emphasis is currently given to contemporary work. The gallery also holds lectures, workshops, demonstrations, concerts and children's events.*

Sales: Work sold

The Space: The art centre is on four floors totalling 938m Screens can be introduced to extend hanging space. The lower ground floor is in two sections with heights at 2.3 and 2.6m and a total wall length of 70m. The Ground Floor has a wall length of 62.5m and a height of 2.8m. The first floor wall length is 79m and height 2.8m with an adjacent multi-purpose space with wall length of 20.9m and height of 2.9m. The second floor wall length is 85.7m with a height of 2.9 rising to 3.2 in the bays.The gallery is equipped with a lift and picture hoist. The lower three floors are air-conditioned regulated by thermo hydrographs. Hanging either by rods or mirror plates. Fully adaptable lighting system uses tungsten halogen spotlights on multi-circuit format.

Exhibiting: [AW][EF] Applications with photographs or slides should be made in writing to Lesley Woodbridge, Assistant Keeper. Commissions are offered depending on grant-aid. The gallery covers all exhibition costs. Commission 15% plus VAT on work sold.

Access: [U][T][L][F] BR Waverley 1 min; Princes Street and all main bus routes 2 mins; Car park 2 mins

City Art Centre: 'Aqua Lapis' exhibition by Nancy Hemenay, 1984
(Photo: Antonia Reeve)

Coleridge

A new gallery and shop specialising in contemporary glass. [Cr]

Address: 47b George Street, Edinburgh EH2 tel 031 220 1305

Contact: Jane Aaronson

Open: Mon-Sat 10-5.30

Policy: A regular stock of fine glass work is held as well as a changing programme of exhibitions which highlight the work of one or more makers. See also Coleridge at 192 Piccadilly, London.

Sales: Work sold

The Space: A large shop.

Access: City centre

Collective Gallery

An artist-run gallery founded in 1984 and recently moved to new premises. [VA,Ph,LA]

Address: 166 High Street, Edinburgh EH1 1QS tel 031 220 1260

Contact: The Collective

Open: Tues-Sat 12.30-5.30

Policy: *'The gallery was founded to provide an opportunity for non-established artists to exhibit their work. We are independent and support artists working in both commercial and experimental areas. We seek to promote and encourage diversity and accessibility and*

Collective Gallery

welcome those pursuing less mainstream areas where work is issue-related or non-object based.' The gallery shows 15 three-week exhibitions a year, about twelve of which are solo shows. Talks and lectures are held on many subjects and visiting artists are asked to talk about their work. Video screenings are also held.

Sales: Work sold; Credit scheme

The Space: The front area is 3x6.5m and 7x2m and 3m high. The back area is 3.5x3m and 3x2.5m and 2.5m high. Access to the gallery is up one flight of steps and the access door is 1.9m high and 0.85m wide. The gallery is lit by spots and daylight which can be screened out.

Exhibiting: [AW] Selection meetings are held twice yearly in the gallery. These meetings are open to all members of the Collective. Membership is currently £6 unwaged/students, £12 low wage, £18 full time. Members are entitled to apply for exhibitions (apart from students) and vote on the forthcoming programme. Applications should be sent to the Administrator with eight slides for a solo show and twelve slides for a group show. The gallery covers cost of insurance, printing and mailing of publicity, list of exhibits and catalogue/card.

Access: [U][T] BR Waverley 5 mins; Bus station 15 mins

Cramond Sculpture Centre

Opened September 1988, this open-air site is a permanent outdoor venue for sculpture. [Sc,Dr,LA]

Address: Moray House College, Cramond Road North, Edinburgh EH4 6JD tel 031 853 1194

Contact: Curator Fiona Byrne-Sutton

Open: Daily 10am-sunset

Policy: Cramond Sculpture Centre will show work in any medium able to be sited outdoors. Site specific, interventionist, time-based and object-based work will all be considered. There are contrasting sites in the grounds, a walled garden, a pond, grass, ruins, woodland. Only contemporary work will be shown and there is a commitment to innovation and experiment. Scottish sculpture will be on show at all times, but the programme will also include national and international exhibitions. Workshops and demonstrations are planned as part of the exhibition programme as is work within the community.

Sales: Work sold

The Space: Contact the Curator for details of all spaces available in the sculpture centre.

Exhibiting: [AW] Artists should send slides, CV and proposal to the curator at any time. Materials and fees will be paid on an individual basis for exhibitions, site-specific work and commissions. The park also meets publicity, insurance, printing and preview costs. Commission is 30%.

Access: [U][T][F] Bus 41 twice hourly from centre of Edinburgh (Mound or Waverley) except Sun ; Bus 18 from Queensferry Street daily; Car park on site

Danish Cultural Institute

A gallery within the institute's Georgian New Town premises. [Pa,Pr,Ph]

Address: 3 Doune Terrace, Edinburgh EH3 6DY tel 031 225 7189

Contact: Director Finn Andersen

Open: Mon-Fri 10-5

Policy: Work by Danish artists shown on a regular basis.

The Space: A gallery on the second floor.

Access: Just north of city centre

Designer Frames & Gallery La Belle Angele

A private gallery and framing shop opened in 1987. [VA,Ph,Cr]

Address: 11 Hasties Close, Cowgate, Edinburgh EH1 1JD tel 031 225 2774

Contact: H. Maboubi

Open: Mon-Fri 10-5, Sat 11-4

Policy: The gallery and shop shows the work of established and young artists in six exhibitions a year, three group and three solo. Talks by exhibiting artists are held.

Sales: Work sold; Credit card

The Space: 52m linear hanging space available in a room 19x19x4m high. Picture rails with nylon and metal rods with uniform white light throughout.

Exhibiting: [AW] Artists should apply in writing. The gallery covers cost of insurance, list of exhibits and catalogue/card. Commission of 33.3% on work sold.

Access: [S] BR 10 mins; Car park 5 mins

Edinburgh City Library

Several spaces within Edinburgh's main public library and a number of community libraries.

Address: George IV Bridge, Edinburgh EH1 1EG tel 031 225 5584

Contact: Exhibitions Organiser Mrs Armstrong

Policy: A variety of temporary exhibitions usually related to a local theme or special book selection.

Access: City centre

Edinburgh College of Art

Two exhibition spaces within Edinburgh College of Art. [VA,Ph,Cr,LA]

Edinburgh College of Art

Address: Lauriston Place EH3 9DF tel 031 229 9311
Contact: Assistant to Vice-Principal (Exhibitions) Mike Docherty
Open: Mon-Fri 10-5, Sat 10-12
Policy: The Sculpture Court and Andrew Grant galleries together show about 30 exhibitions a year, all but two by living artists and ten solo shows. Each exhibition lasts two to three weeks. The exhibition is *'lively, varied and contributes significantly to the college academic programme.'* Though open to the public the majority of visitors are students and teachers. During the Edinburgh Festival however, the college is used as a major public venue and has many more visitors. Talks, seminars, workshops and demonstrations are all held when appropriate. The exhibition programme has no subsidy from the college and is self-financing through hire. The college has a permanent collection of work by past students.
Sales: Sales referred to exhibitor
The Space: The Sculpture Court has 96m linear hanging space and can accommodate large works. The Andrew Grant Gallery has about 25m linear hanging space and is more suitable for smaller works with a 3m maximum height for paintings.
Exhibiting: [AW] Artists should write to the Exhibition Organiser six months in advance, though it is sometimes possible to arrange exhibitions at short notice. Charges for hire of space vary. No commission charges are made. The gallery covers cost of insurance, printing and mailing of publicity, list of exhibits, preview and catalogue card. EPR would be supported.
Access: [U][T][L][F] Buses 23,27,30,45,24; Multi-story car park 5 mins; Near city centre

Edinburgh Filmhouse

A gallery within Edinburgh's quality film house. [Pa,Pr,Dr,Ph,Fi,Vi]
Address: Lothian Road, Edinburgh EH3 9BZ tel 031 228 6382
Contact: Gay Cox
Open: Mon-Sat noon-11pm, Sun 6.30-11
Policy: Recently opened, the gallery shows a regular series of temporary exhibitions focusing on photography.
Sales: Work sold
The Space: One small room and additional wall space in the bar.
Exhibiting: [AW] Write or phone Gay Cox. Gallery takes 15% commission.
Access: [U][T] City centre

English-Speaking Union

A gallery run by the charitable trust the English-Speaking Union. [Pa,Sc,Pr,Cr]
Address: 23 Atholl Crescent, Edinburgh EH3 5HQ tel 031 229 1528
Contact: Director Brian Gorman
Open: Daily except Tues 10-5
Policy: The varied programme of group and solo exhibitions specialises in work by professional contemporary artists working in Scotland. Eight exhibitions are shown a year, each lasting three weeks.
Sales: Work sold
The Space: The gallery has 36.6m linear hanging space interrupted by two doors. Overhead lighting is adjustable and hanging is by rods. There is a restriction of 3m in height.
Exhibiting: [AW] Artists should apply to the Director at least one year in advance. Ask for details of the hire fees and commission charged. The gallery covers cost of printing and mailing of publicity, list of exhibits, preview and a catalogue/card.
Access: [X] BR Haymarket 2 mins; West end of Princes Street 2 mins

Fine Art Society

Commercial gallery in restored Georgian Town House. [Pa,Pr]
Address: 12 Great King Street, Edinburgh EH3 6QL tel 031 556 0305
Open: Mon-Fri 9.30-5.30, Sat 10-1
Policy: Temporary exhibitions mainly by 19th and early 20th artists (particulary Scottish) but the programme also includes selected contemporary artists. There is always a selection of stock available. The Fine Art Society has branches in Glasgow and London.
Sales: Work sold
The Space: Extensive Georgian rooms on three floors.
Access: [S] Just north of city centre

Flying Colours Gallery

Opened in 1986, this private gallery specialises in contemporary British and Italian art. [Pa,Dr]
Address: 35 William Street, Edinburgh EH3 7LW tel 031 225 6776
Contact: Jane Houldsworth
Open: Tues-Fri 11-6, Sat 10-1
Policy: Colourful, accessible works in oil, watercolour, pastel and gouache are exhibited in eight month-long group and solo exhibitions throughout the year. Always a varied stock of contemporary Scottish and Italian pictures. Aiming to broaden the range of people interested in original works of art the gallery looks for work by relatively unknown artists and helps with framing of work. *'We are not an intimidating rich and rare-looking gallery'.*
Sales: Work sold
The Space: Two Georgian shop front rooms with a total of 23.4m linear hanging space along five walls. Height 2.3m up to picture rail. Largest picture accepted (including frame) 1.2x1.5m.
Exhibiting: [AW] Apply in writing with photographs, slides and SAE. The gallery covers partial cost of printing and mailing publicity, list of exhibits, preview and catalogue/card. Commission 33.3% plus VAT.
Access: [F] West end of Edinburgh city centre; BR Haymarket 5 mins, BR Waverley 15 mins

French Institute

An exhibition space within the French Institute's elegant New Town premises and a café in basement with space for small exhibitions. [VA]

Address: 13 Randolph Crescent, Edinburgh EH3 7TT tel 031 225 5366
Contact: Exhibitions Officer Sally Schofield
Open: Mon-Fri 10-5.30
Policy: Temporary exhibitions show the work of French and Scottish artists with French connections in all media. The French Institute organises artists' exchanges with several towns in France. French language classes, recitals and specialist lectures also held. The cafe space shows young artists under 35 who have strong connections with France.
Sales: Work sold
The Space: First-floor drawing room with floor to ceiling window at one end.
Access: [X] West end of city centre

Fruitmarket Gallery

A contemporary art gallery with major funding from the Scottish Arts Council. [VA,Ph,De,Vi,Ar,LA]

Address: 29 Market Street, Edinburgh EH1 1DF tel 031 225 2383
Contact: Director Fiona McLeod,
Open: Tues-Sat, 10-5.30, Sun 1.30-5.30
Policy: *'The gallery aims to create a focal point for contemporary art in Scotland. It hosts major international exhibitions and also tours its own exhibitions throughout the major cultural centres of Britain and Europe. The gallery provides a showcase for home-grown talent with a number of first museum shows for younger artists as well as providing retrospective exhibitions for more established mid-career artists. Historic and thematic shows complement this programme. Non-visual arts activities are actively encouraged as are new and emerging media. An annual 'open' exhibition has been instituted to provide a platform for younger and/or lesser-known artists.'* Talks, discussions and guided tours accompany every exhibition. Workshops introduce a range of practical techniques and skills. Exhibitions attract audiences of up to 30,000. A fully comprehensive strand of outreach activities including community projects, public sculpture and billboard projects take place outwith the confines of the gallery building. The gallery itself is also used for concerts, readings, fashion shows, dance etc.
Sales: Work sold; Credit card; Credit scheme
The Space: Lower gallery is 23.3x9x3.6 high, and the Upper gallery is 23.3x6x2.4 high, with a total of 54.5m linear hanging space and a flexible system of screening for extension. Very large works can be accommodated.
Exhibiting: Artists should contact Lesley Morrison in writing, enclosing slides, photographs and catalogues. The gallery covers all exhibition costs. Commission 30% on work sold.
Access: **[F]** Lower Gallery, **[X]** Upper Gallery Near all city centre bus routes and situated above BR Waverley Station

Fruitmarket Gallery

Galerie Mirages

A new commercial gallery specialising in ethnic art. [Pa,Sc,Pr,Cr]

Address: 46a Raeburn Place, Stockbridge, Edinburgh EH4 1HL tel 031 315 2603
Contact: Partners Sheila Dharinal and Anna Raman, Sheila Dharinal, 105 Warrender Park Road, Edinburgh tel 031 229 1837
Open: Mon-Sat, 1-5, Sun 2-5; Closed Wed
Policy: The gallery runs temporary thematic selling exhibitions of folk/ethnic art. Rugs, pottery, puppets, costume etc. from around the world (India, Japan, Middle East) are the main interest of the gallery, though the work of local and British makers is included when it is felt it integrates with the main theme. Talks and demonstrations are held to illustrate the work. A regular display of stock is sold.
Sales: Work sold
The Space: The main gallery is 100 metres square with movable panel boards, track lighting system with spots and a maximum hanging height of 5 metres. There is an overhead skylight panel covered in muslin to diffuse light.
Exhibiting: **[AW]** Applications to the gallery, which covers cost of insurance, printing and mailing of publicity, preview and display. The commission on work sold is negotiable.
Access: **[S]** Buses to Stockbridge; BR 30 mins

Gladstone's Land

Part of a National Trust for Scotland property, the exhibition space has a seventeenth century painted ceiling, irregular walls and half shuttered windows and shows the work of local artists generally in group exhibitions. [Pa]

Address: Lawnmarket, Edinburgh EH1 2NT tel 031 226 5856
Contact: Sonya Stellar, National Trust for Scotland, Charlotte Square, Edinburgh
Open: Mon-Sat 10-4.30, Sun 2-4.30
The Space: A space of about 19x24 feet with about 38 linear feet, hanging by rods and lighting by spots and natural light.
Exhibiting: Applications to exhibit are accepted. The artist meets all expenses and either pays 25% commission or a hire charge.
Access: City centre

Glassmarket

Craftshop selling studio glass, stained glass, ceramics, wood, knitware and jewellery with occasional exhibitions. [Gl,Ce,Wo,Te,Je]

Address: 25-27 Jeffrey Street, Edinburgh tel 031 557 3517
Open: Mon-Sat 10.30-5.30

Graeme Murray Gallery

A private contemporary art gallery with a specialist publishing programme. [VA,Ph,LA]

Address: 15 Scotland Street, Edinburgh EH3 6PU tel 031 556 6020
Contact: Graeme Murray
Open: Tues-Fri 10-5, Sat 10-1
Policy: The gallery specialises in minimal/conceptual art and shows the work of British, European and American artists with a particular interest in installations created or adapted specially for the gallery space. Work by younger especially local artists is shown as well as more established artists. An international audience is targetted with advertising also aimed at the Edinburgh population.
Sales: Work sold
The Space: A large Georgian room, 3.6m high with windows at either end. A total of 37m linear hanging space (including the stairway).
Exhibiting: **[AW]** Artists may apply in writing to the gallery. The gallery covers cost of insurance, printing of publicity, list of exhibits, preview, transport, mailing out publicity, catalogue/card and artist's expenses. Commission of 30-50% on work sold.
Access: **[X]** BR Waverley Station 10 mins; Bus station 5 mins

Graeme Murray Gallery (Photo: Catriona Grant)

Hanover Fine Art

A commercial gallery which deals in accessible contemporary art. [Pa,Pr,Cr]

Address: 104 Hanover Street, Edinburgh EH tel 031 225 2450
Open: Mon-Fri 10-5.30, Sat 10-4
Policy: Temporary exhibitions change about every four weeks. Painters and makers usually show in large groups, with between twenty and thirty artists showing several small works each.
Sales: Work sold
The Space: An upstairs gallery, not suitable for large works.
Access: City centre; BR Edinburgh 10 mins

Hart Street Gallery

A small commercial gallery in a basement in Edinburgh's New Town. [Pa,Pr]

Address: 19 Hart Street, Edinburgh EH tel 556 7069
Open: Mon-Sat 10-6
Policy: New work shown by contemporary Scottish artists. Stock is always on display and there are occasional temporary exhibitions.
Sales: Work sold
Access: Just north of city centre

HM General Register House

An exhibition space within a government building. [Pr,Ph]

Address: Princes Street, Edinburgh EH2 tel 031 556 6585
Contact: Exhibitions Officer
Open: Mon-Fri 10-4
Policy: All exhibitions mounted are historical and link a theme like 'The Scots in Australia' with photographs, archives and illustrations.
Access: East end of city centre

Inverleith House

Inverleith House, formerly the home of the Scottish National Gallery of Modern Art is located in the 75 acre grounds of Edinburgh's Botanic Garden. [Pa,Sc,Pr,Ph]

Address: Royal Botanic Garden, Edinburgh EH3 5LR tel 031 552 7171
Contact: Exhibitions Officer Paul Nesbitt
Open: Varies
Policy: From 1990 Inverleith House will be a major venue for the curation, display and commissioning of art about nature. It specialises in work which enhances and in turn, benefits from being shown in the unique location of a botanic garden. Works in any medium are shown and outdoor site are available within the garden. Half of the exhibitions each year are originated in-house, particularly those of a specialist nature, and these normally tour. There is an active education programme, leisure learning, and provision for running exhibition related workshops and lectures. Bookshop and cafe/restaurant.
Sales: Work sold; Credit card; Credit scheme
The Space: The main temporary exhibition space

occupies the ground and first floors, comprising seven well-proportioned rooms. Wooden flooring, off-white walls, good natural lighting, track lighting with dimmers, humidity control.

Exhibiting: [AW] Exhibition opportunities normally by invitation. For specific projects and proposals however, please contact the Exhibitions Officer. The Gallery is occasionally available on a hire basis for appropriate events.

Access: Disabled access under development. Free street parking to east and west of Botanic Garden; Buses 23,27 to Inverleith Row

Italian Institute

A gallery within the Italian cultural institute, which moved to the present new premises in the summer of 1988. [Pa,Pr,Ph]

Address: 82 Nicolson Street, Edinburgh EH8 9EW tel 031 668 2232

Contact: Director Alberto Di Mauro

Open: Mon-Fri 9-5

Policy: Temporary exhibitions by Italian artists, artists with an Italian connection or Italian themes. This active cultural centre also promotes and organises Italian theatre, poetry and literary events in Edinburgh. Italian language classes and specialist lectures and recitals also held.

Access: Just south of city centre

Kingfisher Gallery

A small commercial gallery opened in 1987 in a mews house in Edinburgh's New Town. [Pa,Pr]

Address: 5 Northumberland Street Lane N W, Edinburgh EH3 6JL tel 031 557 5454

Contact: Director Leslie Ridgers Gallery Administrator Susan Harvey

Open: Mon-Fri 10-4.30, Sat 10-1

Policy: The gallery shows work by well-established British and international artists, usually in group shows. Temporary exhibitions change monthly.

Sales: Work sold

The Space: Two, domestically proportioned rooms on two floors. Not suitable for large works.

Access: Just north of city centre

Kingfisher Gallery: sculpture by Elizabeth Frink

Malcolm Innes Gallery

A commercial gallery opened in 1981. [VA]

Address: 67 George Street, Edinburgh EH2 2E2 tel 031 226 4151

Contact: Anthony Wood

Open: Mon-Fri 9.30-6 , Sat 10-1

Policy: Specialists in natural history, sporting and Scottish painting, prints and sculpture (historic and contemporary). The gallery normally has seven exhibitions a year and a changing display of work for sale. It also takes part in activities in London and abroad and undertakes framing and restoration.

Sales: Work sold

The Space: A large space with one unbroken wall of 30m and smaller offshoot walls of 15m, 19m, 9m and 6m. Hanging by chain and hooks.

Exhibiting: [AW] Commission 40% plus VAT on work sold and if framing is undertaken this is at cost. The gallery covers all exhibition costs.

Access: [S] Centre of town; BR Waverley 10 mins; Street parking

Moray House College of Education

A wide range and size of exhibitions are mounted sporadically throughout the year. [Pa]

Address: Holyrood Campus, Holyrood Road, Edinburgh EH8 8AQ tel 031 556 8455

Contact: Assistant Principal Mrs P Brown

National Gallery of Scotland

Part of the National Galleries of Scotland. [VA]

Address: The Mound, Edinburgh EH2 2EL tel 031 556 8921

Contact: Keeper Michael Clarke

Open: Mon-Sat 10-5, Sun 2-5, extended during Edinburgh Festival

Policy: The large, elegant building built by William Playfair and just off Princes Street holds Scotland's national collection of historic paintings and drawings. The interior has recently been redesigned to mimic Playfair's original scheme. Small exhibitions focusing on aspects of the permanent collection are held all year round and a major exhibition is usually held every year to coincide with the Edinburgh Festival.

Access: [U][T][L] BR Waverley 2 mins; City centre buses; Street parking

National Library of Scotland

A gallery within Scotland's historic National Library. [Pa,Pr,Ph]

Address: George IV Bridge, Edinburgh EH1 1EW tel 031 226 4531

Contact: Exhibitions Organiser

Open: Mon-Fri 9.30-5, Sat 9.30-1, Sun 2-5

Policy: Most exhibitions are mounted round an historic theme or personality and include books, manuscripts, photographs and artifacts.

The Space: The gallery is on the first floor.

Access: City centre

Netherbow Art Centre

A Church of Scotland arts centre founded in 1972. [VA,Ph,Cr,LA]

Address: 43 High Street, Edinburgh EH1 1SR tel 031 556 9579/556 2647
Contact: Artistic Director Donald Smith
Open: Mon-Sat 10-4.30
Policy: The centre has a well-equipped small theatre which holds performances all year round and is the central space for the Scottish Puppet Festival. The gallery and café show wide-ranging exhibitions with the general public in mind. Activities for schools and community arts groups organised.
Sales: Work sold
The Space: Display on three levels. The main gallery is 6x5.4x3.6 high and there is corridor and café space. Lighting standard 80 and 100 watt spots. No humidity control.
Exhibiting: [AW] Applications to the Artistic Director.
Access: [S] BR 5 mins; Street parking

Open Eye Gallery

A commercial gallery founded in 1982 specialising in contemporary art and craft and also holding stock of early 20th century ceramics and etchings. [VA]

Address: 75-79 Cumberland Street, Edinburgh EH3 6RD tel 031 557 1020
Contact: Directors Thomas and Pamela Wilson
Open: Mon-Fri 10-6, Sat 10-4
Policy: Recently expanded to double its size, Open Eye aims to bring to public attention the work of makers in the field of contemporary art, with particular bias towards the figurative. The gallery holds 17 exhibitions annually which generally show work by two artists working in different mediums, typically a painter and a ceramicist. All exhibitions are originated by the gallery directors. Framing and restoration services are available.
Sales: Work sold; Credit scheme
The Space: Two galleries with 66m linear with suspended brackets and splash spot lights. Glass showcases for display of jewellery and ceramics etc.
Exhibiting: [AW] Artists and makers should write or telephone the gallery to arrange an appointment or should submit slides. Open Eye covers insurance, list of exhibits, preview costs and transport costs of exhibition. Commission 33.3% on work sold.
Access: [F] Buses 23,27,34,24; Near town centre; Parking machine and meter nearby

Portfolio Gallery at Photography Workshop

Portfolio Gallery is part of the Photography Workshop (Edinburgh). [Ph]

Address: 43 Candlemaker Row, Edinburgh EH1 2QB tel 031 220 1911
Contact: Jane Brottlo and Gloria Chalmers
Open: Tues-Sat 10.30-5.30
Policy: Photography Workshop (Edinburgh) opened in July 1988 as a photographic resource centre. Portfolio Gallery programmes twelve exhibitions a year, all of them by living artists. Most exhibitions are originated in Scotland with an emphasis on young and emerging photographers. They are also developing a touring network of non-gallery venues, to introduce new audiences to photography. As well as running the gallery, the workshop also offers open access to a darkroom, print-finishing facilities, specialist bookshop and a quarterly publication *Portfolio Magazine*. An extensive programme of courses and workshops in practical photography is run in conjunction with exhibitions. Seminars and talks tie in local work with national issues. The workshop encourages active membership from all sectors of the photographic community from amateur to professional.
Sales: Work sold; Credit card
The Space: The first-floor gallery is 5x3.8x2.5m high with about 16m linear hanging space. Additional exhibition space of 12m linear is available on the ground floor. Frames are fixed directly to walls. Electric storage heating and lighting of archival quality with true colour rendition. Winding stairs to upstairs gallery prohibits large-scale work. Gallery plans are available.
Exhibiting: [AW] Twelve times a year, through advertisement, photographers are invited to bring portfolios to the workshop. At these times leading curators/exhibitions organisers and photographers/artists are invited to give criticism and advice to young and *'new'* photographers. The gallery hopes in future to commission work from photographers resident in Scotland. The gallery covers most exhibition costs and a fee is paid to exhibitors. Commission 33.3% on work sold. EPR supported.
Access: [X] Buses 2,12; Meter parking in Grassmarket 3 mins; BR 15 mins

Prescote Art & Design

Prescote Art and Design organises exhibitions of the applied arts and design on a consultancy basis. [Cr,Pr,Ph]

Address: 5 Northumberland Street, Edinburgh EH3 6LL tel 031 557 0080
Contact: Ann Hartree
Policy: Exhibitions are normally organised in temporary venues, though Ann Hartree's Georgian house is available for occasional exhibitions. Lectures, presentations etc can also be organised.
Sales: Work sold
The Space: Staircase and drawing room available.
Access: [X] Just north of city centre

Printmakers Workshop

A spacious workshop and gallery within a renovated washhouse. [Pr,Pa]

Address: 23 Union Street, Edinburgh EH1 3LR tel 031 557 2479
Contact: Director Robert Adam
Open: Mon-Sat 10-5.30
Policy: Run as an independent organisation, the Printmakers Workshop puts on a varied selection of exhibitions throughout the year. Most exhibitions are initiated by the workshop though some touring exhibitions are shown. Increasingly, the workshop is

involved in the editioning of prints by well-known Scottish artists, not necessarily printmakers, like John Bellany and Peter Howson.
Sales: Work sold
The Space: A small space in the foyer and a two-room gallery upstairs. Not suitable for very large work.
Exhibiting: Commission 33.3% on work sold.
Access: 5 mins north of city centre's east end

RIAS Gallery

A small gallery within the head office of the Royal Incorporation of Architects Scotland. [Pa,Pr,Dr,Ph]
Address: 15 Rutland Square (off West End Princes Street), Edinburgh EH1 2BE tel 031 229 7205
Contact: Exhibitions Co-ordinator Sarah Fooks
Open: Mon-Fri 9.30-5
Policy: The gallery shows exhibitions related to Scottish architecture and architects as artists. Extensive bookshop.
The Space: A domestic-sized gallery on the first floor of a Georgian townhouse.
Exhibiting: **[AW]** Write to the Exhibitions Co-ordinator for an updated list of exhibitions; enquiries from artists working with architectural subjects welcome.
Access: West end of city centre

Richard Demarco Gallery

A gallery which is 'essentially international in character'. [VA,LA]

RIAS Gallery

Address: Blackfriars Church, Blackfriars, Edinburgh EH1 tel 031 557 0707
Contact: Director Richard Demarco
Open: Mon-Sat 10.30-6
Policy: Richard Demarco is Edinburgh's only arts 'impressario'. He has been involved with performance and particularly the visual arts for 22 years in that city, around the world and particularly in Eastern Europe. This new gallery is currently being renovated, but the exhibition programme is not curtailed.
Sales: Work sold
The Space: Three floors of exhibition space.
Exhibiting: **[AW]** Telephone or write to Richard Demarco or Jane Macallister at the gallery.
Access: City centre, off Royal Mile

Royal Commonwealth Institute

The Institute contains a large gallery showing temporary exhibitions of contemporary Commonwealth art. [Pa]
Address: 8 Rutland Square, Edinburgh EH1 2AS tel 031 229 6668
Open: Mon-Fri 9-5, Sat 10-12 noon (during exhibitions)

Royal Museum of Scotland

The most important component of the National Museums of Scotland, collections are housed in a beautiful Victorian building. [VA,Cr]
Address: Chambers Street, Edinburgh EH1 1JF tel 031 225 7534
Contact: Publicity Officer Vina Oberlander
Open: Mon-Sat 10-5, Sun 2-5
Policy: The museum has extensive collections of decorative arts, ethnography, natural sciences, technology and science. The gigantic greenhouse hall has been recently restored and the rest of the building is well into a programme of refurbishment and reorganisation. Temporary exhibitions relating to museum activities are held throughout the year. Workshops, films and lectures are also held on a regular basis.
Exhibiting: Exhibitions by invitation only.
Access: **[U][T]** City centre, near Royal Mile

Royal Scottish Academy

The Royal Scottish Academy, run by academicians since it was founded in 1826, shows mainly group exhibitions. [VA]
Address: The Mound, Edinburgh EH2 2EL tel 031 225 6671
Contact: Administrative Secretary W T Meikle
Open: Mon-Fri 10-7, Sun 12-5 during exhibitions
Policy: Throughout the year, the gallery shows work by academicians and has always had particular emphasis on painting. The gallery is also hired for major exhibitions by other bodies, eg Scottish National Gallery of Modern Art, Scottish Arts Council, National Museums of Scotland. A show of Scottish students' work is held every spring and an annual exhibition for members every summer. In the last two years the Scottish Society of Artists exhibition has been including time-based and

installation work. About six exhibitions, each running from one to three months, are shown a year. The gallery's permanent collection is of academicians diploma works since 1826. The gallery is financed through commission on sales of members work and sponsorship. A Friends of the Royal Scottish Academy is operated.

Sales: Work sold

The Space: Eight very large Neo-Classical galleries.

Exhibiting: Academy covers printing of publicity, list of exhibits and preview costs for Academy exhibitions. Commission 25% on work sold.

Access: [U][T][L] All buses to centre of Edinburgh; BR Waverley and public car park 5 mins

Scottish Artists

A small commercial gallery specialising in 20th century Scottish art. [Pa,Sc]

Address: 8 Howard Street, Edinburgh EH3 5JP tel 031 556 6337

Open: Mon-Fri 12-4 , Sat 10-1, or by appointment

Policy: The gallery holds twelve exhibitions of Scottish work a year of which eight are solo shows and about half by living artists. As well as temporary exhibitions, there is often a changing display of stock. The gallery also houses an archive on the Scottish painter Joan Eardley.

Sales: Work sold

The Space: Two rooms suitable for domestic-sized work with a total of 40m linear hanging space with hanging by rail, rod and hook system.

Exhibiting: [AW] Applications in writing from Scottish artists only. The gallery covers cost of insurance, printing and mailing of publicity, list of exhibits, catalogue/card and pays fees on commissions by arrangement. The gallery is also available for hire to Scottish artists. Commission 33.3% on work sold.

Access: [F] Beside Canonmills bus stop; BR 25 mins

Scottish Craft Centre

An independent craft centre run on a membership basis in an historic building. [Cr]

Address: 140 Canongate, Edinburgh EH8 8DD tel 031 556 8136

Open: Mon-Sat 10-5.30

Policy: The centre shows the work of Scottish makers working in all media. Very occasional temporary exhibitions are generally large, group shows.

Sales: Work sold

The Space: Exhibition spaces laid out as shop on several floors.

Access: [F] City centre, on Royal Mile

Scottish Gallery

The Scottish Gallery was founded in 1842 and is a loading gallery in contemporary Scottish art and 20th century Scottish painting as well as specialists in contemporary British Crafts. [VA,Cr]

Address: 94 George Street, Edinburgh EH2 3DF tel 031 225 5955

Contact: Director Guy Peploe

Open: Mon-Fri 10-6, Sat 10-1

Policy: Exhibitions change monthly in the four exhibition spaces. In any one year about 30 exhibitions are held each lasting 3-4 weeks. Well over half of these are solo shows and include work by living artists. The gallery represents a number of artists including Barbara Rae, William Crozier, Crawford Adamson, Jim Morrison, Janet Patterson and Rodick Carmichael. Most exhibitions are initiated by the gallery and show a wide range of interests including studio ceramics, jewellery and glass, 20th century and contemporary Scottish paintings and antique and modern prints. Occasional talks and associated events are held.

Sales: Work sold; Credit card

The Space: The total exhibition space is approximately 1212m square metres over four rooms. There is a historic 6x7.5m cupola over the main gallery. Glass showcases available.

Exhibiting: Any individual artist's work is given consideration but exhibitions are by invitation only. Gallery partially covers cost of insurance, printing and mailing of publicity, list of exhibits, cataloge/card and preview. Commission 44% minimum on work sold.

Access: [U][T] Main gallery only. Car park 10 mins; BR Waverley 10 mins

Scottish National Gallery of Modern Art

A part of the National Galleries of Scotland. [VA]

Address: Belford Road, Edinburgh EH4 3DR tel 031 556 8921

Contact: Keeper Richard Calvocoressi

Open: Mon-Sat 10-5, Sun 2-5

Policy: This Georgian building, a converted school, became the new home for the Scottish national collection of modern art in 1984. As well as showing the permanent collection (begun in 1960) of 20th century painting, sculpture and graphic art, the gallery also mounts at least one major exhibition a year, usually to coincide with the Edinburgh Festival. Each exhibition lasts two to three months. Smaller exhibitions surrounding work in the collection are also organised by the gallery.

Access: [U][T][L] BR Haymarket 10 mins; Bus C13; West end of Princes Street 15 mins

Scottish National Portrait Gallery

Part of the National Galleries of Scotland. [VA]

Address: 1 Queen Street, Edinburgh EH2 1JD tel 031 556 8921

Contact: Keeper Dr Duncan Thomson

Open: Mon-Sat 10-5, Sun 2-5

Policy: Scotland's famous faces are shown in the in this custom-built Victorian museum shared with the National Museums of Scotland. In recent years, the gallery has revitalised the national collection of portraits with a programme of commissioning new portraits of well-known Scots by contemporary artists. The gallery also houses the extensive and ever-increasing national collection of photography and there is now a room specially reserved for showing selections from the collection all year round. Several exhibitions are held a year, with a major exhibition to coincide with the Edinburgh Festival.

Access: [U][T][L] BR Waverley 5 mins; Bus station 2 mins; Street parking

Scottish Sculpture Trust

Promoting sculpture in Scotland and Scottish sculpture abroad. [Sc]

Address: Scottish National Gallery of Modern Art, Belford, Edinburgh EH4 3DR KY11 1LR tel 031 556 8921

Contact: Co-ordinator Angela Wrapson, Brunstane House South, Edinburgh EH15 2NQ tel 031 669 8234

Policy: To encourage public interest in and appreciation of sculpture through exhibitions, conferences, commissions, residencies, siting of public art and media.

Seeds Wholefood Café

Cafe with art on the side. [Pa,Dr,Ph,Cr]

Address: 53 West Nicolson Street, Edinburgh EH8 9DB tel 031 667 8673

Contact: F A Winckles

Open: Mon-Sat 10-8

Policy: A diversity of work by local artists shown, mainly paintings and photography. About twelve exhibitions a year, all of them by living artists and most of them solo shows.

Sales: Work sold; Sales referred to exhibitor

The Space: One wall 9m long and 4.5m high. Large window gives good natural light.

Exhibiting: [AW] Artists wishing to exhibit can approach anyone in the café during working hours. Commission 10% (given to charity) on work sold.

Access: [F] BR Waverley 20 mins; Car park 2 mins; many buses

Step Gallery

A small commercial gallery set up in 1988. [VA]

Address: 39 Howe Street, Edinburgh EH3 6TF tel 031 556 1613

Contact: Partners Bill & Laurence Ranson

Open: Mon-Fri 10-6.30, Sat 10-4

Policy: The upper space is devoted to solo or two and three-person shows by established living artists based in Scotland. Young, relatively unknown artists are shown at least twice a year. The lower gallery offers a changing group of paintings and contemporary prints.

Sales: Work sold

The Space: Main gallery is 6.7x4.5x4 and the basement is 6.7x3x3 with a total of 31m linear hanging space. Picture rail and high intensity, low- voltage lighting.

Exhibiting: [AW] Artists and makers should apply in writing enclosing biographical details, photographs and/or slides. The gallery covers cost of insurance, transport, printing and publicity, list of exhibits, preview, mailing of publicity, catalogue/card and is also available for hire (details on request). Commission of 35% on work sold.

Access: [X] BR 15 mins; Just north of city centre

Stills Gallery

A photography gallery run with Scottish Arts Council and Edinburgh District Council funding. [Ph]

Address: 105 High Street, Edinburgh EH1 1SG tel 031 557 1140

Contact: Director Rob Powell

Open: Tues-Sat, 12-6

Policy: The gallery aims *'to encourage photography as an artform and to promote its understanding as a vital and influential medium in contemporary culture through three main areas of activity'*. Those are, exhibitions both national touring and gallery-originated, a lively education programme which includes talks and workshops and the production, commissioning and publication of new work both photographic and textual. Of the 9-10 exhibitions shown each year, approximately half are Stills-initiated and most include work by living artists. Also specialist photographic bookshop.

Sales: Work sold

The Space: The gallery which is 2.1m high and has 51m hanging space is upstairs in an old building in the Royal Mile.

Exhibiting: [AW] Photographers should apply in writing, with slides or other visual material, to the Director. The gallery pays a small fee and commissions new work where budgets permit. The gallery covers all exhibition costs. Commission 30% on work sold.

Access: [X] BR 5 mins; Bus station 15 mins

Talbot Rice Gallery

A university gallery which houses a permanent collection of old master paintings and bronzes, as well as operating a busy temporary exhibition programme. [VA,Ar]

Address: University of Edinburgh, Old College, South Bridge, Edinburgh EH8 9YL tel 031 667 1011 Ext 4308, 4485

Contact: Assistant Curator Bill Hare

Open: 10-5 Mon-Sat

Policy: Founded in 1970, the gallery's commitments to the visual arts in Scotland are to provide a platform for more mature (mainly Scottish) artists to mount major solo exhibitions. Younger artists are encouraged to exhibit in group shows. The gallery also shows at least one major historical show a year. Though the bias is towards Scottish work, the gallery does attract foreign

Stills Gallery: installation of Brian Griffin's exhibition 'Work'

exhibitions. Twelve one-month exhibitions are held annually, a good number originated by the gallery and seminars and courses on the visual arts are also organised. As well as university funding, the gallery receives a grant from the Scottish Arts Council.

Sales: Work sold; Credit card

The Space: Two galleries, upstairs (8.50x11.30x2.35), downstairs (14x12.6x8.22) with a total of 130 linear metres hanging space. Controlled lighting by spots and fluorescent lights and hanging by plates. Work has to be under 3m (or assembled sections) for access. Section of enclosed quadrangle may be used for large sculpture display. There are variously sized 'table-top' glass-covered showcases.

Exhibiting: The gallery covers the cost of insurance, list of exhibits, preview costs, display, transport, printing and mailing publicity and catalogue/card.

Access: [L] City centre; BR Waverley 10 mins

Theatre Workshop

The café walls at this theatre and community arts centre serve as exhibition space. [Pa,Ph]

Address: 34 Hamilton Place, Edinburgh EH3 5AX tel 031 226 5425

Contact: Exhibitions Organiser

Open: Mon-Sat 10-5

Policy: Exhibitions are shown throughout the year. Because of limitations of the space, photography has become the main medium shown.

Sales: Work sold

The Space: Walls of a ground floor café.

Exhibiting: [AW] Contact Theatre Workshop with details.

Access: [S] In Stockbridge, north of city centre

Torrance Gallery

A cosy commercial gallery in a basement. [Pa,Cr]

Address: 29B Dundas Street, Edinburgh EH3 6QQ tel 031 556 6366

Contact: Director Florence Torrance

Open: Mon-Fri 11-6, Sat 10.30-4

Policy: The Torrance shows accessible art mainly by Scottish artists. Exhibitions change regularly and are often group shows of two or three artists in several media (eg jewellery and ceramics shown with paintings).

Sales: Work sold

The Space: Two domestic-sized galleries.

Exhibiting: [AW] Write to the Torrence Gallery.

Access: Just north of city centre

Ware on Earth

A gallery within a shop which specialises in ceramics. [Cr]

Address: 15 Howe Street, Edinburgh EH3 6TE tel 031 558 1276

Contact: Owner Robert Murray Brown

Open: Mon-Fri 10-6, Sat 10-4

Policy: Temporary exhibitions usually highlighting the work of one artist are shown every two months. British and European makers are shown.

Sales: Work sold

Access: Just north of city centre

WASPS Studios Gallery

A gallery within an artists' studio complex. [VA,Cr]

Address: Patriothall, off Hamilton Place, Stockbridge, Edinburgh EH3 5AY tel 031 225 1289

Contact: Resident Administrator Gerry McGowan

Open: Various (mostly afternoons)

Policy: Created in 1987 from the entrance space of a warehouse building now housing studios, the gallery is available primarily for the use of resident artists. However, outside artists are welcome to fill empty slots in the programme.

Sales: Sales referred to exhibitor

The Space: One main room is 12x6x5m and a corridor is12x6m. Hanging is on wires, fluorescent lights.

Exhibiting: Artists must cover all costs including invigilation of the gallery. As the Administrator works on a voluntary basis, there is no system for setting up exhibitions from outside.

Access: [U] Near city centre; BR 20 mins; Street parking

Elgin (Grampian Region)

(SAC) Map1 NJ26

Elgin Museum

A museum and exhibition hall owned and run by the Moray Society, a group with charitable status. [Pa,Sc,Cr]

Address: 1 High Street, Elgin, Moray IV30 1EQ tel 0343 3675

Contact: Assistant Curator Christine Sangster

Open: Reopens 1989

Policy: The exhibitions hall is used for solo and group exhibitions. Major renovations are underway and a permanent temporary exhibition space will be available by summer 1989.

Sales: Sales referred to exhibitor

The Space: The gallery which is 12x6x4m high has 31m linear hanging space with hanging rails at two heights. Unscreened fluorescent lighting without daylight.

Exhibiting: [AW] Artists should write to the Curator. The gallery is currently hired at £7 a day plus electricity.

Access: [U][T] BR Elgin 10 mins; Bus 1 min; Parking next to museum

Ellon (Grampion Region)

(SAC) Map1 NJ93

Tolquhon Gallery

A commercial gallery opened in 1987. [VA,Cr]

Address: Tolquhon, by Tarves, Ellon, Aberdeenshire AB4 0LP tel 06513 2343

Contact: Owners/Directors Donald & Joan Ross

Open: Mon-Sat 1-5, Sun 1-5

Policy: The gallery has regular mixed exhibitions for Spring, Summer and Christmas. Between these, solo shows exhibit a wide range of work by well-known and emerging artists working in Scotland. Ten exhibitions are shown each year, all of them by living artists and at least five of them solo shows. Each exhibition lasts about four weeks. *'Our aim is to create a pleasant ambiance for people to enjoy both in the gallery and in the garden where we exhibit sculpture.'*

Sales: Work sold

The Space: The three main exhibition areas are 4.2x4.5m, 4.1x4.2m and 1.2x3.1m, all with a hanging height of 1.9 metres. Hanging is by picture rods and rail. Spots are mounted in the ceiling on tracks. There is a large attractive garden with trees, shrubs, flowers, grass and a paved area which can be used for sculpture. Gallery plans are available.

Exhibiting: [AW] Exhibition is by invitation but application in person or by letter with CV and slides or photographic material, will be considered. The gallery covers cost of insurance, printing and mailing of publicity, transport, list of exhibits and catalogue/card, preview.

Access: [F] 25 mins by car from Aberdeen; Car park in grounds of gallery

Eyemouth (Borders Region)

(SAC) Map2 NT96

Eyemouth Museum

A museum of folk life run by the Eyemouth Museum Trust.

Address: Auldkirk, Market Place, Eyemouth, Berwickshire TD14 5HE tel 0390 50678

Open: Mon-Sat 10-6 Easter-Oct, Sun 2-6

Policy: This museum of fishing life in Eyemouth holds occasional temporary exhibitions.

Access: Town centre; Car park

Galashiels (Borders Region)

(SAC) Map2 NT27

Christopher Boyd Gallery

A municipal gallery run by Ettrick and Lauderdale District Council. [VA,Ph,Cr]

Address: Old Gala House, Scot Crescent, Galashiels TD1 3JS

Contact: District Curator Ian Brown, Municipal Buildings, High Street, Selkirk tel 0750 20096

Open: Tues-Sat 10-4 , Sun 2-4 April-Oct

Policy: As well as holding a small permanent collection, the gallery plans to show local and national visual art exhibitions in order to encourage interest from the local community. Recitals and lectures held November-March. Six to seven exhibitions are mounted each year.

Sales: Work sold

The Space: The gallery is 9x6x5m high and has 25m linear hanging space and a hanging system with rods and hooks and track spots and floods.

Exhibiting: [AW] Apply in writing at any time to the District Curator, preferably a year in advance. The booking fee is £20 (£30 for groups) and a commission of 15% plus VAT is taken on work sold, but the council covers cost of insurance, printing and mailing of publicity, list of exhibits and catalogue/card.

Access: [X] On A7

Scottish College of Textiles

An exhibition space within this specialist college. [Te]

Address: Netherdale, Galashiels TD1 3HF tel 0896 3351

Contact: Exhibition Organiser Michael Henderson

Open: Weekdays or by arrangement 9-4.30

Policy: The programme reflects the college disciplines, but other fine and applied arts by local artists are also shown.

Sales: Work sold

Access: 1.5 miles from town on south side; Car park

Gartocharn (Strathclyde Region)

(SAC) Map2 NS48

NB Gallery

A small commercial gallery founded in 1972. [Pa,Cr]

Address: School Road, Gartocharn, Alexandria G83 8RT tel 038 983 340

Contact: Mrs W Newton Sealey

Open: Mon-Fri 10-5, Sun 2-5, Closed Christmas-Easter

Policy: *'The gallery was started as an attempt to bring the work of living artists to a wider audience, one which might not otherwise visit a gallery. The aim now is to show visitors to Scotland something more than "tartanalia"'*. The four exhibitions held (each lasting one month) throughout the year show the work of local artists and particularly Scottish landscapes. The gallery holds about six classical music recitals a year.

Sales: Work sold

The Space: The main gallery has about 30m linear of hanging space. Painting size maximum 1x1m. Jewellery display cases and a small outdoor space for sculpture.

Exhibiting: [AW] Contact gallery any time. Commission 33.3% on work sold.

Access: [S] Own car park; Local bus service from commuter rail service at Balloch (2 hourly)

Girvan (Strathclyde Region)

(SAC) Map2 NX19

McKechnie Institute

A municipal art centre managed by Girvan Community Council in association with Kyle and Carrick District Council. [VA,Ph,Cr]

Address: Dalrymple Street, Girvan, Ayrshire KA26 9AE tel 0465 3643

Contact: Hon Curator Margaret McCance

Open: Tues-Sat 10-4; 11-4 Mon in July/Aug

Policy: A diverse selection of temporary exhibitions includes work by local artists and makers, exchange exhibitions with twin towns in Europe and small touring exhibitions. The gallery holds about 14 exhibitions a year, twelve of which include work by living artists. Interest in the gallery is fostered in the community and schools and art classes are held regularly. During the tourist season, exhibitions of local interest and history are mounted.

Sales: Work sold

The Space: Three separate spaces with 24, 28 and 25 linear metres hanging space respectively. Hanging rod

system plus hooks. Victorian wooden framed display case are available.
Exhibiting: [AW] Applications in writing to the Hon Curator. The gallery covers cost of insurance, printing and publicity, list of exhibits, preview and display. The spaces can be hired. Commission 10-15% on work sold.
Access: [U][T] On Ayr-Girvan-Stranraer bus route; BR Girvan 15 mins; Public car park 2 mins

Glasgow (Strathclyde Region)

(SAC) Map2 NS56

90s Gallery

The gallery specialises in Scottish contemporary fine art and design. Also the headquarters of the Scottish Crafts Promotions Association. [Pa,Pr,Cr]

Address: 12 Otago Street, Glasgow G12 8HJ tel 041 339 3158
Contact: Directors Matt and Rona Ewart
Open: Mon-Sat 10-6
Policy: The gallery shows work by Scottish, mainly west coast, artists and designers. Space is reserved for a stock of work which runs alongside a programme of temporary exhibitions. The aim is to *'blur the often artificial distinctions between fine and applied art'* which allows a broad range of work to be displayed. 90% of the work show in the gallery is by association membership which currently stands at about 100. Each month a particular theme is set, or a single artist highlighted. The association provides opportunities which range from export contacts via architects and interiors designers.
Sales: Work sold
The Space: Five separate display areas of, on average, 33 square metres. One area reserved for high-quality craft and design, the rest for fine art. Enquiries welcomed from other galleries for exchange exhibitions.
Exhibiting: [AW] Artists and makers are welcome to apply for details of joining the association.
Access: West end; Underground Kelvinbridge

Annan Gallery

A old-established commercial gallery run by the descendents of the famous Victorian Glasgow photographer of the same name. [Pa,Pr,Ph]

Address: 130 West Campbell, Glasgow G2 4UE tel 041 221 5087
Contact: Director Douglas Annan
Open: Mon-Fri 9-5, Sat 9.30-12.30
Policy: The gallery shows prints and reproductions by well-known Scottish artists. Temporary exhibitions highlighting the work of one or more artists are occasionally held. Original works by various artists are always on show, most of the work tends to be in a traditional style. Also available are prints from the Annan Collection of old photographs
Sales: Work sold
Exhibiting: [AW] Contact the gallery direct with samples or photographs of work.

Art Gallery & Museum, Kelvingrove

One of the finest civic collections in Britain housed in a magnificent, elaborate Victorian building. [VA,Ph,Cr,LA]

Address: Kelvingrove, Glasgow G3 8AG tel 041 357 3929
Contact: Publicity Officer Patricia Bascom
Open: Mon-Sat 10-5, Sun 2-5
Policy: The collection contains paintings of all periods (highlighting Glasgow Boys and Scottish colourists), decorative arts (particularly Glasgow Style), arms and armour, natural history, archaeology and ethnography. Temporary exhibitions are held regularly, as many as four at any one time. Some are based on work and objects held in the permanent collection and others are touring exhibitions. There is a lively education programme and workshops and talks are held regularly.
Access: [U][T] West of city centre; Parking for cars and coaches

Barbizon Gallery

A gallery opened in early 1989 showing contemporary British artists. [VA]

Address: College Lands, High Street, Glasgow G1 tel 041 553 1990
Contact: Directors Lachie Grant & Matt Cavanagh
Sales: Work sold

Barclay Lennie Fine Art Ltd

A commercial gallery founded in 1984. [Pa,Pr,Sc,Cr]

Address: 203 Bath Street, Glasgow G2 4HZ tel 041 226 5413
Contact: Barclay Lennie
Open: Mon-Fri 10-5, Sat 10-1
Policy: The gallery shows 19th and 20th century Scottish artists with an emphasis on local work. While most visitors are from Glasgow, the gallery also has overseas clients. Of the seven temporary exhibitions shown a year, at least three are solo shows. There is always a changing display of stock in the gallery.
Sales: Work sold; Credit card
The Space: Two gallery spaces of 10x8m and 9x6m respectively and a hall area. Daylight is boosted by tungsten lighting. Gallery plans are available.
Exhibiting: [AW] Artists should contact the gallery in person. The gallery covers cost of insurance, and a percentage of printing and mailing of publicity, list of exhibits, preview, catalogue/card. Commission 33.3% plus VAT on work sold.
Access: [X] BR Central and Queen Street 20 mins; Bus station 20 mins

Blythswood Gallery

A commercial gallery opened in 1987. [Pa,Dr,Cr]

Address: 161 West George Street, Glasgow G2 2JJ tel 041 220 5529
Contact: Proprietor Graham Harris
Open: Mon-Fri 10-5.30, Sat 10-1 and by appointment
Policy: As well as the stock of 19th and 20th century Scottish paintings always on display, the gallery also shows five temporary exhibitions a year about half the

pictures on show at any one time are by living artists and all of them concerning Scottish art. Most are group exhibitions centred on a theme like flower paintings, Glasgow Boys or Scottish colourists. The gallery also shows contemporary British ceramics and undertakes framing and restoration. The gallery has a list of clients and friends as well as welcoming the general public.

Sales: Work sold

The Space: Over three separate open-plan areas, the gallery has a total of 44m linear hanging space and is 2.6m high. There is a fixed picture rail and smaller work can be double-hung. Modern track lighting and spots.

Exhibiting: [AW] Applications in writing with photographs or by phone initially but all work must be seen before selected for hanging. The gallery covers cost of insurance, printing and mailing of publicity, list of exhibits, preview and catalogue/card. Commission 40% on work sold.

Access: [X] BR Glasgow Central 2 mins; Underground 2 mins

Collins Gallery

A university gallery showing a wide range of media and issues. [VA,Ar]

Address: University of Strathclyde, Richmond Street, Glasgow G1 1XQ tel 041 552 4400 Ex 4145

Contact: Curator Laura Hamilton

Open: Mon-Fri 10-5, Sat 12-4

Policy: *'Although primarily funded by the University of Strathclyde, the gallery aims to provide an interface between town and gown.'* At least one show a year presents the work of a young artist working in Scotland. Photography is also a major component of the programme as well as the establishment of contacts with artists and galleries abroad. Of the eleven exhibitions held annually, nine show the work of living artists and around two are solo shows. The gallery tours their own exhibitions and is involved with joint exhibition projects with other major galleries and organisations. Lectures, talks, films, readings, recitals and school programmes form an intregal part of the programme.

Sales: Work sold; Credit card

The Space: One large gallery 1212 square metres and with a linear hanging length variable dependent on inclusion of screens. Hanging rods, mirror plate etc. Spot lighting and controlled environment. Work limited to 3m high.

Exhibiting: [AW] Write to the Curator with information and visual material. The gallery hope to pay commissison fees in the future. The gallery covers cost of insurance, printing and publicity, list of exhibits, preview costs, display, transport, mailing out publicity, catalogue/card. Commission of 25% on work sold.

Access: [U][T] City centre; Underground & trains 7 mins; Public car park 2 mins

Compass Gallery

A commercial gallery which has been showing contemporary art in Glasgow for 21 years. [Pa,Pr]

Address: 178 West Regent Street, Glasgow G2 4RL tel 041 221 6370

Contact: Director Cyril Gerber

Open: Mon-Sat 10.30-5.30

Policy: Exhibitions of Scottish and international artists both well-known and emerging. The gallery holds a student exhibition every year after the Scottish art college degree shows. A permanent stock of paintings and prints is always available for viewing.

Sales: Work sold

The Space: Three domestic-sized rooms, not suitable for very large works.

Exhibiting: [AW] Selection is mainly by invitation, but applications are carefully considered. Gallery takes a commission on sales and pays all expenses except delivery in some cases.

Access: [X] City centre; BR Glasgow 10 mins

Cyril Gerber Fine Art

A commercial gallery opened in the eighties. [Pa]

Address: 148 West Regent Street, Glasgow G2 2RQ tel 041 221 3095

Contact: Director Cyril Gerber

Open: Mon-Fri 9.30-5.30, Sat 9.30-12.30

Policy: The gallery deals principally in late 19th to mid 20th century British paintings. Exhibitions derive mainly from changing stock which also includes original prints and art objects.

Access: City centre, BR Glasgow 10 mins

Eastwood House

A house run by Eastwood District Council which is available for hire for exhibitions of paintings, prints or photography. [Pa,Pr,Ph]

Address: Eastwood Park, Giffnock, Glasgow, Strathclyde G46 6UG tel 041 638 1101

Contact: Halls Manager Mrs A J Shaw, Council Offices, Eastwood Park, Rouken Glen Road, Giffnock, Glasgow G46 6UG tel 041 638 1101 ext 226

Policy: Temporary exhibitions and an annual exhibition in the month of October by local residents. Eastwood House is a multi-purpose building, the whole house may be hired or one or two suites.

Sales: Work sold

The Space: The Windsor Suite has three rooms, the Eglinton Suite two rooms with hanging rod system.

Exhibiting: Contact the Halls Department on 041 638 1101 for details of hiring the space.

Access: [X] Bus from Glasgow centre to Eastwood Toll

Fine Art Society

A well-established commercial gallery with branches in Edinburgh and London. [Pa,Pr]

Address: 134 Blythswood Street, Glasgow G2 4EL tel 041 332 4027

Contact: Director Roger Billcliffe

Open: Mon-Fri 9.30-5.30, Sat

Policy: As well as showing a regular stock of 19th and early 20th century Scottish painting, the gallery holds temporary exhibitions throughout the year. They concentrate on the work of 20th century and contemporary artists working in a painterly style. The Scottish colourist tradition is favoured.

Sales: Work sold

The Space: Galleries on three floors decorated in comfortable Edwardian Glasgow Style.
Access: City centre; BR 10 mins

Gatehouse Gallery

Commercial gallery opened in 1988 and situated in a park near a garden centre and butterfly kingdom. [VA,Ce]

Address: Rouken Glen Road, Giffnock, Glasgow G46 7UG tel 041 620 0235
Contact: Anne Mendelow
Open: Mon-Sun 11.30-5.30; closed Tues
Policy: The gallery shows regular exhibitions of paintings, prints, sculpture and ceramics by well-established contemporary artists and by new graduates. Solo exhibitions are planned during each year. The gallery is available for hire by art groups or societies if appropriate (including photographic or textile shows). Its aim is *'to try to encourage the public to buy original work in preference to reproductions'*. It has a permanent stock of paintings by owner Anne Mendelow and offers a framing service. The gallery sells art books and cards.
Sales: Work sold
The Space: Gallery is 8x6m and 3m high with a roof which slopes upwards to skylights. Total linear hanging space is 28m. A 3x3m lobby also has some wall space for hanging. Lighting is by halogen spots and downlighters. A 120 square metre garden lawn surrounded by conifers will be used for outdoor sculpture. Gallery plans are available.
Exhibiting: [AW] The gallery shares insurance, publicity, preview and mailing costs with exhibitors. Commission is 30% plus VAT.
Access: [S] Buses 10,57,45,17 pass outside the gates; BR 15 mins

Glasgow Arts Centre

A gallery within an arts education centre which is part of the local authority further/community education department. [VA,Ph,Cr]

Address: 12 Washington Street, Glasgow G12 8PD tel 041 221 4526
Contact: Exhibitions Organiser Steven Porch
Open: Mon-Fri 10-8, Sat 10-3
Policy: The mixed programme of touring and commissioned exhibitions shows work by both established and younger artists. Members of the centre use the gallery most frequently but the exhibitions also attract the general public. At least twelve exhibitions are held a year, almost all showing the work of living artists.
Sales: The gallery will undertake to sell work or can refer enquiries direct to the exhibitors
The Space: Two galleries are each approximately 12x6x4m high. Total linear hanging space 60 metres with a 2.5 metre restriction on height. Plywood wall surface. Track lighting, floods and spots.
Exhibiting: [AW] Applications welcome at any time which should include portfolio/slides/photographs and CV. Depending on scale of exhibition, a fee is paid on negotiation with the artist. The gallery covers all exhibition costs. No commission charged.
Access: [F][X]

Gatehouse Gallery

Glasgow Print Studio

Founded in 1972 as a non-profit making organisation, the studio has moved to new premises and provides not only exhibition opportunities for printmakers and artists but also extensive workshop facilities. [VA]

Address: 22 King Street, Glasgow G1 5QP tel 041 552 0704
Contact: General Manager John Mackechnie
Open: Mon-Sat 10-5.30
Policy: The open access workshop has facilities for etching, stone and metal plate lithography, screenprinting, relief processes and photography. Evening classes on all media are available to artists and the general public. The studio currently has a membership of over 200 including artists like Adrian Wiszniewski and Elizabeth Blackadder who are best known perhaps for their paintings. Artists from abroad are also welcomed both for exhibition and printmaking. The studio most recently editioned prints by prominent contemporary Scottish artists like John Bellany and Bruce McLean. National and international art fairs have also become part of their regular activities. The gallery holds 12 exhibitions a year, half group and half solo shows. Funded primarily by the Scottish Arts Council and Glasgow District Council, it has become increasingly involved in self-funding through editioning, framing and exhibition sales.
Sales: Work sold; Credit card; Credit scheme
The Space: The spacious gallery has 45m linear hanging space (longest wall 10.5m, height 3m) and track lighting 'Erco' and tungsten halogen wall wash lights.
Exhibiting: [AW] Artists are advised to write first as the gallery is always booked up well in advance. The studio covers cost of insurance, printing of publicity, list of exhibits, preview, mailing of publicity and catalogue/card (sometimes shared) and occasionally covers cost of framing. Commission 33.3% on work sold.
Access: [U][T][L] BR Queen Street 5 mins; BR Central 10 mins; Car park 100 yards

Glasgow School of Art

Two gallery spaces within Glasgow School of Art. [VA,Cr,LA]

Address: 167 Renfrew Street, Glasgow G3 6RQ

tel 041 332 9797

Contact: Exhibitions Co-ordinator

Open: Times vary for each exhibition

Policy: The Mackintosh Gallery is within the main building designed by Charles Rene Mackintosh. Student work is shown throughout the year, as well as touring exhibitions and work by members of staff.

Sales: Work sold

The Space: One large gallery 19x11m, daylight boosted by spotlights. One smaller gallery 15x11m, with artificial lighting.

Exhibiting: **[AW]** Applications in writing to the Exhibitions Co-ordinator.

Access: **[X]** Phone in advance City centre; BR Glasgow 10 mins; Underground Cowcaddens

Haggs Castle Museum

A children's museum in a restored Victorian house. [LA]

Address: 100 St Andrews Drive, Pollokshields, Glasgow G41 4RB tel 041 427 2725

Contact: Assistant Keeper

Open: Mon-Sat 10-5, Sun 2-5

Policy: Both permanent collection and temporary exhibitions are related to children and their interests.

The Space: The temporary exhibition area is 6x9m with 16m linear hanging space.

Exhibiting: **[AW]** Applications to exhibit are accepted, but all exhibitions must be aimed at children and where possible should include items that can be handled. Terms and responsibility for expenses are negotiable.

Access: South side of city

Harbingers

A design gift shop with a small exhibition area. [Pa,Dr,Cr,Je]

Address: 417 Great Western Road, Glasgow G4 9JA tel 041 339 9999

Contact: G Simon and C Docherty

Open: Mon-Sat 10-6

Policy: As well as its permanent selection of ceramics, jewellery, textiles and paintings, the shop mounts a special temporary exhibition every other month. Usually two artists or makers show together, one on the wall and one using the shelf space. As they expand their operations, the young owners intend to introduce group theme exhibitions. Invitations to previews are sent out to all customers of the shop.

Sales: Work sold; Credit card

The Space: The exhibition area has 8m linear hanging space and a height of 2.5m. Large pieces not encouraged. There are low tables, glass shelving and floor space for exhibiting three-dimensional work.

Exhibiting: **[AW]** Artists and makers should write with slides/photos. The shop covers cost of insurance and returns unsold work to artists, all preview costs are shared with the artist. Commission 33.3% on work sold.

Access: **[U][T]** Underground to Kelvinbridge; Street parking; Buses:20,61

Hillhead Underground Gallery

A private gallery in a large cafe setting showing exhibitions of fine and applied art by contemporary Scottish artists. [VA]

Address: 2 Creswell Lane, Glasgow G12 8AA tel 041 339 0968

Contact: Director

Open: Daily 10-5

Sales: Work sold

The Space: The gallery has around 15m linear hanging space.

Exhibiting: **[AW]** Applications accepted, although they are usually booked up well in advance. Commission is 30%.

Hunterian Art Gallery

A gallery built beside the university library to house the university's fine collection of paintings and prints. [VA]

Address: The University, Hillhead Street, Glasgow G12 8QQ tel 041 330 5431

Contact: Curator Pamela Robertson

Open: Mon-Fri 10-5, Sat 9.30-1

Policy: The university owns a superb collection of work by Charles Rennie Mackintosh, Whistler and Scottish painting. It also has Scotland's largest collection of fine art prints, both historic and contemporary. Temporary exhibitions tend to be selected from the gallery's own collection which is too large to show all at the same time.

Access: West end; Underground Hillhead

Hunterian Museum

The Hunterian Museum contains the university's important geological, prehistoric, Roman, ethnographical and numismatic collections. There is a programme of temporary exhibitions. [VA,Ph,Cr]

Address: University of Glasgow, University Avenue, Glasgow G12 8QQ tel 041 330 4221

Contact: Director Professor Frank Willett

Open: Mon-Fri 9.30-5, Sat 9.30-1

Policy: Permanent displays interpret the Museum's collections for the benefit of university students and the general public. Temporary exhibitions highlight important aspects of the collection or are brought in from outside organisations.

The Space: One gallery 9x6m, track lighting, Gallery plans available. Some panels available for hanging.

Exhibiting: **[AW]** Contact Dr J D Bateson for details of current exhibition schedule. Costs to be met by museum might include insurance, transport, publicity, private view, invitations and postage.

Access: **[L]** West end; Underground Hillhead

Images Art Gallery

A commercial gallery founded in 1976. [Pa,Pr,Dr]

Address: 74 Hyndland Road, Glasgow G12 9UT tel 041 334 5311

Contact: C A & E J Sutton

Open: Mon-Fri 9.30-5.30, Sun 9.30-5

Policy: The gallery specialises in 18th and 19th century

Japanese woodblock prints, etchings and drypoints. They have four temporary exhibitions a year lasting four to six weeks, and at least one of them is by a living artist. Framing is done on the premises. There is always a changing display of work on show.
Sales: Work sold; Credit card; Credit scheme
Access: **[F]** BR Hyndland Station 5 mins; Bus 59

Interdec Gallery

A gallery set up in 1988 with the aim of showing art from the Third World as well as young Glasgow artists. [VA,Cr]
Address: Maryhill Burgh Hall, 24 Gairbraid Road, Glasgow tel 041 946 5912
Contact: Owner Ali Abubakar
Sales: Work sold

Kelly Gallery

A gallery founded in 1965 and run by the Royal Glasgow Institute of the Fine Arts. [VA]
Address: 118 Douglas Street, Glasgow G2 4ET tel 041 248 6386
Contact: R C Liddle, 12 Sandyford Place, Glasgow G3 7NE tel 041 248 7411
Open: Mon-Fri 10.30-2, 2.30-5.50, Sat 10-12.30
Policy: *'The gallery's sole function is to enable artists to promote their own exhibitions and is rented out subject to approval of standard.'* The Royal Glasgow Institute was founded in 1861 and promotes open annual exhibitions. It currently has 1500 members. There were 15 exhibitions each lasting two weeks at the gallery last year, eight of which were solo shows.
Sales: Work sold; Sales referred to exhibitor
The Space: Gallery plan available.
Exhibiting: Artists should contact RC Liddle at least one year in advance of proposed date. The charge for hire is £50 per week (two weeks minimum) and 20% commission on sales.
Access: **[F]** Car parks and buses 2 mins; Underground 5 mins; BR Queen Street 15 mins

Lillie Art Gallery

A municipal gallery run by Bearsden and Milngavie District Council with a permanent collection and a temporary exhibitions programme. [VA,Ph,Cr]
Address: Station Road, Milngavie, Glasgow G62 8AQ tel 041 956 2351
Contact: Curator Elizabeth Dent
Open: Tues-Fri 11-5,7-9, Sat,Sun 2-5
Policy: As well as showing aspects of the permanent collection of 20th century Scottish art, the gallery also mounts exhibitions of local art and hires touring exhibitions. Of the 14 exhibitions a year, eleven are by living artists and four are solo shows. Workshops, lectures and demonstrations are regularly organised. There is an artist in residence scheme.
Sales: Work sold
The Space: There are three galleries. Gallery 1 is 425 square metres, Gallery 2 is 160 square metres and Gallery 3 is 80 square metres. Hanging is by hook and rail system. The galleries are lit by spots on tracks and there are blinds to control daylight. Work must be no larger than 2.5m.
Exhibiting: **[AW]** Artists should write to the Curator with details of work, proposed date for exhibition and photographs/slides. The gallery covers cost of insurance, printing and mailing of publicity, list of exhibits and catalogue/card. Commission of 20% on work sold.
Access: **[F]** Car park at gallery; BR Milngavie 3 mins

Main Fine Art

A welcoming commercial gallery which specialises in Scottish contemporary painting. [Pa,Pr]
Address: 16 Gibson Street, Glasgow G12 8NX tel 041 334 8858
Contact: Owners Michael and Lesley Main
Open: Tues-Sat 10-5, Sun 2-5
Policy: Main Fine Art is expanding to another space in Gibson Street while staying on in their current space. As well as a gallery in the Victorian tenement block at 16 Gibson Street, the Mains also run a number of artists' studios.
Sales: Work sold
The Space: A domestic-sized space not suitable for very large work.
Access: West end; Underground Hillhead

Maryhill Arts Centre

Address: 11 Malloch Street, Maryhill, Glasgow G20 8TP tel 041 945 3995
Contact: Jack Henderson

McGavigans

A gallery within a stationery and artists' materials shop. [VA]
Address: 24 Royal Exchange Square, Glasgow G1 3AQ tel 041 221 1011
Contact: Manager
Sales: Work sold

McLellan Galleries

This Victorian gallery space will be refurbished to

Kelly Gallery

international standards by 1990, in order to take major touring shows of contemporary or historical art and to co-incide with the Glasgow Festival. [VA]

Address: 270 Sauchiehall Street, Glasgow G2 3EH

Contact: Tessa Jackson, Glasgow Festival, Glasgow District Council tel 041 227 5699

Open Circle at Hillhead Library

An independent organisation called Open Circle runs a gallery within this public library. [Pa,Pr]

Address: 348 Byres Road, Glasgow G12 8AP

Contact: Ken Palmer tel Ask library for contact number

Open: Mon-Fri 9.30-8, Sat 9.30-1, closed Wed

Policy: Members of Open Circle are asked to exhibit and occasional exhibitions from outside are brought in.

Sales: Work sold

Access: West end

People's Palace

Glasgow's museum of working life opened in 1898. [Pa,Pr,Ph]

Address: Glasgow Green, Glasgow G40 1AT tel 041 554 0223

Contact: Curator Elspeth King

Open: Mon-Sat 10-5, Sun 2-5

Policy: The museum holds collections which relate to trade unionism, industry, social life, religious movements, sport etc. Public art (stained glass and tiles) are particularly interesting features. The young Glasgow artist Ken Currie recently completed a mural project which is the first of its kind in Glasgow in a public building for over 100 years. The gallery holds temporary exhibitions which relate to the collection and has a policy of buying young Glasgow artists' work.

Access: City centre

Scottish Design Centre

Regional office of the Design Council, sponsored by the DTI. [Cr]

Address: 72 St Vincent Street, Glasgow G2 5TN tel 041 221 6121

Open: Mon-Sat 9.30-5

Access: City centre; BR Glasgow 5 mins

Springburn Museum

An independent museum founded in 1986. [Pr,Dr,Ph]

Address: Atlas Square, Ayr Street, Glasgow G21 4BW tel 041 557 1405

Contact: Curator Mark O'Neill

Open: Mon-Fri 10.30-5, Sat 10-4, Sun and bank holidays 2-5

Policy: Six exhibitions shown a year, usually at least one by a living artist. The exhibition space is currently used for locally-inspired shows which reflect both past and present. Arts and crafts classes are held.

The Space: There are 21m linear hanging space. Framed works are hung from hooks on a picture rail. UV filtered spots are used in conjunction with daylight. Possible to show small work only.

Exhibiting: First approach in writing to the Curator. As there is no specific exhibitions policy at the museum yet, details are negotiable.

Access: [U] Buses 45,90,89,8,33; BR Springburn 100 yards; Street parking

Third Eye Centre

For over ten years Third Eye Centre has been developing and expanding its interests and appeal to the community and the specialist audience and the programme includes exhibitions, theatre, poetry, dance, music, performance and video. [VA,LA]

Address: 350 Sauchiehall Street, Glasgow G2 3JD tel 041 332 7521

Contact: Exhibitions Organiser Andrew Nairne

Open: Tues-Sat 10-5.30, Sun 2-5.30

Policy: The policy of the gallery is to present new developments in the visual and performing arts to the widest possible audience. The centre initiates exhibitions and events of particular interest to the local community. Exhibitions tour throughout Scotland, the UK and occasionally abroad. Also bookshop and café.

Sales: Work sold

The Space: Two galleries with 60.5-110m linear hanging space and 40-60.5m linear hanging space plus foyer and café spaces. Direct fixing, spot and day light.

Exhibiting: [AW] Applications enclosing visual material are welcomed although the programme is arrived at largely by invitation. Exhibitions are programmed about a year and a half in advance.

Access: [U][T] City centre; BR Glasgow 15 mins

Transmission

An artist-run gallery with a particular interest in video and live art where Glasgow artists are shown as well as artists from London (Art-in-Ruins) with occasional visits from foreign artists. [VA,LA]

Address: 13-15 Chisholm Street, Trongate, Glasgow G15 HA tel 041 552 4813

Open: Check with gallery for current opening times

Policy: The gallery mainly serves artists with new and unusual ideas who might not otherwise have the opportunity to exhibit.

Sales: Work sold when appropriate

The Space: Two rooms behind a shop-front at ground level. One room has a stone cobbled floor. Both are narrow and not suitable for very large works.

Access: City centre; BR St Enoch Station

Washington Gallery

A commercial gallery in a warehouse setting. [PA,Pr]

Address: 44 Washington Street, Glasgow G3 8AZ tel 041 221 6780

Contact: Owner William Hardie

Open: Mon-Fri 10-5

Policy: Shows mainly 19th & 20th century and some contemporary Scottish art.

Sales: Work sold

The Space: Two rooms, suitable for some very large works.

WASPS Shop & Information Centre

A gallery, shop and information space run by Workshop and Artists' Studio Provision Scotland Ltd. [VA,Ph,Cr]

Address: 26 King Street, Glasgow G1 5QP tel 041 552 0564
Contact: Administrator
Open: Mon-Fri 9-5
Policy: This shop rents hundreds of studio spaces to artists around Scotland at low costs. Through this new 'shop' venture, they hope to give the public a window into what is happening in those studios and the artists an opportunity to sell their work. The gallery and shop will exhibit work made in their studios. All media is represented in a changing display. The shop also provides information and a slide library on artists which enables representatives of trade, industry and commerce to place commissions and sponsorship. WASPS managing director, administrator and marketing officer are all based at this address.
Sales: Work sold
The Space: There are three walls 48, 52 & 21m long and 3.5m high, one wall 3m long and 3m high and two spaces 5m long and 3m high. Maximum picture size is 3mx5m.
Exhibiting: Artists are welcome to apply for studio space to the above address. The gallery however is made available only to WASPS artists.
Access: [F] Underground: St Enoch 5 mins; St Enoch car park 2 mins; BR Central and Queen Street 10 mins

Glenrothes (Fife Region)

(SAC) Map2 NO20

Corridor Gallery

A gallery specialising in photography housed and run by the Fife Institute with funding from Arts in Fife and the Scottish Arts Council. [Ph]

Address: The Fife Institute of Physical & Recreational Education, Viewfield Road, Glenrothes, Fife KY6 2RA tel 0592 771700
Contact: Principal J S Penman
Open: Daily 9-11pm
Policy: The aim of the gallery is to show new work by Scottish photographers, to bridge the gap between amateur and professional photographers and to bring serious photography to the general public. International exhibitions shown occasionally. Workshops and lectures held.
Sales: Sales referred to exhibitor
The Space: The gallery is 25x2x2.5m.
Exhibiting: [AW] Photographers are invited to write to principal with an outline of exhibition which is sent on to the programme co-ordinators. The gallery covers cost of insurance, display and mailing of publicity.
Access: [L] Own public car park; Hourly bus to institute entrance

Greenock (Strathclyde Region)

(SAC) Map2 NS27

Greenock Arts Guild

[VA]

Address: 3 Campbell Street, Greenock PA16 8AP tel 0475 34038
Contact: Daphne Wyllie, 9 McPherson Drive, Gourock tel 0475 32810
Policy: A variety of exhibitions, organised on a voluntary basis.

McLean Museum & Art Gallery

A municipal museum and art gallery run by Inverclyde District Council with a permanent collection of 19th and 20th century European artists and a temporary exhibitions programme. [Pa,Pr,Dr,Ph]

Address: Greenock, Renfrewshire PA16 8JH tel 0475 23741
Contact: Curator Val Boa
Open: Mon-Sat 10-12 & 1-5
Policy: The gallery shows work from the permanent collection as well as exhibitions of contemporary Scottish artists. Exhibitions originated outside the gallery cover a wide range of subjects and artists. The 'Inverclyde Biennial' is an open exhibition organised every two years which usually attracts a large number

WASPS: six artists at 22 King Street Studios

of well and lesser-known artists. The gallery shows nine exhibitions a year, four by living artists and one or two solo shows. Events and educational activities are organised to complement the exhibition programme. The largest space can be used as a lecture theatre. At time of going to press programme effected by redevelopment work on the permanent displays.

Sales: Work sold

The Space: The three exhibition spaces are 12x12x4m high and two are 21x5x5m high. All three have up-to-date lighting systems and are able to take all standard fixings.

Exhibiting: Applications should be directed any time in writing to the Assistant Curator. Commission of 20% on work sold.

Access: Street parking; Bus from Kilblain Street bus station; BR Greenock West 10 mins

Haddington (East Lothian)

(SAC) Map2 NT57

Peter Potter Gallery Trust

A small commercial gallery showing visual arts and crafts. [VA]

Address: 10 The Sands, Haddington, East Lothian EH41 3EY tel 062 082 2080

Contact: Administrator Patricia A Buchanan

Open: Mon-Sat 10-5pm except Thurs 10-2

Policy: Ten exhibitions a year, all of them by living artists. The gallery specialises in pastels, oils, watercolour, ceramics, glass, jewellery, embroidery, designer knitwear. Coffee shop on the premises.

Sales: Work sold

The Space: Gallery One 33x7x2.6m high; Gallery Two 6x6.6x3m high.

Exhibiting: [AW] Send applications to the gallery which covers cost of insurance, printing and mailing of publicity, list of exhibits, preview costs and catalogue/card. Commission 30% on work sold, plus VAT.

Access: [X] Own car parking facilities; On main bus routes from Edinburgh

Hamilton (Strathclyde Region)

(SAC) Map2 NS75

Hamilton District Museum

A local history museum run by Hamilton District Council. [Pa,Ph,Cr,History]

Address: 129 Muir Street, Hamilton ML3 6BJ tel 0698 283981

Contact: Museum Curator Terry F Mackenzie

Open: Mon-Sat 10-12 & 1-5

Policy: The museum has a large permanent collection including local paintings, prints, photographs and costume. Temporary exhibitions on history, science and fine art are held regularly but are most often hired from another agency eg Scottish Museums Council, Scottish Arts Council. Six exhibitions a year are held, at least one being a solo by a living artist. An active education service is operated from the museum.

The Space: The exhibition space is 17x8x4m with about 70m linear hanging space and hanging by chain from rail. Daylight with venetian blinds to part height, UV screened. Three large tungsten chandeliers. Wide range of Edmonds showcases available.

Exhibiting: [AW] Applications in writing to Museum Education Officer.

Access: [X] Large car park in front of museum; BR Hamilton Central 10 mins

Hawick (Borders Region)

(SAC) Map2 NT51

Scott Art Gallery

A gallery run by Roxburgh District Council. [Pa,Pr,Dr,Ph,Cr]

Address: Hawick Museum, Wilton Lodge Park, Roxburghshire TD9 7JL tel 0450 73457

Contact: District Museums Curator Rosi Capper

Open: Mon-Sat 10-5, Sun 2-5 April-Sept; Mon-Fri 1-4, Sun 2-4 Oct-March

Policy: The gallery aims to present a balanced programme of local artists' work, exhibitions by schools, work by outside artists and loan exhibitions from the Scottish Museums Council etc. Ten exhibitions are shown a year, two of them solo exhibitions. Workshops, recitals and educational activities have become a vital part of the gallery's activities.

Sales: Work sold

The Space: The gallery is 17x9.5x2.75m high and has 40m linear hanging space plus a selection of free-standing panels. Hanging rods are used with the option of pinning or mirror-clipping. Spots are suspended from tracks and there are also fluorescent tubes. Heaters and air conditioners have been installed. The gallery has a range of desk-top style cases with a maximum depth of 33mm.

Exhibiting: [AW] Individuals and groups are invited to apply to the Curator preferably a year before they wish to exhibit. The gallery covers all exhibition costs. Commission 10-15% on work sold.

Access: [X] No rail network to Hawick but good bus routes from north and south; 1 mile from town centre; Car park 5 mins

Innerleithen (Lothian Region)

(SAC) Map2 NT33

Malt Loft Gallery, Traquair

A gallery within the historic house of Traquair, still family-owned. [Pa,Cr]

Address: Traquair House, Innerleithen, Peeblesshire EH44 6PW tel 0896 30323

Contact: Owner Flora Maxwell Stuart

Open: Daily 1.30-5.30 April-Sept, Daily 10.30-5.30 July/Aug

Policy: The gardens and rooms of the house are open to the public. Exhibitions by contemporary artists (tapestries to the painted flower) are shown within this historic context, each for six to eight weeks. Both tourists and locals visit exhibitions. There is a programme of artists and makers in residence and painting weekends are organised. Theatre and music recitals are occasionally mounted.

Sales: Work sold

The Space: The gallery is 6.6x5.4m with hanging by rail and hook. Four windows and spot lighting.

Exhibiting: [AW] Write to Flora Maxwell Stuart. Hiring is considered by arrangement. The gallery covers cost of insurance and mailing of publicity. Commission 20% on work sold.

Access: [S] 6 miles east of Peebles on B709; Parking at house

Inverness (Highland Region)

(SAC) Map1 NH64

Culloden Library Mini Gallery

Run by Highland Regional Council, the library gallery was founded in 1985. [VA,Ph,Cr,LA]

Address: Culloden Library, Keppoch Road, Culloden, Inverness IV1 2LL tel 0463 792531

Contact: Branch Librarian Angela Donald

Open: Mon-Wed 10-1,3-5,6-8, Tues, Fri 10-1,3-5

Policy: Regularly changing temporary exhibitions show work mainly by local artists working in all media and styles. The exhibition programme enhances the environment of the library. Talks and workshops are occasionaly organised in conjunction with exhibitions.

Sales: Work sold

The Space: Approximately 20m linear hanging space in the library area and floor space is also available. Works are limited to A1 size.

Exhibiting: [AW] Artists should apply to the Branch Librarian by telephone or in writing. The space can be hired with a charge of 10% commission on all sales. The gallery pays for printing of publicity and list of exhibits.

Access: [U][T] Public transport from Inverness; Free car park

Eden Court Theatre Art Gallery

The gallery is part of a modern entertainments, arts and conference centre serving an area the size of Wales. [VA]

Address: Eden Court Theatre, Bishops Road, Inverness IV3 5SA tel 0463 239841

Contact: Front of House Manager Val Falcon

Open: Mon-Sat 10.30-10

Policy: The visual arts policy is to promote work by professional and amateur local artists and to hire touring exhibitions. Around three out of the twelve exhibitions each year are solo shows. Artists are invited to talk about their work and children's and youth events are held. Though all media are considered, the gallery concentrates on painting.

Sales: Work sold; Credit card

The Space: Two walls 10m, two walls 11m and 1 wall 8m with the height of all walls approximately 2.5m. Hanging system, rod and adjustable hook on hanging rail; natural light and spots. Gallery plans available.

Exhibiting: Applications to Front of House Manager. Selection is made in November for the following year by the selection panel. The space is for hire only occasionally. The gallery covers cost of insurance and mailing of publicity, list of exhibits, half of preview cost. Commission 20% plus VAT on work sold.

Access: [X] BR and bus stations 10 mins; Large private car park

Inverness Museum & Art Gallery

A municipal gallery and museum run by Inverness District Council, holding a small fine art collection of mainly Scottish contemporary works. [VA,Ph,Cr]

Address: Castle Wynd, Inverness IV2 3ED tel 0463 237114

Contact: Curator Catherine Niven

Open: Mon-Sat 10-5

Policy: The gallery shows a wide variety of exhibitions, both fine art and museum related. About 16 shows are held every year, nine of these likely to be the work of living artists. Most of the selling exhibitions are held during the summer months when there is a large tourist audience. Talks, demonstrations, music recitals and children's activities are held regularly.

Sales: Work sold

The Space: The upstairs gallery has 43m linear hanging space with hanging rods. Track lighting is fully controllable. Humidity is monitored and can be adjusted. No lift.

Exhibiting: [AW] Contact the Curator. The gallery is also available for hire at £30 per month. Artists are occasionally paid a commission fee to produce work specially for exhibitions. The gallery covers insurance, printing and publicity, list of exhibits and mailing out of publicity. Commission 25% on work sold.

Access: [X] Town centre; BR Inverness and public car parks 5 mins

Irvine (Strathclyde Region)

(SAC) Map2 NS33

Harbour Arts Centre

A gallery within an arts centre. [VA,Ph,Cr]

Address: 114-116 Harbour Street, Irvine, Ayrshire KA13 6RQ tel 0294 74059

Contact: Jim Clark

Open: Mon-Sat 10.30-4.30, 7-11

Policy: The gallery shows a variety of work from abstract paintings to silk scarves by local, national, amateur and professional artists. New members of the centre always welcome, but facilities are also open to the general public. Twelve exhibitions are shown a year, all of them by living artists. The gallery also holds lectures, a summer school and art classes.

Sales: Work sold

The Space: There are seven hanging walls totalling about 20m linear hanging space. Four display cases 0.9x0.6x1.2m and one 1.2x.9x1.2m are available for jewellery etc and are internally lit. Hanging rails and hooks are used for pictures and the gallery is fully alarmed. Plans are available for exhibitors.

Exhibiting: [AW] Apply to the Director.

Access: [F] BR Station 4 mins

Kilmarnock (Strathclyde Region)

(SAC) Map2 NS43

Dean Castle

A municipal museum run by Kilmarnock and Loudoun District Museums. [VA,Ph,Cr,LA]

Address: Dean Road, Kilmarnock KA3 tel 0563 26401/34580

Contact: Curator James Hunter, Kilmarnock & Loudoun District Museums, Dick Institute, Kilmarnock, KA1 3BU

Open: Daily 12-5

Policy: The permanent collection includes medieval tapestries, armour and early musical instruments. Work by local artists is usually on display. Temporary exhibitions are varied and of the seven held each year, three include work by living artists.

Sales: Work sold; Credit scheme

The Space: The exhibition space is 16x4m with most of the hanging space on island panels.

Exhibiting: The museum covers cost of list of exhibits and mailing of publicity. Commission 20% on work sold.

Access: [X]

Dick Institute

A municipal museum run by Kilmarnock and Loudoun District Council. [VA,Ph,Cr]

Address: Elmbank Avenue, Kilmarnock, Ayrshire KA1 3BU tel 0563 26401

Contact: Curator James Hunter

Open: Mon,Tues,Thurs,Fri 10-8, Wed,Sat 10-5

Policy: Exhibitions are drawn both from the permanent collections (ethnography, archeology, shells and small arms) and the national touring circuit. A range of media and styles are shown both by well-known contemporary artists and local artists. Of the 26 exhibitions shown a year, eleven of them are by living artists and five are solo shows. An exhibition is usually shown for five weeks.

Sales: Work sold; Credit scheme

The Space: The main gallery is 16x10m and hanging space is supplemented by island units. The space is air-conditioned and has controlled lighting. Gallery 2 is 15x4m. Perspex cubes are available for display of crafts etc.

Exhibiting: The gallery covers cost of lists of exhibits and mailing of publicity. Commission 20% on work sold.

Access: [U][T][L][F] Bus station 5 mins; BR 10 mins

Kirkcaldy (Fife Region)

(SAC) Map2 NT29

Kirkcaldy Museum & Art Gallery

A municipal gallery and museum run by the Kirkcaldy District Museums Service with permanent collections of local history and Scottish art with space for temporary exhibitions. [Pa,Pr,Ph,Cr]

Address: War Memorial Gardens, Kirkcaldy, Fife KY1 1YG tel 0592 260732

Open: Mon-Sat 11-5, Sun 2-5

Policy: Though the programme includes non-art exhibitions, the gallery regularly shows contemporary art, particularly group shows and two exhibitions a year are solo shows. The gallery is particularly interested in theme exhibitions or interpreted displays as their audience is not art-specialist based.

Sales: Work sold

The Space: Three rooms upstairs for temporary exhibitions giving a total of 100m linear hanging space.

Exhibiting: The gallery covers cost of insurance and mailing out of publicity.

Access: Next to BR Kirkcaldy

Kirkintilloch (Strathclyde Region)

(SAC) Map2 NS67

Auld Kirk Museum

One of a group of three municipal local history museums run by Strathkelvin District. [Pa,Ph,Cr]

Address: The Cross, Kirkintilloch, Glasgow G66 1AB tel 041 775 1185

Contact: Curator Susan Selwin

Open: Tues,Thurs,Fri 2-5; Sat 10-1,2-5

Policy: The Auld Kirk Museum is open throughout the year with a regular programme of temporary exhibitions concentrating on items of local interest or introducing the community to wider themes. Of the six exhibitions shown annually, two show the work of living artists or makers. Talks and children's activities also held.

Sales: Work sold

The Space: The linear hanging space can be varied with hanging on screens. Edmonds cases available.

Exhibiting: [AW] Contact Curator with slides of work. The gallery covers cost of insurance and printing of publicity. Commission of 15% on work sold.

Access: Car parks 2 mins walk

Kirkwall (Orkney)

(SAC) map1 HY41

Tankerness House Museum

A museum with displays on the island's history. [VA]

Address: Broad Street, Kirkwall KW15 1DH tel 0856 3191

Contact: Curator

Open: Mon-Sat 10.30-12.30 & 1.30-5, Sun 2-5 May-Sept

Policy: Archaeology and local history collections are enhanced by special exhibitions.

Lerwick (Shetland Islands)

(SAC) Map1 HU44

Shetland Museum

A municipal museum and gallery run by the Shetland Islands Council. [Pa,Pr,Dr,Ph,Cr]

Address: Lower Hillhead, Lerwick, Shetland ZE1 0EL tel 0595 5057

Contact: Curator Andrew Williamson

Open: Mon,Wed,Fri 10-7, Tues,Thurs,Sat 10-5

Policy: Within the museum, is an exhibition space which shows mainly painting, photography and drawing. The gallery aims to provide a space for local artists, amateur and professional, and to raise the profile of the visual arts in the community by mounting shows by well-known artists from the rest of Britain. Lectures, talks and films are also held.

Sales: Work sold; Sales referred to exhibitor

The Space: The gallery has 10.3m linear hanging space and additional screens. No large works. There are small desk cabinets and a wall cabinet for display.

Exhibiting: [AW] Artists should apply to the Curator. The gallery covers cost of insurance. Commission 10% on work sold. EPR supported.

Access: [X] Town centre; Public car park adjacent

Leven (Fife Region)

(SAC) Map2 NO30

Loomshop Gallery

A private gallery with regular exhibitions of contemporary Scottish work. [Pa]

Address: 126 Main Street, Lower Largo, Leven KY8 6BP

Open: Tues-Sat 2-4, 6-8

Linlithgow (Lothian Region)

(SAC) Map2 NS97

Portfolio Four

A small commercial gallery showing design, visual art and crafts. [Pa,Je,Ce,De]

Address: 47 High Street, Linlithgow EH49 7ED tel 0506 844445

Contact: Mrs B McLuckie

Open: Mon-Sat 9.30-5.45, Sun noon-6

Policy: The gallery also has a craft shop, framing service and coffee shop.

The Space: Showcases are available, hanging is by rods with spots and natural lighting.

Exhibiting: [AW] The gallery covers mailing, catalogue and private view. Work must be submitted to the gallery and its suitablility assessed. Commission 33.3% on work sold.

Shetland Museum: Art Gallery and Lecture Room

Livingston (Lothian Region)

(SAC) Map2 NT06

Inveralmond Community Education Centre

A varied programme of exhibitions of fine art. [Pa,Sc,Pr]

Address: Community High School, Willowbank, Ladywell, Livingston EH54 6HN tel 0506 38093

Contact: Exhibitions Organiser Hugh Tuckermann

Lochgelly (Fife Region)

(SAC) Map2 NT19

Lochgelly Centre Gallery

The Lochgelly Centre, run by Fife Regional Council Education Committee, houses a sports hall, theatre, art and craft areas and an exhibition area, where exhibitions are held monthly. [VA]

Address: Bank Street, Lochgelly, Fife KY5 9QU tel 0592 780971

Contact: Greg Neilson

Open: Mon-Fri 9-10, Sat,Sun 9-5

The Space: The exhibition area has 25m linear hanging space with an additional 8m linear space on display boards.

Exhibiting: [AW] Applications are welcomed and the gallery takes no commission.

Lumsden (Grampian Region)

(SAC) Map1 NJ44

Scottish Sculpture Workshop

[Sc,Dr]

Address: 1 Main Street, Lumsden, Huntly AB5 4JN tel 046 46 372

Contact: Fred Bush

Open: Daily 10-4

Policy: The workshop is essentially a facility for artists to make sculpture and the gallery mainly shows work made in the workshop.

Sales: Work sold

The Space: A space of 25 square metres with 15m linear hanging space used for showing sculpture and drawings. Hanging is by rail and direct fixing with fluorescent and natural lighting.

Exhibiting: [AW] Applications to exhibit are accepted, commission is 30%, or 20% for members, and the gallery covers insurance, printing and mailing of publicity and an information card.

Access: [U][T] 35 miles west of Aberdeen on Huntly road; Car park

Markinch (Fife Region)

(SAC) Map2 NO20

Arts in Fife, Visual Arts Department

[VA,LA]

Address: Markinch Centre, Bowling Green Road, Markinch, Fife KY7 6BD tel 0592 756633
Contact: Principal Art Officer Bridget Brown
Open: Mon-Fri office hours
Policy: The Arts in Fife, a section of Fife Regional Council's Community Education and Recreation Services, has the aim of encouraging the arts, whether professional performance, exhibitions or community arts. Services include a free regional arts newspaper, music and prints loan libraries.
The Space: Various large and small spaces in mainly non-art community venues, also travelling gallery 'Doorstep Gallery' taking theme based exhibitions on tour of the region and to schools.

Melrose Station Gallery

A commercial gallery set up in 1986 in a complex which includes a restaurant, crafts centre and shop and model railway. [VA,Cr,Ar,LA]
Address: Palma Place, Melrose, Roxburghshire TD6 9PR tel 089 682 2546
Contact: Jean Walley
Open: Daily 10-6, 1 April-31 Oct; Daily 10-5, 1 Nov-31 Dec
Policy: The gallery promotes the work of local artists and makers in particular, though it occasionally shows work from the UK and abroad - Tibetan crafts and Afghan rugs have both been on display. All work shown is by living artists and of the ten exhibitions a year five of them were solo shows.
Sales: Work sold
The Space: The inside space is 10.2x5.9x2.5m high with 23.8m linear hanging space on rods and hooks with full track lighting with dimmer controls. Outside space available on the former station platform 100x10m.
Exhibiting: [AW] Applications in writing. The gallery either charges a hire fee or 45% commission on sales.
Access: [F] There are no trains within 40 miles; Gallery on main bus routes; Crafts centre has own car park

Oban (Strathclyde Region)

(SAC) Map2 NM83

Corran Halls

[Pa]
Address: Esplanade, Oban PA36 5AB tel 0631 2254
Contact: Honorary Secretary
Open: Mon-Sat 10-5
Policy: Small fine and applied art shows organised by the society on a voluntary basis three times a year.

Paisley (Strathclyde Region)

(SAC) Map2 NS46

Museum & Art Gallery

A museum established last century with a famous collection of Paisley shawls and textiles as well as displays on the weaving industry, natural history, ceramics and Scottish paintings. [VA]
Address: High Street, Paisley, Renfrewshire PA1 2BA tel 041 889 3151
Contact: Curator
Open: Mon-Sat 10-5
Policy: A continuous programme of temporary exhibitions ranging from local art societies to *'adventurous'* contemporary work.
Access: West end of town

Paisley Arts Centre

An arts centre showing work by local artists in the foyer space. [VA]
Address: New Street, Paisley PA1 1EZ tel 041 887 1010
Contact: Liz Moran
Exhibiting: [AW] Contact Liz Moran.

Peebles (Borders Region)

(SAC) Map2 NT24

Picture Gallery, Tweeddale Museum

A small gallery run by a local authority museum sevice. [VA,Ph,Cr]
Address: Chambers Institute, High Street, Peebles EH45 8AP tel 0721 20123
Contact: Curator Rosemary Hannay
Open: Mon-Fri 10-5; Sat,Sun 2-5 Easter-Mid-Oct
Policy: A wide-ranging programme including work by local artists and small-scale national touring exhibitions, both contemporary and historical. The gallery shows around ten exhibitions a year - six containg work by living artists and at least two are solo shows.
Sales: Work sold
The Space: The gallery space is 7.2x16.8x4m, with a total of 44m linear hanging space using hanging rods or mirror plates. Overhead skylights for natural light and/or strip lighting. Access by stairs only.
Exhibiting: [AW] Applications from individuals and groups should be sent in writing before October for exhibitions in the following year. The gallery covers cost of insurance and list of exhibits. Commission of 15% on work sold.
Access: [X] Town centre

Perth (Tayside Region)

(SAC) Map2 NO12

Little Gallery

A privately-funded gallery, principaly showing craftwork, but also stocking a range of original prints, paintings and photographs. [Cr,Pr,Pa,Ph]
Address: 90 Canal Street, Perth, Perthshire PH2 8HX
Contact: George F Logan
Open: 9.30-12.30, 1.30-5.30 Mon-Sat; closed Wed
Policy: Very occasional temporary exhibitions. The gallery also has a photographic print processing service, specialising in hand-worked colour printing.
Exhibiting: Exhibitions are held rarely, mainly because of shortage of space, but if approached by an artist wishing to show work, Mr Logan will usually accede, provided that the work is *'of a suitable standard and will appeal to the people of Perth'*.

Perth Museum & Art Gallery

A purpose-built museum with collections of fine art, applied art, archaeology and natural history. [Pa]

Address: George Street, Perth PH1 5LB tel 0738 32488
Contact: Curator
Open: Mon-Sat 10-1,2-5
Policy: A programme of temporary exhibitions is held to enhance the permanent collection.
Access: Town centre; Nearby parking

Perth Theatre Gallery

This repertory theatre uses its foyer and coffee bar space to show temporary exhibitions. [Pa,Pr,Dr,Ph,Cr]

Address: Perth Theatre, 185 High Street, Perth PH11 5UW tel 0738 21031/38123
Contact: Front of House Manager Kenneth McIntosh
Open: Mon-Sat 10am-11pm
Policy: Exibitions show the work of contemporary Scottish artists, both amateur and professional. As well as paintings, batik, collage and embroidery are shown. There are approximately 15 exhibitions a year normally running for three to four weeks each. The exhibition space aims to be self-supporting and occasionally organises exchange shows with other galleries.
Sales: Work sold; Credit card by special arrangement
The Space: The theatre has 26.5m linear hanging space. There is restriction on size and weight and all work must be wall-based. Gravity rods with sliding hooks are used and spot-lighting is adjustable.
Exhibiting: [AW] Apply initially in writing with photographs. The gallery covers cost of insurance, printing and mailing of publicity, list of exhibits, preview and catalogue/card. Commission 30% on work sold.
Access: [X] BR Perth 5 mins; Car parks 5 mins

Selkirk (Borders Region)

(SAC) Map2 NT42

Robson Gallery

A municipal gallery run by Ettrick and Lauderdale District Council. [VA,Ph,Cr]

Address: Halliwells House Museum, Market Place, Selkirk TD7 4AE tel 0750 20096/20054
Contact: District Curator Ian Brown, Municipal Buildings, High Street, Selkirk tel 0750 20096
Open: Mon-Sat 9-5 , Sun 2-4 Easter-Oct; Mon-Fri 2-4.30, Sat & Sun 2-4 Nov-Dec
Policy: The gallery shows the work of professional local artists which ranges from abstract to traditional. Local makers are also encouraged to exhibit. Ten exhibitions are mounted every year. Some are hired touring shows, about 50% are solo shows by living artists and at least one is unrelated to art. Lectures are occasionally held.
Sales: Work sold
The Space: The gallery is 10.2x5.1x2.5m high and has 19.95m linear hanging space with an additional 18.2m linear on screens with hanging from rail using moulding hooks and lighting from track spots. Daylight can be excluded. Heating can be controlled in part.
Exhibiting: [AW] Applications in writing with photographs to the District Curator at any time, preferably a year in advance. There is a booking fee of £20 (£30 for groups) and commission of 15% on work sold, but the council covers cost of insurance, printing and mailing of publicity, list of exhibits and catalogue/card.
Access: [X] On A7

St Andrews (Fife Region)

(SAC) Map2 NO51

Crawford Arts Centre

A mixed programme arts centre, including visual arts, theatre and workshops. [VA,Cr,Ar,Ph,LA]

Address: 93 North Street, St Andrews, Fife KY16 9AL tel 0334 74610
Contact: Director Diana Sykes
Open: Mon-Sat 10-5, Sun 2-5
Policy: *'The aim is to present the best in contemporary and historical art, local, national and international, at a high professional level.'* The widest possible range of visitors from within the community and throughout Scotland are targeted. In addition to its exhibition activities, the centre also runs artist in residence schemes, workshops and evening classes in the fine and applied arts.
Sales: Work sold

Perth Theatre coffee bar and gallery

Crawford Centre for the Arts: The Balcarres Gallery

The Space: There are four galleries with a linear hanging space of 42m, 12m, 9m and 13.5m. Work must not exceed 2.5m in height. Six Edmonds cases, three built-in craft cases and a gravel-covered area outside between the building and street. Hanging by mirror plates. Daylight can be totally excluded, lighting by tungsten spots or fluorescent tubes. Intruder alarms throughout.

Exhibiting: [AW][EF] Artists, makers, sculptors and photographers should contact the Director at any time (planning 9-12 months ahead). A commission is paid for installations which have been commissioned. Terms are flexible and negotiable. The gallery covers the full cost of an exhibition including artist's expenses. Commission on work sold 30%.

Access: [F][S] Town centre; On all main bus routes; Street parking

Stirling (Central Region)

(SAC) Map2 NS79

Rainbow Slides Leisure Centre

A municipal gallery. [Pa,Pr,Ph]

Address: Goosecroft Road, Stirling FK7 tel 0786 50634

Contact: Department of Leisure & Recreation Mark Wells, Stirling District Council, Beechwood House, St Ninians Road, Stirling

Policy: A varied programme of national touring fine art and photography exhibitions, work of local artists and issue-based exhibitions.

The Space: 20 metres linear hanging space. Not suitable for sculpture. Two small display cases.

Stirling Gallery

A commercial gallery. [Pa]

Address: 7 Baker Street, Stirling FK7 1BJ tel 0786 5703

Contact: Director Angus Ogilvie

Open: Tues-Sat 10-5.30

Policy: A continuous programme of contemporary Scottish fine art exhibitions of both younger and more-established artists.

Stonehaven (Grampian Region)

(SAC) Map1 NO88

Riverside Gallery

A small commercial gallery founded in 1982. [Pa,Pr,Dr]

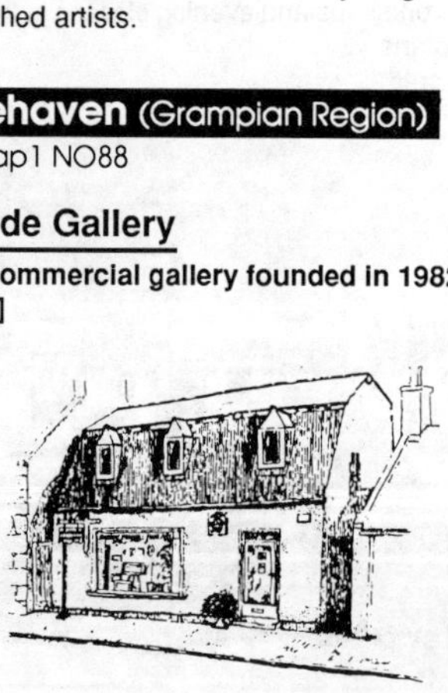

Riverside Gallery

Address: 30a David Street, Stonehaven AB3 2AL tel 0569 63931

Contact: Owner Denis Leiper

Open: Tues-Sat 9.30-12.30, 1.30-5.30

Policy: All work shown in this gallery is by living artists with two solo shows out of four a year. The gallery promotes young artists as well as the more established and aims to build up regular buyers. Talks - Peacock Printmakers of Aberdeen gave the first one on original printmaking - are a recent addition to the programme.

Sales: Work sold

The Space: The gallery has 24m linear hanging space and is 3m high. Paintings must be no larger than 3m square.

Exhibiting: [AW] Artists should apply to the gallery. Cost of insurance, printing and publicity, list of exhibits, preview, mailing of publicity, catalogue/card, is met by the gallery, while other costs may be shared. Commission 33.3% on work sold.

Access: [F] BR Stonehaven 5 mins; Buses pass gallery; Public car park 2 mins

Stornoway (Western Isles)

(SAC) Map1 NB43

An Lanntair

A local art gallery recently set up with funding from the Western Isles Council and the Scottish Arts Council. [VA]

Address: Town Hall, South Beach, Stornoway, Isle of Lewis PA87 tel 0851 3307

Contact: Director Roddy Murray

Open: Mon-Sat 10-6; Closed Wed,Sun

Policy: During the summer when there are many visitors, the gallery shows work by local artists or exhibitions with local relevance. For the rest of the year there is a commitment to making available the most interesting art from the national touring circuit, while promoting Gaelic culture from the Highlands and Islands. Every year has a very mixed programme which has included everything from furniture to photography. Lectures and workshops run on a regular basis. The gallery is available to individuals and groups wishing to set up any such activity.

Sales: Work sold

The Space: Two rooms have 45m linear hanging space and are 3.40m high. Hanging rod system and track-lighting on gantry with spots and floods.

Exhibiting: [AW] An Exhibitions Committee will consider applications by artists which should be accompanied by slides, photographs, CV and statement of intent. The gallery covers cost of insurance, printing and publicity, list of exhibits, preview, transport, mailing of publicity and catalogue/card. Commission 20% on work sold.

Access: [S] Near ferry landing; Public car park nearby

Stranraer (Dumfries and Galloway Region)

(SAC) Map2 NX06

Stranraer Museum

A municipal gallery run by the Wigtown District

Museum Service. [Pa,Pr,Ph]

Address: 55 George Street, Stranraer D69 7JP tel 0776 5088

Contact: Curator Liz Ritchie

Open: Mon-Fri 10-5, Sun 10-1, 2-5

Policy: The gallery aims to show visual art twice a year in their varied exhibition programme. One exhibition is based on local work and the other a hired exhibition. Workshops provided for all exhibitions.

Sales: Sales referred to exhibitor

The Space: The gallery is 500 metres square with suspended, controlled track lighting. Very large work cannot be displayed.

Exhibiting: [AW] Apply to the Curator six months in advance. The gallery covers cost of insurance, printing and mailing of publicity and list of exhibits.

Access: [U][T][L] BR Stranraer 15 mins; Bus stop at museum door; Bus station 10 mins

Strathaven (Strathclyde Region)

(SAC) Map2 NS74

Town Mill Gallery

A gallery within the Town Mill Arts Centre run by Strathaven Arts Guild for community benefit and the promotion of the arts. [VA,Ph,Cr,LA]

Address: Stonehouse Road, Strathaven, Lanarkshire ML10 6LF tel 0357 29411

Contact: Strathaven Arts Guild

Open: Winter 10-5, Summer also 7-9

Policy: The mill was restored as an arts centre in 1976 with modern theatre, large exhibition area, workshops and clubroom and is run on a membership basis. The gallery shows 14 exhibitions a year, almost all by living artists and seven of them solo shows. Craft fairs and antique fairs are also held in the exhibition space. There is also a maker in residence scheme. During the winter art lectures and classes are run from the gallery as well as workshops and outings.

Sales: Sales referred to exhibitor

The Space: A large gallery with craft workshop, foyer and balcony. Plans available to exhibitors. The mill is surrounded by open ground with a public footpath.

Exhibiting: [AW] A telephone call to the Exhibitions Organiser should be followed by an application in writing at least three months in advance. The space is hired at £6 per day plus a 20% commission on work sold over £25.

Access: [U][T][F] Car park adjacent; On A71

Stromness (Orkney)

(SAC) Map1 HY20

Pier Arts Centre

A modern art gallery with a permanent collection housed in two 18th century buildings. [VA]

Address: Victoria Street, Stromness, Orkney KW16 3AA tel 0856 850209

Contact: Director Erlend Brown

Open: Tues-Sat 10.30-12.30, 1.30-5, Sun 2-5 April-Oct

Policy: The collection contains work by Ben Nicholson, Alfred Wallis and Barbara Hepworth. There is a regular programme of temporary exhibitions of contemporary art covering a variety of art forms, both touring and initiated within the gallery.

Sales: Work sold

The Space: Three spaces 3.5x5, 1.8x2.3 and 10.4x2.7m giving a total hanging space of 61 metres.

Exhibiting: [AW] Exhibitions arranged by invitation or application.

Access: Town centre

Stromness Museum

A local history museum with displays on shipping and fishing.

Address: 52 Alfred Street, Stromness, Orkney KW16 tel 085 685 246

Open: Times vary

Policy: Temporary exhibitions held.

Access: Town centre

Thurso (Highland Region)

(SAC) Map1 ND16

Swanson Gallery

A gallery within a library run by Highland Regional Council. [VA,Ph,Cr]

Address: Davidson's Lane, Thurso, Caithness KW14

Contact: Exhibitions Officer Gina Quant, Department of Libraries & Leisure Services, Highland Regional Council, Kinmylies Building, Leachkin Road, Inverness IV7 4BZ tel 0463 234121 ext 448

Open: Mon,Tues,Wed 2-6, Thurs 10-12.30, Fri 2-4 & 6-8, Sat 10.30-1

Policy: *'Due to the isolation of the Highlands, our policy aims to bring into the area a wide range of work by both living and dead artists and makers. Two years ago the region set up a purchase scheme for buying the work of artists living in the area. (See also Wick).*

Sales: Work sold

The Space: Approximately 50 metres wall space and 50 screens. Daylight is excluded and there is track spot lighting.

Exhibiting: [AW] Slides and CVs should be sent to the Exhibitions Officer.

Access: [U][T] Street parking adjacent

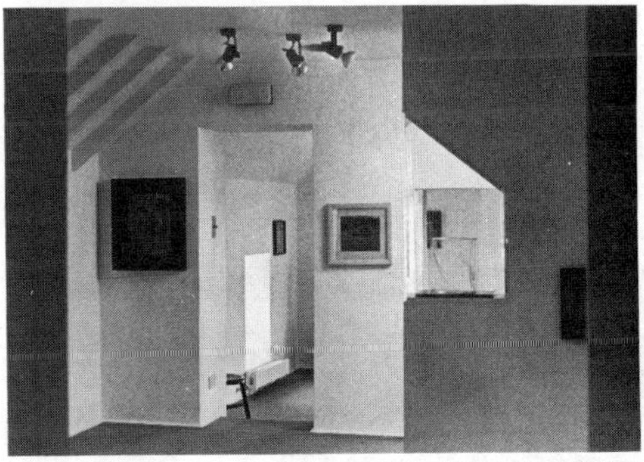

Pier Arts Centre

Wick (Highland)

(SAC) Map1 ND35

Lyth Arts Centre

An arts centre founded in 1977 and funded by the Scottish Arts Council and Highland Regional Council. [VA,Ph,Cr,LA]

Address: Near Wick, Caithness KW1 4UD tel April-Sept 095584 270 by appointment, Oct-Mar 031 226 6424
Contact: William Wilson
Open: Daily 10-6 26, June-6 Sept
Policy: *'Each year the centre mounts a summer exhibition which usually includes a selection of work representing recent developments in the visual arts in Britain, an exhibition which has particular relevence to Scotland, the best local work and several other exhibitions all shown simultaneously for nearly eleven weeks.'* The gallery provides an isolated community the opportunity of seeing contemporary art. The gallery also owns a collection of work by Caithness artists and artists who have worked in the area. Admission is charged.
Sales: Work sold
The Space: The space is flexible and approximately 7,575.75 metres square with overhead track lighting. The outside terrace is available for use.
Exhibiting: [AW] Artists and makers are asked to apply by mid-September for the following year's shows.
Access: [U][T][F] Accessible by car only

St Fergus Gallery

A branch library gallery run by Highland Regional Council. [VA,Ph,Cr]

Address: Sinclair Terrace, Wick, Caithness KW1 5AB
Contact: Exhibitions Officer Gina Quant, Highland Regional Council, Kinmylies Building, Leachkin Road, Inverness tel 0463 234121 ext 448
Open: Mon,Tues,Thurs 2-6, Wed 10-12.30, Fri 2-4 & 6-8, Sat 10.30-1 during exhibitions
Policy: The gallery aims to promote the work of both living and dead artists and makers in an area which would otherwise not be exposed to contemporary art. The range of work shown is diverse in order to cater for many preferences. Two years ago the region set up a purchase scheme to buy work by artists living in the area.
Sales: Work sold

Lyth Arts Centre (Photo: William Wilson)

The Space: Approximately 30m linear wall space and 50 screens. Spots and other tracked lights. Stairs make heavy work difficult.
Exhibiting: [AW] Applications including slides and CV to Exhibitions Officer. The gallery can be hired for £45 per week plus 10% commission on work sold. Exhibition costs are negotiable.
Access: [X] Street parking adjacent

Chapter: 'Gas Mask' by Robert Kennedy, bath stone, 1988 (Photo: Tom Barrance)

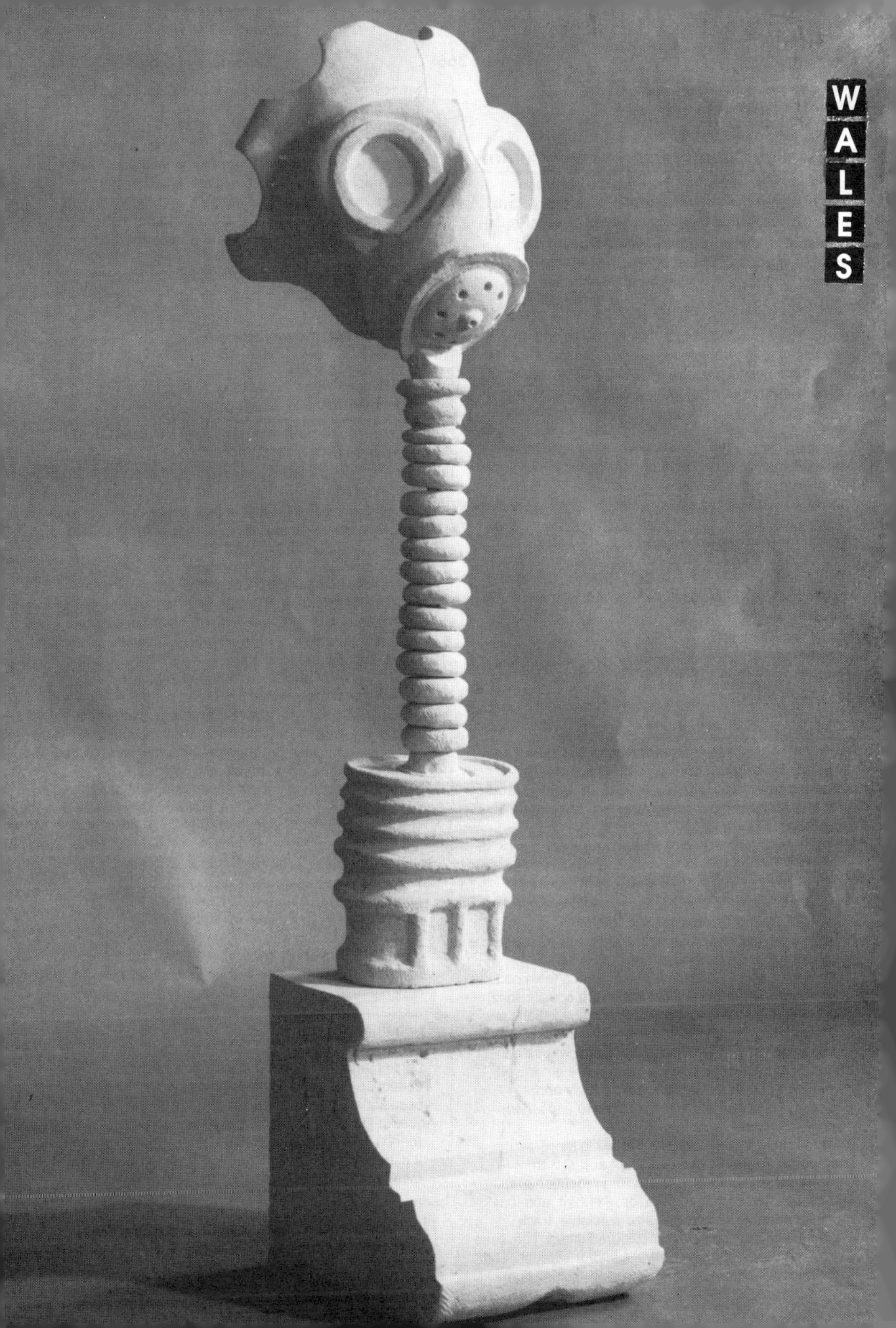

Aberdare (Mid Glamorgan)

(SEWaA) Map4 SO00

Dare Valley Country Park (Visitor Centre)

Exhibition space operating during the summer months within the Visitor Centre of a Country Park run by Cynon Valley Borough Council. [Pa,Pr,Ph,Cr]

Address: Dare Valley Country Park, Aberdare, Mid Glamorgan CF44 7RG tel 0685 874672/883099

Contact: Countryside Officer Dave Protheroe

Open: Mon-Fri 9-5, Sat 10-6, Sun 10-6; closed end September to Easter

Policy: The centre, sited in a Valleys-based country park, attracts 42,000 visitors annually. The exhibition programme encompasses anything which is compatible with the countryside environment, though predominantly these are exhibitions of art and crafts, including solo exhibitions. About four exhibitions are shown during the summer, each lasting for six to eight weeks. Related slide shows, talks, and school visits are also organised.

Sales: Work sold

The Space: Exhibitions shown in the 'balcony area' of the visitor centre.

Exhibiting: [AW] Applications at any time to the Countryside Officer. Gallery only pays for mailing out publicity.

Access: [U][T][X] Aberdare town centre 10 mins; Public car park on site

Abergavenny (Gwent)

(SEWaA) Map4 SO21

Abergavenny Museum

Municipal museum run as Monmouth District Council's Museums Service, with a permanent collection related to local history, archaeology, and rural life, and a regular programme of temporary exhibitions. [Pa,Ph,Cr]

Address: The Castle, Castle Street, Abergavenny, Gwent NP7 5EE tel 0873 4282

Contact: Curator Martin Buckridge

Open: Mon-Sat 11-5, Sun 2-5, closed 1-2 Summer; Mon-Sat 11-4, closed 1-2; closed Sun Winter

Policy: No formal exhibition policy, although a varied programme of exhibitions and events is sought, appropriate to a local history museum in a town popular with tourists. Apart from exhibitions with specific local links, the museum is also interested in exhibitions of contemporary painting and rural crafts which would be of educational value to local schools, for whose benefit talks, demonstrations and workshops are organised whenever possible. *'We try to be as lively and interesting as possible, and will listen to almost any suggestions and ideas.'*

Sales: Work sold; Sales referred to exhibitor

The Space: There are two exhibition areas, with exhibitions on screens in the 5x10m reception area, which has two built-in showcases, 3x1x2m, and four smaller portable showcases also available, track lighting with spots and UV or coloured filters. The Keep is 6.5x10m with hanging on walls and/or screens, and natural lighting from large windows prohibiting light-sensitive exhibits. Gallery plans available. Large lawns in the grounds for outdoor exhibits.

Exhibiting: [AW] Applications to the Curator, describing the exhibition and suggested dates, as far ahead as possible. Gallery covers insurance, printing and mailing out of publicity, and sometimes artists' expenses, though *'much depends on the type and circumstances of the exhibition.'* Fee and expenses sometimes available for demonstrations and workshops. Commission is 20%.

Access: [S][X] Bus station 5 mins; BR Abergavenny 15 mins; Public car park 2 mins

Aberystwyth (Dyfed)

(WWaA) Map4 SN58

Aberystwyth Arts Centre

A large purpose-built arts centre on the campus of Aberystwyth University. [VA,Ph,Cr]

Address: Penglais Hill, Aberystwyth, Dyfed SY23 3DE tel 0970 624278

Contact: Exhibitions Organiser Eve Ropek

Open: Mon-Sat 10-5, also for evening performances in theatre & concert hall; closed Sun

Policy: As well as four main exhibition areas, the arts centre also comprises a concert hall, theatre space, café, and bookshop and crafts shop adjacent to the main gallery space. Of the over 40 exhibitions a year, most feature the work of living artists and makers, and approximately one third are solo exhibitions. To some extent, series of shows are planned to build up the knowledge and interest of the broad but mainly non-art specialised audience, drawn from a wide catchment area of university town and rural farming country. An extensive education programme for adults and children is maintained including residential courses, talks, seminars, workshops and demonstrations. Part of the permanent ceramics collection is always on show in a specially-designed gallery, with regular displays of contemporary ceramics nearby.

Sales: Work sold; Credit card; Credit scheme

The Space: The secure main gallery space is approximately 35x8.5m with 125m linear hanging space. The Ceramics Gallery and ceramics display cases are also fully secure. Two further large display areas, 30x12m and 13x8.5m are in the large foyer space. Other showcases available. A large outdoor concourse area is occasionally used. Gallery plans available.

Exhibiting: [AW] Written applications to the Exhibitions Organiser. The gallery pays for insurance, transport, printing and mail-out of publicity, list of exhibits, catalogue and preview costs. Display costs are occasionally covered. Commission is 20%.

Access: [X] *'We hope to remedy this soon - meanwhile, friendly help always available'.* Buses from town centre, 2 mins; BR Aberystwyth 20 mins walk; Public car park 1 min

National Library of Wales (Gregynog Gallery)

Gallery for temporary exhibitions within the National

Library of Wales, a copyright library which houses a major repository of material relating to Wales. [VA,Ph]

Address: Aberystwyth, Dyfed SY23 3BU tel 0970 623816

Contact: Dr Brynley F Roberts

Open: Mon-Fri 9.30-6, Sat 9.30-5

Policy: The library seeks to display regularly items drawn from its extensive collections. The exhibition programme places emphasis on the visual material in the collections, and exhibitions are regularly mounted on artistic, photographic, cartographic and literary themes, especially on subjects which are considered to be of major significance in the life and history of Wales. The gallery also shows work by contemporary artists and art societies in exhibitions which last between four and six weeks, the majority showing the work of living artists and including solo exhibitions. Numerous visits by schools and other groups are organised.

The Space: Rectangular gallery approx 745 square metres, with 70m of linear hanging space on permanent screens, 2.5m high. UV screens on windows.

Exhibiting: [AW] Applications to the Keeper of Pictures and Maps, Dr D Huw Owen. Gallery covers cost of transport, printing and mailout of publicity, catalogue and list of exhibits, preview costs, and display.

Access: [U][T][L][F] Bus-stop from town centre 5 mins; BR Aberystwyth 20 mins; Car park

Oriel Melyn Wynt/Windmill Gallery

Gallery in converted windmill, showing Victorian & Edwardian watercolours, and some contemporary work with a framing and restoration service. [Pa]

Address: 5 Windmill Court, Upper Eastgate Street, Aberystwyth, Dyfed SA23 2AS tel 0970 615568

Contact: Terry & Dorothy Burgess

Open: Mon-Fri 10-5.30, Sat 10-12.30

University College of Wales (Catherine Lewis Gallery and Print Room)

The gallery is essentially a museum housing Aberystwyth University's graphic art collection and located within the library and used as a reference and teaching collection. [Pr,Dr,Ph]

Address: Hugh Owen Library, University College of Wales, Penglais, Aberystwyth, Dyfed SY23 1HB tel 0970 623339

Contact: Head of Department Alistair Crawford, Visual Art Department, University College of Wales, Llanbadarn Road, Aberyswyth SY23 1HB

Open: Mon-Fri 9.30-5, Sat(term-time) 9.30-12.30; closed Christmas, Easter and bank holidays

Policy: The purpose-built gallery and reference room which stores and exhibits the college collection of graphic art. Exhibitions normally last three months, mostly derived from the collection, but including student exhibitions and exhibitions of graphic art including book illustration from outside the college and collection. The audience is the college community and students though the gallery is open to the public and school visits are organised. *'Proximity to the graphic collections of the National Library of Wales widens the scope. Exhibitions are for scholarship and research rather than entertainment.'*

Sales: Work sold

The Space: Gallery designed for works on paper (also books and small objects), all exhibits are within showcases and displayed without frames. Approx 30 square metres exhibition space, 18.6m linear hanging space. Humidity/UV filtered lighting (no daylight). High-security provision.

Exhibiting: [AW][EF] Applications offering exhibitions of graphic art and photography from outside the College should go to the Head of the Visual Art Department. Gallery covers cost of insurance, catalogue/card or list of exhibits, printing of publicity, and display.

Access: [U][T] Buses from town centre 2 mins; BR Aberystwyth 20 mins; Public car park 2 mins

Ammanford (Dyfed)

(WWaA) Map4 SN61

Anthony Richards Gallery

An artist-run gallery and studio. [Pa]

Address: 38 Quay Street, Ammanford, Dyfed SA18 2EN tel 0269 4959

Contact: Anthony Richards

Open: Irregular, telephone before making a journey

Policy: The gallery, established in 1984, shows changing displays of work for sale rather than separate exhibitions. The majority of works on show are those of the owner (*'representational landscapes and wildlife subjects in acrylics and watercolour'*), though about a quarter of the gallery space is at present available for other artists. Framing service available.

Sales: Work sold

The Space: 16.5x1.5m linear hanging space. Two small glass-fronted cabinets are available for crafts. Track spotlighting and daylight. No environmental controls. *'If it fits through the door, it can fit on a wall'.*

Exhibiting: [AW] The gallery is interested to see work by professional painters rather than amateur artists. Telephone or write to Anthony Richards, and send photographs or bring examples of work to the gallery. At present, the gallery is also interested in good-quality craft work. 10-15% commission on sales, agreements made individually with the artist. Occasionally the gallery can be hired, at negotiable rates.

Access: [F] Very near to town centre, but *'badly signposted'* at present

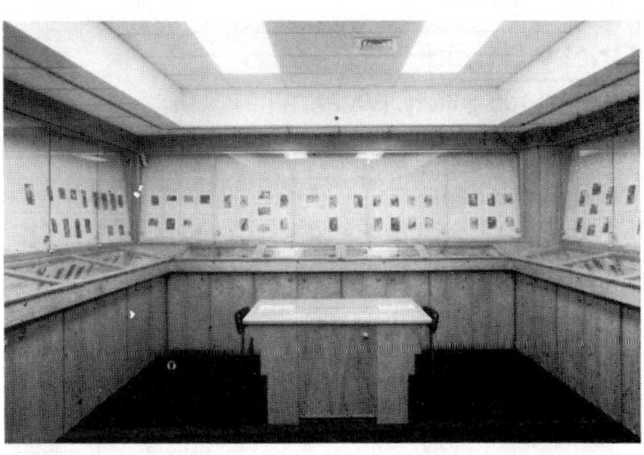

University College of Wales: Catherine Lewis Gallery & Print Room

Beaumaris (Gwynedd)

(NWaA) Map4 SH67

David Hughes Community Centre

Centre in 17th century building adjacent to Beaumaris Castle, showing art exhibitions by local groups and individual artists during the Summer months.

Address: Fford Deg Wen, Llaniestyn, Beaumaris, Anglesey, Gwynedd LL58 8TN tel 0248 810 487
Contact: Hon Secretary K B Williams

Oriel Fach (The Little Gallery)

A commercial gallery showing paintings by local artists. [Pa]

Address: 46A Castle Street, Beaumaris, Anglesey, Gwynedd LL58 8BB tel 0248 810445
Contact: John Joyce
Open: Mon-Fri 10-5; closed 1-2; Wed 10-1 only
Policy: A changing display of work for sale by artists living in Gwynedd.
Sales: Work sold
Exhibiting: [AW] By appointment in person at the gallery. Commission is 25%.
Access: [F] On main street in town centre

Betwys-y-Coed (Gwynedd)

(NWaA) Map4 SH75

Gallery (The)

Crafts shop and commercial art gallery. [VA,Cr]

Address: Holyhead Road, Betwys-y-Coed, Gwynedd LL64 0BH tel 06902 432
Contact: K Rudram
Open: Mon-Sat 9.30-5.30
Policy: Founded in 1976 and housed in a former school, the gallery shows a changing display of mixed work.
Sales: Work sold; Credit card; Credit scheme
Exhibiting: At present the gallery displays work by a selected group of about 25 artists.
Access: [X]

Blaenau Ffestiniog (Gwynedd)

(NWaA) Map4 SH74

Oriel y Ddraig

An artist-run gallery. [VA,Ph,Te]

Address: Unit 2, Diffwys Square, Blaenau Ffestiniog, Gwynedd LL41 tel 0766 831 777
Contact: Pat Clarke
Open: Tue-Sat 9.30-5; closed 1-2; closed Mon
Policy: Shows contemporary work in a wide range of media and styles, with three group exhibitions during the year (including thematic open exhibitions), two solo exhibitions (rarely solo photography exhibitions), the remaining four months of the year exhibiting the work of the gallery's owner, Pat Clarke. Two print racks permanently stock work by about 25 artists. The gallery programme is deliberately uninfluenced by commercial pressures, encouraging unestablished artists and reflecting the interest of the gallery's owners in work which is not always the most easily accessible. Two or three talks, slide shows, poetry readings or music recitals are held in the gallery each year. As the gallery receives no grant aid, the exhibition programme is subsidised by a shop area selling art materials, artists cards, and framing service.
Sales: Work sold
The Space: Downstairs gallery 25 square metres, around 3m high; upstairs gallery 16 square metres, around 2.5m high; 32m linear hanging space overall.
Exhibiting: [AW] Send slides or photographs and CV with SAE to Pat Clarke. Gallery pays for insurance, printing and mailing publicity, list of exhibits, and part of preview costs. The artist is asked for a contribution towards publicity expenses, or alternatively can produce their own publicity. Commission is 25% (20% on work in print racks).
Access: [F]Ground floor **[X]**Upper gallery. BR Blaenau Ffestiniog 2 mins; On bus routes; Public car park adjacent

Brecon (Powys)

(SEWaA) Map4 SO02

Brecknock Museum

Regional history museum run by the local authority, with temporary exhibitions room. Also natural history, art and craft, 19th century court room. [VA,Cr]

Address: Captains Walk, Brecon, Powys LD3 7DW tel 0874 4121
Contact: Curator Don Trueman
Open: Mon-Sat 10-5
Policy: Occasional temporary exhibitions of art and crafts, as well as historical exhibitions.
The Space: Approximate size is 9x10m.
Exhibiting: [AW] Contact the Curator.
Access: [L]

Brecon Library

Library within Powys Libraries & Museums with basement room used for temporary art and crafts exhibitions. [VA,Cr]

Address: Ship Street, Brecon, Powys LD3 9AE tel 0874 3346
Contact: Area Librarian Ken Jones
Open: Mon-Wed & Fri 10-5, Thurs 10-7, Sat 10-12
Policy: The library organises its own temporary exhibitions, but the space is also for hire to individual artists and local societies (free of charge to charitable institutions). See entry for Powys Libraries & Museums, Llandridnod Wells.
The Space: Exhibition room 17x5m with wall display panels, free-standing screens and spotlighting.
Exhibiting: Contact Area Librarian for application details and details of hire charges.

Sable & Hogg Gallery

Small private gallery selling oil paintings, watercolours and prints. [Pa,Pr]

Address: 2 Castle Street, Brecon, Powys LD3 9DD

tel 0874 5901
Contact: Tal Griffiths
Open: Mon-Sat 9.30-5.30; closed Mon & Wed pm

Kiln Gallery

Restaurant, craftshop and post office, with changing display of drawings and paintings by Alex Williams. Second gallery due to open early 1989 with space for other artists. [Pa,Dr]

Address: Honey Cafe, Bronllys, Brecon, Powys LD3 0LH tel 0874 711382
Contact: Alex Williams
Open: Daily 9-7
Sales: Work sold
Access: **[X]** On A438 between Brecon & Hay-on-Wye

Bridgend (Mid Glamorgan)

(SEWaA) Map6 SS97

Nolton Art Gallery

Private gallery, art materials supplier and framing service. [Pa,Pr,Dr]

Address: 66 Nolton Street, Bridgend, Mid Glamorgan CH31 3BP tel 0656 767386
Contact: G L Parkes, 17 Dale View, Cefn Cribbw, Mid Glamorgan tel 0656 745979
Open: Mon-Sat 9-5.30, closed Wed pm
Policy: Founded in 1977, the gallery *'tries to promote a greater awareness of original work instead of the diet of reproductions that the local population has for so long been used to'*. Part of the gallery is reserved for solo and group exhibitions by local artists and others for a fortnight at a time throughout the year. Individual artists may also display one or two works in another part of the gallery reserved for that purpose, plus a changing display of works *'bought in'* by the gallery. Upstairs studio for hire for classes etc.
Sales: Work sold; Credit card
The Space: 5x12x3m with around 35m linear hanging space and spotlights.
Exhibiting: **[AW]** Apply to G L Parkes at gallery. Commission is 25%.
Access: **[F][S]** BR Bridgend 5 mins; Bus station 10 mins.; Public car parks 3 mins

Buckley (Clwyd)

(NWaA) Map4 SJ26

Buckley Library Gallery

Part of Clwyd County Council Library & Museum Service. [VA,Ph,Cr]

Address: Buckley Library, The Precinct, Buckley, Clwyd CH7 2EF tel 0244 550769
Contact: Librarian C Shone
Open: Mon-Fri 9.30-7, Sat 9.30-12.30
Policy: The Clwyd County Council Library & Museum Service policy is to promote awareness of the arts through as varied a programme of exhibitions as possible, including work of local artists and schools, touring exhibitions, artists' residencies etc., making available to the public work that is interesting, educational, entertaining. Exhibitions normally last three weeks, the majority showing work of living artists and makers, including solo exhibitions. The gallery space is also used for other library events.
Sales: Work sold
The Space: 15x8x3m with 14.5m linear hanging space, pinboard with hanging rails with three built-in showcases (available but situated in the lending library on the ground floor) and two movable showcases. Gallery plan available.
Exhibiting: Applications with CV in writing to the Librarian. Library pays for insurance, printing of publicity, list of exhibits. Commission is 20%.
Access: **[X]** Car park adjacent

Builth Wells (Powys)

(SEWaA) Map4 SO05

Wyeside Arts Centre (Wyeside Gallery)

A separate gallery space within an arts centre which also includes theatre and cinema. [VA,Ph,Cr]

Address: Builth Wells, Powys LD2 3BN tel 0982 553668
Contact: Director Jonathon Morgan
Open: Mon-Sat 10.30-4.30; closed Wed
Policy: Wyeside Arts Centre, occupying the former market hall in a country town, is a registered charity. Providing a catholic gallery programme of about ten exhibitions a year, quality and accessibility are its two keynotes, including professional work by artists and makers from the local area, from Wales and beyond, as well as touring exhibitions and local amateur and school groups. The gallery is particularly keen to hear from artists interested in working in residence in the Builth Wells area, or in providing workshops allied to their exhibitions.
Sales: Work sold; Credit card
The Space: Two levels with connecting stairs, with about 40 square metres and 20 square metres and a linear hanging space of 31.8m. Maximum wall height 3.8m, minimum wall height 2.4m. All walls blockboard, spotlights. Alarmed and invigilated. Gallery plans available.
Exhibiting: **[AW][EF]** Apply to the Gallery Selection Committee, which meets three or four times a year. Gallery pays for insurance, transport, printing of publicity and list of exhibits, some artists' expenses. Commission is 20%. The gallery can also be hired, £60 for two weeks. Policy statement available.
Access: **[S]** Directly adjacent to major tourist route; Public car park 2 mins.; On local bus routes

Caernarfon (Gwynedd)

(NWaA) Map4 SH46

Gwynedd Library Service

Library service.

Address: Library Headquarters, County Offices, Caernarfon, Gwynedd LL55 1SH tel 0286 4121 ext 2453
Contact: County Librarian J M Griffiths

Policy: Gwynedd Library Service runs five libraries with special exhibition facilities (listed separately): Blaenau Ffestiniog, Caernarfon, Holyhead, Llandudno, and Llangefni (Oriel Mon). These exhibition spaces are available for staging temporary exhibitions by individual artists (amateur, professional or semi-professional), local art societies or groups, camera clubs etc. Those interested in using the exhibition spaces should contact the relevant person responsible listed for each venue, though a common policy applies: *'The Library Service accepts responsibility for promoting fine arts and crafts and for cultivating public awareness and appreciation of such areas of creative activity. Our significant contribution to such promotion work is the provision of display and exhibition facilities for the work of creative artists. Placed in this context fine art must be narrowed down to include painting, sculpture, drawing and allied art forms, photography and concept art. Performance art and film-making cannot easily be catered for by our necessarily limited facilities.'*

Exhibiting: No fees are charged for the use of the exhibition space, and the library service will prepare posters and simple catalogues. Commission of 15% on sales is charged plus VAT. The staff will not handle sale transactions but will accept reservations and assist potential purchasers in contacting the exhibitor. Exhibitions which are not insured by the exhibitor are subject to *'the practices of the County Council'* which does not accept responsibility for loss or damage to an exhibition during its transit to or from the place of exhibition. Generally, exhibitors are responsible for the transport of exhibitions, and for their assembly and dismantling. However, some assistance can occasionally be provided. A preview may be arranged with the permission of the County Librarian, though refreshments and invitation cards must be provided at the exhibitor's cost. A detailed list of these and other conditions is available from the County Librarian.

Oriel Plas Gwyn Gallery

Private gallery with changing display of mainly local artists. [Pa]

Address: Plas Gwyn, Llanrug, near Caernarfon, Gwynedd LL55 2AQ tel 0286 2619

Contact: Proprietor Richard Humphreys

Open: Open daily 9-9 March-October

Policy: A gallery in a converted 17th century stable, and part of a caravan park, showing a continuous changing display throughout the season of oils and watercolours by local artists, including Richard Humphreys.

Sales: Work sold

The Space: Hanging on pegboard for 70-80 paintings; spotlights.

Exhibiting: [AW] Apply to Richard Humphreys. Gallery pays for printing and mailing publicity, and catalogue/card. Commission is 20%.

Access: [F] On Caernarfon-Llanberis bus route, every 15mins

Caerphilly (Mid Glamorgan)

(SEWaA) Map6 ST18

Coach House Gallery

Artist-run commercial gallery funded in 1988, showing work by artists and makers living and working in Wales. [Pa,Sc,Dr,Ph,Ce,Je,Te]

Address: Mountain Road, Caerphilly, Mid Glamorgan CF8 1HQ tel 0222 863500

Contact: Linda Nottingham

Open: Mon-Sat 10-5, Sun 2-5; Closed Christmas Eve for two weeks

Policy: Exhibitions changing monthly, each displaying work of up to five artists, including one three-dimensional artist or maker, and offering a wide price range. Artists mainly from South Wales, with particular interest in representing the Rhymney Valley, being the only permanent exhibition space in that area.

Sales: Work sold

The Space: Two floors, each 10x5x3m, total of 55m linear hanging space. Hanging from panel pins on battens, and screws into stone walls. Spotlights and good daylight. Two lockable, illuminated glass-fronted cupboards.

Exhibiting: [AW] Apply by letter with slides or photographs, or by appointment in person at the gallery. Will only consider crafts *'of very high standard'*. Gallery pays for insurance, printing and mailing publicity, catalogue/card, and preview costs. Commission is 25%.

Access: [F] Ground floor. Bus station and BR Caerphilly 10 mins

Caldicot (S Gwent)

(SEWaA) Map6 ST48

Tower Gallery

Part of a 14th century tower administered by Monmouth Museums Service. [VA,Ph]

Address: Caldicot Castle, Caldicot, Gwent NP6 4HU tel 0291 420241

Contact: Curator Anne Rainsbury,

Open: Open Mon-Fri 11-5, closed 12.30-1.30; Sat and bank holidays 10-5, closed 1-1.30; Sun 1.30-5, 1 Mar-31 Oct

Policy: About five art and photography exhibitions are mounted during the eight months the castle is open to the public. Gallery established mainly to provide a venue for local artists seeking first exhibition. Now also shows artists from further afield, and formal groups of local artists, photographers, colleges, etc. Regular local following as well as tourist visitors.

Sales: Work sold

The Space: Three rooms, around 4x4m, varying heights, on three floors of castle tower, connected by spiral staircase. Framed work mirror-plated to panelled walls. Track lighting and some daylight, no environmental controls. Limitation on size of work.

Exhibiting: [AW][EF] Apply in writing to Curator, enclosing slides or photographs of current work. Gallery pays for insurance, mailing of publicity, list of exhibits and catalogue/card. Commission is 20% plus VAT on

commission.
Access: [X] Public car park 2 mins

Cardiff (S Glamorgan)

(SEWaA) Map6 ST17

Albany Gallery

Private art gallery founded in 1965, specialising in work by contemporary Welsh artists. [Pa,Pr,Dr]

Address: 74b Albany Road, Cardiff, S Glamorgan CF2 3RS tel 0222 487158
Contact: Mary Yapp & Joan Hughes
Open: Mon-Sat 10.30-5.30
Policy: Regular solo and mixed temporary exhibitions in two rooms on first floor of busy main street, plus changing display of work in stock.
Sales: Work sold; Credit scheme
Access: [X]

Andrew Knight Gallery

Commercial art gallery exhibiting contemporary art. [VA]

Address: 31 Charles Street, Cardiff, S Glamorgan CF1 4EA
Contact: Director Andrew Knight
Open: Tue-Sat 10-5, or by appointment
Policy: Policy to promote a selected number of contemporary artists (these include Harry Holland, Peter Prendergast, Anthony Davies, John Macfarlane), many of whom live and work in Wales, through sales and commissions, both in gallery exhibitions and participation at art fairs UK and abroad. Size of works generally suitable for domestic spaces. *'Target audiences include private individuals (regular buyers, prospective buyers, and those with a committed interest in the visual arts), public collections, and opinion makers.'* About eight exhibitions a year, normally four to six weeks long, majority solo exhibitions, interspersed with occasional mixed displays from permanent stock. Also offers art consultancy services, eg management of commissions and professional advice.
Sales: Work sold; Credit scheme
The Space: Two main gallery spaces (each approximately 16 square metres) and lobby area making a total linear hanging space of 50m. Direct hanging into blockboard clad walls, even fluorescent lighting throughout, no daylight. Gallery plan available.
Exhibiting: Artists usually exhibit by invitation from the gallery, sometimes as result of an application. Before considering new work the gallery likes to see slides of recent work and a CV which should be sent to Andrew Knight. Gallery pays for insurance, printing and mailout of publicity, catalogue/card, and preview costs. Commission negotiable.
Access: [X] BR Cardiff Central 10 mins, Cardiff Queen Street 5 mins; Public car parks 3 mins

Chapter

Gallery in major arts centre, catering for the production and exhibition of visual arts, print, photography, theatre, dance, cinema, music, video and film-making etc., and presenting over 150 public events each month of work by artists of regional and international repute. [VA,Ph,Vi,LA]

Address: Market Road, Canton, Cardiff, S Glamorgan CF5 1QE tel 0222 396061
Contact: Visual Arts Programmer Stuart Cameron
Open: Tues-Sun 12-5, 7-10pm; closed Mon
Policy: Founded in 1971 in a converted school, Chapter is a registered charity. The gallery programmes 24 monthly exhibitions a year with about a third being solo, in all media, but primarily fine art, and is *'committed to showing interesting and challenging work by contemporary artists of regional, national, and international significance. In keeping with the centre's overall artistic policy, the gallery seeks also to address critical involvement with current debate of wider cultural implications (eg social and political) in relation to artistic practice, exhibition and audience. The gallery makes considerable effort to extend its wide audience in relation to specific exhibitions, e.g. community groups, organisations, trade unions etc. Due to a lack of venues in Wales showing such work, the gallery seeks to develop a stronger programme of time-based media/installation work. Frequent activities in relation to exhibitions include talks, debates, workshops, and film and video screenings.*
Sales: Work sold; Credit scheme
The Space: Self-contained alarmed Main Gallery, sub-divided into four interconnected spaces, overall linear hanging space 61m, wall height 3.65m; Second Space 10.7x5.8x3.6m, with 31.3m linear hanging, Second Space Corridor has 17.5m linear hanging, Concourse Wall has 12.2m linear hanging. Fixing with mirrorplates on blockboard walls, tracklighting. Small garden suitable for sculpture.
Exhibiting: [AW][EF] Applications to the Visual Arts Programmer should include CV, captioned visual documentation of work and a visual or written proposal. Applications are accepted at any time but exhibitions

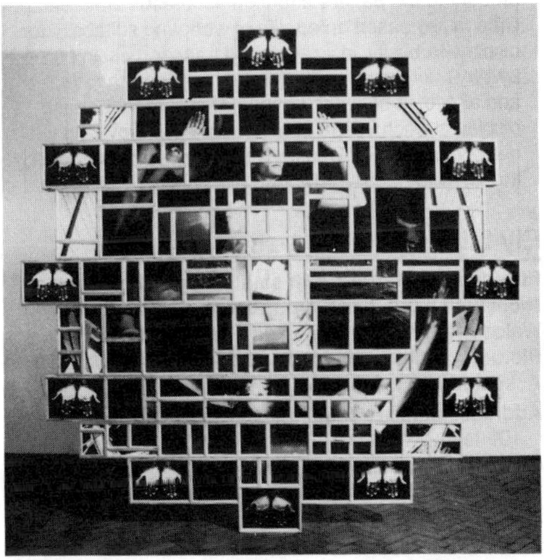

Chapter: 'Icon, Youcon, Wecon' by Graham Ellard from the exhibition 'Transformations', 1988

are programmed 9 to 18 months in advance. The gallery pays for insurance, transport, printing and mailing of publicity, catalogue/list of exhibits, artist's expenses, some installation costs, and preview costs, and can sometimes pay a fee towards production of work tailored specifically to the space. Commission is 25%.

Access: [U][T][F] Buses from city centre 12,14,17,19; BR Cardiff Central 20 mins; Public car park 2 mins

Craft Showcase Network (Welsh Arts Council)

A touring service provided by the Welsh Arts Council. [Cr,Sc]

Address: Craft & Design Department, Welsh Arts Council, Museum Place, Cardiff, S Glamorgan CF1 3NX tel 0222 394711

Contact: Executive Officer Patricia M Harding

Policy: It operates with the co-operation of the network centres, at nine venues around Wales: St David's Concert Hall Cardiff, Newport Museum & Art Gallery, Wrexham Library Arts Centre, Oriel Theatr Clwyd Mold, Rhyl Library Arts Centre, Carmarthen Library, Haverfordwest Library, Caernarfon Library and Llangefni Library (two Mid-Wales venues to be added to Network in 1988/89). Apart from the Showcases in Cardiff, all venues are encouraged to programme displays of local work, in consultation with WAC, as well as toured displays. Work in any one showcase is usually that of an individual rather than group display.

Exhibiting: [AW][EF] Anyone is entitled to apply from anywhere in Great Britain. Work on display is usually for sale, either direct from venue (by prior consultation with Patricia M Harding) or by referral to maker. No commission on sales is charged at this time. Slides of applicants' work are considered by a Selection Panel, one of whose members is the independent researcher responsible for ensuring the contnuity of displays between applicants and other invited artists/makers brought to the panel's attention as a result of research. Criteria are based on quality of work and suitability for display. Publicity, insurance and transport costs borne by WAC, including collection from and return to maker and all transit between venues. Display fee for each display at each venue paid to exhibitors providing full display for any Showcase. Display fees are not paid by the WAC for locally-arranged displays.

Ely Library

Purpose-built library with small separate exhibition room with exhibitions programmed by South East Wales Arts Association as part of their 'Moving Pictures' scheme, see entry for South East Wales Arts Association, Cwmbran.

Address: Grand Avenue, Ely, Cardiff, S Glamorgan CF5 4DF tel 0222 562064

Contact: Senior Branch Librarian John Abraham

Open: Mon 10-1, 2-7, Tues-Fri 10-1,2-6, Sat 9-1, 2-5.30

Policy: To provide an exhibition area that is easily accessible to the local community and schools encouraging new and local artists and allowing space for adult education classes. The exhibitions change monthly.

Sales: Work sold

The Space: The room is about 4x7m using hanging rods and spot lights.

Exhibiting: [AW] Individual artists are responsible for their own insurance and publicity. The room can also be hired for special events.

Access: [F] On bus routes; Street parking

Ffotogallery

Gallery run by the Association of Photographers in Wales, showing changing exhibitions of photographic work from Britain and abroad. [Ph]

Address: 31 Charles Street, Cardiff, S Glamorgan CF1 4EA tel 0222 341667

Contact: Director Christopher Coppock

Open: Mon-Sat 10.30-5.30, closed Sun; closed bank holidays

Policy: The object of the Ffotogallery is *'to promote, maintain, improve and advance education in the knowledge, understanding and appreciation of the Arts and in particular in the medium of photography', through exhibitions, publications, lectures, workshops etc. About ten exhibitions are shown annually, presenting a broad spectrum of photographic work, with both group and solo exhibitions. Some shows originated by the gallery are toured. Whenever possible new work is commissioned by the gallery, forming permanent archive. Regular workshops and full lecture programme. Framing/mounting service.*

Sales: Work sold; Credit scheme

The Space: Gallery on first and second floors, only access stairs. Total of 55m linear hanging space. Direct hanging.

Exhibiting: [AW][EF] Apply to Gallery Director. Programme confirmed one year ahead. Gallery pays for insurance, printing and mailout of publicity, catalogue/card, and preview costs.

Access: [X] BR Cardiff Central and Bus Station 10 mins; Public car parks 2 mins

Frame Shop

Framing business with occasional solo shows in front area of shop.

Address: 17 Pontcanna Street, Pontcanna, Cardiff, S Glamorgan CF1 9HQ tel 0222 345260

Contact: Charles Hallinan

Framework

Framing business with small exhibition space and large window display area usually showing local artists. [Pr,Pa]

Address: 41 Lochaber Street, Roath, Cardiff, S Glamorgan CF2 3LS tel 0222 481336

Contact: Selina and Rory Byrne

Open: Tues-Sat 10-1,2-6

Policy: The gallery sells prints, pictures, hand-painted frames and mirrors.

Sales: Work sold

The Space: Workshop and shop with large windows.

Access: Parking

Gallery (The)

Private art gallery within the showrooms of an interior design consultancy. [Pa,Pr,Sc]

Address: Richard Beere Interiors, 111-117 Woodville Road, Cardiff, S Glamorgan CF2 4DY tel 0222 394131
Contact: Tisch Beere,
Open: Mon-Fri 9-5
Policy: The gallery shows about four special exhibitions a year of paintings and desk size sculptures by contemporary artists, usually group exhibitions but occasionally solo, lasting three to four weeks. At other times, a changing display of work for sale.
Sales: Work sold
The Space: The gallery is about 115 square metres.
Exhibiting: [AW] Apply in writing to Tisch Beere enclosing slides or photographs of work.

Howard Gardens Gallery

Exhibition space in an educational setting. [VA,Ph,Cr,De,LA]

Address: Faculty of Art and Design, S Glamorgan Institute of Higher Education, Howard Gardens, Cardiff, South Glamorgan CF2 1SP tel 0222 551111 ext 5504
Contact: Gallery Secretary Judy Kelly,
Open: Mon-Thurs 9.30-8.30, Fri 9.30-6
Policy: Diverse programme of exhibitions in wide range of media representing the international contemporary arts. *'Encouragement is given to young artists and designers to see and experience standards at national and international level.'* Some associated lectures and performances. Space also used for degree shows.
Sales: Work sold; Credit scheme
The Space: Custom-built gallery of 264 square metres on ground floor of art college with 364 square metres of hanging space on movable floor/ceiling suspended screens. Track lighting and controllable daylight. Three types of secure display cases available. Enclosed courtyard adjacent to gallery. Gallery plans available.
Exhibiting: [AW][EF] Applications (CV and slides/photographs of work) at any time to Gallery Secretary for consideration by the Gallery Committee. Gallery pays for insurance, transport, printing and mailout of publicity, list of exhibits/catalogue, and preview costs. Commission is 25%. Exhibition space also for hire at negotiable rates - contact Mrs E M George.
Access: [F] BR Cardiff Queen Street 5 mins; Buses to Newport Road; Car park; Sign posted from main roads

Llanover Hall Oriel Llanover

Arts centre run by South Glamorgan County Council Educational Authority, offering classes and workshops for all ages.

Address: Romilly Road, Canton, Cardiff, S Glamorgan CF5 1FH tel 0222 342022
Contact: Gallery Director Tony Goble
Open: Mon-Fri 9.30-4 6.30-9, Sat 9.30-12 noon
Policy: Separate exhibition area with regular programme of monthly small exhibitions, with more space available on adjacent main staircase. Programme often features young professional artists from the Cardiff area.
Sales: Work sold; Credit scheme
Exhibiting: Contact the part-time Gallery Director, Tony Goble, or Director, Mary Askey. No commission charged.

Mackintosh Gallery

Framing business with changing display of paintings and prints in front shop area.

Address: 16 Mackintosh Place, Roath, Cardiff, S Glamorgan CF2 4RQ tel 0222 463688
Contact: Mervyn Williams
Open: Mon-Sat 9.30-5.30

Manor House Fine Arts

Private gallery specialising in 19th and 20th century paintings and prints, with only a small proportion of work by living artists, though there are plans to expand this side of the business with a new gallery for contemporary art, including sculpture, opening March 1989. [Pa,Pr]

Address: 73 Pontcanna Street, Cardiff, S Glamorgan CF1 9HS tel 0222 227787
Contact: Steven Hill
Open: Tues,Thurs,Fri & Sat 10.30-5.30
Policy: To make available in Cardiff sensible priced oil paintings, watercolours and prints from 1800 to the present day.
Sales: Work sold; Credit card
The Space: Two well-lit galleries each capable of displaying 40 medium-sized paintings.
Access: City centre 1 mile; Parking

National Museum of Wales (Department of Art)

The museum organises a regular programme of temporary exhibitions (currently restricted by major refurbishments), alongside the permanent display of its art collection and a cabinet display of work by three contemporary makers also changes monthly. [VA,Cr]

Address: Cathays Park, Cardiff, S Glamorgan CF2 3NP tel 0222 397951
Contact: Keeper of Art Timothy Stevens
Open: Tues-Sat 10-5, Sun 2-5
Policy: Exhibitions of contemporary art are also organised by the Museum for the Turner House Gallery (see under Penarth).
Access: [U][T] rear of building, **[L][S]** Free parking by museum

Oriel

Gallery owned and run by the Welsh Arts Council, on ground floor of their bookshop building. [VA,Ph,Cr,LA]

Address: 53 Charles Street, Cardiff, S Glamorgan CF1 4ED tel 0222 395548
Contact: Gallery Manager Joy Goodfellow
Open: Mon-Sat 9-5.30; closed public holidays
Policy: Varied programme of monthly temporary exhibitions, placing an emphasis always on the work of

living practitioners, *'promoting in Cardiff and Wales the understanding and enjoyment of the best of visual arts and crafts, reflecting and aiding the development of visual arts and crafts in and of Wales, and presenting to the people of Cardiff and South East Wales some of the best of the visual arts and crafts from outside Wales.'* School workshops organised for every exhibition. Space occasionally used for evening bookshop readings.

Sales: Work sold; Credit scheme

The Space: Three spaces: 12x6m, 7x2.5m, 3x5m approx. Direct hanging with mirror plates. Lighting by tungsten halogen lamps and spots.

Exhibiting: [AW][EF] Applications to exhibit are placed before Oriel Sub-Committee for consideration. Apply in writing to Gallery Manager, enclosing CV and some visual material, and indicating why you want to show at Oriel. Gallery pays for insurance, transport, printing and mailout of publicity, catalogue/card, list of exhibits, preview costs, display, and artists' expenses. Commission 30% plus VAT.

Access: [X] *'but we do cope.* Centrally situated near all bus routes; BR Cardiff Central 10 mins, BR Cardiff Queen Street 5 mins; Public car parks 2 mins

Riverside Studios

The large first-floor studio and workshop of artists Manuel Cardenas and Catrin Clarke, which is occasionally used for mixed and thematic public exhibitions by invited artists.

Address: 24a Tudor Lane, Riverside, Cardiff, S Glamorgan CF1 8RZ tel 0222 344750

Contact: Manuel Cardenas & Catrin Clarke

Open: Mon-Fri 9-1 2-6 during exhibitions

St David's Hall

Exhibition areas in foyers of 2000-seat concert hall. [VA,Ph,Cr]

Address: The Hayes, Cardiff, S Glamorgan CF1 2SH tel 0222 342611

Contact: Building & Activities Manager Nigel Fraser

Open: Mon-Sat 10-10

Policy: About 20 temporary exhibitions a year, all showing the work of living artists/makers. Policy to exhibit a wide variety of work likely to be of interest to audiences at the concert hall, in particular promoting Welsh artists, both established and new. Exhibitions also mounted to complement events in the auditorium. Venue for six showcases programmed by the Welsh Arts Council Craft Showcase Network (see Welsh Arts Council). Various paintings, sculptures and stained glass on permanent display in foyers.

Sales: Work sold; Credit card; Credit scheme

The Space: Level 2: work fixed to 20 screens, each 2.5x1.3m; fixed exhibition lighting system. Level 4: Wall space 50m long x 1m high.

Exhibiting: [AW][EF] Exhibitions selected by panel which meets twice-yearly. Applicants should contact either the Director or the Building and Activities Manager at any time, preferably by letter. Gallery pays for insurance, printing and mailout of publicity, catalogue, hanging, and preview costs. Commission 25%. Exhibition space also for hire, negotiable terms.

Access: [U][T][L][F] Near all central bus routes; BR Cardiff Central 10 mins; Public car parks 3 mins

Taflen

Sherman Theatre Gallery

'Gallery-cum-restaurant' in performing and film theatre grant aided by the Welsh Arts Council and city/county councils. [Pa,Pr,Dr,Ph]

Address: Sherman Theatre, Senghennydd Road, Cardiff, S Glamorgan CF2 4YE tel 0222 396844

Contact: Front of House Manager Alex Jones

Open: Mon-Sat 10am-10pm, open Sun if performance

Policy: Audience comprises people attending theatre, so exhibitions with particular relevance to centre's main activities preferred. Also shows local professional artists, schools exhibitions etc. Exhibitions last one month minimum.

Sales: Work sold; Credit card

The Space: 30m linear hanging space, direct fixing onto 2m high panels. Spotlights.

Exhibiting: [AW][EF] Apply at any time to Artistic Director, Mike James. Gallery pays for insurance, list of exhibits, part mailout of publicity, and sometimes transport and other artists' expenses. Commission 10%.

Access: [U][T] Main building **[X]** Gallery. BR Cathays Halt 3 mins; Buses 35,73; Car park 5 mins

Taflen

Craft gallery on ground floor of Welsh books and record shop, art gallery in basement. [Pa,Pr,Dr,Ph,Cr]

Address: 12 Duke Street Arcade, Cardiff, S Glamorgan CF1 2AZ tel 0222 227530

Contact: Cen Williams, 19 Dogfield Street, Cathays, Cardiff CF2 4QJ tel 0222 233473

Open: Mon-Sat 10-5.30

Policy: Monthly exhibitions of both established living artists and good young makers from Wales and beyond. Demonstrations to coincide with exhibitions. Also frequently changing display of high-quality crafts in shop area.

Sales: Work sold; Sales referred to exhibitor; Credit card

The Space: Basement: 20m linear hanging space on running panel 1m high, direct fixing with mirrorplates; track lighting. Shop area: 5x1m wall area plus shelving suitable for three-dimensional work.

Exhibiting: [AW] Apply to Cen Williams. Gallery pays for insurance, printing and mailout of publicity, list of exhibits, and preview costs. Commission 33.3%.

Access: [X] BR Cardiff Central 10 mins; Public car parks 5 mins

Things Welsh

Craft and gift shop with small basement gallery showing mixed display of work by local artists. [Pa,Pr]

Address: 3-7 Duke Street Arcade, Cardiff, S Glamorgan CF1 tel 0222 233445

Contact: Kevin Fowler

Open: Mon-Sat 10-5.30

University College Cardiff (Viriamu Jones Gallery)

Large specially-adapted space for temporary exhibitions in concourse, showing predominantly but not exclusively local professional artists. [VA]

Address: University College, Main Building, Park Place, Cardiff, S Glamorgan CF1 3QN tel 0222 874000

Policy: Exhibition programme suspended at time of going to press due to educational cuts and university merger.

Cardigan (Dyfed)

(WWaA) Map4 SN14

Frame by Frame

Gallery and studio run by photographer Graham Holdsworth, showing solo, group and thematic shows by local artists which also stocks frames and artists supplies. [Pa,Pr,Sc]

Address: Black Lion Mews, Cardigan, Dyfed SA43 tel 0239 615121

Contact: Proprietor Graham Holdsworth, Bay View Cottage, St Dogmaels, Cardigan, Dyfed SA43 3DU

Open: Mon-Sat 10-4.30, Tues Oct-March; closed Wed

Sales: Work sold

The Space: The gallery is about 7.5 square metres.

Exhibiting: Contact Graham Holdsworth. Framing and photographic service for exhibitors.

Access: [X]

Carmarthen (Dyfed)

(WWaA) Map4 SN42

Carmarthen Museum

Museum run by Dyfed County Council, reflecting the archaeology, folk life, natural history, culture and environment of the Carmarthen region. [Pa,Pr,Dr,Ph,Cr]

Address: Abergwili, Carmarthen, Dyfed SA31 2JG tel 0267 231691

Contact: Curator C J Delaney

Open: Mon-Sat 10-4.30

Policy: Galleries specially designed to accommodate a varied programme of monthly temporary exhibitions, majority showing work of living artists/makers, plus scientific and historic. Mostly shows touring exhibitions from Wales and beyond, but several initiated annually by museum to show work of professional artists and makers in Wales. Museum's permanent collection also includes work of contemporary artists and makers in West Wales. Organises talks, tours and workshops with exhibitions.

Sales: Work sold; Credit scheme

The Space: Two temporary exhibition galleries with a total of 62m linear hanging space. Direct hanging to blockboard clad walls; showcases. Grade A security conditions also complying with all conservation and display controls. Sculpture has been shown in the Main Hall and the museum grounds. Gallery plan available.

Exhibiting: [AW][EF] Initial application by letter (without slides at this stage) to Chris Delaney, Curator, or Sally E Moss, Assistant Curator. Gallery pays for insurance, printing of publicity, list of exhibits, mailing out of publicity, catalogue/card, preview costs, and transport (though *'some artists have transported their own work'*), Commission 20%.

Access: [U][T][F] On Llandeilo-Carmarthen bus route; BR Carmarthen 60 mins; Own car park

Henry Thomas Gallery (Carmarthenshire College of Technology & Art)

Public art gallery within an educational setting. [VA,Ph,Cr]

Address: Faculty of Art and Design, Job's Well Road, Carmarthen, Dyfed SA31 3HY tel 0267 235855

Contact: Gallery Assistant Alison Lloyd

Open: Mon-Thurs 10am-8pm, Fri 10-4.30

Policy: Broad programme of exhibitions, normally lasting for two weeks, *'evenly balanced between fine art, sculpture, photography, crafts and design'*. Gallery also used for the college's final shows.

Sales: Work sold

The Space: Gallery area 18x5.8m, with 47.6m linear hanging space available on walls and screens; showcases. Direct fixing, fluorescents and tracklighting; humidifiers available, temperature and humidity monitor in gallery.

Exhibiting: [AW][EF] Written applications to Alison Lloyd, Gallery Assistant, or Gareth J Evans, Dean of Faculty. Artists interviewed prior to being offered an exhibition. Early application essential, as programme usually planned two years in advance. Gallery pays for insurance, printing and mailout of publicity, list of exhibits and catalogue/card as well as providing a fee for hire of works. Commission 20%.

Access: [U][T][F] Carmarthen town centre 10 mins; regular bus service from BR Carmarthen and bus depot to college entrance

Chepstow (Gwent)

(SEWaA) Map6 ST59

Chepstow Museum

Gallery for temporary exhibitions within museum run by Monmouth Borough Council dealing predominantly with local history. [Pa,Ph,Cr]

Address: Gwy House, Bridge Street, Chepstow, Gwent NP6 5EZ tel 0291 265981
Contact: Curator Anne Rainsbury
Open: Open Mon-Sat 11-1 2-5, Sun 2-5, 1 Mar-31 Oct; open bank holidays
Policy: Usually five exhibitions during the museum's eight-month opening period, each normally shown for six weeks. In addition to exhibitions which explore contemporary and historical local themes in depth, the programme covers subjects outside the scope of the museum's own collections such as technology and science, natural history and ethnology, as well as art and craft. Particularly interested in professional artists and makers working in the area or on local subjects or related themes, as well as exhibitions of broader interest. Workshops and demonstrations related to exhibitions for children and adults.
Sales: Work sold
The Space: Room area of about 27 square metres with 18.5m linear hanging space; demountable display cases available; tracklighting, no daylight, light levels controlled and monitored. Gallery plan available.
Exhibiting: [AW][EF] Applications at any time for subsequent year to the Curator. Gallery pays for insurance, printing and mailout of publicity, list of exhibits, catalogue/card, and preview costs. Commission is 20% plus VAT on commission.
Access: [U][T] BR Chepstow 5 mins; Public car park 1 min

Old Bell Gallery

Commercial gallery and picture framer. [VA]
Address: Off Bank Street, Chepstow, Gwent NP6 5EN tel 02912 3400
Contact: Proprietor Michael Wadcock
Open: Mon-Sat 9.30-5.30, Wed 9.30-1.30
Policy: Monthly solo contemporary art exhibitions throughout the year, with changing mixed display in separate area. Work exhibited is selected *'without bias, provided that it is professionally presented and good of its kind.'* Occasional talks by artist on exhibition.
Sales: Work sold; Credit card; Credit scheme
The Space: Two galleries, 33m linear hanging space overall; halogen spotlights; showcase for handmade jewellery.
Exhibiting: [AW][EF] Gallery pays for all exhibition costs. Commission is 33.3%. Also agent for sculpture, portrait, and mural commissions. Exhibition space for hire.
Access: [F] Adjacent to free public car park

Picturesque

Framing business also displaying some paintings and prints by local artists. [Pa,Pr]
Address: 16 St Mary Street, Chepstow, Gwent NP6 5EW tel 02912 3000
Contact: Gerry Picton
Open: Mon-Sat 9-5

Workshop Gallery

Commercial art and craft gallery and studio of ceramic artist Ned Heywood. [VA,Ph,Cr]
Address: 13 Lower Church Street, Chepstow, Gwent NP6 5HJ tel 02912 4836
Contact: Owner Ned Heywood
Open: Mon-Sun 2-6, closed Wed
Policy: Varied programme of group exhibitions (usually two or three artists) normally shown for two months, of *'affordable art and craft work with high standards of design, manufacture and integrity.'* Mix of established artists/makers and lesser known newcomers. Target audience *'all who are interested in quality art and craftwork'*, mostly within 50 mile radius.
Sales: Work sold; Credit scheme
The Space: Linear hanging space 20m, height 2.6m.; spotlights and daylight; display stands and wall case; security cameras. Gallery plan available.
Exhibiting: [AW] *'Telephone Ned Heywood to apply. Send photos or slides of work and telephone for comment. Arrange to visit gallery with examples of work'.* Gallery pays for insurance, printing and mailout of publicity, list of exhibits and preview costs. Commission is 30%, with max. £30 commission on any one item.
Access: [X] BR Chepstow 5 mins; Public car park 1 min

Clyro (Powys)

(SEWaA) Map4 SO24

Kilvert Gallery

A private gallery in a Victorian house one time home of the diarist Rev Francis Kilvert (1865-72). [VA,Cr,Ph]
Address: Ashbrook House, Clyro, Nr Hay-on-Wye, Powys HR3 5RZ tel 0497 820831
Contact: Elizabeth Organ & Eugene Fisk
Open: Tues-Sun 10-5
Policy: The owners have converted the two floors of their house into galleries and they present art and craft work in the sense of *'room creating'*, combining paintings and objects in a domestic setting rather than in a gallery context. The policy is to select and promote a number of artists, about 50. Shows work by 20th century artists and some 19th century work. Also organises painting courses and lectures.
Sales: Work sold
The Space: 50m linear hanging space over seven rooms,

Kilvert Gallery (Photo: Cliff Guttridge)

maximum height 2.5m, jewellery display case, small courtyard with stream and large lawn.

Exhibiting: [AW] Apply by letter enclosing photographs with dimensions. Gallery pays for insurance while on premises, shares cost of printing and publicity, catalogues and preview . Commission is 33.3%.

[S] first floor, [X] Second floor. Buses to Hay-on-Wye 1 mile distant; Car park

Connah's Quay (Clwyd)

(NWaA) Map4 SJ26

Connah's Quay Library

Part of Clwyd Libraries and Museum Service.

Address: Wepre Drive, Deeside, Clwyd CH5 4HA tel 0244 830485

Contact: Librarian Sheila Kirby

Open: Mon-Tues, Thurs-Fri 9.30-7, Wed 9.30-1, Sat 9-12

Policy: Clwyd Libraries and Museum Service promotes awareness of the arts through as varied a programme of exhibitions as possible, including work of local artists and schools, touring exhibitions, artists' residencies, making available work that is interesting, educational, entertaining. Exhibitions normally last three to four weeks, the majority showing work by living artists and makers, including solo exhibitions.

Sales: Work sold

Exhibiting: [AW] Apply in writing to the Librarian. Library pays insurance, printing of publicity, list of exhibits and charges 20% commission.

Conwy (Gwynedd)

(NWaA) Map4 SH77

Royal Cambrian Academy of Art

Premises of professional society established in the 1880s.

Address: High Street, Plas Mawr, Conwy, Gwynedd LL32 8DE tel 0492 593413

Contact: Curator/Academy Secretary Leonard Mercer

Open: Daily 10-6 Apr-Sept; 10-4 Oct; Wed-Sun 10-4 Nov,Feb-Mar; closed Dec-Jan

Policy: The 16th century house is open to the public, and presents a regular programme of public art exhibitions and other events, including a major annual Summer Exhibition open to Academy members and non-members.

Cowbridge (S Glamorgan)

(SEWaA) Map6 SS97

John Owen Gallery

Private gallery showing mainly 18th & 19th century paintings, with some contemporary Welsh artists. [Pa,Pr]

Address: Cowbridge Antiques, 55 Eastgate, Cowbridge, S Glamorgan CF7 7EL tel 04463 4774

Contact: John Owen

Open: Mon-Sat 9,30-5.30, Sun 2-5

Old Hall Gallery

Two related exhibition spaces within an adult education centre serving Cowbridge and the Vale of Glamorgan, and Cowbridge Public Library. [Pa,Pr,Dr,Ph,Cr]

Address: Old Hall Community College, High Street, Cowbridge, S Glamorgan CF7 7AH tel 04463 3831

Contact: Principal K James

Open: Mon-Fri 9.30-12,2-4,7-9pm; Sat 10-4; closed Sun

Policy: *'We aim to encourage young artists just completing their degree courses, but also local painters and makers of all ages, whether in societies (eg Glamorgan Guild of Spinners & Weavers) or individually.'* Varied programme of monthly exhibitions, main programme at Old Hall, complementary programme of exhibitions in nearby public library. Crafts workshops held regularly at Old Hall at weekends.

Sales: Work sold

The Space: Linear hanging space around 30m, height 3m; hanging rods.

Exhibiting: [AW] Applications to K James at Old Hall. Exhibition programme selected by hanging committee of Cowbridge Arts Group. Work shown has usually been completed within the past year. Gallery covers cost of insurance, all other costs can be covered in principle by regional grant-aid schemes. Some exhibitors receive exhibiting fee. Commission 10% for main exhibitions, 5% others.

Access: [F] On main Cardiff-Bridgend bus route; Public car parks 2 mins

Watercolour Gallery

Small gallery showing 19th & 20th century watercolours with about 50% by contemporary artists. [Pa]

Address: The Old Wool Barn, Verity Court, Cowbridge, S Glamorgan CF7 7D tel (after hours) 04463 3324

Contact: Rory Allin

Criccieth (Gwynedd)

(NWaA) Map4 SH43

Les Burridge, Framing & Restoration

Framing business opposite Criccieth castle, displaying paintings for sale in the front shop area.

Address: Castle Square, Criccieth, Gwynedd LL52 0DP tel 0766 522803

Contact: Les Burridge

Open: Mon-Sat 9-5.30

Cwmbran (Gwent)

(SEWaA) Map6 ST29

Llantarnam Grange Arts Centre

Regional arts centre with exhibition spaces, other public events, meeting rooms, and coffee shop. [VA,Ph,Cr]

Address: St Davids Road, Cwmbran, Gwent NP44 1PD tel 06333 3321

Contact: Arts Centre Manager Sara Bowie

Open: Mon-Fri 10-4, Sat 10-2

Policy: With 23 different monthly exhibitions annually of work by living artists/makers, the arts centre aims to *'show as wide a range of media as possible and to promote all aspects of the visual arts to a high standard.'* Practical involvement with artists is encouraged through workshops, dayschools and classes coinciding with exhibitions, short artists' residencies in the gallery, involving all age groups from the local community, schools and colleges. Permanent display of ceramics for sale in coffee shop.

Sales: Work sold; Credit scheme

The Space: The main gallery has two rooms: 8x5.5x2.5m, 7x5.5.x2.5m and has 51.3m linear hanging space. Coffee Shop Gallery is L-shaped with 11.6m linear hanging. Third gallery space has two rooms: 8x5.5x2.5m, 5.5x4.3x2.5m with 33.5 linear hanging. Direct fixing and hanging rods, spotlights. Very heavy items not acceptable. Landscape gardens may be suitable for sculpture.

Exhibiting: [AW] [EF] Apply to the Exhibitions Organiser during Oct/Nov for exhibitions during the following year. The gallery pays for insurance, printing and mailout of publicity, list of exhibits, catalogue/card, and preview costs. Commission is 20%.

Access: [U][T][F] BR Cwmbran 5 mins; Public car parks 3 mins; On main bus route to town centre

Moving Pictures

Touring exhibitions service run by South East Wales Arts Association. [VA,Ph,Cr]

Address: South East Wales Arts Association, Victoria Street, Cwmbran, Gwent NP44 3YT tel 06333 75075

Contact: Visual Arts Officer Richard Cox

Policy: Scheme designed as part of its visual arts policy to make available exhibitions for the general public in places either where there is little or no opportunity to see the visual arts, or in places where there are large and broad audiences who might not choose to visit an exhibition even if there was a gallery close by eg libraries, civic centres, leisure centres, schools, hospitals, and *'anywhere that has a good, well-lit, accessible space large enough to show artwork without being compromised by inappropriate or unsympathetic surroundings.'* Organising on average about 75 small-scale shows a year of predominantly but not exclusively *'young emerging artists', the scheme comprises three kinds of exhibitions: Laminated shows, owned and toured by SEWAA, generally photography, prints or drawings, mixed and one-person, 15-25 A1 panels per exhibition. Small and medium-scale framed exhibitions, and larger scale painting and sculpture for suitable venues. Craft work for restricted number of venues with suitable display cases. Work for laminated shows is purchased by SEWAA from the artist.*

Moving Pictures: Ceramics by Carol Anne Davies on show at Islwyn Civic Centre, Gwent (Photo: Tom Barrance)

Sales: Can be negotiated through South East Wales Arts

Exhibiting: [AW][EF] Artists can apply to be considered for this scheme by contacting SEWAA, by sending CV, six slides and SAE. Also *'If you locate a good exhibiting space that complies with our criteria and gain agreement with the host to show work you may qualify for the exhibiting fee'.* In general artists from outside the SEWAA area (South & Mid Glamorgan, Gwent, South Powys) take part in this scheme only by invitation. The scheme is not open to full-time students. Exhibition fees are paid to artists exhibiting in the other two categories: currently £75 solo show, £40 each two-person show, £40 each person showing several pieces in a shared exhibition in a large exhibition area. Exhibitions in the second and third categories must be insured by the artist unless venue offers its own insurance. No commission in most sites.

Dolgellau (Gwynedd)

(NWaA) Map4 SH71

Library Art Gallery

Commercial art gallery in the former library of a Georgian mansion, now a hotel. [VA,Te]

Address: Borthwnog Hall, Bontddu, Dolgellau, Gwynedd LL40 2TT tel 034149 271

Contact: V L Hawes

Open: Daily 10.30-5

Policy: The gallery shows a constantly changing display of work for sale, interspersed with two or three solo or two-person exhibitions during the year, each lasting from three to six weeks. Policy to promote sale of work by Welsh artists or artists resident in Wales, or work with Welsh subject matter. Also shows some sculpture, ceramics, and embroidery. Target audience visitors to hotel and restaurant (predominantly business and professional) and local residents.

Sales: Work sold; Credit scheme

The Space: Approximately 17x4m; hanging on hooks and cord; spotlighting; no environmental controls; picture size limited to 95x85mm.

Exhibiting: [AW] Individual artists should apply to V L Hawes. Gallery pays for preview costs and list of exhibits only. Commission is 33.3%.

Access: [F]

Fishguard (Dyfed)

(WWaA) Map4 SM93

Fishguard Library

Exhibition space in public library run by Cultural Services Department of Dyfed County Council. [VA,Ph,Cr]

Address: High Street, Fishguard, Dyfed SA65 9AR tel 0348 872694

Contact: Rhian Evans

Open: Mon,Thurs 10.30-6.30, Tues,Fri 10.30-6, Wed 10.30-5, Sat 10-12.30; closed 1-2

Policy: Regular programme of exhibitions lasting three to four weeks, all showing work by living artists/makers, in wide range of media, from solo professional exhibitions to work by local schools. Some small touring exhibitions. Special exhibition during Fishguard Festival. Especially interested to invite exhibitors whose work has *'a local flavour and local interest'*.

Sales: Work sold

The Space: Space approximately 9x5m, 2.5m high; direct fixing to blockboard clad walls, hanging rods can also be used; showcase in foyer, 1x4m.

Exhibiting: [AW] Exhibitions are programmed from the County Library at Haverford West, and applicants should contact Eirwyn George, County Library, Dew Street, Haverfordwest, Dyfed (tel 0437 4591 ext 5245). Library pays for list of exhibits only. Commission is 10%. Exhibition space also for hire.

Access: [F]

Talking Point/Man Trafod

Small shop-size commercial art and craft gallery run by silversmith Myles Pepper. [VA,Cr]

Address: 6 West Street, Fishguard, Dyfed SA65 9AE tel 0348 872698

Contact: Myles Pepper, West Wales Arts Centre, Castle Hill, 16 West Street, Fishguard, Dyfed SA65 9AE tel 0348 873867

Open: Mon-Sat 10-5; closed 1-2

Policy: Changing display of work for sale, with a small number of special solo exhibitions, representing *'a selection of the best and the best up-and-coming artists and makers in the country. To have a gallery in such a rural place may seem ridiculous, but I wanted to extend the opportunity for native people to view and collect contemporary art and craft.'* Permanent collection in gallery of work by important contemporary artists such as Kossoff, McLean, Setch.

Sales: Work sold; Credit scheme; Credit card

The Space: Approximately 33m linear hanging space, height 3m; spotlights; size of exhibits limited to around 1square metres; lockable showcases.

Exhibiting: Exhibitors are invited. Nearly all craft items are *'bought in'*. Gallery pays for insurance, printing and mailout of publicity, list of exhibits, and preview costs. Commission is 33.3%.

Access: [F] BR Fishguard Harbour 20 mins; Public car parks 1 min

West Wales Arts Centre

Georgian building adapted for use as an art and craft-based arts centre. [VA,Cr]

Address: Castle Hill, 16 West Street, Fishguard, Dyfed SA65 9AE tel 0348 873867

Contact: Director Myles Pepper

Open: Mon-Sat 10-5; closed 1-2

Policy: The centre was set up *'to encourage and further interest in the arts in general, and especially fine art, craft, and music'*. Continuous changing exhibition of fine art and craft by both established and new artists and makers, with occasional month-long special exhibitions. Recitals, lectures, and other events for all ages, and sale of artists' materials. Accommodation to let to practising artists.

Sales: Work sold; Credit card; Credit scheme

The Space: 60m linear hanging space, height 3m; work limited to 2x1.5m; halogen spots, fluorescents.

Exhibiting: [AW] Send photographs or slides of work and CV to the Director. Centre pays for insurance, printing and mailout of publicity, list of exhibits, catalogue/card, and preview costs. Commission on sales is 33.3%. Most craft items are *'bought in'*.

Access: [S] BR Fishguard Harbour 20 mins; Public car parks 1 min

Workshop Wales Gallery

Gallery in attractive surroundings run by artist-maker John Cleal, with programme of mixed exhibitions of contemporary art and crafts for sale. [Pa,Sc,Cr]

Address: Lower Town, Fishguard, Dyfed SA65 9LY tel 0348 872261

Contact: John & Lel Cleal

Open: 10-5; closed mid-Oct to 1 Mar

Policy: Programme of mixed exhibitions.

Sales: Work sold; Credit card; Credit scheme

The Space: Indoor gallery and outdoor sculpture garden.

Exhibiting: [AW] Telephone John or Lel Cleal.

Access: [F]

Harlech (Gwynedd)

(NWaA) Map4 SH53

Theatr Ardudwy

Theatre which shows temporary exhibitions in the foyer/bar area.

Address: Coleg Harlech, Harlech, Gwynedd LL65 tel 0766 780667

Contact: Valerie Wynne-Williams

Open: Mon-Fri 9am-10pm, Sat-Sun during performances

Haverfordwest (Dyfed)

(WWaA) Map4 SM91

Castle Museum & Art Gallery

Former county museum for the area of Pembrokeshire within Dyfed County, run by Dyfed County Council Cultural Services Department. [VA,Ph,Cr]

Address: Haverfordwest, Pembrokeshire, Dyfed SA61

2EF tel 0437 3708
Contact: Curator R A Kennedy, Pembrokeshire Museums, Scolton Manor Museum, Spittal, Haverfordwest, Pembrokeshire, Dyfed SA62 5QL
Open: Daily 10-5.30; Winter 10-4
Policy: Wide variety of temporary exhibitions in first-floor balcony area, including art and craft, *'with a regional bias'* relating or complementary to the area and the museum's permanent collection. Exhibition policy *'to set a standard and encourage a wider and deeper appreciation, to discover and recognise talent of true worth, and to provide an art-education resource.'* Formerly eight or nine exhibitions a year, half of which were art exhibitions, now much fewer due to public spending cuts. Permanent collection of fine art, topographical art and pottery.
Sales: Work sold
The Space: Balcony area 30x3m, with around 40m linear hanging space (plus 30m on opposite wall for larger works), picture rail/hanging rods, plus extra screens for mirror-plated hanging; large exhibitions can expand onto lower floor; can accommodate large works; upright and *'desk'* showcases available. Lawns suitable for open-air sculpture.
Exhibiting: [AW] Apply to the Curator *'in good time beforehand!'* Museum pays wholly or partially for most exhibition costs except display materials (*'we usually strike a deal with the artist'*) Commission between 10-25%.
Access: [X] BR Haverfordwest and bus station 10 mins; Public car parks 5 mins

Graham Sutherland Gallery

Independent charity housing large permanent collection of work of Graham Sutherland, which also organises special temporary Summer exhibitions of work by other artists 'of international status'.
Address: Picton Castle, The Rhos, Haverfordwest, Dyfed SA62 4AS tel 043 786 296
Contact: Manager Gordon Bennett
Open: Daily 10.30-12.30, 1.30-5 1 Apr-30 Sept; closed Mon except bank holidays

Haverfordwest Library Gallery

Self-contained gallery space in public library run by Dyfed Cultural Services Department. [VA,Ph,Cr]
Address: County Library, Dew Street, Haverfordwest, Dyfed SA61 1SU tel 0437 764591 ext 5242
Contact: Senior Librarian Mary John
Open: Library hours
Policy: Varied programme of touring exhibitions and work by artists in the area, including the library's own annual open art exhibition. About 15 exhibitions a year, normally lasting two or three weeks, over half are solo exhibitions. Policy *'to give exhibiting opportunities to the numerous local artists, and wherever funds allow to introduce new and exciting art to the community. When possible we encourage three-dimensional shows and the work of local craftspeople'.* Gallery also used for society and other public meetings.
Sales: Work sold
The Space: Carpeted circular room about 13m in diameter, about 27m linear hanging; movable hanging rods for up to 100 paintings. The maximum height is 2.5m. Possible extension into foyer area.
Exhibiting: [AW] Contact Senior Librarian in writing or by telephone. Library pays for transport, printing and mailout of publicity, catalogue/card, and preview costs. Commission on sales is 20%.
Access: [F] BR Haverfordwest 5 mins; Own car park

Hawarden (Clwyd)

(NWaA) Map4 SJ36

Hawarden Library

Small exhibition area in public library run by Clwyd County Council Library and Museum Service. [Pa,Ph,Cr]
Address: The Old Rectory, Rectory Lane, Hawarden, Deeside, Clwyd CH5 3NN tel 0244 532926
Contact: Librarian Kathleen Morris
Open: Mon 2-7, Wed 10-1, 2-7, Fri 2-7, Sat 9.30-12.30
Policy: To promote awareness of the arts through as varied a programme of exhibitions as possible, including works of local artists and schools, touring exhibitions, artists in residencies, making available to the public work that is interesting, educational and entertaining.
Sales: Work sold
The Space: 7m wall length; pinboard and picture rail; two spotlights on track.
Exhibiting: [AW] Apply to the Librarian.The Library and Museums Service pays for insurance and printing of publicity and list of exhibits. Commission on sales is 20%.
Access: [F] BR Hawarden 10 mins; Public car park 3 mins, car park adjacent

Holyhead (Gwynedd)

(NWaA) Map4 SH28

Holyhead Library

Part of Gwynedd Library Service. [VA,Ph,Cr]
Address: Newry Fields, Holyhead, Gwynedd LL65 1LA tel 0407 2917
Contact: Branch Librarian Helena Parry
Open: Mon 10-5,Tues 10-7,Wed 10-1,Thurs-Fri 10-7,Sat 10-1
Policy: See entry for Gwynedd Library Service, Caernarfon.
Exhibiting: Two spaces: 8x8.1m, 10x6.1m; some free-standing display boards; spots and natural light; supervised.

Holywell (Clwyd)

(NWaA) Map4 SJ17

Holywell Library

Library run by Clwyd Library Service.
Address: North Road, Holywell, Clwyd CH8 7TQ tel 0352 713157
Contact: Librarian Penny Corbett

Open: Mon-Fri 10-7, Sat 9.30-12.30
Policy: Open-plan library with exhibiting space on two walls with hanging rail, plus space for screens. It exhibits Clwyd Exhibition Service exhibitions and shows of local artists.

Kenfig Hill (Mid Glamorgan)

(SEWaA) Map6 SS88

Kenfig Art Gallery

Changing mixed display of oils, watercolours and prints by local artists also selling artists materials and offering a framing service. [Pa,Pr]
Address: 2 Pisgah Street, Kenfig Hill, Mid Glamorgan CF33 6BY tel 0656 740674
Contact: Mr & Mrs Parkes
Open: Mon-Sat 9-5.30; closed Wed pm
Exhibiting: Commission on sales 25%.

Knighton (Powys)

(SEWaA) Map4 SO27

Old School Gallery

Gallery and arts centre owned and controlled by the Bleddfa Trust, Centre for Caring and the Arts, founded by James Roose-Evans. [VA,Ph,Cr,LA]
Address: Bleddfa, Nr Knighton, Powys LD7 1PA tel 054 781 220
Contact: Gallery Director John Cupper, The Tank House, Weston, Pembridge, Leominster, Herefordshire tel 054 47 540
Open: Wed-Sun 1-5.30
Policy: The Bleddfa Trust is a registered charity whose activities are supported by SEWaA. The gallery, in the former village school, programmes about six month-long exhibitions a year. A year of exhibitions in all possible media and other activities all on one theme (the first was 'Festival of the Tree', and the 1989 theme is 'The Garden'), alternates with a year of exhibitions which vary from month to month. There are many related activities, such as workshops, trails and meals.
Sales: Work sold; Credit scheme
The Space: Gallery is 8x5.5x6m, plus flexible hessian screens and spotlights. Gallery garden suitable for sculpture. Gallery plan available.
Exhibiting: [AW][EF] Apply to Bleddfa Trust via Gallery Director. Exhibitions usually booked at least a year ahead. Gallery covers most exhibition costs, except transport and artists' expenses. Commission is 30%.
Access: [F] No public transport routes; Public parking

Lampeter (Dyfed)

(WWaA) Map4 SN54

St David's University College

Occasional exhibitions held in staff reception rooms.
Address: Lampeter, Dyfed SA40 tel 0570 422351
Contact: Dr Roderick
Open: Mon-Fri 9-5

Theatr Felinfach

Rural theatre and cultural centre, with space for art exhibitions.
Address: Felinfach, Lampeter, Dyfed SA48 8AF tel 0570 470 697

Llanbedrog (Gwynedd)

(NWaA) Map4 SH33

Plas Glyn-y-Weddw Gallery

An 1856 Gothic-style mansion first used as a private art gallery open to the public at the turn of the century, and performing that function again since 1984. [VA,Ph]
Address: Plas Glyn-y-Weddw, Llanbedrog, Pwllheli, Gwynedd LL53 7TT tel 0758 740 763
Contact: Gwyneth & Dafydd ap Tomos
Open: Daily 10-6 including Sun
Policy: Major part of the building (the owners' home) devoted to changing mixed displays of paintings, sculpture and ceramics by contemporary artists, with further rooms devoted to special exhibitions lasting one month. Target audience of 40,000 a year includes holidaymakers, and visitors on art and sketching holidays based at the gallery, but gallery also *'acts as stimulus to the visual arts in North and West Wales'.* Related activities include art courses, talks, demonstrations, concerts, and restaurant, though *'Plas Glyn-y-Weddw is first and foremost an art gallery. Everything that goes on in and around the mansion is intended to enhance the feel and experience of the gallery'.*
Sales: Work sold; Credit card; Credit scheme
The Space: Four furnished rooms and large entrance hall used as galleries; extensive grounds; plan available.
Exhibiting: [AW] Submit applications to the Directors. Gallery covers insurance costs, printing and mailing publicity, list of exhibits, catalogue/card, and preview costs. Commission is 33.3%.

Plas Glyn-y-Weddw: Staircase

Access: [U][T][F] BR Pwllheli 4 miles; Bus route Pwllheli-Llanbedrog hourly; Public car park 2 mins

Llanberis (Gwynedd)

(NWaA) Map4 SH56

Mountain Art

Commercial gallery in Snowdonia specialising in mountain subjects. [Pa,Pr,Dr,Ph]

Address: 64 High Street, Llanberis, Gwynedd LL55 4HA tel 0286 870 925
Contact: Anthony Cain
Open: Mon-Sat 9.30-5.30, closed 1-2; Sun 10-5
Policy: Changing display of prints and watercolours by the owner, plus paintings, prints and photographs for sale by other artists. *'An attempt to fill the hiatus for mountain subject matter in picture galleries in Britain, and to afford an outlet to some of the few artists working in this field in Britain, and hopefully to bring to the attention of the mountain-loving public the work of artists and photographers from around the world'.*
Sales: Work sold
The Space: 25m linear hanging space 2.35m high and track lighting.
Exhibiting: **[AW]** Apply to Anthony Cain either by post or in person with photographs or examples of work (mountain subjects only). Commission on work sold is 33.3%.
Access: **[F]** Buses from Bangor or Caernarfon; Street parking

Museum of the North/Amgueddfa'r Gogledd

The National Museum of Wales' main centre in North Wales, with a programme of varied temporary exhibitions, including fine art drawn from the National Museum's permanent collection, and some contemporary art from North Wales artists and societies (including an artist in residence, Summer 1988).

Address: Llanberis, Gwynedd LL55 4UR tel 0286 870636
Contact: Keeper Dr Dafydd Roberts
Open: Mon-Sat 10-5, Sun 1.30-5 End of May-End of Sept
Exhibiting: Exhibitions by invitation only.
Access: Public car park

Llandeilo (Dyfed)

(WWaA) Map4 SN62

Llandeilo Library

Purpose-built library with exhibition space in foyer and programme of monthly exhibitions.

Address: Crescent Road, Llandeilo, Dyfed SA19 tel 0558 823659
Contact: M Jones tel 0558 822020
Open: Tues & Fri 10-12 1.30-4.30 5-7, Sat 10-12

Raven Gallery and Bookshop

Bookshop and gallery showing the work of Peter John Jones and Kusha Petts, with occasional exhibitions by other artists.

Address: 11 Carmarthen Street, Llandeilo, Dyfed SA19 6AE tel 0558 822976
Contact: Peter John Jones, Ann Mainwaring
Open: Mon-Sat 9.30-5, closed Thurs
Policy: Exhibitions by invited artists.
Sales: Work sold
The Space: Hanging space for 20-25 paintings.
Exhibiting: By invitation only.

Trapp Arts & Crafts Centre

Centre comprising art gallery, craft shop, tea room, demonstration studios and information point. [Pa,Cr]

Address: Trapp, Llandeilo, Dyfed SA19 6TT tel 0269 850 362
Contact: Nigel Card
Open: Daily 11-5.30; closed Mon-Wed, Nov to Easter; open to 7.30 July-Aug
Policy: Gallery shows about six special solo exhibitions annually from April-September, plus changing display of work for sale by local artists. Demonstrations and courses.
Sales: Work sold; Credit card
The Space: Main gallery is 9x5m, exhibition room is 9x4.5m and the exhibition studio is 14x4.5m.
Exhibiting: **[AW]** Apply at any time to Nigel Card. Gallery shares insurance, mailing out publicity, and preview costs. Commission on work sold is 20-25%.
Access: **[X]** No access by public transport

Llandovery (Dyfed)

(WWaA) Map4 SN73

Gallery-on-the-Hill

Artist-run gallery specialising in changing display of contemporary work in leather, wood, ceramics and glass. [Cr]

Address: Pant Farm, Halfway, Llandovery, Dyfed SA20 0SF tel 087482 611
Contact: Tony & Anthea Britnell
Open: daily 10-6
Policy: *'Our policy is to purchase work from the artist, therefore we are most discriminating and really have to believe in and love what we buy. As a large percentage of our visitors are overseas tourists we aim to be as good if not better than what is available in their own countries. Our site is high in the mountains, and we try to give the visitor a special experience, one of peace and tranquillity.*
Sales: Work sold; Credit card
The Space: 4x4.5m with a height of 3.20m and 9m linear hanging space. Rails, sliding systems and spotlights. Additional display space of 30 square metres planned for Summer 89.
Exhibiting: **[AW]** Individual artists should submit 35mm slides or colour prints of their work to Tony and Anthea Britnell. Work purchased from artist before exhibition. *'We do not exhibit traditional work, and look for simplicity and purity of form in the work we carefully choose to show.'*
Access: **[F]** Own transport necessary

Llandrindod Wells (Powys)

(SEWaA) Map4 SO06

Llandrindod Wells Museum

Local history museum run by Powys County Council, with small space used for temporary exhibitions. [Dr,Ph,Te]

Address: Temple Street, Llandrindod Wells, Powys LD1 5DL tel 0597 4513
Contact: Curator Sian Evans
Open: 10-5; closed 1-2
Policy: Mainly *'in house'* exhibitions on local history subjects incorporating the museum collections. Other exhibitions have included display, sale of work and demonstrations by local crafts guilds and local artists.
Sales: Work sold
The Space: The gallery is 5.5x7.5m, wall space limited by windows; fluorescent lighting.
Exhibiting: [AW] Apply to the Curator, at least eight months in advance. *'We encourage displays with some local connection if possible'.*
Access: BR Llandrindod Wells 3 mins

Porticus

Specialist art and craft gallery in restored 1890s building, with exhibition room for regular special displays by individual artists and makers. [Pa,Pr,Cr]

Address: 1 Middleton Street, Llandrindod Wells, Powys LD1 tel 0597 3989
Contact: Rosemary Studman
Open: Mon-Sat 9.30-5.30; closed Wed pm Winter
Sales: Work sold
Access: BR Llandrindod Wells

Powys Libraries & Museums

Library service of Powys. [VA]

Address: Cefrillys Road, Llandrindod Wells, Powys tel 0597 2212
Contact: County Librarian
Policy: There are ten branch libraries with an overall policy to show education, cultural or charitable exhibitions. Crickhowell Branch Library (Silver Street, Crickhowell, Powys tel 0873 810856) has space 7x5.5m with wall and free-standing boards and spotlighting; Builth Wells Branch Library (High Street Builth Wells, Powys tel 0982 552722) has a first floor space of 9x4.8m with wall and free-standing display boards and spotlighting; Hay on Wye Branch Library (Chancery Lane, Hay on Wye, Powys tel 0497 820847 has a ground floor space of 7x5.5m with wall and free-standing display boards and spotlighting: Knighton Branch Library (West Street, Knighton, Powys tel 0547 528778) has a foyer space of 8x5.2m with wall and free-standing display boards and spotlighting where supervision is required; Llanidloes Branch Library (Mount Street, Llanidloes, Powys tel 05512 2855) with a space of 7x5.2m with wall and free-standing boards and spotlighting; Newtown Area Library (Park Lane, Newtown, Powys tel 0686 26934) with a foyer space of 9x3m with free-standing boards; Rhayader Branch Library (West Street, Rhyader, Powys tel 0597 810548) with a foyer space 4.3x4m with free-standing boards; Welshpool Branch Library (Brook Street, Welshpool, Powys tel 0938 3001) has a 12m linear hanging space with free-standing screens and spotlights; Ystradgynlais Branch Library, temperance Lane, Ystradgynlais, Powys tel 0639 845353 has space 6x2.3m and 2.3x2.3m with wall display boards and spot lights. See also entry for Brecon Library.
Exhibiting: [AW] Apply to Librarian at each branch.

Llandudno (Gwynedd)

(NWaA) Map4 SH78

Benards of Llandudno

Private gallery with mixed display of paintings, limited edition prints and reproductions. [Pa,Pr]

Address: Queens Road, Craig-y-Don, Llandudno, Gwynedd LL30 1AZ tel 0492 75852
Contact: Rodney & Malcolm Butterworth
Open: Mon-Sat 9-5.30

Fulmar Gallery

Commercial art gallery specialising in wildlife paintings and limited edition prints. [Pa,Pr,Dr,Ph]

Address: 37 Madoc Street, Llandudno, Gwynedd LL30 2TL tel 0492 79880
Contact: M J Edwards
Open: Mon-Sat 9-5; closed 1-2; closed Wed
Policy: Changing displays of paintings and watercolours, plus about six solo exhibitions annually. Framing service and public talks on framing and conservation.
Sales: Work sold; Credit card
The Space: Maximum size of work which can be exhibited is 1.2x2m.
Exhibiting: [AW] Apply to M J Edwards. Gallery pays for printing of publicity, list of exhibits, and part mailing and preview costs. Commission is 33.3%.
Access: BR Llandudno 5 mins; Bus station 10 mins; Public car park 2 mins

Llandudno Library

Part of Gwynedd Library Service. [VA,Ph,Cr]

Address: Mostyn Street, Llandudno, Gwynedd LL30 2RS tel 0492 860101
Contact: Area Librarian J M Thomas tel 0492 860941
Open: Library open Mon-Tues 10-6,Wed 10-5,Thurs 10-7,Fri 10-6,Sat 10-1
Policy: See entry for Gwynedd Library Service, Caernarfon.
The Space: Separate exhibition space around 6x10m, on first floor, no lift; with four free-standing pegboards 3.5x2.6m and fluorescent and natural lighting unsupervised.
Exhibiting: 15% commission on sales plus VAT.
Access: [X]

Mostyn Art Gallery

Public art gallery originally functioning from 1901-14, renovated and re-opened in 1978 with Welsh Arts Council grant aid as major public gallery of

contemporary art and crafts in North Wales. [VA,Ph,Cr,LA]

Address: 12 Vaughan Street, Llandudno, Gwynedd LL30 1AB tel 0492 79201
Contact: Director Susan Beardmore
Open: Mon-Sat 10.30-5; closed public holidays
Policy: The gallery (which is an independent limited company with charitable status) programmes about ten month-long exhibitions annually of contemporary art and crafts from Britain and abroad, work by artists operating in Wales, and historical exhibitions of fine and applied arts. Some exhibitions originated by the gallery are toured. Regular workshops and classes by artists and makers, discussion groups organised by Friends of the Gallery, and other services provided for local/regional art groups and educational visits. Special displays and changing stock of high-quality crafts for sale in craft shop area.
Sales: Work sold; Credit scheme; credit card
The Space: Gallery one is approximately 8.5x13.5m, gallery two is approximately 15x7.6m with a total linear hanging space of 62m expanding to 100m with modular screens. UV filtration, humidification/air conditioning.
Exhibiting: [AW][EF] Apply by letter to the Director, enclosing slides of work. Gallery covers most exhibition costs. Commission on work sold is 20%. Enquiries about crafts shop and displays to Shop Manager.
Access: [U][T] BR Llandudno 2 mins

Llanelli (Dyfed)

(WWaA) Map4 SN50

Llanelli Borough Library (Nevill Gallery)

Gallery for temporary art exhibitions in public library. [VA,Ph,Cr]

Address: Vaughan Street, Llanelli, Dyfed SA15 3AS tel 0554 773538
Contact: Borough Librarian
Open: 9.30-5
Policy: About fourteen two to three-week exhibitions annually of all forms of art, both local artists and touring exhibitions. Permanent collection of art with local connections. Talks, meetings, workshops, residencies.
Sales: Work sold
The Space: Total of 168m linear hanging with showcases available.
Exhibiting: [AW] Apply one year in advance to D F Griffiths, Borough Librarian. Library covers all exhibition costs except artists' expenses. No commission charged on sales.
Access: [U][T]

Mostyn Art Gallery

Mansion House

Small permanent regional museum and art collection run by Llanelli Library Service, with three rooms used for programme of temporary exhibitions from March to October.

Address: Parc Howard, Felinfoel Road, Llanelli, Dyfed SA15 3LS tel 0554 772029
Contact: Borough Librarian D F Griffiths tel 0554 773538
Open: 9.30-6.30 April-Sept; 10-4.30 Oct-March
Exhibiting: No commission on sales.

Llangefni (Gwynedd)

(NWaA) Map4 SH47

Nant yr Odin

Hotel in 18th century building used for painting holidays, with exhibition space displaying work by local artists. [Pa]

Address: Llanfawr, Llangefni, Anglesey, Gwynedd LL77 7YE tel 0248 723354
Contact: Mr & Mrs Roberts
Open: Hotel hours

Oriel Môn

Part of Gwynedd Library Service. [VA,Ph,Cr]

Address: Central Library, Lon-y-Felin, Llangefni, Anglesey, Gwynedd LL77 7RT tel 0248 750262 ext 226
Contact: Area Librarian Elspeth Mitcheson
Open: Mon 10-7, Tues-Wed 10-5, Thurs 10-6, Fri 10-7
Policy: See entry for Gwynedd Library Service, Caernarfon. Also venue for Welsh Arts Council Craft Showcase Network, see Welsh Arts Council, Cardiff.
The Space: Separate exhibition area 10x6.2m, with six lockable showcases available, adjustable spots and natural light. The space is constantly supervised and alarmed.
Exhibiting: Contact Elspeth Mitcheson.
Access: [F]

Llangennydd (West Glamorgan)

(WWaA) Map6 SS49

Horwood Galleries

Artist-run studio and gallery on 30-acre farm, showing work by the owners and other artists.

Address: Tankey Lake Farm, Llangennydd, Gower, W Glamorgan SA3 1DT
Contact: Judith Horwood & Bob Gammon

Llangollen (Clwyd)

(NWaA) Map4 SJ24

European Centre for Traditional & Regional Cultures (ECTARC)

Gallery for temporary exhibitions within centre devoted to study and promotion of regional cultures, providing information and research facilities, courses, conferences, performances, and permanent displays. [Pa,Ph,Cr]

Address: Parade Street, Llangollen, Clwyd LL20 8RB tel 0978 861514

Contact: Administrator Jenefer Lowe

Open: Mon-Sat 9-5 all year; Sun 12-5 Easter to October

Policy: To house and produce exhibitions on subjects with which centre is concerned. *'We are not an art gallery but have housed such exhibitions on occasion, particularly when the subject matter is of interest to us'.* Gallery aimed at passing and tourist trade, local audience, educational visits, and those with a special interest in traditional cultures. Each exhibition supported by talk, workshop, or weekend course.

Sales: Work sold; Credit card

The Space: Gallery one is 9x5.5m, clad to 2.7m height; no natural light, tracklighting. Gallery two is 5.5x11m, clad, fluorescents; showcases available.

Exhibiting: [AW][EF] Apply to Administrator, preferably in writing, or telephone before visiting. *'We do not take solo shows unless the subject matter is relevant to our aims and activities. If work not suitable, it will be passed on to other county venues.'* Insurance of work covered by gallery, commission 20%. Work occasionally commissioned from artists for in-house exhibitions, in which case all expenses are covered and fee paid.

Access: [U][T][F] Bus link to BR Ruabon, also buses from Wrexham & Bala; Own public car park

Llangollen Library

Public library with wall space for temporary exhibitions. [Pa,Pr,Ph,Cr]

Address: Parade Street, Llangollen, Clwyd LL20 tel 0978 860720

Contact: Branch Librarian C Stafford

Open: Mon-Fri 10-7, closed Thurs; Sat 9.30-12.30

Policy: Regular very mixed programme of art and craft exhibitions, mainly from local sources.

Sales: Work sold

The Space: Wall space around the library, space for display boards in centre of library.

Exhibiting: [AW] Send photos or slides of work to Chris Stafford. Insurance of exhibits covered. Commission on work sold 15%.

Access: [F] Public car parks and buses 2 mins

Llanidloes (Powys)

(SEWaA) Map4 SN98

Studio 13

Exhibition space run by the Comptons Yard Charitable Trust, which promotes cultural and social activities for the benefit of the inhabitants of the Llanidloes area.

Address: 12 Great Oak Street, Llanidloes, Powys SY18 6BU tel 055 12 3402

Contact: Kate Morrison

Open: Variable

Policy: *'Our aim is the promotion of all types of art and crafts; the provision of access to arts and crafts for both the local inhabitants and tourists; and the provision of meeting and workshop space for educational and development activities for all ages'.*

Sales: Work sold

The Space: 10x4x4m with linear hanging space of around 8m, blockboard clad. *'Exhibits need to be carried up two flights of stairs.'* Cafe, children's play area, and studios run by the Trust in same building.

Exhibiting: [AW] The Trust has set out to provide a variety of spaces and amenities available for rent. The exhibition space is for hire for £10 a day. Apply by letter or telephone to Kate Morrison at Studio 13. Commission on sales is 12%.

Access: [X] BR Caersws 7 miles; On Shrewsbury-Aberystwyth bus route; Public car park adjacent

Llantrisant (Mid Glamorgan)

(SEWaA) Map6 ST08

Hill Top Studio

Commercial gallery which is also the restoration studio of its owner. [Pa,Pr]

Address: 56 High Street, Llantrisant, Mid Glamorgan CF7 8BR tel 0443 229015

Contact: Gill Garnham

Open: Thurs-Sun, 10-5

Policy: Changing display of local and antique original paintings (mainly watercolours) and prints, with occasional solo exhibitions of same. *'My gallery is the first step towards bringing art, crafts and visual culture to what has been a decaying but historic town, creating a new market among mainly local people and attracting people from much further afield to see and buy quality items'.* Also sells local crafts and pine furniture.

Sales: Work sold; Sales referred to exhibitor

Hill Top Studio

The Space: Two spaces each 6x1.5m; good natural light and spots.
Exhibiting: Gallery covers most expenses except transport and artist's expenses. Commission 25%.
Access: **[F]** Sporadic bus services; Public car parks

Model House

New regional centre for excellence in craft and design opening spring 1989. A refurbished Victorian workhouse, Model House will function as a visitors centre, offering crafts for sale from the shop and gallery, or direct from makers, visits to makers' studios plus a permanent Royal Mint exhibition, meetings and classes. [VA,Cr]

Address: Bull Ring, Llantrisant, Mid Glamorgan tel 0443 237758
Contact: Director Eileen Townsend Jones
Open: Tues-Sat 10-5, bank holidays; closed Good Friday (opening times to be confirmed when gallery opens)
Policy: *'Small but prestigious'* ground-floor exhibition space within crafts shop. Continuous programme of month-long exhibitions (mainly selling) showing all kinds of three-dimensional work. Limited display space for pictures, although management aim to offer an *'Art for Offices and Public Spaces'* viewing area in first floor multi-purpose room.
Sales: Work sold
The Space: Total shop and gallery area is 465 square metres of which normally 25% available for exhibitions. Spot lighting.
Exhibiting: **[AW]** Contact the Director or Gallery and Shop Manager. The gallery covers the cost of insurance, printing and publicity, list of exhibits, previews and display. Commission to be arranged.
Access: **[U][T][L][F]** 2 miles from M4; Buses from Cardiff 40 mins; Free car parks and on street parking nearby

Llantwit Major (S Glamorgan)

(SEWaA) Map6 SS96

St Donat's Arts Centre

Arts centre in the grounds of St Donat's Castle and Atlantic College, with varied programme of live performances and occasional art and craft exhibitions, including major annual Crafts in Action weekend.

Address: St Donat's Castle, Llantwit Major, S Glamorgan CF6 0WF tel 04465
Contact: Artistic Director David Ambrose
Exhibiting: Telephone for details.

Machynlleth (Powys)

(NWaA) Map4 SH70

Spectrum Gallery

Artist-run town centre gallery showing mainly ceramics plus permanent selling exhibition of old Spanish rural pots and changing display of paintings and one-off clocks by Paul Martinez-Frias. [Pa,Cr]

Address: Maengwyn Street, Machynlleth, Powys SY20 8EB tel 0654 2877
Contact: Paul Martinez-Frias & Pam Taylor
Open: Mon-Sat 10-5
Policy: To promote new talent in the ceramics world either by solo exhibitions or by purchase of selected pieces for show in saleroom displays, against a background of support for established studio potters.
Sales: Work sold; Credit card
The Space: Two ground floor rooms plus a well-lit two-bay cellar suitable for solo exhibitions.
Exhibiting: **[AW]** Ceramicists in particular should present some of their recent work for informal discussions on availability of exhibition space.
Access: Street car parking limited, public car park nearby; Intercity rail link and bus services

Model House

Spectrum Gallery: old Spanish rural pot (Photo: Peter Dobson)

Mancot (Clwyd)

(NWaA) Map4 SJ63

Mancot Library

Library run by Clwyd County Council Library and Museum Service. [Pa,Ph,Cr]

Address: Mancot Lane, Mancot, Clwyd tel 0244 532430
Contact: Librarian Kathleen Morris
Open: Mon,Wed,Fri 10-7, closed 1-2; Tues 12.30-5.30, Sat 9.30-12.30; closed Thurs
Policy: To promote awareness of the arts through as varied a programme of exhibitions as possible, including works of local artists and schools, touring exhibitions, artists in residencies, making available to the public work that is interesting, educational and entertaining.
Sales: Work sold
The Space: Four metres wall length with pinboard.
Exhibiting: **[AW]** Apply in writing to Librarian. Library and Museum Service pays for insurance and printing of publicity and exhibition lists. Commission is 20%.
Access: Car park adjacent

Menai Bridge (Gwynedd)

(NWaA) Map4 SH57

Tegfryn Art Gallery

Private art gallery founded in 1966, showing a mixed display of contemporary work, with occasional special exhibitions.

Address: Cadnant Road, Menai Bridge, Anglesy, Gwynedd LL59 5EW tel 0248 712437
Contact: Gwyn Brown
Open: Daily 10-1, 2-5; closed Mon Oct-March; closed Jan-Feb except by appointment

Merthyr Tydfil (Mid Glamorgan)

(SEWaA) Map4 SO00

Cyfarthfa Castle Museum

Museum and art gallery in 1825 mansion of ironmaster William Crawshay, run by Merthyr Tydfil Borough Council. [Pr,Dr,Ph]

Address: Cyfarthfa Park, Brecon Road, Merthyr Tydfil, Mid Glamorgan CF47 8RE tel 0685 723112
Contact: Curator Nick Mansfield
Open: Mon-Sat 10-6, Sun 2-5; Winter closed 1-2 and earlier in afternoon
Policy: Regular programme of wide ranging temporary exhibitions, including social and industrial history as well as photography, ceramics and art exhibitions, *'trying to reflect the important permanent collections, and the traditions and character of the local community.'* Talks and other evening events.
Sales: Sales referred to exhibitor
The Space: Three areas of 7x5x4m, 14x2x4m and 6x2x2m with 60m linear hanging space; two screen systems and showcases available; UV filters on windows; good security.
Exhibiting: **[AW]** Apply at any time in writing or by telephone to the Curator. Gallery pays for insurance, printing and mail out of publicity. No commission on sales of work.
Access: **[F]** when ramp completed. BR Merthyr Tydfil 20 mins; Bus route from town centre 5 mins; Own public car park

Milford Haven (Dyfed)

(WWaA) Map4 SM90

Torch Theatre

Exhibition space in top foyer of major regional repertory theatre. [VA,Ph,Cr]

Address: St Peter's Road, Milford Haven, Dyfed SA73 2BU tel 06462 4192
Contact: Associate Director/Administration
Open: Mon-Fri 10-8, Sat 10-3
Policy: Regular monthly exhibitions throughout the year, mainly local artists plus schools exhibitions, seen by theatre audiences and other interested people.
Sales: Work sold
The Space: T-shaped space with hanging on rods on six walls.
Exhibiting: **[AW]** Apply to Associate Director, Administration, at least six months in advance. Theatre pays for insurance and list of exhibits. Commission on sales 15%.
Access: BR Milford Haven 5 mins; Public car park 3 mins

Mold (Clwyd)

(NWaA) Map4 SJ26

Clwyd County Art and Exhibition Service

Centralised service organising touring exhibitions of all sizes and all media for a network of county council venues within the county of Clwyd, including Wrexham Library Arts Centre, Oriel Theatr Clwyd and other exhibition spaces and public libraries, as well

Cyfarthfa Castle Museum

as touring its exhibitions outside the county. [VA,Cr,Ph]
Address: County Civic Centre, Mold, Clwyd CH7 6NB tel 0352 2121
Contact: County Arts & Exhibitions Officer Steve Brake

Daniel Owen Centre, Exhibition Room

Temporary exhibitions gallery and small museum display related to Daniel Owen, situated above public library and community centre for Mold. [VA,Ph,Cr]
Address: Daniel Owen Centre, Earl Road, Mold, Clwyd CH7 1AP tel 0352 4791
Contact: Branch Librarian Derwenna Watkin
Open: Mon-Fri 9.30-7, Sat 9.30-12.30
Policy: Regular monthly exhibitions throughout the year, equally divided between touring shows, local and other artists, and local community art and craft exhibitions. *'Target is very definitely the local community. We are encouraging local people to become more involved with the gallery through workshops and other events run by artists, with the aim of exhibiting a higher standard of work and being able to accustom the public to more 'difficult'* work.'.
Sales: Work sold
The Space: First floor space of 15x8.5x3m with 25m linear hanging space plus free-standing screens; mirrorplating to clad walls; spotlights; showcases available. Space occasionally used for meetings, readings, workshops etc.
Exhibiting: **[AW][EF]** Send slides/photos with CV. *'Especially interested in artists who can teach/run workshops, for which they are paid'.* Gallery covers most exhibition costs except display and preview. Commission is 20%.
Access: **[L]** Situated in town centre; Public car parks 5 mins; Nearest BR Flint

Oriel Theatr Clwyd

Gallery spaces in a multi-disciplinary arts centre with two theatre auditoria, film theatre, bookshop, restaurant, bar and conference facilities, administered and financed by Clwyd County Council and the Welsh Arts Council. [VA,Ph,Cr]

Oriel Theatr Clwyd

Address: Theatr Clwyd, Mold, Clwyd CH7 1YA tel 0352 56331
Contact: Assistant Arts and Exhibitions Officer Clare Lilley
Open: Mon-Fri 12am-9pm, Sat 12-9pm, Sun varies
Policy: Regular monthly exhibitions, majority originated by the gallery. Policy change beginning 1989: *'Major emphasis in showing work of new artists in solo or small group shows, plus two large shows of established artists (with historical or theatrical connections), and two community exhibitions. Aim is to provide a forum in North Wales for showing work of younger serious artists alongside an energetic education programme, with artists' residencies and workshops. We are intent on promoting new artists in a difficult cultural climate. We have absolutely no sexual or racial discrimination.'* Also venue for Welsh Arts Council Craft Showcase Network (see Welsh Arts Council, Cardiff).
Sales: Work sold; Credit scheme; Credit card
The Space: Main 'Oriel' Gallery is 43x5.5m with about 70m linear hanging space. Artists fees set at Welsh Arts Council rates. 'Community Gallery' has 30m linear hanging space, some height restrictions. Large grassed area suitable for sculpture.
Exhibiting: **[AW][EF]** Send slides, CV and covering letter. Gallery covers all exhibition costs except display, but stock of frames available for use. 'Community' Gallery also for hire for £15 per week. Commission is 20%.
Access: **[U][T][L]** Public car park 2 mins; Nearest BR Flint 5 miles

Monmouth (Gwent)

(SEWaA) Map4 SO51

Monmouth Museum

Regional museum run by Monmouth Borough Council Museums Service, see also museum entries for Caldicot, Chepstow and Abergavenny.
Address: Priory Street, Monmouth, Gwent NP5 3XA tel 0600 3519
Contact: Museums Officer Andrew Helme
Open: Mon-Sat 10-5, closed 1-2; Sun 2-5
Policy: Temporary exhibition programme includes both exhibitions related to local history and displays of art and crafts, including invited solo shows by established local artists and makers.
Sales: Work sold
The Space: Exhibition screens, maximum 40m, direct fixing, floor area 35 square metres.
Exhibiting: **[AW]** Exhibitors should contact Museums Officer. Museum covers the costs of insurance, printing and publicity. Commission is 20% plus VAT.
Access: **[F]** Ground floor only including exhibition space

Pat Yallup Galleries

Commercial gallery and Pat Yallup's open studio. [VA]
Address: Llandogo, Monmouth, Gwent tel 0594 530940
Contact: Pat Yallup
Policy: Monthly solo contemporary art exhibitions throughout the year, with changing mixed display.
Sales: Work sold

Ranson Art Centre

Commercial art gallery with art materials shop and framing service. [Pr,Dr,Sc,Ph,Cr]

Address: Monk Street, Monmouth, Gwent NP5 3NZ tel 0600 6868
Contact: Ron Ranson
Open: Mon-Fri 10-5, Sat 10-4
Policy: Changing display of work for sale in all media in gallery area. Painting and sculpture modelling demonstrations by exhibiting artists.
Sales: Work sold; Credit card
The Space: Total linear hanging space 39.6m (extension planned); blockboard clad; tracklighting.
Exhibiting: **[AW]** Apply by telephone or letter initially to arrange appointment, usually Mon-Fri 10-5, to Louise Hall at Ranson Art Centre. Exhibition costs discussed individually.
Access: **[S]** Public car parks 3 mins

Nant-y-moel (Mid Glamorgan)

(SEWaA) Map6 SS99

Berwyn Centre

Community theatre and cultural centre for the former mining area of Ogwr, with space for temporary exhibitions. [Pa,Pr,Dr]

Address: Nant-y-moel, Nr Bridgend, Mid Glamorgan tel 0656 840 439
Contact: Administrator Norman Kershaw
Open: Mon,Wed 10-1,2-5, Tues,Fri 2-5,Thurs 10-1,Sat 10-12 noon
Policy: Exhibitions by local artists, plus touring photographic exhibitions.
Sales: Work sold
The Space: Exhibition space is approximately 19x8m, spots on track, hanging is by rail plus some hooks.
Exhibiting: **[AW]** Applications to administrator. Gallery for hire. Commission charged 15%.
Access: **[F]** Bus service from Bridgend 30 min

New Quay (Dyfed)

(WWaA) Map4 SN35

Dyfed Art Galleries

Private gallery showing work by local artists and period paintings. [VA]

Address: Lewis Terrace, New Quay, Dyfed SA45 9PG tel 0545 560654
Contact: B King
Open: Daily 10.30-5.30
Access: **[S]**

Newbridge (Gwent)

(SEWaA) Map6 ST29

Griffin Gallery

Artist-run gallery. [Pa,Pr,Dr]

Address: Tynewydd Terrace, Newbridge, Gwent NP1 4LW tel 0495 247816
Contact: Chris Griffin
Open: Mon-Fri 9.30-5, Sat 9.30-1; closed Wed
Policy: Shows prints and watercolours of the area by the owner, as well as mixed and solo shows by other artists. Picture framing service.
Sales: Work sold
The Space: Very small 5x5m. Suitable for local artists only.
Exhibiting: **[AW]** Gallery shares exhibition costs. Commission is 20%.
Access: **[S]**

Newbridge on Wye (Powys)

(SEWaA) Map4 SO05

Mid-Wales House Craft Shop & Gallery

Private craft shop and gallery with continuous changing display of work, and two main exhibitions each year. [Pa,Sc,Cr]

Address: Newbridge on Wye, Powys LD1 6LY tel 059 789 364
Contact: Rosemary & Peter Studman
Open: Mon-Sat 9.30-5.30; also open Sun pm Easter-Oct
Access: On B4358 Newbridge to Beulah

Newport (Dyfed)

(WWaA) Map4 SN03

Carningli Centre

Centre comprising craft and gift shop, secondhand bookshop and fine arts gallery.

Address: East Street, Newport, Dyfed SA42 0SY tel 0239 820724
Contact: Proprietor C J Field
Open: Daily 9.30-5.30, Wed 9.30-1
Policy: Fine art gallery featuring the works of Royal Miniature Society members including enamel paintings by the resident artist Rita Whitaker. Larger paintings, watercolours and oils, by other well-known artists are also exhibited.
Sales: Work sold; Credit card
The Space: Ground and first floor spaces.
Exhibiting: **[AW]** Artists should contact the gallery in person.
Access: **[F]** Ground floor **[X]** First floor

Gallery (The)

Gallery run by artist Pauline Harries. [Pa,Ce]

Address: Ty Clyd, Long Street, Newport, Dyfed SA42 0TL tel 0239 820404
Contact: Pauline Harries
Open: Mon-Sat 10-5
Policy: Gallery occupies three rooms of a house, showing work by the owner and mixed display of paintings and ceramics by other artists and makers. Occasional special group and solo shows. A selected group of artists from Wales show representational paintings including detailed realism. There is an emphasis on landscape and interiors in a range of painting and drawing media.

Sales: Work sold; Credit scheme
The Space: Not suitable for large paintings.
Exhibiting: [AW] The gallery welcomes applications from professional artists who have considered the gallery's exhibiting policy.
Access: [X]

Newport Museum & Art Gallery

Museum and art gallery run by Newport Borough Council Leisure Services Department, with regular programme of temporary art exhibitions. [VA,Ph,Cr,De]

Address: John Frost Square, Newport, Gwent NP9 1HZ tel 0633 840064
Contact: Exhibitions Officer Felicity Lunn
Open: Mon-Thurs 9.30-5, Fri 9.30-4.30, Sat 9.30-4
Policy: To provide exhibitions and events of the highest standard for the benefit of the people of Newport and visitors to the town. Varied programme of about ten exhibitions annually of five to six weeks duration (both initiated by the museum and touring shows), comprising work by living artists/makers, both prominent locally and nationally and internationally known, photography, graphic design, at least one mixed crafts exhibition, and one exhibition annually relating to local history. Talks, demonstrations and workshops by artists/makers, and other performance events in the gallery. Permanent collections include 18th-20th century British paintings, contemporary prints, studio ceramics. Also venue for Welsh Arts Council Craft Showcase Network (see Welsh Arts Council, Cardiff).
Sales: Work sold; Credit card
The Space: At least 100m linear hanging space available on flexible panels 3m high; direct fixing; track lighting with dimming; full humidity controls. Gallery plan available.
Exhibiting: [AW][EF] *'We are always ready to look at work by artists/makers who submit slides/photographs, but we select contemporary work very carefully, aiming to appeal to our particular audiences as well as benefiting the career of the exhibitor.'* Send visual material to Felicity Lunn, Exhibitions Officer. Gallery covers most exhibition costs. Commission on sales is negotiable.
Access: [L][F] BR Newport 10 mins; Public car park 5 mins

The Gallery: 'Sacrement' by David Tess, oil on canvas, 36"x48", 1983 (Photo: Lightwork)

Rex Moreton Studio

Separate gallery planned for first floor of antique shop which presently also displays paintings and prints, run by photographer Rex Moreton. [Pa,Pr]

Address: Mountjoy Road, Newport, Gwent NP9 2FB tel 0633 67887
Contact: Rex Moreton tel 0633 55078
Open: Tues,Wed,Fri & Sat 10-1 2-5

Sessions House

Gallery on first floor of framing business, showing predominantly solo exhibitions by artists based in the Pembrokeshire area.

Address: East Street, Newport, Dyfed SA42 0SY tel 0239 820853
Contact: Richard Willson
Open: Mon-Sat 9.30-5.30
Exhibiting: [AW] Charge for publicity. 25% commission on sales.

Newtown (Powys)

(NWaA) Map6 SO19

Country Works Gallery

Commercial art gallery in rural location specialising in contemporary country artwork. [VA,Ph,Cr]

Address: Sawmills, Kerry, Newtown, Powys SY16 4NA tel 068 688 434
Contact: Partners Richard & Clare Halstead
Open: Wed-Sun 10.30-6, and bank holidays
Policy: Gallery started with intention of making available contemporary artwork which was not being seen in the area, as well as attracting visitors to the area who have an interest in art and design. Regular monthly exhibitions of paintings, prints and applied arts (often one artist/one maker together), plus changing display of high quality ceramics, basketry, jewellery, prints, etc. *'A great many artists/makers now choose to live in the country, and find their environment affects the work they produce. The title of the gallery reflects this attitude, rather than an interest in wildlife or 'country crafts', and we try to show work which has a freshness and new approach to its subject.'*
Sales: Work sold; Credit card
The Space: Flexible hanging arrangements on stone walls and screens. Total hanging area around 18x2m, with plinths for craftwork, spotlighting and natural light.
Exhibiting: [AW] Interested in work by individual artists/makers. Contact either Richard or Clare Halstead. Initially prefer to see photographs or transparencies of work, or to see artists by appointment (after 5 Wed-Sun). Not usually possible to view work brought without prior appointment. Gallery pays for insurance, printing and mailing of publicity, list of exhibits, and part preview costs. Commission is 33.3% before VAT.

Access: [F] No access by public transport; Own car park

Oriel 31, Davies Memorial Gallery

One of two galleries run by Oriel 31, a registered charity whose aim is to promote the visual arts in Mid Wales. [VA,Ph,Cr]

Address: Davies Memorial Gallery, The Park, Newtown, Powys SY16 2NZ tel 0686 25041
Contact: Director Michael Nixon
Open: Mon-Sat 10-5
Policy: A gallery purpose-built in 1967 and supported by public funds. Twelve month-long exhibitions a year covering the whole range of visual arts, plus a craft exhibition area with lockable display cabinets, where exhibition changes every two months. Also sells wide range of crafts, cards, books etc. (See also Oriel 31, Welshpool).
Sales: Work sold; Credit card; Credit scheme
The Space: Linear hanging space of 47m; no environmental controls.
Exhibiting: [AW][EF] Gallery covers most exhibition costs except artist's expenses. Commission is 25%.
Access: [F] BR Newtown 5 mins; Bus station and public car park adjacent

Neyland (Dyfed)

(SEWaA) Map4 SM90

Neyland Library

Purpose-built public library with separate exhibition room used by local groups of artists.

Address: St Clement's Road, Neyland, Dyfed SA73 1SH tel 0646 600791
Contact: Librarian Mrs Jenkins
Open: Tues & Thurs 3-6, Wed 10-12, 2-5, Fri 2-5, Sat 10-12
The Space: 166 square metres; hanging rods.

Oriel 31: 'They said the war was partly to blame' by Joyce Cairns, oil on board, 84"x96", 1986

Penarth (S Glamorgan)

(SEWaA) Map6 ST17

Turner House

Branch gallery of National Museum of Wales, showing only temporary exhibitions from the museum's collection during 1988/89. [VA]

Address: Plymouth Road, Penarth, S Glamorgan CF6 2DH tel 0222 708870
Contact: Custodian Elizabeth Brace
Open: Tue-Sat 11-12.45, 2-5, Sun 2-5
Access: [S] Ground floor [X] Upstairs. Limited street parking

Penmaenmawr (Gwynedd)

(NWaA) Map4 SH77

Gays Art Gallery

Commercial gallery specialising in oil paintings and watercolours, 1700-1950. [Pa]

Address: Conway Road, Penmaenmawr, Gwynedd LL34 6BH tel 0492 622850
Contact: T W Johns
Open: Mon-Sat 9-5
Access: [F] BR station 5 mins; Own car park

Pontardawe (W Glamorgan)

(WWaA) Map4 SN70

Cross Gallery

Exhibition room within a community centre funded by the West Glamorgan County Council Education Department, offering classes, workshops, advice sessions and room hire for many organisations. [VA,Ph,Cr]

Address: The Cross Community Centre, 1 High Street, Pontardawe, W Glamorgan SA8 4HU tel Pontardawe 863955
Contact: Warden Stephanie Macleod
Open: Mon-Fri 10-4
Policy: A community gallery making art accessible both to the people of the Swansea Valley and the whole of West Glamorgan. Diverse programme of about 24 exhibitions a year by living artists/makers, both solo and group, promoting a percentage of local artists' work as well as artists from further afield. Related workshops whenever possible.
Sales: Work sold
The Space: Separate exhibition room of with about 15.2m linear hanging space on pin boards 1.2 high and a total wall height of 3m.
Exhibiting: [AW][EF] Apply to the Warden. Gallery pays for insurance, printing and mailout of publicity, list of exhibits, catalogue/card. Exhibition contract used. No commission on sales.
Access: [U][T][F] Bus 120 to Pontardawe Cross; Public car parks 2 mins

Pontyclun (Mid Glamorgan)

(SEWaA) Map6 ST08

Art Cetera

Commercial art gallery, picture framer and art supply shop. [VA]

Address: 85 Talbot Road, Talbot Green, Pontyclun, Mid Glamorgan CF7 8AE tel 0443 224567
Contact: V M Hutchins
Open: Mon-Sat 9.30-5.30
Policy: Permanent display of work by South Wales artists, plus special solo and group exhibitions every three months, and thematic summer open exhibition. Policy to promote work of these artists to the general public of the area as well as visitors, and to *'fill a void in the cultural environment of South Wales'*. Occasional demonstrations, seminars and workshops.
Sales: Work sold; Credit card; Credit scheme
The Space: 32m linear hanging space, height 2.67m; hanging from picture rail and wall hooks; natural light and fluorescents.
Exhibiting: [AW] Apply to V M Hutchins. Gallery pays for insurance, printing and mailing of publicity, list of exhibits, catalogue/card, preview costs, and framing. Commission is 30%. Exhibition space also hired out for £240 per week or £40 per day.
Access: [X] Bus X9 from Cardiff; Free car parking

Pontypool (Gwent)

(SEWaA) Map4 SO20

Valley Inheritance

Heritage centre with permanent museum collection and related temporary exhibitions, including some fine art exhibitions.

Address: Torfaen Museum Trust, Park Buildings, Pontypool, Gwent NP4 6JH tel 04955 52036
Contact: Director Adrian Babbidge
Open: Mon-Sat 10-5, Sun 2-5
Policy: Exhibitions relate almost entirely to history, arts and crafts, and the environment of eastern valleys of Gwent (Blaenau, Pontypool, Cwmbran).
Access: [U][T]

Pontypridd (Mid Glamorgan)

(SEWaA) Map6 ST09

Polytechnic of Wales (Y Bont/The Bridge Gallery)

Public exhibition space adjacent to the art department of the Polytechnic of Wales Institute of Higher Education. [VA,Ph,Cr]

Address: Polytechnic of Wales, Pontypridd, Mid Glamorgan CF737 1DL tel 0443 480480 ext 2562
Contact: Head of Visual Arts, Department of Arts & Languages Alan Salisbury
Open: Mon-Fri 9-5 Autumn & Spring terms only
Policy: Exhibition programme includes all media, with *'no veto on style, medium etc. other than those imposed by the size and nature of the space.'* Policy to give students the opportunity to see work of practising, professional artists; to provide a resource in the locality for the exhibition of visual art; to forge links with the local community as a *'shop window'* for the institution. Exhibiting artists usually give lecture and workshops in the college. Most exhibitions are solo and of artists working locally.
Sales: Work sold; Sales referred to exhibitor
The Space: Main space has two facing walls each 9x2.9m; side space has two walls 1.9x2.9m & 3.9x2.9m and rear space one wall 5.1x2.9m. All have direct mirror plating, fluorescents and showcases available. Gallery cannot accommodate large sculpture. There is no direct supervision over the gallery and therefore security is at the risk of the exhibitor.
Exhibiting: *'Unfortunately, with a small number of exhibitions organised a year, it is administratively difficult to deal with large numbers of applications, therefore artists are normally invited to exhibit by the Gallery Organiser'.* Gallery pays for transport (within 40 miles), printing and mailing of publicity, list of exhibits, catalogue/card, and preview costs. No commission on sales.
Access: [U][T] BR Treforest 5 mins; Car park 2 mins

Pontypridd Historical & Cultural Centre

Heritage centre run by Pontypridd Town Council, with space for regular temporary exhibitions. [VA,Ph,Cr]

Address: Bridge Street, Pontypridd, Mid Glamorgan CF37 tel 0443 402077
Contact: Dr Alison Allen
Open: Tues-Sat 9-5, and bank holidays
Policy: Alongside its permanent displays related to local and regional history, the centre programmes regular temporary exhibitions of art, photography and craft from schools, local societies, and invited professionals.
Sales: Work sold; Sales referred to exhibitor
The Space: Up to 50m linear hanging space on flexible free-standing panels with height of 2.6m; spotlights; hanging rods.
Exhibiting: [AW] Apply in first instance to Warwick J S Butler, the Town Clerk, Pontypridd Town Council, Council Offices, Cemetery Road, Glyntaff, Pontypridd CF37 4BE, tel 0443 402810/402794. Centre pays for insurance, printing of publicity and list of exhibits. Commission on sales is 15%.
Access: [U][T][L] BR Pontypridd 8 mins; Bus station and car park 3 mins

Port Talbot (W Glamorgan)

(WWaA) Map6 SS79

Margam Orangery

18th century orangery in country park run by West Glamorgan County Council, used for temporary exhibitions. [Sc,Pa,LA]

Address: Margam Park, Margam, Port Talbot, W Glamorgan SA13 2TJ tel 0639 881635
Contact: Park Director I R Cadogan
Open: Daily 9.30-5.30 Summer; 9.30-4 Winter
Policy: Temporary exhibitions of sculpture and paintings, mostly solo exhibitions, including a sculpture exhibition

throughout the summer. Hitherto related to the activities of the Margam Sculpture Park, the future presence of sculpture in the park, and related residencies and workshops, is at present undetermined. Space also used for tourism-related displays.
Sales: Sales referred to exhibitor
The Space: Exhibition area 32x8m, height 6.9m, one wall suitable for hanging; uneven stone floor.
Exhibiting: [AW] Apply to Park Director. Work considered in relation to existing programme and other proposals. Exhibitions organised as part of the sculpture park programme have all costs covered and exhibition fee paid, commission on sales 10-25%. With other exhibitions agreed to provide visitor attraction, but not part of formal programme, artist is responsible for all costs but no commission is charged by authority.
Access: [U][T] Buses X1,X2,136; BR Port Talbot 3 miles; Car park on site

Porthmadog (Gwynedd)

(NWaA) Map4 SH53

Porthmadog Community Centre

Exhibition space for all kinds of exhibitions, professional shows and trade fairs.

Address: Oakley Wharf, Porthmadog, Gwynedd LL49 tel 0766 513372
Contact: Gwynfor Hughes
The Space: Floor space 9x56m.

Stiwdio Garreg Wen

Commercial artist-run gallery in centre of busy coastal resort showing work by other artists as well as the owner's own work. [VA,Cr]

Address: Snowdon Street, Porthmadog, Gwynedd LL49 9BT tel 076651 3833, 2450
Contact: Rob Piercy, 20 Maes Gerddi, Porthmadog, Gwynedd LL49 9LE
Open: Mon-Sat Easter-Sept, Thurs-Sat Oct-24 Dec; closed Jan-Easter
Policy: Changing display of work for sale, mostly watercolour landscapes by Welsh artists, with occasional solo exhibitions lasting one month. Plans to open second exhibition area during 1989, and eventually *'to create a small art centre in an otherwise barren area art-wise'*.
Sales: Work sold; Credit card; Credit scheme
The Space: Total linear hanging space at present about 33m, height 2.4m; tracklighting; outdoor courtyard.
Exhibiting: [AW] Applications welcome at any time. Work on display is insured. Commission on work sold is 33.3%.
Access: [F] Town centre site

Prestatyn (Clwyd)

(NWaA) Map4 SJ08

Prestatyn Library

Library run by Clwyd Library and Museums Service.

Address: Nant Hall Road, Prestatyn, Clwyd LL19 9LH tel 07456 4841
Contact: Librarian J Beagan
Open: Mon-Tue Thurs-Fri 10-7, Wed 10-5, Sat 9.30-12.30
Policy: Exhibition area in foyer showing occasional touring exhibitions plus work by local artists and makers.
Sales: Work sold
The Space: Screens and showcases available.
Exhibiting: [AW] Continuous rolling programme booked well in advance. The library covers insurance and charges 20% commission.
Access: [F] Bus station & BR Prestatyn 5 mins; Car park 2 min

Presteigne (Powys)

(SEWaA) Map4 SO36

MBCAA Gallery

Gallery run by the Mid-Border Community Arts Association, a voluntary non-profitmaking body whose aim is to bring more arts-based activity to the area. [VA,Ph,Cr]

Address: Shire Hall, Broad Street, Presteigne, Powys LD8 2AD tel 0544 260116
Contact: Chairman S M Stanley tel 0544 267131
Open: Mon-Sat 10-5 during exhibitions
Policy: Growing from the annual Presteigne Festival open art and crafts exhibition, the MBCAA now programmes about six varied temporary exhibitions annually, encouraging young artists as well as presenting major touring exhibitions in all media. School visits and talks by exhibiting artists.
The Space: Georgian building; main gallery and ante room providing about 26m linear hanging space, other rooms also available; high ceilings, natural light and new lighting system; staircase access limits weighty items.
Exhibiting: [AW] Apply to the Chairman, MBCAA, Shire Hall, Presteigne. Gallery unable to finance exhibition costs. Space available for hire, £30 for twelve days, or *'less for young artists'*. Commission on sales 10% for work under £50, 20% for work over £50. Detailed information and conditions of hire available.
Access: [X] Parking adjacent

Pwllheli (Gwynedd)

(NWaA) Map4 SH33

Bodvel Hall Craft Centre

Changing display of craftwork and some paintings and prints for sale.

Address: near Pwllheli, Gwynedd LL53 tel 0758 613386
Contact: G Morris
Open: Daily 10.30-5.30 Easter to end of Sept

Oriel Penlan

Gallery and information centre run by Pwllheli Town Council. [VA,Ph,Cr]

Address: Penlan Street, Pwllheli, Gwynedd LL53

Contact: Ian Roberts, 4 Ffordd y Cob, Pwllheli, Gwynedd
Open: Mon-Sat
Policy: Gallery made available free of charge to any individual, group or bona fide organisation, hence extremely varied programme of around twenty exhibitions annually, of which half are art or craft exhibitions.
Sales: Sales referred to exhibitor
The Space: Gallery is 10x4m with large showcases.
Exhibiting: **[AW]** Gallery available free of charge (*'donation for heating and lighting expected from exhibitors who can afford to contribute'*), no commission on sales.
Access: **[F]** Central location

Queensferry (Clwyd)

(NWaA) Map4 SJ36

Deeside Leisure Centre

Leisure centre with exhibition area adjacent to main foyer.
Address: Chester Road West, Queensferry, Deeside, Clwyd CH5 1SA tel 0244 812311
Contact: Administrator Mr Hogan
Open: Daily 9am-10pm
Exhibiting: 10% commission on sales.

Rhayader (Powys)

(SEWaA) Map4 SN96

Elan Valley Visitor Centre

Award winning visitor centre for spectacular Victorian reservoir, with occasional temporary exhibitions of art and craft, related to artists residencies and Festival of the Countryside during Summer.
Address: near Rhayader, Powys LD6 tel 0597 810898/810880

Rhuddlan (Clwyd)

(NWaA) Map4 SJ07

Rhuddlan Library

Library run by Clwyd Library Service with space for temporary exhibitions.
Address: Vicarage Lane, Rhuddlan, Clwyd LL18 2SF tel 0745 590719
Contact: Branch Librarian Yvonne Davies
Open: Mon,Wed,Fri 10-7, Tues,Thurs 12.30-5.30, Sat 9.30-12.30

Rhyl (Clwyd)

(NWaA) Map4 SJ08

Rhyl Library Museum & Arts Centre

Gallery for temporary exhibitions within combined public library, museum, and arts centre. [VA,Ph,Cr]
Address: Church Street, Rhyl, Clwyd LL18 3AA tel 0745 53814
Contact: Steve Brake, Wrexham Library Arts Centre, Rhosddu Road, Wrexham, Clwyd tel 0978 261932
Open: Mon-Fri 10-5, Sat 10-4.30
Policy: *'Main aim to provide an opportunity for local people to experience first hand all the diverse activities of the art world'.* Regular monthly exhibitions programmed by Clwyd Exhibitions Service. Also venue for Welsh Arts Council Craft Showcase Network (see Welsh Arts Council, Cardiff).
Sales: Work sold
The Space: Linear hanging space 33m, plus 56m on screens, height 2.6m; clad walls, fixing with mirrorplates; fluorescents and spots.
Exhibiting: **[AW][EF]** Apply enclosing CV and slides of work to S Brake. Commission on sales is 20%.
Access: **[U][T][L][F]** BR Rhyl 6 mins; Car park 1 min

Ruabon (Clwyd)

(NWaA) Map4 SJ34

Ruabon Library

Library run by Clwyd Library and Museum Service. [VA,Ph,Cr]
Address: High Street, Ruabon, Clwyd LL14 6NH tel 0978 822002
Contact: Librarian, Cefn Mawr Library Dylan Hughes, Cefn Mawr Library, Plas Kynaston Lane, Cefn Mawr, Wrexham, Clwyd LL14 3AT tel 0978 820938
Open: Mon, Fri 9.30-7, Tues 2-5, Wed 2-7, closed Thurs & Sat
Policy: The library shows Clwyd Library Service exhibitions and local work.
Sales: Work sold
The Space: Exhibition space 8x8m with 4 movable screens and 5 fixed display cases.
Exhibiting: **[AW]** Contact the Librarian. Insurance arranged, library takes 20% commission.
Access: **[F]** Car park adjoining; BR 5 mins

Ruthin (Clwyd)

(NWaA) Map4 SJ15

Ruthin Craft Centre Gallery

Gallery for temporary exhibitions and crafts shop in Ruthin Craft Centre, administered by the Tourism and Leisure Division of Clwyd County Council, providing thirteen studios for makers, restaurant and tourist information point. [Cr,Sc]
Address: Ruthin Craft Centre, Park Road, Ruthin, Clwyd LL15 1BB tel 082 42 5675/4774
Contact: Craft Development Officer Carole Netting
Open: Daily 10-5 Winter; 9-6 Summer
Policy: *'In both exhibition and retail policy the only work to be considered must show substantial elements of both design and making. Our aim is to put before the public the maker in a most professional manner, and support them with quality promotion and marketing. We also believe that encouragement for the development of the crafts can be enhanced by retaining a representation of the highest standard of work in our region'.* Wide ranging monthly crafts exhibitions in main

gallery, both touring and originated in-house, including at least two exhibitions a year toured from Ruthin. Also Studio Eight for additional programme of exhibitions including guilds and community aspects. Exhibition-related lectures and workshops, and summer projects for children.

Sales: Work sold; Credit card

The Space: Main exhibition space is 7x5m, ht 3.5m; Studio 8 is 5.5x4m; craft cases available.

Exhibiting: [AW] Apply to the Craft Development Officer. Gallery covers most exhibition expenses except display and artists' expenses. Commission on sales from exhibitions (not shop) is 20%.

Access: [U][T][F] Bus route 2 mins; Car park on site

St Asaph (Clwyd)

(NWaA) Map4 SJ07

Saint Asaph Library

Library run by Clwyd Library Service.

Address: The Roe, St Asaph, Clwyd LL17 0LU tel 0745 582253

Contact: Branch Librarian Yvonne Davies

Open: Mon,Wed,Fri 9.30-7, Tues,Thurs 12.30-5, Sat 9.30-12.30

Policy: Temporary exhibitions hung on picture rail throughout library.

Swansea (W Glamorgan)

(WWaA) Map6 SS69

Attic Gallery

Commercial contemporary art gallery founded in 1962. [VA]

Address: 61 Wind Street, Swansea, W Glamorgan SA1 1EG tel 0792 53387

Contact: Brenda Bloxam

Open: Mon-Fri 10-5, Sat 10-4

Policy: Changing display of contemporary paintings, original prints and small sculpture, interspersed with about three special month-long exhibitions annually. Gallery originally set up to provide venue for artists working in Wales, but now regularly exhibits work from outside. Policy *'to maintain a wide cross-section of good quality work and to support the artists who provide the work'*. Framing service.

Sales: Work sold; Credit scheme

The Space: Two connected second floor rooms: Room 1 is 4x4m; Room 2 is 5x5m, both with a height of 3m. Linear hanging space 28m; picture rail and hooks; fluorescents and spots; size and weight of work limited by stairs and single door entrance.

Exhibiting: [AW] Contact Brenda Bloxam by telephone for appointment *'rather than just turning up'*. The gallery already regularly promotes the work of 30-40 artists. There is a hanging fee. The costs of an exhibition are shared between artist and gallery. Exhibitions can be framed by the gallery at discount rates. Gallery commission is 33.3%.

Access: [X] BR Swansea 10 mins; Public car parks 5 mins

Glynn Vivian Art Gallery

Municipal art gallery, part of the Museums Service of Swansea City Council. [VA,Ph,Cr,LA]

Address: Alexandra Road, Swansea, W Glamorgan SA1 5DZ tel 0792 655006/651738

Contact: Exhibitions Officer Jennifer A Hallam

Open: Daily 10.30-5.30

Policy: Over 30 temporary exhibitions annually, including contemporary and historical shows of fine art, crafts and photography, with local, national and international origins. Programme combines exhibitions of international significance, solo shows of emerging/mid-career artists, exhibitions of local significance, and exhibitions drawn from the permanent collections of mainly 19th & 20th century fine and applied art. Gallery caters for wide audience, serving both Swansea residents and the wider arts audience. Gallery Education Service organises full programme of workshops/demonstrations for adults and children, tours, lectures, films etc. Association of Friends organise lecture series, and other events.

Sales: Work sold; Credit card; Credit scheme

The Space: All exhibition spaces have blockboarded walls, spotlighting, woodblock floors. The main gallery which has full environmental controls, all daylight excluded is 23x11.2m with 116m linear hanging space. Room 1 has all daylight excluded and is 20x6.9m with 50m linear hanging. Room 2 is 13x6.9m with 10m linear hanging and has windows. Room 4 is 6.9x6.9m with

Attic Gallery

16m linear hanging. The Sculpture Court is a large terraced outdoor display area. Showcases, plinths and screens available.

Exhibiting: [EF] Exhibition proposal, CV, six slides and SAE to be submitted in the first instance to Exhibitions Officer. All applications are then considered together at six-monthly intervals. *'The number of applications far exceeds number of exhibitions possible. The gallery currently books exhibitions two years in advance'.* Most exhibition costs covered by gallery, but *'funding of each individual exhibition agreed between the gallery and artist/exhibition organiser'.* Commission of 25% on sales is added to the gallery purchase fund for works for the collection.

Access: [U][T][L](by prior arrangement only)**[X]**. BR Swansea 5 mins; Bus station 15 mins; Public car parks 10 mins

Mumbles Gallery

Private gallery run by architect Ian Campbell and lacemaker/weaver Janet Campbell.

Address: 618 Mumbles Road, Swansea, W Glamorgan SA3 4EA tel 0792 367102

Contact: Ian & Janet Campbell

Open: Mon-Sat 10-5

Policy: Mixed and solo exhibitions of work by local artists.

The Space: Space of around 115 square metres; shelving and plinths available.

Ocean Gallery

Small private gallery on sea front in Swansea's Maritime Quarter, exhibiting paintings, ceramics and craftwork by mainly Welsh artists. [Pa,Cr]

Address: 1 Ocean Crescent, Maritime Quarter, Swansea, W Glamorgan SA1 1VQ

Contact: A G Upton tel 0792 50332 (home)

Swansea Arts Workshop Gallery

Gallery in converted chapel in Swansea's Maritime Quarter, run on a voluntary basis by artist-members of the Association of Artists and Designers in Wales. [VA,Ph,Cr]

Glynn Vivian Art Gallery: 'Claes Oldenburg with students at the opeining of 'A bottle of notes and some voyages', a Northern Centre for Contemporary Arts touring exhibition (Photo: Graham Matthews)

Address: Gloucester Place, Swansea, W Glamorgan SA1 1TY tel 0792 50821

Contact: Gallery Coordinator Nigel Meager, 148 Overland Road, Mumbles, Swansea SA3 4EU tel 0792 360976

Open: Tues-Sun 12-6 May-Sept; 12-5 Oct-Apr

Policy: Regular monthly exhibitions of current art and craft, often by younger artists/makers, and often with a particular relevance to Swansea or West Wales, reflecting the co-ordinating group of artists. Policy *'by providing an artists'-run gallery, to correct cultural perspective on the visual arts in Swansea and West Wales, and to enable us to act politically as a body of professional artists. The gallery is our public face and point of contact, and we are convinced of the importance of a dialogue between artists and the public'.* Changing display of small art and craft items for sale by Swansea/West Wales artists. Occasional events.

Sales: Work sold

The Space: Exhibition area of 60 square metres with 20m linear hanging space; direct fixing with mirrorplates; track and spot lighting, some natural light. Planned outdoor sculpture area.

Exhibiting: [AW][EF] Make enquiry first to Nigel Meager *'with the warning that few unsolicited applications are likely to succeed'.* Gallery pays for most exhibition costs except display and artists' expenses. Exhibition fee for solo shows only. Commission on sales is 30%.

Access: [F] BR Swansea 15 mins; Bus station & public car parks 10 mins

Taliesin Arts Centre (Ceri Richards Gallery)

Gallery in university arts centre also comprising theatre, bar and bookshop.

Address: Taliesin Arts Centre, University College, Singleton Park, Swansea, W Glamorgan SA2 8PZ tel 0792 295526

Contact: Administrator Eryl Jenkins

Open: Mon 11-3, Tue-Fri 11-7, Sat 12-6

Policy: The gallery shows and sells a selection of work by contemporary artists, also prints and pottery.

Sales: Work sold

The Space: Details available on request.

Exhibiting: [AW] Contact Administrator.

Access: [S] City Mini bus passes main entrance

Treorchy (Mid Glamorgan)

(SEWaA) Map6 SS99

Parc & Dare Theatre

Theatre and concert hall run by Rhondda Borough Council, with function room available for exhibitions.

Address: Station Road, Treorchy, Rhondda, Mid Glamorgan CF42 tel 0443 773112

Contact: Manager Mr Harrison

Open: Mon-Sat 10am-10pm

The Space: 10 square metres.

Usk (Gwent)

(SEWaA) Map4 SO30

Arthouse

Artist-run space in restored stone barn. [Pa,Te,Fu]

Address: Pen-y-parc, Llangibby, near Usk, Gwent NP5 1NY tel 063 349 320

Contact: Susie Martin & Sarah Windrum

Open: Tues-Sun 10-6

Policy: The workshop and display space of painter Susie Martin and tapestry maker Sarah Windrum, who also run classes. The aim is to develop as a centre for other *'likeminded individuals'*, with space for temporary exhibitions.

Sales: Work sold

The Space: Well-lit gallery 5.6x12m.

Exhibiting: **[AW]** Artists and makers are welcome to apply. All work shown in the gallery will incorporate a high degree of traditional skill in whatever medium.

Access: **[X]**

Old Smithy Gallery

Private gallery with framing business and workshop. [Pa,Pr]

Address: Maryport Street, Usk, Gwent NP5 1AE tel 02913 2207

Contact: Brian Sansom

Open: Mon-Fri 9.30-5.15, Sat 9.30-1

Policy: Four exhibitions a year of two weeks duration, both group and solo exhibitions. Otherwise mixed display of paintings, limited edition prints and reproductions.

Welshpool (Powys)

(NWaA) Map4 SJ20

Oriel 31

Art and craft gallery run by Oriel 31, registered charity whose aim is to promote the visual arts in Mid Wales. [VA,Ph,Cr]

Arthouse

Address: 31 High Street, Welshpool, Powys SY21 7JP tel 0938 2990 (after August 1989 - 0938 552990)

Contact: Exhibition Officer Walt Warrilow

Open: Mon-Sat 11-5

Policy: *'We are based in a rural area and cater for widely differing tastes'*. Regular monthly exhibitions of contemporary art and craft/applied art in wide range of media, encouraging work of younger artists/makers, as well as important exhibitions of major figures (eg John Nash, Ivon Hitchens). Some exhibitions originated by the gallery are toured. Some major exhibitions split between Oriel 31 Welshpool and Newtown. Annual regional open exhibition. Special monthly displays in Craft Case, plus changing display of small craft/applied art items for sale. Talks by exhibiting artists, ceramics workshops, life-drawing classes, Association of Friends. (See also Oriel 31, Newtown).

Sales: Work sold; Credit scheme; Credit card

The Space: 11x4.3m, height 2.5m, linear hanging space 27.5m plus stair space; blockboard walls, hanging with mirrorplates; spotlighting; canvas size maximum 2m; showcases, plinths.

Exhibiting: **[AW][EF]** Send slides/photographs to Exhibitions Officer. Exhibiting fee dependent upon media. Gallery covers all exhibition costs except display and artists' expenses. Commission is 25%.

Access: **[X]** BR Welshpool 10 mins; Public car park 3 mins

Wrexham (Clwyd)

(NWaA) Map4 SJ34

Bersham Industrial Heritage Centre

Industrial heritage centre run by Clwyd County Council Library & Museum Service. [Pa,Pr,Ph,Cr]

Address: Bersham, Nr Wrexham, Clwyd LL14 4HT tel 0978 261529

Contact: Curator Ann Lloyd Williams

Open: Tues-Sat 10-4, Sun 2-4; closed 12.30-1.30, closed Mon except bank holidays Easter-Oct; Tues-Fri 10-4, Sat 12.30-3.30; closed 12.30-1.30, closed Sun-Mon Nov-Easter

Policy: The centre interprets the history of the Clywedog Valley and Bersham Ironworks, and its temporary exhibition programme is usually based on either

Oriel 31

industrial or historic topics. However, it does show exhibitions of fine art on industrial or historic themes, and work by artists in residence at the centre. Admission is free.
Sales: Work sold
The Space: 7.2x5.3m, height 2.44m with 35m linear hanging space, spotlighting and controllable natural light, UV filters on all windows. Showcases available.
Exhibiting: **[AW][EF]** Potential exhibitors should submit a CV and slides to the Curator. Exhibitions normally arranged by September for the following 18 months. Centre pays for insurance, transport, printing and mailing publicity, list of exhibits, and preview costs. Commission is 20%.
Access: **[F]** Car park adjacent

Rhosllanerchrugog Library

Library run by Clwyd Library Service.
Address: Princes Road, Rhosllanerchrugog, Nr Wrexham, Clwyd LL14 1AB tel 0978 840328
Contact: Branch Librarian Ann Hughes
Open: Mon Fri 10-7, Tues-Wed 10-5, closed Thurs & Sat
Policy: Purpose-built library with area for exhibition screens. Exhibitions arranged by library, plus Clwyd Library Service touring exhibitions.

Wrexham Library Arts Centre

Major regional arts centre comprising public library, art gallery, meeting rooms and coffee shop. [VA,Ph,Cr]
Address: Rhosddu Road, Wrexham, Clwyd LL11 1AU tel 0978 261932
Contact: Assistant Arts & Exhibitions Officer Shan Evans
Open: Mon-Fri 9.30-6.45, Sat 9.30-5.15
Policy: Regular programme of varied temporary exhibitions including major touring shows and exhibitions organised by the County Exhibitions Service. Also venue for two Welsh Arts Council Craft Showcase Network displays, see Welsh Arts Council, Cardiff.
Sales: Work sold; Credit scheme
The Space: Main gallery and subsidiary 'Foyer' area.
Exhibiting: **[AW][EF]** Apply to the County Arts & Exhibitions Officer, Steve Brake.

Ystradgynlais (W Glamorgan)

(WWaA) Map4 SN71

Oriel Fach

Commercial artist-run gallery. [VA,Cr]
Address: 58 Commercial Street, Ystradgynlais, Swansea Valley, W Glamorgan SA9 1HL tel 0639 843175/849795
Contact: Megan Jones, 9 Heol Derwen, Ystradgynlais SA9 1HL tel 0639 843175
Open: Wed 2-5, Thurs-Fri 10-5, closed 1-2, Sat 10-1
Policy: Mainly a changing display of the paintings of the owner Megan Jones, interspersed with exhibitions of work of other artists three or four times annually. Audience of local people, *'people of the area returning to the locality on holiday'*, and other visitors to the Brecon Beacons. Framing service. Painting workshops for adults and children, craft demonstrations, and poetry readings, usually during the summer.
Sales: Work sold
The Space: The gallery is 10x4m with hanging space for 30-40 'easel-size' paintings; alcoves and window spaces suitable for small sculpture; spotlights.
Exhibiting: **[AW]** Gallery pays for half publicity mailing and preview costs. Commission is 25%. Gallery also for hire, £70 a fortnight, £85 per three weeks, £90 a month.
Access: **[X]** Swansea-Brecon, Neath-Brecon bus routes

Right: Guernsey Museum & Art Gallery (Photo: Guernsey Press Co Ltd)

CHANNEL ISLANDS

Augres (Jersey)

Jersey Museums (Sir Francis Cook Gallery)

Gallery housing the work of the Jersey painter Sir Francis Cook.

Address: Augres, Trinity, Jersey, Channel Islands tel 0534 63333
Contact: Director of Museums Michael Day, 9 Pier Road, St Helier, Jersey, Channel Islands tel 0534 30511
Open: As advertised
Policy: The temporary exhibition gallery shows a wide range of art and history exhibitions. It is also available for hire to individuals or groups.
Sales: Work sometimes for sale
The Space: Main gallery 10x9m with movable screens and low-voltage lighting, smaller gallery 10x7m.
Access: [F] Ground floor only. Free car park 5 mins

St Helier (Jersey)

Studio 18

Commercial gallery showing contemporary work. [Pa,Pr,Ph]

Address: 23a Beresford Street, St Helier, Jersey tel 0534 34920
Open: Mon-Sat 8.30-5.30
Policy: Specialises in painting of the Channel Islands and work by local artists.
Exhibiting: [AW]

St Owen (Jersey)

Saint Heler Galleries

Commercial gallery. [Pa,Pr,Dr]

Address: Les Ormes, Ville au Bas, St Oven, Jersey, Channel Islands tel 0534 82332
Contact: J H Appleby
Open: By appointment only
Policy: Shows work by Jersey artists as well as old master paintings and English paintings and watercolours of the 18th and 19th century.

St Peter Port (Guernsey)

Guernsey Museum & Art Gallery

A local authority museum run by the Ancient Monuments Committee of the States of Guernsey with a permanent collection on the people and history of Guernsey and with an art gallery which also shows temporary exhibitions. [Pa,Pr,Dr,Ce]

Address: Candie Gardens, St Peter Port, Guernsey, Channel Islands tel 0481 26518
Contact: Director Rona Cole
Open: Mon-Sat 10.30-5.30 Summer; Mon-Sat 10.30-4.30 Winter
Policy: Shows primarily the museum's collection of 19th and early 20th century paintings of Guernsey and special exhbitions are held six to seven times a year including Renoir, Miro, Picasso, Mervyn Peake and various touring shows.
The Space: Gallery is 93 square metres with 42.5 m linear hanging space on eight screens and walls.
Exhibiting: [AW] Director.
Access [F] Town centre 5 mins walk

St Peters (Guernsey)

Coach House Gallery

A converted farm building containing a gallery, etching studio, pottery and artists' material shop. [VA,Cr,Ph]

Address: Les Islets, St Peters, Guernsey, Channel Islands tel 0481 65339
Contact: Directors Mrs Lintell
Open: Mon-Sun 11-5; Winter times restricted; closed January
Policy: Temporary exhibitions change monthly.
Sales: Work sold
The Space: Gallery on two floors 32x5m and 5x5m giving a total of 30m linear hanging space, and with direct fixing, spots and natural light.
Exhibiting: [AW] Gallery pays for insurance, publicity, list of exhibits and preview and in special cases share costs of transport and artists' travel. Commission is 33.3%.

Onchan (Isle of Man)

Isle of Man Travelling Gallery

Isle of Man Travelling Gallery is a converted double-decker bus which tours exhibitions to the main population centres on the island and to schools and special events. It is owned and run by Arts in Man (Travelling Gallery), a co-operative set up in 1983 to promote the visual arts on Man and is is the only gallery on the island showing work by contemporary artists. [VA,Ph,Cr,]

Address: tel 0624 75407
Contact: Co-ordinator Norman Sayle, Thalassa, 56 King Edward Road, Onchan, Isle of Man
Open: Tues-Sat 10.30-5
Policy: Four or five exhibitions a year are mounted, showing for four weeks ie one week each in Douglas, Peel, Castletown and Ramsey. It aims to provide exhibition space particularly, but not exclusively, for Manx or Manx-based artists.
Sales: Work sold
The Space: There are 19 specially-designed display boards ranging from 210x60cms to 115x115cms which can be angled or folded to make horizontal surfaces for three-dimensional work. Total linear hanging space is 21m. Upstairs there are overhead opal roof-lights. Downstairs there are side windows with tungsten strip lighting and fan heater. Hanging is by mirror plates. Size of display boards and obvious scale of bus interior limits the size of work shown. A secure perspex showcase 1x1mx75cms is available.
Exhibiting: The gallery hopes to welcome applications in the future. *'We are still catching up on a long backlog of never-exhibited artists based on the Isle of Man.'* The

gallery pays for insurance, publicity, preview costs, display, transport, catalogue and artists' expenses. 15% commission is charged on sales. Supports EPR.

Access: [X] The gallery is parked as near as possible to town centres

Arts councils & regional arts associations

For contacts, addresses and counties covered by the regional arts associations and arts councils see 'Read On...' pages 437-438

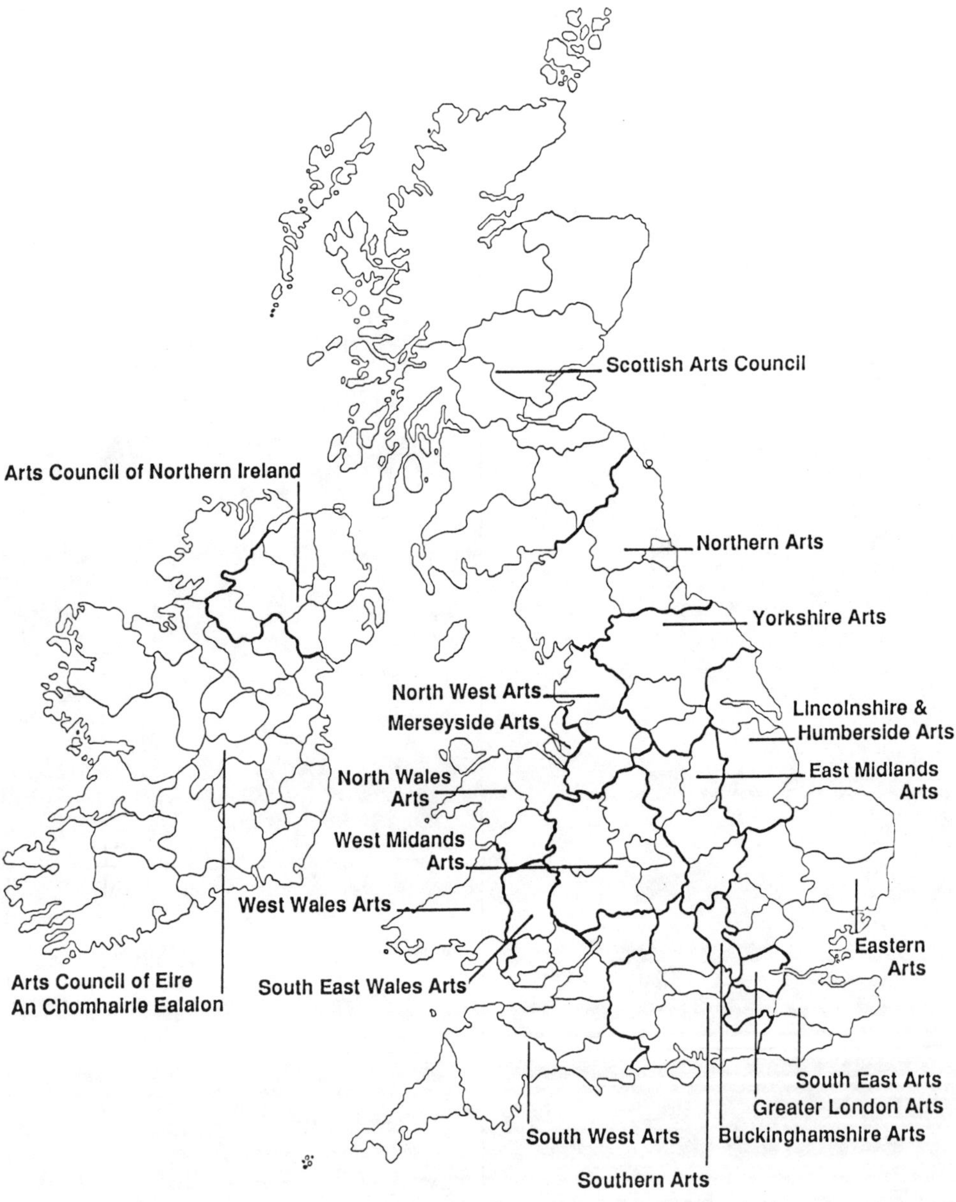

The National Grid

The National Grid provides one system of reference for the whole country which is divided into 100 kilometre (62.5 mile) squares. These are given a two letter reference for England, Scotland and Wales and a single letter reference for Ireland. These major squares are divided into10 kilometre (6.25 mile) squares. These are refered to by a number from 0–9. The National Grid reference is always preceeded by the letter reference of the major square followed by the numbers refering the the smaller squares. For example NT36 is the reference for Dalkeith which lies within the major square NT and is three subdivisions east (from left to right) and six subdivisions north (from bottom to top). A fuller explanation of the National Grid can be found in Ordnance Survey maps.

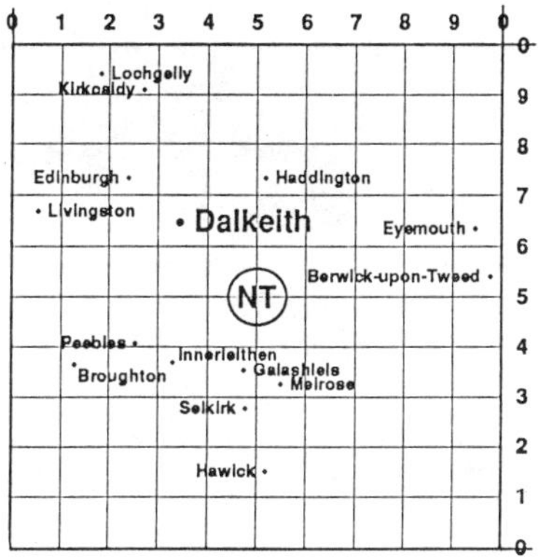

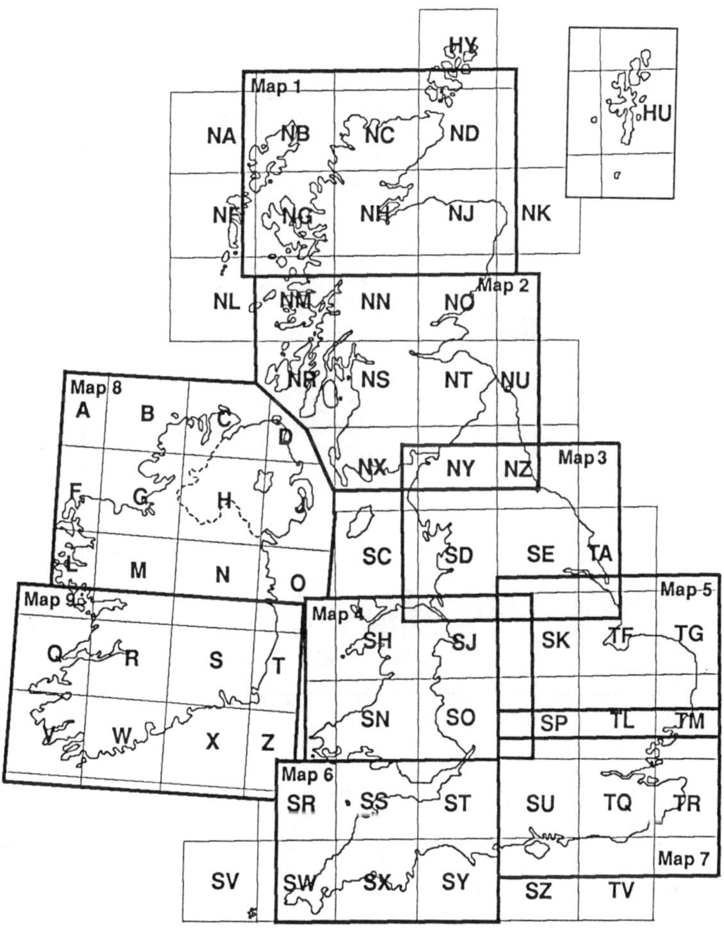

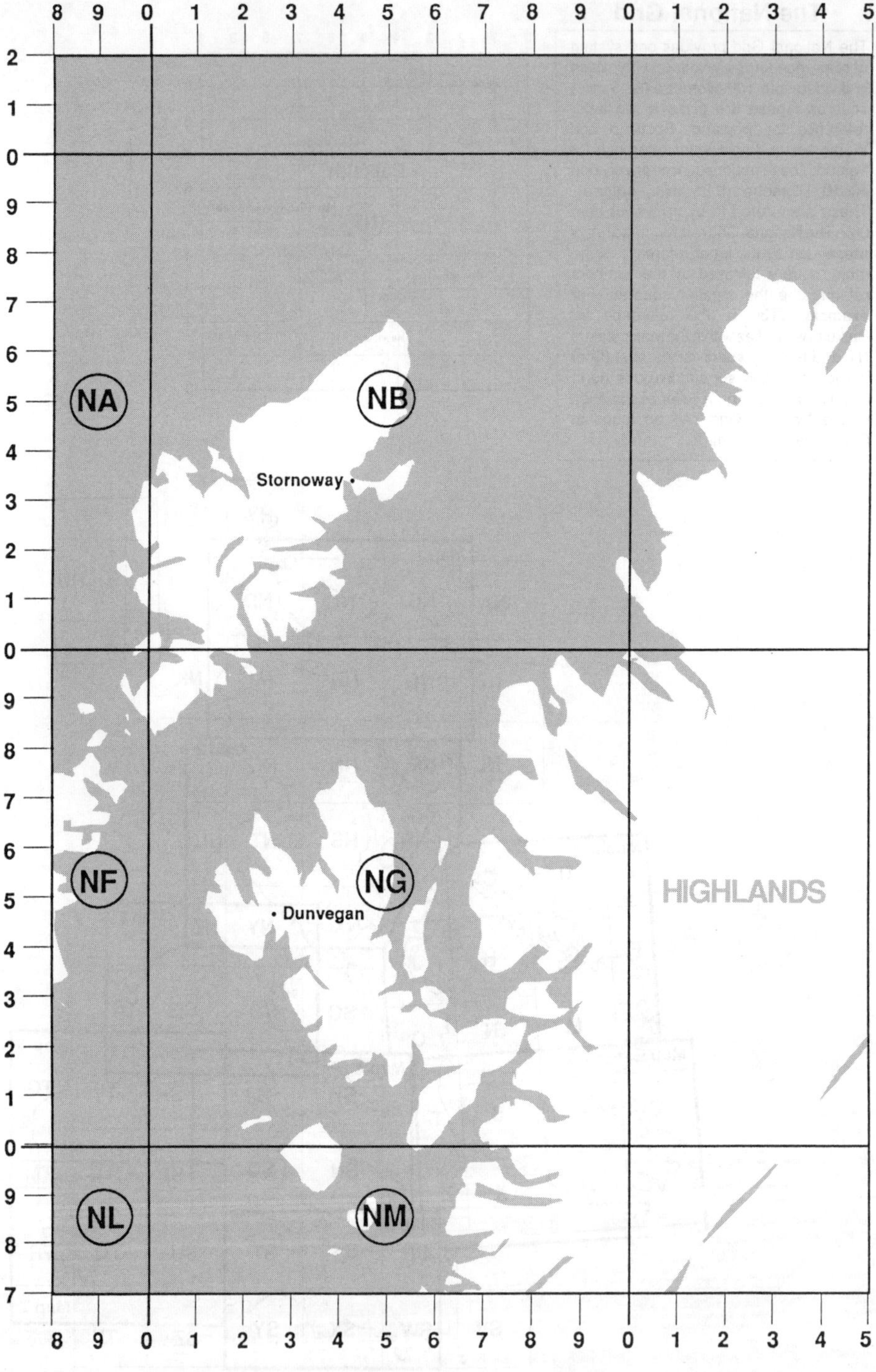
NA
NB
Stornoway
NF
NG
Dunvegan
HIGHLANDS
NL
NM

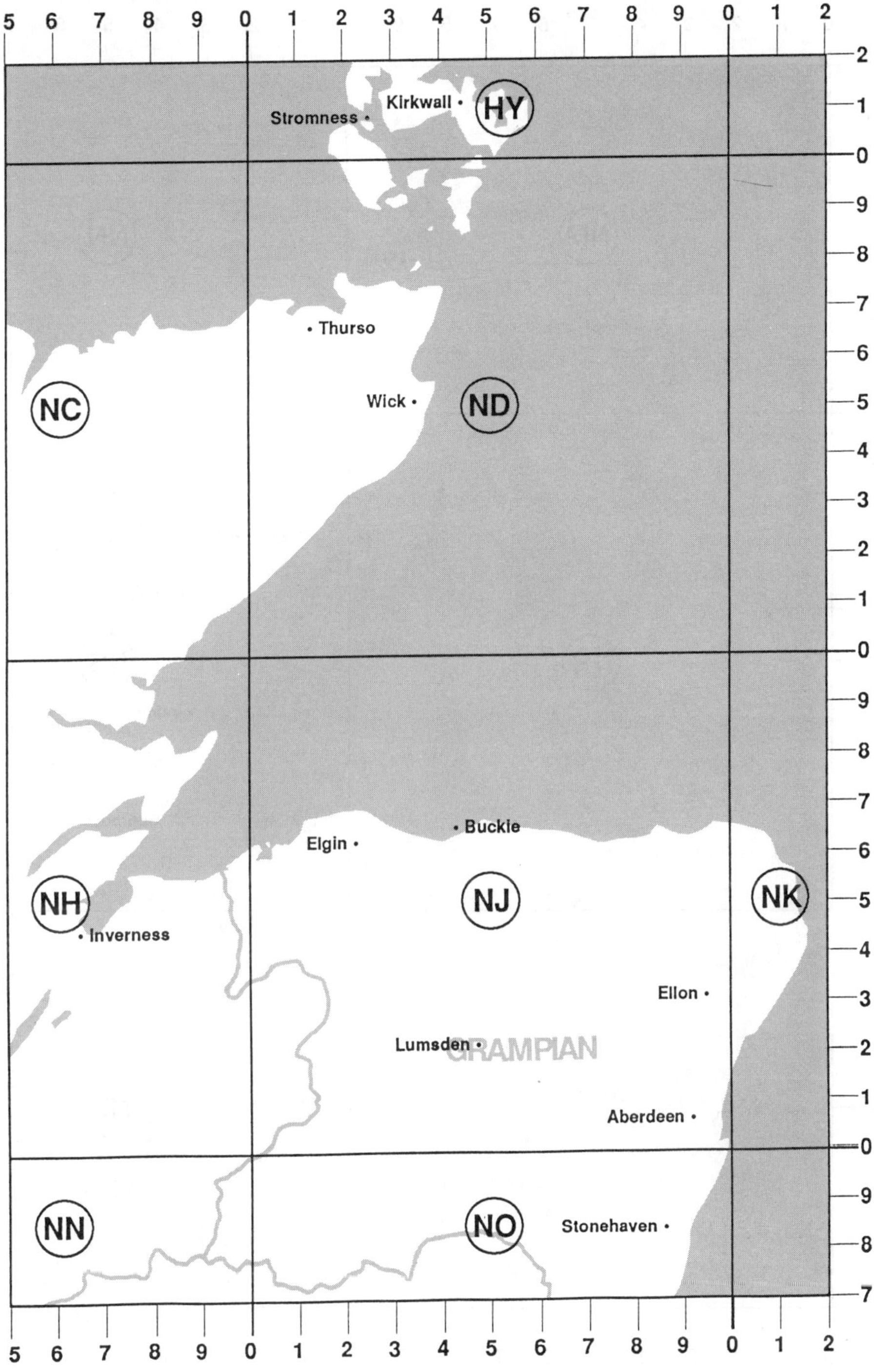
HY
Kirkwall
Stromness
Thurso
Wick
NC
ND
Buckie
Elgin
NH
Inverness
NJ
NK
Ellon
Lumsden
GRAMPIAN
Aberdeen
NN
NO
Stonehaven

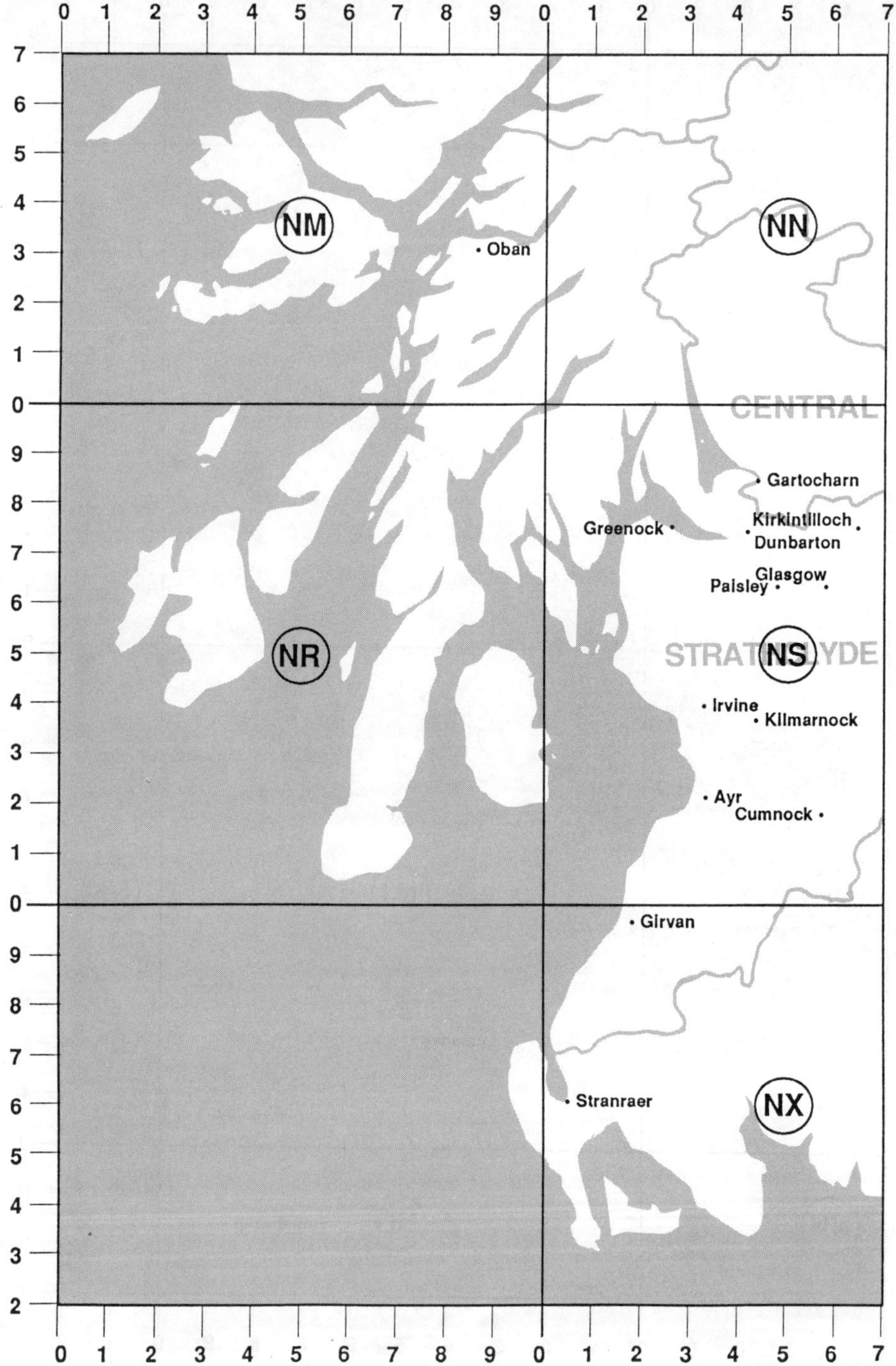
NM
NN
Oban
CENTRAL
Gartocharn
Greenock
Kirkintilloch
Dunbarton
Glasgow
Paisley
NR
STRATHCLYDE
NS
Irvine
Kilmarnock
Ayr
Cumnock
Girvan
Stranraer
NX

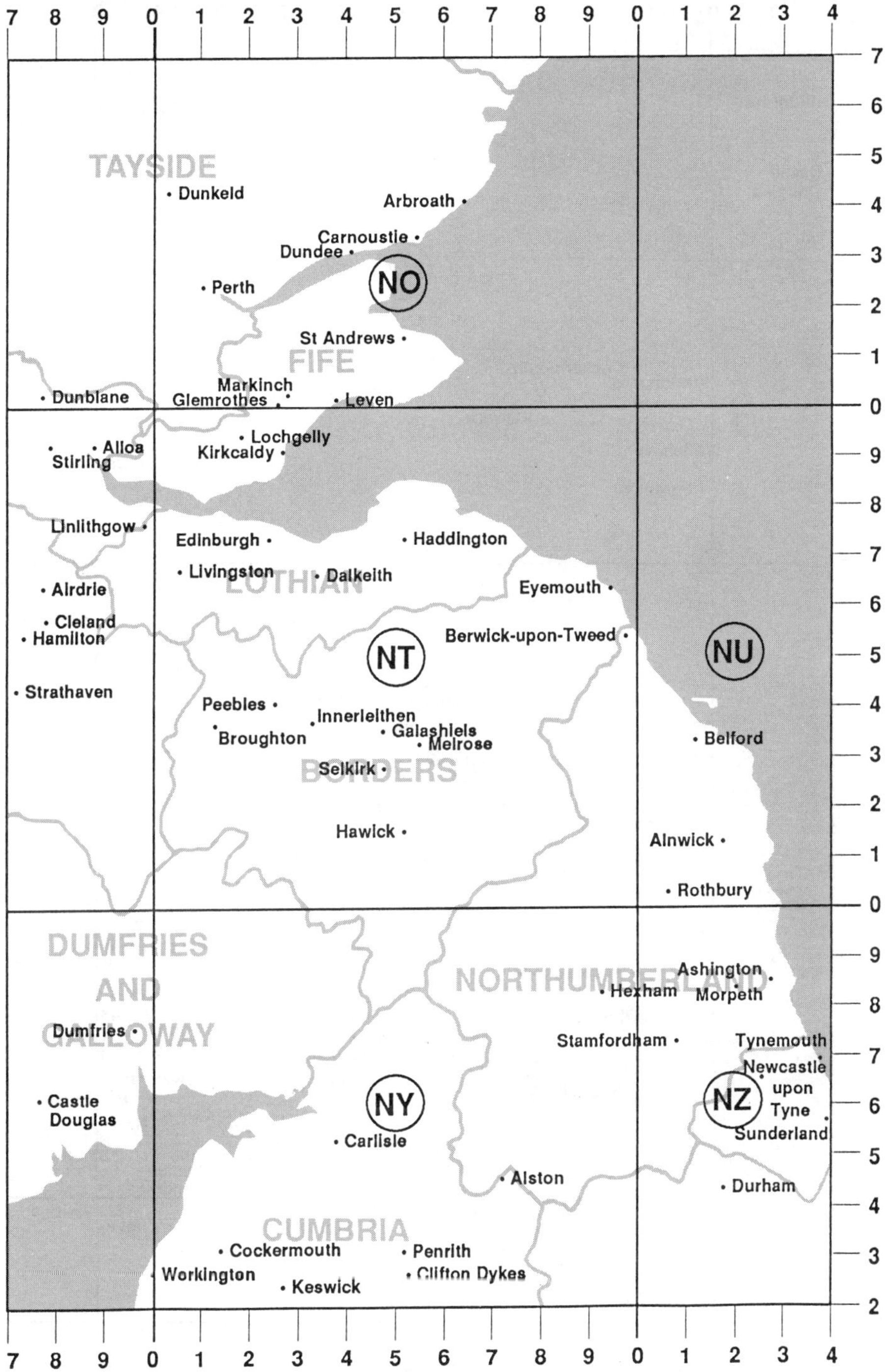
TAYSIDE
Dunkeld
Arbroath
Carnoustie
Dundee
Perth
NO
St Andrews
FIFE
Markinch
Glenrothes
Leven
Dunblane
Lochgelly
Kirkcaldy
Alloa
Stirling
Linlithgow
Edinburgh
Haddington
Livingston
Dalkeith
LOTHIAN
Airdrie
Eyemouth
Cleland
Hamilton
Berwick-upon-Tweed
NT
NU
Strathaven
Peebles
Innerleithen
Broughton
Galashiels
Melrose
Belford
Selkirk
BORDERS
Hawick
Alnwick
Rothbury
DUMFRIES AND GALLOWAY
NORTHUMBERLAND
Ashington
Hexham
Morpeth
Dumfries
Stamfordham
Tynemouth
Newcastle upon Tyne
Castle Douglas
NY
NZ
Sunderland
Carlisle
Alston
Durham
CUMBRIA
Cockermouth
Penrith
Workington
Clifton Dykes
Keswick

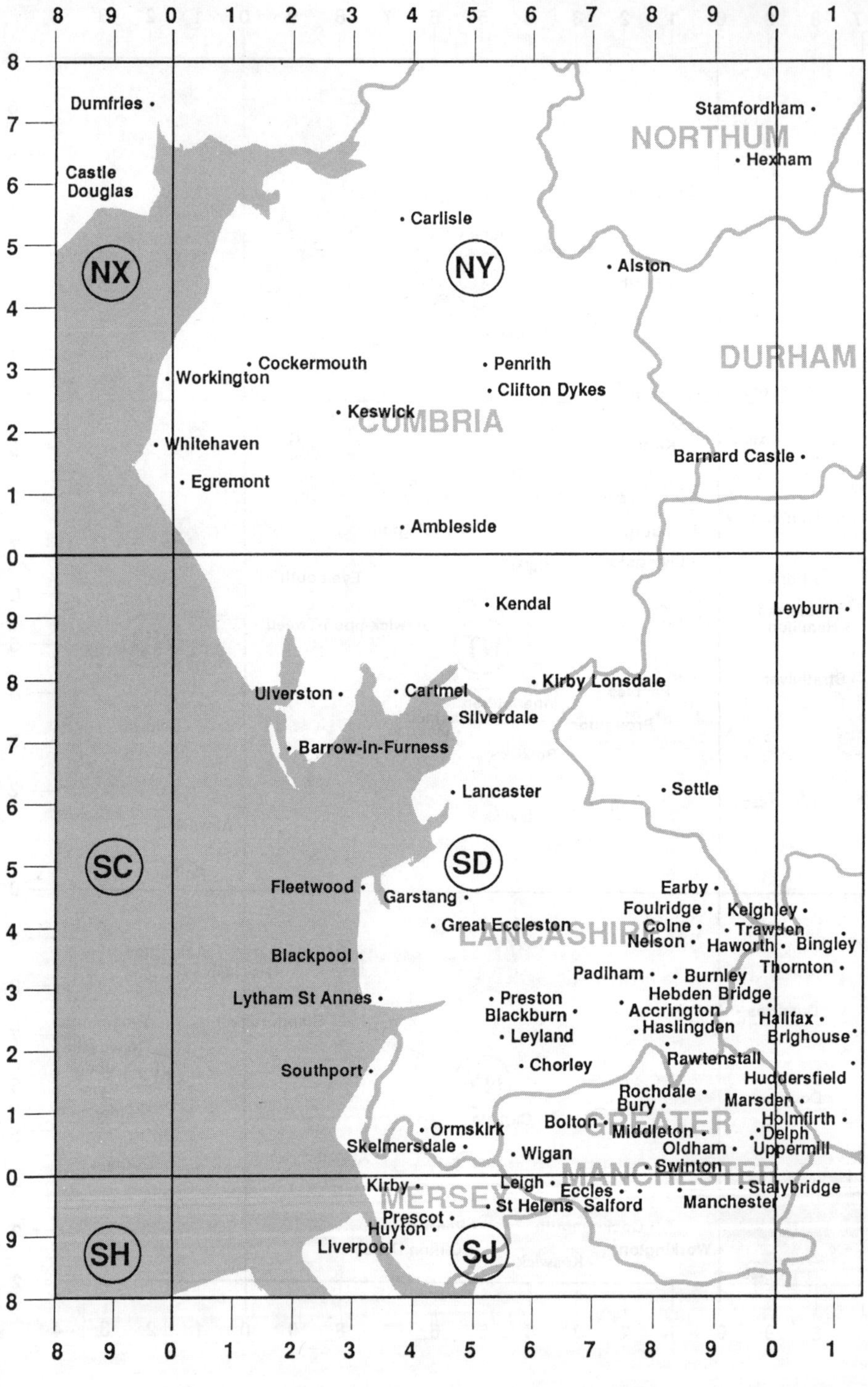
NX
NY
SC
SD
SH
SJ
NORTHUM
DURHAM
CUMBRIA
LANCASHIRE
GREATER MANCHESTER
MERSEY
Dumfries
Castle Douglas
Stamfordham
Hexham
Carlisle
Alston
Cockermouth
Workington
Penrith
Clifton Dykes
Keswick
Whitehaven
Egremont
Barnard Castle
Ambleside
Kendal
Leyburn
Ulverston
Cartmel
Kirby Lonsdale
Silverdale
Barrow-in-Furness
Lancaster
Settle
Fleetwood
Garstang
Earby
Foulridge
Keighley
Great Eccleston
Colne
Trawden
Nelson
Haworth
Bingley
Blackpool
Padiham
Burnley
Thornton
Hebden Bridge
Lytham St Annes
Preston
Blackburn
Accrington
Halifax
Leyland
Haslingden
Brighouse
Southport
Chorley
Rawtenstall
Huddersfield
Rochdale
Bury
Marsden
Bolton
Holmfirth
Ormskirk
Middleton
Delph
Oldham
Uppermill
Skelmersdale
Wigan
Swinton
Kirby
Leigh
Eccles
Stalybridge
Salford
Manchester
St Helens
Prescot
Huyton
Liverpool

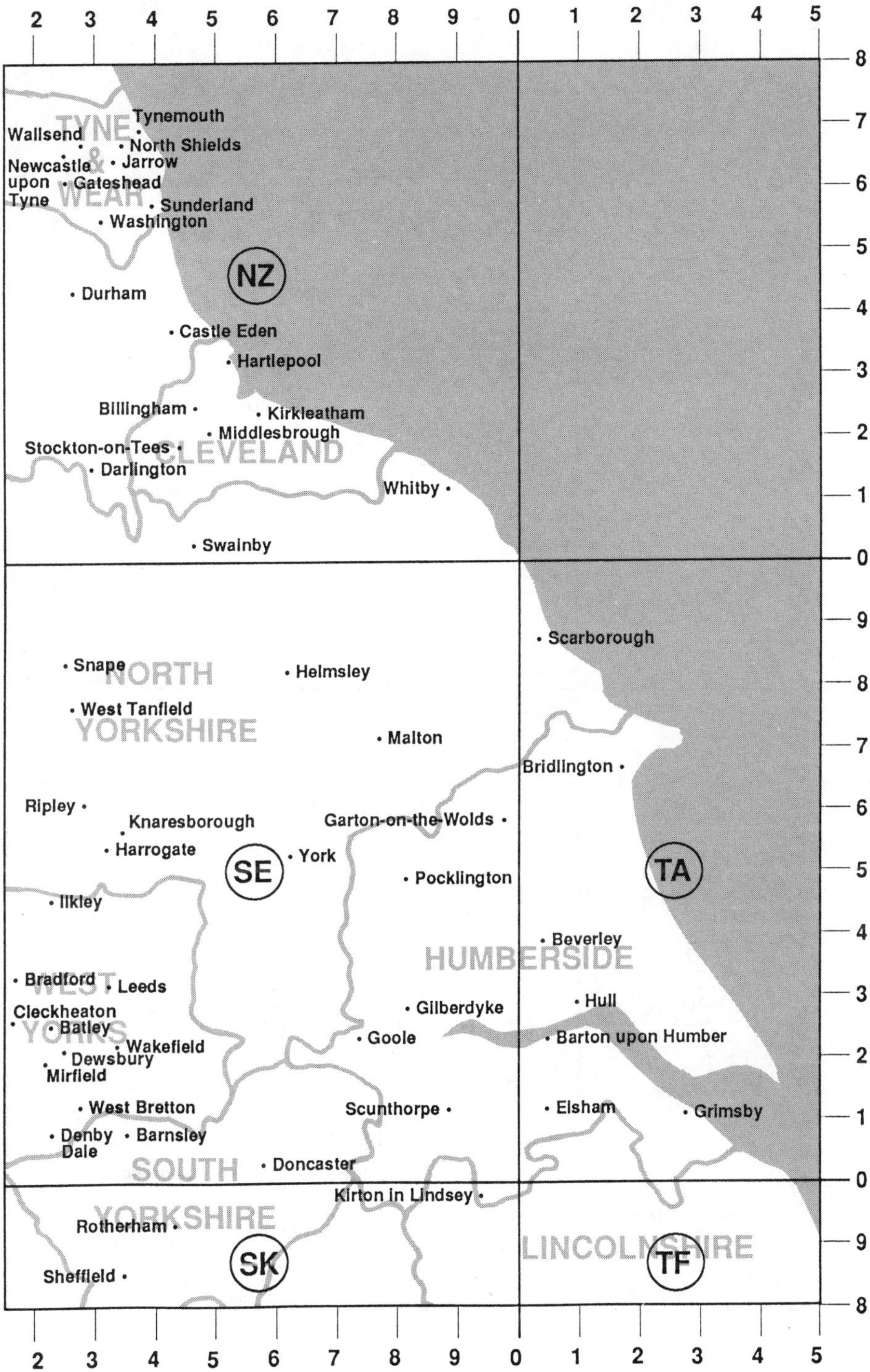

2 3 4 5 6 7 8 9 0 1 2 3 4 5
8 7 6 5 4 3 2 1 0 9 8 7 6 5 4 3 2 1 0 9 8
TYNE & WEAR
Tynemouth
Wallsend
North Shields
Newcastle upon Tyne
Jarrow
Gateshead
Sunderland
Washington
NZ
Durham
Castle Eden
Hartlepool
Billingham
Kirkleatham
Middlesbrough
Stockton-on-Tees
CLEVELAND
Darlington
Whitby
Swainby
Scarborough
Snape
NORTH YORKSHIRE
Helmsley
West Tanfield
Malton
Bridlington
Ripley
Knaresborough
Garton-on-the-Wolds
Harrogate
SE
York
Pocklington
TA
Ilkley
Beverley
HUMBERSIDE
Bradford
Leeds
WEST YORKS
Cleckheaton
Batley
Gilberdyke
Hull
Wakefield
Goole
Barton upon Humber
Dewsbury
Mirfield
West Bretton
Scunthorpe
Elsham
Grimsby
Denby Dale
Barnsley
SOUTH YORKSHIRE
Doncaster
Kirton in Lindsey
Rotherham
SK
LINCOLNSHIRE
TF
Sheffield

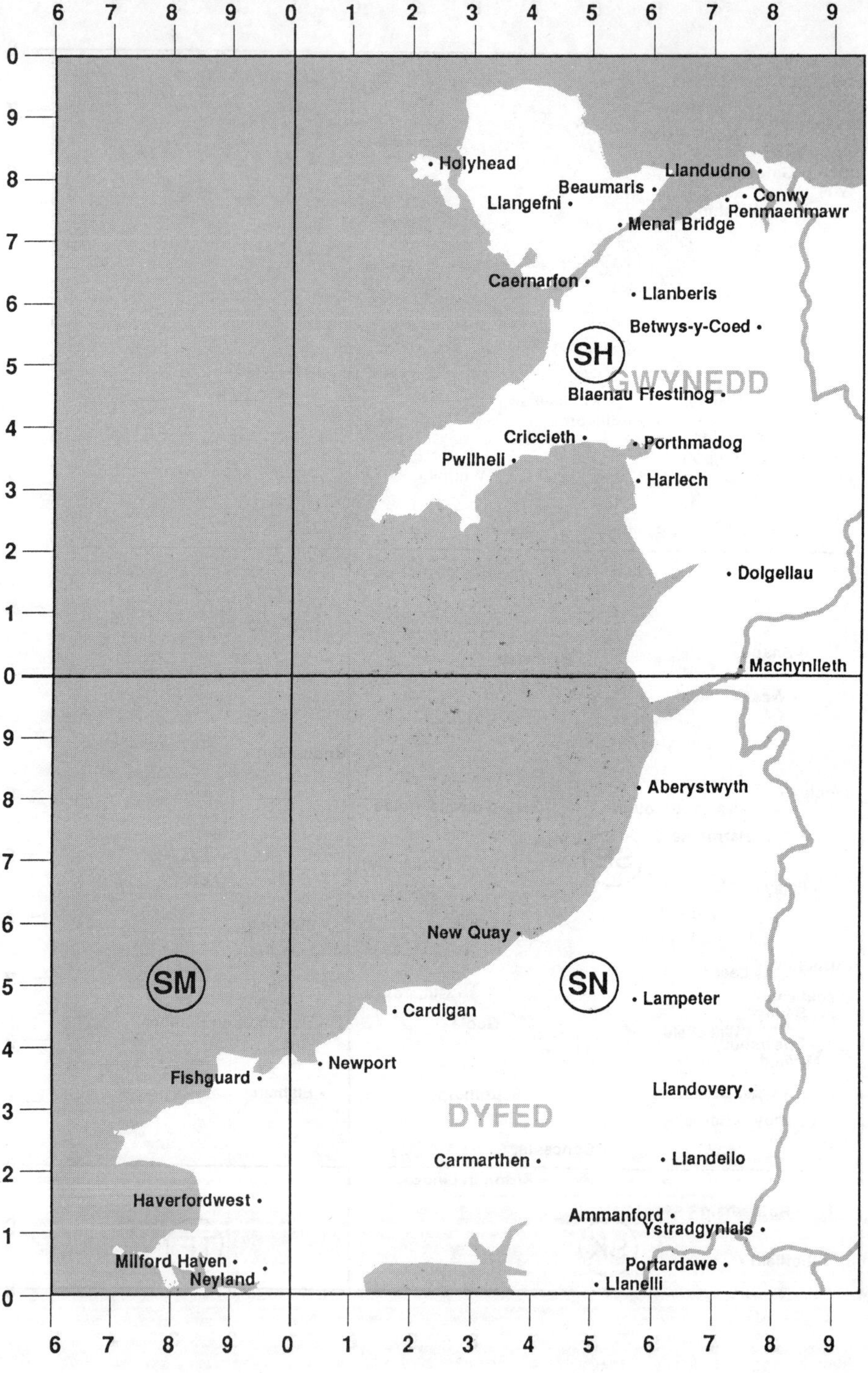

Holyhead
Llandudno
Beaumaris
Llangefni
Conwy
Penmaenmawr
Menai Bridge
Caernarfon
Llanberis
Betwys-y-Coed
SH
GWYNEDD
Blaenau Ffestinog
Criccieth
Porthmadog
Pwllheli
Harlech
Dolgellau
Machynlleth
Aberystwyth
New Quay
SM
SN
Lampeter
Cardigan
Newport
Fishguard
Llandovery
DYFED
Carmarthen
Llandeilo
Haverfordwest
Ammanford
Ystradgynlais
Milford Haven
Neyland
Portardawe
Llanelli

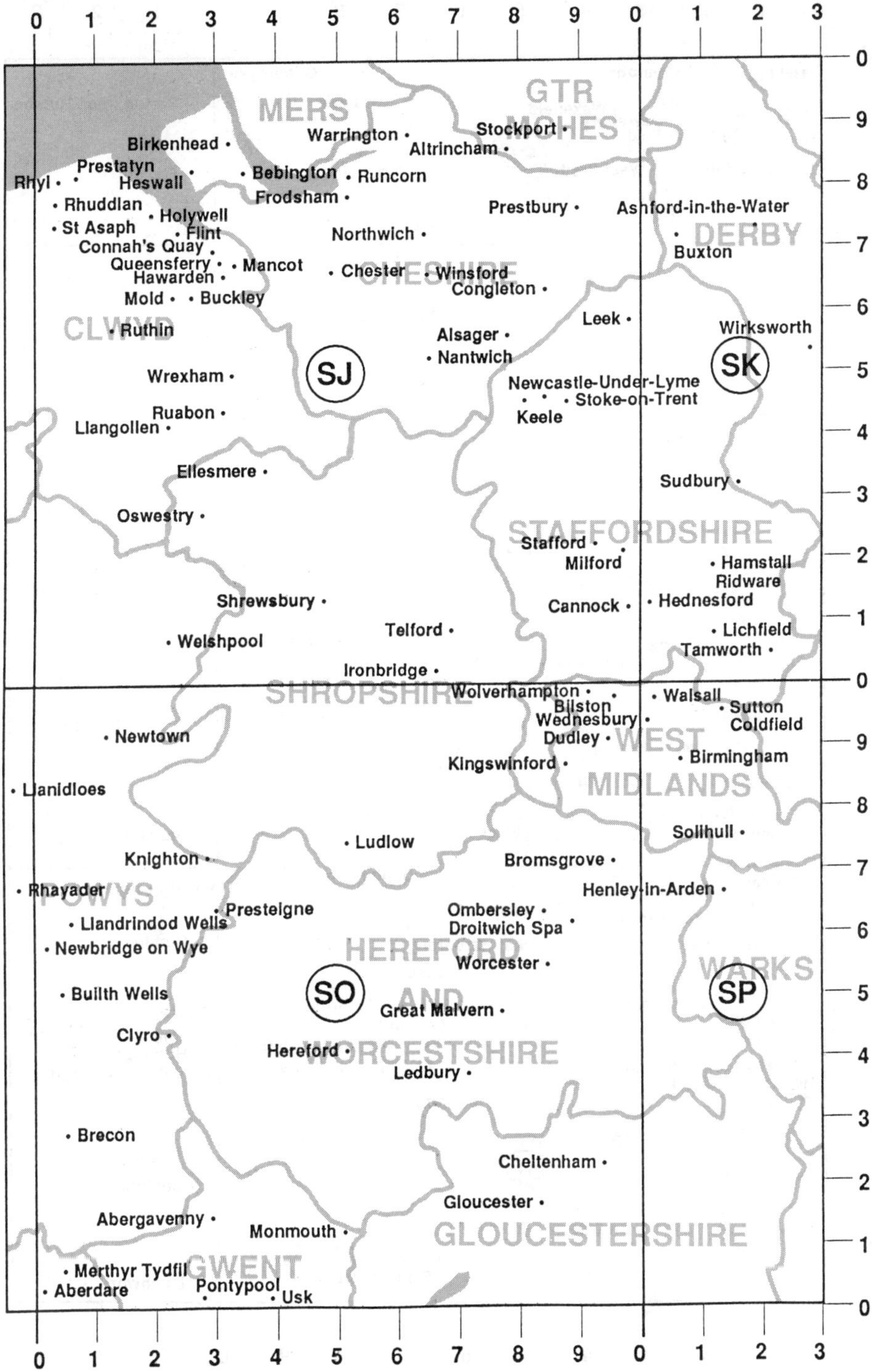
MERS
GTR MCHES
DERBY
CHESHIRE
CLWYD
STAFFORDSHIRE
SHROPSHIRE
WEST MIDLANDS
POWYS
HEREFORD AND WORCESTSHIRE
WARKS
GLOUCESTERSHIRE
GWENT
SJ
SK
SO
SP
Birkenhead
Warrington
Stockport
Altrincham
Prestatyn
Rhyl
Heswall
Bebington
Runcorn
Frodsham
Rhuddlan
Holywell
St Asaph
Flint
Connah's Quay
Queensferry
Hawarden
Mancot
Mold
Buckley
Ruthin
Northwich
Chester
Winsford
Congleton
Prestbury
Ashford-in-the-Water
Buxton
Leek
Wirksworth
Alsager
Nantwich
Wrexham
Newcastle-Under-Lyme
Stoke-on-Trent
Keele
Ruabon
Llangollen
Ellesmere
Sudbury
Oswestry
Stafford
Milford
Hamstall Ridware
Shrewsbury
Cannock
Hednesford
Telford
Lichfield
Welshpool
Tamworth
Ironbridge
Wolverhampton
Bilston
Wednesbury
Walsall
Sutton Coldfield
Newtown
Dudley
Kingswinford
Birmingham
Llanidloes
Solihull
Ludlow
Knighton
Bromsgrove
Rhayader
Henley-in-Arden
Presteigne
Ombersley
Llandrindod Wells
Droitwich Spa
Newbridge on Wye
Worcester
Builth Wells
Great Malvern
Clyro
Hereford
Ledbury
Brecon
Cheltenham
Gloucester
Abergavenny
Monmouth
Merthyr Tydfil
Aberdare
Pontypool
Usk

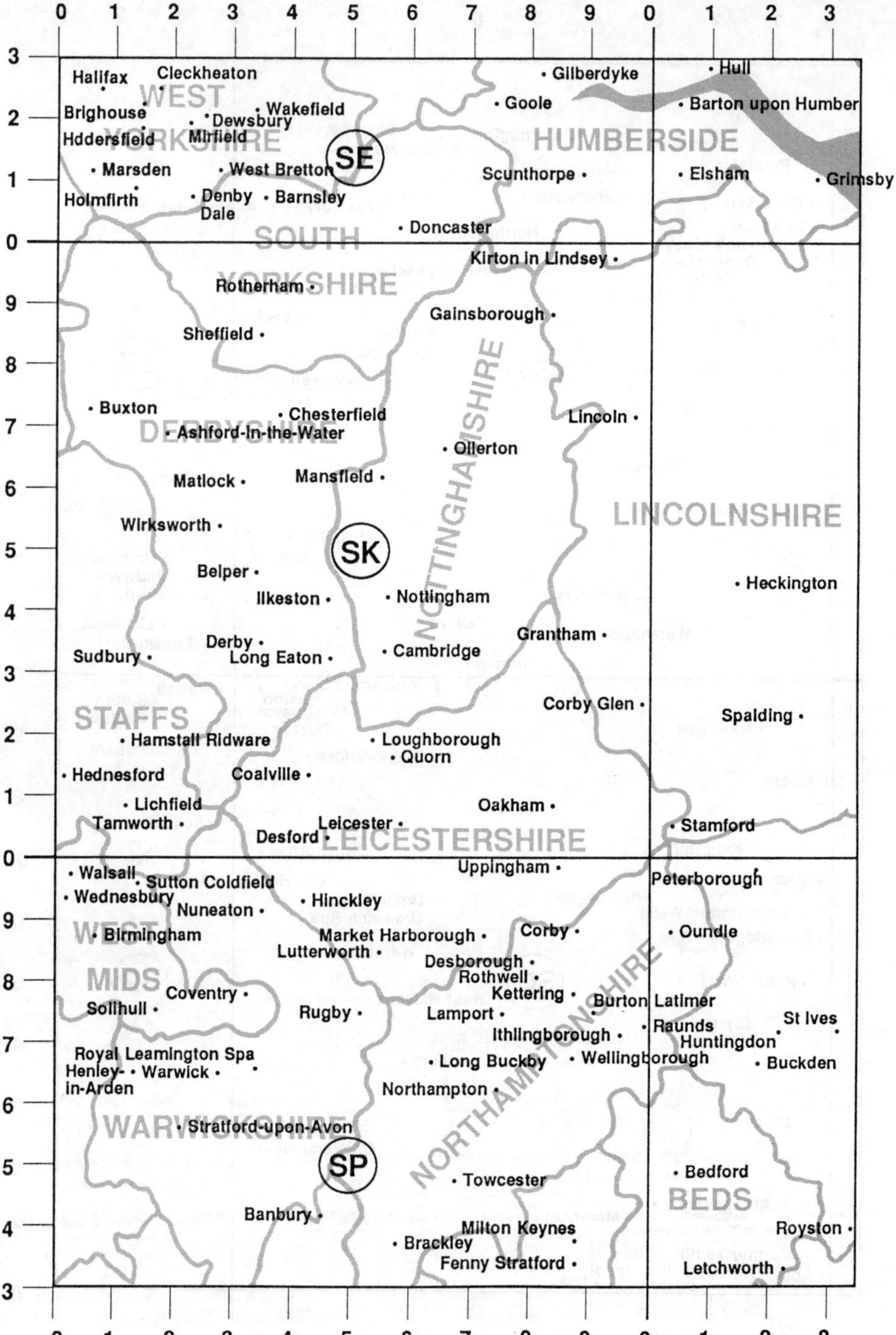
Halifax
Cleckheaton
Brighouse
Hddersfield
Dewsbury
Mirfield
Wakefield
Marsden
West Bretton
Holmfirth
Denby Dale
Barnsley
WEST YORKSHIRE
SE
Gilberdyke
Goole
Hull
Barton upon Humber
HUMBERSIDE
Scunthorpe
Elsham
Grimsby
Doncaster
SOUTH YORKSHIRE
Kirton in Lindsey
Rotherham
Gainsborough
Sheffield
Buxton
Chesterfield
Ashford-in-the-Water
DERBYSHIRE
Lincoln
Ollerton
Matlock
Mansfield
NOTTINGHAMSHIRE
LINCOLNSHIRE
Wirksworth
SK
Belper
Ilkeston
Nottingham
Heckington
Derby
Grantham
Sudbury
Long Eaton
Cambridge
Corby Glen
STAFFS
Spalding
Hamstall Ridware
Loughborough
Quorn
Hednesford
Coalville
Lichfield
Oakham
Tamworth
Leicester
Stamford
Desford
LEICESTERSHIRE
Walsall
Sutton Coldfield
Uppingham
Peterborough
Wednesbury
Hinckley
Nuneaton
Birmingham
Market Harborough
Corby
Oundle
WEST MIDS
Lutterworth
Desborough
Rothwell
Coventry
Kettering
Burton Latimer
Solihull
Rugby
Lamport
Raunds
St Ives
Ithlingborough
Huntingdon
Royal Leamington Spa
Long Buckby
Wellingborough
Buckden
Henley-in-Arden
Warwick
Northampton
WARWICKSHIRE
Stratford-upon-Avon
NORTHAMPTONSHIRE
SP
Bedford
Towcester
BEDS
Banbury
Milton Keynes
Royston
Brackley
Fenny Stratford
Letchworth

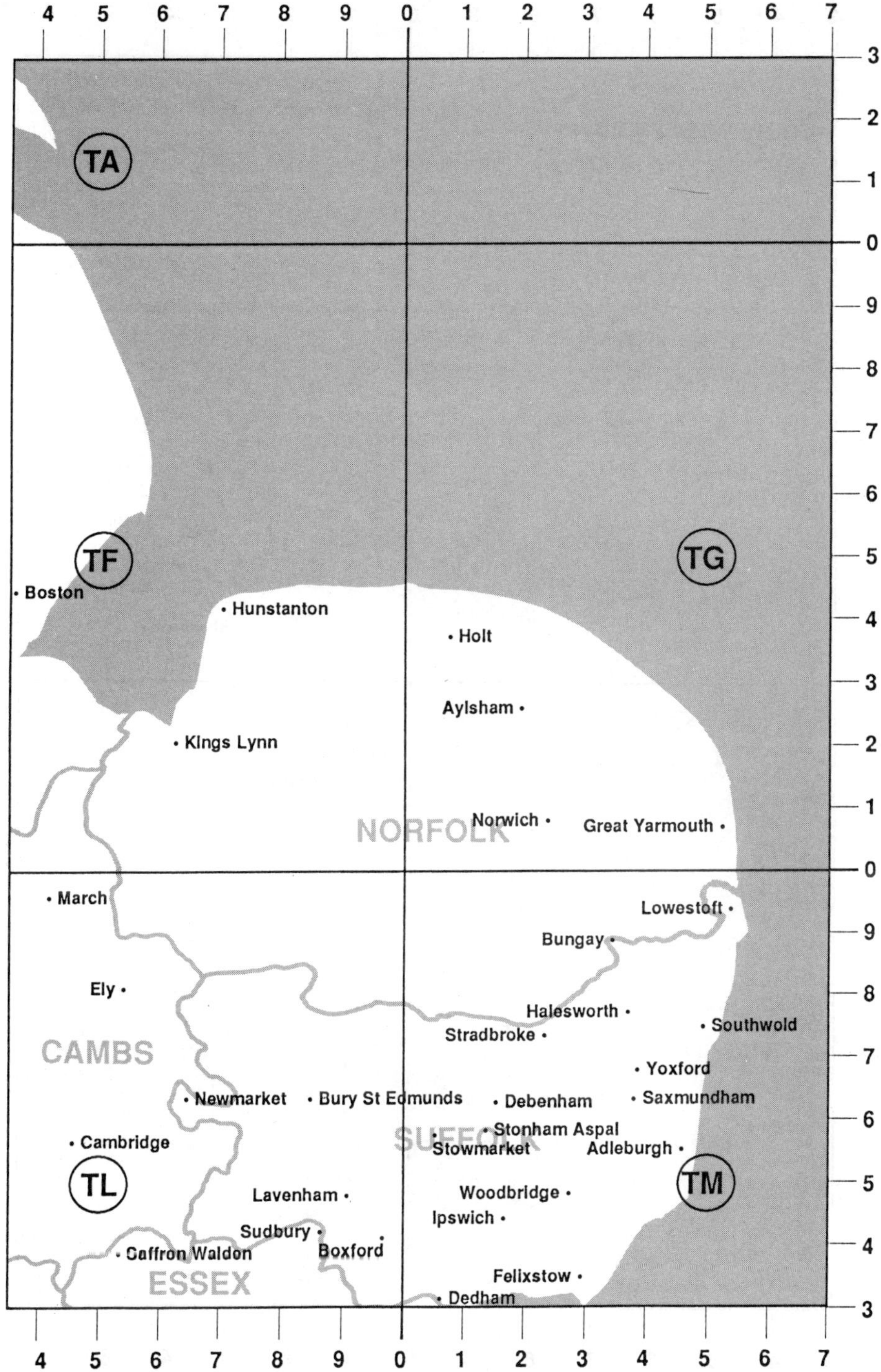
TA
TF
TG
TL
TM
Boston
Hunstanton
Holt
Aylsham
Kings Lynn
Norwich
Great Yarmouth
NORFOLK
March
Lowestoft
Bungay
Ely
Halesworth
Southwold
Stradbroke
CAMBS
Yoxford
Newmarket
Bury St Edmunds
Debenham
Saxmundham
Stonham Aspal
Cambridge
SUFFOLK
Stowmarket
Adleburgh
Lavenham
Woodbridge
Ipswich
Sudbury
Boxford
Saffron Waldon
ESSEX
Felixstow
Dedham

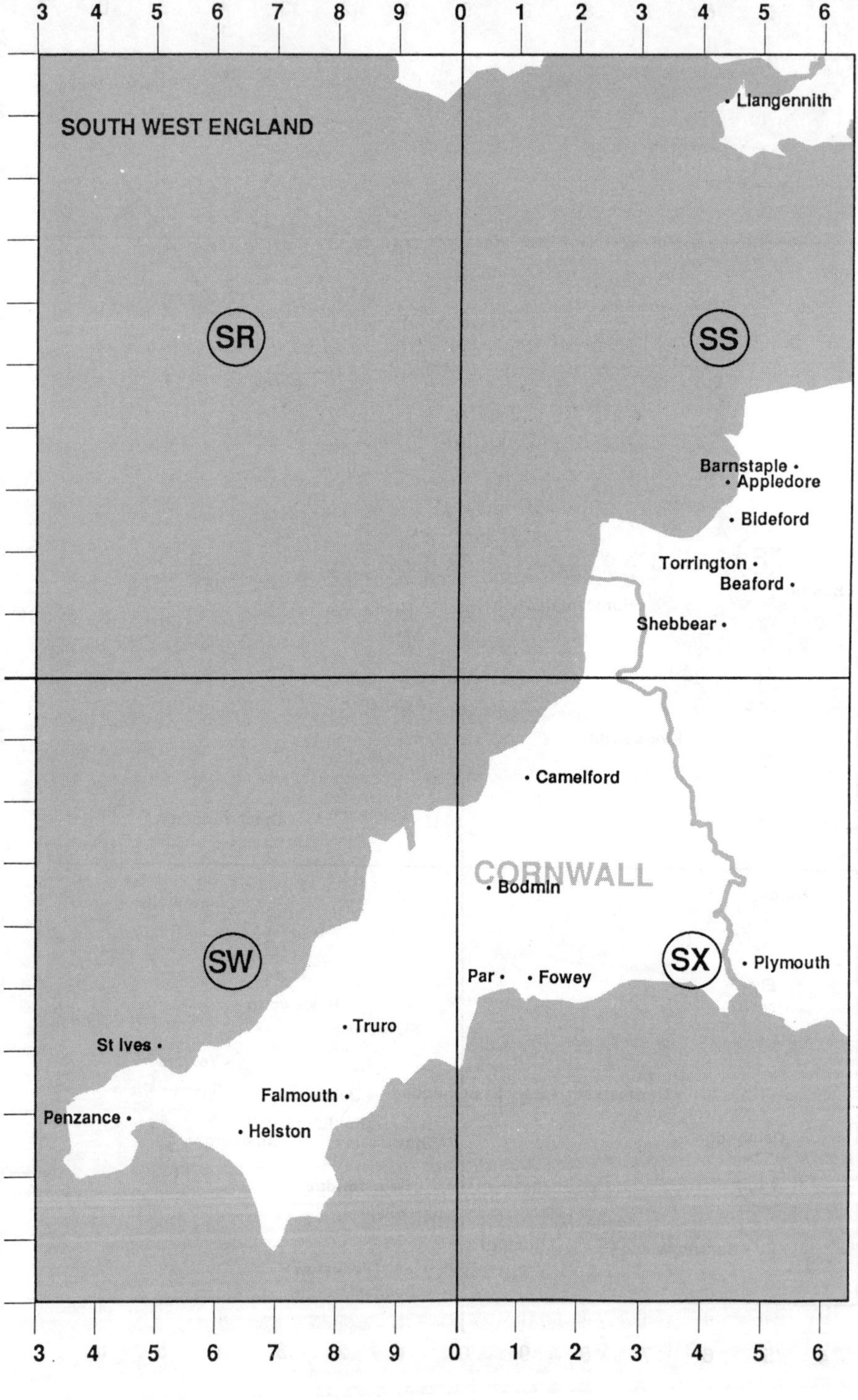
SOUTH WEST ENGLAND
SR
SS
SW
SX
Llangennith
Barnstaple
Appledore
Bideford
Torrington
Beaford
Shebbear
Camelford
CORNWALL
Bodmin
Plymouth
Par
Fowey
Truro
St Ives
Falmouth
Penzance
Helston

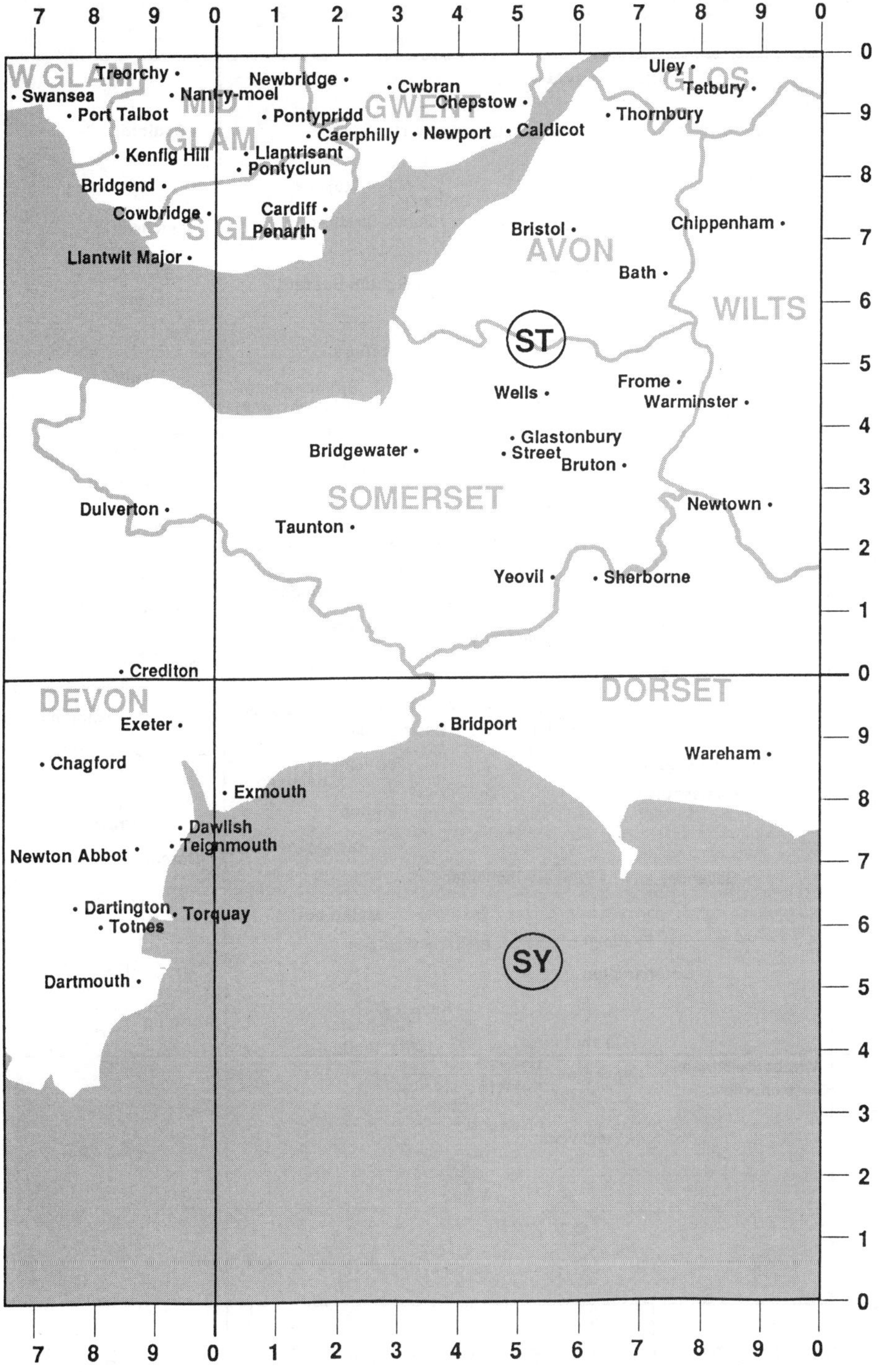
W GLAM
MID GLAM
GWENT
GLOS
S GLAM
AVON
WILTS
SOMERSET
DEVON
DORSET
ST
SY
Treorchy
Swansea
Nant-y-moel
Port Talbot
Kenfig Hill
Bridgend
Cowbridge
Llantwit Major
Newbridge
Pontypridd
Caerphilly
Llantrisant
Pontyclun
Cardiff
Penarth
Cwbran
Chepstow
Newport
Caldicot
Uley
Tetbury
Thornbury
Bristol
Chippenham
Bath
Wells
Frome
Warminster
Glastonbury
Street
Bruton
Bridgewater
Dulverton
Taunton
Newtown
Yeovil
Sherborne
Crediton
Exeter
Bridport
Wareham
Chagford
Exmouth
Dawlish
Teignmouth
Newton Abbot
Dartington
Torquay
Totnes
Dartmouth

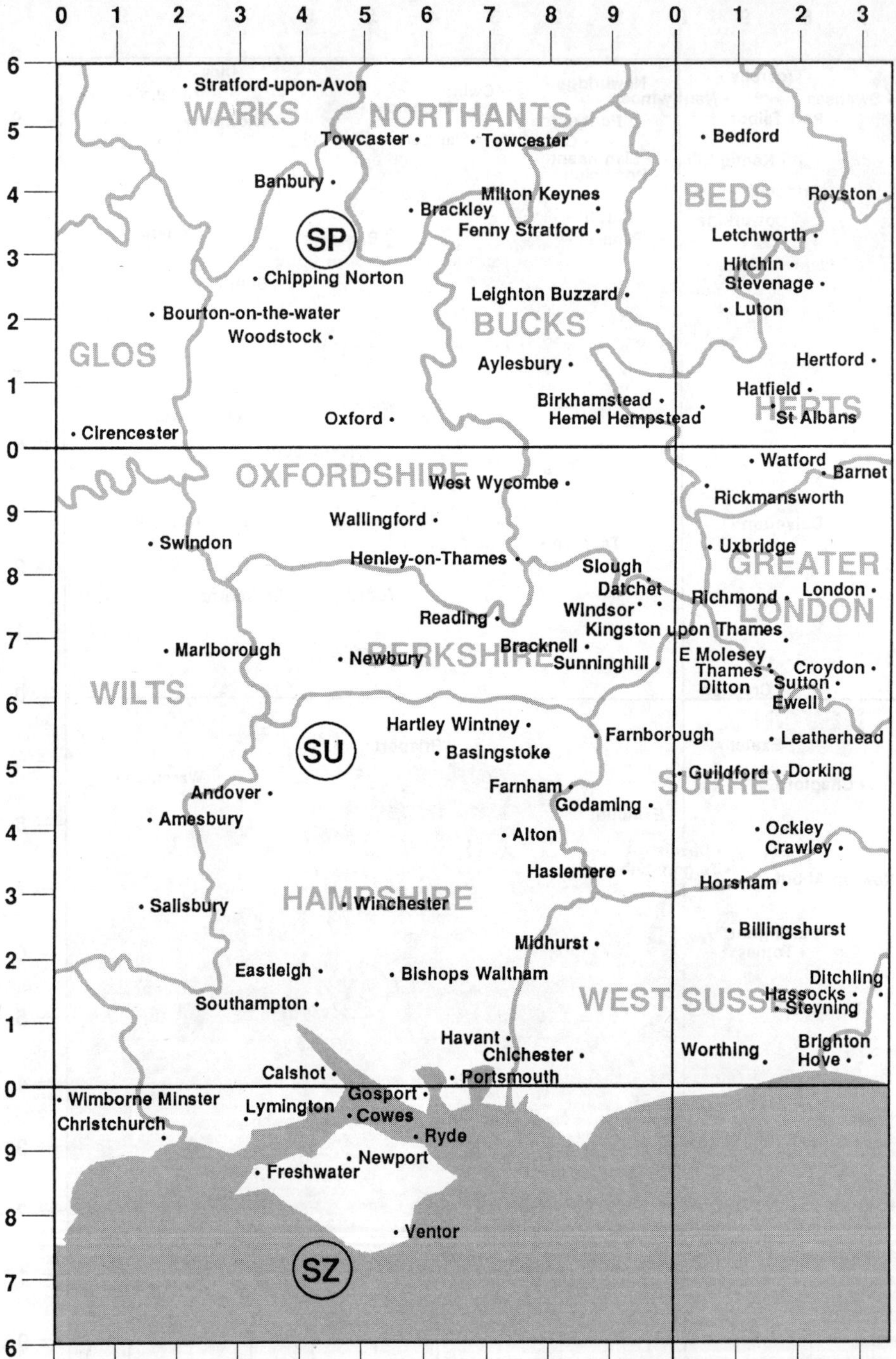
SP
SU
SZ
WARKS
NORTHANTS
BEDS
GLOS
BUCKS
HERTS
OXFORDSHIRE
GREATER LONDON
BERKSHIRE
WILTS
SURREY
HAMPSHIRE
WEST SUSSEX
Stratford-upon-Avon
Towcaster
Towcester
Bedford
Banbury
Milton Keynes
Royston
Brackley
Fenny Stratford
Letchworth
Hitchin
Stevenage
Chipping Norton
Leighton Buzzard
Luton
Bourton-on-the-water
Woodstock
Hertford
Aylesbury
Hatfield
Birkhamstead
Hemel Hempstead
St Albans
Oxford
Cirencester
Watford
Barnet
West Wycombe
Rickmansworth
Wallingford
Swindon
Uxbridge
Henley-on-Thames
Slough
Datchet
Richmond
London
Windsor
Reading
Kingston upon Thames
Marlborough
Bracknell
E Molesey
Newbury
Sunninghill
Thames Ditton
Croydon
Sutton
Ewell
Hartley Wintney
Farnborough
Leatherhead
Basingstoke
Guildford
Dorking
Andover
Farnham
Godaming
Amesbury
Alton
Ockley
Crawley
Haslemere
Horsham
Salisbury
Winchester
Billingshurst
Midhurst
Eastleigh
Bishops Waltham
Ditchling
Hassocks
Southampton
Steyning
Havant
Brighton
Worthing
Chichester
Hove
Calshot
Portsmouth
Wimborne Minster
Gosport
Lymington
Cowes
Christchurch
Ryde
Newport
Freshwater
Ventor

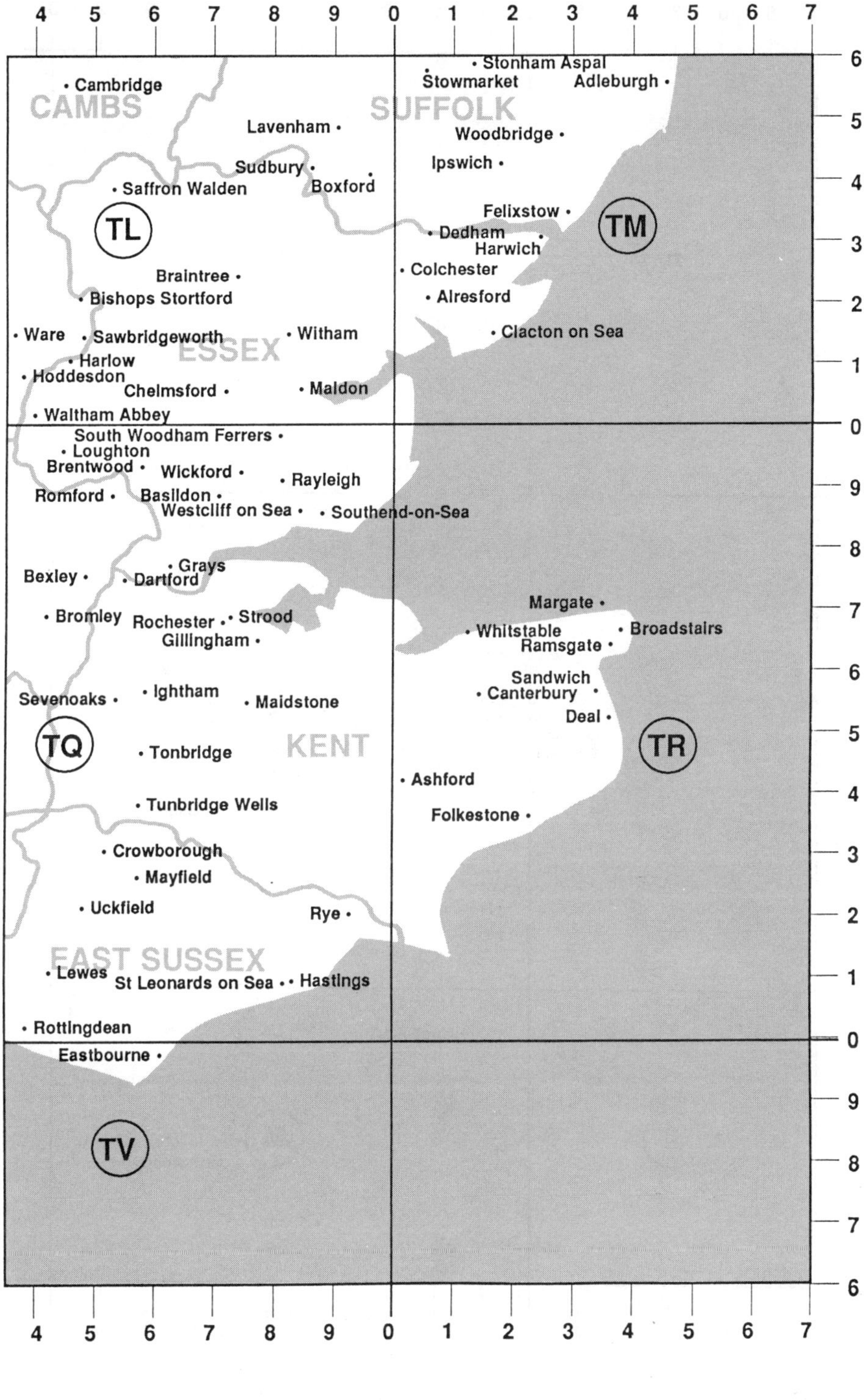
CAMBS
SUFFOLK
ESSEX
KENT
EAST SUSSEX
TL
TM
TQ
TR
TV
Cambridge
Stonham Aspal
Stowmarket
Adleburgh
Lavenham
Woodbridge
Ipswich
Sudbury
Boxford
Saffron Walden
Felixstow
Dedham
Harwich
Braintree
Colchester
Bishops Stortford
Alresford
Ware
Sawbridgeworth
Witham
Clacton on Sea
Harlow
Hoddesdon
Chelmsford
Maldon
Waltham Abbey
South Woodham Ferrers
Loughton
Brentwood
Wickford
Rayleigh
Romford
Basildon
Westcliff on Sea
Southend-on-Sea
Grays
Bexley
Dartford
Margate
Bromley
Rochester
Strood
Whitstable
Broadstairs
Gillingham
Ramsgate
Sandwich
Sevenoaks
Ightham
Maidstone
Canterbury
Deal
Tonbridge
Ashford
Tunbridge Wells
Folkestone
Crowborough
Mayfield
Uckfield
Rye
Lewes
St Leonards on Sea
Hastings
Rottingdean
Eastbourne

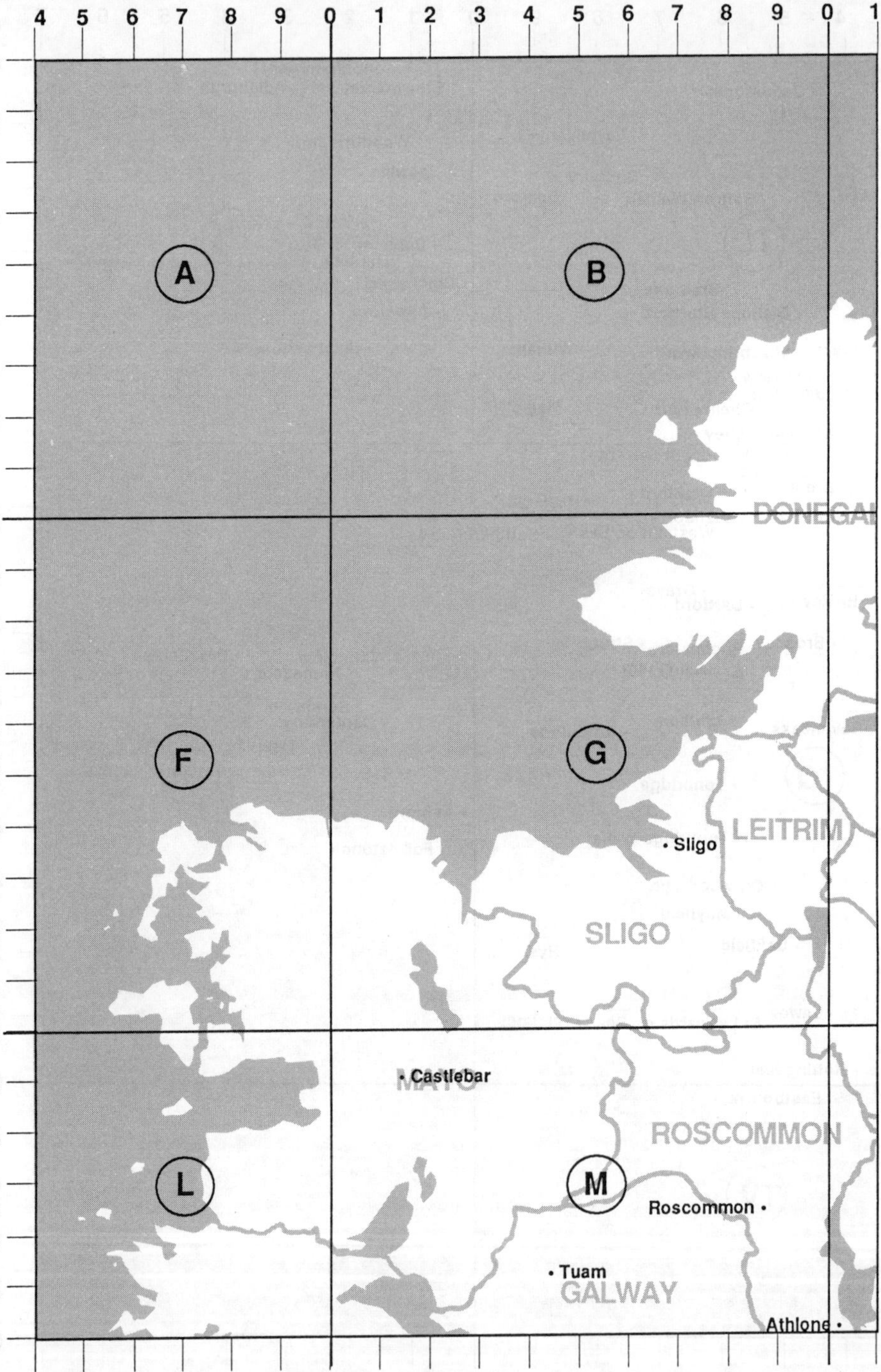
A
B
F
G
L
M
LEITRIM
Sligo
SLIGO
Castlebar
ROSCOMMON
Roscommon
Tuam
GALWAY
Athlone

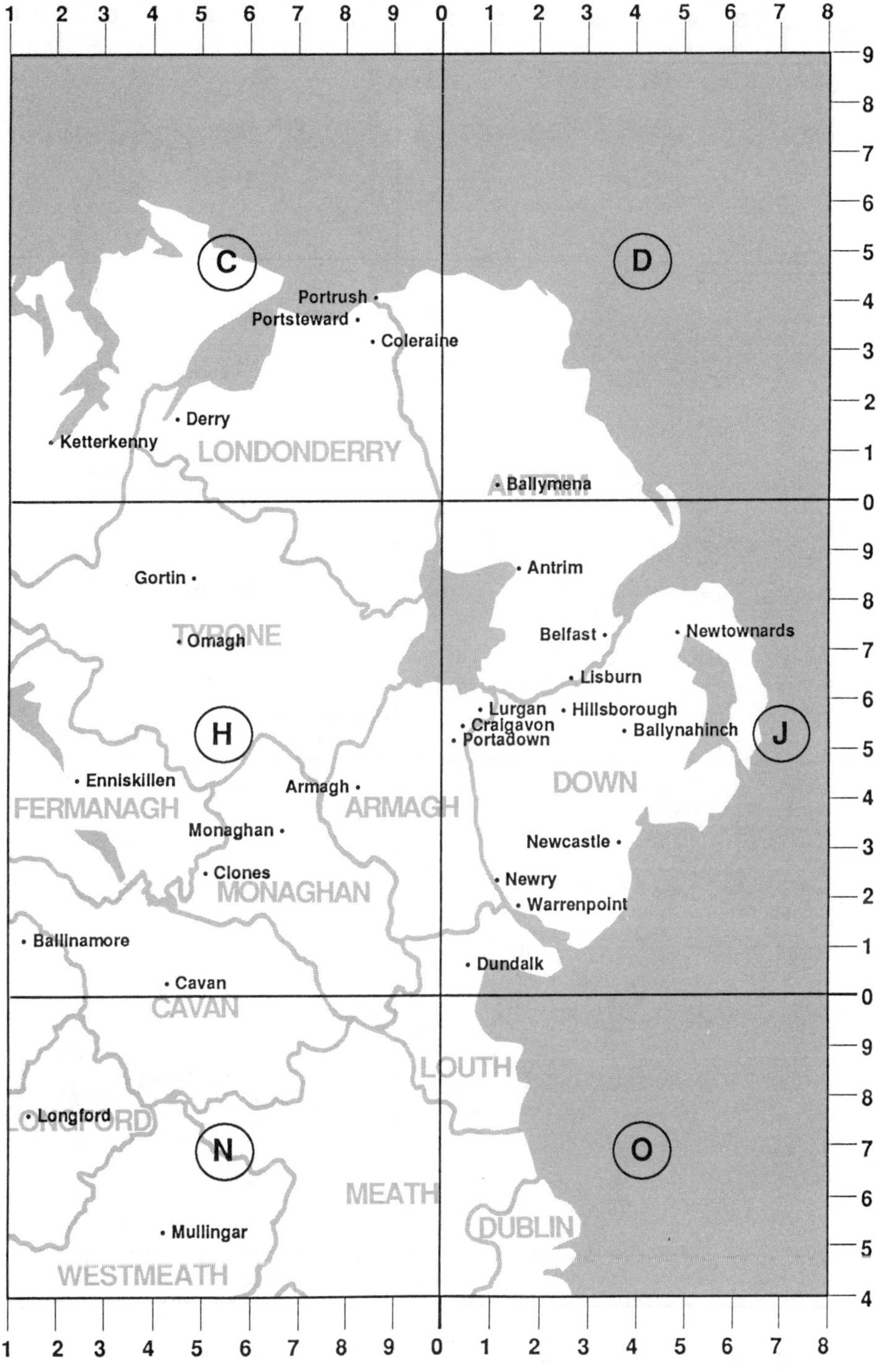
C
D
H
J
N
O
Portrush
Portsteward
Coleraine
Derry
Ketterkenny
LONDONDERRY
ANTRIM
Ballymena
Gortin
Antrim
TYRONE
Omagh
Belfast
Newtownards
Lisburn
Lurgan
Craigavon
Portadown
Hillsborough
Ballynahinch
Enniskillen
FERMANAGH
Armagh
ARMAGH
DOWN
Monaghan
Newcastle
Clones
MONAGHAN
Newry
Warrenpoint
Ballinamore
Dundalk
Cavan
CAVAN
LOUTH
Longford
LONGFORD
MEATH
DUBLIN
Mullingar
WESTMEATH

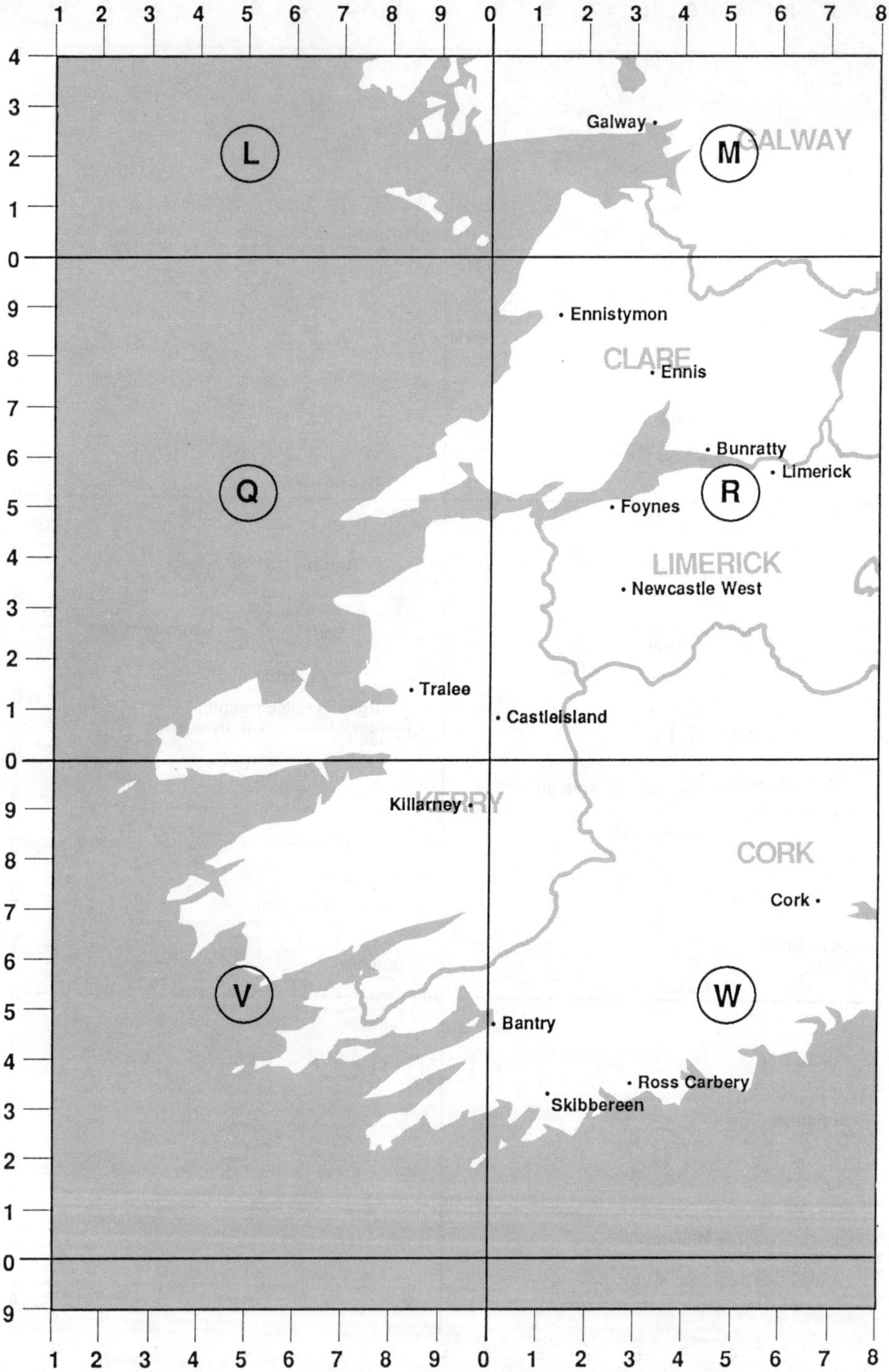
L
M
GALWAY
Galway
Q
R
Ennistymon
CLARE
Ennis
Bunratty
Limerick
Foynes
LIMERICK
Newcastle West
Tralee
Castleisland
KERRY
Killarney
CORK
Cork
V
W
Bantry
Ross Carbery
Skibbereen

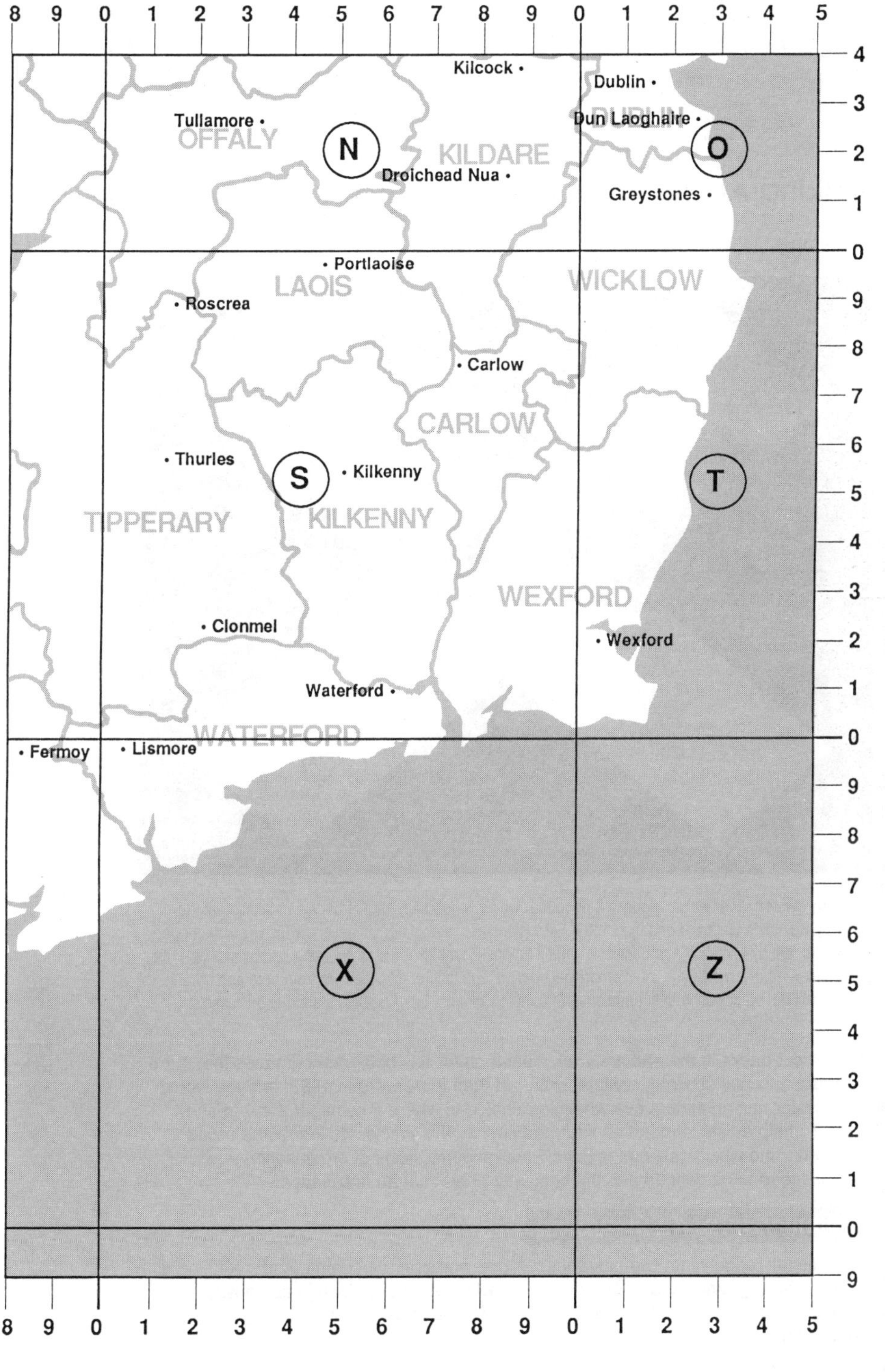
8 9 0 1 2 3 4 5 6 7 8 9 0 1 2 3 4 5
Kilcock
Dublin
Tullamore
DUBLIN
Dun Laoghaire
OFFALY
N
KILDARE
O
Droichead Nua
Greystones
Portlaoise
WICKLOW
LAOIS
Roscrea
Carlow
CARLOW
Thurles
S
Kilkenny
T
TIPPERARY
KILKENNY
WEXFORD
Clonmel
Wexford
Waterford
WATERFORD
Fermoy
Lismore
X
Z
4 3 2 1 0 9 8 7 6 5 4 3 2 1 0 9 8 7 6 5 4 3 2 1 0 9

Making An Informed Choice

by Debbie Duffin

Anthony Wilson, 'that which appears is good that which is good appears', from an installation at the Anthony Reynolds Gallery, London in 1989. Exhibitions at this commercial gallery, which has been open four years, are by invitation and based on what Anthony Reynolds feels *'is right at a particular time'*. The gallery aims *'to place artists in an international context'* and to interest collectors from here and abroad. In 1989, it will be participating in international art fairs in Cologne, Los Angeles, Madrid and Brussels.

Despite cut-backs in the arts generally, research for this book demonstrates that there are more galleries showing contemporary art than there were in 1983, and the would-be exhibitor has an almost overwhelming choice of where they might apply to show work. To help artists to make an informed choice, this article describes the broad categories into which galleries fall, how the responsibilities of organisation and finances tend to be defined and the best way to present an application.

Commercial and Subsidised

Galleries fall roughly into two categories: those who operate commercially, running a business selling artwork, and those galleries which are subsidised in some way – for instance by a local council or arts association for instance – to show a programme of exhibitions.

Some commercial galleries exhibit and sell only contemporary art, whilst others deal in 20th century art as well as promoting and selling work by living artists. Their audience may be relatively small and specialised, although the gallery is usually highly aware of who their market is and the best way to keep them interested. Commercial galleries range from tiny spaces catering for local markets to those promoting a selected number of artists internationally. In the commercial sector, the financial arrangements between gallery and artists will vary, depending on whether the work is likely to sell and the 'risks' the gallery can afford to take. Selection of artists is largely based on whether the gallery thinks it can sell the work or develop a market for it.

Municipal or local authority galleries are subsidised by local or city councils and tend to have permanent collections with perhaps one room used for temporary exhibitions of contemporary art. The main purpose of these galleries is not to sell work but to provide a public facility, and most therefore, don't put selling high on their list of priorities.The degree of freedom and resources available to exhibition organisers or directors varies, as will the division of the exhibition costs. Increasingly, these galleries run educational activities – workshops, talks, residencies etc – which not only engage the general public in the visual arts but also provide some income for the exhibitors and for other artists in the area. Most municipal galleries usually take care of the planning, administration and hanging of exhibitions.

The large number of independent, non-profit making galleries range from small local spaces to large galleries with national or international reputations. Most rely on a combination of public funds, private patronage and business sponsorship. Gallery policy differs considerably. It may be decided by a management committee or be the responsibility of the director or exhibition organiser. Don't assume that independent galleries will always take care of organisation and expenses involved, as this is dependent on the policy and budget of each gallery, and the status of the exhibition. The independent galleries are, however, significant. Unconstrained by commercialism, they can provide opportunities for less established artists and are often in a position to take risks by showing issue-based, controversial or otherwise uncommercial work.

Artists and Issues

Local councils often provide exhibition spaces, although these are often used for meetings, classes, conferences or other events. Policies lean towards the support of work by local artists or on local issues, although exhibitors are likely to have to organise and finance their own exhibition. More councils now organise associated educational activiities – workshops and residencies – in conjunction with exhibitions.

Libraries, which have hundreds of visitors a day, are recognised as a valuable source of exhibition space for artists locally and facilities range from purpose-built galleries to hessian-covered screens in amongst the fiction shelves. They are often more suitable for small works or for two-dimensional work hung on screens or artworks which can be fitted into show cases. Here, the exhibition programme may not be exclusively visual arts, the organiser will have other responsibilities, and if the space is used for other events, an exhibition programme may not be a priority.

In library spaces, artists are usually expected to organise and pay for their show, perhaps paying a hire fee to use the room, although sometimes publicity and other help may be provided. Library space is less likely to be booked up far ahead and many applications are dealt with on a 'first come first served' basis. Libraries can provide a useful first opportunity and, in some parts of the country, a substantial visual arts programme is generated by a network of libraries.

Broadening Audiences

Arts centre galleries and exhibition spaces are places where exhibitions are only one of a number of activities taking place. The exhibition audience is usually drawn from regular users of the centre, and where the gallery is in the foyer or restaurant the exhibition is unlikely to be the event that attracts them to visit.

Exhibitions are also shown in theatres, hospitals and other public places, often in small spaces, like foyers or bar areas, which are only suitable for small wall-hung work. The organisers here – theatre managers, publicity officers, art therapists for instance – are less likely to have a great knowledge of contemporary art and their choice may well be decided by which artists apply to show there.

At the same time there could be a limitation on the content of work suitable for showing in such 'public' spaces – no nudes, polically sensitive or violent images for example. A large audience may be guaranteed but like arts centres, only a small proportion of visitors will come because of the exhibition. Organisation and costs are likely to be the artist's responsibility and selling work is usually not a priority.

Schools, colleges and polytechnics have exhibition spaces, ranging from small foyer areas to large purpose-built galleries. An artist's input into organisation and costs will vary and the audience is likely to be limited to those working or visiting the establishment for another reason. However, with the growth of programmes like artists in schools, exhibitions are often linked with fee-paid visits by artists, makers or photographers.

Artist-run spaces, of which there are a relatively small number, range from a tiny display area in an artist's home or studio where their own work is shown as well as the occasional exhibition by others, to purpose-built galleries run collectively, with or without a paid gallery director. Policies and audiences vary as widely as the spaces themselves. Artists' groups often exchange exhibitions and link their programmes with workshops, demonstrations or events on an occasional or regular basis.

Hiring a Gallery

Over the last five years, more and more galleries for hire have become available.These range from rooms within private houses to large warehouse-type spaces. Some take considerable responsibility for selecting work, organising shows and providing services, others simply let the space on commercial terms to the artist who has to organise, finance and invigilate the exhibition. Some take a commission on sales as well as a hire fee. Usually the audience for each exhibition changes with the artist concerned and attracting people through the door is likely to depend on the artist's own contacts and on their promotional skills.

Attitudes and Specialisations

These are general characteristics not hard-and-fast rules. A commercial gallery may for instance, be prepared to show work for which the market is small and look for funding to support a particular exhibition. Many subsidised galleries are putting a greater emphasis on selling work and this may therefore, affect the choice of work exhibited.

Some galleries have developed clearly-defined policies or specific aims – to promote the work of a particular group, nationality, race or sex – whilst others specialise in photography or ceramics, or a particular subject matter or style of work.

There are those which concentrate on thematic or mixed shows and others who prefer to promote solo shows. Some are especially interested in the work of young or unknown artists whilst others only wish to show the work of the internationally-known, although in both cases, they may wish to show the best work they can.

Some spaces can only accommodate small two-dimensional work while others welcome installations or large-scale work. A community setting might only show work with subject matter of local relevance, an innovative private gallery may pride itself on a policy of showing 'experimental' work.

Making An Informed Choice

Don't waste your time making overtures to a gallery which doesn't generally show work like yours. If you select galleries showing work of a similar nature, subject matter or concerns to yours, your chances of success are much greater.

How do you decide on the type of gallery to look for? The best results will occur if you match up the work you make and your aims and needs with those of the galleries you approach. Start by building up a picture of yourself and your work by answering these questions.

Why do you want to show your work?

If your main aim is to sell, you need a commercial gallery or certainly one which makes positive efforts to sell work on show. If you make 'installation' work the physical nature of the space is of primary importance and you need a gallery which is enthusiastic about your ideas. If you are predominantly interested in what a gallery can do to promote your work, then obviously you need a gallery with an extrovert approach to publicity.

What kind of audience do you wish to attract?

To reach a local audience or serve some social function, choose a local or community-based space. And if the aim of an exhibition is to attract those who can offer you work, for example in education, you may look towards showing in a school, community centre, or polytechnic.

What kind of work do you do?

It is easy to define your work as large or small, abstract or figurative, two or three-dimensional, but how do you define your subject matter or your overriding concerns? Can you identify how your work relates to others, and thus what kind of audience might take an interest in what you are doing? Is your work based in an established tradition or are you working in a relatively new area?

At what stage in your career are you?

If you haven't shown before you may have more chance of success with a small local venue which is committed to showing less established artists whilst if you've already had some shows, you'll need a gallery which will provide you with a more challenging experience.

If you've only been in group shows, try to find a small friendly gallery that will guide you through the experience of a first solo exhibition. But with several small solo exhibitions on your CV, you can afford to be more ambitious and aim for a small group or solo show at a more prestigious gallery. Consider, also, the advantages of getting together with other artists and making a group application to a gallery either for a one-off show or one which is suitable to tour to a number of galleries.

How do you feel about your work at present?

Are you confident or going through a period of doubts and/or changes in your work? Would you feel happy about exhibiting at short notice should the opportunity arise, or do you need time to develop new ideas or images?

Galleries work to very different itme scales, some up to eighteen months or two years in advance, others may offer space much sooner, and a few can offer a slot at very short notice. Are you after an exhibition in the near future or one in two years? The answer to this affects where you apply!

In which part of the country do you want to exhibit?

If the kind of gallery you are looking for happens to be just round the corner, then planning and holding an exhibition is easier, providing the gallery wants to show your work. However, most artists, particularly those working outside big cities, must look further afield.

If you are seeking to show at a gallery outside your area, however, you'll need to pay particular attention to the respective financial and organisational responsibilities of artist and gallery and to be sure, for instance, that the gallery will organise or pay for transportation of your work.

Carol Hughes, 'Your Neighbourhood Watched', a linocut print in 'Black Art: Plotting the Course', an exhibition originated by artist Eddie Chambers for tour to the Bluecoat Gallery Liverpool, Oldham Art Gallery and Wolverhampton Art Gallery during 1988/89. It shows the work of 27 artists of Asian, African or Caribbean origin, many of whom are still at art school or who have recently graduated. Oldham Art Gallery, in an area with a high Asian population, is responsive to ideas from artists and this exhibition has generated many applications from Black and Asian artists to show there. Significantly, the publicity for this exhibition is in Urdu and English and amongst the events accompanying the show was a seminar for art gallery curators in the North West area on integrating Black and Asian artists' work into exhibition programmes.

Having used the *Directory of Exhibition Spaces* to make an initial choice of where you could apply, don't just rely on what's in print. Find out as much as you can about each of the galleries you've shortlisted.

For instance, ask other artists who've exhibited, telephone each gallery and ask for more details, visit and look at publicity for previous and current exhibitions and find out about future plans. This not only helps you to build up a picture of the gallery, but demonstrates to the gallery that you have a professional approach.

Look carefully at each gallery's application procedure and find out how work for exhibitions is selected. If the book doesn't tell you, ask. Most galleries operate their particular system for very good reasons, and since most of them receive far more applications than they can cope with, it is worthwhile making it as easy as possible for them to consider yours. In 1986 for instance, Ikon Gallery in Birmingham got 200 applications from artists, and Darlington Arts Centre 300.

Your chances of serious consideration are greater if you know what the gallery does, that your work is relevant and if you supply the information they ask for in a well-presented application.

Most galleries ask for slides or photographs and a curriculum vitae (CV), and many also require a more extensive written application or proposal. Some prefer postal applications, others ask you to make an appointment with a folio. Some look at applications at any time, others only on particular days; some look at applications at regular intervals, perhaps twice a year.

Selection may be made by the director or exhibition organiser although often there are also selection committees. Some galleries clearly only handle a limited number of artists' work and do not welcome unsolicited applications.

Checklist

- Avoid just turning up at a gallery with your work, it's very unlikely to be looked at on the spot.
- Make sure you have all the material necessary for making applications because you will need several sets of good quality slides and/or photographs (if you can't take them well enough yourself employ a professional), as well as copies of a typed curriculum vitae and statement about your work.
- Applications should be addressed to the current contact, check for out-of-date names beforehand as part of your initial homework.
- Send all the information asked for. Your application is likely to fall by the wayside if a gallery is expected to chase you for omissions.
- Don't send *more* than is requested. It takes time to look through applications and the gallery doesn't usually need more than eight to ten slides or sheafs of additional information to gain a good idea of what you do.
- Pack slides in flat plastic sheet holders as these are more likely to be looked at than those in boxes. Label the sheet with your name and address and the number of slides sent.
- On an accompanying sheet give details of each work, dimensions, medium, date and title and mark which way up slides and photographs should be viewed on an accompanying sheet.
- Make sure you label everything you send with your name as it's very easy for slides, photographs or loose sheets to become separated from the covering letter in a busy office.
- Even if the gallery doesn't ask for a written application, send an accompanying letter.
- Explain why you are interested in exhibiting with the gallery. Point out anything of particular interest whilst keeping your letter short and to the point, as most people won't read more than one side of an A4 sheet.
- Type your application unless your handwriting is exceptionally good. Include a daytime telephone number or indicate where messages can be left.
- Keep a copy of your application and a list of slides submitted.
- Be patient, don't telephone the gallery after only a couple of weeks, many don't acknowledge applications and it will always take some time to go through a large number of applications and make a selection, especially if you are applying in response to a specific deadline. You might, however, telephone to check it has been received.

Success or Failure?

Your application may be turned down for any number of reasons. The gallery may not like your work; it may not fit in with what they are doing; they may already have selected work similar to yours and be trying to provide a balanced programme; it may be that they did like your work but had to select from many such applications or they could just be booked up for the next eighteen months. If you are given a reason, make a note of it as it will be useful with future applications to that gallery or others.

If a gallery says they can't do anything at present but apply again in six months, follow this up, and invite them to your other exhibitions in the meantime.

Seeing the Work

If a gallery is interested in your work they will usually want to see actual artworks. This could mean either taking work to the gallery or a studio visit. When preparing a folio to take to the gallery, select around ten to fifteen works which you feel give a comprehensive view of what you are doing. Don't include too many works which are very similar, but on the other hand, you don't want to give the impression that you skip from style to style.

Present work well by mounting drawings or prints or using a display folio with plastic leaves. Ideally, ask someone else to have a look at it to check that the selection is coherent and makes a good impression. It is also worth practicing talking through your folio to someone, to check that *your* presentation is coherent. You might want to take along a framed work providing it isn't enormous, as well as press cuttings, reviews and catalogues. Don't forget to take a diary so that you can make a note of future meetings or time-schedules for an exhibition.

A studio visit puts a gallery director on your home ground, so make the most of it. Tidy up sufficiently to make sure that work is seen at its best. Try to give an impression of how your work would look in a show – lay it out with enough space between each piece.

If your studio is difficult to find, give directions or a map, put up signs for the day, or arrange to meet at the gate or front entrance. Prepare for a late arrival and allow plenty of time for the meeting even if it might not be needed.

Although a decision is unlikely to be made on the spot, ask for an idea of how long it will be before you know. Be patient, but follow up if you haven't heard after several weeks.

Making Arrangements

Once a gallery has made a definite offer, you'll need to know who is responsible for organising and covering costs of framing, packing, transportation, insurance in transit and at the gallery and for publicity. Will there, for instance, be a card, poster, catalogue, press release and a private view? Who will handle sales and will you recieve a fee for the exhibition?

You also need to be clear about how much commission is taken, how it is calculated and whether it includes VAT.

In terms of the exhibition, establish who is responsible for selecting which works are shown, who will hang the show, how much space you will have and how works will be fixed to the wall.

Will you be expected to invigilate or will you have to arrange and pay others to do it? If an education programme is planned – a lecture on your work, demonstrations for the public or school groups or days working in the gallery – will you be paid? Are there other occasions when you'll need to be at the gallery – a press view, to meet sponsors or the mayor for instance?.

Before finalising arrangements, make sure you are happy about the balance of responsibilities. Do you feel that the arrangement is a fair exchange, can you fulfil your part of the bargain, and, importantly, can you afford the exhibition?

As a rough guide if a gallery states that all organisation and costs are the responsibility of the artist, you would expect to pay little or no commission on sales, perhaps 10% maximum. If these responsiblities and costs are shared you might expect to pay 15-20% commission, if the gallery will bear most of the responsibility and costs, with you framing and transporting the work, you might expect to pay 30-40% commission on sales. If the gallery takes full responsibility, pays all costs and will promote your work widely as well, you would expect them to take 50% and occasionally 60% commission.

Beware of the gallery which expects you to bear too many of the costs and takes a high commission, especially if it is for hire. But if the gallery is prepared to shoulder all responsibilities and overheads, commission will be higher accordingly as the gallery will be doing a great deal to promote and sell your work whilst your responsibility will only be to make the work.

Once you are happy with the agreement, put the details in writing, sending one copy to the gallery and keeping one for yourself. The best way of making an arrangement is to use a contract, either the gallery's or one of your own. The National Artists Association's Draft Contract mentioned in the article on Exhibition Payment Right covers the points which should be agreed prior to an exhibition arrangment.

It is important that both sides agree and the terms for the exhibition are clear from the outset. Having a contract or letters of agreement will minimise misunderstandings and problems later on.

Providing a Focus

Making applications to galleries is time-consuming and may be frustrating and demoralising; the aim of this book is to enable artists to focus on galleries which are likely to be interested in their work. Competition is great, and even the most 'successful' artists are likely to have had negative responses at various points in their careers.

But if exhibiting your work is important to you, you must persevere and learn by your experiences. The more you deal with galleries, the easier it will become to recognise the points where your needs and theirs coincide. Use the exhibiting experience to take you forward in your career and to open up those new opportunities which will help you to develop as an artist, which will enable you to show your work to a wider public or which will provide you with some income from sales.

Exhibition Payment Right

A brief guide for artists and galleries

by Susan Jones

In some of the listings in the *Directory of Exhibition Spaces* the reader will see the phrase 'EPR supported in principle'. Denoting a commitment to the principle that artists should be recompensed for the public showing of their work, the *Directory of Exhibition Spaces* provides the first ever published list of that commitment and it is hoped that by the third edition of the book in around 1991, the principle will have been turned into a nationally-agreed 'Righ't.

Exhibition Payment Right is a proposal similar to Public Lending Right for authors. (Public Lending Right pays authors an annual sum on a sliding scale based on the number of times their books have been borrowed from public libraries, these figures based on sample libraries nationally). Notably, in 1988, Canadian artists won the legal right to be paid EPR when the new Canadian Copyright Bill was passed; EPR schemes also operate in Australia and New Zealand.

The concept of EPR in the UK has developed from a scheme started by the Arts Council in 1979 to provide an Exhibition Showing Fee for artists mounting solo or two-person exhibitions. Fees were set at £100 for a solo exhibition and £50 each for a two-person exhibition. In 1983, the scheme was taken over by the regional arts associations as part of 'devolution' and the fees predominantly stayed the same. In 1985, discussions began between the arts councils and the regional arts associations to review and update the scheme and at this stage, the principle of an Exhibition Payment Right was raised.

In April 1987, the Arts Council and CoRAA (Council of Regional Arts Associations) proposed that EPR should be adopted nationally and that *'The argument for EPR is based on equity - on fairness and justice. All artists, regardless of their medium of expression (whether painters, sculptors or photographers) should benefit from the consumption of their work by the public.... a national guideline for the fee of £250 is to be recommended for 1988'.* (Rory Coonan, Arts Council and CoRAA paper April 1987). It was proposed in that document that the scheme be extended to include group exhibitions.

By the end of 1988, most of the regional arts associations had gone ahead and revised their existing schemes, rather, it seems, than wait for a unified one. With these new schemes however, it is still the case that only some artists receive a fee for exhibitions in publicly-funded galleries. What they have come up with therefore, cannot be called Exhibition Payment Right as artists cannot *by right* claim it, and the total amount allocated by each arts association is not based on an estimation of the annual number of contemporary art exhibitions in their region.

In most cases, the exhibition fee is divided in agreed proportions between gallery and arts association, and there is move towards the use of an exhibition contract as a condition of the arts association contribution.

Exhibition Fees - national and regional variations

In the case of West Midlands Arts, South East Arts, Eastern Arts and Yorkshire Arts, the payment remains at £100, although the conditions for receiving this amount varies. For instance, dependent on whether the gallery showing the exhibition is a client of the regional arts association (West Midlands Arts and Yorkshire Arts) and for solo or two-person shows only (South East Arts), encompassing craft exhibitions (Yorkshire Arts).

North West Arts will contribute £125 per exhibition for up to five artists where the gallery exhibition budget is below £5000, and £150-£250 for those with budgets above this figure, with the aim that the gallery makes the amount up to the £250 minimum fee. They also make provision for exhibitions of more than five artists. South West Arts also operates a sliding scale with £150 per exhibition for galleries with a budget of under £5000, and £200 for those over that figure, both for solo or group exhibitions of longer than three weeks.

Northern Arts has set the fee at £200 from October 1989 which may be divided by the number of contributing artists, although it acknowledges that there *'is a point when it is not administratively cost effective to make payments and this is at the discretion of the gallery.'* Lincolnshire and Humberside Arts also offers £200 at six galleries with others to be added and plans to raise this to £250 in 1989/90. East Midlands Arts, who makes no payments to non-RAA client galleries, is moving towards a fee of £250 for 1989.

Greater London Arts has set a standard rate at £250, Southern Arts recommends £250 and up to £500 for galleries with large budgets and Merseyside Arts proposes to adopt a fee of £300 for 1989.

In Northern Ireland or Scotland, there is not, as yet, any scheme to improve. In the latter, however, although discussions in the past did not lead to the adoption of a scheme, recent developments imply that fees will become an accepted part of the professional gallery/artist relationship in the future.

In Wales the recommended fee of £250 will be implemented in April 1989 with, by 1991, the proviso that *'All Welsh Arts Council revenue client galleries will be required to pay at least a minumum recommended fee (of £250) as a condition of the grant'.*

The Crafts Council has devised a scheme to operate from April 1989 covering exhibitions with no more than four exhibitors in their own gallery with a flat fee of £150 for Gallery 1, and £250 for Gallery 2. The scheme only applies to Crafts Council originated exhibitions.

More Anomalies

There are other variations. Some local authorities have, for some time, been paying exhibition showing fees at higher than the existing £100 rate: the Ferens Gallery in Hull already pays £200, as does the Usher Gallery in Lincoln; the Laing Art Gallery in Newcastle (part of Tyne & Wear Museums Service) pays between £250 and £500, and the Castle Museum in Nottingham £250. The Bluecoat Gallery in Liverpool proposes £300. As yet, there have been no formal consultations by the Arts Council/CoRAA group to the Art Galleries Association, the Museums Association, the National Association of Arts Centres or local authority art departments.

Consultation and Recommendations

In 1988, the Arts Council funded the National Artists Association to run a series of seventeen consultative meetings in England, Scotland, Northern and Southern Ireland, between artists, gallery organisers, local authority officers and other cultural workers to discuss the Arts Council/CoRAA proposals as well as the National Artists Association's draft exhibition contracts. The recommendations drawn out of the meetings were:

1. EPR should be adopted as a Right, applicable without discrimination of any kind throughout Great Britain and Northern Ireland.

2. The definition of EPR – and how it should be applied – should be agreed at national level by arts bodies including government and local government agencies and this definition agreed by artists' and galleries' representaties.

3. EPR should be administered by a national body (or bodies) overseeing a central sum of money set aside for EPR payments.

4. EPR should eventually be incorporated into a form of nationally binding legislation through a statutory instrument such as the British Copyright Act.

5. The central EPR fund, however derived, should be based on an annual review of the number of public exhibitions in Great Britain of work by living artists, and artists covered by the term of copyright as defined by the British Copyright Act.

6. A realistic level of EPR payment should be established at not less than the level proposed by the Arts Council/CoRAA June 1987 document.

7. The central EPR organisation should be independent of existing arts organsiations and answerable to representatives of artists, funding bodies, galleries and other relevant institutions.

8. A standard set of exhibition contracts should be developed and adopted for use with EPR, with terms agreed by all parties involved in the public exhibition of contemporary artworks.

9. The possibility of a form of licencing system to assist the implementation of EPR should be explored.

10. Whatever EPR scheme is developed nationally in Great Britain should be based on reciprocity with other countries operating EPR or analagous schemes.

11. A Standing Conference should be set up on EPR, involving representatives from all the bodies concerned with the implementation and running of an EPR scheme.

In December 1988, the Arts Council, expressed support for the broad principle of a unified scheme applicable throughout Britain, for payment of EPR as a right. It is hoped that this will be followed by agreement from the CoRAA group and that the consultations will be developed and the first Standing Conference be held in 1989.

Background Information

Artists, gallery organisers, local authority arts officers and other cultural workers will find background information on Exhibition Payment Right in the publications and articles listed below:

EPR - Exhibition Payment Right report by Roland Miller for the National Artists Association, available price £7.50 inc p&p from Roland Miller, 49 Stainton Road, Sheffield S11 7AX. This report contains the Arts Council/CoRAA paper and policy papers from regional arts associations, the Welsh Arts Council, the Scottish Arts Council and the National Artists Association's draft exhibition contract.

National Artists Association Draft Exhibition Contract available price £2 from Richard Padwick, 17 Shakespeare Terrace, Sunderland SR2 7JG.

'Payments to Artists for Exhibition of Work' by Roland Miller and Richard Padwick *Artists Newsletter* December 1984, available for 85p from Artists Newsletter Publications, PO Box 23, Sunderland SR4 6DG.

'Payments to Artists for Their Work' by Roland Miller *Artists Newsletter* March 1985, available for 85p from Artists Newsletter Publications, PO Box 23, Sunderland SR4 6DG.

The 'Rights & Status' section of *Artists Newsletter* regularly covers news on EPR developments in this country and elsewhere.

Contact the regional arts associations and arts councils for policy papers on EPR and Exhibition Showing Fees, addresses on page 438

Read On...

Compiled by Susan Jones

Read On... offers users of the *Directory of Exhibition Spaces* an introduction – rather than an exhaustive guide – to the implications of exhibiting and of working with galleries. For ease of use, the booklist has been divided into Exhibiting; Setting up a Gallery; Promoting Exhibitions; Fundraising; Visual Arts and the Visually Impaired and Buying and Collecting.

The books and articles form an introduction to each topic and magazines including *Crafts, Artists Newsletter, Artists & Illustrators* often run articles about the practicalities of exhibiting, sometimes based on artists' experiences, and are worth reading regularly.

The book list is followed by a listing of sources of information on galleries, museums, libraries and local authority visual arts provision and, finally, a contacts and information section.

Exhibiting

Organising Your Own Exhibition - a Guide for Artists by Debbie Duffin, published by ACME, ISBN 0 950692 32 8, price £3.50 inc p&p from Artists Newsletter Publications, PO Box 23, Sunderland SR4 6DG.

This book, essential reading for those intending to initiate exhibitions, covers everything from finding space, finance, timetabling, publicity, promotion, framing, security and insurance, transporting work, hanging an exhibition, the private view, selling your work and how to make the best of an exhibition once it is up. It has been written by artist Debbie Duffin based on her experiences of organising her own and other group exhibitions.

Making Ways - the visual artists guide to surviving and thriving edited by David Butler published by Artic Producers, ISBN 0 907730 04 3, price £8.95 inc p&p from Artists Newsletter Publications, PO Box 23, Sunderland SR4 6DG.

The 'Exhibiting' section covers setting up galleries in artists' own homes and studios as well as specimen contracts for exhibiting, sale and return and copyright licence as well as details on VAT and commission on sales. Also covered are artist-run galleries in studios and elsewhere.

Running a Workshop - Basic business for craftspeople published by the Crafts Council, ISBN 0 903798 80 8, price £3.95.

The section on exhibiting covers venues, budget, reference to organising techniques, press and private views and exhibition follow-up.

Working for Yourself in the Arts and Crafts by Sarah Hosking, published by Kogan Page, ISBN 1 85091 063 4, New edition 1988 price £6.95.

The section on 'The Market Place' deals with the different types of space (municipal, private and commercial, subsidised galleries), how to approach a gallery, leaving work on sale or return, purchase and stipend agreements, contracts, touring, shops, alternative venues, public venues, libraries, hospitals, independent group shows, festivals, fairs and markets, outdoor sites and competitions.

The Artists Directory by Heather Waddell and Richard Layzell published by Art Guide Publications A & C Black, ISBN 0 7136 3039 6, price £8.95.

This well-established book, now in the third edition, contains a number of chapters of interest to artists seeking to exhibit including an 88-page listing of galleries, sheafs of useful addresses, art and the law, buying and selling art, sponsorship and art in public places, the arts councils and regional arts associations and an international section. It was updated in 1988.

'Exhibiting in Public Libraries - Second Class Art Galleries?' by David Briers, *Artists Newsletter* October 1984.

A comprehensive discussion on the pros and cons of using libraries to exhibit in view of the huge audiences using them. Available from Artists Newsletter Publications for 75p inc p&p as above.

'Twelve by Twelve' by Tony Ashton *Artists*

Newsletter, November 1986.

A report on one artist's experience of touring his own exhibition round libraries in the London Borough of Lewisham. Available from Artists Newsletter Publications for 85p inc p&p as above.

'Organising Exhibitions for Non-exhibition Organisers' by Richard Padwick, *Artists Newsletter* December 1983.

Covers in detail the implications of artists setting up and touring their own exhibitions including packing, budgets, time-scales and printing publicity. Available from Artists Newsletter Publications for 85p inc p&p.Some of this article is republishedin *Making Ways* (see above).

'Tyler's Dozen' by Susan Tyler *Crafts* No 94 September/October 1988.

An article looking at the practical arrangements needed to show work, and on what terms, with galleries. It includes interviews with gallery directors and a discussion on the implications of sale or return and contracts. Available from *Crafts* £3.50 (single copy), 8 Waterloo Place, London SW1Y 4AT.

Setting up a Gallery

'The Enterprise Allowance Scheme' by Brian Lewis *Artists Newsletter* June 1984.

Deals with Martine Sayers' experience of the Enterprise Allowance Scheme setting up a small gallery and display space in Yorkshire. Available from Artists Newsletter Publications for 85p inc p&p as above.

'Making it Pay - Gallery Opening' by Gordon Gapper, *Artist's & Illustrator's* No 18, March 1988.

A gallery owner outlines his reasons for setting up a gallery, how he did his homework by looking at how other galleries were set up, funding, finding artists and setting the rate for commission and some hints on reaching the audience. Available from 4th Floor, 4 Brandon Road, London N7 9TP tel 01 609 2177 for £1.75.

Arts for Everyone - guidance on provision for disabled people by Anne Pearson, published by the Carnegie UK Trust & CEH, ISBN 0903 976 15 3.

Contains sections on making arts events and buildings more accessible for disabled people. It includes a section on museums, galleries and arts centres and an appendix on grant-making organisations who, in the past, have given support for projects involving the disabled.

Promoting Exhibitions

Making Ways - the visual artists guide to surviving and thriving edited by David Butler, published by Artic Producers, ISBN 0 907730 04 3, price £8.95 inc p&p from Artists Newsletter Publications, PO Box 23, Sunderland SR4 6DG.

The chapter on 'Promotion' covers in detail how to create publicity items which work and looks at the experiences of several artists' groups and organisers. Dealt with are exhibition invitation cards, leaflets, posters, compiling CVs, dealing with the media and getting into glossy magazines. Also covered is photographing art and craft work for promotional purposes.

Running a Workshop - Basic business for craftspeople produced by the Crafts Council, ISBN 0 903798 80 8, price £3.95 from the Crafts Council, 8 Waterloo Place, London SW1Y 4AT.

The section on publicity covers promotional material, how to obtain press coverage, research on making contacts, timing, plus advertising in specialist journals.

Working For Yourself in the Arts and Crafts by Sarah Hosking, published by Kogan Page, ISBN 1 85091 063 4, price £6.95.

The chapter on 'Marketing and Selling' gives information on presenting yourself and your product, using your expertise, selling, artists' agents, exporting and publicity.

Press Mailing & Contacts Lists published annually by the Arts Council, price £15 inc p&p from the Communications Unit, Arts Council, 105 Piccadilly, London W1V 0AU.

These are compiled for the Arts Council's own use and are broken down into specialist areas as well as region-by-region.

Organising Your Own Exhibition - A Guide for Artists by Debbie Duffin, published by ACME, ISBN 0 950692 32 8, price £3.50 inc p&p from Artitsts Newsletter Publications, PO Box 23, Sunderland SR4 6DG tel 091 567 3589.

The chapter on publicity for an exhibition looks at exhibition listings, advertising, press packs, printed publicity material, cheaper ways of doing publicity, preparing a mailing list and local publicity.

How to Promote Your Own Business - A Guide to Low-Budget Publicity by Jim Dudley, Published by Kogan Page, ISBN 1 85091 230 0, price £5.95.

This book is aimed at small businesses and the author's view of small business is a lot larger than that of most artists and makers. The book is, nevertheless, worthwhile reading for an overview of publicity and includes advertising, public relations, selling, designing and writing advertisements and copy, direct mail, attracting the press and media, financial planning and using an agency.

'Publicity: Collected Articles', a set of seven articles from past issues of *Artists Newsletter.*

Publicity 1 - What's it For?' by Helen Petrie April 1984; 'Publicity 2 - Reaching the Audience' by Susan Jones May 1984; Publicity 3 - Types of

Publicity' by Susan Jones June 1984; Publicity 4 - Radio & TV' by David Briers August 1984; Publicity 5 'Dear Artists Newsletter', October 1984; 'Publicity 6 - The Glossies' by David Briers January 1985; 'How I got into the Glossies' by Judith Richardson Dawes June 1986. Set of articles £2.50 inc p&p from Artists Newsletter Publications, PO Box 23, Sunderland SR4 6DG tel 091 567 3589.

'Making an Application' by Amanda Hare in *Crafts* magazine November/December 1982.

Looks at how to make a CV into something more interesting and for use as promotion. Out of print but possibly available from libraries or regional arts associations.

TMA Marketing Manual Volumes 1-4 by Glyn V Robbins and Peter Verway, published by the Theatrical Management Association between 1982-84.

These reference books can be consulted for particular aspects of promotion, like using 'direct mail' techniques to reach target audiences. (Sending out private view cards for an exhibition is a direct mail shot.)

'The Bottom Line' by Susan Tyler, *Crafts* No 92 May/June 1988.

Introduces marketing - what questions you should ask yourself when trying to market craft work, marketing strategies, some funding possibilities and a book list. Available price £3.50 (single copy) from *Crafts*, 8 Waterloo Place, London SW1Y 4AU tel 01 930 4811.

'The Bottom Line' by Susan Tyler, *Crafts* No 93 July/August 1988.

Looks at marketing for makers with regard to producing effective publicity and some guidelines for dealing with printers. The booklist covers handbooks for those with little previous experience of doing design and art work for printing. Available from *Crafts* price £3.50 as above.

'The Bottom Line' by Susan Tyler, *Crafts* No 94 Sept/Oct 1988.

Looks at press coverage in terms of cutting out all the periodicals which you can't reach through lack of time or money, and at broadening your perspectives of what magazines might help you, at angles for press releases and how to avoid art jargon. Available from *Crafts* price £3.50 as above.

Willings Press Guide an annual publication from Media Publications, ISBN 0611 007185, price £49.

Lists over 11,000 UK publications including contact names and addresses, cost and circulation details. Available in most reference libraries.

A Basic PR Guide by the Directory of Social Change, ISBN 0 907164 17X, price £4.50 inc p&p from Directory of Social Change, Radius Works, Back Lane, London NW3 1HL.

A guide to public relations aimed particularly at the smaller and medium-sized charity, group or association and covering planning public relations, getting local and regional publicity, dealing with journalists, press releases and conferences, dealing with radio and television locally and nationally, stunts and publicity events and how to be more PR conscious.

Fundraising

Raising Money from Trusts edited by Michael Norton published by the Directory of Social Change, ISBN 0 907164 04 8, price £2.95 inc p&p from the Directory of Social Change, Radius Works, Back Lane, London NW3 1HL.

Covers understanding and approaching trusts, writing a fundraising application and a section in which trust directors describe how their trusts operate.

Raising Money from Industry edited by Michael Norton published by the Directory of Social Change, ISBN 0 907164 05 6, price £4.95 inc p&p (new edition autumn 1988) available as above.

A comprehensive guide to getting money from industry, covering the scope and nature of company giving as well as how to set about applying for money.

Raising Money from Government edited by Michael Norton published by the Directory of Social Change, ISBN 0 907164 20X, price £4.50 inc p&p available as above.

Covers getting money from central government, quangos (the Arts Council, Crafts Council etc), and dealing with local government including views of a councillor, a council officer and a grant-seeker.

Industrial Sponsorship and Joint Promotions edited by Michael Norton, published by Directory of Social Change, ISBN 0 907164 07 2, price £.95 inc p&p available as above.

This applies particularly to two forms of joint commercial activity that can be used by charities to raise money. Although the bulk of such schemes occur nationally, there are still opportunities for smaller organisations at regional or local level.

Fundraising Notes - twelve eight-page and twelve-page leaflets produced by the Directory of Social Change covering : setting up as an organisation; planning a capital project; doing research; drawing up a budget, fundraising sources; raising money locally; using MSC; earning money; organising an event; developing a fund-raising strategy; planning an appeal for a capital project and writing an application, price either 50p each or £5 for the set available as above.

The Arts Funding Guide by Anne-Marie Doulton published by the Directory of Social Change, ISBN 0 907164 27 7, price £7.95 inc p&p from the

Directory of Social Change available as above.

A basic guide to fundraising for arts organisations in England, Wales and Scotland with advise on strategies and income-earning. It outlines the policies and activities of the Arts Council, regional arts associations, Crafts Council, the Training Commission and the Visting Arts Office as well as covering local authority funding, grant-making trusts and donations from industry.

Making Ways - the visual artists guide to surviving and thriving edited by David Butler and published by Artic Producers, ISBN 0 907730 04 3, price £8.95 inc p&p from Artists Newsletter Publications, PO Box 23, Sunderland SR4 6DG.

This book contains a chapter on 'Financial Support' which looks at how to approach fundraising; art and non-art sources; MSC schemes which have provided funds for certain projects; co-operatives and sponsorship and includes guidelines on how to find and approach sponsors.

Directory of Grant-Making Trusts published by the Charities Aid Foundation.

This standard reference book on trusts contains: Part 1 a classification of charitable purposes which includes all the principle fields of interest for the allocation of donations made by grant-making trusts; Part 2 lists trusts who've made a donation for a specific purpose and amounts; Part 3 is an alphabetical register of grant-making organisations with basic information as supplied by the trusts; Part 4 contains indexes ie Geographical Index.

Practical Sponsorship by Stuart Turner published by Kogan Page, ISBN 1 85091 245 9, price £12.95.

Looks at the issue from the sponsor's and the recipient's viewpoints, emphasising that both parties should be aware of the other's needs.

'Making it Pay - Sponsorship' by Harriet Lassalle *Artist and Illustrators* No 9 June 1987.

An artist describes her success with gaining sponsorship from businesses for an exhibition and a residency. Available at £1.75 from 4th Floor, 4 Brandon Road, London N7 9TP tel 01 609 2177.

'Sponsorship' by Tony Warner *Artists Newsletter* August 1988.

With the increasing moves towards commercial sponsorship, this article looks at some of the ground rules and practicalities for artists and groups of seeking business sponsorship. Available from Artists Newsletter Publications price 85p as above.

Visual Arts and the Visually Impaired

Talking Touch, a report on a seminar on the use of touch in museums and galleries held at the RNIB. Available price £1.25 inc p&p from the RNIB 224 Great Portland Street, London W1N 6AA.

Covers work in museums here and in France as well as projects undertaken in Nottingham, Leicester and Birmingham plus papers by artist Jefford Horrigan and the London Disability Forum and a bibliography.

Directory of Museums with Facilities for Visually Handicapped People published by the RNIB price £1.25 inc p&p and available as above.

Contains, in county order, 49 museums of all kinds that have permanent 'hands on' displays of art or artefacts, and where efforts have been made to produce braille leaflets, labels and catalogues. This publication will be superceded in 1989 by a book being published by the Museums Association in association with the RNIB.

Touch in Museums and Galleries - Selective Bibliography from the RNIB. This list is available free and is due for update in 1989.

'Art in Touch' by Marcus Weisen Artists *Newsletter December* 1988.

The RNIB's Arts Officer explores the terra incognito of touch in the visual arts. Available from Artists Newsletter Publications price 85p from PO Box 23, Sunderland SR4 6DG.

'In Touch with Reading' by Marcus Weisen *Artists Newsletter* January 1989.

The bibliography for the preceding article divided into catalogues and conference reports and also a description of the Art to Share tours at the V&A Museum in London. Available from Artists Newsletter Publications price 85p as above.

Buying and Collecting

'The Collectors' by Rosemary Hill *Crafts* No 91 March/April 1988.

An interview with Andrew Webb who collects saltglaze pottery. Available from Crafts £3.50 (single copy), 8 Waterloo Place, London SW1 4AT.

'The Collectors' by Rosemary Hill *Crafts* No 92 May/June 1988.

An interview with Susannah Clasen who collects a range of crafts, illustration and furniture and who also commissions work. Available as above.

'The Collectors' by Rosemary Hill *Crafts* No 93 July/August 1988.

Anatol Orient, now partner in Michaelson and Orient, describes his diverse collection of contemporary ceramics. Available as above.

'The Collectors' by Rosemary Hill *Crafts* No 95 November/December 1988.

Lady Gibberd, patron and collector, has an extensive collection of crafts, sculpture, books and jewellery and is keen to support new talent. Available as above.

Contacts and Information

The arts and crafts councils and the regional arts associations offer schemes to assist artists, makers and photographers with their practice. These vary from grants to consultancy and from seminars to information leaflets. Many are now producing booklets and brochures on visual arts provision in the region or in county areas, often linking these with artists' indexes, directories and training schemes. Listed below are addresses and contacts for visual arts, crafts, photography and performance art. See map on page 402 for the areas covered by regional arts associations and arts councils.

Arts Council of Great Britain (*covers England*), 105 Piccadilly, London W1V 0AU tel 01 629 9495. Sandy Nairne Director Visual Arts Department; Barry Lane Photography Officer; Jeni Walwin Performance Art Officer; Rory Coonan Visual Arts Officer(patronage schemes); Sarah Wason Visual Arts Officer (publishing and special projects); vacancy Visual Arts Officer (museums and galleries).

A 'projects' scheme provides grants to organisations and free-lance organisers for projects which are nationally distributed including touring exhibitions, open submission shows and publications. Exhibition franchises have also been developed to encourage galleries to initiate exhibitions of Black and Asian work and there are also opportunities for training for Black administrators and curators.

Crafts Council, 12 Waterloo Place, London SW1Y 4AU tel 01 930 4811. Tony Ford Director; Barclay Price Regional Officer.

Buckinghamshire Arts Association (*covers Buckinghamshire and is a client of East Midlands Arts*), 55 High Street, Aylesbury, Buckinghamshire HP20 1SA tel 0296 34704. Director Shaun Hennessy.

East Midlands Arts (*covers Leicestershire, Northamptonshire, Nottinghamshire and Derbyshire excepting the High Peak District*), Mountfields House, Forest Road, Loughborough, Leicestershire LE11 3HU tel 0509 218292. David Manley Visual Arts Officer; Carol Maund Crafts Officer.

Eastern Arts (*covers Essex, Norfolk, Suffolk, Bedfordshire, Hertfordshire, and Cambridgeshire*), Cherry Hinton Hall, Cherry Hinton Road, Cambridge tel 0223 215355. Jane Heath Visual Arts Officer; Liz Tagg Visual Arts Development Officer; Caroline Sier Crafts Officer; Martin Ayers Film & Photography Officer.

Greater London Arts (*covers Greater London area*), 9 White Lion Street, London N1 9PO tel 01 837 8808. Alan Haydon Visual Arts Officer; Amanda King Photography Officer.

Lincolnshire & Humberside Arts (*covers Lincolnshire and Humberside*), St Hugh's, 23 Newport, Lincoln LN1 3DN tel 0522 533555. Alan Humberstone Visual Arts Officer; Kevin Moore Assistant Visual Arts Officer.

Merseyside Arts (*covers Merseyside and West Lancashire*), Bluecoat Chambers, School Lane, Liverpool L1 3BX tel 051 709 0671. Tony Woof Visual Arts Officer; Rachel Sherratt Crafts Officer.

North West Arts (*covers Lancashire except West Lancashire, Cheshire, Greater Manchester and the High Peak District of Derbyshire*), 12 Harter Street, Manchester M1 6HY tel 061 228 3062. Virginia Tandy Visual Arts Officer; Lyn Barbour Crafts Officer.

Northern Arts (*covers Durham, Cumbria, Northumberland, Cleveland and Tyne & Wear*), 9/10 Osborne Terrace, Newcastle upon Tyne NE2 1NZ tel 091 281 6334. Peter Davies Visual Arts Officer; Laurie Short Crafts Officer; John Bradshaw Photography Officer.

South East Arts (*covers East Sussex, Kent, Surrey excluding Greater London areas*), 10 Mount Ephraim, Tunbridge Wells TN4 8AS tel 0892 515210. Frances Smith Visual Arts & Crafts Officer; Tim Cornish Photography Officer.

South West Arts (*covers Avon, Cornwall, Devon, Dorset except Bournemouth, Christchurch & Poole, Gloucestershire and Somerset*), Bradninch Place, Gandy Street, Exeter EX4 3LS tel 0392 218 188. Christine Ross, Val Millington Visual Arts & Crafts Officers.

Southern Arts (*covers Berkshire, Hampshire, Oxfordshire, West Sussex, Wiltshire, the Isle of Wight and the Bournemouth, Christchurch and Poole areas of Dorset*), 19 Southgate Street, Winchester tel 0962 55099. Hugh Adams Visual Arts Officer; David Kaye Crafts Officer.

West Midlands Arts (*covers West Midlands, Hereford, Worcestershire, Shropshire, Staffordshire and Warwickshire*), 82 Granville Street, Birmingham B1 2LH tel 021 631 3121. Julie Seddon Jones Visual Arts Officer; Helen Doherty Photography Officer; Muriel Fry Crafts Officer.

Yorkshire Arts (*covers North, South and West Yorkshire*), Glydehouse, Glyde Gate, Bradford BD5 0BQ tel 0274 723051. Yvonne Deane Visual Arts Officer; Olivia Stross Crafts Officer; Paul Brookes/Sara Worrall Photography Officer.

Arts Council of Northern Ireland (*covers Northern Ireland*), 181 a Stranmillis Road, Belfast BT9 5DU tel 0232 381591. Brian Ferran Visual Arts Director.

Arts Council of Eire - An Chomhairle Ealaion (*covers Eire*), 70 Merrion Square, Dublin 2 tel Dublin 611840. Medb Ruane Visual Arts Officer.

Crafts Council of Ireland *(covers crafts in Ireland and Northern Ireland)*, The Powerscourt Townhouse Centre, South William Street, Dublin 2 tel Dublin 797368. Sean O'Farrell Crafts Officer.

Scottish Arts Council (*covers Scotland*), 12 Manor Place, Edinburgh EH3 7DO tel 031 226 6051. Art Director Lindsay Gordon; Assistant Art Director Fiona Logue.

Scottish Development Agency (*covers crafts in Scotland*), Rosebery House, Haymarket Terrace, Edinburgh tel 031 337 9595. Negotiations are not yet concluded as to whether the crafts in Scotland will become the responsiblity of the Scottish Arts Council.

Welsh Arts Council (*covers visual arts and crafts in Wales*), Museum Place, Cardiff CF1 3NX tel 0222 394711. Nicholas Pearson Marketing Officer; Roger Le Fevre Crafts Officer.

North Wales Arts (*covers Clwyd, Gwynedd and the Montgomery district of Powys*), 10 Wellfield House, Bangor, Gwynedd tel 0248 353248. V.Clifford Jones Deputy Director.

South East Wales Arts (*Gwent, Mid-Glamorgan and the Radnor and Brecknock districts of Powys*), Victoria Street, Cwmbran, Gwent tel 06333 75075. Richard Cox Visual Arts Officer.

West Wales Arts (*covers Dyfed and West Glamorgan*), Dark Gate, Red Street, Carmarthen, Dyfed tel 0267 234248. Sybil Crouch Deputy Director.

Artists Organisations

National Artists Association c/o Roland Miller Spokesperson, 49 Stainton Road, Sheffield S11 7AX send SAE for membership details.

Design and Artists Copyright Society (DACS) St Mary's Clergy House, 2 Whitechapel Lane, London E1 1ED tel 01 247 1650.

Association of Artists & Designers in Wales (AADW), Gaskell Buildings, Collingdon Road, Cardiff CF1 5EJ tel 0222 407607.

Association of Artists in Ireland, Liberty Hall, Dublin 1 tel Dublin 740529

Artists Collective of Northern Ireland, 22 Lombard Street, Belfast tel 0232 224429

Association of Scottish Artists (ASA) c/o John McCulloch, 4 Gardner Street, Dundee tel 0382 22374; Andy Stenhouse, Edinburgh Sculpture Workshop, Albion Business Centre, 78 Albion Road, Edinburgh EH7; John Clark, Glasgow Sculpture Studios, 85 Hanson Street, Glasgow G31 2HF tel 041 551 0562.

Gallery and Exhibitions Sources

The following list of publications may be worth consulting as they provide some information on galleries, museums, exhibition spaces and local authority arts provision including libraries. The magazines listed are a selection of those which offer free or paid exhibition listings.

1988 British Alternative Theatre Directory published by Conway McGillivray Publishing Ltd

The British Leisure Centre Directory 1988/89 published by John S Turner & Associates Ltd.

British Performing Arts Yearbook 1988 published by Rhinegold Publishing Ltd.

The British Theatre Directory 1987-88 published by Richmond House Publishing Ltd.

The Education Authorities Directory & Annual 1988 published by the School Government Publishing Co Ltd.

Libraries in the UK & the Republic of Ireland 1988 published by the Library Association.

Municipal Year Book & Public Services Directory 1988 published by the Municipal Journal Ltd.

Museums and Art Galleries in Great Britain & Ireland 1988 published by British Leisure Publications.

Museums Yearbook 1988/9 published by the Museums Association.

Public Authorities Directory 1988 published by LGC Communications.

Arts Review Yearbook 1988 published by Starcity.

The Artists Directory published by Art Guide Publications A & C Black (see booklist).

Independent Photography Directory published by the Arts Council (new edition 1989).

Craft Workshops in the English Countryside published by the AA and CoSIRA 1986.

The Crafts Map 1988 published by the Crafts Council and covering selected London and regional galleries selling high-quality crafts.

Art Galleries & Exhibition Spaces in Wales published by the Welsh Arts Council's Art Marketing Information Service 1988.

Handbook for Essex & Suffolk Artists by Jeremy Theophilus to be published by Eastern Arts in 1989.

London: new exhibitions of contemporary art available free from galleries and arts venues in London.

East London Arts available free in London.

Artists Newsletter which is published monthly provides listings of exhibition opportunities, classified exhibition listings and regular up dates to this publication. Details from PO Box 23, Sunderland SR4 6DG tel 091 567 3589.

Artline, an art newspaper, runs gallery listings in the news pages. Details from 3 Garratt Lane, London SW18 tel 01 870 0427.

Art Monthly, published ten times a year, has a free exhibition listings section based on details supplied. Details from 36 Great Russell Street, London WC1 tel 01 580 4168.

Arts Review , issued fortnightly contains an extensive classified gallery listing section divided regionally. Details from 69 Faroe Road, London W14 0EL tel 01 603 7530.

Crafts magazine which is issued six times a year provides gallery listings for its selected galleries and classified gallery listings for others. Details from 8 Waterloo Place, London SW1Y 4AT tel 01 930 4811.

Ceramics Review, issued six times a year provides some free gallery listings as well as small classifieds. Details from 21 Carnaby Street, London W1V 1PH tel 01 439 3377.

Galleries available free in London.

Women Artists Slide Library Journal issued six times a year contains exhibition listings as part of their information service. Details from WASL, Fulham Palace, Bishop's Avenue, London SW6 6EA tel 01 731 7618.

See **'Contacts and Information'** for addresses of the regional arts associations, many of whose magazines provide gallery and exhibition listings.

Advertisers Index

ALL THIS FROM ONE ISSUE OF ARTISTS NEWSLETTER

Please send me the following subscription

Name ______________________

Address ______________________

____

Postcode ______________________

(Annual rate for 12 issues)

☐ UK Individual £9.50

☐ UK Institution £16

☐ Europe, inc. Eire £17

☐ Elsewhere £26

Please make cheques payable to Artic Producers, and send to PO Box 23, Villiers Street, Sunderland SR4 6DG. Telephone 091 5673589

CANDID
CANDID ART & DESIGN FAIR
DECEMBER
BUSINESS DESIGN CENTRE
ISLINGTON
CONTEMPORARY DESIGN FAIRS
SPRING – SUMMER – WINTER
CHELSEA OLD TOWN HALL
SLIDE LIBRARY
DATA SEARCH
ART & DESIGN MARKETING
N.D.I., 144 ESSEX ROAD,
LONDON N18CX
TEL: 01 226 7971
DATA BASE
CANDID
CATALOGUE
VIDEO

- Information
- Advice
- Publications
- Visual Arts Index
- Grant Aid

For further details contact:
The Visual Arts Unit
Lincolnshire & Humberside Arts
St Hugh's
Newport
Lincoln
LN1 3DN
Telephone:
Lincoln (0522) 33555

Lincolnshire & Humberside ARTS

BERLLANDERI SCULPTURE WORKSHOP

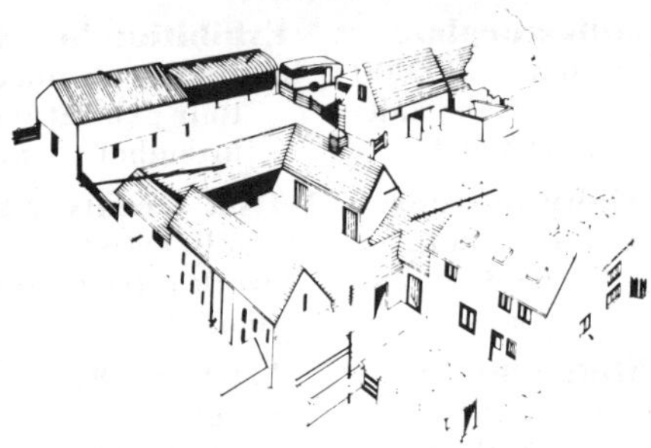

Berllanderi offers a retreat for practicing sculptors from Britain and abroad.

For more information please apply to
Berllanderi Sculpture Workshop, Usk Road, Raglan, Gwent NP5 2HR
Telephone: 0291 690268

North West Arts

SUPPORT FOR ARTISTS & CRAFTSPEOPLE

North West Arts offers grants, advice and encouragement of arts activities in the north west. Its main commitment is to wider access of the arts through exhibition support, residencies, placements in schools and other projects.

If you would like to be included in the artists and/or crafts register of makers and slide index or would like further information, contact the Visual Arts or Crafts Department, North West Arts, 12 Harter Street, Manchester M1 6HY.
☎ 061-228 3062.

North West Arts is the Regional Arts Association for Cheshire (except Ellesmere Port and Halton), Greater Manchester, Lancashire (except West Lancashire) and the High Peak District of Derbyshire.

SCOTTISH SCULPTURE WORKSHOP GALLERY & SCULPTURE WALK

Exhibitions by Workshop Artist and by Invitation
All Applications will be considered
Floor Area 25 sq.m. Hanging space 15 m run

S. S. W. Lumsden,
Huntly, Aberdeenshire AB5 4JN
Tel No. 046 46 372

Cornerhouse

70 Oxford Street
Manchester
M1 5NH
061 228 7621

Three gallery spaces showing twenty exhibitions of contemporary art a year.

Talks, seminars and workshops organised with each exhibition.

Galleries open:
Tues – Sun, 12.00 – 8.00pm.

USHER GALLERY

LINDUM • ROAD • LINCOLN

Tel: Lincoln (0522) 27980

Constantly changing programme of temporary exhibitions.

Permanent collections of fine and decorative arts.

Mondays – Saturdays 10.00 am – 5.30 pm
Sundays 2.30 – 5.00 pm

Lincolnshire County Council Recreational Services

THE PATRICIA WELLS GALLERY

Country House Gallery with a large selection of Paintings and Graphics by Academicians and Leading Artists
Cleansing—Restorations and Framing arranged

SPECIALISTS IN "ONE MAN" EXHIBITIONS

MORTON HOUSE, LOWER MORTON,
THORNBURY, BRISTOL BS12 1RA
Tel: THORNBURY (STD 0454) 412288

An exciting new Gallery in LEICESTER

the City Gallery

90 Granby Street, Leicester

Tel: 0533 540595

Opening April 1989

Artists wishing to exhibit should send 2 slides of their work to the Visual Arts Officer

Frame Hire Scheme
Touring exhibitions to non Gallery venues
Crafts space. Private Hire space
Art magazines, catalogues prints for sale

Leicester City Council   CRAFTS COUNCIL   EAST MIDLANDS Arts

Publications

A CODE OF PRACTICE for INDEPENDENT PHOTOGRAPHY

IF YOU:

- **Exhibit or sell photographs**
- *Work within independent photography*
- **Organise residencies or placements**
- *Publish or commission photographs*

THEN the *Code of Practice for Independent Photography* gives you a set of guidelines and related information to assist in the negotiations and contractual agreements. It doesn't attempt to impose rules and conditions but identifies the respective needs and responsibilities of photographers and organisations and is essential for organisations and groups, funders and sponsors and at all individual photography workers, and, although specifically compiled for independent photography this code is equally valuable to all visual artists and arts organisations. It has been drawn up – after extensive consultations – by Vince Wade for the Independent Film, Video and Photography Association (IFVPA) with funding from the Arts Council.

IT COVERS:

• Employment • Equal Opportunities • Copyright •
• Exhibiting • Commissions • Residencies and Placements •
• Publication • Purchases •

with the relevant legislation and working practices indicating procedures to follow, respective responsibilities, and points for inclusion in negotiations and contracts.

PLUS

- sample fees and rates of pay
- how the new Copyright Act affects photography

A Code of Practice for Independent Photography **by Vince Wade 1989, A5 32pp**
ISBN 0 907730 06 X, price £2.50 UK or £3.00 Ireland, Europe and elsewhere.

From Artists Newsletter Publications, PO Box 23, Sunderland SR4

CLASSIFIED ADVERTS

PHOTOGRAPHIC SERVICES

■ PHOTOGRAPHY OF ART & CRAFT
For exhibition catalogues, publicity material, or for your records. Contact Colin Shaw, 9 Ilfracombe Grove, Green Lane, Coventry CV3 6DX tel 0203 415815.

FRAMING

■ FITTING FRAMES
Friendly, personal, high quality picture framing. We stock a range of plain wooden mouldings which can stain to suit individual artwork, and use conservation materials where requested. Do visit us at Clerkenwell Workshops, Unit 264, 27 Clerkenwell Close, London EC1. Tel 01 251 3101, Monday-Friday 10-6.

■ EXHIBITION FRAMING
Contract or museum quality, hand-made from pine or beech. Your choice of colour and finish. Contact Lindsay or Mark for a quotation at Frameshop, the Exhibition Workshop of Newcastle Arts Centre, 69 Westgate Road, Newcastle upon Tyne. 091 261 0293.

CASTING

■ FIBRE GLASS SCULPTURE CASTING
Services include: bronze, aluminium and stone finishes, mould-making and fabrication. Details from Morrison Frederick, 1 Fawe Street, London E14 6PD. Tel 01 515 4110.

OPPORTUNITIES

■ CRAFT SHOWS BY LEON COLEMAN
Regular sales opportunities for artists and craftworkers including the weekly Wednesday Craft at the Pavilions Shopping Centre Uxbridge. Leon Coleman's Craft Shows, 4 Church Farm Workshops, Hatley St George, Sandy, Bedfordshire SG19 3HR. Tel 0767 51674.

■ ARTSPACE GALLERIES
A regular programme of exhibitions, mainly contemporary fine art. Open Monday to Saturday. Full details from Nina Ashby, Artspace Galleries, 21 Castle Street, Aberdeen AB1 1AJ tel 0224 639539.

PRINTING SERVICES

■ RAVEN PRESS
Catalogues and publicity material, full typesetting off your word-processor disks from £4.00 per A4 side depending on complexity. Contact John Bois at 48 Queen Street, Exeter EX4 3SR. Tel 0392 413508.

SCULPTURE WORKSHOPS

■ BERLLANDERI SCULPTURE WORKSHOP
Berllanderi offers a retreat for practising sculptors. Each has private studio, flat and the use of specialist workshops. For information please apply to Berllanderi Sculpture Workshop, Usk Road, Raglan, Gwent NP5 2HR. Tel 0291 690268.

PHOTOGRAPHY FACILITIES

■ EXETER DARKROOM
Well-equipped darkroom for independent photographers open to the public through a membership scheme. Courses and workshops. Contact James Hadfield, Exeter Darkroom, Exeter & Devon Arts Centre, Bradninch Place, Gandy Street, Exeter EX4 3LS. 0392 432617.

CLASSIFIED ADVERTS

PRINTMAKING FACILITIES

■ **APOLLO ETCHING STUDIO**
has vacancies for members; also day/evening rates, tuition and editioning. 3 Carlton Kings Road, London NW5. Tel 01 485 7750 or 01 485 4928.

■ **GAINSBOROUGH'S HOUSE**
Gainsborough's House Print Workshop has screen printing, intaglio and lithography facilities and courses. Write to Gainsborough's House Print Workshop, Sudbury, Suffolk CO10 6EU tel 0787 72958 for more details.

■ **PEACOCK PRINTMAKERS**
Intaglio, screen printing, relief printing, lithography, process photography and typesetting with facilities for artists through open access. Contract editioning, exhibitions and publishing. Full details from Arthur Watson, Peacock Printmakers, 21 Castle Street, Aberdeen AB1 1AJ 0224 639539.

■ **AADW CARDIFF PRINT WORKSHOP**
Workshop with open access for members with screen printing, intaglio, stone and plate lithography. Some editioning and tuition available. Full information from AADW, Gaskell Buildings, Collingdon Road, Cardiff CF1 5E tel 0222 487607.

■ **WILKEY'S MOOR PRINT WORKSHOP**
This well-established printmaking workshop offers facilities for stone lithography, intaglio and block printing plus summer schools and intensive courses. Contact Michael Honnor, Wilkey's Moor Print Workshop, Ivybridge, Devon tel 0752 8893686.

■ **HOLLAND PARK STUDIO**
50 Queensdale Road, London W11 4SA tel 01 602 1563. Internationally known. Editioning service in intalgio/woodblock. Reasonable rates.

■ **NORTH STAR STUDIOS**
This fine art print workshop has open access use in screen printing, lithography, etching, relief and black and white photography. Also editioning service, evening classes, workshops and summer schools. Details from 65 Ditching Road, Brighton Tel 0273 601041.

■ **HASTINGS ETCHING WORKSHOP**
All facilities including two presses, also classes and courses. Accommodation available. Martin Ware, 74 West Hill Road, St Leonards on Sea, East Sussex, TN38 0NE. Tel 0424 424235.

■ **CHILFORD HALL PRESS**
Professional silkscreen studio. Fine printers, publishers and distributors of contemporary art. Recent editions include:- Helaine Blumenfeld, Cecile Elstein, Terry Frost, Elisabeth Frink, Kip Gresham, Philip Sutton. Contact Chilford Hall Press, Chilford Hall, Balsham Road, Linton, Cambridge. 0223 893544.

PHOTOGRAPHIC SERVICES

■ **THE PROFESSIONAL PHOTOGRAPHIC SERVICE**
For artists in need of quality reproductions, copy slides, colour and b/w prints. Fast, reliable and at competitive prices. For details contact David Jacobson, 31 Cromer Road, Eastville, Bristol BS5 6JU. Tel 0272 511759.

■ **NORTH-WEST PHOTOGRAPHER**
Fast fine art and craft photographs, trannies or prints from Andrew Morris (FRSA), 101 Lake Road, Ambleside LA22 0DB. Tel 05394 32809.

■ **FREELANCE PHOTOGRAPHER**
with understanding of sculptors', painters' and craftspeople's requirements, for portfolios and publications. Paul Rowbottom, 97 Breakspeare Road, Abbots Langley, Watford, Hertfordshire WD5 0GR. Tel Kings Langley 63032.

England

Avon

Bedfordshire

Berkshire

Buckinghamshire

Cambridgeshire

Cheshire

Cleveland

Co Durham

Saddler Gallery

Cornwall

Bodmin:
Cornwall Crafts Association at Pencarrow
Camelford:
North Cornwall Museum & Gallery
Falmouth:
Falmouth Art Gallery
Helston:
Cornwall Crafts Association at Trelowarren
Par:
Mid-Cornwall Galleries
Penzance:
Bread Street Gallery
Jamieson Library
Newlyn Orion Galleries
Trelissick Gallery (Cornwall Crafts Association)
Trelissick Gallery (Newlyn Orion Galleries)
Wolf At The Door
St Ives:
New Craftsman
Penwith Galleries
Salt House Gallery
Wills Lane Gallery
Truro:
County Museum & Art Gallery

Cumbria

Alston:
Gossipgate Gaslight Gallery
Ambleside:
Dexterity
Barrow-in-Furness:
Furness Museum
Carlisle:
Carlisle Museum & Art Gallery
Gossipgate Garden Gallery
Cartmel:
Anvil Gallery
Clifton Dykes:
Wetheriggs
Cockermouth:
Castlegate House
Egremont:
Lowes Court Gallery
Kendal:
Abbot Hall Art Gallery
Brewery Arts Centre (Photographic Gallery)
Keswick:
Keswick Museum & Art Gallery
Lakeland Guild Craft Gallery
Kirkby Lonsdale:
Coach House Contemporary Art
Penrith:
Penrith Museum
Ulverston:
Renaissance Centre
Whitehaven:
Whitehaven Museum & Art Gallery
Workington:
Carnegie Theatre & Arts Centre

Derbyshire

Ashford-in-the-Water:
Tithe Barn Gallery
Buxton:
Buxton Museum & Art Gallery
David Russell
Chesterfield:
Bowling Green Gallery
Chesterfield College of Technology & Arts
Peacock Heritage Centre
Derby:
Art For All
Clock Yard Gallery
Derby Art Gallery
Derby City Council House (Art For All)
Derby City Hospital (Art For All)
Derby Community Arts
Derby Playhouse
Derbyshire College of Higher Education
Green Lane Gallery
Ilkeston Community Hospital (Art For All)
Metro Cinema Gallery
Saint Michael's Gallery
Workshop Gallery
Ilkeston:
Bottle Kiln Gallery
Erewash Museum
Matlock:
Derbyshire Libraries
Sudbury:
Museum of Childhood
Wirksworth:
Gallery, The

Devon

Barnstaple:
Blacksell Arts Centre
Beaford:
Beaford Centre
Chagford:
Chagford Galleries
Crediton:
Red House Arts Centre
Dartington:
Dartington Cider Press Centre
Dartmouth:
Facets
Higher Street Gallery
Simon Drew Gallery
Dawlish:
Porch Galleries
Vivian Gallery
Exeter:
Exeter and Devon Arts Centre
Exeter University (Library)
Northcott Theatre
Royal Albert Memorial Museum
Spacex Gallery
Exmouth:
Exmouth Rolle College Gallery
Newton Abbot:
Devon Guild of Craftsmen
Plymouth:
Barbican Theatre Gallery
Plymouth Arts Centre
Plymouth City Museum & Art Gallery
Plymouth Theatre Royal
Shebbear:
Shebbear College (Little Gallery)
Teignmouth:
Church House Gallery & Ceramic Workshop
Torquay:
Torre Abbey
Torrington:
Plough Theatre
Totnes:
88
Gothic House
Marshall Arts Gallery

Dorset

Bridport:
Symondsbury Gallery
Christchurch:
Red House Museum & Gardens
Sherborne:
Melbury Gallery
Wareham:
Trinity Art Gallery
Wimborne Minster:
Dorset Craft Guild Walford Mill Craft Centre

E Sussex

Brighton:
Brighton College (Burstow Gallery)
Brighton Museum & Art Gallery
Brighton Polytechnic Gallery
Gardner Centre Gallery
Hugo Barclay
Nexus
Pig & Fig
Red Herring Gallery
Studio Shop
Window Gallery
Zap Club
Crowborough:
Green Lane Gallery
Ditchling:
Craftsman Gallery
Eastbourne:
Eastbourne College (Casson Gallery)
Eastbourne Library Gallery
Towner Art Gallery
Hastings:
Hastings Museum & Art Gallery
Stables Theatre Gallery
Horsham:
Christ's Hospital Arts Centre
Horsham Arts Centre Gallery
Hove:
Hove Museum & Art Gallery
Lewes:
Craftwork
Rottingdean:
Grange

Greater Manchester

Lancashire

Leicestershire

Lincolnshire

Suffolk

Aldeburgh:
Peter Pears Gallery
Boxford:
Laurimore Gallery
Bungay:
Bookshop & Gallery
Bury St Edmunds:
Bury St Edmunds Library
Bury St. Edmunds Art Gallery
Chimney Mill Galleries
Saint John's Street Gallery
Debenham:
Debenham Gallery
Halesworth:
Halesworth Gallery
Ipswich:
Area Library Service (Ipswich)
Haste Gallery
John Russell Gallery
Mill Gallery
Wolsey Art Gallery, Christchurch Mansion
Lavenham:
Mill House Gallery
Phoenix Gallery
Lowestoft:
Area Library Service (Lowestoft)
Lowestoft College School of Art & Design Gallery
Suffolk County Council Arts & Libraries
Newmarket:
Bridge Street Gallery
Newmarket Library
Southwold:
Great Eastern Craft Co-operative
Portland Studio
Stonham Aspal:
Caldecott Gallery
Stowmarket:
Museum of East Anglian Life
Stowmarket Library
Sudbury:
Clare Gallery
Gainsborough's House
Quay Gallery
Sudbury Library
Woodbridge:
Deben Gallery
Denis Taplin Gallery
Fraser Gallery
Yoxford:
Yoxford Gallery

Surrey

Dorking:
Spectrum Gallery
E Molesey:
Art Enterprises
Ewell:
Bourne Hall
Farnham:
Johnson Wax Kiln Gallery
New Ashgate Gallery
Redgrave Theatre Gallery
West Surrey College of Art & Design (James Hockey Gallery)
Godalming:
Godalming Museum
Thursley Textile Designs
Waverley Link Plus
Guildford:
Guildford Adult Education Centre (The Gallery)
Guildford House Gallery
Harvey Road Gallery
Jonleigh Gallery
Michael Stewart Fine Art
University of Surrey (Library Gallery)
Haslemere:
Haslemere Educational Museum
Leatherhead:
Thorndike Theatre Gallery
Ockley:
Hannah Peschar Gallery
Thames Ditton:
Fraser Carver Gallery

Tyne & Wear

Gateshead:
Gateshead Central Library
Shipley Art Gallery
Jarrow:
Bede Gallery
Bede Monastry Museum
Newcastle-upon-Tyne:
Café Procop
Calouste Gulbenkian Gallery
Chameleon Gallery
Gallery 7
Greys Gallery
Hatton Gallery
Laing Art Gallery
Newcastle Arts Centre Craftshop
Newcastle Arts Centre Frameshop
Newcastle Central Library
Newcastle Playhouse (New Playhouse Gallery)
Newcastle University Long Gallery
Northern Print
Projects UK
Side Gallery
Newcastle-upon-Tyne:
Newcastle Polytechnic Gallery
North Shields:
Vicarage Cottage Gallery
Wooden Doll
Sunderland:
Northern Centre for Contemporary Art
Sunderland Museum & Art Gallery
Sunderland Polytechnic (Reg Vardy Foundation)
Tynemouth:
Holly House Gallery
Wallsend:
Buddle Arts Centre
Wallsend Heritage Centre
Washington:
Washington Arts Centre

W Midlands

Bilston:
Bilston Museum & Art Gallery
Birmingham:
Birmingham and Midland Institute
Birmingham Art Trust
Birmingham Museum & Art Gallery
Birmingham Polytechnic (Concourse)
Birmingham University (Winterbourne House)
Building Sights
Carleton Gallery
Cave, The
Central Library
Craftspace
Helios Pictures
Ikon
Ikon Touring
Library Exhibition Hall
Midlands Arts Centre
Public Art Commissions Agency
Royal Birmingham Society of Artists
Ten 8 Touring
Coventry:
Centre Crafts
Coventry Polytechnic (Lanchester Gallery)
CRIS Community Arts
Herbert Art Gallery
Koko
Mead Gallery
Museum of British Road Transport
Dudley:
Dudley Art Gallery
Kingswinford:
Broadfield House Glass Museum
Solihull:
Solihull Central Library
Walsall:
Walsall Museum & Art Gallery
Wednesbury:
Wednesbury Museum & Art Gallery
Wolverhampton:
Eagle Works
Wolverhampton Museum & Art Gallery
Wolverhampton Polytechnic

W Sussex

Billingshurst:
Lannards Gallery
Chichester:
David Paul Gallery
Pallant House
West Sussex County Libraries
Hassocks:
Chichester House Gallery
Midhurst:
Tobycraft Gallery
Worthing:
Terrace Gallery

N Ireland

Scotland

Grampion Region

Highland Region

Lothian Region

Orkney

Shetland Islands

Strathclyde Region

Tayside Region

Mid Glamorgan

Powys

S Glamorgan

W Glamorgan

Channel Islands

Guernsey

Jersey

Isle of Man

Isle of Man

Gallery Index

The letter following the town in the Gallery Index indicates the country and the section within which the listing can be found:

- ***E*........England**
- ***I*..........Ireland**
- ***N*........N Ireland**
- ***S*.........Scotland**
- ***W*........Wales**
- ***C*........Channel Islands**
- ***M*........Isle of Man**

A

B

C

G

H

I

J

K

L

M

N

T

Y

Z

Key to codes used in listings

Arts council & regional arts association area

Arts funding bodies responsible for the town:

ACE Arts Council of Eire
ACNI Arts Council of N Ireland
BA Buckinghamshire Arts
EA Eastern Arts
EMA East Midlands Arts
GLA Greater London Arts
LHA Lincolnshire & Humberside
MA Merseyside Arts
NA Northern Arts
NWA North West Arts
NWaA North Wales Arts
SA Southern Arts
SEWaA South West Wales Arts
SWA South West Arts
WMA West Midlands Arts
WWaA West Wales Arts
YA Yorkshire Arts

For contacts and addresses see 'Read On...' pages 437-438.

For a map of arts council and regional arts areas see page 402.

Art forms shown

The codes indicate the main art forms shown by the gallery

VA Visual Arts consisting of:
- **Pa** Painting
- **Dr** Drawing
- **Il** Illustration
- **Pr** Print
- **Sc** Sculpture

Ph Photography
Fl Film
Vi Video
Ho Holography
LA Live Art
Ar Architecture

Cr Craft consisting of:
- **Ce** Ceramics
- **Je** Jewellery
- **Te** Textiles
- **Gl** Glass
- **Wo** Wood
- **Fu** Furniture
- **De** Design
- **Bo** Books

Torrington (Devon)

(SWA) Map6 SS41

Plough Theatre

A gallery space in the foyer of a theatre in a converted pub. [VA,Ph,Cr]

Address: The Plough, Fore Street, Great Torrington, Devon EX38 8HQ tel 0805 22552
Contact: Theatre Director Jenny Neesham
Open: Tues-Sat 10-5 and 6.30-9
Policy: The monthly programme is predominantly work by local artists.
Sales: Work sold
The Space: The gallery has 16m linear hanging space with *'basic lighting', though improvements are 'scheduled'.*
Exhibiting: [AW] Apply to the Director. The theatre provides Insurance, transport, preview, list of exhibits, and artists' expenses. Preview costs split equally between theatre and exhibitor. A commission of 25% is charged on sales.
Access: [U] Town centre location; BR Barnstable

Disabled access

Information on disabled access is based in details supplied by the gallery. Your are advised to check facilities for the disabled prior to a visit.

[U] Unstepped access to the building
[T] Toilet suitable for the disabled
[F] Flat or one-step access to some or all galleries
[L] Lift
[S] 2-5 steps
[X] Many unavoidable steps or dificulties for wheelchair users

Map reference

Codes locate the town on the maps on pages 404–421

Map 1 Northern Scotland pages 404-5
Map 2 Southern Scotland pages 406-7
Map 3 Northern England pages 408-9
Map 4 Wales/West Midlands pages 410-11
Map 5 East Midlands pages 412-13
Map 6 South West England pages 414-15
Map 7 South East England pages 416-17
Map 8 North of Ireland pages 418-19
Map 9 South of Ireland pages 420-421

The code following the map number is the Ordnance Survey National Grid Reference which locates the position of the town within the map and within any map employing the National Grid. *See page 403 Key to Maps.*

Exhibiting

[AW] The gallery welcomes exhibition applications from artists
[EF] The gallery pays a fee to exhibiting artists for allowing public access to their work.

The inclusion of the phrase *'Supports the principle of EPR'* means the gallery agrees with the principle that artists should receive a payment *as of right* for publicly exhibiting their work. See 'Exhibition Payment Right' page 430.

Gallery Update Form

Please use this form (or a photocopy of it) to amend an entry or for a new galllery. The *Directory of Exhibition Spaces* is updated quarterly in the form of a pull-out section in *Artists Newsletter*. These updates will automatically be included in future editions of the *Directory of Exhibition Spaces*.

Name of Gallery ________________

Address of Gallery ________________

Town ________________ County ________________

Postcode ________________ Tel ________________

RAA area (see map on page 402) ________________

Contact: Name ________________ Title ________________

Address for contact (if different from gallery address) ________________

Town ________________

Postcode ________________ Tel ________________

Opening hours ________________

Brief description of what the gallery is ________________

____

____

What art forms does the gallery show? Painting ❑ , Sculpture ❑, Print ❑, Drawing ❑, Illustration ❑, Photography ❑, Architecture ❑, Ceramics ❑, Textiles ❑, Jewellery ❑, Glass ❑, Furniture ❑, Wood ❑, Books ❑, Film ❑, Video ❑, Holography ❑, Installations ❑, Live Art ❑, Other ________________

Brief description of what the gallery does (see 'Policy' in listings for reference) ________________

____

____

____

____

____

Brief Description of the space(s) & facilities available for temporary exhibitions (see 'The Space' in listings) ________________

____

____

____

Brief description of whether and how artists can apply for exhibitions, and financial arrangements with exhibitors (see 'Exhibiting' in listings for reference) ________________

____

____

____

Commission charged on sales ________________%. **Exhibition fee paid to exhibitor(s) Yes/No**

Disabled access to the temporary exhibition galleries from outside: No steps or ramp ❑, one-step ❑, 2-5 steps ❑, Lift ❑, Many unavoidable steps and/or other difficulties for wheelchair users ❑, Toilet suitable for disabled ❑

Access to parking and public transport ________________

____

Please return to:

DES, Artists Newsletter Publications, PO Box 23, Sunderland SR4 6DG Tel 091 567 3589